Contemporary
Literary Criticism

Guide to Gale Literary Criticism Series

For criticism on	Consult these Gale series
Authors now living or who died after December 31, 1999	*CONTEMPORARY LITERARY CRITICISM (CLC)*
Authors who died between 1900 and 1999	*TWENTIETH-CENTURY LITERARY CRITICISM (TCLC)*
Authors who died between 1800 and 1899	*NINETEENTH-CENTURY LITERATURE CRITICISM (NCLC)*
Authors who died between 1400 and 1799	*LITERATURE CRITICISM FROM 1400 TO 1800 (LC)* *SHAKESPEAREAN CRITICISM (SC)*
Authors who died before 1400	*CLASSICAL AND MEDIEVAL LITERATURE CRITICISM (CMLC)*
Authors of books for children and young adults	*CHILDREN'S LITERATURE REVIEW (CLR)*
Dramatists	*DRAMA CRITICISM (DC)*
Poets	*POETRY CRITICISM (PC)*
Short story writers	*SHORT STORY CRITICISM (SSC)*
Literary topics and movements	*HARLEM RENAISSANCE: A GALE CRITICAL COMPANION (HR)* *THE BEAT GENERATION: A GALE CRITICAL COMPANION (BG)* *FEMINISM IN LITERATURE: A GALE CRITICAL COMPANION (FL)* *GOTHIC LITERATURE: A GALE CRITICAL COMPANION (GL)*
Asian American writers of the last two hundred years	*ASIAN AMERICAN LITERATURE (AAL)*
Black writers of the past two hundred years	*BLACK LITERATURE CRITICISM (BLC)* *BLACK LITERATURE CRITICISM SUPPLEMENT (BLCS)* *BLACK LITERATURE CRITICISM: CLASSIC AND EMERGING AUTHORS SINCE 1950 (BLC-2)*
Hispanic writers of the late nineteenth and twentieth centuries	*HISPANIC LITERATURE CRITICISM (HLC)* *HISPANIC LITERATURE CRITICISM SUPPLEMENT (HLCS)*
Native North American writers and orators of the eighteenth, nineteenth, and twentieth centuries	*NATIVE NORTH AMERICAN LITERATURE (NNAL)*
Major authors from the Renaissance to the present	*WORLD LITERATURE CRITICISM, 1500 TO THE PRESENT (WLC)* *WORLD LITERATURE CRITICISM SUPPLEMENT (WLCS)*

Contents

Preface vii

Acknowledgments xi

Preface

Named "one of the twenty-five most distinguished reference titles published during the past twenty-five years" by *Reference Quarterly,* the *Contemporary Literary Criticism (CLC)* series provides readers with critical commentary and general information on more than 3,000 authors from 91 countries now living or who died after December 31, 1999. Before the publication of the first volume of *CLC* in 1973, there was no ongoing digest monitoring scholarly and popular sources of critical opinion and explication of modern literature. *CLC,* therefore, has fulfilled an essential need, particularly since the complexity and variety of contemporary literature makes the function of criticism especially necessary to today's reader.

Scope of the Series

CLC is designed to serve as an introduction to authors of the twenty-first century. Volumes published from 1973 through 1999 covered authors who died after December 31, 1959. Since January 2000, the series has covered authors who are living or who died after December 31, 1999; those who died between 1959 and 2000 are now included in *Twentieth-Century Literary Criticism.* There is minimal duplication of content between series.

Authors are selected for inclusion for a variety of reasons, among them the publication or production of a critically acclaimed new work, the reception of a major literary award, revival of interest in past writings, or the adaptation of a literary work to film or television.

Attention is also given to several other groups of writers—authors of considerable public interest—about whose work criticism is often difficult to locate. These include mystery and science-fiction writers, literary and social critics, world authors, and authors who represent particular ethnic groups.

Each *CLC* volume contains individual essays and reviews selected from hundreds of review periodicals, general magazines, scholarly journals, monographs, and books. Entries include critical evaluations spanning an author's career from its inception to current commentary. Interviews, feature articles, and other works that offer insight into the author's works are also presented. Students, teachers, librarians, and researchers will find that the general critical and biographical material in *CLC* provides them with vital information required to write a term paper, analyze a poem, or lead a book discussion group. In addition, complete bibliographical citations note the original source and all of the information necessary for a term paper footnote or bibliography.

CLC is part of the survey of criticism and world literature that is contained in Gale's *Twentieth-Century Literary Criticism* (*TCLC*), *Nineteenth-Century Literature Criticism* (*NCLC*), *Literature Criticism from 1400 to 1800* (*LC*), *Shakespearean Criticism* (*SC*), and *Classical and Medieval Literature Criticism* (*CMLC*).

Organization of the Book

A *CLC* entry consists of the following elements:

- The **Author Heading** cites the name under which the author most commonly wrote, followed by birth and death dates. If the author wrote consistently under a pseudonym, the pseudonym will be listed in the author heading and the author's actual name given in parentheses on the first line of the biographical and critical information. Also located here are any name variations under which an author wrote, including transliterated forms for authors whose native languages use nonroman alphabets. Uncertain birth or death dates are indicated by question marks. Single-work entries are preceded by a heading that consists of the most common form of the title in English translation (if applicable) and the author's name.

- The **Introduction** contains background information that introduces the reader to the author, work, or topic that is the subject of the entry.

- The list of **Principal Works** is ordered chronologically by date of first publication and lists the most important works by the author. The genre and publication information of each work is given. In the case of works not published in English, a translation of the title is provided as an aid to the reader; the translation is a published translated title or a free translation provided by the compiler of the entry. As a further aid to the reader, a list of **Principal English Translations** is provided for authors who did not publish in English; the list selects those translations most commonly considered the best by critics. Unless otherwise indicated, plays are dated by first performance, not first publication, and the location of the first performance is given, if known. Lists of **Representative Works** discussed in the entry appear with topic entries.

- Reprinted **Criticism** is arranged chronologically in each entry to provide a useful perspective on changes in critical evaluation over time. The critic's name and the date of composition or publication of the critical work are given at the beginning of each piece of criticism. Unsigned criticism is preceded by the title of the source in which it appeared. All titles by the author featured in the text are printed in boldface type. Footnotes are reprinted at the end of each essay or excerpt. In the case of excerpted criticism, only those footnotes that pertain to the excerpted texts are included. Criticism in topic entries is arranged chronologically under a variety of subheadings to facilitate the study of different aspects of the topic.

- A complete **Bibliographical Citation** of the original essay or book precedes each piece of criticism. Citations conform to recommendations set forth in the Modern Language Association of America's *MLA Handbook for Writers of Research Papers,* 7th ed. (2009).

- Critical essays are prefaced by brief **Annotations** describing each piece.

- Whenever possible, a recent **Author Interview** accompanies each entry.

- An annotated bibliography of **Further Reading** appears at the end of each entry and suggests resources for additional study. In some cases, significant essays for which the editors could not obtain reprint rights are included here. Boxed material following the list provides references to other biographical and critical sources on the author in series published by Gale.

Indexes

A **Cumulative Author Index** lists all of the authors who have appeared in a wide variety of reference sources published by Gale, including *CLC*. A complete list of these sources is found facing the first page of the Author Index. The index also includes birth and death dates and cross references between pseudonyms and actual names.

A **Cumulative Topic Index** lists the literary themes and topics treated in the series as well as in *Classical and Medieval Literature Criticism, Literature Criticism from 1400 to 1800, Nineteenth-Century Literature Criticism, Twentieth-Century Literary Criticism, Drama Criticism, Poetry Criticism, Short Story Criticism,* and *Children's Literature Review.*

A **Cumulative Nationality Index** lists all authors featured in *CLC* by nationality, followed by the number of the *CLC* volume in which their entries appear.

An alphabetical **Title Index** accompanies each volume of *CLC*. Listings of titles by authors covered in the given volume are followed by the author's name and the corresponding page numbers where the titles are discussed. English translations of titles published in other languages and variations of titles are cross-referenced to the title under which a work was originally published. Titles of novels, plays, nonfiction books, and poetry, short-story, or essay collections are printed in italics, while individual poems, short stories, and essays are printed in roman type within quotation marks. All titles reviewed in *CLC* and in the other Literary Criticism Series can be found online in the *Gale Literary Index.*

Citing *Contemporary Literary Criticism*

When citing criticism reprinted in the Literary Criticism Series, students should provide complete bibliographic information so that the cited essay can be located in the original print or electronic source. Students who quote directly from reprinted criticism may use any accepted bibliographic format, such as Modern Language Association (MLA) style or University of Chicago Press style. Both the MLA and the University of Chicago formats are acceptable and recognized as being the current standards for citations. It is important, however, to choose one format for all citations; do not mix the two formats within a list of citations.

The examples below follow recommendations for preparing a works cited list set forth in the Modern Language Association of America's *MLA Handbook for Writers of Research Papers,* 7th ed. (New York: MLA, 2009. Print); the first example pertains to material drawn from periodicals, the second to material reprinted from books:

James, Harold. "Narrative Engagement with *Atonement* and *The Blind Assassin.*" *Philosophy and Literature* 29.1 (2005): 130-45. Rpt. in *Contemporary Literary Criticism.* Ed. Jeffrey W. Hunter. Vol. 246. Detroit: Gale, 2008. 188-95. Print.

Wesley, Marilyn C. "Anne Hébert: The Tragic Melodramas." *Canadian Women Writing Fiction.* Ed. Mickey Pearlman. Jackson: UP of Mississippi, 1993. 41-52. Rpt. in *Contemporary Literary Criticism.* Ed. Jeffrey W. Hunter. Vol. 246. Detroit: Gale, 2008. 276-82. Print.

The examples below follow recommendations for preparing a works cited list set forth in *The Chicago Manual of Style,* 16th ed. (Chicago: The University of Chicago Press, 2010); the first example pertains to material drawn from periodicals, the second to material reprinted from books:

James, Harold. "Narrative Engagement with *Atonement* and *The Blind Assassin.*" *Philosophy and Literature* 29, no. 1 (April 2005): 130-45. Reprinted in *Contemporary Literary Criticism.* Vol. 246, edited by Jeffrey W. Hunter, 188-95. Detroit: Gale, 2008.

Wesley, Marilyn C. "Anne Hébert: The Tragic Melodramas." In *Canadian Women Writing Fiction,* edited by Mickey Pearlman, 41-52. Jackson: University Press of Mississippi, 1993. Reprinted in *Contemporary Literary Criticism.* Vol. 246, edited by Jeffrey W. Hunter, 276-82. Detroit: Gale, 2008.

Suggestions Are Welcome

Readers who wish to suggest new features, topics, or authors to appear in future volumes, or who have other suggestions or comments, are cordially invited to call, write, or fax the Product Manager:

Product Manager, Literary Criticism Series
Gale
Cengage Learning
27500 Drake Road
Farmington Hills, MI 48331-3535
1-800-347-4253 (GALE)
Fax: 248-699-8884

Acknowledgments

The editors wish to thank the copyright holders of the criticism included in this volume and the permissions managers of many book and magazine publishing companies for assisting us in securing reproduction rights. Following is a list of copyright holders who have granted us permission to reproduce material in this volume of *CLC*. Every effort has been made to trace copyright, but if omissions have been made, please let us know.

COPYRIGHTED MATERIAL IN *CLC*, VOLUME 390, WAS REPRODUCED FROM THE FOLLOWING PERIODICALS:

American Book Review, v. 30.6, 2009. Copyright © 2009 *American Book Review.* Reproduced by permission of the publisher. —*Anales de la literatura española contemporánea,* v. 24.1-2, 1999. Copyright © 1999 Society of Spanish and Spanish-American Studies. Reproduced by permission of the publisher.—*Arizona Journal of Hispanic Cultural Studies,* v. 5, 2001. Copyright © 2001 *Arizona Journal of Hispanic Cultural Studies.* Reproduced by permission of the publisher.—*Books Abroad,* v. 35.1, 1961; v. 37.4, 1963. All public domain; v. 41.2, 1967; v. 45.1, 1971. Copyright © 1967, 1971 *Books Abroad.* Both reproduced by permission of the publisher.—*Books in Canada,* v. 9.1, 1980; v. 31.9, 2002. Copyright © 1980, 2002 Canadian Review of Books, Ltd. Both reproduced by permission of the publisher.—*Bulletin of Hispanic Studies,* v. 89.6, 2012. Copyright © 2012 Liverpool University Press. Reproduced by permission of the publisher.—*Canadian Literature,* v. 126, 1990 for "Creation Myths in 'Les grandes marées' by Jacques Poulin" by Paul G. Socken. Copyright © 1990 Paul G. Socken. Reproduced by permission of the author.—*Chasqui,* v. 14.1, 1984; v. 19.2, 1990; v. 25.2, 1996. Copyright © 1984, 1990, 1996 *Chasqui.* All reproduced by permission of the publisher.—*España contemporánea,* v. 19.2, 2006 for "*Dos mujeres en Praga*: The Orphaned Child of Juan José Millás" by Patricia Reagan. Copyright © 2006 Patricia Reagan. Reproduced by permission of the author.—*esprit créateur,* v. 48.1, 2008 for "God the Father or Mother Earth?: *Nouvelle France* in Two Quebec Novels of the 1980s" by Susan L. Rosenstreich. Copyright © 2008 Susan L. Rosenstreich. Reproduced by permission of the author.—*Forum for Modern Language Studies,* v. 35.1, 1999. Copyright © 1999 *Forum for Modern Language Studies.* Reproduced by permission of Oxford University Press.—*French Review,* v. 78.1, 2004; v. 79.5, 2006. Copyright © 2004, 2006 American Association of Teachers of French. Both reproduced by permission of the publisher.—*Gestos,* v. 5.9, 1990. Copyright © 1990 *Gestos.* Reproduced by permission of the publisher.—*Hispanic Journal,* v. 6.1, 1984; v. 10.2, 1989. Copyright © 1984, 1989 IUP Indiana University of Pennsylvania. Both reproduced by permission of *Hispanic Journal.*—*Inti: Revista de Literatura Hispanica,* v. 5-6, 1977. Copyright © 1977 Inti Publications. Reproduced by permission of the publisher.—*Latin American Theatre Review,* v. 10.2, 1977; v. 18.1, 1984; v. 46.2, 2013. Copyright © 1977, 1984, 2013 Center of Latin American Studies, University of Kansas. All reproduced by permission of *Latin American Theatre Review.*—*LittéRéalité,* v. 6.1, 1994. Copyright © 1994 *LittéRéalité.* Reproduced by permission of the publisher.—*Massachusetts Review,* v. 36.3, 1995. Copyright © 1995 *Massachusetts Review.* Reproduced by permission of the publisher.—*Mester,* v. 17.1, 1988 for "Historical and Artistic Self-Consciousness in Carballido's *José Guadalupe (las glorias de Posada)*" by Jacqueline Eyring Bixler. Copyright © 1988 Jacqueline Eyring Bixler. Reproduced by permission of the author.—*MLS: Modern Language Studies,* v. 23.4, 1993 for "Feminist Consciousness in the Novel of Lygia Fagundes Telles" by Cristina Ferreira-Pinto. Copyright © 1993 Cristina Ferreira-Pinto. Reproduced by permission of the author.—*RLA: Romance Languages Annual,* v. 6, 1995; v. 9, 1998. Copyright © 1995, 1998 Purdue Research Foundation. Both reproduced by permission of the publisher.—*Romance Notes,* v. 32.2, 1991; v. 48.3, 2008. Copyright © 1991, 2008 *Romance Notes.* Both reproduced by permission of the publisher.—*Studies in Canadian Literature/Études en littérature canadienne,* v. 18.2, 1993; v. 34.2, 2009. Copyright © 1993, 2009 *Studies in Canadian Literature.* Both reproduced by permission of the publisher.—*World Literature Today,* v. 52.2, 1978. Copyright © 1978 *World Literature Today.* Reproduced by permission of the publisher.

COPYRIGHTED MATERIAL IN *CLC*, VOLUME 390, WAS REPRODUCED FROM THE FOLLOWING BOOKS:

Amago, Samuel. From *True Lies: Narrative Self-Consciousness in the Contemporary Spanish Novel.* Bucknell University Press, 2006. Copyright © 2006 Rosemont Publishing and Printing Corporation. Reproduced by permission of Associated University Presses.—Amago, Samuel. From *Generation X Rocks: Contemporary Peninsular Fiction, Film, and Rock Culture.* Ed. Christine Henseler and Randolph D. Pope. Vanderbilt University Press, 2007. Copyright © 2007 Vanderbilt University

Emilio Carballido
1925-2008

(Full name Emilio Carballido Fentanes) Mexican playwright, screenwriter, novelist, and novella and short-story writer.

INTRODUCTION

Emilio Carballido composed more than one hundred plays that blend elements of realism and fantasy. His works display an affinity for the culture of his native Mexico, his interest in psychology, and his fascination with the nature of human relationships. Alternately humorous and poetic, his plays often critique the institutions and politics of traditional Mexican society. Critics have lauded Carballido for his productivity and versatility, and he is considered a central figure in contemporary Mexican theater.

BIOGRAPHICAL INFORMATION

Carballido was born on 22 May 1925 in Córdoba, a city in the Mexican state of Veracruz, to Francisco Carballido, a railroad worker, and Blanca Rosa Fentanes. His parents separated when he was seven years old, and he and his mother moved to Mexico City, where he lived for most of his life. He learned the art of storytelling from his maternal grandmother, who often regaled him with tales from mythology, the Bible, and Mexican history. When he was thirteen, he returned to Córdoba to live with his father for a year. Provincial society and the nearby sea and jungle had a profound effect on him and strongly influenced his later writings. His father's work with the railroad inspired a fascination with trains, images of which recur throughout his writings as a metaphor for change and adventure.

In 1944 Carballido enrolled as a student of English literature at the Universidad Nacional Autónoma de México (UNAM), located in Mexico City. Several of his fellow students also became successful writers, including Rosario Castellanos, Sergio Magaña, and Luisa Josefina Hernández. Carballido earned both a bachelor's and a master's degree from UNAM and worked as an assistant to Fernando Wagner, a prominent actor and film director. In 1946 or 1947 Carballido completed his first full-length play, *Los dos mundos de Alberta* (may be translated as *The Two Worlds of Alberta*), which was never produced or published. His first play to be published was the experimental *La zona intermedia* (published as *The Intermediate Zone*), which was staged in 1950 and appeared in book form the following year.

Also debuting in 1950 was Carballido's comedy *Rosalba y los Llaveros* (may be translated as *Rosalba and the Llavero Family*), first produced at Mexico City's prestigious Palacio de Bellas Artes. The play's resounding success earned Carballido a grant from the Institute of International Education to study for three months in New York City. In 1953 he began teaching at the University of Veracruz, where he also served as assistant director of the theater department. In 1957 he became public relations adviser for the National Ballet of Mexico, which enabled him to travel extensively and familiarize himself with European avant-garde theater and with traditional Asian theater. In the early 1960s the Japanese government sponsored him for a tour of the Far East, where he lectured and learned about the Japanese dramatic form of Kabuki. Carballido also made several visits to Cuba that strengthened his commitment to writing about social issues.

Carballido continued to travel internationally during the next three decades, and his plays were staged and translated around the world. He served as a visiting professor at the University of Pittsburgh and at California State University, Los Angeles, and became director of the School of Dramatic Art at the National Institute of Fine Arts and Literature in Mexico City. During these years Carballido also founded the journal *Tramoya,* was involved in film projects, and mentored a group of young playwrights known as the Nueva Dramaturgia Mexicana (New Mexican Playwrights). In 2002 he suffered a stroke, but he recovered and continued to work and attend public events. The recipient of nearly every major literary prize offered in Mexico, Carballido was inducted into the Mexican Academy of Arts in 2002. He died of a heart attack on 11 February 2008.

MAJOR WORKS

Carballido's early plays combine elements of *costumbrismo,* in which daily provincial life is treated in a realistic fashion, and the expressionistic, experimental style of such modern European playwrights as Jean Cocteau and August Strindberg. In *The Intermediate Zone,* four recently deceased, semi-human characters wait in a kind of limbo for their final judgment, which is contingent on their ability to prove that they were, in fact, true human beings. Characterized by an ironic tone and witty dialog, the comedy *Rosalba and the Llavero Family* features a cosmopolitan mother-daughter duo who unexpectedly show up at their family's home in rural Otatitlán and attempt to rectify family problems involving an illegitimate daughter. First performed in 1956, *La hebra de oro* (published as *The Golden Thread*) is often described as a transitional work in Carballido's career. In the play two elderly women travel to a remote ranch hoping to find a grandson who disappeared many years ago. A stranger endowed with the ability to recreate time, referred to only as the Man in the Kaftan, arrives via radio beam. The Man in the Kaftan ultimately helps the women relive their past and find closure. Although Carballido used special stage effects and mysterious, otherworldly personages in *The Golden Thread,* its characterizations, setting, and dialog evoke a sense of realism.

For his later works Carballido typically combined poetic elements with humor and social commentary. Regarded as one of his most complex plays, *El día que se soltaron los leones* (1963; published as *The Day They Let the Lions Loose*) is a farce that examines questions of individual psychology and criticizes Mexico's political, social, and educational institutions. Set in Mexico City's Chapultepec Park, the play portrays the existential longings of several characters: a repressed spinster in her sixties, a bored housewife longing for a different life, a would-be poet with a penchant for blackmail, and a professor escorting a group of military-school students. *Las cartas de Mozart* (1975; may be translated as *The Mozart Letters*), juxtaposes the dreariness of nineteenth-century Mexico City with the splendor of late-eighteenth-century Europe. A young shopkeeper, Margarita, eager to avoid marrying an older man, uses her entire inheritance to buy several letters written by composer Wolfgang Amadeus Mozart. She and her friend Martín then run away to Europe together. Praised for its poetic use of sea imagery, *Fotografía en la playa* (1979; may be translated as *Photograph on the Beach*) features four generations of a family brought together for a single afternoon on a beach. In its exploration of family tensions and individuals' inner lives, the play depicts various members' attempts to free themselves from family obligations and pressures. The grandmother, believed by her family to be senile, proves to be the only character capable of discerning the real issues concealed under the facade of family unity.

Yo también hablo de la rosa (1966; published as *I Too Speak of the Rose*) has inspired much critical commentary for its innovative style and dense thematic framework. The play concerns a train derailment unintentionally caused by two working-class adolescents exploring a garbage dump while playing hooky from school. Different characters narrate and examine the accident, providing Marxist, Freudian, scientific, and mythological interpretations. The play's structure undermines the concept of a master narrative and suggests that attempts to explain history are bound to be misguided. The monologs presented by the play's main narrator, an enigmatic native woman called the Intermedia, structure the play and provide an intuitive point of view that stresses the mystery inherent in human behavior.

Carballido's diverse body of work also includes *Tiempo de ladrones* (1984; may be translated as *A Time of Thieves*), which focuses on subjects from Mexican history and myth, as well as *Teseo* (1962; published as *Theseus*) and *Medusa* (1966), which treat themes from classical mythology. In addition, he wrote several plays for children, which are collected in *Tres obras para jóvenes* (1998; may be translated as *Three Works for Young People*). Carballido also wrote screenplays, nonfiction works, a short-story collection titled *La caja vacía* (1962; may be translated as *The Empty Box*), and several novellas, of which *El norte* (1958; published as *The Norther*) is generally regarded as his best.

CRITICAL RECEPTION

Carballido's status as a pioneer of contemporary Mexican theater stems from his popularity, his prolific creativity and his influence on younger playwrights. Mexican theater before Carballido tended to be conservative and traditional; he and other dramatists of his generation introduced audiences to the modern themes and technical innovations of European drama. Margaret S. Peden (1968; see Further Reading) discussed how *The Golden Thread* and several of Carballido's other plays employ the experimental ideas of French dramatist Antonin Artaud. Karen Peterson (1977) connected the work of French philosopher and playwright Jean-Paul Sartre to the existentialist themes in Carballido's plays informed by classical mythology, such as *Theseus* and *Medusa.*

Assessments of Carballido's style frequently emphasize the close relationship between form and content in his works. Jacqueline Eyring Bixler (1984) offered a reading of *Photograph on the Beach* and *Un vals sin fin por el planeta* (1970; may be translated as *An Endless Waltz around the Planet*), praising Carballido's ability to match structure, language, and imagery to his thematic intent. Focusing on this same topic in relation to *I Too Speak of the Rose,* Matthew Tremé (2013) observed how the multiple retellings of the train derailment extend Carballido's theme of interpretation and demonstrate the political repercussions of how and by whom a story is reported. In a 1985 essay (see Further Reading), Bixler asserted that Carballido invites the audience "to participate in the production of the work's meaning by challenging it to formulate the conceptual link between the diverse levels of reality."

Carballido's social commentary has been a significant focus for scholars. Eugene R. Skinner (1976) examined several of Carballido's plays to determine the playwright's ideas about the role of art and the artist in society. Discussing three short stories from *The Empty Box,* James J. Troiano (1989) suggested that imagination functions in the tales to provide characters with a means of escaping from their monotonous and painful daily existence. Diana Taylor (1991) analyzed the social critique of Mexican institutions and power structures in *The Day They Let the Lions Loose* and *I Too Speak of the Rose,* contending that the plays treat "culture as an arena for ideological debate." Analyzing *Rosalba and the Llavero Family* and *The Day They Let the Lions Loose* in terms of Carballido's "provocative social critique of patriarchal discourse," Sandra Messinger Cypess (1984) concentrated on women's usurpation of male discourse as a form of rebellion against repressive social values.

Jelena Krstovic

PRINCIPAL WORKS

El triángulo sutil [may be translated as *The Subtle Triangle*]. El Teatro de Recámara, Mexico City. 1948. Performance. (Play)

La triple porfía [may be translated as *The Triple Dispute*]. Aula José Martí, Universidad Nacional Autónoma de México, Mexico City. 1948. Performance. (Play)

Rosalba y los Llaveros [may be translated as *Rosalba and the Llavero Family*]. Palacio de Bellas Artes, Mexico City. 11 Mar. 1950. Performance. (Play)

Escribir, por ejemplo [may be translated as *To Write, for Example*]. Teatro del Caracol, Mexico City. Sept. 1950. Performance. (Play)

La zona intermedia [published as *The Intermediate Zone*]. Teatro Latino, Mexico City. Sept. 1950. Performance. (Play)

La zona intermedia: Auto sacramental y "Escribir, por ejemplo" [may be translated as *The Intermediate Zone: Eucharistic Play and "To Write, for Example"*]. Mexico City: Unión Nacional de Autores, 1951. Print. (Plays)

Felicidad [may be translated as *Happiness*]. Auditorio Reforma, Mexico City. 10 Apr. 1955. Performance. Pub. as *Felicidad: Obra de teatro en tres actos y un epílogo* [may be translated as *Happiness: A Work of Theater in Three Acts and an Epilog*]. Ed. Myra S. Gann. Potsdam: Danzón, 1999. Print. (Play)

Las palabras cruzadas [may be translated as *The Crossword*]. Teatro de la Comedia, Mexico City. June 1955. Performed as *La danza que sueña la tortuga* [may be translated as *The Dance of Which the Turtle Dreams*]. Xalapa, 1955. Performance. Pub. as "La danza que sueña la tortuga." *Teatro mexicano del siglo XX.* Ed. Celestino Gorostiza. Vol. 3. Mexico City: Fondo de Cultura Económica, 1956. Print. (Play)

La hebra de oro [published as *The Golden Thread*]. Auditorio Reforma, Mexico City. 1956. Performance. (Play)

La veleta oxidada [may be translated as *The Rusty Weathercock*]. Mexico City: Los Presentes, 1956. Print. (Novella)

D.F.: 9 obras en un acto [may be translated as *D.F.: 9 One-Act Works*]. Mexico City: Helio México, 1957. Expanded ed. *D.F.: 14 obras en un acto* [may be translated as *D.F.: 14 One-Act Works*]. Xalapa: U Veracruzana, 1962. Expanded ed. *D.F.: 26 obras en un acto* [may be translated as *D.F.: 26 One-Act Works*]. Mexico City: Grijalbo, 1978. Print. (Plays)

La hebra de oro: Auto sacramental en tres jornadas [published as *The Golden Thread*]. Mexico City: Imprenta Universitaria, 1957. Print. (Play)

El norte [published as *The Norther*]. Xalapa: U Veracruzana, 1958. Print. (Novella)

Homenaje a Hidalgo [may be translated as *Homage to Hidalgo*]. Palacio de Bellas Artes, Mexico City. Sept. 1960. Performance. (Play)

Las estatuas de marfil [may be translated as *The Ivory Statues*]. Teatro Basurto, Mexico City. 4 Nov. 1960. Performance. Xalapa: U Veracruzana, 1960. Print. (Play)

El relojero de Córdoba [published as *The Clockmaker from Córdoba*]. El Teatro del Bosque, Mexico City. 11 Nov. 1960. Performance. (Play)

Macario. Adapt. Emilio Carballido and Roberto Gavaldón from "The Third Guest," by B. Traven. Clasa Films Mundiales, 1960. Film. (Screenplay)

*Teatro [may be translated as *Theater*]. Mexico City: Fondo de Cultura Económica, 1960. Print. (Plays)

Trilogía de obras en un acto [may be translated as *Trilogy of Works in One Act*]. Mexico City: Imprenta Universitaria, 1960. Print. (Plays)

Teseo [published as *Theseus*]. Teatro Xola, Mexico City. 19 Oct. 1962. Performance. (Play)

La caja vacía [may be translated as *The Empty Box*]. Mexico City: Fondo de Cultura Económica, 1962. Print. (Short stories)

Un pequeño día de ira [may be translated as *A Short Day's Anger*]. Havana. 15 Aug. 1966. Performance. Havana: Casa de las Américas, 1962. Print. (Play)

El día que se soltaron los leones [published as *The Day They Let the Lions Loose*]. Teatro El Sótano, Havana. June 1963. Performance. (Play)

¡Silencio, pollos pelones, ya les van a echar su maíz! [may be translated as *Be Quiet, You Mangy Chickens, You're Going to Get Your Corn!*]. Teatro del Seguro Social, Ciudad Juárez. 28 Aug. 1963. Performance. (Play)

Las visitaciones del diablo [may be translated as *The Visitations of the Devil*]. Mexico City: Mortiz, 1965. Print. (Novel)

Medusa. Cornell University Theater, Ithaca, 14 Apr. 1966. Performance. Pub. as *Medusa: Obra en cinco actos* [may be translated as *Medusa: A Work in Five Acts*]. Ed. Jeanine Gaucher-Schultz and Alfredo Morales. Englewood Cliffs: Prentice-Hall, 1972. Print. (Play)

Yo también hablo de la rosa [published as *I Too Speak of the Rose*]. Teatro Jiménez Rueda, Mexico City. 16 Apr. 1966. Performance. Mexico City: Instituto Nacional de Bellas Artes, 1966. Print. (Play)

Te juro, Juana, que tengo ganas [may be translated as *I Swear to You, Juana, That I Wanna*]. Monterrey. June 1967. Performance. (Play)

Selaginela. With Gerardo Garza Fausti. Producciones Cinematográfica Teens, 1967. Film. (Screenplay)

Las noticias del día: Coloquio [may be translated as *The News of the Day: Dialog*]. Mexico City: Colección Teatro de Bolsillo, 1968. Print. (Play)

Almanaque de Juárez [may be translated as *The Juárez Almanac*]. Teatro del Bosque, Mexico City. Apr. 1969. Performance. Pub. as *Almanaque de Juárez: Obra en un acto* [may be translated as *The Juárez Almanac: Work in One Act*]. Monterrey: Sierra Madre, 1972. Print. (Play)

Acapulco, los lunes [may be translated as *Acapulco Mondays*]. Teatro Antonio Caso, Mexico City. 30 June 1970. Performance. Pub. as *Acapulco, los lunes: Pieza en un acto* [may be translated as *Acapulco Mondays: Piece in One Act*]. Monterrey: Sierra Madre, 1969. Print. (Play)

Te juro, Juana, que tengo ganas; Yo también hablo de la rosa [may be translated as *I Swear to You, Juana, That I Wanna; I Too Speak of the Rose*]. Mexico City: Novaro, 1970. Print. (Plays)

Un vals sin fin por el planeta [may be translated as *An Endless Waltz around the Planet*]. Teatro Orientación, Mexico City. 1970. Performance. (Play)

Conversation among the Ruins. Trans. Myra Gann. Kalamazoo College, Michigan, 1971. Performed as *Conversación entre las ruinas.* Casa de la Paz, Mexico City. 1989. Performance. (Play)

Felicidad; Un pequeño día de ira [may be translated as *Happiness; A Short Day's Anger*]. Mexico City: UNAM, 1971. Print. (Plays)

Los novios [may be translated as *The Bride and Groom*]. With Gilberto Gazcón. Cinematográfica Jalisco S.A., 1971. Film. (Screenplay)

Teatro joven de México [may be translated as *Young Mexican Theater*]. Ed. Carballido. Mexico City: Novaro, 1973. Print. (Plays)

El arca de Noé: Antología y apostillas de teatro infantil [may be translated as *Noah's Ark: Anthology and Annotations on Children's Theater*]. Ed. Carballido. Mexico City: Secretaría de Educación, 1974. Print. (Children's plays)

Las cartas de Mozart [may be translated as *The Mozart Letters*]. Teatro Jiménez Rueda, Mexico City. 30 Oct. 1975. Performance. (Play)

La güera Rodríguez [may be translated as *The Blonde Rodríguez*]. With Julio Alejandro. Conacite Uno, 1978. Film. (Screenplay)

Tres obras [may be translated as *Three Works*]. Mexico City: Extemporáneos, 1978. Print. (Plays)

Te juro, Juana, que tengo ganas; Yo también hablo de la rosa; Fotografía en la playa [may be translated as *I Swear to You, Juana, That I Wanna; I Too Speak of the Rose; Photograph on the Beach*]. Mexico City: Mexicanos Unidos, 1979. Print. (Plays)

D.F./Distrito Federal. Conacite Uno, 1981. Film. (Screenplay)

†*Tres comedias* [may be translated as *Three Comedies*]. Mexico City: Extemporáneos, 1981. Print. (Plays)

Orinoco. Teatro Gorostiza, Mexico City. 9 Sept. 1982. Performance. (Play)

Más teatro joven de México [may be translated as *More Young Mexican Theater*]. Ed. Carballido. Mexico City: Mexicanos Unidos, 1982. Print. (Plays)

‡*A la epopeya, un gajo: 5 obras dramáticas* [may be translated as *To the Epic, a Segment: 5 Dramatic Works*]. Toluca: U Autónoma del Estado de México, 1983. Print. (Plays)

Tiempo de ladrones [may be translated as *A Time of Thieves*]. Teatro Jiménez Rueda, Mexico City. 1984. Performance. Pub. as *Tiempo de ladrones: La historia de Chucho el Roto* [may be translated as *A Time of Thieves: The History of Chucho el Roto*]. Mexico City: Grijalbo, 1983. Print. (Play)

Fotografía en la playa [may be translated as *Photograph on the Beach*]. Casa de la Paz, Mexico City. Oct. 1984. Performance. (Play)

El tren que corría [may be translated as *The Train That Ran*]. Mexico City: Fondo de Cultura Popular, 1984. Print. (Play)

Ceremonia en el templo del tigre [may be translated as *Ceremony in the Temple of the Tiger*]. Teatro Orientación, Mexico City. 5 Dec. 1985. Performance. Pub. as *Ceremonia en el templo del tigre: Una ficción profética* [may be translated as *Ceremony in the Temple of the Tiger: A Prophetic Fiction*]. Mexico City: Plaza y Valdés, 1994. Print. (Play)

9 obras jóvenes [may be translated as *9 Young Works*]. Ed. Carballido. Mexico City: Mexicanos Unidos, 1985. Print. (Plays)

Orinoco; Las cartas de Mozart; Felicidad [may be translated as *Orinoco; The Mozart Letters; Happiness*]. Mexico City: Mexicanos Unidos, 1985. Print. (Plays)

¡Silencio, pollos pelones, ya les van a echar su maíz!; Un pequeño día de ira; Acapulco, los lunes [may be translated as *Be Quiet, You Mangy Chickens, You're Going to Get Your Corn!; A Short Day's Anger; Acapulco Mondays*]. Mexico City: Mexicanos Unidos, 1985. Print. (Plays)

Teatro para obreros: Antología [may be translated as *Theater for Laborers: Anthology*]. Ed. Carballido. Mexico City: Mexicanos Unidos, 1985. Print. (Plays)

13 veces el D.F. [may be translated as *13 Times the D.F.*]. Mexico City: Mexicanos Unidos, 1985. Pub. as *D.F. Nueva serie: 13 obras en un acto* [may be translated as *D.F. New Series: 13 Works in One Act*]. Mexico City: Grijalbo, 1994. Print. (Plays)

Rosa de dos aromas [published as *A Rose, by Any Other Names*]. Teatro Coyoacán, Mexico City. 18 July 1986. Performance. (Play)

Ceremonia en el templo del tigre; Rosa de dos aromas; Un pequeño día de ira [may be translated as *Ceremony in the Temple of the Tiger; A Rose, by Any Other Names; A Short Day's Anger*]. Mexico City: Mexicanos Unidos, 1986. Print. (Plays)

Vicente y Ramona [may be translated as *Vicente and Ramona*]. Teatro Hidalgo, Colima. 1986. Performance. Colima: Gobierno del Estado de Colima, 1998. Print. (Play)

El censo [may be translated as *The Census*]. Caracas: CELCIT, 1987. Print. (Play)

§*Teatro 2* [may be translated as *Theater 2*]. Mexico City: Fondo de Cultura Económica, 1988. Print. (Plays)

Los esclavos de Estambul [may be translated as *Slaves of Istambul*]. Teatro del Bosque/Julio Castillo, Mexico City. July 1991. Performance. (Play)

La historia de Sputnik y David [may be translated as *The History of Sputnik and David*]. Mexico City: Fondo de Cultura Económica, 1991. Print. (Children's fiction)

La veleta oxidada; El norte; Un error de estilo [may be translated as *The Rusty Weathercock; The Norther; An Error of Style*]. Mexico City: Consejo Nacional para la Cultura y las Artes, 1991. Print. (Novellas)

Teatro de Emilio Carballido [may be translated as *Theater of Emilio Carballido*]. 2 vols. Veracruz: Gobierno del Estado de Veracruz, 1992. Print. (Plays)

Escrito en el cuerpo de la noche [may be translated as *Written on the Body of the Night*]. Teatro Juan Ruiz de Alarcón, Guadalajara. 1994. Performance. (Play)

Flor de abismo [may be translated as *Flower of the Abyss*]. Mexico City: Planeta, 1994. Print. (Novel)

Fotografía en la playa; Soñar la noche; Las cartas de Mozart [may be translated as *Photograph on the Beach; Dreaming the Night; The Mozart Letters*]. Mexico City: Gaceta, 1994. Print. (Plays)

Loros en emergencias [may be translated as *Parrots in Emergencies*]. Mexico City: Fondo de Cultura Económica, 1994. Print. (Children's fiction)

‖*Orinoco, Rosa de dos aromas y otras piezas dramáticas* [may be translated as *Orinoco, A Rose, by Any Other Names, and Other Dramatic Pieces*]. Mexico City: Fondo de Cultura Económica, 1994. Print. (Plays)

Pasaporte con estrellas [may be translated as *Passport with Stars*]. Teatro J. J. Herrera, Xalapa. 21 Oct. 1995. Performance. (Play)

La prisionera [may be translated as *The Prisoner*]. Foro Sor Juana Inés de la Cruz, Mexico City. 11 May 2002. Performance. Tijuana: Caen, 1995. Print. (Play)

Un enorme animal nube [may be translated as *An Enormous Animal Cloud*]. Mexico City: Fondo de Cultura Económica, 1996. Print. (Children's fiction)

El mar y sus misterios [may be translated as *The Sea and Its Mysteries*]. El Teatro del Bosque, Mexico City. 1996. Performance. (Play)

Matrimonio, mortaja y a quien le baja; Las bodas de San Isidro [may be translated as *Marriage, a Shroud and Whom It Diminishes; The Weddings of Saint Isidore*]. Xalapa: U Veracruzana, 1996. Print. (Plays)

Mañanas de abril y mayo [may be translated as *Tomorrows of April and May*]. With Luisa Josefina Hernández. Teatro Orientación, Mexico City. Apr. 1997. Performance. (Play)

Engaño colorido con títeres; Pasaporte con estrellas [may be translated as *Colorful Deceit with Puppets; Passport with Stars*]. Xalapa: U Veracruzana, 1997. Print. (Plays)

Luminaria [may be translated as *Luminary*]. Casa de la Paz, Mexico City. 18 June 1998. Performance. (Play)

Tejer la ronda: 16 obras en un acto [may be translated as *Knitting the Round: 16 Works in One Act*]. Mexico City: Grijalbo, 1998. Print. (Plays)

#*Tres obras para jóvenes* [may be translated as *Three Works for Young People*]. Veracruz: Instituto Veracruzano de Cultura, 1998. Print. (Plays)

Luminaria; Zorros chinos; y La prisionera [may be translated as *Luminary; Chinese Foxes; and The Prisoner*]. Xalapa: U Veracruzana, 2000. Print. (Plays)

El tigre rojo: Drama cinematográfico [may be translated as *The Red Tiger: Cinematographic Drama*]. With Fernando Espejo and Federico Chao. Mérida: U Autónoma de Yucatán, 2000. Print. (Screenplay)

Vicente y Ramona; Algunos cantos del infierno; Las flores del recuerdo [may be translated as *Vicente and Ramona; A Few Songs from Hell; The Flowers of Memory*]. Xalapa: U Veracruzana, 2000. Print. (Plays)

Las manchas en la luna [may be translated as *Blotches on the Moon*]. Teatro La Caja, Xalapa. 1 Apr. 2001. Performance. (Play)

Egeo (el guardagujas) [may be translated as *Aegean (the Switchman)*]. Mexico City: Consejo Nacional para la Cultura y las Artes, 2001. Print. (Novel)

Zorros chinos [may be translated as *Chinese Foxes*]. Teatro Villaurrutia, Mexico City. 2001. Performance. (Play)

Dos llaves y una lanza [may be translated as *Two Keys and a Lance*]. Mexico City: Mexicanos Unidos, 2002. Print. (Novel)

Un error de estilo [may be translated as *An Error of Style*]. Mexico City: Mexicanos Unidos, 2002. Print. (Novella)

Escrito en el cuerpo de la noche [may be translated as *Written on the Body of the Night*]. With Jaime Humberto Hermosillo. Instituto Mexicano de Cinematográfica, 2002. Film. (Screenplay)

El pabellón del doctor Leñaverde [may be translated as *The Pavilion of the Doctor Leñaverde*]. Mexico City: Santillana, 2002. Print. (Children's fiction)

Taller Colima: Seis obras dramáticas [may be translated as *Colima Workshop: Six Dramatic Works*]. Ed. Carballido. Colima: Gobierno del Estado de Colima, 2002. Print. (Plays)

Venus-Quetzalcóatl y cinco cuentos [may be translated as *Venus-Quetzalcóatl and Five Stories*]. Mexico City: Mexicanos Unidos, 2002. Print. (Short stories)

Principal English Translations

The Norther. Trans. Margaret Sayers Peden. Austin: U of Texas P, 1968. Print. Trans. of *El norte.*

**The Golden Thread and Other Plays.* Trans. Peden. Austin: U of Texas P, 1970. Print.

"The Day They Let the Lions Loose." Trans. William I. Oliver. *Voices of Change in the Spanish American Theater: An Anthology.* Ed. and trans. Oliver. Austin: U of Texas P, 1971. 1-46. Print. Trans. of *El día que se soltaron los leones.*

"I Too Speak of the Rose." Trans. Oliver. *The Modern Stage in Latin America: Six Plays.* Ed. George William Woodyard. New York: Dutton, 1971. 289-331. Print. Trans. of *Yo también hablo de la rosa.*

"*Orinoco!* A Play in Two Acts." Trans. Peden. *Latin American Literary Review* 11.23 (1983): 51-83. Print.

"A Rose, by Any Other Names." Trans. Peden. *Modern International Drama* 22.1 (1988): 6-29. Print. Trans. of *Rosa de dos aromas.*

*Includes *The Clockmaker from Córdoba, Rosalba and the Llavero Family,* and *The Day They Let the Lions Loose.*

†Includes *An Endless Waltz around the Planet.*

‡Includes *Homage to Hidalgo* and *Theseus.*

§Includes *The Ivory Statues.*

‖Includes *The Sea and Its Mysteries, Written on the Body of the Night,* and *Slaves of Istanbul.*

#Includes *Tomorrows of April and May.*

**Comprises *The Intermediate Zone, The Clockmaker from Córdoba,* and *Theseus.*

CRITICISM

Helen Rosemary Cole (review date 1961)

SOURCE: Cole, Helen Rosemary. Rev. of *The Norther,* by Emilio Carballido. *Books Abroad* 35.1 (1961): 71. Print.

[*In the following review, Cole provides a plot summary of* The Norther *and characterizes Carballido as a writer "with a good deal of skill."*]

This novel is number three of the attractively illustrated, beautifully printed fiction series of Universidad Veracruzana. Its protagonist, Aristeo, is an opportunistic youngster who frees himself from his undesirable family by turning gigolo. Traveling with his elderly mistress he meets the seashore, comfort, even modest luxury, then complications, and ultimately a moment of liberation from the generous widow and his total past.

Emilio Carballido may offer Françoise Sagan some fair competition. He, too, writes with a good deal of skill.

Manuel Durán (review date 1961)

SOURCE: Durán, Manuel. Rev. of *Teatro,* by Emilio Carballido. *Books Abroad* 35.1 (1961): 172. Print.

[*In the following review, Durán proclaims Carballido as "one of the three most promising young Mexican playwrights." He considers* Medusa *the most ambitious and* Rosalba and the Llavero Family *the most successful of the plays in* Teatro *(1960; may be translated as* Theater*).*]

Emilio Carballido is one of the three most promising young Mexican playwrights (the other two being Sergio Magaña and Héctor Azar). The plays included in this edition (***El relojero de Córdoba, Medusa, Rosalba y los llaveros, El día que se soltaron los leones***) are witty, fast-paced, highly professional. The most ambitious play in this collection is ***Medusa,*** a Mexican recreation of a Greek theme, but by far the most successful play (from the literary viewpoint as well as in terms of box office success) is ***Rosalba y los llaveros,*** one of the best comedies written in Mexico and which, if properly edited, should become an excellent textbook for intermediate Spanish.

Gregory Rabassa (review date 1961)

SOURCE: Rabassa, Gregory. Rev. of *Las estatuas de marfil,* by Emilio Carballido. *Books Abroad* 35.1 (1961): 273-74. Print.

[*In the following review, Rabassa identifies "the ancient battle between the 'practical man' and the artist" as a central theme of* Las estatuas de marfil *(1960; may be translated as* The Ivory Statues*). For Rabassa, the ending leaves a "feeling of futility" and a "sense of fate."*]

More than a "play within a play," this work is really a study of the Mexican theater by means of a dramatic work itself. It deals with an amateur group in the provinces under the direction of a young playwright. Despite the many snide remarks made by the director about the state of the theater in Mexico City, this aspect of the play does not really come off. A more vital theme is the ancient battle between the "practical man" and the artist. The husband of the leading lady is a labor organizer who is opposed to her participation in the small dramatic group. His ultimate weapon is parenthood, and he sees to it that she becomes pregnant and thus cannot perform for the benefit of visiting critics from the capital. The title is derived from a game played by a hanger-on, which consists of assuming the pose of a statue, while the onlookers must guess the material. This ridiculous person really gives us the theme of the play, which deals with the question of role. At the end Sabina, the heroine, realizes that her role is not in the theater and becomes resigned to her position as wife and mother. One has a certain feeling of futility at the end and a sense of fate and circumstance in the determination of one's role.

Pierre Courtines (review date 1963)

SOURCE: Courtines, Pierre. Rev. of *The Empty Box,* by Emilio Carballido. *Books Abroad* 37.4 (1963): 433. Print.

[*In the following review, Courtines provides a generally positive review of* The Empty Box, *arguing that Carballido portrays "the lives, aspirations, happy and sad moments among poor folks as well as lower middle class Mexican families in unusual circumstances."*]

Its title notwithstanding, this book is a collection of ten short stories reflecting the lives, aspirations, happy and sad moments among poor folks as well as lower middle class Mexican families in unusual circumstances. We contemplate the activities, daily or extra-conjugal, of married couples and their efforts to maintain a good front; we encounter honest and not so honest characters. The reader has access to the lovely dreams and illusions of childhood. This volume possesses dramatic as well as stylistic qualities and brings to the fore the literary gifts of its author.

Donald A. Yates (review date 1967)

SOURCE: Yates, Donald A. Rev. of *Las visitaciones del diablo,* by Emilio Carballido. *Books Abroad* 41.2 (1967): 199-200. Print.

[*In the following review, Yates praises* Las visitaciones del diablo *(1965; may be translated as* The Visitations of the Devil*) but calls the novel "a bit too hazy at times to be completely satisfying."*]

There is deception and some mystification in the subtitle which the noted Mexican dramatist, Emilio Carballido, has given to this his third novel. He calls it "Folletín romántico en XV partes." The folletinesque nature of ***Las visitaciones del diablo*** is slight indeed, possibly little more than the explanatory titles applied to the chapters: I. "Paloma: Su llegada a las seis de la tarde"; VI. "Una visita a la fábrica. Regreso en coche, con Paloma." Removing the narrative even further from the realm of the "folletín" is the concise style and the tight control over the prose exercised by Carballido.

Paloma's abbreviated stay at the home of her grandmother and aunt and uncle, the account of her relationship with Lisardo, a nephew of her uncle who comes to live there, the hovering specter of a presence which certain persons in the family believe to be diabolic, are, to be sure, romantic in conception; but they are much too artistically and economically handled to be confused with what is suggested by the adjective in the term "folletín romántico."

The mystification stems from the function Carballido has assigned to his specter of the Devil. This function is not clear, and it should be. The pale and, in one instance, sexually aggressive "thing" that appears and reappears at the house ought to have some specific mien and mission—oneiric, fantastic, psychological, supernatural, or what have you. Lamentably, we cannot pin it down, for Carballido has not given us the subtle artistic hints which allow us to turn the last page and lay the book down, saying, "Of course. *That's* what it was!" It is an interesting performance, though.

Carballido's ***Las visitaciones del diablo*** is much too good to be a "folletín romántico," but a bit too hazy at times to be completely satisfying.

Eric Sellin (review date 1971)

SOURCE: Sellin, Eric. Rev. of *The Golden Thread and Other Plays,* by Emilio Carballido. *Books Abroad* 45.1 (1971): 671. Print.

[*In the following review, Sellin focuses on the surreal elements that "fall naturally within Carballido's purview" and argues that the playwright's work offers "a rich and stirring dramatic experience."*]

A good representation of the work of Mexican playwright Emilio Carballido is now made available to the English-speaking world in the collection entitled ***The Golden Thread and Other Plays,*** translated into good idiomatic English by Margaret Peden. After reading these plays, I wondered how I had gotten along without Carballido all these years, having to make do with pale substitutes like Strindberg, Cocteau, and Ionesco.

In the six plays presented—***The Mirror, The Time and the Place*** (a trilogy), ***The Golden Thread, The Intermediate Zone, The Clockmaker from Córdoba,*** and ***Theseus***—we have a certain consistency of mood which the translator assures us is the trademark of the playwright. In the grotesque surreal world of Carballido, the shadow of death comes and goes with the easy familiarity of an uncle. Relativity, that yardstick of death, forms the dimension and the décor of Carballido's work. For example, in one play, memories come to life in corporeal form, justified logically by the device of a body's preservation in a glacier, and the memories are "consummated" in an eerie representation of necrophilia. The surreal seems to fall naturally within Carballido's purview. His vision accommodates reality, death, and miracles with the same ease with which the Mexican mind reconciles Catholic and Mixtec views of mortality, immortality, and ritual.

Some of Carballido's dreams present substantial challenges to the *metteur en scène.* For instance, the brilliant idea of having time's passage and one's past states of being theatrically rendered by a proliferation of empty skins which are flat and inert one moment but then get up and move about would fail dismally unless correctly implemented.

Carballido's plays read well and—properly produced—surely would provide a rich and stirring dramatic experience in which catharsis might be achieved on both rational and physical levels in a reconciliation of Aristotle and Artaud.

Eugene R. Skinner (essay date 1976)

SOURCE: Skinner, Eugene R. "The Theater of Emilio Carballido: Spinning a Web." *Dramatists in Revolt: The New Latin American Theater.* Ed. Leon F. Lyday and George W. Woodyard. Austin: U of Texas P, 1976. 19-36. Print.

[*In the following essay, Skinner comments on the significance of Carballido's dramatic technique of creating a web of human relationships and discusses the playwright's views on the function of art and the artist. He examines several of Carballido's plays in this light, including* The Intermediate Zone, Rosalba and the Llavero Family, The Golden Thread, *and* I Too Speak of the Rose.]

Emilio Carballido has proved to be one of Mexico's most accomplished writers. He has published outstanding works in both the dramatic and narrative genres, beginning with ***La zona intermedia*** (1948) and extending to his recent short novel ***El sol*** (1970). His work has been recognized nationally and internationally through literary awards, fellowships, tenure of academic positions, and critical studies.[1] His dramatic career coincides with the rapid growth of Mexican theater following World War II, and Margaret S. Peden has identified Carballido's major contribution as the introduction and consistent implementation of "a kind of theatre that may be called fantastic, poetic, surrealistic—or simply non-realistic . . . plays that transcend the specifically realistic and restrictively Mexican to achieve a theatre that can be called modern contemporary and universal."[2] The majority of his plays employ twentieth century Mexico as a scenario; however, this specific reality serves primarily as the raw material from which he fashions a universal image of man. The aim of this study is to define that image, outline its development, and relate it to the techniques employed in its representation. Emphasis will be given to five plays. ***La zona intermedia*** and ***Rosalba y los Llaveros*** exemplify tendencies in his earliest works. ***La hebra de oro*** marks a significant change in his representation of reality, which is further developed in ***Silencio, pollos pelones, ya les van a echar su maíz*** and ***Yo también hablo de la rosa.***

La zona intermedia (***The Intermediate Zone***), Carballido's first published work, affords a concise allegorical image of man. The action of this one-act *auto,* a variant of the traditional morality play concerning Final Judgment, takes place in a spiritual limbo in which the final disposition of "inhumans" is determined. The First Assistant of the Intermediate Zone formulates the distinction between human and inhuman: "Potential, *and* man. He must choose between one thing and another, realizing the worthwhile, rejecting what is not worthwhile. He has a powerful weapon, pain, and he polishes it with the tears of his decisions. ... Man can close his ears to his vocation for something worthy, or something unworthy. He can live between two worlds. He can do evil or good incidentally, unconsciously, like a weak little animal. Then he is lost. He has ceased to be a man." (***The Intermediate Zone,*** pp. 129-130).[3] This concept reveals a basic existentialist position: human existence is equated with potentiality. Unlike an animal that simply *is,* man exists and must create his own being through a process of conscious election. These decisions are made in anguish and suffering, face to face with his ignorance and his limitations. The failure to accept fully this responsibility results in an inhuman existence.

Four mortals are brought into the Zone: the Critic, the Woman, the Little Man, and the Virgin. Each has become an effective theatrical image of an aspect of inhuman existence. These images occupy the extremes of two conceptual axes:

	REASON	FEELING
Active	Critic	Woman
Passive	Little Man	Virgin

All four modes of behavior preclude an authentic existence. Later a fifth character, the Nahual, enters the Zone.

The image of the Critic corresponds to the active overevaluation of a single aspect of human potentiality. He has spent his life criticizing with "impartial reason" the creations of others. With the detachment of an immortal observer, he imposes a rational order on reality that results in his separation from creative participation in existence. He assumes the form of the works that he has judged, a ridiculous mixture of cubist painting and sculpture. Towards the end, he is devoured by the Nahual.

The Woman is characterized as having a mixture of human and feline features. She represents overevaluation of feeling, specifically libidinous desire, which imposes a subjective view on the world converting others into mere objects for satiating her passion. She confesses: "I lost everything human. I was no longer a woman; I was a walking sore, a beast, anything except a woman. I wanted to tear him to pieces" (*The Intermediate Zone,* pp. 133-134). Recognizing that her lover suffered a passion equal to her own, she repents her inhuman condition and finally is considered worthy to proceed to Final Judgment.

The Little Man is old, short, fat, timid, and vacillating. His subservient behavior suggests a defense mechanism against the violence of the world. Within the context of the play, he stands at the opposite extreme to the Critic: whereas the Critic imposed a rational order on the world, the Little Man accepts and bows before any order or will that he encounters. His hiding behind convention results not only in an inauthentic existence, but it also fails to protect him from the world. The Devil asks him if the idea of going to Hell "displeases" him, and he cannot refuse the invitation. Using empty formulas of excessive courtesy, he attempts to avoid conflict and suffering. The Devil simply has him bodily carried off to Hell, and, as he exits, the Devil labels him "amorphous matter," an unrealized potentiality.

The Virgin enters dressed in white and carrying a lily. She, like the Little Man, has avoided active participation in existence. Her life remains uncontaminated, removed from the consciousness of human limitations and indifferent to the desire to overcome these limitations. She has become a passive reflection of nature. She remains in the Intermediate Zone, to fade away slowly and without suffering like the inanimate flower that she has become.

The Nahual is neither human nor inhuman, but rather a curious anachronism: a Mexican Adam before the Fall, completely unconscious of good and evil. His body—half coyote and half human—suggests that his image is fabricated from elements of the Aztec trickster figure, Ueuecoyotl, and from elements of the biblical Adam. His entrance into the Zone is caused by having eaten the Little Man and been unable to digest the crucifix that his victim had been wearing. The act is symbolic of his confrontation with an institutionalized system of values—good vs. evil—that stands in opposition to his previous mode of existence, which was governed by the less abstract polarity of pleasure vs. pain. A further transformation occurs when he ingests the Critic, who tastes like "green apples." The Nahual becomes ill, suffers, and is transformed into the "New Man," Adam after the Fall. Then he is given the opportunity to return to Earth and to create his own human existence.

This contemporary adaptation of the morality play provides a series of images central to the development of Carballido's theater and his most explicit evaluation of the human situation. Of the four mortal types of inauthentic existence, only the Woman possesses any redeeming value. Since she represents libidinous desire, it is evident that the playwright recognizes the primacy of this vital force. With only minor modification, he allows her to proceed to Final Judgment. The other three mortals (Critic, Little Man, and Virgin) are fixed types, incapable of transformation, and are condemned. The Nahual-New Man becomes the central and exemplary figure by virtue of the immensity of his transformation and the degree to which he integrates the other four images. The immortal Nahual, as Ueuecoyotl, is as libidinous as the feline Woman and, as the free-running lightning bolt, is as indifferent to human suffering as is the Virgin of the Flower. During his transformation to the New Man, he physically incorporates the two masculine figures: the Little Man with his crucifix, representing consciousness of an order superior to his own desire, and the Critic, or rational censor of the creative act. Finally, the New Man is returned to Earth where he will embark upon the process of self-creation, elections made in anguish, aware of both his limitations and of his responsibility for these actions, which will realize his potentiality.

Rosalba y los Llaveros (**"Rosalba and the Llaveros"**), a three-act comedy written within two years of *La zona* [*La zona intermedia*], reveals another early tendency in Carballido's theater. Whereas *La zona* is a play of stylized masks that projects within a realm of fantasy archetypal problems of the human situation, *Rosalba* is a comedy of manners providing a realistic depiction of more fully developed characters in a specific context. The action occurs in Otatitlan, Veracruz during the Festival of the Santuario in 1949. The apparent object of ridicule is provincial family life, and the conflict revolves about the differences between the traditional, closed life style of the province and the progressive, open life style of the metropolis. Aurora Llavero de Landa and her daughter Rosalba arrive from Mexico City to visit the family of Aurora's brother, Lorenzo Llavero. Their entrance in the first scene serves to disrupt the strained equilibrium of the provincial family, and, as Rosalba probes the family's unresolved conflicts, the situation increases in complexity, reaching a chaotic climax at the end of act II. Act III provides the necessary scenes of recognition and final resolution.

The major characters are Lorenzo's son, Lázaro Llavero, the victim of traditional values, and Rosalba, the incarnation of progressive values. Lázaro, at the tender age of twelve, had fathered a child by the servant Luz. Ostracized by the family, which projected upon him their repressed libidinous desires, he has internalized their attitude toward sex to the extent that his psychological growth has been arrested. Now, at the age of twenty-six, he works in his father's pharmacy without receiving wages, and he is unable to relate to women in any but a guilt-ridden manner. The stage directions indicate his arrested ego development: "Podría pasar por guapo si no fuera arratonado para moverse. Se ve más joven que su edad."[4] By act II, scene 5, Rosalba has helped Lázaro consciously confront his situation, reject the guilt feelings imposed upon him by the family, and decide to assert his independence. This is the turning point, but further complications arise.

Rosalba, a student of Freudian psychology, at first appears as the light of reason and objectivity necessary to probe the dark recesses of the Llavero family. However, even in the first act there are indications that her analytic approach is exaggerated as she relates how she carried out a detailed clinical study on her own mother for a class in psychopa-

thology (act II, scene 18). Later, Lázaro points to her shortcomings:

LÁZARO:

> Sí, mira, tratas todo sobre esquemas, lo resuelves con principios nuevos, tuyos, pero son principios, ¿no? Y es lo mismo. Quitas los viejos principios para dar nuevos. Vaya, ¿cuál es la diferencia?

ROSALBA:

> ¡Lázaro! ¿Eres anarquista?

LÁZARO:

> No sé. Te he dicho que no le pongo nombres a las cosas.

ROSALBA:

> Sí eres, Lázaro, pero no actúas, no te rebelas. ¿Por qué?[5]

Lázaro, through his failure to objectify his inner feelings, is unable to act. Conversely, Rosalba, through her excessive rationalization, is decisive, but she ignores vital aspects of the situation and is equally unable to cope with it. Frequently her actions are counterproductive.

By act II, scene 31, Rosalba's intervention has alienated Felipe, fiancé of Lázaro's sister Rita. Rosalba, thinking that Rita did not want to marry Felipe, had convinced him that Rita is insane. Now that Felipe has decided to leave, Rita is disconsolate. Not only has Rosalba misconstrued the situation, but she has also misappropriated Rita's prerogative to decide her fate. The budding relationship between Rosalba and Lázaro is also threatened. She finds out that Luz is pregnant and that Lázaro is again suspected to be the father (act II, scene 23). She does not even ask Lázaro if he is the father of the expected child but demands that he apologize to Luz and ask her to remain so that Azalea (Lázaro's daughter by Luz) will have a mother. Azalea takes Rosalba to task, and now even Rosalba begins to suspect that her intervention has been counterproductive.

In act III, scene 12, it is revealed that Lázaro is not the father of the unborn child. He rebels against Lorenzo for suggesting, at Rosalba's instigation, that he marry Luz. Later Lázaro declares that he is leaving home and demands his back wages from his father. Now that Lázaro has asserted his independence, Rosalba comes to accept that her clinical approach has been overevaluated and that she is in love with Lázaro. Their union is prepared by two transformations: his ego is strengthened to the point of being able to free itself from the confining irrational guilt feelings and thus enter actively and consciously into a meaningful relationship with a woman; conversely, Rosalba's discovery of the irrational has allowed her to open herself to something beyond her own ego and form a human relationship with others. For Rosalba, this union produces a "physiological happiness." She has awakened to the emotional aspect of human love, and this puts her in a harmonious relationship with the physical world in general.

Rosalba is fundamentally a comedy of manners, and its treatment of provincial life can be classified as psychological realism. The central conflict involves two antagonistic attitudes towards sex: an irrational repression of sexual desire that impedes the development of a human relationship and a clinically detached approach that also frustrates the creation of a human bond. The first represents a situation in which the ego's development is arrested; the second indicates an overevaluation of the ego.

This conflict is given form in the two main protagonists and is reinforced by other techniques. The surname Llaveros conveys the repressive attitudes of the provincial family, the ones who lock up the sexual instinct. Their house is described as a "vicious circle," the confining circle that Lázaro must break. His father Lorenzo, the comic tyrant, repeatedly commands that the windows be closed. Rosalba, at the end of act II, shouts through the window for the police. Although she is able to bring these repressed conflicts to consciousness, she alone cannot resolve them. However, her cry elicits the necessary assistance in a most unexpected form: Nativitas.

Nativitas, also known as Encarnación de la Cruz, is the only figure in the comedy who approaches the mythological plane. However, her behavior is justified realistically through her characterization as an insane *curandera*. In act I, scene 5, she enters dressed in men's clothes with a red camellia behind her ear. She recites an incantation to rid the house of evil spirits, offers sacramental sweets to the family, and departs. Rosalba's reaction is excessively strong. Here, Nativitas functions primarily as a grotesque mirror for Rosalba, who, with her normal clinical detachment, diagnoses Nativitas's exhibitionism as originating in a frustration of sexual desire. Still, she does not recognize the analogy with her own situation until act II, scene 20. Having confessed that she is really timid, that she considers herself ugly, that her audacious behavior is a compensation for her underevaluation of herself as a woman, she adds: "Hago teatro para los demás, a veces para mí sola, no puedo evitarlo."[6] Like Nativitas, Rosalba tries to draw attention to herself by putting on a show, playing to the hilt her role of the liberated modern woman.

At the beginning of act III, Nativitas appears for the second time. At this point her basic function is to clarify the conflict and foreshadow the eventual union of Rosalba and Lázaro. Illuminated by the full moon, she peers through the window where Rosalba was sitting at the end of act II. Now attired in white sheets, the old *curandera* throws lighted fireworks through the window, awakening everyone in the house and announcing the beginning of the Festival of the Santuario. Next, she offers the following incantation: "¡Guerra a Lucifer y a los leones paganos! ¡Dios nos libre del mal inocente que aseguran que reinando está! Se casa el

rey con la reina mora que a veces canta y a veces llora. Cruz, cruz, cruz. Confiad en la Santísima Encarnación de la Cruz."[7] War is to be waged against Lucifer and the pagan lions, against the rebellious ego (Rosalba), and against the destructive libidinous forces (Luz). The "innocent evil" that has plagued the house is precisely the inability to cope with these two forces. Now, a solution is proposed: the marriage of the king (Lázaro) and the Moorish queen (Rosalba). The triple repetition of "cross," a traditional symbol of union and wholeness, conveys that the marriage is imperative.

Nativitas herself is the Incarnation of the Cross (masculine in act I, scene 5 and feminine in act III, scene 1) and has given birth to a cat, another feline symbol of the libido. It is significant that Nativitas's cat is caged, for this indicates that the libido is no longer destructive. In act III, scene 5, it is revealed that Nativitas gives birth at every full moon and that the last time her "child" was a rat. Thus, she becomes the mother of both Lázaro ("mousy") and Rosalba ("kitten"). She functions both as a mirror for the dramatic action and as a fertility figure representing the source of all creation.

It was the locking up on this vital source of energy that produced the original limiting situation, the stagnation of life in the Llavero family. Rosalba begins the process of liberation, but her distortion of the rational principle creates a new limiting situation, the chaos at the end of act II. Nativitas supplies the synthesis necessary for the creative release of this energy: the formation of meaningful human bonds in which recognition is given to both the rational and irrational forces. Under the sign of the cross, a union can be achieved, not as something static or limiting, but rather as a dynamic equilibrium capable of change and new creativity.

La hebra de oro (***The Golden Thread***) also conveys this image of man as a complex of rational and irrational forces, but it marks a turning point in the development of Carballido's drama. In contrast to ***La zona intermedia***, basically a morality play, ***La hebra de oro*** is a variation on the mystery play, specifically the *auto* of resurrection. It is more closely aligned with the primitive ritual of the cyclic regeneration of vegetation than with the allegorical form of the morality play based on a rational conceptualization of ethical values. ***La hebra de oro*** achieves a greater integration of man and the cosmos. Human potentiality and natural forces are brought together under a single term: energy. Thus, beginning in the late 1950s, Carballido's theater combines a more complex concept and representation of reality.

In a letter to Peden, Carballido himself has recognized the significance of ***La hebra de oro***: "'The Thread' [***The Golden Thread***] is quite important to me; it was the first time I attempted to join a realistic treatment with an imaginative one. ... Before, I wrote works of one genre or the other, but never mixed together."[8] While ***La zona intermedia*** depicts an imaginary world and ***Rosalba*** a realistic environment, they both differ from ***La hebra de oro*** in their separation of the two approaches to drama. *La hebra de oro* effects an interpenetration of the two approaches and produces a more fluid image of reality, in which both the external and the internal facets of the characters are physically projected on the stage.

The realistic context in which the *auto* begins and ends is the hacienda of Ixtla, Mexico in the year 1953. The hacienda belongs to Silvestre Sidel, who has been missing for a number of years. Adela Sidel, Silvestre's paternal grandmother, and her accomplice Rafael have brought Silvestre's maternal grandmother, the ailing Leonor Luna, to the hacienda with the intention of having Leonor die there and taking over Silvestre's estate for themselves.

A basic opposition is established between the two grandmothers: Adela is cold, calculating, and insensitive; Leonor represents maternal compassion. At first Adela is the dominant force, but already in the first act Leonor assumes the initiative as her maternal instinct is awakened. Sibila's child is ill, and Salustio, the *mayordomo* of the estate and Sibila's father-in-law, maintains that nothing can be done for the child because it is possessed by evil spirits. In order to be allowed to care for the child, Leonor must prove to Salustio that she has power over the forces of evil. Therefore, she improvises a ritual against the powers of death.

Leonor's incantations at the end of act I literally open the doors to the supernatural world. First, a radio turns on by itself, emitting bursts of static until the wave lengths of the natural and supernatural realms are brought into tune. Then, a door, sealed by two boards in the form of a cross (X), mysteriously opens. This door parallels the symbolism employed in *Rosalba*. There, Rosalba called for help through a window, and the necessary assistance appeared in the figure of Nativitas. Here, the door, another opening connecting two regions, is reinforced by the sign of a cross, the intersection of opposites. On one side of the door is the living room of the hacienda, the region of consciousness, and on the other side are dark, cavernous passages and a subterranean spring, symbolic of the subconscious. Thus, the opening of the door marks the eruption of the subconscious, or the dream world, into the realm of consciousness, and the Man in the Caftan enters to direct the fantastic episode.

However, the following scenes do not represent a normal dream within the mind of an individual. All the characters present before the fantastic episode (Adela, Leonor, Sibila, the Child, Salustio) are also present after its conclusion, and all of them experience the same events. Also, the natural elements participate in the fantastic episode, specifically the rain and the sprouting of the corn. Thus, this part of the play is more closely related to the collective participation of ritual than to the individual character of dreams. This fantastic episode constitutes the greater part of the play (act II, scene 1 to act III, scene 5) and on the psychological level serves to exteriorize subconscious facets of the major characters through the re-enactment of events from the past.

Thus, instead of a linear development of a conflict, the play consists of a series of recognition scenes that provide an opportunity to reveal and evaluate human behavior.

Adela, born of a poor family, married a wealthy man who suffered from asthma. The marriage was a failure emotionally and financially. She had married for money, but when her husband died he left everything to his son. Adela has an inferiority complex, is paranoiac, and never has established an authentic relationship with anyone. Closed within her own ego, insensitive to the feelings of others, she is alone and ill. Her accomplice Rafael has left, and the only person that cares for Adela is Leonor.

Leonor is very compassionate, but, because of her traditional education, she suffers a physical aversion to sex. After Silvestre's parents died, she raised her grandson. Having internalized the traditional attitude towards sex, she tended to impose it on Silvestre and caused him to flee the hacienda. The Man in the Caftan, playing the role of the young Silvestre, accuses Leonor of not having allowed him to fulfill his desires. Her attitude towards sex impeded the development of Silvestre's ego. Still, her protective maternal instinct saves her, renewing her will to live as she cares for Sibila's child.

Sibila functions as an antithesis to Leonor. She represents animal passion, dominated by immediate physical pleasure, and thus she is analogous to the Woman in *La zona intermedia*. She engaged in intercourse with Silvestre before he left the hacienda. Since then, she has had three children by the *mayordomo*'s son, all of which have died. The maternal instinct is completely absent. Although she abandons her child and runs off with her new lover Rafael, her fate is still in question: both the Devil and her Guardian Angel are seen hovering overhead as she rides off.

The Man in the Caftan, with the aid of his female assistant Mayala, directs the enactment of these recognition scenes. He has a double function: he is the mimetic author of the fantastic episode, directing and commenting upon these scenes, and he himself is a fictional character, enacting the role of the lost grandson Silvestre. In the latter role, he re-creates his own death, lamenting not having realized himself fully: "But I am no longer I, he, Silvestre, but the other, my frustrated possibilities, my nonbeing, the reflection of my broken potentials" (*The Golden Thread,* p. 115).[9] This disjointed farewell, as his unfulfilled desires disintegrate into the void, serves as an exhortation to Leonor. His death returns her to an active role, and reciprocally she gives him a new existence. Picking up the child abandoned by Sibila, Leonor exclaims: "And you, baby, you're not going to cry. You're going to live. You're going to be named Silvestre and you'll have lots of friends, and since you're a little lame, you're not going to be able to get away" (*The Golden Thread,* p. 118). The child's lameness underscores the masculine principle's ultimate dependency on the feminine.

La hebra de oro is not structured upon a linear development of a conflict between realistically delineated characters. Instead, a rythmic pattern of death and regeneration is employed, effecting a sympathetic relationship between the human and cosmic planes. Leonor Luna (feline and lunar characteristics are usually evident in Carballido's libidinous figures) represents the feminine generative principle. At the beginning of act I she is dormant and weak. The reappearance of her lost grandson Silvestre, who is related to seed and rain during the fantastic episode, brings in the masculine fecundating principle. His entrance, death, and absorption awaken Leonor's maternal instincts and finally in act III she gives "birth" to a new Silvestre. In the last scene, this process is given explicit visual expression by the sack of corn: "Something has burst forth in the sack of corn. It has been rising slowly since the beginning of the scene. Now it can be seen clearly: it is stalks of corn, many of them, which stretch upward while Leonor sings" (*The Golden Thread*, p. 119).

Beginning with *La hebra de oro,* these physical effects are fundamental to Carballido's representation of reality.[10] Rather than an illusion of reality like *Rosalba* or a conceptualized fantasy like *La zona intermedia,* his theater becomes magically real: a rhythmic flux of physical sensations that create an archetypal reality. The distinction between reality and illusion is further attenuated in the fantastic episode in which fictional characters (Adela, Leonor, Sibila) represent themselves in their "true" identities; a mimetic author (Man in the Caftan) directs the play within a play, comments upon it, and he himself enacts a fictional role (Silvestre). The total effect of these techniques, which find varied expression in Carballido's later works, is to involve the audience in the spectacle in a more direct and more active manner.

La hebra de oro also develops several images that reveal Carballido's increasingly more complex view of reality. With the threads of his existence—time, space, energy— man fashions his life. "It's like spinning the threads of the spider webs we always have around us" says the Man in the Caftan (*The Golden Thread,* p. 79). The abstract concept of potentiality employed in *La zona intermedia* has become metaphor: a web, fragile and complex, a myriad of interrelated elements spun together as one plays out his existence. The "golden thread" is the spiritual thread that binds our web to that of our fellow man and gives continuity and meaning to our existence. Yet, these threads are not distinct from cosmic forces: energy existing everywhere, taking a multitude of forms, changing, growing, disappearing, and reappearing in the most unexpected ways. The Man in the Caftan may be considered the unfulfilled desires of Silvestre, returning as a spirit to direct the fantastic episode. Still, he returns via a radio magically tuned to a wave length that is spiritual but differing from ordinary radio waves only in frequency. The sky, seen through the living room window of the hacienda, appears as a spider web modeled on a painting by the Mexican

artist Tamayo. Thus, the human and the cosmic planes interpenetrate and are united under the image of a complex and ever-changing web of energy.

Since *La hebra de oro* Carballido's plays have generally depicted a struggle for the liberation of vital creative forces, and the form employed has been the comedy or farce. In his earlier works, the disruptive force was associated with an exaggeration of ego or with traditional mores, represented by specific individuals and within the context of the family. In his later works, this force becomes an institution or society in general.

The one-act farce *Silencio, pollos pelones, ya les van a echar su maíz* (**"Quiet, you mangy mutts, you'll get your bone"**) is an excellent example of Carballido's didactic social theater, presenting a vivid image of social conditions and clearly delineating causal factors. Although political and economic realities are treated, the main object of satire is the institutionalization of charity in the Social Welfare Agency. Charity, while apparently ministering to the needs of the poor, has only a cosmetic effect. It leaves unexplored the causes of poverty and serves to perpetuate the existing system that is based on a dominant-subordinate relationship. Formally the play combines elements of popular satire and epic theater. There are twenty-one characters portrayed by eight actors. Two actors serve as two choruses, providing musical commentary in the popular ballad or *corrido* form. Including transitional devices, there are thirty-six different scenic events with prop and costume changes made in view of the audience. Because of the number of scenes and the frequent transition from representation to commentary, the total effect is not that of illusion but of a rhythmic movement that requires an active, critical response by the audience.

For analytical purposes the farce can be divided into three parts: prologue, story, epilogue. In the prologue, the actors enter uniformly dressed, wearing placards (actor A, B, C; actress A, B, C; chorus D, E). After preliminary banter about the underdeveloped status of Mexican theater, they create the setting of the story through song, maps, and posters. Finally they don, over their uniforms, the costumes of the characters.

The story, an adaptation of Carballido's short story **"La caja vacía"** (**"The empty coffin"**), consists of three major segments. The action of the first segment occurs in a small rural village of Veracruz during the present. Because of the abject poverty in which Porfirio and his family exist, he decides to sign up with some North Americans who collect a wild herb and process it into medicine. A poster, pointing out that 14.4 percent of the state's economically active population works as braceros, directs attention to the economic causes of this situation. Later, at the North American camp, the relationship between the gringo and the Mexican is revealed. The employer, feeling morally superior, labels all the workers cheats. Porfirio, distrusting the gringos' jerry-built tram that crosses to the forest where the plants are gathered, attempts to swim the river. The choruses and characters narrate how he is swept away by the swift current. The final scene depicts the villagers' reaction to the news. Porfirio's death leaves his mother, wife, and daughter completely destitute. One woman, who last year had received government assistance to bury her mother while her husband was laboring in the United States as a bracero, suggests that Porfirio's wife Domitila contact Leonela.

The second segment of the story entails a flashback of one and a half years, and the setting shifts to the state capital. The first scene introduces the central character of the play, Leonela, childless and a widow now for eight years. She runs the Refugio Guadalupano, a private mission for the poor. The name of the mission and a conspicuous portrait of the Virgin of Guadalupe externalize the maternal nature of her role. Leonela's relationship with the poor, however, emphasizes the negative characteristic of dependency as opposed to the nourishing and liberating aspect. Another important motivational factor is the sense of moral superiority that she derives from her role.

Events soon set in motion the revelation of the contradictions inherent in the institution of charity and in the character of Leonela. Her nephew Eustaquio, whom she had raised as her own child, is the government party's candidate for state governor. Short, rapid scenes satirize the rhetoric of the campaign, the fraudulent elections, and the division of the spoils. As assuredly as the electoral process represents no threat to the establishment and the government party, Leonela's appointment as director of social welfare will not eradicate the causes of poverty nor even alleviate the situation of the poor. At first Leonela demands that her staff allow the indigents to present their requests in person. This individualistic approach is countered by Berta, a young professional social worker: "También hay problemas de grupos, no sólo individuales."[11] Berta serves as a rational foil to Leonela as the latter strives to fulfill through a state agency her earlier maternal role. Now, with increased funds and authority, the nature of this role becomes evident:

LEONELA:

> ... ¡Me encanta el don de mando! (*Se queda seria*) ¡Hasta miedo me da ... lo fácilmente que me brota![12]

Although at this time she directs her efforts against the forces of bureaucracy, the satisfaction derived from the exercise of power reinforces the dominant-subordinate relationship that characterized her attitude toward the poor.

After less than two months in office, a decisive conflict occurs. The "leftist press" has exposed how the showers she sent to a remote village that lacked running water ended up in the hands of a hotel enterprise, criticized her use of the Virgin's portrait in a state office, and ridiculed the governor whom Leonela insists on addressing with the diminutive Tiquín. Realizing that she is a political liability, the governor orders her to remove the Virgin's portrait, limit her

activities to bureaucratic forms, and stop treating him as a child. Denied the supports of her positive self-image, she begins to exercise her power in a vindictive manner. In the Welfare Office, she fires her loyal secretary Clementina and labels the poor as ignorant and undeserving of her love.

The third segment returns to the plot begun in the first segment. The scenario now includes both Leonela's office and the rural village. As the unsuccessful search for Porfirio's body continues, Domitila presents her request for assistance. Leonela, now in her second year in office, refuses to provide money for Porfirio's wake. However, Berta, more responsive to Domitila's needs, volunteers to investigate the case. Berta's arrival in the village causes the North Americans to offer Berta 250 pesos so that they will not be implicated in Porfirio's death. She passes the money on to Domitila.

Back in the capital, the following exchange captures the opposing attitudes toward the poor:

LEONELA:

> ... Me hacían creer que era yo buena: idiota, eso era yo. Mi tiempo, mi dinero, todo tirado al pozo. Quisiera yo juntarlo otra vez: abriría mi Refugio de nuevo, nada más para darme el gusto de echarlos a empujones. ¿No les gusta vivir así como viven? ¡Pues que ellos mismos hagan algo!

BERTA:

> Tal vez vayan a hacerlo ... nunca se sabe.[13]
>
> (*Casual*)

Leonela, who had always considered the poor as children incapable of doing anything for themselves, now completely rejects them. Berta, on the contrary, views the poor not only as equals but also as the potential agents for changing the existing system. She rebels against Leonela's refusal to supply additional assistance by sending the most expensive casket she can find.

During Porfirio's wake, the major complication arises from the presence of the luxurious coffin. Aside from the absurd contrast with the humble surroundings, there is no corpse. The death of the ninety-year-old Dalia furnishes a happy resolution. The casket fulfills its normal function, and Porfirio's widow receives a few pesos from Dalia's relatives.

In the epilogue, the actors remove the costumes of the characters and in their commentary make it clear that "No queremos caridad, / sólo queremos justicia."[14] This is followed by a series of petitions, ranging from an increased subsidy for the theater to the release of political prisoners, and ends with the response of the authorities:

TODOS:

> ¡Silencio, pollos pelones,
> ya les van a echar su maíz![15]

The disrespect and unresponsiveness to the just demands of the actors parallels the reaction to the people by the dominant groups within the play: social (Leonela), political (Eustaquio), economic (North Americans). This repetition within the nonfictional frame (prologue, epilogue) underscores the didactic intent and reinforces the fact that the representation is an accurate reflection of reality. Although the solution is not explicitly given, it is clear that justice, not charity, is required, and that if justice is not forthcoming within the system, the people will become the agents for changing the system.

Yo también hablo de la rosa (*I Too Speak of the Rose*) synthesizes earlier thematic concerns and technical achievements of Carballido. This one-act masterpiece further elaborates the concept of human existence as a complex web of interrelationships through a fusion of realistic and poetic techniques, as in *La hebra de oro*. Also, it delineates the repressive effects of ideologies and institutions through popular satire and alternating scenes of commentary and representation, as in *Silencio, pollos pelones, ya les van a echar su maíz.* Finally, it succeeds in realizing both an explicit statement on the function of theater and an exemplary model of total theater.

The action occurs in Mexico City during the present, and the central realistic event is the derailment of a freight train by two adolescents, Toña and Polo. The technique and structure of the play focus the spectator's attention on the process of interpretation rather than on the event itself. There are eighteen basic scenes with twenty-nine characters portrayed by thirteen actors. Transitions are fluid and rapid, effected by lighting and the commentary of the Medium and the Newsboy.

The initial scene establishes a nonrealistic atmosphere. A spot comes up on the Medium, dressed in peasant costume. In her monologue, she conjures up an image of her heart. The heart, like the rose of the play's title, symbolizes human existence, complex and fragile, but also precise and powerful. The Medium herself is an objectification of the social function of theater. In the final lines of her monologue, she outlines the following process: events are perceived and images formulated, and the latter are then communicated and contemplated. The artist provides a representation of the people and their surroundings, an image that is physical and integral as opposed to the abstract and fragmentary analyses employed by scientists and politicians to manipulate reality. With each appearance the Medium's costume becomes increasingly lighter in color until the pure white of the final scene. This externalizes the process of clarification through which art succeeds in transcending the chaos of diverse partial visions in a total concrete image.

During a blackout following the monologue, the event is first presented sensorially: the sound of the derailment, silence, lightning flashes; then the Newsboy: "Get your papers now! Delinquents derail a train!" (*I Too* [*I Too Speak of the Rose*], p. 294).[16] Although apparently a neutral medium for the news, he varies his salespitch according to the version he is vending. The Medium, however, remains constant in her refusal to offer a limited fragmentary interpretation.

Scene 2 provides a realistic representation and employs a linear progression: street scene, derailment, effects of the derailment. The behavior of the young truants is spontaneous. They steal some coins from a public telephone, and then they decide to buy some candy. Their encounters with the Candy Vendor, the Old Woman selling *jícama,* and the young mechanic Maximino develop a contrast between human relationships motivated by self-interest and, in the latter case, mutual respect. Later, at the dump, Toña and Polo give their remaining coins to a Scavenger. Objects that they find, scrap iron and flowers, are seen as gifts for their friend Maxi. In an unpremeditated gesture, they roll a metal tub filled with concrete onto the train tracks. The brief tableau (din of the crash, lightning, Toña and Polo awed by the wreck) suggests the import of the change effected by their actions.

In scene 3 the Medium reads from a Bestiary. Diverse interpretations of human existence are illustrated by animal images. They range from the canine guardian of physical integrity and property rights, the cat watching over man's spiritual integrity, the hen, fish, butterfly, and snake, to the bee that knows "*all* about solar energy and light. Things we don't suspect!" (*I Too,* p. 306). The latter most closely approaches the dramatist's concept of man as an intricate web of interrelationships based upon cosmic energy.

The next five scenes provide brief interpretations of and reactions to the derailment. Commenting upon the newspaper report, a Gentleman identifies poverty as the cause of delinquency. A Lady agrees: "Oh, yes, their poverty's something awful. But they didn't say anything about the trunk murder, huh?" (*I Too,* p. 306). Even if the cause is identified, there is no active response, only the passive consumption of journalistic sensationalism. The Teacher uses the newspaper to illustrate the "dangers of idleness." She, too, refuses to accept any responsibility or attempt to alleviate the problem. Two University Students react with greater sympathy, revealing perhaps a desire to rebel against society. All three responses, however, contrast with that of Maxi. Informed by phone that his friends have been arrested, he immediately requests that his employer give him money and time off so that he can go to the aid of the adolescents. Scene 8 shifts to the dump where the Scavengers and others reap the fruits of the wreck, carrying off sacks of food.

Scene 9 returns to the Medium. She narrates a story that is enacted by two dancers. Living in different towns, they both receive the same command in a dream: to dance and pray *together* at the sanctuary near the house of their brother. They meet in mid-route and, confused by the ambiguous dream, celebrate the rite at the place of their encounter. Each returns home, feeling he has only half-fulfilled the command. The anecdote reflects the image of human existence presented by the play. Man has no foreknowledge of the consequences of his actions. Therefore, primary emphasis is placed upon the process: contradictions should be faced and choices made in a spirit of solidarity with others.

The next seven scenes supply additional interpretations, and the basic opposition is human-vs.-inhuman response. First, we see Toña's mother preparing food and clothing to take to her daughter, and then Polo's mother visits him in prison. Both mothers are confused and vacillate in assigning blame. However, they do reveal a human maternal concern for their children's welfare and establish an obvious contrast with the two following scenes, which employ more elaborate distancing techniques. Both are introduced by the Newsboy: first, he hawks a Freudian analysis holding up papers covered with Rorschachlike ink blots and, later, a Marxist interpretation carrying papers printed in red on black. Each scene includes a narrator (Professor One, Professor Two) who comments upon his version as it is presented by Toña and Polo. The result is the satire of two opposing overrationalizations: the first exaggerating the repression of the libido in the individual, the second stressing the exploitation of the proletariat under capitalism. The three following scenes underscore the inhumanity of the preceding ones by focusing upon the mutual bond of love. Maxi visits Toña in prison. He had come to free his two friends by paying their fines. This is impossible because the derailment has resulted in a half-million-peso "crime." That the real crime is poverty is implied by Toña's expression of solidarity with her fellow inmates, who have violated society's laws in order to live. Toña and Maxi embrace as he vows to carry only Toña's picture in his wallet. What had begun as idol worship on her part and friendship on his part ends in love. A scene at the dump develops a similar bond on the collective level. Here, it assumes a more popular and realistic form, as four Scavengers (two male, two female) celebrate around a fire with food, drink, and song. The earthy language of the songs contrasts strongly with the dehumanizing terminology of analysis employed by the two Professors. The scene concludes with the same gesture as the preceding one: the two couples embrace. Scene 16 returns to the Toña-Maxi plot. On the telephone at the garage, he breaks his engagement with his previous girlfriend and thus prepares the way for his future union with Toña.

Scene 17 restates the theses of the two Professors, adds a third, and requires the audience to make a choice. The Announcer illustrates the theses with three projected images and offers a magnificent prize to those who select the correct interpretation. In addition to the Freudian and Marxist rationalizations (rose petal and rose respectively), we have the weblike fiber of a rose petal seen under a microscope. This is the Medium's image, "primal matter" that is also "energy." The latter thesis destroys the former: there is no

rose, no petal, only "a fusion of miraculous fictions. ... Without the least possibility of rational explanation." (*I Too,* p. 328).

In the transition to the final scene, the Newsboy carries parchmentlike papers imprinted with magical signs and offers *all* the news. This introduces the Medium, now dressed in white, who gives her version. The previous representations by Toña and Polo, commented upon by the two Professors, were basically satires of exaggerated rationalizations, whereas the final scene achieves the total physical effect of ritual. The street scene included by the Professors is eliminated and dramatic intensity heightened as the Medium narrows the focus to the dump, where the change effected by the derailment occurs. As Toña and Polo enter, she explains: "They are changing into all that surrounds them" (*I Too,* p. 328). Their dance harmonizes with and evokes the creative potential of the cosmos. The flowers respond as a Feminine Chorus in a liturgy: "I have strength ... / I have promise ..." (*I Too,* p. 329). The dump itself begins to glow from within, and the Medium adds: "With rhythms such as these we summon and arouse fertility" (*I Too,* p. 329). After the derailment, all the characters in the play embrace, kiss, dance, at first chaotically and finally in a chain, with precise and complex movements. A change from sterility to fertility occurs on all levels: Toña and Polo pass from adolescents to adults (she marries Maxi, he gets his own garage), the situation of the poor shifts temporarily from lack to abundance, and the cosmos itself participates in this realization of creative potential.

Now, instead of commenting upon the representation, the Medium addresses a question to the characters:

MEDIUM:

> (*Asking in the manner of a teacher*)
>
> And now, what about that light from that star— extinguished for so many years?

TOÑA:

> ... It kept flowing into the telescope ... but all it meant to say ... all it meant to reveal ... was the humble existence of the hairy hunter, who was drawn by his friend, the painter, on the walls of an African cave.
>
> [*I Too,* p. 331]

This exchange provides, within the play, a statement on the function of art. The artist produces an image that persists long after the event or person represented ceases to exist. The sole function of the artist is to affirm, through an integral objectification, the existence of his contemporaries as a complex web of creative potential. Thus, the web becomes an image not of entrapment but of liberation, transcending, through a complex yet precise physical representation, the limits imposed by analytical rationalizations of human existence. The play itself is an exemplary realization of this concept of drama, and it clearly demonstrates how greatly Carballido has enriched the allegorical image of man expressed in **La zona intermedia.**

Notes

1. An excellent bibliographical source on Carballido is George W. Woodyard and Leon F. Lyday's "Studies on Latin American Theatre, 1960-1969," *Theatre Documentation* 2 (Fall 1969-Spring 1970): 49-84. More recent items include: Oswaldo A. López's "Crítica de la realidad social mexicana en obras representativas de Emilio Carballido" (Ph.D. dissertation, University of Pittsburgh, 1973); Mary Vázquez-Amaral's "*Yo también hablo de la rosa*: Un estudio crítico," *Revista de la Universidad de México* 27, no. 5 (January 1973): 25-29; Joseph F. Vélez's "Tres aspectos de *El relojero de Córdoba* de Emilio Carballido," *Explicación de textos,* nos. 1-2 (1973), pp. 151-159; and his "Una entrevista con Emilio Carballido," *Latin American Theatre Review,* 7, no. 1 (Fall 1973): 17-24.

2. *The Golden Thread and Other Plays,* trans. Margaret S. Peden (Austin: University of Texas Press, 1970), p. xi.

3. *La zona intermedia,* in *Teatro mexicano contemporáneo,* no. 26 (Mexico City: Unión Nacional de Autores, 1951). The translations provided in the text are from *The Golden Thread and Other Plays,* and the title of the play and page numbers will be indicated in parentheses following the quotation.

4. *Rosalba y los Llaveros,* in Carballido, *Teatro* (Mexico City: Fondo de Cultura Economica, 1960), pp. 151-247. All references to this play are from this edition. Translations provided in the notes are mine: "He could pass as handsome if he were not so mousy. He looks younger than his age" (*Rosalba,* p. 167).

5. LÁZARO:

   > Yeah, look, you treat everything schematically, you decide everything by new principles, yours, but they're principles, right? It's all the same. You do away with old principles to put up new ones. Come on, what's the difference?

   ROSALBA:

   > Lázaro! You're an anarchist!

   LÁZARO:

   > Could be. I've told you I don't label things.

   ROSALBA:

   > Yes you are, Lázaro, but you don't do anything, you don't rebel. Why?

   [*Rosalba,* p. 187]

6. "I put on a show for others, sometimes even for myself; I can't avoid it" (*Rosalba,* p. 241).

7. "War against Lucifer and the pagan lions! God save us from the innocent evil that prevails. The king marries the Moorish queen who sometimes sings and sometimes cries. Cross, Cross, Cross. Have faith in the Holy Cross Incarnate" (*Rosalba,* pp. 222-223).

8. *The Golden Thread and Other Plays,* p. xiii.

9. *La hebra de oro: Auto sacramental en tres jornadas* (Mexico City: Universidad Nacional Autónoma, 1957). The translations provided in the text are from *The Golden Thread and Other Plays,* and the title of the play and page numbers will be indicated in parentheses following the quotations.

10. Margaret S. Peden, "Theory and Practice in Artaud and Carballido," *Modern Drama* 2, no. 2 (September 1968): 132-142.

11. *Silencio, pollos pelones, ya les van a echar su maíz,* in *Teatro mexicano, 1963,* ed. Antonio Magaña Esquivel (Mexico City: Aguilar, 1965). All references to this play are from this edition. Translations provided in the notes are mine: "There are also collective problems, not only personal ones" (*Silencio,* p. 137).

12. *Leonela.* ... I really enjoy ordering people about! (*She becomes serious*) It even frightens me—how easy it is for me! (*Silencio,* p. 139).

13. *Leonela.* ... They made me believe I was good: an idiot, that's what I was. My time, my money, everything wasted. I wish I had it again: I'd open the mission again, just to have the pleasure of booting them out. Don't they like living like they do? Well let them do something for themselves!

   BERTA:

   > (*Casually*) Perhaps they will—you never know.

   [*Silencio,* p. 151]

14. EVERYONE:

   > We don't want charity, we just want justice.

   [*Silencio,* p. 159]

15. EVERYONE:

   > Quiet, you mangy mutts, you'll get your bone!

   [*Silencio,* p. 160]

16. *Yo también hablo de la rosa,* in *Teatro mexicano del Siglo XX* (Mexico City: Fondo de Cultura Económica, 1970), V, 235-275. The translations provided in the text are from William I. Oliver's translation *I Too Speak of the Rose,* in *The Modern Stage in Latin*

America: Six Plays, ed. George W. Woodyard (New York: E. P. Dutton & Co., 1971). The shortened title of the play and page numbers will be indicated in parentheses following the quotation.

Karen Peterson (essay date 1977)

SOURCE: Peterson, Karen. "Existential Irony in Three Carballido Plays." *Latin American Theatre Review* 10.2 (1977): 29-35. Print.

[*In the following essay, Peterson explores similarities among three plays by Carballido—*Medusa, Theseus, *and* The Ivory Statues—*and the plays of French existentialist playwright Jean-Paul Sartre. She notes that Carballido's characters try to escape their circumstances through the choices they make but are ultimately unsuccessful.*]

Emilio Carballido has written many different kinds of plays: one-act vignettes, plays with historical settings, political commentary, and fantasies. The fantasy plays explore the psychological and archetypal delineations of human freedom.[1] *Medusa, Teseo,* and *Las estatuas de marfil,* a trilogy, deal more singlemindedly with the characteristically existential notion of freedom as action, seeking to explore "how far a free agent can escape from his particular situation in his choices."[2] But these three plays include as many styles. *Medusa* is fantastic and heavily symbolic, and *Teseo,* the least complex of the three, is a one-act fantasy. *Las estatuas de marfil* is entirely realistic, but it is the most subtle and difficult. Together, the plays are three variations on a single theme, and Carballido, through symbol and elegantly metaphorical plot, has incorporated the existential irony that is characteristic of Sartre's drama.

In *Medusa,* the protagonist Perseo wants to perform some heroic act. Accordingly, he sets out, with divine guidance, to kill Medusa whom he comes to love and pity. Perseo must choose between not doing a deed he has come to find meaningless and morally questionable, and doing it to accept a definition of himself, though it compromises his freedom. Teseo chooses, at the beginning of his play, to be all that Perseo has become at the end of *Medusa*—opportunistic, amoral, unloving—to escape the ignominious sentimentality and hypocrisy that his father represents in his old age. Teseo also wishes to define himself and his character outside of his surroundings, and explicitly states the implicit aims of Perseo: "I am the son of my own acts."[3] The central characters of *Las estatuas de marfil,* Sabina and César, likewise seek to shape their characters by assuming roles: Sabina wishes to become an actress instead of a housewife, and César, more ambiguously, wants to be a good writer.

The illusory freedom of circumstance is exposed by devastating irony in all three plays. Irony with regard to the expectations of the characters and the situations in which they find themselves is characteristic of the plays of Sartre. Like the heroes of *Les Mains sales* and *Huis Clos,* Perseo comes to disbelieve the heroism of his once intended action, and consciously rejects his fate. Then he is led, by accident, to commit the very acts he has rejected, and to become, because of this, much less free. Teseo, too, is visited by the irony of circumstance: he elects an enormous unseen fate when he chooses Phaedra over Ariadne. He will find himself touched by the feelings and morals he has acted beyond. Teseo compares with César in *Las estatuas de marfil* and with Garcin in *Huis Clos.* All three believe themselves to be acting on a stage much larger than the evident setting: Teseo in the realm of dynasty and power, César in the realm of art, or at least, of the Mexican theatre, and Garcin in the realm of political ideology. Yet each is betrayed by his actions in the visible, immediate setting. Teseo, embracing Phaedra, takes a fate analogous to that of his father; César, inadvertently, becomes the director he does not want to be; and Garcin proves incapable of love or bravery. As in *Medusa,* it is the discrepancy between role and reality that proves the undoing of the characters.

The terrible counterpoint of role, heroism and love in *Medusa* is strikingly close to *Les Mains sales.* Both Hugo and Perseo want to become heroes and seek to act accordingly. Each loves the person he must kill; each rejects the notions of heroism only to commit the act inadvertently. Medusa and Jessica alike condemn the callous and bloody ideal of heroism. Hugo lives to see his deed change shape in the eyes of others. He chooses at the end of the play to identify himself with his legend and not with the personal reality of his action. Perseo, in the end, does the same.

Drama is "acting" as well as action, and role-playing is the most important ironic foil to the real desires and circumstances of the characters in these plays by Carballido just as it is in those of Sartre. In *Medusa,* the paradox of action in the theatre as acting is represented by symbol as well as by the ironies of circumstance that are so much like those of *Les Mains sales.* In *Las estatuas de marfil* Carballido uses theatre as a metaphor for life and explores the complexities of this metaphor more fully than Sartre even in *Huis Clos.*

Marble statuary and monsters, symbols of the lack of freedom imposed by role, are common to all three Carballido plays. In *Teseo,* the minotaur and his labyrinth are figures for Teseo in his hero's role. *Las estatuas de marfil* is named after a game the characters play; the game is in turn the reality of their lives. In *Medusa,* those who look on the monster's hair are literally turned to stone, but the role of hero analogously calcifies the protagonist himself into his role. Perseo questions Medusa about her fate, trying to discover if she petrifies people willfully or not. Wiser than he, she knows the irrelevance of the question. At the end of the play, Perseo tries to use Medusa's head to his own advantage. Turning Acrisio and his court to stone, he inadvertently does the same to his mother. His possession and use of Medusa's head is at once the symbol and irony of his own situation: he has become the thing which he abhorred, condemned, as Medusa had been, to act out his exceptional destiny.

Medusa makes clear that obsession with self-definition ends in the assumption of an imprisoning role. She uses her own case as an example and warning to Perseo, and tries to convince him that love is the only humanly possible way for him to see and know himself. Other characters in the play are monsters like Medusa herself, and have become so because they wished to be different from other men, to see themselves in the shape of an ideal. Dánae, Perseo's mother, is so obsessed with her unrecognized status as "blessed among women" that she is oblivious to the grotesque imitation of that momentary golden rain—her constant tears. Acrisio seems to have turned his inability to guard his daughter into an impotent cult of his own body. Both are caricatures of the human—monsters—in the same way as Medusa and the Gorgone, only they are not as obviously marked. The confusion between the monstrous and the human is all the more evident because the monsters in *Medusa* and *Teseo* behave in a warmly human (if comical) way, whereas the human characters very often are simply parodies of themselves, repeating the same acts over and over.

If the result of role-playing is monstrous and rigid, the origin is equally inhuman. This is explored in both *Las estatuas de marfil* and *Medusa* through the analogy of role and artistic form. In the former, the theatre metaphor, dramatizations, and scenes from other plays are used to show how literary role mirrors life. In *Medusa,* the mirror of Athena's shield is a symbol of the reflections that art and love show to life.

In one scene of Act V of *Medusa,* the court poets are called to immortalize Perseo's deeds. The dialogue between Perseo and the poets is very much like the dialogues on heroism and love between Perseo and Medusa earlier in the play. The poets believe they should universalize Perseo's exploits for all men to experience. Perseo protests that the poet's universal version will not be identical with his own experience, but this is brushed aside. Like Medusa, but in a more clinical fashion, the poets note the murderous character of the hero, and regard as predictable his nausea over the first two "heroic" acts. In fact, none of Perseo's unique emotions interests these poets, and it is tempting to dismiss the scene as a satire.

But in the love scene between Medusa and Perseo in Act IV, both celebrate the universality of their feelings; abandoning the personal, subjective utterances common to such scenes, they speak of themselves and their feelings in the third person. Like Athena's shield, which renders harmless the visible monster Medusa, the mirror of love counteracts the need for self-identification that is its root. The mirror of art, in turn, like love, embraces and defines the universal scope of human possibility without feeling. The posts are not concerned with Perseo's individual feelings because they are common; art defines and limits the actions and circumstances of the hero completely, but without agony or nausea.

Perseo, Teseo, César, and Sabina all believe themselves to be acting on the stage of universals, which is properly the realm of art, or role. Sabina discovers in each new play an ideal new Sabina; Perseo and Teseo become the bloody, cold images of themselves as heroes—their legends; César sacrifices himself and his freedom of action to his artistic ideal.

Through the notion of role, both *Les Mains sales* and *Medusa* expose the loss of human freedom. The exigencies of heroism force both protagonists to forego the personal design of their existence for an impersonal one. The dehumanizing force of role is enlarged by the fact that both men must kill the person whom they love. Carballido extends the essential inhumanity and limitation of role to the realm of art with the symbol of the mirror. In *Huis Clos,* Sartre too adds a symbolic dimension to his commentary on the ironies of role, but unlike the symbols in *Medusa,* the symbols of *Huis Clos* are formal. To represent Hell, Sartre uses a confined stage setting, with a single opening door, and a circular plot.

Huis Clos is a play about the reality and illusions of the characters' visions of themselves and how these define their relations with others—their roles. The "action" of the play is simply a continual theatrical dialogue. The characters must play roles with each other: their situation is dramatic and they have no choice but to play, only a choice of what to play. The three characters discover that Hell is the confines of the room and of their own inter-relationships.

The situation is the same in *Las estatuas de marfil.* The play is about the inter-relationships of the characters; these do not really change in the course of the play, they are only clarified.

Carballido uses the same symbolically confined setting and circular plot here as Sartre in *Huis Clos.* The entire play takes place in two rooms of the Rosas apartment. There is no real division between the bedroom and the living room in the setting; it is only suggested by the lighting. Sabina is never seen out of the apartment. Even the theatre belongs there—her home is the scene of the rehearsals. The two aspects of her life intrude upon each other. The commitments of her married life conflict ultimately with those of the theatre; the theatre intrudes on the bedroom when Sabina comforts herself by acting scenes from a play after her husband has left.

The action begins and ends with the same scene—a cast party at Sabina's home. The small differences in each scene underscore the larger differences. Sabina receives flowers from her husband at the second party—for her true role as wife and mother. The party is obviously less lively; only Mundo, her husband, remarks on this in the first scene.

Sartre uses the theatre metaphor as the framework of the action itself in *Huis Clos*. Carballido's use of it here is more complex. ***Las estatuas de marfil*** is a play about plays, a play composed of fragments from other plays, a play of made-up scenes and games, and a play which ends with a scene composed for a play in the future. This makes the interplay of truth and falsity, reality and illusion, irony and pathos all the more deceptive.

Lucila, Argentina, and Alicia are all variants of Sabina. Each represents a role choice for Sabina, and each is frozen within the confines of the role she represents—like a statue. The opening scene between Lucila and César is an important commentary on the character of Sabina. Lucila is socially pretentious. So is Sabina, and it is part of the "Morel heritage," as Argentina explains it. Lucila presents her infidelity as a drama to César, and what interested her about the adultery was evidently the role of lover rather than love itself. She wanted to feel herself in love, and is forced by the exigencies of role to do all that she does. Sabina adopts the same attitude at the end of Act I; later she reveals that she is interested in acting this particular drama with César. Lastly, Lucila's adultery may correspond to the relationship between César and Sabina. This is not evident to the reader until the end of the play, and is one of the incalculables of it, open to interpretation by actor and director.

Argentina is clearly a model for Sabina, both as wife and mother, and as a Morel. From the first, each Morel, male or female, entertains both artistic pretensions and the longing to leave the city. Each fails, as Sabina will fail. It is perhaps the destiny of each Morel to be "tragado por la selva," as the first one puts it.

Alicia is also a "statue" of Sabina and the opposite of Lucila in social status. She is closely allied to Sabina since they are both of lower class origin, but she is also a parody of Sabina. César suggests that Sabina is "un poco cursi," but Alicia is truly vulgar: inappropriately dressed, unable to hide her feelings for César, ill-behaved, and, most importantly, completely oblivious to the degrading aspects of her potential career as an actress in Mexico City.

Las estatuas de marfil is also a play about plays with an incomplete "play within a play" structure. Two scenes from other plays are used as commentary on the real situation. The first of these Sabina repeats to herself at the end of the first act. Rejecting the attentions of her husband— the reality of love—she acts the role of a woman in love with herself as lover. The scene is the stronger for following Lucila's confession of the same feelings. In the second scene, Sabina struggles to perform the role of an aged actress and cannot master it to César's satisfaction. He demands irony, pride, and dignity in the defeats of a life

that "ella misma se escogió."[4] Sabina is only "lúgubre y gimoteante." At one level, this scene is a figure for Sabina's own inability to measure up to her desire to be a great actress. It may also be a commentary on the last scene of the play. In that scene, Sabina is at one of the low points of the role she has chosen to play. She is given the opportunity to act, presumably, with dignity and pride, accepting her fate. She clings instead to the idea that her child will fulfill the destiny that she herself has given up. As César tries to suggest, this is an illusion. Sabina is not a tragic figure. She has not entirely accepted the realities of her own life if she persists in searching for a way out even in the next generation. She has achieved a certain dignity and light irony in these scenes. She has evidently discovered that César has not told the impresario about her at all. This is clear to the audience from the outset, but Sabina thought she might become an actress in Mexico City simply because she understood that César had mentioned her personally to the impresario. She has been the victim of the contrivances of her husband and of César, and she has, by the end of the play, overcome the hysterics of her initial discovery.

In addition to fragments from other plays, the characters also invent scenes for one another and try to force each other in various ways to assume certain roles. The members of the theatre group try to make César a sort of divine director—a Pygmalion, as Sabina puts it. He resists whenever the role confronts him explicitly—all through Act I, then most clearly when Sabina reveals the extent of her dependence on him for guidance in Act II. He spells out clearly that she must make her own decision. Like Perseo, César rejects the role of hero (director) only to find that circumstances have played him false and he has unconsciously played the role he sought to avoid. As long as the role confronts him in the context of the theatre, he successfully avoids it. But he cannot avoid it in reality. He is the one who dissuades Sabina from an abortion. He makes the decision for her and directs her toward what he believes to be her true role of wife and mother. He does not know that Sabina's conception has not been the ideal sort he described in Act I—a conscious, responsible act. It is dramatic invention, also in Act I, that suggests to Sabina that she might look beyond the confines of her own home to an acting career. It is clear in that scene that César is playing "for himself"; he is describing his own theatrical ambitions, not those of some actress. Yet the scene acquires its own momentum: he is dismayed to discover that Sabina has taken seriously the role he has conjured up, and this confusion lasts through the play.

The two Pygmalions, César and Mundo, play a scene for each other at the end of Act II. Each assumes a stereotypic role: "una brillante exhibición de músculos y de grandiosa virilidad" and "una brillante exhibición de inteligencia."[5] Together they debate the future of Sabina, inconclusively of course. But the irony of the scene is complex. Mundo is clearly aping the role he has refused since Act I—that of tyrannical husband. Yet he has covertly played that role by contriving Sabina's pregnancy. César is aping what has appeared to be his own true role—that of tolerant, liberal bohemian. Yet he has (much more ambiguously) undermined Sabina's position by possibly fathering her child, directing her to seek a career, and then persuading her not to have an abortion. He has essentially acted out the same role as Mundo, and perhaps César and Mundo bear the same sort of relationship to each other that Lucila, Argentina, and Alicia do to Sabina. Each man deceives Sabina, but in a different way, Mundo by the fact of her pregnancy, and César by the scenarios he creates.

The irony does not end there, though. It is clear that Sabina is not a tragic figure. Carballido does not indulge in pathos either, for she is not completely a victim. Each of the Pygmalions is compromised by the circumstances in which he acts. César is unwittingly a "César" or director, and Mundo may be unwittingly a cuckold.

By the end of **Las estatuas de marfil,** the relationships between the main characters have not really changed, but they have been clarified. The false clues have been removed and the reader sees that César and Mundo have been playing the same role all along. César is, for Sabina, a director/husband. She is unable, herself, to decide what she must do, and so she is forced to play a role—ultimately that of wife and mother. César, thinking to apprentice himself humbly to Art, is guilty of arrogance in his private life. His emotional coldness is like the coldness of the two ideal heroes in the other Carballido plays.

Medusa, Teseo, and **Las estatuas de marfil** are closely analogous to the plays of Sartre. The relatively simple circumstantial irony of *Les Mains sales,* **Medusa** and **Teseo**; the symbolism of **Medusa** and *Huis Clos*; and the elegant and subtle irony of game and role in **Las estatuas de marfil** all elaborate the same design.

The characters do not escape their circumstances in their choices, though they try, by adopting role, to act beyond circumstance. Role is the paradigm of eternal damnation: Hell in *Huis Clos*; the generations that hover—unwanted models and unforeseen destinies—about the heroes of all three Carballido plays; and the immortal and inhuman designs of legend and art. As Medusa says, "No hay más que un sitio: el que todos los hombres tienen en el espacio y en el tiempo."[6] Art, statuary, monsters, and games may resemble the human in form, but they lack this essential human characteristic.

Notes

1. Eugene Skinner, "Carballido: Temática y forma de tres autos," *Latin American Theatre Review,* 3/1 (Fall 1969), pp. 37-47.

2. Mary Warnock, *The Philosophy of Sartre* (London, 1965), p. 133.

3. Emilio Carballido, *The Golden Thread and Other Plays,* trans. Margaret Sayers Peden (Austin: University of Texas Press, 1970), p. 215.

4. Emilio Carballido, *Las estatuas de marfil* (Xalapa: Universidad Veracruzana, 1960), p. 58.

5. Ibid., p. 99.

6. Emilio Carballido, *Teatro,* Letras Mexicanas 57 (México: Fondo de Cultura Económica, 1960), p. 110.

James J. Troiano (essay date 1977)

SOURCE: Troiano, James J. "The Grotesque Tradition in *Medusa* by Emilio Carballido." *Inti* 5-6 (1977): 151-56. Print.

[*In the following essay, Troiano places the play* Medusa *in the tradition of the grotesque, pointing out the play's portrayal of a dismal and bizarre world and its thematic use of the "mask and face" and the "ludicrous demon." He argues that Carballido abandons his usual comical tone to leave the audience shocked and stunned instead.*]

Emilio Carballido (1925) very often satirizes imperfections in our society in his comical plays, such as **Rosalba y los Llaveros** (1950) and **El día que se soltaron los leones** (1957). Frank Dauster's statement in reference to **Rosalba y los Llaveros** sums up Carballido's position regarding life's imperfections: "Ni censura ni elogia, sino que se burla con sentido humano, fraternal."[1] Nevertheless, **Medusa** (1958) is a bitter portrayal of the human condition in which Carballido utilizes the grotesque tradition in order to portray his anguished view of the world. The cloak of humor, which is so characteristic of Carballido, is torn away, and a bizarre and suffering world is cast abruptly before the spectator's eyes.

Before analyzing **Medusa,** it is essential to describe the grotesque as a literary tradition. The most fundamental aspect of the grotesque is uncertainty. The author delights in astounding the reader or spectator with completely unexpected events. Apparently tranquil moments often literally explode into terrible nightmares of tension and violence. Wolfgang Kayser writes that "surprise" is a fundamental component of the grotesque tradition.[2] An alien and unpredictable world is presented where life might be compared to walking on the edge of a precipice from which one might fall at any moment. The many shocks and surprises one encounters in the grotesque tradition are created to plunge the spectator into acceptance of the artist's chaotic view of the world.

In addition to the general element of surprise in the grotesque tradition, the world of the grotesque generally involves "the ludicrous demon" and the mask and face theme.

There is very often a purposeful ambiguity in the presentation of the devil or clown in the grotesque tradition. Lee Byron Jennings refers to this kind of confusion with the term "ludicrous demon."[3] Monsters and demons often appear comical and completely innocuous, while harmless or heroic figures are transformed into dangerous and/or ridiculous creatures. This particular component is closely related to the element of uncertainty, which is so basic to the grotesque world. The author hence expends every effort in order to create a world in which man is so estranged from his environment, that he is subject to every surprise or misconception imaginable.

In the grotesque tradition, the author deliberately seeks to stress in his creations unnatural contradictions which exemplify an unpredictable world. One of the most common of these contrasts is the conflict which arises when authentic feelings and desires are pitted against those socially imposed upon the individual; a disparity which produces a virtual distortion of reality. Angela Blanco Amores de Pagella writes: "La máscara que simboliza la vida exterior oprime al pobre rostro, que sufre y soporta la máscara rígida. El rostro es la vida íntima y verdadera, el yo profundo, sin concesiones a lo convencional."[4] This basic conflict is aptly illustrated in a grotesque play appropriately titled *La maschera e il volto* (1913), subtitled "grotesque," by Luigi Chiarelli. Here man is portrayed as constantly forced by society to conceal his true nature by a deceitful mask.

The use of the mask as a figurative symbol is much more satirical than frightening in plays such as *The Mask and the Face*. The mask, however, might be used in a more terrifying manner in what is called "the fantastic grotesque with its oneiric worlds."[5] Terrifying and even lethal identities are exposed in "the fantastic grotesque" when the actual masks or disguises are lifted. In short, the Mexican dramatist presents in *Medusa* a grotesque world filled with shocks, surprises, and innumerable contradictions.

Before analyzing *Medusa*, an outline of Carballido's intricate plot is helpful. King Acrisio of Argos has cast his daughter Dánae into the sea when he refuses to believe that it was Zeus who had impregnated her. King Polidecto of Serifos then protects Dánae and her son Perseo from her father, Acrisio. Polidecto and Dánae become lovers and go to all extremes to hide this fact. On Perseo's twenty-first birthday, the goddess Athena appears to Dánae and orders that Perseo slay Medusa, the monstrous Gorgon. Polidecto and Dánae also demand that Perseo kill his grandfather, Acrisio. Despite Perseo's refusal to execute his grandfather, circumstances lead him to perform this act. Perseo willingly accepts the task of murdering Medusa, but decides against it when he finds a warm and beautiful woman, rather than the monster he has expected. Frustrated in his love for Medusa, however, Perseo is enraged to find that his mother has been impregnated by Polidecto; he then strikes the hypocritical king dead by exposing him to Medusa's uncovered head. Perseo is saddened when Dánae is accidently killed in the same way. A disillusioned and lonely Perseo tells his new wife, Andromeda, in reference to the box which contains Medusa's head: "Aquí guarda todo el amor que me queda" (p. 150).[6]

A grotesque world is envisioned in *Medusa* where nearly every element or occurrence is contradictory and unexpected. One would anticipate, for example, that a father and daughter would share a kind of love or at least tolerance which would bind them together in some way. Nevertheless, Acrisio and Dánae are obsessed throughout the play by a profound hatred. This relentless loathing dominates the character's evey word and action. The intensity and unexpected nature of this relationship provides another example of the grotesque tradition as father and daughter behave in precisely the opposite way from that which one is socially programmed to expect. For example, Dánae states upon encountering her father after many years: "Te escupo también mi odio. Espero que te consumas de rencor impotente y te conviertas en lo que siempre has sido: un viejo gomoso y decrépito, carcomido por pasiones hediondas" (p. 102). Acrisio's response is equally shocking: "Hijo eres una perra. Lamento que vivas aun, y así como te arrojé al mar, te arrojo ahora mi mas profunda maldición" (p. 102). Later he refers to his daughter as "hija de puta" (p. 103). This astonishing depiction of abhorrence repels the spectator, who is catapulted, willingly or unwillingly, into the dramatist's bizarre and grotesque world.

Perseo, in the Greek myth, is the typical fearless hero, who slays dragons and saves maidens. Medusa, on the other hand, is the characteristic monster who savagely destroys all living things without a second thought. Carballido's Perseo behaves as a spoiled and vain child. He egoistically agrees to slay the monster in order to become a hero. The encounter between Medusa and Perseo is a splendid example of the uncertainty of the grotesque world created by the Mexican playwright. The great hero begins to cry out of fear after he encounters Medusa. Unaware that he is speaking to the monster herself, Carballido's Perseo meekly admits his fear: "¡Lloré de miedo! Aquí me tienes; el héroe, llora de miedo porque ve de repente a una muchacha" (p. 109). This is a truly exceptional monster whose relationship to Perseo progresses from that of maternal fondness, to friendship, and then to a lover. Initially, Perseo sheepishly confesses to Medusa: "(como un niño) Quiero ser héroe" (p. 109). She gently informs him of the folly of striving to become superior to one's counterparts, and upholds the general equality of man. Later, Medusa speaks of being transformed from a lovely child to a monster, and thus becoming rejected and despised by everyone because of the jealousy of the gods. Carballido marvelously presents deeply moving and intimate scenes between these two enormously discrepant types, as they communicate their innermost fears and frustrations. Perseo is deeply moved by the suffering Gorgon, who sadly reveals to him: "¿Sabes? Eres el primer hombre en el mundo que llora por Medusa" (p. 121). Finally, Perseo's slaying of Medusa is not the traditional hero indifferently killing a cold, unfeeling monster, but a lover passionately murdering his beloved because the two realize the folly of attempting to fulfill their doomed relationship. Dauster discusses Perseo's necessity to slay Medusa: "Ha matado a Medusa, ha matado a su amor, porque es un amor sin posibilidades de vivir y en vez de dejar que este amor se corrompa como todo lo demás, lo dos prefieren que muera."[7] Carballido astounds spectator and reader alike by adopting a myth concerning a hero's deadly encounter with a monster and completely transforming it to an unexpected and grotesque love story which, as it unfolds, becomes a tragic commentary on the human degradation of family and love, from which no one is exonerated.

One would expect the other Gorgons to be frightening monsters but, as with Medusa and Perseo, Carballido startles the spectators with a completely opposite direction from what would be anticipated. The Gorgons are actually very similar to Jennings' view of "the ludicrous demon." These monsters are not portrayed as snarling, killing, or plotting, as are Dánae, Polidecto, and the gods. A bizarre situation awaits the audience as the curtain falls in *Act IV,* for Carballido's frightening Gorgons behave like old women very much taken up with a game of cards. In contrast to almost all other characters in **Medusa,** these are good-natured and happy people. A grotesque world is presented here in which the heroic is childish, the classical villain is a hero, and the monsters are innocuous and even delightful. In **Medusa,** no one and nothing is what it seems to be.

The grotesque mask functions as both a satirical and frightening element in **Medusa.** Nearly all the characters conceal their true feelings and selfish intentions. Dánae and Polidecto are the most extreme examples of masqueraders. These two characters continually camouflage their true actions behind a veil of deceit. The two make love frequently, but constantly attempt to hide their actions with elaborate devices. They contrive to have guards posted to assure that no one enters Dánae's quarters, supposedly not even King Polidecto himself. They also agree not to use the intimate "tú" form of speech when anyone is near. At one point, Dánae exclaims with horror to Polidecto: "Estamos tuteando," as Perseo is about to enter. This is all particularly absurd since Perseo categorically denounces his mother and lover for the intimate relationship which they painstakingly strive to conceal. The mask becomes reality to the characters, as does madness to Henry IV in Pirandello's play, which is also interpreted as grotesque by Kayser.[8] Henry becomes enslaved by his fictive mask of madness, as Carballido's two lovers seem to believe their farce. Polidecto and Dánae exert themselves to maintain a pure facade for Dánae, feigning that she is untouched by

human hands, and enjoyed only by Zeus. The gods, too, wear masks in this play. The greedy Atenea wants Medusa slain not because the monster has killed innocent victims, but because the Gorgon's oracle is taking business away from hers. Polidecto and Dánae desire to have Acrisio murdered not really because he had cruelly cast Dánae and her son into the sea, but because they want to take material advantage of the wealthy island of Argos where Acrisio rules. Carballido uses the satirical mask in these instances to present a grotesque world, where truth is disguised and actual character and motives are impossible to distinguish.

In addition to these examples of the satirical use of the mask, the play has supernatural overtones. This aspect of the grotesque coincides with Kayser's description of "the fantastic grotesque." Carballido utilizes and transforms the portion of the Medusa myth in which people who look directly upon the Gorgon are converted into stone. In the Mexican's version of the myth, however, it is Medusa's exposed body, not her face, which causes petrifaction. Carballido stresses the fact that the corruption is on the inside, and not the exterior of Medusa. The Gorgon herself reveals to Perseo: "mi pelo ... mi melena, está aquí adentro. La siento moverse. Ella es el horror, es la que petrifica. Si yo estuviera descubierta, tú serías ya tu propio monumento" (p. 111). Once again a variation of the mask and face theme is presented, for here the true corruption of man is hidden. Even Medusa, the best character in the play, hides her true nature behind a deceitful mask, a condition forced upon her by the envious gods. In this bleak, grotesque work, a world is exposed which is inhabited by characters similar to Dante's depiction of the classical monster Geryon: harmless, charming in appearance, and yet ready to strike the lethal blow. Medusa suffers greatly because of her horrendous condition, but even Perseo's love for her is useless in the face of it. No one is saved in this, Carballido's bleakest and most pessimistic work.

Initially, it might seem perplexing that Carballido wrote such a bizarre and grotesque work as **Medusa,** since his plays have been known to be basically lighthearted farces, such as **Rosalba y los Llaveros** and **El día que se soltaron los leones.** The seeds which blossomed into **Medusa** were, however, always there. Carballido has always been aware of, and concerned for, the flaws of society. **Rosalba y los Llaveros,** a comedy of customs, is the framework for criticism of life in rural Mexico. **El día que se soltaron los leones** is a fantastic and comical play which points out the absurdities of contemporary society. **El relojero de Córdoba** (1958), like **Medusa,** re elaborates old material to attack many negative aspects of our time: wrong values, the distortion of justice, commercialism, and the like. The tone of **El relojero de Córdoba** is generally more farcical than **Medusa,** but the themes are basically the same.

The characters also mirror the author's social consciousness, for even in the lighter plays, such as **El día que se** *soltaron los leones* and *Rosalba y los Llaveros,* they are frustrated and in conflict with their environment. Ana and the poet, in the former play, speak of the lack of fulfillment in their lives and their alienation from society. Lázaro and Rita, in the latter work, are both tortured by their thwarted and sheltered lives. Carlos Solórzano observes the unhappiness of characters created by Carballido when he speaks of: ". . . un ambiente de marcada tristeza que no se desgarra nada, sino que mantiene a los personajes en un medio tono de angustia psicológica tristemente soportada."[9] The characters are products of a highly sensitive man, who sees and feels the many tragic aspects of life, and attempts to communicate this concern through his art. Carballido's humor is an ironic humor which cloaks the writer's concern for the many imperfections of contemporary society. Carballido's situation corresponds in this instance to Lord Byron, who writes in *Don Juan,* Canto the Fourth: "And if I laugh at any mortal thing, 'Tis that I may not weep; and if I weep, It is that our nature cannot always bring itself to apathy."[10] Carballido's laughter is transformed into weeping in *Medusa* in very much the same way his Perseo mourns for the death of the enchanting Gorgon.

In short, Emilio Carballido presents an uncharacteristically dismal world in *Medusa.* The basic elements of surprise, "the mask and the face," and "the ludicrous demon," all defined as essential aspects of the grotesque tradition, are utilized by the author. *Medusa* is a play in which Carballido has decided to no longer entertain his audience by satirizing the many flaws of society, but instead to stun and shock them, as if in hope that one Promethean blow might end all the horror and injustice in the world.

Notes

1. Frank Dauster, "El teatro de Emilio Carballido," *La palabra y el hombre,* (Veracruz), 23, (July-Sept. 1962), p. 372.

2. Wolfgang Kayser, *The Grotesque in Art and Literature,* (Bloomington, Indiana: Indiana University Press, 1963), pp. 184-185.

3. Lee Byron Jennings, *The Ludicrous Demon: Aspects of the Grotesque in German Post-Romantic Prose,* (Berkeley and Los Angeles, California: University of California Press, 1963), p. 11: "Death or the devil very often puts on a fool's garb, or the clown becomes a demon."

4. Angela Blanco Amores de Pagella, *Nuevos temas en el teatro argentino: La influencia europea,* (Buenos Aires: Editorial Huemel, S.A., 1965), p. 74.

5. Kayser, p. 186.

6. All quotations from Carballido's plays are taken from the anthology *Teatro de Emilio Carballido,* (Mexico: Fondo de Cultura Económica, 1960).

7. Dauster, p. 381.

8. Luigi Pirandello, *Henry IV* in *Naked Masks,* ed. Eric Bentley, (New York: Dutton, 1952).

9. Carlos Solórzano, *El teatro latinoamericano en el siglo xx,* (Mexico: Editorial Pornaca, 1964), p. 176.

10. Lord Byron, *Don Juan,* ed. Leslie Marchand, (Cambridge and Boston: Riverside Press, 1958), Canto the Fourth, p. 136.

Jacqueline Eyring Bixler (essay date 1984)

SOURCE: Bixler, Jacqueline Eyring. "The Family Portrait: Dramatic Contextuality in Emilio Carballido's *Un vals sin fin sobre el planeta* and *Fotografía en la playa.*" *Chasqui* 14.1 (1984): 66-85. Print.

[*In the following essay, Bixler concentrates on the correlation between form and content in two plays by Carballido. She examines how the plays focus on members of a family during a finite period of time and how their interconnected and sometimes converging plots emphasize the complexity of human relationships.*]

During his thirty-five-year reign as Mexico's most versatile and prolific dramatist, Emilio Carballido has created virtually every conceivable form of theatre, from pure fantasy to strict realism, from light comedy to plays of serious and explicit social protest.[1] Despite a total production of nearly one hundred works, Carballido continues to impress his audience and readers with his ability to devise the dramatic form that will best correspond to the thematic content of each new piece. In two plays of the 1970's—*Fotografía en la playa* (1977)[2] and *Un vals sin fin sobre el planeta* (1970)[3]—Carballido creates a dramatic family portrait by capturing one day in the lives of two large, provincial families. He slowly interweaves the life threads of the various family members into a polylinear web that complements his thematic focus on the complexity and ambiguity of human relationships. The image of the *tejido,* the web that unites all men despite individual differences, is not new to Carballido's theatre nor to the critical study of his work.[4] *Fotografía en la playa* and *Un vals sin fin sobre el planeta,* however, represent the efforts of a more mature and technically innovative dramatist who now expresses that continuing concern with interrelationships through dramatic contexture rather than through explicit dialogue or conspicuous on-stage imagery. The combination of thematic subtlety and structural complexity invite the reader/spectator to discover for himself the contextural patterns that lie behind the deceiving stillness of these two family portraits.

Contrary to Aristotelian notions concerning the primacy and the development of plot, Carballido offers in each of these plays a rather static situation, with a minimum of plot and therefore little causal development from beginning to end. Rather than the one major plot line characteristic of conventional drama, Carballido develops several different plot lines by observing the actions of various characters at a given moment (a synchronic or vertical movement), instead of following the development of one or two characters over a certain period of time (a diachronic or horizontal development). Accordingly, there is no single direction to the play's movement, but rather a number of short lines that crisscross and weave a web of interpersonal relationships. This particular structure corresponds to what Marvin Rosenberg calls the "contextual drama," wherein "the tensions of context, rather than direction, of vertical depth, rather than horizontal movement, become important."[5] Tensions increase within a situation already in existence when the play begins rather than arising as a result of any horizontal development. A closer look at the two works in question will illustrate their contextuality as well as Carballido's adaptation of form to content.

At first glance, *Un vals sin fin sobre el planeta* appears to be traditionally structured, an impression produced by the play's formal division into several separate scenes, all of which follow a temporal progression from one morning to the next. Under the surface, however, lies an intricate network of human relationships, composed of lines that cross one another and extend indefinitely into the future. Through constantly shifting character combinations and a subconscious dream sequence, Carballido reveals the changes that occur in this network as a result of a single incident—the arrival of two young peddlers to the Moredia household. Unknowingly, these two visitors act as a catalyst in causing desires, which were previously subconscious or repressed, to surface within the family.

Aside from the arrival of the peddlers and the reaction that they inadvertently cause in the family, there is very little plot development. Nevertheless, the illusion of a changing situation is created by the continuous physical movement of the characters on stage. Family members, guests, and neighbors move constantly in and out of the spotlight as the dramatist presents every possible combination of characters. Only scenes IV and VI, during which the young Carlos is left alone to develop a more intimate relationship with his new friends, are relatively motionless. Each of the other five scenes contains as many as eighteen changes, as characters move continually on and off the stage. This changing of character combinations not only produces a sense of movement, which decompensates in part for the lack of dramatic action, but also suggests visually the idea of a web of human relationships in constant flux.

Scene I introduces this network of relationships and suggests some of the tensions located therein. A minor mishap—the escape of Carlos' goat—reveals conflicts already in existence within the family before the peddlers arrive. Carlos, a sensitive 14-year-old, is delighted when the goat collides with Guille, his 22-year-old stepmother. Carlos' resentment of Guille is due in part to his father's obvious preference for her over him and also to the memory he holds of his dead mother; his father, Víctor, was already living with Guille when his first wife died. Guille responds to Carlos' hostility by encouraging Víctor to send the goat to the butcher. Carlos' two middle-aged spinster aunts, Aminta and Rocío, show that their own sympathies lie with their nephew. Víctor's role in the household proves to be a paternal one, as demonstrated by the fact that even his two sisters call him "Papá." While seeming to focus on the chaos caused by Carlos' goat, this first scene presents the family relationships and also reveals some of the tensions that exist among them: Carlos' resentment of Guille; her reciprocal dislike for Carlos; the spinsters' servile role in the house; and, finally, Víctor's role as mediator and father to all.

The second scene portrays the arrival of the two peddlers and their reception into the Moredia household. Their unexpected appearance, a seemingly insignificant event, is actually the catalyst for the rest of the play, as all of the family's subsequent actions revolve around their guests. According to Robert Corrigan, apparently meaningless incidents are often the key to non-linear drama: "We see the drama and the complexity of the seemingly trivial, inconsequential, and the simple that is the very tissue of the human situation."[6] Every member of the family, with the exception of Guille, is overwhelmed by the young couple's charm, good looks, and adventurous spirit. When Gabriel and Consuelo tell the family the sad tale of their lives, any suspicion or resistance that might have remained quickly disappears. They speak sadly of their life in Mexico City with a tyrannical father and of their abandoned, ailing mother in Chiapas, whom they wish to join. The money they hope to receive in exchange for Consuelo's jewelry will be used to purchase their train tickets. Despite slight discrepancies between the versions that Gabriel and Consuelo offer of their situation, no one ever questions the validity of their story, and all but Guille resolve to help the strangers as much as possible. Carlos persuades his father to buy the jewelry, for which Víctor voluntarily pays three times what they ask. Rocío and Aminta invite them to dinner and later prepare a room for them to spend the night. Impressed by the youths' sincerity, and particularly by Consuelo's beauty, Víctor later gives them train tickets, while Guille stands back in helpless rage and jealousy.

During the remainder of the play, Gabriel and Consuelo unknowingly produce a radical, yet almost invisible change in the family. The candor and adventurousness shared by the youths infuse the family with a desire for the same kind of freedom. As the family members become more and more painfully conscious of these once buried desires, the lines of the family network begin to extend outward. As Elder Olson explains, the lines of polylinear drama may extend in one of three directions: they may converge, diverge, or run parallel to one another. *Un vals sin fin ... [Un vals sin fin por el planeta*] is clearly a case of divergence, which Olson defines as "the stemming of separate lines from a single cause."[7] Instead of causing the family's lives to converge toward a point of union, the peddlers' visit prompts them to extend outward in search of individual freedom. The play's structural movement, coupled with the pre-existing web of relationships, suggests the following pattern:

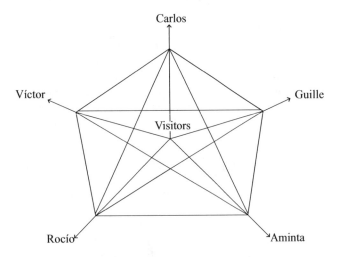

Carlos

Víctor   Guille

Visitors

Rocío   Aminta

This star-shaped pattern reinforces structurally the *tejido* motif so characteristic of Carballido's work. In addition to the five lines that diverge from a common center, the pattern contains other lines that interweave among and connect with those diverging lines to create a complex web. The crossing and connecting points of the various lines represent the tensions and conflicts that arise as a result of the different concept that each character has of freedom.

Not until the end of the play does the family fully realize how much the visit has affected their lives. At this point, Carballido presents a dream sequence in which all of the characters reveal their most hidden thoughts and desires. To create the illusion of a dream world, Carballido directs the actors to move continually about the stage as if sleepwalking:

> [...] aparece toda la familia, inmóvil, como un coro de sonámbulos. Todos descalzos, ausentes. Carlos viste solamente un pantalón blanco que le queda algo corto. Los demás, ropa de dormir. Entran deslizándose, de dos puntos distintos, Gabriel y Consuelo: traen maletas, visten ropa normal. Caminan entre la familia, como si ésta no existiera. [...] Los huéspedes caminan despacio entre la familia, normalmente; van, vienen, se entrecruzan, juntos o separados. No se detendrán, tampoco expressarán relación alguna.[8]

Carballido recreates visually in this scene the same idea of the web that he has presented structurally throughout the play. The continual crisscrossing of the lines strengthens the network while at the same time the characters' conflicting attitudes threaten to pull it apart. The threads extend outward as the members try to disengage themselves from the web, but their ties with other threads continually prevent them from obtaining complete independence. Although there seems to be little possibility of liberty in the near future, the characters all realize that they have been permanently changed by the visit. Aware now of what they have been missing in life, they cannot return to their former existence:

Rocío:

> Hay el arte, y hay el baile, y tantas cosas tan divinas que nada más vemos de lejos ...

Carlos:

> Hay trenes, aventuras ...

Aminta:

> Hay personas que pasan y son preciosas, dan ganas de verlas mucho tiempo, de que nunca se vayan y duerman en nuestras camas ...

Rocío:

> Gente que se ríe a carcajadas y corre y baila de un lado a otro de la tierra, y le suceden cosas, huye, siente, sufre, y todo cuanto le pasa tiene significado, importa y es intenso ...
>
> [...]

Aminta:

> Y los días en sus vidas son distintos, pueden reconocer un día de otro ...

Rocío:

> Quién sabe cómo, llegan y nos trastornan, nos vuelven al revés ...

Aminta:

> Y soñamos con ellos ...

Rocío:

> Y es tan difícil, siempre, hallar con quién soñar ...

Aminta:

> Y los sueños también son realidades. Después de soñar algo, ya no somos los mismos.

(pp. 73-74)

These two sisters, once relatively happy with their peaceful existence in Víctor's house, now realize that their life has been uneventful and therefore meaningless. In this shared dream, they revolt against Víctor's domination of their lives: "Queremos sufrir lo que se nos dé la gana, no lo que tú decidas" (p. 69). Although the sisters share the urge to be free, each has somewhat different hopes with regard to the future. At 42, Aminta no longer hopes to marry, but Rocío, ten years her junior, still secretly entertains thoughts of marriage. Through their conversations with the peddlers, the sisters gradually reveal that their spinsterhood is due not to a lack of suitors but rather to Víctor's overruling "protection." Yet while he can effectively prevent them from marrying, he cannot destroy their secret desires.[9] In lifting and hugging the guests' suitcases they openly embrace the idea of freedom. But even in this world of dreams, Víctor continues to thwart their goal:

VÍCTOR:

>   Y es la casa dormida, la casa sobre mis hombros ... La casa con sus sueños que se entrecruzan ...

AMINTA:

>   Y tú decides siempre cómo acaban los sueños.

VÍCTOR:

>   Proteger a las hermanas, ver crecer a los hijos, que sean fuertes, que entiendan ... Y decidir por todos, decidir ...

>   (p. 67)

Víctor produces an ambivalent reaction of antipathy and sympathy in the audience, the former through his jealous protection and consequent repression of his sisters, and the latter through his affection and endless generosity. While his intentions are undoubtedly good, he remains entirely oblivious to the tensions and unhappiness that he himself has created in the family. His firm belief, for example, in a double moral standard and in the existence of two separate universes, one masculine and the other feminine, is actually the cause of many of their problems: Rocío and Aminta's mounting discontent, Carlos' resentment of Guille, and Guille's own frustration as a helpless and jealous wife.

Although Guille is at 22 already a wife and a mother, she is incapable of cooking, cleaning house, or even dressing the three children she has had with Víctor. Instead of trying to help her, the others either make light of her complaints or ignore her completely. Throughout the peddlers' stay, Guille occupies a marginal position, ignored and excluded by the rest:

>   GUILLE *va a salir hacia la cocina: se oye un coro de carcajadas de las tres mujeres.* GUILLE *se detiene; vuelve melancólicamente a la sala y se sienta, con una mano en el collar. Oscuridad.*

>   (p. 32)

The reader/spectator comes to sympathize with her situation when he comprehends that her disagreeable nature is clearly the result of loneliness and insecurity. Víctor barely pays attention to her, and when he does it is almost invariably in the form of a sexual advance. Guille suffers this treatment in silent rage and jealousy until the dream scene, wherein she finally vents her frustrations:

[...] voy a sanar cuando hayan cambiado un poco las cosas y se hayan ido esas mujeres, tus hermanas. Son muy buenas, sí, pero no las aguanto! Me ven como una inútil, soy idiota, no sé hacer nada, pues míralas cacareando, como gallinas alborotadas, por ese tipo. Guisan riquísimo, ¿verdad? Pues tú vas a comer lo que yo haga, te guste o no. Ya aprenderé. Ya sabré manejar la casa. Cuando me zafe de ellas.

>   (p. 70)

Guille's situation, like that of Aminta and Rocío, involves a struggle for self-assertion and self-determination. The peddlers' visit prompts her to seek these goals by causing her to experience envy along with frustration over her own helplessness. As she finally exclaims to her sleeping mate, "Estoy harta de no ser nadie. Hoy fue la última gota" (pp. 67-68).

Although Consuelo and Gabriel's visit changes all of the characters in one way or another, Carlos is clearly the one most profoundly affected by their presence. In what could be considered a mythic journey, Carlos enters, with the help of his new friends, into the fascinating world of adulthood. After their departure, he is no longer the child he was yesterday:

ERASTO:

>   Vamos luego a la vía, ¿no?

>   (CARLOS *niega.*)

ERASTO:

>   ¿Por qué no?

CARLOS:

>   (*Le hace seña de que se calle.*) Shh ...

ERASTO:

>   ¿Por qué?

CARLOS:

>   Sh ... (*Y le hace seña de que se aleje.*)

ERASTO:

>   ¿Pues qué tanto ... haces?

CARLOS:

>   Acordándome ...

>   (*Sale* ERASTO. CARLOS *se queda muy ausente, escribiendo suavemente en el suelo, con un dedo.*)

>   *TELON*

>   (p. 76)

Carlos' rejection of his friend and his attempt to recapture the previous day suggest the profound effect that the peddlers have had upon his life.[10] Gabriel and Consuelo unknowingly cause this change to occur in Carlos by introducing him to the adult world of sex, freedom, and movement. They open the door to sexuality by arousing his curiousity with all the mysteries surrounding their own relationship. The boy begins to suspect that Gabriel and Consuelo's association is not really of fraternal nature when Consuelo recites her verses about "la bella suicida" to the family. From the cryptic comments exchanged between the peddlers, Carlos, along with the audience, deduces that Gabriel once saved Consuelo from an attempted suicide. A subsequent examination of the contents of Consuelo's purse creates suspicions not only in Carlos but also in Gabriel, who becomes jealous and distrustful upon spotting the name of Consuelo's ex-lover in her notebook, Thus, Carlos is not the only one puzzled by Consuelo's impulsive and irrational behavior:

CONSUELO:

¿Qué, pues?

GABRIEL:

Contigo . . . siempre quedan dudas.

CONSUELO:

¿Por esto?

GABRIEL:

Por todo. Me das una versión de cualquier cosa, luego otra, luego otra . . .

(pp. 48-49)

Through enigmatic conversations such as the above, Carlos begins to sense the ambiguities that underlie the adult, sexual world.

During his passage into adolescence, Carlos undergoes not only a mental change with regard to sex but also an important physical change, which is due primarily to his own physical attraction to Consuelo. Like his father, the young boy is captivated by her charm and beauty. After Víctor presents the guests with trail tickets, Consuelo bewilders Carlos by kissing him on the mouth. Later that night, the boy sleeps fitfully, as he dreams of boarding the train with Consuelo for some unknown destination. When he finally appears in the dream scene, Carlos admits embarrassingly to his guests, "Soñaba con ustedes y me chorrié todo . . ." (p. 67). Now physically and mentally aware of the adult world and of the adventures awaiting him beyond the small town of Córdoba, Carlos can no longer stand still and allow life to pass by him.

Although Víctor maintains his sisters in a slavish existence, he recognizes that Carlos, as a part of "el universo masculino," requires a certain amount of liberty. He demonstrates this male-to-male understanding during the dream scene, when he takes Carlos aside to warn him of life's temptations and of restraints of binding relationships. According to Víctor, life is like a moving train, an endless series of changing relationships:

> [. . .] tú ves, vamos pasando, vamos yéndonos juntos en esta casa, nos vamos alejando unos de otros, ¿y qué sabemos, en realidad? Una verdad es este movimiento, esta especie de tren sin fin en que vamos todos, estos carros que a veces cambian de vía . . .

(p. 74)

Víctor appropriately chooses the train as a metaphor of life's movement and resulting changes. A recurrent image throughout the play, the train becomes symbolic, as in two other Carballido plays,—*Conversación entre las ruinas* and *Yo también hablo de la rosa*—of adventure and progressive change. One of Carlos' favorite pastimes is to watch the trains from the energy tower as they arrive and depart again for unknown destinations. Before the peddlers' visit, he was content simply to observe the train, but now Carlos wants to be a part of the train and of the excitement and movement it embodies. Significantly, Carlos' passage into adolescence occurs as a result of a dream involving an exciting train journey with Consuelo. Like Víctor's description of "carros que a veces cambian de vía," Carlos has changed tracks from childhood to adolescence.

Gabriel and Consuelo supplement Víctor's philosophy on movement and freedom by showing Carlos their importance in the fulfillment of one's future. When Carlos begs his new friends to extend their stay in Córdoba, Consuelo explains that immobility or hesitation only result in doubts over what the future *might* have been: "Y si aquí nos quedáramos, sin movernos, quien sabe mañana dónde habríamos llegado, ni quiénes seríamos" (p. 64). Yet Carlos is just beginning to explore the world around him and must first orient himself to his exact position on this earth. After the peddlers have boarded the train, Carlos climbs onto the platform, spreads his arms, and begins to spin slowly like a weather vane:

CARLOS:

> Arriba, en algún sitio, hay la estrella Polar y la Cruz del Sur. Sé que son puntos de referencia en este viaje, en esta fuga, en esta carrera loca. No sé reconocerlas todavía, no las veo. A la derecha hay un océano: el Atlántico; a la izquierda otro océano: el Pacífico. Bajo mis pies, el centro mismo de este mundo. En derredor, la superficie toda, toda, toda del planeta . . .

(p. 75)

Carlos' rotating movement, coupled with the waltz playing in the background, underscores the title of the play and the idea of movement. The title actually derives from a poem by Ramón López Velarde, which Consuelo recites as her own for the family and which includes the verse "valsando un vals sin fin por el planeta." The play's title, the recital of the poem itself, the characters' physical movement on the stage, and the general theme of movement all support the dramatist's idea of a world of human relationships in constant flux.

Due to the major mental and physical changes that Carlos undergoes, the play lends itself well to a mythic interpretation. Carlos' experiences with the guests suggest a series of initiatory events. The first meeting with the visitors, his discovery of their true relationship, the lessons on freedom and change, his own sexual attraction to Consuelo, and, finally, the dream all suggest a mythic passage into adulthood. The only drawback in subjecting this work to a mythic interpretation is that in doing so one would virtually have to ignore the development of the other family members. A focus on Carlos' passage into adulthood and thereby on one single character would, by necessity, neglect the play's contextual structure. While Carlos' experience is clearly the most noticeable and the most significant, every member of the family is radically changed by the peddlers' visit. Carballido focuses not on the development of one single person but rather on the changing situation of an entire family.

With the exception of the final visionary scene, Carballido treats his characters and his material in a realistic manner. According to Marvin Rosenberg, the creator of a contextual work can choose to protray his characters either realistically or non-realistically.[11] In *Un vals sin fin sobre el planeta*, the dramatist, through careful psychological observation, makes his characters seem "real," even though they develop in dimension rather than in direction. By choosing this realistic, dimensional portrayal of characters, Carballido, much like his predecessor Anton Chekhov, is able to study the movement of many interweaving planes of human behavior, and the tensions located therein, during one particular day in the characters' lives.

Fotografía en la playa displays many of the same structural characteristics and thematic concerns found in *Un vals sin fin sobre el planeta.* Even the material is basically the same, as Carballido examines once again the inner and outer lives of a large provincial family during the course of one day. In this second family portrait, he weaves an even more complex web by gradually revealing an underlying pattern of divergence beneath the more superficial pattern of convergence. The play's multilinear structure, the two-dimensional pattern of the web, and the recurrent image of the sea complement each other in conveying the idea that life, while brief, is complex and ambiguous.

Although Carballido subtitles *Fotografía en la playa* "obra en dos actos," the play's structure is even less traditional than that of *Un vals sin fin sobre el planeta.* Besides the division into two acts, which serves only to indicate a change of setting from the house patio to the beach, the play contains no other scenic divisions. This lack of exter-

nal structuring increases the vertical depth of the work and produces the sensation of simultaneity, as the spectator is unaware of any passage of time. In fact, time seems to stand still while Carballido explores the many interpersonal relationships that exist within a large family. As in *Un vals sin fin sobre el planeta,* there is little causal development of events. Instead, the dramatist creates once again the impression of ongoing movement through the constant movement of the characters on stage as they enter and leave the camera's focus. Due to the far greater number of characters in *Fotografía en la playa,* this pattern of movement becomes more complex as the dramatist's possibilities of character combinations increase. The family itself consists of four different generations:[12]

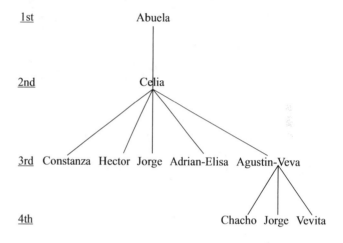

The cast is further enlarged by several servants and friends of the family: Nelly, Héctor's student and Jorge's lover; Adolfo, Vevita's current boyfriend; Luis, Héctor's new friend; the photographer; and two maids, Benita and Patricia, who actually create a great deal of the play's movement by repeatedly crossing the stage with cots and blankets as they try to accomodate the guests. Their frequent appearance on stage and confused movements reflect visually the turbulence and confusion that lie beneath a seemingly peaceful reunion of the family. In this play, however, those hidden problems do not emerge as a result of unknown and unexpected visitors, but rather as a result of what appears to be a happy family reunion. The family members have come together once again on this particular day, and in doing so, bring to the surface problems and tensions that had been buried or forgotten since the last gathering.

The contextual nature of the play is established shortly after the curtain rises, as the characters begin arriving for a brief reunion. Abuela, Celia, and Constanza all reside at the site of the get-together, which appears to be Veracruz due to the frequent reference to the *norte*—the cold winter wind that strikes the eastern coast of Mexico. Adrián, after serving a six-month sentence for embezzlement, has recently moved in with the three women. His wife, Elisa, arrives later in the day to visit him for the first time since

his release. Héctor, Jorge, and Nelly, all of whom live in
Mexico City, have already been at the family home for
several days when the play begins. The group is complete
when Agustín arrives with his family soon after the play
commences. From this moment on, the play moves quickly as new character combinations evolve and dissolve on
stage and Carballido presents in rapid succession a series
of interrelationships and the tensions and conflicts that
exist within each one. All polylinear forms develop, as
Robert Corrigan explains, "not through a predetermined
subject and plot, but through an increasingly intense and
revealing series of emotional states."[13]

Unlike *Un vals sin fin sobre el planeta,* with its network
of diverging lines, *Fotografía en la playa* displays a pattern of convergence. Two main events cause the lines to
converge. The first is the basic situation presented in the
play—the family reunion—, an event which brings all of
the independent family lives together at a common point.
The second event is the taking of the family portrait. At the
end of the play, a photographer gathers the family together
in front of his lens to create a lasting impression of their
reunion. The photograph serves as a final converging point
for lies which, once the photo is taken, will continue in
their former, independent direction. Even Celia seems to
sense the impermanence of this reunion:

CELIA:

> Una vez más, mientras lo permita el destino, toda la fa-
> milia está reunida. Bueno, faltan algunos nietos, y hay
> aquí gente que no nos toca de nada, pero vamos a quedar
> unidos en un retrato. Qué hermoso es eso.[14]

By the end of the play, when this portrait is finally taken, it
is apparent to all, characters and audience alike, that their
convergence or reunion is superficial and impermanent,
and that their lives will only unite momentarily in the photograph. It becomes increasingly evident throughout the
play that those same lines that appear to be converging
are actually diverging as the family members continue to
follow their own separate paths, all of which extend outward toward freedom from family obligations and responsibilities.

As the play progresses, the reader/spectator becomes more
and more aware of the characters' true nature, which is, for
the most part, hermetic and egotistic. Even Abuela, who is
probably the most likable of the characters, prefers to keep
to her own little world of past memories. She often feigns
deafness, blindness, and even senility as a means of isolating herself from the rest of the family. Second-generation
Celia cares more about soap operas and the conservation
of her fading beauty than she does about the welfare of
her own children. She is, for instance, completely unaware
of her daughter Constanza's unhappiness. She discloses
her ignorance of the problem after Héctor proposes that
Constanza take a vacation from her family responsibilities:
"Hijo mío, Constanza nació para vivir así, con nosotras.

Obsérvala: siempre está feliz" (p. 235). The weight of maintaining the house and taking care of Abuela and Celia, along
with a growing fear of spinsterhood, prompts Constanza to
seek freedom from her family ties. Like Rocío and Aminta
of the preceding play, she is determined to break away from
the family, even though she realizes that her chances of
happiness are slim. During the reunion, Constanza asks
her brothers for help and understanding and discovers that
they, too, do not want to be burdened with family responsibilities. Agustín, concerned only with maintaining his own
family's high standard of living, is unwilling to settle for a
less lucrative position in Veracruz. Adrián is too involved
with his own personal failure and too weak to be of any
help. It was, in fact, Constanza who bailed him out of jail
with her own money. Héctor is at first unwilling to sacrifice
his free and easy life as a bachelor and professor in Mexico
City. At the end of the play, when he suddenly offers to
move into the family house and thereby relieve Constanze
of her duties, it is only because he wishes to be near his new
friend Luis. The younger members of the family—Jorge,
Vevita, and Chacho—are also in the process of trying to
assert themselves and break away from the family, be it
through their dress, vulgar language, or sexuality.

The egocentricity of the entire family is most obvious in
the final scene, in which the photographer prepares to take
their picture. Following Chacho's suggestion that they all
think of something pleasant, each family member secretly
enjoys thoughts of personal pleasure:

CHACHO:

> Piensen algo agradable, para que saquen buena cara.
> (*Breve silencio inmóvil. Crece el rumor del mar.*)

FOTÓGRAFO:

> Uno ...
> (*Los rostros de todos van tomando una expresión especial
> "para retrato."*)

PATRICIA:

> Mi día completo es mío, nadie me ordena tonterías.

ELISA:

> No llorar, no tener miedo. Hay música de baile.

VEVITA:

> Un espejo muy grande.

CELIA:

> Mi piel tersa y sin manchas, mi cuello lindo, como en-
> tonces ...

ADOLFO:

> Ya pusieron mi nombre en la puerta de la oficina.

CHACHO:

> Les gusto a las mujeres, caigo bien, puedo ser lo que quiera.

AGUSTÍN:

Me acuerdo de esos ensueños tontos, de juventud, y no me duelen.

VEVA:

Tener algo.

ABUELA:

Recordar . . .

(pp. 237-238)

This passage is strikingly similar to the dream sequence of *Un vals sin fin sobre el planeta,* as Carballido again stops time and penetrates the subconscious world of his characters showing that even while united before the camera lens, the family members continue to pursue their egotistic dreams and goals.

Although the characters show very little genuine interest in one another's lives, preferring to follow their own separate paths, there are two members of the family—Abuela and Héctor—who provide the family, and consequently the play, with a subtle, overall sense of unity. As the eldest member of the family, Abuela functions within their small world as a central character. Since she no longer pursues any personal goals, she is more of a static figure around which the others revolve in pursuit of their individual dreams. She prefers to enjoy memories of the past—her betrothal, her former house, her long, flowing hair—as she sits back and observes all that occurs in the present. From her lofty position as family matriarch, Abuela perceives all of the family's actions. As she herself admits, the others often disregard her observations of their behavior as signs of madness: "Como, según ellos, estoy idiota, no me doy cuenta de nada" (p. 171). Yet her true alertness is shown by the fact that despite her poor eyesight—she fails to recognize Agustín when he arrives—nothing escapes her:

La abuela no ha perdido una coma de toda la escenita, sin disimular su atención y haciendo ruidos significativos de vez en cuando. Ahora, vuelve a jugar con la arena.

(p. 230)

The extent of Abuela's awareness approaches omniscience as she gradually reveals all that she knows about her family. She functions not only as a historian of the past but also as the main source of information concerning the present. Abuela is, for example, the only one who knows that Constanza frequently escapes to the street corner to call her lover, or that Constanza even has a lover. Furthermore, she is somehow aware of the fact that while Nelly came as Héctor's guest she is actually Jorge's bed partner. As Abuela explains, her ubiquity is not limited to the daytime, but rather extends through the night:

[. . .] Benditos sean los que duermen. (*Pela chícharos.*) Es muy triste perder el sueño, pasar la noche como alma en pena, dando vueltas en la cama, hasta oír cantar los gallos . . . Dar vueltas por la casa, caminar cuando todos duermen y oírnos dar suspiros como de alma en pena, rezar rosarios hasta que están llamando a misa y pasan por la calle los lecheros . . . Benditos los que duermen.

(p. 170)

Although the other family members regard her infantile behavior and her morbid remarks as signs of advancing senility, the reader/spectator can easily see that Abuela is the only member of the family who is entirely conscious of the world around her, or in the words of Margaret Peden, "la vidente de la pieza."[15] Abuela is the only character who is not totally involved in pursuing egotistic dreams and, therefore, is the only one able to perceive the disunity that lies beneath the superficial layer of familial harmony. Her central position as matriarch and her role as family historian and informant combine to provide a certain amount of unity to an otherwise fragmented presentation of the family.

As spokesman of Carballido's philosophies on life, Héctor unites the play thematically by making the characters' common situation apparent to the reader or spectator. His frequent comments on the web, the sea, and life's changing design show that the characters, in spite of their individual differences are part of a universal pattern. The train of *Un vals sin fin sobre el planeta* is replaced here by the sea, an image that Héctor employs to describe metaphorically life's complexity and changeability. Early in the play, he explains to Nelly that life consists of a texture of cells in continual transformation:

Imagínate: el cuerpo está cambiando constantemente; los tejidos no cesan de transformarse. Si en este instante parpadeas, el ojo sufre cambios bioquímicos, y los abres y ya es otro organismo diferente. . . .

(p. 175)

Like the dramatist who created him, Héctor understands that life involves constant changes. Furthermore, he is aware that reality, like the sea, is not always as one perceives it to be:

Lo que vemos, todo, es una especie de fantasía. No es cierto que esté quieto, ni que así sea. Cualquier cosa que vemos, es como el mar.

(p. 175)

Man's existence, like the ocean water, is often turbulent beneath its deceivingly calm surface. Through philosophical observations such as these, Héctor unites the family, and consequently the various threads of the play, by showing the characters all to be a part of a larger design.

Héctor's ideas on the illusive nature of reality are closely related to the play's structural duality. While the action of reuniting creates the illusion of convergence, behind all the hugs and pleasantries the characters' lives are actually diverging as they seek freedom from family obligations and responsibilities. The final scene, similar to the oneiric sequence of *Un vals sin fin sobre el planeta,* reinforces this contrast between illusion and reality, between feigned contentment and hidden desires. Even as the characters smile and hug one another, they continue in their minds to follow their own egotistic goals and desires.

In addition to highlighting the contrast between illusion and reality, the photograph taken near the end of the play also underscores Héctor's idea of a universe in constant transition. The role of the photograph in detaining and preserving one particular moment in time is explained in an earlier Carballido play, *Almanaque de Juárez,* wherein the Fotógrafo explains:

> [...] Así hacemos cada fotografía. La Historia es un proceso semejante, fenómeno de luces y de sombras y de sales que fijan gestos aislados para guardarlos en la memoria colectiva. La luz que emana de los gestos de un hombre sirve para fijarlos, para dejarnos una imagen que perdure. ...[16]

In *Fotografía en la playa,* however, Carballido shows that despite the permanent image represented by the photograph, the world will continue to change after the portrait is taken. He demonstrates, through the following disparity between the characters' fixed expression of happiness and the accompanying monologue, that the photograph is nothing but an illusion of permanence:

FOTÓGRAFO:

> Dos ...
>
> (*Desde este momento, los rostros de todos quedan ya sonrientes, estereotipados ligeramente, fijos, rostros de fotografía. No corresponderán las expresiones con lo que se diga.*)

JORGE:

> Despue de lo de Nelly, que afectó tanto a mi tío, yo seguí trabajando, ganando más. Ya me iba a recibir. La Dientona, como le decía Nelly a María de Lourdes, visitaba a todos mis tíos y hacía proyectos. Y los míos, mis planes, se cumplían. Empezaban a verse un poquito vacíos, un poco tristes. Pero ya no había más. Chacho se había casado, también Vevita ... Ya me tocaba a mí. Fue cuando vino mi accidente. Iba en motocicleta, no sentía nada, ni me di cuenta casi; volví la cara, se me venía algo encima. Y de repente, yo ya no estaba aquí.

NELLY:

> Al empezar la curva, alguien gritó. Era un paisaje prodigioso, eso veníamos viendo, los Alpes. Ya supe por qué gritaron, no supe quién. Después, muy poco claramente, llegué a entender que tenía yo la cara despedazada, lo decían en francés, y que a causa del golpe podía yo quedar

ciega, o paralítica, si viviera. Estuve oyendo quejidos mucho tiempo: eran los míos.

> [...]

CONSTANZA:

> (*Quedo.*) Las dos solas aquí en la casa. Viendo esta foto, contando los difuntos. Las dos quedamos todavía, la abuela y yo. Pero la foto ha ido borrándose poco a poco.
>
> (*Luz muy intensa, blanca, por un instante. Luego, se va volviendo una luz amarilla, cada vez más opaca y borrosa.*)
>
> (*Sube el ruido del mar.*)

> TELÓN (pp. 238-240)

While the characters remain absolutely still on stage, as if preserved forever in that cheerful state, their voices reveal that the ensuing years actually brought with them many changes. Carballido suddenly projects his audience into the future as Jorge, Nelly, Adrián, and Benita all describe their deaths and Abuela and Constanza their solitude. Gradually, by means of special lighting, the dramatist makes those on stage fade out, just as the photograph will fade with passing time. When the curtain finally falls, all that remains is the sound of the sea, which continues to move as life goes on. The rising and persistent sound of the water stands in contrast to the fading of the photograph. In fact, as a result of this juxtaposition of sea and portrait, the water appears to be a contributing force in the gradual eradication of the characters, a phenomenon that was suggested in one of Héctor's earlier observations:

> [...] Si sigue uno viendo y viendo, se va uno borrando, se va quedando en blanco. Eso nada más pasa con el mar: me borro, ya no soy yo.

> (pp. 209-210)

The continuing sound of the sea suggests, therefore, the ongoing process of life as it changes and eventually erases the lives of those in the photograph.

Carballido gradually prepares his audience for the tragic end of his characters by means of various staging devices. Act I, for instance, ends with a scene that corresponds in technique to the final protrait scene. Nelly is happily singing and dancing to a recorded French poem when the dramatist abruptly ends her movements:

> (*Queda en pose de vedette, sonriendo ... Oscuridad repentina. Un fogonazo fotográfico deja verla un instante más. Oscuridad.*)

> (p. 208)

By detaining her actions and enveloping her in complete darkness, the dramatist foreshadows the tragic end that awaits this vivacious girl in Europe. Likewise, the accompanying flash of the camera presages the final beach scene, in which the photographer attempts to create an image that will still survive long after destiny has changed the lives of the characters.

In addition to the sea, two other natural elements—the wind and the clouds—are used to suggest impending change. Throughout the second act, Carballido creates the illusion of passing clouds by means of changing light patterns. The alternate periods of light and darkness produced by the clouds' movement reflect on a visual scale the movement that occurs within the family, their changing lives, and their passage through periods of happiness and sadness. The coming *norte,* which will occasion a drastic change in the weather, also conveys the idea of imminent change. The ominous presence of these elements—the clouds, the wind, and the sea—helps to prepare the reader or spectator for a tragic conclusion by serving as a natural representation of the same turbulence that lies within the family. Just as the coming *norte* will bring changes in the weather, the audience knows that the future will likewise bring changes in the family. The two central images of the play—the sea and the photograph—reinforce the idea that change is inevitable. In this opposition between transition and permanence, the latter must eventually succumb; the sound of the sea will persist long after the photograph has faded and vanished.

Due to the greater number of characters and to the existence of two opposing structural patterns—one converging toward a common point and the other diverging in many different directions—, the structure of **Fotografía en la playa** is more intricate and at the same time less conventional than that of **Un vals sin fin sobre el planeta.** Aside from this difference in degree of complexity and technical movement, which is not the product of any causal development of events but rather of the movement created by tensions and emotions deep within the two family structures. These works may easily remind the reader/spectator of the polylinear dramas of Anton Chekhov, about whom Robert Corrigan observes: "Because Chekhov is more concerned with the inner lives of his characters and is not interested in presenting an action, his plays seem lifeless, timeless, static."[17] Marvin Rosenberg makes a similar comment when he discusses the challenge that non-linear drama poses to the dramatist: "The materials ... reside in the aimless, unclimactic multiplicity of emotional life."[18] The real challenge of the contextual drama appears to lie, then in capturing and mainting the reader/spectator's attention and interest. Carballido accomplishes this in both plays through the continuous movement of the characters on stage and through the consequent variation of character combinations and audience perspectives. The incomplete, fragmented view that he presents each family, along with the slow surfacing of hidden conflicts and tensions, maintains the audience's attention throughout the play, thus compensating for the lack of plot and other traditional interest-creating devices.

Above all, the contextuality of these two plays is highly effective in expressing the idea of life as a complex and

continually changing pattern. This is, as Rosenberg suggests, the goal of all non-linear drama, which "sets out to recognize the ambiguity of all human behavior rather than the chain-link effects of isolated acts."[19] The fact that Carballido is now able to convey on a structural level what he previously communicated only through dialogue and imagery demonstrates his progress toward total integration of form and content. In both works, Mexico's premier dramatist has woven structural, symbolic, and thematic threads into a richly textured dramatic web and microcosm of that universal web known as life.

Notes

1. For the most conclusive study to date on Carballido's theatrical output, see Margaret Sayers Peden, *Emilio Carballido* (Boston: Twayne, 1980), which encompasses all of his work, both narrative and dramatic, from his beginning in the late 1940's to 1974. My own unpublished dissertation, "Theory and Technique in Selected Plays of Emilio Carballido (1968-1978)," University of Kansas, 1980, treats the seven plays that Carballido wrote between 1968 and 1978. Another general study on Carballido is by Mary Vásquez-Amaral, *El teatro de Emilio Carballido (1950-1965)* (Mexico: B. Costa-Amic, Editor, 1974).

2. *Fotografía en la playa* was begun in Madrid on October 1, 1974, and finished in Mexico City on June 12, 1977. The play has not, to my knowledge, ever been performed on stage.

3. Although Carballido began writing *Un vals sin fin sobre el planeta* in May 1957, he did not finish it until February 22, 1970. The play's subject matter will not be new to some of his readers. The short story "Los huéspedes," a part of the colleciton *La caja vacía,* is a narrative version of the same story enacted in *Un vals sin fin sobre el planeta.* The same situation also serves as the basis for *La danza que sueña la tortuga* (1954), a play which, although written three years before the commencement of *Un vals sin fin sobre el planeta,* could be considered its sequel since it deals with the same family, only four years later. *Un vals sin fin ...* was first staged in 1970 by Carballido himself.

4. The *tejido* is a central image in two of Carballido's best-known plays, *Yo también hablo de la rosa* (1965) and *La hebra de oro* (1955), wherein it also functions as a symbol of the complexity of the real world and of man's relationships with others. For a thorough critical discussion of this image see Eugene Skinner, in "The Theater of Emilio Carballido: Spinning a Web," *Dramatists in Revolt,* eds. Leon F. Lyday and George W. Woodyard (Austin: University of Texas Press, 1976), who writes of how Carballido "elaborates the concept of human existence as a complex web of interrelationships through a fusion of realistic and poetic techniques" (p. 31). What is

new in these two plays is not the idea of the *tejido* itself, but rather the creation of a structural web to match that pre-existing conceptual web.

5. Marvin Rosenberg, "A Metaphor for Dramatic Form," in *Perspectives on Drama,* eds. James L. Calderwood and Harold E. Toliver (New York: Oxford University Press, 1968), p. 107.

6. Robert W. Corrigan, "The Plays of Chekhov," in *The Context and Craft of Drama: Critical Essays on the Nature of Drama and Theatre,* eds. Robert W. Corrigan and James L. Rosenberg (San Francisco: Chandler Publishing Co., 1964), p. 155. Chekhovian criticism in general and certain plays, such as *The Cherry Orchard* and *Uncle Vanya,* offered many insights into the contextual nature of these two dramas by Carballido.

7. Elder Olson, "The Elements of Drama: Plot," in *Perspectives on Drama,* p. 291

8. Emilio Carballido, *Un vals sin fin sobre el planeta,* in *Tres comedias* (Mexico: Ed. Extemporáneos, 1981), pp. 66-67.

All subsequent quotes will proceed from the same source.

9. This growing need to determine their own lives ultimately leads the sisters to a state of relative independence in the sequel *La danza que sueña la tortuga,* wherein, four years later, Rocío and Aminta run a small general store attached to the family house. Nevertheless, their hopes of complete independence disappear forever when Víctor destroys what will most likely be Rocío's last chance of marrying.

10. In the narrative version of the play, "Los huéspedes," Carlos reveals more openly his own awareness of this change in his life:

    ... tal vez él era otro; algo había cambiado y le ponía una distancia entre "anoche" y "ahora."

    Emilio Carballido, "Los huéspedes," from the collection *La caja vacía* (Mexico: Fondo de Cultura Económica, 1962), p. 37

11. Rosenberg, pp. 107-108.

12. Margaret Sayers Peden, "Emilio Carballido: *Fotografía en la playa,*" *Texto Crítico,* Ano IV, No. 10 (mayo-agosto 1978), 15-22, places Jorge as the son of Jorge, Celia's dead son, in her generational scheme (p. 17). The following passage, however, suggests that Jorge is in fact the son of Veva and Agustín:

CONSTANZA:

   (*Entra.*) Yo pensé que podíamos estar tres mujeres en un cuarto ...

VEVA:

   ¿Y esa otra, la que anda detrás de mi Jorge?

                                        (p. 190)

13. Corrigan, pp. 150-151.

14. Emilio Carballido, *Fotografía en la playa* (Mexico: Editores Mexicanos Unidos, 1980), pp. 230-231.

15. Peden, p. 19.

16. Emilio Carballido, *Almanaque de Juárez* (Nuevo León, Monterrey: Ediciones Sierra Madre, 1972), p. 11.

17. Corrigan, p. 147.

18. Rosenberg, p. 107.

19. Rosenberg, p. 106.

Jacqueline Eyring Bixler (essay date 1984)

SOURCE: Bixler, Jacqueline Eyring. "Myth and Romance in Emilio Carballido's *Conversación entre las ruinas.*" *Hispanic Journal* 6.1 (1984): 21-35. Print.

[*In the following essay, Bixler analyzes Carballido's use of myth. She argues that myth is "just one more dramatic form with which Carballido experiments in his own quest for other ways to express the problems and experiences of modern man."*]

In two of his early works—*Medusa* (1960) and *Teseo* (1962)—Mexican playwright Emilio Carballido found artistic inspiration in classical Greek mythology.[1] In a more recent work, *Conversación entre las ruinas* (1969), the same dramatist builds upon the foundation of broader archetypal patterns, or myths which have been repeated by all mankind time and time again over the centuries. Although the play clearly takes place in the Mexico of the 1950's, Carballido creates, by following basic mythic patterns, a work that transcends both spatial and temporal limitations. Two complementary theories on myth—Frye's myth of romance and Eliade's rites of initiation—enable the reader to discover these universal patterns beneath what appears on the surface to be a highly personal, enigmatic situation. By recreating basic myths within a twentieth-century frame, Carballido presents a drama which every spectator or reader may experience as his own, and in doing so, uncovers once again the inseparable link that exists between art and life.

The Princeton Encyclopedia of Poetics defines myth as "a story or a complex of story elements taken as expressing, and therefore as implicitly symbolizing, certain deep-lying aspects of human existence."[2] The reader or viewer subconsciously recognizes the myth on the basis of primordial images and archetypes which are present within the work as well as within man's collective unconscious. Yet myth extends beyond symbol in the sense that one myth may contain any number of symbols, which are then arranged into stories or patterns of action.[3]

Within the realm of literature, Northrop Frye identifies three different forms of myth—undisplaced myth, realism, and romance—which, when viewed together, comprise what he calls "a world of myth, an abstract or purely literary world of fictional and thematic design."[4] These three literary forms, repeated through the centuries and universally recognized, have themselves become basic mythic structures. Undisplaced myth, generally concerned with gods, demons, and the metaphorical identification of natural phenomena, is the most primitive form of the three. In the realistic mode, mythic patterns are more difficult to identify because of the emphasis on the story's content or representation rather than on its shape. Somewhere in between these two poles lies romance, which Frye defines as "the tendency to suggest implicit mythical patterns in a world more closely associated with human experience."[5] Here the supernatural and the sacred of undisplaced myth become both secular and more credible. Yet, romance never becomes entirely realistic. As Frye explains, romance tends to "displace myth in a human direction and yet, in contrast to 'realism,' to conventionalize content in an idealized direction."[6]

The presence of romance in *Conversación entre las ruinas* is suggested by the fact that Carballido creates an entirely human situation in which mythic patterns are only implied. The play fits somewhere in between undisplaced myth and realism since it does not deal directly with the world of gods, demons, or supernatural events, nor does it present an entirely realistic situation. The play's poetical, mythological language, along with certain ambiguous actions, produces a sense of vagueness which suggests something beyond realism, yet within the realm of romance. In addition to this inherent ambiguity, *Conversación* also displays a structural and a thematic organization very similar to those which Frye identifies as the basic elements of romance.

As the title implies, *Conversación entre las ruinas* involves a long conversation between two characters. The *ruinas*, their memories of the past, form the basis for this long, one-act dialogue. The play contains virtually no dramatic action; it begins with Anarda's arrival one afternoon at Antonio's hut in the Oaxacan jungle and ends that same night with her violent death. The conversation that the two characters maintain between these two framing actions is a mutual attempt to explain and perhaps even justify their past actions and feelings. Because there are only three characters—the third is Enedina, Antonio's servant and companion—and since the play is primarily a discussion between the two principal characters, there is very little characterization beyond what they reveal of themselves in the course of their conversation. During their encounter, the audience learns that Anarda is the beautiful daughter of a once-famous poet and the wife of César, a powerful Mexican *político*. Antonio, formerly an aspiring young poet and Anarda's admirer, has fled to the jungle to escape from his own failure. Believing Anarda to be ill-used by César, Antonio tried to murder him, failed, and consequently fled. Anarda, who now believes herself to be in love with Antonio, has followed him to the jungle with the intention of either remaining there with him or persuading him to return with her to civilization. During the conversation, however, both realize that all that once joined them in the past has now fallen into ruins.

Antonio and Anarda's personal, contemplative reexamination of the past is characterized by one of the primary elements of romance, which is, according to Frye, "a persistent nostalgia, the search for some kind of imaginative golden age in time or space."[7] Here, two star-crossed lovers search in the past for lost ideals, ideals which, having been shattered, can never be recovered. This attempt to recapture an idyllic past produces a constant shifting between two temporal levels, which Frye identifies as another basic feature of romance: "one the time of the narrative action, the other a much more deliberate and creative time in which hidden truths are eventually brought to life."[8] By conversing in the present, Antonio and Anarda succeed in recreating and reliving the past, most of which they were previously unaware.

In addition to this nostalgic tone and form, the themes of sexuality, violence and the opposition between good and evil interweave in *Conversación* to produce the basic patterns of romance. In typical romance, a love story must be established before the themes of violence and sexuality can be introduced. The love story of *Conversación* begins in the past. As a young poet, Antonio visited the house of Anarda's father, and gradually grew to worship his beautiful daughter. Later, a disparity between the type of love each one felt for the other kept them from consummating their love. Instead of developing a physical love for Anarda, Antonio idolized her, and consequently placed her on a pedestal far above himself—". . . la diosa, Titania, lo eterno Femenino, tú sobre un pedestal."[9] Partly because of this respectful distance on Antonio's part, and more so because of Anarda's need for love, she finally fell into the arms of a mutual friend.

Since the separation brought on by Antonio's attempt on César's life, Antonio and Anarda's mutual estimation has changed; while she has fallen in his estimation, he has risen in hers. Antonio now rejects Anarda, considering her to be an inextricable part of the evil world from which he has tried to escape. During Antonio's absence, Anarda has formed an idealistic image of him and has decided that she loves him. She has, in fact, come to the jungle with the hope of consummating the relationship and thus regaining his love. Antonio, however, calmly rejects her amorous advances. This disparity in their esteem and desire for each other keeps the love story from being resolved happily. Unlike most romances, *Conversación* ends with violence and death instead of reunion and/or marriage.

Violence, like love and sexuality, is a theme of both the past and the present. In effect, all three themes are interrelated and dependent upon one another. Love was the cause of the violence of the past; Antonio attempted to kill César in order to save his "Titania." This violent act is in turn the cause of the violence that finally occurs in the present. The one reason why Antonio can no longer love Anarda is that she stopped him from killing the husband whom she claimed to despise. In the present level of action, a cyclical pattern develops through the recurrence of violence and Antonio's subsequent realization that he does indeed love Anarda. Although he is determined never to forgive her for defending César, another act of violence, similar to the previous one, finally unleashes Antonio's repressed feelings. The outburst occurs when Enedina decides to save Antonio, just as he thought he would save Anarda in the past. Enedina worships Antonio as her master and healer. He has cured her physically of a skin disease and spiritually of the hatred she once felt toward the husband who had abandoned her in the jungle. Enedina sees Anarda as a threat to the object of her devotion, as she is convinced that Anarda has come to take Antonio away from one place where he has found peace. With the intention of saving him, Enedina picks up the butcher knife and repeatedly stabs Anarda until Antonio succeeds in pushing her away. Just as Anarda suddenly and inexplicably protected the husband she claimed to hate, Antonio now protects the woman whom he has just rejected forever. Although the same pattern of action repeats itself, Antonio appears to be too late to save her; as the curtain falls Anarda is dying. These two similar acts— Antonio's attack on César and Enedina's attack on Anarda—in past and present, are the only real actions, either discussed or enacted, in the play, standing in sharp contrast to the contemplative nature of the rest of the work. The parallel between the two actions is almost too obvious to be credible. Through them, however, the dramatist expresses the inseparable link that exists between love and violence, and the cyclical pattern that they form, a pattern in which one follows the other in an endless cycle. At the end of the play, Anarda expresses the fear that they have both been "víctimas de algún rito espantoso" (p. 43).

The interwoven themes of love, sexuality, and violence form part of a more general theme of romance—the opposition of two contrasting worlds, one desirable and the other undesirable. In *Conversación,* the opposition is seen on both a human and a non-human level, in the representation of the physical world and in the portrayal of the characters as either heroes or villains. According to Frye, this "polarization of ideal and abhorrent worlds" later leads to the motifs of ascent and descent as the characters move between the opposing worlds.[10] The desirable world should be a "world associated with happiness, security and peace; the emphasis is often thrown on childhood or on an innocent or pre-genital period of youth."[11] The abhorrent world, on the other hand, should be a "world of exciting adventures, but adventures which involve separation, loneliness, pain and the threat of more pain."[12] A

similar polarity develops in both the past and the present in *Conversación,* with a human and a physical representation of both worlds within each time period. The following diagram illustrates the different levels on which this opposition exists:

PAST

Ideal world	vs.	*Abhorrent world*
Antonio		César
Train		Anarda's house

PRESENT

Ideal world	vs.	*Abhorrent world*
Antonio		Anarda
Jungle		Civilization, world of past experience

In the play itself, the only physical world actually represented on stage is the jungle, and the only human representation of the opposing worlds is in the form of Antonio and Anarda. The other sides of the conflict take form through this dialogue. Throughout their discussion of the past, Antonio and Anarda refer many times to the selling of a certain train and to the house of Anarda's father. These two elements gradually come to symbolize on a physical level the opposition of the past. The house represents the corrupt, immoral world of César and the rest of Mexico. The train is a concrete symbol of all that Antonio had hoped, and failed, to save—"el movimiento, la vida, la tradición" (p. 24). César, who eventually fell from political grace during Antonio's absence, has sold the train to other corrupt politicians in order to save himself from financial ruin, and the train and tracks have since been dismantled. As a result, the whole region has lost its movement and only means of communication. Antonio hates César even more now for having destroyed that life-giving force—"Odio, odio, qué furia, mi pueblo, mi tren, mi gente, mi viaje amado, mi ruta de la magia, de las revelaciones, qué odio, qué furia" (p. 40). Whereas the train represents movement and vitality, the house of Anarda's family represents just the opposite— decadence and stagnation. Although once a famous poet, Anarda's father is now an alcoholic, a bigamist, and a mute—a product of moral and physical deterioration. After losing his poetic talent, he was forced to sell himself out to politicians such as César in order to avoid total financial ruin. The house itself is a visual image of decadence. Antonio recalls, ". . . un patio muy—abandonado, con la gran fuente seca, macetas mustias, naranjos raquíticos; había rosales, había—musgo, yerbajos, unos andamios viejos . . ." (p. 21). The physical decadence, combined with the moral decadence of this large family, creates a picture very reminiscent of *Cien años de soledad*. As Antonio explains to Enedina, "había muchas leyendas de él, y de Anarda y de . . . la casa. De todos los hijos de él [el padre de Anarda]. Una familia enorme. Muchos hijos del viejo, sus nueras, sus nietos y sobrinos . . . Eran como un gran mundo, un universo aparte con sus leyes" (p. 20). Anarda herself realizes that her own husband is responsible for having maintained and perpetuated this abhorrent world of chaos and immorality:

ANARDA:

> Mantuvo a mi familia, comimos todos, bebimos, en la casa siguió la vida igual y el viejo pudo seguir bebiendo, seguir viendo en silencio la ruina que había hecho con tantos hijos locos, brillantes, ingeniosos, tanto talento inútil, traviesos como príncipes, flores de invernadero, inútiles y vagos, viciosos, bellos, lóbregos ... (*Pausa*) ¿Tú crees en el demonio? Quiero decir, en una fuerza externa de sombra y desequilibrio, que al tocarla nos deja muertos por dentro, vendidos para siempre al desorden, a la fealdad y al caos. ¿Crees?

> (p. 42)

César is the "demonio" that has polluted the house and, on a symbolic level, all of Mexico with corruption and immorality. Antonio, as the human representatitve of the desirable world, hoped that by killing César he would save them all: "Pensaba en remediar un mal social, y César era el mal encarnado" (p. 28). Frank Dauster supports this view of César as a human representative of evil: "el ataque no fue sólo a César, el marido, sino al mal, como elemento integrador de la sociedad humana. Antonio quiso matar el mal, y fracasó."[13]

Having failed in his heroic efforts, Antonio flees to the jungle, an idyllic, primordial world, where he discovers a peaceful existence. But with Anarda's arrival he must confront once again the undesirable world. The difference, though, is that Anarda, in her attempt to take Antonio back to civilization, corruption and evil, now serves as the representative of that world. In the present, the two worlds are more amply represented on a physical scale by the jungle and the civilized world. The present opposition occurs, therefore, between Antonio and Anarda—between the peaceful, innocent world of the jungle and the evil world of past experience.

With respect to the movement of ascent and descent so commonly found in romance, Antonio has risen while Anarda has fallen. Antonio is currently established in what can easily be considered a higher world—the primeval, innocent world of the jungle. The lower world was a place of exciting adventure, as Frye suggests, but adventures which brought Antonio pain, loneliness, and separation. The separation that he suffered at that time was not only from Anarda but also from himself:

ANTONIO:

> ... Y era—irreal—esa *distancia*, esa—separación. De todo. Yo, moviéndome, percibiéndome como un títere en un mundo deliberado, sentir era algo *diferido*, era material para hablar. Era—nada. No era. Fuga. Irrealidad. Un actor (que era yo) en un mundo pintado, escrito, proyectado. Un mundo de palabras y descripciones, lo masticaba yo como un molino, lo reducía a una pulpa de palabras.

> (p. 33)

Antonio experienced a form of self-alienation, in which he now sees himself as an actor following conventional roles from the worlds of painting, literature, and film. In the jungle, however, he attempts to uncover his true identity, an identity free from conventions. In learning more about himself, he also finds that words have an unnecessary, and often deceptive role in man's life: "me callé. Y así ... empecé a—ver. A ver. Y a oír" (p. 13). Frye observes that "with ascent themes, identity grows through the casting off of whatever conceals or frustrates it."[14] In this case, Antonio must rid himself of conventions before he can uncover his own identity. Those around him in the jungle have also contributed to his new identity and peace of mind: "Aquí, al menos, son distintos. Menos complejos, que equivale a decir más puros" (p. 16). In this lonely and simple world he has found the peace and well-being that he had searched for in vain amidst the conventionalisms of the other world.

The ascent that Antonio experiences from one world to another, and the accompanying change of identity, correspond closely to discoveries made by Mircea Eliade in his study of initiatory rites. Eliade defines initiation as a process of birth, death, and finally rebirth:

> The central movement of every initiation is represented by the ceremony symbolizing the death of the novice and his return to the fellowship of the living. But he returns to life a new man, assuming another mode of being. Initiatory death signifies the end at once of childhood, of ignorance, and of the profane condition.[15]

Eliade describes a passage from one world to another, from a profane world to a sacred world, a passage in which the initiate must die spiritually in the first world in order to gain access to the second. Although Eliade's study is based on the rites of primitive religions, he concludes by extending these patterns to modern existence: "Initiation lies at the core of any genuine human life ... Any genuine human life implies profound crisis, ordeals, suffering, loss and reconquest of self, 'death and resurrection.'"[16] Not unlike the initiates of primitive societies, Antonio passes from a state of youthful innocence, through a period of suffering, and finally arrives at a state of spiritual peace. His journey to the jungle represents, on a symbolic level, his passage to manhood. He can now look back and contemplate the stages that led him to his initiation into life:

ANTONIO:

> Fue todo tan irreal ...

ANARDA:

> ¿Lo que le hiciste?

ANTONIO:

> No. Eso fue real. En tercera persona, pero real ...

ANARDA:

> ¿Lo que—lo—lo que pasó después—conmigo?

ANTONIO:

> No. Eso fue en primera persona, pero real. Antes. Todo. Mira: conocerte. No: antes: mis amigos, escribir. No: antes: cambiar de voz y verme en el espejo, verme las manos. Enamorarme y sufrir.

(p. 32)

Retreating through time, Antonio relives the changes of puberty and the experiences of adolescence, which in turn led to suffering and to the final formation of a new man.

Anarda, on the other hand, undergoes no initiation, and therefore cannot ascend to a new level of existence. It is clear from the start that she is too much a part of the lower world to remain peacefully here in the jungle with Antonio. The transition is impossible, in part due to her inability to leave behind the conventions of the other world. Everything in the jungle seems unreal to her and she can only relate to her new surroundings through literary conventions:

ANARDA:

> (se ríe) Cocodrilos. Nada es cierto. Ni tú ni yo ni—venir a visitarte aquí, a la selva. Con orquídeas y cocodrilos. Kipling y Joseph Conrad corren entre los árboles, tomando notas en sus libretas. Y tarántulas. Y el relámpago verde de los loros. . . .

(p. 10)

A major factor in the occurrence of Antonio's own initiation is, in fact, his discovery of Anarda's true position with regard to the two worlds. This revelation comes about when Antonio attempts to kill César. As Frank Dauster explains, "al intentar matar a César, vio cómo Anarda también formaba parte del mismo mundo, cómo defendía al marido, cómo ella también estaba corrompida."[17] In the present, Antonio reminds Anarda that she is physically chained to the other world, first as mistress of the family house, and second as another one of César's possessions: "un pacto con el demonio: recuperar la casa, recuperar las joyas . . . tu alma a cambio de todo" (p. 42). In Antonio's eyes, Anarda will always be inextricably linked to César and the evil world that he embodies: "la imagen pura del mal, nuestro sistema político encarnado, el ladrón, el íntimo de los fuertes . . . nuestra historia encarnada, tu marido, tu César" (p. 39). The repetition of the possessive "tu" emphasizes Anarda's unbreakable tie with the lower world.

Along with the general romance themes of love, sexuality, violence, ascent and descent, *Conversación entre las ruinas* displays a structure very similar to that of Frye's myth of romance. In typical romance, the hero passes through six stages: 1) birth; 2) innocent youth; 3) the quest; 4) maintenance of the innocent world against the assault of experience; 5) contemplative withdrawal from experience; and 6) return to solitude.[18] Obviously, the hero cannot pass through all of these stages during the time allowed for a one-act play. In order to compensate for this, Carballido varies the structure somewhat by having stages one through

three occur in the past before the play even begins. Only the fourth and fifth stages actually take place during Anarda's visit. Carballido also varies the normal pattern by attaching no importance to the hero's birth, which in typical romance is usually of mysterious origin. The end of the hero's journey, the sixth phrase, is also left to the reader/spectator's imagination, as Carballido offers no definite resolution to the action. The standard romance usually concludes with marriage and/or the discovery of the long-sought ideal. In *Conversación,* however, the reader/spectator is left to decide whether Anarda will really die and, if she does, whether Antonio will remain in the jungle or continue his search elsewhere for an authentic existence.

The reader/spectator learns of stage two, innocent youth, and stage three, the quest, through Antonio's conversation with Anarda. The key elements of the second phase are, according to Frye, innocence and some form of sexual barrier. Antonio describes with what innocent expectations he and his friends first went to Anarda's house, with the hope of publishing some of her father's poetry:

> . . . Imaginábamos . . . muchas cosas. ¿Cómo sería? ¿Cómo sería su casa, por dentro? Queríamos verla. Casa de nobles, de duques, tiene un escudo en piedra sobre la entrada. . . .

(p. 21)

Upon falling in love with Anarda, Antonio creates his own sexual barrier by considering her to be far above himself. But his "Titania" finally falls from her pedestal when Antonio sees her make love to his friend Wally. At this point, Antonio's innocence begins to disappear with the advent of similar revelations. Mircea Eliade notes the importance of these major discoveries in the passage from adolescence to manhood: "The initiate becomes another man because he has had a crucial revelation of the world and life."[19]

The end of innocence is contiguous with Frye's third stage—the quest—, and with Eliade's initiation or spiritual death. In his definition of the quest, Frye states that it "tends to limit itself to a sequence of minor adventures leading up to a major or climactic adventure."[20] This initiatory period usually contains three consecutive stages of its own: conflict (*agon*), death struggle (*pathos*), and discovery (*anagnorisis*). The first step, the conflict, consists of preliminary minor adventures. These are, for Antonio, the many afternoons spent with Anarda, during which they play intimate, verbal games. The games are imaginary adventures, yet at the same time, filled with secret emotions. One game, for example, consists of imagining what person and which two books each would take if he or she were to be shipwrecked on a desert island. Other real adventures include short trips on the train, their "ruta de la magia, de las revelaciones" (p. 40).

Antonio's intimacy with Anarda finally leads to confessions of the cruel and perverted way in which César uses her. There revelations, and the accompanying loss of innocence, move Antonio on to the death struggle, in which he hopes to save his "Titania" by killing César. According to Frye, the death struggle should be "a crucial struggle, usually some kind of battle in which either hero, foe, or both must die."[21] But in this case, due to Anarda's intervention in the struggle, neither hero nor foe dies.

Although neither one dies physically, Antonio suffers the spiritual death described by Eliade upon experiencing the death of his youthful innocence and ignorance. Antonio's discovery, or *anagnorisis,* consists of further revelations brought on by the quest. The most shocking discovery is to find that Anarda belongs to the evil world of César. After seeing Anarda defend her husband, Antonio realizes that he has not been a hero after all, but merely an actor trying to fill a hero's role. He has failed in his quest because he has based it on false ideals. He suffers upon discovering his own self-deception and upon seeing all that he once worshipped—poetry, the train, and Anarda—fall into the realm of the abhorrent world. Antonio flees not only from the law but also from the ruins of his ideals.

The fourth and fifth stages of the hero's journey take place during the present level of action. Carballido once again makes a slight deviation from the normal pattern by reversing the order of the two phases. In *Conversación,* the contemplative withdrawal from experience actually takes place before the protection of the innocent world from the assault of experience. When the play begins, Antonio is already in the stage of contemplative withdrawal. This phase should be, according to Frye, a "contemplative ... sequel to action," in which the hero enjoys a "reflective, idyllic view of experience from above."[22] After fleeing from his crime and his own deception, Antonio is now able to step back and reflect calmly upon his past actions. In this contemplative state he has risen above his actions to the point where he can now see them through a different light. He explains to Anarda, "ahora siento de otro modo. Veo lejos muchas cosas. Ya no están vivas, se han vuelto—temas de conversación" (p. 24). Anarda, still seeing everything through a conventional light, compares their situation to a painting that they once shared, a painting that serves as a visual image of the play's title:

ANARDA:

> ¿De quién era ese cuadro? Una mujer y un joven conversando en medio de una casa despedazada, con un desierto azul en torno ...

ANTONIO:

> Conversando y tomando té. De Chirico. ¿Quieres un té, para que nada falte?

> (p. 25)

Antonio and Anarda, like the woman and the young man of the painting, are conversing amidst the ruins of the past. In his solitude, Antonio has been able to rise above these ruins and live in peace, but with the arrival of Anarda he is forced to confront once again the world of past experience.

Now in the fifth stage (Frye's fourth), the hero must protect the integrity of the innocent world against the assault of experience. According to Frye, the "happier society" should be more or less visible throughout this state.[23] Even though Antonio lives without any of the comforts of civilization, he is clearly at peace with those around him. He almost seems to commune with the natural world that surrounds him:

ANTONIO:

> El río ... verdoso, frío, más bien oscuro, con reflejos, lleno de ramos que cuelgan. Unos monos brincaban cerca de mí ... Nos hicimos muecas, huyeron ... Había sapos y ranas interprentando música ... Así estaba el río.

> (p. 23)

The world of experience threatens this primordial haven in the person of Anarda and in the vivid memories of the past that she carries with her. Antonio can no longer reflect passively upon the past; he must confront it once again, emotionally and physically. Reminded of his failure to kill César and thereby halt the destruction of the train, Antonio unleashes feelings of hatred that he believed to have overcome—"odio, odio, qué furia. ..." Although Antonio now realizes that he has not fully conquered the past, he stands firm against the advances of Anarda. He does not allow her to bathe with him in the river nor does he show any inclination to sleep with her. When Anarda finally asks him to forgive her for the past, Antonio answers that he can forgive everything except her having come to him, her having reminded him of the past:

ANTONIO:

> Yo, perdonarte, yo. Por ... ¿por qué? No hay nada que perdonar. Ya no pensaba en—todo eso. Ya no quería—lo que entonces. Ya no quería librarte, ni salvar nada—ni—hacer gestos inútiles ni—hablar. Ya no quería matar. A nadie. ¿Perdón ...? ¿Por haber venido? Eso ya no es tan fácil de perdonar.

> (p. 45)

If not for Enedina's violent reaction to their conversation, Antonio would have succeeded in overcoming Anarda, and with her, the world of past experience. But with the attack on Anarda, the old cycle of love violence love begins anew. The innocent world dissolves and Antonio is forced to admit his love for her. In both past and present, Antonio fails in his efforts to destroy the abhorrent world, first in his struggle with César, and then with Anarda.

In addition to the more evident mythic pattern found in the play's themes and structure, the audience or reader experiences a vague, yet pervading, mythic atmosphere. The jungle setting contributes to this feeling by imparting a sense of timelessness to the situation. Anarda compares her journey through the jungle to a passage back through time—"en Cosalapa empieza la tierra de los vestidos sin forma, sin época" (p. 7). The timeless nature of the play is accompanied by ambiguous words and actions. So much of the play is left unclear or unanswered that the reader/

spectator finds himself turning to universal patterns for the answers to his questions. In his study of romance as archetype, John Vickery observes that the romance reader's experience is normally a "gradual accrual of meaning as the reader follows a trail of hints and artistically incomplete bits of information."[24] Another critic describes the "sense of a story at once primeval and eternal lurking beneath the surface of the action."[25] The mythic patterns become more discernible to the observer when he steps back from the work and is able to see the experiences of Antonio as experiences of his own and of all men. Without the underlying presence of archetypal patterns, the play would lose a great deal of its force by appearing to be nothing but a sketchy relationship between two star-crossed lovers. With the discovery of these patterns, however, it becomes clear that the play is concerned not only with Antonio and Anarda, but with men everywhere who have at some point in their lives experienced an initiatory journey similar to that which Antonio undergoes.

Conversación entre las ruinas is not only a dramatic representation of certain basic aspects of human existence, but also a play concerned with the nature of art as a reflection of that existence. References to artistic forms, such as painting, sculpture, and literature, are scattered throughout the play. The majority of the references to painting and sculpture are associated with the house of Anarda's father and with the relationship that existed in the past between Antonio and Anarda. The house itself is a decaying museum of art, filled with works which, when seen together, lend a sense of timelessness to the house:

ANTONIO:

> ... en la sala había un órgano de iglesia, unos muebles imperio, una alfombra francesa sobre el piso de ladrillos, un gran espejo, unas vitrinas llenas de piezas arqueológicas, piezas muy bellas, cuadros, un gran paisaje de Clausell, unos dibujos de Tamayo, y unas litografías firmadas, de Picasso, y un retrato del viejo, pintado por Orozco cuando ambos eran jóvenes ... y un dibujito de Kandinsky. ...

(p. 22)

These pieces of art are among those that entered into the lives of Antonio and Anarda, and those that formed, along with literature, the basis of the conventional world in which they moved. In their present attempt to explain past actions and emotions, Antonio and Anarda repeatedly refer to painting and to romance literature—*The Tempest, A Midsummer Night's Dream,* and the writings of Kipling and Conrad. The numerous references to classical romance, in particular, serve to highlight the romance pattern of the play in which they appear.

The literary motif is carried further when Antonio refers to himself as an actor of conventional roles: "Fuga. Irrealidad. Un actor (que era yo) en un mundo pintado, escrito, proyectado. Un mundo de palabras y descripciones ..."

(p. 33). Antonio finally realizes that his past actions were not his own, but rather borrowed from the conventions of painting, literature, and film. Once convinced that he had discovered an authentic existence in the jungle, he is surprised to find himself still acting: "¿Qué dije? ¿Ves? El histrión, en beneficio tuyo. El simulacro del odio: y no le odio, estoy actuando" (p. 31). In his role as an actor, Antonio compares himself specifically with two Shakespearean characters—Bottom of *A Midsummer Night's Dream* and Miranda of *The Tempest.* In the past, his role was similar to that of Bottom, and in the present he identifies with Miranda. As the common, naive Bottom falls in love with the fairy queen Titania, so Antonio fell in love with Anarda. Later, Antonio is rudely awakened from his dream in a way similar to that in which Bottom is roused from his "dream." In both plays the two men perform their roles within a wider, more universal drama. In the present, Antonio identifies with Miranda, who, shipwrecked on a desert island with only her father, encounters other men for the first time. But whereas Miranda exclaims "How beauteous mankind is!" upon meeting this evil group of tyrants, assassins, and thieves, Antonio has already experienced the outside world and can only admit, "quisiera ... no burlarme del grito de Miranda" (p. 16). These direct references to Shakespeare and to Antonio as an actor place the play within the realm of theatre and, on a broader scale, within the realm of romance. The two books that Antonio chose to take with him to the jungle reinforce even further the archetypal nature of this play: *War and Peace* and the complete works of Shakespeare, both universal works concerned with the eternal struggle between good and evil and with other basic aspects of human experience.

Viewed in the light of myth, *Conversación entre las ruinas* is a play concerned with man's existence and with the function of art as an inseparable part of that existence. The structural and thematic organization of the play, along with the numerous references to classical romance, clearly place the work within the broader realm of romance. The scope of *Conversación* is, therefore, not limited to political corruption in twentieth-century Mexico or to the problems of two ill-fated lovers. The play reaches beyond personal and national concerns in its portrayal of the eternal struggle between good and evil, the endless cycle of love and violence, and finally, the passage of man from innocent youth to adult awareness, or what Eliade identifies as the rite of birth, death and rebirth. Yet Carballido's play is more than just a copy of preexisting, mythic patterns. In *Conversación,* he has expressed his own, twentieth-century version of romance. The myth itself becomes demythified in the sense that the hero ultimately fails in his attempt to fulfill mythic roles. Even after rejecting these conventional roles, the hero, or in this case the anti-hero, still fails in his search for an authentic existence. Myth is, therefore, just one more dramatic form with which Carballido experiments in his own quest for other ways to express the problems and experiences of modern man.

Notes

1. For works on Carballido's use of Greek myth, see: Mary Vázquez Amaral, "Dos mitos: Medusa y Teseo," in her book, *El teatro de Emilio Carballido (1950-1965)* (México: B. Costa-Amic, 1974), pp. 77-97, and Tamara Holzapfel, "A Mexican Medusa," *Modern Drama,* XII, No. 3 (Dec., 1969), 231-37. Other, more general studies concerning the presence of classical myth in Mexican theatre are: Margaret S. Peden, "Greek Myth in Contemporary Mexican Theatre," *Modern Drama,* XII, No. 3 (Dec., 1969), 221-30; Antonio Magaña-Esquivel, "El teatro griego de moda en México," *El Nacional,* 695 (Mexico, July 24, 1960); and Bert Edward Patrick, "Classical Mythology in Twentieth-Century Mexican Drama," Ph.D. diss., University of Missouri, 1972.

2. *The Princeton Encyclopedia of Poetics,* Alex Preminger, ed. (Princeton: Princeton University Press, 1965), p. 538.

3. One of the clearest treatments of archetype is offered by Philip Wheelwright in his *Metaphor and Reality* (Bloomington: Indiana University Press, 1962). See the chapter entitled "The Archetypal Symbol," pp. 111-28, and the following chapter, "On the Verge of Myth," pp. 129-152, where he moves from archetype to myth.

4. Northrop Frye, *Anatomy of Criticism: Four Essays* (Princeton: Princeton University Press, 1957), p. 136.

5. Frye, pp. 139-140.

6. Frye, p. 137.

7. Frye, p. 186.

8. Northrop Frye, *The Secular Scripture: A Study of the Structure of Romance* (Cambridge: Harvard University Press, 1976), p. 136.

9. Emilio Carballido, ed *Conversación entre las ruinas,* unpublished manuscript, 1969, p. 36. All subsequent quotes will be from the same source. The play was first seen on stage in translation (*Conversation among the Ruins,* trans. Margaret S. Peden), in 1971 at Kalamazoo College, Michigan.

10. Frye, *The Secular Scripture,* p. 80.

11. Frye, *The Secular Scripture,* p. 53.

12. *Ibid.,* p. 53.

13. Frank N. Dauster, "El teatro de Emilio Carballido," in his *Ensayos sobre el teatro hispanoamericano* (México: SepSetentas, 1975) p. 186.

14. Frye, *The Secular Scripture,* p. 140.

15. Mircea Eliade, *Rites and Symbols of Initiation: The Mysteries of Birth and Rebirth* (New York: Harper and Row, 1958), p. xii.

16. Eliade, p. 135.

17. Dauster, p. 186.

18. Frye, *Anatomy,* pp. 198-202.

19. Eliade, p. 1.

20. Frye, *Anatomy,* p. 187.

21. *Ibid.*

22. Frye, *Anatomy,* p. 202.

23. Frye, *Anatomy,* p. 200.

24. John B. Vickery, "*The Golden Bough*: Impact and Archetype," in *Myth and Symbol,* ed. Bernice Slote (Lincoln: University of Nebraska Press, 1963), p. 188.

25. Robert Heilman, "*The Turn of the Screw* as Poem," in *Five Approaches of Literary Criticism,* ed. Wilbur Scott (New York: Collier MacMillan, 1962), pp. 288-89.

Sandra Messinger Cypess (essay date 1984)

SOURCE: Cypess, Sandra Messinger. "I, Too, Speak: 'Female' Discourse in Carballido's Plays." *Latin American Theatre Review* 18.1 (1984): 45-52. Print.

[*In the following essay, Cypess analyzes how the handling of women's speech in* Rosalba and the Llavero Family *and* The Day They Let the Lions Loose *contributes to Carballido's social critique of patriarchal discourse. She notes that the former play depicts Rosalba as a "false androgyne" who imitates male language and that the latter disparages traditional language through the character of the repressed spinster, thus calling attention to the arbitrary nature of social conventions.*]

Yo también hablo de la rosa, Carballido's one-act play, has one of the more provocative titles of the many suggestive works by Mexico's well-known contemporary playwright. It serves as a good example of Julia Kristeva's "croisement de surfaces textuelles."[1] The title refers not only to Villaurrutia's poem and to Sor Juana's famous sonnet, but suggests a polysemy of the image of rose, and a multiplicity of signification in general. Margaret Sayers Peden calls it the most important one-act play written by Carballido and one of his best works of any length.[2] I would like to play with this title in order to initiate an examination of the speech act as Carballido has shaped it for his female characters, since one aspect of his central theme of social criticism is his treatment of the status of women in Mexican society. On the thematic level, I shall also relate female discourse to *La rosa*'s [*Yo también hablo de la rosa*] philosophical exploration of the meaning of existence and the nature of reality as a union of reason and emotion.

Mexican society can be considered a patriarchy, since it is a society whose driving principles are those of Fatherness, which is power, authority, discipline, maleness.[3] In this scheme, women are generally silent figures, submissive to the patriarchal powers which govern their lives, whether it be the fathers of the family, of the Church, or of the body politic. Since the one who has power in society controls discourse, men have been portrayed in the active role of speaker or director of action, with women generally the listeners or receivers of directions. In focusing on the particular ways Carballido's women characters relate to discourse, I shall refer to the concepts developed by the French social historian Michel Foucault.

The multiplicity of elements which come into play in various discursive practices are elaborated by Foucault in "The Discourse on Language," found as an appendix to *The Archaeology of Knowledge*. In that coherent analysis of the conventions which govern the production of discourse, Foucault names three principles—exclusion, limitation and appropriation—which are active on the exterior level for the control and delimitation of discourse. Let us consider Foucault's description of the rules of exclusion since they pertain to the sexual and political spheres of discourses that are the focus of this paper:

> In a society such as our own we all know the rules of *exclusion*. The most obvious and familiar of these concerns what is prohibited. We know perfectly well that we are not free to say just anything, that we cannot simply speak of anything, when we like or where we like; not just anyone, finally, may speak of just anything. We have three types of prohibition, covering objects, ritual with its surrounding circumstances, the privileged or exclusive right to speak of a particular subject; these prohibitions interrelate, reinforce, and complement each other, forming a complex web, continually subject to modification. ... In appearance, speech may well be of little account, but the prohibitions surrounding it soon reveal its links with desire and power.[4]

Foucault reminds us that this system of rules within which discourse is enclosed is an expression of a culture and handed down from generation to generation. For Mexican society, as has been noted above, women are not usually privileged to be speaking subjects, but rather, are objects described or manipulated. Carballido explores the restraints placed upon women in their exercise of the speech act as well as their rebelliousness against the rules of exclusion. It is important to note that among Carballido's women characters there are individuals whose discourse breaks the rules of prohibition and exclusion, just as there are traditionally submissive Latin females. Woman as object is clearly personified in Emma's treatment by Mario in *Felicidad,* or Juana's role in *Te juro, Juana, que tengo ganas,* or in Margarita's treatment by her mother and aunt in *Las cartas de Mozart*; an examination of any number of other works shows that patriarchal exploitation of women is present to varying degrees and is related to Carballido's overall concern for social reform. It is also thematically and structurally significant that Carballido does not treat patriarchal exploitation in a stereotyped way. Rather, in consonance with the polysemous nature of signification, the patriarchy is diversely represented: by the traditional father figure—a Mario or a Diógenes—as well as by fe-

males who accept and transmit patriarchal values by their own actions, as represented by the mother and aunt of *Las cartas de Mozart* or the aunt in *El día que se soltaron los leones.* In this study, I have chosen to focus on the discursive practices of two of the women who appear to rebel actively against society's accepted patterns of female discourse: Rosalba of *Rosalba y los Llaveros* and Ana of *El día que se soltaron los leones.*

In one of the only articles to date to focus on linguistic function in *Rosalba y los Llaveros,* Solomon Tilles explores the manner in which words are utilized by the female protagonist as an instrument to stimulate change in the lives of others. Tilles mentions the question of communication, or "el choque entre el hablar de Rosalba y el no hablar de los demás" as one of the themes of the play.[5] In my reading I would say that discursive practices within the context of Mexican society are one of the major subjects of exploration in the play. The Llaveros as a family have accepted totally the rules of exclusion, as described by Foucault above, and have refrained from entering into discourse because of the constraints of prohibition. Rosalba's use of discourse, on the contrary, breaks the rules of exclusion and forces a change in their silence which then leads them to the use of words and actions. In the contrast between Rosalba and the Llaveros, Carballido draws attention to the system of rules within which discourse is enclosed in Mexican society, and its links with desire and power. The following analysis of dialogue will verify this hypothesis.[6]

In examining the discourse of the female protagonist, Rosalba, it becomes immediately evident that her speech is characterized by none of the traditional restrictions and prohibitions surrounding female vocal behavior. She is not afraid to speak about anything, from the sacred—her own mother—to the sexual, including the illicit relations of members of her family. The unorthodox nature of her speech patterns is verified by the shocked reactions of her listeners, whose responses remind us of the rules and restrictions that society generally applies to female speakers. It is not only that Rosalba uses forbidden words, such as "prostituta" (208), but that she dares to ask questions unbecoming to a young woman:

ROSALBA:

> Tía, ¿Lázaro y Lucha, son amantes?

LOLA:

> Rosalba, ¡qué preguntas para una señorita: No sé como tu madre te permite!

(195)

Rosalba's mother, however, has no control over her daughter, a situation more in consonance with typical mother-son relationships than with mother-daughter ties. Indeed, Rosalba's discourse, as it relates to the systems of exclusion and constraints outlined by Foucault, identifies her use of language with accepted patterns of masculine behavior. That Carballido is consciously encouraging this aspect of Rosalba's characterization is evident from the following comment of Rosalba to Lázaro: "Es muy fácil que te olvides de que soy una muchacha" (174). While that line provokes laughter, since on the visual level it is not easy to forget that Rosalba is a young woman, nevertheless, on the level of verbal discourse, Rosalba does indeed speak the language associated with maleness and power in her society. A careful examination of the text reveals that until the final scenes, Rosalba is identified with patriarchal class structure and values. As she tells Lázaro: "Soy gente 'culta,' ves? Así estoy clasificada" (173). Also, Lorenzo, the father of the family, identifies Rosalba with his own pattern of behavior: "Casi en todo he visto que pensamos muy similarmente" (208). To think similarly to the head of the family is to be identified with the patriarchy. It is pertinent at this point to remember that previously Lorenzo had been called "un viejo tirano" (171) in his role as patriarch of the family. Although this phrase may apply ironically to Lorenzo, it seems clear that Carballido is exploring the nature of the family as a microcosm of the patriarchal system. In addition, Rosalba is identified with logos, or speech, a traditionally masculine characteristic:

LÁZARO:

(*a* ROSALBA)—Hablar. Eso te gusta siempre.

(219)

Furthermore, Rosalba comes from the city, a place associated with masculine power, as opposed to the country, or rural area, traditionally considered feminine space.[7] Thus, Carballido has created the rather unusual situation that the masculine characteristics of authority, reason, and analysis are personified in a female figure; Rosalba as signifier may be female from the visual perspective, but from the auditory aspect—how she sounds and her use of discourse—she is marked as masculine.

It is interesting to note that in their analyses of Rosalba as a character, both Tilles and Eugene Skinner identify her as a "liberated modern woman."[8] It is this characterization that I would like to oppose on the basis of Rosalba's use of discourse which is associated in the text, as I have shown, with patriarchal discursive practices. While Skinner associates Rosalba with "excessive rationalization," he does not identify that characteristic as traditionally "masculine"; nevertheless, he does note that Rosalba is linked with Nativitas, observing that the latter "functions as a grotesque mirror for Rosalba" (24). In that regard, it should be remembered that when Nativitas first appears on stage in Act I, scene 5, she is dressed in men's clothing, a semiotic device that leads us to consider that there are discrepancies in normal signifier/signified relations. In other words, Nativitas as a visual sign here signifies male, though her content is female; conversely, Rosalba as a visual signifier is female, though her content (discourse) is male.

Tilles also identifies Rosalba with the word, and equates her with Lázaro in that both are rational creatures, while he contrasts Rosalba with Rita on the basis of Rita's feminine behavior: "Rita, como mujer, es esencialmente irracional y obra sobre la base de las emociones. Sus palabras no representan ni una profunda verdad psicológica ni un hecho sino un estado de ánimo. Rosalba, porque no comprende esta distinción, se equivoca al obrar enérgicamente sobre la base de los desahogos de Rita" (Tilles, 43). Tilles' observation seems to support the distinction Rosalba-rational-masculine, on the one hand, and Rita-emotional-female on the other. Yet his final commentary stresses that Rosalba is "una muchacha cualquiera" (43). The conclusion I would suggest, however, is that Rosalba's way with words for most of the play is patriarchal, and in that vein works neither with Lázaro nor Rita. As long as Rosalba used the discourse of patriarchy, she did not accomplish her goals: neither Rita nor Lázaro nor Rosalba appear satisfied with the results of her interference in their lives.

Rosalba's discursive practices are criticized because she usurps the rights of others; she speaks to Felipe about Rita's feelings instead of giving Rita the opportunity to face Felipe directly; she assumes Lázaro is the father of Luz's unborn child instead of facing him directly, posing the question and listening to his response. In order for Rosalba to find her own individual voice, instead of mimicking the patriarchy, she first has to detach herself from the realm of the Fathers, and unite with the realm of the Mothers, or the emotions, because it has been the female aspect of her self that she has denied. As Rosalba finally admits to Lázaro, she has not acted true to her own inner voice, but imitated another pattern: "Hago teatro para los demás, a veces para mí sola, no puedo evitarlo" (223). Once Rosalba recognizes, however, that the voice she has been accustomed to using is "theatrical" or contrived, then her subsequent use of discourse works in a positive way. Instead of serving as the instrument of separation for Felipe and Rita, Rita and Felipe are encouraged to meet together. When Felipe and Rita do communicate with each other, instead of having Rosalba as an intermediary, they reach a state of union. When Rosalba faces Lázaro in the final scene, she is a changed woman, a reborn individual who no longer speaks to exercise power. She is conscious of the need to speak as a form of communion, not confrontation: "Estoy contenta y quiero hablar bien, lucirme" (228). She now shines, and fits into her name "Rosalba," or rosy dawn, because she has transcended the limits imposed by analytical rationalization of human existence (to paraphrase Eugene Skinner's analysis of *La rosa*).[9] In Rosalba, then, as in *La rosa,* Carballido affirms that a holistic approach, a union of the "masculine" and "feminine" in traditional terms, or of reason and emotion, succeeds while a mono-thematic perspective leads only to failure.

Rosalba as a character is not a mere catalyst, but instead undergoes a process of transformation herself through the experiences of discourse. Her usurpation of masculine discourse and patriarchal values, which transformed her into a false androgyne, shows how language can trap—not liberate—us.[10] The dominance of the patriarchy imposes male values on females, creating images of women that are male-oriented, as Rosalba symbolizes so well. Rosalba's disavowal of her previous discursive practices and her espousal of "lucid discourse" ('quiero hablar bien, lucirme' [228]), marks the shift from authoritarian, patriarchal values to liberating, life-affirming values.

Still energetic and active at the play's end, Rosalba has shed the old stereotypes and has been rejuvenated, as noted in her last comment: "Todo mundo es joven en realidad. Vámonos" (228-229). Her call to action is cast in a plural form, and refers to herself and Lázaro, whose hand she holds, as well as to the other newly formed couple, Rita and Felipe. The formation of these couples signifies that there has been a shift from individual separations to a union of opposites: Rita, the Hispanic with Felipe, the Indian, Rosalba of the Word with Lázaro the silent one. As Carballido has emphasized in the majority of his dramatic works, the polarities of reason/emotion, universal/particular, objective/subjective, male/female should be united. Rosalba's final "vámonos" can be considered a call to a new social order in which discourse is not used to control others, but to unite with others. ***Rosalba y los Llaveros*** ends, not only as a humorous and entertaining play, but it also offers a provocative social critique of patriarchal discourse.

The same quest for liberating discourse which Rosalba experiences can be found in ***El día que se soltaron los leones***.[11] In contrast to Rosalba, Ana is a woman in her sixties who never strayed beyond the confines of her socially accepted role as submissive niece to the head of her family, in this case the Aunt. In the process of the play's development, however, Ana, like Rosalba before her, ultimately represents a new pattern of discourse.

Initially, Ana experiences language as a form of oppression and enslavement because she is considered the inferior member of the discursive dialogue and is forced to always agree with her aunt. In acquiescing to her aunt—"diciendo siempre que sí"—Ana has a fixed role in what Foucault termed the fellowship of discourse (225). Within that closed society, "the roles of speaking and listening were not interchangeable" (265), just as they were not in the aunt's home. The aunt, who is identified with "gobiernos, jefes, teorías" (226), is thus another signifier for patriarchal society. When Ana escapes from her aunt's home—or the world of patriarchal values—into the forest of emotions and fantasy, Ana discovers that she has the power to exercise discourse without repeating the words and actions of her past models. Ana realizes the destructiveness of her previously submissive role in discourse: "Yo he perdido tanto diciendo siempre que sí" (265). In rejecting the patriarchal values of the rationalist world Ana steps beyond the limits of restrictive, stereotyped patterns of female behav-

ior. She rejects her aunt's world and chooses to live with the lions in the zoo. As Peden comments: "It is inevitable that Ana would elect to live among the 'caged' lions and devote the remainder of her life to educating children who only think they are free to be wholly free. It is appropriate, too, that it is the search for her beloved pet that leads her from the confinement of the spiritual cage of her aunt's apartment to the freedom of the literal cage of the big cats" (133). Carballido has once again pointed to the ambiguity of appearance and reality, or the polysemous nature of the signifier. Just as Rosalba-woman signified male discourse, Ana caged with the lions signifies freedom of discourse. For the first time, she is beyond the control of the patriarchy with its rules and restrictions; she is free to speak, to direct her discourse to others.

As Peden has observed above, Ana has chosen to educate children "who only think they are free to be wholly free." Yet an examination of her discourse shows that it is characterized by invective; she yells at the children, calling them "niños tarados, niños idiotas," and "niños gusanos, niños imbéciles" (273). One might well question how the use of such words will raise the consciousness of the children to whom they are directed. Her verbal attack against the children shows that Ana functions outside the systems of rules and societal restrictions governing the production of discourse. By hurling insults at the children, Ana attacks the proprieties of the society from which she has escaped. Perhaps Luis Rafael Sánchez' comment on the use of vulgarities (lo soez) is also pertinent here: "Lo soez es la transgresión del cultivo social, es el desprecio o la ignorancia del repertorio de normas, gentilezas, gracias y respetos, que integran la convivencia."[12]

Ana's abusive words are equivalent to "lo soez" as described by Sánchez in that both are signs of transgressive acts for the speakers. Ana had previously been the victim of a manipulative, authoritarian moral code and its concomitant restrictive discursive practices. Her present discursive transgressions now reveal her disdain for that society and her liberation from it. As Foucault reminds us in his "Conclusion" to *The Archaeology of Knowledge*, "To speak is to do something other than to express what one thinks . . ." (p. 209). When Ana speaks to the children, her discourse breaks the rules and procedures whereby speech is traditionally controlled, selected, organized and redistributed (See Foucault, 216), thereby bringing to light the existence of these rules and their restrictions. She brings to the level of consciousness for the children, and for the reader, the generally unconscious system within which discursive practices function. Ana's comment about her verbal attack against the children reveals she is conscious, too, of the role of her discourse:

ANA:

> Les grito así para que aprendan. ¿Usted cree que entiendan por qué les grito?

EL HOMBRE:

Ahora no. Más tarde.

ANA:

Mejor . . .

(273)

Ana, freed from patriarchal values, uses her discourse to liberate others, to lead them to the realization that it is possible to break the rules of restriction, prohibition, and exclusion. Ana in the lion's cage, speaking freely, is an audiovisual sign that contradicts the patriarchal rules which were outlined in my initial citation from Foucault's study: "We know perfectly well that we are not free to say just anything, that we cannot simply speak of anything, when we like or where we like; not just anyone, finally, may speak of just anything." As we have seen in the discursive practices of Rosalba and Ana, however, this traditional system which has been institutionalized and authorized through generations of use can be challenged and transgressed, or, in more positive terms, transformed to allow for a liberation of restrictions. In that way, new speakers, new circumstances, new ideas are possible. Like Ana, we may have to wait for this message to be understood, and for discursive practices to change. In the meantime, Carballido's humanistic dramatic world will help lead the way. He acknowledges the presence and reality of social conventions, yet with humor and insight, shows the inherent arbitrariness and stereotypic nonsense of past generations regarding these discursive practices.

Notes

A shortened form of this paper was first presented at the Second Annual Conference of Foreign Languages and Literatures at Rollins College, March 1984.

1. Kristeva, "Bakhtine, le mot, le dialogue, et le roman," *Critique* 239 (avril, 1967), 439.

2. Peden, *Emilio Carballido* (Boston: Twayne, 1980), p. 50.

3. For a discussion of patriarchy, see Sheila Ruth, "Sexism, Patriarchy, and Feminism," in *Women and Men: The Consequences of Power,* ed. Dana V. Heller and Robin Ann Sheets (Cincinnati: Office of Women's Studies, 1976), p. 56. See also Lynne B. Iglitzin, "The Patriarchal Heritage," in Iglitzin and Ross, eds. *Women in the World: A Comparative Study* (Santa Barbara and Oxford: Clio Books, 1976), pp. 7-24.

4. Foucault, *The Archaeology of Knowledge,* trans. A. M. Sheridan (New York: Pantheon, 1970), p. 216.

5. See "La importancia de la 'palabra' en *Rosalba y los Llaveros,*" *Latin American Theatre Review,* 8/2 (Spring 1975), 40.

6. All references in the text to *Rosalba y los Llaveros* are based on the edition found in Emilio Carballido, *Teatro* (México: Fondo de Cultura Económica, 1965).

7. Sherry Ortner, "Is Female to Male as Nature Is to Culture?" in *Women, Culture, and Society,* eds. Michelle Rosaldo and Louise Lamphere, (Palo Alto: Stanford University Press, 1974). For other developments of these polar associations of masculine and feminine, see Jungian works, such as Jung's own *Man and His Symbols,* as well as Erich Neumann, *The Great Mother: An Analysis of the Archetype,* Bolingen Series XLVIII, trans. Ralph Manheim (Princeton: Princeton University Press, 1963); Ernesto Sábato, "Fin de una era masculina" in *El escritor y sus fantasmas* (Buenos Aires: Aguilar, 1963); Hernán Vidal, *Maria Luisa Bombal: La feminidad enajenada* (Gerona: Colección Aubi, 1976).

8. See Tilles, note 5; Eugene Skinner, "The Theater of Emilio Carballido: Spinning a Web," eds. Leon Lyday and George Woodyard, *Dramatists in Revolt* (Austin: University of Texas Press, 1976), 19-36.

9. See Skinner's interpretation of *La rosa,* 31-35.

10. For some critics, like Carolyn Heilbrun in *Toward a Recognition of Androgyny,* androgyny means a reconciliation of masculine and feminine characteristics to create a whole or complete individual. Recently, feminist critics have rejected the term on the basis that "masculine" and "feminine" have both been defined by patriarchal culture, so "androgyny" does not refer to a true union of opposites.

11. All references to *El día que se soltaron los leones* are based on the edition found in *Teatro,* note 6 above.

12. "Apuntación mínima de lo soez," *Literature and Popular Culture in the Hispanic World. A Symposium.* ed. Rose S. Minc (Gaithersburg, MD.: Hispamérica, 1981), 14.

Jacqueline Eyring Bixler (essay date 1988)

SOURCE: Bixler, Jacqueline Eyring. "Historical and Artistic Self-Consciousness in Carballido's *José Guadalupe (las glorias de Posada)."* *Mester* 17.1 (1988): 15-27. Print.

[*In the following essay, Bixler proposes that Carballido employs the strategies of "metatheatre" through self-referential structure and themes.*]

In an attempt to provide a working definition of the popular term "metatheatre," Susan Wittig posits that *"all* artistic drama [as opposed to popular drama] is metatheatre, drama cast in a self-conscious medium" (453).[1] In addition to self-consciousness, or the drama's own awareness of itself as art, she lists deliberate theatricality as a basic characteristic of metatheatre. The inward turn of this form of theatre calls the audience's attention to the work's internal creative process rather than to any social reality that may exist outside the play. In short, as critic Silvio Gaggi explains, self-referential art "calls attention to its own construction and makes itself as art a part of the content of the work" (45). A recent Mexican play, *José Guadalupe (las glorias de Posada),* written by Emilio Carballido in 1976, meets this definition of metatheatre in both structure and theme.[2] The dramatist employs a series of plays-within-a-play as well as certain non-illusory devices to highlight the play's intrinsic theatricality. Furthermore, he emphasizes the work's metatheatrical structure and self-referential nature by foregrounding the concept of artistic creativity, and more specifically, the role of art in the interpretation and preservation of history. While paying tribute to one of Mexico's greatest yet least-known artists, Carballido underscores the similar way in which art and theatre revive, re-create, and transmit past history to the public.

Over the past four decades, Mexico's most prolific dramatist has produced a multitude of plays that traverse the gamut of dramatic styles, from macabre fantasy to strict provincial realism, from allegorical farce to works of explicit social protest. While the content of his plays varies almost as much as the form, Carballido has displayed over the years a steady interest in the history of his own country, particularly in the years of and surrounding the regime of Porfirio Díaz. In *Homenaje a Hidalgo,* which premiered in 1960 and later in an extended version in 1966, Carballido pays a spectacular tribute to the founder of the Mexican Independence movement. Three years later, he extends similar homage to Benito Juárez, first Indian president and father of the Reforma, in his epic *Almanaque de Juárez* (1969). More recently, he again returned to the 19th-century in *Tiempo de ladrones. La historia de Chucho el Roto* (1984), a highly acclaimed re-creation of the now legendary bandit-hero Chucho el Roto. Among these historically-based dramas, *José Guadalupe (las glorias de Posada)* stands out as the most theatrically self-conscious, the most challenging for the potential director and the most panoramic in its sweeping view of pre-revolutionary Mexico. Rather than focus on any one historical personage, the dramatist captures the spirit of an entire nation at a tumultuous moment of upheaval and transition. In music-hall fashion, the author presents a series of sketches which together communicate the socio-political situation, customs and prevailing mood of turn-of-the-century Mexico. The source of the title and of Carballido's dramatic inspiration is José Guadalupe Posada (1952-1913), known as "el ilustrador de la vida mexicana," a popular engraver and lithographer who captured and recorded in his illustrations that particular epoch. Large projections of Posada's illustrations serve throughout the revue as a visual backdrop to the dramatic action as well as a tribute to the artist's work. The historical reality that Posada re-created in his increasingly famous rough sketches is even further stylized in Carballido's dramatic revue, so that the audience is actually twice removed from the initial reality. In other words, art refers back to art, which only then refers to an extratextual, historical reality. Carballido's unusual combination of history and art conveys not only their very interdependence but also his own personal concern with the role art plays in preserving and relaying our history.

The play's metatheatrical structure derives in great measure from Carballido's adaptation of Brechtian structure and distancing techniques, both of which may also be appreciated to varying degrees in his other historical pieces. Aside from their ultimate socio-political objectives, Epic, or Brechtian, works are a perfect example of metatheatre in the sense that they destroy any illusion of reality by making a conscious effort to expose their own theatricality. This purposeful destruction of illusion is commonly achieved through the juxtaposition of incongruous elements on stage, sudden transitions between contrasting episodes and the use of non-realistic lighting and setting. Carballido further increases the play's theatricality and simultaneously reduces any illusion of reality by relying heavily on farce, opera, dance and caricature—all artistic forms that stylize the work's historical base. As a result, the spectator is distanced from the work and obliged to regard each episode as a dramatized image of real life, an image deliberately defamiliarized by means of non-realistic acting styles and staging techniques.

Whereas Brecht used similar devices to make the audience aware of extratextual social and political imbalances, Carballido draws on them to emphasize the revue's awareness of itself as an artistic entity. Unlike other Carballido plays with a distinctly Brechtian flavor—*¡Silencio, pollos pelones, ya les van a echar su maíz!, Un pequeño día de ira* and *Almanaque de Juárez*—*José Guadalupe* does not contain any explicit socio-political criticism or objectives.[3] The dramatist appears to be more concerned here with the aesthetic value of theatre as used in the communication and preservation of history, withholding any personal judgment he may have regarding that history and its impact on present-day Mexico.

Although Carballido subtitles the play "una revista," its structure is very much like Brecht's idea of *montage,* wherein "the various episodes of a play create a collective effect by accumulation but can be enjoyed separately as well" (Alter, 130). *José Guadalupe* consists of a series of sketches, which are experienced as independent events yet governed and linked by the thematic relationship between art and history. A program, included in the text and presumably to be distributed among the spectators, prepares the reader or audience for a dramatic potpourri:

PROGRAMA

1. Obertura
2. José Guadalupe (1)
3. La rosa de Hong Kong (rumba)
4. Los dos catrines (juguete cómico)
5. El chalequero
6. Las catástrofes
7. José Guadalupe (2)

8. Los 41
9. Soñar (melodrama)
10. El obelisco de Luxor (romanza)
11. La Bejarano
12. Caperucita Roja (cuento)
13. Las lavanderas
14. José Guadalupe (3)
15. Calaveras

Accordingly, Carballido presents a series a vignettes, or plays-within-a-play, each radically different from the next in both content and style. As Wittig explains, the play-within-a-play, the most common device of metatheatre, signals to the audience the theatricality of the entire work:

> The reduction of the dramatic situation to a framed, re-fracted miniature of itself calls the audience's attention immediately to the stage, the *medium* of the dramatic presentation; to the theatricality, rather than to the reality of the play, ... to the artifice of life.

(451)

This statement echoes and clarifies Lionel Abel's oft-quoted definition of metatheatre as "theatre pieces about life seen as already theatricalized" (60). In other words, metatheatre makes no attempt to create the illusion of reality, but rather treats life as if it were already theatricalized. This is definitely true in the case of *José Guadalupe,* wherein Carballido develops his own dramatized images from those which Posada had already stylized in his illustrations. These theatricalized images are then strung together to form a variety show of musical, dramatic and narrative scenes.

While the various sketches range widely in topic, style and effect, the general presence of José Guadalupe Posada provides the play's structural and thematic unity through his dual function as both off-stage historical personage—present only in his artwork—and on-stage character. While Posada's 19th-century drawings serve as a constant visual background to Carballido's dramatic sketches, Posada, the on-stage artist, unifies the revue through three appearances on stage in which he expounds on the nature and function of art. A brief description of the twelve non-Posada scenes conveys the dramatic diversity and metatheatrical nature of the work and suggests that withouth the presence of Posada as both historical artist and on-stage character the play would be highly fragmented and most probably incomprehensible.

The first such scene, "La rosa de Hong Kong (rumba)," has a disorienting effect on the audience because of its brevity and combination of disparate elements. Three kimono-clad women appear abruptly, sing a vulgar rumba and just as suddenly abandon the stage. The only apparent justification for this bizarre scene is the enlarged Posada illustration of Oriental women projected in the background. While the exotic, stylized nature of the costumes and song contrasts sharply with the stark realism of the previous scene—wherein Posada humbly introduces himself—, the mere presence of one of his illustrations makes "La rosa de Hong Kong" an integral part of the whole. Indeed, the fusion of contrasting elements characterizes the entire revue. In this particular segment, for instance, the audience, led by the costumes and the projected illustration to expect an Oriental song, is disoriented by the sound of a popular, slightly obscene rumba:

> Soy flor de loto,
> flor de pecado;
> prueba la vida,
> prueba mis labios;
> yo no respondo
> si sale caro.
> [...]
> Ay, papacito,
> lo digo en serio.

(3)

Although each scene is totally unrelated to the next, the transitions between sketches are remarkably rapid and effective. Without interrupting the action on stage, the dramatist indicates scenic shifts through abrupt changes in illustration, lighting and music. "La rosa de Hong Kong" leads directly into "Los dos catrines," for example, when a waltz and a print of the Alameda promenade replace the rumba and illustration of the Oriental girls. "Los dos catrines" differs radically from the preceding scene in style as well as content. After Posada's narrative introductory monologue and the musicality of the "Obertura" and "La rosa de Hong Kong," Carballido finally shifts here into the dramatic mode with what he labels a "juguete cómico." To prevent any possible illusion of reality, the dramatist prefaces the scene with a highly stylized "cuadro plástico":

> Recortado en triplay formando un marco como las porta-das de Posada, y con la firma y todo de Vanegas Arroyo, los personajes hacen cuadro plástico. El título dice: "Los dos catrines. Juguete cómico."

(8)

Carballido uses this living portrait not only to distance his audience by making the scene's non-relaistic intent evident from the start, but also to give credit to Antonio Vanegas Arroyo, editor and Posada's long-time employer. The play itself portrays the comic efforts of two dandies to win the love of the young and silly Hipsipila. The combination of slapstick action and exaggerated character types offers a very entertaining scene while still retaining the stylized atmosphere established by the "cuadro plástico." This farcical piece functions in the revue not only as a humorous reflection on the customs of 19th-century Mexico but also as a metatheatrical recreation of the *sainete,* a popular dramatic style of that period.

A sudden change in lighting shifts the audience from the humorous to the shockingly macabre in "El Chalequero." As the scene opens, El Chalequero, an infamous rapist and throat-slasher of the day, prepares to leave his latest victim. His monologue is characterized throughout by a mixture of poetic and brutal images: "Ni gritó: gorgotea nomás. Como el arroyo, o el ojo de agua" (10). A tremendous sense of brutality is created through the six different illustrations of slain women that appear at intervals during the scene. El Chalequero's dark form, silhouetted against the backstage lights, enhances the mythic overtones of his monologue. He describes the sexual act, for instance, as the entrance into a dark earthen well: "... Como el fondo de un pozo ... Un lodo aquí, hasta las ingles ... Un lodo espeso, calientito ..." (9). While the documentary aspect of the prints particularizes El Chalequero, the mythic thread of his monologue suggests universality. Once again, Carballido creates distance between the stage and his audience with this disturbing mixture of poetry and horror, myth and history.

As El Chalequero retreats into the darkness, pandemonium breaks loose on the stage with the opening of scene 6, "Las catástrofes":

> De golpe, entran corriendo y gritando todos, en ropa de dormir o en ropa interior de la época. Dos caen y empiezan a cantar un *alabado*.
>
> Mientras: se despliegan por todos lados los grabados catastróficos [...].
>
> Percusiones frecuentes.
>
> Hablan todos.
>
> (10)

Carballido dramatizes here the turn of the century, the age of Naturalism, during which man believed himself to be the helpless victim of natural forces. Ten large illustrations of various catastrophic events—in which victims flee from flood, fire, earthquake and comets—portray their fear of Nature's/God's wrath. Beneath the illustrations, the characters gather to pray and lament their helplessness. Yet when one of them miraculously produces a bottle of whiskey from his pocket, the others promptly abandon their *alabados* in favor of a drink, while a young girl in the group sings an obscene song. As in the preceding scenes, Carballido produces a mixed, alienating reaction in his audience by showing the victims to be at once worthy of compassion and morally corrupt.

After the second appearance of José Guadalupe, the variety show continues with a scene portraying "Los 41," a notorious group of transvestites and homosexuals who were arrested during a private party. Three prints depicting their detention and subsequent deportation to the Yucatán accompany the dialogue, which is itself a blend of music, song and prose. Once again, the audience finds itself torn between pity and mirth as the actors alternately complain about their humiliating persecution and boast of the beautiful dresses they wore to the ill-fated party:

> Mi traje tan precioso,
> llegado de París,
> y el día que lo estrenaba

> ¡me pasa este desliz!
> [...]
> Iremos con los yaquis,
> con otros despojados,
> y con los ofendidos
> y con los humillados.
>
> Todo porque en la fiesta
> me puse este vestido.
> Yo ya me lo pensaba:
> mejor no haber venido.
>
> (16-17)

Scene 9, "Soñar (melodrama)," is one of the few in this series of plays-within-a-play that contain an obvious thematic development. In this short piece, the dramatist gives a melodramatic treatment to the eternal opposition between dream and reality as an archbishop effectively prevents Angélica, a beautiful but lower-class orphan, from marrying his illegitimate son, Gabriel. After Angélica makes a lengthy confession of their love, the priest, no longer able to control his own lust, kisses her brutally on the mouth. The girl's escape from this horrible reality is depicted by two Posada prints of "La joven suicida," which show her leaping from the cathedral tower. Following the projection of these two images, Posada's portrait of Emile Zola appears with an engraved quotation from *Le Rêve*:

> Salía ella del sueño para entrar en la realidad. Aquel pórtico de luz cruda se abría sobre el mundo que ignoraba.
>
> (22)

The priest and Angélica are both forced by cruel revelations of the real world to abandon their religious dreams, his of saintliness and hers of a visitation from the Archangel Gabriel. Although the theme of dream and reality is well-developed, the melodramatic nature of the piece and non-realistic setting (the only stagecraft is a projected illustration of an altar) keep the scene in line with the non-illusory character of the other episodes.

The tenth segment, "El obelisco de Luxor," is similar to "La rosa de Hong Kong" in the sense that both are short pieces of musical verse and that neither bears any obvious relation to Mexican reality. A young man plays an Oriental tune on the piano while a young woman sings of the Luxor obelisk. Aside from the four Posada lithographs of Middle-Eastern subjects that appear in the background, the scene shows no connection with those that precede or follow it. The content of the poem itself, however, reflects the revue's underlying concern with history:

> Supo de guerras y de glorias,
> supo de historia, supo de amor,
> y es más eterno que la historia
> el obelisco de Luxor.
>
> (23)

A visual symbol of eternity, the obelisk has witnessed and withstood all forms of disaster and all acts of mankind. Yet, unlike history, the obelisk cannot be transformed, erased or forgotten by man.

Another jolting transition occurs when "La Bejarano," a scene as cruel and horrifying as "El Chalequero," follows directly upon the pleasant music and song of "El obelisco de Luxor." A famous criminal of the day, La Bejarano's name became synonymous with child abuse. While her monologue does not share the mythic qualities of El Chalequero's, the two scenes are quite alike in form and technique. The same backstage lighting is used to create a somber, silhouette effect as La Bejarano, standing over her abused daughter, delivers a lengthy monologue. Posada's illustrations of the famous crimes are not projected in either "El Chalequero" or "La Bejarano" until the middle or end of the scene, thereby forcing the audience to focus its attention on the monologue. Although La Bejarano explains that the beatings are to prevent her daughter from becoming a whore like herself, the audience detects in her speech and actions a desperate plea for respect and control:

> [...] Es necesario que alguien nos respete. ¡Es necesario tener algún poder, sobre alguien! Es necesario que alguien nos tema. Es necesario, alguna vez, sentir, sentir algo, en medio de este borrón eterno, de esta magulladora eterna, sentir intensamente, sentir. ...

> (24)

While horrified by La Bejarano's unrelenting cruelty, the audience at the same time comprehends her irreversible fate of hunger, misery and humiliation in an equally brutal society.

With the opening of scene 12, "Caperucita Roja (cuento)," the audience shifts again from brutal reality to playful fantasy. Occupying nearly a quarter of the entire script, this play-within-a-play dramatizes and recreates the popular story of Little Red Riding Hood. In the style of "Los dos catrines," the dramatist deliberately gives the piece a stylized appearance by having the actors form a "cuadro plástico" in front of a cover illustration bearing the title and the editor's name. An overture precedes the action and establishes the operatic nature of the dramatization. All but the shortest lines are sung by the actors, who play multiple roles, using masks and disguises for quick character changes. An opening aria sung by Porfirio Díaz sets the satirical tone of the sketch:

> (*Entra* Porfirio Díaz, *muy solemne. Es el presidente de la República y se le nota.*)

P. D.:

> Sepan, ciudadanos
> de este país. Sepan, personas.
> Oigan con atención y sepan.
> Oigan.
> La Presidencia de la República informa
> que una última acción de caza
> terminó con todos los lobos
> que durante tanto tiempo infestaban

> los bosques frondosos de nuestra República.
> La Presidencia de la República informa
> que han sido exterminados los lobos.
> Leñadores y niños ya pueden ir al bosque.
> La Presidencia informa:
> se acabaron los lobos.

> (25)

The subsequent story of Caperucita Roja and the wolf refutes, of course, Díaz's confident and reassuring speech. Besides the inclusion of the dictator, Carballido makes other comical variations in the well-known story: the grandmother is a nasty *suegra* who has been exiled to the forest by a possessive daughter-in-law; Caperucita herself is a rebellious teenager, more interested in sex and hallucinatory mushrooms than in a visit to grandmother's house; finally, the wolf hunters (Díaz's men) discover that the sleeping old woman is really a wolf only when they try to steal her belongings, including her fur coat. Aside from its operatic style, the episode shares many of the farcical and non-illusory features of "Los dos catrines": slapstick humor, exaggeration of character traits and frenzied physical action, all of which allow the audience to laugh and enjoy from a safe distance.

Scene 13, "Las lavanderas," opens with a discussion among three women washing clothes in the river and ends with a celebration of the Mexican Revolution, which was the last major topic of Posada's art before his death in 1913. As the three *lavanderas* comment on the newborn Revolution, a young woman dressed as a soldier enters dancing dreamily to a festive polka and establishes herself as a human symbol of the struggle against oppression:

La Que Bailaba:

> Yo soy el trueno que rueda por las montañas y va comunicándose como temblor de tierra; soy el cometa que anuncia cataclismos: trenes dinamitados, puentes hundidos, fuegos, incendios. (*Las otras tres sacan ropa de sus cestas, se visten ahora de soldaderas. Las otras tres bailan oníricamenta ahora, mientras ésta habla.*)

La Que Bailaba:

> Soy el alud, el torrente de rocas que barre todo. Soy una fuerza natural, soy el fermento de las catástrofes largamente guardado en el corazón de los hombres.

> (36)

The four female soldiers communicate, through images of nature's violence and their coordinated dance, the uniting of the *pueblo* against the forces of tyranny and injustice. At the end of the piece, the remaining actors enter on stage to join the Revolution, which now consists of a realistic polka and boastful *corridos* in which the actors glorify great revolutionary leaders like Villa and Carranza. Thus, in one short scene, Carballido is able to depict the birth and spread of the Revolution and at the same time the end of an era in Mexican history.

Following a final monologue by Posada, the revue ends with a skit entitled "Calaveras," named after the artist's most well-known series of illustrations. Justino Fernández describes these skeletal sketches as a representation of Posada's "vision and interpretation of the other world, of a fantastic world beyond that embodies, transformed and transfigured, this world of daily life and history" (142). The dream-like atmosphere of "Las lavanderas" resumes when the actors, all wearing skull masks of characters whom they have portrayed throughout the revue, dance dreamily to a festive, tropical tune. As the music becomes more lively, Posada, now also wearing a skull mask, joins in the dance and in the recital of "versos de calavera." When he and the others finally exit, all that remains on stage is a printing press, which suddenly sends Posada prints flying all over the stage as the final curtain falls.

The printing press itself functions not only as a piece of on-stage machinery, but also as a concrete symbol of artistic productivity. Occupying a central position on stage, the machine is always visible to the audience, and the rhythmic sound it produces while printing copies of Posada's illustrations is audible throughout the play. When Posada himself is not physically present, the constant activity of the press helps to remind the audience of the artist's general presence behind the revue, while the on-stage production of art reinforces the underlying theme of artistic creativity.

This particular theme is expressed not only through the presence of the press and the projected prints, but also through the repeated appearance of Posada, who, in his three monologues, conveys his philosophy on the nature and purpose of art. In doing so, he unites thematically the rest of the revue, which is itself a product of his and Carballido's combined artistic inspiration. In his first appearance, Posada establishes his own creative capacities. A musical overture accompanies the rhythmic sound of the press as the artist produces copies of his illustrations. Suddenly, a group of characters springs from behind the press as if newly created by the illustrator's hand:

> Un desfile de personajes brota de detrás de la imprenta; giran en torno a ella y se transforman en otros: todos, conforme a los grabados del artista. Podrán ser unos en blanco y negro, otros en color.
>
> (1)

This opening action at once establishes the image of Posada as a creator of characters, both historical and fictitious, as well as his artistic license to transform reality.

In a lengthy description of his work, Posada humbly presents himself as an artist of the *pueblo,* as one who sees his duty as that of providing the people with an easily understood interpretation of their daily reality:

> Hago la Realidad y la pongo en las manos del pueblo, contradictoria como es, múltiple como es; pues nada

más el Arte puede tratar de todo: de la infinita gama, de los extremos intocables e idénticos, de los muertos, de los vivos, de la trivialidad cotidiana, de lo que miro como visión dentro de mis ojos, de lo que miro fuera, de profecías, delirios, magias y tradiciones, de lo que las generaciones heredan; de las noticias ultramarinas. De los rebeldes. De la lucha de hoy. De lo que mira y juzga el pueblo. Porque el pueblo nos juzga. Y en mi trabajo y en mi vida, soy un artista. Y soy el Pueblo.

> (2)

As an artistic re-creator of the reality that surrounds him, Posada is reminiscent of La Intermediaria of Carballido's *Yo también hablo de la rosa,* who likewise describes her role as that of an artistic medium for the expression of daily reality:

> Todos los días llegan noticias. Toman todas las formas: suenan, relampaguean, se hacen explícitas o pueriles, se entrelazan, germinan. Llegan noticias, las recibo, las comunico, las asimilo, las contemplo.
>
> (94)

La Intermediaria, through her poetic interpretation of a train derailment, and Posada, through his re-creation of 19th-century Mexican reality, both serve as creative media, by means of which daily reality takes on new forms and perspectives. Posada himself is consciously aware of his role as a creative artist, as one who creates a new reality on the basis of familiar images:

> También hago retratos: de la gente que veo del diario por las calles, de personajes de la política y de la Historia. También hago ... cuentos, leyendas, fantasías. Crímenes, chascarrillos. Ilustraciones para versos y para letras de canciones, para noticias que nos llegan de aquí y del extranjero. Hago la Realidad en imágenes y eso es, a fin de cuentas, un trabajo de artista.
>
> (2)

During this introduction, the spectator, the direct recipient of Posada's monologue, adopts the role of the *pueblo,* the recipient of Posada's artwork. The audience's new identity becomes more explicit when the artist's newly-created characters reappear on stage and distribute among the spectators copies of his prints. As a result of this actor-audience contact, the latter necessarily becomes more directly involved in the revue. This involvement is, nevertheless, more intellectual in nature, any possible emotional participation having been precluded by the previously mentioned distancing techniques.

During his second appearance, in scene 7, Posada speaks in more detail about the art of engraving and lithography. The audience is suddenly no longer just the general *pueblo* but rather a group of small children watching him work through the shop window:

> [...] muchos niños vienen a curiosear por los vidrios. [...] Se nota que les gusta lo que hago, aparte de la curiosidad.

Me pongo luego a dar explicaciones en voz alta, para que
me oigan ellos, ya que ellos no preguntan, me oigan y
sepan como se hace esto. Trabajo en plomo y en zinc.
También uso a veces el cobre [. . .].

(14)

Following an explanation of the materials and instruments
with which he works, Posada confesses that of his many
young observers he is particularly fond of three—Gerardo
Murillo, José Clemente Orozco, and Diego Rivera—all of
whom, inspired by their first master, went on to create their
own artistic monuments.

Posada's third and final monologue occurs during old age,
at the end of his artistic cycle. The passage of time is
evident in the old artist's forgetting of his own work, his
more contemplative attitude and his anticipation of death.
Although he speaks of death as something that man must
accept as a natural occurrence, he nonetheless hopes that
somehow he will live on in the minds of the people. This
discussion of death and eternal memory leads naturally into
the "calavera" scene, in which Posada dons a skull mask
and joins the other skeletal figures in a ritualistic dance of
death. In his own "verso de calavera," Posada describes
himself as a monument of art and poetry:

Tuve la mirada abierta
a todo cuanto veía,
mis ojos fueron la puerta
por donde el mundo venía,
mi mano con línea experta
en el papel imprimía
la infinita realidad:
fue toda mi propiedad.
Mi recuerdo dejo al viento.
Mi nombre es un monumento
de papeles y poesía.

(39)

Posada's memory is indeed present throughout the play in
many different forms: the projected illustrations, the printing press and distributed copies of his prints, and finally,
the appearances made by the fictionalized artist himself.
The whole revue, in fact, could be easily summed up as a
dramatic dedication to Posada's memory, an effort on the
part of Carballido to rescue Posada from oblivion.[4]

But *José Guadalupe* is more than just a commemoration
of Posada's work and 19th-century Mexico. It is a play
about art in general and in its many forms, among them the
theatre. The play's own self-consciousness as art is evident
on one level in the artwork of Posada and on another in the
dramaturgy of Carballido. Both artists are plainly aware
of their role in providing the *pueblo*-audience fresh new
images of reality. With the help of his engraving tools,
Posada was able to re-create reality and render it easily
comprehensible to all. Carballido does the same, only
with theatrical tools. Through the use of such non-realistic
forms as farce, opera and dance, and through special visual
effects, Carballido presents an even more stylized version

of the same reality that Posada re-created in his illustrations. Both Posada and Carballido, in making the real
world fascinatingly new and poetic, have succeeded in
preserving their nation's history by transforming it into a
lasting and tangible art.

While the presence of Posada—in the illustrations, the
printing press, and the on-stage character—serves to express the play's thematic self-consciousness, the use of
the Epic form produces its theatricality, its structural self-
consciousness as art. The idea of the *revista* and its division
into numerous plays-within-a-play emphasize the metatheatrical nature of *José Guadalupe,* its overt effort to
dramatize life. The lack of traditional plot and suspense,
combined with certain distancing techniques characteristic
of Brechtian theatre, produces an emotional disorientation
and detachment in the audience, whose attention is drawn
instead to the play's metatheatrical process, which begins
with images of Mexican reality and ends with a highly
transformed and theatricalized version of that same reality.
In transferring Mexican history to the stage, Carballido
reasserts his conviction that life is inherently theatrical.
Wittig supports this interdependence between theatre and
life when she states that "it is the metaphor of the theatre—
dramatized action—that makes the metaphors of life—lived
action—endurable, visible, conscious" (454). *José Guadalupe* is evidence of Carballido's own continuing belief that
art, and more specifically theatre, is the most viable vehicle
in the expression of history and of life in general.

Notes

1. To distinguish "artistic drama" from "popular drama,"
   Wittig explains that " 'popular' discourse is discourse
   conscious only of its message, while esthetic discourse is discourse conscious of itself as a made
   thing, a system of human signs that demand recognition as *signs,* not as natural phenomena" (454).

2. Unfortunately, *José Guadalupe* has to date been neither published nor staged. In a letter dated February
   11, 1981, Carballido explains: "*José Guadalupe* has
   never been produced. It is very expensive and after
   the first try they did failed, everyone has forgotten the
   thing."

3. In a prior essay, I examined Carballido's adoption and
   adaptation of Brechtian techniques in *Almanaque de
   Juárez.* While the earlier play does share certain technical characteristics with *José Guadalupe,* its ultimate
   goal is more Brechtian in nature, as Carballido draws
   explicit parallels between current socio-political conditions and those that existed over a century ago.

4. Notwithstanding his popularity while alive, Posada
   was quickly forgotten by a nation swept up in the
   chaos of the Revolution:

   A pesar de su vida fecunda y de su inagotable talento,
   murió pobre en la fría mañana del 20 de enero de 1913.
   La historia que se escribió en los años que siguieron a

su muerte no quiso franquearle sus puertas; José Guadalupe Posada "fue sepultado en una fosa de sexta clase en el Panteón de Dolores; sus restos, que nadie reclamó, fueron arrojados sieta años después a la fosa común en compañía de otras calaveras anónimas."

(Rodríguez Santillán, 3)

Works Cited

Abel, Lionel. *Metatheatre. A New View of Dramatic Form.* New York: Hill and Wang, 1963.

Alter, Maria P. "Bertolt Brecht and the Noh Drama." *Modern Drama* 11:2 (1968): 122-31.

Bixler, Jacqueline Eyring. "Emilio Carballido and the Epic Theatre: *Almanaque de Juárez.*" *Crítica Hispánica* 2:1 (1980): 13-28.

Carballido, Emilio. *José Guadalupe (las glorias de Posada).* Unpublished ms., 1976.

———. *Yo también hablo de la rosa.* Mexico: Editorial Novaro, 1970.

Fernández, Justino. *A Guide to Mexican Art. From Its Beginnings to the Present.* Trans. Joshua C. Taylor. Chicago: University of Chicago Press, 1969.

Gaggi, Silvio. "Brecht, Pirandello, and Two Traditions of Self-Critical Art." *Theatre Quarterly* 8.32 (1979): 42-6.

Rodríguez Santillán, Jesús. "Posada, grabador del pueblo." *Revista mexicana de cultura* Feb 24, 1980: 3.

Wittig, Susan. "Toward a Semiotic Theory of the Drama." *Educational Theatre Journal* 26 (1974): 441-54.

James J. Troiano (essay date 1989)

SOURCE: Troiano, James J. "Illusory Worlds in Three Stories by Emilio Carballido." *Hispanic Journal* 10.2 (1989): 63-79. Print.

[*In the following essay, Troiano discusses three short stories from Carballido's collection* The Empty Box, *analyzing how each tale develops the theme of a character's escape from a monotonous daily existence into a world of illusion.*]

The Mexican author Emilio Carballido (1925) wrote an excellent volume of short stories entitled *La caja vacía* (1962). Margaret Peden points out that although Carballido is known primarily as a dramatist, he also has published four novels in addition to the collection of short stories (9). Peden also ponders: "Considering their quality, one wonders why Carballido has not returned to the short story form" (55). Thomas Gullason wrote that the short story was not a very respected medium in the 1960's: "both short story and short story writer are clearly underrated, even ignored, by professional and academic critics, publishers, some literary artists, and by general readers (13). This attitude toward the short story and more importantly Car-

ballido's remarkable continued success as a dramatist help to explain the author's diminished interest in the short story.

This paper will treat three of the stories: **"Los huéspedes," "Danza antigua,"** and **"La desterrada."** All three stories deal with characters who escape from their monotonous, shabby existences into illusory worlds. The main character in **"Los huéspedes"** discovers two young companions who help give substance to his magical reveries, the grandmother in **"Danza antigua"** creates a chimerical world which is accidently destroyed by her innocent granddaughter, the woman in **"La desterrada"** recreates an ideal past in which her daydreaming grandson is an eager companion. One significant experience in each situation has profound effects on the protagonist.

The central character in **"Los huéspedes"** is a young man named Carlos. He departs from the tedium of daily existence by use of his prolific imagination. One day an encounter with an enchanting young woman named Consuelo and her companion Gabriel add a special magic to Carlos' imaginary world. The beguiling visitors enthrall all members of Carlos' household, with the possible exception of his stepmother, Guille.

"Los huéspedes" begins with a description of flying insects that struggle toward the light, but quickly lose strength and perish. This symbol of man groping to find meaning in life symbolizes the struggles of most characters in *La caja vacía.* Carlos himself does not really know how he feels about the bugs, and yet his own attempts to find something better in life are analogous to the plight of the insects.

Carlos is a dreamer, and when his father threatens to cook the boy's pet goat, Carlos' imagination soars beyond the struggling insects and prosaic reality, accompanied by his loyal pet:

> Por la mente le cruzaron imágenes aventureras: un joven audaz, con su atado al hombro, desafiando tormentas y distancias, acompañados por el fiel animal. Otra imagen: la lluvia, torrencial, el muchacho abrazando al chivo en el fondo de la gruta; los dos fugitivos tiemblan, un rayo cae cerca, pero no van a volver allá.
>
> (19)

Carlos creates an adventurous world as his imagination filters out anything which is unpleasant or tedious. This selective vision helps to explain his enjoyment of the harpist's music while he is repelled by the harpist's deformed body and twisted hands:

> El arpista, contrahecho, con sus manos torcidas y el instrumento al hombro iba a desayunarse al mercadito. A Carlos le gustaba oírlo, pero le daba horror verle las manos alrevesadas volando sobre las cuerdas.
>
> (20)

The propensity toward beauty prepares the reader also for Carlos' fascination with the lovely and imaginative enchantress Consuelo. The music lifted Carlos to an ideal Veracruz:

> El son lo arrebató a un Veracruz perfecto, con el mar, los cocos, la delicia del mar ... Aunque estaba tan flaco que sujetaba el calzón con los puros huesos, en su imaginación no le daba vergüenza desnudarse; allí era más robusto, así saltaba al agua, a salvar aquella figurita lejana (¿millonaria, artista de cine?) que movía los brazos y gritaba. Olas, olas, él audaz, y el chivo nadando tras él. ...

> (20, 21)

Later, before a second encounter with Consuelo, Carlos will once again feel joy upon hearing the music and horror at viewing the player. The boy's perfect world will thus welcome the beauteous Consuelo, but shun the unfortunate harpist.

At first Consuelo was merely an intruding shadow of reality ejecting Carlos from his chimerical vision of Veracruz. This enchanting creature will soon enhance the boy's imaginary world as he accompanies her in her fantasies. The stunning Consuelo also constantly propels herself from tedious reality and is willing to have Carlos or anyone so disposed as a companion.

Significantly, in Carlos' initial encounter with Consuelo, she is depicted as "la sombra" (21). It is in the shadowy world of dreams and fantasy that Consuelo and Carlos will be comrades. When she first attempts to sell him earrings, Carlos' reply is a perfunctory no: "No, gracias—contestó automáticamente" (21). Upon observing her, however, Carlos is quickly impressed by both her height and beauty: "¡Qué bonita era ella! Alta, un poquito más que el joven" (21). Carlos soon enlists himself as a supporter both Consuelo and her companion as he attempts to convince his aunt, sister, and stepmother of the worth of Consuelo's jewelry. It is obvious that he is apparently taken more with Consuelo than anything else: "Ella es muy alta. Son simpáticos" (22).

The story is a fascinating portrait of the tedium of living in a small town where every place and person is boringly familiar. Everyone in the household is beside himself with excitement with the prospect of the young couple returning to the house with their wares, and each fears that Victor, the father, might miss everything by taking his customary nap. The author relates the pure enchantment as everyone views the attractive duo:

> Rocío y Aminta se bebían con los ojos a Gabriel. Victor no perdía una sola de las palabras de Consuelo, y asentía a cada momento: —Es muy cierto, señorita—. O: —Tiene usted mucha razón.

> (26-27)

They were invited to dine and stay over with Carlos' family as the boy was not alone in being enthralled with the two strangers.

Carlos is so enthusiastic about the visitors that he finds himself completely incapable of depicting his effervescent condition:

> Carlos no respiraba casi. ¿Cuál era el adjetivo? No sabía decirlo ni para sí mismo, no se atrevia a calificarlos. Quería decir: "¡qué buenos son!," o ¡qué simpáticos son!," pero sólo pensaba "¡qué son!," y los tres puntitos los llenaba con un sentimiento cálido, que le oprimía el estómago como el miedo y lo hacía enrojecer cuando creía que los había contemplado demasiado.

> (27)

Victor happily paid three times the value of the jewelry offered by Consuelo and Gabriel. Real magic penetrated the walls and seeped through the cracks of every corner which the young guests brushed against.

Carlos' new friend, Consuelo, also has a prolific imagination and this factor helps explain in part his fascination with her. In the following examples Consuelo shows herself to be a storyteller, claims to be a poet, has definite histrionic talent, and is indeed a siren who awakens Carlos to his first sexual desires.

Consuelo and Gabriel relate a sad tale in which they are the children of a poor, sickly mother and a cruel delegate from Corzo. The father apparently does not wish that they see this woman, whom he never married. The children, however, courageously flee and attempt to arrive in Mexico City to help their mother. Their tragic plight further impresses the family and later Victor purchases their tickets for Mexico, because "Quise mucho a mi madre" (33). Victor's act of generosity overwhelms Carlos as the boy kisses and embraces his father.

After dessert the girl recites some very melancholy verses which describe a very young beautiful girl who commits suicide. Sympathy and respect further blossom for the lovely girl. The bewitching Consuelo enjoys drawing attention to herself. By her poetry or descriptions of her life she continually attempts to have people admire and be attracted to her. Occasionally, she creates bizarre outbursts and always finds ready audiences. On one occasion she begins dancing and displaying her legs on the railroad track and suddenly shouts in a way Carballido portrays as "salvaje, feroz" (30). Gabriel and Carlos are startled as she replies: "¿No les dan ganas de gritar, a veces?" (30) Consuelo is able to transcend the prosaic world from which she continually tries to flee.

Her dramatic skills are further evident as she precipitates a crowd gathering by throwing herself to the ground and shouting: "¡me pega mi marido, me pega mi marido" (34). The furious Gabriel angrily responds: "¡Loca, payasa, párate, que va a venir la gente!" (34) Consuelo further mortifies her young companion with: "¡No me pegues, no me pegues!" (34) After the crowd assembles, Consuelo calmly gets off the ground and runs off with her two loyal followers

Carlos and Gabriel. The girl is a kind of Quijote who magnetically draws disciples to whatever temporary aberration happens to effect her at the moment.

Carlos' sexual impulses are awakened by the stunning Consuelo when she takes his hand: "Consuelo ... le había tomado el brazo como a un compañero, como a un hombre" (34). Because of his inexperience and youth, Carlos finds it difficult to reconcile these first sexual feelings with the real world. It is therefore no great surprise that the lovely and mysterious visitor accompanies Carlos in his dream world, as he awakens to puberty.

Carlos dreams of searching for the goat with Consuelo who, as she did that very evening: "Lo tomo del brazo, como a un hombre" (35). The youth finds himself surrounded by flashing lights, bars, and smiling prostitutes. The women display their breasts. Carlos took Consuelo by her waist as a train passed quickly by. Sensual and sexual images abound as Carlos awakens in a state characterized between bewildered and excited. He feels ashamed of the soiled sheets.

Harsh reality enters in with the morning sun as Carlos faces the departure of his dear friends. Guille, the stepmother, attempts to disillusion Carlos and everyone, however. Her cold and indifferent reaction toward Consuelo's and Gabriel's farewell was a precursor to her attempt to destroy the enchantment of the visit. The return home finds Guille: "... triunfal, con el libro en la mano" (37). The stepmother gleefully reveals that Consuelo was not the author of the poetry which she had claimed to have written. Guille was confident that by having found the source of Consuelo's plagiarism she had also proved that the girl was a complete fraud. The stepmother was indeed certain that the tale of the cruel father and the sickly mother was deceitful as well as the idea that they were brother and sister. Guille clearly believed that the two were runaways.

Carlos, the idealistic dreamer, is not daunted. He dramatically rejects the stepmother's attempt to impair his splendid fantasy with meager speculation and tedious reality. The marvelous pair made his monotonous life a little more beautiful and exciting and he will take that with him and ignore the rest. He will listen once more to the heavenly music and ignore from whence it comes. His brusque response to Guille's mere utterance of mundane possibilities is a stunning: "¿Y qué?" (38) which he immediately repeats to the surprised family. Alone the boy ponders the implications of the discovery and the experience:

> Todo sería mentira? Estaba aquella carta arrugada, estaban los otros versos ... ¿Y qué? Había algo más, mejor que esa historia que habían cantado, había otra cosa pero ya no sabía cuál.
>
> (38)

As Carlos continues to contemplate the encounter, the adjective he searches for finally comes forth: "¡Qué her-

mosos son! ¡Qué hermosos son!" (39) The youth then came to fully feel what the episode meant to him:

> Era tan sincero, tan profundo, que le dolía. Volvió a cerrar los ojos, y así se quedó, en la sombra, reconstruyendo, corrigiendo, reviviendo, prolongando.
>
> (39)

His experience with Consuelo and Gabriel has now transcended reality. Carlos will be comforted by this magic moment and Guille's words ring meaningless. From the depths of Carlos' dull existence has come something special which he can reconstruct and re-enter whenever he wishes. Consuelo came to him as a 'sombra' and she will now remain with him as part of his chimerical world. The two bewitching visitors will accompany Carlos wherever he goes and for as long as he lives.

"Danza antigua" concerns a old woman who longs for the distant past when she was younger and filled with beauty and vitality. The grandmother's inability to accept reality precipitates hostility toward the grandaughter she once cherished. Carballido skillfully unfolds the tale as the reader is drawn progressively into the mystery of how this transformation from love to hostility toward the young girl, Palmira, transpired. The narration alternates between occurrences in the past and present, which underscores the sharp contrast between deep initial affection and later profound hostility toward the child. The reader thus becomes increasingly aware of the grandmother's disturbed behaviour and more mystified by the mysterious motive.

The reader is immediately propelled into the situation as Palmira's weary mother Hilaria returns home only to be met by her weeping mother who bewails: "Palmira y sus retobos, sus groserías. La haragana Palmira" (71). The child frustratingly attempts to claim her innocence. The grandmother alleges that the child stuck her tongue out at her, while Palmira insists that the act was directed toward another child. Grandmother is victorious and Palmira is punished but the extent of grandmother's joy at this victory makes Hilaria ponder the wisdom and justice of her decision:

> Pero Hilaria estaba harta de ser juez. Algo en el gozo de la vieja parecía sugerir la injusticia consumada, y allá en el rincón seguía Palmira, sollozando exageradamente y viéndolas de reojo, con rencor. Y sin embargo, siempre es más fácil regañar a una hija que a una madre.
>
> (72)

The reader becomes progressively allured into the bizarre domestic situation as Carballido tantalizes the reader with more baffling details regarding the relationship between Palmira and her heartless grandmother. The question to ponder is why does the transformation occur in which a favored and even spoiled granddaughter becomes so despised and abused. Hilaria is subjected to listening to a barrage of accusations by the grandmother and repeated denials by the girl. Carballido makes it clear that the weary Hilaria is continually forced to observe and judge the grandmother's venomous condemnations of Palmira.

Hilaria's mother cleans, cooks, and cares for the children. This allows the widowed Hilaria to be able to work in order to sustain her family. Palmira's mother realizes that it is a difficult age for both her mother and daughter, but remains perplexed by this sudden and dramatic alteration in the relationship of the two. Palmira feels that the problem is that her grandmother simply does not love her:

> —¿Y por qué no va a quererte?
>
> —No sé.
>
> Pero había algo en el tono.
>
> —¿No sabes?
>
> —Antes te quería mucho.

> (73)

Hilaria reflects on the way in which the two loved each other as perfectly as any grandmother and granddaughter might. The child would save little gifts and the grandmother would preserve them in a special box. The grandmother would in turn rescue any special sweets which she might encounter so that she might present them to Palmira. As the past and present intermingle, the reader is increasingly perplexed as he attempts to understand how such a loving relationship could be so brutally transformed into one so hostile. Moreover, what could a child possibly do to precipitate such extreme and bizarre hostility? The mother's interrogation of the child is interrupted by the prying grandmother which further clouds Hilaria's and the reader's confidence in the veracity of the old woman's attacks against Palmira. That very evening in which the reader is catapulted into their lives, the grandmother takes pleasure in seizing a sweet which the child was about to enjoy. The grandmother delights in confiscating from Palmira what she had previously saved for her. How could a symbol of love become so blatantly twisted into a grotesque act of hatred? Carballido reveals the truth at the end but gradually prepares the reader with insightful details with regard to the grandmother's peculiar behaviour.

The grandmother so overflows with venomous sentiments toward her granddaughter that she does not find satisfaction in pouring these feelings out to Hilaria, as she finds a much more sympathetic listener in her son Efraín. He not only believes in and accepts his mother's hatred of the child but begins to partake in it himself. Efraín halfheartedly offers that she stay with him although the expense of feeding and caring for her as well as his mother's general dissatisfaction with life would make her a rather distasteful housemate for his wife. Guilt regarding this situation as well as frustration in an attempt to find steady employment are ignited by a considerable amount of alcohol propelling Efraín into a frenzied act of violence against Palmira.

Hilaria was in the movies with one child when she heard the extraordinary news that Palmira was hiding out at a neighbor's house. Efraín had entered the children's room in a blind rage and terrorized both young girls. He started whipping the half-naked Palmira and chased her down the streets until she finally found refuge. In his warped reasoning, Efraín may have hoped that by beating the child his mother would stop complaining and continue to live with Hilaria. When Hilaria returned home, Efraín's frustrated attempts to explain belt wounds on little girls were exercises in futility and Hilaria decided to expel the mother from the house. Carballido splendidly captures the moment when the weeping mother leaves her daughter's home:

> Cuando salió la anciana era bien tarde, pero casi nadie en la calle dejó de disfrutar el espectáculo. Balcones y ventanas, con absoluta indiscreción, se llenaron de ojos que miraban al hombre silencioso, cargado de maletas y bolsas, y a la vieja que iba junto a él, a tropezones, con la cara escondida en un pañuelo, dando algunos chillidos entre sollozo y sollozo. Hilaria gemía contra la puerta, sin atreverse a ver cómo su madre iba marchando cuesta abajo. Lola y thayo también lloraban, encharcando sus almohadas, porque se había ido la abuela. Sólo Palmira, fingiéndose dormida, permaneció con los ojos secos.

> (81-82)

All the neighbors view the spectacle as Carballido emphasizes both the tedium and gossip which dominate the small town. One is reminded of the powerful climatic scene in García Marquéz's masterful tale "La siesta del martes": the strong and indigent woman whose son was labeled as a thief and murderer faces the local townfolk who gaze at her every movement. The woman in **"Danza antigua"** is a direct opposite with regard to nobility of character, but is equally interesting. Noteworthy is that Palmira stays dry eyed throughout the compelling scene. The brave young girl must accept more household responsibilities without her grandmother's being there, but she has been freed from suffering the effects of a bitter hatred which she was too young to begin to understand.

Immediately prior to the expulsion of the grandmother, Carballido reveals the one climatic moment in which this loving relationship is transformed into detestation, but the author does present glimpses throughout the story of the grandmother's strange distancing from reality. In the middle of the night she awakens her daughter with weeping:

> —Mamá, ¿qué tienes?
>
> —Nada.
>
> Mamá, ¿por qué lloras?
>
> —Por nada, por nada. Duérmete.
>
> Callaron un momento. Después la anciana preguntó, con voz tenue:
>
> —¿Te acuerdas, hija, qué bonita era yo?
>
> —Si, mamá—. Extrañada, soñolienta.

—¿Te acuerdas de tus tías? Ninguna era tan. . . .

—Calló, volvió a llorar.

(75)

Unexpectedly, this obsession with death and old age pre-cipitated the grandmother's hostility toward Palmira. In order to alleviate her suffering caused by the ravages of time, she secretly closeted herself in a chimerical world where she was once again young and beautiful. Reality was more unbearable to the grandmother than to Carlos in **"Los huéspedes"** for he at least had the dreams of youth with the possibilities of escape to the future to help combat the tedium and poverty which surrounded him. The grand-mother in **"Danza antigua"** had nothing more than old fantasies and the past. The innocent grandchild accidently stumbled upon the grandmother in the midst of an elaborate chimera. The old woman has been an active participant in a ritualistic fantasy in which she reconstructs her youth. She was dressed in an old withered and once beautiful night-gown surrounded by admiring 'fantasmas' suitors from her past. This is a classic example of Todorov's definition of the multiplication of personality as the grandmother imagines reliving her youth in her old and decrepit body:

> The multiplication of personality, taken literally, is an immediate consequence of the possible transition between matter and mind: we are several persons mentally, we become so physically.

(116)

This kind of clandestine fantasy was evidently repeated to give the grandmother solace from the cruelty of reality and time.

Carballido describes in detail the grandmother's tragic "danza antigua" and Palmira's untimely entrance:

> Y así entró a la cocina, sin hacer ruido, y vio a la abuela, jorobadita y arrugada, con su largo vestido en blanco y negro, su chal de lana, entre la luz verdosa que se iba, vio a la abuela brincar con las enaguas levantadas y las canillas descubiertas, una media torcida y otra cayéndosele, bai-lando y canturreando por la pieza, sonriendo, coque-teando, saludando algún par de fantasmas que se perdían en un rincón. Palmira no pensó que fuera chistoso exacta-mente. (Aunque tenía gracia . . .) No pensó nada, más bien, sintió profundamente algo como placer, por la anciana contenta, y también lo contrario, una intuición oscura de despojo.

(80)

The bewildered Palmira pondered what she saw and then: "Y todo eso sentido, no pensado, salió en forma de risa" (81). The innocent child had no idea of the significance of what she had just observed. Her initial reaction was a collage of feelings ranging from pleasure to sadness. The grandmother furiously grabbed the child and angrily struck her for the first time ever. She then accused Palmira of spying on her. The grandmother's fanciful journey was brusquely interrupted and she was unable to deal with the embarrassment of revealing her own sorrowful needs and the girl in her youth and naiveté fell victim to the grand-mother's frustration and rage against time and the destruc-tion of all that is mortal. Her elaborate and very personal chimera came brutally stumbling down and the innocent Palmira was the one who was the unwittlingly culpable intruder. Seeing the young girl gaping in wonder at her had the same effect on the grandmother as if she had stared at her old and decayed image through an enormous mirror of truth. A magical and mystical escape was transformed into a terrifying nightmare. Palmira was thus castigated and punished for this unfortunate occurrence which she could not but partly comprehend or begin to communicate. The grandmother was unable to reveal the true motive for her sudden hatred of Palmira for it would expose her secret fantasy which might be interpreted as lunacy. The grand-mother's reluctance to accept and admit her need to escape from reality is similar to the situation discussed by David Gordon:

> What connections can be established, then, between liter-ary art and the unconscious: the most obvious is by the way of the work's own dramatized insight into uncon-scious processes, as when the writer creates characters who are shown to resist (perhaps only partially up to a point) the recognition of certain wishes and fears apparent to the reader.

(XV)

In **"Los huéspedes,"** Carlos' flights of fantasy will be reinforced by his continuous reconstruction of the magical world nurtured by Consuelo and Gabriel. In sharp contrast, the grandmother's real and chimerical worlds were unal-terably impaired by this accident of fate. The true pleasure and effectiveness of the grandmother's flight from unbear-able reality was violently smashed by a guiltless and con-fused child.

"La desterrada" is another story which depicts the rela-tionship between a grandmother, Leonor, and her grand-child. In sharp contrast to **"Danza antigua,"** however, the two are tied to each other by Leonor's glowing remem-brances of the past which allows them both to escape from the squalor of smothering reality. They consequently are forced to participate in a harsh destruction of the fantasy so intricately weaved by the grandmother. Raucus lan-guage and a clangorous din composed of penetrating whis-tles and hostile shouting permeate the apartment building where the grandmother and grandson live. In addition, a boxing ring surrounds the unfortunate woman's home and intensifies the brutality of the environs. As with Carlos in **"Los huéspedes"** and the grandmother in **"Danza antigua,"** Leonor feels herself isolated from a hostile en-vironment. Her daughter accepts the situation with more stoicism than Leonor, who in contemplating the boxing matches: "no podía dejar de imaginarse que dos hombres se pegaban allá, hasta sangrarse, hasta medio matarse" (115). Leonor fabricates an escape from the violence below by creating a haven of plants and flowers to elevate her from her present circumstances in Mexico City. Her younger sensitive grandchild anxiously participates in a more beautiful world which she lovingly brings into existence. Carballido describes the sharp contrast between the two children from Leonor's point of view: "El nieto menor era el más bueno, él que más la quería. El mayor se creía independiente, no hacía caso nunca. Y era respondón, sarcástico" (116). The older boy seems to enjoy the harsh sounds emanating from the boxing and wrestling matches below, but the younger desperately holds on to Leonor and takes flight transported by her prolific imagination.

The physical environment of the house and neighborhood is stifling to the grandmother as it is to the central characters in **"Los huéspedes"** and **"Danza antigua"**:

> La vivienda era chica y el barrio no era bueno. Los vecinos: obreros, empleados pobres, solteronas retorcidas; abajo, la familia del capitán. Leonor hubiera querido ver la calle, tener un balcón siquiera una ventanita, pero las piezas daban a ese pasillo angosto, descubierto, pozo de luz para ellos y para los de abajo, a los cuales podían ver siempre, sin inclinarse siquiera sobre el barandal, y a los cuales oían siempre quisieran o no.
>
> (116)

Leonor finds the need to construct a kind of bucolic paradise to assist in elevating her away from the overt squalor of her surroundings:

> El pasillo y el barandal eran un bosque, un intrincado invernadero, con plantas que parecía imposible ver aclimatadas en esta altura seca de la ciudad. Tenía, por ejemplo, dos huacales de orquídeas, a los que conseguía ver florear una vez al año; los helechos crecían tan frondosos como en una gruta, había macetas con yerbas de olor, para usar en la cocina: yerbabuena, épazote, culantro, acuyo (que aquí en México le decían ycrba santa).
>
> (117)

It soon becomes obvious that Leonor strives to recreate her childhood in Otitlán which represents to her all that is innocent and beautiful. Crime and blasphemy cause Leonor to seek refuge in the rusty walls of her memory. The plants and flowers are a shrine to her remembrance of the past. The town represents, as did the dance to the grandmother in **"Danza antigua"** all the splendor and glory of yesteryear: "Y con el nombre del pueblo venían las amistades, la casa propia, y el esposo vivo, el río, la juventud" (118). Leonor desperately needs the enchantment of the misty recollection of all this in order to tolerate the repressive environment in which reality tyranically reigns.

The marvelous relationship with her nephew clashes sharply with **"Danza antigua"** in which the grandmother conceals her secret chimera because of personal shame and anguish. In **"La desterrada"** Leonor enchants the boy with old songs which her mother used to sing to her. The grandson memorizes the ballads and yearns to escape to magical Otatitlán with his marvelous grandmother. He asks Leonor to lead him away: "Cuéntame de tu casa" (120). The grandson also needs refuge from the screaming blare of harsh reality:

> "Tu casa" era aquella grande, en Otatitlán. "Tu casa" en realidad eran la juventud, la familia dispersa, la tierra caliente, y el pozo y el gran árbol de mango. La invitaba a hablar el nieto y Leonor se lanzaba a aquellos años; su memoria giraba lentamente, viendo todo, deteniéndose al azar en algún punto.
>
> (120)

Leonor's past weaves a magical spell like a favorite fairy tale for the boy. Her chimerical realm is even more fascinating for its ties to reality.

The noisy and vulgar family below complains that the plants leak on their apartment. Leonor is unable to respond to her daughter's suggestion that they sell the plants: "Leonor no dijo nada. ¡Vender las plantas!" (120). The undersized enclosed prison in which she lives becomes bearable only because of the meaningful plants. To sell them would be a rejection of her past and an acceptance of the concrete and artificial world which surrounds her. Carballido gradually reveals fragments of Leonor's past as the reader begins to share with the loving grandson his fascination for Leonor's former life and dreams.

Tragedy and sadness were also very evident in Leonor's past. Her mother died when she was thirty five years old and her first fiancee was drowned. She married another, but Leonor seemed to remember her first love with tender passion. The grandmother communicates fervently all aspects of her past to the sensitive child. In addition, Carballido masterfully presents the child's reaction to Leonor's narrative. He finds it strange, for example, that the grandmother, who is so very old, would have ever had a mother: "Al nieto se le hacía raro oírla decir 'mi mamá'" (118). The boy longs to understand and escape into his grandmother's distant world, but finds himself chained in part to his own limited experience. When informed about the drowned fiancee, the child is astonished to observe that his grandmother still weeps for something which occurred so very long ago. He asks if she cried a great deal: "Y las lágrimas corrían de nuevo sobre las arrugas, sorprendiendo y lacerando al niño" (121). The deep, touching communication between those two alienated figures makes this story perhaps the most sensitive and best-developed of the Carballido collection. The two intimately share Leonor's past and this relationship makes the climatic harsh collision with reality ever more violent.

The urgent need for finances sets in motion the grandmother's return to Otatitlán. The failure to receive rent payments from the tenants living in her childhood home precipitates Leonor's necessity to make a personal visit. Only the grandmother and her younger grandson are not tied to duties in Mexico and thus are free to visit Otatitlán. The fanciful location which Leonor depicted before bed time and always bordered on the phantasmagorical must face the harsh glow of reality. Leonor's mystical tales are woven so well that the sensitive reader feels the same combination of fear and excitement as do Leonor and her loyal follower:

> La vieja y el niño sentían un miedo creciente: él, porque nunca había viajado; ella porque iba a regresar. ¡Otatitlán! Ahora sus relatos al nieto se volvían más vivos, parecían proyectarse al futuro inmediato y no al pasado indefinido. El niño casi creía que iba a conocer a todas aquellas gentes pretéritas y difuntas.
>
> (124)

The boy is the first to wince because of the cruel burning glare of reality as nothing seems to glow nearly as brightly as that created by the prolific Leonor. Carballido reveals the initial descriptions the jubilant grandmother recited to the boy:

> Papaloapam quiere decir "río de las mariposas" dijo la abuela alguna vez. Y él esperaba ver una corriente azul, llena con los vuelos multicolores de grandes animales.
>
> (124)

The park at night was portrayed as having sweet smells and bright lights and young lovers. Leonor's portrayed lively saint's day carnivals with games and dances. The masses of people included drunks and prostitutes which provoked the sensitive boy to remark: "¿No es muy feo todo eso, abuelita?" "No, hijo. Es divino" (125). All of Otatitlán sparkled wonderfully for Leonor as all recollections embodied the joy and magnificence of youth. Her past had become as mythical to Leonor as to her young grandson. Reality would ultimately collide even more violently against the seasoned dream weaver Leonor than against the inexperienced young dreamer.

Upon arrival at Papaloapam the boy immediately inquired about the whereabouts of the butterflies. The actual river did not begin to measure up to the boy's view of a stretch of water permeated with innummerable multicolored butterflies. Carballido effectively portrays how Leonor is much too engrossed in her own reverie to be awakened by this harbinger of reality delivered by the grandson: "Pero ella no lo oía, perdida en la corriente parduzca de sensaciones y recuerdos" (126). An air of decay, however, radiates the area, which precipitates Leonor's tears. This symbol of the ravaging of her adolesence and dreams is her first genuine awakening to the indifferent chill of reality. In addition, economic necessity forces the two to take a delapidated bus rather than more costly and enticing boats which the disappointed child: "contempló con codicia" (126). The symbol of Leonor's encounter with faded dreams and impending death becomes progressively more distinct throughout the final section of the story. These lugubrious representations creak and bellow with the power of Quevedo's "Miré los muros de la patria mía" as all signs in Otatitlán become tarnished by rust and corrosion.

Upon entering the center of town, Leonor is struck even more harshly by the brutal contrast between her past and how she remembered it and the present Otatitlán. Carballido strikingly describes the acute physical torment of viewing her village which is a mere fraction of her deep physical anguish:

> La luz de mediatarde se desplomaba dolorosamente sobre los ojos. Entrecerrándolos, vio la iglesia, el palacio municipal ... ¿Y los árboles? Fue como una puñalada: en vez del kiosko viejo había otro, muy feo, una estructura de cemento chata y sin gracia. Surgía en medio de un espacio vacío y descuidado, no había flores, y en vez de los racimos de globos luminosos, unos postes largos y funcionales sostenían un fruto único y sin encanto.
>
> (126-127)

All romance and splendor are lost in this purely functional setting. From the rusty old bus which transported her to Otatitlán to the smelly, rotting river Leonor finds her illusory work smashed into tiny fragments and the initial pain is described as being pierced with a knife. A more lasting hurt follows Leonor's early anguish.

Leonor discovers that she is as alienated in Otatitlán as she was in Mexico City. The innumerable changes which are soon apparent in buildings and landscape disorient her, and she is soon forced to ask directions in her own hometown. Leonor's godmother has difficulty in recognizing her as the protagonist feels herself to be a stranger in her own land:

> Era como otro pueblo: las pocas cosas reconocibles estaban estragadas o renovadas y no había rostros amigos; muertos y ruinas: el pueblo había sufrido una carcoma, por dondequiera había rastros de una lenta y minuciosa catástrofe. Algunas ancianas, sobrevivientes también, eran como espejos o ecos: las mismas arrugas, los mismos recuerdos, la misma nostalgia.
>
> (127)

Some solace is encountered with these old friends who cling to the same memories of the past which have horrified Leonor for so long. The boy finds that the grandmother's dreams are not as unique as he originally thought: "Desde un rincón, el niño las oía con fastidio, cinco ancianas diciendo las mismas cosas que siempre decía la abuela" (127). The group mourned for Leonor's drowned fiancee, one old woman sang one of Leonor's old songs in a harsh voice. Sad and joyful anecdotes were told and recounted. Leonor had rediscovered her old village, but it existed only in old memories. The protagonist was now indeed exiled from the present and future and her life inhabited a dark dusty corner in the long ago.

The grandson became increasingly irritable because the fairy land which he had dreamed about became more and more like a musty portrait of relentless time. Leonor's childhood home symbolizes even more clearly the crumbling of her dreams and youth:

No había cortinas en las ventanas; donde había sido la sala estaba un tendejón y la gente salía y entraba con los pies sucios. Las piezas vacías y desvencijadas, los muros descascarados, los suelos carcomidos; donde fue la recámara de Alma, aquel cuartito azul y rosa, había una bodega de granos, olía a humedad y una rata se dejó ver por un momento. El patio era una extensión salvaje y abandonada.

(128)

Leonor weeps as she views her delapidated home. Nothing remains the same from her bedroom to the trees outside. Obliterated dreams are nearly impossible to communicate so Leonor merely attempts to explain her weeping with the statement: "Es que todo ha cambiado tanto. Esta era mi recámara, aquélla la de mi hija ... Todo ha cambiado ..." (129). Only the boy can begin to fathom the depth of her anguish for he has soared with her to the heights of her fantasies and now must accompany Leonor in her fall.

There is no solace even with the dead in Otatitlán as the cementary disorients the returning pilgrim. The engravings on her parent's tombs are barely legible and it is impossible to even find her first fiancee's grave. Leonor wonders isolated among the dead as well as the living. Vegetation hides the various graves as she is once again completely disoriented. Leonor resigns herself to placing flowers at an unknown grave and receives no satisfaction from that resigned symbolic act: "Gozó por un instante imaginando la grata sorpresa de los deudos, después comprendió que aquel sepulcro viejo no le importaba a nadie, ni a ella misma" (129). What was to be Leonor's lost paradise is nothing more than a grotesque version of her past where everyone and everything is blatantly marred by the savage indifference of time.

Upon her return to Mexico City, Leonor suffers yet another cruel and frighteningly symbolic episode. She is suddenly attacked by an inebriated passerby who "tal vez la confundió con otra persona, tal vez lo ofendió la pulcritud de la anciana" (130). Her uncertain and yet meaningful feelings toward the episode help to explain the significance with regard to the protagonist:

No lo pensó, pero supo vagamente que aquélla era la agresión de un lugar al que no pertenecía, que aquello formaba parte de los edificios altos y pobres, del distinto hablar de la gente, de los siempre amenazantes vehículos.

(130)

Leonor does indeed view herself as "la desterrada" for she feels alienated in both Mexico City and Otatitlán. She walks both alone in and estranged from her surroundings. Leonor's sole comfort was in the Otatitlán of her youth which is entombed in a hidden, labyrinthian burial ground.

Leonor realizes that what she imagined to actually be part of the real world was merely illusion. With her return home

Leonor has become similar to the hopeless people describe by D. W. Winnicot: "We find the individuals live creatively and feel that life is worth living or else that they cannot live creatively and are doubtful about the value of living" (71). The plants and flowers were her way of keeping Otatitlán and her youth alive, but with her new awareness Leonor becomes fully transformed. Carballido masterfully portrays the transfigured Leonor's retrospection after her epiphany in Otatitlán:

El agua caía en los tinacos y el patio era un simulacro de aquel otro que ya no existía en ninguna parte. Viendo al cielo, oyó al nieto canturrear la canción de "La palma." Algo había perdido sentido, tal vez la voluntad. Por un instante, pensó en tantos recuerdos que había depositado en la pequeña cabeza. ¿Qué pasaría con ellos? ¿Qué valía un recuerdo, qué significaba? La realidad era ésta: una vieja indiferente viendo al cielo, ruido de agua en tinacos, un dolor curioso "como el de una planta arrancada, con las raíces al aire," pensó. Vagamente pensó también en la muerte, y en quién iría después a cuidar las plantas. Ahora la cansaba mucho regar. La cansaba todo, profundamente. Por un momento pensó que la cansaba vivir.

(130)

Leonor's plants had represented all the purity and vitality of her youth. She now feels that her nurturing of shrubs and herbs to keep her past alive has been a deception. The former joy of observing the blossoming of flowers and viewing them emit life has now become a gloomy reminder of the folly of her illusory past. She consequently sells some and gives others away. Only the child understands the true meaning of the tragic act as he closets himself behind the door and weeps. The last words by Leonor to the boy in the story are: "Ya es muy tarde" (131). This brief statement symbolizes the fact that now that her dreams are shattered there is only death to wait for.

* * *

In conclusion, Carballido has proven with this excellent volume to be a master of the short story. His tales splendidly capture the essence of the characters and the distinctive enchantment of small towns with the same poignancy of masters of this genre and theme, such as García Márquez and Rulfo. In each of these stories Carballido weaves tales in which characters escape their tedious poverty stricken lives by creating magical worlds. The jarring clash with reality effects each character, all of them unique individuals, as they react to the disharmony in their own singular fashion. Carballido always stressed the importance of the individual in his theatrical masterpieces such as *Medusa* (1959). *El día que se soltaron los leones* (1959), *El relojero de Córdoba* (1959). In these short stories as in the above-mentioned plays, each personality is etched with detailed precision as Carballido creates little gems filled with beauty and insight. A reading of *La caja vacía* will surely convince the reader of the great dramatist Carballido's prowess as a short story writer.

Works Cited

Carballido, Emilio. *La caja vacía.* Mexico: Fondo de Cultura Económica, 1982.

———. *Teatro.* Mexico: Fondo de Cultura Económica, 1976.

Gordon, David J. *Literary Art and the Unconscious.* Baton Rouge: Louisiana State University Press, 1976.

Gullason, Thomas. "The Short Story: An Underrated Art" in *Short Story Theories.* Edited by Charles E. May. Ohio: Ohio Univ. Press, 1976.

Peden, Margaret Sayers. *Emilio Carballido.* Boston: Twayne Publishers, 1980.

Todorov, Tzvetzan. *The Fantastic: A Structural Approach to a Literary Genre.* Cleveland: Case Western Univ. Press, 1973.

Winnicott, D. W. *Playing and Reality.* N.Y.: Basic Books, Inc., 1971.

Jacqueline Eyring Bixler (essay date 1990)

SOURCE: Bixler, Jacqueline Eyring. "Carballido's *Acapulco, los lunes* and the Darker Side of Comedy." *Chasqui* 19.2 (1990): 3-11. Print.

[*In the following essay, Bixler finds* Acapulco, los lunes *(1969; may be translated as* Acapulco Mondays*) to be a "bleak" and "dark" drama. She argues that although the play "is fairly didactic in its dramatic revelation of moral and physical decadence, the author proposes no remedy. Instead, he leaves the spectator with confusing moral questions and no direction in which to turn."*]

Now in his fifth decade of playwriting, Emilio Carballido, widely recognized as Mexico's reigning king of comedy, has created nearly one hundred dramatic works, including full-length plays, one-acts, and children's theatre, most of which resist facile classification into dramatic genres.[1] Nonetheless, Carballido has a curious penchant for generic subtitles, which inevitably influence not only the production and enactment of the play, but also the audience's expectations and subsequent perception of the performance. Four of his full-length pieces, for instance, are subtitled "farsa": *El día que se soltaron los leones* (1957); *¡Silencio, pollos pelones, ya les van a traer su maíz!* (1963); *Te juro, Juana, que tengo ganas* (1965); and *Acapulco, los lunes* (1969). Yet, with the possible exception of *Te juro, Juana,* which is considerably lighter in tone, this subtitle is indeed a misnomer, for these so-called "farsas" extend well beyond traditional notions of the genre in their seriousness of purpose, dark undertones, and strong emotional impact on the audience. Given the tremendous popularity and commercial success of Carballido's full-length comedies, it is curious that, with the exception of *El día que se soltaron los leones,* relatively little has been written about this farcical foursome.[2] This lack of critical attention may be explained by the unexpected complexity of their dramatic fabric as much as by the fact that while farce is an audience's delight, it has long been scorned by critics as an inferior brand of comedy.[3] Strictly speaking, however, these plays do not fit the standard definition of the genre. Contrary to the expectations of simplicity, slapstick, and easy laughter that their subtitle engenders, these pieces "farsas" bewilder and confuse their audience by wedding comedy and tragedy, satire and social criticism, and by producing such disparate reactions as laughter and despair.

Due to the rapid disintegration of traditional standards and values that has occurred throughout the twentieth century, it has become increasingly difficult to classify dramatic works as either pure comedy or pure tragedy. In an effort to reflect these changes in man's principles and morals, Carballido, like Pinter, Brecht, Albee, and others, has produced plays that defy and deny the traditional definition of comedy by mixing diverse genres and emotions: the comic with the tragic, the moral with the immoral, the noble with the ignoble. As a result, modern comedy is, as Robert Corrigan describes it, "a special kind of comedy, a grotesque kind of comedy, which makes us laugh with a lump in our throats" (*Comedy*, 10). In an attempt to label this dramatic hybrid, contemporary theorists and philosophers have coined denominations such as "tragicomedy" and "dark comedy," which, despite their paradoxical ring, encompass the blend of darkness and sunshine, sobriety and absurdity that pervades Carballido's so-called "farsas."

Written in 1969, *Acapulco, los lunes* is the most recent of Carballido's full-length "farsas."[4] Although it has received the least critical attention of the four plays listed above, it best portrays the admixture of diversion, didacticism, and pathos present in these would-be farces.[5] On a superficial level, this lengthy one-act does indeed fulfill the audience's expectations of farce by providing certain basic mechanisms associated with the genre: the accelerated pace of the action, the stock nature of the characters, and the low humor.[6] Nevertheless, the play's farcical frame conceals a tone and a basic philosophy which soon lead the audience well beyond the pleasures of simple comedy and into the perplexing emotional experience of tragicomedy. The fusion of farcical form and non-farcical themes indeed creates an uncomfortable situation for the spectator, who finds him or herself stranded between the ironic detachment of comedy and the sympathy of tragedy. In this brutal demythification of Acapulco's glittery paradise and of the "Mexican miracle," Carballido treats his spectators to the bewildering experience of making them laugh while at the same time forcing them to recognize their own moral ambivalence and weaknesses. As Frank Dauster notes, "la obra es una de las más fuertes de Carballido en su rechazo de toda la mitología oficial de Acapulco y el turismo" (187). In the same vein, Margaret Peden describes *Acapulco* as "a bitter and pessimistic play" (116). A closer examination of the work reveals that *Acapulco, los lunes,* and by extension *El día que se soltaron los leones* and *¡Silencio, pollos pelones . . . !* [*¡Silencio, pollos pelones, ya les van a echar su maíz!*], far surpasses the facile laughter of traditional farce and quickly plunges its audience into the ambiguous and troublesome realm of modern dark comedy, whose main objective is precisely that of emotionally confusing the spectators and thus obliging them to reflect upon themselves as members of the very same society besieged by the dramatist.

On a structural level, *Acapulco, los lunes* indeed fulfills the basic expectations engendered by its subtitle. Farce is, as Robert Corrigan explains, "a surrealistic art [. . .] an art of flat surfaces and of images. Like a giant collage, it is composed of violent juxtapositions and disparate patterns having no continuity" (*Theatre,* 68). Accordingly, Carballido offers not a smoothly flowing plot, but rather a loose concatenation of scenes in which he depicts the daily lives of natives and non-natives alike. The play has no real beginning or end, opening in the midst of a Hollywood-style movie-set escapade complete with gunshots and a loose tiger and ending without ever really resolving the characters' psychological or moral problems. The "violent juxtaposition" prescribed by Corrigan resides in the play's constant alternation between two entirely different groups of characters, one of whom elicits the audience's pity, the other its scorn.

The first group consists of three American expatriates and a Mexican gigolo who struggle to survive what they call "los lunes de Acapulco," or the days when there are few tourists to support the local economy. Liuba, an aging, sex-starved German-American zoologist, survives by offering guided tours of a hotel menagerie that she herself has created. Myra, an ex-stewardess from San Francisco, scrapes by as a part-time model. Another young American, Alvin, currently unemployed, has fled to Mexico to escape the Vietnam draft. At a movie set, Alvin and Myra meet the native Lucio Coronado, a trickster who feeds off the wealthy tourists. In subsequent adventures, Lucio initiates his new pals into his own means of survival, among them deception, theft, and prostitution. Alvin and Myra, increasingly afraid of becoming implicated in Lucio's schemes, ultimately denounce him to the police. When the final curtain falls, Lucio remains in jail, while the others have found new ways of surviving the Acapulco Mondays: Liuba is now cook and guide on a glass-bottomed boat; Myra has become a prosperous lady of the night; and Alvin has also apparently turned to prostitution by accepting his own latent homosexuality. The characters' financial woes have been resolved, yet their moral and existential dilemma remains not only unresolved but unresolvable.

Whereas the three Americans and Lucio are highly individualized characters, the second group, composed of tourists, is characterized collectively. They comprise the more comic side of this dark comedy as they flock to Acapulco to shake their inhibitions and to live, if just for a few days,

their wildest fantasies. In the opening stage directions, Carballido states that the tourists should be of an archetypal and hyperbolic nature: "Los turistas serán arquetípicos. No es posible evitar la caricatura: los turistas reales son caricatura en su mayor porcentaje. Es preferible exagerla hasta el exceso" (164). Accordingly, the tourists who soon emerge on stage are obvious stereotypes—wealthy, aging, gullible, and desperately in search of excitement. Their amorphous character is accentuated by the fact that they appear almost exclusively as a chorus:

TODOS:

¡Fin de semana eterno! Acapulco sin lunes.

—Siempre anochece en sábado y amanece en domingo para el brunch en la alberca, para el trago en la playa.

—Pero además, no es caro.

—Pueden comprarse tragos y siempre hay experiencias.

VARIOS:

Excitante.

VARIOS:

Muy excitante.

MUCHOS:

Excitante, excitante.

TODOS:

Aquí es muy excitante.

UNO:

El muchacho en la playa da servicio especial.

TODOS:

Excitante.

(175)

Carballido employs a collective voice to convey the tourists' hedonistic desires and at the same time creates an ironic effect by using the chorus of ancient tragedy to highlight the drama's comic surface rather than its tragic undertones.

While the tourists' frenzied pleasure-seeking is appropriately farcical, the difficulties shared by the main characters— Liuba, Myra, and Alvin—add a darker side to the comedy. Their life, unlike the frivolous, carefree style of the tourists, is one of never-ending Mondays. As Liuba explains, "Las vacaciones, los fines de semana. Pero llegan los lunes y duran. Los largos lunes de Acapulco. Esto . . . se vuelve un pueblo, nos quedamos los raros, los descastados, los nativos, los pobres [. . .]" (227). Whereas the tourists' main preoccupation is the search for excitement, whether it be in the form of alcohol, cheap sex, or other bargains, the three expatriates are concerned only with the source of their next meal. The spectator cannot help but feel compassion upon seeing Alvin's futile attempts to become an adult and to confront his own homosexuality, Myra's desperate search for a meaningful identity, and Liuba's pathetic begging for human companionship. The play's binary focus on two distinct groups reinforces this comic/tragic contrast while at the same time producing an uncomfortable and bewildering emotional experience for the audience, who alternately laughs and laments. In fact, the work's dramatic tension arises not as a result of any concern over the characters' future, but rather from the constant shifting and confusion in the spectator's emotions. In this darker form of comedy, as Charney notes, an "uncertainty of tone is cultivated by the author to produce a bewildering, if not also painful experience, as the play shifts unpredictably between the farcical and the tragic, and no way is offered to bridge the discontinuity" (106). The play maintains the discomfort by alternating between the amusing schemes of Lucio and his cohorts and dialogue among the three American outcasts. The only point of convergence between the two groups is Lucio, who, albeit a native, is equally desperate to survive and who periodically brings them together as part of his roguish schemes.

Carballido is well aware of the fundamental role of a quicksilver tone in creating the desired uneasiness in the audience. As he explains in another one of his bittersweet comedies, *¡Silencio, pollos pelones ... !*, "La obra es una farsa. Lo cual no impide que los momentos patéticos deban serlo sin vacilación alguna ... Las salidas de tono romperán el patetismo pero también lo acentuarán" (96). In other words, he believes that this game of tonal ping-pong not only breaks the somber mood of the play but also serves to highlight it through contrast. Complementary to this notion is Styan's belief that the fluctuating focus present in dark comedy adds to the play's overall emotional impact: "The dark drama is exciting because one pattern of feeling, dramatized perhaps by one character or group of characters, is countered by a contrary pattern from an opposite character or group" (265). By shifting back and forth between the absurdity of the tourists and the true pathos of the three primary characters, Carballido achieves this contrast of light and dark patterns and thus maintains the dramatic tension.

The play's dual focus is further highlighted by the bilingual dialogue that results when natives and non-natives make futile attempts to communicate with one another. Besides creating humorous effects and an atmosphere of misunderstanding and confusion, the mixture of Spanish and English adds an authentic touch to the play. While the action and the characters are for the most part highly exaggerated, the language is realistic and essential to the revelation of the serious ideas underlying this farcical shell.

In his famous study on laughter, Henri Bergson contends that the audience is only able to laugh after it has distanced itself sufficiently from the object of its laughter: "Step aside, look upon life as a disinterested spectator: many a

drama will turn into a comedy" (63). In order to distance himself from the play, the spectator must first be made to feel superior to those on stage, after which the dramatic irony of superiority prevents him from feeling either compassion or sympathy for the characters. Nevertheless, the binary focus of *Acapulco, los lunes* on both tourists and non-tourists creates a problem in terms of this psychological distance, for while the tourists' trivial problems are highly risible, it is not easy to laugh at the very real problems that Liuba, Myra, and Alvin encounter daily in their struggle to survive. Through the effective use of stereotypes and exaggeration, the dramatist makes the tourists appear utterly ridiculous, thereby enabling the spectator to view them scornfully from a position of superiority. One of Lucio's female victims, for instance, is described by the dramatist as "una Turista viejona. Ella viste de noche, algo en texturas metálicas y color vívido, poco adecuado para su edad y su figura [...]" (186). Neither the author nor the spectator feels any pity whatsoever as these wealthy, materialistic tourists suffer one deception after another at the hands of tricksters like Lucio. At one point in the play, Lucio and Myra con a couple of naive *gringos* into buying a pair of exotic birds. Only after one of the birds loses its beak do the victims realize that their precious toucans are really made of paper maché and that their so-called health permit is actually a permit for entry into grade school.

Carballido facilitates the audience's psychological removal from the stage not only through the absurdity of the situations and the exaggeration of character types, but also through the deliberate distortion of the dramatic illusion of reality in terms of tempo and setting. He sets a fast pace by presenting in rapid succession a number of short scenes and by keeping the stagecraft as simple as possible. Instead of specifying formal scenic divisions that would break the flow of the action, the dramatist uses abrupt shifts in lighting and music to indicate changes of time and setting. A trio of rock musicians and the flashing of neon lights, for example, frequently signal the appearance of the tourists. In this fashion, the author produces a change of scene as well as a complete shift in mood and atmosphere. He states in the opening stage directions that the stagecraft must be kept as simple as possible so that these changes can be effected quickly and unobtrusively:

> Toda la obra deberá fluir sin interrupción, con cambios rápidos, y evidentes, a los que ayudarán los mismos actores. [...] Cuando está presente el mar el foro deberá estar casi vacío y habrá ciclorama muy luminoso, u oscuro y con estrellas que brillen. Lo demás tendrá siempre sugerencias de selva, de vegetación tropical. Las jaulas serán carros que salgan con mucha facilidad y sin ruido. Las mesas y sillas de playa o cabaret las cargarán con naturalidad los meseros.

(164)

The limited number of stage objects and the fact that they are carried on stage by the actors themselves combine to destroy any possible illusion of reality. This deliberate lack of realism, coupled with the exaggeration of action and character, makes the spectator constantly aware that he is watching a highly stylized version of daily life in Acapulco.

In his study on the psychology of farce, Eric Bentley states that "the speeding up of movements has a psychological and moral effect, namely, that of making actions seem abstract and automatic when in real life they would be concrete and subject to free will" ("Psychology," xx). With the exception of Lucio and the three expatriates, Carballido reduces his characters to puppet-like figures, whose actions and emotional responses are so exaggerated as to appear mechanical. As Esslin notes, "In farce, events develop with the relentless mechanical precision of a machine and the characters appear as mere cogs" (71). Through the distortion of both action and emotion, the dramatist conveys the tourists' lack of free will and their condition as puppets in an absurd, unrelenting system.

Yet, despite the puppet-like figures, the exaggeration of pace and mood, and the purposeful destruction of the illusion of reality, these farcical underpinnings are but a backdrop to the grave moral and metaphysical questions that belie the play's subtitle. Beyond the patent demythification of Mexico's tropical paradise and the exposé of the victim-victimizer relationship that exists between natives and non-natives, Carballido expresses preoccupations that transcend the limits of time and geographical borders: modern man's search for an identity and his raison d'etre, the moral corruption of society, and the consequent backward evolution of man and society. These serious issues counteract whatever humor might be derived from the frenzied pleasure-seeking and absurd antics of the tourists and comprise the dark note that permeates and dominates the text.

In addition to the special problems that each of the *gringos* experiences, all three suffer a lack of direction and identity. Throughout the play they frequently ask themselves questions of an existential nature, such as Who am I? Why am I here? Where am I going? Although each one desires to escape some dark event in his or her past, they fear what the future may bring. For Alvin, it is an avoidance of the draft and of his own repressed homosexuality. He is haunted by the guilt-ridden memory of a young friend who committed suicide when Alvin refused to be his lover. Myra fled both her job with the airlines and her country when two fellow stewardesses died in a plane crash. She not only fears the past but also the future, not knowing who she is nor where she is going: "Y es esta misma sensación, algo como … '¿para qué?,' o como '¿por qué?,' o como '¿quién soy?'" (201). In a desperate attempt to establish a meaningful identity for herself, Myra pretends to be a Vietnam war widow, even though it is pathetically clear to all that she is lying. Considerably older than the other two, Liuba's case is even more pitiful. As she feels herself losing her youth and attractiveness, she

seeks sex as a means of retaining what little youth she still possesses. Most of her speech is characterized by a *carpe diem* motif that reflects this preoccupation with physical decay. During one of her menagerie tours, for instance, she explains:

LIUBA:

[…] Esta, la cascabel, mata por desintegración de los tejidos. Podría decirse que mata como el Tiempo.

EL TURISTA:

¿Como el tiempo?

LIUBA:

Sí. Porque el Tiempo nos desintegra … Usted, por ejemplo, ve a la señora. […] Tuvo su cara fresca, pétalos de flor en cada rinconcito del cuerpo, del rostro … Y un veneno se filtra en los tejidos y va quedando esto […].

(179-180)

As is customary in Carballido's theatre, the dramatist uses one of the characters as spokesperson of his own personal concerns. In this case, he employs Liuba to convey the disturbing concept of the backward evolution of mankind. As Margaret Peden points out, "Liuba's function, rather than being directly involved, is more that of a commentary that questions our accepted lines of demarcation between the animal and human worlds" (113). In the insensitive and dehumanized world in which she lives, Liuba more readily identifies with the animals in her menagerie than with her fellow human beings. Furthermore, the constant fusion of human and animal images in her philosophical commentary suggests that there is little difference between the two worlds in today's society.

The existential problems that plague Myra, Liuba, and Alvin have a disturbing effect on the spectator, who has been (mis)led by the subtitle to anticipate only amusing characters and situations. Yet even more unsettling than these philosophical questions are the moral questions that arise as a result of the actions of the main characters. As the play progresses, Liuba's metaphorical comments extend from the disintegrating effects of age and time to an invisible and broader evil—the moral decay of mankind. Upon witnessing this dehumanized, dog-eat-dog world in which they move, the audience is urged to reassess its own moral values. One knows that the deeds of Lucio, Liuba, Myra, and Alvin are immoral, yet at the same time one sympathizes with their need to survive. This onset of moral doubts is common in tragicomedy for, as Mathew Winston explains, "the violent combination of opposing extremes unsettles us so that we do not know how to respond. Our emotional and intelectual reactions become confused; this in turn disturbs our certainty of moral and social values and challenges our sense of a secure norm" (273). Carballido unsettles his spectators by making them unsure whether to laugh or cry, condone or condemn, and by denying them a secure norm to which they can refer. Not one of the characters fits the audience's idea of moral normalcy. Its moral standards are confused even further by the fact that the one noble action of the play is, ironically, performed by Lucio, whom the spectator has already dismissed as a shameless rogue. In one of the final scenes, Lucio sucks the poison from the infected leg of a fellow prisoner. After seeing him cheat, drug, and rob numerous victims, the audience is bewildered by this sudden act of unrequited kindness toward a fellow human being and forced to re-evaluate not only its own moral stance toward Lucio but also the overall moral atmosphere of the play as a whole.

While the dramatic conflict is clearly that of victim vs. victimizer, the have-nots vs. the haves, the spectator's perception changes throughout the play as to who exactly is the victim and who the victimizer. The audience begins by sympathizing with Myra and Alvin and their daily struggle to survive and to establish an identity for themselves, yet by the end of the play we realize that they have succeeded only at the expense of Lucio. For while they decry and ultimately denounce his means of survival, they willingly accept part of the money thus gained. In the words of Peden, Myra and Alvin are finally perceived as "odious— weak, parasitical, unprincipled, and disloyal" (116). Lucio, on the other hand, is ultimately recognized as the victim, not only of his so-called friends Myra and Alvin, but also of society. Like many of his compatriots, Lucio's family lost its land to developers and he was forced to leave the family farm and to adopt other means of survival. While the audience can hardly condone his actions, it can appreciate his generosity and honesty. Unlike Myra and Alvin, he accepts himself for what he is—a pimp, thief, and racketeer. In a world in which traditional moral values and standards have been turned topsy-turvy, Lucio is the anti-hero par excellence of modern comedy, a lower-class character whom we come to admire despite his moral shortcomings.

Through the words of Liuba and the actions of the other main characters, Carballido presents the bleak notion that man acts according to his environment, an idea that is reinforced when one of the other prisoners tries to explain to Lucio his own reluctance to help their sick cellmate: "Te digo que nos vuelven. Yo estoy aquí por culpa de unos cabrones ... ¿Crees que por mi gusto soy lo que soy?" (250). The implicit proposition that man must adapt himself to the society in which he lives pertains to the general theme of backward evolution. In one of her more prophetic moments, Liuba envisions man as "un pez sin ojos":

> Evolución ... Y se le borran los ojos al pez del río sub-
> terráneo, se le convierten en manchas insensibles ... Por-
> que los ojos no hacen falta cuando no hay luz.
>
> (194-195)

Liuba's poetic description of human decadence neatly captures the theme of devolution that underlies the entire play. Through her, Carballido conveys the grim message that man's social and moral condition is in a state of regression,

not toward a golden age, but back to "la edad de hierro," an age well described in a cabaret song performed toward the end of the play:

> Porque es la Edad de Hierro.
> No cesa el sufrimiento de los hombres,
> no cesan sus trabajos y miserias en el día
> ni su corrupción por la noche.
> Porque es la Edad de Hierro.
> Los bienes se entremezclan con los males,
> no es el padre semejante a su hijo
> ni el hijo al padre,
> ni el huésped a su huésped,
> ni el amigo al amigo,
> y no es el hermano amado por su hermano.
> Porque es la Edad de Hierro.
> Los unos saquean las ciudades de los otros.
> No hay piedad, ni justicia, ni acciones buenas
> y el violento y el inicuo son respetados.
> ¡Si hubiese muerto antes, o nacido después!
>
> (237)

In short, Carballido presents a bleak situation for which there is no apparent solution. The play's conclusion, in which the chorus of tourists chants the names of popular mixed drinks, seems trite and purposeless, but when considered within the context of the entire play it reaffirms the *carpe diem* philosophy advocated by Liuba: the brevity of life, the finality of death, and man's need to enjoy, while he may, the few pleasures remaining in life.

Although **Acapulco, los lunes** is fairly didactic in its dramatic revelation of moral and physical decadence, the author proposes no remedy. Instead, he leaves the spectator with confusing moral questions and no direction in which to turn. As Winston explains, the dark humorist evades because he himself has no answer: "His perception of inseparable complexities and unresolvable antitheses keeps him from advocating or hoping for any reform" (270). This two-toned twilight drama is, therefore, designed to be a theatre of paradox, whose very objective is to present through its own dramatic ambivalence the complexity and ambiguity of human behavior. If there is any final message at all in the play it is that this is the way the world is today and that we the spectators, like Lucio, Liuba, Myra, and Alvin, must learn to live accordingly. Again, Winston states: "We do not know how to react to the literary work any more than the characters know how to cope with their world. We find ourselves in the same confused and problematical situations as the characters ... Which is precisely where the author wants us to be" (284). In the final analysis, the subtitle "farsa" merely describes the thin comic surface of **Acapulco, los lunes**. It serves, at the same time, as a thin façade for a much darker drama and as a curtain with which the dramatist drapes in laughter his own pessimism and despair.

Notes

1. The generic classification of Carballido's theatre has been a persistent problem for critics of his work. In

one of the few books devoted to his dramaturgy, Margaret Sayers Peden observes that "because of Carballido's variety and diversity, we can arrive at no satisfactory groupings of plays based on the division between realism and fantasy, on structure or technique, or on subject matter. The plays, then, will be considered in approximately chronological order [. . .]," a system which she herself admits is "not entirely satisfactory" (90). In a more recent study focused on his later plays, I accept from the start the impossibility of classifying his works and treat them instead as plays that contain contradictory and at times irreconcilable elements.

2. While all four of these plays have been mentioned in general studies of Carballido's theatre, no individual attention has been granted to them with the exception of *El día que se soltaron los leones,* which Eugene Skinner treats as an existential adaptation of the allegorical *auto* in his "Carballido: Temática y forma de tres autos." Diana Taylor focuses on images of freedom and confinement as well as the use of farce as a means of discourse in her "Mad World, Mad Hope: Carballido's *El día que se soltaron los leones,*" while Oswaldo Augusto López examines the work's sociopolitical implications in his essay "Crítica a las limitaciones del individuo (*El día que se soltaron los leones*)."

3. Most critics seem to believe that farce is limited to amusing confusions and that it has no real conflict or characters of stature and significance. Allardyce Nicoll, for one, explains that since the word "farce" derives etymologicaly from the Latin "farcire" for "to stuff," the term signifies a type of drama "stuffed with low humor and extravagant wit" (87). In the same vein, Barbara Cannings suggests a lack of purpose and significance when she states that the subjects of the genre are "the accidents of humdrum existence" (558) and that "farces poke fun at someone or everyone, but with no particular axe to grind" (559). Bernard Grebanier, Maurice Charney, and Edwin Wilson echo this philosophy when they state, respectively, that "Nobody is expected to take the story seriously" (291), that farce is "unintellectual, unpsychological, and uncomplex" (97), and that "Farce has no intellectual pretensions, but aims rather at entertainment and provoking laughter" (189-90).

4. I specify here "full-length" because, in addition to the four titles mentioned above, Carballido also has a number of brief one-acts that he has labelled "farsas": "El espejo (1)"; "Paso de madrugada"; "Un cuento de Navidad"; and "Hoy canta el fénix en nuestro gallinero," all of which may be found in his collection *D.F. 26 obras en un acto,* except for "Hoy canta . . . ," which forms part of the collection *A la epopeya un gajo.*

5. In an interview with Joseph Vélez, Carballido expressed his belief that farce is far more effective than a purely didactic theatre in making the audience gain consciousness and reflect upon itself: "hay otro tipo de teatro que sí es el que funciona, que es un teatro de tipo catártico, como las farsas, donde por medio de la risa, por medio de cierto tipo de funcionamientos humanos desaforados [se muestra] un tipo de conducta, de ideología, de funcionamiento social [. . .] un tipo de farsa con una fuerte actitud de compromiso social" (Vélez, 18). This comment would, however, suggest that Carballido has a broader and less traditional view of a genre that is not normally associated with social consciousness-raising.

6. For the purposes of this study, we will presuppose that the intended audience is a typical audience composed of middle to upper-class Mexicans, who no doubt applaud the antics of playboy Lucio while condemning the denunciation of his "crimes" by killjoys Alvin and Myra and laughing with abandon at the tourists.

Works Cited

Bentley, Eric. *The Life of the Drama.* New York: Atheneum, 1964.

———, ed. "The Psychology of Farce." *Let's Get a Divorce and Other Plays.* New York: Hill and Wang, 1958. vii-xx.

Bergson, Henri. "Laughter." *Comedy.* Ed. Wylie Sypher. Garden City, NY: Doubleday, 1956.

Bixler, Jacqueline Eyring. "A Theatre of Contradictions: The Recent Works of Emilio Carballido." *Latin American Theatre Review* 18.2 (1985): 57-65.

Cannings, Barbara. "Towards a Definition of Farce as a Literary Genre." *Modern Language Review* 56.4 (1961): 558-60.

Carballido, Emilio. *Acapulco, los lunes.* In *Tres obras.* Mexico: Editorial Extemporáneos, 1978a.

———. *¡Silencio, pollos pelones, ya les van a echar su maíz!* In *Tres obras.* Mexico: Editorial Extemporáneos, 1978.

———. *D.F. 26 obras en un acto.* Mexico: Editorial Grijalbo, 1978.

———. *A la epopeya un gajo.* Mexico: Universidad Autónoma del Estado de México, 1983.

Charney, Maurice. *Comedy High and Low. An Introduction to the Experience of Comedy.* New York: Oxford UP, 1978.

Corrigan, Robert, ed. *Comedy: Meaning and Form.* San Francisco: Chandler Pub. Co., 1965.

———. *The Theatre in Search of a Fix.* New York: Delta, 1973.

Dauster, Frank N. "El teatro de Emilio Carballido." *Ensayos sobre teatro hispanoamericano*. Mexico: SepSetentas, 1975. 143-88.

Esslin, Martin. *An Anatomy of Drama*. New York: Hill and Wang, 1976.

Grebanier, Bernard. *Playwriting: How to Write for the Theatre*. New York: Thomas Y. Crowell Co., 1961.

Holtan, Orley I. *Introduction to Theatre: A Mirror to Nature*. Englewood Cliffs, NJ: Prentice-Hall, 1976.

López, Oswaldo Augusto. "Crítica a las limitaciones del individuo (*El día que se soltaron los leones*)." *Explicación de Textos Literarios* 3 (1975): 151-59.

Nicoll, Allardyce. *The Theory of Drama*. New York: Benjamin Blom, 1966.

Peden, Margaret Sayers. *Emilio Carballido*. Boston: Twayne, 1980.

Skinner, Eugene R. "Carballido: Temática y forma de tres autos." *Latin American Theatre Review* 3.1 (1969): 37-47.

Styan, J. L. *The Dark Comedy. The Development of Modern Comic Tragedy*. 2nd ed. London: Cambridge UP, 1968.

Taylor, Diana. "Mad World, Mad Hope: Carballido's *El día que se soltaron los leones*." *Latin American Theatre Review* 20.2 (1987): 67-76.

Vélez, Joseph F. "Una entrevista con Emilio Carballido." *Latin American Theatre Review* 7.1 (1973): 17-24.

Wilson, Edwin. *The Theater Experience*. New York: McGraw-Hill, 1976.

Winston, Mathew. "'Humour noir' and Black Humor." *Veins of Humor*. Ed. Harry Levin. Cambridge: Harvard UP, 1972. 269-84.

Judith Ishmael Bisset and Howard Blanning (essay date 1990)

SOURCE: Bisset, Judith Ishmael, and Howard Blanning. "Visualizing Carballido's *Orinoco*: The Play in Two Imagined Performances." *Gestos* 5.9 (1990): 65-74. Print.

[*In the following essay, Bisset and Blanning present two interpretations of* Orinoco *(1982). Bisset "explores how a reader or spectator will perceive" the play; Blanning "constructs a 'virtual performance'" in which the reader "can and may become the interpreter of the text in a real performance."*]

I

The following discussions are both possible readings of Emilio Carballido's ***Orinoco***. Judith Bissett, a professor of language and literature, begins with the text and applies a specific model to construct a reading whose purpose is to create at least one possible dramatic world for a reader and, perhaps, future spectator. This reading must remain on the imaginary stage of the mind even as it explores how a reader or spectator will perceive it. Howard Blanning, a director and playwright, also begins with the text and constructs a "virtual performance" which takes on life in the imagination. Yet, the reader in this case can and may become the interpreter of the text in a real performance.

All plays may be, and often are, approached as either written or staged performance. According to Jean Alter, these two categories should not be separated. Total theater is both text and performance and must be examined as a real or visualized process of transition. Often a reader may not have the opportunity to experience a play as "staged text," that is, "the totality of verbal signs which appears as such in both text and performance." Nevertheless, it is always possible to treat a play as "total text," or "a graphic notation of a performance"—an imagined, visualized staging, or "virtual performance" (Alter 113-116).

Readers, when transformed into mental spectators, are capable of creating as many "possible worlds'" on the stage of their dramatic imaginations as a true spectator might find when observing several performances of the same text. Discovering the reader or mental spectator's response to a text becomes a problem if the critic interested in theatrical reception must contemplate many imagined variations of the dramatic world. However, Una Chaudhuri posits that if, for example, Brechtian drama contains structures designed to direct spectator response, it is possible to examine theatrical reception in other forms of modern drama by identifying structures with a similar purpose (286-287).

In an analysis of *Equus* by Peter Shaffer, Chaudhuri demonstrates that reader/spectator response to the work occurrs on two levels, ". . . corresponding to the two kinds of reality Artaud mentions ('direct, everyday' and "archetypal dangerous')" (295). Describing how this happens, Chaudhuri states, "The spectator is carried into the drama by the former, the mechanism of his involvement being the galvanizing of popular myths and cliches; the drama is carried into the spectator by the latter, the mechanism being the horse archetype as realized and defined in the play" (295). It is precisely this type of process which should involve the spectator in Carballido's ***Orinoco,*** and assist in the creation of a possible reader's imagined performance. Although, as Jean Alter has emphasized in a discussion of the processes which take place as a text becomes performance, the imagined or virtual staging of a work cannot provide a perfect framework for the final, actual performance. An imagined performance will always remain just that even when it serves as a step in the transformation of the text from literature into theatrical event.

Our purpose here is to describe the steps which go into creating a virtual performance of ***Orinoco*** by examining the way the reader/spectator enters into and receives the drama through the process which makes it possible to visualize the play. Because it is not feasible to present an entire play here, I propose to concentrate on selected, but significant, elements in the text which might aid in the creation of a more complete reading.

It is obvious, as J. L. Styan points out, that "a play must communicate or it is not a play at all" (1). The criticism of drama is, according to Styan, "... the study of how the stage compels its audience to be involved in its actual processes. The spectator interprets and so contributes to and finally becomes the play, whose image is all and only in his mind" (4). For Chaudhuri this act of communication takes place on two levels. When confronted with a contemporary piece like *Equus,* it is important to discover the difference between what a play ... says (or seems to say) and what it does to the spectator" (290). *Equus* first draws the spectator in through the "... myth of Freudian psychology" (289). The play tells a story of madness and its treatment which is part of the fabric of our culture. However, it is the frequent appearance of the archetyepal image of a horse which causes the audience to "experience" the action on stage. The horse depicted on stage is, for the audience, a symbol of "... psychological associations, developed over the course of historical human experience ..." (293).

Orinoco elicits spectator response in much the same way as *Equus.* Like many of Carballido's works, this play treats a realistic theme within a fantastic or magical structure. In a description of the tension between reality and fantasy in *Orinoco,* Matías Montes Huidobro states, "La textura eminentemente realista del dialogo, ... se transforma de pronto en imágenes fantásticas, sin necesidad de mayor ornamentación que la sorpresa misma del texto" (13). On one level, *Orinoco* tells the story of two women, Mina and Fifi, who are stranded on a boat unexpectedly steaming up river without a captain at the helm. The women are cabaret performers who have not had much sucess in the past and must now travel to a remote area to entertain workers at an oil camp. The play takes place on the day Mina and Fifi discover that no one except a wounded black man is on the boat. The wheel is tied and the engines are running, but there is no real indication that anyone is going to return. When the women question the black man, who never appears on stage, they are told that a fight occured that night before. After a bout of heavy drinking, the boat's crew had threatened to assault Mina and Fifi. However, Salome, the black deckhand, threw each man overboard. thereby saving the two from harm. As they proceed up the river, the women pass the time talking about their lives, rehearsing an act or attempting to find a way out of the situation. By the end of the day, the boat's engines have stopped and it is really adrift, now floating down river away from the job Mina had acquired for them at the camp.

This "realistic" story is framed by fantastic events and circumstances. For example, the logbook that the charac-

ters hope will help them is filled with nonsense. Salomé who is supposedly a strong, masculine figure has a feminine name, and is physically absent. The audience receives only a description of his physique and a second-hand account of his unusual prowess. The stage directions themselves set up the fantastic atmosphere in which the action takes place. Dawn in the opening scene, is described as "unreal," "inverosimil" by the playwright who also calls for a light to be burning in the empty pilot house.

It is the "real" story-line which draws the spectator into the fantasy world Carballido creates in the play. However, there is one element operating on both levels that allows the drama to enter the spectator: the river. Like the archetypal horse in *Equus,* the river is a constant presence. It is a part of the story being told, but it involves the spectators in the action on a more intimate level because it is the symbol of a timeless, shared experience. In his analysis of the play, Montes Huidobro identifies the river and the boat, the Stella Maris, with both life and death (25). Yet, the image of the river, reinforced by other images of water, is more powerful than that of the boat itself. The river makes possible the mythical journey characters and spectators alike experience as they create and respond to the dramatic world of *Orinoco.* Mina and Fifi are traveling, as Montes Huidobro points out, toward the river Styx, a journey forever present in the collective mind. Jung states that: Born of springs, rivers lakes, and seas, man at death comes to the waters of the river Styx and there embarks on the 'night sea journey.' Those black waters of death are the water of life, for death with its cold embrace is the material womb, just as the sea devours the sun but brings it forth again." (218) The women in *Orinoco* find themselves on a river at dawn, the moment of rebirth, and realize that their sojourn must continue as evening approaches, the moment of death. Yet, it is at night that Fifi reaffirms her commitment to life even as Mina, older and closer in time and desire to death, tells her that there is little hope.

Because the river is the most potent structuring element in the play, a potential director or reader should concentrate with care on the transformation of its image from text to performance, or in this case, virtual performance. Every play that is read not as literature but as possible performance, must, Jean Alter asserts, go through two phases which, "... generate two different referential activities. During the first phase, before actual staging begins (or, rarely during the staging process but before it is completed), a text must be read (studied); at that time, continuously or intermittently, it is attributed one or several virtual performances in the mind of the reader/director. During the second phase, as staging progresses toward its final form, the virtual performances both lead to, and are erased by, the eventual actual performance." (120)

Alter also emphasizes that in actual performance, no traces of the virtual performance remain even though at least one virtual performance does take place. However, if a reader, or potential director, identifies those elements in a play which draw the play into the spectator, it may be possible to discover aspects in a virtual performance necessary to the successful presentation of an actual performance and therefore integral parts of both phases of transformation. Although a reader must take into consideration several processes as a text is visualized or converted into performance, I will focus on two mechanisms in particular: verbal signs (contained within the dialogue) and staging signs (contained either in the stage directions or provided through other processes like the construction of a set). The virtual performance will emerge through an examination of the verbal and staging signs evident in the written text and through the identification of visualized possible signs suggested by the reading.

According to Alter, there are five types of transformations that occur when verbal signs encounter staging signs: confirmation (referents of culturally coded staging signs and verbal signs coded within the text coincide); reinforcement (staging signs stress the referent of verbal signs); restriction (selective reinforcement of one of several referents presented in ambiguous verbal signs thereby resticting the referential potentialities of the text); diversion (the shifting of verbal referents through the use of optional staging signs); and subversion (the use of staging signs opposite to the referent of the verbal sign) (134-138). A director might use any one of the above-mentioned transformations in creating a performance of **Orinoco.** Yet, the image of the river present in the written text should cause the reader/ spectator or even director to emphasize its presence in the verbal and stagings signs of the virtual performance. This image of water, of the river, should be reinforced as it is transformed.

Alter stresses that the process of reinforcement can yield poor results if care is not taken to guard against falling into weak confirmation or reinforcements that call attention primarily to the performance thereby destroying the tension between text and performance. Reinforcement is most successful, ". . . when complex networks of signs are considered, a stress laid on particular referent may entail a contrast with referents which are merely confirmed; partial or total structures of the play are then modified; and the tension between text and performance grows." (135) By stressing the river as archetypal symbol rather than as a "real" water way with symbolic qualities in the text, a reader/spectator can structure several layers of tension into a visualized presentation. At the same time, this reinforcement provides the virtual performance with the element that causes the reader/spectator involvement in the work from text to performance. That is, staging and verbal signs refering to the river and other images of water must be stressed while signs refering to the boat, the "real-world" journey and occupation of the characters may be either confirmed or altered in such a way that they will reinforce the river's image.

After describing the characters, Carballido provides two stage directions, or written staging signs, describing the boat and the dawn. Those that concern the boat can be confirmed in an imagined stage set. The reader might visualize the set just as depicted: We can see a portion of the bow. There are two doors, each to a cabin, as the boat accepts a few passengers. Also visible are a section of the deck and a companionway that leads to the bridge deck and pilot house" (52). On the other hand, it is possible to stress the fact that the boat is only an extension of the water which carries it along. The boat might be surrounded and overshadowed by visual references to water, however, not to the point of caricature. The sounds of birds and music which are called for in further stage directions could be replaced by a subtle sound of water. Of course, one would avoid using Sam Shepard's technique for involving an audience in the action of *Fool for Love,* that is, placing a speaker under every seat.

Stage directions for portraying dawn as Mina and Fifi see it need little reinforcement. Carballido says, "The play opens at the moment of an unreal tropical dawn: clouds, streaks of color in the sky, the whole gamut of fiery splendor. Then dazzling light" (52). Verbal signs provided by Mina and Fifi transfer these staging directions to the virtual performance. Due to their reference to dawn on the water—the beginning of life—and therefore the river's function in the collective mind, these signs should also appear in the actual performance. Lighting can underscore Mina's description of the black clouds of birds which she first identifies as buzzards eating dead animals. Lighting can call attention to certain aspects of Mina's portrayal of the colors she sees in the sky: red like blood and grey like ashes. These images reinforce the image of the river as the vehicle which transports man into the realm of darkness and death, then provides new life at the beginning of each day.

Other verbal signs concerning the river as archetype and life and death that should be reinforced occur in the poem fragment recited by Mina and a story told by Fifi. The poem is "Mundo Nuevo Orinoco" by Juan Liscano and along with references to plants and animals establishes the connection between the river and life itself: "A woman's life is like a river / winding to the waiting sea. / for every "joy." that life delivers / the sea is whispering "ecstasy!" / Hear the sea sing, negra, / bear the sea sing." (80).

Fifi's story traces the history of flax blossoms cut to make fiber for cloth which was later used for paper and books finally, ending up in a fire. Each ending, according to Fifi, representing a new beginning—even as sparks the blossoms continue their cycle. These verbal signs within the dialogue both emphasize the river's significance as shared experience and underline those aspects of its image which can be reinforced visually through the use of color, the red of dawn and the black of night.

There are many other verbal and staging signs in the play which can be identified as elements that will cause the spectator to experience the play through reception of images of the river. For example, the characters themselves can be reinforced both in casting and costuming to involve the spectator even further. Nina is described as old and no longer attractive. She commits suicide symbolically by throwing her cup overboard. She has no hope for the future and almost embraces death. Perhaps Mina knows that her action has no meaning because death is so near. Fifi is young, romantic and optimistic. Even in the face of darkness and impending disaster, she believes that they have a future. Mina identifies herself, at dawn, with endings and dark colors. Fifi does not. She sees, instead, beginnings and light. This contrast could be emphasized visually through physical type and color of costume to alter the women, transforming their referents. The spectator should receive them as part of the river, as part of its significance in the play and in life, rather than as two women trapped on a river.

This reading has been applied to only a fragment of the text and functions as an invitation to other reader/spectators to continue until a complete, virtual performance can be achieved. As the virtual performance is constructed using the process indicated above, it is hoped that all those elements which contribute to a total experience of the work can be identified and used to analyze reader and possible-spectator response on all levels.

II

Very few plays are so specific that there is only one way to conceive of them in production. Even the most faithful devotion to what is thought to be a playwright's intention may, in the hands of two different directors, result in two significantly different presentations—and even readings—of the script. Plays are usually wrought for the stage rather than written for the page, and, as Bissett suggests, seldom can a reading of a work match the potential of its staging, no matter how vivid the reader's imagination. Yet, a reading *can* be an imagined performance. It is critical for the director of a play to read and study the script in exactly the manner Bissett suggests. However, eventually the director must incorporate another method of visualizing the play in order to understand the logic and truths within the works *as they would be represented in an actual performance.* In other words, while a play may seek to represent a vision of life much larger than the space in which it performs, the director must also understand that the performance of a play is itself a reality *precisely* as large and as long as the space and time it takes to perform.

In visualizing the *staging* of a play, there are often "facts" in the script that do not appear so significant during a reading. Yet, they can have an enormous effect when seen and heard. One of the best examples of this occurs in the opening of Act II of Chekhov's *The Cherry Orchard,* as we hear Charlotte speak thoughtfully to herself: "When I was a little girl my father and mother used to go about from one country fair to another, giving performances, and very good ones too. I used to do the *salto mortale* and all sorts of tricks. When papa and mamma died an old German lady adopted me and educated me. Good! When I grew up I became a governess. But where I come from and who I am, I haven't a notion. Who my parents were—very likely they weren't married—I don't know. (Taking a cucumber from her pocket and beginning to eat it.) I don't know anything about it. (A pause.) I long to talk so, and have no one to talk to, I have no friends or relations" (523). Soft, sad and gentle as this speech may be, the "fact" of the matter is that the audience will hear the last part of it in between the sounds of the character munching a cucumber. The reality of the speech and the environment (in the cherry orchard itself) may present the *reader* with a mental image that is responsive to what Charlotte says; the *viewer* on the other hand, will be likely to remember the speech *and* the cucumber.

Such devices may be referred to as *forced* visualizations, and are used by playwrights to qualify and, on occasion, contradict other elements of the play, as well as to give the audience a sense of understanding, of knowledge that the characters do not have. Perhaps the best example of this in **Orinoco** is the riverboat on the water in the tropical sunrise. As the play begins, I am given a very distinct picture and context within which the lines and action are to occur. There is water all around, and (just as important) it is flowing water. And as I read, I hear and see in the background an old boat deck on a vast expanse of water bordered by jungles. The sound of the boat's engines no less than the dialogue itself underscores how they are slicing and pushing upstream. Indeed, *I* know before Fifi and Mina when the engines stop and they begin to drift/flow downstream, because I stop hearing the sound of the engines and hear only the two women and nature.

Salomé is another example of a forced visualization: as I think of these two women drifting alone down the river, the playwright has one of them recall Salomé. They are *not* alone. Salome is on the boat as well . . . but, he is also pretty predictably out of the action (as indeed he remains). In fact, Salomé may be one of the more important *visual* elements in the imagined play, next only to the women and the river. He also provides us with an example of how one can have an easier time visualizing by treating the play as a truth.

A typical analysis of **Orinoco** might quite conceivably ask what Carballido's purpose was in including the never-seen Salomé in the play as he did. Much may be learned by such an inquiry, but much may also be lost in terms of feeling the dynamics of the situation in which the characters find themselves. However, if instead of asking such a question, we accept the fact that Salomé IS in the play and that he is a part of the truth of the situation we are watching, the dynamics of the play stay dynamic, and never become pedagogic. He is there, in the cabin, just out of our sight but not out of Mina's and Fifi's. Then, like good detectives, we can deduce certain circumstances that are critical to what we see and understand as we go through the play.

Salomé is flamboyantly gallant and attracted to Fifi, as we gather from his swimming ashore to get flowers. He is also attractive to the women, especially Fifi, and is different from the other men on the boat if only by his name: he is a beautiful man with a beautiful name and a beautiful way about him. He is also magnificently strong and willing to defend boldly, as we may reasonably assume by his having dispatched the entire rest of the crew before they could rape the women. But there is something else about Salomé, something which doesn't dawn on us until the end of the play, and perhaps not even then.

Fifi may seem beyond belief at times in her ability to see the bright and possible amid all the dim and dreadful, and as they float with the current away from the mining camp, she plays almost no attention to Nina's concern about Rico getting even for them not showing up for their jobs, in spite of Nina's vivid description of Rico. Therefore, as she speaks her last line: "We're on our way. And the best is yet to come!" (83), it would be easy to hear in those words the naive optimism of a fool. For if they don't drift out to sea, Rico's men will probably eventually catch up with them.

Yet, it isn't likely that they will drift out to sea; we know that because they tell us so when they describe the channels and bends in the river. And if Rico's men were to catch up with them? ... Well, we can't be certain what would happen, but the last time a bunch of men (eight) sought to do them harm, all the men died: Salomé killed them. And Salomé will be with them for a least as long as they are on the boat.

There is nothing in the script that guarantees Salomé will remain with them, or that Rico will really put much effort into tracking down the two women (after all, the whole *boat* never showed up, not just Mina and Fifi). Salomé creates a bit more of a sense of balance for Fifi's half-full and Mina's half-empty cups, and threatens the possibility that things *might* turn out well. Because Salomé is of great value, in an actual performance, I would reinforce his function within the play. To involve the audience through this character's "presence," I would put the door to where Salome is recovering center stage, and I would have many of Mina and Fifi's scenes split so that the door was visually between them frequently. Finally, and simply, after the last line I would have all but three lights fade, leaving one on Mina, one on Fifi, and one on the door, leaving three pools of light onstage. If I really wanted to push the point, I would give Salomé's light about an extra half-second as I faded them all out.

This reading, like Bissett's, does not deal with the a complete text. However, it also represents an effort to contrib-

ute to a more effective experience of the play during a process which can transform it into performance.[1]

Note

1. Because only one of the readers knows Spanish, an English translation of *Orinoco* was used so that both readings could be based on the same text.

Works Cited

Alter, Jean. "From Text to Performance." *Poetics Today* 2.3 (1981): 113-39.

Carballido, Emilio. "Orinoco." Trans. Margaret Sayers Peden. *Latin American Literary Review* 9.23 (1983): 51-83.

Chaudhuri, Una. "The Spectator in Drama/Drama in the Spectator." *Modern Drama* 27.3 (1984): 281-98.

Chekhov, Anton. *The Collected Works*. New York: Walter J. Black, Inc., 1929.

Jung, C. G. *The Collected Works*. Eds. Sir Herbert Read, Michael Fordam, Gerhard Adler, William McGuire. 2nd ed. Vol. 5. Princeton, New Jersey: Princeton University Press, 1967. 20 vols.

Montes Huidobro, Matías. "Zambullida en el *Orinoco* de Carballido." *Latin American Theatre Review* 15.2 (1982): 13-25.

Styan, J. L. *Drama, Stage and Audience*. London: Cambridge University Press, 1975.

Diana Taylor (essay date 1991)

SOURCE: Taylor, Diana. "Theatre and Transculturation: Emilio Carballido." *Theatre of Crisis: Drama and Politics in Latin America*. Lexington: UP of Kentucky, 1991. 148-80. Print.

[*In the following essay, Taylor considers the political content of* The Day They Let the Lions Loose *and* I Too Speak of the Rose. *She argues that the former play exposes the "network of power structures, institutions, and traditions" that oppresses individuals in Mexico and that the latter explores the role of theater, discourse, and epistemology in Mexican culture.*]

Readers of Latin American theatre may be surprised to find a chapter on Emilio Carballido (born 1925 in Mexico) in a study of theatre of crisis.[1] Carballido's plays, especially the two emphasized here—*El día que se soltaron los leones* (*The Day They Let the Lions Loose*, 1957), and *Yo también hablo de la rosa* (*I Too Speak of the Rose*, 1965)—are playful and expansive, calling for elaborate and complicated sets, large casts, bright colors, and music. These plays do not seem to belong to a violent, grotesque world of oppression and crisis. No one overtly torments or tortures anyone else; death comes only to those who deserve it. Compared with much Latin American drama in general and with all the other plays included here in particular, Carballido's theatre seems joyful, almost optimistic. This is no "poor" theatre; there is no call to action associated with "revolutionary" theatre. Nor are Carballido's plays "committed," "popular," or didactic in any straightforward sense. But commentators will be deceived by Carballido's playfulness if they do not recognize that these plays speak to revolution; they are profoundly "popular" as I defined the term in chapter 1; they offer a liberating vision of Mexican culture which evades the tugs of the West and yet resists the temptation to fall back onto some native traditionalism.

Carballido's theatre is deceptively frivolous; it deceives both in style and in subject matter. In part, this is because Carballido openly questions the *efficacy* of didactic theatre. Although he calls **Lions** [***The Day They Let the Lions Loose***] "a didactic farce ... with a strong social commitment, a reflection on the 'Third World,'" he asks whether univocal, agitational theatre does more than simply convert the converted (Velez, "Entrevista"). The political impact of his work, he would argue, lies in the breadth of the audience receptive to his work, rather than in the directness of the message itself. In his theatrical production of more than one hundred plays since 1946 he has addressed a wide variety of audiences. He is Mexico's best known and most influential playwright, head of the theatre department at the National University of Veracruz and founder and editor of Mexico's largest theatre journal, *Tramoya*. He has a broad student and intellectual following; he holds regular workshops in playwriting throughout the country; he has the works of young playwrights published and produced yearly in conjunction with the publishing house Editores Mexicanos Unidos. He also has a wide middle-class appeal; he has written theatre for children; and in 1984 he compiled a volume of theatre for workers.

Perhaps a more important reason that commentators have been deceived by Carballido's theatre, however, is that his focus—culture—has been underestimated by Third World theorists and practitioners concerned primarily with Mexico's pressing economic and political problems. Though culture is generally considered important in the context of revolutionary change (as attested by the very concept of "cultural revolution"), people usually think of it as something that happens after the revolution. Carballido, however, recognizes the importance of counterhegemonic cultural activity as *fundamental* to a people's struggle for liberation.[2] He not only examines the role of theatre in a Third World country such as Mexico in which individuals feel oppressed and marginal, obliterated by foreign rulers, policies, ideologies, and art forms; he also points to a way of coming out of the crisis that involves recasting the indigenous self as *central* to Mexico's quest for identity, self-representation, history, and knowledge.

The strategies that Carballido proposes to liberate Mexico from its position as dependent and peripheral vis-à-vis First World powers are not military; they call for neither war nor revolution. Rather, he emphasizes that in spite of its long history of colonization, Mexican culture (and the same holds true for other Latin American cultures) is neither moribund nor a poor imitation of a foreign original. It is an energetic, vital, ongoing activity: the absorption and selection of foreign ideas and influences received through the centuries; the merging of the received cultural material with ideas and world views deriving from its autochthonous traditions; the transformation of this material into an original, creative, culturally specific product. In other words, Carballido goes beyond the binary self/other frame imposed on economically underdeveloped countries by colonization to explore the independent development of a cultural heritage that is tied into but not subservient or inferior to the global cultural development. Using foreign material, he argues, need not be merely derivative borrowing on the part of economically underdeveloped countries but ongoing, intercultural reciprocity. What would Western theatre be without Aristotelian tragedy, Stanislavski's method acting, or the transcultural raids of Artaud and Brecht? By rethinking culture, Mexicans and Latin Americans can rethink their relationship with the dominant powers, for culture "is not a thing ... but a relationship."[3] Hence, rather than continue to internalize the colonizer and accept the external view of themselves as *inferior others* (let alone the other terms of self-hatred used, as we have seen, by Mexican playwrights such as Usigli and Gorostiza), Mexicans can see their world from their own perspective; they can stop seeing themselves as excentric to their own history, their present, their future.

Carballido's concentration on culture as an arena for ideological debate does not imply that he ignores the very real political and economic problems facing Mexico and Mexicans either in the 1960s or today. Anyone carefully analyzing his work would realize that the social, political, and philosophical questions posed by his plays are as critical and as urgent as those in more apparently serious Latin American drama. The confrontation between individuals and society, for all Carballido's humor, proves as life-threatening in **Lions** or **Rose** [***I Too Speak of the Rose***] as in Triana's *Night of the Assassins* and Wolff's *Paper Flowers*. But by focusing on culture "not only as a way of seeing the world, but also as a way of making and changing it" (Dirlik, 14), Carballido offers other than military solutions in the perennial struggle for liberation. Culture, he proposes, not only participates in systems of domination but can also provide a way out of them. In ***The Day They Let the Lions Loose,*** Carballido lays bare the network of power structures, institutions, and traditions that oppress individual existence and suppress identity in Mexico. In ***I Too Speak of the Rose,*** he indicates how rethinking culture and repositioning the indigenous self as central in it can provide strategies to liberate the dominated from the restrictive hegemonic/counterhegemonic binary.

CAGES, BIG AND SMALL: *THE DAY THEY LET THE LIONS LOOSE*

The farcical nature of *Lions* is immediately apparent in Carballido's stage design calling for "painted trees" and lions "played by two actors per lion."[4] The play opens with a dialogue between the Aunt and the Neighbor. The invalid Aunt suffers from "a most unusual pain" that has plagued her since puberty: "It runs up my back, then it grabs me around the shoulders, after that it digs into my joints, and when it goes away for a bit it comes back around my heart!" (7). The Neighbor has left her child tied up, attacked by rats and screaming for liberation, in order to tend to the ailing woman. The Aunt constantly shouts for her sixty-seven-year-old niece Ana, whose position in the household resembles that of a maid rather than a relative. Ana prepares tea, talking to and caressing the cat she keeps without the Aunt's knowledge or consent. The Aunt, fed up with waiting for her tea, enters the kitchen, finds Ana with the cat, and throws the cat out of the house. Ana, after a second's hesitation, leaves the house to look for the cat. Her search takes her to the lake in Chapultepec Park, where she meets the Man, a hungry, outcast poet. Together they capture a swan from the lake and roast it over a fire for breakfast. In another part of Chapultepec Park, the Teacher leads his military cadets through the zoo. While the instructor pauses briefly to chat with his fiancée, the Young Girl, the students throw stones at the animals and engage them in a rock fight. One mischievous student, López Vélez, hits the Young Girl; then, afraid of the Teacher's punishment, he opens the lions' cage and runs away. The lions escape to where Ana and the Man are preparing their meal and frighten them into taking refuge in the trees. The Woman, a widowed housewife who inadvertently stumbles upon the scene, faints when she sees the lions. Ana comes out of hiding and chides the lions for threatening to devour first the roasted swan and then the Woman. The first act ends as Ana, the Man, and the Woman share a meal in the company of the peaceful lions.

In the second act the police and the Teacher begin their pursuit of the lions and, by extension, of Ana, the Man, and the Woman as accomplices, but the fugitives escape to the island in the middle of the lake. In the confusion the Teacher is wounded by police bullets—intended for the lions—and dies.

In the third act, Carballido juxtaposes the confusion of the police activity (sirens, megaphones, searchlights) with the intimate conversations of Ana, the Man, and the Woman, in which they question the pressures, fears, and attitudes that have skewed their lives. The Woman realizes that she has "belonged" to someone all her life—first her parents, then her husband—and that she has never done anything for or by herself. Still, she cannot live without her role as housewife, even when there are no children or husband to take care of, so she decides to go back to her house and the only role she knows. Setting off in a rowboat, she tips into the water and is rescued by the child López Vélez, whose bravery is rewarded with a medal. The police begin their attack on the island. In order to escape, Ana and the Man ride the lions back to the mainland. Hemmed in by police, they run toward the lions' cage. Ana and the lions enter the cage, but the police catch the Man at the door. When he claims to have captured the lions and returned them to their cage, he is rewarded with a job as zoo keeper. Ana opts to live in the cage with the lions, even though she learns from the Neighbor that her Aunt has died and bequeathed her the house. As the play closes, Ana knits a sweater for a baby bear and converses with the Man, who now wears a uniform. She warns him to beware of institutionalization. She screams insults at the military cadets as their new teacher leads them through the zoo.

Lions juxtaposes two worlds which, though apparently contradictory and mutually exclusive, are very much the same. The first world is the Aunt's house, a constricted, restrictive domestic prison. Like Triana's characters, Ana is a grownup child, a sixty-seven-year-old woman who has been infantilized and controlled all her life. The oppression she experiences at the hands of her Aunt is not overtly violent, but as Carballido signals throughout, there are different kinds of violence. Some kinds do not look like violence, and some people might argue that they are not. Of the two paradigms of violence I set forth in chapter 1— crisis and oppression—Carballido focuses particularly on the latter, which is at times less easy to identify than the former. The use of language is an example: the Aunt calls Ana "Anita," the diminutive, which in Mexico is usually an affectionate way of addressing a loved one but in this case forms part of the Aunt's exploitation of her niece; it is somewhat akin to calling adult black men "Boy." The power exercised on the body is another. Ana's body is literally shrouded in custom; she has dressed in black mourning since she can remember: "If it isn't one relative, it's another. I wore mourning for six years for my parents; for my sister, three. Aunts, uncles, nephews, and nieces, two years each. Six months for first cousins; and for close friends of the family, three months. I've gotten used to black" (24). She has never understood her body or her sexuality. Like a prepubescent child, she ponders the mysteries of life: "I don't believe people really do all those things."[5] She danced once when she was young and pretty, and even then her Aunt pinched her, hissing that she would get back at her (25). The play also depicts the power and violence associated with censorship, surveillance, and control. Ana has never been allowed to read things of her own choosing, to go where she wanted to, to eat the things she liked; she has never had friends or, until now, a pet. She has suffered violence in the name of love. As the Aunt tells her, "You always kill the thing you love" (31). This, then, is the kind of violence described by Emmanuel Levinas (21): "Violence does not consist so much in injuring and annihilating persons as in interrupting their continuity, making them play roles in which they no longer recognize themselves, making them betray not only commitments but their own substance, making them carry out actions that will destroy every possibility for action." Carballido compares the Aunt's controlling "love" for Ana with the violence of forcing people to accept lifestyles incompatible with their own needs and nature. "Imagine," says the Man to Ana, "giving a farm to a tribe of gypsies, or what's worse, forcing those gypsies to *work* that farm" (30). What could be crueler than pressuring gypsies into settling down to till the soil?

Carballido does not mythify the stifling oppression of Ana's existence by suggesting that freedom and hope reside elsewhere. On the contrary, the second world, the park that Ana flees to, is as repressive as the situation she has tried to leave behind. The park *seems* freer; the trees, the lake, the "early morning light," the mist, the swan going by, "exaggeratedly delicate and poetic—reminiscent of Pavlova and Tchaikovsky" (5). But Carballido warns rather than seduces us through these images. This is no magic realism; the oppression and violence are real enough. Instead of the house, we have Chapultepec Park with its famous gates; instead of the Aunt's *tinaco* or water tank, the artificial cement-lined Chapultepec lake; instead of cats, lions living in a cage.[6] Instead of a censoring Aunt, there is the Teacher telling the youngsters what they can know; instead of Ana's black dress there are the military uniforms of the children. The Neighbor's child is tied up; the schoolchildren are threatened with court martial. So even though the Aunt's home seems more repressive than the magical outdoors, the opposition between oppression and liberty is more complex than a straightforward inside/outside dichotomy. Ultimately, there is little difference between inside and outside, since the characters cannot escape from the social constraints that hamper or work against their needs and their nature. The idea of choice collapses if both options are identical; the possibility of differentiation or individuation is belied by the fact that only a few characters—those who defy the totalizing system—have proper names.

Carballido's depiction of power and oppression indicate that they are not localizable in any one spot, institution, or person. The Aunt, Neighbor, Teacher, police are not individually responsible for the oppression; they *all* are, in conjunction. The power associated with the inside—domesticity, family, home, education, religion, and custom—reinforces and is in turn reinforced by the power of the outside with its educational, scientific, religious, military, and governmental institutions. In this play, Carballido is suggesting something very similar to Foucault's statement: "Power must be analyzed as something which circulates, or rather as something which only functions in the form of a chain. It is never localized here or there, never in anyone's hands. ... Power is employed and exercised through a net-like organization" (*Power/Knowledge,* 98). But Carballido is not referring to abstract power; he is

decoding the particular configuration of forces at work in Mexico.

Set in modern Mexico City, *Lions* evokes centuries of destructive displays of power. The area of Chapultepec, where most of the action takes place, has historically been the scene of brutal confrontation; it indicates not only the sacrifice of the individual in modern Mexico but sacrifice as a persistent theme in Mexican history. Ana and the Man realize that the ground they sit on is "slightly rotten."[7] The ground, the leaves, the air, the water retain the memory of violent, unnatural deaths. The absurd attack by the police on the island that harbors the fugitives, though staged in a highly theatrical, fanciful manner, recalls the Spaniards' siege of the island of Tenochtitlán, approximately on the same spot, in 1521. It recalls the bitter "Battle of Chapultepec" in 1847, when school-aged children—military cadets like the children in Carballido's play—died defending Chapultepec hill from the invading United States army (a statue commemorating the "Boy Heroes" stands in the park today). Moreover, Chapultepec Castle, overlooking the park, symbolizes the French domination of Mexico, inhabited as it was by the French-appointed imperial couple, Maximilian and Carlota, in 1864.

The domination of Ana by her Aunt and the violence suffered by the Neighbor's child do not constitute isolated acts of silencing and annihilation; rather, they indicate the perennial sacrifice of individuals trapped in a violent history. Yet this history is justified in the name of future rewards. Ana recalls her mother's saying before she died in 1899 that the "twentieth century was going to be marvellous!" (29). The Aunt justifies exploiting her niece by telling her that a "young girl's future is simply charged with promises" (31), and after all, she will inherit the house. The Man clings to the belief that his present hunger and misfortune somehow make sense in the cosmic order of things: "There are millions of people who sacrifice everything, and carefully construct the future of mankind, which others will enjoy two hundred years from now" (38). In pre-Hispanic times the shedding of human blood was considered necessary to keep the universe functioning by ensuring that the god Huitzilopchtli would have the strength to conquer the stars and usher in the new day. In present-day Mexico, where the government's austerity programs rest exclusively on the backs of the middle and poor classes, the notion of sacrifice expands to keep the many suffering to protect the few.

But power does not simply lie in the hands of the few; it is supported by ideologies. In this play, Carballido clearly refers to the positivist and evolutionary theories that have shaped Mexican thought since the end of the nineteenth century. His portrayal of the Teacher parodies the *científicos* or "scientists" under Porfirio Díaz, who argued that social institutions were fundamental in obtaining and maintaining the social order needed for progress.[8] Like the positivists in general, the Teacher emphasizes the importance of education by dutifully drilling his pupils. He echoes the belief in evolutionary (rather than revolutionary) change; in rationality, in social progress: "The zoological scale is perfectly graduated and it ends with the rational animals—men" (14). The irony, of course, is that the education he imparts to his pupils is not the kind that broadens their intellectual scope and sharpens their critical awareness. On the contrary, he insists that there is only one right answer to every question—his. When a student offers another answer, one given him by his father, the Teacher responds: "Would you kindly tell your father that he's talking nonsense" (15). He has the correct words to supplant the children's faulty vocabulary, preferably in Latin or Greek. And though he speaks of an evolutionary, zoological scale, it is clearly a finite, totalizing system; it ends with "man."

It becomes increasingly clear that this "scientific" education serves to elevate the foreign over the local and the "cultured" over the "primitive" in a manner characteristic of colonialism. It controls the children by objectifying and reducing them to dots on an evolutionary scale; further, it consolidates a political system based on centralized knowledge and surveillance of the population. "You are a homo sapiens," the Teacher tells his pupil, "a mammiferous vertibrate. The particular facts of your life are on file in the civil register and the archives of the school. At this moment you are undergoing a process of domestication but you will be locked up in a cage at the first sign of bestiality" (14). Knowledge is certainly power, not the knowledge ostensibly being passed from Teacher to pupil but the real political power exerted by identifying, locating, classifying, and "domesticating" a population. It is a process that objectifies the individual, and although it differs radically from the persecution analyzed by Griselda Gambaro's work, this too is the antithesis of individuation. It is an education that empowers the political system rather than the individual. The Teacher notes that "the more people know, the harder it is to control them. . . . The ideal system would be: nobody learns things they don't have to know."[9]

The education imposed by the Teacher is not only alien to the children's backgrounds but hostile to it. The extent to which positivist thinking has molded modern Mexican thought (more fully developed by Carballido in *Rose*) can be briefly summed up here. By basing itself on "scientific" and, more specifically, biological premises, positivism can treat racial and sexual prejudices as fact. The effects of Darwinism and theories of natural selection in Latin America, Harold Davis explains in his *Latin American Thought* (104), led to the development of theories of superior races: "The superior 'race' was often thought of as Portuguese or Spanish." Given the fact that 80 percent of Mexico's population is of mixed race, predominantly a mixture of indigenous and Hispanic peoples, the results of these theories on the nation's population are devastating. Moreover, combined with the *malinchismo* I noted in chapter 1, whereby racial self-hatred is conflated with a hatred of women (symbolized by Cortés's lover/translator Mal-

inche), these racial theories have particularly damaging effects on the female population—doubly despised as women and as *mestizas*. When Carballido, in *Rose,* centers Mexican self-knowledge and identity in the person of a *mestizo* woman, a *mujer de pueblo,* he is fighting the sexism and racism pseudoscientifically grounded in the positivist theories.

Positivist theories also intensified the Mexican feeling of inferiority in other areas, specifically politics and economy. Positivism emphasizes institutions as central to social development and progress. The Teacher inanely confesses to his girlfriend: "It's nice working for an institution like this. Everything one could need—and discipline to boot!" (16). However, as Davis points out, the "Latin American sense of political inferiority" derives "from the failure to develop institutions of constitutional democratic government"; he concludes that a "sense of failure to achieve the economic prosperity promised by independence leaders increased the poignancy of political failure" (104-5). The theories offered by positivism, as applied in Latin America, legitimated conservative, elitist policies, the "evolutionary" rather than "revolutionary" answers to political, social, and economic problems.

It is important to indicate that Carballido also recognizes the dangers of the seductive, "positive" aspects of power, not just of its negative and oppressive ones. As Foucault notes in *Power/Knowledge* (59), "Power would be a fragile thing if its only function were to repress, if it worked only through the mode of censorship, exclusion, blockage and repression . . . exercising itself only in a negative way." The "knowledge" generated by the *científicos* in Mexico is a product of and in turn reproduces systems of power. The arts too, Carballido points out, function largely to celebrate power. In *Lions,* the tune the Man whistles changes from an expression of spontaneity and liberty when it becomes the background music for the "Intermission with Music," which in turn (and without interruption) flows directly into the "music of persecution" that opens Act 2[10] and intensifies into the "Prelude to the Nautical Battle" in Act 3 (41). Likewise, the lions' dance of liberty in Act 1 evolves into the dance between the Man and the Woman in Act 2, and later the police dance as they circle in on their fugitives. The persecution scene closes triumphantly with the "March of the Captured Lions" (44). (The representation of dramatic conflict through dance echos pre-Hispanic forms, the combined spectacle made up of dance, song, and representation.) Poetry, too, has been co-opted. As the Man relates, he himself is a poet who composed verses for the September 15 independence celebrations, yet he distinguishes himself from the "immortal bards" who serve another purpose, metamorphosed as they are into public figures, frozen as objects in the famous busts that line the Avenue of the Poets in Chapultepec Park. Finally, photography, as Carballido represents it, has ceased being an art form altogether and merely serves as an instrument of state disinformation. A newspaper photographer who covers the confrontation between the authorities and society's "bestial" elements (Ana, the Man, the lions) photographs the Teacher's corpse, and the official version of the Teacher's death—summed up in the caption to the photograph—demonstrates the complicity of art and power: although the bullet wounds suggest otherwise, the Chief, the Policeman, and the Photographer concur: "He was killed by the lions" (35).

Perhaps the appealing aspects of power are ultimately more dangerous than the oppressive ones. Fame and glory are seductive. The Man quotes one of the immortal poets, boasting of "certain birds that can cross the swamp and never soil their feathers" (11), but he is not one of them. At the end of the play he locks himself out of the natural cycle by trying to cash in on the economically and spiritually bankrupt system. Wearing a uniform, he waits for the authorities to honor their promise of a salary and prize money. He confesses to Ana: "I used to feel the seasons change in my veins—but not any longer" (46). Ana, through the bars of her cage, gently warns him to "beware" (45). The same seduction of heroism wins the young boy, López Vélez, back to the system. He alone was capable of defying the Teacher, but he becomes submissive under the glory showered on him for rescuing the Woman from drowning. Even though the Woman was not in fact in danger of her life, the young boy is photographed and turned into a *Niño Heroe* like the ones already honored in the park. The irony is not only that concepts of "heroism" and "honor" are now as worn and worthless as the Man's uniform but that one of the few named characters loses his name, becoming an anonymous, albeit prestigious, Boy Hero.

The world that Carballido depicts in *Lions* is the same lethal world I explore throughout this study. Like Buenaventura's inferno and Gambaro's terrorized state, this world also offers its members two choices, death or oppression—which, of course, is no choice, since choosing the first precludes life altogether and the second also leads to annihilation. For Carballido the problem lies in the contradiction that power systems can be seductive, fraudulent, corrupting, oppressive, and lethal, yet people cannot find "truth" and "reality" or sustain a viable existence outside them. Life in a cage, shouting insults at children "so they'll learn" (46), hardly seems the answer to Mexico's problems. And Ana's appeals to justice in some nebulous future—"One of these days you'll all be in cages while we lions run around loose, roaring through the streets"—only reactivate the utopian solutions that we have seen fail throughout the course of the play. Her inability to come up with a different response only accentuates the lack of real options, the absence of viable, life-affirming spaces. These are felt only as absence, as lack, in the totalizing structure. What I believe Carballido is saying about power, truth, reality, and self-determination is that they cannot be understood as lying outside or beyond the realms of social systems; it is within social systems on all their many levels

that these issues must be fought out. There is no elsewhere, no outside, no beyond, no place free of political exigencies where truth and freedom can be found. Again, this is an idea that was later theorized by Foucault: "Truth isn't outside power, or lacking in power . . . truth isn't the reward of free spirits, the child of protracted solitude, nor the privilege of those who have liberated themselves. . . . Truth is a thing of this world" (*Power/Knowledge,* 131). The hope, then, lies not in Ana's distant "one day" but precisely in the title, "the day they let the lions loose." On that day Ana chose an authentic (and thus liberating) action over her previous acts of subjugation, thereby rupturing her restrictive world: she said no to her Aunt, recognizing that "I've lost so much always saying yes" (39). For Ana, that day becomes important not in historic terms but within her personal context. The oppressed must change their position within the system, even if that means becoming marginals, like Ana. We are all involved in the network of power—not just the police, the government officials, the Teacher but also the oppressed themselves. As Ana finally realizes, she has allowed herself to be used: "Right now I feel responsible for everything" (39). The Man says, "We're all of us responsible for our parents, our relatives, and our leaders" (39). Aunts, governments, bosses, theories—"they're all surgeons, butchers, amputating parts of our bodies, our minds, our actions."[11]

In *Lions,* Carballido only indirectly points to what will become the dominant theme of *Rose*: the epistemic grids determining the relationship between the world and the consciousness perceiving it. The dialogues between Ana and the Man pose epistemological questions about knowing in "totalities" of holistic thinking as opposed to knowing in parts or "details" (31) of pluralistic thought. The fashion in which the characters present the subject is straightforward. Ana believes that the "natural" way of perceiving experience lies in pluralistic thought, knowing in parts. The lions, like all cats, Ana tells the Man, "look at me as a combination of smells and sizes and feelings." Her cat, she says, "used to look at me in little bits, never all at once" (31). The Man claims that humans also know in parts. The multiple perspectives, however, never add up to any knowable, totalizable whole. Those who claim to know it all and submit, as the Teacher does, that "everything is known" (15) are in fact supporting totalizing structures and, as in this case, authoritarian institutions. Carballido here, and more directly in his depiction of orality in *Rose,* seems to propose the opposite of Claude Lévi-Strauss's "the savage mind totalizes" (*The Savage Mind,* 245) or Walter Ong's more polite "the oral mind totalizes" (175) For Carballido, the officials representing government and educational institutions are the ones who impose totalizing world views. This totalizing, from Carballido's perspective, characterizes hegemonic thought more than it does the so-called primitivism of savages (whether felines or semiliterate populations). Neither the animals nor the Poet nor Ana herself thinks in terms of totalities.

There are two points worth noting in regard to Carballido's epistemology, one political, one philosophical. Totalizing or universalizing is not only a hegemonic practice but is key to maintaining the hegemonic culture as central, as exemplary, as the model to be emulated. In order to escape Western hegemony, Carballido proposes a nonhegemonic approach to cultural activity. His aim is not to fight hegemonic practices by replacing one universalizing system with another but to find a way of thinking that does not ape or parody Western thought. Hence, he proposes that people know in parts, which make up a plurality of experiences that will forever elude closure or finality. Throughout *Lions,* he progresses from the particular (Ana, cat, cage) to the social (oppression); in this way he combats the hegemonic propensity of "imposing universals of whatever kind upon the particular" (Dirlik, 50). Moreover, I think Carballido's philosophical as well as political views reflect the inductive method: no matter what the Teacher claims, we cannot know everything, we do not have answers to all questions. Even the Teacher, as he lies dying, admits that his theories did not prepare him for life's many mysteries: "I don't understand anything. Everything seems so strange" (28). *Lions* points to an infinitely more complex concept of existence than any theory or perspective can comprehend, to dimensions of reality which, as the Medium warns us later in *Rose,* "we cannot even begin to suspect." A totalizing approach to thought, like the discourse that maintains it, tries to absorb and classify knowledge to sustain itself. The attempt to reduce the infinite to the finite explains not only the intellectual subjugation we see throughout the play but also the distortion of reality required to support the fictitious framework. Carballido humorously underlines the arrogance of, and ultimately the danger posed by, those who pretend to understand existence "in totality" and maintain that "everything that happens in the world is clear and intelligible" (15).

I Too Speak of the Rose: A Discourse on Discourse

Carballido's *I Too Speak of the Rose* (1965) probes the role of theatre, in itself a cultural activity and an instrument of communication, in a totalizing political system. Theatre, as Austin E. Quigley points out in *The Modern Stage and Other Worlds* (53), "invites audiences not just to receive entertainment and instruction but to participate in an inquiry that questions both what we know and how we know it—an inquiry that also helps us recognize the complex dependence of our knowledge on our ways of knowing both in the world of the theatre and in the worlds beyond it." *Rose* focuses on the convergence of different, and changing, modes of perception. Carballido is not interested so much in events (plot) as in the discourses that shape those events and endow them with meaning.

Rose opens with a peasant woman, the Medium, sitting downstage center, talking in a quiet, introspective voice about knowledge. Her opening speech establishes that she is a *mestiza,* physically and ideologically a mix of indigenous and Spanish elements. She speaks Spanish, but her language conveys the poetic accumulation of images and the repetitive singsong quality of oral languages that rely on poetic devices for recalling information. Her particular use of Spanish, then, bespeaks the coexistence of another language alive within it; it is an odd, poetic bilingualism that simultaneously transmits two cultural codes. She retains oral sources of knowledge; she remembers stories handed down to her by word of mouth. But her oral knowledge is mixed with her knowledge of books and texts; both traditions come together in her, and her heart, that potent "central ventrical" (47), commingles them and pumps new life throughout the complex, hybrid organism. Her imagery identifies her as a Mexican from Mexico City: old Tenochtitlán. The allusions she makes to the city's pre-Columbian network of channels also describes modern Mexico City with its intricate freeways and *vías*. Only after she locates herself within an oral network of communication whereby she receives, stores, contemplates, and transmits information does Carballido proceed with the action.

The events, in fact, are minimal. Throughout the play only one thing happens: two lower-class children (Polo, aged twelve, and Toña, fourteen), who are playing in a garbage dump, derail a passing train. The antecedents as well are few. Polo is not in school because he does not have any shoes, and his mother cannot afford to buy them until the following week; children are not allowed into his classroom without shoes. Toña has decided not to go to school because she has not done her homework. They tamper with the public telephones looking for change; they flip the coins they find with a candy vendor, lose the coins, win them back, buy some candy, and give a few pennies to a passing vagrant. They meet their friend Maximino, who offers them money for school, but they turn it down to play by the dump: "We might find something. You can see the train go by" (49). The children dance around, joke, and pick things up. One of the things they find is a tub full of cement, used and discarded by some builders. On impulse, they roll the tub onto the tracks as the train approaches. The stage lights flash frantically as the audience hears a thundering crash. The lights go out, and in a second we hear the newsboy running through the theatre, crying out the headlines.

The newsboy reappears several times as the headlines change, alternately casting the children as vagrants, as schizophrenics, as proletarians. Throughout, the play juxtaposes interpretations of the crash, offering only a few hints regarding the fate of the characters. After the derailment, the terrified children stay where they are; the police take them to jail, where Polo's mother visits him and Maximino visits Toña. The play suggests that Maximino and Toña become romantically attached. At the end, the Medium asks us enigmatically: "Do you know how Polo came to own his own garage? And what Toña's marriage was like? . . . that's another story."[12]

The rest of the twenty-one scenes focus on the process and significance of interpretation, on the construction of meaning, on discourses. Four times, beginning with the first scene and ending with the last, the Medium speaks about knowledge and ways of knowing. The play's twenty-eight characters comment on the derailment in scattered scenes. Toña and Polo's school Teacher refers to her pupils as truants and blames their parents. The university students applaud what they view as an anarchistic act. The Emcee discusses three representations of the rose—the petal, the whole flower, and the microscopic fiber—and asks the audience to identify the "correct" image of the rose.

Carballido's *Rose* undertakes an examination of various discourses in relation to the various world views they propose. Like the rose of the title, which Carballido depicts as a complicated and interconnected conglomeration, inextricable from (and inconceivable without) its multiple parts (stalk, petals, fibers), the play is made up of numerous yet irreducible viewpoints and interpretations. Each ties into the creation of a new subject. Like the Emcee (or Locutor) who playfully separates the rose into three isolated images or "parts"—the rosebud, the petal, the microscopic view of the petal's tissue—the end product or composition of the subject matter under discussion is in part shaped by the discursive enunciation of it. We might well ask, looking at the Emcee's three illustrations, whether in fact we are looking at the same subject matter at all. The way the question is framed in a sense determines what we see and, hence, the "answer."

Because *Rose* raises so many issues, many of which exceed the scope of my particular analysis, it may be helpful to indicate what I am looking at. First, I examine the several interpretations and what they say about the speakers/knowers and about their relationship to the known and to their world. Then I focus on the politics and power of the various discourses in structuring and legitimating world views, in defining culture, in privileging perspectives, in imposing distinctions between the so-called First World producers of culture and cultural products and Third World importers, "imitators," and recipients of theories. Last, I signal the extent to which these distinctions are misleading, not so much because they are wrong as because they are reductive. Instead of a simple, one-directional process by which dependent countries "import" cultural *products* (that is, static objects) from First World nations, Carballido shows the ongoing, vital activity of transculturation. Unlike the Emcee, I do not suggest that we choose or privilege one view, dismissing all others as "false." On the contrary, the artificial rupture of the multifaceted into isolated parts only proves that no one of them can exist in isolation. While *Lions* calls attention to false totalities, *Rose* cautions against radical separations. In both, Carballido suggests that the multiple parts coexist and together give a far more complete outlook on reality. The microscopic closeup of the tissue is unrecognizable as a rose.

And who, as the Emcee himself suggests, can conceive of a rose without its petals?

First, then, I turn to the various epistemic grids presented in *Rose,* the "what we know and how we know it" (as posited by Quigley). The differences in perception, culminating in the play's conflicting interpretations, is the aspect most studied by the various commentators. Sandra Cypess has studied the patterns of "male" and "female" discourse in *Rose,* emphasizing the relationship between power and discursive practice in a patriarchal society such as Mexico ("I, Too, Speak," 45). For George Woodyard (1976, quoted by R. A. Kerr, 57), the Medium, the play's central figure, "is always the link between the rational and the irrational." However, an important dimension that has not been discussed, which I think is fundamental to our understanding of the cultural specificity and the political repercussions of the play, involves the distinct discursive and perceptual modes stemming from different epistemic grids—orality and literacy. Carballido presents a double confrontation of the literate and oral spheres. The two first come together *horizontally* in the original conquest and colonization of Mexico, when the literate, foreign culture imposed itself on the oral, indigenous one. Here, we can see the impact of one culture on another as an example of transculturation whereby cultural material passes from one society to another. However, Carballido also presents the confrontation *vertically,* as the literate culture cements its domination to produce a stratified society in which the lower classes are either semiliterate or illiterate.[13]

In *Rose,* Carballido explicitly links discourse to perception: we talk about what we know, and what we know depends to a large extent on our experience within language. In opposition to the play's two professors, who use Cartesian logic to expound European theories of consciousness and being-in-the-world, Carballido presents the Medium, wearing a rebozo "like a peasant woman" and telling story after story. The philosophical schools that shape the professors' perception and the literacy that maintains it do not by and large form the traditions within which most Mexicans have lived and, to different degrees, continue to live. In a country like Mexico, characterized by the coexistence of literate and primary oral cultures, consciousness and discourse change according to how people receive, store, and transmit information and knowledge.[14] As the play begins, the audience, sitting in almost total darkness, listens to the Medium relating the things she knows: "I know many things!" She receives information and transmits it; knowledge is a fluid, ongoing, reciprocal exchange. She compares knowledge to her heart, which pumps blood through channels, each somehow connected to another. As she narrates what she knows—herbs, faces, crowds, rocks, books, pages, illusions, roads, events—it becomes clear that her source is the collective, orally transmitted knowledge handed down from generation to generation. The Medium gives special importance to the two major kinds of messages, news and interpretation, that

Jan Vansina, in *Oral Tradition as History,* considers central to oral transmission. The Medium passes on "news," a word that she shouts out at the end of her first monologue, ushering in the thunderous crash of the train accident. The word "news" also introduces the newsboy shouting the headlines immediately following the crash. But while she is directly tied into the immediate, sensational world of "news," the Medium is far more concerned with the interpretation and meaning of the events she transmits. Following her opening monologue, the sound of the crash, and the newsboy's shouts, the play proceeds with the scene leading up to the derailment of the train and the multiple interpretations that follow.

The play flashes a series of interpretations past the audience, only a few of which can briefly be summed up here. For the Freudian professor (55-57), the derailment is symptomatic of the children's repressed sexuality, which culminates in destructive impulses. A psychologist's job, he says, is one of decoding the unconscious in order to render it conscious: "It is our duty to make the patient aware of them [traumatic nuclei] and thus guide him until he discovers for himself the secret reasons which lie hidden behind his impulses, the unconscious controls, the frustration of our acts, very much in the manner of some sort of explicit formulation. ... Let us take, for example, this terrible act, difficult to understand, when one tries to explain it as a conscious and rational deed. Two adolescents derail a train. Well, it just so happens that there are certain antecedent factors which will permit us to explain concretely the hidden, submerged impulses ... we will see how the *whole* matter becomes logical and coherent." He then steps aside as the children act through their original scenario again, but this time according to his direction. "Now," he tells the audience as the children speak new words only vaguely similar to their original dialogue, "I want you to observe the symbolic content of that phrase." The entire scene changes, including the dump and the garbage. As the stage directions indicate, "now in the various plants and objects are distinct sexual configurations. ... Polo picks up the broken piece of the engine. It now has a very suspicious shape." While the children push the tub of cement onto the railroad tracks, the Freudian has them chanting.

POLO:

    Incest! Libido! Maximino!

TOÑA:

    Defloration! Maximino! Father!

POLO AND TOÑA:

    Womb! Jealousy! Crime!

The psychologist concludes his presentation with a self-satisfied "Psychology! Whenever a man's conduct appears to be inexplicable ... psychology will lay it bare!"

For the Marxist professor (57), the act bespeaks the "extreme results" of extreme economic contradictions: "We are all of us witnesses of the event commented upon so extensively in the press. It is without any question a clear expression of class struggle. Protagonists: two children of the proletariat." He too directs the entire scene again. He emphasizes that the children are not in school, that they are undernourished, badly dressed, barefoot victims of all the social ills "typical" of "underdeveloped countries." The "answer" to the children's almost hopeless predicament, for the Marxist, lies in their hero worship of their friend and role model Maximino, "an authentic representative of his class: exploited, socially responsible, self-sacrificing, incorruptible, fraternal, vigorous, alert. By his example, he plants within these children the highest ideals and principles." This too, however, involves an act of decoding; Maximino's face is frozen in ideology and in his "expression the children can read his disappointment at how corrupt syndicalism has betrayed the workers to the power of capitalism." As the children push the tub of cement onto the tracks, the Marxist has them declaiming.

POLO:

    Fear is the springboard of all revolutions.

TOÑA:

    One must fell a certain number of trees in order to preserve the forest.

For the university students reading the newspaper, the derailment constitutes a gratuitous, anarchistic, and hence "inspired" act. For the Señor and Señora waiting for the bus (52), the derailment only substantiates what they think already: "Little savages, that's what they are. All of them. They're all a bunch of savages." This *malinchismo* or self-hatred substitutes for any insightful social critique. After concluding that "these people are criminal from the day they are born" and that they look forty years old, the Señor and Señora dismiss the children as barbaric and misery as "awful." They are more interested in the grisly and sensational news of a "trunk murder." For Polo's schoolteacher (52), the crime is due to "idleness," "stupidity," and "lack of civil spirit." For the owner of the train, the vandalism represents a loss of five million pesos. For Polo's mother, the whole thing is the fault of the father's alcoholism, child beating, and irresponsibility. For Toña's mother (54), the death of Toña's father is the cause of her actions. The derailment itself and the children's role in it are completely incomprehensible to her; it is all an economic nightmare: "I mean, why would they keep her locked up? Fat chance she'll ever pay for that train." And upon hearing that Toña *is* locked up, presumably "to keep her from doing it again," the mother responds, "As if she were going to go around derailing trains."[15] For the hungry scavengers who pick up food from the overturned train, the accident is a miracle of good fortune. All these perspectives fit together like petals on a rose, orchestrated by Carballido's other central image, the beating heart. There are no breaks in the action; the scenes pulse by the audience at a rhythmic pace.

In terms of time and staging devices, however, three perspectives claim preeminence. They are juxtaposed as three perceptual hypotheses during the Emcee's game show, and they correspond to the epistemic positions of the Freudian, the Marxist, and the Medium respectively. For the professor of psychology only the individual, the petal, matters. For the professor of economy only the collective totality, the rose, has significance. The Medium's "interpretation" (if we can even call it that) defies all pretense of objectivity: the children, she says, turn into "everything that surrounds them: they *become* the dump, the flowers, the clouds, amazement, joy ... and they understand ... they see! That's what happened" (60). But the play not only depicts different modes of perception in isolation and conjunction; it also refers us to the sources and traditions that make such modes of perception possible, and it points to the sociopolitical implications of the different positions.

The Medium's knowledge, we come to understand, represents a mode of perception different in kind and origin from the "scientific," objective knowledge posited by the professors. Her epistemological framework is primarily oral. Much of what she knows springs from an unwritten tradition, conserved by memory and passed on by word of mouth: "I also retain memories, memories which once belonged to my grandmother, my mother or my friends ... many of which they, in turn, heard from friends and old, old people" (47).[16] Yet she is a transcultured being, a hybrid of two cultural traditions. She also knows books and pages "in the style of Dürer, or of certain botanical and zoological illustrations of the German school of the nineteenth century, or of any old Mexican codices—perhaps all three" (51). Her mixture of orality and borderline literacy is a product of the history of conquest, and in turn it produces and feeds into a wide social network of cultural *mestizaje* (or hybridization), establishing her central position in it as much as literacy shapes that of the professors.

The play's most immediate distinction between oral and literate cultures lies in the relationship between knower and objects of knowledge. The Medium's knowledge cannot be called "objective"—empirically verifiable or *out there* in the world, outside or disconnected from herself as knower. Unlike the professors with their methodological and causal framework, she does not aspire to the Cartesian ideal of objectivity. From her first line in her first speech, the Medium approaches knowledge reflexively, comparing it to her heart, which, with its "canals that flow back and forth" (47), connects her with the rest of the world. As the fluidity of her speech shows, her way of knowing is anything but isolating or reductive; each idea opens a way to another, defying the possibility of conclusion. Her thinking progresses not systematically or linearly but rather through association; hence, she is incapable of interpretation in its strictest sense of formulating facts, ideas, impressions into a systematic whole.[17] She receives information; she contemplates and assimilates it; she stores knowledge in her memory; she comments on it and transmits it verbally.

Because she is not separate from what she knows, she is a subject, not an object, in a world of other subjects. The professors' way of knowing is eccentric in that they stand outside and removed from the source of their knowledge and information, which now in the literate society lies out there, in books and newspapers. Writing stores knowledge, and people write books in isolation. In contrast, we witness in the Medium's role the supreme importance of the speaker in an oral culture: if either the speaker or the audience is not present, there is no communication. Knowledge, kept alive by storytelling, avoids the dangers of reification. It is always fresh, its relevance assured by the presence of the speaker and the audience. If the subject were not of interest, they would not be listening. The physical presence of the professors is gratuitous in that they only read or speak what has already been prepared in writing. Individual scholars do not have to be together with their readers in order for the material to be communicated. They maintain a peripheral, alienated position in both the acquisition and transmission of their knowledge.

It is important to recognize the degree to which individuals' experience of themselves as knowing subjects or, conversely, as known objects, affects their experience of the world. Marx used the term "alienation" to describe the plight of the individual as subject in an objective and objectifying system. Alienation, then, is not an existential given but a product of the relationship between knower and known. Freud's theories challenge the individual's capacity to know, particularly to know her- or himself. He divides experience into several psychic structures—id, ego, superego—with unconscious and often unknowable links between them. The way we know affects the way we are. It need not surprise us that terms like the "divided self" and "alienation" have become commonplace in the twentieth century. The separation between knower and known, coupled with the inordinate value granted to the known over the knower, changes and reduces and fragments human experience. What Donald M. Lowe points out in *History of Bourgeois Perception* (105) about a bourgeois, literate society becomes even more acute in the era of rapidly advancing technology: "Being-in-the-world, under the pressure of visuality and objective reason, divided and turned in upon itself. Bourgeois society was highly compartmentalized; thus the articulation of the self took place in all the many spaces and times of that world. However, there was always more of the self than what could be realized in all those compartmentalized experiences. As a result, the person was disembodied into mind, body, emotion and sexuality. Each was a part of the person; but together they did not constitute a whole being."

Ironically, then, while literacy allows us to know more as well as more accurately, with greater abstraction and sophistication, it simultaneously widens the gap between knower and known.[18] The professors see the children as alienated, estranged from their "true" libidinal or proletarian "reality." But I maintain that Toña and Polo, chosen to illustrate theories, are frozen into the Sartrean "being-as-object"—alienated not in their lived experience as the professors argue but in the very act of "being-looked-at" (Sartre, *Being,* 344, 353). Discourse creates its own reality in the very act of framing the subject matter. This is not to suggest that the professors do not offer important readings of the situation. As Toña's crush on Maximino shows us, her adolescent sexual fantasies are revved up (to echo the Freudian professor's motorcycle analogy). And no one would dispute or underemphasize the poverty or the educational, economic, and social disadvantage of these children. However, the children are neither "neurotic" nor "alienated." They would not recognize themselves or what occurred at the dump in the professors' representations any more than they recognize themselves in the mug shots that make them look like forty-year-old hardened criminals. The problem arises because each professor, in his own way, "universalizes the self-conscious dissolution of the bourgeois subject" (Sangari, 157), creating an idiosyncratic reality and a meaning more in keeping with their society than with the children's situation. Hence, the political repercussions of discursive framing are multiple and long-term: the intellectuals, represented here as professors of psychology and economy, are alienated from the situation they are supposed to illuminate. Their alienation results in their distortion of reality, a misrepresentation of themselves and others that justifies or complies with oppression. As Edward Said (25) notes, the rift between intellectuals and society can result in "the regulated, not to say calculated, irrelevance of criticism." Yet the irrelevance of discourses does not mean they are dismissible or *benign.* They contribute to the marginalization and objectification of their subject—in this case the children. The ministers of education, Carballido makes clear enough in *Lions* and *Rose,* can intellectualize and legitimize hegemony.

The fact that reality—even the professors' so-called "objective" reality—is idiosyncratic indicates that all realities, as constructs, are in some way a product of our way of knowing, even when we become victims in our objectifying system. While the professors speak as if there were one "Truth" (a different one for each, of course) and claim "objectivity" in analyzing it, the play repeatedly reminds us to beware of the very idea of objectivity. The concept describes a particular system of human interactions both with others and with the world around them—but that system, like all others, changes and evolves. There is not one truth but many, with many centers. The newspapers reflect the changing perception of reality in a literate culture; the notion of objectivity quickly disappears. Even though the words on the paper are forever fixed—"objects" imbued with a certain authority because they are there, on the page—the many versions, each claiming truth, one replacing another in rapid succession, show the plurality of experience. The problem with written words is that they can outlive their context; they can become wrong, not in themselves but when they no longer speak to lived experience.

The Medium's perspective, in contrast with the professors', allows for change. The Freudian professor speaks of the children's "hidden guilt and desires for self-punishment" (55), which ultimately could be used to explain or justify whatever violent things befall them. Who can argue with self-destruction? (Then, of course, we remember that they are children in the hands of the Mexican police.) He compares the dump to human nature: "I don't believe that it is necessary to point out that by nature there exists within each and every one of us a veritable garbage dump!" (56). Again, who can argue with nature? The Marxist professor is also totalizing and essentialist: he says that "man is Economy. ... There is nothing inexplicable in this act. It is typical of its class" (57).[19] The Medium's explanation, however enigmatic or inadequate, includes the vital concept of change: the children were *turning into* everything around them, they *became* part of it all. Her interpretation may elude us, but therein lies its power. The professors fix and objectify the children; they use them as examples to show the profundity of their thought and the strength of their theories and tradition. But as long as the children can evade being "classified" on a psychological, economic, or zoological scale, they maintain their identity as living subjects, active players in their continuing *historia*—as story, as history.

The Medium's subjective or reflexive relationship to knowledge, as opposed to the professors' "objective" approach, poses a question of sources of knowledge as well. The authority substantiating the Medium's position stems primarily from an internalized oral tradition, while the professors rely on external material: ongoing research and book learning. This does not imply that the Medium (any more than the professors) represents the original sources of knowledge. She, as Medium (mediator), functions as a vehicle or channel (*vía*) of thought as much as they. Her source does differ, however; her information is founded in collective wisdom, old wives' tales, "common knowledge" handed down through the generations.[20] The information passed on by the professors has individual sources, as demonstrated by the very terms "Freudian" psychologist and "Marxist" economist. The Medium's knowledge is unspecialized, though broader in scope. While she knows "books, pages, illusions," she also understands little-known aspects of popular culture such as herbal healing. Unfettered by the limitations of objectivity, she freely moves in realms of belief—the healer's "cure" or *limpia*, for example—that scientific thought would discard as manifestations of the occult or magic. This freedom, in turn, animates the world and the universe, which she approaches anagogically, through the mystical reading of signs that only superficially resembles literacy: "They are looking at signs like children learning the alphabet. They are looking at arrows that point out directions, paths. They are searching for crossroad signs," (60). I say "superficially" because the signs-as-signifiers do not correspond to specific sounds or objects. The children are free to interpret them as they like.

Faced with such radically diverse world views and ontologies, our awareness of the implications of the differences in perception becomes key. It is not a question of choosing between perceptions, as the Emcee proposes, or privileging orality over literacy. The point is not to add the widespread misrepresentation or mystification of Third World subjects. Rather, it becomes critical to understand how our experience changes according to what and how we know, so that we can in turn change or modify that experience. "Each head is a universe" says the motto, and if Carballido rejects anything at all, it is only the arrogance and ignorance in those who presume that "whatever seems inexplicable in human behavior . . . can be explained!"[21] Framed as they are in the world of the play, the professors' worlds seem small and static. Carballido depicts them in a humorous, almost farcical manner, and we laugh not because they are wrong but because they are reductive. Everything that is unique and individual about people and situations is boiled down to the lowest common denominator. The Freudian uses language not to open up channels of communication, as the Medium does, but to obliterate distinctions. Telephones, motorcycles, horses, dreams of flight, he tells us, are all sexual symbols, all signs of the same signifier. The Marxist too equates man (with a small *m*) to Economy (with a capital *E*) as though they were the same thing. Both professors are incapable of addressing individuality and lived experience. Their use of interpretation recalls Sontag's argument that "the task of interpretation is virtually one of translation. The interpreter says, Look, don't you see that X is really—or, really means—A? That Y is really B? That Z is really C?" (*Interpretation,* 15). Though Carballido's Freudian claims to focus on the individual, he objectifies the "common man" into the "common patient." For Carballido's Marxist, the human face freezes into a text reflecting ideology. Neither of them satisfactorily explains the accident or proposes solutions to the problems they have identified.

But what about the Medium? Does she explain the derailment? Why the special authority Carballido seems to grant her, and what does it consist of? Her speech may be ambiguous or mysterious but never farcical. The cosmos illuminated by the Medium is more miraculous and inclusive and yet certainly no more *real* or *true* than the world of the professors. The brevity and opacity of her "interpretation" of the accident, along with her peremptory dismissal of the question—"that was all" (172)—does not "answer" any questions. On the contrary, it dissuades us from privileging her explanation over the professors.' She refuses to give answers, to say the last word, to anticipate or precipitate an ending to the stories. She commands such a substantial amount of stage time not because she is right but because she is vital, not objectively as an answer but subjectively as

a presence. She tells stories in both meanings of the word *historia,* story and history. She represents the consciousness and memory of a race—its history—kept alive by the very act of speaking. As such, she commands all our attention because, in an oral tradition, when the speaker stops, the *historia* ends. This double dimension lends her her paradoxical character: she is firmly planted in the soil but also transcends it. Within the dramatic structure, she is central to the workings of the play. Metaphorically, her consciousness is central to Mexican thought if Mexico is to avoid aping modern European thinking.

Rooted in orality, the Medium's vision encompasses past, present, and future. While oral tradition as defined by Vansina (27) refers to "oral statements spoken, sung or called out on musical instruments" for more than one generation, Vansina also specifies that oral statements are not necessarily about the past. This is important to note, given that oral traditions are generally considered (by Ong and others) "conservative." While orality is necessarily "conservative"—if by that word we mean "conserving in memory"—it is a mistake to think of these societies as politically conservative. Jean Franco has stressed that "the secret weapon of the Indian group [during the colonial period] was the oral tradition in the native language. Indeed the most significant feature of colonial culture is this differentiation within the production process itself, between an oral culture dependent on community and a written culture, which was overwhelmingly associated with domination" ("Dependency Theory," 68). The Medium draws from that independent heritage and combines the stories from the past with her recently acquired knowledge. Her perspective cannot be viewed as regressive or nostalgic for two main reasons. First, the word "nostalgia" suggests a discontinuity, a break between past and present, which we do not have in the play. Second, there is no backward impetus, no archaeological intent to recuperate a lost past. It is crucial to recognize that the Medium, then, does not represent an escape from the present into Mexico's pre-Hispanic traditions. Such a move would be as suicidal—politically and culturally—as surrendering to the First World. Fortunately, as Carballido illustrates, the choice goes beyond those two options. The story the Medium narrates about the "two who dreamed," her third monologue in the play, illustrates how Mexico's indigenous past flows into and is part of its contemporary situation.

It is the story of two men who lived in different villages, Chalco and Chalma. One version, the Medium tells us, says they were twins, another that they were brothers, another that they were friends; we as audience have no way of knowing for certain. Be that as it may, each of them, in their separate villages and at exactly the same time, dreamed of a prodigious figure instructing him to go to the other's town and, together with the other, pray before the sanctuary next to his house. Both men awoke, walked toward the other town, and met halfway. "Each in turn told the other his dream and they were identical . . . like a mirror with two contradictory images." They do not know how to interpret the dream, or which town to go to. They flip a coin (much like the children in the play), which falls in a crack: " 'It is a sign,' they said, and so they made camp on the very spot and waited for another sign . . . another dream. . . . The sign never came, and so they decided to fulfill their command right there where they were. It was a barren place covered with weeds and rocks" (the dump?), which they cleared and on which they built a "very small church." The men, wearing the garments of their pre-Hispanic ancestors, "had a few drinks of mescal and then they danced and prayed. They danced in that complicated rhythm that had been passed down to them from their fathers. They prayed the prayers they had learnt from childhood. Two tired, dirty men decorated with feathers and mirrors danced and prayed in the nocturnal ambiguity of that wilderness without answers. . . . Their time was up and they knew no better way of satisfying the whims of the arbitrary being that had spoken to them in their dreams" (54).

The story of the two who dreamed spans from the ritualistic sung-dance of Mexico's pre-Hispanic past to the contemporary scene—the dump where the children dance, play, and flip their coins, the dump where the scavengers drink their tequila at night and sing their songs about yet another rose, the rose of Castille. The ritual the men perform recalls Mircea Eliade's description (*Sacred,* 27-28) of the archaic practice of invoking divine or supernatural guidance: "some *sign* suffices to indicate the sacredness of a place. . . . When no sign manifests itself, it is *provoked*" to "*show* what place is fit to receive the sanctuary or the village" (Eliade's emphasis). However, this in no way suggests that pre-Hispanic ritual can somehow solve the present situation in which the men find themselves.[22] What the play suggests, rather, is that generation after generation, people have tried to interpret the inexplicable—what the ancients would call the sacred; most 20th-century people, the "arbitrary." The dance the men perform as part of a holy rite resembles yet differs from the children's dance, and differs too from the professors' "explanation" of the dance. To the Freudian the dance represents "the mutual release and discharge of libido" (56); to the Marxist it is an example of "those dances with which capitalism manages to corrupt the true spirit of the people" (57). Carballido juxtaposes the various forms of dance to illustrate how the very concept and meaning of the activity changes according to the context. In *Rose,* the past forms a part of the present which opens up into some unknown, unforetold future. Through memory and imagination the Medium spans past and present. She holds, too, a promise for the future: more stories will be revealed; more will be known in the telling. Her sense of lived time—as opposed to chronological, "objective" time—is both retrospective and prospective. The past is incorporated into a lived present both in her memory and in the blood that flows through her veins that resemble the pre-Hispanic waterways of Tenochtitlán. By means of images and allusions she integrates the pre-Columbian past with modern Mexico in each of her four speeches. Her narration, the act of speaking itself, situates her as the living link in an ongoing series of *historias.* She does not allude to the concept of progress or to future fulfillment, the triumphalist reading of history offered by the Man in *The Day They Let the Lions Loose.* Rather, time unfolds story after story.

TRANSCULTURATION

The story of the "two who dreamed" provides Carballido with a framework within which to examine the concept of tradition, hegemonically and counterhegemonically. The men's feathers and mirrors, like the Medium's rebozo, dangerously border on the folkloric. As I noted in chapter 1, perpetuating a dead or dying tradition as a museum piece or a tourist attraction, often under the auspices of a Ministry of Culture, proves as artificial and alienating as imposing totally foreign cultures. It also contributes to what Dirlik (26) calls "hegemonic culturalism," a way of seeing culture as a "thing," autonomous from social activity and lived experiences: "An irrefutable tradition that defines the center of history is crucial to ruling-class history, and so is the presentation of that tradition as prior to everyday life." If culture in the Third World could be reduced to feathers and mirrors, mariachi bands and magic realism, the hegemonic cultures would not need to emphasize and fight for the centrality of a Western canon. The point, as Carballido illustrates, is that while the pre-Hispanic world is dead and buried, the traditions that have grown out of it are neither dead nor reified; they have survived by transforming and adapting to living societies. In the image offered by the play, the light from the star shining on the cavemen reaches our telescopes and illuminates our present, even though the star itself may be dead. The difference would be that while the starlight remains in its "pure" or unadulterated essence, culture survives by adulteration, by "impurely" mixing with other cultural elements. The dances, the songs, the prayers inherited from pre-Hispanic times change as the society does. The divine being is now an arbitrary being. The barren ground is now a dump; the garbage once had a use, and the children (much to everyone's shock) find new uses for things. The scavenger's house is constructed of some boards he found, some broken boxes, and "sheet metal I stole from the chicken coop over there." "It may be poor and rickety," he admits, "but I'll tell you one thing about my house, it's warm" (59). These useless, displaced remnants of past structures undergo change as they become part of a new, useful structure. Carballido does not depict this changing tradition and culture romantically; he shows dumps, derailments, and thefts as well as song and dance. Again, the point is not that culture is a museum piece of "folklore" but that it is vital. The process of cultural change, as the garbage humorously illustrates, is one of loss, selection, recuperation, recycling. Cultural products, like garbage, are the byproducts of living, changing societies: products are tried out, discarded, added to, displaced, replaced, rediscovered, and made over by combining the new with the old.

In short, what Carballido demonstrates in *Rose* is the process of cultural change, loss, and rejuvenation that Fernando Ortiz, in the 1940s, called "transculturation," a three-stage process consisting of the acquisition of new cultural material from a foreign culture, the loss or displacement of one's own, and the creation of new cultural phenomena. Angel Rama, in *Transculturación narrativa en América Látina* (33), points out in his commentary on Ortiz's theory that his is very much a Latin American perspective in that "it reveals the resistance to considering one's traditional culture, receiving the impact of the foreign culture that will modify it, as merely a passive or even inferior entity, destined to major losses without the possibility of creative response." For Rama, expanding on the three-step process, Ortiz does not sufficiently emphasize selectivity and inventiveness in transculturation. After all, cultures do not borrow indiscriminately; like the scavenger, one takes only what one needs. Latin American theatre, Rama notes, did not appropriate the Broadway musical. What it did appropriate were the absurdist, grotesque, and fragmented techniques that reflect a sense of Latin America's chaotic reality as well as more socially oriented dramatic techniques, associated with Piscator and Brecht, to help change the sociopolitical situations. Moreover, when these techniques were borrowed, they were radically altered by their new context. *Rose* is a fine example of the selectivity and inventiveness that Rama writes of, as well as what he calls the "rediscovery" of "primitive values almost forgotten within one's own cultural system that are capable of standing up to the erosion of transculturation" (39). Rama, then, speaks of four stages in the process—loss, selectivity, rediscovery, and incorporation—all of which take place simultaneously.[23]

Let us briefly look at *I Too Speak of the Rose* from the perspective of transculturation. The "borrowings" are obvious, and not just in terms of the Freudian psychology and the Marxist economic theories so prevalent in Mexico around the time the play appeared. There are theatrical borrowings as well. Carballido himself calls the play a *loa,* which is both a short piece (usually one act) presented before a full-length play and a "hymn of praise" (47), a genre which, though common from the Golden Age to the nineteenth century, gradually went out of fashion in the twentieth. The narrator and the episodic structure seem Brechtian; the ritualistic elements, including the final scene, Artaudian. However, looking at the parts separately is misleading. Although *Rose* has Brechtian elements, this is no Brechtian play, as some commentators claim.[24] Looking at the Medium in the light of her own tradition, rather than through Western theories, we see that her role as narrator stems from her experience in an oral culture. Speaking rhythmically in the darkness, the Medium tells us, she can hear her heart, though her sense of sight is blurred. Moreover, we as audience experience that tradition in *her* terms, not ours. Like the Medium, we sit in darkness; we hear, but we can hardly see. Her speech draws us in, en-

veloping rather than distancing us, awakening us to the beauty and fluidity of her language. Carballido places us in the same physical position before her as we would assume before a bard; her scenes are intimate, quiet, introspective, or reflective. As Walter Ong (73) states: "The way in which the word is experienced is always momentous in psychic life. The centering action of sound (the field of sound is not spread out before me but is all around me) affects man's sense of the cosmos. For oral cultures, the cosmos is an ongoing event with man at its center." This experience, then, is profoundly different from that of the audience in Brecht's theatre. Brecht advocates leaving the house lights up to create an informal music-hall atmosphere in which people feel comfortable smoking, laughing, and commenting on the action.

The oral tradition also explains the episodic plot in *Rose.* As in Brechtian theatre, some of the twenty-one scenes seem strung together arbitrarily; one could change the order without significantly changing our experience of the play. However, the episodes are not Brechtian if we accept Brecht's own description (201) of episodic plots: "The individual episodes have to be knotted together in such a way that the knots are easily noticed. The episodes must not succeed one another indistinguishably but must give a chance to interpose our judgment. ... To this end it is best to agree to use titles." The episodic structure in *Rose* is not meant to distance us. Though episodic, the scenes derive their structure from the narrative sequence characteristic of the oral tradition. The Medium is telling us the story; from her opening monologue, she knows how Toña and Polo's particular story unravels—"but more of that later" (47), she tells us, or "that's another story" (54). The misreading of the episodic plot lies in the insistence on labeling the episodic "Brechtian" rather than recognizing that Brecht's "epic" theatre picks up ("borrows") from the oral tradition. As Ong (144) states: "What made a good epic poet was, among other things of course, first, tacit acceptance of the fact that episodic structure was the only way and the totally natural way of imagining and handling lengthy narrative. ... Strict plot for lengthy narrative comes with writing." Brecht himself was the first to admit that "stylistically speaking, there is nothing at all new about the epic theatre" (75), that he had used techniques and ideas from Asiatic theatre, medieval mystery plays, Spanish classical theatre, Jesuit theatre, and many more sources. Brecht, in fact, is one of the greatest examples of the vitality, selection, and innovation associated with intercultural exchange. However, what makes him *Brechtian* is his particular use of the acquired materials. What makes Carballido *non-Brechtian* is his particular use of *his.*

The same applies to the play's ritual elements. The story of "the two who dreamed" and the final scene of the play are not Artaudian because they invoke ritual; rather, Artaud is "ritualistic" because he invokes, even mystifies, Mexican indigenous rites. For Artaud the non-Western is the "true culture [that] operates exaltation and force. . . . In Mexico, since we were talking about Mexico, there is no art: things are made for use. And the world is in perpetual exaltation" (*Double,* 10-11). Carballido, on the other hand, does not mystify Mexico's past or, like Artaud, take suicidal risks to recuperate it.[25] Rather, more in the manner we have associated with transculturation, he "rediscovers" (Rama's term) and incorporates the past into the present. The ritual, we noted, does not point toward the past; it relates the experience of two men trying to function appropriately in an inexplicable wilderness devoid of supernatural or divine guidance, drawing from the traditions they have at hand. Moreover, Carballido's ritual dance linking the characters at the end of the play is not an ahistorical or nostalgic return to ritual community. It is a historically accurate depiction of what Kumkum Sangari (158) calls the cultural heterogeneity of Latin America: "The simultaneity of the heterogeneous is a matter of historical sedimentation that results from the physical coexistence over time of different ethnic groups. . . . Simultaneity is the restless product of a long history of miscegenation, assimilation, and syncretization *as well as* of conflict, contradiction, and cultural violence" (Sangari's emphasis).

Carballido's conscious use of foreign material is evident in *Rose.* As we have seen, he juxtaposes two traditions, two ways of knowing: orality and literacy. The theatrical techniques he uses to depict those two epistemic grids are also different, necessarily different, for what we know depends on how we know it. We would not understand what an oral tradition consists of if we only listened to the Freudian or Marxist expounding on it. Carballido, in the darkened theatre, recreates the situation in which an audience depends on its sense of hearing for its information and knowledge. The Medium, sitting quietly, relates. The literate world is portrayed through representation (rather than narration), emphasizing our visual sense by means of more openly theatrical scenes involving the professors, the Teacher, the Emcee. The action is fast paced, noisy, full of children's antics, bombast, pomposity—wonderfully visual and humorous as the stage becomes full of sexual shapes and revolutionary slogans. These theatrical scenes can be described in terms of Brechtian distanciation, for the stereotypical situations and the caricatured figures keep us out. They depict the alienation produced and reproduced by the theories themselves, and what better way to depict alienation than through Brecht's alienating techniques or "A-effect"? Carballido's use of distanciation in these particular scenes serves Brecht's original intention of sharpening our critical awareness. In opposition to the way we perceive in the Medium's company, these scenes are asking us to know something different, and in a different manner. What do we learn from the theatrical juxtaposition of these two worlds? Through the professors and the Teacher (endorsed ministers of education), through all their rhetoric and manipulation, we see the grim socioeconomic context in which the children live. The children grow up in poor,

single-mother homes; they play in garbage, miss school, and seem destined at best to borderline literacy. To paraphrase the Marxist, this is unfortunately "typical" of the class that Carballido portrays. While the professors and the Teacher notice the problem and paint it in the darkest, most hopeless light, they seem unable to improve the situation. Their attitudes, instead of helping the children, only subject them to further violence, the violence of misinterpretation and reification. The children clearly do not recognize themselves in the professors' depictions, the Teacher's harangue, the newspaper headlines and photographs. They, as individuals, become "objects" of interpretation in a larger scheme of things, pawns to be pushed and pulled in political debate. Public attention focuses not on them but on the "event," the sensational derailment, in order to ignore what Paul Ricoeur in *History and Truth* (226) calls "the violence of exploitation." As Ricoeur makes clear, "battles are events, so are riots; but poverty and the dying poor are not events."

The Medium, on the other hand, never once alludes to the children's poverty. She is not insensitive to their poor living conditions; she too lives in an environment pervaded by smells of "smoke and stale food" (47), but she does not turn it into a metaphor to explain something else— repressed unconscious thoughts or a capitalist economy of waste. Through her vision, we understand the relativity of the junkyard. It is not only an unmitigated disaster of filth and trash, as the professors see it, equated by the Freudian with human nature and by the Marxist with capitalism. The children go there because it is fun; they find things. The Medium neither equates nor interprets; she simply places the issue in a broader context. By means of her consciousness, past flows into present. What we regarded as junk when it lay on the ground out of context now regains meaning. The piece of metal Polo picks up has a history: "This came out of a mine. . . . It formed part of a machine" (172). Toña and Polo are poor, but as they realize, they are healthy, productive, and capable of love. The Medium does not lock them into a theory; she opens up the realms of possibility, indicating more and more stories: "And do you know how Polo came to own his own garage? And what Toña's marriage was like? Well . . . that's another story" (153). For her, then, the catastrophic derailment is not a cause for alarm but an opportunity for rethinking history—past, present, and future—and for repositioning the hitherto marginalized both outside and within society.

Perhaps Carballido's most important political insight in *Rose,* however, is not his recognition of diversity or of cultural heterogeneity and simultaneity. Clearly, there are many different ways of seeing the world. Carballido's central image of the rose is itself the most obvious example of the plurality of interpretation. The rose appears in the title, in the scavenger's love song, in the play's enveloping structure, in the psychologist's description of the self. In the epigram, Carballido quotes lines from two Mexican poet-playwrights, Xavier Villaurrutia's "But mine is not the frigid rose," and Sor Juana Inés de la Cruz's "Portent of our human architecture." In the Emcee's game show the rose is portrayed from three representative perspectives: rose, petal, tissue, and the Emcee asks his audience if they are looking at "the image of a flower of the dicotyledonous bush of the rosaceous family" or "one of those divine roses which, among cultured and refined people, is taken as the favorite symbol of the human architecture. ... Our job here is to reject quite definitely and conclusively all false images" (59). Clearly, however, the rose is one of the most complex and ambiguous of images; it stands for both "heavenly perfection and earthly passion; the flower is both Time and Eternity, life and death, fertility and virginity" (Cooper, 141). The rose heart is also an important pre-Columbian symbol of life in the Nahua tradition (Amaral, 155). What needs stressing, however, is that aside from the fascinating diversity, the rival and conflicting versions struggle to win out. For all his facetiousness, the Emcee is not just joking when he says that "there are three [images] and only one is authentic. The other two should be stricken from the books so that they will be forgotten forever. And any person who divulges them should be pursued by law. All those who believe in these false images should be suppressed and isolated! Kept under constant surveillance" (59). In the context of the game show, with its promise of a "magnificent prize" to the person who identifies the one true image, the Emcee's words are humorous. When placed in the context of Mexican history, however, the hegemonic discourse and its articulation and valorization of the "true" did in fact result in the isolation, suppression, and erasure of the "barbaric."

Carballido's strategy in this play (and others) lies not in replacing but in displacing the hegemonic discourse. He inverts the practice that has so long marginalized the *mestizo,* the female, the indigenous, the non-Castilian, and the non-Western in Mexico. In terms of stage time, the Medium dominates the action; she is central to the workings of the play. By making her central, Carballido not only legitimates the indigenous, oral traditions of Mexico but also situates woman as a positive, life-giving, and liberating force in the nation's history—a move that openly defies Mexico's *malinchismo,* or self-hatred, and misogyny. Women, even more than men, have been associated with the oral tradition because they have been denied access to education and positions of *author*ity considerably longer than indigenous males.[26]

Carballido also gives Mexicans back their own language. Instead of Castilian Spanish the children's expressions *órale, no se me raje, re fácil, ¡Quihubo!, cuate* situate us firmly in the streets of Mexico City. Mexicans, too, speak of the rose, in their own way.

Moving the marginalized from the periphery of the known universe to its center in itself constitutes an important, liberating, historical *act,* for by the same move the Eurocentric (the professors) recedes, reduced in importance.[27]

Changing the relationship between the marginal and the dominant changes history, for as Hayden White points out in *Tropics of Discourse* (94), histories "are not only about events but also about the possible set of relationships that those events can be demonstrated to figure." I go into the subject of the struggle for history in the next chapter; here it is sufficient to note that Carballido depicts the derailment in order to propose various ways that the event figures in divergent discourses. Framing the derailment in different ways, gives it different meanings, which then become the basis for different world views. Reclaiming the events in an indigenous discourse makes the articulating, speaking self central to history. This move becomes obvious in any theatrical production of the play—quite simply, the more time the Medium is onstage, the less time there is for the professors. Clearly, in *Rose* the Medium "steals the show." Dominating our attention, she is the presence that was perceived as absence in *Lions.* Here, right in the center of Mexico's systems and traditions, is the spirit and language of a people that has managed to survive both the cages and the hegemonic system. But the political repercussions of the displacement of Western thought to the periphery, where it is allowed to coexist and intermingle with the non-Western traditions without eclipsing them, is truly significant. Perhaps it surprises no one that the Medium's interpretations are no more valid or correct than those of the professors; no one would expect them to be. But to maintain that the most advanced Western theories of individual and economic development are no more real or valid than those of the Medium is indeed extraordinary. The professors' theories appear irrelevant, if not downright hostile, to the reality they are supposed to be illuminating. By making the Medium central, the play makes them marginal to Mexican reality. Marginality, I stated in chapter 1, is *positional.* Now the professors are irrelevant *and* marginal. And although the *científicos* have long dominated the Mexican scene, *Rose* illustrates that the professors are no more correct than the Medium. However, as Carballido stresses by introducing the story of the "two who dreamed," life in Mexico did not start with the Conquest, nor did it end there. Although the professors seemingly deny the possibility of change, Mexico is changing. What seems static, fixed, hopeless (a single petal of the rose) must be understood as part of a larger, multifaceted conglomerate. The liberating strategy does not lie only in military prowess; perhaps more urgently, it lies in reclaiming center stage in one's own culture, one's traditions, one's history.

What will come of Carballido's political vision? Can it ever be more than a vision? Can it help Mexico and Mexicans find nonviolent ways out of their political and social chaos? The "two who dreamed" would tell us from their experience that it is impossible to know the results of one's action. The Freudian professor (like the Octavio Paz of *The Labyrinth of Solitude*) would call Mexico a hopelessly schizophrenic country: mother Malinche's seduction by father Cortés has created a traumatized, self-hating brood. For the Marxist, Mexico is an underdeveloped country on the brink of open class warfare. For the Medium, Mexico is a miracle of creative energy that has survived centuries of oppression and kleptocracy. Carballido's vision, like the Medium's, transforms the discordant notes of Mexico's many dissonances into a *loa,* a hymn of praise.

Notes

1. Emilio Carballido was born in Córdoba, Veracruz, in 1925; the family moved to Mexico City in 1926. He began writing plays in 1946, and premiered his first major play, *Rosalba y los Llaveros* (Rosalba and the Llaveros) in 1950. Since then he has written more than a hundred plays; his major ones include *La hebra de oro* (1957, trans. by M. S. Peden, *The Golden Thread and Other Plays,* 1971), *El día que se soltaron los leones* (1957; Oliver's translation of *The Day They Let the Lions Loose* appeared in his 1971 *Voices of Change*), *El relojero de Córdoba* (1960, trans. by M. S. Peden as *The Clockmaker from Cordoba* in *The Golden Thread*), *Un pequeño día de ira* (1961, trans. by M. S. Peden as *Short Day's Anger,* 1975), *Medusa* (1960), *Te juro Juana* (1965), *Yo también hablo de la rosa* (1965, trans. by Oliver in Woodyard's 1971 *The Modern State in Latin America*), *Orinoco* (1979), *Ceremonia en el templo del tigre* (1983), and *La rosa de dos aromas* (1986). Carballido won the Casa de las Americas award in 1962 for *Un pequeño día de ira,* as well as numerous other awards. His plays have been translated into English, French, Italian, Russian, Czech, Norwegian, and other languages. Carballido currently lives in Mexico City.

2. Arif Dirlik, in "Culturalism as Hegemonic Ideology and Liberating Practice" (13), verbalizes a position similar to Carballido's when he insists on the importance of studying culture as a "liberating" practice and "argues the radicalism of cultural activity against efforts to subsume the question of culture within other, seemingly more radical activities upon which individuals attempting to change the world have increasingly focused their attention. In a world where economic necessity and political crisis confront us daily, this argument may seem superfluous or even self-indulgent. This is especially the case where the question of culture relates to the non-Western world where millions of lives await the urgent resolution of practical problems for their survival. Yet I will argue in the face of necessity that the realm of culture, as the realm of activity that is bound up with the most fundamental epistemological questions, demands priority of attention."

3. Dirlik (14), who, in turn, is paraphrasing E. P. Thompson.

4. Translations from *The Day They Let the Lions Loose* (in Oliver's *Voices of Change*) and *I Too Speak of the Rose* (in Woodyard's *The Modern Stage in Latin America*) are by William I. Oliver except as otherwise noted; page numbers cite these editions.

5. This is my translation. Oliver's "I don't think people are the way they say" misses the sexual innuendos of Carballido's original: "Yo no creo que las gentes hagan esas cosas que dicen" (233; page numbers of the Spanish correspond to *Teatro,* the Fondo de Cultural Económica edition of three Carballido plays).

6. In 1880, Cunninghame Graham observed a phenomenon foreshadowing Carballido's play: "The giant cypresses, tall even in the time of Moctezuma, the castle of Chapultepec upon its rock ... did not interest me so much as a small courtyard, in which, ironed and guarded, a band of Indians ... were kept confined ... their demeanour less reassuring than that of the tigers in the cage hard by" (116).

7. My translation of Carballido's "huele a orilla de lago, a tierra levemente podrida" (263); Oliver has "it smells of rotting leaves" (37).

8. See Davis, *Latin American Thought,* chap. 5, for a study of positivism in Latin America.

9. My translation of Carballido's "Entre más sabe la gente, más difícil resulta disciplinarla" (241), erroneously translated by Oliver as "The more people you know, the more difficult it is to keep order" (15). Carballido is referring here to an uneasy contradiction in Mexico's educational system. On one hand, the government is obliged and theoretically "committed" to provide an education for its population. Schools and universities are free in Mexico, and the large national universities are "autonomous," meaning that the government cannot send in police or directly influence their functioning. But like the Teacher, the government finds itself in the situation of having to educate people who are potentially threatening to its continued existence. Its way of solving this contradiction without directly meddling with university education has been to unionize the university workers—janitors, watchmen, and the like. When the political situation becomes heated, this union goes on strike, and the universities must be shut down for lack of personnel.

10. "Musica de la persecución" (246), not "percussive music" as Oliver has it (20).

11. My translation. I approve of Oliver's substitution of "we" in Carballido's original "they are surgeons, butchers" (39) insofar as the scene emphasizes that we (as victims and outcasts) are responsible for our leaders; however, the original distinction between "we" and "they" is an important one in that we are

responsible for our roles as *victims* but not as butchers—we are not the oppressors.

12. Oliver's translation (331) except that he has "what Toña's wedding looked like."

13. I am indebted to my colleague Raul Bueno for the observation of the double dynamic of the oral/literate paradigm. Though the vertical class tensions are evident throughout the chapter, I concentrate on the horizontal aspect because *Rose* provides an example of the passage of cultural material from one society to another, which is at issue throughout this work.

14. Ong defines primary orality as "the orality of cultures untouched by literacy" (6) and says of its coexistence with literacy: "Today primary oral culture in the strict sense hardly exists, since every culture knows of writing and has some experience of its effects. Still, to varying degrees many cultures and subcultures, even in a high-technology ambiance, preserve much of the mind-set of primary orality" (11).

15. My translation. In the original, the mother implies that Toña is not about to go around derailing trains for the rest of her life, whereas Oliver's translation, "Oh, well, if she's going to go on derailing trains ..." (54) seems to leave that possibility open.

16. I disagree with Kerr's reading (52) of these lines as Jungian, a product of the "collective unconscious" manifesting itself through the dreams and visions of the individual psyche. Rather, I think Carballido is referring here to a much more concrete social process, the transmission of knowledge and cultural traditions from one generation to another through speech.

17. I hasten to add, with Susan Sontag: "Of course, I don't mean interpretation in the broadest sense in which Nietzsche (rightly) says, 'There are no facts, only interpretations.' By interpretation, I mean here a conscious act of the mind which illustrates a certain code, certain 'rules' of interpretation" (*Interpretation,* 15).

18. See M. M. Bober, *Karl Marx's Interpretation of History,* 5.

19. My translation of "man is Economy." Oliver's "Man is economy" misses some of Carballido's humor.

20. For an interesting essay on "common sense," see Geertz, "Common Sense as a Cultural System," in *Local Knowledge.*

21. My translation.

22. Alice Lakwena's "Holy Spirit Movement" in Uganda in 1987 graphically illustrates the devastating consequences of relying on ritual to solve violent social crisis. Her warriors, armed only with stones, felt that the ritual preparation for combat made them impervious to attack from the heavily armed enemy. An interview with one of her followers describes their beliefs: "If you throw a 'stone' grenade it will explode. I threw them in battle but it was difficult to tell if they worked because other people were throwing real grenades. ... This woman [Lakwena] can reach Kampala because when they are moving the NRA do not see the Holy Spirit soldiers. That happens. ... People in ambush will sleep as you pass." This, the soldier explains, is because the soldiers rub over themselves a powder made of burned squirrel bones, which makes them invisible. An eyewitness report of a battle, however, saw things differently: "They [the Holy Spirit Movement] came in three groups totalling around 500 men and women singing religious hymns ... they were received by a shower of bullets from the NRA soldiers who had taken cover," and nearly half the group were killed or captured (qtd. in Uganda's *New Vision* 26 (Oct. 1987): 1-11.

23. Transculturation is also discussed by Carl Weber in a 1989 article, "AC/TC: Currents of Theatrical Exchange." Weber seems unaware of the earlier uses of the term as I outline them here, stating that the word "is as new as the phenomenon" of international arts festivals dating from the 1950s onward (11). He notes that "the trend labeled 'transculturation' has, indeed, pervaded [the media] on a global scale. ... 'Western,' which in this context means European or North American ideology, its values, structure, and contents are inscribed in the predominant models of performance accepted by most contemporary societies, models that partly ingest, partly destroy indigenous cultural values and forms" (12). However, Weber does accept that the process is not merely one-directional and that original, culturally specific art forms can develop from it: "Even when early efforts still bordered on copies, soon the models became infused and mediated with native literary and/ or performance tradition" (18).

24. Kerr (53) associates the Medium with Brecht's narrators and asserts that, like them, she functions to distance the audience from the action: "The fact that she evokes the other scenes avoids any semblance of reality in her representation. She transforms the spectator into an observer, rather than participant, of the action. These elements, and the effects of distancing that they produce, represent the theatrical norms that we associate with Brecht's epic theatre."

25. See Artaud's *México y Viaje al país de los Tarahumaras* (Fondo Cultura Económica) or the extract "Concerning a Journey to the Land of the Tarahumaras" in the *Artaud Anthology.*

26. The fluidity I have associated with orality is also, according to Josette Féral (550), a characteristic of

feminine discourse, which is "closer to the liquid (and therefore intangible) state of fluids rather than contained in the rigid system of solids."

27. Dirlik (26) makes a similar observation in discussing E. P. Thompson's *Making of the Working Class*: "The centering of the working class must necessarily be accompanied by the 'decentering' of the ruling, hegemonic class, since the two groups by definition make contradictory claims upon history."

Bibliography

EMILIO CARBALLIDO

SELECTED PLAYS

El día que se soltaron los leones. Emilio Carballido: Teatro. Mexico City: Fondo de Cultura Económica, 1960, 1976, 1979.

———. Trans. William I. Oliver as *The Day They Let the Lions Loose, Voices of Change in the Spanish American Theatre.* Austin: Univ. of Texas Press, 1971.

Yo también hablo de la rosa. Revista de Bellas Artes 6 (Nov./Dec. 1965): 5-22.

———. *I Too Speak of the Rose.* Oliver translation. George Woodyard, ed., *The Modern Stage in Latin America: Six Plays.* New York: E. P. Dutton, 1971.

OTHER WORKS CITED

Artaud, Antonin. *Artaud Anthology,* ed. Jack Hirschman. San Francisco: City Lights Books, 1965.

———. *México y Viaje al país de los Tarahumaras,* prologue by Luis Mario Schneider (Mexico City: Fondo de Cultura Económica, 1984).

———. *The Theater and Its Double.* Trans. Mary Caroline Richards. New York: Grove Press, 1958.

Bober, M. M. *Karl Marx's Interpretation of History.* New York: Norton, 1965.

Brecht, Bertolt. *Brecht on Theatre: The Development of an Aesthetic.* Trans. John Willett. New York: Hill & Wang, 1957; 1964.

Cooper, J. C. *An Illustrated Encyclopedia of Traditional Symbols.* London: Thames & Hudson, 1984.

Cypess, Sandra Messinger. "I, Too, Speak: 'Female' Discourse in Carballido's Plays." *Latin American Theatre Review,* 18, no. 1 (Fall 1984): 45-52.

Davis, Harold Eugene. *Latin American Thought: A Historical Introduction.* Baton Rouge: Louisiana State Univ. Press, 1972.

Dirlik, Arif. "Culturism as Hegemonic Ideology and Liberating Practice." *Cultural Critique,* 6 (Spring 1987): 13-50.

Eliade, Mircea. *The Sacred and the Profane.* Trans. William R. Trask. New York: Harcourt Brace Jovanovich, 1959.

Féral, Josette. "Writing and Displacement: Women in Theatre." Trans. Barbara Kerslake. *Modern Drama* 27, no. 4 (1984): 549-63.

Foucault, Michel. *Power/Knowledge.* Trans. Colin Gordon, Leo Marshall, John Mepham, and Kate Soper. New York: Panther, 1980.

Franco, Jean. "Dependency Theory and Literary History: The Case of Latin America." *Minnesota Review* 5 (1975): 65-80.

Geertz, Clifford. *Local Knowledge.* New York: Basic Books. 1983.

Graham, R. B. Cunninghame. *Selected Writings of Cunninghame Graham.* Cedric Watts, ed. East Brunswick, N.J.: Associated Univ. Presses, 1981.

Kerr, R. A. "La función de la Intermediaria en *Yo también hablo de la rosa.*" *Latin American Theatre Review* 12, no. 2 (1978): 51-60.

Levinas, Emmanuel. *Totality and Infinity.* Trans. Alphonso Lingis. Pittsburgh, Pa.: Duquesne Univ. Press, 1979.

Lowe, Donald M. *History of Bourgeois Perception.* Chicago: Univ. of Chicago Press, 1982.

Ong, Walter J. *Orality and Literacy: The Technologizing of the Word.* London: Methuen, 1984.

Quigley, Austin E. *The Modern Stage and Other Worlds.* London: Methuen, 1985.

Rama, Angel. *Transculturación narrativa en América Latina.* Mexico City: Siglo XXI, 1982.

Ricoeur, Paul. *History and Truth.* Trans. Charles A. Kelbley. Evanston, Ill.: Northwestern Univ. Press, 1965.

Said, Edward W. *The World, the Text, and the Critic.* Cambridge, Mass.: Harvard Univ. Press, 1983.

Sangari, Kumkum. "The Politics of the Possible." *Cultural Critique* 7 (Fall 1987): 157-86.

Sartre, Jean-Paul. *Being and Nothingness.* Trans. Hazel E. Barnes. New York: Washington Square Press, 1969.

Sontag, Susan. *Against Interpretation.* New York: Dell, 1966.

Vansina, Jan. *Oral Tradition as History.* Madison: Univ. of Wisconsin Press, 1985.

Vásquez Amaral, Mary. *El teatro de Emilio Carballido (1950-1965)*. Mexico City: 1974.

Vélez, Joseph F. "Una entrevista con Emilio Carballido." *Latin American Theatre Review* 7 (Fall 1973): 17-24.

Weber, Carl. "AC/TC: Currents of Theatrical Exchange." *Performing Arts Journal* 33/34 (1989): 11-21.

White, Hayden. *Tropics of Discourse*. Baltimore, Md.: Johns Hopkins Univ. Press, 1986.

Matthew Tremé (essay date 2013)

SOURCE: Tremé, Matthew. "The Beginnings, Means, and Ends of Interpretation in *Yo también hablo de la rosa*." *Latin American Theatre Review* 46.2 (2013): 25-38. Print.

[*In the following essay, Tremé demonstrates how Carballido's handling of dramatic style and structure in* I Too Speak of the Rose *reinforces the play's main themes and supports the author's "central preoccupation with the impossibility of imposing any one master narrative."*]

Any essay on Emilio Carballido's play **Yo también hablo de la rosa** would necessarily have to be a dialogue not just with the work itself, but also with the many different interpretations that have been posited over the years by various literary critics. This situation, far from being in any way an imposition, is actually quite apropos in the context of the play itself and in light of the multiple interpretations that have been generated since its debut. The central theme of this work, as has been repeated time and again and which it is not my intention to refute here, at least not in its entirety, is the way in which any action can be framed by multiple interpretative discourses that seek to claim or uncover its ontologically inherent "truth." Even the most cursory analysis of this play could discover the failings of any claim to a so-called objective revealing of the ardently sought truth or reason behind the derailment caused by Polo and Toña. My intention, then, is not to enter into this non-debate about why they placed a tub of concrete on the train tracks. To clarify, the term non-debate characterizes this aspect of the play not because no serious concerns are at issue here, but because of the work's central preoccupation with the impossibility of imposing any one master narrative, as Jacqueline Bixler points out in her book on Carballido, and thus the impossibility of definitively answering the question of why the children committed this deed. Rather than speculate further about why this tragic action was performed by these two children, this essay explores the ways in which the dramatic structure of the play, as assembled by the dramatist himself and opposed to the often identified Medium-as-narrator character, constitutes a fusion of the acts of creation and interpretation, one which underscores the work as a whole and has important repercussions for our understanding of the interpretative acts that are so salient in the analysis of this play. We shall see how the perception generated by and within this play is directly tied to its narrative modality as a dramatic work of art and the questions of representation that consequently arise from this confluence of genres.

Beginning as Locus of Interpretation

Although it is true that the events are minimal and in fact it could even be affirmed that there is only one action that occurs in this play (i.e. the derailment of the train), it is suggestive that the train wreck occupies a space of non-interpretation. There is no exhaustive reflection, either by the play's characters or its critics, on the consequences of this action in and of itself, which is to say that it is generally accepted to be simply a trigger for an interpretative act that looks for reasons and causes, not outcomes. In other words, it is an artistic mechanism that unleashes the representation of a series of narrative nodes that chronologically precede it and which, although they endow it with meaning, are themselves taken to be more meaningful. Rather than being seen as an event worthy of analysis, its worth resides in its ability to conjure up the events that lead up to it, specifically as represented in the four different versions of Polo and Toña's morning. The train wreck, which is represented five times in the play, is loaded with force not because of what it means, but because of what the events that precipitate it mean. As Bert States describes, therein lies the allure of theater:

> In short, the deep appeal of drama, as the art of catastrophe, is that behind anything you *do* or *are* at a particular moment stands the causal pyramid of your life—all its choices, givens, accidents, mistakes—and, it turns out, the causal pyramids of everyone with whom you have crossed paths. Your *now* is the product of a unique lifetime of *thens* and *others*.
>
> (63-64)

So, if behind every great catastrophe on stage there is a chain of factors both causal and accidental leading to it, the critical interest in the four versions of Polo and Toña's story in **Yo también hablo de la rosa** can certainly be explained as the need to define and analyze this pyramid described by States and whose broad base offers a much larger field of play than its narrow top.

In many ways, then, this play is a reflection on beginnings. The questions of beginnings and ends and how to get from one to the other, and in what direction and with what consequences, permeate the entire work. As we shall see, many more beginnings are implied than just those represented in the four versions of the derailment's antecedents. For example, if we were to search for the first of the many types of beginnings present here, we would logically have to begin with the title, which is the formal beginning of any text, and which, in this case, is directly followed by the playwright's classification of his play as a *loa*. The title evokes a verbal act, which could be one of narration or interpretation and is clearly a response to some other speech act that precedes it.

The ambiguity of this title (Who is this "I"? What does he or she say about the rose? Who else has spoken about the rose "too"?) speaks volumes to us about the play that follows. It posits from the beginning of **Rosa** [*Yo también hablo de la rosa*] as written text or staged representation the importance, and the inherent difficulty, of fixing a beginning, which, as Edward Said states, "is by no means a simple proposition, since in choosing a beginning [an author] confers upon it a certain status based on its ability to intend the whole of what follows from it" (50). In this case, the title, as the threshold or entrance to the play, stands in stark contrast to its immediately subsequent classification as a *loa,* which was a Golden Age prologue, usually in the form of praise in verse and preceding a comedy. So, from the title, which is the formal beginning of any work, and in this case is some sort of reference to dueling, oblique, and sequential narrations or interpretations whose specific content is neither here nor there and whose referenciality, furthermore, points to a moment *in media res* (which, as Said points out, is a beginning with the burden of the pretense that it is not one), we pass to the definition of the play as a whole as a prologue, a beginning before the true beginning of the real show. This formal aperture of the play places in the foreground the problematical nature of beginnings, middles, and ends and clearly merits a deeper analysis.

This preoccupation with beginnings goes on to manifest itself in the formal structuring of the play. As has been previously stated, the train wreck is represented five times in the play, once after the Medium's introductory monologue and then in each of the four versions of Polo and Toña's actions. Strikingly, the first representation of the derailment breaks with a strictly chronological presentation of events by preceding its own causes and antecedents. By structuring his play so, Carballido deprives the derailment of the privileged status to which it could lay claim as the climax (or in Aristotelian terms, the peripety or sudden reversal of fortune) in a more linear presentation. In breaking with a more explicitly realist style of chronological unfolding of events, the dramatist exposes the presence of formal manipulation in the creation of his drama, in this case emphasizing the importance of beginnings in any tale even though, and in this example specifically because, they are not presented chronologically.

Before examining more fully the consequences of the playwright's conscious decision to put the would-be climax first, a further analysis of exactly what a beginning is and why and how it is important is in order. In his book on this subject, titled *Beginnings,* Edward Said studies this concept from many different perspectives, be it an author's intention as that which precedes the actual act of writing, or in the work of art itself as that which commences, opens, or serves as the point of departure. Regardless of whether we are speaking about textual or pre- or extra-textual beginnings, the designation of a beginning as such can only be made retrospectively and is made to specifically "designate, clarify or define a *later* time, place or action" (5).

That being said, the force of a beginning radiates from its two defining attributes: it is powerful because it comes first and because something important happens at a later junction of time or space that makes it relevant now. Moreover, it is endowed with force precisely by these pressing conditions of the present, as Said states:

> For one rarely searches for beginnings unless the present matters a great deal; this is as true of comedy as of tragedy. It is my present urgency, the here and now, that will enable me to establish the sequence of beginning-middle-end and to transform it from a distant object—located 'there'— into the subject of my reasoning. So conceived and fashioned, time and space yield a sequence authorized by a wish for either immanent or surface significance.

> (42)

This act of naming as such a beginning, which is notably located in the past, from the distant or even not-so-distant present is temporally framed by a representational process; any notion of beginning is a fictional construct. In this regard, Said identifies it as "the first step in the intentional production of meaning" (5). That is to say, it is an interpretative action that by definition projects itself in such a way that it necessarily implies a hierarchization or valorization of an action, whether tragic or comedic, and its antecedents. In *Yo también hablo de la rosa,* then, its narrative structure is a hermeneutic gesture; it is in no way casual that Carballido presents the end before the beginning. So, even though Margaret Sayers Peden states that "the play is not about the train wreck" (50), maybe, in a way, it is. On the one hand, placing it first is part of a narrative strategy whose nonconsecutive organization will condition our interest in Polo and Toña's story and will predispose us to underscore those elements that will explain the outcome that we have already witnessed. On the other hand, the fact that we will approach everything that follows (or, viewed chronologically, precedes) with the full knowledge that it will be important predisposes us to look for meaning where we would have perhaps only done so retrospectively. Although the author has inverted the order of events, the beginning, as Said states, will continue to be the most fertile raw material for the discovery of the densest nodes of meaning and, consequently, of interpretation.

But let's take this idea one step further: in Carballido's play, the top of States' pyramid of concatenation of events (the derailment) is the narrative beginning of the drama, the place from which every interpretative gesture and all search for cause and meaning is derived. Hence, here the narrative beginning of the play, and not the causal origins of the derailment, becomes important as the first act of interpretation. The former is, in reality, the beginning of all hermeneutic causality, not only of the interpretations generated in the play by its myriad of characters, who like the spectator look for cause after becoming aware of the derailment, but also of those elaborated by the play's critics. In other words, by being presented first, the end is made the beginning; what Said claims we cannot select or discard, this urgency of the present, has been claimed as a beginning by the author. This was a choice that was made for, not by, us; it is the one element that throughout the play neither changes nor is reinterpreted. This fictional construction of the end-as-beginning, this creative act of the playwright as artist, makes another statement about beginnings that in a certain way coincides with the criticism that this play has generally generated: discourse can be willfully manipulated to produce a desired effect, in this case to spark the multiple hypotheses made about this action.

BETWEEN NARRATION AND DRAMATIZATION

As Jacqueline Bixler astutely points out, *Yo también hablo de la rosa* is a play that defies generic categorization; nevertheless, approaching it as a tragedy in the Aristotelian sense can be helpful to see how its dramatic structure is intimately tied to my claim here that interpretation is cardinally generated in the formal structure laid down by its author. Bert States, in *The Pleasure of the Play,* a contemporary re-reading of tragedy, starts with the premise that mimesis in tragedy is the imitation of an action, which he defines as "any sequence of events which is complete and whole (with a beginning, a middle, and an end) and possesses a certain magnitude" (59). For our purposes here, the question that arises is that of what, then, would be the action imitated by this play. I hold that it cannot be the train wreck per se, because if we accept that Aristotle's "main point about [an action] is that it should represent a single change to good or bad fortune" (58), the effects of the derailment are far too ambiguous, and indeed largely too ignored, to be what this play is "about." It is too unclear what, if any, punishment is meted out to the children as a result of their action. But, as I hinted at above, in a way the play *is* about the train wreck, albeit in a roundabout one. The rearranging of the beginning, middle, and end, together with the infusion of certain narrative qualities (i.e. flashforward or flashback; temporal and spatial jumps that today we would refer to as cinematic) in the dramatic structure of the play, point us in another direction than the one indicated by the surface plot of this drama.

The tragic plot, with its peripety and subsequent recognition, traditionally moves in such a way that the action is dictated by complication and then its denouement, all the while defined by its likelihood, as States calls it, which is to say its probability within the range of all possible human actions. According to States, the recognition, or unconcealment as he labels it, is the central component of action: "Unconcealment is a continuous process in the play, for even when things seem to be more in doubt, more questionable, the play is moving, however obliquely, toward its master unconcealment, and this unconcealment is what gives force and depth to all dramatic speech" (66-67). With the reordering of these two key components in *Rosa* and its presentation of the denouement before its

complication, the telling of events, and not the events themselves, becomes the central object of dramatic action. By breaking the conventional rhythm of plot, the play comes to be about not the story of the derailment, but rather how that story is told. As we have seen, it is about how the telling of a story can have an embedded interpretation.

By placing the spectator in a position where the outcome is known from the outset, Carballido situates us somewhere between mimesis and diegesis, between drama and narrative. On this matter, John Kronik writes:

> In brief, dramatic representation ostensibly involves no description, no commentary, no point of view, no frame, no inside and outside, no shifts of perspective. Stated another way, the difference between drama and narration is the difference between experience and the reflection on experience, between present event and past time, between immediacy and mediation, between a tale that tells itself and a story that has a storyteller.

(26)

Being placed somewhere in between these genres is somewhat uncomfortable for the spectator, as the direct and unmediated world created by classical drama offered a stable representation of an action that is notably absent here. In his article, Kronik analyzes this "mixing of modes" in several Latin American plays, concluding that a heightened narrative component in a drama creates a metatheatrical dimension that destabilizes the position of the spectator. Laid bare the craft behind the onstage representation, the mimetic illusion breaks down and forces the spectator to recognize the artifice that produces it. The spectator is no longer watching "something," but rather something "about" something.

These preliminary observations on the play between mimetic and narrative representation can lead us to approach *Rosa* in the light of what States posits as "the question of how it is that mimesis can be an end in itself and adapt itself to other ends as well" (16). To do so, we shall now turn to the four versions of the derailment's antecedents.

TRUTH ACCORDING TO VERSION

The repetition of the initial scene in which Polo and Toña appear—the beginnings of the derailment as it were—as employed has a distinct discursive quality that allows us to reflect on the ways in which a story can be told and what that telling means. These four versions have been examined by almost every critic of the play, but generally taking into account their function as discourses of interpretation, separated from the narrative or representational questions that they put in tension and which will be the subject of our interest here. While it is true that the competition between the versions is nothing less than a battle in which each tries to impose its view as superior to the others, nevertheless, they all share a common characteristic: they are positioned somewhere between drama and narration, between action and reflection as proffered by Kronik, with consequences that we will now examine.

Any analysis of the four versions should naturally begin with the first one. It is generally granted ontological supremacy over the other versions, probably because it comes first in the play and it wears a mask of authenticity. The natural, we could even say realist, language that the children use here contrasts sharply with the obvious manipulation and codification of their language in the subsequent versions and makes it figure as the "real" story, the one against which all other versions must be judged. Moreover, the absence of an obvious, internal narrator framing the onstage action markedly bolsters the idea that this first version is the original enactment of how events played out on that fateful morning. This lack of narrative framing combined with the manifest absence of the veneers of interpretation that characterize the three reenactments is a dramatic sleight of hand meant to coerce spectators into believing that they are one step closer to the action. Frank Dauster goes so far as to claim that we witness this first version of events exactly how it happened (*Ensayos* 176), while Priscilla Meléndez grants it primacy by referring to the "triple recreation" that it spawns and which consists of re-reading incidents that we have already witnessed (313). Diana Taylor, likewise, gives the first version a free pass; that is to say, she also exempts it from critical scrutiny: "In terms of time and staging devices, however, three perspectives claim preeminence. They are juxtaposed as three perceptual hypotheses during the Emcee's game show, and they correspond to the epistemic positions of the Freudian, the Marxist, and the Medium respectively" (165).

But, if we agree with Said's claim that the designation of a beginning is by definition a heuristic act of election (of selecting and discarding), we must accept that this first version has also gone through a process of interpretation, even though it tries to hide the machinery that has been employed in its creation. We could say that its perspective, in part, corresponds to the epistemic position of the artist. We do not view the morning in its entirety, in real time; after a blackout Polo and Toña reappear onstage, at the dump that is the site of the accident. The implication is that the dramatist as storyteller must have left out details, because he judged them to be either unimportant or cumbersome. Either way, this cannot be a neutral or transparent version of Polo and Toña's actions, however much it may seem so when we compare it to the versions proffered by the Professors and the Medium. Indeed, this is the trap that it sets. It is not present to serve entirely or exclusively as an objective contrast to the other three versions, although it does, in part, fulfill that function, but with a few important caveats.

To begin, the spectator's appreciation of this version is conditioned by the playwright's authorial gesture of put-

ting the derailment before the events that lead up to it, establishing a field of play that has been consciously and conspicuously manipulated. We can assume that when the peripheral characters (i.e. the newsboy, the teacher, the university students, the parents, etc.) speak of the accident and speculate about its causes, they do so knowing that it has happened (in the past) and thus do so retrospectively. In order to put spectators in the characters' position, which is to say, in a position from which we too can retroactively find meaning in the derailment, Carballido gives us the accident first, so we approach it just like all of the characters who read about it in the paper or hear about it secondhand. We, and they, know the event through its outcome first. For this reason, the first representation cannot be neutral. We know where it is going to finish, so we ask ourselves what the importance of each action is as we watch. We are no less guilty of seeing causality in these beginnings than the Professors or the Medium, and, arguably, no less right or wrong.

Moreover, this first version is deceptive precisely because it appears to be purely mimetic. Its naturalness and, more importantly, its likelihood within the range of possible human actions stabilize its representation for the spectator. We can enjoy it because it lulls us into believing that what we see is what we get. As Priscilla Meléndez states, we get a representation that does not appear to be tinged by ulterior motives; it is primarily descriptive (313). The other three versions, which are striking because they are reenactments and as such challenge what we may have naively seen and accepted as truth, put the narrative dimension of the drama in the foreground by employing other characters as onstage narrators. These scenes are startling because we have made assumptions or interpretations based on the first version that we saw; we don't expect the children to act like this, and they are obviously acting. Gone is the natural air of the first version; Polo and Toña are obviously taking direction and reading from a script as characters, not just as actors.

Here Carballido achieves the destabilization of spectatorship alluded to by Kronik and brought about by the surfacing of a metatheatrical dimension to his play. The ironic use of Freudian or Marxist discourse in the Professors' versions and the cryptic, mystic discourse in the Medium's version draw our attention to the fact that we are no longer watching "something"; we are watching something "about" something. The spectator cannot watch passively; we must make an attempt to get to the bottom of why these scenes are being re-represented and why they have changed.

Ultimately, the only way to reconcile these four disparate versions of the derailment's beginnings is to link them to the greater concerns of artistic creation and interpretation that are central to the work at large. Tellingly, the Professors and the Medium frame the original version not through an analytical discourse per se but through a restaging of the initial story, returning us to our initial observations here about text reception as interpretation versus the interpretation implied and embedded in artistic creation. In all three re-enactments, the onstage representation breaks down; the foregrounding of the narrative retelling of the initial scene, with an onstage director/narrator no less, produces an estrangement with the realization that the characters are acting. The central theme put forth is that the telling of any story can be manipulated as a means to an end, whether we are aware of it or not. Let us consider as an example this dialogue in the first version between Polo and Toña, after he has given all of their money to the Scavenger:

Toña:

>   ¿Le diste todo?

Polo:

>   Pues sí.

Toña:

>   ¡Te pidió un quintito! Ay, qué tarugo.

Polo:

>   ¡Pues, tú dijiste que le diera!

Toña:

>   Pero no todo. Te pidió un quintito.

Polo:

>   Loca y además coda.

(Carballido, *Yo también* [*Yo también hablo de la rosa*] 139)

In the restaging directed by the Marxist Professor, there is no mention whatsoever of this exchange. The Freudian Professor prefaces his scene by stating that certain antecedent factors will allow him to present his explanation, the implication being that he will select what is most suitable and will discard that which is not convenient. We can assume that this preamble applies also to the Marxist, whose scene follows the Freudian Professor, and that he leaves out this dialogue purposefully, as it undermines the whole idea of class solidarity that is the basis of his rationalization of the derailment. This omnipresent suggestion, that underlying any act of creation or enunciation can be found a process of selection and exclusion, finds other, less subtle, manifestations in the play, such as when the Teacher reads to Polo's classmates:

>   (*Lee.*) Los delincuentes juveniles quedaron inmóviles junto a la vía, viendo su obra. Fueron capturados fácilmente. (*Asiente, busca otro trozo ejemplar.*) Debe culparse también al abandono de los padres (*Asiente.*) que dejan a sus hijos entregados a la vagancia, y al descuido de los maes ... (*Calla. Dobla el periódico.*) Pues ya lo saben, eso pasó.

(146)

She only partially replicates her source material, manipulating its content as need be. Her reading of the newspaper for her class is metonymical of the play as a whole, of the ways in which knowledge is generated and received, extracted and manipulated to all kinds of ends. And as with the three reenactments, here the gaze of the spectator is drawn to the storyteller and not the story. By being made completely visible, the interpretative filter of narration as reflection makes us take pause by distancing us from the show on stage and requiring us to decide which, if any, of these dueling versions of the same event can speak some truth to us.

How to End

Since we started with beginnings, it is only fitting that we should end with endings. As Edward Said states, the beginning implies the end, so any analysis of beginnings and their means must include their ends. In our effort here to see intention in method, we have seen several instances of ends defined as objectives or aims. The end of the multiple reenactments, as we have just seen, is to reveal how the interplay of representation and narration can destabilize the play's mimetic illusion through their rivalry, thus making a statement about truth and deception in art. Another example of ends would be Carballido's putting the ending first to foist upon us the recognition that everything that followed would therefore be important.

However, I do not mean to end with this type of end. Rather, we shall examine the end as conclusion, as that which closes, for as much as *Yo también hablo de la rosa* is about beginnings, it is also about endings. The circular structure of the play leaves us without the classical tying up of all of the loose ends. The Medium, whose reenactment brings the play to a close but does not necessarily close the story of Polo and Toña, teases the spectator with the end that she knows we want, but she does not give it to us: "(*A gritos.*) ¿Saben cómo muy pronto sucedió un cambio sorprendente? ¿Y saben cómo Polo llegó a instalar un taller? ¿Y cómo fue el matrimonio de Toña? [...] Ésa ... ya es otra historia" (174-75). These words resonate because we have heard them before, at the end of the Medium's third monologue, which is the story of the two brothers who had the same dream: "(*Empieza a retirarse. Casi al salir se vuelve.*) ¿Y saben lo que pasó con el terreno que los dos hombres desmontaron y limpiaron para bailar? (*Calla. Ve a todos. Semisonríe con malicia.*) Ésa ya es otra historia. (*Sale rápidamente.*)" (152-53). In both of these cases, our desire for a neat ending to the story is frustrated by the Medium, whose malicious smile in the first instance and dramatic pause in the second show just how consciously she is toying with us. The story of the brothers seems strange to us, like an odd puzzle whose presence in the play is disconcerting. Interestingly, both Roy Kerr and Priscilla Meléndez, in their respective articles on this play, point out the need to "decipher" the puzzle of the Medium's third monologue, the former noting that neither the brothers nor the spectators can manage to find a logical answer and the latter going so far as to affirm that "[l]a inserción de esta narración tiene como base el acto de descifrarla, es decir, de interpretarla tanto en términos de los propios soñadores como de su pertinencia—si hay alguna—en el drama" (311).

Let us take up this common thread sustained by both critics—that this story demands an interpretation—and furthermore, the idea that its inclusion in the play must also be accounted for somehow, although Meléndez herself seems skeptical of this proposition. In light of all of our reflection here on the question of interpretation's beginnings, means, and ends, obviously it is not much of a stretch to say that the story's insertion in this drama is just one more part of the puzzle that is constructed by the manipulation of form in the telling of a tale. These demands that the story and its presence in the drama be explained are intimately tied to one explicit, troublesome fact: this story (and, ultimately, the play itself) has no ending. The Medium recognizes the power she holds as a storyteller by waiting until she is almost offstage to address our eagerness to know what happens to the brothers. If their tale is mind-boggling to the spectator, it is precisely because she does not tell us how it ends. Without the end, without States' master unconcealment of the plot, we do not know what importance to grant to the details that have been narrated by the Medium and pantomimed by the dancers. We are left with nothing but questions. Is it important that the brothers could have been twins or maybe not even brothers at all, just two friends? What importance does the fact that it is physically impossible for the two brothers to be present at the same time in each other's house have? Is the solution that they have found adequate? If not, what are its consequences?

Without Aristotle's peripety and recognition, we can make neither head nor tail of this story, and maybe that is just its point. If we are angry with the Medium for teasing us by dangling resolution before us, it is because what she is withholding is not another story, but rather the end of this one. Without a conclusion, without Said's pressing urgency of the now that authorizes the beginning, the tale of the two brothers is bereft of all meaning. Inasmuch as a beginning only has meaning endowed by the end that it precipitates, any attempt to interpret the significance of the brothers' actions is doomed to failure because we cannot know what they mean if we do not know where they lead. The same also holds true for the Medium's bestiary. Why does she describe a seemingly random list of animals and their characteristics? Are the specific animals that she has chosen somehow relevant to Polo and Toña's situation? Does the order in which they are presented matter? How is this bestiary in any way relevant to the play? Clearly Carballido is trying to push us into explaining what cannot be explained. The bestiary seems to point to a hyperactive search for meaning that can be juxtaposed neatly against the story of the brothers and the ways in which it prods us

to uncover its hidden meaning. Ultimately, the Medium's allusions to the various versions that exist of the brothers' story come to nothing, because with no conclusion it is impossible to ascertain the value of their possible discrepancies. Consequently, here we have the opposite of Carballido's putting the end first at the play's opening; just as the author can rearrange his drama's plot to impose interpretation on and by us as we have seen, so too can he impede it through willful manipulation. Then, as much as the brothers' tale is about what Meléndez calls the inconclusive and the absence of answers (312), it is also about the inseparability of beginnings and endings.

THE CURTAIN FALLS

In the end, there is no real denouement in *Yo también hablo de la rosa,* no master unconcealment, no untying of the knots tied by the plot. Indeed, if it were not for the progressively ordered choreography of the dance and the ever brightening lights that accompany it, the end would be wholly anti-climactic. In spite of the fact that the Medium tempts us with hints sprinkled here and there and although the curtain does ultimately fall, the play does not really have an end. It goes back to the beginning and ends with yet another version of the beginning, the Medium's reenactment. We do at least get to the end that she hinted at in her first monologue: "si todos los corazones sonaran en voz alta . . . Pero de eso no hay que hablar todavía" (129). At the curtain, the growing light, like pulsating heartbeats, returns us to the beginning and leaves the mystery of life, whose end cannot be known, unsolved.

This enigmatic state of affairs at the close can be reconciled with our experience as spectators by taking into account the position sustained here that this play is not really about Polo and Toña's story in and of itself. *Yo también hablo de la rosa* is, as countless critics have pointed out, about interpretation and how it can be willfully manipulative and must necessarily be partial. I am certainly as guilty as everyone else for selecting what I wanted to discuss and leaving out the rest. But as we have seen, interpretation is not just a function of reception; it can likewise be embedded in the gestation and transmission of art. For this very reason, any apparent transparency that a story may purport or be purported to have is a sham, as fictional as the story is as the imitation of an action. There is always manipulation of the raw material from which any story is constructed. Consequently, truth becomes a function of representation, be it dramatic or narrative. It is a fictional construct, which is to say that actions cannot reveal truths; only through their telling can a claim of truth be offered or postulated.

Works Consulted

Bixler, Jacqueline E. *Convention and Transgression: The Theatre of Emilio Carballido.* Lewisburg, PA: Bucknell UP, 1997. Print.

Carballido, Emilio. *I Too Speak of the Rose*. Trans. William I. Oliver. *Drama and Theatre* 8.1 (Fall 1969): 47-60. Print.

———. *Yo también hablo de la rosa. 9 dramaturgos hispanoamericanos*. Vol. 3. Ed. Frank Dauster, Leon Lyday, and George Woodyard. Ottawa: Girol Books, 1983. Print.

Cypess, Sandra Messinger. "I, Too, Speak: 'Female' Discourse in Carballido's Plays." *Latin American Theatre Review* 18.1 (1984): 45-53. Print.

Dauster, Frank. "Carballido y el teatro de la liberación." *Alba de América* 7.12-13 (1989): 205-20. Print.

———. *Ensayos sobre teatro hispanoamericano*. Mexico: SepSetentas, 1975. Print.

Kerr, Roy. "La función de la Intermediaria en *Yo también hablo de la rosa*." *Latin American Theatre Review* 12.1 (1978): 51-60. Print.

Kronik, John. "Invasions from Outer Space: Narration and Dramatic Art in Spanish America." *Latin American Theatre Review* 26.2 (1993): 25-48. Print.

Mélendez, Priscilla. "La interpretación como metáfora o la metáfora de la interpretación." *Alba de América* 7.12-13 (1989): 305-17. Print.

Peden, Margaret Sayers. *Emilio Carballido*. Boston: Twayne, 1980. Print.

Said, Edward W. *Beginnings. Intention and Method*. New York: Columbia UP, 1985. Print.

Skinner, Eugene R. "The Theater of Emilio Carballido: Spinning a Web." *Dramatists in Revolt*. Ed. Leon F. Lyday and George Woodyard. Austin: U of Texas P, 1976. 19-36. Print.

States, Bert O. *The Pleasure of the Play*. Ithaca, NY: Cornell UP, 1994. Print.

Taylor, Diana. "Theatre and Transculturation: Emilio Carballido." *Theatre of Crisis: Drama and Politics in Latin America*. Lexington: UP of Kentucky, 1991. 148-80. Print.

Vázquez-Amaral, Mary. "*Yo también hablo de la rosa* de Emilio Carballido. Un estudio crítico." *Revista de la Universidad de México* 27.5 (1973): 25-9. Print.

Vélez, Joseph F. "Una entrevista con Emilio Carballido." *Latin American Theatre Review* 7.1 (1973): 17-24. Print.

FURTHER READING

Bibliographies

De Toro, Fernando, and Peter Roster. "Carballido, Emilio." *Bibliografía del teatro hispanoamericano contemporáneo (1900-1980)*. Vol. 1. Frankfurt: Verlag Klaus Dieter Vervuert, 1985. 60-4. Print.
    Provides a useful bibliography of Carballido's dramatic work up to 1980. Not available in English.

Peden, Margaret Sayers. "Emilio Carballido, curriculum operum." *Latin American Theatre Review* 1.1 (1967): 38-49. Print.
    Offers a chronological listing of Carballido's work up to 1967.

Biographies

Bixler, Jacqueline E. *Convention and Transgression: The Theatre of Emilio Carballido*. Lewisburg: Bucknell UP, 1997. Print.
    Studies the evolution of Carballido's theatrical works over several decades. Bixler includes a bibliography of published and unpublished plays, as well as secondary works.

Peden, Margaret Sayers. *Emilio Carballido*. Boston: Twayne, 1980. Print.
    Addresses Carballido's theatrical works, short stories, and prose fiction written before 1977.

Criticism

Bixler, Jacqueline Eyring. "Freedom and Fantasy: A Structural Approach to the Fantastic in Carballido's *Las cartas de Mozart*." *Latin American Theatre Review* 14.1 (1980): 15-23. Print.
    Considers *The Mozart Letters* in terms of Tzvetan Todorov's theory of the literary fantastic.

———. "A Theatre of Contradictions: The Recent Works of Emilio Carballido." *Latin American Theatre Review* 18.2 (1985): 57-65. Print.
    Argues that, for Carballido, audience participation is essential in establishing a link between a play's various levels of fantasy and reality.

Cypess, Sandra Messinger. "Changing Configurations of Power from the Perspective of Mexican Drama." *Ideologies and Literature* 2.2 (1987): 109-23. Print.
    Assesses the power struggle in Carballido's play *Ceremonia en el templo del tigre* (1985; may be translated as *Ceremony in the Temple of the Tiger*) as constituting both national and international players who seek to undermine hierarchical and authoritarian societies.

Dauster, Frank. "*Fotografía en la playa: Rosalba* Thirty Years Later." *In Retrospect: Essays on Latin American Literature (in Memory of Willis Knapp Jones).* Ed. Elizabeth S. Rogers and Timothy J. Rogers. York: Spanish Lit., 1987. 115-20. Print.

> Questions categorization by earlier critics of Carballido's *Photograph on the Beach* and *Rosalba and the Llavero Family* as "realistic" and re-examines the plays in order to account for their unrealistic elements.

Moretta, Eugene L. "Spanish American Theatre of the 50's and 60's: Critical Perspectives on Role Playing." *Latin American Theatre Review* 13.2 (1980): 5-30. Print.

> Analyzes role-playing in Carballido's play *Medusa* as a means of personal denial of the protagonist's twentieth-century reality. Moretta explores the use of role-playing in *Medusa* together with other Latin American plays.

Peden, Margaret S. "Theory and Practice in Artaud and Carballido." *Modern Drama* 11.2 (1968): 132-42. Print.

> Discusses how Carballido's plays typify French dramatist Antonin Artaud's notion of "total theater," in which reality and fantasy mingle, special effects abound, and language is more important than character or action.

Taylor, Diana. "Mad World, Mad Hope: Carballido's *El día que se soltaron los leones.*" *Latin American Theatre Review* 20.2 (1987): 67-76. Print.

> Proposes Carballido's seemingly "frivolous" play *The Day They Let the Lions Loose* as a serious piece that poses social, political, and philosophical questions and concerns.

Additional information on Carballido's life and works is contained in the following sources published by Gale: *Contemporary Authors,* **Vols. 33-36R;** *Contemporary Authors New Revision Series,* **Vols. 54, 87;** *Contemporary World Writers,* **Ed. 2;** *Dictionary of Literary Biography,* **Vol. 305;** *Drama for Students,* **Vol. 4;** *Encyclopedia of World Literature in the 20th Century,* **Ed. 3;** *Hispanic Writers,* **Ed. 1;** *Latin American Writers***; and** *Literature Resource Center.*

Juan José Millás
1946-

Spanish novelist, novella and short-story writer, essayist, and journalist.

INTRODUCTION

Juan José Millás's fiction explores such themes as identity formation, the perception and manipulation of reality, and the role of writing in making sense of modern life. A member of the Generation of 1968—a group of Spanish authors that also includes Luis Goytisolo, Eduardo Mendoza, Rosa Montero, and Julio Llamazares—Millás reacted against social realism, which downplayed literary form to promote political and social goals. In addition to writing novels, novellas, and short stories, Millás is a journalist and a television and radio host. Commentators have praised his inventiveness, experimentation, and distinctive combination of journalism and fiction.

BIOGRAPHICAL INFORMATION

Millás was born on 31 January 1946 in Valencia, Spain, the fourth of nine children of Vicente Millás and Candida García Millás. The family moved to Madrid in 1952 and settled in the working-class suburb of Prosperidad. Millás attended local schools and later studied philosophy and literature at the Universidad Complutense de Madrid, working at a post office to support himself. Finding the university too politically conservative and old-fashioned, he dropped out and dedicated his free time to independent reading and writing. His first published work, the novella *Cerbero son las sombras* (1975; may be translated as *Cerberus Are the Shadows*), won the 1974 Sésamo Prize. With the novel *El desorden de tu nombre* (1988; published as *The Disorder of Your Name*), he became a best-selling author.

Millás's other accolades include the prestigious Nadal Prize for his novel *La soledad era esto* (1990; published as *That Was Loneliness*); the 2002 Primavera Award for *Dos mujeres en Praga* (2002; may be translated as *Two Women in Prague*); the Francisco Cerecedo Prize for journalism in 2005; the 2007 Planet Prize for *El mundo* (2007; may be translated as *The World*), a metafictional novel about Millás's relocation to Madrid during his childhood; and the 2008 National Novel Prize. He has received honorary degrees from the Universidad de Turín and the Universidad de Oviedo. The author of a weekly newspaper column in *El País* since the early 1990s, Millás is known for his "articuentos," short articles that combine elements of journalism

and short stories to comment on topics ranging from politics and social justice to popular culture. These works have been collected in *Articuentos* (2001) and *Articuentos completos* (2011; may be translated as *Complete Articuentos*). Millás's other collections of journalism include *María y Mercedes: Dos relatos sobre el trabajo y la vida familiar* (2005; may be translated as *María and Mercedes: Two Stories about Work and Family*) and *Todo son preguntas* (2005; may be translated as *All Are Questions*), in which he discusses photography. Millás hosts "La ventana," a radio show, and a weekly Spanish television program that focuses on word definitions. After his first marriage ended in divorce, Millás married psychologist Isabel Menéndez in 1987. He has two children and lives in Madrid.

MAJOR WORKS

Millás's early novels examine the aftermath of the Spanish Civil War. The anonymous narrator of *Cerberus Are the Shadows* lives in a grim basement apartment and tells the tragic story of his family's migration from a coastal town to a gloomy home in Madrid. The novel universalizes the family's alienation from society by offering few temporal, spatial, or historical parameters. *Visión del ahogado* (1977; may be translated as *Vision of the Drowned Man*) is set in Madrid in the 1960s and 1970s and traces the frantic flight of a man named Luis after he stabs a policeman at a subway stop. Luis is estranged from his wife, Julia, who is now living with his former friend, Jorge. Through flashbacks, the narrator gradually reveals Luis and Julia's violent sexual history. Millás creates parallels between the couple's degraded personal relationship and the social and political turmoil that affected a generation of Spaniards who lived through Francisco Franco's dictatorship, as well as between the police manhunt for Luis and each character's moral struggles. *El jardín vacío* (1981; may be translated as *The Empty Garden*) develops a similar correlation between personal and national memory. The novel follows a man obsessed with figuring out his true identity who decides to visit his senile mother. His wanderings through decaying Madrid streets in hopes of reconstructing his past recall Spain's efforts to unearth long-concealed truths about its Francoist history.

The Disorder of Your Name offers the first extensive treatment of one of Millás's trademark motifs, writing about writing. In this novel, Julio Orgaz—a divorced publishing executive and would-be writer—meets a woman named Laura in a park as he is leaving his psychoanalyst's office, and they fall in love. Laura turns out to be the wife of Julio's psychoanalyst, Carlos Rodó, whom they kill. Julio impedes the publication of a book of short stories by Orlando Azcárate, and fantasizes about murdering the gifted young writer and passing the book off as his own. He eventually begins writing by imagining a double who writes short stories. The novel concludes with one of these stories, "El desorden de tu nombre," which is revealed to be the main narrative. *That Was Loneliness* follows Elena Rincón, a bored, disconnected, middle-aged woman who smokes hashish and whose husband is cheating on her. Elena examines the diaries of her recently deceased mother and learns of various similarities between them. She also hires a private detective to spy on her husband. As she reads her mother's diaries and the detective's detailed reports, Elena begins to reevaluate and transform her life: she starts keeping her own diary, cuts back on smoking, leaves her husband, and asks the detective to report on her instead. Millás leaves the ending open to the possibility that Elena might succeed in recreating herself.

El orden alfabético (1998; may be translated as *The Alphabetical Order*) is a fantasy novel in which the young narrator, Julio, opposes his father by ignoring a cherished encyclopedia collection. His father warns Julio that if he does not read, all the books in their house will fly away, leaving the family without words. Julio discovers a secret realm where disappeared words go and travels back and forth between it and the real world. As all words begin to vanish, society grinds to a halt. When printed material begins to decompose and physical referents to ideas disappear, people have trouble communicating. In the second half of the novel, Julio is an adult obsessed with the fact that his reality and identity are contingent upon the manipulation of language. He chooses to retreat into the safety of the strict alphabetical order of his father's encyclopedias.

Two Women in Prague tells the story of Álvaro Abril, a young writer struggling to compose his second novel. Luz Acaso, a mysterious woman at the end of her life, hires him to write her biography, but everything she tells him is invented. The novel comments on loneliness, incomplete communication, and the blurring of fact and fiction in the modern media. *Laura y Julio* (2006; published as *Laura and Julio*) is the story of a contemporary marriage. The title characters live in an apartment next to that of Manuel, a writer, who seems to be coming between them. After Manuel is hit by a car and falls into a coma, Laura asks Julio to leave. While he tries to figure out what to do with his life, Julio becomes involved with his brother's ex-wife and her daughter. He also spies on Laura from Manuel's apartment, which provides him with a new perspective on his situation. The novel emphasizes the vulnerability of relationships and the ease with which people can be persuaded to alter their opinions of one another. In *La mujer loca* (2014; may be translated as *The Madwoman*), Julia studies grammar at night because she wants to impress a philologist with whom she has fallen in love. The words

she investigates present existential issues that she must try to solve. It is revealed that Julia is a character in a book that Millás is trying to write. The author's presence becomes increasingly conspicuous in the text until he takes it over, and the reader realizes that the novel is actually about Millás's alter ego, a novelist who is suffering from writer's block.

CRITICAL RECEPTION

Reviewers have focused on Millás's investigation of identity, praising his compelling explorations of psychology, his suggestive critiques of the chaos of urban life, and his imaginative engagement with critical theory. Barbara Gordon (1994) probed issues of identity and doubling in *Cerberus Are the Shadows,* identifying parallels between poverty and violence on the family and national levels in post-Franco Spain. Discussing modern disaffection, identity formation, and the symbolic importance of writing in several of Millás's novels, Samuel Amago (2006) noted that storytelling often mitigates the characters' despair, uncertainty, and emotional turmoil.

Several critics have studied issues of identity in *That Was Loneliness.* While commending Millás's "commentary on contemporary mores and on the emptiness of existence," Edward H. Friedman (1997) nevertheless found the protagonist's metamorphosis "somewhat illusory." He asserted that Elena is largely responsible for her own solitude, having purposely isolated herself from friends and family. In the essay "Juan José Millás' *La soledad era esto* and the Process of Subjectivity," Yaw Agawu-Kakraba (1999) discussed the permutations of Elena's identity, emphasizing the role of writing in her self-transformation. Amago (2007) examined the novel's "poetics of disaffection that functions as a critical response to economic, social and political discontent" and compared the author's use of "narrative self-consciousness" to that typically used by Generation X authors in the service of social critique.

Some scholars have considered Millás's works within the context of contemporary literature and theory. In his essay "Desire, Psychoanalysis, and Violence: Juan José Millas' *El desorden de tu nombre*," Agawu-Kakraba (1999) explicated references to French psychoanalyst Jacques Lacan's concepts of desire and doubling in *The Disorder of Your Name.* He suggested that Julio serves as Carlos's double and that Orlando functions as Julio's. Irene Andres-Suárez and Ana Casas (2009; see Further Reading) edited an important collection of Spanish-language essays that primarily concern the metafictional and transgeneric aspects of Millás's writing. Dale Knickerbocker (2003) studied Millás's use of self-reflexive narrative techniques and mentally disturbed protagonists in *The Disorder of Your Name* and other works. He argued that the author is primarily focused on exploring "the internal contradictions of the Spanish collective unconscious." Carter Smith (2012) considered

Millás's representation of the manipulation of language in *The Alphabetical Order*, aligning the novel's themes with those of Portuguese author José Saramago's *The Cave* (2000). Fernando Valls (2003; see Further Reading) offered an analysis of the relationship between Millás's journalism and fiction.

Jelena Krstovic

PRINCIPAL WORKS

Cerbero son las sombras [may be translated as *Cerberus Are the Shadows*]. Madrid: Espejo, 1975. Print. (Novella)

Visión del ahogado [may be translated as *Vision of the Drowned Man*]. Madrid: Alfaguara, 1977. Print. (Novel)

El jardín vacío [may be translated as *The Empty Garden*]. Madrid: Legasa, 1981. Print. (Novel)

Papel mojado [may be translated as *Wet Paper*]. Madrid: Anaya, 1983. Print. (Novella)

Letra muerta [may be translated as *Dead Letter*]. Madrid: Alfaguara, 1984. Print. (Novella)

El desorden de tu nombre [published as *The Disorder of Your Name*]. Madrid: Alfaguara, 1988. Print. (Novel)

La soledad era esto [published as *That Was Loneliness*]. Barcelona: Destino, 1990. Print. (Novel)

Volver a casa [may be translated as *Back Home*]. Barcelona: Destino, 1990. Print. (Novel)

Primavera de luto y otros cuentos [may be translated as *Spring Mourning and Other Stories*]. Barcelona: Destino, 1992. Print. (Short stories)

Ella imagina [may be translated as *She Imagines*]. Madrid: Alfaguara, 1994. Print. (Novel)

Algo que te concierne [may be translated as *Something That Concerns You*]. Madrid: El País/Aguilar, 1995. Print. (Essays)

Tonto, muerto, bastardo e invisible [may be translated as *Dumb, Dead, Illegitimate, and Invisible*]. Madrid: Alfaguara, 1995. Print. (Novel)

Cuentos a la intemperie [may be translated as *Weather Stories*]. Madrid: Acento, 1997. Print. (Short stories)

El orden alfabético [may be translated as *The Alphabetical Order*]. Madrid: Alfaguara, 1998. Print. (Novel)

Tres novelas cortas [may be translated as *Three Novellas*]. Madrid: Santillana, 1998. Print. (Novellas)

La viuda incompetente y otros cuentos [may be translated as *Incompetent Widow and Other Stories*]. Barcelona: Plaza y Janés, 1998. Print. (Short stories)

No mires debajo de la cama [may be translated as *Do Not Look under the Bed*]. Madrid: Alfaguara, 1999. Print. (Novel)

Cuerpo y prótesis [may be translated as *Body and Prothesis*]. Madrid: País, 2000. Print. (Journalism)

*Articuentos. Barcelona: Alba, 2001. Print. (Journalism)

Números pares, impares e idiotas [may be translated as *Even, Odd, and Idiot Numbers*]. Barcelona: Alba, 2001. Print. (Short stories)

Dos mujeres en Praga [may be translated as *Two Women in Prague*]. Madrid: Espasa, 2002. Print. (Novel)

Cuentos adúlteros desorientados [may be translated as *Adulterers Disoriented Stories*]. Barcelona: Lumen, 2003. Print. (Short stories)

Hay algo que no es como me dicen [may be translated as *There Is Something That It Is Not How They Tell It to Me*]. Madrid: Aguilar, 2004. Print. (Journalism)

María y Mercedes: Dos relatos sobre el trabajo y la vida familiar [may be translated as *María and Mercedes: Two Stories about Work and Family*]. Barcelona: Península, 2005. Print. (Journalism)

El ojo de la cerradura [may be translated as *The Eye to the Keyhole*]. Barcelona: Península, 2005. Print. (Journalism)

Sombras sobre sombras [may be translated as *Shadows on Shadows*]. Barcelona: Península, 2005. Print. (Essays)

Todo son preguntas [may be translated as *All Are Questions*]. Barcelona: Península, 2005. Print. (Journalism)

Laura y Julio [published as *Laura and Julio*]. Barcelona: Seix Barral, 2006. Print. (Novel)

El mundo [may be translated as *The World*]. Barcelona: Planeta, 2007. Print. (Novel)

Los objetos nos llaman [may be translated as *The Objects Call Us*]. Barcelona: Seix Barral, 2008. Print. (Short stories)

Lo que sé de los hombrecillos [may be translated as *I Know about the Little Men*]. Barcelona: Seix Barral, 2010. Print. (Novel)

Articuentos completos [may be translated as *Complete Articuentos*]. Barcelona: Seix Barral, 2011. Print. (Journalism)

Vidas al límite [may be translated as *Harsh Times*]. Barcelona: Seix Barral, 2012. Print. (Essays)

La mujer loca [may be translated as *The Madwoman*].
Barcelona: Seix Barral, 2014. Print. (Novel)

Principal English Translations

The Disorder of Your Name. Trans. Allison Beely. London:
Allison and Busby, 2000. Print. Trans. of *El desorden
de tu nombre.*

That Was Loneliness. Trans. Beely. London: Allison and
Busby, 2000. Print. Trans. of *La soledad era esto.*

Personality Disorders and Other Stories. Trans. Gregory
B. Kaplan. New York: MLA, 2007. Print.

Laura and Julio. Trans. Bernard Jones. London: White
Night, 2012. Print. Trans. of *Laura y Julio.*

*The title of this work is a word coined by Millás to describe his short articles
that combine elements of journalism and short stories.

CRITICISM

Barbara Gordon (essay date 1994)

SOURCE: Gordon, Barbara. "Doubles and Identity in
Juan José Millás's *Cerbero son las sombras.*" *RLA: Romance Languages Annual* 6 (1995): 486-91. Print.

[*In the following essay, originally presented at a conference in 1994, Gordon examines the theme of identity and
the motif of doubling in Millás's* Cerberus Are the Shadows. *According to Gordon, the narrator's autoeroticism,
his interdependent relationship with his father, and his
sadomasochistic tendencies contribute to the novel's portrait of displacement, oppression, and poverty in 1950s
Spain.*]

The political history of Spain since the beginning of the
nineteenth century is a prolonged tale of scisms and fac-
tions, rivalries and civil war. In 1806, Carlos IV allowed
Napoleon to use the peninsula as a passageway for his
troops, and Napoleon declared Spain part of his empire.
At that same time, Carlos was dealing with domestic disputes with his wife, María Luisa, and her power-seeking
lover, Manuel Godoy. Wedged between Napoleon and
Godoy, Carlos bestowed the crown upon his son Fernando
VII, who initiated a rebellion against Godoy. The War of
Independence began in 1808, and in 1812 the progressive
Constitution of Cádiz was signed. Not until 1814 did Fernando expel the French and return to power. Later, the
Liberals regained control and the French returned. The
"década ominosa" (1824-1833) marks the bloody, perse-
cutory return of Fernando's absolute power. Universities
closed and *tauromaquia* schools opened. Upon Fernando's
death in 1833, the Carlist wars began in the battle for
sovereignty between Isabel, Fernando's two-year old
daughter, and Don Carlos, his brother. These wars continued through the Romantic period and writers of the time

were forced to abandon their native country because of
political persecutions. Larra's metaphor of Madrid as a
cemetery summarized the *Weltanshauung* of Spain's intellectuals and their desire to leave behind the battleground,
whatever the consequences. In the mid-twentieth century
the Spanish Civil War again split this country and its inhabitants into two parts, and Spain witnessed its own suicide. The end of the war lead to the inner breakdown of
Spain's survivors and initiated the internal battle for identity and a struggle with *soledad* in the aftermath of the three-
year conflict Franco inaugurated on that July day of 1936.

After the war, many Spaniards found it necessary to leave
their rural lifestyle in search of a healthier economic atmosphere in Spain's metropolis; therefore, in the years following the war, coastal families emigrated en masse to the
capital. The resulting depression assumed two faces: the
more obvious, economic hardship caught its reflection in
the fragile condition of the Spanish psyche. The dictatorship left the dissenting half of Spain under political condemnation that forced many into seclusion.

This forced isolation is one of the faces of *soledad,* which
represents not only loneliness, but sadness—a nostalgia
for what life could have been and a longing for what it
still might be. This is the *soledad* Juan José Millás refers to
when he says:

> La soledad siempre tiene dos caras. Quiere decir que la
> soledad es un espacio necesario que hay que defender, y
> otra cosa es cuando la soledad es impuesta. Y en este
> sentido la sociedad española se siente que en los últimos
> años con la incorporación—digamos al mundo—ha em-
> pezado a sufrir un tipo de soledad que antes no conocía.
> Madrid es una ciudad muy dura.

(Millás, Interview)

Though Millás defends the ambiguity of the setting of
Cerbero son las sombras, his first novel, the mythical
space he creates is undeniably similar to Madrid in the
fifties. The city itself demonstrates the protagonist's inner
turmoil. An external, initially undefined oppressor compels
a family to leave the coast and travel to Madrid. Without
documentation—and thus without identity—a man and
woman with three children board a train in search of psychological freedom and rest in Madrid—a battered city that
does not recognize them. The narrator provides no particu-
lars as to the reasons for their flight, but according to Millás
"la peripecia exterior (la forma en que huyen) puede ser una
metáfora de algo interior" (qtd. in Gutiérrez 25).

Cerbero son las sombras is based on a young man's attempt to justify his existence after the disturbing experiences he undergoes during his youth. The novel consists of
a letter the boy composes to his father detailing his perception of the family's plight. Upon arriving in Madrid, the
family members install themselves in a dilapidated apartment, using their meager resources to pay several month's
rent in advance. During their time there, the younger son,

Jacinto, attempts an escape and dies as a result. The father arranges a meeting with an acquaintance to acquire money in order to leave Madrid, but fails in his attempt. The psychological trauma and fear of disclosure brought on by his debacle cause him to lose control of himself. He strikes his head against a brick wall until he tears his ear to shreds and nearly loses consciousness.

At this point in their story, the narrator takes over the paternal role while his father suffers from an infection due to his self-inflicted injuries. The mother acts as guardian of their secret life. She refuses to allow the others to know of Jacinto's death, and she belittles her husband while confiding in her son, the narrator. He, however, identifies with his father and feels that listening to her means betraying his father and, ultimately, himself. When finally they receive some financial assistance, the narrator cannot bear to continue living anonymously. He steals some of the money and escapes to another run-down *pensión* where he sits and writes to his father. When he is not writing, he pokes small pieces of wire into the sides of some rats he captures.

This letter—which details the protagonist's feelings about his family and the life he has just abandoned—enables the reader to understand that the degradation of this family's grotesque existence is due to *soledad* and lack of personal identity. The father in *Cerbero* [*Cerbero son las sombras*] personifies both mental and physical instability. The young man despises the weakness he witnesses in his father because he recognizes that same weakness in himself. Millás's characters are practically mirror images of one another—their fear and *soledad* ally them: "Querido padre: Es posible que en el fondo tu problema, como el mío, no haya sido más que un problema de soledad" (*Cerbero* 9). This initial glimpse into the problem of a shared *soledad* demonstrates just one of the many examples of doubles in this novel. In *A Psychoanalytic Study of the Double in Literature,* Robert Rogers identifies three types of doubles from his readings of world literature: manifest, latent, and baroque. The manifest double is "some rather antithetical self, usually a guardian angel or tempting devil" (2) as seen so often in literature, film, and theater. When Tymms says that "Superficially, doubles are among the facile, and less reputable devices in fiction" (qtd. in Rogers 31), Rogers quickly points out that this refers only to manifest doubles. He agrees that the manifest double is inherently limited: "A crucial drawback lies in the reader's awareness that some kind of decomposition is being represented" (31).

The latent double, on the other hand, is implicit rather than explicit: Rogers says: "We may sense this division, but it is not mentioned by the author, and none of the characters exhibits any direct awareness of it" (4). These doubles often elude even the author because of their subtlety. The baroque double, a term coined by Jorge Luis Borges, draws on a flagrant overuse of identical characters or personalities duplicated *ad infinitum*. The characters in *Cer-*

bero son las sombras reflect Rogers's manifest and latent doubles.

The first of these doubles in *Cerbero* is the father and the son, the author of the letter. The narrator identifies with his father after his father's injury and proceeds to take over the patriarchal role. He writes about the experience of reattaching his father's ear and the role he then plays as caregiver:

> Yo mismo me encargué de desnudarte antes de meterte en la cama, pero no pienses que esto me afectó demasiado, pues la relación padre-hijo se había trastocado en el cuarto de baño, si no antes, y sólo experimenté las sensaciones ambiguas y encontradas que debe de experimentar todo adulto que cuida a su pesar de otro adulto, al que las costumbres sociales le han obligado a amar, y del que respeta todo, incluso su pudor. . . . Yo, entretanto, te cubría con la manta y te decía en voz baja y vergonzosa palabras suaves, como tú mismo habías hecho conmigo de pequeño, cuando me acometían fiebres altas y me colocabas la mano en la frente, mientras le quitabas importancia al asunto con la voz.

(60-61)

At this time the family is practically penniless, since no one is able to leave the house to secure a job. They are obligated to depend on the charity of former friends who share their same political plight, and who are financially more stable. The father secretly assigns to his son the task of seeking assistance from an ex-lover named Bárbara. The idea of meeting his father's former lover "me enervaba hasta el punto de que, sin darme cuenta, iba poco a poco convirtiéndome en ti" (87). He imagines an amorous encounter with her in which she would pay for the hotel room. Though he realizes his identification with his father stems from the *soledad* that the two share, it also comes from the *soledad* that results from the loneliness of living in hiding.

The son sets out to find Bárbara's apartment with instructions to speak only to her. Ignoring the advice, when a man answers the door, he asks for Bárbara. She tells him to wait for her in the bar across the street. As he sits in a booth daydreaming about her, she emerges from the portal of the building, and while crossing the street, is struck and killed by a car. The sight of the blood seeping from her head grotesquely obscures the narrator's vision of a love affair. Shaken and trembling, the son returns to the apartment and, unwilling to reveal the truth, tells his father he could not locate her. This first solo venture into the streets of Madrid disillusions him and forces him to recognize the inhospitable environment he inhabits.

Because of the harshness of their situation, the father and son are bound to each other. And because the son is the father's double, any move to abandon him would be in essence an abandonment of self—a suicide. The son cannot live without the father because they have become one, and the mutual emotional attachment is impossible to break without dire consequences. The fear they experience reappears throughout the novel. They are doubled in a non-verbal bond: "Entonces te sentía como un desprendimiento de mi ser, convirtiéndome de esta forma en tu causa y a ti en mi resultado" (104-05).

This bond between father and son does not carry over to mother and son where there exists a genuine lack of *cariño*. The son sees the mother's manipulation of the father and considers it a personal affront. His sterile relationship with his mother imitates the lack of intimacy between his parents:

> Por fin, tras una vuelta por un extraño laberinto, la habitación en la que mamá y tú os acostabais juntos, y os abrazabais tal vez con esa sensación contradictoria que te obliga a odiar a la persona que amas, y que a mí me ha enseñado que el odio no es más que una forma de conocimiento que en general no aprovechamos a causa de una deficiencia congénita, que nos conduce siempre del lado de las equívocas palabras.
>
> (52)

The mother's attempts to sever the tie between her husband and son prove useless because these characters share the same psyche. One night as the mother confides in her son, she says: "Lo peor de tu padre es que ha vuelto siempre contra sí mismo el odio que sentía por los demás; le faltan arrestos para vivir y sacar adelante a los suyos" (84). Of these nightly conversations he writes

> no pude evitar que pusiera en marcha la máquina de soltar confidencias, ... cuyo único objeto era, sin duda, desprestigiarte ante mis ojos, y pasar a ocupar ella el puesto de heroína.
>
> (68)

Her manipulation of the son fails because he sees himself projected in his father and understands the grasp she has on her husband. This cruel, possessive woman blames her husband for all of the disgraces that befall them, and though filled with remorse, the narrator comes to the conclusion that he will never be free while his mother lives. He comprehends, finally, his father's relationship with her:

> Y este admitir mi propia contradicción me llevaba también a comprender mejor tus sentimientos con respecto a mamá, pues sin duda ella encarnaba todo cuanto habías tratado de destruir; entonces tu permanencia junto a ella revelaba una fisura cuya explicación sería la fidelidad inconsciente de tu corazón a unas formas de vida que habían alimentado tus primeros años y con las que aún mantenías relaciones a través de la vagina de mi madre.
>
> (146-47)

The son hates his mother and denies her his love; he loves his father but denies him respect. These conflicting emotions reveal themselves in his own self-love and self-hate demonstrated through narcissism and sado-masochism.

The classic story of Echo's tragic love for Narcissus is the main constituent of narcissism and its grotesque companion, masochism. According to Rogers, the ego is a subject but can view itself as an object and thereby analyze, criticize, observe, and treat itself as an object: "So the ego can be split; it splits itself during a number of its functions— temporarily at least" (18, 19). Freud discusses narcissism as an investment of libido in ego. Ego is the rational part of the psyche, developing and borrowing from the id's psychic energy but discharging energy when the situation is appropriate—when the pleasure must be temporarily suspended. Libido is the energy itself and the source of mental activities such as thinking, remembering and problem-solving as well as for sexual drives.

Further examples of doubles include the evidence seen in the narrator's sadism and masochism. Otto Rank's theories on the double focus on the narcissistic self, and follow the Freudian idea of repressed sexual desire along with the Jungian desire for rebirth. C. F. Keppler explains Rank's suggestion that:

> an erotic component is concealed within the first self's hatred for the second, eroticism which is really auto-eroticism, infantile narcissism carried forward into adult life. The heroes of *Doppelgänger*-stories, like the authors who create them, are capable of love only for themselves. ...
>
> (Keppler 184)

More than simple "self love," Rank refers to a "sexual attachment" (184). Narcissism then raises questions about identity since the subject determines whether the object deserves the right to exist. The narcissist cannot bear the thought of the second self's "inevitable process of decay" (184), which explains "the emergence of a genuine death-wish toward the second self out of the original, and always central, motivation of auto-eroticism" (184). Suicide answers the need for self-preservation, but according to Rank, "to the true narcissist, slaying the treasured self is as unthinkable as watching the decay is unbearable" (185). In order to resolve this dilemma, the first self must split off from the second before destroying it. The issues of narcissism, auto-eroticism, and sado-masochism in *Cerbero* demonstrate the protagonist's desire to destroy his opponent, which of course is himself.

Narcissism is evidence of the search for the other, and the young man finds that search both difficult and desirable. From the beginning of the story we detect the narrator's self-love: "estaba yo junto a la ventana de mi cuarto amando mi rostro en un pequeño espejo ..." (28-29). When his sister observes him washing up one afternoon, he admits his narcissistic behavior:

> Normalmente nunca tardaba más de dos minutos en esta operación, pero el hecho de sentirme observado me incitaba a actuar con una morosidad narcisista, que prolongaba cada gesto hasta más allá de lo necesario.
>
> (174)

This attitude of self-love coincides with the narrator's feelings of self-hate that come in the form of sado-masochism and masturbation.

Millás reflects the family's situation with the inclusion of the rats in the narrative, which are doubles of the characters themselves. When the narrator feels trapped and alone like the caged rats, he says he is

> obligado a introducir finísimos alambres por entre los barrotes de las jaulas, para herirlos levemente. Y entonces, adelantándome unos momentos al instante, los estoy viendo ya lamerse las pequeñísimas úlceras que les he producido.
>
> (12)

He realizes that the pain inflicted upon the rats parallels his own suffering and feels justified tormenting them because he is one of them. As he composes the letter, the female rats are preparing to give birth and are warring against the males. The narrator then identifies with the newborn rats when he says: "Quiero ver a sus hijos, lampiños y ciegos, que también son mamíferos como yo" (10).

Trying to extract the other that is within him becomes the object of the narrator's behavior. He imagines for himself a lover and on numerous occasions engages in self-stimulation to satisfy his sexual drives:

> cuando pienso en mi amor y lo imagino como un bello desnudo de mujer de bello gesto en la boca y en los ojos, ... y luego vuelve y besa hasta el rincón más solo de mi cuerpo, y milagrosamente ha encontrado el resorte, y yo me muevo levantándome sobre ella, y con todas las fuerzas de mi voluntad recorro su piel y sus cabellos sin que nadie me empuje desde el exterior, como si fuera libre de estar en sus rodillas, de acariciar su espalda, de volver la mirada hacia sus ojos y de hundirme otra vez entre sus piernas libándole la vida, mientras la mía escapa por las ingles en dirección a nadie. ...
>
> (24)

Masturbation vindicates the narrator as he admits that

> al jugar con mi cuerpo de un modo tan tipificado por las leyes eternas que hasta tenía un nombre y, por lo tanto, pensaba yo, un largo historial, que en cierto modo me justificaba.
>
> (157)

Auto-eroticism also demonstrates masochistic behavior because of the sexual excitement and satisfaction derived from the humilliation associated with the act. A negative side to the sexual pleasure he seeks is wrought with *soledad*:

> Luego incliné lentamente mi cuerpo hacia la almohada en una especie de rito encaminado a hacer el amor conmigo mismo por el puro placer de aumentar el cansancio a que me había sometido la jornada. No hay soledad total si el agotamiento físico no es completo. Incluso pienso que ambos son la misma cosa bajo ropajes diferentes, pues es bien cierto que los dos conducen a la lenta y minuciosa destrucción del cuerpo que nos ha tocado en suerte con una maestría tal que hace sospechar al entendimiento que

no hay forma posible de diálogo con nuestro propio ser, que no esté basada en su mutilación.

> (66)

The masochistic manner in which he treats the rats proves his identification with them: "yo pondré mi cara a la altura de las jaulas, porque por la noche suelen atacarse, y me hacen sentir un extraño placer con sus peleas" (103). This strange pleasure derived from pain and violence demonstrates the desperate situation in which the young man finds himself. He arrives at the point in his life that even his imaginary love becomes the object of violence:

> el comportamiento de mi imaginario amor había modificado nuestras relaciones hasta el punto de que me obligaba a descargar sobre su cuerpo una agresividad que jamás hubiera sospechado en mí, y que no estaba exenta de un placer. ...
>
> (136)

Since he imagines this relationship, the true object of his violence is himself. Thus we have another example of sado-masochism because of the violence he inflicts on others who are nothing more than projections of himself.

This violence comes out in full force against the helpless rats he keeps confined. The rats are restless because the females are preparing to give birth. The males lie in wait to devour the young, but the narrator refuses to separate them. For the male to devour the offspring is natural, but nature is subverted in this novel. The females here are the ones who devour their young, just as the narrator's mother feasts upon her own children.

After the son escapes from home, the authorities discover his parents and take them into custody and continue searching for him and his brother, Jacinto. Moments before they locate the narrator in the *pensión*:

> las hembras cogen a sus pequeños entre las patas delanteras y se los van comiendo lentamente. Primero la cabeza, luego el resto de esa pequeña realidad lampiña, ciega, tan precaria como esta realidad algo más grande que soy yo, que enseguida voy a ser atrapado por las redes de quienes me persiguen.
>
> (191)

That the narrator tells of the females devouring their young demonstrates again his feelings toward his mother and her relationship not only to him but also to his brother. For the narrator, Jacinto becomes an idol to worship because he has escaped the cage that holds them all prisoner. Jacinto's role as a Christ figure is another manifestation of doubles.

Jacinto is one of two characters with a name to identify him (the other is Rosa, the younger sister who is relatively unaware of the circumstances around her.) When the family arrives at their new apartment, the *soledad* stemming from monotony and familiarity collapses for a short time.

Jacinto and his brother have to share a bed but they sleep back to back so as not to have to face the difficulties enshrouded in each other's eyes. The narrator says:

> Solíamos dormir espalda contra espalda para evitar complicaciones; y aunque al principio creo que nos resultaba vergonzoso que nuestros cuerpos se encontraran en el centro de la cama, la costumbre acabó por devolvernos a la soledad, y a las dos semanas actuábamos cada uno en nuestro lado como si el cuarto y la cama fuesen de uno solo.

(19)

Jacinto, though the younger of the two boys, realizes that survival depends upon deserting the family. He proposes to his brother that they both leave, but that if the protagonist does not want to go, Jacinto will go alone. In this respect Jacinto and his brother are opposites. Jacinto tries to be strong and break the chains of familial obligation in order to survive, but his brother is too weak to attempt the escape. Alone, Jacinto casually leaves the kitchen after an unsatisfying meal and closes the front door. His brother reveals to their parents that Jacinto will not be returning. After three days, Jacinto is located. He lacked the courage needed to escape and hid under the bed he shared with his brother. He never made a sound while he lay freezing and hungry for three days and three nights.

Here is evidence of distorted versions of the Jonah, Lazarus, and Christ stories. Jonah disappeared into the ocean: "For as Jonas was three days and three nights in the whale's belly; so shall the Son of man be three days and three nights in the heart of the earth" (Matt. 12: 40). But the jaws of the fish never release Jacinto from their grasp. Lazarus lies dead in his tomb, awaiting Christ's saving powers to raise him. After four days "he that was dead came forth, bound hand and foot with grave clothes: and his face was bound about with a napkin" (John 11:44). He arises from the dead and lives to die again at some later date. But Jacinto never fully sheds the burial shroud; he does not recover. And finally Jacinto's experience parallels Christ's own resurrection after three days in the tomb. Jacinto, unlike the others, spends his three days uncovered, unanointed, unlamented. The narrator employs religious images whenever he refers to Jacinto.

Besides the religious symbolism, a mythological character appears in conjunction with Jacinto. The mother places the moribund boy into an unused room and there attempts to nurse him back to health. No one enters the locked sanctuary except her. It is a sacred room guarded by Cerberus, the monstrous three-headed dog that guards the gates of Hades. The protagonist's mission—gain entrance into Jacinto's crypt—echos Virgil's description of the mythical Cerberus:

> These regions echo with the triple-throated
> bark of the giant Cerberus, who crouches,
> enormous, in a cavern facing them.

> The Sibyl, seeing that his neck is bristling
> with snakes, throws him a honeyed cake of wheat
> with drugs that bring on sleep. His triple mouths
> yawn wide with rapid hunger as he clutches
> the cake she cast. His giant back falls slack
> along the ground; his bulk takes all the cave.
> And when the beast is buried under sleep,
> Aeneas gains the entrance swiftly, leaves
> the riverbank from which no one returns.

(6.550-61)

The reference to the mother's "ojos de medusa" (134) suggests that she is the echo of Cerberus. The mother facilitates the son's discovery of what lies in Hades by feigning sleep in order to share the burden and fashion a triangle of conspiracy with Jacinto at the top: "Cerbero descansaba vigilando con una de sus cabezas (las otras dos dormían y tú te desangrabas) al visitante hostil, o al forastero desprovisto de los venenos convencionales" (*Cerbero* 50). She like the beast is the guardian of ultimate knowledge of the depths of hell. This inferno represents the internal one the narrator experiences, and she symbolically holds the key to his self-knowledge. Just as Virgil says that Aeneas "leaves the riverbank from which no one returns" (6.561) so the narrator will never be able to return to innocence and ignorance once he discovers his brother's death.

Millás does not disclose how long Jacinto lives but long after his death, the mother continues to enter his room with the largest portions of their meager supplies. The narrator genuflects before Jacinto's door each time he passes, occasionally tapping on it. Jacinto never responds. Finally he steals the key from his mother, looks into Jacinto's room and to his surprise, he encounters no one, just a lingering stench of perfume and death. In the armoire lies Jacinto, covered by a white linen and anointed with perfume: "Allí estaba mi hermano, en posición horizontal sobre un entrepaño. ... Tenía las manos colocadas sobre el pecho, tal como las estampas cristianas muestran a los que mueren en gracia de Dios; sólo que mi hermano no tenía aureola ni tampoco una sonrisa dulce" (129-30).

After discovering his brother's death, the narrator fears his own imminent death, and throughout his retelling of the story, he realizes his duplicity and understands the reality of his lost identity. He recounts fears of his own imminent death: "Y yo tenía miedo aquellas noches de que los años acabaran sorprendiéndome acostado junto a mi asesino (que no era otro que yo mismo, nacido en un desdoblamiento impuesto por la soledad) ..." (136-37). He is unraveled, shattered and irreparable.

In order to avoid his assassin and establish himself as a living entity, the narrator turns to the act of writing. He confesses that he continues writing the letter to his father out of curiosity. Uncertain of where this "mal iniciado diálogo entre mi memoria y yo" (62) will lead him, he continues to write as he watches the battle raging between the male and female rats. Violence associated with writing appears in many novels of postwar Spain. To write is to empower with abilities one lacks in mind and character. Writing is not only a defense but a personal justification of identity. The need for identity profoundly affects the protagonist of this novel as well as the other characters. He sees himself only as a reflection of his father, a truth that erodes his integrity. He writes of his concerns: "Querido padre: hoy renunciaría a todo lo que he escrito si estos papeles no fueran el único refugio de mi identidad. No tengo a dónde ir ni qué hacer. No sé quién soy hasta que leo esta espiral, que palabra a palabra me vomita y completa mis rasgos línea a línea" (152).

The narrator hides within his writing. He creates a text based upon a reality, itself based upon a falsehood. His family lives a fabricated life secreted away somewhere in Madrid. With a pen he could change their history to fit his personal needs:

> Renunciar a lo escrito y comenzar de nuevo, acordándome en cada palabra de vuestra suerte, daría lugar a un documento distinto, en el que yo me reconocería con menos vergüenza que con la que me reconozco en éste, sobre todo ahora que la evidencia de los hechos impide a mi imaginación otorgaros un final menos desastroso.
>
> (154)

The young man's history is indelible. His mother may deny his perspective, but no one can erase his existence. He creates with a pen the identity he lacks.

The written word doubles the author because it is the projection of himself. Millás says that "en el acto físico de escribir ya se produce una duplicidad porque en el momento en que uno escribe, hay dos sujetos: está el escritor, Fulano de Tal, y está el narrador. Esa duplicidad metaforiza esa otra duplicidad interna" (Interview). The young man in *Cerbero* reads about the capture of his family in the newspaper. He finds this article disturbing and at the same time, comforting: "A mí esto de encontrarme con mi propio apellido en letra impresa me produce una sensación de otredad que me libera en parte de la tensa situación que soportan mis nervios" (165). Fear, however, motivates the continuation of the narration until his capture: "En las últimas horas no he parado de escribirte, padre. Temo que al dejar el lápiz suceda una catástrofe" (76). The catastrophe occurs precisely at the end of the novel when the boy finds himself captured, and—like the rats in the cage—devoured simply because he exists. His father's political actions have made him a victim, and while he shares none of the culpability, he suffers all of the consequences.

Millás's characters suffered identity crises manifested through their duplicity while hostages within their own home. Spain's doubling during this time appears in its treatment of political prisoners. Despite the reforms taking place after 1951, Spain remained very much divided. According to Richard Herr, in the early fifties, the Civil Guard, oppressors of their dissenting brothers, began withdrawing themselves from obvious public places. In spite of a general feeling of peace and dictatorial rest, "prisoners still serving sentences for political crimes prior to 1951 could testify that it [Spain] was a police state nevertheless" (238). The succeeding decades introduced affordable higher education and an end to food rationing. Since the death of Franco in 1975, Spain has suffered another identity crisis as it has tried to recoup lost time and become a European cultural center. Millás acknowledges that the dictatorship surfaces in his novels: "La dictadura era la consecuencia de una guerra, y eso está en mi literatura. ... La gente de mi generación por necesidad ha combatido una dictadura. Ese es un fenómeno no en que funcionó el odio ni el rencor pero sí como información de la propia existencia" (Interview). Journalist Santos Sanz Villanueva asserts that writers after the dictatorship are now required to reflect "de manera distanciada sobre las consecuencias recientes de un compromiso que ... ha concluido en ámbitos que van del desencanto al fracaso" (3). These writers necessarily include in their works symbols and doubles from that period of oppression.

Works Cited

Gutiérrez, Fabián. *Cómo leer a Juan José Millás.* Madrid: Júcar, 1992.

Herr, Richard. *An Historical Essay on Modern Spain.* Berkeley: U of California P, 1974.

Keppler, C. F. *The Literature of the Second Self.* Tucson: U of Arizona P, 1972.

Millás, Juan José. *Cerbero son las sombras.* Madrid: Alfaguara, 1975.

———. Personal interview. 26 August 1992.

Rogers, Robert. *A Psychoanalytic Study of the Double in Literature.* Detroit: Wayne State UP, 1970.

Sanz Villanueva, Santos. "Una realidad en la última novela española." *Insula* (Aug.-Sept. 1989): 3-4.

Virgil. *The Aeneid of Virgil.* Trans. Allen Mendelbaum. Berkeley: U of California P, 1981.

Edward H. Friedman (essay date 1997)

SOURCE: Friedman, Edward H. "Defining Solitude: Juan José Millás's *La soledad era esto.*" *RLA: Romance Languages Annual* 9 (1998): 492-95. Print.

[*In the following essay, originally presented at a conference in 1997, Friedman analyzes* That Was Loneliness *as a novel about contemporary alienation. He concludes that Millás's "rhetoric of solitude is affected" in that the protagonist chooses to be alone and to isolate herself from her family.*]

La soledad era esto by Juan José Millás (b. 1946, Valencia) is a novel that takes a number of chances and, as we will argue here, that may produce a wide range of readings. The major character is a woman, Elena Rincón, whose vision of self and circumstance is presented through both third-person and first-person narration and into whose story are interposed unmediated documents by others. The theme of solitude, explicitly introduced in the title, offers a focus for what could be termed a double evaluation: Elena's scrutiny of her life and the reader's scrutiny of Elena. There is no question that Millás hopes to explore experiences and situations that are distinctly related to women. This rather bold artistic choice puts him in a vulnerable position, given that his depiction of feminine sensibility may be filtered through his own gender identification. It must be noted, however, that *La soledad era esto* was the winner of the 1990 Premio Nadal, Spain's most prestigious prize for a novel, and that the judges will have read it blindly, that is, presumably without knowing the name (or the sex) of the author. My contention—obviously without the benefit of this "blindness"—is that Millás successfully conveys solitude but, in doing so, sacrifices significance. *La soledad era esto* may be more a commentary on contemporary mores and on the emptiness of existence than on feminine sensibility. A genuinely feminist text, I would argue (while recognizing the problematic nature of the word *genuinely*), would endeavor to portray a woman's solitude with greater sensitivity to the dignity of the individual and to the causes of her isolation. After a brief examination of Millás's novel, I would like to underscore the difference to which I have alluded by comparing the ideological scope of *La soledad era esto* to that of Kate Chopin's *The Awakening,* a text that projects solitude in what is, for me, a more consistent and meaningful way.

In *La soledad era esto,* Millás accentuates the solitude of his protagonist both through her personal experiences and through a narrative structure that calls attention to itself. The third-person narration of the first part shifts to the first-person in the second part. Elena Rincón finds a group of notebooks, or diaries, kept by her mother, the notice of whose death opens the text and who was exactly Elena's age—forty-three—at the time of the writing. Selected diary entries are intercalated into the text, as are reports made by a detective whom Elena hires (anonymously) to report on her husband's activities and then on her own. Signs of estrangement appear from the beginning. The narrator refers to the fragile ties between Elena and her mother Mercedes ("para Elena su madre estaba muerta desde hacía mucho tiempo," 14), and Elena elects not to attend the funeral. The pattern is duplicated in the relationship with her newly married daughter, also named Mercedes, with whom she has only negligible contact. Elena's marriage to Enrique Acosta is hardly secure; an increasing sense of distance between them motivates her to have a private investigator follow Enrique. She employs the investigator as if she were the assistant to a man who wished

to leave his identity unknown. She seems to enjoy keeping the detective in the dark, and she finally asks him—ironically—to keep track of Enrique's wife. Her meeting with her sister and brother at the home of their deceased mother is a disagreeable experience, but on this occasion she discovers the diaries, which obviously were not meant for her consumption. The mother explains that, through much of her life, she has had an intimate mental relationship with her "antipode," named Elena. As a type of objective correlative to her existential malaise, Elena suffers from some kind of digestive ailment, and the diaries disclose that her mother also had long-term medical problems that she did not reveal to her family. The investigator corroborates Elena's suspicions that her husband is having an affair after trailing Enrique and his secretary on a trip. Elena's reaction borders on indifference.

The story continues in the second part through the direct discourse of Elena, who includes additional passages from her mother's notebooks and the investigator's report on her activities, with commentaries on each. Enrique informs Elena that their daughter is pregnant, and, troubled by the lack of rapport, she visits Mercedes. Their conversation does little to improve the lines of communication. Enrique invites Elena to accompany him on a trip to Brussels, and—reliving, to a degree, a journey of discovery revealed in her mother's diary—Elena decides to end her marriage. She returns to Madrid alone, determined to begin a new life. Enrique unapologetically accepts her decision, and he writes that he would prefer that their interaction be limited to the sharing of good news. When shopping for items for her relocation, Elena is attacked by a man on the street and saved by the investigator, who receives a stab wound. In her role as employer, she berates him for having gone beyond the call of duty and suggests that he may have fallen in love with his charge. The detective dismisses himself from the assignment but vows to keep looking after Elena, whom he believes needs protection from the party who initiated the investigation. In the final chapter, Elena is established in the new apartment. She has changed her hairstyle and, it would seem, her way of life. She has called Mercedes to invite her to lunch, but her daughter is about to leave on vacation. Elena views this as a liberation of sorts, a respite from the inevitable need to confront adversities of the past. As she writes, she sits in the armchair that she retrieved from her mother's home. She remarks that her intestinal pain has disappeared, "y noto su ausencia como la ausencia de la melena cada vez que inclino la cabeza" (181). Her account ends precisely in this moment of transition and of apparent peace.

In Elena Rincón, Millás creates a character who is out of touch with those around her. Elena is detached from her mother, her siblings, her husband, and her daughter, in short, detached from life. She has material comforts, but joy and fulfillment are absent from her daily existence. She smokes hashish, but neither dulled senses nor expanded awareness seems to be the result. She connects only with the investigator, whom she deceives with respect to her identity (and his mission). In this case, solitude and emptiness are synonymous. Elena defines her solitude in this way:

> ... encontrarte de súbito en el mundo como si acabaras de llegar de otro planeta del que no sabes por qué has sido expulsada. ... La soledad es una amputación no visible, pero tan eficaz como si te arrancaran la vista y el oído y así, aislada de todas las sensaciones exteriores, de todos los puntos de referencia, y sólo con el tacto y la memoria, tuvieras que reconstruir el mundo, el mundo que has de habitar y que te habita.

> (133-34)

There is a certain ambivalence projected in the text as to how to "read" Elena Rincón. The ambivalence hinges, I would submit, on the issue of responsibility. To what extent does the character control her destiny, and to what extent is she a victim?

Without question, *La soledad era esto* reflects a cyclical pattern of withdrawal, of estrangement. Natural bonding, most prominently between mother and daughter, does not take place. Elena remains aloof, alienated from a mother who also feels alone in the universe and from a daughter reluctant to announce her impending maternity. Having married at a relatively early age, Elena lives without goals, without motivation, and without the intimacy, both physical and emotional, that she had enjoyed with Enrique. The hashish that she smokes with some regularity becomes a symbol of her walking through life in a daze, of going through the motions, as it were. The private notebooks articulate what she has long intuited, that her mother associated her with an opposing nature, a direct opposition, or antipode; there is more than a name that links the two Mercedes, grandmother and granddaughter. The reader is not privy to details of Elena's childhood or to her psychology of parenting, but one can sense that she has reenacted the drama of her youth—with the roles reversed—with her own daughter. Although the past is constantly juxtaposed to the present, Millás's novel surveys the effects rather than the roots of solitude. In the terminology of social determinism, it could be said that heredity is a given and environment an enigma in *La soledad era esto.* It seems clear that Elena, in one way or another, is out of control, but her passivity—her feeling of helplessness, of desperation—cannot necessarily be attributed to restraints placed upon her, as opposed to restraints that she places upon herself. She has the intelligence and the means to undertake new ventures, to lead a constructive existence, but, as the investigator's reports emphasize, in ironic fashion, there is a superficial quality of her routine. The spark has gone out of her marriage, but the coldness and virtual silence between the partners obviously precedes Enrique's affair with his secretary. Whether justifiably or not, Enrique is unwilling to see himself as the agent of the breakup. He responds to the separation in a letter, in which he comments:

> También yo tengo derecho a que se respete el modo de vida que he elegido, y en ese modo de vida no tienen cabida las tragedias, ni las molestias intestinales ni los dolores de cabeza; mucho menos, las grandes preguntas acerca de la existencia o la angustia por ignorar adónde vamos o de dónde venimos. No entiendo nada acerca de esas cuestiones que dejaron de interesarme mucho antes de atravesar la barrera de la madurez.

> (169)

While the letter does not run over with sensitivity or compassion, the reader may sense that the remoteness has multiple, and long-term, causes.

Just as Millás makes the determination to foreground the story (and the discourse) of a female protagonist, he frames the narrative with ambiguities, with curiously open spaces. Equally interestingly, he is anything but reticent about casting Elena in a negative light. In one sense, the character seems fated from birth to lead a life filled with tension. Her mother has scripted her into a scenario marked by alterity, difference, conflict. A similar tension informs Elena's meeting with her sister. Even more striking, perhaps, is her inability to establish lines of communication with her husband and her daughter, who are extremely close. The protagonist's refusal to attend her mother's funeral is an immediate indication that the author is working in a gray area from the perspective of judgment. The reader may vacillate between sympathy for and condemnation of Elena's attitude and actions. The complex narrative focalization provides an analogue of the equivocal tone:

> Finalmente decidió que no iría al entierro. Enrique podría decir que había pasado muy mala noche y que durante la madrugada había padecido un cólico. Ella quiso venir a pesar de todo, pero yo no se lo permití, debería explicar a todo el mundo, aunque ni su hermana ni su hija, Mercedes las dos, llegaran a creérselo.

> (23)

(Note the onomastic imbalance, the battalion of Mercedes against the "antipodal" Elena.) On one hand, then, lies a destiny that seems to point to inescapable alienation. On the other is a present that would seem to belie the innately tragic, that is, a present replete with possibilities for a bright, hardworking, and caring woman. Millás inserts into the literary equation the dialectics of agency and agent. He juxtaposes a natural repetition—fate, if you will—with individual initiative, or free will. In essence, he invites the reader to judge Elena Rincón, but the final judgment may be out of sync with the "vita nuova" theme of the closing chapter.

There is nothing about the depiction of Enrique or of the three Mercedes that would especially draw the reader toward them, but it is significant to recognize that Elena possesses few endearing attributes. Her characterization foregrounds self-centeredness. The effort to seek a reconciliation with her daughter is half-hearted, at best, and she is relieved when Mercedes's vacation will delay their meeting; this expression of relief comes on the next to the last page of the narrative, after the change of residence. By the same token, she seems more committed to verifying her husband's indiscretions than to saving their marriage. Indifference is a factor on both sides, warmth a factor on neither. Elena's dealings with the private investigator prompt her to invent a persona through which to transmit the tasks. The voice that she adopts is stylized, arrogant, and ultimately a bit absurd. The negotiation takes an unusual turn when Elena makes herself the object of the investigation, and in the end she is reduced to chastising the detective for coming to her rescue when she is mugged: "Su misión . . . no consiste en proteger a Elena Rincón de agresiones callejeras, sino en seguirla allá donde vaya e informarnos después de sus movimientos" (176). She continues:

> El informe es excesivamente corto, como si intentara ocultarnos algunos de los movimientos realizados por la investigada. Empezamos a tener la impresión de que a usted le gusta demasiado esa mujer y quizá tengamos que prescindir de sus servicios.

(176)

Elena is a woman with time on her hands, and her utilization of this time, it would seem, leaves something to be desired. It would be difficult to maintain that she comes to terms with the past or that she drafts a substantive program for the future. Nonetheless, she does make a break, and the ending is open.

In my opinion, *La soledad era esto* reaches an impasse, or a blind alley, with regard to determinism. The rationale—the ideological bases—of solitude are not inscribed into the text. If Elena Rincón is a victim of destiny, the value of her decisions is severely limited. If she is able to mold her destiny, the insubstantiality of her behavior shows through. It is, arguably, easier for the reader to see the author emplotting parallel circumstances and narrative variations than to see the protagonist in search of answers to fundamental and profound questions about her identity and about her place in the world. As a consequence, the novel portrays the effects of solitude but fails, to a great degree, to address its causes. The creation of an atmosphere of emptiness is a strength of *La soledad era esto,* but readers may wonder if emptiness here is more the result of missed opportunities than of an overriding, and abject, moral climate.

In what follows, I will enter two dangerous—some would say potentially "fallacious"—critical areas, intentionality and prescription, and I will attempt to transgress only minimally. I am less concerned with Juan José Millás than with the *implied author* of the novel, whom I "read" as wanting to present the central character at a crucial moment in her life. Elena's decision to leave Enrique and to begin anew is designed, I believe, to flow seamlessly from the events that precede the decision, but the apparent climax—the trip to Brussels—seems to involve a change of scenery rather

than a change of heart. It is hard to observe an evolution in Elena's thought or outlook, and it is hard to specify a precise direction that the new life will take. In short, it is not necessarily evident that increased self-knowledge is a product of the process that the reader has witnessed, yet neither is it evident that the novel's message is inescapable emptiness. While Millás appears to employ the motif of the character who at first floats through life and who then achieves insights that lead to a radical transformation of perspective, metamorphosis in *La soledad era esto* is somewhat illusory. If one chooses to be alone—or chooses not to pursue means of reconciliation—the rhetoric of solitude is affected. Millás is adept at evoking a particular milieu and the desolation that it inspires, but Elena Rincón's solitude operates in a vacuum, so to speak, despite the author's recourse to conventions that might suggest otherwise.

There is a critical paradigm—look at Pardo Bazán reading Galdós, for example—in which analysis takes the form of an implicit "The work in question would be better had the author done *this* instead of *that*." While I generally dislike, and distrust, this model—preferring to concentrate on what is there over what is not there and on criteria established by the author, not the critic—I find myself questioning a number of the narrative decisions made by Millás. The most basic is, of course, the treatment of solitude per se. Secondly, I do not understand the value of the shift in point of view, which is engaging from the structural dimension but whose value on the conceptual level eludes me. I do not see the merit of the many coincidences. The eerie effect produced by repetition of names is undermined by the forced correspondence in ages; Elena and her mother (at the time she wrote the diary entries) are the same age, as are Enrique and the detective. I find it unusual also that Millás would choose to emphasize the fact that Elena goes for a time without shaving one of her legs—she was waxing them when she received the notification of her mother's death—and that this detail makes its way into the investigator's report. Perhaps it is intended to serve as part of a frame, since Elena celebrates her independence by cutting her hair, but I am not sure that the discomfort I feel on reading these passages (and, to cite another example, Enrique's reference to a conversation that he had with his elderly father about masturbation) is a *meaningful* discomfort, a means of entry into the order of ideas in the novel. I would point, as well, to the diary entries themselves. There is no question that the mother's commentary is moving and dramatic, but it is, at the same time, overly literary and unnatural, in the sense that it plays too conveniently into the other plot—into Elena's story—and into the analogical scheme. The words are geared toward what the reader needs to know rather than toward the formulation of a unique and verisimilar voice. Note the following passage, for example:

> El parto más difícil fue el de Elena, que es la que más disgustos me da. Mi marido dice que discutimos tanto porque somos iguales de carácter. Pero yo digo que este

diario, o lo que sea, no es para hablar de los hijos. A los hijos los quiero y los atiendo, pero como tema de conversación prefiero el páncreas.

(51)

Solitude is the *dominant* (v. Jakobson), the unifying element around which the narrative is constructed. When Millás introduces the title phrase into the text, he stresses Elena Rincón's sensation that she is living in suspended animation, that she is disconnected from the world, that she is painfully alone. Nevertheless, this detachment takes the form neither of helpless passivity nor of worthwhile activity. Millás fills the space between the old life and the new with a trivial pursuit—an upper-middle-class game of espionage—that demeans the protagonist and reduces the impact of the transition. The semiotics of change is manifested in a haircut, as contrasted with Elena's expression of relief that she will not have to confront her daughter. It seems to me that, within the parameters of the plot, the author must select stasis or movement for his character, and I would contend that he allows Elena Rincón to rest uncomfortably in the middle.

There is a remarkable resemblance between **La soledad era esto** and Kate Chopin's *The Awakening,* first published in 1899. The "awakening" of Edna Pontellier, Chopin's protagonist, takes place before the narrative begins, and the story shows the realization or the effects of Edna's detachment from those around her. Edna is a flawed character, and her flaws give the author a mediating space from which to examine such issues as protocols of matrimony, idealized love, feminine stereotypes, self-determination, and women and language. Chopin distinguishes between a surface structure of prosperity and fulfillment and a deep structure of dissatisfaction and inner turmoil. It is not my purpose here to analyze *The Awakening,* nor do I wish to advocate an irresponsible use of comparisons—I believe that I understand the message of Borges's "Pierre Menard"—but I would like to propose that Chopin succeeds in doing what Millás leaves on dubious ground. *The Awakening* is supremely ironic, and—for me, this is the most significant difference between the two novels—its ambiguities are *meaningful,* logical, justifiable on all levels of story and discourse, that is, and paradoxically, internally consistent. Edna Pontellier is trapped *in* and *by* society, *in* and *by* language, *in* and *by* gender. The symbolism of *The Awakening* is densely textured, richly inflected, and impressively open, in part because—unlike Elena Rincón—Edna Pontellier is both a victim and a character who can be held responsible for her actions. It is not so much the clarity of the messages but the coherence of the message systems that differentiates the two novels. It is the difference, I believe, between ambition and achievement.

Works Cited

Chopin, Kate. *The Awakening.* Ed. Nancy A. Walker. Boston: St. Martin's, 1993.

Jakobson, Roman. "The Dominant." *Twentieth-Century Literary Theory: A Reader.* Ed. K. M. Newton. London: Macmillan, 1988. 26-30.

Millás, Juan José. *La soledad era esto.* Barcelona: Destino, 1994.

Pardo Bazán, Emilia. "*Tristana.*" *Nuevo Teatro Crítico* 2.17 (May 1892): 77-90.

Yaw Agawu-Kakraba (essay date 1999)

SOURCE: Agawu-Kakraba, Yaw. "Juan José Millás' *La soledad era esto* and the Process of Subjectivity." *Forum for Modern Language Studies* 35.1 (1999): 81-94. Print.

[*In the following essay, Agawu-Kakraba evaluates Elena's reinvention of herself and her rediscovery of personal power in Millás's* That Was Loneliness. *Agawu-Kakraba scrutinizes Elena's efforts to differentiate herself from her mother and her husband, and traces the effects of her transformation, including the limitations it places on the structure of the novel.*]

Various schools of thought in the twentieth century such as psychoanalysis, existentialism, surrealism, structuralism, poststructuralism and postmodernism have contended with the question of the subject or the self in which different formulations of the self have evolved. Indeed, the subject has undergone a complex process of differentiation in social and cultural theory to the extent that one finds, for instance, Lévi-Strauss using linguistics to do structural exercises on myths in order to comprehend the parallels beyond knowledge or agency in the human subject. Karl Marx finds the making of history outside voluntary human agency, by social forces. For Ferdinand Saussure, language exists prior to its speaker and has the ability to constitute the speaker at the instance of its enunciation.[1]

In their discussion of subjectivity, Jean Paul-Sartre and Michel Foucault also advance theories of the self. In *Being and Nothingness,* Sartre talks about self-creation as the moment of consciousness in which values or meanings are inserted into the world (Part II, Chapters 1, 2, 5). Sartre moved closer to a balanced relationship of self and world in *Critique of Dialectical Reason.* However, the self in this case continues to be based on fleeting consciousness. If Sartre conceived of self-constitution as the internal experience of consciousness, Foucault strives to understand it as fundamental to normative discourses, social codes, and systems of knowledge. Foucault's "mode of subjection (mode d'assujetissement), that is, the way in which people are invited or incited to recognize their moral obligations"[2] is a system of governance divided into four categories: "technologies of production," "technologies of sign systems," "technologies of power," and "technologies of self."[3]

The last two of these categories, "technologies of power" and "technologies of self," are germane to my attempt to read Juan José Millás' *La soledad era esto* in which the protagonist of the novel makes a conscious effort at self-constitution and identification. While "technologies of power" mould subjects as a means of subordinating individuals and bringing them to define themselves in specific ways, "technologies of self" are utilised by individuals as a way of transforming their conditions into those of a more autonomous sense of contentment.[4] The last phase of Foucault's theory of the subject that he calls ethics, presented in 1980, in which a concerted effort is made to understand the contingency of self-constitution, a genuine search for an ethics, is applicable to the protagonist in Millás' *La soledad era esto.* The purpose of this study is to examine how the novel engages the issue of subjectivity in which, as an individual, the protagonist Elena Rincón plays the dual role of being exposed to certain roles and structures defined by institutions of power, discourse, and theories of the person, and the construction of a self fixed to her own identity by a consciousness of self-knowledge. I want to argue that Elena displays a rather naive disposition to "technologies of power" in her bid to undermine alterities and heterogeneities when she attempts to generate resistance to an established social order from which she has profited. The protagonist's desire to redefine her identity in which she transforms herself into an individual who upholds certain moral, ethical, and even political values, is flawed because she fails to acknowledge the fact that, a priori, the invitation to recognise one's moral responsibilities in itself takes place only within the confines of what Foucault calls "mode of subjection" ("How We Behave," p. 67). Put differently, the technologies of governance, which are mechanisms through which the collective is managed and subsequently manages itself, make it impossible for one to develop a complete ethical identity.

La soledad era esto, winner of the prestigious Premio Nadal in 1990, is the story of Elena Rincón, who, upon the death of her mother, undergoes a slow metamorphosis through which she realises that she can obtain her liberation only by learning how to deal with solitude. That is to say, solitude becomes the progenitor of the realisation of the self as agent capable of attaining self-awareness in spite of social confinement. Idealists in their youth, both Elena and her husband, Enrique Acosta, participated in student movements at the university dedicated to bringing about democratic change. The end of the authoritarian Franco regime meant the establishment of another system in which the likes of Acosta occupy important positions. With the radical social restructuring of the post-Franco era in which economic prosperity and political freedom become the norm, a new class of citizens emerges. As the detective whom Elena hires puts it, members of this class:

> Me hicieron la revolución, como quien dice, y luego se largaron a ocupar despachos y consejos de administración y direcciones generales desde las que han perdido la memoria de la gente como yo. Son los que fueron siempre,

unos señoritos, pero conservan de aquel paréntesis de sus vidas el gusto por el hachís o por la cocaína.

(p. 92)

The new post-Franco urban landscape that the detective portrays, framed by sociopolitical and economic correctness, becomes the backdrop against which the reader notices the factors that constitute the structures that determine the self in contemporary Spain.

The account of the life and death of Elena's mother suggests that, living under the Francoist government, the mother has been forced to recondition herself by interiorising and exteriorising the values spelled out within an ideologically-minded regime that sought social conformity with the hope of creating a unique Spanish society.[5] But being circumscribed by the Francoist institutions of power mitigates against the classic tension that John Stuart Mill in *On Liberty* believes is critical in the relation between the individual and the state. He notes the importance of a "necessarily antagonistic" relationship between "subjects, or some classes of subjects, and the government" that generates an indispensable relationship between "liberty and authority," "society [and] the individual" (p. 59). The constantly shifting position between the interiorisation and exteriorisation of the Francoist values creates a situation for Elena's mother in which her essence becomes decentred. In fact, as one proceeds to read Elena's mother's diaries with her, so does one surmise that the body of the protagonist's mother has been proscribed completely from her inner essence. After drawing an impressive portrait of how parts of her body represent different sections of the community within which she lives ("las uñas de mis pies son la periferia de mi barrio. Por eso están rotas y deformes [. . .]. Mi cuello parece un callejón que comunica dos zonas desiertas" [p. 49]), the mother concludes: "Por mi cuerpo no se puede ni andar de sucio que está y el Ayuntamiento no hace nada por arreglarlo" (p. 49). Elena's mother's lack of happiness because of her acceptance of the social structures within which she finds herself hostage and her psychological malaise lead to an intense physical discomfort. She resorts to drugs and alcohol, and finally she rediscovers a subjectivity that she hopes would promote a personal liberation.

The death of Elena's mother, coupled with the diaries she finds in her mother's apartment, forces the protagonist to reflect on her life as she notices a rather surprising mirror-like image with her mother. The mother's apparent discovery of a selfhood prompts Elena to come to terms with her past and present life. She re-examines her life and also uses the services of a detective to spy on her and Enrique. The idea is to provide Elena with a dimension of herself that may escape her. In short, the mother's story and history will eventually become the blueprint for Elena's quest for a spiritual, moral and psychological liberation.

Elena's self-analysis of her situation, her mother's diary, and the detective's reports enable her to develop a singularity that supposedly undermines the discursive authority embedded in the newly-established social codes. The result is an apparent total rebirth for Elena. She separates from her husband and sets the stage for a new life that she hopes will bring about a radical transformation of her selfhood. Elena's decision to subvert the hitherto rigid tradition of marriage and motherhood in her bid to attain what can be termed a Sartrean self-creation, or, in Foucault's terms, self-constitution that attempts to locate a ground for personal freedom, reminds us of Jacques Derrida's notion of singularity. In his discussion of singularity, Derrida transforms the traditional notions of the self-reflexive, self-determining subject when he conceives of agency as singularity in which an individual can subvert authority. For Derrida, singularity not only entails the signatures the individual leaves as traces designed to subvert the authority of existing categories, but also signals one's ability to define simultaneously one's difference as well as to expose oneself to irreducible alterity and heterogeneity in social life. While singularity raises the spectre of the individual's ability to subvert authority, it simultaneously locates the individual within factors that are beyond its limits. Elena's belief that she has discovered the tools necessary for a self-constitution that fails to acknowledge its connection with the outside world is thus fraught with problems since self-constitution, as the inner experience of consciousness, invariably takes into account social codes and normative discourses. In addition, as Derrida has argued, any subjective agency capable of engaging an ethics engendering a responsibility without resorting to rationalist or humanist notions of self-constitution must contend with the concept of intentionality. Derrida believes that traditional ideals of self-knowledge about one's intentions cannot bring about a coherent self or a consistent notion of the self. As a result, it is imperative to confront the most unpredictable elements within those old ideals and generate fresh positions capable of entertaining the issues of value and ethical responsibility. For Derrida, whatever is ascribed to intentionality must be contrasted with some variety of forces that are not controlled by intention, a kind of non-self embedded within the self that is basically a Kantian empirical self.[6] But the realisation of the subject's intention can be effected only when it makes its particularity an object of desire which can be easily overlooked since the realised intention becomes accessible to the public. The individual's attainment of intentionality and desire thus becomes public knowledge that robs the self of the ability to engage in an enterprise that is singular, personal, and devoid of outside interference.

As law students at the university of Madrid, Elena's and Enrique's desires and intention to work against the Francoist dictatorship become public knowledge, thanks to the private detective's excellent work. By the same token, their shift from leftist militants to shameless upper middle-class consumers becomes apparent to the reader through Elena's brother Juan's description of their social status:

—Yo [...] nunca te he entendido bien, Elena. A tu marido tampoco. Y, sin embargo, recuerdo que en un tiempo os tuve muy idealizados. Representabais lo que más que se podía ser en esta vida. Estoy hablando de hace muchos años, cuando en casa se os criticaba por meteros en cosas políticas. Bueno, será mejor que no hable de esto. Pero, mira, yo no te entiendo, de verdad. Has tenido siempre lo que has querido: de joven, la revolución; ahora el dinero. ¿De qué te quejas?

(p. 136)

Clearly, both Elena and Enrique have realised their desires and have become rationally selfish consumers in post-Franco Spain. Ironically, however, the fulfilment of their desires also frustrates their intentionality, especially if one is to believe that intentionality is fundamentally a construction in which agents link desire to targeted objectives, which then implement intention outside the subject and necessitate an unworking of fulfilments. Unlike Enrique Acosta, Elena comes to terms with the Cartesian bind and opts for the viewpoint that, as an individual, what is crucial is not the fate of specific objects of desire but her understanding that she can continue to shape intentions in view of what is realised and in view of the interests that ensure that certain realisations are desired.

The death of Elena's mother signals the juncture at which Elena's subjective crisis comes to a head. Prior to her mother's death, Elena already manifests symptoms that can be said to represent the affluent middle-class "nouveau riche" woman: married to a man who ostensibly makes a fortune in his business deals, Elena does not have to work. The private detective puts it well when he says: "Elena Rincón podrá ser una mezcla de ama de casa contemporánea y mujer liberada que no soporta las imposiciones de un trabajo regular" (p. 93). But financial security is not enough. To pass her time, she constantly smokes marijuana and when faced with insomnia, a few shots of whisky or cognac come in handy. However, it is difficult to know whether Elena's recourse to drugs and alcohol is the result of her physical malaise and psychological and moral depression. One thing is clear, however. The protagonist is in constant physical distress. Elena's recourse to hashish and alcohol eerily echoes her late mother's experiences. She indirectly invites the reader to see her as a reflection of her mother during a meeting with her siblings, Juan and Mercedes, to decide what to do with their mother's house. The numerous cheap cognac bottles that Elena discovers in one of her mother's wardrobes and the contents of her mother's personal diaries reveal a parallel between mother and daughter.

In one of her entries, Elena's mother relates a story that her own mother told her when she was young. The entry indicates that every one has an antipode who experiences the same things that the individual experiences. Although the mother acknowledges the impossibility of encountering one's antipode, she decides to name her opposite Elena, a name that she subsequently gives to her daughter (p. 61). While the mother intends to play a game, she underlines what Wolgang Iser calls the "doubling of fictionality." According to Iser,

> The lack of any transcendental reference and the impossibility of any overarching third dimension show literary fictionality to be marked by an ineradicable duality, and indeed this is the source of its operational power. Since the duality cannot be unified, the origin of the split eludes capture, and yet it remains present as the driving force that constantly seeks to bring separated entities together.

> (p. 80)

Elena's mother is right when she signals the impossibility of converging with her antipode because her opposite escapes containment. But at the same time, her insistent allusion to her antipode paradoxically has the power to bring her even closer. Unaware that her own daughter could be her opposite, Elena's mother unknowingly paints her daughter's portrait:[7]

> Algunas tardes, cuando comprendo que estoy bebiendo más coñá de la cuenta, pienso que a lo mejor es cosa de mi antípoda, de Elena, que se ha alcoholizado por no saber hacer frente a los momentos difíciles de la vida, como este de la soledad que nos ha tocado vivir a las dos en la vejez. Me da pena porque se está destruyendo, aunque a lo mejor en una de estas se suicida y me hace descansar a mí también.

> (pp. 61-2)

This diary entry is important because it lays emphasis on the fundamental crisis that mother and daughter face: solitude and the subsequent interrogation of one's subjectivity. Most importantly, it reflects for the mother a core of her self that can be viewed in the mirror self. Iser discovers that as their own doppelgängers, "human beings are at best differential, traveling between their various roles that supplant and modify one another. Roles are not disguises with which to fulfil pragmatic ends; they are means of enabling the self to be other than each individual role. Being oneself therefore means being able to double oneself" (pp. 80-1). For Iser, the question of duality arises as a result of the individual's "decentered position" in which one's "existence is incontestable, but at the same time is inaccessible to [one]" (p. 81). The significance of the mother's invention of a doppelgänger is striking. Like an actor, she identifies with her antipode, a nonexistent entity, in order for her to be able to constitute herself in accordance with that personification. Put differently, her boundary-crossing is designed to discover herself outside of herself. Elena's mother's invention—her identification—fits what Iser believes the essence of doubling: "identifying oneself with a phantom in order to bring it to life entails no longer being what one was, even if the new shape is partially conditioned by what one was before" (p. 81). Having abandoned her parched and wasted body, she must of necessity identify herself with her double. However, she paradoxically

hopes that her opposite would also manifest some of the symptoms she has:

> Permanecí durante mucho rato en el cuarto de baño, sin llegar a desmayarme, aunque tengo cierta facilidad para ello, sobre todo desde que Elena, mi antípoda, se ha dado al alcohol y a las pastillas. Tuve un pensamiento extraño que quizá perteneciera a mi antípoda, que estaría en ese instante en otro hotel contrario al mío temblando de miedo como yo.

> (p. 102)

The mother's wishes suggest that she does not really believe that her absent antipode potentially could have qualities that she lacks. Helmuth Plessner has noted that "given the disposition of being a doppelgänger—a structure which allows the human being any kind of self-understanding—, does by no means imply that the one half of the other is to be seen as 'by nature' the better. The doppelgänger merely has the possibility of making it so" (p. 235).[8] The mother is either unwilling or unable to construct her opposite in such a manner that the opposite acquires qualities that are superior because she recognises that, as mother, her existence cannot be authenticated since she is separated from herself: "Lo malo es vivir lejos de una misma, que es como vivo yo desde hace años" (p. 128). She cannot in real terms fathom her being. The image that she constructs of herself in the form of her antipode lacks substance in so far as she is convinced that she possesses her self through it. The fundamental difference between Elena and her mother becomes apparent. Unlike her mother, Elena recognises the limitations of her subjectivity and is willing to articulate them in order to evolve a singularity capable of subverting authority and emancipating the self from extraneous social factors.

The point at which Elena takes the narrative reins into her own hands reflects the moment when she begins a gradual and systematic transformation of the self. It also marks a shift that echoes Foucault's idea of self-constitution in the context of morality in which one forms "oneself as an ethical subject." For him,

> [a] history of the way in which individuals are urged to constitute themselves as subjects of moral conduct would be concerned with the models proposed for setting up and developing relationships with the self, for self-reflection, self-knowledge, self-examination, for the decipherment of the self by oneself, for the transformations that one seeks to accomplish with oneself as object.

> (*The Use of Pleasure*, p. 29)

The shift from an omniscient third-person narrator in the first half of the novel to a first-person narrative voice—that of Elena's in the second half—is not accidental. The switch indicates a change from the "descriptive," narrated from the point of view of the omniscient narrator, to the "experiential," in which Elena self-represents the transformation that she is undergoing. By the same token, the role of the private detective shifts. The interpolation of the detective's reports within Elena's text is important for the protagonist because those reports enable her to sketch the contours of her new self perceived through the mirror of another. For that matter, Elena insists that, rather than sticking to the rules of his profession by reporting cryptically his findings, the detective should engage in a kind of narrative that is more introspective. By demanding a more profound examination, scrutiny, and reflection of her self perceived through the looking-glass of another—the private investigator—Elena is ready to autoanalyse her own subjectivity and her intent on initiating a transformation.

The chronicle of Elena's transformation and new self-constitution as individual takes place through the simultaneous act of speaking directly to her readers and the inscription of that discourse in a diary. The act of writing her own life mirrors that of her mother because the traces of her signature seem to be inserted within the margins of her mother's chronicle. Both mother and daughter embark on the same metaphorical journey:

> He comprado un conjunto de pequeños cuadernos, cosidos con grapas, que se parecen mucho a los que utilizó mi madre para llevar a cabo un raro e incompleto diario que, tras su muerte, fue a parar a mis manos. Mi vida discurre apaciblemente entre la lectura de su diario y la redacción del mío.

> (p. 108)

Elena's act of writing her diary is important. Writing for her becomes a creative mechanism and, as in the case of her mother, a substantiation of the attempt to leave part of herself to posterity.[9] But there is a crucial distinction between Elena and her mother. While her mother makes no conscious effort to redefine her subjectivity and resigns her fate to a Madrid that she calls "este barrio roto" (p. 48), Elena's writing indirectly reinforces her desire to reconstitute herself. For that matter, Elena jettisons what for a long time has defined the core of her existence with her husband. When she moves out and finds her own apartment, she intends to initiate a completely new life:

> Y comprendí también que no regresaría a casa, no porque me fuese a morir, como mi madre cuando recibió la visita de su antípoda, sino porque iba a acelerar el proceso de convertirme en otra para encontrar al fin mi propio infierno y descansar.

> (p. 161)

Elena in this instance seeks recourse to language and battles with self-constitution through the control of an enunciative statement. Her enunciation is more or less a confessional that is a discursive practice. However, Elena does not have any illusions that her transformation in personhood, her new subjectivity, is going to be an easy one:

> En cualquier caso, estos días, dedicados a resolver las cuestiones prácticas de mi próxima existencia, me han hecho reflexionar un poco sobre mis inclinaciones bur-

guesas y me he visto obligada a darle la razón a Enrique en algunas cosas. No viviría en cualquier sitio ni sin unas comodidades mínimas, a las que ya estoy acostumbrada, pero tampoco estoy dispuesta a que el disfrute de tales comodidades constituya el precio de no saber quién soy ni dónde están mis intereses.

> (pp. 162-3)

Although she does not display a radical departure from the bourgeois taste that she has acquired, Elena believes that the act of turning back on what had hitherto constituted her mode of existence, even if limited, does not compromise her new subjectivity. That new subjectivity is spelled out when Elena realises for the first time that her physical discomfort has vanished entirely:

> En estos momentos siento que la rareza intestinal ha desaparecido y noto su ausencia como la ausencia de la melena cada vez que inclino la cabeza. *Hay dos hombres discutiendo en la calle, frente a mi terraza; forman parte de esa sociedad, de esa máquina que Enrique, mi marido, representaba tan bien.* Viven dentro de una pesadilla de la que se sienten artífices. Cuando despierten de ese sueño, les llevaré una vida de ventaja.

> (p. 181 [my italics])

Elena's rediscovery of self in which apparently she escapes from the discursive practices that frame her husband and others, implies for the protagonist a forming of herself as an ethical subject. It also implies a self-constitution within the confines of Foucault's elaboration of the term in which the theorist notes that it is imperative to "look for the forms and modalities of the relation to self by which the individual constitutes and recognizes himself *qua* subject" (*The Use of Pleasure,* p. 6). Elena's self-constitution could be likened to an inner experience of consciousness in which she believes her situation involves social, emotional, spiritual and psychological emancipation. On the other hand, she finds her daughter, Mercedes, just like her father, incapable of coming to terms with her own identy by realising that as individuals they are "subject to someone else by control and dependence; and tied to [their] own identity by a conscience or self-knowledge" (Foucault, p. 778). In other words, Elena thinks that Mercedes and Enrique are trapped within a social structure that inhibits their freedom and ability to recognise the need for self-transformation. In his discussion of transformation of selfhood, Charles Altieri spells out the end result of subjectivity. He observes that

> The crucial issue for subjectivity is no longer the necessary struggle against determining itself but the possibility of understanding what provides transitions among intentions and dictates the subject's sense of directed agency. It is precisely this shift which enables us to explain why in most cases we do not actually feel any loss when intentions are realized; instead we feel the need to adapt to the situation thus produced.

> (p. 88)

Elena's apparent rediscovery of self, her new agency, forcefully echoes Altieri's exegesis of self-transformation. Consequently, one can now understand why, although prior to the discovery of her new subjectivity Elena feels a sense of guilt for not being "motherly" to her daughter, she does not really feel any loss once she achieves her liberation. She notes:

> He telefoneado a mi hija con intención de invitarla a comer, pero me ha dicho que mañana mismo sale de vacaciones y que tenía que prepararlo todo. No quería verme y para mí ha sido una liberación, pues todavía no tengo mucho que decirle.

> (p. 180)

In contrast with her daughter, Elena is ready to adapt to her new situation:

> En los próximos meses, su bulto y el mío crecerán de forma paralela, *pero el mío, aquel a través del cual me naceré, crece hacia la posibilidad de una vida nueva, diferente,* mientras que el suyo crece hacia la repetición mecánica de lo que ha visto hacer en otros. Mercedes no ha advertido aún que es mujer y que esa condición implica un mandato al que tarde o temprano hay que enfrentarse si queremos que esa vida continúe mereciendo la pena.

> (p. 180 [my italics])

Elena's observations are crucial. They raise the spectre of the woman condemned to live under certain inflexible social codes and forced to tread mechanically the difficult path that other women have trodden. At the same time, they confirm an earlier reflection on her past when she puts the effects of hashish in perspective:

> Con el hachís me pasó algo parecido, porque gracias a él tuve acceso a una percepción diferente de la realidad y me ayudó a escapar de las cárceles en las que suelen caer las mujeres, en general, y en la que estaba destinada a mí, en particular. El hachís me ayudó a ver la trampa, como diría Enrique, que se esconde debajo de las cosas, pero me proporcionó también un sinfín de desarreglos que conducían a un modo de autodestrucción que desde esta nueva perspectiva me resulta incomprensible.

> (p. 171)

The clarity she attains from avoiding the effects of drugs and alcohol allows Elena to put things in perspective. Like any other woman, she also is trapped within an undefined prison constructed by a male-dominated world. Part of that undetermined prison is revealed in the patronising nature of the relationship between Elena and Enrique as revealed in a conversation in which Elena asks Enrique if he thinks they are vulgar because of their lifestyle and the abandonment of their socialist cause. As if to suggest that Elena lacks the intellectual ability to reflect on themselves, Enrique, in a patronising fashion, attempts to exonerate Elena and assumes full responsibility for their actions (pp. 68-9). Most importantly, however, Elena's belief that she has found a new life suggests a discovery of an enunciative

statement in which, having wrestled with self-constitution, she manipulates the symbols and the systematised rules of formation that had hitherto shaped the formation of herself.

Unlike her mother and her daughter, Elena opts for a conversion in her beliefs. She shatters her former convictions to the extent that she succeeds in transforming her ontology and the content of those beliefs. Elena's new beliefs remind us of Jacques Schlanger's assertion that "there is a conversion, a thorough transformation in our beliefs and, very often, in the conduct of our lives when we abandon beliefs that have been very important to us and we start holding new beliefs, beliefs that are sometimes opposed to the beliefs we have discarded because of them" (p. 124). As to be expected, Enrique does not undergo the same kind of conversion. As mentioned earlier, Enrique and his daughter Mercedes are still imprisoned within the universe from which Elena believes she has escaped.[10] As a result, Elena's new subjectivity from which she interrogates the ethics of her past life is completely at odds with Enrique's. While Elena has now discovered a distinct kind of vocabulary to define her new self, her husband still holds on to the old paradigm. As a matter of fact, Bakhtin's affirmation that within the polyphonic novel it is conceivable for characters' discordant social vocabularies to interact "dialogically" to produce an exchange in which "each language reveals to the other what it did not know about itself, and in which new insights are produced that neither wholly contained before," does not apply to Elena and her husband.[11] The dialogic interaction between them does not yield the appropriate insights that enable them to contemplate each other's positions. This is so because while Enrique's existence is still defined by the post-Francoist society in which greed, corruption, and political manoeuvring are the status quo, Elena, on the other hand believes she has now attained a subjectivity, a level of consciousness, that is in direct conflict with the norms that define Enrique. The dialogic tension between Elena and her husband, which becomes transparent in Enrique's letter to her, suggests that unlike Elena whose language now reflects a new self-consciousness, Enrique is still imprisoned within a language that is limited by cultural/social circumstances. In one of their conversations in which Elena attempts to interrogate their past activities, the gap between husband and wife becomes obvious: "—Hay cosas—respondí—que no guardan relación con el dinero. Tú y yo hemos vivido de esas cosas en otro tiempo" (p. 160). In response, Enrique makes it clear that he is not ready to change the status quo: "—Mira, Elena, en esa época teníamos impulsos, pero carecíamos de ideas. Yo ahora tengo ideas, estoy lleno de ideas que se alimentan con dinero o con los atributos del dinero y no pienso renunciar a ellas porque son mi razón de ser" (p. 160). The assumption that an engagement in a dialogic exchange engenders the ability to see the social field and the fortuitous character of all cultural paradigms—hegemonic and subversive alike—does not hold true for

Enrique. For Elena, however, dialogism implies a more pronounced revelation of the other side of the spectrum that she once inhabited.

Elena's notion of agency opens new demands for another subjectivity but it is somewhat limiting because the individual act must be located within an identical configuration of forces maintained by broader cultural determinants. The question to be asked is whether Elena can, in fact, evolve a self-constitution in isolation from the technologies of power that seem to determine the social mores to which she is intricately tied. Put differently, can one really discover what she calls "una vida nueva" (p. 180) in which one is able to transform oneself in order to allow for greater rationality and autonomy? To answer this question, one must take into consideration the fact that the deep self is a cultural invention. As Foucault has shown, the need for self-discovery prompts us to look for therapies and confessional practices that provide exceptional access into our lives since, by virtue of our culture's mode of enunciation and techniques of self-formation, we are more easily responsive to its management techniques and "normalising" practices.[12] If one is to give credence to Foucault's idea that determinative power is dispersed among a limitless number of sites where knowledge and power intersect, and that this dispersal is part of a "totalising" process which is an integral part of life in the modern economy of confession, control and surveillance, with coercion becoming less a matter of the state's policing power and more a matter of the internalising of vocabularies by individuals, then one can conclude that Elena's attempt at self-constitution is limited. That is to say, Elena's new selfhood is not as progressive as she would want the readers of her diaries to believe since the enactment of this selfhood finds site within a sociohistorical condition that provides inadequate resources for the implementation of a personal subjectivity. Indeed, the mere fact that she still relies on her husband's monthly allowance suggests a dependence on a system from which she so desperately wants to escape. Irrespective of Elena's naive understanding of subject formation in society and particularly so in post-Franco Spain, she nevertheless evolves a personal identity cognisant of its abilities to undermine alterities and heterogeneities. The result is a transformation in which Elena constitutes herself as an ethical subject that is willing to resist an established social order from which she has profited.

Notes

1. In "The Jewish Question," Karl Marx offers a critique of the liberal solution to the project of human emancipation. He contends that the liberal interpretation of emancipation is flawed because it is confined to political freedom. Marx proposes instead a kind of liberation that encompasses civil society as well as politics, the private sphere as well as the public. The structuralist anthropology of Claude Lévi-Strauss suggests that one can conceive of myths as a problem-solving mechanism, adjusted to context in divers ways but always going back to the persistent issues of human existence—principally the structures of law and taboo that circumscribe institutions such as marriage, the family, tribal identity, and so forth (*Tristes Tropiques*). Like many poststructuralists, Foucault persuasively addresses the problem of the theoretical subject in "Truth and Power" (pp. 109-33). Referring to what he calls the "space" of postmodernism, Fredric Jameson advocates a radical new "space" that undermines all attempts at self-location, of referential self-coordination. He proposes new categories of thought, an "aesthetic of cognitive mapping" that enhances "a breakthrough to some as yet unimaginable new mode of representing [...] in which we may again begin to grasp our positioning as individual and collective subjects and regain a capacity to act and struggle" (p. 92). For Saussure's contention that language is a system that defines the subject, see *Course in General Linguistics*.

2. See Foucault's "How We Behave" (pp. 66-7).

3. See Foucault's "Technologies of the Self" (p. 18).

4. See Foucault's "Technologies of the Self" (p. 18).

5. In order to rediscover what they call the essential origins that constituted an authentic Spanish essence, the Franco government, like other totalitarian regimes such as Hitler's Germany and Mussolini's Italy, resorted to myth and propaganda. The Francoist use of myth, as I show in my *Demythification in the Fiction of Miguel Delibes* (pp. 6, 7, 151), deployed myth as a will to power and domination of Spaniards who were forced to conform to officially sanctioned cultural values.

6. See Altieri's study (especially p. 144), in which he explores the Derridean concept of intentionality which is linked to the Kantian notion of the empirical self.

7. There is no indication at this point that the mother believes that her daughter, Elena, is her opposite. In her final entry, however, for some inexplicable reason, she identifies her daughter as her antipode. But Elena disputes the certainty of that assertion and suggests that her mother could have confused her with her real opposite, a woman whom Elena claims she saw in a hotel lobby on a visit to Brussels with Enrique: "En realidad, me estaba confundiendo con su antípoda, lo que por un lado resulta halagador y, por otro, terrible. Además, me he acordado de que en la recepción del hotel vi a una mujer que parecía a mí y con un vestido que quizá fue mío en otro tiempo" (pp. 157-8). On that basis, she concludes that that woman could have been her opposite as well as her mother's: "Tal vez sea mi antípoda, tal vez se haya escapado de su lugar geométrico para venir a anunciarnos

nuestra muerte, la mía y la de ella [mi madre]" (p. 158). The fact that the mysterious woman could be the opposite of both the protagonist and her mother suggests the strong mirror-like image and affinity between the three, to the extent that each duplicates the other.

8. Cited from Iser (p. 80).

9. One cannot help recalling Sartre's notion (in _What Is Literature?_, p. 165) that writing is a form of doing and "doing reveals being. Each gesture traces out new forms on the earth. Each technique, each tool, is a way that opens upon the world; things have as many aspects as there are ways of using them. We are no longer with those who want to possess the world, but with those who want to change it."

10. Enrique's letter to Elena in which he simultaneously sympathises with Elena and condemns her actions reflects the position from which he is speaking. His actions are framed by different factors. Cates Baldrige notes that "whenever a character in a novel speaks, he or she reveals a perspective on reality shaped by concrete cultural factors such as class, occupation, gender, or generation, meaning that when fictional persons interact, what really comes into proximity and often into conflict are the various self-interested and partial descriptions of the social system they articulate" (p. 12). Enrique articulates a social system that he has profited from. On the other hand, Elena will enunciate a discourse that transcends those factors that hitherto had shaped her essence.

11. To some extent, it can be argued that _La soledad era esto_ is a polyphonic novel. Bakhtin defines such a novel, in which those figures whose social perspectives oppose those of the narrator, as one in which "a character's word about himself and his world is just as fully weighted as the author's _not only [as] objects of authorial discourse but also [as] subjects of their own directly signifying discourse_" (p. 7). While Millás is no self-styled social realist, one wonders if on some level the author might be advocating the moral and spiritual transformation that Elena undergoes.

12. In _The History of Sexuality_, Foucault examines the development of a science of sexuality and its normalising force over us.

Works Cited

Agawu-Kakraba, Yaw, _Demythification in the Fiction of Miguel Delibes_ (New York, 1996).

Altieri, Charles, "Intentionality without Interiority: Wittgenstein and the Dynamics of Subjective Agency," in: _Transformations in Personhood and Culture after Theory_,

ed. Christie McDonald & Gary Wihl (University Park, 1994), pp. 85-116.

Bakhtin, Mikhail, _Problems of Dostoevsky's Poetics_, ed. & trans. Caryl Emerson (Minneapolis, 1984).

Baldridge, Cates, _The Dialogics of Dissent in the English Novel_ (Hanover, 1994).

Derrida, Jacques, _Limited Inc_, trans. Gerald Graff (Evanston, 1988).

Foucault, Michel, _The History of Sexuality. An Introduction_, Vol. 1 (New York, 1980).

———, "How We Behave," _Vanity Fair_ (November, 1983), 66-7.

———, _Technologies of the Self: A Seminar with Michel Foucault_, ed. Luther H. Martin (London, 1988).

———, "Truth and Power" in: _Power/Knowledge: Selected Interviews and Other Writings, 1972-1977_, ed. Colin Gordon, trans. Colin Gordon et al. (New York, 1980).

———, _The Use of Pleasure_, trans. Robert Hurley (New York, 1985).

Iser, Wolfgang, _The Fictive and the Imaginary. Charting Literary Anthropology_ (Baltimore, 1993).

Jameson, Fredric, "Postmodernism; or, The Cultural Logic of Late Capitalism," _New Left Review_ 146 (1984), 53-92.

Lévi-Strauss, Claude, _Tristes Tropiques_, trans. John Russell (London, 1961).

Marx, Karl, "The Jewish Question," in: _Selected Essays_, trans. H. J. Stenning (Freeport, 1968).

Mill, John Stuart, _On Liberty_ (Harmondsworth, 1974).

Millás, Juan José, _La soledad era esto_ (Barcelona, 1990).

Plessner, Helmuth, "Soziale Rolle und menschliche Natur" in: _Gesammelte Schriften_, X, ed. Günter Dux (Frankfurt, 1985).

Poster, Mark, _Critical Theory and Poststructuralism_ (Ithaca, 1989).

Saussure, Ferdinand de, _Course in General Linguistics_, trans. Wade Baskin (London, 1974).

Sartre, Jean-Paul, _Being and Nothingness: An Essay in Phenomenological Ontology_, trans. Hazel E. Barnes (New York, 1964).

———, _Critique of Dialectical Reason_, trans. Alan Sheridan-Smith (London, 1976).

———, _What Is Literature?_, trans. Bernard Frechtman (New York, 1966).

Schlanger, Jacques, "Changing One's Beliefs," in: _Transformations in Personhood and Culture after Theory_, ed.

Christie McDonald & Gary Wihl (University Park, 1994), pp. 117-31.

Yaw Agawu-Kakraba (essay date 1999)

SOURCE: Agawu-Kakraba, Yaw. "Desire, Psychoanalysis, and Violence: Juan José Millas' *El desorden de tu nombre." Anales de la literatura española contemporánea* 24.1-2 (1999): 17-34. Print.

[*In the following essay, Agawu-Kakraba discusses the various manifestations and implications of desire in Millás's* The Disorder of Your Name, *referencing Jacques Lacan's theory of desire and doubling. Agawu-Kakraba focuses on the "mimic game" played by the protagonist and the author as each of them writes his respective novel.*]

In *Deceit, Desire, and the Novel,* René Girard indicates that desire is "triangular" with a structure based on three components: the agent who desires, the object of this agent's desire, and the agent who serves as the "model" or "mediator" of the desire. Girard provides the reason why the mimetic subject wittingly or unwittingly constructs models, mediators, and masters who are superior to him/herself: because the mimetic subject suffers from an "ontological sickness," because he/she secretly wants to appropriate the "being" of the "Other," the mimetic subject demonstrates an insistent pursuit for transcendence. Girard reiterates the mimetic subject's quest for "being" in *Violence and the Sacred* when he suggests that because the model is someone who possesses a plenitude of being, the mimetic subject by attempting to imitate the desires of the model demonstrates a lack of being (204). He further asserts that mimetic desire unquestionably involves rivalry, conflict, and violence. He writes: "mimetism is a source of continual conflict. By making one man's desire into a replica of another man's desire, it invariably leads to rivalry; and rivalry in turn transforms desire into violence" (235). Elsewhere, Girard notes that "[t]o imitate the desires of someone else is to turn this someone else into a rival as well as a model. From the convergence of two or more desires on the same object, conflict must necessarily arise" (*"To Double Business Bound": Essays on Literature, Mimesis, and Anthropology* 140).

The Girardian conception of desire can be applied to Juan José Millas' protagonist, Julio Orgaz, in *El desorden de tu nombre* (1988). The purpose of this study is not only to demonstrate how germane the Girardian model of "triangular" desire is to Millas' text, but also to show how the self-reflecting nature of the novel aids in the structural configuration of the text to the extent that the reader notices an affinity between the *poiesis,* the process of creating the text, and the apparent realization of desire on the part of the characters that populate the text. I also intend to argue that desire, psychoanalysis, and violence are all circumscribed by a cyclical and transitory temperament. As

B. Barrat has shown, to talk psychoanalytically is to come into confrontation with the conditions of the human subject and its desire. Such desire and, indeed, the subject's every activity, including even "its metadiscursive functioning" Barrat argues, are confined by an illusoriness that is fixed to and "constrained by the determinacy of the sociocultural totality, the system of discourse that constitutes the possibilities of all thinking and speaking" (17).

An influential and successful executive in a publishing house, Julio is tormented by the persistent recollection of his deceased lover, Teresa Zagro, and the dissatisfaction from his failure to be an accomplished novelist. His weekly appointments with a psychoanalyst, Dr. Carlos Rodó, and his clandestine escapades with the latter's wife, Laura, reveal an intense desire to possess the psychoanalyst's object of desire, Laura, and the very "being" of Carlos Rodó. A triangular desire occurs when Julio demonstrates an unrelenting pursuit for transcendence by constructing Carlos Rodó as his model and covets Laura who, subsequently, becomes an object of desire for both men. A second triangular desire also emerges when Julio comes into contact with the work of a talented young writer, Orlando Azcárate. Julio admires and envies Orlando Azcárate's work to the extent that he appropriates the writer's fictions and reads them to Laura. The triangular desire, in this case, is on the artistic level. The sophistication of Orlando Azcárate's fiction becomes the object desired, and Orlando Azcárate is transformed into a model that Julio unconsciously desires to imitate in order to fulfill partially his desire for artistic creation and recognition. The complexity of the novel becomes evident with yet another triangular desire when the reader realizes that the psychoanalyst who is supposed to help Julio also demonstrates a desire to possess the being of his patient. In other words, faced with the stark reality of losing his wife, Rodó envies Julio's apparent reckless and carefree attitude in dealing with his lover, Laura, and indirectly wishes to imitate Julio in order to regain his wife's love. The psychoanalyst thus displays what Albert Bandura calls the "social cognitive theory" in which a "utilitarian imitator" notices the consequences of others' deeds and then duplicates those actions that end up in outcomes that he or she considers rewarding. Put differently, as analyst Carlos Rodó comes to occupy the place of the Other by inserting himself in a preexisting process, a recurrent, extensive process of messages that demand responses in reversed form.

Julio's sessions with his psychoanalyst reveal to the reader the protagonist's emotional and psychological infirmity.[1] His decision to see a psychoanalyst, on the advice of his doctor, is precipitated by a series of factors: his divorce at age forty, the accidental death of his lover, Teresa, and a topsy-turvy state in which he hears constantly the hymn, "La Internacional." The reader gains access to the protagonist's turbulent and unstable psychological condition in the first few chapters when Julio begins to read a novel that his deceased lover gave him two years earlier. As in the case of Miguel Delibes' protagonist, Carmen, in *Cinco horas con Mario* who finds underlined paragraphs in the Bible that her defunct husband, Mario, used to read, so does Julio encounter certain sections of the novel underlined. While for Carmen, Mario's underlined passages give her the chance to explore what conceivably could have been her husband's thoughts (communication between the couple was almost nonexistent while Mario was alive), in the case of Millás' protagonist, however, the portions of the novel that Teresa highlights generate a number of effects on him. As he reads the novel, Julio begins to undergo a rather strange experience that could be likened to the fantastic (20). The rather abnormal external forces that seem to regulate an ordinary space—Julio's apartment, soon manifest themselves in his physical condition: "En ese instante la ocupación alcanzaba ya a todos los territorios de su ser . . . Se incorporó aterrado e intentó gritar qué pasa ahí, pero su garganta estaba bloqueada y sólo pudo articular la frase con el pensamiento" (20). Julio's bizarre experience takes another turn when, in his attempt to recall Teresa's appearance, he ends up transposing Laura's face on Teresa's, thus producing a mutation.[2] What is significant in Julio's feverish state is the access the reader gains to his desire to become a successful writer, and the fact that Teresa has served indirectly as his muse in his effort to explore different dimensions of his yet unwritten novel. In fact, Julio literally and metaphorically drinks from the fountain that Teresa provides in order to emerge as a writer of extraordinary caliber. The mutual dependence between the two is evident in some of their clandestine encounters in bars for the retired:

> Elegían para sus encuentros bares de jubilados o de jóvenes, y en ellos ocurrían milagros; el primero de ellos consistía en la infatigable elocuencia de Julio, que de vez en cuando se detenía unos instantes para saborear su ingenio, dar un trago, y degustar el brillo de los ojos cautivos de Teresa. Pero de vez en cuando, sobre todo, Teresa alzaba su mano—escondida hasta entonces debajo de la mesa—y le ofrecía con los dedos el producto de una secreción enloquecedora, acaecida en las profundidades de su falda, que Julio lamía con actitud contemplativa, en una suerte de arrebato místico.

(23)

The shared satisfaction that both Teresa and Julio evidently desire to obtain from each other is, however, unfulfilled. For Teresa, the frequent encounters between her and Julio that invariably end up in explosive sexual experiences, are designed to offer her a deeper meaning of love and the essence of her being. However, as the narrator indicates, she fails to take into account the vital ingredients that circumscribe all such sexual encounters: their ephemeral condition and the agony involved. Teresa's realization that her relationship with Julio provides only guilt and anguish precipitates her search for yet another relationship in which she hopes to satisfy her angst for ontological transcendence. It is in her persistent quest for that elusive ideal that she meets her tragic death.

In Julio's case, the inability to transform his verbal eloquence obtained from conversations with Teresa into a textual masterpiece manifested in a novel, propels him to rediscover yet another muse in the form and shape of the deceased Teresa. Thus, the mental and psychological transmutation that takes place in his mind in which he fuses Teresa and Laura is intended to capture that slippery genie that can engender the fulfillment of his desire for literary accomplishment. To some extent, Julio believes he has found that muse in Laura. In a session with his psychoanalyst, he notes: "Si Teresa y yo hubiéramos seguido juntos, si no hubiera muerto, tal vez yo habría llegado a escribir algo, ella me provocaba intelectualmente . . . No sé . . . El caso es que conozco a otra mujer—de la que no le he hablado todavía—que, sin parecerse a Teresa, da a veces la impresión de ser su reencarnación" (55). Elsewhere he asserts: "Las imágenes de ambas se superponían, como dos transparencias fatales, haciéndome saber que Teresa se manifiesta en Laura, que Teresa ha ocupado los ojos y gestos y la risa de Laura para mostrar que aún está aquí . . . (56). In fact, there is evidence that as Julio concludes that Laura is indeed the reincarnation of Teresa, he regains his ability to write (56). The kind of writing that Julio does, however, is framed by his own personal experiences in which his objects of desire play central roles. Put differently, the novel in the hands of the reader, as well as the one that the protagonist aspires and purports to write, are both conditioned by a mirror-like image in which Julio plays the dual role of creator created. Consequently, Julio's sessions with Carlos Rodó are of vital importance in this creative and created process because, supposedly, by getting to the core of the protagonist's essence, the reader sees the simultaneous unfolding of two parallel texts: Millás' and Julio's. Julio's sessions with Carlos Rodó are also important because aside from highlighting the fact that characters in the novel constantly demonstrate an insistent pursuit for transcendence, the meetings reveal various dimensions of the relationship between the analyst, Carlos Rodó and his analysand, Julio.

Julio's insistence in wanting to be a recognized writer is the result of a crisis situation that reveals to him a sense of finitude, mortality, imperfection, and the lack of being. The fact that he has fulfilled part of his professional ambition in the publishing house does not yield a desired satisfaction:

> En la empresa me han dado una prima de gestión y me han recomendado para un puesto importante. Llevo ocho o nueve meses detrás de ese puesto; he perpetrado durante ese tiempo más intrigas que en toda mi vida, y al fin lo he conseguido. Pero la noticia no me ha proporcionado el placer que cabía esperar.

(54)

Consequently, he must seek out a model to imitate in the literary world since he spells out clearly his ambition: "le he hablado de mis ambiciones de juventud, de mi deseo de llegar a escribir y del continuo aplazamiento de este proyecto, que aún no he desechado" (54-55). Curiously, however, instead of imitating Orlando Azcárate, Julio rather dismisses Orlando Azcárate's *La Vida en el Armario*, attempts to stifle its publication, and finally appropriates the stories as his own and recounts them to Laura between intervals of their love making. To the extent that he takes up some of Orlando Azcárate's stories indicates Julio's acknowledgment of Orlando Azcárate's novelistic qualities. In fact, it can be argued that Julio's sole aim in inviting Orlando Azcárate to lunch is not to discuss the young writer's book but rather to access Orlando Azcárate's mind and imitate indirectly the attributes that have endeared the young writer's work to him. Needless to say, the encounter between the two in an expensive restaurant that Julio had chosen, highlights Julio's inferiority. Instead of meeting a submissive unpublished young writer, Orlando Azcárate turns out to be someone with a remarkable plenitude of being. In fact, the roles between the powerful editor/publisher and the unknown writer are radically inverted:

> En esto se acercó el maître y preguntó si alguno de los dos era don Orlando Azcárate.
>
> —Soy yo—dijo el joven escritor.
>
> —Le llaman al teléfono.
>
> Cuando Julio se quedó solo comprendió que había perdido los papeles. Todo estaba invertido; hasta la llamada telefónica, que por importancia jerárquica le habría correspondido a él, le había sido arrebatada por el joven autor.
>
> (91-92)

An obvious rivalry emerges between Julio and Orlando Azcárate to the extent that Julio contemplates violence towards his object of desire. His initial impulse is to murder the young writer and appropriate Orlando Azcárate's text as his own: "Julio pensó en asesinar a Orlando Azcárate. Podía llevarlo a cualquier lugar apartado y golpearlo hasta darle muerte. Luego publicaría *La vida en el Armario* como si fuera suyo. Pero ya no era posible; el original había pasado por el comité de lectura" (89). While it is plausible to suggest that Julio could not have committed the homicide because Orlando Azcárate's text is already being reviewed, it must be mentioned that as mimetic subject, Julio's relation to the conflict with Orlando Azcárate in which Julio suffers an inherent inferiority, implies an indifference. In underlining the essential ambivalence that emerges when one man makes another person's desire into one's own, Girard notes that "[t]he subject has no wish to triumph completely over the rival; he has no wish for the rival to triumph completely over him. In the first event, the object would fall to him, but it would have lost all value. In the second event, the object would attain infinite

value, but it would be forever outside his reach" (*Things Hidden since the Foundation of World* 361). In order to ascertain that Orlando Azcárate does not "triumph completely over him," Julio decides that his evaluation of the young writer's work should be carefully written: "Acodado en la barra, comenzó a pensar en el tono que debería usar para escribir el informe sobre el libro del joven escritor. Tenía que ser lo suficientemente cruel como para evitar su publicación, pero lo bastante inteligente como para cubrirse las espaldas en el caso de que otra editorial lo editara con éxito" (93). From all indication, it seems as if the mimetic subject has defeated the rival. However, the said triumph does not generate a lasting satisfaction of desire obtained in victory. Although Julio succeeds in blocking the publication of Orlando Azcárate's work by virtue of his new post as director general of production, he continues to seek a model to imitate in his bid to write his yet to be written novel. In other words, although Julio has succeeded in stifling Orlando Azcárate's text, the inherent lack that he displays from the outset as an unaccomplished writer persists.

The relationship between Julio and his psychoanalyst also evokes another triangular desire. Contrary to the reader's expectation that the sessions between Julio, the analysand and Carlos Rodó, the analyst, would yield a hidden dimension of the protagonist's self to himself as well as his analyst, those meetings rather highlight the psychoanalyst's persistent quest for transcendence in which he unconsciously erects his client as a model. One of the constitutive elements involved in the relationship between the analyst and the analysand, as Lacan notes, is that of transference.[3] In "Au-delà du principe de réalité" (*Ecrits: A Selection* 83-85), Lacan recapitulates the analytic process from the point of view of the *imago* and transference as a change of place (*Übertragung*) for the image that proceeds from the analysand to the analyst. The analysand confers tangible form to his/her essence and achieves that essence through an image that vitalizes him/her. The analysand not only etches the attributes of his/her image onto that of the analyst but also misrecognizes that image because of ignorance of either the image's constitution or of its importance. Nevertheless, the psychoanalyst reflects back the image and thus restores the unity that the analysand over time has lost in its dimension as imaginary and not real. The question to be asked, however, is whether Carlos Rodó will respect the ethics of his profession by conforming to the Lacanian idea that the analyst must provide the analysand "the pure mirror of an unruffled surface" (*Ecrits: A Selection* 15) by acting as if he/she were dead in order to enable the analysand to expose his/her own destiny. The obvious answer to this question is *no* because if, as Lacan puts it, each time a speech act is enacted there is transference in which the unconscious that precedes analysis almost always is represented by a preconscious one, then Carlos Rodó's evaluation of his patient's desire, ostensibly elaborated on a preconscious level, suggests that the relationship between him and his client raise ethical problems. His patient's desire is clear to him:

> Por lo que se refería a Julio Orgaz, *estaba claro que, inconscientemente, en algún lugar oscuro de su laberíntica conciencia, sabía quien era Laura, y, al intentar conquistarla, lo que pretendía no era otra cosa que ocupar el puesto de su psicoanalista.* Este es un deseo normal en cualquier paciente; otra cosa es que tuviera oportunidad de realizarlo, aunque fuera de un modo parcial.

(72; my emphasis)

Freud had dealt earlier with the question of transference in *Beyond the Pleasure Principle* when he noted that transference is the presence of the past in the present, an experience that the analyst can neither prevent or spare the analysand from. Another form of the presence of the past is a repetition (*Wiederholung*) that implies a reliving (*wiedererleben*). The analyst must compel the analysand "to reexperience some portion (*ein Stück*) of his forgotten life" (19). But it is precisely in the performance of his duties as analyst, as facilitator for Julio to relive his past that Carlos Rodó finds himself enmeshed in a love story that hits close to home.[4] That is to say, while the ethics of his profession demand that he returns the image through which Julio's displaced unity is restored, Carlos Rodó short-circuits the analytic process by being an accomplice in the drama being played out in his office. The analytic process in itself, as Lacan informs us in "Intervention on the Transference," creates an obstacle (Freud calls it *das Hindernis*) because the move toward subjectivation on the analysand's part is contingent on the analyst's response. Because such transference (conceived as a twofold relationship of image to image) mitigates against the very process of transference, intersubjective truth is problematized to the extent that transference obstructs the dialectical experience between analyst and analysand. The culprit, Lacan believes, is the imaginary in the intersubjective relation (*Ecrits* 215-26).

If, by its very nature, the analytic process, as Lacan conceptualizes it, is fraught with the problem of obtaining intersubjective truth, then the dialectic between Julio and his analyst is doubly prone to an impossible approximation to the locus of truth. This is not only because his intuition tells him that he is a player in the drama that Julio unfolds in his office, but also because he renounces one of the fundamental principles of the psychoanalytic process: abandoning his prior knowledge and assuming the role of a "layman" in order to acquire textual knowledge embedded in the analysand's speech. In his discussion of the knowledge (savoir) and the subject, Lacan advances the Freudian subject and unconscious knowledge by suggesting that the analyst's desire is circumscribed by a double choice in which, in the first place, irrespective of the referential knowledge (savoir) the analyst already possesses, he or she will make a conscious effort not to know it. Referring to what Freud says in *Die Frage der Laienanalyse*

(1926), Lacan also concludes that the analyst is a *Laie* (layman). That means that he/she does not seek recourse to his prior training or knowledge but rather learns to appropriate the kind of knowledge (savoir) that is embedded in language that emanates from the analysand's speech, that is, textual knowledge. The second choice open to the analyst is one in which whatever he/she does not know of the supposed textual knowledge (savoir), will become eventually available to him/her since the enthusiasm of not knowing the first choice engenders the second. The idea is that through speech, a literal knowledge (savoir littéral) emerges, and the analyst, through the analytic process, may perceptibly gain a piece of knowledge, provided that he/she is not merely a fool or a "clerk" but a "layman." Carlos Rodó blocks the analytic process because, rather than assuming the position of "knowledge without a subject" in order to enhance his patient's ultimate cure in which the analysand would cease to demand an answer to his problems, he adheres to the position of the "subject supposed to know," i.e., the analyst, in order to protect his own desires and interest in reclaiming his wife's love.

Carlos Rodó's intention to abandon his client and pass him on to another colleague of his, as well as his decision to engage the services of an older psychoanalyst that he used to see in the past, mark the moment when he begins a desperate effort to regain his wife. But most importantly, his objective reveals his own double status as analyst and analysand. Having failed to offer Julio the "pure mirror of an unruffled surface," Carlos Rodó finds it imperative to seek out his former, more experienced psychoanalyst, who will incidentally furnish him with the services that he so woefully failed to provide his client.

The meeting between Carlos Rodó and his former psychoanalyst is crucial not only because the discussion between the two raises the theoretical fine points of psychoanalysis, but also because Carlos Rodó reveals in this session his awareness that he has short-circuited Julio by not providing the kind of professional assistance that he has been trained to offer. Acknowledging the fact that he surmised that Laura is Julio's object of desire and that Julio intends to take his place, he confesses: "sé que mi actitud es, profesionalmente hablando, insostenible" (118). Elsewhere he observes: "Sospecho, por tanto, que de algún modo sutil yo mismo he alentado, en contra de mis intereses, la relación entre ambos" (119). His lack of professional ethics has a selfish motive because he claims that Julio's relentless expression of his desire for Laura arouses sentiments for his wife that hitherto, he had failed to demonstrate. The reader notices the contrast between Carlos Rodó and his psychoanalyst. Unlike the former who fails to return his client's image to him in order to restore his unity, lost over time, the latter avoids the temptation of an imposing or seductive presence. Instead, the older psychoanalyst offers Carlos Rodó the mirror through which his client, although unwilling, sees a reflection of himself.[5] For the psychoanalyst, Carlos Rodó is not really in love with his wife Laura but rather with his patient since Julio is a mirror-image of himself:

> Fíjese: los dos tienen edades parecidas, los dos poseen un grado de ambición social y profesional importante, en ambos existen indicios de un remordimiento general que ninguno reconoce, y los dos parecen estar locamente enamorado de la misma mujer. Oyéndole hablar, cuando describía a su paciente e interpretaba sus impulsos, yo tenía la impresión de que usted hablaba de sí mismo. *Su paciente es su espejo.* Me ha dicho que estaba a punto de alcanzar un puesto de mucho poder en la editorial en la que trabaja y eso pasa justo en el momento en el que usted está a punto de alcanzar un puesto de mucho poder en la sanidad pública. Piense en ello.

(122; my emphasis)

In what is essentially the Lacanian notion of the analytic game of bridge in which the analysand eventually dramatizes his own existence, the older psychoanalyst leaves the cards for Rodó's destiny exposed on the table. Indeed, Rodó's analyst reminds us of Lacan's "Audelà du 'Principe de realité'" in which the theorist tries to convey the Freudian technique of a blank page. For Lacan, the silent image of the psychoanalyst is a blank page on which are etched signs of the image that energize the talking, agonizing subject. By virtue of the enunciation emanating from the subject's image, the analyst provides the subject a mirror in which finally the subject can recognize himself/herself in the unity of his/her ego, established at last. As readers, we can now put Carlos Rodo's conflict in perspective. His desire for Julio is one of mimetic desire in which his client's desire for social recognition and artistic ambition, coupled with his desire for Laura, become a blueprint worth imitating. The tension between Carlos Rodó and Julio is thus a rivalry in which Rodó makes Julio's desire into a replica of his own desire. As mimetic agent, Carlos Rodó prizes self-sufficiency. The most indisputable indication of his lack of self-sufficiency is to feel a desire towards what Julio stands for. However, from the sessions between Julio and Carlos Rodó, we realize that the psychoanalyst's model, who is also the object of desire, embodies an auspicious form of narcissism. Carlos Rodó's desire is nevertheless, self-defeating because a mimetic subjugation to Julio ensures that he can never successfully realize the fundamental desire for individual autonomy. The contradictory notion of desire is evident because Julio, who embodies the self that Carlos Rodó wants to acquire, also experiences desire. Since desire aspires to self-sufficiency neither Julio nor Carlos Rodó really possesses it.

Carlos Rodó's aim to seek self-sufficiency by imitating Julio whom he erroneously believes possesses the self he wants to acquire, thus precipitates the psychoanalyst's resolution to pursue with vigor his wife and the position at the city council: "Lo primero que tenía que hacer era ... ordenar su vida. Es decir, no olvidar que en el éxito profesional obtenido a lo largo de los últimos años Laura había jugado un papel estabilizador importante. Debía recuperarla, y recuperarla con la misma fascinación que sentía cuando su paciente le hablaba de ella" (72). The parallel between Carlos Rodó and Julio is clear. Laura becomes the object of desire for both men. However, Carlos Rodó's intention to reappropriate his wife, as demonstrated above, comes rather late. As a matter of fact, prior to the above declaration, Laura has already fantasized her husband's death and concludes that she must use him as a scapegoat in her crisis. Her crisis is one in which as subject, she suffers an essential indeterminacy or lack. In an entry in her secret diary, Laura notes:

> Desde que nos casamos toda nuestra vida se ha organizado en función de sus intereses, de su carrera. Yo he ido renunciando poco a poco a mis aspiraciones para facilitarle a él las cosas y ahora que empieza a triunfar soy incapaz de ver qué parte de ese triunfo me correspondería a mí. Claro, que yo podría haber hecho como otras compañeras que se casaron y no por eso dejaron de trabajar. Pero Carlos, muy sutilmente, me fue reduciendo a esta condición de ama de casa quejumbrosa, justo la imagen de mujer que más odio.

(40-41)

Laura's assertions not only call forth similar sentiments that Elena Rincón expresses in ***La soledad era esto*** (1990), another novel by Millás, but also a quest in wanting to find out what constitutes her personal identity. Laura's basic problem is that of coming up with an answer to the question "Who am I" in a relationship in which she feels that she has lived a lie in order to see her husband's career flourish to the detriment of her own (41). As is the case of Elena Rincón, solitude has become the progenitor of Laura's existence to the extent that no response can be found to her existential questions by exclusively contemplating that solitude. In the absence of an answer, she imagines that a response is to be found in the eyes of another—Julio. In fact, the real object of Laura's desire or quest occupies a range of possibilities that include recognition, self-esteem, and the love and approval from Julio.

Laura's decision to use her husband as a scapegoat manifests itself prior to the act of poisoning him with an overdose of tranquilizers. Rodó's murder takes place on a fantasy level before it is actually effected. While cleaning her husband's office that he uses as a consulting room, Laura fantasizes her husband's death: "Al salir del rencor entró en la fantasía de que se quedaba viuda. La llamaban por teléfono del hospital en el que trabajaba Carlos y le decían que su marido estaba muy mal. ... Lo había matado un infarto" (39 40). The act of fantasizing, Wolfgang Iser observes, is the product of unfulfilled desire. In his discussion of the various definitions of fantasy, Iser notes that "[n]o matter how different the contexts and related definitions may be, all reveal fantasy as an event: It runs counter to imperfection, it changes the world it enters, it roams round the mind, or it offers the mirror image of frustrated desires" (172).

Laura's apparent involvement in her husband's death demonstrates clearly what happens in those moments of general conflict in which human beings incidentally imitate each other and end up by blaming certain individuals for the existence of disorder. From the dynamics of the conflict, a scapegoat emerges, and the mob makes him/her accountable for the chaos. The group portrays the victim as a sign of crisis, and this portrayal of responsibility invests the victim with great power, since to be accountable for an event, one must have had the power to have caused it.[6] Obviously, both Laura and Julio view Carlos Rodó as the one responsible for the existence of their disorder, their inability to carry out their clandestine trysts in the open. The emotional/amorous tensions that both lovers are forced to hide in order not to produce a scandal for the husband, as well as Laura's daughter, propel them to seek a scapegoat that they believe is responsible for their chaos. However, the issues of conflict, desire, and violence for both Laura and Carlos Rodó are all evanescent since the infliction of violence on a scapegoat only leads to an illusoriness that promotes the urge to reaccentuate actions that can only become a cyclical phenomenon. In other words, the fulfillment of desire that is predicated on the use of violence provides only fleeting satisfaction. Once that gratification ends, the need to resort to yet another form of violence emerges irrespective of the psychotherapeutic devices used to contain that impulse.

While Millás' novel explores the various dimensions of desire and violence, perhaps what makes the text appealing is the strong correlation between the main story line as told by Millás, and Julio's indirect rendition of his own life story which he seeks to textualize in his yet unwritten novel. The reader notices a complementary relationship between Millás' process of creating his text and the mirroring image that reflects Julio's attempts to realize his desire for artistic creation/recognition in which he duplicates the implied author's *poiesis* that incidentally revolves around Julio's life. In a metafictional mode, Millás' text therefore, informs consciously the reader of the structure that defines the novel.

What can be considered a *mise-en-abyme,* a kind of reduplication in which the part that mirrors relates in equation of similitude to the whole that contains it, defines the evolution of Julio's text. In one of his sessions with his psychoanalyst, Julio spells out what constitutes the beginning of his novel:

> Ya tengo un buen principio: imaginemos a un sujeto maduro que un día, inopinadamente, comienza a escuchar "La Internacional." Y que eso le lleva, como a mí, al diván de un psicoanalista. Y del diván del psicoanalista pasa a los brazos de una mujer que conoce en un parque. Y esa mujer es otra distinta de la que aparenta ser. Y el sujeto …
>
> (58)

Julio proposes to construct his novel in parallel correspondence with his own life. The reader notices a subtle un-

raveling of both the implied author's novel as well as that which constitutes the structure of Julio's own novel. The naming of Julio's narrative process theorizes and effects simultaneously the protagonist's lived experience. Thus, what is supposed to be an inventive endeavor on a creative level is nothing more than a meta-descriptive phenomenon of the already lived: Julio's life. Elaborating more on this novel, the protagonist notes: "Esa novela horada mi existencia y de ella aprendo que *el lugar de usted y el mío, por poner un ejemplo sencillo, son fácilmente intercambiables*" (58; my emphasis). Aside from the fact that Julio already shares the psychoanalyst's wife with him, thus highlighting the veracity of his assertion, this statement also underlines the transference inherent in the relationship between the analysand and analyst.

The entire novel engages in a kind of mimic game through which the main story line explicates a triangular desire in which the protagonist, consciously aware of his role in this game, occupies the position of both character and author within a text that has already set the ground rules for its creation. In contrast with a self-reflective text like André Gide's *Journal des faux-monnayeurs* in which, within the novel, the reader is informed that the subject of Edouard's novel, also entitled *Les faux-monnayeurs,* is Gide's effort to impose order and meaning on events, Millás' text makes no attempt to warn the reader of the protagonist's endeavor to wrest the narrative events from the implied author. Neither does it seem to bother Millás that his own fictional invention has leaped out literally from the text to become a collaborator, a writing narrator, who displaces him and supplants the original structural framework of the implied author's novel, *El desorden de tu nombre* with his own unwritten novel, *El desorden de tu nombre.* The reader is left with the uncertainty as to which of the two authors, the implied author (Millás) or the protagonist-narrator-author (Julio) has rights to the title of the novel within the novel. Curiously, however, while the implied author engages in the painstaking labor of literary creation, Julio instead constructs his novel in his imagination and allows the birth of his novel to be given by an imaginary writer:

> Al tercer whisky, encendió el televisor, se tumbó en el sofá y se quedó dormido observando al escritor imaginario (él mismo), que desarrollaba sobre las cuartillas la trama precisa y compleja del *El desorden de tu nombre.* Al protagonista lo matan entre el paciente y la mujer, dijo antes de perder la conciencia.
>
> (169)

Not only does the imaginary writer attain the unfulfilled desire on Julio's part to write his magnum opus, but the contents of the novel also reflect the triangular desire that has circumscribed the relationship between Julio, Carlos Rodó, and Laura. Indeed, it can be argued that Julio's imaginary writer could not have written until Julio had defined the terms under which the imaginary writer would write. In one of his sessions with Carlos Rodó, Julio dramatizes the plot of his story: "Se trata de un sujeto como yo que se analiza con un sujeto como usted y que se enamora de una mujer del psicoanalista, o sea, de usted. A partir de esta situación, el relato puede evolucionar en varias direcciones" (129). When Carlos Rodó offers a possible outgrowth of Julio's story by suggesting that "[e]l psicoanalista y su esposa saben lo que ocurre; el paciente no" (129), Julio immediately discounts that possibility and establishes in clear terms who is in charge of the narrative: "—¡Bah!, esa posibilidad la he descartado, porque yo, además del narrador, soy el protagonista y comprenderá que no iba a dejarme a mí mismo en ese lugar de imbécil" (129). This kind of exegesis on the craft of fiction is the one that Julio expects his imaginary writer to employ. Julio insinuates that his imaginary scribe can function only by playing by his rules:

> Me refiero a las novelas que no he escrito, naturalmente. Para mí, sin embargo, poseen un cierto grado de existencia, como si, una vez pensadas, comenzaran a desarrollarse a espaldas de mi voluntad, o como si alguien estuviera escribiéndolas por indicación mía en ese otro lugar que yace oculto bajo los sucesos de la vida diaria.
>
> (125)

As a result, when Julio returns home from visiting Laura in order to be informed about Carlos Rodó's death, he is confident that his imaginary scribe would have finished writing his novel because he sees a parallel convergence between the real and the imaginary. As Laura painstakingly recounts the violent act of Carlos Rodó's death, so does Julio see the dramatic evolution of his novel: "Julio permanecía algo perplejo, como asustado de que la realidad se pudiera moldear tan fácilmente en función de sus intereses" (171). Faced with the coincidence between the real and the fictive, Julio exclaims: "—Pero esto es lo que pasaba en mi novela, en *El desorden de tu nombre*" (171). Laura's innocent response "—es que esta historia nuestra, amor, es como una novela" (171) only goes to buttress Julio's belief that individuals live a life that is too linked with the apparently superficial without speculating on the fantastic. He notes that "he entrado en contacto con el otro lado de las cosas" (126). Within the margin of the real that is intricately linked with the fantastic, Julio is certain to find the final product of his work: "Abrió el portal, entró en el ascensor, apretó el botón correspondiente, y entonces tuvo la absoluta seguridad de que cuando llegara al apartamento encontraría sobre su mesa de trabajo una novela manuscrita, completamente terminada, que llevaba por título *El desorden de tu nombre*" (172).[7]

While both Julio and Laura are ecstatic that they have fulfilled in different ways their desires, the question to be asked is whether those desires can sustain a relationship that is the product of violence. If we are to accept Girard's belief that "desire is, finally, the first to acquire a knowledge about itself that it finds unbearable" and has the tendency to "misunderstand," "forget" and "deceive itself" (*Things Hidden since the Foundation of the World* 327), then it is plausible that Julio's and Laura's desires be ephemeral. In fact, the title of Julio's manuscript, *El desorden de tu nombre,* reflects the significance of the fusion of both Teresa and Laura. Instead of restoring the protagonist's lack of being, a disorder is created in which neither of the two women really succeeds in naming the unnameable: the transformation of the imagined and the fantasized from an unconscious state into a palpable textual product that is capable of rescuing Julio from the doldrums of literary obscurity into the open glare of literary success. The supposed temporary restoration of Laura's and the protagonist's emotional and psychological disorder, as well as the fulfillment of their desire, are tempered by the reality that circumscribes all desires and violent acts: their evanescence and cyclic nature.

Notes

1. In his excellent study, "The Pleasures of Oedipal Discontent and *El desorden de tu nombre,* by Juan José Millás García." Vance Holloway also examines the issue of psychoanalysis. He asserts that *El desorden de tu nombre* can be read as narrative that combines two competing models of psychoanalysis. He notes: "Accordingly, psychoanalysis is part of the story as well as being thematically foregrounded, as the protagonist and his analyst provide the reader with narrative models of human subject struggling to reconcile primary drives, desires and social obligations." Elsewhere he adds: "Consequently, *El desorden de tu nombre* can be read as a narrative incorporating two contesting models of psychoanalysis. According to one possible reading, Millás' novel is a story of the protagonist's ego. However, *El desorden de tu nombre* also suggests another, antithetical interpretation that challenges the notions of protagonist progress and therapeutic success. This alternative reading underscores psychoanalysis as a means of comprehending the fragmentary, intersubjective nature of the human subject . . ." (33). While Holloway is interested in highlighting the two psychoanalytic schools of thought that seem to be competing in Millás' text, my main motive in exploring the psychoanalytic dimension of *El desorden de tu nombre* is to examine how the psychoanalytic process is linked with desire and how the quest for unfulfilled desire leads to violence. I agree, however, with Holloway's belief that an alternative reading of the novel underscores the fragmentary intersubjectivity of the human subject. Indeed, the notion of indeterminacy and lack is what precipitates both Julio and Carlos Rodó to seek recourse to the analytic process in order to restore an ego that has been fractured and truncated by a narcissistic desire for self-fulfilment.

2. Holloway indicates that the mutation/transformation that takes place in Julio's delirium suggests a narcissistic desire on a linguistic level in which the Lacanian Other manifests itself. He suggests that since Teresa's last name, Zagro, is a palindrome of Julio's last name, Orgaz, both Teresa and Julio are reflections of each other (35). One can argue, however, that rather than being reflections of each other, they both share something in common: an intense desire for determinacy and ontological transcendence.

3. See *The Seminar of Jacques Lacan. Book I: Freud's Papers on Technique, 1953-54* (109).

4. Julio makes a conscious effort to obliterate his past in order to live in the present and the future. Indeed, the persistent hearing of "La Internacional" is an indirect realization of a past unresolved psychological situation. For Holloway, Mella, a possible *Doppelgänger* of Julio, also links Julio with the past, a past that symbolically becomes present when Julio encounters Mella and gets from him a coat that reflects the fashionable tastes of the present (39).

5. In spite of the fact that the older psychoanalyst seems to implement the classic psychotherapeutic technique aimed at helping Carlos Rodó, one cannot help but speculate on the ironic dimension involved in Millás' treatment of psychoanalysis. The novelist subverts overtly high culture by having Julio and Laura, symbols of popular and low culture outwit the psychoanalyst at his own game.

6. See Girard's *Violence and the Sacred.*

7. One can recall Carmen Martín Gaite's protagonist in *El cuarto de atrás* who wakes up from a deep sleep to discover a completed manuscript that contains the details of the conversation between herself and her nocturnal visitor who apparently helped craft the manuscript.

Works Consulted

Agawu-Kakraba, Yaw. "Germán Sánchez Espeso's *Narciso*: Murderous Desire, Paradoxical Narcissism, and Narrative Narcissism." *Revista Canadiense de Estudios Hispánicos* 20.3 (1996): 519-29.

Bandura, Albert. *Aggression: A Social Learning Analysis.* Englewood Cliffs, N.J.: Prentice Hall, 1973.

———. *Psychological Modeling: Conflicting Theories.* Chicago: Aldine-Atherton, 1971.

Barrat, Barnaby B. *Psychoanalysis and the Postmodern Impulse.* Baltimore: Johns Hopkins UP, 1993.

Delibes, Miguel. *Cinco horas con Mario.* Barcelona: Destino, 1966.

Freud, Sigmund. *Beyond the Pleasure Principle.* Ed. James Strachey. *The Standard Edition of the Complete Psychological Works of Sigmund Freud.* London: Hogarth, 1962. Vol. 18.

Gide, André. *Journal des faux-monnayeurs.* Paris: Gallimard, 1927.

Girard, René. *Deceit, Desire, and the Novel.* Baltimore: Johns Hopkins UP, 1965.

———. "Narcissism: The Freudian Myth Demythified by Proust." Ed. Alan Roland. *Psychoanalysis, Creativity, and Literature.* New York: Columbia UP, 1978. 293-311.

———. *"To Double Business Bound": Essays on Literature, Mimesis, and Anthropology.* Baltimore: Johns Hopkins UP, 1978.

———. *Things Hidden since the Foundation of the World.* Trans. Stephen Bann and Michael Meteer. Stanford: Stanford UP, 1978.

———. *Violence and the Sacred.* Trans. Patrick Gregory. Baltimore: Johns Hopkins UP, 1977.

Holloway, Vance R. "The Pleasures of Oedipal Discontent and *El desorden de tu nombre,* by Juan José Millás García." *Revista Canadiense de Estudios Hispánicos* 18.1 (1993): 31-47.

Iser, Wolfgang. *The Fictive and the Imaginary. Charting Literary Anthropology.* Baltimore: Johns Hopkins UP, 1993.

Lacan, Jacques. *Ecrits: A Selection.* Trans. Alan Sheridan. New York: Norton, 1981.

———. *The Seminar of Jacques Lacan. Book I: Freud's Papers on Technique, 1953-54.* Ed. Jacques-Alain Miller. Trans. Sylvana Tomaselli. New York: Norton, 1988.

Martín Gaite, Carmen. *El cuarto de atrás.* Barcelona: Destino, 1978.

Millás, Juan José. *El desorden de tu nombre.* Madrid: Alfaguara, 1988.

———. *La soledad era esto.* Madrid: Alfaguara, 1990.

Paisley, Livington. *Models of Desire. René Girard and the Psychology of Mimesis.* Baltimore: Johns Hopkins UP, 1992.

Phillipe, Julien. *Jacques Lacan's Return to Freud. The Real, the Symbolic, and the Imaginary.* Trans. Devra Beck Simiu. New York: New York UP, 1994.

Brad Epps (essay date 2001)

SOURCE: Epps, Brad. "Battered Bodies and Inadequate Meanings: Violence and Disenchantment in Juan José

Millás's *Visión del ahogado*." *Arizona Journal of Hispanic Cultural Studies* 5 (2001): 25-53. Print.

[*In the following essay, Epps offers a rhetorical analysis of* Vision of the Drowned Man, *arguing that the work engages with* "a moment in Spanish cultural history marked by the transition from dictatorship to democracy and characterized by change as well as continuity, expectation as well as frustration." *Epps suggests that the novel demonstrates both the* "oppressive force" *and the democratic promise of disenchantment.*]

> Desde una perfecta adecuación con la realidad, uno hará otras cosas, pero no escribirá.
>
>   Juan José Millás

AN INADEQUATE INTRODUCTION

It is treacherous, no doubt, to take a literary text as the measure of a society: as treacherous, if not more so, as taking a family as the measure of a nation. Treachery, moreover, is scarcely gainsaid by invoking a social text to match a literary text or national sites to go with domestic sites. Such rhetorical plays, involving parallelisms and analogies, matches, correspondences, marriages, concordances, and other relations, are fairly standard fare for a wide range of realist-inspired, empirically oriented, mimetically fashioned endeavors; but they persist even in many of the most linguistically attuned endeavors as well. These rhetorical plays, however, are perhaps at their most intense when one endeavor meets another, when realism, understood broadly, recognizes its own language, or rhetoric. Contemporary cultural critique, including cultural studies, is a case in point; for with its studied skepticism, its semiotic sophistication, and its contextual sensitivity, it grapples with nothing less than the meeting of rhetoric and reality and, within that, with the problem of adequation. It seeks, that is, to provide an *adequate reading* of social, historical, and political reality even as it disputes the very viability of an adequate reading (in part because it reads reality as susceptible only to readings, in the plural). Put a bit differently, it problematizes the *relations* between rhetoric and reality, words and things, texts and societies, families and nations, even as it sustains, extends, and alters them. Racked with paradox, cultural critique is treacherous because, even though it often debunks literary critique, it indicates, however ambivalently, that it too can never be *completely* adequate.

Flirting with treachery, I want to take a literary text, Juan José Millás's **Visión del ahogado** (**Vision of the Drowned Man**), as a particularly *inadequate* measure of contemporary Spanish society. Paying special attention to the avatars of violence, I want to consider how Millás's text, published in 1977, reflects, represents, or corresponds to a moment in Spanish cultural history marked by the transition from dictatorship to democracy and characterized by change as well as continuity, expectation as well as frustration. I want to do so, furthermore, in recognition of the general *inade-*

quacy of such concepts as reflection, representation, and correspondence, many of which are crucial, in turn, to the concept of democracy. Interestingly, Millás's text makes only weak reference to the Spanish political situation—democratic, dictatorial, or otherwise—and is more explicitly concerned with the breakdown of reference as such, the loss of stable foundations, and the collapse of absolute truth: in short, with the crisis of adequation. And yet, as I will be arguing, the crisis of adequation bears not only on democracy, but also on what has come to be known, in Spain and elsewhere, as (the) disenchantment, *el desencanto*. José-Carlos Mainer has noted the lability, indeed the *subjectivity,* of such epistemic markers as "transition," "disenchantment," and "democratic affirmation," connoting respectively, for him, mere descriptive asepsis, militant irritation, or dogged optimism (11). All of these markers, to varying degrees and to varying ends, figure in my reading of (in)adequation for the not so simple reason that, as I have already indicated, no one marker is adequate to the diversity, let alone the totality, of my object of critique.

A somewhat awkward, erudite term, "adequation" '*adecuación*' appears a number of times in Millás's text, almost always in introspective or reflective passages. For example, towards the beginning of the text, the narrator states that "la adecuación de Julia (the main female character) con el mundo resultaba natural y perfecta" (18). But this "natural and perfect" adequation is here a function of oblivion, of the absence of memory. A bit later, the narrator speaks of Jorge's (one of the two main male characters) "adecuación con las cosas" (25). In this case, adequation is presented as a function of sadness and internalized prohibition or repression. Later still, the narrator, adopting a sort of free indirect discourse, speaks of yet another instance of "adequation," or rather "inadequation," with respect to the third main character, Luis, "El Vitaminas" (49-50).[1] Here, the accent falls more explicitly on inadequation, with time itself presented as an inadequate measure of sickness as well as of some forms of work and language. All three main characters are implicated, then, in the problem of (in)adequation. And a problem it is indeed. For all three instances of adequation, different as one is from the other, involve oblivion or repression or illness, that is to say, either a forgetting of the *misery* of history or a sad, sick accommodation or resignation to it. Whether taken together or separately, these instances of adequation are far from easy; but that may be just the point. Adequation, particularly an adequation that is "natural and perfect," may be possible, sad to say, only through an act of oblivion, prohibition, or repression, through a kind of (self)-violence. I will return to all of this in greater detail, but for the moment suffice it to say that in Millás's text adequation—its successes and failures, its crises and problems, its bearings on democracy and disenchantment—is bound up in violence, both symbolic and real. What is more, although the narrator presents adequation as something personal (implicating Julia, Jorge, and Luis), it is also deeply political, implicating the "things" of the world. The absence of direct political meaning does not preclude its indirect presence, quite the contrary.

In a certain sense, adequation functions as a democratic concept, bespeaking equality, equivalence, and equalization (Lat. *adaequatus,* past participle of *adaequare,* to equalize; *aequus,* equal). In a certain sense: for in another sense, adequation functions as a decidedly less than democratic concept, bespeaking an equality less free than forced. I am referring, of course, to the principle of adequation effectively deployed by the Francoist state, where equality, and for that matter freedom, continued to be important signifiers, whatever the reality thereby signified. Of course, if adequation can bespeak a *totalitarian* equalization, inadequation, once put into play sociopolitically, does not necessarily bespeak inequality or the non-viability of democratic representation. Adequation and inadequation are thus not *related* in a stable, mutually opposing manner, one always "better" or "worse" than the other; instead, they are related ambivalently. In English, in fact, adequation and adequacy are the stuff of deconstructionist dreams: "adequate" means both "satisfactory and suitable" and "barely satisfactory or sufficient." And although "adequate" does not correspond neatly to "adecuado," although one word is not a truly adequate translation—or is only an adequate translation—of the other, ambivalence attends "(in)adecuación" as well. As Millás's text indicates, it is an ambivalence of ethical and political dimensions, an ambivalence that may be treacherous, but that is not necessarily devastating, and that may even be quite promising. To put it more clearly (or less ambivalently), the ambivalence is such that adequation *may* signify political inequality, non-representationality, and even violence, while inadequation *may* signify, if not exactly the opposite, something like an opportunity for democracy itself.

The democratic opportunity that I find in and around inadequation is not easy and is certainly not the social effect of some positive, straightforward literary message. If anything, **Visión del ahogado** indicates the devastating dangers of adequation *and* its collapse instead of the promising possibilities of inadequation (or of the suspension of the adequate/inadequate pair altogether). And yet, the novel also indicates the perils of fighting the crisis of adequation as well as, indeed, the perilous opportunities of accepting it. These opportunities and possibilities, admittedly beyond the novel, are not of my imagination alone. Gianni Vattimo sees in the dissolution of strong metaphysical concepts— and adequation is surely among them—an occasion for a resignified reality whose values are *not* domination, homogeneity, and centrality. Ernesto Laclau and Chantal Mouffe see the dissolution of tight universal concepts and "the decentring and autonomy of [...] different discourses and struggles, the multiplication of antagonisms and the construction of a plurality of spaces" (193) as an occasion for an open, "unsutured" society whose values are discontinu-

ity, contingency, and difference. In a rhetorical flourish indebted to Lacan, Laclau and Mouffe speak of the "impossibility of society," in the sense of some utterly unified and self-same order, and argue, out of impossibility, for a radically democratic society of diversity and plurality. For them, as for Vattimo, failure to accept the dissolution of strong notions of society, failure to accept a certain inadequation or non-correspondence, can have devastating effects: from unbridled strife to totalitarian control. Lest this all seem too theoretical and inopportune, we might recall that civil strife and totalitarian control—operant terms in any modern society—are especially resonant in Spain during the so-called Transition. Associated at the most extreme with an expansive terrorism and a resutured Francoism, civil strife and totalitarian control are specters of a past ever ready to return, or to *continue,* in the present.

One of the reasons it is treacherous to take one thing as the measure of another is that it can entail a violent denial of difference. Truth, after all, has long been reasoned as an effect of adequation—*adequatio intelectui ad rem*—and true adequation, to loop the loop, has long been "reasoned" as gentle, spontaneous, and self-evident, as "natural." And yet, there is something else in "truth," "reason," and "adequation," something less than gentle. Spun a bit sharply, if the fit is not easy, it can be forced. Adequation can thus be an act and effect of violence, a coercive equalization that is often as not the residue of hierarchization. This holds most clearly for the violence of the totalitarian state, but it also holds for the violence of ETA (Euskadi ta Askatasuna) and GRAPO (Grupo de Resistencia Antifascista Primero de Octubre). Both ETA and GRAPO claim to have the truth, to represent the people, to act in a way that corresponds to reality: violence matching, and purportedly bettering, violence. Insofar as relations of equivalence or interchangeability are here at issue, it bears noting that one violence is *not* necessarily the *same* as another and that the violence of GAL (Grupo Antiterrorista de Liberación) is particularly troubling because it issues from within the democratic state apparatus itself. The existence of GAL points to the continuity of totalitarian tactics in democratic times and thus casts doubt on the *difference* between one system and the other. And yet, as significant as the violence of and against the state is, there are obviously other modes of violence as well. One is the violence of the self and against one's self, a violence that does not issue, at least not directly, from some external site, but that instead issues, or appears to issue, from within. Another is the violence of the home, the family, a violence of privacy and domesticity that is often, but certainly not always, sexual in scope. These last two modes of violence—self-violence and domestic violence—figure prominently in Millás's text as relatively internal and intimate problems of (in)adequation: relative to what passes for more public, socially visible, and historically momentous problems. Turning now to the literary text, we may turn, if only (in)adequately, to something socially significant as well.

LITTLE STORIES

Hacía tiempo que había concluido que en el fondo de las decisiones importantes no había grandeza o virtud, sino una puerta falsa que conducía al desengaño.

(*Visión del ahogado* 58)

Visión del ahogado is not, by most measures, a story of great significance. It contains few specific historical and political references, few "important" names and dates, and little, if anything, "transcendent." Published in the wake of Franco, it makes no mention of the dictator except through topographical allusion: his presence is sustained, but displaced, in the repeated place name, Caudillo de España. Published, moreover, in the year of peaceful general elections and the Law of Political Reform, it does not narrate the struggle for political power, the plight of the working class, or the machinations of the rich and powerful. Nor does it narrate—depending on the narrative's chronology—the depletion of Francoism or the intricacies of the transition to democracy. Instead, it centers on petty crime, rather sordid affairs, adolescent obsessions, and small-minded pranks. Indeed, the smallness of the narrative is reinforced by the vagueness of the temporal markers. The action, at its most recent, may take place during the transition, but it seems much more probable, according to calculations by Gonzalo Sobejano and Robert Spires (100), that it takes place in the last years of Francoism, sometime between 1973 and 1975. Through a careful reconstruction and reordering of the temporal markers—a reference to a political assassination, the average age of students, vividly vague memories—it is possible to affirm that the text *cannot* be about the disenchantment because the action takes place *before* the disenchantment, at least as historically codified. For that matter, according to the same history, even the text's date of publication is prior to the disenchantment. And yet, it is just such historical precision around what is ultimately a sentiment, impression, mood, or sensation that begs to be questioned. Disenchantment precedes and exceeds any discrete chronology; *the* disenchantment, in contrast, purports to crystallize and signal something "in the air," to name a *Zeitgeist.* As such, it is symptomatic of an anxiety regarding historical definition.

The disenchantment or *el desencanto*—with the definite article in Spanish as prominent as it is unobtrusive—effectively validates a "before" and an "after" that is in some respects strangely comforting. Enchantment, that is, is saved even as it is negated, consigned to a time when change for the better was still thought to be possible. Of course, one of the more uncomfortable effects of disenchantment is that it casts the enchanted time as benighted. In that sense, the enchanted time, as a sort of lost anteriority, is also profoundly false: an illusion or a pathetic innocence, a deception or a lie. So while the disenchantment appeals to a chronology of change it also signals a *diffuse continuity*—or as Spires calls it, a "discursive continuity" (96)—from a "then" to a "now" by which things do *not*

change, at least not for the better. As Spires so discerningly observes:

> the strategy to blur temporal boundaries suggests that the imprint of a watchtower system is as much in evidence in the infancy of the Spanish democracy as it was during the maturity of the Franco dictatorship.

(101)

Interestingly, such organic or generational markers as "infancy" and "maturity" are problematized by the text's insistence on adolescence, itself a *transitional* time as momentous as it is petty. Published in a time that many consider momentous, and narrating a time that is necessarily *before* the time of publication, *Visión del ahogado* relates moments whose pettiness, profuse and discontinuous, disrupts any sense of a story, or history, that depends on neatly definable disruptions:

> El tiempo transcurría con gran profusión de acontecimientos íntimos y con algún que otro suceso exterior (la aparición de un nuevo modelo de la casa Seat, la ascensión inesperada de un equipo de segunda a la primera división, y también el asesinato del presidente Kennedy, católico y anticomunista, que tenía los hombros muy anchos y la sonrisa muy brillante), que, como más tarde se comprobaría, *tampoco sirvieron para crear una conciencia cronológicamente ordenada en la que los aconteceres externos estuvieran registrados con un carácter sucesivo.* Los hechos, como las personas, se debatían entre la identidad y el apelmazamiento.

(193, emphasis mine)

The intimate events of Millás's text are not those of some Unamunian *intrahistoria,* nor are the external events those of some grand history: political assassination, sporting upsets, and marketing innovations seem to be strung haphazardly together. If there is a *grand récit* here it is, ironically, in the disruption, if not collapse, of the *grand récit,* whether intimate and interior or public and exterior.

And yet, among the plays of irony, the smallness of Millás's story is the sign of its weakened grandeur. This might suggest that small signifies grand, or grandly, but *Visión del ahogado* is not about the hidden greatness of lowly individuals, the honor of petty thieves, or the magic of debased lovers. And it is certainly not about the latent heroism of the common citizen. It appears to hold no humanist moral, no utopian message, and no redemptive lesson. Indeed what it is about, if anything, is the debilitation of humanism, utopianism, and redemption in general. What it is also about, as I have indicated, is the debilitation of the very principle of adequation that allows us to say that a text is "about" anything at all. Anything, including nothing: for in the crisis of adequation we cannot even say that the text is "about" nothing. Death itself, that once grand signifier of nothingness, is here weakened to such an extent that it signifies nothing so grand as release or resolution or transformation.

The text ends with a small-time robber—Luis, "El Vitaminas"—brought back from the edge of death only to be thrown into jail:

> estaba en que se iba a morir, en que se ahogaba. Pero un médico ha dicho que se va a joder, que un lavado de estómago y listo.

(238)

The clinical, cynical tenor of this closing comment, made by the meddlesome doorman of the building where "El Vitaminas" is finally discovered, indicates to what extent the vision of the drowned man announced in the title of the text is not a true illumination, even a truly profane one. Hallucinatory and sick, "El Vitaminas" does not die; he is just fucked over.

Still, it is possible to recast the most derisive and flippant of comments into something serious and profound. In that sense, if *Visión del ahogado* is "about" the death of grandeur, it is about quite a bit. As if to drive this home, the text contains lengthy, dense, and far from straightforward reflections on life, liberty, and love; sadness, suffering, and fear; language and consciousness; aging and death. As Constantino Bértolo and Esther Cuadrat have noted, there is more than a trace of Juan Benet and, through him, of William Faulkner in Millás's dense reflectiveness. The effect is, however, quite different; for in Millás's text, identifiable political events and precise historical moments are not merely washed away by smaller stories, they are also belittled, as it were, by a certain philosophically reflective grandeur that is, however, neither as consistent nor as dense as Benet's. Sobejano qualifies Millás's text, with all its conversations, as monologic or, more precisely, as "plurimonologic" (207), a quality that brings to mind Benet's much-touted grand style. But Benet's grand style seems to saturate his texts; it is the same for one character as well as another, one event as well as another (*Inspiración* 78). Millás's style, in contrast, is far from grand or is only *intermittently* grand, punctuated as it is by easily recognizable commonplaces and all too common situations. Even though Millás has spoken of Madrid as "territorio mítico" (Rosenberg 154), the Spanish capital is not of the same order as Yoknapatawpha or Región, and its reality, its presence on maps not of the author's making, drags down the more grandly reflective moments.[2] Just as the passages of reflective grandeur may belittle rather than elevate the few precise historical and political events present in the text, the passages that narrate small and rather sordid events belittle the moments of grand reflection. Millás himself, in an interview published in the late 1980s, says that *Visión del ahogado* oscillates between narration and reflection (**"En fin"** 22), a point that virtually all of his critics corroborate. He goes on to say that he has attempted to diminish reflection in subsequent texts, accentuating instead "narrative technique." The contrast between reflection and narrative technique is instructive, but no less instructive are the author's assertions that "la

reflexión sirve muchas veces para disimular carencias de oficio" (**"En fin"** 22) and that "el oficio puede utilizarse a veces para tapar carencias" (Rosenberg 143). These extratextual assertions dovetail the narrative's self-reflective concern with falsity, simulation, masquerade, and lack, each one feeding into and off the other.

In *Visión* [*Visión del ahogado*], lack is prolific: lack of talent, intelligence, expertise, faith, commitment, endurance, health, love, and communication, lack of adequate relations. If lack spurs desire, it also spurs simulation, the desire for simulation, the simulation of desire. If lack constitutes a form of truth, it also constitutes forms of falsity, the lack of truth. All of the characters of *Visión,* without exception, give testimony to the vagaries of lack; all are creatures of simulation and simulacra, acting as if in accord with pre-scripted roles and incapable of any "experience" that is not surrounded by quotation marks. True things of fiction, all reflect not just problems of social history but also problems of narrative technique, of storytelling. And the problems of telling a story, whatever the author states, are not limited to the presence or absence of reflection alone. Ponderous as the moments of reflection are in Millás's text, they are part and parcel of the story here told. As I have suggested, it is a little story, little in its weak, reflective grandeur. It centers, in classically triangular style, on three people, two men and a woman. After having robbed a pharmacy and wounded a policeman, Luis, "El Vitaminas," hides out in the boiler room of the building where his estranged wife, Julia, lives with their young daughter. Soaked with rain, cold, lonely, and increasingly delirious, Luis reflects, almost in spite of himself, on his past. In the meantime, as Luis shivers with fever, in the apartment above him Julia and Jorge go hot and cold, talking, avoiding talking, and having violent sex. Outside, the search for Luis involves a number of less prominent personages. They include policemen; inspectors; the doorman of the apartment building who is a retired member of the Guardia Civil ("El Ratón"); a barman ("El Cojo"); and Jesús Villar, the husband of Rosario, a woman with whom Luis had regular sexual encounters in the school bathroom when he was a teenager. Interrogated by the police, Villar makes a series of calls to throw off the investigation and toy with and defer Luis's capture. Villar is eventually found and beaten by the police. Luis, babbling incoherently in a corner of the womb-like room in which he has hidden, is also found by the police. Julia, engaged by the police to assist them, is present when Luis is caught. Jorge, however, is absent, having left Julia, Luis, and the entire situation in a final act of frustration and failure. This, in broad strokes, and minus the reflection, is the story that Millás tells. It does not, in itself, seem especially significant. Of course, as I have suggested, the semblance of insignificance may be precisely the point.

Ignacio-Javier López, in one of the few sustained readings of the text, sees the story in familiar terms of adultery and quest, a "conjugación de quijotismo y bovarismo" (38).

Sobejano, in contrast, underscores the story's strangeness (*extrañeza*), its senses of estrangement. Indeed, Sobejano detects a strangeness of expression in all of Millás's texts that, for him, "corresponds perfectly" to the strangeness of themes and the estrangement of human consciousness (196). Though López raises interesting questions, Sobejano is, in my opinion, closer to the truth, if for no other reason than that truth is here the uncanny effect of the persistence and return of something familiar, yet (partially) lost. "Something familiar" might be Franco and Francoism, continuing, for many, even after their apparent disappearance, continuing, moreover, in the act of writing and publishing *after* Franco's death a tale that may very well take place *before* it. More generally, and hence more disturbingly, "something familiar" might be anything that forms part of a familiar story, a tradition, a family. Millás's text, profuse in quasi-philosophical reflection and sparse in social, historical, and political reference, does relate some strangely familiar things. Among them is the persistence of violence, discipline, and punishment that may imply the return, or persistence, in a time of transition, of the norms of social control. Millás's text does not partake of the newer, sexier projections of Spain that accompany the move to democracy; it does not bring to mind the *Movida* or the *Destape*; it does not present something wild, ecstatic, glamorous, campy, or kitsch. Instead, it stays with what has not quite changed: the routines of daily work, the presence of the police, the eyes and ears of others. This is not to say that the text acknowledges no social change whatsoever. In what may be an allusion to the 1973 assassination of Luis Carrero Blanco, a principal Francoist *continuista*, "El Vitaminas" apostrophizes the occupants of an armored police jeep: "aún recuerdo cuando gozabais de tal impunidad que no necesitabais viajar enrejados" (49). Nor is it to say that the text acknowledges no sort of political struggle. Jorge, seeing the crowd at the entrance to the metro where "El Vitaminas" has injured a man, reflects:

> el conjunto recordaba sin esfuerzo a un grupo de manifestantes que portara una pancarta incomprensible y desproporcionada.
>
> (13)

But the references to the vulnerability of the police and the power of demonstrations—to what may be taken as the signs of political change—do not change the fact that while the meaning of the crowd is incomprehensible, the meaning of the police is reinforced.

The persistence and return of a policed reality should not be underestimated. *Visión del ahogado* is, as Sobejano notes, a work of close interiors and ever-vigilant exteriors. Even more, it shows how vigilance is interiorized, domesticated, and, as Spires remarks, "popularized," uncoupled from a centralizing state apparatus and brought into play with popular culture (100). The most insistent indication of the "domestication" of vigilance is Julia's bathroom mirror, its tain flecked in such a way that it recalls a key-

hole. The surface of reflection—so important to, but also against, narration—is chipped in a way that calls forth an illusory depth and opacity, at once titillating and threatening. Standing naked before the mirror, Julia sees both herself and a blind spot from which she can imagine that she is seen. Jorge sees something similar, and yet is more annoyed than excited. The difference between Jorge's and Julia's reaction is touched by the difference of gender, a ritualized difference to which I will return.[3] For the moment, what is important is the extended play of vision and blindness, of voyeurism, paranoia, and civil espionage. Jorge watches Julia and "El Vitaminas," who watch him in turn, and each is watched, or believes himself or herself to be watched, by others, most intensely the police and their minions. More devastatingly, each character watches, *almost blindly,* him or herself. Millás's "scopic regime" does not have the dystopic intensity of Orwell's or the pan-optic rigor of Foucault's reading of Bentham, but it is arguably more chilling for being more strangely familiar. Millás's presentation of the scopic owes much to the less than grand formulations of reality found in detective and police narrative. Yet, it is the evocation of the everyday and, more exactly, of the persistence of the past in the present that marks *Visión*. The text's epigraph, attributed to John Le Carré, reinforces this idea: "Fue de nosotros de quienes aprendieron el secreto de la vida: hacerse viejo sin hacerse mejor." Things do not get better; they just get older.

The epigraph is well chosen, adequate, that is, to the story of inadequation and inadequacy that follows. In both, progression appears more powerful than progress, and aging, not ethics, is the gauge of narrative development. Historical movement is similarly implicated, textualized in terms of decay, decline, and degeneration. The latter is an especially intriguing term, one that reverberates in a variety of ways. Degeneration may be a general phenomenon, but according to a number of Millás's critics it is the feature of a particular *generation*. For Sobejano, the characters featured in *Visión del ahogado* are "los desplazados del 60," adults who came of age in the 1960s and who, torn between apathy and anarchy, bore witness to an advanced, decrepit Francoism (208). By coming of age, Sobejano means "going through" adolescence, the "age" in life that Millás's characters remember most vividly. Both Jorge and Luis, "El Vitaminas," are all but obsessed with adolescence, a *sexually tumultuous* period marked by possibility and opportunity, frustration and failure. Generational coordinates abound. Constantino Bértolo, to whom the novel is dedicated, declares that

> *Visión del ahogado* es una novela generacional, la novela de una generación fracasada y aplastada por sus propias falsedades internas como por la degeneración y fraude moral de la sociedad en la que ha crecido.
>
> (*Papel* 203)

Sobejano, for his part, sees the text as a "*cuadro de una generación* frustrada que mira hacia atrás para comprobar su inerte prolongación en un presente sin esperanza" (209, emphasis original). The generation to which Bértolo and Sobejano refer comes of age, in short, in the shadow of Franco: *a man who grows older without getting better* and, what is more, a man who grows weaker without losing power.

Leaving aside the Spanish penchant for generational terms (few histories of literature rely as heavily as the Spanish on "generation"), Sobejano hits on something crucial when he describes the present as hopeless. Inasmuch as the date of the narration (1973-75) approximates the date of its composition and publication (1977), the present to which Sobejano refers is far from stable. It is also, one might think, far from hopeless, a transitional, *politically tumultuous* period of possibility and opportunity, of potential *regeneration*. And yet, if the experience of adolescence is any indication, the upshot of so much possibility and opportunity is failure and frustration, disenchantment. On this score, Sobejano is emphatic:

> El significado de **Visión** no sería otro que el fracaso de las relaciones amorosas y amistosas: *la angustia de* un *convivir* inauténtico.

> (208, emphasis original)

The failure of human relations and the anguish of an inauthentic community: what Sobejano points to is a crisis of adequation or adequate relationality that, far from constituting an opportunity for something positive, generates only negativity. Violence, sadness, melancholy, despair, anger, and aggression are the principal forms of negativity that Millás's text showcases. Violence, anger and aggression are perhaps more socially visible, more spectacular, but, as Millás indicates, they are often mixed up in sadness, despair, and melancholy. Sadness, violence, and so on are the signs not just of some nebulous human condition but also of a certain—though perhaps ultimately equally nebulous—generation. Take, for example, the previously noted sadness and suffering of Jorge:

> su adecuación con las cosas y sus escasas tentativas de entendimiento con el mundo se habían producido siempre por vía de la tristeza.

> (25)

Sadness may have been a sin in the Middle Ages, but in the Modern age it has become a tremulous virtue, a sign that the subject is in tune with the sad truth of reality. Through Jorge, Millás's text shares a notion of reality whose exponents include Benjamin, Adorno, and, however differently, Benet, and that suggests that to know reality is to know sadness, suffering, and pain. And yet, the text also indicates that the truth-value of sadness and pain goes the way of the truth-value of death—emptied, as indicated, of grandeur. Jorge's "adequation with things" may have "always" occurred through sadness, but what the narrator signals is that this adequation is no longer functional, that what was "always" adequate is so no longer. Coopted as an emotion-

al response, sadness is no longer an adequate measure of truth and reality.

Jorge's situation is not unique. "El Vitaminas's" suffering, pain, and sadness are likewise undermined. After all, it is with regards to "El Vitaminas" that we read that the mythical, let alone redemptive, dimension of sadness and pain is defunct. The narrator ponders:

> de qué manera habían perdido estos sucesos cualquier posible relación con lo mitificable—lo que se nombra triste y doloroso—hasta convertirse en visión espantosa [...] era una cuestión adyacente tal como preguntarse en dónde pudo conseguir el muerto cuerda tan eficaz.

> (71)

Indeed, the narrative voice is so incisive that no sooner does it assert the inoperability of the relation between the quotidian and the mythic (as in allegory) than it asserts that this assertion is itself ancillary, like wondering, after the fact, about the efficacy of suicide. The last remark is not a throwaway. A principle of adequation, founded on sadness, suffering, and pain, is not replaced with a principle of efficiency, but endures—in its inefficiency, its inadequacy—as something frightful. Fright and fear pervade **Visión del ahogado,** though they too are styled as the emotional effects of Millás's version of the culture industry.[4] They are not, at any rate, incidental. In a short book on the Transition published in 1980, Juan Luis Cebrián underscores the importance of fear. Cebrián describes:

> un miedo tanto mayor y tanto más acusado cuanto más desaparece el temor de los representantes del antiguo régimen, cuanto más reverdecen las antiguas formas, los antiguos modos y los antiguos objetivos del gobernar. El miedo se enseñorea hoy de la actualidad española.

> (9)

For Cebrián, fear is the emotional mark of the Transition. For Millás, in an interview with José María Marco published in 1988, however, fear is the emotional mark of Francoism, of a time apparently before. *Apparently* before, because fear is a dominant factor of many of the novels that Millás writes after Franco's death, indeed well after the Transition itself, deep in the midst of democracy. **Visión del ahogado,** published in the midst of the Transition, remains, however, special. In it, as in Cebrián's work, fear is a function of a past that *remains and returns* in the present and that shapes the future. At the same time, fear is a function of the past as it passes into something else, a function, that is, of oblivion and loss. *Fear is a function both of continuity and change,* permanence and impermanence. This spins a number of ways: one may fear that people, things, and relations *do not change*; that the truth of reality is sadly the same as it ever was; that the transition from dictatorship to democracy is more rhetorical than real. Alternatively, one may fear that people and things *have changed* so much that no relation is viable, let alone adequate; that truth cannot be measured even in terms of sadness and suffering; that the transition from dictatorship to democracy has rendered the dream of a better society a frustrating failure. There are, needless to say, other fears, other modes of sadness and violence: fears not only of past and present Francoists, Communists, Social Democrats, and so on, but also of less politicized subjects not so readily related to anything grand. Millás's "little" story, shot through with reflections, is about nothing if not the (in)adequacy of relations and the treacherous interplay of sadness, fear, and violence generated therein. Having touched on sadness and fear, it is to violence that I will now turn.

NAMES, BODIES, AND OTHER DAMAGED GOODS

Men have always fought their misery with dreams. Although dreams were once powerful, they have been made puerile by the movies, radio and newspapers. Among many betrayals, this one is the worst.

Nathaniel West, *Miss Lonelyhearts*

It is tempting to say that the only adequate relation is one that recognizes its inadequacy. Tempting, it is also too easy; for within the very text that is a inadequate measure of Spanish society, there is at least one character who struggles to accept, indeed to accentuate, his inadequacy in a desperate effort to salvage something he can call his own. Inadequacy and inadequation are, for this character, the stuff of a *negative authenticity,* shot through with gestures of ritualized mortification and fraught with yearnings for an authenticity more traditionally positive (one need only think of the authenticity of the ascetic). Perhaps not surprisingly, the character in question is the most self-violent in the text, physically sick and close to madness: Luis, a.k.a. "El Vitaminas." To be sure, "El Vitaminas" is also violent towards others (he wounds a policeman), but what *characterizes* him is a centripetal decline, a desperate, increasingly inner-directed movement of destruction. It is as if "El Vitaminas" believed that by destroying himself he could save himself; as if by beating himself he could overcome the distance between people, words, and things. As Bértolo observes, "El Vitaminas's" only desire is for self-destruction, but that too is a trap (*Papel* 204). Self-destruction is a trap, *Visión* indicates, because so many others have performed it to such an extent that it has become part of an appallingly predictable script, a pose, and a cliché. It is not enough to seek a devastation to match the devastating truth of reality; nor is it enough to accept inadequacy as adequate to (a negative) authenticity: in *Visión del ahogado,* self-destruction, willful though it may be, has gone the way of sadness, suffering, and death.

Part of the problem with self-destruction, at least as it is presented here, is that it refuses to relinquish a sense of redemption and, more intricately, a sense of the self. "El Vitaminas's" self-destruction is thus vitiated, ironically, by the presence of codes of conduct and reason, Christian, capitalist, and so on:

la suya es una memoria competitiva y cristiana que fía a la voluntad lo que no puede alcanzar con la inteligencia. De ahí que continúe, a su pesar, buscando las pruebas de una superación que haga más llevadero su desastre.

(205)

Furthermore, "El Vitaminas's" desire for self-destruction is a desire for the destruction of an *inauthentic* self, a destruction that would recapture or redeem an authentic self. In contrast to the text's epigraph, "El Vitaminas" appears to hold on to an idea of progress even as he lets himself go; it is as if he believed that he could make himself better by making himself worse. But if "El Vitaminas" seeks adequation (a sad and suffering self to match a sad and suffering reality); if he attempts to accept his inadequacy as adequate to authenticity; if he strives to redeem himself by destroying himself, that does not mean that he has got at reality, its truth. In fact, even as the text suggests that "El Vitaminas" is close to the truth of reality, it stresses that he is still very far away. The following is illustrative:

Con las manos apoyadas en la reja metálica que rodea el amplio complejo deportivo, husmea el aire, registra la interrupción momentánea de la lluvia, gira la cabeza a izquierda y derecha comprobando con la barbilla la humedad de sus hombros: intenta protegerse a cualquier precio de la realidad. Y esta incapacidad que ahora le impide aceptar como propia la actual experiencia le conduce una y otra vez desordenadamente a ese sucedáneo de la experiencia que es la memoria. Descubre el barrio por cuyos laberintos hubo de destilar una adolescencia inútil. La escasa gente que se cruza con él son los representantes de todo aquello que el Vitaminas no quiso para sí.

(49)

Grasping a fence, "El Vitaminas" struggles not to move to the other side but to remain away, symbolically speaking, to guard himself from reality. He is incapable of doing so, however, and also incapable of accepting (his) present experience as his own. Cebrián's present fear and Sobejano's present hopelessness come together in "El Vitaminas's" dilemma. Unwilling to be like other people, he cannot "really" be himself; unable to accept reality, he is unable to deny it.

So presented, "El Vitaminas" is a creature of the culture industry, where commodification serializes and annuls personal experience. Throughout *Visión,* characters reproduce gestures, words, and even emotions seen in movies as if they were their own; they replay, again as if they were their own, the sentiments and rhythms of popular songs. For example, translated lines from a song by Simon and Garfunkel are incorporated into the body of the narrative:

las palabras de los profetas, dice ["El Vitaminas"] como quien escuchara una guitarra, están escritas en las paredes de los subterráneos y en los vestíbulos de las casas baratas.

(202)

Memory, far from providing access to experience, is instead a substitute or "sucedáneo" for it. What is worse, experience itself is unreliable, its immediacy spurious, its intimacy fraudulent. Nowhere is this more apparent than in the intensification of "El Vitaminas's" sickness and his attempt to make sense of it:

> El resultado es desastroso: apenas ha conseguido musitar dos oraciones que se despegan muy ligeramente del lenguaje oficial y establecido. Además no significan nada. Pero ¿es que significa algo su modo de actuar? Tal vez resida ahí la clave del asunto, dice, e inmediatamente: qué clave, qué asunto, qué residencia. Las frases hechas le rodean y desprestigian su actitud.

(204)

Everything, it seems, has been said, everything thought, everything felt. It is not just that, as Martha Miranda maintains, the characters pretend to be what they are not (527), but that, outside of pretense, they are not anything at all. This holds for Jorge and Julia as well, but for Luis, "El Vitaminas," it has a special force, manifested not only in his bodily discomfort but also in the very name by which he is known. Names, like everything else, are popularized, commercialized, and officialized to the point of banality. So stifling is this lack of originality that nicknames become desperately feeble attempts to give the name an elusive body and to rescue the authenticity of the sign. If "Luis" is the official, duly registered name of the man sought by the police, the nickname might just be a way to elude "officiality" while preserving a sign of the self.

In *Visión del ahogado,* nicknames abound: "El Ratón," "El Lefa," "El Cojo" and, most importantly, "El Vitaminas." They also seem adequate to the person so named: "El Ratón" (the "Rat") is the ever vigilant doorman; "El Lefa" (slang for ejaculated semen) is Jorge's and Luis's sexually furtive schoolmate who dies at a young age; and "El Cojo" is a barman with a limp. In the case of Luis, the nickname, "El Vitaminas" ("Vitamins" or "Mr. Vitamin"), is ironically motivated, insofar as the sickly Luis is "reinforced" in name only. Or rather, the nickname impossibly supplies the body with the physical force that it is missing. Whichever way it may be, there is something telling about the adequation of *nickname* and body. For in all cases, the physicality signified by these nicknames is itself defective or damaged and signals, in turn, the impossibility of a *perfect* adequation between word and thing, name and body. What is most adequately named is the *imperfect* body:

> Luis amaba como pocas cosas su cara de tuberculoso que era, al tiempo que una advertencia—tal vez una amenaza—, la señal evidente de una distinción que hasta el momento había funcionado.

(80)

Imperfect as this is, it *is* something. Jorge, on the other hand, does not have anything visibly "wrong" with him and yet does not have anything that is "rightfully" his.

> Seguramente Jorge ignoraba que quien no se deja motejar hace de su propio nombre el peor de los motes, por cuanto

al confiar en él toda posible referencia a su persona admite al mismo tiempo que nada de destacar hay en ella, ni siquiera un ligero estrabismo, una imperceptible cojera o una disposición original de los dientes; nada excepto la paz mediocre que se adivina tras los nombres todos.

(80)

So ill and imperfect is the signifying relation that authenticity and originality, that refreshing other side of banality, are here the accidental attribute of a set of teeth.

There may well be something more expansive in the "mediocre peace" that the narrator finds behind all names, be it the peace of the Francoist establishment, celebrated with pomp in 1964 as "25 Years of Peace," or the peace of the Transition. For all their undeniable differences, both modes of peace may not be just mediocre, but deceptive as well. And part of their deceptiveness, a critical part, is violence. Again, even at its most reflective, the text does not expound on peace and violence in some grandly historical sense, but remains focused instead on the small story of a small group of characters. Theirs is the peace and violence that is at issue, and as with the grander senses there are undeniable differences in these smaller senses as well. Although "El Vitaminas" is the object of public concern, sought by the police and certain civilian collaborators, and although he is considered to be armed and dangerous, he is not necessarily the most violent. The most outwardly violent character, the one whose aggressiveness is most morosely detailed, is Jorge, the former friend of "El Vitaminas" and current lover of "El Vitaminas's" estranged wife, Julia. This may seem paradoxical, for this outwardly violent character is depicted, in large measure, inside the home. The outward violence is here domestic violence, the violence that lies behind the mediocre peace that lies, in turn, behind so many seemingly fine proper names. Domestic violence has only recently been recognized in Spain as a legitimate social and political problem. As Anny Brooksbank Jones notes, it is not until 1984, years after *Visión* appears, that statistics on domestic violence in Spain were collected. Jones cites a number of reports and affirms, in a way that intersects compellingly with Millás's novel, that "domestic violence aids the smoother functioning of [the social] order" (97). Of course, the social order that so smoothly functions is one founded, as Jones implies, on force. And when the social order does not function smoothly, when violence "inhabits" the streets and even the police—as fearful forces of social order—are subject to fear, often as not the domestic order is adduced as being either too violent or, indeed, not violent enough.

Again and again, away from the streets and in the close space of the home, in what Millás has called an "oquedad moral" (Rosenberg 153), Jorge beats Julia. He beats her as he has sex with her, in order to have sex with her. Along with the violent yearnings for authenticity, Millás's text is steeped in violent masculine yearnings for femininity. Jorge is not alone. Jesús Villar—whose wife had sexual relations with "El Vitaminas" when they were in high school—fantasizes about hitting his wife in the face with an ashtray. The violent yearnings run through "El Vitaminas" too, though they run more explicitly through Jorge. What "El Vitaminas" and Jorge yearn for is a woman they both "have" yet cannot have, a woman adequate to their needs, demands, and desires. Haunted by the past and rocked with yearning, both men end up leaving the same woman; but only Jorge is depicted as doing so after engaging (her) repeatedly in violently abusive sex. The difference is significant, though in both cases the sexual relation seems, as Lacan might put it, impossible.[5] Its impossibility, or inadequacy, does not issue in anything very promising, but rather in forms of violence—one directed largely inwards, the other largely outwards—that would overcome ('*superar*' 205) impossibility and inadequacy alike. Something similarly unpromising goes for the social relation, in part because sexual relations *are* social relations. But the difference between one man and another man, let alone the difference between them and the woman, is, I repeat, significant. "El Vitaminas's" attempt to accept impossibility and inadequacy entails doing violence against himself. This is so largely because it is actually an attempt *not* to accept impossibility and inadequacy, but rather, through a play of established negations, to make them good; it is not for anything that the narrator describes "El Vitaminas's" memory as "competitiva y cristiana" (205). "El Vitaminas's" attempt is arguably more involute than Jorge's, but it is not for that reason more troubling. For what Jorge attempts is to overcome inadequacy and impossibility, not simply by accepting or denying them, but by mastering them, willing and guaranteeing them. It is he, more than anyone else in the story, who tries *to make things fit by force.*

Force, for Jorge, assumes the form of sexual violence. In *Visión del ahogado,* sexual violence is at once coupled to, and displaced from, self-violence. It functions as yet another attempt to overcome impossibility and inadequacy (even by *willing* impossibility and inadequacy to be) and as yet another attempt to save the distance between people, words, and things (even by *willing* the distance to be). What Millás's text indicates is how the attempt to save such distance can become mired in destruction, how the refusal or inability to give up the ghost of adequation can become ghastly. This fearful vision, beyond sadness and suffering, assumes a variety of forms and is at once masked and exacerbated in consumer capitalism, where new and original products nourish the ever-expanding banality of experience. "Es como si no fuéramos capaces de alimentarnos con nuestra propia experiencia" (210-11), declares Jorge, caught between the hyper-mediated tyranny of mass culture and the nostalgia for direct, non-mediated experience. With food for experience as well as for thought alienated and mass-produced, the subject grows grave with its own insubstantiality:

> Donde debía haber carne, no hay más que un vacío atravesado por el viento. Alcanza [Jorge] como mucho, a ver

> pequeños jirones, algunos trozos putrefactos pegados a la osamenta de su vida. Un esquema sin cuerpo.

> (220)

The specter of such material consumption, the vision of the rotten remnants of a once full flesh, stands in stark contrast to the promise of longevity, youth, beauty, and bodily gratification that characterizes the modern market. It also stands in contrast, and yet strangely subtends, the promise of fulfillment through sex.

It is important to keep in mind that the promises shadowed forth in *Visión del ahogado* are not gender neutral. When Jorge hits and penetrates Julia, he is striking out at an image of his own inadequacy. This is not to deny Julia's materiality (textually figured as it is), but it is to underscore that her body is, *for Jorge,* a masculine fantasy or phantasm (again, textually figured). The text indicates as much, but it also indicates that Jorge is not exactly aware of the phantasmatic nature of what is, for him, Julia's body: a body he projects onto and over hers, a body of his making, a body, in short, that is "his." This is the body that Jorge attempts both to affirm and to deny by striking out against it. He attempts to affirm it, violently, as the site of something substantive, true, and real; and he attempts to deny it, violently, as something phantasmatically of his making. In a state of generalized inadequacy and inadequation, then, Jorge strikes out, attempting to make Julia lie in for a truth that has lost both grounds and objects. Again, the text suggests that Jorge may not understand this, but that it is not for want of trying. Jorge, though not physically ill like "El Vitaminas," is nonetheless consumed by a feverish intellectual activity. Julia, on the other hand, remains for the most part impassive,

> tranquilamente instalada en una especie de debilidad que la exime de intentar cualquier iniciativa. Aunque por otra parte no hay ninguna iniciativa que tomar.

> (220)

The contrast between activity and passivity, insight and ignorance, masculinity and femininity is only partially undercut by the assertion that there is no action, no initiative, to be had. As Jorge and, perhaps, the narrative voice understand it, there is no action to be had *by Julia.*

Jorge appears to believe that he, unlike Julia, can grasp the "reality" of the situation, empty and factitious though it may be:

> Jorge, por el contrario, se encuentra sometido a una gran actividad interior. Comprende que en cierto modo se ha hecho cargo de la situación porque el guión exige de él una palabra, un gesto, algo que establezca por su parte lo que ya ha quedado establecido por parte de Julia.

> (220)

What Jorge understands, if anything, is that his innermost acts, his words and gestures, are pre-scripted and externally imposed; he understands, that is, a diffuse but powerful *imperative to understand*. And part of this imperative, a dangerously essential part, is that Jorge don a mask of meaning and be a man. Julia's part, already obscurely established, is to play the willing victim whose alluring body will fill in (for) the fulsome emptiness that Jorge dreads (the "vision" of the drowned man, of "El Vitaminas"). And yet, early in the narrative, the feminine fullness for which Jorge yearns is presented as a fantastic sham. Julia's memories and desires of peace and happiness, her own innermost activities, recall, for instance,

> algunas secuelas habituales ya en algunos anuncios encargados de promocionar un suavizante para el cabello o un abrillantador de dientes.

(36)

They recall Adorno's assertion that

> the most intimate reactions of human beings have been so thoroughly reified that the idea of anything specific to themselves now persists only as an utterly abstract notion: personality scarcely signifies anything more than shining white teeth and freedom from body odor and emotions.

(167)

Reified intimacy, like banal originality, marks Julia as a thoroughly modern woman, one about whom there is little to be understood, as Jorge might put it, except, once more, the mediocre peace behind her name.

Mediocre as such peace may be, it is not what characterizes Julia. Moved by anger rather than complacency, she too seeks to understand not heady metaphysical problems such as the ends of life, but something tantalizingly closer to home:

> Entretanto medita y se pregunta no por el objeto de su vida, sino por la intención inmediata de sucesos [...] a través de los cuales se reconoce, y que actúan a manera de acotaciones en un texto cuyo único asunto parece ser la dentellada atroz del tiempo.

(35-36)

Like Jorge, Julia understands that she is prompted to act in a text not of her own making. There is, of course, an authorial incision here: Jorge and Julia, as if they were the heirs of Unamuno's Augusto Pérez, confront their confinement in a script signed by Juan José Millás. But there is something even more incisive: time, aggressively personalized, leaves the atrocious, figurative mark of its teeth—"la dentellada atroz"—on the text. We might wonder, after Adorno, if these teeth are not rotten with the beguiling gleam of progress. Regardless, the estrangement of experience, the specter of emptiness, and the inadequacy of signification all contribute to make the female body so (in)significant a thing for Jorge. That the body is thought to be a thing, if not the Thing, to be seized in the name of truth points to what is at stake in the breakdown of linguistic confidence. For if truth has long been an

effect of the adequation of thought to thing in language, it does not simply turn into falsity when adequation is reckoned inadequate. Instead, truth persists, but as a shadow of its former self, as a memory of a time when truth was (thought to be) adequately produced and maintained.

With Julia, the problem of truth is linked, fearfully, to the persistence of memory. Here, an adequate solution seems to be the erasure of thought itself. It is in this light that we can return to the question of Julia's adequation:

> La adecuación de Julia con el mundo resultaba natural y perfecta, ya que el olvido de la existencia de un horario no nacía de la erosión de una memoria perezosa, sino de la ausencia de cualquier tipo de memoria.

(18)

The absence of memory—and thus of history, human time, and the more banal schedule, or "*horario*," of day to day life—is alone capable of a natural, perfect, and true adequation. But while truth may paradoxically be "recalled" as oblivion in Millás's text, it nonetheless persists as a memory that is archaic in its own right. Or at least truth persists as a *fantasy* of archaic memory, a fantasy that is, moreover, sexual in scope. Troubled by the memory of an adolescence that, "como el cadáver de Dios" (96), inhabits the heart of maturity, Jorge seeks to "lose" or "forget" himself in the eroticized body of Julia. Such ecstatic oblivion, though hardly novel, is inflected with a significant difference:

> Ignora [Jorge] que el olvido de Julia procede de una memoria centenaria. No sabe del tumulto, ni del rumor de voces que se escuchan tras los ojos cerrados de su amiga. El aprieta y olvida.

(43-44)

The narrative voice, quite masculine itself, "knows" and "remembers" what Jorge does not.[6] The result is a disjunction between Jorge's ignorance and oblivion and Julia's, a disjunction effected through the agency of something supposedly engendered long ago.

Carter Smith, in a Bakhtinian reading of the text, argues that two chronotopes, one bio-historical and the other abstract and ahistorical "enter into a conflicting, dialectic relationship" (698). I agree, but would add that the conflicting temporal relationship is dramatized as a conflicting heterosexual relationship, duly given to triangulation and homosociality, with Jorge and Luis playing off each other. Stereotype, convention, and normativity, by which something historical is shaped into something ahistorical, are here critical. In *Visión del ahogado* an allegedly age-old memory returns, strangely full of forgetting, to a woman. But not to just any woman, for Julia is a mother. This is perhaps most evident in the description of Julia's recollection of her husband: "la imagen de su marido se ha ido haciendo sitio en un interespacio amniótico de su memoria" (37). The "amniotic interspace" is itself an image that gives, as it were, maternal body to memory. Mysteriously disjoining Jorge and Julia even as they join in the sexual act, the age-old, archaic memory to which the narrator refers is thus that of the mother in general.[7] She is, it seems, a mother held "responsible" for the inadequacies of truth and signification. Such responsibility carries a high price. For Julia, cast in the role of the hopelessly responsible mother, is repeatedly beaten while her daughter watches on. The narrator stresses the observant presence of the daughter on several occasions (88, 151, 181), as if the spectacle of sexual violence required not merely a spectator, but one who will "learn" from what she sees. What the little girl presumably sees, and what we read, is an act of sex that slips, not quite seamlessly, in and out of rape. Even if Julia and Jorge's sexual encounters are not read as rape, but as consensual sadomasochism, the violence persists.

Now, the fact that Julia is a mother and that Jorge beats her while her baby girl watches intensifies the force of the act. For in beating Julia's *maternal* body, Jorge is beating, in psychoanalytic terms, the symbolic site of the reproduction of the symbolic itself. He is also beating a woman. True, she is not a "real" woman, he not a "real" man, but rather they are textual effects, things of writing and reading. Their relationship, we can remind ourselves, is not really related to us, their violence not ours. So read, the writing is safely in place, comfortably incommensurate with other places, our places, be they the home, the street, or the chambers of government. The violence of (in)adequation in the text may be put in its place as peacefully inadequate to us, to our peace as well as to our violence. In a sense it really is; textual violence is never adequate to the violence outside the text, regardless of how we respond to the assertion that there is no outside-text. And yet, the inadequation of one to another does not mean that there is no relation or that mimesis is utterly inoperative. In *Visión del ahogado,* where the characters seem to intimate that they are characters and that, in many respects, we all are too, relations assume some violent forms, so much so that *relationality per se seems suffused with violence.* Textual violence is and is not real violence, but across the divide violence persists. Perhaps such violence persists, like truth, in the place of truth, a diffuse and intense memory in its own right: "Con los dedos [Julia] busca a través del dolor la memoria de los golpes" (87). Perhaps violence is, as the text suggests, the *only* truth to be remembered, and forgotten, the only truth that never fails to make a return. This is not to say that truth, as violence, returns always and in the same way to everyone. In fact, amid the mundane figures of contemporary Madrid, violence and truth haunt Julia in especially acute ways:

> determinados fantasmas no son sino la huella de una hábil manipulación efectuada por el miedo sobre su memoria más antigua de las cosas. Pero siente el temor, o la repulsa, de ser depositaria de unos fantasmas que ya tuvo su madre, que se repetirán en su hija, y que a ella le parecen

> las señales que marcan la distancia entre la corrupción y el deterioro.

(62)

What Julia finds so fearful is the idea that she is a repository of phantasms that mark her within a matrilineal chain. Something cyclical, inescapable, and fatalistic is hereby signaled, but there is more. In the *distance* between her mother and her daughter, a past decay (or corruption) and an anticipated decay, Julia senses that truth would have a body still. And the body that truth here would have is cut in violent contradiction, a body thought, willed, and desired as both living and dead. It is along these lines that Jorge takes, or would take, Julia's body as the last adequate measure of truth, as the repository of the phantasms *she* so fears. In saying that her body is cut in contradiction, I mean that Jorge's attempt to take it as the measure of something vitally true damages if not destroys it. Lest this dynamic seem unique to Jorge and Julia, we might remember that Julia is not the only woman subjected to violence in *Visión del ahogado.* Before her, there was Rosario, the object of "El Vitaminas's" adolescent anguish. What "El Vitaminas" fantasized then, like what Jorge fantasizes now, is nothing less than the destructive certainty of masculine identity:

> alentaba el deseo de destrozar la vida de Rosario en beneficio del macho inseguro que en su interior buscaba afianzarse con la desgracia ajena.

(154)

Weaving between Julia, Rosario, Jorge, and "El Vitaminas," between adolescence and maturity, past and present, Millás's text points to the violent repetitiveness of sexual knowledge. Violence is here fundamental, because it maintains and even generates contradiction at the same time that it aims to overcome it. Gender too appears to be fundamental. What thereby obtains, in a chiasmus too tempting to resist, is something like the violence of gender and the gender of violence. Exploring the ties between violence and gender, a number of feminists have pointed out the historically established tendency to engender the body in the feminine and truth—in such abstract forms as thought, mind, and spirit—in the masculine. According to this history, men create with their mind and imagination while women create with their body: or more succinctly, men produce, culturally, and women reproduce, naturally. The primacy of maternity is readily apparent in this history, not merely as a feminine matter, but as a masculine idea as well. With regards to Julia, the phantasms that she fears as the archaic fate of femininity are, historically speaking, the phantasms of masculinity. These phantasms mark her body as a violently (in)adequate reserve of masculine truth. Indeed, the idea of the feminine body as a repository of truth—simultaneously holding and withholding meaning—seems here untenable outside of violence. To put it more concisely, in *Visión del ahogado,* Jorge cannot think of (or desire) Julia outside of violence. In one scene after another, one beating after another, Millás's text is on this point implacable: "La violencia delata la falta de sustancia. O la sustituye" (181). Violence discloses the lack of substance. Or it substitutes it, replaces it, takes its place.

To substitute a lack of substance does not necessarily mean that something is made good; instead, it may imply a dizzying replication of lack, a simulation. And yet, despite so much emptiness and falsity, it is important to note that violence discloses not so much the insubstantiality of the desired object (Julia, as objectified by Jorge and the narrator) as the insubstantiality of the desiring subject (Jorge). In *Visión del ahogado,* in short, violence substitutes a historically constructed, peculiarly masculine lack. Through violence, the inadequacy of meaning and the lightness of being that hound Jorge, far from being resolved, are made all the more unbearable:

> Jorge la persigue [a Julia] a través del reducido espacio y golpea con precisión los lugares más deseados de su cuerpo desnudo: toma venganza de una adolescencia determinada por aquellas caderas indiferentes a su dolor profundo; y crece su violencia al tiempo que también, de algún modo, el objeto sobre el que la descarga; y así el cuerpo de Julia pierde o recupera sus límites al ritmo de su identidad, que con la crecida de los golpes atraviesa en sucesión los posibles modelos de todo aquello con lo que Jorge no ha concebido nunca otras relaciones que las basadas en la violencia o la transgresión.

(88)

In the close, domestic space of the apartment, Jorge pursues, beats, and penetrates Julia with willful precision. And as he beats her, as he moves to master her, she, or more precisely her body, grows. Rising and falling in her body, her identity is rhythmically coupled to his violence, created and destroyed by it, over and over. Coupled to violence himself, Jorge may indeed be of limited ideas, but these ideas are not, unfortunately, limited to him. The scene of violence is here almost primal in its intensity, and belies a disturbingly irresolute tension within the home itself. For it is as if domesticity, symbolized as the placid and productive heart of culture, were unable to relinquish a wildness that it deems its other: as if Jorge had to brutalize Julia to make her fit for the home.

There is a profound domestic dilemma in *Visión del ahogado.* Jorge takes the place, sexually at least, of Julia's sick and delinquent husband. It is not the typical adulterous affair because "El Vitaminas" actually encourages Jorge, his healthy and aggressive childhood friend, to take his place. While Sobejano touches on the text's relation to realism (205), it is López who, as previously noted, situates Millás's text within a realist tradition of adultery that includes Clarín, Eça de Queirós, Flaubert, Tolstoy, Galdós, and Fontane (40). López's reading is compelling, but what I read is not so much the maintenance of literary traditions and established narrative frames as their violent simula-

tion. Millás's text, in other words, has more to do with the wrenching of tradition and the collapse of master narratives so dear to postmodernity than it does with the mimetic totalization and "virile maturity" that Georg Lukács finds in the realist novel (71).[8] In Millás's novel, virility and maturity are adolescent illusions, fierce substitutes for a profound ontological emptiness. Adultery, betrayal, and crime are not situated and signified within a stable frame; instead, they are set impossibly loose in a world made mean with masculine meaning.

But if *Visión del ahogado* comes close to laying bare the violence of established masculinity and of male-ordered domesticity, it is not by refiguring meaning within a feminist frame and even less by appealing to "positive role models." Julia, for example, repeatedly validates the violence against her as the only tangible value she knows:

> Para Julia, que con los mismos gestos con los que intenta defenderse procura asimismo provocar nuevos golpes, aquello no deja de ser también en cierto modo una reivindicación: el dolor reivindica sus pechos y los dos abanicos de sus nalgas, y su pelo, que se le cruza por delante del rostro y le ayuda a sentirse bella y codiciada.

(88-89)

Such instances of complicity recur repeatedly in Millás's text, as if there were some masochistic truth about women beneath all the violence. I submit however that this particular truth constitutes yet another instance of masculine anxiety before the inadequacy of truth in general. Moreover, the crisis of masculinity in which the subject melancholically fixates on the body as the refuge of lost meaning is shot through with the (dis)ordering of truth:

> el desorden nuevo advertido por alguna parte de su ser en una de las mínimas terrazas se convertía bajo la sospecha en un desorden lógico (como si el orden, el número o la causa tuvieran un fundamento razonable); es decir, en un desorden motivado.

(116)

For Millás, as the title of a later text, *El desorden de tu nombre,* indicates, the enigmatically motivated disorder is perhaps first and foremost the disorder of the name: another name, an other's name, your name. And the disorder of the name—the sign of the self—is of course often thought to be adequate to the disorder of the body: the treacherous site, or repository, of truth.

AN INADEQUATE CONCLUSION

la literatura es, de un lado, imposible, y de otro, necesaria.

Millás, **"Literatura y necesidad"**

la literatura sólo puede llegar a ser posible en la medida en que se vuelve imposible.

Millás, **"Literatura y realidad"**

It may seem strange that violence and disorder become the only truly adequate measure of truth. A disorderly word for a disorderly world, a disordered name for a disordered body: adequation, broken down, does not disappear, but seems to engender breakage. If *Visión del ahogado* is *any* indication, the breakdown of strong metaphysical concepts such as adequation, so crucial to truth, can have fearful repercussions, not so much because truth is untethered and set adrift, but because it is pieced (together) as broken. Broken down, truth persists, and returns, as breakdown and breakage; disordered, it persists and returns as disorder. The "rabiosa voluntad de desorden" (64) that Jorge experiences as he hits Julia across the face—while her infant daughter watches on—is therefore not just an attempt to disrupt the order of an already "broken" home; rather, it is an attempt to make a "private" (dis)order adequate to the more "public" (dis)order that Jorge encounters in the street. In this sense, Jorge's act, far from going against the dominant (dis)order, conforms to it. What is ironic is that Jorge, in one reflective passage after another, criticizes conformity, particularly as it is embodied, in his eyes, in Julia. But while Julia's use of popular American and Mexican love songs may be a symptom of conformity, Jorge's use of violence is itself a symptom of conformity, especially since the all too well-established violence he uses is sexual and domestic in order. I use the word "order" deliberately because Jorge's rabid will for disorder, inasmuch as it is manifested in an eroticized assault on Julia, is inseparable from a will to order. Slapping Julia across the face, he may keep her from fully facing him (and himself from fully facing her) as an autonomous, equal subject, but he does not achieve the disorder that he wills. After all, disorder, at least when understood in terms of violent subjugation, paradoxically replicates established order, the subjugation and violence that subtend it.

According to Gianni Vattimo, in an age of disenchantment, characterized by the absence of foundations, "the only possible foundation for the predominance of an order of meaning is force" (*Transparent* 95). It is worth tarrying with the word "foundation." Vattimo does not "mean" that an order of meaning is impossible without force, or that meaning is always violent, but rather that the attempt to *found* an order of meaning, to *ground* it once and for all, is unthinkable outside of force. The danger of disenchantment is the danger of groundlessness, of a lack of foundations, and the danger of groundlessness is that it may issue in the will to deny groundlessness and reassert foundations by force. In many respects the danger of disenchantment resembles the danger of full adequation, of taking one name, concept, thing, or person for another, of making them all fit, of denying inadequation. I have already indicated how the denial of inadequation is far from straightforward and may involve, paradoxically, an *apparent* acceptance of inadequation or a will to disorder as the only adequate response to an inadequate world. Different as they are, neither "El Vitaminas" nor Jorge gives up the ghost of adequation and

neither gives up violence, whether directed primarily towards the self or towards another. I do not mean to suggest that one *can* ever fully give up the ghost of adequation or that it is a principle that *can* be cast off like a worn garment, but rather that the violent turns of (in)adequation are crucial to the foundation of an order of meaning.

From the idea that a predominant order of meaning is founded by force it is only a small jump to the idea that the predominant meaning of order is force, that the meaning of order, its *truth,* is forced, violent, and hence at bottom even disordered. The idea that the meaning of order is at bottom disorder is bound to the idea that there is no bottom, or foundation, outside force. This is most apparent in the order of Francoism, and less apparent in the order that follows Francoism, and arguably even less apparent in the order of the home. At its most wily, the Francoist order, totalitarian in scope, fosters the illusion of peace, of being on firm, "natural" foundations. The order after Francoism, democratic in scope, is considerably more complex, particularly in the so-called Transition. Foundation here assumes the form of a democratic constitution and its ratification, both occurring *after* the publication of *Visión.* The democratic constitution is a far cry from the commanding voice, however legally inscribed, of the lifetime leader. Still, as forceful a document as the new constitution is, it would be naive to read it as if other forces—ranging from the police, the military, and state-sponsored terrorism to capitalism—were not also at work. The troubling side of disenchantment is that little if anything can get better (only older) and that the old order and its disorders merely continue in new guises. The order of the home, spanning political regimes, is, as noted, especially important.

Focusing on the violence of the home without losing sight of the violence of the street, *Visión del ahogado* comprises an indictment of the domestic order. True, in Millás's rendition, the domestic order is broken from the outset, with Jorge not exactly filling in for the absent husband and father. Some readers might take comfort, I suppose, in the fact that the home so violently depicted is not that of a faithfully married couple and might imagine that there would be no violence if the home were whole "as it should be." They might imagine that the true domestic order is an order founded not on the historical forces of domestication by which women and children are subjugated. They might imagine an order that held, once upon a time, when marriages did not break, at least not in a publicly, legally sanctioned way (divorce was not permitted until 1981); when women's rights were an oxymoron; and when adultery *really* mattered, morally and juridically. They might imagine a happy family, a stable home, peaceful without being mediocre. What they might thus imagine, of course, is the Francoist family, its idealized version at any rate, the one propped up and propagated with slogans, set phrases, and laws. However accurate such imaginings may be, for many Spaniards, the very idea of the happy, stable family continued to arouse suspicion during and after the Transition. Indeed, it is possible, I believe, to read the broken domestic scene in Millás's text in the light of the official version of domesticity. Whatever the case, Millás's text does not stage violence only in the street, but in the home, suggesting an imbrication of sites.

Calling for the need "to broaden the domain of the exercise of democratic rights beyond the limited traditional field of 'citizenship,'" Laclau and Mouffe question "the very idea of a natural domain of the 'private'" (185). In addition, they assert that "neo-conservative discourse today is exerting itself to restrict the domain of the political and to reaffirm the field of the private" (185). Part of the democratic process, they contend, is the opening of sites traditionally held to be beyond or outside democracy such as the home and, indeed, the body. Lest this democratic opening be taken as absolute, Laclau and Mouffe argue that democracy does not dispense with a certain closure. Accordingly, they set a principle of equivalence, by which all sites are equalized, alongside a principle of autonomy, by which sites remain different, in a mutually limiting way (185) that is particularly resonant for Spain. Drawing from the work of Claude Lefort, Laclau and Mouffe declare that

> the radical difference which a democratic society introduces is that the site of power becomes an empty space; the reference to the transcendent guarantor disappears, and with it the substantial unity of society. As a consequence a split occurs between the instance of power, knowledge, and the law, and their foundations are no longer assured.

> (186)

The result, they continue, is "an unending process of questioning" (186) that was by definition inoperable under Franco and only partially operable after the so-called consolidation of democracy. The problem, Laclau and Mouffe concede, is that the unending process of questioning, the splitting of established bonds, and the dissolution of foundations are not accepted without question and can generate a wide array of reactive responses. One such response is nostalgia, from both the right ("Con Franco vivíamos mejor") and, more complexly, the left ("Contra Franco vivíamos mejor"). Another response, connected to nostalgia, is violence, be it in the attempt, from a variety of political positions, to reassert unity and foundations or indeed in the attempt to disseminate splitting and dissolution. If the former is a case of ordered disorder, the second is a case of disorder ordered, in the sense that disorder is willed; both, as indicated, perpetuate a principle of adequation. But whether it be nostalgia, violence, some combination thereof, or something else altogether, the space that Franco leaves behind is neither discretely public nor private.[9]

Emptiness is not easily tolerated in the Western tradition. Running against plenitude and fulfillment, in both the religious and the erotic sense, emptiness can motivate penetration, occupation, inhabitation, expansion, colonization,

and so on. If democracy introduces a radical difference, and if that difference takes the form of—or maybe even takes place in—an empty space of power, it is not a difference long-lived—if it ever truly existed. For the Transition in Spain is in many respects closer to a *ruptura pactada* than to a *ruptura democrática,* closer to a planned or bargained break than a radically democratic break. The bargained break, whose aim was to ensure continuity and, as Tom Lewis puts it, "to gain breathing space for the new government by involving the Left parties in stemming the rising tide of strike activities and popular unrest" (173), was thus not really a "break" at all. Then again, the idea of a break that is truly one, of a reversal unmarked by what is being reversed, may itself be a function of enchantment, that is to say an illusion. Be that as it may, as Lewis rightly notes, "[t]alk of a *ruptura democrática* after the end of 1977 became stigmatized as immature political fantasy" (174). So one break becomes immature and fantastic—and these terms, along with the violence implicit in so many ruptures and breaks, swirl throughout Millás's text—while the other, the break that is not one, becomes mature and realistic, indeed real. But breaks do not need to be absolute, let alone clean, in order to be breaks: a *ruptura democrática* does not necessarily imply a denial of all historical continuity nor entail any more fantasies than a *ruptura pactada.* At any rate, the *ruptura pactada* was in the eyes of many less a break than a patching over of a potentially unbearable gap: the gap—or as Laclau and Mouffe would have it, the empty space—of democracy. This situation did not go unnoticed and gave way to a more temporally acute sense of disenchantment.

The disenchantment in the wake of Franco and in the midst of a transition to a newly (re)constituted society is, among other things, the effect of an intolerance of the radical difference that democracy might introduce. In the same sweep, it is the effect of a rush to fill in an ostensibly empty space of power with the same old thing or with something similar to it. The rush seems to be conditioned by the fear of an even swifter return of totalitarianism, of *absolutely* the same old thing, and by the fear of *different* totalizing systems. Franco may be as much a ghost of the empty space of power as Stalin, and it is perhaps not surprising that neither can be recuperated, in the person of one of their followers, as a guarantor of any social wholeness that is not totalitarian. This is important, for

> with totalitarianism, rather than designating a vacant site, power seeks to make itself material in an organ which assumes itself to be representative of a unitary people. Under the pretext of achieving the unity of the people, the social division made visible by the logic of democracy is thereupon denied.

> (Laclau 187)

The democracy that is constituted through these specters does not, however, simply accept social division or respect the vacancy of power. It too strives for a kind of fulfillment.

In the "broken" home which one man has left only to be replaced by another, the situation is uncannily like that of the nation. A site of power is vacated (Luis, "El Vitaminas," leaves), a difference is introduced (Julia is alone with her daughter), and a new guarantor of power arrives (Jorge). But what Jorge guarantees, in the use of force, is the previously mentioned *impossibility* of sexual relation. This raises some interesting paradoxes. Laclau and Mouffe's notion of the impossibility of society, by which they mean that society is not possible as a closed, complete, and utterly unified totality is here germane. Rather than accepting and managing impossibility, rather than accepting the vacancy so ambivalently signified by "El Vitaminas," Jorge strives to deny it, seeking instead a relation that is ordered under him. Or disordered: for the relation that Jorge imagines as possible is one founded on force, ordered in and as disorder, planned to fail:

> Jorge [. . .] no tenía nada que planificar, excepto el fracaso. Ordenar el fracaso, disponer adecuadamente sus partes y digerirlo luego día a día.
>
> (227)

Ordering failure, it might seem that Jorge does indeed accept the impossibility of a totally sutured, fixed, and non-antagonistic relation, but what he does is strive, through the willful use of force, to make that impossibility "his." *Ordering* failure and *willing* disorder is not the same as accepting or managing them. Quite the contrary, it is as if Jorge, intimating the impossibility of utterly unified sexual and social relations, sought to make his breakage adequate to a more extensive breakage that comes to him only in images of violence.

Millás's text is an inadequate measure of Spanish society. Shot through with references to fraud, failure, falsity, inauthenticity, simulation, and insubstantiality, it is a fractured testament to the pervasive disenchantment associated with the dissolution, not only of systems of total stability and projects of political redemption, but of truth and meaning as well. It is also a chronicle of violence: a disenchanted violence that arises in the breakdown of an adequate notion of truth and that is itself perhaps the frightful last gasp of adequation whose tone is tellingly manly. The same (masculine) privileges and prerogatives that are presumably without substance or objective grounds are reasserted by Jorge but also by "El Vitaminas," in and as violence. Theirs is not the violence of terrorism and the state-sponsored terrorist "resistance" to terrorism, but the violence of everyday life: the petty, banal, domestic strife of a society seemingly bereft of struggles more grandiose. It is in these "little stories" that grand historical projects, including the project of democracy, are tested. They are tested inadequately and for their own inadequacy, for their inability to saturate the social field as well as for their inability to discount little stories and their "personal" and "private" concerns. The democratic project, for instance, must grapple with the fact that these small stories, however told, are neither identical to it nor entirely different from it. It is in this tension, perhaps, that there lies something significant and, just possibly, promising for us all.

But what is the promise, for democracy, of disenchantment? I have perhaps belabored the dangers of disenchantment—understood as the dissolution of, among other things, a principle of adequation—as they pertain not only to Francoism but also to a good deal of anti-Francoism. The dangers include the violence of (re)founding a dominant order of meaning (in which a lack of foundations is forcefully denied) or of guaranteeing disorder as a dominant order of meaning (in which a lack of foundations becomes the adequate "justification" of a free play of forces). *Visión del ahogado* is in many respects an account of disenchantment (if not of *the* disenchantment), where the absence of foundations issues in the loss of socially constructive bonds. There is, however, another way of reading the text, one that takes disenchantment, for all its negativity, as holding a certain promise. Vindicating such weakened, humanist-laden terms as "compassion" and "solidarity," Vattimo claims that disenchantment need not find its truth in oppressive force, whether exercised against the other, the self, or both. For him, disenchantment—and this I believe is important for the fate of the term in contemporary Spanish thought in general—includes:

> the recognition that there are no objective structures, values or laws and that everything is posited, created by man (at least in the realm of meaning).
>
> (*Transparent* 97)

And created by woman, I might add. For one of the things that Millás's text stages is the violent refusal, on the part of Jorge (and perhaps the narrator), to recognize Julia as creative of any meaning that does not issue from the culture industry and/or phantasmatic conceptions of the maternal body. Disenchantment extends to the so-called private, domestic sphere, but need not, as it does in the text before us, extend only as force and frustration. As Vattimo says, disenchantment

> can be understood neither as the grasp of a true structure of reality, nor [. . .] as a 'transposition' into a world of undisguised relations, that is of pure relations of forces.
>
> (*Transparent* 99)

Indeed, "to the extent that it takes responsibility for the creation of meaning, disenchantment assumes the form of a decision for non-violence" (*Transparent* 94-95). And to the extent that the meaning that it creates does not ground itself, its truth, in a principle of strict adequation, disenchantment becomes the site of democratic opportunity, fractured and fluctuant in the home as in the street as in the text.

* * *

To be sure, meaning, so configured, may still seem quite grand. As such, it gives the lie to my claim that *Visión* is a small story holding no utopian message or redemptive lesson. This is not necessarily a "good thing." There is a risk—if that is indeed the way of putting it—of extracting a new enchantment from disenchantment. Taking a clue from *Visión,* there is also a risk of resuscitating the "drowned" and offering not just the opportunity for another, better way of living but also for another, more effective way of getting fucked over, of fucking over. And so the new enchantment that may be adumbrated in Vattimo's "opportune" reading of disenchantment, *pace* Vattimo, and in my extension of it to Millás's text, may harbor an opportunity for yet more disenchantment, more "adolescent" fantasies and "adult" failures, more violence. To the extent that it takes responsibility for the creation of meaning, disenchantment *does not perforce* assume the form of a decision for non-violence. Much as it pains me to suggest it, responsibility may itself be an inadequate principle, even, or especially, when it bears on the creation of meaning, all of which does not mean, in this swirling play of meanings grand and small, that responsibility can be simply thrown aside. Things, I would submit, are considerably more complex, more treacherous even, and require a good deal of vigilance: which can also be quite treacherous. This, at least, is the meaning for which I, however inadequately, take responsibility.

Notes

1. For Luis,

   > el tiempo es un privilegio de clase que ni sucede ni dura, porque durar denota, más que una adecuación entre existir y ser, un trasiego confuso de ambas categorías, cuyo enredo conduce finalmente a la renuncia de las dos. Dura, verbigracia, una enfermedad no atendida, un trabajo improvento, o este discurso mío cuyo final espera nadie para ni aplaudirlo ni censurarlo.

   (49-50)

   Time is inadequate because some things it tries to measure are simply too complex.

2. The relative lack of specific historical markers does not mean that there is a lack of specificity altogether. For Smith,

   > a very specific urban space in *Visión* (a blue-collar neighborhood in a northern quadrant of the city) is the locus for the tensions and contradictions in the novel.

   (697)

   It is interesting, however, that this "very specific urban space" is not named.

3. Julia's moment of oblivious, "perfect and natural" adequation with the world takes place before the mirror, in the "rutinaria comprobación de su belleza" (17). It is as if the contemplation of her own beauty blinded Julia to everything else: "ella no se sentía

vinculada al recuerdo ni a la evocación, sino más bien a su propia imagen" (20).

4. Whether it is "El Vitaminas's" fear of capture or Julia's "miedo antiguo que conservaba aún como reliquia de la adolescencia" (19), fear, overlaid with desire, saturates the text. The irruption of "El Vitaminas" into Jorge's sphere of activity is one of those events that:

   > si bien no suceden cada día ni cada hora suceden en todo caso con la frecuencia necesaria como para acabar por tomarle miedo al mundo en general y a la calle en particular.

   (12)

5. Lacan's claim that "il n'y a pas de rapport sexuel" (35) should be read against a horizon of ideal reciprocity, correspondence, unity, and adequation. *That* sexual relation is impossible.

6. Jorge's and Luis's memories are explicitly related, while Julia's are only suggested through the memories of the men. Memory is thus given narrative content in masculine terms. López is right to read the omniscient narrating voice as masculine and as being close to Jorge's and to describe Julia as a desired object or voiceless, unsaid subject (44).

7. Kristeva's highly problematic theorization of the archaic mother—as what cannot be seized by rational thought yet undergirds signification—is appurtenant to Millás's figurations of femininity. Expanding on the Lacanian notion of the real as bound to death, Kristeva suggests that the mother bears the chore of delivering the real into the symbolic, and hence of bringing life to death and death into life. Of course, such a suggestion can have devastating consequences.

8. For Lukács, the novel as the art form of "virile maturity,"

   > means that the completeness of the novel's world, if seen objectively, is an imperfection, and if subjectively experienced, it amounts to resignation.

   (71)

   In *Visión del ahogado,* "virile maturity" is an adolescent fantasy and the very notions of objective vision and subjective experience are violently unhinged.

9. The death of a dictatorial father does not lend itself to indisputable mourning because the father in question is not indisputably loved and perhaps not even indisputably hated (one may have loved to hate him). Unlike Hitler and Mussolini, Franco escapes retributive justice and, however pathetic his protracted agony, finds instead the symbolic sweetness of slipping "naturally" into death. To mourn Franco thus

entails mourning the conditions and circumstances of his demise. Given the circumstances of Franco's death, melancholia is almost a constitutional risk.

Works Cited

Adorno, Theodor W. and Max Horkheimer. *Dialectic of Enlightenment.* Trans. John Cumming. New York: Continuum, 1987.

Benet, Juan. *La inspiración y el estilo.* Madrid: Revista de Occidente, 1966.

Bértolo Cadenas, Constantino. Apéndice. *Papel mojado.* By Juan José Millás. Madrid: Anaya, 1983. 183-223.

Cabañas, Pilar. "Materiales gaseosos: Entrevista con Juan José Millás." *Cuadernos Hispanoamericanos* 580 (1998): 103-20.

Cebrián, Juan Luis. *La España que bosteza: Apuntes para una historia crítica de la Transición.* Madrid: Taurus, 1980.

Cuadrat, Esther. "Una aproximación al mundo novelístico de Juan José Millás." *Cuadernos Hispanoamericanos* 541-542 (1995): 207-16.

Jones, Anny Brooksbank. *Women in Contemporary Spain.* Manchester: Manchester UP, 1997.

Kristeva, Julia. *Soleil noir: Dépression et mélancolie.* Paris: Gallimard, 1987.

Lacan, Jacques. *Le Seminaire XX-Encore.* Paris: Seuil, 1975.

Laclau, Ernesto and Chantal Mouffe. *Hegemony and Socialist Strategy: Towards a Radical Democratic Politics.* London: Verso, 1985.

Lewis, Tom. "Aesthetics and Politics." Afterword to *Critical Practices in Post-Franco Spain.* Eds. Silvia L. López, Jenaro Talens, and Darío Villanueva. Minneapolis: U of Minnesota P, 1994. 160-82.

López, Ignacio-Javier. "Novela y realidad: En torno a la estructura de *Visión del ahogado* de Juan José Millás." *Anales de Literatura Española Contemporánea* 13 (1988): 37-54.

Lukács, Georg. *The Theory of the Novel: A Historico-Philosophical Essay on the Forms of Great Epic Literature.* Trans. Anna Bostock. Cambridge: MIT P, 1973.

Mainer, José-Carlos. "1975-1985: Los poderes del pasado." *La cultura española en el posfranquismo: Diez años de cine, cultura y literatura (1975-1985).* Madrid: Playor, 1988. 11-26.

Marco, José María. "En fin … Entrevista con Juan José Millás." *Quimera* 81 (1988): 20-6.

Millás, Juan José. "Literatura y necesidad." *Revista de Occidente* (1998): 185-91.

———. "Literatura y realidad." *Revista de Occidente* 85 (1988): 122-25.

———. *Visión del ahogado.* Barcelona: Destino, 1989.

Miranda, Martha Isabel. "El lenguaje cinematográfico de la acción en la narrativa de Juan José Millás." *Revista Hispánica Moderna* 47.2 (1994): 526-32.

Rosenberg, John R. "Entre el oficio y la obsesión: Una entrevista con Juan José Millás." *Anales de la Literatura Española Contemporánea* 21 (1996): 143-60.

Smith, Carter E. "Between Two Chronotopes: Space and Time in Juan José Millás's *Visión del ahogado*." *Romance Languages Annual* 9 (1998): 697-703.

Sobejano, Gonzalo. "Juan José Millás: Fabulador de la extrañeza." *Nuevos y novismos: Algunas perspectivas críticas sobre la narrativa española desde la década de los 60.* Eds. Ricardo Landeira & Luis T. González-del-Valle. Boulder: Society of Spanish and Spanish American Studies, 1987. 195-215.

Spires, Robert C. *Post-Totalitarian Spanish Fiction.* Columbia: U of Missouri P, 1996.

Vattimo, Gianni. *The End of Modernity.* Trans. Jon R. Snyder. Baltimore: The Johns Hopkins UP, 1991.

———. *The Transparent Society.* Trans. David Webb. Baltimore: The Johns Hopkins UP, 1992.

Dale Knickerbocker (essay date 2003)

SOURCE: Knickerbocker, Dale. "*El desorden de tu nombre.*" *Juan José Millás: The Obsessive-Compulsive Aesthetic.* New York: Lang, 2003. 39-62. Print.

[*In the following essay, Knickerbocker studies Millás's use of metafictional narrative techniques and mentally disturbed protagonists in* The Disorder of Your Name *and other works. He argues that Millás is primarily focused on exploring "the internal contradictions of the Spanish collective unconscious."*]

> Visto así, parece absurdo que los hombres nos empeñemos en la búsqueda de un destino propio o de una identidad definitiva. Si de verdad tuviésemos identidad, no necesitaríamos tantos papeles (certificados, carnés, pasaportes, etcétera) para mostrarla. En fin.
>
> Juan José Millás, *El desorden de tu nombre*

DN [*El desorden de tu nombre*] relates the story of aspiring author Julio Orgaz, executive in a large publishing house, and his affair with Laura who, unbeknownst to him, is the wife of Julio's psychoanalyst, Carlos Rodó.[1] On the moral level, Julio undergoes an identity crisis as a result of several psychological trauma: his rejection by a former lover, Teresa Zagro, who then dies in an automobile accident; his divorce and the guilt he feels over abandoning his wife and child; and a mid-life crisis aggravated by the fact that, at age forty-three, he has still not achieved his goal of becoming a published author. The protagonist becomes obsessed with forging a new identity for himself, one based on his desires to achieve corporate advancement, success as an author, and possession of Laura. By the end of the novel, Julio has apparently achieved his professional, creative, and amorous goals: in addition to the completion of a manuscript titled *El desorden de tu nombre,* he conquers Laura, who kills her husband to be with him, and he is promoted to a position created specifically for him, above even the one he coveted. Julio has apparently created a new identity; however, this success is ironically subverted for the reader, who knows that Julio has achieved it by the unethical rejection of a manuscript he knew to be worthy of publication, the cynical adoption of a modern image based only on the imitation of the clothes and affectations of an acquaintance, and a less than admirable desire to supplant his amorous and professional rivals. Furthermore, his success necessitates turning his back on his family and social origins. Thus, neither his means nor his motives are presented as a positive model. From the perspective of his novelistic trajectory, *DN* constitutes a milestone in Millás's work, as he selects for the first time a truly bizarre, neurotic and highly ironic protagonist, a type that will become the hallmark of his obsessive-compulsive narrative. The author himself has commented that through Julio "En *El desorden de tu nombre* aparecen casi todas las obsesiones que le acompañan a un escritor en el proceso de elaboración de una novela [. . .]" (Marco 22). While obsession itself is not explicitly thematized in *DN* as it will be in later works, Millás's two obsessively ruminated main themes, identity and social criticism, predominate. These are developed and supported by a core of secondary preoccupations: alienation, the metafictional theme of writing, life as semiotic endeavor, success and failure, and the tenuous line between reality and fantasy, or life and death.

The effects of Julio's personal and cultural environment upon him and his attempts achieve some control over these circumstances are played out on the screen of narrative; in *DN,* as in all the novels examined in this study, the symptomology of the protagonist's neuroses or psychoses allow the reader to discern the causes of the mental illness. These sign/symptoms in turn serve as the vehicle for the works' social commentary. On an allegorical level, both Julio and Carlos may be seen as collective characters, as a "reduction of the alien collective to the valorized individual biography" (Jameson 30). Their social and sexual desires therefore constitute "allegories of desire [. . .] whose master narrative is the story of desire itself" (Jameson 67). These desires are channeled by the social structures of late capitalism, resulting in Carlos and Julio's unscrupu-

lous behavior in their drive for wealth, fame, and power. On a thematic level, Millás utilizes the characters of both Julio and Carlos to implicitly criticize the generation of Spaniards to which he himself belongs, who were beginning to occupy positions of power at the time of the writing of *DN,*[2] a critique that will also be of primary import in *SE* [*La soledad era esto*], *TMBI* [*Tonto, muerto, bastardo e invisible*] and *OA* [*El orden alfabético*]. Moreover, on the level of the historically determined political unconscious, it is possible to conjecture that the writing of this novel responds to class guilt experienced by the collective to which Millás himself belongs and that, at least in part, the writing of this work, and its formal and thematic characteristics, constitute a working-through of that guilt.

It is significant that, after being a central figure in Millás's only novel written before the death of Franco, *no father figure will receive anything more than a passing mention in the author's work until 1995.* This suppression of the paternal may be interpreted as Millás's individual manifestation of a much more wide-spread repression of conflicting emotions toward the dictator by the Spanish people. A justified hatred of a political figure deeply identified with the paternal function of lawgiver could give rise to emotions of guilt upon feeling relief and joy upon his death. Such ambivalence could well cause both a supression of the paternal in *DN* and later works and a narrative symptomology designed to allay the anxiety that such a repression creates: the repressed returns as an obsessive-compulsive aesthetic.

This deep-seated Freudian allegorical master narrative may also be seen in Julio's contemptuous attitude toward his mother, as the son feels a need to lower the standing of the "false" mother in order to claim his true birthright: in Julio's case, professional, economic, and artistic success. This allegory too leads us to an anagogical reading: the protagonist's disdain for the mother who reminds him of his humble social origins (a Millasian "obsession" repeated in other works) is a class fantasy, a particular literary manifestation of the class guilt felt by many members of the author's generation.

DN is perhaps Millás's most self-reflexive work.[3] As Julio experiences the events recounted, he occasionally observes an alter ego seated at the desk in his apartment, writing the text of what will become upon its completion the novel itself. In addition to the presence of the *mise en abyme* author, the plots of nine short stories or novels (including *DN* itself) are described.[4] These are either the protagonist's own projects or are written by a talented young author, Orlando Azcárate, whose work Julio is assigned to evaluate, and whose career he will undermine out of envy. Julio also appraises these stories, as Azcárate does with the protagonist's projected novel. Yet another author figure is present, the protagonist's former schoolmate Ricardo Mella, a writer of best-selling adventure novels, who is now dying of cancer. Laura also writes, maintaining a diary in which, in addition to relating her thoughts and impressions, she plays at combining fragments of pairs of word to create new ones. All these metafictional elements will be seen to contribute to Millás's elaboration of the identity theme, as the novel portrays Julio's drive to construct a new, solid subjectivity for himself as a metafictional attempt to *escribirse.*

On a formal or stylistic level, the compulsive reiteration of motifs increases in importance as both a structural device and in the development of *DN*'s thematics. It is also in *DN* that Millás solidifies the set of motif types that will be used as sign/symptoms in future works. Several motifs point to the causes of Julio's psychological aberrations, while others suggest obsessive-compulsive thought or behavior on the part of the protagonist, such as parataxis, epistemophilia and phobia. The protagonist repeatedly suffers auditory and olfactory hallucinations, hearing the socialist anthem *La Internacional* and smelling his mother's broth. These sign/symptoms point to the sources of his guilt feelings, thus serving to elaborate the novel's social criticism. Corporal, spatial, and doubling motifs possess a metaphoric function in developing the theme of identity, as do several metafictional motifs.[5] In the denouement, the work's themes are masterfully bound together as obsession is revealed as informing the work, not only on the moral levels of characterization, theme, style and structure, but on the anagogical level as well.

The failure of Julio's relationship with Teresa, her traumatic death and the loneliness they provoke send him into a deep depression.[6] The repetition of the age motif provides evidence that Julio is beginning to suffer a mid-life crisis: his sudden, radical change in wardrobe inspired by Ricardo Mella and his incipient womanizing constitute behavior stereotypical of such a crisis.[7] As is the case with the protagonists of Millás's next four novels, the loner Julio is alienated (more by choice than by circumstance) not only from his family but from society in general and his peers in particular. His first encounter with Laura plants in him a seed of hope that will result in his urge to forge a new identity: "Pronto comprendió que no se iba a morir o al menos no iba a ser enterrado, porque los síntomas que anunciaban su fin no tenían las trazas de resolverse en un cadáver. Por el contrario, advirtió que estaba falleciendo para convertirse en otro [...]" (35). Julio also possesses at least two alter egos: Carlos, and the other self into which the protagonist himself is evolving. Despite his optimism, his underlying psychological problems have not disappeared, but have merely been repressed, only to return as symptoms. Adding to these origins of his neuroses is the fact that his new identity entails the rejection of his son, his mother, and his class origins, all of which he now sees as vulgar.[8] In one example, the narrator describes the following reflections of Julio: "podía verse unos años atrás de la mano de un niño-su hijo-que por entonces era portador de un deseo innombrable [...] Pero el parque era otro, como otros eran los afectos y las ambiciones y la mirada

de taladrar la vida" (68). Nonetheless, upon seeing a father and son together "sintió en la conciencia un arrepentimiento leve, relacionado con su hijo, pero lo anuló con la promesa de un futuro espléndido, ahora que iba a ganar mucho dinero [...]" (190). Such rejection occasions guilt that must be repressed-and eventually reappear, a process that manifests itself in the reiteration of the signs/symptoms *remordimiento, arrepentimiento* and *culpa.*

JULIO'S SYMPTOMS

While Julio is not an obsessive-compulsive personality, he does display certain traits that will be accentuated in later Millasian characters. *Ansiedad,* the principal symptom of obsessive-compulsive disorder, significantly appears for the first time as a reiterated motif, as do *inquietud, angustia, nervios, congoja, tensión* and *desazón.*[9] While not yet indicative of an obsessive-compulsive personality in clinical terms, the presence of these motifs demonstrates a move in that direction: the protagonist's feelings for Laura, his erotic "obsession," come close to the clinical sense of the term, as he feels an anxiety when he is not with her that can only be assuaged by her presence, which itself provides only temporary relief. Julio feels "ansiedad" (9), "desamparo" (9) and "desazón" (11) due to her absence; as soon as they meet, "Julio sintió en seguida que sus nervios se aflojaban, pues la conversación le proporcionaba una suerte de paz [...]" (12), an effect later repeated (15). Just as formalized repetition is the fundamental characteristic of compulsive ceremonies, their meetings are described as "reproducciones más o menos exactas" of the first one (12). Furthermore, the narrator describes on several occasions Julio's impression that their love and actions together seemed to originate "al margen" (10), "a espaldas" (13) or "ajeno a su voluntad" (16). While this is certainly a metafictional allusion to the "author" seated at Julio's writing desk, it also describes the nature of obsessive thoughts and compulsive activities, which are normally experienced as ego-syntonic or involuntarily. The protagonist also describes his love for Laura in relation to anxiety: "la angustia, que se trenzaba con la felicidad para dar lugar al producto al que ambos se referían con el nombre del amor" (26); "la angustia no atenuaba su dicha; la reforzaba más bien o incluso la hacía posible hasta el punto en que Julio no podía imaginar aquella historia sino como el efecto de una carencia, cuya manifestación más elocuente consistía en ese grado controlable de desasosiego" (29). Julio's relationship with Teresa, for whom Laura is a substitute, is described in similar terms: "Fue una época rara en la que la felicidad y la angustia se trenzaban entre sí como las partes de un todo que llamaban amor" (23).

The protagonist also displays an epistemophilic drive that serves as a vehicle for the theme of life as semiotic endeavor. Julio believes that "La presencia oscura de Teresa [...] estimulaba en él el deseo de establecer conexiones lógicas entre asuntos difíciles de unir sin la colaboración de esa sustancia que segregan los afectos" (24). In the context of this statement, it becomes clear that sexual desire and the desire for greater understanding are intimately and even inextricably intertwined, as the following observation concerning his relationship with Teresa could apply equally to his epistemophilia: "la vida es eso [...] una loca carrera hacia un objeto que siempre queda más allá; en ocasiones, más allá de la muerte" (31). He frequently suffers from fevers that alter his perception of reality, and believes that this mental state creates *agujeros* or *rendijas* that provide him privileged insight into *el otro lado de las cosas* or *de la vida*: the first time this occurs, "Julio supo que estaba viviendo uno de esos instantes en los que los objetos menos dignos de atención adquieren una relevancia inusitada" (52).[10] This "other side" is a polysemic, reiterated sign/symptom that at times seems to signify a realm of greater understanding, and at others, death. The protagonist complains that: "Vivimos una vida demasiado pegada a lo aparente, a lo manifiesto, a lo que sucede o parece suceder" (140). It is in these moments of ironic enlightenment that he is able to interpret repeated inanimate objects such as *objetos* or *muebles* as *signos*: "Observó el dormitorio y tuvo la impresión de que todo el conjunto-incluido él-había sido separado de un proceso general para convertirse en una unidad autónoma situada al otro lado de donde sucedían las cosas [...] Julio llegó a pensar que en la otra realidad-la realidad real-estaban muertos ya desde el principio de los siglos" (50-1).[11] These signs are compulsively referred to as possessing a *misterio* or *secreto* that is *oculto, clandestino,* or *oscuro.*[12] In these states, Julio believes himself able to delineate the *conexiones* or *hilos,* imbricated in a *marco* of *puntos de referencia,* that compose the hidden *red* of signification.[13] The reiterated mention of *miradas* or *observación* suggests a scopophilic drive, frequently present in cases of obsession, to visually decipher these signs of reality.[14] *Coincidencias* and *casualidades* are also mentioned recurringly during the narrative; these are invariably interpreted as possessing significance, as examples of *sincronía.*[15] In a similar manner, he frequently grants certain ideas the priveleged status of *premonición* or *presentimiento,* considering them as bearing a significance in relation to future events.[16]

In addition to his anxiety and epistemophilic proclivities, Julio frequently displays tendencies toward superstitious, parataxic thought, albeit to a more limited extent than later Millasian protagonists. In one instance, "comenzó a sentir una opresión en un punto del pecho y supo en seguida que se trataba de un ataque de angustia del que intentó defenderse con los mecanismos que solía utilizar en tales casos" (27). When Julio and Teresa's relationship nears its end and he suspects she is seeing another man, her tardiness in arriving at a date in a movie theater causes him anxiety, which he diminishes through parataxic activity: "comenzó a sentir que la butaca vacía era la prueba más palpable de su infidelidad, por lo que conjuró el error de la cita realizando dos o tres actos supersticiosos con los dedos" (30). Julio also possesses the following superstitious conviction

concerning Ricardo's cancer: "Si le tocaba a uno [de su generación] ya no podía tocar a los otros. De manera que se encontraba a salvo" (187). These examples of parataxis are underscore by the repeated mention of the motifs *superstición* and *sobrenatural.*[17]

The effort to deepen his understanding of the diverse aspects of his life in order to control them relates epistemophilia to parataxic thought in their earliest appearance in a Millasian protagonist. The narrator suggests that Julio sees a cause and effect relationship between understanding and the control of one's environment that brings success: "De modo que las cosas parecían engarzarse con cierto sentido o, al menos, dirigidas a un fin que ponía en relación diferentes fragmentos de su vida" (36). As he gains insight, he takes action he thinks will provide the desired results: "Luego cambió de lugar algunos muebles en el apartamento e imprimió a su trabajo un ritmo diferente-más eficaz, pero también más frío-que le valió un ascenso en pocos meses" (36). But perhaps the moment that best exemplifies the relationship between the desire for understanding and the compulsion to control his circumstances is the following:

> [...] comprendió que la realidad inmediata, la más familiar, la de todos los días, estaba llena de rendijas por las que un temperamento como el suyo podía penetrar para observar las cosas desde el otro lado. Esas rendijas estaban hábilmente camufladas por las costumbres, por las normas, por los hábitos de comportamiento. Pero de vez en cuando se mostraban como una herida, como una boca abierta-a través de una taza de caldo o de una reencarnación-y uno podía entrar en el laberinto al que daba acceso y manejar desde sus túneles la vida como un muñeco de guiñol.
>
> (187)

As mentioned in the introduction, the obsessive-compulsive personality nearly always suffers from phobias. In this respect, Julio corresponds to the clinical profile, as the description of his feelings toward his pet canary demonstrates: "[estaba] dominado por un temor supersticioso que otorgaba al canario algún poder sobrenatural" (19).[18] When Laura comes to Julio's apartment to make love for the first time the canary begins to chirp so loudly that he nearly drowns out their conversation. Julio believes that "'el pájaro está cantando 'La Internacional'" (121). He takes the bird out of its cage, crushes it, and tells Laura that it must have had a heart attack. Far from distressing her, she later admits that the act excited her, in what constitutes the first metaphoric manifestation of the conflicting drives of *eros* and *thanatos* together. As they make love, "Ella de vez en cuando abría los ojos unos instantes para observar el cadáver del pájaro [...] El animal le confirmaba que la muerte es posible, poniendo al descubierto la precariedad de los principales puntos de referencia de su vida. Y ello le permitía también gozar de aquello que le estaba pasando y que parecía un sueño [...]" (123).[19] The mention of reference points and the blurring of the line between reality and dream also point to the theme of life as semiosis.

IDENTITY AND ALTER EGO

Julio's desire to create the identity of a successful executive, author, and conqueror of women involves a process of internal doubling or *desdoblamiento,* demonstrated in his creation of the author alter ego seen seated at his writing desk. Julio will also be seen at one time or another as having a *doppelgänger* relationship with several individuals: Teresa Zagro, Carlos Rodó, Orlando Azcárate and Ricardo Mella, each of whom will execute a different function with respect to Julio's unstable identity. The work's reiteration of the mirror and *otro* motifs supports this doubling.[20] Millás also employs the repetition of a series of corporal motifs that are generally perceived as the definitive signifieds of individual identities, such as the face, eyes, and the body itself, apparently to suggest the solidity and permanence or specificity of identity.[21] Furthermore, specific characteristics are repeatedly associated with the identity of certain individuals: Laura's attractive *melena,* for example, or Carlos's bald spot and dandruff.[22] The author then metaphorically and ironically undermines the concept of fixed identity suggested by these conventional signs: roles, attitudes, and even bodies will be blurred, usurped, or exchanged as the boundaries of subjectivity are transgressed. The effect will be to subvert any notion of a stable, unitary identity in favor of a more postmodern, fragmentary concept of subjectivity; for as critics such as Vance R. Holloway have noted, *DN* "render[s] problematic the notion of the unified human subject as a fundamental hermeneutic truth" (32).[23] Spatial motifs are also used as metaphors of identity, as subjectivity is referred to as a *sitio, territorio, lugar, espacio,* or *zona*; however, these mysterious zones or spaces in the interior of one's self, while endlessly explored, are never successfully mapped, their coordinates as transient as blowing sands.[24] Even Millás's choice of heterodiegetic, non-focalized narrator metaphorically subverts the bounds of identity, allowing the reader to see events from the perspective of different characters. The work also includes chapters told from the points of view of both Carlos and Laura, enhancing this effect.[25]

The permeability of the borders of the protagonist's identity is first suggested when he feels himself to be possessed by the spirit of Teresa Zagro, whose surname's palindromic relationship to Orgaz playfully suggests a mirror relationship between the two. The occupation of one body by the personality of another, whether as a character's fantasy or a possible reality within the fictional world presented, is a metaphor of this permeability, and the fact that the boundaries crossed include those of gender (both types of events will become increasingly common in the author's fiction) augments this transgression. Julio, in a fevered state which he believes allows him access to the "other side," fantasizes or hallucinates the internalization of the

former object of his desire: "advertía un movimiento de ocupación que el interior del apartamento registraba [. . .] En seguida todo el ambiente-incluidas las oquedades de su pecho-pareció habitado por una presencia calculadora que daba la impresión de actuar con algún fin determinado" (21).[26] Julio picks up a book Teresa had left him and begins to read it, finding in it passages underlined that are of no apparent importance. It is suggested that the occupying presence is that of Teresa when the epistemophilic protagonist goes "en busca de una clave secreta que justificara el subrayado" (21), an act that intensifies the occupation: "En ese instante la ocupación alcanzaba ya a todos los territorios de su ser" (22). In a humorous turn of events, Julio even imagines his pet bird to be occupied by Teresa. He later describes this experience as "sobrenatural": "He oído decir que los muertos gastan bromas de este tipo [. . .]" (61). Another day, the physically and emotionally exhausted protagonist, contemplating his failures as husband, father, lover and above all writer, "se sentía invadido por la mujer aquella, poseído por su imagen y troceado por su ausencia, ausencia que [. . .] equivalía a una mutilación íntima [. . .]" (92). The passage implies that the object of Julio's affections serves to fill an absence inside him. While on the surface this may simply seem to refer to his missing her, or to the absence of her love, the fact that he feels she fills his *oquedades* or hollow cavities may also be seen as suggesting that Julio's introjection of this other is meant to fill his lack of identity.

Another facet of the self-other relationship that appears in the novel is that of social and familial roles and expectations. Laura experiences a dream in which she had lost all contact with her mother some twenty years earlier. A television show manages to locate the parent, now bed ridden and moribund, and invites the daughter to a televised re-union. However, when the two meet, "Ambas se miraban a los ojos y simultáneamente comprendían que se trataba de un error; ni la anciana moribunda era la madre ni Laura la hija. Pero las dos establecían con la mirada el pacto destinado a no decepcionar a los numerosos espectadores— quizá a no decepcionarse a sí mismas—y se abrazaban llorando de emoción" (42).[27] The dream metaphorically implies that the identities of mother and daughter are not specific and unique to any two subjects, but rather are social constructs, a function of social roles and expectations. But the false other fulfills a need—not only for the audience, but for the two subjects involved, whose acceptance of the simulacra signals that a substitute fulfills the role as well as any original.

The identities of Teresa and Laura are also repeatedly confused in the protagonist's consciousness. In a fevered state, Julio tells his psychoanalyst that Laura "sin parecerse a Teresa, da a veces la impresión de ser su reencarnación" (61), describing to him an occasion when

> [. . .] los rostros de Teresa y de Laura [. . .] comenzaron a
> confundirse en mi recuerdo. Las imágenes de ambas se

superponían [...] haciéndome saber que Teresa se mani-
festaba en Laura, que Teresa ha ocupado los ojos y los
gestos y la risa de Laura para mostrar que aún está aquí y
que es posible retomar nuestra historia en otro cuerpo.
Recuerdo ahora que una de las primeras veces que vi a
esta mujer, a Laura, tuve la impresión de que venía a mí
desde el otro lado de las cosas. Y desde que he compren-
dido esto soy algo diferente.

(61)

Millás uses Julio's apparently bizarre thoughts, in which
the images of Teresa and Laura become confused, to metaphorically suggest the chimeric nature of identity. Ironically, Julio even considers the realization that Teresa is
manifesting herself in Laura an epiphany that modifies
his own identity, as the clever double sense of "algo"
(somewhat different or *something* different) implies. He
describes Laura as "como un recodo, como una ramifica-
ción de Teresa" (91);[28] in another instance, the protagonist
"Cerró los ojos y evocó el rostro de Teresa. Cuando sintió
que tenía sus principales rasgos dibujados, éstos sufrieron
una leve mutación, un imperceptible cambio en su disposición, y alumbraron el rostro de Laura. Durante un tiempo
difícil de medir ambos rostros jugaron a superimponerse
como si fueran dos apariencias diferentes de la misma
persona" (22-23). In yet another moment, he relates to
Rodó that "El domingo pasado [...] ella [Laura] dejó de
ser Teresa en algún momento, pero puede volver a serlo en
cualquier instante [...] es un misterio que guarda relación
con ese lado de la realidad que no podemos ver ni domi-
nar" (142-3).

But it is evident that, for Julio, Laura is not only a copy
of Teresa, but the two are interchangeable. Julio also displays interest in another Laura, Ricardo Mella's wife;
the eponymy implies that, from Julio's perspective, these
two would be interchangeable as well. In addition, Julio
intends to pursue a relationship with his secretary Rosa,
undermining the singularity of his love for Laura. For the
protagonist, the female object of desire is a non-discreet
entity, possessing no individual subjectivity: "Estos días
pasados, mientras hacía el amor con Laura, mientras la
penetraba, tenía la impresión de que su vagina se comuni-
caba, por conductos ocultos, con todas las vaginas de todas
las mujeres pasadas, presentes y futuras [...] el río en el
que se sumergía mi pene" (144). Beyond the utilitarian
misogyny of this viewpoint, the passage metaphorically
suggests a model of subjectivity in which the self's relationship to the other is entirely narcissistic. As Holloway
has noted, Teresa and Laura, the objects of Julio's desire,
correspond to Lacan's concept of the *objet petit a*: they are
as mirrors in which the protagonist sees his only true erotic
object, his own image (35). He perceives Laura's eyes,
since antiquity considered mirrors of the soul, "más de
órganos de ver o de mirarse, un símbolo de la nostalgia,
una huella de su propio pasado en la que parecía posible
descansar al fin" (77). To Julio, her eyes do not represent or
reflect her subjectivity but traces of his own past, his own

identity. The protagonist himself confirms this reading in a
session with Carlos: "yo me enamoro de las mujeres pen-
sando que tienen algo de lo que yo carezco, pero que sin
embargo me concierne. En realidad, todas las mujeres que
miro parecen guardar fragmentos de algo que me perte-
nece; ocasionalmente, en una de ellas se produce la suma
de todas esas partes y entonces me enamoro" (143). He
does not see in his love objects a unique subject, but rather
part of himself, and considers how many fragments of his
own identity he perceives in her the measure of a woman's
attractiveness. Only when she possesses enough of "him"
does he fall in love. Furthermore, the images of self that
he sees are fleeting and volatile: "eso que era tan visible
desaparece, se volatiza y aparece gratuitamente en otra"
(143); Julio then feels compelled out of an "afán de com-
pletud" to repeat the process (143). These descriptions,
and the scenes in which not only the boundaries of identity
but those between the living and the dead (and in the case
of Teresa's occupation of the bird, even distinct species)
are transgressed, are not just the hallucinations or fantasies
of a febrile or disturbed mind, but metaphors suggesting
the proteic, precarious, fluid, non-discrete nature of identity. This in turn suggests the impossibility of Julio's project, the creation of a stable, defined subjectivity.

This impossibility is symbolically related to the need to/
impossibility of a full understanding of reality, of an absolute correspondence between signifier and signified, and
hence to Julio's epistemophilia, for as he tells Laura: "Tú
perteneces al otro lado de las cosas y gracias a ti puedo
comunicarme con ese lado de la vida" (76). The "other
side" may be Teresa and death, or a realm of greater com-
prehension; what is certain is that Laura is *not* merely
Laura. The possibility or "meaning" of meaning itself on
"this side" would therefore seem to coincide with Jacques
Derrida's concept of dissemination, as proposed in the
introduction to this study.

Carlos also perceives Laura's multiplicity, as the following
fragment in which he observes her illustrates:

> [...] era un rostro sin alma, un recipiente hermoso y so-
> segado dispuesto a albergar de forma sucesiva individua-
> lidades diferentes, personalidades alternativas, nombres
> varios.
>
> Podría ser Teresa, por ejemplo [...] Pero podría ser tam-
> bién su propia esposa, Laura, aunque una Laura diferente
> de la que me hablaba Julio Orgaz.

(79)

Even Laura herself seems to intuit a temporariness in her
own subjectivity, which she interprets as an evolutionary
process: "Laura [...] sintió que se estaba convirtiendo en
otra; sintió, más bien, que la realidad regresaba y se intro-
ducía en su existencia" (123-4). Her penchant for word-
play, for combining the parts of two different words to
form two new ones (sometimes semantically significant,
other times without meaning) is a metaphor of the lack of

correspondence between signifier and signified; between name, physical appearance and identity-the novel's title is itself a metaphor of this lack of correspondence.[29]

The nature of the relationship between psychoanalyst and patient allows Millás to present further speculative models for the nature of subjectivity.[30] The author creates numerous parallels between Julio and Carlos: in addition to being approximately the same age, Rodó is the embodiment of the blind, ruthless professional ambition that also characterizes the identity-in-formation that Julio creates. These similarities and the analyst-analysand relationship permit Millás implicitly to take advantage of the processes of transference and countertransference that psychonalysis posits as part of the curative process. Julio's quest for identity begins after Teresa's death and his divorce, approximately at the same time he begins hearing *La Internacional* and seeing Rodó. This coincidence may imply that, to some degree, the protagonist's development may be due to a transference identification, a phenonenon defined by Moore and Fine as "The [largely unconscious] displacement of feelings, thoughts, and behavior, originally experienced in relation to significant figures during childhood, onto a person involved in a current interpersonal relationship [...] in the psychoanalytic situation transference is apt to appear with particular clarity and intensity" (196). Julio himself confirms this: "No ignoro que usted representa para mí sucesivas figuras de autoridad cuyo vínculo todavía no he conseguido romper" (147). Julio also yearns to replace the analyst, desiring possession of Rodó's wife, a relationship of which the analyst is aware although the patient is not. The analyst observes that "Por lo que se refería a Julio Orgaz, estaba claro que, inconscientemente [...] sabía quién era Laura y al intentar conquistarla, lo que pretendía no era otra cosa que ocupar el puesto de su psicoanalista. Éste era un deseo normal en cualquier paciente [...]" (80).

The analyst-analysand relationship itself is doubled or mirrored, as Rodó's own psychoanalyst and mentor points out the similarities between Carlos and Julio, suggesting that a clear-cut case of countertransference exists. This process, according to Moore and Fine, "is narrowly defined as a specific reaction to the patient's transference" in which "an analyst's feelings and attitudes toward a patient are derived from earlier situations in the analyst's life that have been displaced onto the patient [...] It is likely to appear when the analyst identifies with the patient [...]" (47). As Rodó's analyst observes:

> Fíjese: los dos tienen edades parecidas, los dos poseen un grado de ambición social y profesional importante, en ambos existen índices de un remordimiento general que ninguno reconoce, y los dos parecen estar locamente enamorados de la misma mujer. Oyéndole hablar, cuando describía a su paciente e interpretaba sus impulsos, yo tenía la impresión de que usted hablaba de sí mismo. Su paciente es su espejo.

(137-8)

Carlos recognizes that the mirror may reflect in both directions, that countertransferrence may exist: "O, lo que es peor, he sufrido un proceso de identificación con este paciente; algo hay en su locura que concierne a la mía, algo de su pasado se relaciona con mi historia; yo he contribuido sin saberlo—o sin querer saberlo—a levantar esta trampa en la que estamos metidos los tres, los cuatro, si incluimos a la difunta Teresa" (80). In fact, the psychoanalyst's countertransferrence identification with Julio is so strong that he confesses to his analyst having adopted or reproduced his patient's desire, believing that he has come to love his wife through listening to his patient talk about her: "desde que Julio Orgaz comenzó a hablarme de Laura, yo ya no pude prescindir de sus palabras. Poco a poco fui enamorándome de mi propia mujer [...] él es el vínculo que todavía me une a Laura; me he enamorado de ella a través de sus palabras" (135). Whether the two are involved in transference, countertransference, or identification, their similarities in age, socioeconomic ambitions, sexual objectives, and above all their common remorse, serve as the sources of the characters' anxiety.

The therapist disagrees with Rodó's analysis, proposing that his specular relationship with Julio is narcissistic in nature: "lo que yo he oído es que de quien está realmente enamorado es de su paciente" (138). Not only does Millás employ the concepts of transferrence and contertransferrence as the basis of this mutual specular subject-alter ego relationship, by doing so he offers another hypothetical model of the role of the other in the continuous process of subject formation. According to this model, each man narcissistically sees himself in the mirror of the other, each imitates himself imitating the other, as if the two were perfectly aligned mirrors returning the same image to each other over and over. This portrayal of the two men metaphorically undermines the logocentric concept of identity by suggesting the interchangeability of the two, an interpretation that Julio himself proposes to Carlos:

> Usted, por ejemplo, se cree que es mi psicoanalista y yo me creo que soy su paciente [...] Laura se cree que para mí es Laura, cuando en realidad es Teresa; ignoro a quién se dirige cuando me habla a mí, pero seguro que no es a Julio Orgaz. [...] Lo cierto es que su lugar y el mío, por poner un ejemplo, son perfectamente intercambiables. [...] Usted acepta la posibilidad de curarme y yo la de ser curado [...] De ese modo, el dinero circula [...] Pero esta relación [...] puede modificarse en un instante y de forma tan gratuita como surgió. Hay veces que todo está bien [...] y, sin embargo, en cuestión de segundos, me convierto en otro, aunque los demás [...] me sigan viendo como el anterior. ¿Qué ha ocurrido? Pues he entrado en contacto con el otro lado de las cosas

(140-1)

This fragment, in which Julio's claim of becoming an "other" metaphorically undermines the concept of a stable subjectivity, also recalls Laura's dream of the reunion with her "mother" on the television program in suggesting the importance of social roles in identity formation.

Julio's relationship to Orlando Azcárate is also one of role usurpation.[31] Julio envies Azcárate's talent and claims the author's writings as his own to impress Laura; ironically, her hearty approbation is Julio's first literary "success." As was the case with his psychiatrist, the protagonist's other possesses what he desires: in the former case, the object of his sexual appetite, and in the latter, literary talent. Julio invites Orlando to lunch to discuss his manuscript; when the aspiring author refuses to adopt the fawning, servile attitude that Julio expects of him, the protagonist becomes intoxicated, angry and depressed at his own failures. His behavior gives rise to the two repeated sign/symptoms of guilt: during the meal he begins to hear the silverware producing the strains of *La Internacional.* When he returns home, he believes he smells broth, and even imagines that the canary is in league against him with his furnishings:

> Cuando entró en su apartamento tuvo la impresión de que reinaba allí una paz siniestra [...] Olía a caldo. Encendió el televisor y le quitó el sonido. [...] No estaba ligado sentimentalmente a aquel espacio, a aquellos muebles. Todo le era a la vez ajeno y familiar; ajeno por la evidente hostilidad que cada uno de los objetos mostraba hacia él, pero familiar porque esos objetos formaban parte de su historia como el olor a caldo o la compañía muda del televisor.

(105)

In order to relieve his anxiety, he once again imagines the author seated at his desk: "¿Qué mejor venganza que escribir una buena novela?" (106). The parallel drawn by the protagonist between the writing of a novel and taking vengeance; i.e., an emotional release, suggests that the activity is used to decrease anxiety. Ultimately, Julio will keep the young writer's collection of short stories from being published by his company, thus destroying or at least delaying Azcárate's career.

The influence that Orgaz's other-self Ricardo Mella will have upon his evolving character is suggested by his surname: the verb *mellar* means to cause a fissure in a solid object and break off a part. Perhaps even more significantly, the expression *hacer mella* means to cause a profound impression or effect on someone. While the young, poor Azcárate possesses the talent that Julio envies, Mella is a popular, economically successful writer of travel and adventure stories. Although Julio considers his writings superficial, he is jealous of his success. As previously mentioned, Ricardo's status as one of Julio's others is suggested by the fact that his wife is also named Laura and that Julio clearly desires her; this parallel is reinforced by an observation Mella makes about her that reminds the reader of both Teresa and Laura: "siempre parece que acaba de llegar de otro sitio al que el resto de los mortales no tuviéramos acceso" (160). When Julio, while again suffering/enjoying a fever that changes/augments his perception of reality, encounters Ricardo on the street, the latter invites him home for drinks and cocaine. Julio's description to

Carlos of his relationship to Mella, the only friend mentioned in the novel, suggests his alienation from his contemporaries: "nos hemos tenido siempre cierta prevención. Hemos pasado la vida huyéndonos [...]" (186). The narrator also describes Ricardo from Julio's point of view:

> Era un sujeto de su edad que, pese a haber perdido el pelo, conservaba un aire como de adolescente envejecido. Vestía pantalones vaqueros y una camiseta con los colores del arco iris, sobre la que llevaba una chaqueta blanca, de hilo, bastante arrugada; los zapatos eran amarillos. [...] había evitado su contacto, en parte porque despertaba en él la envidia del escritor inédito y, en parte, porque despreciaba su manera de vestir y su literatura.

(157)

As an intoxicated Julio leaves Mella's apartment, he realizes he has forgotten his raincoat, causing an equally inebriated Ricardo to give him his sport coat. Ricardo indeed seems to cause a "fissure" in the protagonist's identity and make an impression upon him, provoking a profound change in his behavior. Ironically, Julio will imitate Ricardo's fashionable, modern ways, a change that will contribute to his promotion at the publishing house. He also adopts the affectation of calling Laura "mi vida," explaining that "Ya ves, cuando era joven no podía decir mi vida, porque con lo de la revolución y todo eso resultaba un poco extemporáneo. He sido un joven muy austero, pero ahora me voy a comprar una camiseta como la de Ricardo Mella y voy a ir a trabajar con su chaqueta moderna. Y a Rosa, que es mi secretaria, la llamaré mi vida todo el tiempo" (166). On the thematic level of the *sign,* Julio's rejection of the symbolically interrelated motifs of revolution, austerity, his mother's broth, and the *Internacional*; and his adoption of affectations that he previously disdained, are implicitly criticized here, as he embodies a certain type of conscienceless *trepas* or social climber. On an anagogical level, these elements also hint at the collective class guilt proposed in this study as underlying Millás's obsessive-compulsive aesthetic.

Despite the success of Julio's new modern style, the reader perceives the irony: the protagonist is imitating a model he previously disdained, becoming an almost ridiculously stereotypical male mid-life crisis figure. The superficial nature of these changes implies the inauthenticity of the identity assumed; the ease with which such changes are made by Julio and accepted by others metaphorically indicates the provisional nature of identity.

ESCRIBIR AS *ESCRIBIRSE*: JULIO'S WRITER ALTER EGO

The author figure that Julio imagines seated at his writing desk, and who he is certain will produce a novel called *El desorden de tu nombre* chronicling the protagonist's experiences, could most obviously be interpreted as a metafictional allusion to the extratextual author Millás himself. However, Millás's penchant for having his characters create alter egos for themselves in times of psychological stress suggests two other possible interpretations. It may be that Julio feels compelled to write, yet is unable to do so out of fear of failure. This paralyzing fear causes him to fantasize an alter ego to write for him, thereby divesting himself *psychologically* of responsibility for any possible failure; this would also be consistent with the obsessive's penchant for mistaking thinking for doing. Alternatively, the figure may be seen not only as the product of his imagination, but also as a self-deception, as a result of Julio's repression of the fact that he does *physically* write it, behavior consistent with the protagonist's gestalt. It is, after all, Julio's story that is being written, in accordance with Julio's needs and desires, and he ultimately achieves all his goals. Julio could thus be interpreted as a literary ancestor of Jesús, the protagonist of **TMBI,** who fantasizes the *tonto, muerto, bastardo* and *invisible* alter egos that are nonetheless quite real to him.

Julio's splitting of himself into two also constitutes a metaphor of his increasing self-alienation, an alienation characteristic of his relationship with his other selves as he evolves into a "success." The following fragment appears to support this possibility: "el Julio imaginario era ya para el Julio real el personaje de una historia de amor y de adulterio [...] fijó la vista en su mesa de trabajo [...] y se imaginó sentado en ella [...] se sintió repleto de gratitud hacia sí mismo" (93). He would not feel gratitude toward himself if he were not the one writing. This allows him to state to his psychoanalyst with total certainty that he will find the finished manuscript on his desk: "a veces tengo premoniciones, atisbos de cosas que ya han sucedido en una dimensión diferente, pero que todavía no se han reflejado en esta otra. Por ejemplo, [...] que, al llegar a casa, voy a encontrarme la novela escrita encima de la mesa" (148). Once again, Millás creates a delightful ambiguity: the other dimension seems to allude to the flesh-and-blood author; but at the same time, one must recall that Julio believes in an *otro lado de las cosas* where deeper truths may be found, truths for which it is the writer's job to search. This interpretation is underscored when, after making love, Laura asks Julio who he is, he affirms: "Yo soy el que nos escribe, el que nos narra" (74).

The narrator first mentions Julio seeing the writer as the protagonist suffers from a fever: "Observó su mesa de trabajo, donde un escritor imaginario (él mismo) rellenaba de cuentos geniales un mazo de cuartillas [...]" (19). However, it later becomes clear that this other self has existed for quite some time: "Con Teresa Zagro [...] Julio daba muestras de un ingenio un poco sorprendente, considerando al menos que sus energías creadoras habían estado dirigidas hasta entonces a alimentar a ese escritor imaginario (él mismo), de cuyo futuro parecía depender su vida" (24). It is interesting that the first two descriptions of this double both affirm that it is he himself; this is also reiterated in this double's final appearance, confirming the interpretation that Julio is in fact physically writing a novel (192). The fact that his future depends upon this writer can

be interpreted in two ways: either metafictionally (the protagonist's literal existence as a fictional character in the novel) or as a figurative, hyperbolic statement originating in the protagonist's mind and transmitted by the narrator. In the former reading, if the extratextual author Millás decides not to write the novel, Julio will indeed not exist on paper; according to the latter, Julio sees his life *as an author* at stake.

Julio frequently expresses the impression that the events of his life, and even his love for Teresa, are outside his willful control, as when he speaks of his writing to Carlos: "Me refiero a las novelas que no he escrito [...] para mí, sin embargo, poseen un cierto grado de realidad, como si, una vez pensadas, comenzaran a desarrollarse a espaldas de mi voluntad, o como si alguien estuviera escribiéndolas por indicación mía en ese otro lugar que yace oculto bajo los sucesos de la vida diaria" (140).[32] In the same way that the writer figure has been considered metafictional in nature, this feeling has been seen as an allusion to the flesh-and-blood author who wrote the novel. However, it may also be interpreted psychologically, as being consistent with an obsessive-compulsive personality disorder. Despite the fact that writing is seen as part of his struggle to achieve control over his existence (and thereby achieve professional, literary and amorous success), Julio cannot control his need to write, as if the impulse were coming from outside himself, and would therefore be ego syntonic. The fact that this makes him feel out of control of his own life metaphorically displays the fundamental paradox that underlies this disorder. The metafictional allusion is hence a polysemic sign/symptom also suggesting Julio's psychological tendency toward the obsessive, reinforcing the concept of writing as the compulsive expression of obsessive thought.

In light of the fact that Julio sees his other self writing on no less than seven occasions and that this alter ego is mentioned even more often, it is fair to claim that he is obsessed with writing in the clinical sense: the protagonist imagines the writer figure in moments of stress, his appearance exercises a calming effect, and Julio's need to ruminate about writing is not an impulse that he is able to control. Upon his return home from his unsuccessful, frustrating lunch with Orlando Azcárate, he "observó la mesa de trabajo y se imaginó escribiendo esa novela [...] ya empezaba a resolverse en su cabeza [...]" (106). It is at this time that the idea occurs to him to have the adulterous couple kill off the psychoanalyst husband: "La idea lo tranquilizó, pensó incluso ponerse a escribir en ese momento, pero decidió que sería mejor dormir unas horas" (106). This anxiety reduction is characteristic of obsessive-compulsive disorder. Julio's descriptions of why he needs to write seem to confirm that he is compelled to do so to reduce anxiety produced by life:

> Llevo años mirándome ahí, sentado, con la paciencia de un sabio, con la vocación de un sacerdote. Y esa imagen me salva, me libera de los estados de ansiedad, me da la

paz que necesito frente a las humillaciones de la vida diaria, me coloca, en fin, en un espacio diferente a aquel en el que actúan los otros. Los otros, de quienes no entiendo muchas cosas, pero de quienes no comprendo, sobre todo, cómo soportan la vida si no escriben.

(65)

Writing constitutes for Julio the answer to the most fundamental question upon which he repeatedly reflects: "cómo, en fin, se defiende del terrorismo de la existencia cotidiana [...]" (66). In the same vein, the narrator implies a cause and effect relationship between the traumatic loss of Teresa, his desire to replace her with Laura, and the writer's goals in writing: "el escritor imaginario que, sentado frente a su mesa de trabajo, escribía una novela suya titulada *El desorden de tu nombre,* pues ese sería su argumento, una tupida trama capaz de tapar el agujero producido por la desaparición del otro nombre-el de Teresa-y de aliviar la distancia que todavía le separaba de Laura" (167).

Writing is furthermore portrayed as a manifestation of epistemophilia: "yo estoy sentado, escribo, me hago sabio. Así me veo, así soporto la existencia diaria. [...] Todo ello [la actividad cotidiana] no tiene otra función que la de alimentar a ese sujeto que se pasa el día sobre mi mesa de trabajo, escribiendo la historia de un incrédulo que padece de una alucinación auditiva de carácter marxista" (64). It is interesting that Millás himself has expressed an identical opinion concerning the relationship between writing and understanding: "la literatura consiste, precisamente, en escribir lo que uno no sabe" (Cabañas 104). Not only is writing presented as an effort to understand deep truths, but above all to achieve a deeper understanding of self, of identity-Julio's (and Millás's) primary theme/obsession: "Todos [los escritores] creen conocer la novela de su vida, pero lo cierto es que apenas saben algo de la mujer con la que duermen. La información que tenemos de nosotros mismos es tan parcial como la de un personaje de novela" (62-3). Thus, it would be consistent to read the following statement made by Julio not only as a metafictional reference to the extratextual author, but as a metaphorical statement explaining his relationship with his writer alter ego: "ese escritor es el que sabe cosas de mí que yo ignoro, pero que me conciernen" (66).

The relationship between writing, the other, and the constitution of identity has been implicit in Millás's earlier novels: one may think of the young protagonist of *CS* [*Cerbero son las sombras*], for example, or the diary of Hermano Turis of *LM* [*Letra muerta*]. Indeed, one could see these two protagonists' writings as expressing their obsessions (the boy's relationship with his father; Turis's relationship with the Organization). However, in *DN,* the use of a psychologically aberrant protagonist for the first time allows Millás new, more metaphorical avenues of experimentation with these ideas. Julio's fear of failure motivates him to create an alter ego who takes the risk of delving into the secrets of subjectivity through writing. In

this way, *escribir* as *escribirse* becomes a much more prominent preoccupation, and will be at the heart of the next novel examined, *SE.*

SOCIAL CRITICISM

After meeting Laura, Julio begins the construction of a new self obsessed with attaining *triunfo* or *éxito* in three arenas by ruthlessly eliminating anyone he perceives as professional (his superior at work), literary (Orlando Azcárate) or sexual (Carlos Rodó) competition.[33] Thematically, Millás presents his social and generational criticism through the figures of Orgaz and Rodó, whose similarities to the protagonist have already been discussed. This social content also betrays, on an anagogical level, the presence of class guilt concerning the abandonment on the part of this generation of the socialist ideals of class struggle in favor of the satisfaction of their own personal desires for wealth and power.

Since Julio's aspirations require him to abandon his child and reject his mother and humble socioeconomic origins, his guilt manifests itself as the repeated intrusion of the thought of his mother's home-made broth, or the belief that he smells it when this is clearly unlikely.[34] This motif appears for the first time when his mother comes to prepare him home-made chicken broth during his illness: "percibió un olor antiguo, íntimamente ligado a su existencia y enquistado sin duda en lo más profundo de su memoria olfativa [...] hizo un gesto de rechazo [...]" (51). When his mother describes its healthful contents, "La enumeración de los ingredientes no hizo sino aumentar el rechazo de Julio [...] tenía la impresión de que la mano de su madre había disuelto en él la esencia misma de toda la historia familiar; el olor evocaba algo cercano, pero oculto [...]" (52). It is a scent that "remitía al pasado, pero al pasado más rancio, más mohoso, al abandono en la zona más oscura y húmeda de su memoria" (68). It is a past he clearly associates with the low standard of living on which he blames his own mediocrity or "damaged intelligence," motivating him even to the extreme of seeing in his mother a "carrier of evil":

> Con semejante fuerza surgió en él la evocación de lo familiar al oler el caldo. Pero la evocación ya no era protectora [...] por el contrario, presentaba signos de enemistad al aparecer convertida en el depósito de aquella arqueología personal, cuya sustancia había actuado con mayor eficacia en la desertización de su dañada inteligencia. De este modo su madre-concreción personal de esa sustancia-se transformaba en una madre falsa que ocultaba bajo una apariencia bondadosa su condición de portadora del mal.

(53)

Julio associates the mental images the scent evokes with the home's working-class furnishings, metonymic of his humble origins: their "cuarto de estar con mesa camilla, sillas de tapicería desflecada y televisor en blanco y negro sobre estantería vulgar de escasos volúmenes encuadernados en piel" (52). The circumstances that cause him to smell or think of the broth indicate that these symptomatic intrusions upon his consciousness are motivated by guilt. These instances occur, for example, after the lunch meeting in which Julio unsuccessfully attempts to get Orlando Azcárate to humbly curry favor with him in turn for his manuscript's acceptance, and after Julio convinces his company's chief executive to cancel plans for its publication. His desire to forget the socioeconomic environment from which he wishes to escape at one point leads him to fantasize a comparison in which his life is a tree "cuyas ramas representaban los diferentes sucesos que habían dado forma a su vida actual. Imaginó que tenía el poder necesario para podar aquellas ramas que no le gustaban: la de su matrimonio, o aquella otra por la que discurría la savia que había dado forma a su ambición de escritor y a su fracaso consecuente" (91).

The auditory hallucination of hearing the socialist hymn *La Internacional,* metonymically related to class struggle and solidarity, also occurs in moments that make clear the symptom's origins in guilt. It reminds him of his more idealistic youth, the music "haciendo caminar a Julio, que asistía al espectáculo con los ojos desorbitados, tras de antiguas banderas y olvidados impulsos" (35). Julio himself declares that the song "siempre [. . .] me emociona como en los primeros días de mi juventud" (62). Interestingly, one of the reasons he finds it so bothersome is that "me incapacita para pensar sobre el significado de las cosas" (191); that is, it interferes with his epistemophilic drive. In addition to appearing together with the broth smell when his mother originally serves it to him and in the two situations cited above, he experiences it while ignoring an unemployed man asking him for a cigarette at a traffic light, while thinking disdainfully how vulgar is a statement made by a waiter concerning a young couple's sex life; and at the novel's end when he realizes that Carlos is dead, Laura conquered, his new position secured, and the novel written. In a humorous twist, in this final moment, he is not hallucinating: the song is being whistled by a humble street cleaner. It is also worth note that, as Julio becomes increasingly unscrupulous and successful, both symptoms recur with increasing frequency. Ultimately, he becomes so self-centered, so unfeeling that, upon learning that Ricardo Mella is soon to die of cancer, his only reaction is to think (in an appropriately superstitious, parataxic manner): "¡Qué suerte tengo que no me ha tocado a mí! Consideraba que la enfermedad de Ricardo Mella era una especie de fatalidad, de lotería, en la que cada uno de los miembros de su generación llevaba varios números. Si le tocaba a uno, ya no podía tocarle [sic] a los otros. De manera que se encontraba a salvo" (187).

As noted above, there are many similarities between Julio Orgaz and Carlos Rodó that make the latter an alter ego of the former in his process of identity formation: they are approximately the same age, both desire Laura and are extremely ambitious. It is this latter characteristic that is used by Millás as a signifier of what is wrong with his generation as it rises to positions of power, and by extension, of the corruption and *amiguismo* plaguing Spain in general. Carlos, already in line to be named head of all health services in the city, ultimately aspires to a cabinet-level position in the Ministry of Health. And he is willing to go to any lengths to achieve his goal: "se le sugirió a Carlos Rodó la realización de un par de mezquindades y de cinco o seis trampas, dirigidas contra colegas suyos, que él aceptó" (131). Carlos's character is most clearly seen when the narrator allows the reader access to his thoughts as the psychoanalyst considers how he has arrived at his present situation:

> Años de estudios, de contactos, de oposiciones, de análisis, años de inteligente y devastador trabajo político, para que al final la existencia empiece a hacer agua por el sitio por el que menos se podía esperar. Años, pues, dedicados a una razonable acumulación de poder personal que ahora carece de sentido sin el soporte del amor, del amor, abandonado a los rigores de la juventud, como el valor moral, como el conjunto de principios bajo los cuales llegué a pensar que debería organizarse la vida. [. . .] años de renuncia; años, en fin, de intercambio, de venta, años de mezquindad, de entrega, de cinismo, que seguramente han llegado a convertirme en lo que más podía detestar.
>
> (80-81)

Carlos, like Julio, cannot avoid moments of remorse over what he has become. The guilt experienced by these characters, who represent a collective, communicates the deep sense of class guilt that informs the work.

THE DENOUEMENT

The novel's denouement artfully makes use of the threads of reiterated motifs to weave together the themes of identity and social criticism. Before entering the meeting in which the chief executive will officially promote him, Julio decides to redecorate, to modernize his office to go along with the new modern image his clothes project: "Ese archivador parece un ataúd [. . .] Y las cortinas [. . .] me recuerdan a las que había en la salita de estar de mis padres" (179). What he rejects is significant: the file cabinet/*ataúd* must be removed because it represents death, a thought that the middle-aged Julio wishes to repress. Rejecting the curtains is a form of repression as well: he does not wish to be reminded of the humble origins he so desires to bury in his past and subconscious. Julio, who had already expressed interest in Ricardo Mella's wife (enough to notice that she was wearing no undergarments beneath her clothes) begins to notice, desire and flirt with Rosa, his secretary, "en cuyos ojos comenzaba a abrirse una promesa" (189). Just as the superficial change of wardrobe and furnishings constitute mere ornamental covers for the unfillable *agujero* or *vacío* at the core of his existence, signalling the inauthenticity of his new identity, his supposed love for Laura is revealed to be inauthentic: in the same way that she is simply a substitute for Teresa, she can be replaced by Mella's Laura or Rosa. Ultimately, they are all just mirrors in which the narcissistic Julio sees reflections of himself.

Julio's conversion into a triumphant predator is completed when, during his meeting with the director and the company's chief executive: "Julio escuchaba la conversación con una actitud distante y reflexiva como si hablaran de otro. Sabía que se referían a él, pero él estaba instalado ya en el otro lado de las cosas, de manera que el director general y el presidente tan sólo podían ver el decorado. Pero el decorado bastaba para triunfar" (181). This point of view is undermined, as the protagonist's process of self-creation is portrayed as self alienating in the metaphoric "actitud distante," an interpretation that Julio himself later confirms: "Al pasar frente a su propio reflejo, en un escaparate, tardó unas décimas de segundo en reconocerse, lo que interpretó como un síntoma de buen agüero. Para triunfar, pensó, hay que ser un poco ajeno a uno" (190). On the moral level, Julio's difficulty in recognizing himself constitutes not only a metaphor of his ironic lack of self-knowledge and of the increasing self-alienation caused by his drive for success, but also of the inherently split nature of subjectivity: one cannot see one's self without the help of a mirror, but the image (like the titular disordered name) will never *be* the subject. The fact that the executives can only appraise Julio's external attributes and yet that is all that is needed for him to triumph suggests to the reader the superficial hence inauthentic nature of Julio's success, thus criticizing both his means of achieving it and the power structures in Spanish society that foment and reward such behavior. Julio, however, ironically interprets his successes as evidence of his superior insight, an insight that leads him to believe parataxically that he possesses the omnipotent power to control reality: "La realidad, de repente, parecía una masa dócil de moldear entre sus manos. Tuvo la impresión de que podía hacer con ella lo que le viniera en gana, de que le bastaría pensar una cosa para que ésta, inmediatamente, se cumpliera" (183).[35] The product of Julio's process of subjetivity is held up to the readers not as a success, but as a moral failure: at the end of the meeting, he looks at his boss and thinks "Un año más, se dijo, y me sentaré en tu sillón, hijo de puta" (182). Despite the criticism of the inauthenticity of Julio's subjectivity, there is nothing in the work that would suggest the possibility of any authenticity. Moreover, the use of the decoration, reflection, and self-alienation motifs once again suggests anxiety provoked by class guilt.

Part of the novel's irony consists of the fact that the protagonist believes himself to be very self-aware, carefully polishing his new image, when in fact the reader sees him as a man going through a stereotypical mid-life crisis and as an increasingly despicable person. This dramatic irony is augmented by the fact that Julio, supposedly writing the novel he is living, is the last to find out that Laura is his psychoanalyst's wife. Indeed, in an earlier session with

Carlos, when Julio enumerates the possible plot twists for the romantic triangle, Rodó points out that he had omitted/repressed one possibility: that both the analyst and the wife were aware that the lover was his analysand, but that the patient himself did not, an option Julio is quick to reject because "no iba a dejarme a mí mismo en ese lugar de imbécil" (145).

After killing her husband, Laura calls Julio and invites him to her residence. When he arrives at Laura's door, he discovers that it is also Carlos Rodó's home. Not only is he unaware that he finds himself precisely in the "lugar de imbécil" mentioned above, he believes that the coincidence corresponds to his newfound superior understanding: "La coincidencia era, sin duda, una de esas rendijas que se abren a veces sobre la superficie tersa y dura de la realidad" (192). This metaphoric example of epistemophilia is accompanied by fevered, irrational thought betraying parataxic symptomology, as his successes cause him to believe that he can mold reality to suit his desires and ambitions. He is furthermore convinced that his deceased ex-lover has crossed the barrier between life and death to occupy Laura's person: "Julio permanecía algo perplejo, como asustado de que la realidad se pudiera moldear tan fácilmente en función de sus intereses. Es obra de Teresa, pensó, de Teresa Zagro, que ahora se disfraza de viuda para mí" (193-4). When Laura happily tells him they have their whole life together, his response reiterates the metaphoric erasure of the borders between identities: "Toda la vida, amor, la nuestra y la de otros. Toda la vida-respondió Julio enfebrecido" (194).

Julio leaves her apartment as a new dawn breaks, a symbol of his optimistic hopes for their new life together: "Cuando salió a la calle estaba amaneciendo. El rosicler, se dijo, qué palabra, qué vida, que rarísimo es todo; no tengo culpa, ni memoria ni culpa, somos una pasta moldeable y protéica-otra palabra-; protéica debe venir de prótesis; lo que no es prótesis es plagio. Pero qué amor, qué amor el de Laura y el mío. Y qué novela" (194). "Proteic" indeed describes his identity, and his association of this word with "prosthesis," a reiterated motif of enormous import in later novels, is significant. As something false, a simulacra not part of the original organism, the prosthesis metaphorically suggests the inauthentic nature of the identity he has developed. This passage furthermore suggests that all subjectivity is both proteic and prosthetic: a prosthesis is a replacement for something that is lacking. Lacking any fixed identity, with an existential *agujero* at his core, Julio fills the emptiness inside with images of, or reflected in, his alter egos, mistakenly believing them to be his own. Millás utilizes the specific nature of these images to create his social criticism, ironically subverting the protagonist's professional, literary and amorous successes by making evident that he has become a predator. The use of the characters Julio and Carlos as vehicles of social and generational criticism foreshadow *SE*'s Elena Rincón and her husband Enrique, as well as *TMBI*'s protagonist Jesús and his acquaintance Luis. Julio has repressed all memory and feels no blame-neither for turning his back on his family, nor for his lack of solidarity with the class from which he came. He will not escape being reminded: in the novel's humorous ending, Julio hears a street sweeper whistling a tune, and stops to ask him what it is (possibly to reassure himself that he is not hallucinating). When informed that it is indeed *La Internacional*: "entonces tuvo la absoluta seguridad de que cuando llegara al apartamento encontraría sobre su mesa de trabajo una novela manuscrita, completamente terminada, que llevaba por título *El desorden de tu nombre*" (195).[36]

In *DN,* Millás for the first time makes use of a protagonist whose abnormal psychology manifests sexual and material desires through an obsessive-compulsive narrative symptomology. Julio's psyche thus functions as the screen on which class fantasies are played out, fantasies which, when analyzed in light of this symptomology, offer a fascinating pathology not only of the individual protagonist, but of the society which channels his desire. The collective characters Carlos and Julio subvert the protagonist's above-cited assertion that "where there is no memory, there can be no guilt": on the contrary, their own symptomology and, on an anagogical level, the novel itself demonstrate that, while memory and guilt can be repressed, they always return as symptoms. These symptoms are manifested on the moral level in the development of characters, and on the anagogical level in the symptomology of the work's obsessive-compulsive aesthetic. In this case, the suppression of any father figure hints at a subconscious guilt over the death of the Father/Franco, and the text reveals a distinct sense of class guilt. In *SE,* similar psychic trauma and social pressures will be experienced by the protagonist Elena Rincón, and she and her husband will place in evidence once again the internal contradictions of the Spanish collective unconscious of the period.

Notes

1. *El desorden de tu nombre* is Millás's most critically commented novel. See the reviews by Randolph Pope, José María Marco and Gonzalo Sobejano, as well as Constantino Bértolo's "Introducción" and the articles by Esther Cuadrat, Rebeca Gutiérrez and Vance R. Holloway. Also important are Sobejano's "Sobre la novela y el cuento dentro de una novela," "Novela y metanovela," Marta Isabel Miranda's "El lenguaje cinematográfico," and the dissertations by Colvin and Abbott.

2. This aspect has also been commented upon by Pope, Miranda ("Lenguaje"), Cuadrat, Abbott and Holloway, among others.

3. Sobejano, following Robert Spires, classifies this work and *SE* as "metanovelas de la escritura" ("Novela y metanovela" 5), and proposes that the interpolation of short stories represents a "pugna del género largo por vencer al género breve" and the "triunfo de áquel sobre éste" ("Sobre la novela" 73). With respect to the presence of the intratextual author, Holloway concludes that the protagonist's "finding" of the manuscript at the novel's end is "an ultimate act of narrative and existential self-affirmation [in which] Julio even thinks that he has written himself" (37).

4. Interestingly, several of the stories glossed have been published by Millás in the collection *Primavera de luto.* These include "La vida en el armario," which appears in *Primavera* as "Una carencia íntima"; an untitled story very similar to "La conferencia," and another tale that corresponds to "El pequeño cadáver de R. J."

5. Other repeated motifs appearing for the first time in this novel, albeit lacking in thematic significance, include the television (pp. 42, 64, 105, 121, 154, 169, 176, 192) and the telephone (19, 33, 34, 39, 41-43, 48, 49, 58, 73, 90, 102, 103, 113, 116, 126, 155, 165, 167, 173, 174, 177, 191), both of which will play a key role in *VC*. It is interesting that several items mentioned yet not reiterated in this novel will become central sign/symptoms in later works. These include compulsion (114) or obsession (174) themselves, masturbation (171), control (98), a phobia of Sundays (35), a shoebox in which a child keeps his most valuable possessions, boxes (*caja* or *estuche*) in general (87, 120, 148), prostheses (194), disguises or masks (176), and metamorphoses (35).

6. This novel, along with *SE* and *VC,* has been published as a trilogy titled *La trilogía de la soledad. Soledad* is a minor reiterated motif in *DN,* appearing on pp. 12, 27, 32, 33, 50, 108.

7. The preoccupation with aging is seen on pp. 17, 21, 23, 34, 48, 84, 91, 100-102, 117, 128, 137, 153, 154, 157, 158, 162, 166, 170, 172. A preoccupation with death is also present in the reiteration of the *muerte* (20, 21, 31, 33, 35, 42, 46, 61, 65, 66, 72, 73, 79, 122, 123, 146, 148, 149, 154, 165-167, 174, 186, 191) and *cadáver* (35, 51, 73, 122, 123, 149, 153, 193) motifs, although not to as great an extent as in the author's later obsessive novels, where the conflict between the *eros* survival drive and the death impulse of *thanatos* plays a significant role.

8. Julio is unaware of the vulgarity of his own actions, adding to the work's dramatic irony. The vulgarity motif appears on pp. 134, 153, and 181, and is symbolically related to *menesterosidad* (25, 68) and the *cotidiano* (56, 64-66, 114), all of which are repugnant to Julio himself.

9. One or more of these motifs are present on pp. 9-11, 14, 16, 23, 26-30, 35, 37-40, 65, 67, 69, 70, 73, 75, 115, 126, 127, 139 and 169. Commonly occuring

somatic symptoms are also present as recurring motifs, although not to the extent seen in later works. These include *dolor* (17, 18, 35, 48, 50, 129, 148), anxiety-induced *sudor* (18, 20, 37, 103, 153, 175), *llanto* at inappropriate times (34, 44, 126, 153, 182) and *enfermedades* in general (15, 17, 18, 35, 45, 47-49, 53, 54, 59, 81, 90, 124, 161, 164, 166, 187, 190, 193). *Locura* (34, 62, 77, 80, 102, 143, 175), *miedo* and *temor* (20, 22, 48, 74, 113, 116, 125) could also be seen as contributing to this theme.

10. Holloway interestingly equates *el otro lado* to the Lacanian Other (34). Fevers are mentioned on pp. 15, 18-20, 23, 36, 47, 53, 67, 69, 70, 72, 75, 90, 92, 99, 155, 158, 194; *agujeros* or *rendijas* on 167, 184 and 192; and *el otro lado/más allá de las cosas/de la vida* on 36, 43, 50, 61, 76, 101, 113, 140, 141, 143, 165, 179, 182, 183 and 185. At these moments, reality appears irreal or fictitious and the other side more real: such *irrealidad* is present on pp. 20, 40, 51, 52, 72, 80, 98, 100, 101, 115, 119, 121, 123, 146-148, 153, 157, 158, 179, 183, 183, 192 and 194.

11. *Objeto* appears on pp. 14, 82, 105, 125 and 144; *muebles* on 30, 36, 52, 81, 84, 87, 89, 93, 105, 114, 132, 161, 166, 167 and 189.

12. *Misterio, secreto, oculto, clandestino,* or *oscuro* are seen on pp. 10, 13, 14, 21, 40, 52, 54, 64, 67, 80, 140, 144, 160, 175, 181 and 189.

13. *Signos, conexiones, hilos, marco, red* or *puntos de referencia* occur on pp. 9, 12, 24, 33, 36, 74, 79, 81 and 123.

14. *Mirada* or *observación* are present on pp. 11, 14, 16, 18, 19, 24, 28, 37, 38, 42, 45, 50, 64, 65, 68, 69, 71, 72, 75, 77, 78, 92, 98, 99, 106, 107, 109, 111, 112, 117, 119, 121-123, 133, 134, 152, 154, 156, 161, 164, 167, 175, 185 and 192. In later works, these motifs will frequently take on a sexual, voyeuristic nature.

15. *Coincidencias* (192) and *casualidades* (15) are also mentioned during the narrative; these are interpreted by Julio as possessing significance, as examples of *sincronía* (11).

16. In a similar manner, he frequently grants certain ideas the privileged status of *premonición* or *presentimiento* (148, 171, 172, 190), considering them as bearing a significance in relation to future events. The rumination of *palabras,* a metaphor of the need to understand and the impossibility of doing so, is seen on pp. 12, 23, 25-27, 32, 40, 46, 51, 53, 77, 108, 109, 135, 157, 176, 177 and 194.

17. *Superstición* is mentioned on pp. 19, 20 and 30; *sobrenatural* on 61.

18. *Pájaro* or *canario* appears on pp. 18, 19, 22, 36, 47, 48, 61, 66, 72, 73, 75, 91, 92, 94, 95, 105, 108, 120-123, 139, 166, 167 and 190.

19. It is also worthy of note that Julio treats her body as if it were a mannekin to be manipulated: Julio "Utilizó su cuerpo para crear complicadas arquitecturas" (123). This foreshadows the mannekin's extremely important role in *VC, TMBI* and *OA*. Their sexual relationship is also somewhat sadomasochistic, a leitmotif seen in *VA* and that will reoccur in both *TMBI* and *OA*.

20. The other is present on pp. 37, 46, 60, 66, 69, 92, 123, 133, 141, 143, 160, 182, 192 and 194.

21. The *cara* or *rostro* is mentioned on pp. 10, 17, 23, 37, 41, 48, 50, 61, 68, 70, 71, 74, 78, 79, 81, 88, 102, 103, 111, 119, 121-123, 129, 138, 153, 154, 168, 187, 190; *ojos* on 11, 16, 19, 22-25, 28, 35, 42, 50, 61, 68-70, 75, 78, 82, 92, 93, 109, 118, 121, 123, 143, 154-156, 158, 171, 179, 180 and 189; and *cuerpo* or *corporal* on 9-11, 17, 18, 26, 27, 29, 31, 32, 35, 36, 52, 63, 69, 74, 77, 82, 87, 88, 90, 93, 119, 120, 122, 123, 132, 155, 158, 161 and 172. *Labios* or *boca* might also be seen as executing this function, and occur on pp. 11, 16, 28, 31, 69, 78, 93, 121, 123, 184, 185, 187. *Pecho* is another recurring somatic motif (16, 21, 22, 25, 27, 35, 38, 70, 74, 76, 119, 120, 122, 155, 159); however, it is presented as the site where Julio feels the physical manifestations of obsessive anxiety.

22. Laura's *melena* is present on pp. 11, 38, 41, 71, 74, 78, 119, 144, 153, 186 and 187; Carlos's bald spot and dandruff on 65, 68, 151 and 175. On the importance of physical appearance in the work, see Abbott's dissertation.

23. Critics agree that *DN* subverts the notion of a monadic identity. On this point, see also Abbott and Gutiérrez.

24. *Sitio, territorio, lugar, espacio,* or *zona* are mentioned on pp. 10, 22, 24-26, 30, 31, 40, 50, 56, 64-66, 70, 71, 74, 80, 82, 85, 88, 105, 108, 125-127, 16, 140-142, 145, 146, 148, 150, 153, 157, 160, 165, 167 and 186; *interior* on 39, 40, 46, 50, 72, 87-89, 114, 117, 125, 161, 174, 176 and 192.

25. I use here the terminology proposed by Gérard Genette in his *Narrative Discourse: An Essay in Method.* He defines heterodiegetic narrative as one in which "the narrator [is] absent from the story he tells" (244); this is opposed to homodiegetic narrative, in which "the narrator [is] present as a character in the story he tells" (245). A nonfocalized narrative is one in which "the narrator knows more than the character, or more exactly *says* more than any of the characters knows" (189; original emphasis). This type of

focalization stands in contrast both to internal focalization, in which a character narrates and is thus limited to relating knowledge he or she could know, and the external focalization characteristic of objectivist or behaviorist narrative, in which the narrator is never allowed to know or present characters' thoughts (189).

26. This supposed "invasion" of Julio's body by Teresa foreshadows the protagonist of *VC,* who believes he takes on the physical attributes of a woman while masturbating.

27. This may be an allusion to the program, popular at the time, "¿Quién sabe dónde?." Television will become an extremely important motif in *VC* and *OA*. In both works it will be seen as creating a false sense of community that simply feeds individual alienation, and as providing false images as models of subjectivity.

28. This confusion also occurs on p. 36; on 76 he compares the tone of voice they use when making love; on 86 he compares their way of laughing; and on 119, their common habit of playing with their hair in exactly the same way.

29. Laura's wordplay and the palindromic relationship has been noted by many critics, typically as a metaphor of the uncertain nature of identity. See for example Holloway and Abbott. Colvin proposes that it forms part of Millás's overall attempt to demonstrate "the corrupt state of language as it fails to carry specific meaning" (27).

30. Holloway has offered several interesting hypotheses concerning the meaning of Millás's use of the psychoanalytic situation. He raises the possibility that "The novel's story can be read as an elaboration of the Oedipal allegory" (32), with Carlos in the paternal role. He also posits that the novel "can be read as a narrative incorporating two contesting models of psychoanalysis [...] therapy geared toward the empowerment of the protagonist's ego. [...] [and] psychoanalysis as a means of comprehending the fragmentary, intersubjective nature of the human subject [...] which can never attain a final, integrated resolution" (33).

31. Holloway asserts that Orgaz, Azcárate and Mella's names are all exmples of "disordering" and notes that "all share mental, physical and occupational characteristics" (35). Abbott believes that Azcárate "is one of two 'winks' with which the author, Millás, inserts himself into the novel" (169).

32. See also pp. 10, 13, 16.

33. The recurrent sign/symptoms *triunfo* or *éxito* are found on pp. 45, 54, 60, 62, 79, 92, 104, 131, 135, 138, 141, 142, 157, 182, 185 and 190; Julio also demonstrates fear of *fracaso* on 40, 91, 92, 142 and 147. The competition between the writers Julio and Orlando foreshadows the relationship between Juan and José in *VC.*

34. The *olor a caldo* motif is found on pp. 51-53 (the only time he has any apparent reason to smell it), 68, 69, 153, 184 and 185.

35. Julio's belief in his omnipotence foreshadows Jesús's even more exaggerated parataxic thought in *TMBI.*

36. Critics generally agree that the denouement is meant as a moral criticism of conscienceless ambition, corruption and an abandonment by Millás's generation of the ideals of social justice. Abbott curiously reacts to this interpretation by asserting that "The criticism [...] has read Julio's rise to power as false because it is based upon misprojections, duplicitous discourse, and mere wardrobe changes" based on "a dichotomous set up of reality [...] versus appearance" (58). I believe this is a misreading of the critics: while scholarship has indeed noted that Millás once again employs such a dichotomy, it has been interpreted as criticizing Julio's *means,* not as denying the "reality" of his successes. The ending's irony questions the moral value of such "success," not its reality.

Bibliography

Works by Juan José Millás García

El desorden de tu nombre. Barcelona: Destino, 1988.

Letra muerta. Madrid: Alfaguara, 1983.

El orden alfabético. Madrid: Alfaguara, 1998.

Primavera de luto y otros cuentos. Barcelona: Destino, 1989.

La soledad era esto. Barcelona: Destino, 1990.

Tonto, muerto, bastardo e invisible. Madrid: Alfaguara, 1995.

Critical and Theoretical Texts

Abbott, Annie R. *Transitional Discourses: The (Psycho) Somatic Fiction of Juan José Millás.* Diss. U Illinois, 1998. Ann Arbor: DAIA, 1999. DA9912181.

Bértolo Cadenas, Constantino. "Introducción a la narrativa española actual." *Revista de Occidente* 98-99 (July-Aug. 1989): 29-60.

Cabañas, Pilar. "Materiales gaseosos: Entrevista con Juan José Millás." *Cuadernos Hispanoamericanos* 580 (Oct. 1988): 103-20.

Colvin, Robert Lloyd. "The Denaturing of Experience in Four Novels by Juan José Millás." Diss. Vanderbilt U, 1997. Ann Arbor: DAIA, 1998. DA9815585.

Cuadrat, Esther. "Una aproximación al mundo novelístico de Juan José Millás." *Cuadernos Hispanoamericanos* 580 (Oct. 1988): 103-20.

Genette, Gérard. *Narrative Discourse: An Essay in Method.* 1972. Trans. Jane E. Lewin. Ithaca: Cornell UP, 1980.

Gutiérrez, Rebeca. "Teorías que cohabitan con la ficción: Síntomas posmodernos en *El desorden de tu nombre* de Juan José Millás." *Romance Languages Annual* 9 (1997): 526-28.

Holloway, Vance R. "The Pleasures of Oedipal Discontent and *El desorden de tu nombre,* by Juan José Millás García." *Revista Canadiense de Estudios Hispánicos* 18.1 (Fall 1993): 31-47.

Jameson, Fredric. *The Political Unconscious: Narrative as a Socially Symbolic Act.* Ithaca: Cornell UP, 1981.

———. *Postmodernism, or The Cultural Logic of Late Capitalism.* Durham: Duke UP, 1991.

Marco, José María. "El éxito se paga." Rev. of *El desorden de tu nombre,* by Juan José Millás. *Quimera* 76 (1988): 67.

———. "En fin: Una entrevista con Juan José Millás." *Quimera* 81 (sept. 1988) 20-6.

Miranda, Marta Isabel. "El lenguaje cinematográfico de la acción en la narrativa de Juan José Millás." *Revista Hispánica Moderna* 47.2 (Dec. 1994): 526-42.

Pope, Randolph. Review of *El desorden de tu nombre,* by Juan José Millás. *España Contemporánea* 3.2 (Fall 1990): 148-50.

Sobejano, Gonzalo. Rev. of *El desorden de tu nombre,* by Juan José Millás. *Ínsula* 504 (Dec. 1988): 21-2.

———. "Novela y metanovela en España." *Ínsula* 512-513 (Aug.-Sep. 1989): 4-6.

———. "Sobre la novela y el cuento dentro de la novela." *Lucanor* 2 (Dec. 1988): 73-93.

Spires, Robert. *Beyond the Metafictional Mode. Directions in the Modern Spanish Novel.* London: Methuen, and Lexington: UP of Kentucky, 1984.

———. *Post-Totalitarian Fiction.* Columbia: U of Missouri P, 1996.

Patricia Reagan (essay date 2006)

SOURCE: Reagan, Patricia. "*Dos mujeres en Praga*: The Orphaned Child of Juan José Millás." *España contemporánea* 19.2 (2006): 27-42. Print.

[*In the following essay, Reagan explores the metaphor of adoption and orphanhood in* Two Women in Prague. *She argues that Millás's conception of orphanhood functions as a metaphor for authorship.*]

In his 2002 novel, *Dos mujeres en Praga,* Juan José Millás creates a crisis of identity for the majority of his protagonists by exploring the ways in which they are orphaned or have orphaned others in their lives. But, in point of fact, not one of them is without parents, nor have any of them given up their own children. And so, the classic definition of orphan as that of a person or child whose parents are absent does not apply.

Millás' novel, the central conflict of which is the ways in which we are adopted and orphaned or adopt and orphan others, needs a new concept of orphanhood—that of the auto-orphan, a state of self-inflicted abandonment, which emerges as a result of a variety of crises of identity experienced by the characters of the novel.

As Luz Acaso, nears her death, she seeks an author, Álvaro Abril, to undertake the project of writing her life. In the course of several meetings with Abril she adopts different fictional identities for herself, each of which present paths she did not actually choose in life. Consequently, the "truth" of her identity is never fully known, as it is hidden in a well-developed web of lies including a feigned widowhood and more importantly, a claim that as a teenager she gave a baby up for adoption. Despite the fact that she admits to being a liar, Álvaro's sense of disconnection from others leads him to believe that he himself was adopted as a child, and over time, that Luz is in fact his birth mother. Through these encounters and others, the sense of loneliness and isolation that the characters experience, create a fertile ground for the seeds of auto-orphanhood to take root.

The notion of adoption/orphanhood develops into a unique multi-layered metaphor, treated directly through plots and subplots, as it becomes a central theme of the interviews between Álvaro and Luz, and for each of them in their personal lives. The novel also contains an intercalated story, a letter from Álvaro to his mother, and a non-fiction research report, all of which deal with adoption as well. The unnamed narrator of *Dos mujeres en Praga* is a professional non-fiction writer whose role it is to piece the different fragments and stories together to "write" the novel and create a coherent story from the fragments of Luz's life. Álvaro, Luz and the narrator all inflict upon themselves a state of auto-orphanhood as they disassociate from a real yet incomplete identity and begin the construction of a new identity, as an orphan. Even as the characters take on their new state of auto-orphanhood, the narrator discovers on a metafictional level that the act of writing leads to an "orphanhood" of the work from its author. Writing is a birth process and after laboring over the novel, the text is ripped from the author, and given to the reader who adopts the text as his or her own.

The complexity of *Dos mujeres en Praga* can be understood more completely through an analysis of the various layers of the adoption/orphanhood metaphor. Despite the novel's publication in 2002 it has received little critical attention. My analysis engages in a close reading of the novel, informed more generally by an understanding of adoption in literature as well as other fiction by Juan José Millás. One of few published pieces on the novel, Joanne Lucena's short conference paper, "*Dos mujeres en Praga*: Alegoría del proceso de escritura," demonstrates the way in which the various modes of self-referential writing come together to question the limits between fiction and reality in the novel. As one element of her analysis of metafiction, Lucena shows how the narrator links authorship to parenthood as an example of metafiction in the text. Lucena cites the passage in the novel, "del mismo modo que hay padres adoptivos más legítimos que los verdaderos, hay autores que no se merecen los libros que han escrito. Es muy difícil ser padre, o ser autor" (Millás 130), concluding that, "Esta metáfora se puede relacionar directamente con la de los procesos de escribir, que forma parte del elemento metafictivo del texto al indicar la futilidad de buscar una paternidad, un origen que ancle el contenido y el significado" (138). Clearly, as Lucena's analysis reveals, the connection between authorship and parenthood contributes to the novel's allegory of the writing process. While her argument is a starting point, my analysis establishes that this connection is not simply an example of the writing process but rather the driving force of the entire novel. To demonstrate this, I will first look briefly at adoption in literature and in contemporary psychological and sociological studies. Then, I will use general criticism of Millás' earlier fiction to demonstrate how *Dos mujeres en Praga* fits into his broader critical preoccupations. By using Tzvetan Todorov's and Jacques Derrida's theories of absence as a critical basis for my textual analysis of the adoption/orphanhood metaphor, I will explore at this point the novel's three main characters, Álvaro, Luz and the narrator to show how each character formulates a conceptualization of their own identity based on his or her own auto-orphanhood. Finally, I will explore the role of the narrator and author in the metafictional level of the text.

Adoption is not a new subject matter in literature. Marianne Novy's study *Imagining Adoption: Essays on Literature and Culture* contains a wide range of essays dealing with literary works in which adoption plays a significant role. In her introduction, Novy discusses mythical cases of adoption such as *Oedipus,* later examples such as *Silas Marner* and *Great Expectations,* as well as more contemporary examples such as *Pigs in Heaven*. She asserts that adoption has figured heavily in literature because "adoption plots dramatize cultural tension about definitions of family and the importance of heredity" (2). As Novy shows, adoption literature often focuses on the identity construction of isolated characters.[1] Outside of literature, adoption studies have only recently gained momentum. Adam Pertman's *Adoption Nation: How the Adoption Revolution Is Transforming America,* argues that the silence in society concerning adoption often contributes to feelings of insecurity amongst the adopted. "Adoption has been considered off-limits for so long, both by individuals and society as a whole, that until very recently studies have not been devised, census questions have not been asked, surveys have not been conducted. There is no national organization or branch of government that keeps track of adoptions" (7).[2] Pertman further makes the case that both adoptive parents and legislation encourage silent acceptance by adopted individuals.

John Triseliotis, in one of few early adoption studies, interviewed a small group of highly conflicted individuals who revealed a relatively high level of unhappiness. The participants "Attributed their general unhappiness to dissatisfaction, to poor family relationships, lack of close links with their parents and a failure to develop a sense of attachment and belonging" (77). More specifically, several individuals talked of experiencing a sense of 'emptiness,' 'isolation' or 'vacuum'; of feeling 'false,' 'not being a whole or real person,' 'depressed and unhappy,' 'tense and anxious,' 'not coping,' 'unable to get close to people,' among other feelings (Triseliotis 82). In summary, the adopted individual feels isolated, disconnected and incomplete.

The lack of identity and community, difficulty in uncovering one's true self and general sense of unhappiness in cases of real adoption/orphanhood relate directly to the auto-orphanhood that characterizes *Dos mujeres en Praga.* As Branka Kalenic Ramsak indicates, Millás' novel "se trata de la ausencia de amor o del eterno anhelo inalcanzable que deja a los protagonistas inseguros, solitarios, angustiados de su existencia cotidiana" (135). This lack of love and the definitive feelings of anguish provoke the protagonists to self inflict a state of auto-orphanhood. Similarly, Freud's theory of the family romance considers this concept that I have named auto-orphanhood:

> There are only too many occasions on which a child is slighted, or at least *feels* he has been slighted, on which he feels he is not receiving the whole of his parents' love, and, most of all, on which he feels regrets at having to share it with brothers and sisters. His sense that his own affection is not being fully reciprocated then finds a vent in the idea, often consciously recollected later from early childhood, of being a step-child or an adopted child.
>
> (237-38)

Basing her ideas on the Freudian concept, Novy concludes, as well, that "for most people—nonadopted people—the fantasy of discovering that they were adopted and can be reunited with a different family elsewhere is a way of dealing with negative feelings about their parents" (2). The adopted person has the ability not only to construct an image of the person he or she wants to be, starting from his or her origin, but also the right to change that image, which is why the adoption fantasy works so well for the novel's characters.[3] In this sense, the adopted individual can create and manipulate his or her identity in the same way that a novel is a created and manipulated fictional construction. The adoption/orphanhood metaphor in *Dos mujeres en Praga* demonstrates both levels.

Criticism of Millás' prior work focuses on his preoccupation with identity construction. Dale F. Knickerbocker concludes, "Cada acercamiento millasiano al concepto de la identidad es un experimento distinto, cuya meta es indagar las posibilidades aparentemente inagotables que ofrece" ("Identidad" 561). Millás' various identity experiments all share the same basic starting point: "La identidad implica siempre un enfrentamiento con la realidad circundante, a partir del cual un personaje, conscientemente o no, construye, adopta o halla un otro-yo" (Knickerbocker "Identidad" 561). Knickerbocker's article prefigures Millás' new experiment in self-discovery with the phrase "adopta . . . un otro-yo," and applies directly to *Dos mujeres en Praga* as well when he states: "Millasian characters fear, dislike and shun human contact, do not feel part of any collective, and are generally considered by others (including the readers) to be eccentrics" (Knickerbocker *Obsessive* 18). Thus, *Dos mujeres en Praga* can be considered a new Millás experiment in the search for identity, completely in keeping with his previous fiction.

Indeed, two other critics have also used the word orphan to describe Millás' protagonists. Miguel Catalán concludes: "El sentimiento que se cuela por los escasos resquicios de la fascinadora mirada ajena de Millás es siempre un sentimiento de orfandad, de separación injustificada del resto del mundo, y, principalmente, de los familiares más próximos" (3). Thus, Catalán associates alienation with orphanhood, in Millás' fiction. In addition, Pepa Anastasio applies Catalán's conclusion to her discussion of Millás' *El orden alfabético,* associating the protagonist's feelings of anguish described as orphanhood with Millás's negative worldview. She says, "El sentimiento de orfandad del protagonista puede entenderse en el contexto de la negación de Dios por la razón" (196).[4] For both Catalán and Anastasio, to be or to feel like an orphan in Millás' fiction is not simply to be parentless, but rather to be wracked with an existential angst. Moreover, Knickerbocker concludes that each of the five novels preceding *Dos mujeres en Praga* have protagonists who suffer the same feelings of alienation. He determines: "The representation of identity in each of these works treated here may be seen as different linguistic, aesthetic experiments with others, alter egos, each pair of which constitutes a metaphor of the inherently split, self-alienated subject itself" (*Obsessive* 24). It follows that the "self-alienated" subject to which Knickerbocker refers is fundamentally equivalent to the self-inflicted auto-orphanhood in *Dos mujeres en Praga.* In this way, Millás' protagonists *auto-orphan* or *self-alienate* in order to be able to *un-identify* themselves from their origins. In order to reconstruct a different identity each character must be reborn as part of the process of recreating his or her new self-determined identity, which always necessarily ends up

being one of isolation or absence, but in point of fact, disassociation leads to self-(de)-actualization.[5]

Millás' writing of orphanhood in *Dos mujeres en Praga* is propelled by the same sense of absence felt by the process of identity construction. Todorov's analysis of Henry James' short fiction reveals a similar phenomenon in his analysis of James. He writes, "James' tales are based on the quest for an absolute and absent cause . . . Everything in the story owes its presence, in the last analysis, to it. But it is absent and we set off in quest of it" (75). The same can be said of adoption/orphanhood in *Dos mujeres en Praga.* The protagonists feel the force of absence, resulting in a self-imposition of orphanhood. Todorov also discusses James' view of the author in his work, which parallels the metafictional level of the metaphor in Millás' novel.[6] For James, "The author's life is only an appearance, a contingency, an accident; it is an inessential presence. The work of art is the truth to be sought after, even if there is no hope of finding it" (94). Thus, for James, the work of art stands alone. Millás' novel, as it is orphaned from its author is just that, a separate, stand-alone work of art. The novel's parent, the author, makes only a brief "appearance."

In the novel, then, the sense of a lack of origin and of absence leads the characters to try to re-create their identities after auto-orphaning themselves. Through this process of self-alienation each character discovers a hole in himself or herself, what Derrida calls the lack of center, which he defines as "a presence—*eidos, arché, telos, energeia, ousia, aletheia*" ('form, origin, purpose, energy, being, truth') (879). Derrida identifies that a rupture of this presence has occurred, leaving man center-less as a result of "the totality of an era" (880). Thus, the orphanhood of modern man can be seen as a self-inflicted sense of loss. Orphanhood describes the disease while presenting auto-orphanhood as the proposed cure. The textual center, the motivating force of the novel is the lack of a core, manifested in the individual dilemmas of Álvaro and Luz, and the creation of the narrator propelled by the necessity to create as a response to existential angst and lack of origin, a feeling shared by the novel's protagonists.

I would like to look carefully now at the three protagonists of *Dos mujeres en Praga*—Álvaro, Luz and the narrator. The first reference to orphanin in the text is in Álvaro's phone conversation with a prostitute, whom he has called after reading her ad of herself as a "viuda madura" (37). In the course of the conversation she asks if he is alone: "¿Como un viudo?" to which he answers "Como un huérfano" (38). The prostitute seems to understand Álvaro's feeling of isolation: "Pues una viuda y un huérfano tienen muchas cosas en común" (38). The prostitute's offhand remark becomes a strand enmeshing Luz and Álvaro. Indeed, Luz had claimed in her first meeting with Álvaro to be a widow, although she reveals later that she is not. As Álvaro elaborates the orphan/widow feeling by describing his own insecurity, he adopts his own alienation.

Although he is not an orphan of happenstance, Álvaro demonstrates traits of an orphan, revealing an obsession with the ghosts of his past. The narrator connects Álvaro's specters with literature: "Sabía por sus lecturas literarias que estamos condenados a tropezar con aquello de lo que huimos y comenzaba a sospechar que los fantasmas eran seres reales" (40). Tying these loose threads together, the narrator calls attention to the fact that lack and centerlessness are spun out in different ways in literature. When the prostitute arrives, Álvaro realizes: "sin duda era el fantasma que él mismo había reclamado por teléfono unos minutos antes: era su madre muerta" (41). Thus, the prostitute momentarily converts his absence into a live presence. Subsequently, Álvaro reveals his desire to watch the prostitute bathe herself and he explains that as a child he used to watch his mother bathe from the dirty clothesbasket. At the end of the chaste encounter with the prostitute, a confession is wrung from both parties. She is no more a widow than he is an orphan. Yet, his auto-orphanhood is a way to free himself from the psychological torment he feels for having desired his mother as a child. In order to reconstruct a satisfactory self-identity Álvaro releases himself from his past and from his Oedipal guilt. This unfolds later in a phone conversation with the narrator. He reports that he has always had the suspicion that he was adopted based on overhearing his mother state, "Estoy arrepentida, ahora no volvería a hacerlo" (113) on the phone. The narrator tries to convince Álvaro of the inconclusiveness of the sentence, although Álvaro is unswayed. The significance of the event with the prostitute is revealed later in the novel, although it is this incipient event that weaves the weft of Álvaro's life into the warp of Luz's. The scene establishes Álvaro's obsession with his disconnected self, even as he begins to believe his own lies.

In Álvaro's ensuing interview with Luz, during which she confesses that she is not a widow but rather that she gave a child up for adoption when she was fifteen, he finds confirmation of his feeling of loss. While we have seen that in Millás' fiction, identity can be reshaped when ties are cut with the past we must consider how this should be interpreted in terms of *Dos mujeres en Praga.* The key lies in the fact that Luz neither gave a child up for adoption nor was Álvaro really adopted. Luz is making up for a life never lived while Álvaro is rejecting the ties to his actual family. The two have found the adoption/orphanhood metaphor as a way to describe their desired absence. In order to rebuild an identity different from their own, they must first stitch together a story of adoption/orphanhood in order to have a familial tie from which to dissociate. Both Álvaro and Luz are in a self-inflicted state of bereavement. Álvaro longs for his "birth" mother (who never existed) and Luz yearns for her lost child (whom she never bore).

As these fictions develop during Luz's life-story interviews, the narrator is simultaneously developing a report based on "real" adoption cases. This report provides a non-fictional level in contrast with Álvaro's false-biography writing, which serves to blur the line between truth/lies, non-fiction/fiction. The narrator's real report is seen to have an effect on the false claims of Luz. Indeed, it is his report that Luz hears from her car stereo and which provokes the confession that she gave her child up for adoption, subsequently leading Álvaro to the improbable conclusion that he could be Luz's son. Luz's lies combined with Álvaro's real encounter with a prostitute compound Álvaro's self-inflicted orphanhood. Fact and fiction are both juxtaposed and superimposed beyond distinction while truth and lies are both shown to be catalysts of the other. María José, Luz's room-mate (and the other of the "dos mujeres" in the novel) contributes to this juxtaposition by calling Álvaro and pretending to be a nun at the hospital where María Luz de Acaso gave him up for adoption. Her lie is yet another untruth disguised as truth, which affects the narrator, prompting him to go to the clinic to investigate María José's claim. Just as the author's report of real adoption fuels Luz's lies, María José's lie affects the narrator's real investigation. The narrator finds himself so swept up in the fantasy that in spite of his skepticism towards that which Álvaro's asserts, he is compelled to abandon his "real" report to study auto-orphans. He admits, "Ahora solo me interesaban los falsos adoptados" (140). He is drawn to validate fantasy with reality and vice versa.

Luz's meetings with Álvaro follow a continuing pattern of claims and retractions. In her admission of her deceit she says, "Me impresionó tanto que hice mío el problema de esas pobres mujeres a las que les arrebataron el bebé nada más nacer. Pero se trataba de una mentira que no era una mentira, porque mientras la contaba era verdad. ¿Puede usted entender esto, que una cosa sea al mismo tiempo mentira y verdad?" (69-70). In justifying her lies she describes real feelings. By claiming to have lost a baby to adoption, her lack will be better understood in her biography. Even after Luz confesses, Álvaro maintains his own lie that he is Luz's son, indicating that he does understand how a lie can sometimes be true. Luz betrays her awareness of her deceitful personality when she promises to tell Álvaro the truth in their final interview. However, at this point in the novel, we recognize that the concept of truth has been completely deconstructed and has in fact become meaningless. Luz's confessions remain questionable, when she admits in her final interview that she is a prostitute and that the various lies she has told Álvaro constitute the lives of others. Furthermore, she claims to have maintained a long relationship with a married man who had given his child up for adoption. Thus, Luz's declarations, whether true or not, are based on fact, which makes her self-determined identity only partially fiction.

In this way, Luz's fictions relate to the task of the novelist in that her comment. "mientras la contaba era verdad" (70) parallels the relationship of the author with his text. Through the novel's multi-tiered structure, in which Millás writes a novel about a narrator telling the story of a writer constructing another's identity in a false biography, it is revealed that the absolute truth is irrelevant in fiction. The writer (author, narrator, and biographer) constructs identities in the same way that the novel's characters reconstruct identities—as fictions grounded in truth. In other words, if the reader can understand Luz's angst by means of her false assertion at having orphaned a child, then the "truth" of her life becomes irrelevant within that fiction. Furthermore, a novel's characters are always orphaned from a true origin (before the text) or a future one (beyond the text). The task of the reader is to construct origins for the novel's characters, in a sense, to read a novel is to adopt a child. The adoptive parents (readers) know only what the child (novel) chooses to tell them. Thus, the adoption/ orphanhood metaphor can bring the attentive reader to question individual character's lives within fiction, the author's relationship with his or her fiction, and the role of the reader's perspective when approaching the text.[7] In this way, the inaccessibility of absolute truth is affirmed.

In comparison to what seems to be the narrator's real investigations, Luz's false biography (not included in the novel) will appear to be more fictional than the novel that contains it, although both are equally constructed (un)truths. The struggling narrator can only write the novel that we read by combining bits and pieces of fictional and non-fictional accounts including Luz's biography interviews, Álvaro's obsessions and the *novela zurda* that María José is trying to write. Yet, all of the pieces constitute a unity within the fiction of the novel. ***Dos mujeres en Praga,*** is not seamless, indeed, the art of the novel lies in its outward demonstration of the interwoven processes of spinning truth into fiction. The novel gives the reader the sensation that he or she is undergoes the same thought processes as those of the author while writing a novel. Yet, the novel is still separated from Millás, and his intentions in writing are not as important as those of the reader of his estranged novel.

Just as ***Dos mujeres en Praga*** constructs both a multi-layered and fragmented novel in which the various narrative threads intertwine, the narrator demonstrates that reality is sometimes ordered through coincidences, recognizing this as the basis of his own writing: "Quizá el mundo se sostiene sobre una red invisible de casualidades. Si un fragmento de esa red queda al descubierto ante tus ojos, cómo evitar la tentación de tirar el hilo" (63). Thus, he shows that borne out of coincidences is the possibility to make sense of the world and create order. Out of the random acts of happenstance Luz and Álvaro are able to order their lives. Even the narrator is drawn in after Luz (Fina to the narrator) chooses him to be Álvaro's fictional father. We also see this need to create order at a book signing, when a boy reveals that his father looks uncannily like the narrator, so much so that he comes to call the narrator "stepbrother." This encounter provokes the narrator to think: "Supongamos, me dije, que ese hombre y yo fuéramos realmente hermanos gemelos y que nuestros padres nos hubieran

separado al entregarnos en adopción a dos familias distintas" (78). He even imagines that reuniting with his long-lost twin brother would explain "esa sensación de estar inacabado, inconcluso, que me ha acompañado a lo largo de la vida" (78). The narrator finds comfort in his auto-orphanhood, a way to understand his sense of incompleteness in life. The narrator is able to direct his lack in a productive way—he uses the experience as a motivation to begin a report on adoption, and eventually to "write" the novel. Before writing he goes to observe his "brother" from a distance and is able to understand how others perceive him.

Another example of the adoption/orphanhood metaphor that draws attention to the importance of coincidences, is the short story intercalated within the novel, entitled *Nadie.*[8] The narrator writes this story for the newspaper in the midst of his adoption research. In the story, Luisa contacts Luis Rodó by phone stating, "Soy Luisa, la hija de Antonia" (81). This conversation brings back the memory of Antonia, Luis's lover from twenty years ago and the possibility that Luisa might be his child. Luis realizes that Luisa could give meaning to his mediocre life: "Llevaba años esperando aquella llamada, sufriendo anticipadamente por ella ..." (83). But, after meeting Luisa and going to her apartment, which in another incident of chance Luis discovers to be the same apartment where his romantic encounters with Antonia took place, Luisa reveals that he is not her father. Sex ensues, leaving Luis with the same empty feeling he suffered with Antonia, only now he becomes obsessed with the possibility that he left Luisa pregnant with his child. Thus, his circle of lack continues, and twenty years later Luis shows himself to be incapable of learning from the past. When his wife asks with whom he had lunch, he responds "nadie," demonstrating the insignificance of the impossible unlived other life, and generating the title of the story.

The intertwining coincidences of the plots of the short story and the novel become even more complicated. Luisa of *Nadie* has a problem with her left eye, just as María José does. The narrator also admits to the reader that a portion of *Nadie* is autobiographical, an adulterous relationship and the loss of a child, continuing to blur the line separating fiction and reality. At the same time, the narrator has a "real" daughter, although he is not entirely convinced that she is his. He has an argument with his ex-wife in which he yells: "Sé perfectamente lo que hago porque es mi hija" (99). Her response is, "¿Estás seguro?" (99), which she later tries to pass off as a joke. He suggests that the possibility of his daughter having a "real" father could explain his estranged relationship with her. Finally, the narrator admits that he desires the uncertainty of the false life over the realities of his current life: "Cómo me gustaría ahora que todo fuera cierto: que yo fuera adoptado y que hubiera tenido un hijo con aquella mujer de la que no he vuelto a tener noticias en todos estos años" (100). In this way, we see that his own dissatisfaction with his real life (adultery, unknown children, bad relationships with his real children, general angst, his family relationships, etc.) causes his self-imposed auto-orphanhood, which he is in a better position himself to understand through Álvaro's and Luz's stories. At the same time, *Nadie* and the novel as a whole question the everyday chance that constitutes reality. Fiction is shown to intermingle with the possibilities of our unlived lives, when the narrator proclaims: "La vida está llena de novelas" (144).

Finally, as coincidence would have it, *Nadie* is the reason that the narrator and Álvaro have continued contact. After reading *Nadie,* Alvaro writes the narrator an e-mail which links the metaphor of adoption/orphanhood to the metafictional layer: "Me gustó *Nadie,* me gustó mucho *Nadie.* Todo ese juego entre la realidad y la ficción, la ambigüedad sobre si ella es hija o no de él ... Me interesa mucho el asunto de la autoría en la obra de arte, que quizá no sea muy distinto del de la paternidad. ¿Somos hijos de nuestros padres? ¿Somos los autores de nuestras obras ...?" (101). In his e-mail Álvaro directly references both layers of the adoption metaphor, leading the narrator to his own conclusion, that perhaps Álvaro is his "nadie," his long-lost son. For the narrator, to be Álvaro's father, is one of those lies "que merecerían ser verdades" (117) indicating an appropriation of Luz's idea of "mientras la contaba era verdad" (70). Álvaro repeats the same comparison of adoption with authorship from his e-mail in his subsequent interview with Luz, specifically referring to his first novel *El parque.* He proclaims that just as he is orphaned, so is his novel: "Hay escritores que creen haber escrito lo que publican ... *El parque* es hija mía como yo soy hijo de mis padres" (129). Álvaro finds himself in doubt over the origins of this writing just as he doubts his human origins. Indeed, it is actually Álvaro who leads the narrator to understand the metaphor and to write the novel. The narrator concludes: "Entonces comprendí lo que intentaba decirme acerca de la autoría. Del mismo modo que hay padres adoptivos más legítimos que los verdaderos, hay autores que no se merecen los libros que han escrito" (130). From this understanding, the narrator arrives at an important conclusion that helps him transition from reporter to novelist, a change he has wanted to make since abandoning the adoption report to his interest in "falsos adoptados." The metaphor itself has enabled the narrator to write.

The narrator admits that Luz (Fina) has helped him understand that his failure as fiction writer is a direct result of his attempt to isolate his own reality from his fiction, which he learns is impossible (161). Feeling defenseless when he is confronted with joining the two together, the narrator explains:

> Yo siempre había trabajado con materiales reales y sabía de qué manera manipularlos para alcanzar el significado o la dirección que convenía a mis intereses. Mi experiencia con la ficción, en cambio, se reducía a aquel cuento, *Nadie,* en el que incluí por otra parte tantos elementos autobiográficos que en cierto modo era también un repor-

taje disimulado. No sabía, en fin, de qué manera se defiende uno de lo irreal.

(164)

Although his realization concerning fact and fiction comes at the nadir in his well being he learns that fiction is not isolated from reality and that his role as a writer of fiction is to bring the two elements together simultaneously. With this realization he is finally able to write his novel.

The role of the narrator as a writer also brings us to question the role of the author in *Dos mujeres en Praga.* Michel Foucault's article, "What Is an Author?" contradicts Roland Barthes' conceptualization of the author's death by maintaining that the concept of author persists in the text as an open space. He concludes: "It is not enough, however, to repeat the empty affirmation that the author has disappeared ... we must locate the space left empty by the author's disappearance, follow the distribution of gaps and breaches, and watch for the openings that this disappearance uncovers" (892). In the open space of the absent author in *Dos mujeres en Praga* the reader discovers a lack of origin, mirroring the case of an orphaned child. Through an analysis of the metaphor of adoption/orphanhood in *Dos mujeres en Praga* we can deduce that the aesthetic value of the novel itself is in its absent center. In Millás' novel, the space left empty by the disappearance of the author from the center of the text is a dramatization of the separation itself. The author is a birth parent, and while not truly dead, his own life, experiences and perspectives contribute to the *nature* of his child, his novel. The reader adopts the waif and *nurtures* it with his or her own life and experiences. Each reader will have an individualized relationship with this adopted child. Although many critics would have us question the nature of the author, *Dos mujeres en Praga* dramatizes that, as Foucault indicates, he is an absent origin, in the same way that an orphaned child has both a true and absent origin. Derrida's ruptured center coincides with Barthes' dead author, demonstrating that the dilemma of absence in contemporary society is manifested in *Dos mujeres en Praga* on these same two levels, converting Millás novel into a reflection of contemporary society.

The narrator of *Dos mujeres en Praga* joins various genres together into a solid example of truth-questioning postmodern Spanish fiction: the short story *Nadie,* Alvaro's strange epistle to his non-mother, the reports of adoption, Alvaro's interviews with Luz and the narrator's own bringing together of all of these parts. Each of the novel's fragments contributes to the adoption/orphanhood metaphor. At the very end of the novel, the reader bears witness to Luz's request that the narrator be the executor of her meager estate and, in essence, her story, her life.[9] In this way, the narrator's account begins and the novel ends at the same point. This also characterizes the relationship of the author with his fiction: for one brief moment, the novel is his; after its birth he looses it instantaneously in a forced orphanhood, his moment of parenthood already past. Thus, the metaphor of adoption/orphanhood not only unifies textual elements of *Dos mujeres en Praga* but also functions as a metaphor for authorship. Millás has birthed a perfect child, an orphan many readers will happily adopt.

Notes

1. As Novy indicates, this sense of isolation can be attributed to a lack of community amongst the adopted or their adoptive parents. As a result, the feeling of isolation is not limited to a fragmented identity but is extended to include social isolation. Novy writes: Unlike many minority groups, neither adoptees nor adoptive parents necessarily grow up among, raise children with, or wish to socialize with others in their category ... Because their relation to adoption has been associated with loss and even with stigma, adoptees and adoptive and birth parents have generally been, for the most part, isolated and fragmented (5).

2. This trend has now changed dramatically since Pertman's 2000 study. Support groups and social groups for adoptive parents and for their children are now quite prevalent. Special groups for adopting families are also gaining popularity such as support groups for parents of children adopted from specific regions. For example, Richmond, VA has at least 4 groups: Adoptive Families Del Sol (families who have adopted from Latin America), Coordinators 2 (Birth parent & adoptee support), Families of the China Moon (families who have adopted from China), and Families for Russian/Ukrainian Adoption of Central VA.

3. One of the essays in Novy's book is by Nancy Gish who analyzes the Scottish poet, Jackie Kay, Gish demonstrates that Kay, as an adopted person constructs and modifies her image at will as Freud demonstrates is the advantage to the adoption fantasy. For Gish, Kay's work gains importance and complexity through her changeable sense of identity. "The possibilities for the adopted person to constantly re-invent themselves are endless. To study Kay's work is to explore relations of adoption, identity, language and voice ... The 'I' who speaks may be neither the lyric 'I' of the author speaking as a traditional unitary self nor the dramatic 'I' of the author's fictional constructions. Rather, it may be both self and other, a voicing of internal multiplicity" (180).

4. Citing the quote from Catalán, Pepa Anastasio discusses the difference between the disassociated adult and the secure child who still feels connected with his origin (195). She cites an example from *El orden alfabético,* in which young Julio, confronted with his grandfather's death, begins to fears losing his father

before arriving at "una edad en la que no le necesitaría: siempre me ha dado miedo la orfandad" (28). As we see in *El orden alfabético,* in Julio's imaginary world the loss of words and communication leads to the dehumanization and animalization of man. This loss of language results in an uncertain identity for Julio and an existential orphanhood, because of the lack of reason.

5. Millás himself discusses his conceptualization of identity construction in an interview with Katarzyna Olga Beilin. He believes that it is common for young people (*jóvenes*) to question their individuality and whether it is possible to have "una identidad propia o si es posible aceptar como propia la que se ha heredado o la que se ha imitado" (123). This is exemplified in "Primavera de luto" in the collection of the same name published in 1989. The protagonist in the story, Elena, begins to search for her own identity after her husband's death. Upon cutting her hair she feels as if she has witnessed her rebirth, but at the same time she realizes that to be valid her change must be more than superficial. As Knickerbocker concludes: "Elena tiene que desprenderse de todo lo que le recuerde al pasado; sobre todo en cuanto a relaciones familiares o sentimentales" ("Identidad" 568).

6. Todorov demonstrates the way in which James reverses the traditional view of psychological criticism that the author is actually the absent cause of the text.

7. Oftentimes, the reader searches for the origin of an author's work, by comparing new fiction to earlier examples of novels by the same author. For example, Knickerbocker demonstrates that Millás's "El pequeño cadáver de R. J.," also from the collection *Primavera de luto,* plays with the idea of author, narrator, identity and ownership of text. In "El pequeño cadáver de R. J.," R. J. publishes, with permission, a text originally written by the narrator. Later, the two switch papers in a conference leading to the success of R.J. and to the demise of the narrator. Knickerbocker compares their relationship to that of Cain and Abel. In the story, the narrator is ultimately destroyed by his other, R. J. ("Identidad" 564). R. J. represents the text itself that becomes a living being, existing beyond the reaches of its narrator or author. It is also an intertextual reference to Roland Barthes's, "The Death of the Author" (Knickerbocker "Identidad" 564). In this way we see that Millás demonstrates a consistent questioning of the role of the narrator and author. The origins of *Dos mujeres en Praga* can be found in earlier works written by Millás.

8. Although it is customary to put the titles of short stories in quotation marks, in *Dos mujeres en Praga* the title, *Nadie* is italicized. I have chosen to do the same.

9. The last words of the novel explain this as the narrator's task. He is left as the executor of Luz's meager estate, but more importantly with the task of telling her story: "La cuestión, en fin, es que me había convertido en el albacea o ejecutor (qué palabras, por cierto) de aquel curiosos testamento que dejaba los escasos bienes de Luz Acaso—el piso de Praga y una cuenta de ahorro—a Álvaro Abril y a María José. Era evidente que para llevar a cabo ese reparto no hacía falta un albacea, pero sí un narrador, un narrado que al contar los últimos días de Luz Acaso tuviera, sin comprender por qué la impresión de ordenar su propia vida."

Works Cited

Anastasio, Pepa. "*El orden alfabético* de Juan José Millás: Salvación por la palabra." *Monographic Review* 17 (2001): 187-205.

Beilin, Katarzyna Olga. "Vivir de la huida." *Confluencia* 17:1 (2001): 117-28.

Catalán, Miguel. "Lógica y solipsismo en la obra de Juan José Millás." *Espéculo: Revista de estudios literarios* 6 (1997): 1-3.

Deans, Hill. "File It under "L" for Love Child." *Imagining Adoption: Essays on Literature and Culture.* Ed. Marianne Novy. Ann Arbor: U of Michigan P, 2001: 231-50.

Derrida, Jacques. "Structure, Sign and Play." *The Critical Tradition.* Ed. David H. Richter. Boston: Bedford, 1998: 878-89.

Foucault, Michel. "What Is an Author?" *The Critical Tradition.* Ed. David H. Richter. Boston: Bedford, 1998: 889-900.

Freud, Sigmund. "Family Romances." *Standard Edition,* 9. Trans. James Strachey. London: Butler and Tanner Ltd, 1959: 237-41.

Gish, Nancy. "Adoption, Identity and Voice." *Imagining Adoption: Essays on Literature and Culture.* Ed. Marianne Novy. Ann Arbor: U of Michigan P, 2001: 171-92.

Kalenic Ramsak, Branka. "Las llamadas perdidas de 'Dos mujeres en Praga' (Manuel Rivas y Juan José Millás)." *'El amor, esa palabra . . .': El amor en la novela española contemporánea de fin de milenio.* Eds. Anna-Sophia Buck and Irene Gastón Sierra. Madrid: Iberoamericana, 2005: 129-40.

Knickerbocker, Dale F. "Identidad y otredad en *Primavera de luto* de Juan José Millás." *Letras Peninsulares* 13:2-3 (2000-2001): 561-79.

———. *Juan José Millás: The Obsessive-Compulsive Aesthetic.* New York: Peter Lang, 2003.

Lucena, Joanne. "*Dos mujeres en Praga*: Alegoría del proceso de escritura." *Selected Proceedings of the Pennsylvania Foreign Language Conference.* Ed. Gregorio C. Martín. New Kensington: Grelin P, 2003: 133-39.

Millás García, Juan José. *Dos mujeres en Praga.* Madrid: Espasa Calpe, 2002.

———. *El orden alfabético.* Madrid: Alfaguara, 1998.

———. *Primavera de luto y otros cuentos.* Colección Áncora y Delfín 656. Barcelona: Destino, 1989.

Novy, Marianne. *Imagining Adoption: Essays on Literature and Culture.* Ann Arbor: U of Michigan P, 2001.

Pertman, Adam. *Adoption Nation: How the Adoption Revolution Is Transforming America.* New York: Basic, 2000.

Todorov, Tzvetan. "The Structural Analysis of Literature: The Tales of Henry James." *Structuralism: An Introduction.* Ed. David Robey. Oxford: Clarendon P, 1973: 73-103.

Triseliotis, John. *The Search of Origins: The Experiences of Adopted People.* London: Routledge & Kegan Paul, 1973.

VanStavern, Jan. "A Junction of Amends." *Imagining Adoption: Essays on Literature and Culture.* Ed. Marianne Novy. Ann Arbor: U of Michigan P, 2001: 151-70.

Wimsatt, W. K., and Beardsley, Monroe C. "The Intentional Fallacy." *The Critical Tradition.* Ed. David H. Richter. Boston: Bedford, 1998: 748-57.

Samuel Amago (essay date 2006)

SOURCE: Amago, Samuel. "Mapping the Storied Self: Consciousness and Cartography in the Novels of Juan José Millás." *True Lies: Narrative Self-Consciousness in the Contemporary Spanish Novel.* Lewisburg: Bucknell UP, 2006. 65-94. Print.

[*In the following essay, Amago analyzes the role of narration in identity formation and in the ordering of reality in Millás's novels. Amago traces the theme of the "redemptive powers" of the writing process in Millás's works of the 1970s through his 2002 novel,* Two Women in Prague.]

Juan José Millás is among the most popular and critically acclaimed authors writing in Spain today. Among other literary awards, he has won the prestigious Nadal Prize for *La soledad era esto* [**This Was Solitude**] (1990) and the Primavera Prize for *Dos mujeres en Praga* [**Two Women in Prague**] (2002). He is the author of more than thirteen novels, and seven collections of short stories and essays, and has been a regular contributor in the Spanish press. Among the principal themes of his fiction are the individual's alienation by contemporary society and his or her search for a more authentic existence; the exploration of the processes of constructing and representing personal identity; and the examination of the writer's attempt to represent reality through writing. This chapter addresses the self-conscious dimensions of Millás's fiction and how the author uses narrative self-consciousness as a strategy by which his protagonists and narrators are able either to articulate themselves or be articulated, and thereby come to terms with their various experiences of societal, familial, and existential estrangement. In the novels of Juan José Millás, narrative functions as a symbolic cartographic act by which his characters are able to find their points of reference and orient themselves within their geographical, spiritual, and personal territories.

Millás uses metafiction as a metaphor that represents the human struggle not only to make sense of the world, but also to form personal identity. Like Lucía, the protagonist of Rosa Montero's *La hija del caníbal,* Millás's characters see identity as a slippery, indeterminate thing. The protagonist of Millás's classic novel *El desorden de tu nombre* [**The Disorder of Your Name**] (1986), articulates the quintessence of Millás's conception of personal identity: "[P]arece absurdo que los hombres nos empeñemos en la búsqueda de un destino propio o de una identidad definida. Si de verdad tuviésemos identidad, no necesitaríamos tantos papeles (certificados, carnés, pasaportes, etcétera) para mostrarla" (126). [It seems absurd that we should insist on searching for a particular destiny or a definite identity. If we really had an identity, we wouldn't need so many papers (certificates, cards, passports, etcetera) in order to prove it.]

In his later story **"El pequeño cadáver de R. J.,"** [**The Little Corpse of R. J.**] which appears in the collection, *Primavera de luto y otros cuentos* [**Spring of Mourning and Other Tales**] (1992), the disgruntled narrator characterizes identity with similarly skeptical language:

> No comprendo la loca carrera de los hombres en busca de un destino personal que no existe o de una individualidad que, en el mejor de los casos, es un mero artificio incapaz de tapar la falta de sustancia que, como un agujero, nos traspasa. La propia identidad, y sus pobres distintivos, no pasa de ser, en mi opinión, una ingeniosa construcción verbal, útil para crear sociedades, establecer jerarquías y levantar así edificios, trazar autopistas o plantar semáforos.

> (12-13)

> [I don't understand the crazy efforts of people searching for a personal destiny that doesn't exist or for an individuality that, in even the best of cases, is nothing but an artifice incapable of covering the lack of substance that, like a hole, runs right through us. In my opinion, identity, along with all of its outward signs, is nothing more than an ingenious verbal construction useful for creating societies, establishing hierarchies and thus erecting buildings, sketching out highways and planting streetlights.]

For the characters that people Millás's world, identity is an ingenious verbal construction that hides existential emptiness. Yet, while his characters are often mystified by their ever-changing relationship to their surroundings, these same characters use narrative as the device through which they attempt to arrive at a sort of personal peace through their varying experiences of diegesis, either as authors, narrators, and organizers of the discourse or simply as narrative objects.

MILLÁS'S EARLY FICTION

Just a perfunctory look at a few of Millás's novels published in the 1970s and 1980s demonstrates the thematic and structural importance of narrative self-consciousness to his oeuvre. In these early works, the narrative process has redemptive powers for protagonists and narrators alike. *El desorden de tu nombre,* for example, concludes with the protagonist's realization that he is the protagonist of the novel we are reading. He is finally able to take comfort, not so much from his romantic success with Laura or his sessions of psychoanalysis, as from the thought that when he gets back to his apartment, this novel will be waiting for him on his table:

> Julio sonrió para sus adentros. Abrió el portal, entró en el ascensor, apretó el botón correspondiente, y entonces tuvo la absoluta seguridad de que cuando llegara al apartamento encontraría sobre su mesa de trabajo una novela manuscrita, completamente terminada, que llevaba por título *El desorden de tu nombre.*

> (1986, 172)

> [Julio smiled to himself. He opened the front door, entered the elevator, pressed the appropriate button, and then felt the absolute certainty that when he entered the apartment he would find on his desk the manuscript of a novel, completely finished, that carried the title *The Disorder of Your Name.*]

Whether or not Julio Orgaz is the author of his own novel remains unclear, but the notion that he might be the protagonist of a novel about himself gives him a sense of security. Being written about, it seems, gives him enough of a comforting sense of stability that he is able to give up his counseling (although, in an interesting twist, his psychologist, who happens to be Julio's lover, has in fact been murdered by his wife). While Julio is unable to write his own novel, he sees writing as the key to personal understanding and success: "[T]riunfar, tal vez, era escribir, era escribir. Era escribir un libro que articulara lo que sé y lo que ignoro" (Millás 1986, 57). [To triumph, perhaps, was to write, to write. It was to write a book that would articulate what I know and what I don't know.]

If the information that we have about ourselves, including our identity, takes the form of narrative, then the processes of collecting and representing personal identity will also coincide with the processes of writing. As Julio states from the outset, "La información que tenemos de nosotros mismos es tan parcial como la de un personaje de novela" (57). [The information that we have about ourselves is just as partial as that of a character in a novel.] Our privileged point of view about our own lives, he suggests, does not allow us any more information about ourselves than we might have about a character in a work of fiction. Thus, his efforts to write his own novel titled *El desorden de tu nombre* correspond to his desire to take control of his life and write some sense into it. Although he is at first unnerved by the uncomfortable coincidence between his own reality and the fictional world of his novel, it is only when he finally realizes that he is living a novel that he finds a resolution to his personal crisis: "Pero qué amor, qué amor el de Laura y el mío. Y qué novela" (172). [What a love, what a love Laura and I have. And what a novel.]

To look at one's life as if it were a novel is a reassuring way to deal with personal estrangement while putting order into the human experience. In most novels, after all, everything has a purpose; events happen for a reason; and there is an author who has created the world according to a plan. As Millás himself has stated in an interview: "[I]t is true that literature is a representation of reality, or a metaphor of reality, but literature and reality are autonomous territories, they have their own laws. In reality everything is contingent, while in literature everything is necessary" (Cabañas 1998, 106). Thus, whereas literature may pretend to represent reality, it differs in a fundamental way: in fiction, things happen for a reason, while in real life things do not necessarily follow any sort of order. If Julio can think of his life as a narrative, then maybe he can find some meaning in it, for he sees that there is a comforting degree of order in the literary text that is not replicated in nature.

An earlier, Borgesian metafictional novel is Millás's **Papel mojado** [**Wet Paper**] (1983). Fabián Gutiérrez has indicated that it is with this work that we begin to see "the appearance of writer protagonists" (1992, 37) in Millás's fiction. As in **El desorden de tu nombre,** the resolution of the novel's plot is achieved through the actual completion of the narration, at which point the "narrator" discovers that he is in fact the protagonist of the novel written by his dead friend, a novel that he had stolen from him upon his death.

Millás's next novel, **Letra muerta** [**Dead Letter**] (1984), documents the efforts of a narrator named Turis as he represents the process by which he comes to terms with his current position as a "resentido social" [misanthrope] who has been duped into joining the Catholic Church as a lay religious brother. Throughout part 1 of the novel, he reflects upon his experiences, writing what he resignedly considers the useless scribblings that give the novel its title (81). In part 2, however, he comes to understand his situation through the reading and writing of his diary, and finally realizes that the recuperation and reading of his "dead letter" has allowed him to find a progressive meaning or direction ("sentido progresivo") for his existence (95). Robert Baah has written that the novel suggests that "literary discourse can achieve sufficiency only when

it engages with reality" (1993, 17). In this way, reading and writing complement lived experience in the making of meaning: "[L]a lectura ordenada de estos cuadernos, que en ese sentido han funcionado a modo de sumario, fue alumbrando con cierta lentitud una serie de conclusiones a las que un hipotético lector, algo más inteligente y menos implicado que yo en estos sucesos, habría llegado con la sola lectura de la primera parte" (Millás 1984, 129). [The ordered reading of these notebooks, which in that respect have functioned as a kind of summary, highlighted a series of conclusions that a hypothetical reader, more intelligent and less implicated in these events than myself, probably would have figured out just by reading the first part.] Part 2 represents the novel's turning point, in which the resolution of the tension is linked to the act of writing. The narrator's uses of expressions such as "sentido progresivo" [progressive sense] and "lectura ordenada" [ordered reading] point to the power of narrative to give meaning and order to a personal reality that was previously only a series of "fluctuating emotional states." This understanding of self is provisional, however, and Turis is only able to say that he has arrived at "casi la categoría de la certidumbre" (129) [almost the category of certainty]. More satisfying, perhaps, is the fact that he is able to find an antidote for his existential malaise through the writing and rereading of his story. From the beginning, Millás's fiction has always linked writing and living. **Letra muerta** offers one of several examples of a narrator who comes to believe that what he has written can be more important than what he has lived, for narrative can give order to the chaos of life.

MAPPING THE SPACE OF SELF: *LA SOLEDAD ERA ESTO*

In Millás's fiction published during the 1990s and 2000s we can see a developing emphasis on narrative as a symbolic act. In particular, in his novels **La soledad era esto** (1990), **Volver a casa** [**Returning Home**] (1990), **Tonto, muerto, bastardo e invisible** [**Dumb, Dead, Bastard and Invisible**] (1995), and **Dos mujeres en Praga** (2002) narrative self-consciousness not only draws attention to the complex nature of representing reality, but also functions dramatically as an antidote for the protagonists' existential malaise and feelings of estrangement.[1] In the following sections, I analyze these four novels in terms of their strategic use of cartographic imagery, which is linked to a self-conscious emphasis on the dynamics of narrative creation.

Let me introduce my discussion of **La soledad era esto** with a brief mention of Graham Huggan's *Territorial Disputes* (1994). In it the author discusses the symbolic importance of maps in literature. Huggan indicates that maps are useful representations of the real world, precisely because they are "conceptual models containing the essence of some generalization about reality" (4). Futher, citing Christopher Board, Huggan points out that it is because they are conceptual models that "maps are useful analytical tools which help investigators to see the real world in a new light, or even to allow them an entirely new view of reality" (4).

Huggan addresses how maps "are frequently used as metaphors in literary texts, usually of structure (arrangement, containment) or of control (organization, coercion)" (24), although in twentieth-century fiction, as he emphasizes, the map "has often tended to function as a metaphor of the appearance of control rather than of its actual exercise" (25).

In *La soledad era esto,* narrative is a symbolic cartographic act through which Elena Rincón is able to chart her space of self and thereby achieve a comforting resolution to the crisis occasioned by the death of her mother. Like many of Millás's protagonists, Elena is estranged: she remains ignorant of her daughter's pregnancy and she is alienated from her increasingly distant husband, whom she suspects of having an affair. Having anonymously hired a private investigator to follow her philandering husband, she finds that her suspicions were true, but is uninterested finally in the investigator's findings. Instead, she employs the detective to follow *her,* again anonymously. Curiously, it is the private investigator's reports on her own activities that intrigue Elena, and finally, through her readings of his briefs—what amounts to a "novel" written about herself by a hired narrator—her mother's diaries, and her own diary writing, she is able to realize a positive sort of personal transformation or epiphany that parallels the novel's epigraph, which is taken from Kafka's *Metamorphosis.*

Much of Elena's anxiety comes from within; her sense of estrangement is in many respects self-induced and springs from a crisis of personal identity and familial estrangement. As she confesses in the second part of the novel, she sees identity as a precarious, indefinite thing:

> A veces pienso que la identidad es algo precario, que se puede caer de uno como el pelo que se desprende cuando nos lavamos la cabeza y desaparece por el sumidero de la bañera en direcciones que ignoramos. [...] Por eso me da miedo salir, por si no me reconocen al volver y me quedo sin identidad.

> (Millás 1990a, 154-55)

> [Sometimes I think that identity is something precarious that could fall off like the hair that comes out when you shampoo and that disappears down the drain of the bathtub to unknown places ... that is why I'm afraid to go out, just in case they don't recognize me when I return and I end up without an identity.]

Elena Rincón, much like Lucía Romero in Montero's *La hija del caníbal,* sees identity as something fragile that can dissolve unexpectedly. The solitude to which the novel's title alludes is the solitude that comes with Elena's sense of alienation and anomie, and her subsequent search for a personal, inner understanding as she undergoes her transformation. The novel's first part is narrated from a third-person, omniscient point of view. Elena has two roles in this part, as she is both protagonist and reader. Throughout the novel, she reads two texts: her mother's diary and the

reports about herself written by Enrique Acosta, the private investigator she has hired to follow her. Elena is the thematic link between all of the manuscripts that make up the novel: her mother's diaries, her own diaries, the investigator's reports, and the novel itself; all these texts are similar in that they are about her in some way.

Elena is not interested merely in being observed, although she does sometimes take comfort in knowing that her private detective is watching her, particularly after he intervenes to thwart a mugger. Because he is a narrator of her story, she attempts to maintain a distant relationship with him, although she misses him when he is absent (150). Acosta's reports interest Elena, and soon she undertakes to improve them, since she finds them lacking in subjective depth: "[H]ay en ellos una gran pulcritud sintáctica, pero son excesivamente contenidos, como si el investigador, que, no lo olvidemos, es el que narra, estuviera apresado en el interior de un corsé lleno de fórmulas y frases hechas de las que no pudiera desprenderse" (82). [They have a great syntactic neatness, but they are too contained, as if the investigator, whom, we should not forget, is the one who is narrating, were imprisoned inside a corset full of formulas and set phrases from which he could not free himself.] Throughout the novel, the investigator's reports are transcribed into the body of the novel's discourse. These reports are coupled with Elena's *literary* criticism of them, a common characteristic of contemporary metafiction, which seeks to break down "the distinctions between 'creation' and 'criticism' and merges them into the concepts of 'interpretation' and 'deconstruction'" (Waugh 1984, 6). Elena's directions to the investigator are narrative, not substantive, and have little to do with his actual investigation, for she is more interested in the story than in the actual inquiry. As the novel progresses, she comes to occupy three positions vis-à-vis the narrative: she is the object of the narrative, a critic of it, and a writing subject. As she reads the textual representation of herself, she attempts to understand herself better through a critical interpretation of it, and is able finally to take on the role of author.

Significantly, the reader discovers near the middle of the novel that the private investigator, Acosta, is not just a gumshoe, but also an aspiring writer. In compliance with Elena's wishes and obeying his own writerly inclinations, he abandons the objectivity of his previous investigations and allows himself to become more subjective in his reports. The reader can detect a gradual change in Elena as she begins to depend upon her "author," who, in the beginning, appears better able to articulate her than she can herself. Taking into account Elena's statement near the conclusion of the novel, we should view narrative as a symbolic cartographic act: "[L]o cierto es que el detective ha comenzado a funcionar como un punto de referencia del que difícilmente podría prescindir en este momento" (Millás, 1990a, 177-78). [The truth is that the detective has begun to function like a point of reference that I really couldn't do without at this moment.] The protagonist,

Elena, previously lacked concrete points of reference, and it is her detective/narrator who serves as a symbolic compass: his reports are a chart by which Elena is able to map herself.

Elena's personal transformation is linked to reading and writing. Her process of self-knowledge begins with her mother's diaries and the private investigator's reports on her own activities. Toward the end of the first part the narrator links this process to the Kafka work that gives the novel its epigraph:

> [P]ensó que durante los últimos años también ella había sido un raro insecto que, al contrario del de Kafka, comenzaba a recuperar su antigua imagen antes de morir, antes de que los otros le mataran. El pensamiento consiguió excitarla, pues intuyó que si conseguía regresar de esa metamorfosis las cosas serían diferentes.
>
> (99)

> [She thought that during the last couple of years she, too, had been a strange insect that, contrary to Kafka's, began to recuperate its old image before dying, before the others killed it. This thought excited her because she intuited that if she were able to reverse that metamorphosis things would be different.]

It is not coincidental that Elena turns to the world of literature for a symbol for her own transformation, for she is, first and foremost, a reader. What is significant about her choice of "The Metamorphosis" is that in Kafka's text, the narrator's physical transformation leads not only to a total alienation from his family and surroundings, but ultimately to his own death, locked in his bedroom. Elena's is an ironic reversal of this negative trajectory, and as the novel progresses, she sheds the psychological and physical symptoms of her alienation in order finally to reintegrate herself into the world. The novel ends not in darkness, but with the promising light of future possibilities pouring through her window.

The second part of *La soledad era esto* is narrated from the first-person point of view and marks a major turning point as Elena effectively takes control of her own story. Flush with the power to take active control of her own life narrative, she writes, "Me encuentro en el principio de algo que no sé definir, pero que se resume en la impresión de haber tomado las riendas de mi vida" (107). [I find myself at the beginning of something I don't know how to define, but that can be summarized as an impression of having taken the reins of my life.] Although her new efforts as narrator help her achieve self-realization, she continues to rely heavily on Enrique Acosta's briefs to fill in the blank spaces:

> Como al detective le he encargado ser muy subjetivo, dice cosas de mí que yo ignoraba y eso, además de divertirme mucho, me reconstruye un poco, me articula, me devuelve una imagen unitaria y sólida de mí misma, pues ahora veo que gran parte de mi desazón anterior provenía del hecho de percibirme como un ser fragmentado cuyos intereses estuvieran dispersos o colocados en lugares que no me concernían.
>
> (109)

> [As I've told the detective to be subjective, he now says things about me that I didn't know. This not only entertains me but also reconstructs me a bit, it articulates me, it gives me back a unified solid image of myself, and I see now that my previous anxiety came from the fact that I perceived myself as a fragmented being whose interests were dispersed or placed in locations that didn't concern me.]

Thus, being the object of the detective's narrative has the effect of reconstructing her self-image, of restoring the illusion of a unified solid identity.

Writing is the principal thematic and structural conceit of *La soledad era esto.* Elena's efforts as a writer not only constitute the second part of the text as she writes it into existence, but she is also aware that her body is a text that can be written and consequently understood. She comes to believe that, without her narrative, there would be no Elena Rincón: "Pese a la firmeza de mis propósitos, llevo varios días sin acudir a este diario y eso me proporciona la rara sensación de no existir" (115). [Despite the firmness of my resolve, it has been several days since I spent time on this diary, which gives me the strange sensation of not existing.] This explicit link between story and self links Millás's work with that of the other authors included in *True Lies.* Elena Rincón self-consciously acknowledges the narrative logic of personal identity, and her tale shows that "to be without stories means … to be without memories, which means something like being without a self" (Young and Saver 2001, 74).

Much like the narrator of *Letra muerta,* Elena depends on narrative to constitute her self. It is significant, then, that she uses cartographic terminology throughout the novel when she describes the act of writing: "[U]n diario de este tipo es una suerte de mapa esquemático en el que se relatan los aspectos más sobresalientes de la propia vida. Sin embargo, en mi imaginación, el diario es la vida misma" (Millás 1990a, 115). [A diary of this type is a kind of schematic map in which the most noteworthy aspects of life are related. Nevertheless, in my imagination, the diary is life itself.] Elena Rincón not only equates writing and living, but she imagines a somewhat paradoxical absolute equivalence of the two.

The impossibility of arriving at the perfect correspondence of map (diary) and territory (life or body) brings to mind Borges's tale "Del rigor en la ciencia" [The Rigor of Science], which allegorizes the absurdity of such an enterprise. Referring indirectly perhaps to Borges's story, Elena writes, "Alguna vez leí algo acerca de quienes confunden el territorio con la representación del territorio (el mapa); tal vez eso es lo que me sucede, tal vez por eso tengo la impresión de no haber existido los días pasados" (115). [At some point I read something about people who confuse the territory with the representation of the territory (the map); perhaps that is what is happening to me; maybe that's why I have the impression of not existing in past days.]

In his essay "A Misreading of Maps," Bruno Bosteels illustrates the importance of Borges to our contemporary understanding of the map as a symbol. Referring to Borges's "Del rigor en la ciencia" and "Magias parciales del *Quijote*" [Partial Magic of the *Quixote*], the author points out that "Whenever a map *is* the territory, cartography is useless or, in any case, without semiotic value as a sign" (1996, 121). The value of the map, in other words, is its ability to translate massive geography into readable signs that stand for real places. Cartography is useful precisely because it does not represent exactly the territory it purports to represent. What is notable about Borges's tale is that "the dream of total mimesis ... becomes a self-destructive nightmare" (Bosteels, 1996, 121). Elena never actually attempts a perfect representation of herself through writing, but narrative is important because, like a map, it represents "the embodiment of a middle ground through which human beings bestow meaning upon their material environment" (Bosteels 1996, 115-16). Quoting the semanticist Alfred Korzybski, Bosteels indicates that "The map is *not* the territory it represents, but, if correct, it has a *similar structure* to the territory, which accounts for its usefulness" (115, italics in original). Elena's story is not her life, but her diary/map is useful in that it allows her to navigate not only the exterior space of her surroundings, but also her own space of self.

In many of his tales, Borges emphasizes the absurdity of human attempts to represent and understand reality. In "Del rigor de la ciencia," the map represents paradigmatically this very human endeavor. In a valuable collection of essays, *The Nature of Maps* (1976), Arthur H. Robinson and Barbara Bartz Petchenik engage with the popularity and usefulness of maps in general. The authors indicate that historically maps have represented a comforting method of understanding the world that surrounds us:

> As we experience space, and construct representations of it, we know that it will be continuous. Everything is somewhere, and no matter what other characteristics objects share, they *always* share relative location, that is, spatiality; hence the desirability of equating knowledge with space [as in "mapping things out scientifically"], an intellectual space. This assures an organization and a basis for predictability, which are shared by absolutely everyone. This proposition appears to be so fundamental that apparently it is simply adopted a priori.

(4)

Maps give us predictive power in the physical world. In *La soledad era esto,* Elena looks to narrative as a map that will give her a continuous knowledge of her self and the space that she inhabits. In her mother's diary, the body is described as a geographical space, characterized either with the complications of continents or the solitude of islands (Millás 1990a, 118). Cartographic imagery constitutes the symbolic syllogism that is the novel: The body is a territory (and the territory is a body), and writing functions as a

map. But, although the narrator implies that narration is the key to the cartography of the body, she simultaneously draws attention to the limitations of this invention: "Esta ciudad es un cuerpo visible, pero la visibilidad no es necesariamente un atributo de lo real. Quizá no exista ni existamos nosotros" (130). [This city is a visible body, but visibility is not necessarily an attribute of the real. Perhaps it doesn't exist and we don't exist.] Elena, like Borges, understands that the map is not a perfect metaphor, and she recognizes that our understanding of the universe is provisional at best.

In an essay on the limitations of cartography entitled, "Cities without Maps," Iain Chambers writes that "the very idea of the map, with its implicit dependence upon the survey of a stable terrain, fixed referents and measurement, seems to contradict the palpable flux and fluidity of metropolitan life and cosmopolitan movement" (2000, 188). The map, in other words, serves to navigate the dynamic spaces of a city, but it cannot reflect the contradictions and complexity of a living, breathing metropolis—that is, its reality. A map cannot explain or contain the entire territory to which it corresponds. The map "permits us to grasp an outline, a shape, some sort of location, but not the contexts, cultures, histories, languages, experiences, desires and hopes that course through the urban body. The latter pierce the logic of topography and spill over the edges of the map" (188). The map is not a perfect metaphor for reality, but the limitations of cartography draw attention to the very issues that arise in the examination of literary texts: reality in its many forms is much too broad to be encompassed by a text. Reality will always spill over the edges of the map—or, in our case, the text—and tend to escape perfect representation. Elena quite obviously cannot map her subjectivity in its totality, but the symbol of the map still serves as a guide or outline by which she might trace the shape of her personal world.

Regardless of the limitations of representation, the appearance of control is still useful as a counterbalance to existential angst. As Robinson and Bartz Petchenik point out, although the map is not *the* territory, it is *a* territory, and consequently "it may be meaningful to employ a variety of transformations to retain particular relationships from one territory to the other. Reality and language must, therefore, *both* be converted into some kinds of spaces before one can be mapped on the other" (1976, 5-6, italics in original). Reality, in other words, must be distorted in order to be mapped. But the map is a territory with its own internal logic that serves to understand better that reality. Language, then, must also take into account the distortion inherent in the cartographic process. This is the dynamic with which Millás's narrators struggle.

In *La soledad era esto,* the implicit and explicit link between geographical terminology and the human body represents the text's point of symbolic cohesion: if, as her mother had written, the body is a geographical space, then perhaps what Elena has been lacking is a map by which to navigate that space; she lacks a map with points of reference. Like Julio in *El desorden de tu nombre,* Elena repeats that her life lacks concrete definition: "¿Qué tengo yo que certifique lo que he sido, lo que ahora soy, si soy algo?" (Millás 1990a, 127). [What do I have that verifies what I have been, what I am now, if I am anything?] The only thing she really has, she confesses, is the hashish that she is trying to quit; the clock and easy chair she inherited from her mother; and, most importantly, the diary in which she begins to chart the processes of her emotional and personal self-discovery. Near the conclusion of the work, Elena reaches a sort of epiphany and begins to answer the question that arises from the novel's title: "What is solitude, really?"

> [L]a soledad era esto: encontrarte de súbito en el mundo como si acabaras de llegar de otro planeta del que no sabes por qué has sido expulsada. [...] La soledad es una amputación no visible, pero tan eficaz como si te arrancaran la vista y el oído y así, aislada de todas las sensaciones exteriores, de todos los puntos de referencia, y sólo con el tacto y la memoria, tuvieras que reconstruir el mundo, el mundo que has de habitar y que te habita. ¿Qué había en esto de literario, qué había de divertido?
>
> (133-34)

> [Solitude was this: finding yourself in the world as if you had just arrived from another planet from which you had been expelled for unknown reasons. ... Solitude is an invisible amputation, but one that is as effective as if they were to take away your sight and hearing and thus, isolated from all exterior sensations, from all points of reference, and equipped only with your sense of touch and your memory, you would have to reconstruct your world, the world you would inhabit and that would inhabit you. What was so literary about that? What was fun about that?]

Solitude is suddenly finding oneself alone in the world, estranged and without points of reference. Symbolically blind and deaf, Elena must feel her way about by relying on her memory. Writing is the key to this process.

Her own diary helps Elena to map her identity, and the efforts of her private investigator help complete that identity. To be the object of an externally generated narrative allows her to feel more "real." His briefs, she finds, justify and certify her very existence, and give her the power to reconstruct her life:

> De estos informes, por banales que resulten, no puedo prescindir porque certifican mi existencia, pero también porque la seguridad de que alguien me mira me da fuerzas para moverme de un lado a otro en esta durísima tarea de construir mi propia vida. Nunca terminamos de hacernos; estos días tengo la impresión de estar frente a mí como un escultor frente a una roca de la que ha de eliminar todo cuanto no sea substancial.
>
> (163)

> [These reports, banal as they may be, are impossible for me to do without because they certify my existence, but

also because the security that someone is watching me gives me the power to work on this very difficult task of constructing my own life. We never finish making ourselves; these days I feel like I'm standing in front of myself like a sculptor in front of a rock from which she must eliminate everything but that which is essential.]

Jacques Lacan has written that the process of self-knowing is a constant and ever-changing struggle that can have no final conclusion. The novels of Millás dramatize the many different stages of this process and demonstrate that human identity is never perfectly complete. Just as Borges's map cannot encompass every aspect of the territory that it tries to represent, so is a definitive representation of the self impossible. If we take into account Lacan's idea that we cannot ever really *know* who we are, since the subject (our "self" or "I") is always undergoing the process of coming into being, then Millás's characters demonstrate that it is the struggle to know ourselves that characterizes us as humans. But in *La soledad era esto*— and elsewhere in Millás's work—writing and being written function not only as devices of self-exploration, but also as comforting methods of coping with the bleaker relativism of postmodern worldviews such as Lacan's, which view humans as transitory "beings" floating unmoored in a world of nothingness. To know oneself truly may be impossible, but Millás nonetheless points to the redemptive power of narrative.[2]

Javier Marías writes that Elena is a woman that "*wants to be narrated,* that is, she wants to be objectified and subjectified at the same time and become in a way a fictional character, as if only through that process or transformation could she know herself or, if you prefer, *recognize herself*" (1995, 45, italics in the original). It is this struggle to come to terms with a subjectivity in constant flux, to recognize and understand oneself by peering into the mirror of the text (a desire that is wrapped up in narration), to be written as both subject and object of a text (and perhaps even fictionalized) that represents the novel's main symbolic and dramatic driving force. Elena finally concludes that perhaps she will never be able to map precisely her space of self. But in the novel's final pages, she takes the impossibility of an absolute correspondence of map and territory, text and self, as a possibility for freedom and relief: "Ahora que no tengo coordenadas, que he perdido todos los puntos de referencia, la tarde del domingo me parece un lugar para el descanso" (Millás 1990a, 172), [Now that I don't have coordinates and have lost all my points of reference, Sunday afternoon seems like a nice place to rest.]

URBAN SPACES AND PERSONAL PLACES: *VOLVER A CASA*

Published in the same year, *Volver a casa* (1990) is similar to *La soledad era esto* in that its protagonist suddenly finds himself without any points of reference and therefore experiences an existential crisis. Juan Estrade is estranged from his spouse, life, and society at large. When his identical twin brother José, a famous novelist, disappears, Juan comes to Madrid from Barcelona to investigate. His return to his hometown after so many years leads him to question his life, his identity, and his place in the world. Like Elena in *La soledad era esto,* Juan's personal evolution can be traced through the novel's geographical language. Indeed, Juan sees identity as precarious and unstable, but the narrator expands on Elena's formulation, linking explicitly geographical space with personal space:

> Comparó la evolución de la ciudad en la que había vivido en otro tiempo con su propio territorio corporal y afectivo, y dedujo que las ciudades y los cuerpos poseían una identidad precaria, inestable, pues cuando alcanzaban el punto en el que parecían ser una cosa, un movimiento subterráneo los convertía en otra, aunque era una mutación tan sutil, tan insensible, que podía pasar inadvertida a una mirada perezosa.

> (Millás 1990b, 21-22)

> [He compared the evolution of the city in which he had lived in another time with his own corporal and affective territory, and decided that cities and bodies possessed a precarious, unstable identity, because just when they reached the point of seeming like one thing, a subterranean movement would change them into something else, although it was such a subtle mutation, so imperceptible, that it could escape a lazy glance.]

Juan's crisis of identity is compounded by the fact that, as young men, he and his brother swapped their identities along with everything that came with them: their professional pursuits, their mother's favor, and, in a particularly difficult twist, Juan's girlfriend, Laura.[3] As a result, Juan views the life that he made for himself later in Barcelona as a fake, but, after so many years, he is unable to acclimate himself fully to being back in Madrid. He is thus characterized as a piece of a puzzle that does not fit with the whole: "Y ahora estaba en la ciudad que debía haber sido suya y venía de ver a la mujer en quien su vida habría encontrado un complemento, pero también en este espacio funcionaba como una pieza que no acababa de encajar con precisión" (Millás 1990b, 39). [And now he was in the city that should have been his and he was returning from seeing the woman in whom his life would have found its complement, but also in this space he functioned like a piece that wouldn't fit with precision.]

Juan, like many Millás characters, lacks points of reference to navigate his physical space. As he steers his way through the spaces of his memory and personal geography, he fixes on his ex-girlfriend Laura, who has since married his brother, José. Laura becomes a possible point of reference: "[L]a figura de Laura constituía un elemento de referencia estable, como el horizonte para un marinero" (117). [The image of Laura constituted an element of stable reference, like the horizon for a sailor.] Romantic love is not the answer to Juan's problems, however. His problem is that he lacks "un espacio propio" (46) [a space of his own], for even after he and his brother have traded identities again, he still cannot find happiness. In this respect, the

novel is fundamentally different from *La soledad era esto,* since, unlike Elena, he is unable to find his "espacio propio" through narrative. While the novel that he purports to write is the novel that he is already living—a work entitled *Volver a casa*—he never sits down to write, preferring instead to revel in the fame and recognition that his twin brother has won for him by writing critically acclaimed novels in his name. The work ends ambiguously, although it appears as though Juan has (perhaps symbolically) committed suicide, taking the place of the wax figure of himself (or of his identical twin brother) in the suggestively named Museum of Desperation.

The question of unstable identities is reflected in the novel's structure. In particular, there is a metafictional frame break in the final chapter in which Millás himself appears in a televised roundtable discussion of Juan's publicity stunt. (After a final swap of identities, Juan had posed as José and had appeared at an interview wearing a mask, declaring that he planned to become a superhero-like "masked writer.") During the televised discussion, the fictional Millás inexplicably starts crying, and when another writer accuses *him* of attempting to steal some publicity, too, Millás punches him in the mouth. After a cut to a commercial, someone comes up with a theory that Juan Estrade and Millás are perhaps conspiring together (241). This play between the "real" author and his fictionally represented persona within the novel appears in recent novels by Javier Marías, Rosa Montero, and Javier Cercas, all of whom make a sustained use of this ambiguous interplay between an extradiegetic "reality" and the purely "fictional" world of the diegesis. This narrative trick functions superficially as a playful wink at the reader while introducing a deeper hermeneutic confusion that problematizes clear-cut distinctions between fact and fiction, reality and make-believe. It is perhaps not a coincidence that the two brothers of *Volver a casa,* Juan and José, each represent one-half of Millás's own given name: Juan José.

In *El desorden de tu nombre,* Julio derives a sense of existential satisfaction from the fact that he is the protagonist of a novel, while in *Letra muerta* Turis seeks through writing a way of understanding himself and his new, unfamiliar situation. We can see in Elena a combination of these two things, as she finds that both writing and being written offer a concrete, comforting counterbalance to her personal feelings of instability and dissatisfying experience of reality. In *Volver a casa,* however, the protagonist seems to be the object of a more cruel sort of authorial joke, as he is alternately the protagonist of his brother's sadistic game/novel and the unwilling object of Millás's own novel. In the end, "returning home" is not a nostalgic return to the comforts of childhood, but rather a vertiginous existential meditation on the indeterminate nature of personal identity.

TONTO, MUERTO, BASTARDO E INVISIBLE

In Millás's intriguingly odd novel, *Tonto, muerto, bastardo e invisible* (1995), the protagonist is bored with his situation in life. Having lost his job as the director of human resources at a paper manufacturing company, Jesús decides to construct for himself a new identity. He puts on a fake mustache, takes a new apartment, begins to frequent the local sex shop, and finally divorces his wife in order to run away—in a final flight into fiction—to Denmark with his favorite stripper, an Asian prostitute whom he calls Gretel to his Hansel. Jesús's nihilistic worldview is most probably the result of his numbingly banal life among the "social democrats," a term with pejorative connotations that he uses to describe the bourgeois drones who live and work in the contemporary Spanish workplace.[4] As he begins to construct (indeed, write) his own alternative reality, the narrator becomes more adept at seeing through the artifice and banality that surrounds him.

Having quit his job and taken on a new identity, Jesús is suddenly able to see through his surroundings and recognize the artificiality that characterizes the world of which he once formed a part. Jesús grows more dissatisfied with his surroundings, and in a search for his peculiar idea of authenticity he begins to inhabit the periphery of society, wandering the streets, frequenting sex shops, and visiting psychics. His new critical vision allows him to invert more traditional perceptions of the world, and he yearns to amputate himself from reality, since reality is nothing but another part of a body (Millás 1995, 93).

The language that Jesús uses to describe the process of reintegrating his identity is based upon the same kind of vocabulary that characterizes many of Millás novels: reality is fragmented and chaotic, and the novel represents his attempts to make sense of the chaos. His rambling, disorganized discourse reflects a crisis of his subjectivity: "[M]e parecía que la vida era un conjunto de fragmentos como los que forman los cristales de un vaso roto sobre el suelo, y esos pedazos han comenzado a aproximarse como cuando pasas la película de un desastre al revés, se encuentran los fragmentos, digo, y forman un sujeto que soy yo, un hombre articulado, una geografía definida de la que se puede levantar un mapa" (165). [It seemed to me that life was a pile of fragments like the shards from a broken glass on the floor, and that those pieces had begun to come together like when you watch a disaster movie backward: I'm saying that there are fragments, and that they form a subject that is I, an articulated man, a defined geography from which you can construct a map.] This is only one part of a sentence that spans an entire page. He continues to describe the reintegration of his fragmented self and the usefulness of the map metaphor: "[S]abemos dónde están colocados sus bordes y dónde termina el órgano y comienza la prótesis, porque ahora sé que mi identidad o mi personalidad, qué palabra, era una prótesis con la que intenté sustituir la función de la inteligencia" (165). [We know where the borders are and where the organ ends and where the prosthesis begins, because now I know that my identity or my personality—what a word—was a prosthesis with which I had tried to substitute the function of my

intelligence.] Thus, the idea of the map allows Jesús to identify the borders and limits that outline his self in a process that is linked to the intelligence that he previously squandered as an administrator of human resources at a paper factory. The physical paper is now linked to the subjective process of writing a personal narrative. Jesús continues on this theme in the same extended sentence, referring to "un papel en el que los otros escribían su vida porque tenían una novela de ella y sabían desde donde la debían contar y en qué persona, no yo" (165) [the paper on which the others wrote their life because they had a novel about it and they knew from where they had to tell it and in what person, not I].

Psychoanalytic theory is an ever-present subtext in Millás's fiction. In *Tonto, muerto, bastardo e invisible,* Jesús's psychological struggle exemplifies Lacan's formulation of the conflict between the ego's unachievable goal of a unified identity and the unconscious acknowledgment of the subject's own "fragmented body" (Lacan 1977, 4) to which I referred briefly in my discussion of *La soledad era esto.* Jesús is aware that any homogenous vision of himself (of his "I") will necessarily be a product of his imagination and his intelligence. Consequently, he describes identity in artificial terms as a prosthesis. Jesús's case is illustrative of the way in which Millás's protagonists are possessed of an extraordinary insight not only into their own psyches but also into the world that surrounds them. While these characters explore the processes and dynamics of their written texts, they simultaneously use those processes to examine the workings of their own consciousnesses.

Millás's novels tap into larger issues of the importance of narrative to our understanding of human consciousness. Jesús exemplifies how narrative infiltrates every aspect of our lived cognitive experience, and demonstrates how "conscious experience is not merely linked to the number and variety of personal stories we construct with each other within a cultural frame but is also consumed by them" (Fireman, McVay, and Flanagan 2003, 3). While narrative gives meaning to Jesús's conscious experience, that experience is simultaneously, like our own, consumed by narrative. Like the narrator of Nuria Amat's *Todos somos Kafka,* Jesús struggles to stave off the disintegration of his personality by engaging directly with the narratives that constitute his self. He recognizes a conflict between the fragmentation of his personality and a desire for unity, and finally decides that writing can help him to arrive at a cohesive, whole self: "Creo que comprendí de súbito que la escritura es un cuerpo lleno de órganos de todas las medidas, quizá por eso antiguamente los libros se encuadernaban en piel" (178). [I think I understood suddenly that writing is a body full of organs of all sizes; maybe that is why they used to bind books in leather.] Jesús decides to construct a new textual body, written on paper that, properly bound, would provide a space for the emergence "de una anatomía fisiológica o patológica, en fin, no sé, con la que identificarme" (178) [of a physiological or pathological anatomy with which, I don't know, I might identify myself].

Jesús begins writing himself on the Sunday that his crisis began (181), and as he continues to construct his narrative, he begins to realize that his words give order to his existence: "A medida que las palabras se ordenaban, formando un cuerpo que no había podido ni soñar que existiera, mi existencia iba adquiriendo un orden insospechado y funcional" (181-82). [As the words ordered themselves, forming a body that I could never have dreamed to exist, my existence began to acquire an unsuspected functional order.] Each narrative fragment that he transcribes functions as a part of an organic, living, whole: "[L]a escritura era un cuerpo complejo" (82). [Writing was a complex body.] For Jesús, narrative is the only route to authenticity. But, like the protagonist of Amat's *Todos somos Kafka,* he eventually loses touch with reality, and his sense of self finally loses its coherence. The fictions he has created begin to wash away his previous identity, and an invented persona supplants his real persona: "[Y]o dejé de ser Jesús y me transformé en Olegario, un héroe de novela" (193). [I stopped being Jesús and I became Olegario, a novelistic hero.]

Only by first narrating and then reading himself is Jesús able to understand both his actions and his personality, and although from our perspective he is still a borderline case, he is nevertheless able to make conclusions based upon his written self, conclusions that only reinforce his earlier suspicions that his previous life as a cog in the capitalistic "social democrat" machine was an inauthentic and soul-deadening one. His new identity may be artificially generated, but it is authentic in that it provides him with a very real alternative to a more profoundly false, negative existence in the bureaucratic, capitalistic world of contemporary Madrid. Paradoxically, it is through his flights of fantasy and role-playing that Jesús attempts to infuse his life with "un poco de realidad" (197). [a little reality]. What Jesús needed, he realizes finally, was a story: "La gente como yo necesitaba amuletos, pócimas, cuentos en general, para abrirse camino en la vida, y para comprenderla" (202). [People like me needed amulets, concoctions, stories in general, to find our paths in life and to be able to understand it.]

LOST IN MADRID WITHOUT A MAP: *DOS MUJERES EN PRAGA*

In an article published in *El País,* Juan José Millás writes that the story of the Tower of Babel continues to have an important symbolic value in the contemporary world. He posits that the destruction of the tower was a watershed event in the story of humanity: "[I]t was an instant in which our reality was broken into a thousand pieces, like a porcelain vase, and thus began the history of the fragment . . . before the construction of that damned tower, nature had the coherence of a literary tale" (Millás 2002b). Millás offers that it was when the Tower of Babel fell that

human beings lost their ability to comprehend reality or themselves.

The fundamentally unknowable nature of the universe and our fragmented experience of reality is a common theme in much of Millás's fiction. In this section, I will analyze his novel *Dos mujeres en Praga* in terms of its dramatization of the narrative process, and how the novel itself—through a self-conscious insistence upon its own coming into being—represents metaphorically the relationship between fiction and reality. Before the Tower of Babel, nature may have had the coherence of a literary work, and *Dos mujeres en Praga* attempts to answer the question of how we might restore some semblance of order to our perception of reality.

Like many of Millás's protagonists, the characters of *Dos mujeres en Praga* all suffer from various degrees of estrangement and find themselves searching for points of reference. Álvaro Abril, for example, has effectively prostituted himself professionally; having written a critically acclaimed novel, he has resigned himself to selling his services as a writer for hire. His intriguing customer Luz is apparently a prostitute herself, and is either a pathological liar or a born novelist. Her quirky new friend María José, (despite her stubborn insistence on learning to write a "left-handed" novel) seems to be—along with the unnamed narrator—one of the most emotionally stable characters of the work. Álvaro and Luz suffer from a more generalized anxiety that they do not really belong anywhere. As Álvaro states on the third page, "Yo no estoy seguro de que las cosas sucedan unas detrás de otras. Con frecuencia suceden antes las que en el orden cronológico aparecen después" (Millás 2002a, 9). [I'm not sure that things happen one after the other. Often things that were supposed to happen first chronologically happen later.] The novel traces the process by which each of these characters finds personal meaning in the narrative act, and it is the act of narration that holds the novel and its characters together.

In *Dos mujeres en Praga,* the metafictional process of constructing the narrative not only brings all the novel's characters together in the first place, but also allows each one to come to terms with his or her own experiences of reality. Like Elena in *La soledad era esto,* Luz Acaso wants to be narrated. Luz visits Álvaro Abril's office at Talleres Literarios, a biography-for-a-fee firm. Through his efforts to put Luz's story to paper, Álvaro discovers important clues about his own possible origins and personal identity. Similarly, through *his* narration of these personal narratives (Luz's and Álvaro's) the narrator is able finally to order his own life. In the final paragraph of the novel, he acknowledges explicitly the importance of the narrative act in creating order:

> Era evidente que para llevar a cabo ese reparto no hacía falta un albacea, pero sí un narrador, un narrador que al contar los últimos días de Luz Acaso tuviera, sin comprender por qué, la impresión de ordenar su propia vida.

(230)

[It was evident that in order to accomplish the execution of the will, they didn't need an executor but rather a narrator, a narrator who, upon relating the final days of Luz Acaso, would have, without knowing why, the impression of ordering his own life.]

In stark contrast to these lost characters is the concrete geographical orientation of the world they inhabit. The reader becomes quickly aware that Millás has gone to great lengths to establish a very specific geographical setting for *Dos mujeres en Praga,* as the narrator carefully and continuously mentions specific geographic areas and locales, beginning in the first chapter. Four pages into the novel, for example, he situates Álvaro's office with noteworthy geographic specificity:

> La sede de Talleres Literarios estaba situada al fondo de un callejón de chalets antiguos que arrancaba en Alfonso XIII, cerca de López de Hoyos, e iba a morir violentamente contra el parapeto metálico de un ramal de la M-30. A la entrada del callejón, llamado Francisco Expósito, había una señal de tráfico con el símbolo de calle cortada.
>
> (11)

> [The head office of Literary Workshops was situated at the end of a small street of older houses that began on Alfonso XIII, near López de Hoyos, and died violently against the metallic parapet of a branch of the M-30. At the entrance of the alley, called Francisco Expósito, there was a traffic sign that indicated that the street was closed.]

As in most of Millás's works, the novel takes place in northeast Madrid in the neighborhood known as "Prosperidad." The narrator later points out that Literary Workshops is located approximately four blocks east of the Parque de Berlín, where the protagonist of Millás's *El desorden de tu nombre* most often met his lover. The reader is told that Luz lives just south of the Parque de Berlín, which is near the Chamartín train station behind the Auditorio Nacional on Príncipe de Vergara. Álvaro lives on Corazón de María, which runs perpendicular to López de Hoyos, very near Luz's house. The narrator himself mentions that he lives on Calle Alcalá, near the Plaza de Manuel Becerra, not far south from where Luz and Álvaro live. His supposed twin lives even further south, near the intersection of Doctor Esquerdo and Pez Volador, just east of the Retiro park and Atocha.

But, although the text is very exact in its description of physical settings, the novel's characters wander through their environment lost without points of reference. For some characters, this disjunction between real and imaginary space is voluntary: María José provides the title of the novel, assigning the name "Praga" to Luz's home in Madrid. While her choice of Prague is in keeping with the geographic imagery of the novel, it represents for her an invented "espacio físico singular" (22) [a singular physical space] where she might write her left-handed novel. Similarly, she is obsessed with the idea of lumbago precisely because of its geographic sonority. "[S]uena como el nombre de una geografía mítica" (18) [It sounds like the name

of a mythical geography], she says during her first visit to Luz's flat.

Dos mujeres [***Dos mujeres en Praga***] demonstrates a more skeptical approach to the representation of reality than we see in many other novels by Millás. The novel's structure and themes serve to create a hermeneutic confusion, which is introduced thematically by Luz's frequent falsifications of her life's story. Structurally, the unreliable nature of representation comes to the fore most emphatically through the narrator's sly manipulations of point of view. In chapter 3, for example, Álvaro goes to a party where, quite unexpectedly for the reader, he meets the previously invisible narrator of the novel. Up to this point, the novel is narrated in the third person, but suddenly, while the narrator describes Álvaro's entrance and his awkward wanderings as he searches for someone with whom to interact, the narrator slips for the first time into the first-person singular to say that Álvaro's boss "hablaba conmigo" (28) [was talking with me]. The effects of this ingenious device are disconcerting, since it undermines the normal conventions of the third-person discourse, forcing the reader to reexamine his or her suspension of disbelief. The sudden appearance of a first-person narrator this far into the novel serves as a warning to the reader, who so far has taken for granted the narrative point of view and everything for which it traditionally stands: objectivity, truth, and neutrality. It is here that the reader is forced to realize that things are definitely not what they seem in the novel, and significantly, we learn soon thereafter that Luz's story has probably been invented in its entirety.

The narrator's surprise appearance in this chapter also has important ramifications for the plot, since it raises thematic questions about how the narrator can possibly describe so clearly and with so much detail events that he has not witnessed. For example, when their conversation at the cocktail party has concluded, the reader is hard-pressed to discern how the narrator is able to describe so closely Álvaro's feelings at the time that he experiences them. At the party, for example, the narrator describes in detail his movements and thoughts for the remainder of his short visit (31).

A similarly surprising shift of narrative voice appears in chapter 5, while Luz Acaso sits in her car, waiting for her appointment with Álvaro. As she listens to the radio—an activity described with what can only be characterized as an omniscient sort of third-person point of view—the narrator suddenly inserts himself into the discourse, using the first-person form of the preterit:

> Al día siguiente, Luz Acaso llegó a Talleres Literarios a las doce menos diez y se quedó dentro del coche, escuchando la radio, para hacer tiempo hasta las doce. El programa de la radio trataba sobre la adopción y me habían invitado para que contara algún caso. Hablé de madres que entregaron a sus hijos en adopción al nacer y que después de muchos años decidieron buscarlos para verles el rostro. También conté [otras] historias.
>
> (47)

[The next day, Luz Acaso arrived to Literary Workshops at ten minutes to twelve and stayed in her car, listening to the radio to kill time until noon. The radio program was about adoption and they had invited me to talk about a case. I spoke about mothers who had given up their infant children for adoption and that had later decided to seek them out in order to see their faces. I also told other stories.]

In a further twist, Luz later uses this information (which she has heard on the radio from the narrator of the novel) in order to turn it into an invented story of her life for Álvaro to write into her biography. This invention in turn makes Álvaro begin to suspect that she may be his birth mother. Much of the novel's narrative tension is derived from a carefully structured discourse that teases the reader with a movement back and forth between the narrator's statements about things he could not possibly have seen and the resolution of the confusion in the following chapter.

The plot of *Dos mujeres* deals almost exclusively with the various characters' attempts to reach some final result: the narrator writes his novel, Álvaro writes his biography of Luz, María José tries to get perspective on her novel on the so-called lumbago or "l'um bago." The novel, then, is composed of the various processes of these various narrative works in different stages of coming into being, as all these characters strive to make sense of the disparate experiences that make up their lives. The work's interest lies in that all these characters are interconnected not only socially or thematically, but also structurally, so that when their stories are woven together they become a novel themselves. The narrator, therefore, functions as a compiler who orders all the information he has received from his various sources.

María José offers the most dubious material, and her story represents perhaps the greatest interpretive challenge. The narrator confesses that it was not easy for him to distinguish between truth and fiction:

[N]o me fue fácil distinguir lo verdadero de lo falso. Tampoco supe si en su cabeza estas categorías permanecían separadas. Procuré, a la hora de seleccionar unos hechos y desestimar otros, aplicar el sentido común—mi sentido común—, lo que quizá significa que este relato es la suma de dos invenciones (de tres, si contamos el material aportado por Álvaro). Lo interesante es que todos los materiales, pese a su procedencia, siempre fueron compatibles.

(105)

[It was not easy for me to distinguish the real from the false. Nor was I sure whether she viewed those categories as separate. I tried, at the time of selecting certain happenings and leaving others out, to apply common sense—my common sense—which perhaps means that this tale is the sum of two inventions (of three, if we count the material provided by Álvaro). What is interesting is that all these materials, in spite of where they came from, were always compatible.]

In many ways, the narrator's position vis-à-vis his subject mirrors the reader's position facing the novel itself. It is nearly impossible to distinguish convincingly between fact and fiction, because both enjoy an equal status within the various texts that constitute the novel.

Millás's protagonists are searchers who strive to put together the fragmented pieces of their world, and it is only through narration that they are sometimes able to do so. While life is imperfect, literature has an internal logic, and for Millás's protagonists, the written text represents a reassuring metaphor for the universe. In the absence of order in the world, at the very least they may find comfort in the comprehensible nature of the creation of literary works.

As the narrator wonders, "Quizá la red sobre la que se sostiene la realidad es pura retórica. La realidad no necesita sostenerse sobre ninguna red: ella es la red. Pero nosotros sí que necesitamos la invención. Necesitamos creer que las cosas suceden unas detrás de otras y que las primeras son causa de las segundas" (116). [Perhaps the web upon which reality rests is purely rhetorical. Reality doesn't need to rest on any web: it is the web. But we do need invention. We need to believe that things happen one after another and that the first ones cause those that come later.] Significantly, this statement comes near the center of the novel's 230 pages. The centrality of its placement reflects its importance in understanding the novel, since this is what *Dos mujeres* is about: reality, the narrator pronounces, is what we make it. In order to make sense of the world that surrounds us, we need to believe that things happen in an ordered fashion. But the narrator, like his postmodern readers, recognizes that the order we put to our experience of reality is an arbitrary creation of illusion; it is a comforting metaphor that hides the sometimes disconcerting absence of an authoritative master narrative. It is only in the creation of these narrative illusions that the narrator seems to take solace and even find pleasure. The universe may be, as Borges famously wrote, an "infinito juego de azares" (Borges 1956, 75), [an infinite game of chance], but in the world of *Dos mujeres,* we can still enjoy the creation of our life's illusions and take consolation in the writing.

The narrator points out that "la vida está llena de novelas" (Millás 2002a, 144). [life is full of novels]. If indeed life is like a novel, then perhaps we can understand reality by using the same tools we use to interpret fiction. The novel itself, with its constant self-reflexivity, seems to embody this idea. The novel cries out that it is fiction, but it also tells us that fiction is just like reality, and reality is just like fiction. And fiction is important to our experience of everyday reality. As Álvaro says in his humorous letter to his mother, written at the request of his editor, "Los libros justifican mi existencia del mismo modo que a mí me habría gustado ser la justificación de la tuya. Todo es escritura, como verás" (193). [Books justify my existence in the same way that I would have liked to have been the

justification of yours. Everything is narrative, as you will
see.]

After reading Alvaro's letter to his mother, the narrator is
surprised by the mixture of reality and fiction that it offers,
but he comes to an important realization after its reading.
As we can see also in the recent novels of authors such as
Javier Marías, Javier Cercas, and Rosa Montero, the narrator of **Dos mujeres** realizes that all writing involves a
mixing of reality and fiction:

> Comprendí que toda escritura es una mezcla diabólica de
> las dos cosas, con independencia de la etiqueta que figure
> en el encabezamiento. La materia de mis reportajes era tan
> ficticia como la de la *carta a la madre* de Álvaro, o la de la
> carta a la madre era tan real como la de mis reportajes. Se
> podía decir de las dos formas porque todo era mentira y
> verdad al mismo tiempo. Todo es mentira y verdad de
> forma simultánea, Dios mío.
>
> (209-10)

> [I understood that all writing is a diabolical mix of the two
> things, regardless of the label that appeared in the heading.
> The material of my reports was just as fictitious as the
> *letter to his mother* that Álvaro wrote, or his letter to his
> mother was just as true as one of my reports. You could
> say it both ways because everything was lies and truth at
> the same time. Everything is lies and truth simultaneously.
> My God.]

As we see in many contemporary works of Spanish metafiction, the narrator explicitly draws attention to his task,
which is comprised mainly of weaving these varied stories
into one coherent whole. These various ends that he attempts to tie together often seem too coincidental, as he
remembers, there is a "red de coincidencias sobre la que se
sostiene la realidad y que a veces, por causas que desco-
nocemos, se queda al descubierto, como los árboles cuando
se retira la niebla" (115) [web of coincidences upon which
reality relies and that sometimes, for causes that we will
never know, is suddenly discovered, like trees when the
mist recedes]. Nevertheless, he is always forthright about
the indeterminacy of his sources and the admittedly subjective and individual method that he uses to tie them together. After all, he uses his own common sense to put
together the narrative pieces of the novel, and therefore
his story is perhaps doubly unreliable. The question that
he poses to himself might just as well be directed to the
reader: "¿Cómo saber la verdad?" (104). [How to know the
truth?] The truth, he seems to suggest, is only as good as
the words that we use to represent it.

But just because everything contains simultaneously a
mixture of fiction and truth does not mean that we must
despair at the lack of certainty and absolutes in the world.
In the novels of Juan José Millás, what makes life bearable
are the stories we tell about ourselves, the stories in which
we play a part, the stories that make us who we are. In a
universe perhaps devoid of existential certainty, we can
still seek comfort in storytelling. Literature, after all, im-

poses the "imaginative order of its conventions on the
disorder of life" (Pike 1981, 137). For the narrators and
protagonists that people Millás's fictional world, metafiction is the map that leads them to understand not only the
trappings of artistic representation, but also themselves
and their relation to the world they inhabit. As Álvaro
tells Luz during their first meeting, "[L]a vida, de ser
algo, es eso: un relato, un cuento que siempre merece la
pena ser contado" (Millás 2002a, 9). [Life, if it is anything,
is that: a story, a tale that is always worth telling.]

The disjuncture between physical and emotional space
provides the novel's principal dramatic tension. As the
novel progresses, it becomes clear that only the narrative
act will offer the characters a meaningful point of reference
from which to make sense of their surroundings and their
place in the world. Life, Álvaro asserts, is like a novel, but
it is up to us to organize the events and assign them significance. The only thing one has to do is "tomarlo y orde-
narlo" (35) [take it and give it order].

Notes

I owe the title of the "Mapping the Space" section to
Matthew J. Marr, whose essay, "Mapping the Space of
Self: Cartography and the Narrative Act in Esther Tusquets's *El mismo mar de todos los veranos*," analyzes
how a narrator who "resides in a space of uncertainty
and alienation" (2004, 228) seeks through writing a way
"to define spatially ... the here-and-now of her own condition, the geography of the self" (218). Marr argues that
Tusquets's novel "presents a protagonist who, despite her
much-studied predisposition to process reality through the
illusory filter of myth and literary fantasy ... emerges
periodically in a conscious struggle to chart and comprehend the 'geography' of the external world, the space
within whose chaotic flux she finds herself immersed"
(218). He persuasively concludes that the text therefore
represents a kind of "cognitive map" (a term borrowed
from Fredric Jameson), by which the implied author is
"able to lay claim to a more cogent glimpse into the intricacies of her authentic reality" (229). These are very much
the same dynamics that come into play in Millás's fiction,
especially in *La soledad era esto*.

1. Millás's *El orden alfabético* [Alphabetical Order]
   (1998) and *No mires debajo de la cama* [Don't
   Look under the Bed] (1999) are also metafictional
   novels. The former, for example, is a sort of metafictional fantasy in which the letters of the alphabet
   progressively disappear, causing havoc in the world.
   The novel cleverly describes a fantastic reality that
   begins to unravel as the linguistic symbols used to
   describe it disappear. As the signifiers disappear, the
   world becomes a chaotic, shapeless mass. The novel
   is narrated from the point of view of a young boy
   who, we find out in the second part, is in fact insane.
   The latter novel deals with Elena Rincón, a judge

living in Madrid, who falls in love with a woman she sees on the metro who is reading a novel called *No mires debajo de la cama.* The novel's discourse is split; on the one hand, we have Elena's experience and that of her beloved Teresa; on the other hand, interspersed throughout the novel are chapters taken from the fictional novel of the same name, which is narrated from the point of view of people's shoes.

2. In an interview with Gutiérrez Flórez, Millás mentions the fundamental importance of writing in constructing personal identity, and how his own writing is a personal necessity: "I keep writing in order to keep constructing myself" (Gutiérrez Flórez 1992, 10).

3. Thomas Franz discusses in greater detail the theme of the double in Millás, noting that the novelist resembles Unamuno in his exploration of how personal identity is linked to a literary act (1996, 131). Franz concentrates his study on the theme of the double in Unamuno's *Niebla, Abel Sánchez,* and *El otro* and compares them to Millás's own treatment of the theme in *Volver a casa* (1990). According to Franz, the main difference between Millás and Unamuno is that in Millás the metaphysical component of the protagonists' struggles has disappeared, although the characters of his novels continue to search for the answers to important questions: "[W]hat we have in *Volver a casa* is a strong evocation of certain Unamunian premises that are explored fully in their epistemological frame, but definitively secularized insofar as their refusal to explore the metaphysical dimension" (1996, 140).

4. Dale Knickerbocker points out that *Tonto, muerto, bastardo e invisible* has a dual structure, based upon the protagonist's alienation from his surroundings and upon an acute social criticism of Spanish society in the early nineties: "[T]his work constitutes a convincing commentary on the insuperable situation of the individual in a society that is more and more inhumane and dehumanizing" (1997, 230).

References

Amat, Nuria. 1993. *Todos somos Kafka.* Madrid: Muchnik.

Baah, Robert. 1993. "Ficción, historia y autoridad: Juan José Millás y el narrador inconstante en *Letra muerta.*" *Mester* 22, no. 1:9-18.

Borges, Jorge Luis. 1956. *Ficciones.* Buenos Aires: Emecé Editores.

Bosteels, Bruno. 1996. "A Misreading of Maps: The Politics of Cartography in Marxism and Poststructuralism." In *Signs of Change: Premodern, Modern, Postmodern,* edited by S. Barker, 109-38. Albany: SUNY Press.

Cabañas, Pilar. 1998. "Materiales gaseosos: Entrevista con Juan José Millás." *Cuadernos Hispanoamericanos* 580:03-20.

Chambers, Iain. 2004. "Cities without Maps." In *From Space to Place and Back Again: Reflections on the Condition of Postmodernity,* edited by J. Bird, 188-98. London: Routledge.

Fireman, Gary D., Ted E. McVay Jr., and Owen J. Flanagan. 2003. Introduction to *Narrative and Consciousness: Literature, Psychology, and the Brain,* 3-13. Oxford: Oxford University Press.

Franz, Thomas R. "Envidia y existencia en Millás y Unamuno." *Revista Canadiense de Estudios Hispánicos* 21, no. 1:131-42.

Gutiérrez Flórez, Fabián. 1992. *Cómo leer a Juan José Millás.* Madrid: Ediciones Júcar.

Huggan, Graham. 1994. *Territorial Disputes: Maps and Mapping Strategies in Contemporary Canadian and Australian Fiction.* Toronto: University of Toronto Press.

Knickerbocker, Dale F. 1997. "Búsqueda del ser auténtico y crítica social en *Tonto, muerto, bastardo e invisible.*" *Anales de la Literatura Española Contemporánea* 22, no. 2:195-96, 211-33.

Lacan, Jacques. 1977. "The Mirror Stage as Formative of the Function of the I as Revealed in Psychoanalytic Experience." In *Écrits,* 1-7. New York: W. W. Norton.

Marías, Javier. 1995. "La huella del animal." *Vuelta* 19, no. 220:43-5.

Marr, Matthew J. 2004. "Mapping the Space of Self: Cartography and the Narrative Act in Esther Tusquets's *El mismo mar de todos los veranos.*" *Anales de la Literatura Española Contemporánea* 29, no. 1:217-33.

Millás, Juan José. 1984. *Letra muerta.* Madrid: Alfaguara.

———. 1986. *El desorden de tu nombre.* Madrid: Ediciones Alfaguara.

———. 1990a. *La soledad era esto.* Barcelona: Ediciones Destino.

———. 1990b. *Volver a casa.* Barcelona: Destino.

———. 1992. *Primavera de luto y otros cuentos.* Barcelona: Ediciones Destino.

———. 1995. *Tonto, muerto, bastardo e invisible.* Madrid: Alfaguara.

———. 2002a. *Dos mujeres en Praga.* Madrid: Espasa Calpe.

———. 2002b. "La extraña pareja: Una mente única." *El País Digital,* August 28. http://elpais.es/.

Montero, Rosa. 1997. *La hija del caníbal.* Madrid: Espasa Calpe.

Pike, Burton. 1981. *The Image of the City in Modern Literature.* Princeton, NJ: Princeton University Press.

Robinson, Arthur H., and Barbara Bartz Petchenik. 1976. *The Nature of Maps: Essays toward Understanding Maps and Mapping.* Chicago, IL: University of Chicago Press.

Waugh, Patricia. 1984. *Metafiction: The Theory and Practice of Self-Conscious Fiction.* London: Methuen.

Young, Kay, and Jeffrey L. Saver. 2001. "The Neurology of Narrative." *SubStance* 94-95:72-84.

Samuel Amago (essay date 2007)

SOURCE: Amago, Samuel. "Can Anyone Rock like We Do? Or, How the Gen X Aesthetic Transcends the Age of the Writer." *Generation X Rocks: Contemporary Peninsular Fiction, Film, and Rock Culture.* Ed. Christine Henseler and Randolph D. Pope. Nashville: Vanderbilt UP, 2007. 59-77. Print.

[*In the following essay, Amago identifies thematic connections between* That Was Loneliness *and works by younger Spanish Generation X authors. He points out that, like many Generation-X slacker characters, Millás's Elena is alienated, abuses drugs and alcohol, tries to understand reality through writing, and attempts to construct a more authentic identity for herself.*]

Criticism of the emerging canon of Generation X writers has emphasized the importance of a sex, drugs and rock and roll aesthetic linked to Anglo-American popular culture. What has tended to elude study is the prevalence of controlled substances in works by previous generations of Spanish novelists. Indeed, some of the foundational works of the post-Franco period are steeped in their own drug culture. Juan Goytisolo's *La reivindicación del Conde don Julián* (1970), for example, cannot be understood fully without a consideration of the importance of hashish to the narrator's ever-deteriorating mental state, while in Carmen Martín Gaite's *El cuarto de atrás* (1978), the hallucinogenic pills that C. ingests with the Man in Black play an important structural role. These novels' adversarial critical stances vis-à-vis some of the most ingrained commonplaces of Spanish cultural history make them fine models for the Gen X project of the 1990s, which on both sides of the Atlantic has taken an iconoclastic approach to cultural tradition.

Inspired in part by Robert Spires's recent article, "Depolarization and the New Spanish Fiction at the Millennium," in which the author problematizes generational shibboleths, this essay investigates how the Generation X aesthetic that came to the fore in the early 1990s might be profitably expanded to include work by writers born in the 1940s and 1950s. In the following pages, I explore some of the points of contact between younger Gen X writers and the more "mature" (Gracia 238) generation of Spanish writers that continues to write and publish alongside them—authors such as Nuria Amat (b. 1950), Carlos Cañeque (b. 1957), Juan Madrid (b. 1947), Eduardo Mendoza (b. 1943), Juan José Millás (b. 1947), Antonio Muñoz Molina (b. 1956), and Manuel Rivas (b. 1957). From this admittedly broad and varied range of writers—all of whom have drawn in one way or another upon some of the styles and themes that we now associate with Gen X literature—I focus here on Juan José Millás and Carlos Cañeque because of the critical acknowledgment that they received in the 1990s both in the form of the Premio Nadal—a prize that served to legitimize at least two Gen X authors—and that they continue to receive in the pages of academic journals and scholarly monographs.

Juan José Millás is routinely recognized as one of the most popular and critically acclaimed authors writing in Spain today, sharing his position on the bestseller lists with younger writers such as Lucía Etxebarria, Ray Loriga, and José Ángel Mañas. Among other literary awards, he won the Nadal prize for *La soledad era esto* in 1990, and the Premio Primavera for *Dos mujeres en Praga* (2002). He is the author of more than thirteen novels, seven collections of short stories and essays, and he has been a regular contributor in the Spanish press. Carlos Cañeque has not enjoyed the same kind of success as some of his contemporaries, although he has recently begun to receive deserved critical attention for his first novel, *Quién* (Premio Nadal 1997) (Amago; Kunz). Cañeque has since published two other novels with major Spanish publishing houses, *Muertos de amor* (1999) and *Conductas desviadas* (2002); two books of nonfiction: *Dios en América* (1988) and *Conversaciones sobre Borges* (1995); and two books about Borges for children, *El pequeño Borges imagina el Quijote* (2003) and *El pequeño Borges imagina la Biblia* (2002); and several co-edited scholarly volumes.

Taking as my point of departure these two Premio Nadal-winning novels of the 1990s, Millás's *La soledad era esto* (1990) and Cañeque's *Quién* (1997), I argue that the aesthetic that we have come to associate with Gen X is not entirely unique to younger authors such as Mañas, Etxebarria, and Loriga, but rather, that this aesthetic transcends the chronological paradigm of the literary generation and brings together a wide group of writers of varying ages who published novels in the 1990s. Like the Gen X writers with whom they share the pages of literary supplements and academic journals, older authors like Millás and Cañeque draw upon sex, drugs, rock and roll, and literary criticism as methods not only to reexamine our contemporary experience of reality but also to propose new ways of representing it through the use of self-conscious narrative strategies, a critical examination of "canonical" texts, the fusion of popular and literary cultures, and the exploitation of a 1990s poetics of disaffection that functions as a critical response to economic, social and political discontent.

While my purpose here is not to define the Generation X aesthetic or to explain its provenance—critics such as Toni Dorca, Christine Henseler, Jason Klodt, and María Pao have made important contributions on this theme already in the Peninsular context—I should like to offer a brief synthesis of some of the themes and forms that have come to be associated with Gen X fiction in order to analyze later the work of Millás and Cañeque within the larger literary context of the 1990s. In addition to the sex, drugs, and rock and roll paradigm I mention above, Gen X narrative is typified by some of the following themes: a sometimes nihilistic stance of resistance to dominant cultures; marginalization and estrangement, either self-imposed or imposed by society; inability or unwillingness to engage in meaningful social intercourse with partners and/or peers; vitriolic antiestablishment attitude, often in terms of a perceived or desired generational conflict and/or misunderstanding; emphasis on achieving or maintaining personal authenticity, usually through oppositional strategies of identification; slackerism, boredom, depression and self-pity; protracted interest in the materiality of the body; and a well-articulated awareness and acknowledgment of foreign literatures and cinematic traditions. Related to these themes are narrative forms that may be called a poetics of disaffection: ironic commentary on the trappings of literary representation; critical distance; complexity; fragmentation; use of vernacular language and emphasis on dialogue (and, conversely, a predominance of first-person narration); intertextuality, usually through references to popular culture, rock music and punk; self-referentiality; intermingling of reality and fiction / abstraction from reality; drug and alcohol abuse as structuring elements; communal production through multiple narrators and/or the illusion of collaborative literary production; open-ended resolutions (Dorca; Gracia; Henseler; Pao; Ulrich and Harris).

In the following two sections, I discuss *La soledad era esto* and *Quién* in terms of these Gen X poetics of disaffection and propose that many of the formal and thematic characteristics that exemplify youth narrative of the 1990s transcend the "Generation X" moniker and in fact infiltrate much of contemporary Spanish literary production by writers born not just in the 1960s and 1970s, but also in the 1940s and 1950s.

LA SOLEDAD ERA ESTO

In a music review published in the *New Yorker*, Sasha Frere-Jones writes that "rock bands, like people, are living longer" (94). Discussing several big ticket rock concerts of 2004, Frere-Jones points to the continuing success and relevance of aging rock stars and bands such as Bob Dylan, REM, The Pixies, U2 and David Bowie, who have continued to tour

and release popular, critically acclaimed albums well into and beyond middle age. To varying degrees, these musicians represent important influences on subsequent popular music and literature and have been involved in contemporary inter-generational cultural production. We may recall, for example, the collaboration between Pearl Jam and Neil Young—the de facto elder statesman of grunge—on his "Mirror Ball" album released in 1995, a record that demonstrated how two generations of rock musicians might collaborate and challenge each other in the production of a recording that, for lack of better words, really rocked. Similarly, Spanish novelists born in the 1940s and 1950s such as Rosa Montero, Manuel Rivas, Antonio Muñoz Molina, Carlos Cañeque and Juan José Millás have all continued to rock the literary establishment in novels published coetaneously with those produced by a younger generation of writers by pushing the limits of the novelistic genre; engaging critically with conventional ideas about high and low brow cultural production; self-consciously exploring the boundaries between reality and fiction, self and other, and received notions of literary tradition.

Juan José Millás, whose novels can be read and understood within the context of Gen X narratives of the 1990s, is, like Neil Young, an elder statesman of the same kind of anomy and alienation that pervades transatlantic cultural production of the 1990s. Among the principal themes of his fiction are the individual's alienation by contemporary society and his or her search for a more authentic existence; the exploration of the processes of constructing and representing personal identity; and the examination of the writer's attempt to understand reality through writing. I begin this essay with *La soledad era esto* because of the critical acknowledgement it received with the Premio Nadal and because the novel appeared at the beginning of what would later become the Gen X decade. Millás's stature in the Spanish literary world makes him a propitious beginning example of how older writers can rock just as hard as we do. *La soledad era esto* in particular shares many thematic and structural elements—an emphasis on drugs and rock and roll, a fragmented multivocal discourse, a marginalized slacker protagonist, protracted generational and familial estrangement, social and mental disconnection—with Gen X works written around the same time in the United States and Spain, and consequently serves to demonstrate how this aesthetic permeates Spanish narrative of the 1990s regardless of the age of the writer.

La soledad era esto, like many other Millás novels and many Gen X works of fiction, is about alienation and the search for personal authenticity. The protagonist, Elena Rincón, is estranged from her surroundings: she remains ignorant of her grown daughter's pregnancy and is at odds with her increasingly distant husband, whom she suspects of having an affair. Perhaps because she has no profession, Elena spends most of her days smoking hashish and strolling about her northeast Madrid neighborhood known as "Prosperidad." Elena is not only disconnected from her daughter and her husband, but she also avoids family responsibilities upon the death of her mother and thereby creates further emotional distance from her brother and sister.

Elena Rincón is an angsty, neurotic forty-year-old who meanders without points of reference through her geographic and personal spaces. The free indirect style of the novel's first part focalizes on her consciousness as she struggles to come to terms with her self-imposed solitude and estrangement. Having just learned of her mother's death, Elena becomes aware of generational continuity and conflict through the reading of her mother's diary, and although she realizes that she shares more with her mother than she thought, she eschews meaningful contact with her daughter in order to submerge herself in her own personal development. Like Lucía Etxebarria's protagonists in *Amor, curiosidad, prozac y dudas* (1997) and *Beatriz y los cuerpos celestes* (1998) published later in the decade, Millás's novel explores the ebb and flow of a feminine subjectivity and "the estranging effects of individual autonomy and the failure of intimacy" (Klodt 3), all the while embracing the Gen X notion that depression, introspection, and solitude may be cathartic methods of walking a path to possible redemption. *La soledad era esto* documents the process of Elena's gradual personal metamorphosis as she comes to terms with her alienation, following the pattern of the Kafka tale from which Millás draws his epigraph. From monstrous disaffection Elena seeks to become more authentically human and finally come to terms with her self-imposed solitude and alienation.

Millás's novel is composed of a variety of textual elements: Elena's mother's diaries, her own diaries, reports from the private detective she has hired, a letter from her husband, and a transmogrified Beatles song. In part one, Elena is both protagonist and reader; she is the object of the overarching narrative of the novel in which she has a more passive role while she reads her mother's diaries and the detective's reports. In part two, Elena assumes the role of narrator of this novel about herself, creating her own discourse from her own point of view while commenting directly upon the construction of the other narratives that comprise the text. Elena's disjointed experience of reality is reflected in the fragmented discourse that communicates her story. Her interior life is documented by an impersonal, unknown omniscient narrator, while her movements in the city are painstakingly recorded by the private detective she had hired earlier to follow her husband. This personal and textual fragmentation also reflects the generational separation that Elena perpetuates by distancing herself from her better-adjusted daughter, her mother before she died, and her brother and sister.

Acknowledging that she is alienated from her own life (20) and from the lives of her family (146), Elena is trapped in a self-perpetuating downward spiral of drug and alcohol abuse that further exacerbates her alienation and misanthropy. As she points out variously throughout the novel, hashish (sometimes combined with whisky) allows her to control the images that comprise her life (94) and alter in some way her reality: "sometimes a joint modifies my vision of reality. The bad thing is that lately it accentuates the reality I'm trying to escape from" (153).[1] Nevertheless, she does assign marijuana a positive role in her personal transformation, saying that "thanks to hashish I was able to access a new perception of reality and escape from the prison that awaits so many women" (177). At the same time, however, Elena realizes that her drug use was also an important part of her self-destructive behavior and she consequently vows to stop smoking so much. Related to her drug habit are Elena's hygiene and intestinal problems. After attending the burial of her mother, Elena wanders through the streets of Madrid, unshowered and unshaven. She has not showered or shaved her left leg in several days because of a mental association she has created between her mother's passing and the bathroom. Elena's hygienic tics reflect the total loss of symmetry and order from Elena's perception of space and time, while simultaneously pointing to the extent to which she embodies a slacker/stoner persona. In the novel's final chapters, the detective she has hired to follow her and write reports about her activities notices that she must have quit smoking so much weed because of her improved personal hygiene and physical appearance, two common casualties suffered by the habitual stoner.[2]

Elena's excessive use of hashish is linked structurally to the Beatles' tune, "Lucy in the Sky with Diamonds," a song that has been commonly associated with the drug culture of the 1960s.[3] The song is imbedded in the novel's first part, and the fact that the tune appears here translated into Spanish points to a nearly unconscious appropriation of British-American rock music by contemporary Spanish culture. As she enjoys a beer at a cafeteria, the sound system pipes in the Beatles song that she translates mentally. In Elena's mind, the lyrics cross national and linguistic boundaries to become immediately relevant to her own situation, and while the song initially improves her mood, Elena quickly loses her sense of well being as all the images that constitute her perception of reality become confused. As her ability to distinguish between what is real and unreal begins to collapse, she realizes that she is literally living in a world like that of the Beatles song. Elena wanders through a nearby neighborhood and sees juxtaposed images that whirl through her brain: her unshaved leg, the wet streets, a broken streetlight, a plastic minister, a marmalade river with caramel boats, the cadaver of her mother wrapped in green and yellow cellophane (32). This schizophrenic apparition of images is a technique exploited by many Gen X writers, especially Loriga (*Tokio ya no nos quiere* 1999), and serves to represent emblematically the conflicting facets of her fragmented perception of reality. This collapse of reality and fiction—a melding of psychedelic song imagery, quotidian Madrid, and reminders of personal loss—

lead Elena back to her previous nihilistic vision of a "reality condemned to death" (**Soledad** [**La soledad era esto**] 30). Searching for a bathroom to relieve her chronic colic, she enters a kindergarten and passes out with her underwear around her ankles. This is perhaps the lowest point to which Elena will fall, and from this moment to the end of the novel she struggles to reconcile her slacker attitude, the generational conflict that she has constructed between herself and her daughter and dead mother, her unwillingness to settle things with her husband, and her growing self-awareness and reconciliation with her previous identity crisis.

What distinguishes Elena's alienation from that of a younger generation is that she devotes much of her social criticism not to a previous generation but to the corruption that she sees in her own cohort. While her critical stance does not approximate the vitriol that characterizes Jesús, the narrator of Millás's **Tonto, muerto, bastardo e invisible** (1995)—another novel that picks up and amplifies Gen X static—her identity crisis is very similar.[4] Elena, for her part, is appalled by people like her husband, a low-level government bureaucrat who has been embezzling funds and investing them abroad. He is a cynical, self-identified sell-out (86-87) who has given up his youthful idealism in favor of making money. Elena's husband has become a corporate phony much like the television studio executive played by Ben Stiller in *Reality Bites* (1994), who packages the images of youthful idealism for an MTV-style television show. Elena's husband, on the other hand, cynically acknowledges that he no longer has to identify with the losers in the struggle between the classes because he has become a winner. Having worked his way up in the ranks of corporate Spain, he now believes that the very corruption that he has come to embrace is an important, even necessary, part of any system (122). While Elena finds his attitude disgusting, she also realizes that he, at the very least, may rely on his status within this corrupt socio-economic system as a way to certify his existence and define himself (128), while she has no such method of self-definition. Elena Rincón is a woman without qualities, and faced with forming a part of a corrupt, diseased social order, she chooses to opt out rather than sell-out. As a reader of Kafka's *Metamorphosis,* Elena seeks to reconcile her inner and outer selves and achieve personal authenticity, while her husband picks up the story and rereads it, not from the perspective of the victim Gregor Samsa, but from the point of view of Gregor's family and his boss (86-87) in order to understand his own newfound position as a "winner" in the contemporary class struggle.[5]

As she herself indicates in the second part of the novel, Elena views her husband and daughter as if they were two fragments of her identity that have been separated from her being. Consequently, she regards her life as useless and mutilated (117), her experience of the world is a collection of unrelated fragments. The solitude to which the novel's title alludes is a direct result of Elena's sense of generational and economic alienation and subsequent search for a personal, inner understanding as she undergoes her transformation. Solitude, she says, is an amputation that she can barely perceive (135), a fragmentation of the body and the body politic.

Much like the reader finds in Mañas's *Historias del Kronen,* the protagonist of **La soledad era esto** inhabits a markedly specific geographical and cultural milieu that is contemporary Madrid. Taking into account the geographic language (concrete street names and numerous cartographic references) that pervades Millás's text, it becomes apparent that the key to Elena's eventual metamorphosis will be the dual activities of reading and writing, both of which function as symbolic cartographic acts that orient and situate Elena in a more concrete physical and emotional space and allow her to reconstruct her own identity through an oppositional strategy of self-identification: she is *not* like her husband, she is *not* like her mother, she is *not* like her daughter.

Having discovered that her husband has been cheating on her and that she does not really care after all, Elena hires a private detective to follow and write reports of her activities. These reports form an important part of the novel's discourse, and as she becomes more comfortable with her narrator for hire, Elena begins her *literary* criticism of them. This technique represents a key characteristic of postmodern metafiction, which seeks to break down "the distinctions between 'creation' and 'criticism' and merges them into the concepts of 'interpretation' and 'deconstruction'" (Waugh 6). Although she does not reach the extreme of Antonio López, the protagonist of Cañeque's *Quién,* Elena's role in the novel becomes that of an alienated critic who attempts to create something through criticism. A careful reading of the work reveals that as her story continues, Elena's directions to the investigator become increasingly narrative—indeed, critical. With the help of her private investigator, Elena goes about the work of self-centeredly and self-consciously producing what ultimately amounts to a novel about herself. The private investigator's third-person narrative complements her own first-person account of her life. This illusion of collaborative critical production functions as an important structuring principle; it is a method of de-centering the self and converting it into a text that may be read, interpreted, commented upon and understood. Gen X narrative culture, as Traci Carroll writes in an intriguing discussion of *Beavis and Butt-Head* and *Mystery Science Theater 3000,* draws heavily upon this kind of communal critical production. Carroll notes that one of the main thematic concerns of Gen X writing and criticism has to do with "making something out of nothing, of creating something out of an ever-shrinking economic security that is perceived as a nothing, an empty set, an 'X'" (Carroll 201). Alienated from her family, her husband, her society in general, and having no economic opportunities or adequate social alternatives of her own, Elena is similarly forced to fashion a new self out of nothing by cobbling together all of the various texts that are, in some way, about her.

As she goes about the business of re-writing her self, Elena essentially promotes her private investigator into a narrator-for-hire, and thus she becomes both an object of investigation and a discerning critical subject. This self-conscious collapse of traditional distinctions between subject and object effectively transforms Elena Rincón into her own shrink while complicating the tradition of the noir P.I. This self-conscious game between subject and object is very much a part of the postmodern narrative culture of the 1990s, in which conventional hard-and-fast binary distinctions are complicated in order to draw attention to the importance of multiple perspectives to the representation and interpretation of reality.

Carroll writes that, in many ways, "Generation X rhetoric reproduces Beat generation clichés about white alienation, but instead of taking the alienated artist as its emblem, Gen X culture focuses on the textual consumer—the alienated critic" (205). Much criticism of Gen X culture points to the widespread dearth of economic opportunities, the dehumanizing effects of some aspects of postmodern cultures, and the ills of contemporary social, cultural and economic reality as generative causes of its generational anomy. Faced with selling out like her husband, Elena chooses to take control of her life (180), find an apartment, and stop smoking so much weed. She realizes that perhaps no one ever really finishes constructing his or her personal identity (166), and that perhaps identity is *supposed* to be tenuous (156, 159). Like the younger generation that would come of age in the 1990s, Elena Rincón must come to terms with the idea that perhaps our identities are composed of nothing more than a seemingly random conglomeration of stories, sound bites, songs and film clips. Although Millás suggests that personal identity is provisional, the novel nevertheless ends with a possibly positive open-ended conclusion in which Elena takes control of this novel about herself and begins the introspective, contemplative life of a writer. But she still does not appear to have found a job.

QUIÉN

Carlos Cañeque is a titular professor of political science at the Autonomous University of Barcelona, but the bulk of his published work is literary. While he has only recently begun to be recognized for his fiction, the author's first novel, *Quién,* is particularly noteworthy because of its ingenious engagement with many of the commonplaces of literary postmodernism. Further, the novel represents an important example of how Jorge Luis Borges has grown in importance in the contemporary Spanish literary sphere. Its biting irony, humor and pure enjoyability make the novel arguably Cañeque's best work to date, in spite of the fact that his two subsequent novels touch on some of the same themes—the literary marketplace, social estrangement, narcissistic nihilism, narrative self-consciousness—

and the protagonists of *Quién* appear in his later novel, *Muertos de amor.*

Quién not only appeared in the midst of the Gen X decade—three years after José Ángel Mañas was chosen as a finalist for *Historias del Kronen* in 1994 and one year before Lucía Etxebarria won the award for *Beatriz y los cuerpos celestes* in 1998—and the novel embodies much of the alienation and anomy that typifies 1990s narrative fiction. In these ways, the novel represents a prime example of how the Gen X aesthetic has tended to transcend generational taxonomies, bringing together writers born in the 1940s, 1950s, 1960s and 1970s as they use sex, drugs, rock and roll and literary criticism to represent their multiple experiences of contemporary reality.

Quién shares many formal characteristics with the tradition of Gen X novels written by younger writers. Its defeated nihilistic protagonist, Antonio López, is very much like Mañas's narrator Carlos of *Historias del Kronen* in his egocentric misanthropy, antiestablishment attitude, and acute critical acumen—while Carlos is well-versed in the language of cinema and film criticism, Antonio is a well-read professor and critic of literature. In addition, *Quién* offers a protracted ironic commentary on the many traditions of literary representation through a carefully constructed critical distance that brings the novel in line with many other Gen X works. This self-conscious distance is created through the use of multiple and mutually aware narrators, critics, scholars and readers, all of whose voices converge in the novel in order to create the illusion of a collaborative literary production. Indeed, *Quién* is about creation through criticism; all of the voices that appear in the novel belong to critics of one kind or another. Cañeque's work shares with the youth narrative of the 1990s a formal complexity derived through fragmentation, self-conscious intertexuality, and use of drugs and alcohol as important structuring elements.

Quién is made up of first person stream of consciousness; third person omniscient points of view; transcripts of conversations; letters; scholarly prologues to critical editions of the novel; fictional reviews of *Quién* taken from newspapers and scholarly articles; and footnotes which comment upon the novel even while it is being "constructed." There are at least three possible narrators: Antonio López, Gustavo Horacio Gilabert, and Luis López (Antonio's estranged brother), although many other narrative voices appear throughout. Composed of such varied textual elements, the novel's title alludes to the indeterminacy that characterizes the entire narrative: Who is the real author of this novel?

Antonio López, the first person narrator of chapter one and ostensibly the novel's principal protagonist, is a defeated, unsuccessful, nihilistic college professor trapped in what he characterizes as a loveless marriage. Nevertheless, this numbingly banal married life is useful to Antonio in at least one way, as it allows him the peace and quiet he needs in order to begin his novel (25). Many of the work's un-numbered sections deal directly with Antonio's narcissis-tic desire to write something that will save him from his "painful anonymity" (14), for he believes that to publish a great novel represents his only chance for personal re-demption. Antonio constantly reiterates that the only way to escape his spiritual and emotional malaise would be to write a critically acclaimed novel, but, as *Quién* progresses, it becomes increasingly apparent that he lacks the willpower and focus necessary for the completion of his project. The novel therefore becomes the documen-tation of both his desultory preparations and, to a lesser degree, his actual writing of the novel, in spite of the fact that he believes that he arrived much too late to the distri-bution of literary *savoir faire* (12-13).

Antonio López's novel will be about an older book editor named Gustavo Horacio Gilabert, who is in turn writing a novel about a failed college professor named Antonio López, who is writing a book about a book editor named Gilabert, and so on. Regardless of who narrates, however, it is clear from the beginning that Antonio is a loser in just about every sense of the word, and is very poorly suited to his profession as a scholar of literature. Recalling Beck's iconic Gen X anthem, "Loser," from 1994, Antonio is a self-conscious "perdedor" who pins his hopes on a novel that he will never write. He has many ideas for titles, possible plot lines and scenarios for a work that will in essence be an extended Borges tale, but he knows that his dream is perhaps unattainable: he confesses that the terri-ble process of writing the novel will probably result finally in making him a "definitive loser" (89).

The novel that Antonio writes—basically a diary that documents his desire to write the novel and his various ideas as to what it could be about—is peppered with ad-missions and justifications as to his own laziness: "today I have arrived at the conclusion that I am extraordinarily lazy" (120); "only the lazy can contemplate the world as it truly is" (123); and he even proposes that "absolute relaxation" might be gainfully declared the new national pastime (124). Antonio's slacker attitude is related perhaps to the fact that he has failed so miserably as an academic. For example, his book on Borges titled, *La morfología de los cuentos de Borges* [A Morphology of the Stories of Borges] has sold only 116 copies in ten years. In a passage that may be read as a critique of scholarly publishing in general, Antonio suggests that authors such as himself be cited and fined for taking advantage of a system that re-quires a book for tenure; only by imposing a fine would the authors of scholarly books stop writing unnecessary works (95). And for academics who insist on continuing to write books even after they have been fined, he suggests a man-datory jail sentence, although he admits that even then "the imbeciles would probably keep writing [. . .] To produce a book without a readership is a capricious extravagance that, like water dripping into water, calls for oblivion"

(95). Antonio's protagonist/narrator Gilabert, for his part, criticizes the commercialism of the publishing industry on a radio show whose transcript is included as part of *Quién*'s discourse. He likens his own project to Marcel Duchamp's ready-mades: by making Antonio López the author of his book, Gilabert says that he seeks to problem-atize deep-seated notions about authorship and artistic cre-ation (227-32).

The painfully self-conscious Antonio López is completely unable to engage in meaningful social intercourse with his wife, his family, his coworkers or even his character/narrator Gilabert. The disaffected distance that he creates between himself and the world places him squarely into the more masculine discourses of Gen X literature of which *Historias del Kronen* is a prime example. Antonio refers to his life with his ever-suffering wife as a "simula-crum of happiness" (24) that only barely dissembles a marital routine based upon "matrimonial hatred" (88). Their lovemaking is a mind-numbing mechanical activity that produces only boredom (41-42). Similarly, Antonio's professional life is completely bereft of meaning. He teach-es the classics, works by Homer, Virgil and Dante that over the years have become more and more boring: "everyday their works become more boring because what I read day after day from my rancid notes is boring" (42).

Antonio also disdains his father for his one-dimensional bourgeois life (65) and deems his brother "an insipid un-interesting character, a bourgeois conservative who 'plays the system'" (62), just like Elena Rincón's husband and any one of the older pro/antagonists that appear in novels such as *Historias del Kronen*. Perhaps not surprisingly, a third-person narrator (who may or may not be Gilabert) traces Antonio's disaffection and perceived estrangement from his family to his young adulthood when he began smoking hashish habitually and listening to early sym-phonic rock. Drugs, after all, have become a cornerstone of the thematic triad that has traditionally been understood to comprise Gen X cultural identity. Antonio, again like Loriga's and Mañas's characters, is only able to meaning-fully communicate with *anyone* via the consumption of large quantities of drugs. He smokes hashish and/or swal-lows poppers before having sex with his wife, and he is only able to reconcile himself with his father after slipping him some LSD during a trip they took together a few years before (66). Drugs represent for Antonio the only viable access to authenticity and communication with his father (67). At an academic conference devoted to the work of Borges, an overdose of hashish allows Antonio to finally converse with his hero on a hotel balcony (102-3), al-though having swallowed massive doses of the stuff, he begins to hallucinate that Borges can fly. Controlled sub-stances are arguably the only *real* thing in Antonio's life. One of his favorite rituals involves soaking in a hot bath while smoking a joint, listening to jazz musician Bill Evans under the watchful eye of a poster featuring Marilyn Monroe. These are the essential elements that comprise his "growing philosophy of laziness and sloth" (23) on which he disserts so often. Faced from the beginning with personal and professional failure, Antonio always opts for a good soak in the tub.

At the same time that drugs and alcohol allow Antonio to suffer his way through dissatisfying social encounters, professional failures, and familial estrangement, hashish offers him a heightened perception that, coupled with poppers (amyl nitrate) and his many literary readings, allows him to confront his literary forebears in the novel's antepenultimate chapter. Just before his death, Antonio participates in dreamlike conversations between Cide Hamete Benengeli, Avellaneda, Cervantes, Don Quixote, Pierre Menard, Unamuno, and Augusto Pérez and converses with his own character/author Gilabert, who plays Don Quixote to his Sancho. Virtually the entire tradition of Spanish self-referential writing appears in this chapter, alongside the authors and characters of great works from the western canon. Gilabert becomes Virgil and Antonio is Dante, and at the gates of hell they see various sinners playing with a globe; nearby are Fernando Savater and E. M. Cioran, while Charles Foster Kane repeats "Rosebud" over and over, accompanied by several characters from Dante's *Inferno*-Pier della Vigna, Ugolino and Ruggieri degli Ubaldini. In this respect, I would say that *Quién* is markedly different from much of the work of younger writers of the 1990s who draw upon more rigorously contemporary cultural referents in the construction of their narratives. Cañeque most often draws upon the classics of world literature and largely leaves contemporary cinematic and popular literary references out.

When Antonio wins the prestigious "Galaxia" prize for his novel—in spite of the fact that he never entered the competition—he dies of a heart attack. Having fortified himself with tranquilizers washed down with whisky in order to make it through the stultifying pleasantries of a literary dinner, when his name is announced as the winner of the "Galaxia" prize, Antonio expires. His final words are, "this is a bad joke . . . I never presented . . . a . . . novel . . . to any . . . fucking prize competition" (36). It later becomes apparent that his girlfriend Teresa had collected his diaries and notes, put them together in manuscript form, and submitted them to the competition as a novel. Thus, not only are Antonio and Gilabert alternately posited as possible authors throughout the text, but Teresa's editorial instincts and savvy are also required for the completion of Antonio's manuscript. Further, with a Unamunian twist, the novel ends with the possibility that Antonio's brother may in fact be the "true" author of the text. Cañeque himself is also drawn into the game of authorial identities, for he appears in several of the novel's footnotes to proffer an erudite quip or two. It is the collaboration and exchange between multiple mutually-aware narrators that conspire together and against each other that gives the novel its form. Because no one author rises above any other to claim ultimate responsibility for the text, *Quién* functions also as a critique of conventional notions of authorship.

Quién can be read as a philippic against academe, the publishing industry, yuppies and the bourgeoisie, authorship, religion and marriage. In this way, Cañeque's novel is very much of its time. Antonio holds back none of his invective, and even criticizes Nietzsche, the ultimate iconoclast, for his formulation of the superman, what he calls "the most naive utopia conceived in the history of humanity" (115), and he describes Dante's poetry as a combination of a "hippy and Don Juan" (118).[16] Indeed, his antipathy is very reminiscent of any one of the hypercritical Gen Xers portrayed in *Reality Bites* or Kevin Smith's *Clerks* (1994), or (again) Carlos of *Historias*. But *Quién* is not all vinegar and vitriol. It is at once an entertaining ode to literature and the literary life and a critical attempt to demystify Literature in general and put some fun back into the critical process. As Patricia Waugh reminds us, contemporary metafictional novels seek to "[examine] the old rules in order to discover new possibilities of the game" (42). *Quién* is a game in which metafiction is stretched to its extremes, parodying all metafictional texts, premodern, modern and postmodern, in order to draw attention to the creative process and the dynamic nature of the reader's reconstruction of the written text.

Criticism has become a creative vehicle that textual consumers may use in order to deconstruct traditional discourses and, in the process, build new ones from the rubble. As Traci Carroll affirms, "rather than trickling down to the culture at large from the vantage point of the university, critical thinking both inside and outside centers of learning derives from a postmodern aesthetic of creative textual consumption" (206). These novels by Millás and Cañeque demonstrate how anyone can become a writer, a critic, a literary creator, regardless of their academic formation, social status, or professional success. Millás offers a sensitive reflection on the power of narrative in one woman's reconstruction of her life, while Cañeque's novel takes a more extreme, decidedly masculine approach to the representation and repudiation of the western academic establishment and literary tradition. Carlos Cañeque shows how even a graduate education does not guarantee success in the contemporary world. The postmodern aesthetics of creative textual consumption serve, in the end, as a reassuring alternative to pure nihilistic fatalism: "Doubtful about the possibility of a profound political shift, Gen X criticism is nevertheless an attempt to respond to our culture with intelligence, wit, hope, and a sense of fun" (Carroll 206).

HOW THE GEN X AESTHETIC TRANSCENDS THE AGE OF THE WRITER

In his introduction to the section on narrative in the first supplement to the *Historia y crítica de la literatura española. Los nuevos nombres: 1975-2000*, Jordi Gracia asserts that while they are certainly newer and younger, there really is no difference between Gen X writers—Mañas, Etxebarria, Loriga, et al—and the more mature writers born in the 1940s and 50s (known also as the generation of 1968) that preceded their appearance on the literary scene (Gracia 237-38). While Gracia acknowledges the thematic and formal diversity of contemporary Spanish literary production, he nevertheless lumps Gen X writers together with older authors such as Mendoza, Muñoz Molina, Rivas, Montero and Millás.

Am I advocating the same kind of undiscriminating association of all writers of the 1990s? My answer is a qualified, "not exactly." Returning to Robert Spires's essay on "Depolarization," the author points out, rightly I think, that the whole idea of the literary generation has a propensity to be problematic because it tends "to be simultaneously all-exclusive and all-inclusive" (485). On the one hand, as the essays included in this volume attest, even those members who are associated with a generation from the very beginning often "convey ethical attitudes and narrative styles that are both similar to and in conflict with not only those of other designated members, but also those of several writers born within the same decades but not generally recognized as charter members of the category" (486). To prove his point, Spires mentions first the divergent styles and themes that separate the work of Etxebarria, for example, from the "blatantly sexist discourses found in Mañas and Loriga" (486). Spires devotes the bulk of his study to the work of Javier Cercas (b. 1962) and José Ángel Mañas, two writers born within the parameters that normally define Generation X, but whose work is, on the surface, very different. The tricky thing about the literary generation—a "disputable classificatory term" (Epps 723) to begin with—is that

> once the initial membership has been determined, the tendency is to create closed societies; a given writer either is or is not considered a member, new constituents are almost never admitted, and old ones are seldom rejected. Once the designation is assigned, the category usually becomes all-exclusive.
>
> (Spires 485-86)

This second point about exclusion brings me back to the issue that I have sought to address here. By looking beyond the canonical group of young Gen X writers, I have explored how the Gen X aesthetic can be seen to function in the work of other writers not immediately associated with that generation. Through their critical use of the interrelated themes of literature, criticism, music, sex and drugs, Juan José Millás and Carlos Cañeque participate in the oppositional cultural work of 1990s fiction along with a cadre of younger writers such as Etxebarria, Loriga and Mañas. Nor are Millás and Cañeque alone; I think that it is safe to say that the Gen X aesthetic can transcend the age and personae of the writers who embrace it. Juan Madrid's novel *Días contados* (1993), for example, and Manuel Vázquez Montalbán's *El estrangulador* (1994)

arguably stand out also for their explorations of the Gen X violence, death, and criminality that characterize some of the most well-known fiction of Mañas and Loriga.

In spite of the fact that Elena Rincón and Antonio López are in their forties, both are self-absorbed slackers who are perhaps even more confused about their situation in life than are their twenty-year-old counterparts. But rather than dwell in a space of nihilism and defeatism, both characters embrace their status as losers and turn their disaffection into literature. The dynamic, indeterminate nature of Antonio's novel explores new possibilities for the game of writing fiction even while it exposes the arbitrary nature of traditional notions of authorship. Similarly, by decentering her own narrative and incorporating multiple points of view into her discourse, Elena succeeds in constructing a viable alternative to her unfulfilling identity as the trophy wife of a morally corrupt executive. From their marginalized positions outside of mainstream economic, political, academic and familial cultures, Elena Rincón and Antonio López search for the same kind of personal authenticity that has variously obsessed younger Gen X characters. Their hair is just a little grayer.

Notes

1. It is worth remembering also that Millás is fond of Freudian allusions. Elena's rejection of socially established notions of cleanliness and good grooming may also be read as symptoms of a late anal expulsive stage of her personal development as she comes to terms with her changing, marginalized place in society.

2. In a recent interview with *Uncut* magazine, Paul McCartney finally admitted that "Day Tripper" was about acid and that it was "pretty obvious" that "Lucy in the Sky with Diamonds" was inspired by LSD ("Sir Paul Reveals Beatles Drug Use").

3. Jesús's nihilistic world-view springs from his dissatisfying, trite existence in a society populated by people he calls "social democrats," a term with pejorative connotations that he uses to describe any one of the bourgeois drones who live and work in the contemporary Spanish workplace. Dale Knickerbocker has pointed to the dual structure of *Tonto, muerto, bastardo e invisible,* which is based upon the protagonist's alienation from his surroundings and an acute social criticism of an inhumane, dehumanizing Spanish society of the early nineties (230).

4. In this respect, Elena's sell-out husband is much like José Antonio, the cousin of Carlos's mother in *Historias del Kronen,* whom the narrator describes as "one of the finest of the 1968 vintage, a millionaire owner of a publishing company affiliated with the Communist Party" (162).

5. To avoid prolixity, I have chosen to leave out the rest of the novel's implicit and explicit intertextual

references, criticisms and critiques of the literary tradition simply because the novel is filled with them.

Works Cited

Amago, Samuel. *True Lies: Narrative Self-Consciousness in the Contemporary Spanish Novel.* Lewisburg: Bucknell University Press, 2006.

Cañeque, Carlos. *Conductas desviadas.* Madrid: Espasa-Calpe, 2002.

———. *Conversaciones sobre Borges.* Barcelona: Destino, 1995.

———. *Dios en América: Una aproximación al conservadurismo político-religioso en los Estados Unidos.* Barcelona: Ediciones Península, 1988.

———. *Muertos de amor.* Barcelona: Destino, 1999.

———. *El pequeño Borges imagina el Quijote.* Barcelona: Zendrera Zariquiey, 2003.

———. *El pequeño Borges imagina la Biblia.* Barcelona: Sirpus, 2002.

———. *Quién.* Barcelona: Destino, 1997.

Carroll, Traci. "Talking out of School: Academia Meets Generation X." *GenXegesis: Essays on "Alternative" Youth (Sub) Culture.* Ed. John M. Ulrich and Andrea L. Harris. Madison: University of Wisconsin Press, 2003. 199-220.

Dorca, Toni. "Joven narrativa en la España de los noventa: La generación X." *Revista de Estudios Hispánicos* 31 (1997): 309-24.

Epps, Brad. "Spanish Prose, 1975-2002." *The Cambridge History of Spanish Literature.* Ed. David T. Gies. Cambridge: Cambridge University Press, 2004. 705-23.

Frere-Jones, Sasha. "When I'm Sixty-Four: Aging Rockers Onstage." *New Yorker* 17 January 2005: 94-5.

Goytisolo, Juan. *Reivindicación del Conde don Julián.* Madrid: Cátedra, 1995.

Gracia, Jordi. "Prosa narrativa." *Historia y crítica de la literatura española. Los nuevos nombres: 1975-2000. Primer suplemento.* Ed. Jordi Gracia. Vol. 9/1. Barcelona: Crítica, 2000: 208-54.

Haynesworth, Leslie. "'Alternative' Music and the Oppositional Potential of Generation X Culture." *GenXegesis.* Ed. John M. Ulrich and Andrea L. Harris. Madison: University of Wisconsin Press, 2003. 41-58.

Henseler, Christine. "Pop, Punk, and Rock & Roll Writers: José Ángel Mañas, Ray Loriga, and Lucía Etxebarria Redefine the Literary Canon." *Hispania* 87.4 (2004): 692-702.

Klodt, Jason Edward. "Sex, Drugs, and Self-Destruction: Reading Decadence and Identity in Spain's Youth Narrative." Diss. Michigan State University, 2003.

Knickerbocker, Dale F. "Búsqueda del ser auténtico y crítica social en *Tonto, muerto, bastardo e invisible.*" *Anales de la Literatura Española Contemporánea* 22.2 (1997): 15-16, 211-33.

Kunz, Marco. "*Quién*: Cañeque, Borges y las paradojas de la metaficción." *Iberoamericana* 4.15 (2004): 61-77.

Loriga, Ray. *Tokio ya no nos quiere.* Barcelona: Plaza & Janés, 1999.

Mañas, José Ángel. *Historias del Kronen.* Barcelona: Ediciones Destino, 1994.

Martín Gaite, Carmen. *El cuarto de atrás.* Barcelona: Destino, 2001.

Millás, Juan José. *Dos mujeres en Praga.* Madrid: Espasa Calpe, 2002.

———. *La soledad era esto.* Barcelona: Ediciones Destino, 1990.

———. *Tonto, muerto, bastardo e invisible.* Madrid: Alfaguara, 1995.

Pao, María T. "Sex, Drugs, and Rock & Roll: *Historias del Kronen* as Blank Fiction." *Anales de la Literatura Española Contemporánea* 27.2 (2002): 245-60.

"Sir Paul Reveals Beatles Drug Use." (Wednesday, 2 June, 2005): *BBC News UK Edition.* 2 June 2005. <http://news.bbc.co.uk/1/hi/entertainment/music/3769511.stm>.

Spires, Robert C. "Depolarization and the New Spanish Fiction at the Millennium." *Anales de la Literatura Española Contemporánea* 30.1-2 (2005): 485-512.

Ulrich, John M., and Andrea L. Harris, Ed. *GenXegesis: Essays on "Alternative" Youth (Sub) Culture.* Madison: University of Wisconsin Press, 2003.

Waugh, Patricia. *Metafiction: The Theory and Practice of Self-Conscious Fiction.* London: Methuen, 1984.

Carter Smith (essay date 2012)

SOURCE: Smith, Carter. "Like Prisoners in a Cave: A Problematic Search for Identity and Truth in Two Peninsular Novels." *Bulletin of Hispanic Studies* 89.6 (2012): 615-25. Print.

[*In the following essay, Smith studies the manipulation of reality in contemporary society in Millás's* The Alphabetical Order *and José Saramago's* The Cave. *Smith suggests that Millás exposes the mechanisms of language that enable mass media to shape individual identity and to alter perceptions of reality.*]

In Book VII of *The Republic,* Plato presents a rather bleak allegory of man's existence. We are all, he posits, like prisoners in a cave, strapped into chairs, unable to move, and surrounded by darkness. The only access to ourselves and to the world outside comes from the observation of shadows on the wall we are forced to face—images manipulated by a few men behind us who dance figures in front of a fire (Grube 1992: 186-87). Indeed, what we prisoners are obliged to watch are images of images. Because we can have no real knowledge of the objects these images reflect, we understand as real what are mere shadows, distortions caused by the idiosyncrasies of our mental vision or those of the reflecting medium.

Many argue that little has changed for contemporary society, in that we still do not see reality as it is, but rather as it is represented to us. We do not see things directly and we are attached to the illusion because it constitutes our world and gives meaning to our particular existence. Indeed, as Jean Baudrillard taught us, all forms of communication are based on the production and consumption of signs. Thus there is no separation between 'reality' and symbolic representation. Therefore, identity can be manipulated by those who control the production of the signs we take as real. More recently, Manuel Castells expanded on the critique of Baudrillard. He agrees that '[a]ll realities are communicated through symbols. And, in human, interactive communication, regardless of the medium, all symbols are somewhat displaced in relationship to their assigned semantic meaning.' He goes on to claim that, 'In a sense, all reality is virtually perceived' (1996: 373). Today, a post-industrial, global network society creates the figures, the objects, whose reflections we see. It is a system that generates what Castells calls 'real virtuality.' A system 'in which reality itself (that is, people's material/symbolic existence) is entirely captured, fully immersed in a virtual image setting, [...], in which appearances are not just on the screen through which experience is communicated, but they become the experience' (1996: 373).

Given the seductive, manipulative, and illusory power of the symbolic system described above, are there, then, any possible spaces of agency for the average citizen? Can a true knowledge of one's own identity be achieved in spite of the 'real virtuality' that constitutes our experiences? Do alienation and exploitation in the post-industrial society doom us to experience reality like the subjects in Plato's cave? These questions are central to the recent works of two Peninsular novels, *El orden alfabético* (1998) by Juan José Millás (Spain) and *A caverna* (2000) by José Saramago (Portugal).[1]

The essay at hand addresses the questions above through an analysis of these two novels by Millás and Saramago. In the face of manipulative and, at times, monolithic urban spaces (an unnamed city in the neo-liberal Spain of the 1990s in *El orden alfabético* and the all-encompassing *Centro,* a commercial mall, in *A caverna*), these novelists

have written perceptive and penetrating critiques of economic and social discourses of power that dictate interpersonal relations and communication (*El orden alfabético*), and even the means of economic survival (*A caverna*). The novels critique a world in which the human condition becomes abject and worthless by means of the spectacle of modernity, with its media that play on the ignorance of those who cannot discern the shadows from the real. The present analysis will show that these critiques are based, in part, on the Classical need for a transcendental signifier with which to regain a sense of identity and belonging. Millás addresses this search for subjectivity through the reconstruction of the alphabetical (i.e. symbolic) order while Saramago romantically recovers the figure of an independent and free-thinking artisan, still intimately connected to the work and product he produces. Of interest also is how both novels dialogue, either directly or implicitly, with Plato's allegory of the Cave from *The Republic* in their representation and critique of the global, post-industrial society and its forces of production as an unreal, spectacular centre where historical and material reality and identity are manufactured daily for our consumption.[2]

Juan José Millás (b. Valencia, 1946) is a well-known novelist and journalist in Spain. During his career he has garnered several important literary honours, including the prestigious Premio Nadal in 1990 for his novel *La soledad era esto.* He is also familiar to many Spaniards because of his writing for *El País* and other important national newspapers in which he has written articles that comment on daily life: the fiction of reality and the reality of fiction. His work as a journalist informs much of his novelistic writing, and the general influence of the mass media in the creation of what is accepted as daily reality is an important theme in the novel to be addressed.

El orden alfabético presents a world in which language is unstable and in constant flux. The urban environment portrayed in the novel is one without a transcendental signifier, in which signs literally float and meaning gives way to mystery. Within such an unstable language system, one's identity (created in great part by language) is denied the opportunity to affirm a sense of reality. The reader, then, is confronted with a world of diminished humanity, of the anonymous and superfluous, of human isolation and fragility: all elements to be read in Millás's work.

In the first half of the novel the main character, a young boy named Julio, rebels against his father by refusing to take an interest in the family's cherished encyclopedia collection. The father's response is that if the boy persists in his refusal to read, one day all of the books in the house will take flight, like birds, and the family will be left without words. This is exactly what comes to pass. During several days of fevers and delirium due to infected tonsils the young protagonist discovers a parallel universe where the printed word has taken flight from homes, schools, hospitals, street signs and more. This creates a great deal of chaos—classes are cancelled due to the lack of reading material, people get lost driving around in a city without signs, patients are unable to read drug prescriptions—and the situation inevitably worsens. After a few days all printed material begins to die, fall to earth and decompose, causing the loss of certain letters in the alphabet, and eventually of complete words. When these words disappear, so do their signifiers and, thus, language directly and negatively affects reality. Since language constitutes episteme (that is, what we understand as knowledge and its discourses) the disappearance of words directly affects the nature of our being and existence. It will be shown later, through the novel's main character, that the obverse is also true: that the text creates 'reality' as well.

Julio travels back and forth between the two worlds as his illness ebbs and flows, but his experience on 'the other side of the world,' as he puts it, has shown him the importance of each object in its synchronic relations that construct the discourses of reality. He begins to take more of an interest in the side of the world that is not disintegrating, and begins to perceive the important role that human beings play in the relational and differential system of signs that creates language and meaning.[3] He also comes to believe that the only way to save the other side of reality, now in a state of utter deterioration, is by rebuilding a map of reality with his father's encyclopedia 'por cuyas páginas desfilaba todo lo existente' (Millás 1998: 85). Beginning with the first volume, with the letter 'A,' he would reconstruct reality. Starting with the first word, 'ábaco,' the others would necessarily fall in line. If he could just stay in the other side of reality long enough he knew he would see 'aparecer de nuevo, los bolígrafos, [...], los cinturones, las cucarachas, las mesas ...' (148).

The first half of the novel ends with the main character attempting to reconstruct by hand, letter by letter, the decaying universe where language and, therefore, the ability to name and understand reality are being lost. In the second part, the narrative voice abruptly changes from the first person to an omniscient narrator who begins to describe Julio's present situation, now grown up, on his own, and living once again in the world of books and tables. Nonetheless, the experiences in his youth have profoundly marked Julio's existence. The aforementioned change in narrative voice signals a loss of identity for the main character. The reader is introduced to a man obsessed with the knowledge that his material reality is nothing more than a world created for him. Because of the experiences in his youth, he has learned how easy it is to manipulate language and signs and how intimately involved they are in the creation of identity.

This obsession is validated when, for an assignment related to his work, Julio discovers in the centre of the city what he reports as the production centre of reality. He is assigned to write an article about an interactive television studio where the public is invited to choose between vari-

ous possible endings for television shows. What he discovers is a contemporary echo of Plato's Cave allegory as presented in the introduction of this essay. While the invited guests watch the different versions projected on the television screen in front of them, they are asked to choose, by pulling certain handles, the version they believe more appropriately ends a particular episode. Julio '[o]bservó los movimientos expertos de su vecina comprendiendo en seguida que desde aquel garaje se piloteaba la realidad como un avión. Más que eso: *aquél era un centro de producción de realidad* cuyo género llegaba a cada domicilio a través de la pantalla como el agua a través del grifo' (1998: 246, emphasis added). What is more, he is convinced that the city must be full of rooms like this where small groups of people are deciding at that very instant which part of the world should remain and which should be discarded. Instead of the wall of the cave, the images manipulated by others are projected now onto the television screen. Julio has discovered the free-floating, unstable language system that constructs arbitrary, post-modern realities. In her study of Millás's novel, Pepa Anastasio highlights these forces of production of the unreal. She points out that in the interactive television studio the adult Julio is presented with yet another proof that, just as he had sensed as a youth, the world is in a process of 'reality-unmaking' ('desrealización') in which the real becomes invisible and that which is fiction can be manipulated literally by hand to become the real (2001: 198).

Identity, for the novel's main character, is constituted by multiple discourses, but all are either pre-packaged, unintelligible, or imaginary. Habits of consumption dictate the type of food and entertainment to choose, the make-up of the imaginary family Julio creates in his mind, and even how he mourns the death of a family member. Through Julio, Millás constructs a post-modern subject for whom, as Antonio Sobejano-Morán has stated, language no longer serves to communicate an external, transcendental reality. The humanist concept that placed man at the centre of his universe gives way to a post-modern concept of the individual founded in intertextual play, in the word without an original or real referent (1991: 104). As referred to previously, this is the communication system that generates 'real virtuality'; a system in which reality is fully immersed in the world of make believe and in which appearances become the actual experience (Castells 1996: 372-75).

At the end of the novel, Julio, unable to bear this manipulation of reality in his world, seeks refuge in the only order that presents him with any sense of stability. His experiences have shown him that reality, far from having an inherent unity in itself, requires the projection of an order. In this case, the alphabetical order attributes a coherence to that which, otherwise, would be nothing more than a conglomeration of arbitrary signs. He returns to his father's encyclopedia and enters the volume 'H,' for 'hombre.' Here, among a multitude of others, he waits for an Adam-like God to come along and name him, thus bestowing upon him identity and, consequently, confirming his existence. '¿Qué haces aquí?—preguntó un desconocido. / Espero una voz que me nombre y me rescate de esta situación tumultuosa. ¿Y tú? / Yo también' (Millás 1998: 267).

In this final scene, Julio leaves behind the culture of real virtuality associated with the network society where history, identity, are 'first organized according to the availability of visual materials, then submitted to the computerized possibility of selecting seconds of frames to be pieced together, or split apart, according to specific discourses' (Castells 1996: 462). He instead returns to the word with ontological power. In order to escape the manipulation inherent in the 'centre for the production of reality' Julio seeks refuge in the most highly organized example of the symbolic order, in the authoritative catalogue of knowledge deemed important.[4] With this novel, Millás hints at a return to the origins of language, to an Adamic process of naming and identifying, in order to comprehend and apprehend a sense of order and identity. Julio is placed into the symbolic dimension of language that links subjects together in one action. If we are indeed prisoners in Plato's cave, this novel reveals to us the mechanisms of language that can incarcerate and produce the shadows taken for the real.[5]

The year that Millás published *El orden alfabético* was the year that José Saramago (b. Azinhaga, 1922), was awarded the Nobel Prize for Literature. *A caverna* was his first novel to be published after receiving the award, and there was great anticipation for its release. The novel completes a trilogy of narratives, the first two instalments represented by the novels *Ensaio sobre a cegueira* (1995) and *Todos os nomes* (1997). These three works form a triptych reflecting what Teresa Cristina Cerdeira da Silva has called 'humanity's quest for meaning in the midst of its end-of-millennium crisis' (cf. Klobucka 2001: xv). *A caverna*, like Millás's novel, presents a world that is quickly disintegrating. Yet, this time, instead of language, the reader is witness to the extinction of a way of life.

The novel tells the story of Cipriano Algor, an ageing, traditional potter who lives with his daughter and son-in-law in a backward village outside a large, expanding urban area. He sells his products to the nameless *Centro,* a new model city with entertainment, recreational, and residential facilities located in the nearby, urban area. Cipriano's daughter Marta is married to Marcial Gacho, a security guard for the *Centro.* This particular job requires him to be gone from home for a week at a time. So, he hopes to become a resident guard, which would allow him to live with his family at the *Centro* and end the tiresome cycle of their periodic separations. As the narrative unfolds, the relocation of the entire family to the *Centro* is one of the main concerns and, indeed, later becomes a question of survival and a moral dilemma when the move takes place.

In her introduction to a volume of articles focusing on the works of Saramago, Anna Klobucka has noted that in *A*

caverna, 'the apparent location of the Center within the surrounding urban fabric is at several points challenged by the narrative discourse, where the Center is implied to absorb and contain, and even to replace, the city itself, as it constantly expands its voracious and far-reaching periphery' (2001: xvi). In order to convince his father-in-law that he should leave the village and come to the *Centro* with him and Marta, Marcial attempts to describe it. 'Creio que a melhor explicaçaõ, do Centro ainda seria considerálo como uma cidade dentro de outra cidade. [...] O que há é o mesmo que se encontra numa cidade qualquer, lojas, pessoas que passam, que compram, que conversam, que comem, que se distraem, que trabalham' (Saramago 2000: 258). In Saramago's novel there is no end to the illusions of the gigantic commercial *Centro* where everything one needs in order to live is just one short elevator ride (up or down) away. The *Centro* is itself the city, which, as we shall see, has been relegated to a ghostly existence.

For a brief period, the family's transfer actually takes place. As was hinted at above, the pressure to leave the village for the city has been exercised not only by Marcial, but also by the *Centro,* since its commercial representatives have cancelled Cipriano's contract. They do not want to market his pottery because the demand for such items is already met through the use of synthetic materials. This implies the abandonment of the old man's traditional way of life and manufacture. What is more, Cipriano must accustom himself to living in an environment where everything is already there. Nothing need be created or searched for by the inhabitants since the *Centro* provides for all and controls all. *A caverna* presents many elements of urban dystopia in the figure of the *Centro* and contrasts them with a transcendental signifier, with a sense of identity and place in the character of Cipriano and his profession. Klobucka, again, points out that 'the dystopia represented by the sinister, Big Brotherish *Centro* is contrasted with the utopian space of Cipriano's homestead, which is organically fused with the potter's workplace' (2001: xvi). The novel's representation of Cipriano's living and working space insists on its almost impossibly anachronistic nature and draws the reader's focus to the intimate relationship between the artisan, his work and his product:

> Já se tinha visto como o barro é amassado aqui de mais atersanal das maneiras, já se tinha visto como são rústicos e quase primitivos estes tornos, já se tinha visto como o forno lá fora conserva traços de inadmissível antiguidade numa época moderna, a qual, não obstante os escandalosos defeitos e intolerâncias que a caracterizam, teve a benevolência de admitir até agora a existência de uma olaria como esta quando existe un Centro como aquele.

(Saramago 2000: 147)

While the shadow of the shopping mall looms over the entire novel, the dichotomy between the *Centro* and Cipriano's homestead fuels the tension between the post-industrial global society we live today and a mode of local and particular existence which works to resist the totalitarian forces of globalism.

As was stated earlier, Marcial is awarded the position of resident guard and the family moves to the *Centro*. Shortly after their arrival the news spreads of an intriguing secret being kept in the complex; of something found underneath the *Centro*. As a security guard, Marcial knows what it is, but cannot reveal anything to his wife and father-in-law. Cipriano defies orders one evening by sneaking out and going down to the entrance of a cave-like area under construction below the *Centro* where his son-in-law is standing guard. Marcial stops him initially but in the end acquiesces, gives Cipriano a lantern, and lets him enter to see what the authorities have been so keen to conceal. The old man makes his way down a gentle slope dimly lit by the light of a fire burning at the top. At the bottom there are six human corpses, tied by their legs and necks to a stone bench so that they are facing a wall. The bodies are still distinguishable as three men and three women but their eyes have completely rotted away.

When he returns to where Marcial is waiting, Cipriano says that although the bodies are palpable—he has touched one of them—they are not real and that they are somehow a reflection of the world outside. The corpses are to be identified with himself, Marcial, Marta, the inhabitants of the *Centro,* perhaps with the whole world. The fear and angst depicted in this scene are reminiscent of Baudrillard's discussion regarding the power of the simulacra that does not serve to reflect a profound reality nor to refute its existence. Rather, it brings one to the realization that deep down 'truth' never existed, that only the simulacrum ever existed. These images that Cipriano discovered were in essence not images, such as an original model would have made them, but perfect simulacra, 'forever radiant with their own fascination' (Baudrillard 1994: 5).[6] After this discovery Cipriano is determined not to spend another day in the *Centro,* so all three decide to leave, no matter how uncertain the prospects outside might be. When they have made some progress on their journey, they recall a sign on the front façade of the *Centro.* This recollection constitutes the last sentence of Saramago's novel:

> BREVEMENTE, ABERTURA AO PÚBLICO DA CAVERNA DE PLATÃO, ATRACÇÃO EXCLUSIVA, ÚNICA NO MUNDO, COMPRE JÁ SUA ENTRADA

> (2000: 350)

—another cave within the Cave.

Saramago's reference to Plato's Cave allegory could not be more explicit. Those who live in the *Centro* are doomed to live a life of shadows. Indeed, as Cipriano insinuates, we are victims, perhaps even prisoners of a system that ultimately marginalizes and alienates. It has gained such control of daily life that it is practically impossible to differentiate between the shadows on the wall and the

'real' that exists, to continue with Saramago's imagery, outside the mall. The urban saturation of the *Centro* brings about the disappearance of the public and private space. By connecting the *Centro* and Plato's Cave, Saramago is able to bring to light the dichotomy of the sphere of consumption (the Mall, the spectacle) versus the sphere of production (class exploitation and the alienation hidden from the surface). The potter's workshop and village, in turn, represent a way of life which is less and less under our control as in the world today, slowly even the traditional capitalist working class, is systematically being erased, or hidden away in the Third World. The cave in Millás's text is less physically present yet no less insidious. The manufactured real that we experience daily via mass media and advanced technology in the post-industrial world becomes part of the fabric of what we accept as real and from which we create identity.

The reader of Millás's work is presented with these manipulative economic and symbolic systems that saturate the public and private sphere. However, we are also encouraged to recognize these discourses and the daily appropriation of their language (i.e. the mass media and its identity creation, the habits of consumption we are encouraged to adopt as central to our existence), and to critique their manipulative powers. As Millás himself has opined, 'Tengo la impresión de que vivimos en un mundo donde al lenguaje se le trata cada vez peor y por lo tanto hay menos capacidad de pensar. Entonces somos una sociedad más fácil de manipular, incapaz de comprender lo que lee y escucha' (Posadas 1999). For the fictional character Julio, though he apparently loses touch with reality in seeking refuge in his father's encyclopedia collection, his choice is rather logical. The encyclopedia represents everything that post-modern manipulation and fragmentation rejects, for indeed a centring, an (alphabetical/symbolic) order, is a precondition for being a social agent.[7]

Saramago's novel seems to express a desire to recover the intimate relationship between creator and creation in the face of globalization. Cipriano's discovery of the bodies underneath the *Centro,* chained in place and forced to watch a manufactured reality, opens his eyes to the fact that there are no more truths. An initial reading of the novel's final image of the rickety old truck of an old, unemployed potter, advancing towards an uncertain new life in an unknown location seems to present a darker, more disillusioned end. A closer reading of this last image, however, points to a transformation of the very place from which the truth is produced. Cipriano's escape from the *Centro,* along with his family, highlights the fragmentation, the loss of depth and identity that is inherent in the post-modern world, and calls into question what it means to speak from the centre of life where de-centredness is guaranteed. This final scene underlines Homi Bhabha's assertion that, in the search to locate the forces of cultural production, 'it is only through a structure of splitting and displacement [...] that the architecture of the new historical subject emerges at the limits of representation itself' (1994: 217). Spaces of potential agency are to be found in both a local and a global perspective.[8]

This diaspora, at the end of the novel, projects the hope for a morally responsible and forward-thinking community. Cipriano and his family, upon escaping their cave, represent the possibility of becoming accustomed to the light, of eventually grasping reality well enough to see the simulacra for the illusion it is and then to assist their fellow cave-dwellers in seeing the truth.[9] In a post-industrial society, the search for identity is 'the defense of the subject, in its personality and in its culture, against the logic of apparatuses and markets' (Touraine, cf. Castells 1996: 23). While the main characters of these novels defend the subject in their own way, each defence, as problematic as it may be, provides a map that, in turn, may present a route for our escape from the Cave.

Notes

1. All textual citations used in this essay come from *El orden alfabético,* Madrid: Grupo Santillana de Ediciones, 1998; and *A caverna,* Lisbon: Editorial Caminho, 2000. Translations into English, unless otherwise noted, are those of this author.

2. Providing examples of these spectacular, urban spaces is not a difficult task. One thinks immediately of the 'mega malls' in Edmonton, Canada, and Bloomington, Minnesota. Also coming to mind would be Disneyland, and the entire city of Las Vegas: two great simulacra. These examples are no longer, however, restricted to on-land phenomena. A North American entrepreneur, by the name of Norm Nixon, is currently fanfaring the imminent launch of the so-called 'Freedom Ship,' or 'City at Sea,' from the coast of Florida. This would be the largest ocean-going vessel ever built, containing helipads, shopping precincts, multi-million dollar apartments and a K-12 school system. It is both a symbolic and a material bastion of free-floating market forces. References here to such spaces of capitalism are particularly relevant to this essay and, as will be seen, to the analysis of Saramago's novel.

3. This concept of the synchronic and arbitrary relationship between the sign and the signifier comes, of course, from Ferdinand de Saussure and the seminal work *Course in General Linguistics.*

4. In Lacanian thought, the symbolic order works in tension with the imaginary order and the Real. Julio's taking refuge in the laws and restrictions that control our desire and the rules of communication is, as will be discussed later, ironic.

5. Later in the episode of the Cave, Plato considers the following: 'When one of [the prisoners was freed and suddenly compelled to stand up, turn his head, walk,

and look up towards the light, he'd be pained and dazzled and unable to see the things whose shadows he'd seen before.' If someone told him that what he now looked at was closer to reality and the truth of things, he would 'be at a loss and [...] he'd believe that the things he saw earlier were truer than the ones he was now being shown' (Grube 1992: 187-88). Though Julio turns away from the light and flees into the stability of the alphabetical order, Millás presents literature's potential to realize the function of the philosopher who is able to escape the cave. The prisoner's 'contemplation of the heavens dissolves the perspective of the city, the laws of which now seem to be mere conventions with no natural status' (Bloom 1968: 308). I will return to this point later in the essay.

6. Here Baudrillard is discussing the fear that iconoclasts had (have) in their relation with the Idea of God. Iconoclasts feared the icon 'precisely because they predicted this omnipotence of simulacra, the faculty simulacra have of effacing God from the conscience of man, and the destructive [...] truth they allow to appear—that [...] God never existed, that only the simulacrum ever existed. [...] If they could have believed that these images only obfuscated or masked the Platonic Idea of God, there would have been no reason to destroy them. One can live with the idea of distorted truth. But their [...] despair came from the idea that the image didn't conceal anything at all' (1994: 4-5).

7. Dale Knickerbocker's reading of the final scene in Millás's novel is much more pessimistic. Analysing the work based on characteristics of obsessive-compulsive disorder, he sees Julio's retreat into the alphabetical order as an 'obsessional device.' Words and thoughts take on magical powers and expiate any need for action. 'This belief then contributes to further alienation of the individual as (s)he distances him/herself from society and societal responsibilities' (2003: 16). This analysis is insightful and instructive towards an understanding of the main character as he 'apparently loses all contact with external reality' (2003: 273). However, it is also a case of Millás creating dramatic irony. While Julio does not openly recognize his dementia, the juxtaposition of the fantasy world he creates with the real contemporary Spain at the time of the novel's publication provides an ironic distancing for the reader and a convenient vehicle for Millás's criticism of neo-liberalism and its alienating consumerism. This, again, allows the author to emphasize literature's capacity to expose the economic and social discourses of power that can enslave the average citizen.

8. Castells proclaims a radical transformation of the concepts of space and time in the twenty-first century. As 'localities become disembodied from their

cultural, historical, geographic meaning,' they are reintegrated into the communication system and create a 'space of flow that substitutes for the space of place. Time is erased [. . .] when the past, present, and future can be programmed to interact with each other in the same message,' thus creating 'timeless time' (1996: 375). This is the material foundation of a new culture that, yes, transcends the symbolic power of an individual or group, but also includes their diversity and allows for the creation of new dimensions of human life.

9. Axel Schönberger (2001) connects the end of the novel with Plato's *Politeia,* in which man is urged to always strive for justice and to live an average, simple life; to choose the 'aurea mediocritas.' In that way he will always be happy. Cipriano and the others choose to leave the capitalistic consumer paradise of the *Centro* for a simple yet authentic life. While I am drawn to Schönberger's more idealistic reading, in the end of Saramago's novel one could just as easily hear echoes of Paul Virilio's nihilistic assessment of the great migratory movements of this twenty-first century. 'The nomads are the poor. We are moving towards a category of people who are nowhere at home.' Virilio predicts the 'end of mankind as a work force in favor of the machine. [. . .] The end of mankind as producer, the end of mankind as progenitor [. . .] the end of humanity' (2002: 71).

Works Cited

Anastasio, Pepa, 2001. '*El orden alfabético* por Juan José Millás: Salvación por la palabra,' in *Monographic Review/ Revista Monográfica,* 17: 187-205.

Baudrillard, Jean, 1994. *Simulacra and Simulation,* trans. Sheila Faria Glaser (Ann Arbor: University of Michigan Press).

Bhabha, Homi, 1994. *Location of Culture* (New York: Routledge).

Bloom, Allan, 1968. *The Republic of Plato* (New York: Basic Books).

Castells, Manuel, 1996. *The Rise of the Network Society* (Cambridge, MA: Blackwell Publishers).

Grube, G. M. A. (trans.), 1992. *Plato. Republic.* Revised C. D. C. Reeve. (Indianapolis, IN, and Cambridge, MA: Hackett Publishing Company, Inc.).

Klobucka, Anna, 2001. 'Introduction: Saramago's World,' in *Portuguese Literary & Cultural Studies,* 6 (Spring): xi-xxi.

Knickerbocker, Dale, 2003. *Juan José Millás: The Obsessive-Compulsive Aesthetic* (New York: Peter Lang Publishing).

Millás, Juan José, 1998. *El orden alfabético* (Madrid: Grupo Santillana de Ediciones).

Posadas, Claudia, 1999. 'La palabra es un órgano de la vision: Entrevista con Juan José Millás,' in *Siempre* 2407. Available at: http://www.m323.com.mx/SIEMPRE/2407/Cultura/Cultura1.html (accessed 19 January 2010).

Rollason, Christopher, 2004. 'Globalisation and Particularism in the Work of José Saramago: The Symbolism of the Shopping Mall in *A caverna,*' in *Global Neo-Imperialism and National Resistance: Approaches from Postcolonial Studies,* ed. Belén Martín Lucas and Ana Bingas López (Vigo: Servicio de Publicacións da Universidade de Vigo), pp. 207-16.

Saramago, José, 2000. *A caverna* (Lisboa: Editorial Caminho).

———, 2002. *The Cave.* Trans. Margaret Costa (London: The Harvill Press).

Schönberger, Axel, 2001. 'Zur function des platonischen Höhlengleichnisses in José Saramagos Roman *A caverna,*' in *Studien zur brasilianischen undportugiesischen Literatur* (Frankfurt, Germany: Domus Editoria Europaea), pp. 149-75.

Sobejano-Morán, Antonio, 1991. 'Poética de la postmodernidad,' in *Revista de Estudios Hispánicos,* 25, 1 (January): 95-108.

Virilio, Paul, and Sylvère Lotringer, 2002. *Crepuscular Dawn.* Trans. Mike Taormina (Los Angeles, CA: *Semiotext(e)*).

FURTHER READING

Criticism

Andres-Suárez, Irene, and Ana Casas, eds. *Juan José Millás: Grand séminaire, Universidad de Neuchatel, 9-11 de mayo de 2000.* Zaragoza: Libros, 2009. Print.

A comprehensive collection of essays about Millás, primarily exploring the metafictional and transgeneric nature of his work. Andres-Suárez and Casas also include a detailed bibliography covering works published through 2007. Not available in English.

Franz, Thomas R. "Envidia y existencia en Millás y Unamuno." *Revista canadiense de estudios hispánicos* 21.1 (1996): 131-42. Print.

Compares Millás's novel *Volver a casa* (1990; may be translated as *Back Home*) with works by Miguel de Unamuno. According to Franz, Millás suggests that human existence is the result of a literary act. Not available in English.

García Gutiérrez, Mercedes. "*Laura y Julio*: La individualidad en la otredad." *Bulletin of Hispanic Studies* 88.5 (2011): 545-52. Print.

> Analyzes the importance of space in *Laura and Julio*. García Gutiérrez argues that the multiplicity of space in the novel plays an important role in the process of subject formation. Not available in English.

Valls, Fernando. *La realidad inventada: Análisis crítico de la novela española actual.* Barcelona: Crítica, 2003. Print.

> Traces Millás's formulation of ideas from his journalistic articles to his later novels. Valls's essay is one of few to explore Millás's narrative journalism. Not available in English.

Additional information on Millás's life and works is contained in the following sources published by Gale: *Dictionary of Literary Biography,* **Vol. 322; and** *Literature Resource Center.*

Jacques Poulin
1937-

Canadian novelist.

INTRODUCTION

Jacques Poulin is noted for his novels dealing with Canadian and North American identity. His works, which have attracted critical acclaim in English translation as well as in the original French, explore topics as varied as nature, technology, art and creativity, the loss of innocence, and Quebecois sociopolitics, as well as the relationship between language, writing, and communication. Many of his novels feature a male writer struggling with questions of personal, creative, and national identity. Commentators have characterized Poulin's literary style as intimate, precise, and quietly comic.

BIOGRAPHICAL INFORMATION

Poulin was born on 23 September 1937 in Saint-Gédéon-de-Beauce, Quebec, the second of the seven children of Jeanne d'Arc Grondin and Roger Poulin, a general store manager. Poulin received a classical education at the Séminaire de Saint-Georges, where his classmates included Roch Carrier, the future author and national librarian of Canada. After being dismissed from the institution for distributing wine for the Mass among his fellow students, Poulin continued his studies at the Séminaire de Saint-Nicolet, graduating in 1957. He then entered a bilingual arts program at the Université Laval in Quebec City, studying psychology and literature. After qualifying for a license in counseling in 1960, he worked in the university's psychology department as a research assistant until 1962. He received his bachelor of arts degree in 1964. By the following year, he had decided to pursue a professional writing career.

In 1967, Poulin began working as a counselor at the Collège Notre-Dame-de-Bellevue in Quebec City. He published his first book, a short novel titled *Mon cheval pour un royaume* (published as *My Horse for a Kingdom*) in the same year. Two thematic sequels, *Jimmy* (1969) and *Le coeur de la baleine bleue* (1970; published as *The Heart of the Blue Whale*), completed a loosely constructed trilogy that was later translated and published collectively as *The Jimmy Trilogy* (1979), which introduced his work to English-speaking readers. From 1970 to 1973, Poulin worked as a translator for the Canadian government. Thereafter, he concentrated on his writing, but he contin-

ued to do freelance translation work for various publications, including the *Dictionary of Canadian Biography*.

In 1974, Poulin published his fourth novel, *Faites de beaux rêves* (may be translated as *Sweet Dreams*), which won the Prix de La Presse, the first of many literary prizes he received. Four years later, he won the Governor General's Award for French-language fiction for his novel *Les grandes marées* (1978; published as *Spring Tides*). *Volkswagen Blues,* arguably his most-discussed and widely read book, followed in 1984. *Le vieux chagrin* (1989; published as *Mr. Blue*) won the Prix Québec-Paris (1989) and the Prix France-Québec-Jean-Hamelin (1991). Poulin has received multiple awards in recognition of his achievements, including the Quebec government's Prix Athanase-David in 1995, the Canada Council's Molson Prize in 2000, and the Fondation Emile-Nelligan's Prix Gilles-Corbeil in 2008. In the early 1990s, Poulin moved to Paris, where he lived for fifteen years before returning to Quebec. He currently resides in Quebec City.

MAJOR WORKS

Poulin's first novel, *My Horse for a Kingdom,* prefigures much of his later work in its poetic, dreamlike setting and its thematic focus on Quebecois identity and the power of language. Set in Quebec City, the work is narrated by Pierre Delisle, a young, indecisive writer fascinated with both the beauty of the surrounding cityscape and the terrorist activities of the Front de Libération du Québec (FLQ), a radical Quebecois separatist group. Pierre's narration, which consists of his recollections of the events leading up to his injury in a bombing carried out by the FLQ, features detailed descriptions of the landmarks of Quebec City, as well as metafictional reveries on the nature of literary creation. *Jimmy,* the second novel of the Jimmy trilogy, also focuses on the inner life of a confused, obsessive youth, this time an eleven-year-old child who retreats into fantasy amid the breakdown of his family. The redemptive power of beauty, a common theme in both novels, is also central to the trilogy's final installment, *The Heart of the Blue Whale,* about a man whose life changes radically after he receives a heart transplant from a fifteen-year-old girl.

Like the Jimmy trilogy, *Sweet Dreams* is dreamlike in tone, imparting mythic and symbolic resonance to its portrayal of relations among three people attending the Grand Prix du Canada auto race, where the juxtaposition of human and mechanical movement provides an important narrative motif. *Spring Tides* tells the story of Teddy Bear, a comic-strip translator living alone on a deserted island, where he intends to compose a novel about the influence of France and the United States on Quebecois identity. His happy seclusion is disrupted when his boss, who periodically flies in to pick up Teddy's translations, begins to send him various guests, who eventually form a small community on the island. Teddy's inability to maintain an idyllic isolation is implicitly equated with Quebec's relationship to the surrounding world. The novel is among Poulin's most formally adventurous works, incorporating various typographical experiments into its episodic, comic-strip-like structure.

Volkswagen Blues expands upon Poulin's earlier concern with Quebec's relationship to other cultures and challenges the narratives established by European colonizers. Inspired by Jack Kerouac's novel *On the Road* (1957), the narrative focuses on Jack Waterman, a blocked writer who takes a road trip across North America to find his brother. Along the way, he is joined by an enigmatic woman of mixed Innu and European ancestry, and as they pass through Canada and the United States, their discussion frequently turns to the European discovery and colonization of North America, as seen from the perspectives of both a settler and an indigenous inhabitant. As with much of Poulin's work, *Volkswagen Blues* is self-referential and displays an abiding interest in the nature of language and verbal communication. Literary references and allusions abound, and various authors, including Kerouac, Saul Bellow, and Ernest Hemingway, appear as minor characters. At the end of his journey, Jack finds that his brother, who suffers from amnesia and degenerative paralysis, can no longer recognize him. Jack parts ways with his companion and returns to Quebec, disillusioned but enlightened and able to write again. A later novel, *La traduction est une histoire d'amour* (2006; published as *Translation Is a Love Affair*), is narrated by Marine, a young translator who befriends Waterman, the protagonist of *Volkswagen Blues,* who now appears as an old man. The novel blends Marine's contemplative reveries on the nature of literary translation with the recounting of a fabulistic mystery plot in which she and Jack become involved.

CRITICAL RECEPTION

Critics of Poulin's work have examined its treatment of Quebecois history and culture, often focusing on the Quiet Revolution, a period of intense sociopolitical upheaval during the 1960s and 1970s following the death of Premier Maurice Duplessis and the end of Catholic rule in Quebec. Gilles Labrie (2006) contended that *Spring Tides* serves as an indirect commentary on the social consequences of the Quiet Revolution, and Edith Biegler Vandervoort (2011) asserted that the portrayal of masculinity in *Volkswagen*

Blues reflects shifting conceptions of gender in the Quiet Revolution's aftermath.

Scholars have assessed the postcolonial and postmodern elements of Poulin's novels. Roger Hyman (1999; see Further Reading) analyzed postmodernism in *Volkswagen Blues,* arguing that it contains an embedded warning against the destructive power of monolithic conceptions of history, such as gave rise to the Holocaust. Commentators have discussed cultural and historical topics in the context of concern with language and literature. Anne Marie Miraglia (1994; see Further Reading) considered the significance of intertextuality to the themes of *Volkswagen Blues,* presenting the novel as Poulin's distinctively Quebecois rewriting of various American fictional works, including Kerouac's *On the Road,* Bellow's *The Adventures of Augie March* (1953), and Jack London's *The Valley of the Moon* (1913). Robert Sapp (2008) explored the relationship between language and cultural identity in *Volkswagen Blues.*

Poulin's fiction has attracted comparisons to works by other writers, particularly works by Canadian authors about Quebec. Philip Stratford (1990) studied Poulin's *Spring Tides* alongside Matt Cohen's novel *Wooden Hunters* (1975) in an attempt to identify the distinctive qualities of French-Canadian and English-Canadian fiction. Adam Paul Weisman (1995) designated *Volkswagen Blues* and Henry David Thoreau's *A Yankee in Canada* (1866) as examples of a postcolonial cultural process called "imaginative colonization," in which "one North American culture imagines the other not on that culture's own particular terms, but as a feature of its own historical self-understanding." Beatrice Guenther (2007) compared *Volkswagen Blues* and *Translation Is a Love Affair* to two novels by Lise Gauvin in terms of their portrayals of the culture, history, and geography of Quebec. Susan L. Rosenstreich (2008) considered the thematic treatment of historical origins in *Volkswagen Blues* alongside that in Anne Hébert's novel *The First Garden* (1988).

James Overholtzer

PRINCIPAL WORKS

*Mon cheval pour un royaume [published as *My Horse for a Kingdom*]. Montreal: Jour, 1967. Print. (Novel)

*Jimmy. Montreal: Jour, 1969. Print. (Novel)

*Le coeur de la baleine bleue [published as *The Heart of the Blue Whale*]. Montreal: Jour, 1970. Print. (Novel)

Faites de beaux rêves [may be translated as *Sweet Dreams*]. Montreal: Actuelle, 1974. Print. (Novel)

Les grandes marées [published as *Spring Tides*]. Montreal: Leméac, 1978. Print. (Novel)

Volkswagen Blues. Montreal: Québec/Amérique, 1984. Print. (Novel)

Le vieux chagrin [published as *Mr. Blue*]. Montreal: Leméac, 1989. Print. (Novel)

La tournée d'automne [published as *Autumn Rounds*]. Montreal: Leméac, 1993. Print. (Novel)

Chat sauvage [published as *Wild Cat*]. Montreal: Leméac, 1998. Print. (Novel)

Les yeux bleus de Mistassini [published as *My Sister's Blue Eyes*]. Montréal: Leméac, 2002. Print. (Novel)

La traduction est une histoire d'amour [published as *Translation Is a Love Affair*]. Montréal: Leméac, 2006. Print. (Novel)

L'anglais n'est pas une langue magique [may be translated as *English Is Not a Magic Language*]. Montréal: Leméac, 2009. Print. (Novel)

L'homme de la Saskatchewan [may be translated as *Man of Saskatchewan*]. Montréal: Leméac, 2011. Print. (Novel)

Un jukebox dans la tête [may be translated as *A Jukebox in the Head*]. Montréal: Leméac, 2015. Print. (Novel)

Principal English Translations

†*The Jimmy Trilogy.* Trans. Sheila Fischman. Toronto: House of Anansi, 1979. Print.

Spring Tides. Trans. Fischman. Toronto: House of Anansi, 1986. Print. Trans. of *Les grandes marées.*

Volkswagen Blues. Trans. Fischman. Toronto: McClelland and Stewart, 1988. Print.

Mr. Blue. Trans. Fischman. Montreal: Véhicule, 1993. Print. Trans. of *Le vieux chagrin.*

Autumn Rounds. Trans. Fischman. Toronto: Cormorant, 2002. Print. Trans. of *La tournée d'automne.*

Wild Cat. Trans. Fischman. Toronto: Cormorant, 2003. Print. Trans. of *Chat sauvage.*

My Sister's Blue Eyes. Trans. Fischman. Toronto: Cormorant, 2007. Print. Trans. of *Les yeux bleus de Mistassini.*

Translation Is a Love Affair. Trans. Fischman. New York: Archipelago, 2009. Print. Trans. of *La traduction est une histoire d'amour.*

*These novels form the Jimmy trilogy.

†Includes the English translations *My Horse for a Kingdom, Jimmy,* and *The Heart of the Blue Whale.*

CRITICISM

Wayne Grady (review date 1980)

SOURCE: Grady, Wayne. "Accent on the Soul." Rev. of *The Jimmy Trilogy,* by Jacques Poulin. *Books in Canada* 9.1 (1980): 14-15. Print.

[*In the following review, Grady assesses Poulin's Jimmy trilogy, finding that the novels exhibit "the grace and style of poetry as well as the more immediate impact of expository prose." Grady contends that the series distinguishes Poulin from his fellow Quebecois writers and establishes him as "a profoundly contemplative and analytical novelist."*]

In 1973 Sheila Fischman wrote in the *Supplement to the Oxford Companion to Canadian History and Literature* that Jacques Poulin (1937-) was "a very important, unjustly neglected young writer." Now she herself has helped to correct that imbalance by translating Poulin's first three novels—*My Horse for a Kingdom* (1967), *Jimmy* (1969), and *The Heart of the Blue Whale* (1971)—and presenting them in a single volume as a trilogy. And she would seem to have proven her point: *The Jimmy Trilogy* is a clear indication that Jacques Poulin is a fine Quebec writer of whom English readers now can sit up and take notice.

What distinguishes Poulin—and indeed all the best Quebec novelists, among them Hubert Aquin, Roch Carrier, Jaques Godbout, Anne Hébert—is that he has a soul as well as a brain, and that he is concerned about the health of his soul more than about his sanity, and I mean this without the obvious reference to Catholicism. Poulin has struggled to combine philosophical enquiry with the more ordinary kinds of inquisitiveness, and the result is a series of novels with the grace and style of poetry as well as the more immediate impact of expository prose.

Of the three novels, *Jimmy* (which is also its French title) is central in more than just the literal sense (a tribute to Fischman's deep insight into the inner workings of the books as much as into their skin of language). First of all it is one of a very few novels told through a child's point of view that can hold an adult's attention. Jimmy is a precocious, Salinger-like 11-year-old who lives with his parents in a cottage on a beach near Quebec City. Papou, his papa, works in the psychiatric ward of Quebec's Hôtel-Dieu (French writers are so lucky: imagine having a culture with such built-in symbolism as a hospital called Hôtel-Dieu). Mamie, Jimmy's mama, has a miscarriage that affects her mind, making her more child-like in some ways than Jimmy, and Papou retreats to his attic study to write a book about Hemingway (and here's an intriguing sign: Papa Hemingway is cropping up in Quebec literature in some of the oddest ways; he's also in Godbout's *Dragon Island*).

Jimmy, as a result, is left almost entirely alone, except for the old English commodore in the next cottage, and as his child's natural fantasy-world (TV-inspired, for the most part) gradually melds with the mundane, the prose takes on an eerie quality that is both recognizably innocent and deeply disturbing. In the end, when Jimmy imagines that the cottage has broken away from its pilings and its English neighbours to float down the St. Lawrence with Jimmy at its helm, the fantasy assumes a political dimension that, in 1969, is also foreboding.

The first novel, **My Horse for a Kingdom,** is little more than a 50-page short story, but its reverberations with the other two novels inflate it to something approaching a novella. Pierre Delisle is Jimmy grown up—there is much talk of his "carapace," his tough outer shell that corresponds to the stone walls of Old Quebec City. Pierre is an anarchist, but only in a quasi-political sense: ridding Quebec of foreign domination is merely a metaphor for cleansing his own soul. When he plants a bomb on a statue of an English soldier near the Portes St. Louis he is himself wounded in the explosion, and becomes the central image of the third novel—a wounded bird in the cage that is Quebec City.

The main character in the final third of the trilogy, **The Heart of the Blue Whale,** is Noël, a 30-year-old writer who, while working on a novel about a boy named Jimmy, has had a heart transplant. His new heart—the wounded bird within the rib cage—is both tender (the donor was a 15-year-old girl killed in a motorcycle accident) and an image of the death that lurks in us all. The metaphor is borrowed from a poem by Saint-Denys Garneau, "*Cage d'oiseau,*" which begins (in F. R. Scott's translation):

I am a bird cage
A cage of bone
With a bird

The bird in the cage of bone
Is death building its nest

But it doesn't stop there, for these novels are essentially revolutionary, as this passage from **The Heart of the Blue Whale** attests:

I closed my eyes to forget the Americans. I saw the walls of Old Quebec. On rue des Remparts, at the level of the former Grand Séminaire, someone has written on the grey wall—once in red and once in black—REVOLUTION. I like it when people write on walls, on houses, on sidewalks, in the street, everywhere. In any case, I like words. What escaped me was the relationships between things. Léo Ferré said that poets wrote out their rebellion with the claws of birds; there was a new thing living in my chest, a thing Saint-Denys Garneau had described as a bird; Goethe said that ideas have doves' claws.

In short, Jacques Poulin emerges from Quebec in much the same way that Mikhail Bulgakov, (whom he resembles, and who, by the way, wrote a novel called *Heart of a Dog* in 1925) once emerged from the Soviet Union: a profound-

ly contemplative and analytical novelist, whose control of language, imagery, and theme makes him, as Sheila Fischman observed, a major writer. He is, moreover, necessary to anyone interested in the soul of Quebec.

Paul G. Socken (essay date 1990)

SOURCE: Socken, Paul G. "Creation Myths in 'Les grandes marées' by Jacques Poulin." *Canadian Literature* 126 (1990): 185-90. Print.

[*In the following essay, Socken reads* Spring Tides *as a novel that uses biblical creation myths for ironic purposes, creating a parody of divine destruction, not creation, by European cultures. Socken contends that Poulin contrasts the dehumanizing nature of European culture with native mythology, which represents what the author considers a cyclical, not destructive, vision of life.*]

Les Grandes marées pits a modern, verbal, intellectual, and collective culture against a primitive, non-verbal, instinctive, and individualistic one. The first is inherently superficial and implies the victory of technology over humanism; the second is ostensibly at its mercy and rendered impotent. An initial reading, therefore, reveals a scathing satire of contemporary society. A closer examination, however, gives pause for further reflection.

The surface structure of the novel is clearly an ironic version of the biblical story of creation. There is also a deeper structure, a reprise of primitive non-biblical myths of creation, which suggests a second level of meaning.

The parallels to the biblical text are numerous and apparent. The general situation itself mirrors the biblical account: a superior—a man's boss—takes a certain young man by helicopter to an island he owns and leaves him there, alone, where he hopes his employee, called Teddy Bear, will be happy. The boss, known only as le Patron, comes from Le Soleil (a newspaper he owns). Eventually, he brings him a young female companion and, later, other people with whom he is to share the island.

The chapters are numbered, like the Bible story, and code names ("nom de code," p. 9)[1] and signs ("Des signes derrière le vitre," p. 9) suggest hidden meaning and invite interpretation. Names such as Matousalem, Hagar, and Eden (p. 149) are transparently biblical. The novel contains parables, like the Bible, in the form of a poem (chap. 40), and allegories (the whale and the squid in chapter 39, and the treasure chest in chapter 26). The language, too, is biblical in tone ("Au commencement, il était seul dans l'îsle," p. 9), with many specific borrowings ("le paradis terrestre," pp. 14, 34; and "La Terre promise," p. 171). Finally, the novel ends with an exile, as the young man is banished from the island, echoing the Bible story of Adam's fall from grace.

What is striking about the novel, however, is not so much the similarities with the Bible, as the irony that creates a critical distance between the two accounts. The effect is to deflate the grandeur and majesty associated with the biblical text.

The boss is clearly not God, as he himself affirms: "Je ne me prends pas pour Dieu le Père . . ." (p. 54). The Patron's humble disclaimer is superfluous, as the narrator's description of him at the beginning of the novel had made abundantly clear: "Court de taille, pansu et chauve, il marchait à grandes enjambées, le regard fixé au sol, le visage empourpré, et il croisa son employé sans le voir" (p. 10). One of the later inhabitants of the island reverts to monkey language (pp. 151-52), which is a sophisticated irony, as it introduces a kind of reverse evolution into the "biblical" story. At the end of the novel, the employee is banished from the island, not by God, but by his fellow man (chap. 43). The Bible, like all creation stories, "describe[s] the creation of the earth as being accomplished before that of man. . . ."[2] The novel, here too, is at variance with the biblical text, as the focus is on man alone.

Les Grandes marées is, then, on one level, an ironic version of the Bible story. It is really a social, not a religious, document. The parody that results is the story of a destruction, not a creation, made all the more telling because it masquerades as the biblical creation. *Les Grandes marées* uses the ironic parallel with the Bible story as a starting point to parody modern society. The intellectual, technological, collectivist and verbal aspects of modern culture are its targets.

Teddy Bear's companions on the island, all brought by "le Patron" to make him "happy," consist of a professor of cartoon strips from the Sorbonne, known as Professor Mocassin, an author from Montreal, an efficiency expert, a doctor, and a community organizer. None of them has a name, but rather, they are known by their generic titles.

The critique of the intellectual set is as humorous as it is biting. The author rewrites the first sentence of his projected novel, and does not know what his book is all about (p. 135). Professor Mocassin, he of the Sorbonne, plans to write the definitive book on human nature, based on the pattern of pathways on the island (pp. 138-39), but "ses travaux avaient abouti à une impasse" (p. 192), the pun on pathways and impasse adding a playful note. The futility of intellectual endeavour, its lack of focus and goals, are attacked with zest. The Patron's wife, known only as "Tête Heureuse," joins the group and offers herself, in turn, to the professor and the author. Both reject her in favour of their work, an ironic comment on intellectuals who supposedly reject life for their "art" (chap. 34).

The arrival on the island of both the "animateur" (p. 161) and the efficiency expert, called "l'Homme Ordinaire" (p. 124)—a modern version of Everyman?—is announced on the telex machine by "Fiches signalétiques." In this way,

nothing of the person is first revealed to us. They are presented as statistics, facts, details, devoid of real humanity, as, indeed, they are shown to be.

The "animateur" has the "insulaires réunis" (p. 167) all sit in a circle so that each can feel the "bio-énergie" of the group. The author is excited momentarily as he claims to feel something. It turns out to be a "petite roche" he is sitting on (p. 168). The cumulative effect of these portraits and scenes is to satirize and undermine the role and importance of intellectuals. When Teddy is informed that he is to leave the island, l'Homme Ordinaire says that "on a réfléchi tous ensemble . . ." (p. 196). This collective thinking is a form of tyranny which leaves no room for the individual. This is a story about a group of people that thinks it has all the answers, and one man, infinitely more appealing, who isn't even sure what the question is.

The satire on intellectuals can be seen as one element in a broader attack on the nature of society produced by an intellectual élite. Everything about the society imposed on Teddy Bear is rationalized, mathematical, technological, and dehumanized. Conditioned by the society he left, he is accustomed to attempting to accomplish things by rules and mathematical perfection. The result is failure. He attempts a recipe, following a mathematical formula: "Il s'était livré à des calculs inutiles et avait perdu son temps" (p. 43). Moving from one house to the other on the island is undertaken in exactly ten trips with accompanying lists ("16. Les Dix Voyages"). Tête Heureuse gives Teddy Bear a massage by following a precise list in her manual ("19. Le massage du sportif"). The "Animateur's" book claims that social relations depend on the first four minutes of two person's meeting (p. 166). All of this sage counsel comes from experts' books on the subject. In fact, all their knowledge seems to come to them from such sources: Teddy learns to play tennis from a book (p. 20) and his companion, Marie, learns about birds from a guide (p. 55).

The world of the novel, in which all knowledge comes in lists from guides and manuals, and in which everything is measured, counted, and quantified, is dominated by machines. Technology is king; or rather, prince. "Le Prince" is the name of a tennis machine on the island whose game surpasses any human's: "Grâce à son cerveau électronique, le Prince avait un jeu dont la perfection dépassait les possibilités humaines . . ." (p. 107). Finally, Man is replaced by Machine. Teddy had been hired to translate comic strips for the Patron's chain of newspapers. He learns, near the end of the novel, that his translations had never been used. He had been replaced by a translating machine, Atan. Atan, one step beyond Adam, is the New Man, Machine-Man, the victory of technology over humanity.

Science and technology, in the form of helicopters, translating machines, tennis machines, and "experts" of all kinds, displace traditional values and signal a new, dehumanized order. The Patron prides himself on being called "Le poète de la finance" (p. 50). In the New Order, poetry is practical and quantifiable. Similarly, people don't have names, but animals and things do: "Pouchkine" is a ship (p. 68) and "Matousalem" is a cat. Jet Ranger, Puss'n Boots, Harrap's, Terry et les pirates, Dunlop, Wilson, Maxply, and Fred Perry are some of the names that are found in the novel. The dehumanization of modern culture is vividly and repeatedly depicted as proper names accumulate and attach themselves, not to characters, but to everything from comic-strip characters to animal foods. If people, in this novelistic world, have lost their individualism and, therefore, their identity, the manufactured items of a materialistic society gain instantaneous recognition and fill the void. One may even suggest that the latter displaces the former. In a novel about genesis and origins, Man is, ironically, seen to be surrounded by, and utterly dependent on, the products of technological existence, rather than on natural sources.

The dehumanizing nature of the New Order is powerfully rendered through the treatment of language in the novel. The replacement of a conscientious translator, who capably weighs every nuance, as Teddy does, by a machine, constitutes an eloquent statement about modern, technological life and values. It is the most dramatic, but only one, of many uses of language to make the same point. Teddy Bear is obsessed by language. It is absolutely central to his life and to the life of the novel. He is concerned with questions of meaning and etymology (p. 34) and totally committed to finding an exact translation (chap. 18). In an exquisite irony, the world of men is shown to be dehumanized, whereas the words come to Teddy "comme des invités qui ont oublié l'heure; ils le tenaient éveillé une bonne partie de la nuit" (p. 15). In this inversion of values, it is the words that are his true companions.

Yet, in every other instance, language is seen to be inadequate, debased, and the object of ridicule. The author is portrayed as having nothing to say, and the professor, who is deaf, cannot stop talking (chap. 21). Communication through language proves futile. The author says "Fuck" and the professor hears "phoque" (pp. 97-98). L'Homme Ordinaire, the efficiency expert, calls "une séance de *dynamique* de groupe" a "séance de *dynamite* de groupe" (p. 166) and "des moyens *audio*-visuels," "des moyens *idiots*-visuels" (p. 188; emphasis added). The Patron buys the deaf professor a hearing aid, but the instructions are in Japanese, which no one understands (chap. 28). Once tried, the machine is found to be useless. A doctor is brought to the island to examine Teddy, but his vocabulary is so technical that he has difficulty communicating with his patient (chap. 33).

As a result, the novel points to a world beyond words, suggesting potential for profound non-verbal communication. Teddy and Marie do not speak a great deal with each other, but one of their most meaningful encounters is "une conversation muette. Ils se parlaient avec leurs yeux et leurs mains ..." (p. 73).

This silent, unspoken, and non-verbal truth is at the very heart of the novel. The satire of modern mores is only one aspect of this complex novel. An alternative reality is evoked, one which is more basic, primitive, and instinctive. Teddy defines for Marie what is important to him: "C'est quand, dans les yeux des gens, parfois, on voit passer quelque chose. Une sorte d'éclair qui brille, une sorte de chaleur. C'est une chose que j'aime beaucoup" (p. 176). The idea that there exists a profound meaning within, an inner life of real value, is suggested at various points in a number of different ways. Teddy had once told his brother that "les amis des chats avaient probablement dans leur inconscient une zone de sérénité totale, comme il en existait peut-être au fond de la mer ..." (pp. 25-26). The island itself, on which the action of the novel is played out, is "grand comme ma main" (p. 116), if one does not count the interior which is "aussi impénétrable que la jungle de l'Amazone" (p. 116). This "forêt de l'intérieur" is described as "mystérieuse et sauvage" (p. 60). In addition, Marie quotes one of Van Gogh's letters in which he writes of "un grand foyer dans son âme et personne ne vient jamais s'y chauffer" (p. 84). The sea, the island, the people on it, and others, as implied by the reference to Van Gogh, possess a mysterious, unnamed, inner life, which is quite distinct from the society which is the object of Poulin's satire.

The world alluded to corresponds to the one associated with primitive man. Indeed, parallels with primitive non-biblical mythology can be found throughout. In the novel, in spite of the levity and satire, an atmosphere of high seriousness remains at the core. Basic questions are broached. Teddy and Marie discuss "[l]e sens de la vie et le sens du travail ..." (p. 95). The group decides that its members are neither French nor American, but the question, "Alors qui êtes-vous?" (p. 99), posed by the professor from the Sorbonne, is never answered. This gravity is perfectly in keeping with archaic myths: "Creation myths are of a different class from other myths ... for when they are told there is always a certain *solemnity* that gives them a central importance; they convey a mood which implies that what is said will concern the basic things of existence. ..."[3]

The presence of cats, too, is eminently reminiscent of the world of mythology. Both Teddy and Marie have cats. The cat is, at once, among the most prevalent, and the most mysterious figures, in world mythology: "Le symbolisme du chat est très hétérogène, oscillant entre les tendances bénéfiques et maléfiques. ..."[4] Immediately after the major revelation of the novel, that Teddy's translations have never been used (chap. 36), there is a one-line chapter (p. 174) announcing a litter of three cats. The number three is fraught with meaning for the archaic mentality: "In ritual, to repeat an action or phrase three times is to emphasize what is being done or said to the point of irrevocability."[5] In Greek mythology, too, the number is significant: "To the Pythagoreans, three was the perfect number because it had a beginning, a middle and an end. For similar reasons, it was the symbol of Deity as Creator."[6] The combination of the symbolism of the cat, with the number three, suggests a magical world that stands in stark contrast to the one satirized. In addition, it connotes a counterpoint to the biblical story of creation, a different tale of creation, less known and more mysterious.

The ritualistic number three is not limited to the litter of kittens. It is linked to another important mythological theme—that of food and cooking. Teddy meticulously gathers and arranges ingredients to bake a pie. The recipe is divided into three parts and there are three ingredients for the crust (p. 41). The other ingredients must be boiled for three minutes (p. 45). Food is central to mythological man: "Toute alimentation est transsubstantation . . . l'acte alimentaire confirme la réalité des substances. Car l'intériorisation aide à postuler une intériorité."[7] Milk and honey[8] are archetypal foods in myth and both are present in ***Les Grandes marées***.[9] The idea of food as substantiating the notion of an inner reality coincides perfectly with the major thrust of the novel, as we have demonstrated. The search for and establishment of a truth beyond the one apprehended by contemporary culture lie at the very heart of the novel.

The omnipresence of water in the novel, and its prominence in the title, are related to the dominant motifs. Water is associated with creation and rebirth: "Si les eaux précèdent la création, il est bien évident qu'elles demeurent présentes pour la recréation."[10] In addition, bodies of water, as opposed to rain, are considered feminine: "l'eau première, l'eau naissante de la terre et de l'aube blanche est feminine: la terre est ici associée à la lune, comme un symbole de fécondité accompli. . . ."[11] The moon, indeed the full moon, and moonlight, are present throughout the novel (pp. 15, 16, 23, 117, 118, 124).

If water represents the themes of genesis and creativity in the novel, it also embodies the language of silence to which Teddy aspires: "L'eau est la maîtresse du langage fluide, du langage sans heurt, du lagage continu, continué, du langage qui assouplit le rhythme, qui donne une matière uniforme à des rhythmes différents."[12] The presence of water everywhere—the action takes place on an island—suggests that this special kind of communication is accessible: "L'eau est aussi un modèle de calme et de silence . . . L'eau vit comme un grand silence matérialisé . . . Il semble que, pour bien comprende le silence, notre âme ait besoin de voir *quelque chose* qui se taise; pour être sûre du repos, elle a besoin de sentir près d'elle un grand être naturel qui dorme."[13] Here, too, as with the symbol of the cat, the ritualistic number three, and the ceremonial food preparation, the water imagery evokes a hidden, primitive reality that is superior to the one portrayed in the novel. This alternative world is ancient and innocent, however, precisely because it is uncorrupted by modern man.

At one point, Teddy and Marie walk to a neighbouring island at low tide, only to be turned away by a man with a gun (chap. 13). At the end of the novel, when he is banished, Teddy swims to the same island, where he discovers the man: "Le vieux n'était pas vivant: il avait la peau dure comme la pierre" (p. 201). The novel closes with these words. Again, potent and mysterious symbolism associated with the world of mythology is presented. Teddy must clearly establish himself again on this new island, which is to say that his world must be recreated: "Settlement in a new, unknown, uncultivated country is equivalent to an act of Creation."[14] In addition, creation associated with death is omnipresent in world mythology: "It is not possible to create something without destroying something else at the same time. . . ."[15] This relationship seems to be universally acknowledged: ". . . a violent death as a precondition of life reborn is a theme which runs through nearly all early religions."[16] The end of the novel, then, implies the beginning of a new cycle of creation:

> The Germanic and Hindu concepts point to a cyclic event, namely that there is a constant rhythm of successive creation and destruction. Not much will be really changed; the beginning is always wonderful and towards the end this world slowly decays, evil and the forces of decadence slowly prevailing until the final catastrophe, and then everything emerges again in the vernal beauty of a new possibility for life.[17]

The Judaeo-Christian world view, expressed in the Bible, is basically eschatological—tending toward an end of the world—where the "Germanic and Hindu" concepts are cyclical. The novel contains both, but prefers the second.

That the man's skin feels like stone, too, is significant: "Dans la tradition, la pierre occupe une place de choix. Il existe entre l'âme et la pierre un rapport étroit . . . Ce n'est sans doute pas un hasard si la Pierre philosophale du symbolisme alchimique est l'instrument de la régénération."[18] The union of the figure of death and of stone indicates a rebirth into a new life.

It may be implied that the new life, which is to begin, will be merely the setting into motion of another cycle that is destined to decay and die. There remains, however, Teddy's implicit search for an alternate life of meaning based on a hidden, deeper, more fulfilling truth than sustains conventional society. Must that dream, associated with an instinctive, non-verbal, and primitive society, necessarily be subverted by a more "enlightened" view as society evolves? To that question, the novel responds with silence.

Notes

1. Jacques Poulin, *Les Grandes Marées* (Montreal: Leméac, 1986). All references are to this edition of the novel.

2. S. G. F. Brandon, *Creation Legends of the Ancient Near East* (London: Hodder and Stoughton, 1963), 2.

3. Marie-Louise Von Franz, *Patterns of Creativity Mirrored in Creation Myths* (Dallas: Spring Publications, 1972), 5.

4. Jean Chevalier et Alain Gheerbrant, *Dictionnaire des symboles* (Paris: Seghers, 1969), 178.

5. Desmond Varley, *Seven: The Number of Creation* (London: G. Bell and Sons, 1976), 29.

6. Varley, 29.

7. Gilbert Durand, *Les Structures anthropologiques de l'imaginaire* (Paris: Bordas, 1969), 293.

8. Durand, 294, 296.

9. E.g., pp. 23, 34, 147.

10. Chevalier, 226.

11. Chevalier, 228.

12. Gaston Bachelard, *L'Eau et les rêves* (Paris: Librairie José Corti, 1976), 250.

13. Bachelard, 258.

14. Mircea Eliade, *The Myth of the Eternal Return* (Princeton, 1974), 10.

15. Von Franz, 96.

16. Philip Freund, *Myths of Creation* (London: W. H. Allen, 1964), 55.

17. Von Franz, 221.

18. Chevalier, 600-01.

Philip Stratford (essay date 1990)

SOURCE: Stratford, Philip. "No Clear Strait of Anian: Comparing Jacques Poulin and Matt Cohen." *Studies on Canadian Literature: Introductory and Critical Essays.* Ed. Arnold E. Davidson. New York: MLA, 1990. 296-308. Print.

[*In the following essay, Stratford compares* Spring Tides *to Matt Cohen's* Wooden Hunters, *citing the two novels as representative examples of French-Canadian and English-Canadian fiction, respectively. Stratford notes dissimilarities and affinities between the novels in order to draw conclusions about the distinctive qualities of the two literary traditions from which they emerged.*]

In a book called *All the Polarities* I tried to balance conflicting views about Canadian literature. The poles are represented by pioneer comparatist Ronald Sutherland, who subscribes to the mainstream theory, and sociologist Jean-Charles Falardeau, who proposes what one might call, still

using geographical terms, the theory of the great divide. Sutherland contends that between Canadian literatures in French and English there exists a strong current of similarity. "French-Canadian and English-Canadian novels of the twentieth century," he writes in *Second Image,* "have traced a single basic line of ideological development, creating a whole spectrum of common images, attitudes and ideas" (23). In contrast, Falardeau, in *Notre société et son roman,* contends that the two literatures are diametrically opposed. "English-Canadian literature," he says, "finds its basic tensions along a horizontal axis, studying man and his milieu or man and society. French-Canadian, on the contrary, is situated along a vertical axis where relations between man and his destiny or man and the absolute predominate" (58). These antithetical views are not new; they are nearly as old as Canada itself. Just a few years after Confederation, Ontario novelist William Kirby wrote that he hoped the two literary traditions of France and England would be united "in one great floodstream of Canadian literature" (268), while at the same time Québec's first prime minister, man of letters Pierre-Joseph-Olivier Chauveau, opined that the literatures of the two groups were so estranged that they reminded him of the double-spiral staircase at the Château de Chambord, which two people can mount without ever meeting until they reach the top (335).

In my own study I tried to test these hypotheses by comparing a dozen well-known contemporary novels. I compared Hugh MacLennan's *Two Solitudes,* for example, with *Bonheur d'occasion,* by Gabrielle Roy; Sinclair Ross's *As for Me and My House* with André Langevin's *Poussière sur la ville*; Margaret Laurence's *Diviners* with Anne Hébert's *Kamouraska*; I also paired novels by Alice Munro, Robert Kroetsch, and Margaret Atwood with ones by Marie-Claire Blais, Roch Carrier, and Hubert Aquin. I found much evidence to support both Sutherland's and Falardeau's theories and came to the median conclusion (an island in mid-mainstream, straddling the divide) that in comparing novels in Canada's two official languages, one would have to respect poles of difference as well as the axis of similarity—hence my title.

Perhaps in the long run I found more differences than likenesses. After analyzing the six pairs of novels, I tried to codify my results into general definitions of what the typical English-Canadian novel and the typical *roman québécois* seemed to be. Here, in abbreviated form, are the main features of those definitions:

> The English-Canadian novel tends to be the story of something that happened to someone in a distinct time and place. Its sense of historical realism is heightened by the treatment of characters as individuals and by attention to detail. The reader is persuaded to identify with the hero by reference to the minutiae of that character's life. Symbolism is seldom explicit, rarely emerging more clearly than as the presence of a certain atmosphere. The upshot of the story is frequently moralistic, although its impact is

usually diffuse. The role of the novelist is not to universalize but to particularize; that of the reader to learn to side with the eccentric hero.

And now a look at the other side:

> *Le roman québécois* is a tale not generally tied to a specific time or place. The sense of historical realism is replaced by an intensely personal and present apprehension of reality, heightened by a sparse and selective use of detail. Characters tend to be representative or symbolic. The reader is urged to enter intimately and uncritically into the hero's state of mind, sharing the character's daydreams and nightmares. Symbolism has free rein and replaces moral suasion. The role of the novelist is to convert the raw material into captivating patterns; the role of the reader is to submit.

The novels that provided me these deductions were mainly written in the 1960s or before, and their authors are well-established figures. What I would like to do in the present essay is to test the continuing validity of the definitions by pushing on to examine works by younger, less well known writers from the following generation, namely Matt Cohen and Jacques Poulin.

Cohen is an inventive, energetic writer who has published eight novels and four collections of short stories since 1969. While his style varies widely from short to long fiction, *Wooden Hunters,* his fifth novel, can be taken to represent a writer whom W. H. New calls "the most accomplished of the young experimental stylists" (262). Poulin is a little older, and although he began to write at about the same time, he has been less prolific (in the same period he has published six novels). He is considered, by Laurent Mailhot among others, to be "a very important, unjustly neglected young writer" (675). *Les grandes marées* is his fifth novel also and won the Governor General's Award for fiction in 1978.

My choice of these two novels is not fortuitous. For a comparison to have some chance of success, the two sides must initially share some common ground, and more than chalk and cheese. In this case the common ground is the setting of the novels, for in each work the author has chosen an island, a distinctive geographical space that strongly influences its inhabitants and thus the character of the fiction. So the first step in the comparison must be to reconnoiter these islands.

Apart from size they are quite similar, set along a north-south axis with habitations at either end, a road or path linking them across an interior wilderness. Cohen's island is much bigger; it is situated in the Queen Charlottes in the Pacific Ocean off the coast of British Columbia; it has a summer population of six hundred, which drops to half that in winter, a logging town at its north end joined by a rough road to an airstrip at the south, with some Indian villages midway on the east side. Poulin's island, Ile Ma-

dame, lies in the St. Lawrence River off the northeast shore of Ile d'Orléans; it is only two kilometers long and to begin with has a caretaker population of one; a large house at its north end is joined by a path to a cottage at the south, with a tennis court midway; a helicopter can land at either end, if the tides are favorable.

Already the intricate play of sameness and difference begins to draw us deeper, for these novels are not only on but about islands. The first sentence in *Les grandes marées,* "In the beginning he was alone on the island," sets the right Crusoe-like, Genesis context. In the end "he" is forced to leave the island, swimming off into the cold St. Lawrence, where he meets death. In between, the tale develops like *Ten Little Indians* in reverse. To start, there is only one, Teddy Bear, code name for *traducteur de bandes dessinées* (T. D. B., hence Teddy Bear), a translator of comic strips. He has been offered this island retreat by his employer, a vigorous entrepreneur who owns a chain of Québec newspapers. The "boss" is the deus ex machina of the novel; his machine is the private helicopter he pilots from Montréal every Saturday with provisions for Teddy and a fresh batch of comics to translate. His sole aim, he says, is to make people happy, and to this end he ferries in a series of companions for wistful Teddy until eventually the island paradise is overpopulated with ten people, a chihuahua, and five cats. The islanders (as they are now called) turn on Teddy and expel him.

The first companion the boss provides for his island Adam is a girl, Marie, who climbs down a ladder out of the air with a tabby for the translator's old tom. Next the boss introduces his wife, code named Featherhead, to play mother hen to the young couple. He then supplies intellectual companionship in the persons of the "Author," a surly Québec nationalist, and Professor Mocassin, a Sorbonne anthropologist who is an expert in the history and aesthetics of the comic strip. As an antidote, the next visitor is known simply as the "Ordinary Man." He is followed by the "Organizer," a specialist in group dynamics; by a visit from a doctor; and finally, since things are obviously not going well, by a thaumaturge, Old Gélisol, whose primitive therapy consists in holding a patient on his lap in a rocking chair and exuding heat.

From this brief description it is immediately apparent that we are not dealing directly with the ordinary world. The *Pushkin* goes by in the channel, the lights shine from the opposite shore, the boss flies off to board meetings in Québec City and inspection tours of plants at Rimouski and Sept-Iles, but life on the island goes on in its own fantastic way, hardly more real than life on the island of the Katzenjammer Kids. The style of the narrative is in fact closely related to the comics. With the possible exception of Teddy and Marie, all the characters have comic strip traits. Professor Mocassin, with his glasses on the end of his nose, his hearing problems, and his absent-mindedness, is explicitly modeled on Professor Tournesol in the well-known Belgian comic albums *Tintin.* The others, with their nicknames, their tics, and their caricatural features, also resemble the population of the funnies. They have allegorical status and represent various types and attitudes, all of them incapable of alleviating the translator's essential solitude. Their dialogue is succinct, its movement erratic; it bobs like comic strip balloons, and the novel progresses in forty-three brief chapters like weekly installments. A convention of unreality is clearly established, and the novelty of fantasy is its staple. At one point Teddy's actions follow the sequence of the narrative but it turns out that he has imperceptibly crossed a threshold and dreams the close of the episode. It is that kind of fiction.

In *All the Polarities* I discovered that the Québec novels examined made little attempt "to create a convincing external view of reality or to reflect the autonomous, believable world" (98). More recent works by the same authors—Aquin's *Neige noire,* Hébert's *Héloïse,* Carrier's *La dame qui avait des chaînes aux chevilles,* Blais's *Visions d'Anna*—still take us swiftly into the depths of the characters' psyches, without introduction or explication, present us with surreal images of their traumas, make us privileged observers of their most intimate dreams (or, for that generation, perhaps we should say nightmares). In the 1970s the delirium grew somewhat less intense. Although there has always been a manic gleam of black humor in Québec fiction, with Poulin some of the blackness dissolves, the humor becomes gentler, more pervasive, and relaxes into drollery and nonsense. One can observe the same phenomenon in works by some of Poulin's contemporaries, in Michel Tremblay's novels, in Yves Beauchemin's *Le matou,* in Jacques Godbout's later fictions, and in Louise Mauheux-Forcier's stories. But whether comedy or tragedy predominates, whether nightmare or fantasy, the premise and logic of this fiction seems to be that of dream.

Trying to differentiate more specifically between the two types of fiction written in Canada, I observed in the definitions that English-Canadian novels were basically wedded to realism and paid great attention to detail. Unlike some of his antecedents, Poulin writes abundantly detailed fiction. His characters' states of mind and heart are not delivered directly in the typically abstract vocabulary of Québec fiction but are displayed in conjunction with a set of facts and objects completely exterior to them. But how are these details presented? Often by lists: the contents of Marie's suitcase, for example; a list of what was carried on ten trips from the North House on the island to the South House; the reproduction, verbatim and typographically, of telescripter messages, of signs, of a recipe for graham cracker pie; one chapter is completely devoted, in instruction-manual prose, to advice on how to deliver the best forehand and backhand strokes in tennis. The world of objects coexists with the world of the characters but in dislocation. The objects are not natural projections of the human but have a strange, separate existence, like the contents of

Winnie's handbag in Beckett's *Happy Days,* or the isolated units in Ionesco's stilted verbal universe.

Cohen's universe is detailed in a different way. Here is an example, chosen at random:

> He reached into his pocket, to find the candle he had taken from the kitchen. The jacket was new, or at least different, a blue-black serge jacket from Harry Jones's infinite supply to replace the one that had been torn in the explosion last night. This one had all its pockets still intact. In one of them he had found a yellowed ferry ticket, both departure and destination erased by age. He set the candle on the sill beside the bottle, and started searching around in the pockets again, this time for tobacco and papers.
>
> (95)

Nothing special is happening here, yet unlike the eccentrically autonomous objects in Poulin's fiction, these commonplace items are related in time to character or plot. The new jacket harks back to the old one, reminding us of a central incident in the story, the blowing up of an old logging camp tractor; the mention of its previous owner recalls Johnny Tulip's family; the faded ticket emphasizes the remoteness of the island setting; even the insignificant candle stub appears half a dozen times in the next few pages as Johnny walks through the sleeping house holding it up to illumine now this room, now that, each one evoking a different set of memories. Cohen's use of detail is tendentious; Poulin's, discontinuous. Cohen's is continental, Poulin's, islanded. The details in Cohen's fiction relate to the past, are connected to memory, form part of a history. Poulin's, in contrast, are atemporal. Typically, Québec fiction tends to be first-person, present-tense narration; *Les grandes marées* is told in the third person and the past tense, but the presentation of detail produces the typical effect: details exist, odd and surprising, in a timeless present, like objects in a dream.

The same is true of character. Take the two enigmatic heroines, for example. Laurel Hobson of *Wooden Hunters* has more than a full name; she has a past. Part of it is obscured by drugs and alcohol, but she does relive memories of parents and childhood and of her life with her Indian lover, Johnny Tulip, and his family. In fact, a good half of what we know of her is provided by reminiscence, and her story makes up almost half the novel. But Marie, her equivalent in *Les grandes marées,* has no surname (none of the characters do) and no appreciable past either. All we know of her background is that her father liked hunting and her mother was a long-distance swimmer. No question is raised about her past; she exists self-substantial, her mystery intact, in and for the present, like the objects in Poulin's tale. She arrives, in fact, as an answer to Teddy's fantasizing:

> Teddy pensait à une autre personne: une fille; elle n'existait pas dans la réalité, mais ses traits et son allure commençaient à se fixer dans sa tête.
>
> (15)

Teddy was thinking about someone else too: a girl. She didn't exist in reality, but her features and appearance were beginning to take shape in his mind.

(13)

She arrives from the air and disappears into the sea.

In each novel one of the main interests is romantic. I have referred to Poulin's hero, Teddy the translator; now a few words about Calvin, Cohen's male protagonist. Like Teddy he is a newcomer to the island; we are initiated to it and to its inhabitants through his eyes. Perhaps because he fills the role of initiate and initiator, he is not a strong character, a witness rather than an actor, and more a foil to Laurel than an equal partner, although at the end of the novel he has a chance to prove himself, as does Teddy.

There are the same number of secondary characters in the two novels, but Cohen's are more fleshed out. Here, the role of deus ex machina is played by C. W. Smith, once a Montana grain merchant who now owns the hotel at the north end of the island, the setting for some monumental brawls and the shootout that closes the work. Like 'the boss' in *Les grandes marées,* he is the prime mover, although not from concern for others' happiness but from jealousy and, as ugly American, by greed. His collusion with government officials and the timber company to arrange the logging off of ancestral Indian burial grounds, and his brutal affair with the Indian waitress, Mary Gail, are the specific reasons for the growing enmity he inspires, but his malevolence, unlike the boss's benevolence, is not simply given: he is accorded two full chapters in which to explain himself. Johnny Tulip—Laurel's former lover, Mary Gail's brother, and a representative of Indian rights—is also given two chapters, and other less important characters are provided with proper names and particular histories, unlike the cleverly stylized characters of Poulin's fiction.

The convention behind Cohen's novel is obviously realism. But what kind? Interestingly enough, Cohen's variation displays some attributes of Québec fiction. Eschewing stock-in-trade realism, he does not simply depict characters from the outside or detail stream-of-consciousness responses but penetrates deeper, revealing half-states of thought, emotion, dream, sensual perception, physical sensation, and visceral reaction. Some of the phrases in my definition of the typical *roman québécois* referring to the re-creation of a state of mind, "an intensely personal and present apprehension of reality," could be applied accurately to Cohen's style. Since style dictates subject as much as the other way around, the novel contains many scenes of violence suited to display primitive reactions. In chapter 1, for instance, Calvin's first night on the island, the lovers shoot a deer by night, a flashlight strapped to the rifle barrel to blind the animal; they haul it back to the campsite, string it up, and butcher it in graphic detail. Later they wade through a rushing stream netting salmon, gut them, and make love on the bank, smeared with blood and eggs. Every chapter has its quota of drunkenness, fighting, or sex, giving the narration its headlong impetus.

But despite the physical violence, the narrative turbulence, the frequent use of dreams, and a nonrational bias that frequently presents the characters in a state of semistupor, the premise and progress remain realistic. The characters, even minor ones, are treated as individuals, not types. Their lives are inscribed in space and time and contribute to the general history of the island. However eccentric they are or however briefly they are evoked, they intermesh in a credible way; they belong, although perhaps reluctantly and marginally, to a recognizable society. They are thus situated in the central realistic tradition that nourishes nearly all English-Canadian novelists from Laurence, Robertson Davies, Munro, and Atwood to Rudy Wiebe, Jack Hodgins, W. P. Kinsella, and Kroetsch.

Were we to compare these major contemporary English-speaking novelists with one another, the variety of their styles and the novelty of their experimentation within the central tradition would invite examination. But when we compare them with Québec writers, no matter what characteristics they may at first seem to share with their francophone counterparts, in the long run it is their common traits that predominate and the essential difference between the two groups that demands commentary. The difference in the case at hand is as great as that between the two islands, the crude, untamed West Coast island I have just described and that other island in the St. Lawrence, where characters are ciphers, where domestic objects have a life of their own, where events follow a dreamlike development, where references to the real world tend to be cultural or literary, where sex is flirtatious and whimsical, where the only violence is verbal.

Islands are places that encourage introspection and self-discovery: witness Margaret Atwood's *Surfacing* or Marian Engel's *Bear*. They can also contain communities whose existence is threatened from inside or outside: for Canadian examples, see Félix Leclerc's *Le fou de l'île,* Jacques Godbout's *L'île au dragon,* or Hodgins's *Invention of the World*. The private and public significance of life on the two islands will be the theme of the closing part of this comparison.

Poulin's parable seems to focus chiefly on introspection. In line with Falardeau's statement about the verticality of Québec fiction, it is Teddy's destiny and the meaning of his life that most concern us. At first he uses the island merely as a retreat. With Marie's arrival, however, the couple begin to discover the island's unique character—"This place is heaven on earth!" (28) Marie asserts—and they try to live to its rhythms and respect its ecological integrity, agreeing to leave it "exactly as it is" (49). The intrusion of the other characters, however, seems to shrink their *paradis terrestre*; halfway through the book Marie complains: "There's starting to be too many people" (96). Indeed, no island is inviolate, and near the end the Organizer bids Teddy consider the wisdom of Donne's "No man is an island" and join in the group dynamics. But Teddy refuses to reveal his private thoughts; since he will not play, he is first ostracized, then physically expelled, forced into the water and obliged to swim across to the next island, Ile aux Ruaux, uninhabited except for the petrified remains of an old man, a former caretaker.

Even before his expulsion, Teddy has suffered several grave disillusionments. First he discovers that the translations he had been doing for the boss were never published; they had been replaced by ones done by an electronic brain: end of career. Then Marie leaves: end of romance. Finally he learns from the others that although they accept the notion that marginal people may be useful, they consider him not aggressive enough and "outside the margin" (164).

So the novel, like other tales embedded in the main narrative (one of the Hermit of Ile Saint-Barnabé, another of a fight between a cachalot and a giant squid), has an unhappy ending. As far as fiction means anything, what does this tale mean? On a global level it may be a pessimistic commentary on the future of life on an overcrowded planet. On a more local level it may refer, again pessimistically, to the political hopes of the islanded nation of Québec. Ecologically speaking, the message is clear: the islanders do not leave the island exactly as they found it. But I think these social interpretations are less important than a more personal, philosophical one.

The isolated island translator (*island* and *isolated* have the same root) is the writer in the modern world. Teddy is absorbed in his work (the novel contains many examples of the finesse required in translation), but his art is undervalued and his skills prove to be obsolescent. His chief qualities—his meticulousness, his adaptability, and his gentleness (one might say his humanity)—are belittled and rejected. He is betrayed by his lover, his employer, his friends. Growing numbness in his right hand and arm signifies a withdrawal of power and perhaps life. The reader is forced to conclude that, for T. D. B., Donne was probably wrong: we are not "all part of the main"; rather, in Arnold's sad words, "We mortal millions live alone / ... [enisled in] / The unplumbed, salt, estranging sea." Or, to give the thought a contemporary Canadian expression, in Ken Norris's words, "we will only / ever know islands, for we cannot help / but be them" (102).

The conclusion to Cohen's novel is complex but not so distressing. Calvin, Teddy's counterpart and newcomer to the island, is likewise involved in a search for the self, but he is not estranged or expelled; he is finally accepted. At first he feels "like a scientist on a new planet" (16). The island's wildness has overtones of a northern Eden (a common British Columbian theme), and its fertility and fresh-

ness make him think of the continent to the east, where he comes from, as "a place that could no longer renew itself ... a vast conglomerate city of doomed smokestacks and concrete" (14). By exposure to this new environment, but even more by the mediation of Laurel, he gradually becomes acclimatized. Laurel's experience precedes his. Six years earlier, under the guidance of Johnny Tulip, she had shaken off the influence of her too rational mapmaker father and has gained some of the intuitive knowledge of island ways possessed by Johnny and his family. Calvin thinks of her as having been "turned wild by this island and ... imparting the same thing to him" (2) in their love-making. In fact, her choice of Calvin over Johnny when she discovers she is carrying Calvin's child, and her decision to stay and have the baby on the island consolidate Calvin's integration—as does the fact that he risks his life to save Johnny when C. W. Smith goes on a rampage and tries to shoot the Indian. In the closing pages Laurel anticipates living off the land with Calvin: "In the spring they would explore the coast, live on mussels and clams, make salads of wild peas and plantain" (218). Johnny's blind old mother, who has second sight, predicts a good future for Laurel. She salutes the unvanquished strength of Johnny's spirit. All in all, it is an upbeat ending.

But although it may be much less gloomy than the close of *Les grandes marées*, it is not unconditionally optimistic. The ecological issue is a constant concern throughout the novel. In contrast to Laurel's and Calvin's readiness to adopt island ways, there is a powerful threat of exploitation. "Pretty soon they'll take down the whole island" (66), says Johnny morosely, and his act of protest, blowing up the logging company's caterpillar tractor, is a futile gesture unlikely to stem "the ultimate if narrow triumph of technology over this wild island" (193). C. W. Smith personifies accommodation to the forces of exploitation and destruction. "You'd think it was the end of the world just because we were going to cut down a few trees" (158), he says. His death—he is killed by a bullet from his own rifle—is a minor victory but only a temporary reprieve.

Behind the ecological issue, of course, is the even graver one of the destruction of the Indian way of life. The community, divided into loggers and Indians, teeters on the brink of conflict, and it is the news that, in opening a new road, the loggers have blown up mortuary poles at the old Indian village that sparks the final melee. More than this, Johnny's poor health and drunkenness, his sister Victoria's sickness and suicide, his mother's blindness (which the Vancouver doctors are unable to cure), and Mary Gail's seduction by C. W., all point to decline and degradation. The fact that Laurel is accepted into Johnny Tulip's family almost as a replacement for Victoria is taken as a positive sign, but despite that kinship and her appreciation of the Indian character and gifts—Mary Gail's warmth (she generates heat like Old Gélisol), Johnny's forest skills, his mother's clairvoyance—the future of the

Indians looks grim. In his own vision of the future, Johnny sees himself turned into wood. "They wouldn't know whether to bury him or throw him away" (42). So although there is personal fulfillment for some of the characters at the end of *Wooden Hunters,* the progressive note is undercut by skepticism.

Perhaps in the final analysis the main difference between the endings of the two novels is one of emphasis. But emphasis is style, and style is all. One can say that in their conclusions these two books touch on the same themes and content—violation of the island as sanctuary, growing aggression among island inhabitants, triumph of technology over humanity, a measure of personal defeat. In the English novel, however, we are concerned about several characters and points of view and are left pondering the fate of the couple, the family, the community, the island as a place of human habitation, whereas in the French work we close the book absorbed in metaphysical speculation about the hero's solitary destiny. The difference in emphasis seems to validate Falardeau's distinction: the French novel *is* more preoccupied with relations "between man and his destiny or man and the absolute," while the English novel *is* concerned chiefly with "man and his milieu or man and society."

What conclusion can one draw after this cursory comparison of two books, two writers, two types of novel? In **Les grandes marées** the "Author" speaks of his ambition to write the great novel of America. "The French novel deals more with ideas," he explains, "while the American novel deals with action. Now, we are French in America, or Americans of French descent, if you prefer. We in Quebec, then, have the opportunity to write a novel that will be the product of both the French and the American tendencies" (141). He may be on the right track, but, from present evidence, the realization of his theory is a thing of the future. For despite the fact that young Québec writers do seem, like their English-Canadian counterparts, to be assimilating traits from the opposite culture, and despite striking similarities (such as the fictional islands), the two literary traditions remain as distinct as the regions of the country where the novels are set. The first conclusion to be drawn, then, is that readers in the United States must not make the mistake of viewing Canadian literature as univalent. Canadians are learning to live this difficult and stimulating duality, and those who study Canadian literature must learn to respect the diversity too. Second, neither the French nor the English expression of Canadian reality is exclusive; rather, the two views are complementary, and the investigation of their complex relations is arduous but rewarding. Earle Birney's "Pacific Door" comments poetically on the task involved and suggests an alternative to the dichotomy represented by Arnold and Donne:

Here Spaniards and Vancouver's boatmen scrawled
the problem that is ours and yours
that there is no clear strait of Anian
to lead us easy back to Europe

that men are isled in ocean or in ice
and only joined by long endeavour to be joined. ...

(142)

Works Cited

Aquin, Hubert. *Neige Noire.* Montréal: Cercle du Livre de France, 1974. *Hamlet's Twin.* Trans. Sheila Fischman. Toronto: McClelland, 1974.

Arnold, Matthew. "To Marguerite." *Norton Anthology of Poetry.* Ed. Arthur M. Eastman et al. New York: Norton, 1970. 820-21.

Atwood, Margaret. *Surfacing.* Toronto: McClelland, 1972.

Beauchemin, Yves. *Le matou.* Montréal: Québec/Amérique, 1981. *The Alley Cat.* Trans. Sheila Fischman. Toronto: McClelland, 1981.

Birney, Earle. *Selected Poems.* Toronto: Oxford UP, 1966.

Blais, Marie-Claire. *Visions d'Anna.* Montréal: Stanké, 1982. *Anna's World.* Trans. Sheila Fischman. Toronto: Lester and Orpen Dennys, 1984.

Carrier, Roch. *La dame qui avait des chaînes aux chevilles.* Montréal: Stanké, 1981. *Lady with Chains.* Trans. Sheila Fischman. Toronto: Anansi, 1984.

Chauveau, Pierre-Joseph-Olivier. *L'instruction publique au Canada: Précis historique et statistique.* Québec: Augustin Côté, 1876.

Cohen, Matt. *Wooden Hunters.* 1975. Toronto: McClelland, 1984.

Engel, Marian. *Bear.* Toronto: McClelland, 1976.

Falardeau, Jean-Charles. *Notre société et son roman.* Montréal: HMH-Hurtubise, 1967.

Godbout, Jacques. *L'île au dragon.* Paris: Seuil, 1976. *Dragon Island.* Trans. David Ellis. Toronto: Musson, 1978.

Hébert, Anne. *Héloïse.* Paris: Seuil, 1980. *Heloise.* Trans. Sheila Fischman. Toronto: Stoddart, 1982.

———. *Kamouraska.* Paris: Seuil, 1970. *Kamouraska.* Trans. Norman Shapiro. Toronto: Paperjacks, 1974.

Hodgins, Jack. *The Invention of the World.* Toronto: Macmillan, 1976.

Kirby, William. *The Golden Dog.* 1877. New York: American Publishers, n.d.

Langevin, André. *Poussière sur la ville.* Montréal: Cercle du Livre de France, 1953. *Dust over the City.* Trans. John Latrobe and Robert Gottlieb. Toronto: McClelland, 1955.

Laurence, Margaret. *The Diviners.* Toronto: McClelland, 1974.

Leclerc, Félix. *Le fou de l'île.* Paris: Denoël, 1958. *The Madman, the Kite and the Island.* Trans. Philip Stratford. Ottawa: Oberon, 1976.

MacLennan, Hugh. *Two Solitudes.* Toronto: Macmillan, 1945.

Mailhot, Laurent. "Jacques Poulin." *The Oxford Companion to Canadian Literature.* Ed. William Toye. Toronto: Oxford UP, 1983. 675-76.

New, W. H. "Fiction." *Literary History of Canada.* Ed. C. F. Klinck. 2nd ed. Toronto: U of Toronto P, 1976. 233-83.

Norris, Ken. *Islands.* Kingston: Quarry, 1986.

Poulin, Jacques. *Les grandes marées.* Montréal: Leméac, 1978. *Springtides.* Trans. Sheila Fischman. Toronto: Anansi, 1986.

Ross, Sinclair. *As for Me and My House.* 1941. Toronto: McClelland, 1957.

Roy, Gabrielle. *Bonheur d'occasion.* Montréal: Société des Editions Pascal, 1945.

Stratford, Philip. *All the Polarities: Comparative Studies in Contemporary Canadian Novels in French and English.* Toronto: ECW, 1986.

Sutherland, Ronald. *Second Image: Comparative Studies in Québec/Canadian Literature.* Toronto: New, 1971.

Paul G. Socken (essay date 1993)

SOURCE: Socken, Paul G. "Water Imagery in the Novels of Jacques Poulin." *Studies in Canadian Literature/Études en littérature canadienne* 18.2 (1993): 156-67. Print.

[*In the following essay, Socken contends that Poulin has sought individual and social unity throughout his career and that he often chooses water imagery to represent that pursuit. Socken notes that among the images Poulin uses is water as a vehicle of transformation, as a life force and healer or purifier, and as a potentially threatening element.*]

Amongst the most common images in Jacques Poulin's novelistic universe is that of water. Its meaning is so highly charged that even its rare absence signals an important lack. Gaston Bachelard's study of water imagery is an acknowledged classic whose relevance is timeless. A reading of the Poulian corpus taking into account Bachelard's analysis[1] will reveal the centrality of this image to Poulin's novels and its significance.

According to Bachelard, water is one of the most difficult images to categorize, but it does appear to be, above all else,

> un être total, elle a un corps, une âme, une voix. Plus qu'aucun autre élément peut- être, l'eau est une réalité poétique complète. Une poétique de l'eau, malgré la va-

riété de ses spectacles, est assurée d'une unité. L'eau doit suggérer au poète une obligation nouvelle: l'unité d'élément.

(22-23)

Poulin's writing is, in fact, a search for unity, both within the self and beyond, and so the omnipresent water imagery perfectly and naturally expresses that search. I will study the Poulian corpus in chronological order to demonstrate the subtle differences in the use of the symbol in the seven novels.

Mon Cheval pour un royaume (1967) is a novel about personal and social frustration and imprisonment. The protagonist, Pierre Delisle—man really is an island—is in prison for radical political activism. Political dissatisfaction mirrors personal dissatisfaction as Pierre cannot relate to those around him. In keeping with this theme, there are no natural bodies of water in the novel, except for the water in which one of the characters, Simon, drowns himself.

Virtually all other water appears in the form of tears, rain and the imaginary liquid state of his companion, Nathalie "qui commence à déborder" (104). The "solidity" of people and things, their imposing physical being, seems to be an obstacle to their harmonious contact,[2] and so Pierre imagines her flowing out beyond herself, reaching him and touching him as would a body of water. The fact that the contact is imaginary only serves further to underline the lack of relationships between the characters.[3] The restaurant Pierre frequents is called L'Aquarium, suggesting water that is contained, not in its natural setting. The novel concerns itself with personal and cultural frustration, psychological and physical imprisonment, and the absence of natural sources of water reflects that tension, the tears and rain suggesting the melancholia of the protagonist's state of mind.

Poulin introduces the notion of the rain in ***Mon Cheval pour un royaume*** as blue (10, 188, 189, 190), grey (188), and another time as "une pluie jaune, terreuse, terreuse et froide" (168). Water that takes on the colour of the sky or the earth, for example, is not merely decorative in the novel, but suggests an important metaphoric reality:

> Les valeurs sensuelle—et non plus les sensations—étant attachées à des substances donnent des correspondances qui ne trompent pas. Ainsi les parfums verts comme les prairies sont évidemment des parfum frais; ce sont des chairs fraîches et lustrées, des chairs pleines comme des chairs d'enfant. Toute la correpondance est soutenue par l'eau primitive, par une eau charnelle, par l'élément universel, des chairs pleines comme des chairs d'enfant. Toute la correspondance est soutenue par l'eau primitive, par une eau charnelle, par l'élément universel.

(46-47)

Water has the power to take on the properties of the world around it, to evoke powerful associations and to participate in the protagonist's search. Water imagery here, and in the subsequent novels, is an active element, virtually a companion to the protagonist. Pierre may feel "walled in" personally and politically, but the imagery expresses a desire for fluidity, for a blending of elements, for an ideal world of harmony. The novel embodies the dichotomy of isolation and inclusion in its water imagery.

With *Jimmy* (1969), a novel dominated by water imagery from beginning to end, water is explicitly linked to dreams: "Beaucoup d'eau dans son rêve et le rêve se jette dans la mer" (10); "À marée haute, on dort bien, on rêve mieux" (21). For Bachelard, the link between dreams and water is important:

> Si la rêverie s'attache à la réalité, elle l'humanise, elle l'agrandit, elle la magnifie. Toutes les propriétés du réel, dès qu'elles sont rêvées, deviennent des qualités héroïques. Ainsi, pour la rêveries de l'eau, l'eau devient l'héroïne de la douceur et de la pureté. La matière rêvée ne reste donc pas objective, on peut dire vraiment qu'elle s'évhémérisme.[4]
>
> (205)

Water imagery in Poulin is not only a participant in the protagonist's quest, as we have seen in *Mon Cheval pour un royaume,* but a vehicle for transforming reality, a preparatory element in an idealized vision of the world. Jimmy's world is corrupt and collapsing, as symbolized by the rotting piles on which his house stands in the river. The imagined flood at the end of the novel, and the transformation of the house into an ark, translate the desire for the recreation of the world, the regeneration of a failed world into a new one of greater potential. The water imagery and the dream together fuse to form the vision.

Towards this vision of an ideal world of unity and harmony, water is combined again with other elements, here with fire and sky. Jimmy says that "tu pourrais croire que toute la voie lactée se reflète dans l'eau" (92-93). He notes that "sur la rive sud, à Saint-Nicolas, ou quelque part, il y a un autre feu de grève et il se reflète dans l'eau" (89) and that "la marée qui monte doucement dans le noir ... menace d'éteindre le feu et toutes les histoires" (40).

Bachelard makes the point that "dans le règne des matières, on ne trouvera rien de plus contraire que l'eau et le feu. L'eau et le feu donnent peut-être la seule contradiction vraiment substantielle" (133). Yet even these innately contradictory elements can be combined: "Si le Soleil est le glorieux époux de la Mer, il faudra qu'à la dimension de la libation, l'eau "se donne" au feu, il faudra que le feu "prenne" l'eau" (Bachelard 134). Bachelard terms this combination "un épithalame [i.e. poem] pour le mariage des deux éléments" (134). Thus, the association of sky, earth and fire, with water, suggests the ultimate union of harmonious elements towards which the Poulian universe strives and in which water is the central link.

In *Jimmy,* the vision is internalized as the protagonist proclaims "L'eau me rentre" (75) and associates "l'eau de la mer et les yeux" (80). This process of internalization foreshadows the later novels and points to a vital relationship between the world and the inner being.

The dream, then, links the material world and the idealized world, as the sky and earth, fire and earth, earth and water and water and the self are incorporated into one another in the world of the imagination. Bachelard states that "L'être qui sort de l'eau est un reflet qui peu à peu se matérialise: il est une image avant d'être un être, il est un désir avant d'être une image" (Bachelard 49). The Bachelardian notion of the desire preceding the image and the image the being is a perfect summary of Poulin's novelistic world. The dreamed-of ideal world waits to be born as the vision is elaborated and the desire constantly reformulated.

Focused as it is entirely on questions of life and death, *Le Coeur de la baleine bleue* (1970) portrays water as the vehicle of the "bateau fantôme": "Il tombait une lourde pluie d'automne que le nordet plaquait aussitôt contre la vitre. ... On ne voyait pas la côte de Lévis et on entendait par intervalles mugir la sirène d'un bateau fantôme" (25). References to the "bateau fantôme" appear as well in *Mon Cheval pour un royaume* (81) and *Le Vieux Chagrin* (Chapter 31). Bachelard explains this preoccupation with the ship of death as an adventure of the soul:

> Ainsi, l'adieu au bord de la mer est à la fois le plus déchirant et le plus littéraire des adieux. Sa poésie exploite un vieux fonds de rêve et d'héroïsme. Il réveille sans doute en nous le échos les plus douloureux. Tout un côté de notre âme nocturne s'explique par le mythe de la mort conçue comme un départ sur l'eau. Les inversions sont, pour le rêveur, continu-elles entre ce départ et la mort. Pour certains rêveurs, l'eau est le mouvement nouveau qui nous invite au voyage jamais fait. Ce départ matérialisé nous enlève à la matière de la terre.
>
> (103)

The protagonist, Noël, has had a heart transplant and is intensely conscious of the fine line between life and death, and so water, "la plus maternelle des morts" (Bachelard 100), becomes associated here with images of death.

The protagonist's apartment in Quebec City overlooks the St. Lawrence. That mighty waterway forms a backdrop to the novel, and most of the water imagery appears in the form of ice. A series of boats are described as "prisonniers de la glace" (60-61), two "traversiers" are "immobiles au milieu des glaces" (101), and much of the discussion in the novel takes place between Noël, and Bill, an ice-hockey player, about their passionate interest in that most Canadian sport. Just as Noël feels obsessed with thoughts of death, trapped between life and death, the water is frozen into ice, reflecting the main character's feeling of helplessness. The life-force is immobile, all movement suspended.

The opposite phenomenon occurs when water joins with earth to form mud: "alors commence l'expérience de la "liason," le long rêve de la "liason." Ce pouvoir de lier substantivement, par la communauté de liens intimes, l'ouvrier en rêvant sa tâche, l'attribue tantôt à la terre, tantôt à l'eau" (143). When Pierre dreams of the world reborn after the explosion in *Mon Cheval pour un royaume,* he is "à plat ventre dans la vase fraîche" (175). Before the "flood" in *Jimmy,* three of the characters try to re-build the world themselves in the sand: "Lucy, Jenny, et la nageuse de longue distance sont en train de construire tout un village avec des maisons, des routes, un pont, un garage, une église et tout" (89). Bachelard explains the mixture of earth and water as a form of creation: "Les vrais travailleurs sont ceux qui ont mis "à la pâte." Ils ont la volonté opérante, la volonté manuelle. Cette volonté très spéciale est visible aux ligatures de la main ... Si Bouddha a cent bras, c'est qu'il est pétrisseur" (146-147). The frustration of immobility is expressed by the image of ice, but the desire to recreate the world in keeping with the ideal is translated by the image of the union of earth and water.

In *Le Coeur de la baleine bleue,* Noël's attachment to life is still expressed through water imagery in spite of the predominant images of ice. When his doctor advises him to move, Noël responds "que je tenais autant à voir le fleuve qu'à ma vie, que je préférais courir le risque" (66). And when he finally accepts the inevitability of his death, that, too, is expressed in a similar way: "Alors j'ai compris que la douceur était le sentier qui menait à la mort et aussi que la mort était comme un fleuve" (144). As Noël is about to die, his friend, Simon, says to him "Je la [la porte] laisse ouverte pour que tu entendes la marée" (200). Whether it is water on which the "bateau fantôme" floats, the ice in which boats are trapped, or the water which travels towards death, the water imagery in this novel about death is complex as it reflects Noël's angst about the relationship between life and death.

However, the novel concerns itself equally with the *acceptance* of death as it does about death itself, about understanding as much as about fact. For that reason, water imagery, as we saw in *Jimmy,* is internalized and becomes a force within the individual: "Le coeur battait tranquillement et je me laissai envahir petit à petit par le sommeil qui semblait monter du fond de moi comme une grande marée" (18-19). The inner voyage towards an understanding of the self is expressed in similar terms: "Quand vous voyagez à l'intérieur de vous-même, les courants vous entraînent fatalement vers votre enfance" (147). Bachelard refers to subterranean water as "cette eau intérieure" (203) and suggests that in the realm of the poetic imagination it has the power to purify the ground under which it flows. In the same way, Poulin's internalization of the image suggests healing on a personal level. As Bachelard succinctly puts it, "L'eau dans son symbolisme, sait tout réunir" (203). The very course of coming to terms with life, and with death, finds expression in this same image. Poulin's

novels until *Le Vieux Chagrin* are about process, not result, and the complexity of water imagery serves to reflect the intricacies of that process.

Faites de beaux rêves (1974), which takes place on a course for race cars in Quebec, is the least introspective of the novels, the most pessimistic, and has much less water imagery than the other novels. It is as if, after staring death in the face in the previous novel, Poulin needed to distance himself from such intensely personal confrontations. The result is a novel that is more despairing precisely because it avoids the central issues that make Poulin's novelistic universe seductive, albeit bittersweet in tone.

The only references to water are Jane's mention of her brother's death by drowning (164), Amadou's immersing himself in the river (49-50), and the recounting of the Indian legend of America born of the waters (139).

Drowning occurs in several of the novels (cf *Le Coeur de la baleine bleue* 100) and emphasizes the polyvalence of the image of water. It is a life-force, a healer, a purifer, but it is also potentially threatening. Like life itself, which it symbolises more than any other single image, it is complex and mysterious, embodying contrary aspects of nature and human nature.

The protagonist, Amadou, nicknamed Madou, like Poulin's other protagonists, searches for meaning, but he is trapped and terribly frustrated by the environment in which he finds himself. The racetrack, and the monitoring of the race, symbolize the futility of his life and of those in whose company he finds himself.

It is revealing that the only sustained image of water in the novel, other than the Indian legend, is one in which Amadou immerses himself in the river, to the dismay of his brother. The water is cold:

> Elle était même frette. Elle était frette en calvair, je n'ai pas osé me baigner. Je suis resté au bord et je me suis lavé la figure. Mais mon frère Madou est entré dans l'eau comme si c'était le Gulf-Stream. Il s'est même assis au fond de la rivière, il avait de l'eau jusqu'au cou et je pense qu'il est resté là à peu près une demi-heure.
>
> (49-50)

Bachelard comments that the water of the river is a purifying force:

> À l'eau pure on demande donc primitivement une pureté à la fois active et substantielle. Par la purification, on participe à une force féconde, rénovatrice, polyvalente ... La meilleure preuve de cette puissance intime, c'est qu'elle appartient à chaque goutte du liquide. Innombrables sont les textes où la purification apparaît comme une simple aspersion.
>
> (193)

The contrasting reactions of Amadou and his brother are striking. The water is too cold for Théo, but Amadou immerses himself and remains in the water as if a rite were being acted out. In the novel most dominated by frustation, futility and despair, the protagonist seeks out an active ritual of spiritual cleansing. His immersion takes on the qualities of a personal encounter with the primitive life-force in a quest for meaning.

The Indian legend of the creation of America in *Faites de Beaux Rêves* recounts that the earth once had no people:

> L'espace, aussi loin que vous pouvez voir devant vous, était rempli par un vaste océan. Il n'y avait pas de soleil ni de lune ni d'étoiles, de sorte que la lumière n'existait pas et que tout était ténèbres. Au-dessus du vaste océan se trouvait un grand vide d'air.

> (136)

The waters are called "les eaux sombres" (138). It is here that "la Femme Céleste" falls to the floor of the waters, brings earth, and creates "une grande île que l'on appelle maintenant l'Amérique du Nord" (139). This "generic" creation story contains the primordial elements of virtually all creation stories, including the essential ingredient of water.[5] That there is a creation story at all in this novel is noteworthy. Its presence betrays a need for regeneration, new beginnings, hope for a better future. Just as the ritual "bath" suggests the potential for spiritual rebirth on the personal level, the Indian legend evokes the same longing on a cosmic level.

Les Grandes Marées (1978) is a satiric look at society and its failings, given the ideals of unity, harmony and sensitivity that Poulin has set out in his previous writing. The novel treats water imagery, not with the reverence it commands in the earlier and following novels, but with irony, as befits the context. "Ilots de verdure" are plants in office buildings (13), the sun's reflection on the water appears as a picture on a man's shirt (125), and the protagonist dreams that he and his brother are on an island together—Alcatraz (140). In addition, the tides, instead of bringing refreshing waves of cleansing water, are associated with all the problematic characters brought to the island ("Tout le monde est arrivé dans l'île au moment des grandes marées" 162).

An even greater irony is that the story does unfold on an island and that the protagonist's solitude, surrounded by the waters of the St. Lawrence, holds real promise for a new life, a genesis unmistakably akin to the biblical one. The renewal is not to be, and the situation ends up as nothing more than failed potential. The protagonist's companion, Marie, enters the water "en s'aspergeant" (37), which, we have seen above, is a ritual act, and swims fearlessly in the waters surrounding the island. Bachelard calls the swimmer "un héros précoce" (218) and observes that "le saut dans la mer ravive, plus que tout autre événement physique, les échos d'une initiation dangereuse" (222). The protagonist, Teddy Bear, on the other hand, less "heroic" and therefore more subject to the vicissitudes of life, does not really swim until he is exiled from the

island by the crass intruders when he must make his way to another island retreat (199).

If the absence of water reveals a spiritual lack, as it does in *Faites de Beaux Rêves,* its presence, then, does not necessarily guarantee the realization of the Poulian ideals. Quite the contrary in *Les Grandes Marées.* All of which is preparatory to *Volkswagen Blues* (1984), in which water imagery appears in its most ambiguous and polyvalent (varied) form. Water is linked in this novel with annihilation of the Indians of North America, and yet constitutes an indispensable part of the protagonist's search for meaning and for the self. So much so that his very name, Jack Waterman, incorporates the elemental substance.

La Grande Sauterelle, Jack's companion, who is partly Indian, points out to him the Indians' tragic fate: "Pendant de nombreuses années, tous les Indiens qui passaient par la vallée de la rivière Illinois firent un détour afin d'éviter le Roher, car c'était un endroit habité par la mort et par les esprits de la tribu qui avait été exterminée" (116). As la Grande Sauterelle reveals the history of the various Indian peoples, it becomes clear that their demise is always associated with bodies of water. One massacre took place "sur les bords de la rivière Washita" (206), another at Sand Creek, "un ruisseau qui se trouve à 70 kilomètres du Fort Lyon" (205), and the final Indian defeat "au bord d'un ruisseau qui s'appelle Wounded Knee" (207). Bachelard recognizes this link between waters and death:

> Eau silencieuse, eau sombre, eau dormante, autant de leçons matérielles pour une méditation sur la mort. Mais ce n'est pas la leçon d'une mort héraclitéenne, d'une mort qui nous emporte au loin avec le vourant, comme un courant. c'est la leçon d'une mort immobile, d'une mort en profondeur, d'une mort qui demeure avec nous, près de nous, en nous.

> (96)

In fact, this meditation on death opens Jack's eyes to the realities of North American history and allows him to begin his search for meaning within himself. The ideal world he had been looking for across America does not exist beyond the self, either in the past or in the present. This point is tellingly made by an old woman whom Jack and la Grande Sauterelle meet:

> Elle disait qu'elle chantait maintenant pour réchauffer le coeur des hommes et des femmes qui, un jour, avaient possédé une maison, des parents et des amis quelque part sur le vaste territoire de l'Amérique et qui, après avoir tout perdu, avaient été emportés par le courant et étaient venus échouer sur les bords du Pacifique.

> (279)

The Indians' loss is generalized as part of the condition of modern man whose dreams for a better world have ended in failure. Jack's quest is doomed in the material, topographical sense, but leads him back to his own, inner resources.

It is only as the novel ends that Jack's inner search truly begins, but that search is alluded to, again through the medium of water imagery. All of chapter fifteen concerns Jack's withdrawal into himself, in which he cuts himself off completely from the world. That state is called "le complexe du Scaphandrier" which compares it to a diver who isolates himself in a diver's suit at the ocean's depths. In addition, as pointed out above, Jack's very name is associated with water, suggesting that his identity is linked with that image. At the end of the novel, as he prepares to return to Quebec, and his companion will stay in San Francisco to find herself, which will be in effect an exploration of the self for both, la Grande Sauterelle cites Daniel Boone: "Je me sens parfois comme une feuille sur un torrent. Elle peut tournoyer, tourbillonner et se retourner, mais elle va toujours vers l'avant" (289). Here the water imagery and the inner state are clearly associated. All the waterways of the novel, great and small, become internalised to carry the protagonists on their currents towards the realities of the inner self. They had to travel the continent's rivers to discover that the only one that matters is the one that leads them back to themselves.

Le Vieux Chagrin (1989) combines the major themes of the previous novels and does so through the inevitable and necessary water imagery.

All of the novels are about a protagonist's quest for the authentic, inner self, and this is never more true than it is here. They are also studies of frustrated writers attempting to express themselves, as every protagonist, except Jimmy, is a writer. (Jimmy's father is a writer.) And they all search for the "royaume" of the first novel, a world of peace, harmony and unity which eludes them. *Le Vieux Chagrin* achieves a synthesis of these issues.

It is established from the beginning that this is a novel centered on water as the protagonist makes the point repeatedly that his house had been moved from the city and was the only one "au milieu da la baie" (10). The other major site in the novel is a cave which is located "tout à fait au bout de la baie, près d'une petite crique sablonneuse" (13). In addition, absolutely every aspect of the novel, including the most ostensibly minor ones, is associated with the waters: the preface is a poem called "Le Fleuve caché"; Jim, the protagonist, consoles la Petite, his adopted daughter, with a song titled "L'Eau Vive."

This is a novel of revelations, all of which involve the water. Jim's brother talks to him about Jim's idealized woman, Marika, the elusive inhabitant of the cave, as the two men cross the St. Lawrence: "Nous étions rendus au milieu du fleuve et il soufflait une petite brise rafraîchissante. C'était un de ces moments où l'on a le sentiment que tout est parfait et où l'on voudrait que le temps s'arrête" (70-71). Jim finds the "paradis terrestre" for a fleeting moment, a place of perfect harmony and inspirational beauty, in Venice, a city on the water (Chapter 29). La Petite tells Jim about her discovery of her real parents and their indifference to her when they are beside the river: "je crois bien que le fleuve, tout à côté de nous, le vieux fleuve qui, pendant trois siècles et demi, avait entendu les confidences de tout un peuple, retenait son souffle lui aussi" (135).

That this vital image is attached to the profound personal and global aspirations of the protagonist is anticipated by Bachelard:

> Fort de cette connaissance d'une profondeur dans un élément matériel, le lecteur comprendra enfin que l'eau est aussi un type de destin, non plus seulement le vain destin des images foyantes, le vain destin d'un rêve qui ne s'achève pas, mais un destin essentiel qui métamorphose sans cesse la substance de l'être.
>
> (8)

Water is the constant companion of most Poulian "heroes" because of its association in the imagination with the very essence of what it is to be human and to be searching for meaning.

Meaning in the Poulian fictional universe is irrevocably associated with writing, and this is a novel about writing as much as it is about anything else. Not only is writing linked here to the expression of the authentic self, to consoling oneself for the sadness in life and to reconciling oneself to the world and to others, writing and water imagery are intimately related. Jim's fear of not being able to write is compared to "un vieux puits asséché" (81) and he always writes facing the river: "Il [le fleuve] donnait, me semblait-il, un peu de force et de régularité à ma pauvre inspiration" (47).

Bachelard calls water "la maîtresse du langage fluide" (250), explaining that language and water are fundamentally the same: "la liquidité est, d'après nous, le désir même du langage. Le langage veut couler. Il coule naturellement" (251). Water speaks, as does language, and what it speaks of is the very idea of the Poulian ethic: "L'eau aussi est une vaste unité. Elle harmonise les cloches du crapaud et du merle. Du moins une oreille poétisée ramène à l'unité des voix discordantes quand elle se soumet au chant de l'eau comme à un son fondamental" (260). The writer searches for his "voice"; that is, the truth about himself and the world, beside the waters, because the two must be harmonized, the one in concert with the other:

> les voix de l'eau sont à peine métaphoriques, que le langage des eaux est une réalité poétique directe, que les ruisseaux et les fleuves sonorisent avec une étrange fidelité les paysages muets, que les eaux bruissantes apprennent aux oiseaux et aux hommes à chanter, à parler, à redire, et qu'il y a en somme continuité entre la parole de l'eau et la parole humaine.
>
> (22)

The writer and the waters exist in a symbiotic relationship as nature and human nature complement one another and nourish one another spiritually and artistically.

The Poulian adventure, which crosses boundaries of time and space, only to find itself most deeply involved in issues rooted in the self, is inextricably linked to water imagery. The unity Poulin seeks for the world and for the self, the search for meaning in life and in death, the place of writing and the role of the writer are fundamentally and intricately linked to the waters. The great dream of the human imagination, says Bachelard, is that of the "substance valorisée," be it the waters or the word, which holds the key to life, which reveals the mighty secret:

> C'est la loi même de la rêverie de puissance: tenir sous un petit volume, dans le creux de la main, le moyen d'une domination universelle. C'est, sous la forme concrète, le même idéal que la connaissance du mot clef, du petit mot, qui permet de découvrir le plus caché des secrets.

(194)

Notes

1. *L'Eau et les rêves, Essai sur l'imagination de la matière,* Paris: Librairie José Corti, 1987. All quotations taken from this edition with page numbers in brackets following the quotation.

2. He imagines himself as a stone in the river with the water passing over him (60) and he describes himself as a being walled in by his "carapace."

3. Rain, while natural, is associated with "des larmes cosmiques," with "l'eau-mère du chagrin humain, la matière de la mélancolie" (Bachelard 89).

4. évhémérisme: "doctrine pour laquelle les dieux du paganisme sont des personnages humains divinisés après leur mort," Robert, 1976, 644.

5. Eliade, Mircea, *Patterns in Comparative Religion,* Meridian Books, Cleveland and New York, 1970, 212.

David Walker (essay date 1994)

SOURCE: Walker, David. "The Role of the Incipits in Poulin's *Le vieux chagrin.*" *LittéRéalité* 6.1 (1994): 97-107. Print.

[In the following essay, Walker considers the role of the incipits—the opening words of a text, including epigraphs, chapter titles, and first sentences—in Mr. Blue *in relation to the novel's overall narrative. Walker explores how these textual fragments "interact both with the content of the story . . . and with the formal organisation of the narrative."]*

> Encompassing the complexity of existence in the modern world demands a technique of ellipsis, of condensation.
>
> Milan Kundera, *Art of the Novel*

The potential importance of pre-narrative and narrative beginnings, or "incipits" in the signifying process has been underlined by a number of writers and critics. Louis Aragon, for example, held that a text was in large measure determined by its first sentence.[1] Harry Levin affirms the close relationship of title and text, describing this relationship as "synecdochic" in nature.[2] The similarity of the operations of an incipit to those of the "construction en abyme" has been signalled by Raymond Jean[3] and by Jean Ricardou, for whom "le début d'un livre agence souvent un raccourci de son fonctionnement."[4] These comments challenge the more traditional view of the incipits as subordinate to and simply illustrative of the signifying processes presented in the macro-text. A "générative" approach on the other hand confers upon these opening fragments—title, epigraph, chapter title, initial sentence—a principal role in the *production* of textual meaning.

Jacques Poulin's seventh novel, *Le Vieux Chagrin,*[5] offers a particularly fine example of the dynamic interaction between incipits and the narrative they introduce. Increasingly Poulin's novels have been characterized by a highly compressed style resulting from a tenacious struggle—often explicitly invoked in the novels—to find the "right" word. As the strategy of lexical condensation adopted by Poulin is also that which leads to the successful operation of an incipit—by permitting more complex interactions with the macro-text—his works offer a privileged area for the investigation of these textual beginnings.

In *Le Vieux Chagrin* a close re-reading of the incipits is authorized by an important episode in the novel. Here the writer-protagonist (Jim) comments upon the significance of the title of Hemingway's short story, *Big Two Hearted River.* Jim's explicitly figurative reading of the title gives us a better understanding not just of this particular short story but also of the American novelist's life and *oeuvre.* As well, the interpretation is relevant to the situation of the protagonist himself and of the character (La Petite) for whose benefit he has performed this *explication.* By extension, Jim's "lesson" is useful to the reader of *Le Vieux Chagrin,* suggesting the relevance of a similar analysis of the novel's own title and of other textual beginnings. While the following examination of the incipits does not claim the definitiveness of Jim's interpretation—he is after all seeking to give guidance to a psychologically scarred adolescent—nonetheless it is clear that these micro-texts, beginning with the title, are key indicators of the signifying processes at work in the novel.

I. PRE-NARRATIVE INCIPITS

TITLE: LE VIEUX CHAGRIN

The title appears at first simply to perform two of the conventional functions[6] attributed to this incipit, the *nominative* (by designating a "character" in the novel—Jim's ageing cat), and the *thematic* (by signalling the emotional complex animating—and immobilizing—the protagonist). But the very merging of these two functions into a single unit has important implications. Most evidently, it provides an exemplary instance of lexical condensation, one of whose effects is to bring together disparate elements: the animal and the human, nature and culture, instinct and artifice. As well, this interweaving of character and theme in the title mirrors the work's blending of realism and dream in a narrative which seeks to harmonize the conscious and the unconscious. For if in the novel "Chagrin" is always only Jim's cat, each naming occurrence invests the text with the repressed and displaced *trace* of the deep distress ("le chagrin") which is Jim's other constant companion.

"*Le Vieux*"

Both the article and the adjective in the title demonstrate a similar layering effect to that noted in the substantive. The definite article, for example, designates simultaneously the particular and the general and thus anticipates a narrative which, although ostensibly grounded in the concrete and the individual, is regularly absorbed into the uncanny and the oneiric.

The adjective "vieux" transposes into temporal terms the same layering effect. Most obviously, the adjective designates a *linear* temporality thematized for example in Jim's relationship with the teenaged "Petite." The adjective also emphasizes the longstanding and obsessive nature of Jim's distress, thereby anticipating the numerous narrative analepses during which the protagonist will relive—and perhaps exorcize—the pain of his traumatic abandonment by his wife. "Vieux" also initiates a *cyclical* temporality based upon recurrence. Jim's pain is "le [même] vieux chagrin" which returns throughout our individual and collective history. The protagonist's situation is thus transposable from the particular to the general: his "chagrin" is as old as literature itself, and the adjective designates it as a recurring constant in human experience.

"*Cha(t)grin*"

A final layer of signifying potential is embedded in the substantive's graphic and phonetic word-play. Here the incipit foregrounds its status as language, and thus as artifice. This consciousness of origins implies a self-reflexivity which will be realized in the text by a meta-fictional narrative in which the protagonist is a novelist attempting to write "une histoire d'amour," a story which in its revised form may well be entitled "*Le Vieux Chagrin.*"

Epigraph

CONVERSATION

(Sur le pas de la porte, avec bonhomie)

Comment ça va sur la terre?
—Ça va, ça va, ça va bien.
Les petits chiens sont-ils prospères?

—Mon Dieu, oui merci bien.
Et les nuages?
—Ça flotte.
Et les volcans?
—Ça mijote.
Et les fleuves?
—Ça s'écoule.
Et le temps?
—Ça se déroule.
Et votre âme?
—Elle est malade.
Le printemps était trop vert
Elle a mangé trop de salade.

Jean Tardieu, "Le Fleuve caché"

Both fragment and a complete text, the epigraph permits comparisons to be drawn with the novel, not only in terms of content—*fleuve, temps, âme, printemps* will reappear in the narrative, as will the poem's theme of disillusionment—but more interestingly in terms of formal signifying strategies. Tardieu's poem, for example, interweaves a highly mimetic text—dialogue, familiar diction, literal imagery—and one whose strangeness borders on the surreal: the mysterious questioner, the evolution of the imagery towards ever greater figurative weight, culminating in the total evacuation of realism in the final verses ("le printemps était trop vert / Elle [l'âme] a mangé trop de salade"). This juxtaposition of representativity and anti-realism will be echoed in the novel by the blending of a resolutely realist narrative (Jim/Chagrin/Bungalow/La Petite) with an anti-realist narrative (les traces de pas/la caverne/Marie K.—Marika) characterized by indeterminacy, *invraisemblance,* and other indications of the workings of dream and the unconscious.

Like the title, therefore, the epigraph conflates representativity and anti-realism. In so doing it mirrors a similar signifying procedure at work in the novel. Moreover, like the title, the epigraph refuses to hide its origin in language and clearly foregrounds its status as artifice. Through its constant recourse to the traditional norms of poetic diction—rhyme, rhythm, lexical repetition—the poem proclaims its rootedness in linguistic convention. As noted earlier this self-awareness is enacted in the novel by means of a meta-fictional narrative of which writing itself is the subject.

II. Narrative Incipits: The First Chapter

Title: "Les Traces de Pas"

As with the pre-narrative incipits the first chapter's title performs the conventional functions of naming an important narrative element and designating an essential theme: the quest for the ideal love object which begins with Jim's discovery of the footprints on the river's shore.

As with the title and epigraph, however, the incipit interacts with the narrative in more subtle and complex ways. The very implausibility of these footprints—they are exactly Jim's size but cannot be his (p. 9)—endows the "traces de pas" with an ambiguous status: are they "real" or fantasized? This ambiguity will be echoed in the text by a double narrative in which realist and antirealist threads are seamlessly interwoven. *Traces* (literally) of a presence that is never actualized but always deferred, the footprints are the key indicator of the solipsistic nature of the protagonist's quest: "Marika n'existait pas vraiment, elle n'était que la projection d'un désir, une partie de moi-même..." (p. 153).

The chapter title can be viewed also as indicative of the existence of a self-conscious (reflexive) dimension in the text. Neither totally outside nor fully within the narrative (Who in fact narrates these rubrics?), the chapter title arrests the narrative flow by focusing the reader's interpretive attention upon an element which will later reappear within the narrative. The rubric functions therefore as a semiotic counterpoint to the narrative's mimetic linearity. Sign of an authorial presence within the narrative, the chapter title is another indicator of the text's status as artefact and of its origin in writing. This dimension of self-reference, as noted earlier, will be echoed in the novel by a meta-fictional narrative thread.

THE FIRST SENTENCE: "*LE PRINTEMPS ÉTAIT ARRIVÉ*"

This concise opening sentence recapitulates the work of the pre-narrative incipits and anticipates the activity of the narrative which follows. By reintroducing the vernal allusion of the epigraph ("le printemps était trop vert"), the first sentence immediately tempers the conventional spring-time associations—rebirth hope, love, fertility—and signals a situation in which these positive values are under threat.

The springtime reference also imports into the narrative the double temporal structure already noted in the title ("vieux"): time in the novel is both linear and cyclical. Temporal linearity guarantees the representativity of the narrative (its "realism"), while time viewed as recurrence invests the work with symbolic potential, transforming the individual and finite into the universal and eternal.

The use of the pluperfect tense in the opening sentence is significant. The process delineated in Tardieu's poem— spring-time contributing to the sickness of the soul—is already underway and the naively positive vernal associations are already undermined. The incipit thus anticipates the failure of the protagonist's quest. Nonetheless, the positive connotation of "printemps" will be actualized in the less exalted but relatively optimistic second ending of the novel: the adoption of "la Petite."

The use of the pluperfect tense also inscribes in the narrative a past temporal dimension (the arrival of spring) which determines the present. This presence of the past is actualized in the narrative by the numerous analepses invoking decisive past experiences, whether of childhood (p. 10-11), of ephemeral happiness (p. 130-2), or of traumatic

pain, as represented by the numerous flashbacks to the departure of Jim's wife.

"*LA CAVERNE*" AND "*LA MAISON*"

The opening chapter concludes with two descriptions, that of the cave to which the mysterious footprints lead the protagonist, and that of Jim's house, "une maison hétéroclite et dotée de plusieurs styles..." (p. 10). Echoing the operation of the incipits, these initial descriptions are characterized by condensation and layering. Both appear rooted in representativity, yet both transcend the mimetic and reveal a marked tendency towards both anti-realism and reflexivity.

The description of the cave, for example, is highly concrete and yet certain details impart a metaphorical dimension to this space. The protagonist's very entry into the cave—"en se faufilant par une brèche très étroite" (p. 9)—invests this space with an erotic dimension and evokes certain symbolic connotations of the cave (woman, the womb). That Jim's relation with this cave goes back to his childhood, and that he detects in the cave "l'âme de quelqu'un" (p. 10) confer upon this space associations that far transcend a merely naturalistic description.

This undermining of the representational is furthered by the fact that the cave is above all a *literary* space. *The 1001 Nights* is the only object discovered in the cave, and it is the memory of this book which will remain strongest in Jim's mind after his first visit to the cave and which will interrupt his own writing (p. 11). The "caverne" is thus closely linked to the metafictional dimension of a text in which writing itself is narrativized.

The description of the protagonist's house introduces another apparently representative object which functions both metaphorically and self-reflexively. A number of details undermine the naturalistic nature of the description: the allusion to "son aspect un peu étrange" (p. 10); the explicit reference to the house as "la maison de mon enfance" (p. 10); and perhaps most significantly, the ritualistic crossing of the house from one side of the river to another, a passage with which Jim imaginatively identifies (p. 11).

It is, however, the *structure* of the house which most clearly portrays the non-representational nature of the description. The house is a tri-level space with each level clearly distinct from the other. The main floor, for example, is reserved for the activities of everyday life; the second floor is explicitly associated with childhood and dream (the family bedrooms) and revery ("la galerie vitrée"). The third floor attic is of course the space of *writing,* the space where language and imagination appropriate and synthesize the data of experience garnered from the rest of the house and from the world outside. The description of the house is therefore figurative as well as representational: its construction mirrors the various levels of the narrator's experience of life. In addition to this important metaphorical component, the description of the house functions reflexively—as a *mise en abyme*—by mirroring the work's tripartite narrative structure: representative, anti-realist, and metafictional.

INCIPITS AND THE NARRATIVE

Although the description of the protagonist's house offers perhaps the clearest example of the specular relationship between incipit and text, *all* the "beginnings" studied here possess a similar layering structure, the result of radical lexical condensation. The incipits constitute emblematic verbal structures whose (vertical) integration is projected on to the (horizontal) narrative in the form of three distinct but intertwined narrative threads:

> 1. a representative narrative—the mimetically based recounting of Jim's conscious interaction with the external world;
>
> 2. an anti-realist narrative—the metaphor-centred narrative whose principal elements (the footprints, the cave, Marie K.—Marika) are generated by dream and other workings of the unconscious;
>
> 3. a metafictional narrative—the story of the writing by the protagonist of a novel (this novel?).

These narratives, although distinct, are permeable one to the other, and numerous transpositions and cross-overs occur throughout the novel. Bungalow, for example, arrives in Jim's kitchen as if in response to an invitation to Marika that Jim has recently left in the cave. Jim for his part will regularly transpose into his novel elements of his "real-life" experience. And Marika, while integral to the anti-realist narrative, will by her absence both inspire and block Jim in his writing. This interweaving of diverse narrative threads corresponds to the radical tendency towards condensation which characterizes the incipits. Both incipit and narrative seek integration and harmonization. Both aim at reducing *difference* while simultaneously affirming its presence.

THE INCIPITS AND EXPERIENCE

In examining the operation of the incipits in **Le Vieux Chagrin,** we have noted how these fragments interact both with the content of the story (nominative and thematic functions) and with the formal organisation of the narrative. The radical condensation of meaning characteristic of the incipits is mirrored by the interweaving of various narrative "threads," each corresponding to a layer of meaning discernible in the incipits. Both incipit and narrative reveal a centripetal tendency towards integration and harmonization. This impulse towards unifying disparate elements can be interpreted as reflecting an aesthetic *parti pris* favouring a Hemingwayesque economy of verbal resources. Indeed, Jim's comments on the aphorism "A coeur vaillant, rien d'impossible" summarizes, on the phrastic level, what appears to be the poulinien textual ideal: "C'était une phrase

courte, dépouillée, bien ramassée, et on ne pouvait pas enlever ni déplacer un mot. Elle avait toutes les qualités qui plaisaient au vieux Hémingway" (p. 89).

Our analysis has been confined thus far to an investigation of certain formal and stylistic traits of the novel. The total exclusion of an "existential" dimension to this study of the incipits would however be a mistake. While most of Jim's reflections upon literature are related to formal and stylistic considerations, the writer-protagonist also affirms explicitly—if somewhat sheepishly, as such declarations are hardly fashionable—his belief in an extra-textual mission for his writings: "... je nourrissais l'ambition naïve et démesurée de contribuer, par l'écriture, à l'avènement d'un monde nouveau ..." (p. 139). This potential for literature to effect change in the "real world" is in fact actualized by "La Petite," whose gradual recovery is in part due to her reading of Jim's work: "Mais quand j'ai lu tes livres, c'est comme si on m'avait donné la permission d'être moins agressive ..." (p. 139).

This validation of the experiential in literature suggests another less formalist basis for the workings of the incipits. The tendency of these textual fragments to integrate disparate elements can be seen as a product of *desire,* the verbal expression of an existential quest for unity. Both Jim and "La Petite" are attempting to heal the wounds of past experience which have left them in a state of inner conflict and fragmentation: "... nous étions tous les deux emmurés en nous-mêmes et occupés à recoller les morceaux de notre passé" (p. 120). From this perspective the textual penchant for condensation and integration constitutes a displaced expression of a profound desire for self-reconciliation and for a more harmonious relationship with the world.

The ultimate outcome of this quest for the unity and integration of the self remains ambiguous. On the one hand there is defeat. Jim fails in his pursuit of the ideal love object: Marika remains absent, at most a "silhouette," at best "un rêve magnifique." Jim also fails to write his novel about love.

And yet there are victories: Jim and "La Petite" will form an alliance and struggle together in their search for harmony. Jim will begin a new version of a love story ("il y a des choses qui s'en viennent" p. 136), integrating elements of his earlier effort. These are small but real steps forward. And above all, there is a *textual* victory, one in which the triumph over fragmentation is demonstrable, a victory most convincingly achieved in the complex and productive activity of the incipits.

Notes

1. Louis Aragon, *Je n'ai jamais appris à écrire ou les incipit* (Geneva: Editions d'Art Albert Skira, 1969), p. 145.

2. Harry Levin, "The Title as Literary Genre," *Modern Language Review* 72 (1971), xxiv.

3. Raymond Jean, "Commencements romanesques," in *Positions et oppositions sur le roman contemporain* (Paris: Editions Klincksiek, 1971), p. 138-39.

4. Jean Ricardou, "La Bataille de la phrase," *Poétique* 274 (1970), p. 231.

5. Jacques Poulin, *Le Vieux Chagrin* (Montréal: Leméac, 1989).

6. Richard Sawyer, "Fictional Titles: A Classification," *The University of Toronto Quarterly* 60: 3 (Spring 1991), p. 374-88.

Adam Paul Weisman (essay date 1995)

SOURCE: Weisman, Adam Paul. "Postcolonialism in North America: Imaginative Colonization in Henry David Thoreau's *A Yankee in Canada* and Jacques Poulin's *Volkswagen Blues*." *Massachusetts Review* 36.3 (1995): 477-500. Print.

[*In the following essay, Weisman considers the postcolonial themes of* Volkswagen Blues *alongside those of Thoreau's travelog* A Yankee in Canada. *Weisman cites both works as examples of "imaginative colonization," by means of which the cultural landscape of one former colonial society of North America is appropriated by another.*]

Since the early 1960s and especially during the past decade, much of the world's literature has been under review from the critical perspective of postcolonialism. Postcolonialism is, as its name suggests, the study of what happens to peoples, cultures, or nations after they have been liberated from the bonds of European colonialism. However, the basic paradigm for the study of literature from a postcolonial point of view puts much more emphasis on the "colonial" than it does on the "post," since it argues that the exploitative power imbalance of colonialism persists long after the nominal work of decolonization has been accomplished.

Most postcolonial theory focuses upon the strategies employed by cultures that perceive themselves as victimized to subvert the dominating culture, but the domination-to-subversion paradigm effectively describes only one type of postcolonial relationship, that in which the former colonizer remains palpably ascendent over the formerly colonized. In this way, the binary model for postcolonialism tends to reinscribe the colonial—not the postcolonial—power dynamic. To this day, postcolonial literary theory remains most comfortable where the postcolonial power dynamic between former colonizer and formerly colonized most closely resembles the colonial power dynamic.

But there is another postcolonial relationship that needs to be studied, and that is the connection between nations, formerly colonies, that are no longer mediated by the original colonizing power. This situation is becoming more prevalent as former colonies grow in power and self-confidence to the point where they begin to assert themselves as potential colonizers. This model is of special interest to North Americans, because it describes the relationship between Canada and the United States. Neither Canada nor the United States remains under the political, economic, or cultural sway of Great Britain and neither North American nation has ever successfully colonized the other. Yet both nations are products of the same American Revolution and the relationship between the Canadian colonies of British North America and the Thirteen Colonies of America has taken place entirely under the rubric of postcolonialism. In short, there is no context *other* than the postcolonial in which the literary and cultural relationship between Canada and the United States can be explored.

This paper explores one literary response to the postcolonial situation in North America that is visible in both American and French Canadian literature. I call it "imaginative colonization," and it occurs in texts where one North American culture imagines the other not on that culture's own particular terms, but as a feature of its own historical self-understanding. In Henry David Thoreau's travelogue, *A Yankee in Canada* (1866), French Canada becomes as much a colony of the United States' revolutionary cultural mythological landscape at midcentury as it was a colony of Britain. In *Volkswagen Blues* (1984), Jacques Poulin performs a selective recuperation of French Canadian history that allows him to reimagine all of North America as the cultural property of 17th and 18th century *voyageurs,* a legacy passed on to the French Canadians of the late 20th century. Imaginative colonialism attests that one means by which "the other" has been known in North America is through an act of literary appropriation that imaginatively mirrors the process of colonization.

In late September of 1850 Thoreau set out with his friend Ellery Channing and nearly 1500 other Bostonians on a package tour to Montreal and Québec offered by the Fitchburg Railroad for seven dollars.[1] At the time of his trip Thoreau was 33 years old, yet he had never travelled farther south from his home in Concord than Philadelphia, or further north than Mt. Katahdin in Maine. In fact, Thoreau's trip to Canada East was the only trip he ever took to a foreign country and his only practical experience with a language other than English.[2]

Unlike most of his other excursions, Thoreau did not make significant preparations for French Canada. Although he ultimately became quite expert on the history of the exploration of Canada by the French, Thoreau did not start this course of reading until after he returned from his 1850 trip. It was also in November of that year that Thoreau began the notebook that ultimately became the published record of his Canadian visit, *A Yankee in Canada.* Within two years he wrote 70 pages about French Canada, combining his own experiences with direct reference to the published works of 45 other discoverers, explorers, and travellers.[3]

It was not until 1866, four years after Thoreau's death, that *A Yankee in Canada* finally appeared as a book, bound together with Thoreau's "anti-slavery and reform papers," including "Slavery in Massachusetts" (1854) and "Civil Disobedience," which was originally published as "Resistance to Civil Government" in 1849. Although the title of the volume featured *A Yankee in Canada,* it is Thoreau's essays on slavery and civil disobedience that have found the most avid readers over the years, and in the 1893 edition of Thoreau's complete works, *A Yankee in Canada* was "demoted" from a titular work to one of Thoreau's several "excursions." This is not surprising, as critics have been almost universally scornful of *A Yankee in Canada,* rating it the least inspired of Thoreau's excursions.[4] This sentiment was shared by the author himself who wrote his friend Harrison Blake: "I do not wonder that you do not like my Canada story. It concerns me little, and it is probably not worth the time it took to tell it. Yet I had absolutely no design whatever in my mind, but simply to report what I saw. I have inserted all of myself that was implicated, or made the excursion."[5]

Thoreau may have had nothing in mind but first-person reportage when he wrote *A Yankee in Canada,* but there are many reasons for the student of Thoreau's oeuvre to be more appreciative of this under-studied work and even to defend its original placement at the head of a volume of anti-slavery and reform papers. One way to look at Thoreau's writing in the decade between the beginning of his sojourn at Walden Pond in 1845 and the publication of "Slavery in Massachusetts" is through the lens of the author's related preoccupations with imperialism and colonialism. Wherever he turned at mid-century Thoreau discovered these twin abuses of power. In the 1840s the United States waged a war of conquest against Mexico that led to the annexation of Texas in 1848. In the American South the internal colonization of slavery spread to new territories, with the Fugitive Slave Law of 1850 extending its grasp even into the abolitionist territory of New England. And north of America, in the two Canadas, North Americans still lived under the colonial rule of the British Empire—as if the American Revolution had never been fought and won.

Thoreau's writing at this time is an extended, unplanned trilogy about imperialism in North America; imperialism through the human colonialism of slavery, through the militant annexationist sentiment of manifest destiny, and finally through the traditional New World colonialism of the British Empire. From this point of view there is much sense in binding together Thoreau's personal testament of his protest of the Mexican War and slavery with his lecture on the Fugitive Slave Law and his personal sojourn among the conquered and colonized people of French Canada.

And while "Resistance to Civil Government" and "Slavery in Massachusetts" have proven more durable canonical works than *A Yankee in Canada,* that does not change the fact that *A Yankee in Canada* is the one occasion in Thoreau's corpus where his engagement with the issues he raised goes beyond the intellectual. In Canada Thoreau came closer to experiencing the imperialism and colonialism he so eschewed than he ever did before or after. The title of *A Yankee in Canada* is not accidental: the work is Thoreau's dispatch from the belly of the beast.

Thoreau's observations of Canada East in 1850 fall into the common American pattern of kinship and alienation toward French Canadians. Thoreau desires to see the *Canadiens* as fellow, hardy colonists of North America, often by praising their *voyageur* ancestors of the 17th and 18th centuries: "The Canadians of those days, at least, possessed a roving spirit of adventure which carried them further, in exposure to hardship and danger, than ever the New England colonist went. ..."[6] Yet he cannot make peace with what he sees as French Canadian complicity in the evil colonialism of Great Britain in the present: "They are very far from a revolution; have no quarrel with Church or State, but their vice and their virtue is content." (60).

This two-minded reaction to French Canadian culture fits an American pattern set by the colonial rebels of the 1770s. In October of 1774 the Continental Congress, partially in response to the passage that June of the Québec Act,[7] addressed a letter to "the people of Great Britain" deploring, among other things, the establishing in Canada of "a religion that has deluged your island in blood, and dispersed impiety, bigotry, persecution, murder and rebellion through every part of the world."[8] Several days after drafting this nakedly anti-*Canadian* letter, the Continental Congress dispatched another, this time addressed "Aux Habitants de la Province de Québec." Unsurprisingly, this letter was far more flattering of French Canadians, imploring them to join their "amis et concitoyens" in the rebellion against Great Britain and suggesting that Catholicism and Protestantism could coexist peacefully in North America on the model of the Swiss Cantons.[9] There are virtually no 19th- or 20th-century French Canadian histories of the revolutionary period that neglect to condemn either the hypocrisy, or in some versions the outright stupidity, of the Continental Congress in sending two such contradictory letters.[10] For, of course, the French Canadians read both and by the time of the American colonials' invasion of Canada a year later, they were understandably skeptical of their intentions toward Canada. As historian Francois-Xavier Garneau opined in 1848, "Cette déclaration ... était donc fort inconsidérée; elle ne produisait aucun bien en Angleterre, et fit perdre peut-être le Canada à la cause de la confédération."[11] [This declaration was extremely ill-advised, produced no good will in England, and was perhaps the very thing that lost French Canada to the cause of North American confederation.]

By contrast, American histories of the Revolution from Thoreau's time make no mention of colonial double-dealing with Canada. In 1857, Benson Lossing wrote that the *habitants* "were cordially invited to join their Anglo-American neighbors ... but having very little sympathy in language, religion, or social conditions ... they refused and were necessarily considered supporters of the royal cause."[12] This is, of course, inaccurate, as many French Canadians remained sympathetic to the colonial cause despite the letters of 1774 and many did fight in support of the invading troops of Richard Montgomery, Benedict Arnold, and Ethan Allen. To explain this, school historian Salma Hale ignores the letters of 1774 entirely and focuses instead on Montgomery's proclamation to the city of Montreal in 1775 "that the property, rights, and religion of every individual should be sacredly respected." Hale concludes that "[b]y his benevolence and address, he gained the affections of the Canadians, many of whom joined his standard."[13] Ultimately, French Canadian histories of Thoreau's time, while they evince little love for the British Empire, still make the American invasion seem very close to a war of conquest. By contrast, most 19th-century American histories continue to advance the theory that the *habitants* were sympathetic to the American cause, but were either bought into neutrality by the Québec Act, cowed into it by a Catholic Church complicit with the British Empire, or both.

After the American Revolution, no Canadian historian ever again considers the possibility that the United States might be invading its northern neighbor with the best interests of Canadians in mind. The War of 1812 is painted as an American war of conquest and nothing more; American meddling on the border during the rebellions in Upper and Lower Canada in 1837 is an uninvited nuisance, as is the annexation agitation of 1849. By midcentury, most visitors to Canada, including Charles Dickens from England, Alexis de Tocqueville from France, and the American historian George Bancroft, recognized that Canada was a viable democracy advancing not by revolution, but by a process of evolution within the increasingly flexible bounds of British imperial institutions. De Tocqueville even went so far as to analogize the two North American cultures: "[t]he French of America are to the French of France as the Americans are to the English ... the spirit of equality and democracy is alive there [in French Canada] as in the United States, although it is not so rationalistic."[14]

Thoreau did not see things this way during his visit, and his copious criticisms of French Canadian Catholicism and political and social backwardness in *A Yankee in Canada* have their origin in his conviction that French Canadians have missed the North American revolution that would have made them free. Thoreau is mortified to learn that French Canadians speak only French and to discover that he is "in fact ... in a foreign country" (32-33). To him French Canada is a nation of peasants (76-77) who fairly represent "their ancestors in Normandy a thou-

sand years ago" (60), and he doubts "if there are any more simple and unsophisticated Catholics anywhere" (48). All of this Thoreau attributes to the pernicious influence of British colonialism and its military presence in Canada. As Edmund G. Berry explains, "[h]ere is the real New Englander of the Revolution speaking. ... His tone is exactly that of hundreds of men in the small towns of New England seventy years before. ..."[15]

In short, Thoreau unabashedly advances a liberating revolutionary imperative for North America that was understandable in 1775, but inapplicable to the evolutionary Canada of 1850. Yet Thoreau seems not to be able to pull himself out of the 18th century and ends up sounding more like a nativistic colonial rebel than a credible critic of mid-19th-century North America:

> A New Englander would naturally be a bad citizen, probably a rebel, there,—certainly if he were already a rebel at home. I suspect that a poor man who is not servile is a much rarer phenomenon there and in England than in the Northern United States. ... What makes the United States government, on the whole, more tolerable,—I mean for us lucky white men,—is the fact that there is so much less of government with us ... but in Canada you are reminded of the government every day. It parades itself before you. It is not content to be the servant, but will be the master.

(76-78)

Thoreau's blunt assertion of American governmental and social superiority is certainly tempered by deliberate overstatement and the self-effacing qualification, "for us lucky white men," but it still fairly represents the degree to which Thoreau's thinking about North American culture was rooted in a late 18th-century revolutionary imperative that is nonsynchronous with the evolutionary state of the democratic Canada East of 1850. Without being deliberately ironic, Thoreau reveals the degree to which his understanding of political and social progress is in fact grounded in and limited to the revolutionary ideology of 1775.

Thoreau is 70 years behind the times ideologically, but it remains to be pointed out that Thoreau's imaginative colonization of Canada is not an anomalous occurrence, but a feature of the postcolonial thinking that marked American writing in Thoreau's time. Only recently have some literary critics begun to question the most persistent area of American literary exceptionalism, that which insists that "the appreciation of American writing depends upon our keeping it separate from the rest of the world."[16] Because the United States in Thoreau's time, the era of Manifest Destiny, is more readily perceived as the consummate New World colonial power, it has been easy to disregard the degree to which references to its colonial past were still essential to American literature's understanding of the culture of which it was both a creator and constituent part. Lawrence Buell advances precisely this theory with regard to the United States' postcolonial relationship to Great

Britain during the American Renaissance, but Buell's theory is perhaps even more applicable to the United States' relationship to Canada.[17] Since the two North American nations are inextricably linked by their colonial pasts and by the American Revolution, which set them on their separate paths of political and social development, there is virtually no other context in which to compare the United States and Canada apart from the postcolonial. This is borne out, as I have shown, both by American historiography of the first half of the 19th century and by comparative cultural works like *A Yankee in Canada,* which can only understand Canada as a feature of the postcolonial history and development of the United States. A perfect example of this postcolonial myopia being Francis Parkman's assertion in his history of North America that the significance of Wolfe's triumph over Montcalm on the Plains of Abraham in 1759 was that it began the history of the United States, not Canada; an arguable but still fundamentally counterintuitive claim.[18]

Thoreau's 19th-century travelogue and Poulin's postmodern novel, *Volkswagen Blues* are 118 years apart in publication, from different literary genres; their authors are held at a distance not only by time but by a national border and a language. Yet there is also much that unites these two examples of imaginative colonization across the national and cultural lines of North America. Both are works predicated upon the importance of the cross-border, cross-cultural journey, and both evince a belief in the knowability of the North American "other." Both Poulin and Thoreau know the territory they write about, and their writing places great value on the presentation of precise detail to drive this point home. Both *A Yankee in Canada* and *Volkswagen Blues* make an integral use of intertextuality, linking the personal experiences of travel of their authors (or those of the travelling characters they create) to the writing of others who have travelled the route before them. And finally, both works emerge from locales, one a nation the other a province in a larger national confederation, that have waged significant battles for political decolonization prior to their publication. So while it is true that *A Yankee in Canada* and *Volkswagen Blues* are from different nations and centuries, they are also from similar historical and developmental epochs within those different countries.

Volkswagen Blues is a deceptively simple novel telling a straight-ahead story that is little more than a national switch on *A Yankee in Canada*: two French Canadian characters take an economy vacation in the United States, travelling in a Volkswagen camper. Jack Waterman, the pen-name (the pun is intended) of a middle-aged French Canadian novelist who lives in Québec City, owns the Volkswagen and is driving east toward Gaspé, hoping to find some clues as to the whereabouts of his brother, Théo, who disappeared more than a decade before. The last correspondence Jack had from Théo is a postcard from Gaspé inscribed with a mysterious message in archaic handwriting. On the way to Gaspé, Jack picks up a hitch-hiker, a young woman who is *Métisse,* half Indian and half French Canadian, and goes by the name, La Grande Sauterelle, a French translation of her Montagnais Indian name. La Grande Sauterelle decides to join Jack in his search for his brother, and they follow the meager clues they have from Gaspé all the way to San Francisco, where they find Théo. Along the way, they visit well-known touristic sights, meet interesting (and even famous) people and, in completing their journey, learn something about the United States, about the relationship of the United States to Canada, and about themselves, for as Thoreau said, no matter how far we wander, "it is only ourselves we report."[19]

As with Thoreau's travelogue, there is much more to *Volkswagen Blues* than the day-to-day journeying of its characters. *Volkswagen Blues* raises important and complex questions of symbolism by using postmodern techniques of intertextuality and extratextuality and by the blurring of the lines between the accepted conventions of "fiction" and "reality." In this way, Poulin creates a novel that is less a self-contained work than a living node at the intersection of current ideas about North American identity and French Canadian mythology and history. For example, *Volkswagen Blues* has an extra-textual cartographic element that piques the reader's curiosity before he has even begun reading. Poulin's novel is preceded by a simple map of Canada and the United States, but with the names of the two countries omitted, though the states and provinces are delineated. What is not delineated is the border between Canada and the United States. Marked upon the map is the route taken by Poulin's travellers from Gaspé in the easternmost part of Québec, to San Francisco, via the St. Lawrence River, the Great Lakes, the Mississippi River, and, finally, the Oregon Trail. Place names and geographic features are named, some in English and some in French, but it is not immediately clear what linguistic logic is being used. It is as if English-speaking settlers left their mark upon the surface of the continent in the form of individual place names, but the continent itself, its mountain ranges (marked *"Rocheuses"*) for example, is French, as are its pioneering destinations, *Californie* and *Oregon.* But the most important fact may be the borderlessness and overwhelming blankness of most of the map, which gives it an unexplored, pre-national feel.

Volkswagen Blues is also laced through with a dense web of intertextuality that puts it in dialogue both with historical events in the exploration of the North American continent and with the development of an historiography and a mythology surrounding those events. For example, the Bay of Gaspé is the place where, in 1534, Jacques Cartier erected a cross in the name of God and France, thereby inaugurating the French history of North America. This is, appropriately, where Jack and La Grande Sauterelle's trip begins, but it also emerges that Théo's postcard from Gaspé is merely a photocopy of the text of Cartier's speech at the placing of the cross in 1534. Thus Jack's personal search for his brother is transformed into a postmodern historical mystery in which the sleuth, like Oedipa Maas in Thomas Pynchon's *The Crying of Lot 49,* must become an amateur historian in order to unravel the clues at hand. Of course, this means that the reader will also receive a selective historical education in reading the novel, in much the same way that the author must have educated himself in preparation for its writing. This forms a perfect parallel to the intertextual experience of *A Yankee in Canada,* which comprises not only Thoreau's personal observations of Canada East, but the fruits of his research into its history, geography, and ecology with reference to 45 other published sources on Canada. According to Anne Marie Miraglia's count, **Volkswagen Blues** has no less than 40 significant intertexts sustaining it, of which nine are extensively discussed or physically present in the novel itself.[20]

In a final turn of postmodern textual self-awareness, La Grande Sauterelle gives a crucial speech on the holism of the reading experience:

> Il ne faut pas juger les livres un par un. Je veux dire: il ne faut pas les voir comme des choses indépendantes. Un livre n'est jamais complet en lui-même; si on veut le comprendre, il faut le mettre en rapport avec d'autres livres, non seulement avec des livres du même auteur, mais aussi avec des livres écrits par d'autres personnes. Ce que l'on croit être un livre n'est la plupart du temps qu'une partie d'un autre livre plus vaste auquel plusieurs auteurs ont collaboré sans le savoir.[21]

> [You shouldn't judge books one by one. I mean, you mustn't see them as independent objects. A book is never complete in itself; to understand it you must put it in relation to other books, not just books by the same author, but also books written by other people. What we think is a book most of the time is only part of another, vaster book that a number of authors have collaborated on without knowing it.]

(Fischman, 122)

Thus it is with deliberate irony that a *Métisse*—herself the physical evidence of the mixing of the European and native populations in North America—advances the philosophy of literary *métissage* or mixing that sanctions the intertextuality of both **Volkswagen Blues** and *A Yankee in Canada.* It also explains, in part, the mixing of the westwarding experience of the French and French Canadian *voyageurs,* which begins with Cartier in Gaspé in 1534, with that of the American pioneers on the Oregon Trail. In the map of **Volkswagen Blues,** the former flows seamlessly into the latter as the St. Lawrence flows into the Great Lakes and the Great Lakes into the rivers that feed the Mississippi.

Thoreau's *A Yankee in Canada* is driven by the author's desire to "go a little way behind that word *Canadense*" (93), to ferret out the truth of French Canadian ideology and to recast it in terms of the American cultural mythology of the Revolution. Similarly, Poulin's **Volkswagen Blues** seeks to strip away the accumulated layers of cul-

tural mythology and national ideology that sustain French Canada and the United States and to discover, beneath it all, a single myth that explains the development of North America. Poulin finds his philosopher's stone in the myth of the *voyageur,* the solitary French or French Canadian explorer and advance agent of the fur trade who, with reckless abandon, launched himself into the interior of North America in search of pelts and ended up making a tenuous separate peace with the native tribes of the continent, largely by intermarrying with them.[22] All of the elements of this myth are present in Poulin's novel, right down to the *voyageur's* quasi-imperialist or colonialist lack of interest in anything but adventure and acquisition.

In **Volkswagen Blues,** Jack Waterman, La Grande Sauterelle, and especially Jack's brother, Théo, are *voyageur* figures. In fact, Jack reveals to La Grande Sauterelle that in their youthful games, Théo played the role of his personal hero, the roguish Etienne Brûlé (65-66), the historical prototype for the cultural myth of the *voyageur.* As Jack recounts in a flashback, Brûlé came to New France with Champlain in 1608 at the age of 16, was the first of the French to learn the languages of the Indians and to adopt their way of life, while exploring the region of the Great Lakes and the interior of what is now Canada and the United States. Poulin sets the scene for this valorization of the *voyageur* while Jack and La Grande Sauterelle are still in Québec City; after they have returned from Gaspé, but, not coincidentally, before they launch their own exploration of America. La Grande Sauterelle tracks down a book on Jack's shelves, *La Pénétration du continent américain par les Canadiens français, 1763-1846* (1939) by Benoît Brouillette, that speaks of the French Canadian origins of St. Louis, where she suspects Théo may have gone. As Jack and La Grande Sauterelle's discussion of the book reveals, "[l]'auteur [Brouillette] semblait avoir une grande estime pour eux" (45), "they" being the later, post-Brûlé generations of *voyageurs* of the period covered by Brouillette's history. Unsurprisingly, both Jack and La Grande Sauterelle also admire the *voyageurs,* he because of positive associations with his brother and youthful play, she because, "[e]lle trouvait ... que leur conduite avec les Indiens était acceptable, compte tenu des moeurs de l'époque. Même chose pour les trappeurs et les coureurs de bois: en général ils s'étaient mieux comportés à l'égard des Indiens, d'après elle, que ceux qui avaient exercé les mêmes occupations du côté américain" (46). ["She also thought that they had behaved acceptably toward the Indians, given the customs of the time. Same thing for the trappers and the *coureurs de bois*: in general, they had treated the Indians better, in her opinion, than their American counterparts" (Fischman, 34).]

Poulin sets the scene for an historical/mythological showdown on the treatment of native peoples between the first *Canadiens* and pioneering Americans, but this showdown never materializes, as **Volkswagen Blues** reveals more details about Brûlé which are not so flattering and which explain his virtual expulsion from the canon of heroes by later French Canadian historians. In fact, Brûlé has been underrated as an explorer by the 20th century. Although Parkman dubbed him the "pioneer of pioneers,"[23] French Canadian historians, many of whom have been clergymen, have been more concerned with his sexual license and apparent preference for the "savage" Indian way of life. As if this weren't bad enough from a Catholic standpoint, Brûlé is also seen by many as the first French Canadian traitor, as it was he who piloted the troops of the British Admiral Kirk from Tadoussac to Québec, setting up the attack that led to the fall of that city in 1629.

As *Volkswagen Blues* develops our understanding of what kind of explorer Brûlé was, so our opinion of Jack's unseen brother is complicated, since the two are parallel. The unmitigated praise for the later *voyageurs* of Brouillette's nationalist history gives way to Percy Robinson's opinion of Brûlé in *Toronto during the French Régime* (1933), which La Grande Sauterelle borrows from a library in Toronto. Robinson notes that Brûlé was a traitor, that his contemporaries do not speak well of him and that, for unknown transgressions, his life ended when he was killed and eaten in 1632 by the Huron Indians with whom he lived after his final break with Champlain in 1629.[24] Soon after this Brûlé-laden interlude, Jack and La Grande Sauterelle learn that Théo was arrested while in Toronto and that among his possessions at the time was a revolver. Suddenly, Théo is much less appealing to the reader, who is not surprised when Jack later reveals that "Théo, comme les pionniers, était absolument *convaincu qu'il était capable de faire tout ce qu'il voulait*" [italics in original] (137). ["Théo, like the pioneers, was *absolutely convinced that he could do whatever he wanted*" (Fischman, 98).]

In giving a central role to the ultimate historical *voyageur* (Brûlé), the history and mythology that surrounds him, and one of his modern reincarnations (Théo), Poulin launches *Volkswagen Blues* into a major French Canadian historical and cultural debate. At the heart of this debate is a fundamental question of identity: who are the French Canadian people of the 20th century and what should they be called? Poulin seems to agree with Brouillette that they are the descendants of *voyageurs* and are best called "*Canadiens.*" But this line of argument, as Poulin's novel immediately reveals, is fraught with historical danger. To assume the identity of or to associate oneself with the *voyageurs* is to take responsibility for a legacy of European colonialism that, if less injurious to the native peoples of the 16th and 17th centuries, was still based upon Théo's egocentric conviction that he could do whatever he wanted—with a revolver to back him up. This attitude runs counter to the oft-expressed postcolonial ideal that cultures once colonized themselves never seek to colonize others.[25] Although this claim is contradicted by the historical and political reality of North America in the 19th and 20th centuries,[26] it has remained a central tenet of much French Canadian cultural mythology; expressed as the idea that

the French Canadians are too multiply colonized and powerless ever to seek to colonize anybody else. As Laurent Girouard wrote in 1963, "... il n'y a jamais eu de Canada français. Nous n'étions que des isolés sur un immense territoire occupé et exploité par les étrangers."[27] [there never was any such thing as French Canada. We were never anything but castaways in an immense expanse of territory, occupied and exploited by foreigners.] Hence the pervasive myth that all French Canada aspires to culturally is merely "*la survivance,*" or survival.

This myth is in stark contrast to Poulin's self-stated "projet de roman" for *Volkswagen Blues,* which is "quelque chose comme: agrandir, élargir la conscience américaine des Québécois."[28] [something like: to enlarge, to broaden the American identity of the French Canadians.] Recently, some literary critics and social historians have begun to reconsider the strict French Canada-as-victim idea. For example, Linda Hutcheon has written that "the precolonial history of the French in Québec was an imperialist one ... the French were the first imperial force in what is now Canada, and that too cannot be forgotten—without risking bad faith. This is not to deny ... the very real sense of cultural dispossession and social alienation in Québec; but history cannot be conveniently ignored."[29] Other writers, including Miraglia and the social scientist Jean Morisset, have stressed the degree to which the recuperation of the history and myth of the *voyageur* leads to the possibility, and even the desirability, of the physical reappropriation of the American continent, of what I am calling imaginative colonization. As Miraglia puts it, the French Canadian novel of *américanité* in Poulin's vision must "... vivre à la fois sa francité et son américanité; il faudrait commencer par se réapproprier le continent américain en le parcourant dans le temps et dans l'espace."[30] [to live at the same time its Frenchness and its Americaness; to do so it must begin by reappropriating the American continent by travelling throughout it in both time and space.] Morisset, writing after the publication of *Volkswagen Blues* but not about the novel itself, also emphasizes the degree to which he who controls the myth of identity controls everything.[31] It is Morisset's contention that French Canadians have been far too timid about acknowledging the power and sweep of their continental history and the implications it has for their identity in the late 20th century.

This is another point at which *Volkswagen Blues* and *A Yankee in Canada* are closer together than they may at first seem: both appear at junctures in their respective provincial and national developments at which the political aspect of the decolonizing mission is mostly completed and the rise to national power confirmed. It is at this point that New World cultures, through their literatures as through their political structures, can begin to confront the rest of the world as potential colonizers, which is how the latter-day *voyageurs* of *Volkswagen Blues* confront the United States. The primary difference between the United States of Thoreau and the Québec of Poulin is that Québec remains a province in a larger national confederation, while the United States of 1850 as an independent nation embarked upon an overt program of continental colonization. This is a major difference, as many of those who continue to see Québec as a second-class colony, including the separatist Bloc Québécois that is now the official opposition in the Canadian federal government, see Québec's provincial status in an overwhelmingly English-speaking nation as incontrovertible prima facie evidence of its ongoing colonial mistreatment.

It is this problem in postcolonial cultures that Simon During addresses in his distinction between groups that are "postcolonized" and those that are "postcolonizing."[32] Groups fitting under the former rubric are the usual focus of postcolonial literary theory; nations or cultures that, even after the technical act of political decolonization has been completed, remain in a second-class or subjugated posture in relation to the former colonizer. They are, in During's phrase, "heirs to undone culture." Places like Québec may fit better under the second heading, as nations or cultures that are heirs to the work of colonizing.

This is the case with the United States' and Canada's internal colonization of both native peoples and slaves, but it is also possible to see Québec as a nascent postcolonizing culture (even if it is not an independent nation), if not in its essence then with regard to the recent strengthening of its position within the Canadian confederation. For there is much strong evidence that speaks to the health and strength not only of Québec's cultural independence, but its political autonomy as well. Business interests within Québec controlled by non-Québécois fell from 38 percent to 26 percent between 1979 and 1982, and Québec invested 20 times as much abroad in 1984 as it did in 1960.[33] Québec has put in power separatist political parties at both the provincial level (the *Parti québécois* of René Lévesque in 1976) and the national level (Lucien Bouchard's *Bloc québécois* in 1993). Excluding caretaker prime ministers, there has not been a Canadian federal government led by a non-Québécois or Quebecker since 1968, and today both the prime minister and the leader of the opposition are francophones hailing from Québec. Québec has established 25 of its own ambassadorial agencies in 14 foreign countries since the 1960s, including the influential Délégation générale du Québec in Paris.[34] Since 1931 the percentage of people speaking French as their *langue maternelle* has increased, and Québec has passed and enforced restrictive language laws, like Bill 101 in 1977, that have made the non-French-speakers of Québec feel like a conquered and colonized people.[35] Meanwhile, French-language publishing in Québec has boomed; the province produced four times as many novels in French between 1978 and 1982 as it did between 1962 and 1965, and its authors,[36] Poulin among them, have begun to imagine the day when they will conquer the literary markets

of the United States. One can still use the cliché of Pierre Vallières in 1968—that Canada is a triply colonized sub-sub-sub colony[37]—but one should not expect to do so without receiving a stiff counter-argument based on at least some of the points I have mentioned here.

What Poulin's novel strongly suggests through its selective recuperation of *voyageur* history and its valorization of *métissage* is a unity of destiny among French Canadians and native peoples in North America that has as its representative, its ambassador to the future, the *Métis,* whom Jack praises as "quelque chose de neuf, quelque chose qui commence" (224). La Grande Sauterelle's own view of history serves to unite the French Canadian and the Indian in a similar exploratory mission. As she explains to Jack, "il paraît que les Indiens sont venus de l'Asie et qu'ils sont arrivés en Amérique par un pont de glace qui recouvrait le détroit de Béring. On est arrivés par l'Ouest et vous êtes arrivés par l'Est" (28). ["And apparently the Indians came from Asia and reached America by means of an ice bridge that used to cover the Bering Strait. We came from the West and you came from the East" (Fischman, 23).]

In his challenging study of French Canadian identity in the 20th century, Morisset also equates French Canadians and Indians as peoples native to North America who were forcibly displaced by multiple waves of first British and then American colonialism. In Morisset's view of history, the first "nations" with claims to the Americas were those of Latin America (Brazil and Mexico) and the native peoples of North America.[38] What this theory elides, of course, is the imperial or colonial venture that brought the French to the New World in the first place. Although it is a point particularly difficult for Americans to grasp, Morisset, like Poulin and Brouillette, does not see the relevance of that fact after the point in North American history when the French Canadians were dispossessed by the French and had intermarried extensively with the native populations of North America. After this point, as La Grande Sauterelle's anecdotal view of history is meant to suggest, French Canadians (whom Morisset very pointedly calls "*Canadiens*"), and Indians can both be seen as non-antagonistic residents of the New World, neither of whom are sustained by the colonial connection to Europe. Morisset does not argue that *Canadiens* and Indians are the same, merely that their role in North America after the conquest of 1759 is the same: groups indigenous to the continent who are under programmatic assault by British and American colonialism in North America.

This is Morisset's point of departure for arguing a territorial imperative not unlike Poulin's idea of imaginative colonization through physical reappropriation of the continent. For it is the coming together of the agendas of selective historical recuperation and physical appropriation that leads to imaginative colonization. In order to possess their "country," *Canadiens* must do precisely what Poulin has them do in ***Volkswagen Blues***: join with the *Métis* who are spiritually, and in many cases physically, their flesh and blood, abandon the idea of political retrenchment in the province of Québec, and reconquer the American continent.[39] Despite his choice of words, Morisset, like Poulin, does not see this as a military venture, but rather as an imaginative one. Morisset performs *"une annexion"* of North American history and culture that has been suggested by Canadian writers as diverse as Leonard Cohen, in his early postmodern classic, *Beautiful Losers* (1966), and Victor-Lévy Beaulieu in his Beat-inspired *"essai-poulet," Jack Kerouac* (1972).

In lacing the United States through with *Canadien* history and language and figuratively undergirding it with the *voyageur* map, Poulin creates a literary example of Morisset's contention that "Enlevons le Canadien et l'Indien de la littérature de l'Amérique du Nord Britannique, il n'en reste à peu près plus rien."[40] [Take the French Canadian and the Indian out of the literature of British North America and there's hardly anything left of it anymore.] La Grande Sauterelle makes much the same point explaining the origins of Fort Laramie in Wyoming, which was named for a 19th century trapper, Jacques Laramée. In Laramée's time, according to La Grande Sauterelle, "tout ce territoire et peut-être même tout l'Ouest américain ... était inondé de Canadiens français. ... Ils vivaient avec les Indiennes et souvent ils avaient eux-mêmes du sang indien" (202). ["all that territory and maybe even the entire American West was flooded with French Canadians. ... They lived with Indian women and many had Indian blood themselves" (Fischman, 145).] Historical *métissage* links the Canadien and the Indian permanently and inseparably, literary *métissage*—Poulin's postmodern ability to break down the boundaries of textual and cartographic history—allows Poulin to assert the primacy of the *Canadien* "Légende de l'Amérique" over that of the American. Outside of Detroit Jack hears a French song on the radio that celebrates "le chemin d'Amérique" and the narrator chimes in, "L'Amérique! Chaque fois qu'il entendait prononcer ce mot, Jack sentait bouger quelque chose au milieu des brumes qui obscurcissaient son cerveau. ... C'était une idée enveloppée de souvenirs très anciens—une idée qu'il appelait le 'Grand Rêve de l'Amérique'" (100). Soon after, Jack's reverie is checked by the realization that "Avec le temps, le 'Grand Rêve de l'Amérique' s'était brisé en miettes comme tous les rêves, mais il renaissait de temps à autre comme un feu couvait sous la cendre. ... Et parfois, en traversant l'Amérique, les voyageurs retrouvaient des parcelles du vieux rêve qui avaient été éparpillées ici et là ..." (101). ["America! Every time he heard the word Jack felt something stir in the fog that muddled his brain. ... It was an idea wrapped in ancient memories—an idea he called the 'Great Dream of America.' ... In time, the 'Great Dream of America' had been shattered like all other dreams, but from time to time it was revived, like a fire smouldering under the ashes. ... And sometimes, travellers crossing America found traces of the old dream scattered here and there ..." (Fischman, 73-74).]

It is difficult for American readers to grasp the degree to which Jack's sentiments represent an imaginative colonization of the United States, for there are few concepts with which the literary American reader is more familiar and comfortable than "the American dream." But the American dream translated into French as "le Grand Rêve de l'Amérique" is not what Jack is talking about, and the evidence, like the bits of the dream itself, is strewn about the America that is both the subject and text of *Volkswagen Blues.* Through a French Canadian lens, Poulin's novel refocuses the American map, the westward pioneering trail, a score of specific locations from Detroit to Fort Laramie, and the fundamentally American authors, such as Jack Kerouac and Saul Bellow, to whom the novel pays homage. It would be a mistake to assume, after all this, that "le Grand Rêve de l'Amérique" is a translation *into* French. In fact, Poulin makes it clear that, to the contrary, "le Grand Rêve de l'Amérique" cannot be translated *out* of French.

Poulin asserts that though the dream is smashed, it can, from time to time, be rediscovered by *"les voyageurs."* In Sheila Fischman's translation of *Volkswagen Blues, les voyageurs* becomes "travellers."[41] But the question isn't whether "travellers" is an acceptable translation of *"voyageurs"* according to the dictionary, but whether *voyageurs,* understood in light of all the historical and mythological weight with which Poulin invests it in *Volkswagen Blues,* is even translatable. This is a real question, not a nicety, as we must remember that Poulin is himself a professional translator, well aware of the difficulties of that art. As a postmodernist, Poulin is also fully capable of bringing the question of translation into play in a novel that is in large measure about the understanding of North America through French Canadian culture. To the American reader, this re-understanding of North America may seem like a kind of cultural translation, but it is, more precisely, an act of appropriation.

For evidence of this one need go no further than the title of the novel, *Volkswagen Blues,* which is immediately accessible to the anglophone reader and might even be construed as English. But is it English and is it translatable? "Volkswagen" is a German word, but the Volkswagen automobile, as a cultural artifact, is readily understood in North America and by no other name than Volkswagen. Blues, as in "blues music," is of American origin, but is, like Volkswagen, understood in many cultures. The translation of "blues" in an English-to-French dictionary, for example, is "blues."[42] Thus it is likely that *Volkswagen Blues* is not precisely what it at first appears to be to an American, a French Canadian, or even a German. Most of all, like "le Grand Rêve de l'Amérique" and *"voyageurs,"* it defies translation.[43] In confronting what appears to be familiar in *Volkswagen Blues,* whether it is St. Louis or "le Grand Rêve de l'Amérique," the American reader confronts an untranslatable (but not un-understandable) French Canadian cultural mythology of North America—"la Légende de l'Amérique." The mythology may be familiar to Americans, but it is not translated: it is annexed, appropriated. ***Volkswagen Blues*** represents "une parcelle du territoire littéraire américain que Poulin revendique comme le sien."[44] [a bit of American literary territory which Poulin claims as his own.] In his imaginative colonization of North America in ***Volkswagen Blues,*** Poulin—like the original pioneers of the continent, like Étienne Brûlé, and like Théo—"était absolument convaincu qu'il était capable de faire tout ce qu'il voulait."

Notes

1. The excursion of Bostonians that Thoreau joined was significant enough to make news in Canada. On 23 September the *Montreal Gazette* reported the imminent arrival of "Our Neighbours From Boston" and stated, "We may prepare for a throng in our streets and public spaces." On the 27th the *Gazette* followed up with the announcement of the arrival of almost 1200 Bostonians and remarked, "We have not seen such a crowd for a long time, as was formed by the confluence of the streams of our fellow-citizens running down, and that of our American friends setting upward to the town." On the 28th, with the arrival of the final American tourists, the *Gazette* lamented "the unusual dullness of our city just now" and feared inclement weather would create "rather an unfavorable impression on their minds."

2. Before the Act of Union in 1840, Canada East was known as Lower Canada (Bas-Canada). With Confederation in 1867, Canada East became the province of Québec.

3. John Aldrich Christie, *Thoreau as World Traveler* (New York: Columbia UP, 1965), 95-99.

4. A list of works primarily concerned with or containing chapters devoted to *A Yankee in Canada* includes Sidney Poger, "Thoreau as Yankee in Canada" in *American Transcendental Quarterly,* v. 14 (1972), 174-77; Edmund Berry, "A Yankee in Canada" in *The Dalhousie Review,* v. xxiii, n. 1 (April, 1943), 68-74; Lawrence Willson, "Thoreau and the French in Canada" in *Revue de l'Université d'Ottawa,* v. 29, n. 3 (Juillet-Septembre, 1959), 281-97 and "Thoreau's Canadian Notebook in *The Huntington Library Quarterly,* v.xxii, no. 3 (May, 1959), 179-200; James Doyle, *North of America* (Toronto: ECW Press, 1983), 32-39; Walter Harding and Michael Meyer, *The New Thoreau Handbook* (New York: New York UP, 1980), 46-48; and Stephen Adams, "Thoreau Catching Cold" in *ESQ,* v. 25, n. 4 (1979), 224-34. Stephen Fink considers "A Canadian Journey" in the larger context of Thoreau's publication history and commercial aspirations in Chapter 9 of his *Prophet in the Marketplace: Thoreau's Development as a Professional Writer* (Princeton: Princeton UP, 1992).

5. Thoreau to Harrison Blake (27 Feb. 1853) in F. B. Sanborn, editor, *Familiar Letters of Henry David Thoreau* (Boston: Houghton Mifflin, 1894).

6. Henry David Thoreau, *A Yankee in Canada* (Boston: Houghton Mifflin, 1888), 40. Further references are made parenthetically in the text.

7. The Québec Act of 22 June 1774, one of those branded "intolerable" by the American colonists, legalized the Catholic Church in Québec, allowed it the freedom to tithe, restored the traditional borders of the province, eliminated loyalty oaths that barred Catholics from holding office, and reinstated French civil law while preserving British criminal codes. For the importance of the Québec Act see Gustave Lanctôt, *Le Canada et la Révolution Américaine* (Montréal: Librairie Beauchemin, 1965), 29-56 and Francois-Xavier Garneau, *Histoire du Canada* (Québec: Fréchette et Frère, 1848), 364-78.

8. "To the people of Great-Britain" (5 Sept. 1774) reprinted in Lanctôt, *Le Canada et la Révolution Américaine,* 279.

9. "Aux Habitants de la Province de Québec" (26 Octobre 1774) reprinted in Lanctôt, *Le Canada et la Révolution Américaine,* 290.

10. In his 1877 history Hubert Larue reports: "De son côté, le congrès américain, par ses lettres pleines de duperies et de fausses réprésentations, ne manqua pas de s'aliéner l'esprit de la population." [For its part, the Continental Congress, due to its letters full of deceptions and false representations, never missed a chance to alienate the French population of Canada.] Hubert Larue, *Histoire Populaire du Canada* (Québec: Blumhart et Cie., 1877), 177. Garneau, the great French Canadian historian of the 19th century, is even more incensed: "Ce langage n'eut été que fanatique, si ceux qui le tenaient eussent été sérieux; il était insensé et puérile dans la bouche d'hommes qui songeaient déjà à inviter les Canadiens à se joindre à leur cause (Garneau, 378). [The language of the Continental Congress was that of the fanatic, if those who were maintaining this position are to be taken seriously; such words were insane and childish in the mouths of men who had already expressed a desire to invite the French Canadians to join their cause.] For a more contemporary view, see Lanctôt, *Le Canada et la Révolution Américaine,* 48.

11. Garneau, 378.

12. Benson Lossing, *A History of the United States* (New York: Mason Bros., 1857), 239.

13. Salma Hale, *History of the United States* (New York: Charles Wiley, 1825), 175. Hale's history won a prize in 1825 from the American Academy of Belles Lettres as the best history for use in schools. See

Ruth Miller Elson, *Guardians of Tradition* (Lincoln: U of Nebraska Press, 1964), 406.

14. Alexis de Tocqueville, *Journey to America,* translated by George Lawrence, edited by J. P. Mayer (New Haven, Yale UP, 1960), 189-90.

15. Edmund G. Berry, "Thoreau in Canada" in *The Dalhousie Review,* v. xxiii, n. 1 (April, 1943), 71.

16. William Spengemann, *A Mirror for Americanists* (Hanover: University Press of New England, 1989), 141.

17. Buell writes: "[a]lthough the 13 American colonies never experienced anything like the political/military domination colonial India did, the extent of cultural colonization by the mother country, from epistemology to aesthetics to dietetics, was on the whole much more comprehensive. ..." Lawrence Buell, "American Literary Emergence as a Postcolonial Phenomenon" in *American Literary History,* v. 4, n. 3 (1992), 415.

18. Francis Parkman, *France and England in North America,* vol. ix, part 2 (New York: Frederick Ungar, 1965), 408.

19. Thoreau, *The Journal of Henry David Thoreau,* v. ix, edited by Bradford Torrey and Francis H. Allen (Salt Lake City: Gibbs. M. Smith, 1984), 104.

20. Miraglia's count includes "chansons, tableaux, films, photos, livres historiques et, bien sûr, romans. Leurs origines sont françaises, québécoises, américaines et indiennes." Anne Marie Miraglia, *L'écriture de l'Autre chez Jacques Poulin* (Québec: Les Éditions Balzac, 1993), 121.

21. Jacques Poulin, *Volkswagen Blues* (Montréal: Éditions Québec/Amérique, 1989), 169. Further citations made parenthetically in the text.

22. Thoreau shows a similar inclination to see the French Canadian *voyageur* as the American pioneer par excellence: "... the Greeks, with all their wood and river gods, were not so qualified to name the natural features of a country, as the ancestors of these French Canadians; and if any people had a right to substitute their own for the Indian names, it was they. They have preceded the pioneer on our own frontiers, and named the *prairie* for us" (52). Thoreau also cites numerous historians on the tendency of the French Canadians to adopt the Indian way of life: "while the descendants of the Pilgrims are teaching the English to make pegged boots, the descendants of the French in Canada are wearing Indian moccasins still." Thoreau goes on to describe the more amicable bond between the French Canadians and native peoples: "The French, to their credit be it said, to a certain extent respected the Indians as a separate and independent people, and spoke of them and contrasted themselves with them as the English have never done. They not ony went to war with them as allies, but they lived at home with them as neighbors. ... The impression made on me was, that the French Canadians were even sharing the fate of the Indians, or at least gradually disappearing in what is called the Saxon current" (61-62).

23. Francis Parkman, *Pioneers of France in the New World,* part ii (Boston: Little Brown, 1899), 226.

24. Consul Wilshire Butterfield, *History of Brûlé's Discoveries and Explorations, 1610-1626* (Cleveland: Helman-Taylor, 1898), 120-23.

25. "Post-colonial inversions of imperial formations ... do not overturn or invert the dominant order to become dominant in their turn, but to question the foundations of the ontologies and epistemological systems which would see such binary structures as inescapable." Helen Tiffin, "Post-Colonial Literatures and Counter-Discourse in *Kunapipi,* v. ix, n. 3 (1987), 32.

26. For information on Canadian colonialism as governmental policy in the 20th century see two works by Robin Winks, *The Relevance of Canadian History* (Toronto: Macmillan, 1979), 63-64 and *Canadian-West Indian Union: A Forty-Year Minuet* in *The University of London Institute of Commonwealth Studies Commonwealth Papers,* v. xi (London: Athlone Press, 1968), 7-8.

27. Laurent Girouard, "Notre littérature de colonie," in *Parti Pris,* v. i. n. 3 (décembre 1963), 30. On the English side, Margaret Atwood, for example, states that Canada can be seen through its literature as "a collective victim." Margaret Atwood, *Survival* (Toronto: Anansi, 1972), 36.

28. Poulin quoted by François Vasseur and Michelle Roy in *Nuit Blanche,* n. 14 (juin, juillet, août 1984), 50.

29. Linda Hutcheon, "'Circling the Downspout of Empire': Post-colonial and Postmodern Ironies" in *Splitting Images: Contemporary Canadian Ironies* (Toronto: Oxford UP, 1991), 73.

30. Miraglia, 181.

31. Jean Morisset, *L'Identité usurpée, vol. i: L'Amérique écartée* (Montréal: Éditions Nouvelle Optique, 1985), 12.

32. Simon During, "Postmodernism or Postcolonialism?" in *Landfall* 155 (Sept., 1985), 369-70.

33. For figures on Québecois control of Québec businesses see Paul-André Linteau, René Durocher,

Jean-Claude Ronbert, and François Ricard, *Histoire du Québec contemporain: Le Québec depuis 1930* (Montréal: Boréal, 1986), 419. See also Jorge Niosi's *Canadian Capitalism,* translated by Robert Chodos (Toronto: James Lorimer, 1981). For figures on foreign investment see Linteau, 420 and Niosi, 60.

34. Linteau, 672-75.

35. Linteau, 545.

36. Linteau, 698.

37. Pierre Vallières, *Nègres blancs d'Amérique* (Montréal: Parti Pris, 1968), 334.

38. Morisset, 14-15.

39. Morisset states, "Il s'agit ni plus ni moins d'une Reconquête de l'Ego Collectif à travers une Géographie et une identité écartées" (12).

40. Morisset, xvi.

41. Poulin, *Volkswagen Blues,* translated by Sheila Fischman (Toronto: McClelland and Steward, 1988), 74.

42. See, for example, the *Harper Collins French Dictionary* (London: Harper Collins, 1990).

43. I am indebted to Prof. Marc Shell and to Kate Matwychuk for my understanding of the complexities of the title of *Volkswagen Blues.*

44. Jean-Pierre Lapointe, "Sur la piste américaine" in *Voix et Images,* v. xv, n. 1 (automne, 1989), 27.

Jack Illingworth (review date 2002)

SOURCE: Illingworth, Jack. "'Same Character and Same Character Trait.'" Rev. of *Autumn Rounds,* by Jacques Poulin. *Books in Canada* 31.9 (2002): 8. Print.

[*In the following review, Illingworth praises the "extraordinarily light and genial" prose of* La tournée d'automne *(1993; published as* Autumn Rounds*), arguing that the novel's dialog helps Poulin establish "a feeling of unforced intimacy" with his readers. Illingworth contends that fans of Poulin's previous novels "will find* Autumn Rounds *to be a fresh tour of his old ground; those who are new to his work will find it enchanting."*]

All of Jacques Poulin's novels are the same; all of them are different. This critical truism has long been applied to the works of this distinguished Québecois novelist and translator, for all of his novels are stories of detached, literate, wandering men, who travel across North America, meet their ideal feminine companion, while working through a socially-relevant problem. Anglophone readers may remember his *Volkswagen Blues,* which uses this formula to explore, among other things, the displacement of the

First Nations in contemporary Quebec, the moral dilemmas of the history of French North America, and the ethics of sibling responsibility. ***Autumn Rounds,*** Sheila Fischman's recent translation of Poulin's 1993 novel ***La Tournée d'automne,*** continues to develop this pattern, with remarkable results.

Autumn Rounds is among Poulin's most introspective novels. It is the story of an aging man, known simply as "the Driver," who leaves his Québec city home several times each year to tour the north shore of the St. Lawrence in his bookmobile. The Driver is a solitary fellow, with few friends and almost no family. Afraid of the decrepitude which will come with old age, the Driver has resolved to asphyxiate himself at the end of his summer rounds, preferring to die in his beloved van, on his own terms.

Just before his trip begins, however, the Driver meets Marie, a French woman of his own age who manages an itinerant troupe of acrobats and musicians. The Driver is quietly smitten by Marie, and, happily, her group intends to spend the subsequent weeks touring the Driver's usual haunts. Their travels frequently coincide, and Marie often opts to leave her troupe's school bus and travel in the Driver's bookmobile. The relationship develops slowly, for Poulin's characters are reserved types who shy away from aggressive romance or unprompted self-revelation. Marie and the Driver talk about their favourite books, the beauty of Quebec's landscape, and, with great reticence, about the terrors of aging. On their travels they encounter a host of rural readers who eagerly accept the Driver's books—and even the rejected, unpublished manuscripts that the Driver circulates as a service to Quebec's less successful writers. They also enjoy a couple of meetings with Jack, a kind of author's stand-in who makes rumbustious pronouncements on matters of literary taste and is overjoyed about *Le Devoir's* comment that "'In book after book [...] he gives us the same character with the same character traits.'" Jack also provides Poulin's readers with a brief list of their author's literary touchstones: Raymond Carver, Ernest Hemingway, John Fante, Gabrielle Roy, Boris Vian, Jack Kerouac, Richard Ford. Poulin's own style owes much to all of these writers, and as such is ideally suited to his emotive Québecois road tales.

At the beginning of their tour, Marie is involved in a relationship with Slim, her troupe's tightrope walker. One would expect some nasty scenes of vehement jealousy, but this isn't Poulin's style; Marie shifts her allegiances gradually, with a minimum of hand-wringing and without petty competition on the part of the men. It is tempting to criticize Poulin for leaving his readers with next to no idea of how Slim feels about the loss of his lover, but this is a simple consequence of the author's favoured way of treating love. Poulin seems to believe so wholeheartedly in the inevitability of passion that he refuses to bother with scenes of emotional posturing. Marie and the Driver appear to be a perfect, natural couple, and they slide into their roles slowly, with a minimum of fuss or authorial comment. Only the Driver's plans for suicide warrant discussion, and even that matter is approached calmly, as though he were contemplating something as mundane as the purchase of a trailer for his bookmobile.

Poulin's prose is extraordinarily light and genial, and this is what makes his fiction work so well. He creates a feeling of unforced intimacy that effaces the artifice of the narrative voice, allowing him to make use of symbolism that would otherwise feel pretentious or clumsy. His characters have a tendency to turn didactic, but they never become offensive, and their dialogue has a rough verve that keeps it free of the affected speechifying that too often creeps into all but the best novels of ideas.

Sheila Fischman, a Governor General's Award nominee for her work in translation, is consistently graceful here. Poulin's French is simple and unaffected, full of subtle modulations of tone, and Fischman has always been skilled at carrying these distinctions into fluid, readable English. Her long career has enabled her to translate almost any work of Francophone fiction into a wholly satisfying English novel; *Autumn Rounds* is no exception.

Strangely, comparisons between *Autumn Rounds* and other Poulin novels such as *Volkswagen Blues* are almost impossible. His talent as a writer is great enough that, no matter how often he recycles his favoured plot and characters, each book will always be unique. Superficially, *Volkswagen Blues* was a "bigger" book, packed with the kind of historical and nationalist critique that academics enthuse about. *Autumn Rounds* is a much subtler novel, one that appears to operate on an entirely personal level, but which nonetheless gently gathers a love of Québec's landscape, history, and culture into its understated autumnal romance. Those who have travelled with Poulin before will find *Autumn Rounds* to be a fresh tour of his old ground; those who are new to his work will find it enchanting.

Ritt Deitz (review date 2004)

SOURCE: Deitz, Ritt. Rev. of *Les yeux bleus de Mistassini,* by Jacques Poulin. *French Review* 78.1 (2004): 204-06. Print.

[*In the following review, Deitz discusses Poulin's weaving of plot, imagery, and characters throughout his novels, noting that the narrator of* Les yeux bleus de Mistassini *(2002; published as* My Sister's Blue Eyes*) is Jimmy, the protagonist of an earlier novel. Dietz concludes that Poulin needs to broaden the world he is presenting in his novels.*]

Each of Poulin's novels reveals a world slightly different from the previous one, yet composed of the same materials. Despite some variety in character and locale, cherished themes and objects return: hot chocolate, cats, interrupted naps in sleeping bags, Volkswagen minibuses, Formula One racing, tennis, Quebec City, thoughts of suicide. These are the building blocks of a fictional universe, a larger story in ten books thus far.

The story is so coherent, in fact, that with its most recent installment, Poulin's world seems to be turning in on itself. *Les Yeux bleus de Mistassini* is narrated by Jimmy, the protagonist of Poulin's early novel of the same name. Now an adult, Jimmy befriends Jack Waterman, the hero of Poulin's known novel, *Volkswagen Blues.* An aging writer, Jack has a dementia problem and an idiosyncratic bookstore in Old Quebec. Jimmy ends up managing the bookstore and hoping to become a writer himself. He also takes a soul-searching trip to Europe, living in a Volkswagen minibus in Paris before finally returning to Quebec—the trip, the vehicle and the place of return all classic Poulin touchstones. Mistassini is Jimmy's mysterious younger sister, who joins her brother in an unusually symbiotic relationship, faithful to her role in Jimmy's mind as the spritelike muse who leaves as unexpectedly as she appears.

Intertextuality is nothing new to Poulin—his earlier novels are full of references to writers—but *Les Yeux bleus* [*Les yeux bleus de Mistassini*] is the first to build so directly on the imagined lives of his own previous characters. *Volkswagen Blues* remains the main point of reference. That novel ends as Jack finds his long-lost brother Théo in San Francisco, wheelchair-bound, glassy-eyed and unable to identify Jack. In *Les Yeux bleus,* an older Jack alludes to this episode: "[C]'est une maladie [. . .] pernicieuse. Ça ne se guérit pas, ça ne peut que s'aggraver avec le temps" (58). References to *Volkswagen Blues* abound, but as a book Jack Waterman has written himself. "[V]ous avez écrit un peu partout," says Jimmy, "sur le bord des routes et dans les campings, quand vous êtes allé en Californie avec le minibus Volkswagen." Jack's editor, also in the room, adds, "Le livre se vend encore très bien" (66).

As in other Poulin books, fears of loss pervade the narrator's thoughts. While stuck in Paris traffic after watching Sampras lose at Roland Garros, Pascarolo lose at Le Mans and Villeneuve finish fourth at the Magny-Cours speedway, Jimmy is exhausted: "J'étais aux prises avec l'idée démoralisante que mes héros, dans le domaine sportif, étaient en déclin" (129). Likewise, when Jimmy admits to his mentor, "J'ai peur d'appartenir à cette race de fous qui aime davantage les mots que les choses" (177), one realizes Jimmy's major anxiety about writing: it threatens his physical connection with the real world and its experiential joy. Words risk becoming the dominant *thing* in his life: "Je commençais à prendre conscience qu'entre les mots et moi se nouaient des liens qui risquaient de durer longtemps et peut-être même d'occuper une place trop grande dans ma vie" (55).

The newest element in this novel is Mistassini herself. Poulin's books routinely feature restless, catlike women who exist primarily to provoke desire and nostalgia in the narrating male character, but the affection these two show each other is uncomfortably erotic. Once, when she is kissing her brother, a small confetti star falls from her face and lands on his. "[P]our me l'enlever," he says, "elle humecta le bout de son index qu'elle passa ensuite très délicatement sur ma lèvre" (70). When the girl he calls "ma petite sœur, la moitié de mon âme" (70) massages him in the shower (his having attracted her with artificial moans of pain), the intimacy between them borders on incestuous. Jimmy's explanation comes off as overly dramatic, a clichéd understatement: "Nous ne suivions pas les mêmes règles que tout le monde" (173). Narration like this makes one wonder, not why these sibling characters are so touchy, or why recycled characters still fret over the power of words in their lives—but whether it isn't time for Jacques Poulin, back in Quebec City after a decade in Paris, to think about expanding his horizons.

Gilles Labrie (essay date 2006)

SOURCE: Labrie, Gilles. "Quebec's Quiet Revolution in Jacques Poulin's *Les grandes marées*." *French Review* 79.5 (2006): 1037-48. Print.

[*In the following essay, Labrie contends that* Spring Tides *functions as a veiled commentary on the societal changes in Quebec brought about by the Quiet Revolution.*]

Jacques Godbout, writing about the 1960s and early 1970s in Quebec, states that

> Ce que tout jeune écrivain québécois devrait savoir, c'est [. . .] que ce n'est pas lui qui écrit ses livres [. . .] et qu'il n'y a au Québec qu'Un seul Ecrivain: NOUS TOUS. Un écrivain québécois ne peut chercher à exister en dehors du texte [national] québécois, il lui faut participer à l'entreprise collective [. . .]

(150)

Similarly, in Jacques Poulin's *Les Yeux bleus de Mistassini,* published in 2002, the narrator says that the character Jack Waterman, a writer, also believes that literature is a collective enterprise: "il échafaudait lui-même une théorie suivant laquelle les œuvres littéraires étaient, contrairement aux apparences, le fruit d'un travail collectif" (41). On first reading, Jacques Poulin's 1978 novel *Les Grandes Marées,* though clearly set in Quebec, does not appear to contain many overt references to the society and culture of the 1960s and 1970s or to the transformations taking place in Quebec society. Although the novel seems to deal entirely with universal themes, a closer reading reveals it to be a fictional representation of Quebec's Quiet Revolution in the 1960s and 1970s.

Most readers do not perceive a great degree of "Québecness" in the novel because of its minimalist style and lack of direct allusions to issues of the day. There are, however, some obvious clues: the novel is set on the *île Madame,* a small island not far from Quebec City and the *île d'Orléans.* The main character, Teddy Bear, translates cartoons from English into French for the Quebec City newspaper *Le Soleil.* When his boss, the *patron,* asks how he could make him happy, Teddy replies: "Vous n'auriez pas une île déserte?" (14). His boss does, and while Teddy is living on the island, every month at the time of the highest tides, the boss brings new characters to the island in hopes of making Teddy happy. A young woman, Marie, arrives first, providing companionship, followed by *Tête Heureuse,* the *patron*'s wife, the intellectuals Professor Mocassin and the Author, a Québécois novelist. *L'Homme Ordinaire,* the management specialist, appears next, followed by the specialist in communication. Finally the group excludes Teddy and banishes him from the island because he is sick and unable to work.

THE QUIET REVOLUTION

Contemporary Quebec history is often divided into three parts: the period before the Quiet Revolution, the Quiet Revolution itself, and the period after the Quiet Revolution (*Si je me souviens bien* 213). The period before the Quiet Revolution is characterized by the conservative government of Maurice Duplessis in power from 1944 to 1959. Duplessis's death in 1959, and the subsequent election of the liberal Jean Lesage government in 1960, mark the beginning of the Quiet Revolution (*Si je me souviens bien* 217-18). In a strict sense, the Quiet Revolution refers to the period of reforms that took place between 1960 and 1966. In a broader sense, the term characterizes the decades of the 1960s and 1970s.

The Quiet Revolution is part of a worldwide period of change marked in the United States by the Civil Rights Movement, the Vietnam War, and a cultural and sexual revolution. In Quebec, the main goal is "le rattrapage," "catching-up," the desire to accelerate the modernization of Quebec (Linteau, *Histoire* 421). This is a period of major social change. In health, human services and education, the Quebec government replaces the Catholic Church which had controlled these institutions since their creation. A major reform of education makes the system more accessible to all. On the economic level, electricity is nationalized, Hydro-Quebec is created as well as a major pension fund (*Si je me souviens bien* 215). Equally important, a concerted effort (signaled by Jean Lesage's 1962 campaign slogan "Maîtres chez nous") to promote francophone majority access to positions of influence in the economy and society up to then controlled by the Anglophone minority, is largely successful (Linteau, *Histoire* 421-22). These changes and Montreal's selection as the site of the 1967 World's Fair inspired a new attitude, a new way of seeing and being in the citizens of Quebec. "Pendant ces années, il régnait au Québec un climat d'optimisme et une confiance en soi collective, jusqu'alors inconnue. On pouvait croire que tout était possible et que l'avenir ne pouvait être que prometteur" (*Si je me souviens bien* 215).

The year 1960 thus marks the beginning of a new era that "has to be represented as a founding myth, a break from an alienated past" (Marshall 48). In *Les Grandes Marées* the reference to a new myth representing the Quiet Revolution appears in its opening sentence: "Au commencement il était seul dans l'île (9)," an imitation, perhaps even a parody, of the first line of Genesis "Au commencement, Dieu créa le ciel et la terre." Other reminders throughout the novel reinforce the idea that this is a secular retelling of the myth of the Garden of Eden. Sometimes the Garden of Eden is mentioned explicitly, as when Marie points out, "C'est le paradis terrestre, ici!" (34). The Author, speaking of the island, adds: "Quand le boss m'en a parlé, il m'a dit que c'était comme le paradis terrestre ou à peu près et qu'il n'y avait pas de meilleur endroit pour écrire un livre" (116). Later the *patron* tells Teddy in reference to Marie's arrival: "Evidemment, je ne me prends pas pour Dieu le Père et je ne me suis pas dit: 'Il n'est pas bon que l'homme soit seul' ou quelque chose du genre, mais j'ai pensé que vous auriez plus de chances d'être heureux à deux" (54). Obviously, though, that is precisely what the *patron* is doing, even when he paraphrases Genesis 2, 18: "Il n'est pas bon que l'homme soit seul. Il faut que je lui fasse une aide qui lui soit assortie." Later Teddy mentions *Eden Blues* (149), a song by Moustaki sung by Edith Piaf, which foreshadows his own fate: as Adam was banished from the Garden of Eden, so, too, is Teddy from the *île Madame* (Socken 50). All of these references to the Garden of Eden, the Judeo-Christian myth of the origin of the world, alert the reader that *Les Grandes Marées* represents a new beginning, the new world of Quebec's Quiet Revolution. And just as it did for Adam, in the beginning everything goes well for Teddy. After Marie's arrival, Teddy claims that he has never been happier: "je ne me suis jamais senti aussi bien de toute ma vie" (60).

WOMEN

Tête Heureuse, the second woman to arrive on the island, is the new woman of the Quiet Revolution or rather a parody of one. In pre-Quiet-Revolution Quebec, the role of every woman was to be very Catholic in having lots of babies. The aim was to increase the French-Catholic population and thus political power to forestall assimilation into an Anglophone Quebec (Marshall 209). This policy kept women in subservient positions until passage of a law in 1964 providing equality of husband and wife. But with the rise of feminism starting in 1970, women in Quebec demanded much more:

> autonomy, self-definition and equality between the sexes. Many people thought sexual equality had been won with the right to vote in provincial elections in 1940 and the law on the legal capacity of women in 1964. The new feminism exposed such "equality" for what it was: women had been granted rights, but there was no real equality [...].

Economically and socially, women were still dependent on men. Feminist critiques revealed the extent of that dependence, and the degree to which women desired autonomy. This new concept of autonomy placed individual growth before self-sacrifice, a revolutionary idea in Quebec, where sacrifice was almost synonymous with femininity. Autonomy meant that a woman could plan her own life [...]

(Dumont 356)

Tête Heureuse embodies these demands, for the *patron*'s wife has, as Teddy observes, a great sense of liberty (88). Though still described as a *mère poule* (137), she no longer is the mother hen cackling about a large brood of children like women of earlier times. Rather, flaunting her newly-found feminine independence, she provides comfort for the men on the island in such non-traditional ways as massages and sexual favors. Of course, she also differs from traditional Quebec women in that she pursues her own well-being (157). *Tête Heureuse* has no children and there are none on the island, which reflects the changing birth rate in Quebec from among the highest in the world before 1960 (3.86 children per woman on average) to among the lowest after 1960 (2.09 by 1970 and 1.75 in 1975), with serious political and social implications for the future of Quebec. A birth rate of 2.10 is required to maintain the population. Today the birth rate is 1.4 (Lacoursière 528).

LANGUAGE

The issues concerning the preeminence of French in Quebec arise in part because of this declining birthrate and in part because of increasing immigration of speakers of languages other than French or English. Before 1977, immigrants coming to Quebec could choose English or French-language schools for their children. Because English is the predominant language of North America, a great many of them chose English. This choice, and their attendant affiliation with the Anglophone population, raised fears that Montreal would eventually become an English-speaking city with francophones as its minority (Linteau, "La Question linguistique" 71).

In fact, the immigrants' choice of English thus appeared to threaten the survival of francophones throughout Quebec because, with the decline of Catholicism—a core value of pre-Quiet-Revolution French-Canadian identity—the French language became increasingly important to francophones as the one remaining central element of identity. Accordingly, from 1969 to 1977, three language laws were passed culminating with Bill 101, the Charter of the French Language, which made French the official language of Quebec and the language of government, schools and work. Since its passage in 1977, the Charter of the French Language has remained controversial, but the French language itself has become the base of Québécois identity for everyone living in Quebec (*Si je me souviens bien* 218).

The novel reflects this importance of language during the Quiet Revolution. Teddy translates American cartoons into French and frequently discusses the nuances of meaning of different words and the importance of using language precisely to translate difficult passages accurately. The text of a sign in the *Maison du Sud,* the older of the two houses on the island, welcoming survivors of shipwrecks, is in French only, reflecting the language practice in effect until 1969. However, that year Canadian Prime Minister Pierre Elliot Trudeau passed a law making federal institutions bilingual; accordingly, the map in the machine room in the *Maison du Nord* contains warnings about the dangers of navigation in the vicinity of the island in both French and English, reflecting the new bilingual policy.

Since the passage of The Charter of the French Language of 1977, every item sold in Quebec must include instructions in French; however, the professor's *bille auditive* has instructions in Japanese only, which no one can read. There the novel makes the point that this is a reasonable law: it protects citizens from unscrupulous companies neglecting to provide instructions in French, the language of the majority in Quebec.

THE NEW ELITES

Whereas before the Quiet Revolution the traditional elites included the priest, the lawyer, the doctor, and the notary public, the new elites are the intellectual, the manager, the technocrat, and the entrepreneur, all of them characters in ***Les Grandes Marées.*** The intellectual elite of the Quiet Revolution is represented by university professors and experts in law, engineering, and accounting as well as communication. The French Professor Mocassin and the Author are the intellectuals the *patron* brings to the island because he believes Teddy needs to interact with people on an intellectual plane. However, neither of the two is able to do so effectively. Professor Mocassin, for example, is an expert in cartoons. But because he pedantically deals with minutia, no intellectual exchange occurs between him and Teddy, the translator of cartoons.

Managers, representing the emerging commercial elite, become increasingly important as the number of francophone companies increases and as more and more francophones are recruited to fill management positions in non-francophone companies (Linteau, *Histoire* 555-57). The *Homme Ordinaire,* the manager par excellence, turns the island into a camp where all chores are performed on schedule: communal meals take place at fixed times, buildings and tennis courts are maintained scrupulously, and all islanders have to perform housework. But, because he, too, belongs to the elite, the *Homme Ordinaire* feels he deserves special privileges. So he conducts a survey of the work the islanders do to see who should have a room in the *Maison du Nord.* Not surprisingly, because Marie answers that she reads, an occupation he considers non-productive, he takes over her room (139-40).

The period of the Quiet Revolution is also known as the *Age de la parole,* a time when a quiescent Quebec population regains its voice, when strata of the society who had never spoken suddenly speak out (Vautier 167; Rioux 112). The novel parodies this development when the communicator encourages everyone to speak: however, instead of encouraging conversation, all he frees is the aggression of the Author who insists on taking over Teddy's house.

The *patron,* the ultimate example of the new entrepreneurial class, has the power to play god. The real-life model for the *patron* in ***Les Grandes Marées*** is Paul Desmarais, the CEO of the Power Corporation, a large industrial and financial empire, and the rising star among the entrepreneurial class that developed in the wake of the new spirit in Quebec after 1960 (L'Italien-Savard 9; Linteau, *Histoire* 559). Desmarais started his career by transforming the failing bus company he inherited from his father into the base of his expanding empire. The *patron* also has inherited a failing company from his father: "Mon père m'avait donné une petite compagnie d'autobus qui était au bord de la faillite" (52). The *patron* describes how he built his empire like Desmarais on the basis of this company. The *patron's* colonial cap—"Son crâne chauve était abrité du soleil par un casque colonial" (126)—symbolizes the political ties he exploited to achieve his power as had Desmarais, a friend of then Prime Minister Pierre Elliot Trudeau and not of the pro-independence *Parti Québécois,* hence colonial in the eyes of many Québécois (Fraser 238-39).

The *patron* wants to make everyone happy; yet, at the end of the story when Teddy is living on the beach, about to be banished from the island, and desperately needs his help, the *patron* is vacationing in Florida and never comes to assist him. The *patron* is essentially a God-like figure who abrogates his responsibility. The novel parodies and ridicules the importance and self-importance of these new elites whose interests are served by the Quiet Revolution, but who in their self-serving and callous way ruthlessly displace both Marie and Teddy.

RELIGION, POLITICS, AND INDEPENDENCE

In Marcel Rioux's description of the pre-Quiet-Revolution myth, Quebec society rests on "the Catholic religion, the French language, the parish, the extended family, a high birth rate, and a docile labor force (240). The novel makes allusions to some of these elements: although Catholicism and the Church had been central to the future of the pre-1960 society, religious practice and ritual appear in the novel only as a parody of the new deities—technology, politics and government—and as a symbol of the desire for independence.

The Quiet Revolution had replaced the myth of agriculture, religion, and the French language with the new myth of technology, and legitimized the aspirations of the new middle class (McRoberts 103). Early in the story the description of the *île Madame* establishes the setting as a metaphor for the story about to be told. On the island there is only one path, the path that leads to the center, to the tennis court and the Prince, the god of perfection, the exemplar of the new way, of the new myth technology.

> l'île mesurait un peu plus de deux kilomètres de largeur; sa superficie totale était de deux cent soixante-six acres [...]. Mais il n'y avait pas tant d'espace libre à la vérité car l'intérieur était presque entièrement recouvert par une forêt trop dense pour qu'il fût agréable d'y pénétrer. Un seul et unique sentier allait d'un bout à l'autre de l'île en passant par le court de tennis qui se trouvait au centre.

> (*Les Grandes Marées* 15-16)

The Prince, the marvel of technology, is a tennis-playing automaton. Teddy first goes off to play tennis with the Prince in a chapter titled "Le Cérémonial" (19). According to *Le Petit Robert*, the word refers to the rules for ceremonies but also has a second meaning referring to the book containing the liturgical rules for religious ceremonies. This meaning transforms Teddy's game with the Prince into a religious ritual. Furthermore, the Prince's skill is superhuman: "Grâce à son cerveau électronique, le Prince avait un jeu dont la perfection dépassait les possibilités humaines, et Teddy, même au meilleur de sa forme, ne pouvait songer à rivaliser d'adresse avec lui" (107). The narrator then describes Teddy's experience of playing tennis against the Prince as a mystical experience.

> Le traducteur sentait confusément que ses bras, ses jambes et finalement son corps en entier était envahi par une sorte de chaleur ou d'énergie, mentale et physique à la fois, qui l'élevait au-dessus de ses capacités ordinaires et lui permettait ainsi d'accéder à un univers de bien-être où chacun de ses muscles obéissait à la plus petite stimulation de son cerveau et où ce cerveau lui-même fonctionnait en parfaite harmonie avec celui du Prince.

> (107)

On other occasions Teddy's religious experiences derive from meditation on the deity. For example, one day when Teddy is ill and unable to play, Marie finds him watching the Prince. The narrator then points out that "Elle comprit qu'il jouait mentalement et qu'il mettait la même application que si le match eut été réel" (163). Technology has replaced religion, an important part of pre-Quiet-Revolution Quebec, just as the court at the center of the island has replaced the church at the center of every village in Quebec.

Pierre Hébert, in comparing Poulin to his favorite author Hemingway, says of the latter that he possesses "cette grande vertu de feindre de raconter une chose [...] pour en dire une autre, autrement plus importante. C'est au lecteur de faire ce *déplacement* de sens, car le narrateur lui, se limite à créer des *occasions* de sens" (113). Poulin employs precisely this technique when he calls his tennis-

playing automaton "the Prince," which immediately brings to mind Machiavelli's book by the same title. Rightly so, for Teddy's mystical experiences are ultimately even more closely related to politics than they are to technology. This is the period of the creation of the pro-independence *Parti Québécois* in 1968 and its electoral victory in 1976 under René Lévesque, a time when for many people politics in Quebec were lively and lived intensely.

Before the Quiet Revolution, the Church controlled education and human services and provided one of the few career paths open to francophones in Quebec. Beginning with the Quiet Revolution and the expansion of the Quebec government, politics and government rapidly became the career path of choice, for jobs in business did not become available in significant numbers until after 1977 when French became the language of work in Quebec (Guindon 64). It is ironic that during the Quiet Revolution, young people went into politics and government with the same fervor and passion to transform society and save the world as they had previously entered the Church. As represented in the novel, during the Quiet Revolution politics had replaced religion and government had replaced church, but the intensity and faith were the same: Teddy's mystical experience and meditation represent the intense engagement of many individuals in politics and government and parodies that displaced fervor and belief.

Teddy's mystical relationship with the Prince also reflects the dream of an independent Quebec. By referring to his tennis-playing automaton as the Prince, Poulin associates Quebec's lack of sovereignty to that of Renaissance Italy during the papacy of Rodrigo Borgia (Pope Alexander VI, 1492-1504), who was determined to unify Italy's city states under the rule of his illegitimate son Cesare. In *The Prince*, Cesare serves Niccolo Machiavelli as the model of the perfect ruler determined to bring an end to political rivalries that made the country the victim of incursions by neighboring kings (Adams xiv-xv). Teddy's ecstasy and feelings of complete harmony with the Prince symbolize his desire for a sovereign Quebec state similar to Prince Cesare Borgia's dream of a united independent Italy.

THE FLQ

Machiavelli's work justifies whatever means the Prince might use to free Italy from foreign powers: the citizens of Quebec, however, rejected political violence. In October 1970 a cell of the Quebec Liberation Front (FLQ), a radical Marxist group, kidnapped the British government representative James Cross and Pierre Laporte, a minister in the Quebec government. These events and Laporte's murder a few days later caused the citizens of Quebec to reject terrorism (*Si je me souviens bien* 215-16). Not surprisingly, Poulin's work reflects these developments. In his first novel, ***Mon Cheval pour un royaume,*** the narrator is a member of a terrorist group. He participates in a terrorist act by blowing up the statue of the British General James Wolfe commemorating his conquest of Quebec in 1759 on the Plains of Abraham in Quebec City. ***Les Grandes Marées,*** on the other hand, makes no mention of the radical left because as a result of the October crisis of 1970, terrorism had lost all popular support.

IDENTITY

The independence movement also contributed to a change in *Québécois* identity. According to Guy Rocher, "l'histoire, qu'elle soit racontée dans des mythes, des légendes, des contes ou des études savantes, sert à fonder, nourrir, rafraîchir, corriger la mémoire collective" (*Si je me souviens bien* 11). History, the collective memory, furnishes the stuff for constructing identity; this identity changes, however, as history is revisited (*Si je me souviens bien* 12). Until 1760, Canada was a French colony. After the British conquest, it remained a British colony until Confederation, the creation of the modern Canadian state in 1867. In post-Conquest Quebec, the challenge for the French-speaking Canadians was survival by resisting assimilation into English-speaking North America. In Quebec, this struggle against assimilation was enhanced by developing the people's pride in their French origins through teaching the history of New France (*Si je me souviens bien* 13). This connection to France as a buttress against an English-speaking North America persisted, though by the 1960s, Quebec had been cut off from France for two centuries. It received a tremendous boost with de Gaulle's 1967 visit when he reestablished this connection with his speech in Montreal (*Si je me souviens bien* 11-13). "C'est une immense émotion qui remplit mon cœur en voyant devant moi la ville de Montréal, française. Au nom du vieux pays, au nom de la France, je vous salue de tout mon cœur." After reaffirming the unbroken connection between Quebec and France, de Gaulle's speech addresses the issue of Quebec's desire for independence by comparing his arrival in Montreal to his return to Paris in 1944 when France regained its sovereignty. "Je vais vous confier un secret que vous ne répéterez pas. Ce soir ici et tout le long de ma route je me trouvais dans une même atmosphère que celle de la Libération." He closed his speech with his vision of Quebec's independence "Vive le Québec Libre!" After 1968 and the creation of the *Parti Québécois,* a party determined to achieve independence for Quebec, citizens had to decide where they stood in regard to independence. Very quickly a new Quebec identity emerged that for a good number of people took the place of their Canadian identity (*Si je me souviens bien* 168-69). Today, most people in Quebec call themselves *Québécois,* whether they support independence or not: *Québécois* identity is first and foremost.

Poulin's work reflects these issues of identity during the Quiet Revolution. In his first novel, ***Mon Cheval pour un royaume,*** published in 1967, the narrator refers to Canadians, not *Québécois,* when he speaks of the blood spilled for the British Empire: "du sang que Les Canadiens ont versé pour l'Empire" (160). It is interesting to note that ***Les Grandes Marées*** contains references to Jacques Cartier's three voyages (89) to establish the French roots of Quebec without a single mention of the British Regime. But American-ness and the connection with the United States is also an important part of the debate on Quebec identity during the Quiet Revolution. "For Quebec [...] 'America' represents a possible identity, a possible extension of itself ('*Américanité*' as opposed to identities centered on Quebec), and in time ('*rattrapage*'/'catching up'), a leap-frogging over the restrictive and limiting Canadian state" (Marshall 48-49). American-ness also suggests a connection to the French-Canadian "coureur de bois," the nomadic and free early explorer of the North American continent (Miraglia 181).

In ***Les Grandes Marées*** the connections to France and America are mirrored by the two intellectuals, the French professor Mocassin, and the Author, who dreams of the American West and the Pony Express and wants to write the great North American novel. When the Professor states "j'ai l'impression de retrouver ici un coin de la France" (99) he echoes de Gaulle's speech at the city hall in Montreal. De Gaulle had spoken of the people of Quebec as "les Français du Canada"; he had also spoken of "Les Français de part et d'autre de l'Atlantique." However, in answer to the Professor's statement the Author replies: "On n'est pas des Français!" "Alors qui êtes-vous?" asks the Professor. "On cherche" (99), the Author answers. Later, speaking of the great American novel he is writing, he insists that:

> le roman français s'intéresse plutôt aux idées, tandis que le roman américain s'intéresse davantage à l'action. Or, nous sommes des Français d'Amérique, ou des Américains d'origine française, si vous aimez mieux. Nous avons donc la possibilité, au Québec, d'écrire un roman qui sera le produit de la tendance française et de la tendance américaine.

(170)

These claims connect *Québécois* identity to both France and America.

EXCLUSION AND EXPULSION

Poulin's most serious issue growing out of the Quiet Revolution is the fate of the individual. In time Teddy learns that, since his arrival on the *île Madame,* the *patron* has never used his translations but relies instead on a computerized translation system. "Le patron a acheté un cerveau électronique. Il coûte un prix fou, mais il traduit les bandes dessinées en deux minutes. Il s'appelle Atan" (173). Obviously, Teddy has been replaced by the technology he adores. Moreover, the new elites eventually banish him from the island. When he demands to know why, Professor Mocassin tells him: "La répartition ne prévoit rien pour ceux qui sont affligés d'une incapacité physique temporaire ou permanente" (197). The Author adds: "Les temps s'annoncent plus difficiles [...] et comme vous n'êtes plus capable de travailler..." (198).

Teddy eventually finds his way to the neighboring island, *île aux Ruaux,* and again sees the man at the edge of the woods that he and Marie had noticed on an earlier visit. Upon closer examination, Teddy realises that "le vieux n'était pas vivant: il avait la peau dure comme la pierre" (201). At this point, the reader remembers that earlier, when the doctor checked the numbness in Teddy's hand, he told him that he suffered from a relatively new disease of which little is known. "Le principal symptôme est une diminution graduelle de la température du corps. Certains spécialistes ont parlé d'une forme d'hypothermie spontanée [...]. J'ai vu un cas semblable l'an dernier à l'*île aux Ruaux.* [...] On dirait que c'est le milieu ambiant qui envahit l'organisme" (157). The old man who has now died is the same old man the *patron* kicked off the island because he was old and sick and whom Teddy replaced at the beginning of the story; Teddy thus confronts his own end in the old man turned to stone. Their fate cautions about the brutality and mercilessness of the new myth growing out of the Quiet Revolution, and that for those like Teddy and the old man, who supposedly have outlived their usefulness, it leads to exclusion and death.

* * *

It should now be clear that what was happening in Quebec during the Quiet Revolution is the subtext of *Les Grandes Marées.* But like all utopian fictions, even parodies thereof, Poulin's story is a cautionary tale, for the novel does not represent the agenda of the movers and shakers of the Quiet Revolution who were interested in modernization, development, technocracy and technology. Rather, it exposes the dangers of this new society: its vicious exclusion of some of the members of the community. In particular, Marie's mythic story of Sabra, a young woman offered as a sacrifice to appease the fire-spewing monster and save the city, foreshadows the ending of *Les Grandes Marées* (77). Modern societies consider such sacrificial myths barbaric, but Sabra's story does suggest that what the movers and shakers do to Teddy and the old man is equally barbaric and a blind spot in their vision of the new society.

Poulin has written five novels since the publication of *Les Grandes Marées,* but none of them has explored in such detail Quebec's Quiet Revolution. What they do explore, usually under the guise of love stories, are some of the themes of the 1960s and 1970s—*Québécois* identity, memory, and independence.

Works Cited

Adams, Robert M. Historical Introduction. *The Prince.* By Niccolo Machiavelli. Trans. and ed. Robert M. Adams. New York: Norton, 1977. vii-xvi.

De Gaulle, Charles. "Vive le Québec Libre." 24 Juillet 1967. *Archives de Radio-Canada.* March 31, 2004. <http://archives.radio-canada.ca>.

Dumont, Micheline et al. *Quebec Women: A History.* Trans. Roger Gannon and Rosalind Gill. Toronto: The Women's Press, 1987.

Fraser, Matthew. *Quebec Inc.: French Canadian Entrepreneurs and the New Business Elite.* Toronto: Key Porter Books, 1987.

Godbout, Jacques. *Le Réformiste: Textes tranquilles.* Montréal: Quinze, 1975.

Guindon, Hubert. *Quebec Society: Tradition, Modernity, and Nationhood.* Toronto: U of Toronto P, 1988.

Hébert, Pierre. *Jacques Poulin: La création d'un espace amoureux.* Ottawa: Presses de l'université d'Ottawa, 1997.

Lacoursière, Jacques, et al. *Canada-Québec: Synthèse historique 1534-2000.* Québec: Septentrion, 2001.

La Sainte Bible. Traduite en français sous la direction de L'Ecole Biblique de Jérusalem. Paris: Cerf, 1956.

Linteau, Paul-André et al. *Histoire du Québec contemporain.* Vol. 2. Montréal: Boréal, 1989.

————. "La Question linguistique de 1960 à nos jours." *Langue et identité: Le français et les francophones d'Amérique du Nord.* Ed. Noël Corbett. Québec: Presses de l'Université Laval, 1990. 65-76.

L'Italien-Savard, Isabelle. *Isabelle L'Italien-Savard présente Les Grandes marées de Jacques Poulin.* Montréal: Leméac, 2000.

Marshall, Bill. *Quebec National Cinema.* Montreal: McGill-Queen's UP, 2001.

McRoberts, Kenneth, and Dale Postgate. *Quebec: Social Change and Political Crisis.* Toronto: McClelland and Stewart, 1976.

Miraglia, Anne Marie. *L'Ecriture de l'autre chez Jacques Poulin.* Candiac: Balzac, 1993.

Poulin, Jacques. *Les Grandes Marées.* Montréal: Leméac, 1978.

————. *Les Yeux bleus de Mistassini.* Montréal, Paris: Leméac, Actes Sud, 2002.

————. *Mon Cheval pour un royaume.* Montréal: Leméac, 1987.

Rioux, Marcel. *La Question du Québec.* Montréal: Typo, 1987.

Si je me souviens bien = As I Recall: Regards sur l'histoire. Dirigé par l'Institut de recherche en politiques publiques avec John Meisel, Guy Rocher, Arthur Silver. Montréal: IRPP, 1999.

Socken, Paul G. *The Myth of the Lost Paradise in the Novels of Jacques Poulin.* Toronto: Associated UP, 1993.

Vautier, Marie. *New World Myth: Postmodernism and Postcolonialism in Canadian Fiction.* Montreal: McGill-Queen's UP, 1998.

Beatrice Guenther (essay date 2007)

SOURCE: Guenther, Beatrice. "Land and Cityscape[1] in Lise Gauvin's and Jacques Poulin's Narratives: Between Cultural Memory and *l'invention du quotidien.*" *Land and Landscape in Francographic Literature: Remapping Uncertain Territories.* Ed. Magali Compan and Katarzyna Pieprzak. Newcastle upon Tyne: Cambridge Scholars, 2007. 60-87. Print.

[*In the following essay, Guenther examines* Volkswagen Blues *and* Translation Is a Love Affair *alongside Gauvin's novels* Letters from an Other *(1984) and* Un automne à Paris *(2005), addressing the ways in which each author handles the Quebecois cityscape and Quebec's place within its historical, cultural, and geographical context.*]

In Jacques Poulin's **Volkswagen Blues,** (1984) the two protagonists find themselves during the early part of their voyage on the banks of the Saint-Lawrence River, gazing out across the Thousand Islands. We learn: "Quelque part au milieu du fleuve, une frontière imaginaire séparait le Canada et les Etats-Unis" [somewhere in the middle of the river, an imaginary border separated Canada from the United States][2] (56-7).[3] The laconic statement suggests that the description of place is hardly unproblematic or easily mapped. The reference to an imaginary border separating Canada and the U.S. seems to posit a commonality linking the two nations and even hints at the potential shakiness of a clearly identifiable national distinction particular to Canada. In this quotation, the difference between the two nations is hardly a given, hardly grounded in the land. While the insight into the constructedness of (national) geography is hardly new, one is nonetheless led to ask oneself how the protagonists' quest across North America from la Gaspésie to San Francisco will be meaningful in this narrative—to what extent and how this "road novel" will map the North American continent for its readers. If the American and Canadian landscapes are seen to merge, how will a Québécois writer define Québec's place within his protagonists' trajectory?

Lise Gauvin's *Lettres d'une autre,* [*Letters of/from Another*] also published in 1984, draws on the travel motif as well, but it does so in a very different way—by rewriting Montesquieu's *Lettres persanes* (1721) and translating the clash of French and "Persian" perspectives into a Québécois encounter. In Gauvin's epistolary novel, focused on one single character's impressions and commentary, Montesquieu's harem-bound Roxane is transformed into a foreign doctoral student determined to evaluate life and culture in

Quebec by exploring the province and its North American context. Roxane's academic stay in Quebec includes short excursions to New York City and, especially, other regions in Canada, and these outings are staged as a series of initiations allowing her to identify gradually Quebec's place within the Canadian (federal) context.

Both works were written in the 1980's, in short, about twenty years after *la Révolution Tranquille,* characterized traditionally, if perhaps a little too liturgically, as a watershed moment in Quebec history.[4] The *Révolution Tranquille* has often been characterized as the moment when Québécois society broke with the holy trinity of rurality, religion, and (French) language rights that was meant to act as a bulwark to protect the cultural identity of French-speaking Canadians caught in a British hegemony. In standard accounts of Québec's history, the Revolution of the 1960's is associated, then, with the turn toward a more urban, modern, even "postcolonial" form of life—and this shift is accompanied by a nationalist rhetoric where the link between cultural identity and territory motivates the push toward political sovereignty for the province. While contemporary historians such as Jocelyn Létourneau and Gérard Bouchard have begun to question if the "national" legend of the leap within the space of six years from a rural-based, colonized identity to an industrialized, decolonized one should be accepted at face value,[5] in these two literary texts of the mid-1980's, the neatly binary periodization of Québécois history in pre- and post-*Révolution Tranquille* still seems to hold true.

Both Gauvin's and Poulin's poetics of landscape do not simply privilege representations of modern, that is, urban space, however. In fact, the two writers make use of the travel motif in order to explore through their protagonists' experiences the coexistence of the rural and urban spaces on the continent. The preoccupation with a more rural, traditional space can perhaps be linked to the failure of the sovereignty myth in 1980 to lead to Quebec's territorial and political autonomy. Nonetheless, this emphasis on exploring and representing the continent also does foreground both writers' concern with the "legibility" of space—the connection between place and cultural memory. The contrast of **Volkswagen Blues** and *Lettres d'une autre* will allow us, then—through their *décalage* of twenty years from the Quiet Revolution—to evaluate how the representation of "national" space negotiates the tension between conflicting accounts of Québécois memory and identity.

The fact, moreover, that Gauvin and Poulin both publish in 2006 what one might loosely call sequels to their earlier narratives will allow us to evaluate if and how a poetics of (politicized) landscape has evolved in the past twenty years. In *Un automne à Paris* [*An Autumn in Paris*], Gauvin uses a journalistic form in order to capture her perceptions of the Parisian cityscape, which acts as a backdrop to her informal inquiry into how the French "Metropolitans" perceive and represent Québécois culture. In **La traduction est** *une histoire d'amour* [*Translation Is a Love Story*], by contrast, Jacques Poulin places his earlier protagonist, Jack Waterman, in a new scenario concentrated on Quebec City and the nearby, quite rural Ile d'Orléans. The question linking a poetics with the politics of landscape is of special interest in that the two recent works precede by a short margin Quebec's change in status within the Canadian Confederation in November 2006: its official status as "nation within a united Canada."[6]

READING THE LANDSCAPE IN THE 1980'S: CONFLICTING FICTIONS OF "*L'AMÉRICANITÉ*"

Lise Gauvin's *Lettres d'une autre* poses the dilemma of a stranger to Québécois culture attempting to decipher the physical clues around her, in particular the significance of these clues vis-à-vis a Québécois politics of identity. While visiting Quebec City, Roxane is struck by the architectural contradictions marking the city's skyline, where the Hilton tower vies with the Château Frontenac for control over the "*silhouette de Québec*" [the cityscape of Quebec] (30).[7] For Roxane, this cityscape is implicitly connected to a general philosophical scission defining the Quebec of the 80's:

> Les tenants du patrimoine, d'une part, n'en finissent plus de rapailler tout ce qui peut avoir quelque valeur historique, ethnologique ou architecturale. Les adeptes du modernisme, d'autre part, [...] invectivent à qui mieux mieux ceux dont la vision passe nécessairement par ce qu'ils appellent les œillères des lucarnes folkloriques.
>
> (18)

> [The supporters of the national heritage movement, on the one hand, never give up collecting anything that might have some historical, ethnological or architectural value. The modernism enthusiasts, on the other hand, hurl abuse, each one louder than the next, at those whose vision passes—they claim—through the blinkers of folklore's dormer windows.]

While Roxane detaches herself explicitly from either position—attributing to each a sense of guilt she associates with the "*réflexe du colonisé*" [the colonized's reflex] (19)—her narrative sets out to discover in contemporary Quebec the clues of the province's cultural heritage.

In Poulin's *Volkswagen Blues,* the link between space and cultural memory seems quite different from *Lettres d'une autre*. The two protagonists, a writer and a Métisse, do not limit themselves to the territory of Quebec. Instead, Poulin uses the quest for a lost brother as a frame to highlight the intersection of U.S. and Canadian histories by having his protagonists travel in the footsteps of the early French explorers and the pioneers of the Oregon Trail. Many critics have commented on the *américanité* of Poulin's work, and, among them, Jean-Pierre Lapointe highlights the multivalence of the term:

> ... [la notion d'américanité] décrit l'attraction centripète de la civilisation étatsunienne et se confond avec le phé-

nomène d'américanisation de la culture québécoise. Mais le mot peut recouvrir un sens beaucoup plus large, fondé sur l'appartenance continentale, sur la participation au temps et à l'espace du Nouveau Monde, sur un déterminisme tellurique distinct, qui apparente les Québécois aux Brésiliens et aux Cubains tout autant qu'aux Américains.[8]

> [The notion of *américanité* describes the centripetal attraction exerted by U.S. civilization and it merges with the phenomenon of Americanization prevalent in Québécois culture. But the word can also hide a much broader meaning, one founded on the sense of continental belonging, the participation in the New World's time and space, the distinct telluric determinism, which forges links, connecting the Québécois with the Brazilians, the Cubans as much as with the Americans.]

In the case of Poulin's *Volkswagen Blues,* the protagonists excavate details about the histories of mainstream "heroes," such as Jacques Cartier, Etienne Brûlé, and Buffalo Bill—a venture suggesting a "continental" rather than "national" perspective on spatial and cultural memory.

The novel's ending may seem to caution against a straightforward celebration of *l'américanité*. The writer's brother, Théo, who had decided to settle in the United States and who is the ostensible goal of the quest, makes an appearance at the end of the novel, unable to walk, speak or even to remember his brother. This character's destiny is often read as a symbol of the loss of memory, roots, even the faculty of (French) speech associated with the Québécois' exodus to the United States. If this example is taken on its own, it seems to make a case for the need to withdraw into the protective confines of the Francophone province,[9] and, indeed, the protagonist, Jack, does choose to return to Quebec at the end of the text.[10]

Nonetheless, such a narrow representation of the Francophone presence in North America is debunked in the novel through the multiple references to the 17th-century explorers discovering the Ohio Valley, the Mississippi, and Louisiana, not to mention the Francophone settlers in St. Louis and even further west, the references to Laramie. Indeed, even Jack's decision to return to Quebec is not simply coded as a flight back to a familiar home. His own experiences have led him to conceptualize (somewhat humorously) a culturally modified imaginary:

> [...] il souriait malgré tout à la pensée qu'il y avait, quelque part dans l'immensité de l'Amérique, un lieu secret où les dieux des Indiens et les autres dieux étaient rassemblés et tenaient conseil dans le but de veiller sur lui et d'éclairer sa route.
>
> (320)

> [Despite everything, he smiled, however, at the thought that there was, somewhere in the immensity of America, a secret place where the gods of the Indians and other gods were meeting and holding counsel with the goal of watching over him and scouting out his route.]

Poulin's choice of a Métisse protagonist also seems to signal a more open-ended approach to Québécois identity. Jack's part Montagnaise, part French-Canadian companion adopts for a time San Francisco, where her own status as Métisse no longer marks her as other [285]:

> [La grande Sauterelle] voulait rester un certain temps à San Francisco: elle pensait que cette ville où les races semblaient vivre en harmonie, était un bon endroit pour essayer de faire l'unité et de se réconcilier avec elle-même.
>
> (317-18)

> [La Grande Sauterelle [Big Grasshopper] wanted to stay a little longer in San Francisco. She thought that this city, where the races seemed to live in harmony, was a good place to try to create unity and to be at peace with herself.]

It is in this city, associated with American icons such as Jack Kerouac and the Beat generation, that la Grande Sauterelle finally loses her sense of being an outsider that has haunted her in Quebec. She stumbles, in fact, across a strangely familiar and yet profoundly different double of her own identity (284). The half-Chinese, half-Mexican young librarian symbolizes the potential of a new community without sacrificing the diversity of hybrid identities.

* * *

Despite the differences in setting, Poulin's and Gauvin's works do share certain characteristics. Both choose to integrate the focus of an "Other" in order to displace and rework cultural commonplaces. Gauvin's Roxane demystifies, for instance, the feminist emancipation of the Québécoises, noting drily that Persian women would hardly accept behavior such as the use of physical attributes in order to succeed in the business world. Gauvin's use of the Other as filter helps to unsettle too comfortable, perhaps even self-indulgent perceptions of the Québécois community.

By contrast, la Grande Sauterelle's function in *Volkswagen Blues* is to show up the ellipses and hidden violence of the European narrative of conquest, "heroism" and identity. In Poulin's novel, the two characters first inspect a map of 17th-century New France which expands from the arctic regions to Mexico and which reaches west to the Rockies.

> Mais il y avait aussi une autre carte géographique, tout aussi impressionnante, qui montrait une Amérique du Nord avant l'arrivée des Blancs; la carte était jalonnée de noms de tribus indiennes, des noms que l'homme connaissait: les Cris, les Montagnais, les Iroquois, les Sioux, les Cheyennes, les Comanches, les Apaches, mais également une grande quantité de noms dont il n'avait jamais entendu parler de toute sa vie ...
>
> (19)

> [But there was also another map, just as impressive, which displayed a North America before the arrival of the whites; the map was marked out by the names of Indian tribes,

names that the man knew: Cris, Montagnais, Iroquois, Sioux, Cheyennes, Comanches, Apaches, but also a large quantity of names which he had never heard of in all his life.]

Throughout the novel, la Grande Sauterelle pushes her companion to distance himself from his fascination with European conquest legends by drawing attention to the generally overlooked markers of her own (partial) heritage connecting her with First Nations cultures. In short, both Roxane and la Grande Sauterelle make visible and debunk stereotypes that feed an ethnocentric self-satisfaction. Through the integration of the "Others'" perceptions, the self-evident truths associated with Québécois territorial rights (Poulin) or even modernity (Gauvin)—two tenets of the *Révolution Tranquille*—are nuanced, even called into question by both narratives.

The fascination with "reading" space for cultural clues connects Poulin's *Volkswagen Blues* with Gauvin's *Lettres d'une autre* as well. To what extent does this quest to read and thereby mark the North American landscape participate in the process outlined by Pierre Nora's *Lieux de mémoire*? For Pierre Nora, the *lieux de mémoire* are limited to places, objects, and commemorative events that self-consciously rework and reshape cultural memory.[11] The examples of such "realms of memory" described in his monumental, multi-authored work highlight the multiple layers of memories that transform the meanings associated with the historical spaces commemorating France's cultural icons of identity. To cite one example: for Nora's team, an exhibit celebrating France's colonial prowess takes on new meanings even before the *Exposition coloniale* is realized because of the shifts in leadership shaping this commemorative space. In effect, Nora highlights a tension in the realms of memory; he points out that the *raison-d'être* of the *lieux de mémoire* is to stop time, to counter forgetting, to infuse with a maximum of meaning a minimum of signs.[12] He also argues that despite this explicit function, such an enterprise shows up a paradoxical quality that limits the capacity of commemoration to fix a culture's patrimony:

> [...] c'est ce qui les rend passionnants, que les lieux de mémoire ne vivent que de leur aptitude à la métamorphose, dans l'incessant rebondissement de leurs significations et le buissonnement imprévisible de leurs ramifications.
>
> (38)

> [... what makes the realms of memory fascinating is the fact that they only live through their aptitude to metamorphose, through the unceasing revival of their meanings, and the unforeseeable branching out of their ramifications.]

Volkswagen Blues is quite clearly organized around the excavation of memories hidden on the North American continent. The trajectory of the protagonist's quest begins in Gaspé, commemorating (in popular parlance, at least) the first presence of Europeans in "Canada" with the arrival of Jacques Cartier in 1534.[13] In contrast to Nora's project, Poulin's characters are not engaged explicitly in the reconstruction of their roots. Their travels lead them from the settlements of the East Coast through the Great Lakes region (Toronto, Detroit, Chicago) to the Mississippi and beyond to the Oregon Trail and California, and they seem to discover historical landmarks that seem quite self-explanatory. In short, on the surface, the discovery of the *lieux de mémoire* is framed as a by-product of the voyage—subordinate to the personal quest for a missing brother.

The opening chapter does demonstrate, however, how Poulin throws into relief the shifting significance of spaces marked by memory. The protagonist is located at the "origin" of Québécois history, as he enters into the museum meant to commemorate the arrival of the French on the North American continent. Jack's attempt to find a specialist who might help him decipher a copy of Jacques Cartier's description of marking New France with a cross, of claiming the land for the French throne, is met with incomprehension. He is confronted instead by a museum employee unable and disinterested in identifying the copy of the 16th-century text. The commemoration of the French claim to Canada seems irrelevant in this 20th-century world. The "guardian" of memory is engrossed instead by Superman cartoons rather than by the artifacts surrounding him (16). Clearly, this example is a polemic about the americanization (not the *américanité*) of Québécois culture and the loss of collective memory such a process brings about. Ironically, this polemic is supplemented by a second perspective when it is the Montagnais employee who is better informed about the museum exhibits than her young white counterpart. Her role as cleaning lady in the museum has familiarized her with its artifacts and allows her to act as guide to the protagonist.

This framing of the historical object emphasizes the continued significance of Cartier's text, although there is a rather important shift in its meaning. Clearly, the heritage of Cartier's cross lives on by re-establishing the hierarchy of the European and Aboriginal societies. In addition to representing a critique of the social hierarchy limiting the woman's career options, this moment makes clear the metamorphosis of the *lieux de mémoire* identified by Nora, even if this metamorphosis is marked less as a commemoration than as a critique. Supplementing this example of the transformed survival of cultural memory is the reference to the two maps delineating the North American continent—one European, the other reconstructing the diversity of the different First Nations. The *lieu de mémoire* of Cartier's first steps on North American soil becomes the place of intersecting and conflicting historical meaning.[14]

In this road novel, the juxtaposition of the *lieux de mémoire* serves a double function. On the one hand, the journey is used to frame the *Bildung* of the protagonists; their spatial quest is matched by their search for texts that can provide depth to their experiences. They discover the presence of

Francophone settlers in unexpected locations, as in St-Charles, a suburb of St-Louis, or in Laramie. On the Oregon Trail in the Rockies, for instance, they are able to match their knowledge of *The Oregon Trail Revisited* with the stone markers bearing the names of the pioneers whose path they had been following and whose journals they were reading (235). La Grande Sauterelle reads the biographies of North American explorers and settlers in order to make sense of the landscape. In fact, the novel incorporates excerpts, songs, and even photographs as a way to reinforce the transmission of knowledge in the text.

Equally important, however, is the use of the voyage motif that leads to an *Anti-Bildung*—an unlearning of preconceptions. Jack's hero worship of the "*coureurs de bois*" [(illegal, often romanticized) French trappers] is gradually dismantled. Early on in the novel, his belief that Etienne Brûlé—associated with the territory around Toronto—was an exceptional explorer perfectly integrated into Indian culture is replaced by la Grande Sauterelle's research, which highlights the explorer's estrangement from both the Québécois and First Nations' cultures (82). Indeed, the demystification of the conquest narratives and of the myth of the self-sufficient, self-made hero serves as a preliminary stage for Jack's own detachment from his hero worship of his brother, not to mention from his own unthinking internalization of such values. He begins to reflect on the bankruptcy of a great "*rêve d'Amérique*," [dream of America] which idealizes the seekers of gold and spices (109).

Jack is not the only character who learns to nuance his unquestioning belief in the heritage stories of his childhood. While la Grande Sauterelle's main function is often to counter the Eurocentric accounts of North American history, her displacements across the continent lead her to confront aspects of the First Nation cultures which resist idealization as well. The passage by the "*Rocher de la Famine*" [Starvation's Rock] in Illinois draws attention to the violence between the First Nations—to the extermination of one tribe by others (125-26). As the journey progresses, la Grande Sauterelle learns to detach herself from her automatic polemic against white culture, as in "La Mitrailleuse Gatling," [the Gatling machine-gun] where she misreads the machine-gun as artifact displayed in the museum at Fort Laramie (222). Although the violence of the settlers against the Aboriginals is not questioned in this novel, the episode calls attention to the non-transparence of symbolic or historical objects; the machine-gun is demystified as a technological error, never used in battle against the indigenous peoples of the Western states. The episode suggests the need for an attention to detail that undercuts a shorthand form of a reductive, binary symbolism, supposedly distinguishing clearly oppressors from their victims.

La Grande Sauterelle's *Anti-Bildung* is also staged when she undertakes a quest to discover her roots through a pilgrimage to the grave of a particularly famous chief,

Thayendanegea or Joseph Brant;[15] she enacts the ritual of sleeping near his grave in an attempt to open herself up to ancestral visions. The attempt to turn back to a lost heritage is ironically debunked as la Grande Sauterelle admits the next morning that she experienced nothing. The demystification of a rooted or "natural" *lieu de mémoire* does not only occur through la Grande Sauterelle's experience of disappointment. She has also claimed a link to an ancestor who is not a cipher of "pure" Amerindian stock. Joseph Brant was himself associated with the British government and traveled to Great Britain. The return to an untainted past and lost practices is represented here as impossible and, in fact, at odds with la Grande Sauterelle's own status as Métisse.

Through the juxtaposition of the two protagonists' quests for a sense of community underpinning their North American pilgrimage—mediated either through the search for a lost brother[16] or through the broader search of one's effaced forbears—the *lieux de mémoire* in Poulin's ***Volkswagen Blues*** function in two ways. First, they act as a trigger to unearth and decipher lost or effaced histories, and second—in a contradictory manner—as signposts leading to the demystification of one's mythologized origins. This demystification targets both the mainstream, nationalist history glorifying the "originary" French presence on North American soil as well as an uncritical, idealized elaboration of the dispossessed Amerindian peoples.

* * *

Despite the temporal context it shares with Poulin's ***Volkswagen Blues***, *Lettres d'une autre* frames the "legible" connection between space and national identity in a more explicitly contemporary way. Her Persian protagonist starts out by validating the importance of the struggle for Quebec's political sovereignty and, in fact, critiques the political apathy of the Québécois, caused by a post-referendum (1980) blues. In this text, the (political) landscape that the foreign-born Roxane sets out to discover and describe resolutely belongs to the late twentieth century. Rather than re-enacting the explorers' or pioneers' voyage across the continent, this protagonist travels in a focused and rapid way from one city to another—poised less to conjure up the cityscapes unfolding before her than to track the effect of these spaces on the interactions taking place between Canadian Anglophones and Francophones.[17] The spatial descriptions are sketched in shorthand. The flight to Vancouver, for instance, leads her to detach herself from the federal government's "propaganda," indoctrinating the Québécois with the belief that Canada's unity is a natural concept—that the Rocky Mountains are anchored in the internal landscape of each Québécois citizen:

> [j'étais] endoctrinée par la propagande fédérale voulant que les Rocheuses et la Colombie-Britannique fassent partie du paysage intérieur de tout citoyen montréalais ou québécois.

> (55)

> [(I was) indoctrinated by federal propaganda which claimed that the Rockies and British Columbia were part of the interior landscape of any Montréal or Québec citizen.]

Vancouver's urban space is evoked briefly through allusions to Stanley Park and English Bay, and this emphasis on the British colonial influence is clearly polemical—not the pretext for investigating the plural histories intersecting in a place name or monument—as was the case for Poulin.

The description of the West Coast setting nicely supplements the main point of Roxane's letter about Vancouver. Roxane's primary reason for travelling to Vancouver is to investigate the newly formed *Association internationale des études canadiennes* and, more largely, to evaluate the state of the policy on Canadian bilingualism—a policy, incidentally, already demystified during her flight before even arriving in Vancouver: "[…] les hôtesses [communiquaient] en français entre elles et en anglais avec le public" [the stewardesses communicated in French amongst themselves and in English with the public] (56). Despite the diverse origins of Neo-Canadians, the Anglophone—one could even say, British—influence on the culture in the Canadian West remains pervasive:

> La discrétion est de mise dans ce lieu jadis peuplé par les plus royalistes des immigrants anglophones et maintenant envahi par des gens d'origines diverses dont l'attitude s'est calquée sur celle des premiers habitants. Les Italiens ont gardé leur élégance mais sont devenus peu bavards.

> (57)

> [Discretion is a requirement in this place populated by the most royalist of anglophone immigrants and now overrun by people of various origins whose attitude modelled that of the first inhabitants. The Italians have kept their elegance but have become less talkative.]

It is, however, Roxane's analysis of her fellow literary critics that leads her to recognize the threats posed to Quebec by a federal policy of national unity. The anecdotes concerning monolingual participants unable and unwilling to engage seriously with their Québécois counterparts already highlight the marginalization of a Francophone perspective in Canada (59). It is, moreover, the decision to label Québécois writers as Canadian that leads, in Roxane's opinion, to the misrepresentation of their cultural significance:

> Les plus contestataires des écrivains québécois s'y trouvent savamment couplés à leur collègues anglophones, associés malgré eux à la fiction d'une culture et d'une littérature canadiennes.

> (61)

> [The Quebecois writers with the strongest anti-establishment sentiments find themselves intelligently paired with their Anglophone colleagues, and linked despite themselves to the fiction of a Canadian culture and literature.]

Roxane's conclusions are hardly different when she describes Manitoba—a province with strong historical ties to Canadian *Francophonie*. She informs her friend back in "Persia" of the fate of Manitoba when the 1890 School Act repealed the right of Manitoba children to an Anglophone or Francophone schooling—a ruling re-enacted in 1979 when the attempt to apply the policy of bilingualism to Manitoba's legislation on education is met with strong opposition (121). For Roxane, the provincial politics of Manitoba reveal a commitment to effacing *la francophonie* from the Canadian landscape:

> La question du Manitoba dépasse largement celle de la langue. C'est à l'existence même des francophones qu'on en a, dans la mesure où cette existence, pour se maintenir, doit s'assortir d'un certain nombre de pouvoirs ou de droits.
>
> (121)

> [The question of Manitoba surpasses largely that of language. We are concerned with the very existence of the Francophones, since this existence has to be accompanied by a certain amount of powers or rights in order to maintain itself.]

In this text, Manitoban space serves to symbolize the repetition of history—the threat to Francophone survival.

Lettres d'une autre does not simply denounce the bad faith of Anglophone Canadians toward Quebec, although this is certainly a strong component of this epistolary novel. The protagonist's fascination with Québécois identity reaches an impasse when she wonders:

> La spécificité serait-elle une notion purement passéiste, un assortiment de symboles figés, devenus caricaturaux à force d'usage exclusif et répété.
>
> (35)

> [Would [cultural] specificity be a backward-looking notion, a collage of fixed symbols that have become caricatures due to their exclusive and repeated use.]

Roxane attempts to understand the deep split in Québécois society between the traditionalists desiring to protect their heritage and the modernists who fear the paralysis resulting from a static politics of identity, which would emphasize the need for continuity with the past. Her letters effectively demystify both extremes. On the one hand, she debunks the simplistic materialism of traditionalists who equate their cultural heritage with the collection of rustic furniture. Her visit to the quaint, old-fashioned Ile d'Orléans leads her to discover a celebration of St-Jean-Baptiste day (Quebec's "national" holiday), devoid of any true historical significance. Her satiric description lambastes the natives' lukewarm congregation around a bonfire, their beer-drinking ritual around a plastic tent—and this on land named in honor of one of the first seigneurs of New France. The commemoration of Québécois heritage

has turned into an empty, pointless and cliché'd North American ritual.

At the other end of the spectrum, we find the "modern" preoccupation with experiencing and producing change—a preoccupation that in this text is coded as an American trait, as becomes clear when Roxane visits New York City. Roxane's experiences in SoHo lead her to conclude that in this city, one's sense of coinciding perfectly with one's epoch is matched by the recognition that one can also modify the contours of this epoch at will (37). New York is represented as existing beyond parochialism and has become "*le lieudit de l'universel*" [the so-called locality of the universal] (37), not forced to suspend itself continually over the question of its own cultural specificity (41). While in New York, Roxane debunks the rhetoric associated with the importance of defining one's cultural specificity:

> La spécificité obligée des Québécois est comme la réponse à une aggression constante qu'on pourrait formuler ainsi: si vous voulez être, soyez, mais spécifiques [. . .] Qui suppose un regard qui fige et réifie l'autre, le transforme en objet.
>
> (41)

> [The compulsory cultural specificity of the Quebecois is like the response to a constant agression that we could describe as such: if you want to be, be, but be specific . . . He who supposes a look that freezes or reifies the other, transforms him into an object.]

And yet, the fascination with this urban space par excellence is soon marked by a growing anxiety. The cultural dynamism of New York City leads to an acceleration of change that undermines both the existence of memory or heritage as well as the novelty of new fashions in the present. Roxane writes:

> On est ainsi voué à l'anachronisme permanent. A peine ont-ils été consacrés que les minimalistes sont déjà passés [. . .].
>
> (39)

> [As such we are doomed to permanent anachronism. Having been just barely consecrated [established], the minimalists are already passé.]

While an approach focused exclusively on the symbols of a lost past has been criticized quite explicitly, the rapid succession of styles and fashions does not represent a satisfying solution to the dilemma of understanding a culture either. Roxane's description of the cityscape of Quebec translates explicitly the worry over indiscriminate change that alters and deforms a cultural heritage. In fact, Roxane's first experience of Quebec's "national" capital—the cradle of Champlain's New France—reveals a Quebec no different from other commercial centers in North America. The letter opens with an ironic reference to the icons of New France. The world of the "*coureurs de bois*" has ceded to a banal station for the bus line, Voyageur (27). Roxane next transcribes her first impressions of Quebec City:

> Après avoir dépassé un pont ultramoderne nommé en l'honneur d'un ministre assassiné, l'autobus traverse les quartiers résidentiels de Sainte-Foy avant de s'arrêter à un immense centre commercial où la densité des voitures indique éloquemment la quantité des transactions qui s'y traitent [...] La ville de Québec serait-elle une vaste banlieue au coeur rythmé par l'ampleur de son pouvoir d'achat?
>
> (29)

> [After having passed an ultramodern bridge named in honor of an assassinated minister [Pierre Laporte], the bus drives through the residential neighborhoods of Sainte-Foy before stopping at a huge shopping center where the dense accumulation of cars shows eloquently the quantity of transactions taking place there. ... Could the city of Quebec have become a vast suburb whose heart is paced by the scope of its buying power?]

Montreal's urban landscape is, of course, even more closely affiliated with that of New York City. We read that Montreal attracts Roxane and that she is never bored in this city "*de la presque Amérique*" [this city of almost America] (99). Nonetheless, the description of this cityscape emphasizes the fragmentation and effect of an eclectic bric-à-brac that dominates the city's horizon.[18] This "*architecture de situation*" [architecture of a given moment (for a given occasion)] which escapes the imprint of a consecrated culture or institutionalized system also is characterized by a "*babélien des signes*" [an incomprehensible Babel of signs]—where changes in style and indiscriminate hybridity seems yoked to the loss of communicable meaning (87).

This incoherence of eclectic styles in the name of situational, dynamic architecture is echoed in the art scene where an artistic happening connects performance with a market ambiance. Roxane concludes drily: "[...] le spectaculaire l'emporte trop souvent sur le spectacle, le cliché sur la recherche, le procédé sur la découverte" [the spectacular wins too often over the spectacle, the cliché over research, process over discovery] (91). If artists privilege the discontinuous and the fragment, it seems that art ends up being societal rather than social—setting its sights on "deciphering/parodying" the marks of civilization or disconcerting its readers rather than reconceptualizing its projects (92). For Roxane—and, it seems, for *Lettres d'une autre*—the question turns around the issue for whom and for what one is ultimately writing: "Ecrire, créer: pour qui? Pour quoi? Quels sont les enjeux de la culture dans un quasi-pays menacé de lente disparition?" [To write, to create: For whom? For what? What are the cultural stakes in a quasi-country, threatened by slow disappearance?] (97). The self-referential experimentations with the fragment and with humor are clearly secondary to such an engaged artistic production.

In *Lettres d'une autre,* the protagonist explores solutions to the dilemma of choosing a traditionalist or a modernist approach to (Québécois) identity by refusing to adopt one ideological position or its opposite. She tempers the modernist project when she distances herself from an all-inclusive celebration of globalization:

> L'effacement des cultures n'est-il pas l'un des problèmes angoissants du monde contemporain? L'utopie du village planétaire ne recouvre-t-elle pas une forme à peine déguisée de discours centriste et uniformisant?
>
> (141)

> [Isn't the erasure of cultures one of the most angst-producing issues of the contemporary world? Doesn't the utopia of the world village signify a slightly veiled centrist and homogenizing discourse?]

Where the traditionalists place a premium on the needs of the community, its historical continuity, the modernists privilege the dynamism and solipsism of an individual's iconoclasm. In *Lettres d'une autre,* the dichotomy of self and community is figured more fluidly—and this already in New York City. Roxane recognizes that she is a "foreign element" in the wash of the crowds, but she also realizes that by participating in that throng, she has also become part of the economy of the whole.

In the domain of cultural production in Quebec, Roxane is particularly fascinated by the strategies used by the "*écrivaines au feminin*" [(women) authors writing in the feminine].[19] Rather than adopting a commemorative, culturally conservative agenda or the celebration of a free, dynamic individualism, the contemporary feminist writers work at balancing the "je" [I] and "nous" [us] in their writings—creating the difficult rapport between autobiography and fiction, the singular and the collective (24). A key to reading Gauvin's *Lettres d'une autre* as an enactment of such a strategy is hinted at toward the end of the epistolary novel when Roxane describes the effect of such "singular/plural" writing meant to displace the gaze and represent a simultaneously familiar and different world. The singular/plural split sheds new light on Gauvin's strategy of drawing on intertextuality to transform a familiar text and to use a protagonist who reproduces and transforms a familiar landscape. Indeed, Roxane writes:

> A preuve aussi les textes de celles qu je nomme mes amies qui, par le biais d'un je qui se pose souvent dans l'humilité institutionnelle du journal ou de la lettre, arrivent à gauchir les codes, tant littéraires que sociaux, et à faire advenir *l'Existence* [...].
>
> (134)

> [Take also as proof, for instance, the texts by those whom I call my (female) friends who—by using the "I" which manifests itself in the institutional humility of the diary or the letter—often succeed in warping [subverting] literary as well as social codes, (who succeed) in making *Existence* happen [...].]

The attempt to balance the singular and plural perspectives or to check the extremes of traditionalism and modernism also manifests itself in a rhetoric of space and, fittingly, connects Gauvin's and Poulin's works explicitly. Roxane alludes directly to *Volkswagen Blues* at the very end of her last letter by contrasting the French and American influences on a Québécois sense of identity:

> De plus en plus sensibles aux clichés, [les Québécois] savent qu'entre la France paternaliste, toujours un peu intéressée, et l'Amérique des Big Macs chaque jour plus gros et moins chers, ils n'ont pas à choisir. A travers l'Amérique du normal et du banal, ils apprennent à reconnaître celle de l'insolite et des marges. Comme les personnages du dernier roman de Poulin, *Volkswagen Blues,* ils dessinent leurs itinéraires, tracent leurs réseaux, cherchent à inventer les signes de leur lecture.
>
> (142)

> [More and more sensitive to clichés, the Québécois know that between paternalistic France, always somewhat self-interested, and the America of the Big Macs, each day larger and less expensive, they do not have to choose. Through the America of the normal and the banal, they learn to recognize the America of of the unusual and marginal. Much like the characters in Poulin's last novel, *Volkswagen Blues,* they sketch out their own itineraries, trace their networks, seek to invent the signs of their reading.]

Roxane notes that the Québécois reject a "singular" America in favor of a pluri-dimensional South America. A French politics of power and exhibitionism is passed over in favor of a local eccentricity to be discovered in certain (unnamed) Parisian neighborhoods. Here, even the relation of Québécois sameness and international difference moves past a poetics of insularity by drawing on a more nuanced representation of geographical affiliation.

For Roxane, her own itinerary means refusing to choose either landscape or cityscape—refusing to be trapped by the valorization of a Pre-*Révolution Tranquille,* privileging the *terroir* [soil, rural region] or by a post-*Révolution Tranquille* celebration of urban experience. For this cultural observer, both spaces (Montreal and l'Ile d'Orléans) appeal to her. In contrast to her Québécois colleagues and friends, she feels at ease on the asphalt of Montreal streets as she does surrounded by the Saint Lawrence and the rusticity of the island. It is fitting that this epistolary novel stages the integration of this foreigner into the narrative of *Québécité*; the Persian becomes a *Québécoise d'adoption.* Much like Poulin's *Volkswagen Blues, Lettres d'une autre* refuses a rhetoric of origins that would equate (national) identity with ethnicity.

Poulin and Gauvin do use different strategies in order to represent links between space and national identity. Whereas Poulin uses *lieux de mémoire* which evoke plural historical meanings, such "realms of memory" are not elaborated upon in Gauvin's *Lettres d'une autre.* In Gauvin's text, the cityscapes are more in flux, caught in a modern dynamic of transformation. What does link the two narratives, however, is the attempt to structure the trajectory of the protagonists through the frame of a North American context. The characters' experience of space fluctuates between personal impressions and the evocation—however flawed, incomplete or even contradictory—of a broader geography of collective identity. For Poulin, this means debunking a nationalist mythology whereas Gauvin's narrative demystifies both a politics of nostalgia as well as a postmodern celebration of discontinuous change.

A RHETORIC OF (DAILY) LOCATEDNESS: TEMPERING THE NATIONALIST MYTH

Twenty odd years later, this broad narrative sweep has narrowed in focus—both in Gauvin's *Un automne à Paris* [*An Autumn in Paris*] (2006) and in Poulin's *La traduction est une histoire d'amour* [*Translation Is a Love Story*] (2006). Poulin's *La traduction* is particularly marked by the return to a more local perspective. In this text about the development of a new friendship between the writer, Jack Waterman, and the narrator, a youthful translator of his work, the Québécoise Marine of Irish origin, the plot centers primarily on the contrast of and connection between rural l'Ile d'Orléans and nearby Quebec City. Moreover, the decrypting of a historical subject hidden beneath the physicality of a landscape which drove *Volkswagen Blues* forward is reduced to a narrative of personal origins. While Jack and Marine do draw attention to the marginalized history of Anglophone immigrants within the Francophone province—both in the Eastern Townships, a Loyalist-American stronghold, and on Grosse-Ile, the quarantine island located to the northeast of Quebec and l'Ile d'Orléans,[20] we learn more about Marine's own troubled heritage. After traveling in Geneva and the south of France, Marine returns to Quebec City and seeks out a local cemetery, in which is located the tombstone designating the official final resting-place of her mother; only Marine knows that this marker also commemorates the secret grave of her younger sister.

The general drift of the novel does not lie in excavating marginalized histories problematizing or enriching a more official Québécois history. The cityscape of Quebec in this later novel sets the scene for a detective intrigue where the apartment buildings, corner grocery stores, and streets function as the backdrop for the two protagonists attempting to aid an adolescent stranger glimpsed from a distance on the top of a neighboring apartment building. In the act of deciphering this mystery, the references to the city function as orientation points rather than as a pretext for evoking the city's or the province's Francophone legacy:

> On trouvait bien un garage Auto Place dans la rue d'Aiguillon, non loin de la Tour du Faubourg [...].
>
> (90)[21]

[One did indeed find a garage "Auto Place" in the Aiguil-lon Street, not far from the Tower du Faubourg [...].]

Rather than nuancing one's understanding of the multiple layers of historical significance embedded in the land- and cityscape, this text ends by conjuring up a different temporality—that of an earthly paradise. Having freed the adolescent, Limoilou, and provided her with a new home for the moment, Marine concludes the novel with the following description:

C'était l'été des Indiens, la température avait soudain re-monté [...] Je jetai un coup d'oeil vers le haut de la côte par la porte du solarium. Pour tout dire, je n'aurais pas été surprise de voir le renard roux, ou même la biche aux chevilles de mannequin, descendre le chemin de terre en trottinant pour aller se joindre au cortège de la fille et des deux chats.

(132)

[It was Indian summer; the temperature had suddenly risen again [...] I glanced toward the top of the hill through the door of the solarium. Actually, I wouldn't have been surprised to see the red fox or even the deer with the model-like ankles, descend the dirt path trotting in order to join the procession of the girl and the two cats.]

This earthly, nature-bound paradise creates a new sense of community between three strangers otherwise devoid of family ties. Moreover, it doesn't force the characters to choose between the rural charms of l'Ile d'Orléans or the contemporary cityscape, which provides its own charm:

La basse-ville sommeillait encore. L'autoroute Dufferin avec ses lampadaires orangés était déserte et je ne vis que trois ou quatre voitures au carrefour du boulevard Charest et de La Couronne.

(104)

[The lower city was still dozing. The Dufferin Autoroute with its orange-tinted street lamps was deserted, and I only saw three or four cars at the intersection of Charest and La Couronne.]

The snapshots provided of Quebec City resolutely ignore the hackneyed views of the Château Frontenac or the panorama onto the Saint Lawrence River. The images foreground instead the functional but also familiar city.

In his novel, focused on a meaningful world located in a (perhaps timeless) present, the possibility of a community of adoption is undergirded by the ideal of the possibility of translation, the communicability of meaning through a vehicle of difference. Jack acknowledges the ability of Marine to reproduce in English the "*petite musique*" [little music] of his French prose (27) and, in fact, the act of translation is coded as an expression of human connectedness. Language is able to overcome the dispossession of exile (87) and, in the quotation of Kafka's Milena, cited in the novel, translation communicates an intimacy born of language:

Chaque jour, pour être fidèle à votre texte, mes mots épous-sent les courbes de votre écriture, à la manière d'une amante qui se blottit dans les bras de son amoureux.

(113)

[Each day, in order to be faithful to your text, my words marry the curves of your writing in the manner of a (fe-male) lover who nestles in the arms of her lover.]

In Poulin's and Gauvin's most recent narratives, the commemoration of national or continental space gives way to an approach more closely affiliated with Michel de Certeau's *L'invention du quotidien*. Rather than attempting to reconstruct as well as problematize a "panoramic" narrative that would blend a representative geography with historical significance, both contemporary texts highlight the experience of the city—either as the attempt to make use of the cityscape in order to track a particular mystery or, in Gauvin's case, as a *flâneur* interested in taking the pulse of the city—a venture that distances itself completely from an exploration of Parisian monuments and famous places (Gauvin 9). Gauvin's fascination with the "*flots d'images*" [stream of images] or "*bribes de vie arrachées de justesse*" [fragments of life just barely snatched in time] privileges Certeau's take on daily practices and, in particular, urban space—where it is the footsteps of city inhabitants interacting with the streets and architectural barriers that help create a city rather than the rational, commemorative organization of that space. Certeau notes in his introduction to *L'invention du quotidien* that he will focus on the tactics of consumers—individuals who are not simply passive cogs in a larger economic system. His comments on the act of reading actually have a particular relevance for the relation between the characters and the land- and cityscape they inhabit:

Un monde différent (celui du lecteur) s'introduit dans la place de l'auteur. Cette mutation rend le texte habitable à la manière d'un appartement loué. Elle transforme la pro-priété de l'autre en lieu emprunté, un moment, par un passant. Les locataires opèrent une mutation semblable dans l'appartement qu'ils meublent de leurs gestes et de leurs souvenirs [...].[22]

[A different world (that of the reader) is introduced in the place of the author's. This change makes the text habitable like that of a rented apartment. [This change] transforms the property of the author into a borrowed space, a moment [borrowed] by a passerby. The tenants carry out a similar change in the apartment which they furnish with their gestures and their memories [...].]

The passage of the characters through the space of the city enacts this same mutation.

How are we to understand Gauvin's shift in perspective—her fascination with a Parisian rather than "purely" Québécois cityscape? How does the Parisian backdrop function in this later text? At one level, Gauvin is simply inventing a more individual, intellectual (and more interesting) form of tourism—a personal map of Paris.

Returning to her hotel via Marguerite Duras' rue St-Bénoît and the rue des Grands-Augustins, made famous through Balzac's *Le chef-d'oeuvre inconnu* and Picasso's *Guernica*, she notes:

> A Paris, chaque immeuble a le souvenir plus ou moins secret, plus ou moins affiché des écrivains et artistes qui l'ont habité. Et les pierres de servir de témoins à ceux qui tentent, au présent, de faire exister la vie dans les mots.
>
> (39)

> [In Paris, each building has a more or less secret memory, more or less displayed, of the writers and artists who have inhabited it. And the stones serve as witnesses to those who try in the present to make it live through words.]

Not surprisingly, we hear echoes of Baudelaire's *flâneur* in this work—the fascination with the experience of being lost in a crowd, of fixing on a passerby, simply pursuing a fleeting or contingent moment. Gauvin's own work is composed, in effect, of "[c]es instantanés parisiens, tableaux en miniatures" [Parisian snapshots, paintings en miniature] (29). In addition to this less commercial or monumental tourism, Gauvin privileges the public spaces of cafés where she can observe the interactions between coffee-house *habitués*. Much like her predecessor Balzac, she establishes a loose codification of café culture—a form of marginal Parisian history composed of "*clins d'œil*" [winks] rather than a masterful gaze:

> L'existence des cafés parisiens est un savant dosage de permanence et d'imprévisibilité. [. . .] Il en est à Paris des cafés comme des quartiers. Chacun a sa tradition, sa culture, diraient les sociologues, ses spécialités et ses rites. [. . .] Les cafés sont parmi les repères les plus stables de la ville, telles les inscriptions qui en jalonnent les parcours.
>
> (81-83)

> [The existence of Parisian cafes is a skillful dose of permanence and unpredictability. [. . .] In Paris, there are cafes as there are neighborhoods. Each has its own tradition, the sociologists would say its culture, its specialties and its rituals. [. . .] The cafes are among the most stable landmarks of the city, much like the inscriptions marking out a route.]

Gauvin's fascination with a less official or documented Paris' landscape is not simply the pretext for displaying an insider's knowledge of Parisian space and history. Her autobiographical narrator finds herself located between a contemporary cityscape and her own journalistic impressions from a previous stay, which had emphasized the unchanging familiarity of the city: "*Je retrouve Paris comme si je l'avais quittée la veille. La ville change peu et lentement*" [I find Paris again as if I had left it yesterday. The city changes little and slowly] (18). Through a "*mise en abîme*," the present narrator is, however, precisely unable to re-experience her earlier self's masterful certainty that Paris was transparent to her. The contemporary narrator sets out to rediscover her earlier "*flâneries*" from over a decade ago, in particular, her discovery of a street performer

from "Barbarie." During her earlier stay, the street performer had charmed her with his natural grace and unexpected "installation" (19). As she recognizes later in her three-month stay, this quest for the street performer, which will remain unfulfilled, is linked to the desire to superpose an older image on a present one, "*de revivre une antériorité révolue et, ce faisant, d'arrêter le temps*" [to live again a bygone anteriority and, by doing so, to stop time] (87).

The narrator's preoccupation with her memories of a new city does not lead to a complete bracketing of Québécois issues. In fact, the narrative highlights an "ex-centric" view of Québécois culture, one that rejects a straightforward equation of territory and identity. The pretext for the narrator's stay in Paris is her role as visiting professor of Québécois literature. Not surprisingly, she is troubled by the lack of knowledge concerning Québécois and, indeed, Francophone culture among the Parisians (43). In fact, she notes that with the exception of the Québécois bookstore, "*le livre québécois reste introuvable sur la place de Paris*" [the Quebecois book is nowhere to be found on the Paris' square] (33). When there is a conference on Quebec Studies, it is the East European scholars who seem to contribute the most compelling insights into Quebec—for instance, the contradictory representations of the *Révolution Tranquille* in Aquin's works, the analysis of the self-made man (as Napoleon) or Cinderella as manifestations of the American dream in Québécois writings, the contrast of Québécois, French, and Spanish discourse on migrant writing. Whereas the protagonist is fascinated by the traces of Québécois culture to be discovered in Paris, she remains rather pessimistic about the value of such perceptions.

> La ville représente dans l'imaginaire de plusieurs Québécois le double inversé de ce que signifient le Québec et le Canada pour les Français.
>
> (64)

> [The city represents in the imaginary of several Québécois the inverted double of what Quebec and Canada signify for the French.]

If the Québécois see in the Old World a prestigious *antériorité*, the European perspective highlights Canada as a "mythic place," making possible the most elaborate hopes. The narrator concludes tartly that it is time to put aside the clichés and stereotypes and recognize that Quebec is not simply a landscape of wide open spaces, forests, and winter—that the rural universe has little by little been replaced by an urban population (65). While the narrator is interested in the Parisian cityscape, this space is not to be taken as the diametrical opposite of Québécois space.

An alternative to such a stereotypical take on intercultural difference takes place in three different ways in this narrative. Rather than assuming that a physical visit to Quebec will eliminate any preconceptions, the narrator undertakes a demystification of ahistorical, uninformed clichés about Quebec through critical discourse. Countering the French cinematic journals' dismissal of Denys Arcand's 2004 film, *Les invasions barbares,* as cliché'd in its own right, Gauvin turns the lens back on the French critics to point out that Arcand hadn't set his sights on "renewing" cinema and that his concern is first and foremost to track a certain disarray in the hearts and bodies of his characters (15). The second approach seems even more constructive. In her own course, which, incidentally, only attracts twelve students, she notes with satisfaction how her students move from a rather complete ignorance of writers in Quebec (notably, with the exception of Jacques Poulin), to an enthusiasm for the Québécois classics. Poulin's ***Volkswagen Blues*** resonates particularly with the students, even if there is a general lack of knowledge about the many historical references. Gauvin seems to suggest that it is the literary landscape rather than the physical experience of travel that most effectively debunks the simplistic clichés concerning Canadian and Québécois spaces.

Toward the end of her stay in Paris, the protagonist does end up pursuing a narrative of origins when she attempts to retrace the steps of a distant ancestor, one of the 17th-century *Filles du Roy* [Daughters of the King], sent by Louis XIV to help populate the colonial space of New France. The protagonist does not seem primarily concerned with reconstructing a national narrative, meant to affirm Quebec's rootedness within French soil. She writes of her personal ancestor with special attention given to her experiences *au féminin*:

> J'ai envie de retrouver sa trace, de mettre mes pas dans les siens, de rêver sa vie [...] Quels antécédents négatifs pouvait avoir une orpheline de seize ans? Quelles étaient ses peurs, ses appréhensions devant l'aventure qui s'offrait à elle? Dans le voyage à rebours que j'accomplis maintenant, son image m'aide à apprivoiser cette 'terra incognita' qui s'appelle Paris.
>
> (103)
>
> [I want to find her trace, place my steps in hers, dream her life [...] What negative previous history could an orphan of sixteen years possibly have had? What were her fears, her apprehensions facing the adventure that was offering itself to her? During the voyage that I am accomplishing now in reverse, her image helps me to tame this "terra incognita" which is called Paris.]

In effect, the protagonist highlights the solidarity between women—the bond connecting two migrants located in foreign space.

The protagonist's "*voyage à rebours*" [voyage in reverse] undoes the unidirectional link between Paris and Quebec, and this is, in fact, the third strategy used by the narrator to undo the stereotype of Otherness fixing both French and Québécois identity as immutable and mythological. This third strategy connects the narrator's exploration of an unofficial, personal Paris with her demystification of a necessary link between physical territory and cultural identity.[23] As Gauvin's narrator walks through the streets

of Paris, the Parisian neighborhoods are remapped as part of a Québécois literary landscape. Interspersed throughout the narrative, the descriptions of four neighborhoods—associated with the notable Québécois writers, Anne Hébert, Gaston Miron, Marie-Claire Blais, and Jacques Poulin—act as a subtext, foregrounding the link between emigration and (Québécois) writing as well as the recognition that it is the former "colonists" who—by settling in Paris—have transformed the quintessentially French cityscape. At the cour du Rohan, the narrator recalls the existence of a *salon de thé* [tea salon] where she had frequently met with Anne Hébert (45). The curved silhouette of a passerby triggers in the protagonist the recollection of a neighborhood characterized as Miron's—he had often frequented it. The contrast of Marie-Claire Blais' modest apartment dominated by an impressively severe typewriter is countered by Poulin's XXe *arrondissement* space transformed by panels of cloth into an imaginary ship's cabin or camping car. Miron does privilege his experience of life in the French capital:

> on y parle français! Il signifiait par là qu'il n'avait plus à se demander, devant chaque mot ou chaque expression utilisée, s'il s'agissait ou non d'un calque de l'anglais.
>
> (61)
>
> [one speaks French there! He meant that he no longer had to ask himself before each word or expression, if it was or not an exact copy of the English.]

Nonetheless, that privileging of life in Paris is not to be equated with the transformation of Québécois writers into French ones. As she wanders around the streets of Paris, she notes:

> L'ombre de Miron habite toujours Paris. Quelle n'avait pas été ma surprise, lors d'un voyage précédent, de lire un extrait d'un de ses poèmes reproduit dans une bouche de métro.
>
> (63)
>
> [Miron's shadow still lives in Paris. How surprised I was during a previous trip to read an excerpt of one of his poems reproduced at a metro entrance.]

Ultimately, more is at stake in this remapping of Paris as part of Quebec's literary landscape. In contrast to the 1980's texts, where the travel motif was linked to excavating lost traces or to unearthing an authentic, hidden culture or even the threats to its continued survival, in this recently published text the protagonist highlights a more personal dimension to the act of voyaging:

> Tout voyage est un recommencement, une remise en cause de soi et de son rapport au monde, un arrachement au confort et au conformisme des habitudes, à la sécurité routinière. Tout voyage comporte le risque d'un départ définitif, et pour ceux qui restent, de l'abandon ou de l'oubli [...] Le risque, comment ne pas le prendre lorsque en contrepartie se dessinent avec une netteté exemplaire, à

la manière d'icebergs fascinants et inéluctables, les para-
mètres de son propre parcours.

(106)

[Each voyage is a beginning over, a calling into question of
oneself and one's relation to the world, a tearing oneself
away from comfort and the tendency to conform to habits,
to routine security. Each voyage includes the risk of a definitive departure and for those that stay, the risk of being
abandoned and forgotten. [...] How can one not take the
risk when—in a contrasting view—the parameters of one's
own journey are sketched out in an exemplary clarity, much
like fascinating and ineluctable icebergs.]

What replaces the concern to identify one's cultural specificity or to mark out one's own territory is the desire to
detach oneself from daily habits of thought and routine
certainties. The act of writing, coextensive with that of
travel, is no longer treated as the literary expression for a
collective but rather as the process of transforming the
ordinary into an act of seeing, of vision.

Notes

1. While the term "cityscape" is defined by the Webster
   dictionary as a view, photograph or painting of a city
   (or a part of a town), I use the term to designate two
   aspects: the image of the city as it appears against the
   horizon and the general or overall (physical) impression made by a larger city.

   *Encarta Webster's Dictionary of the English Lan-
   guage* (N.Y.: Bloomsbury, 1999, 2004).

2. Unless otherwise acknowledged, all translations are
   my own.

3. Page numbers for all citations from Jacques Poulin,
   Volkswagen Blues (Montréal: Léméac, 1984) are
   placed parenthetically after the citation.

4. Gérard Bouchard, *La nation québécoise au futur et
   au passé* (Montréal, vlb éditeur, 1999).

   Jocelyn Létourneau, *Passer à l'avenir. Histoire,
   mémoire, identité dans le Québec d'aujourd'hui*
   (Montréal: Boréal, 2000).

   While Létourneau continues to assert the importance
   of *La Révolution Tranquille,* he seems to emphasize
   the symbolic historical function of the period as a
   means to decenter an English Canadian historio-
   graphical approach. Where, within a "great English
   Canadian narrative," the Conquest of 1759 might
   have been interpreted "as a virtual liberation of the
   French" or a "blessing," he argues that the Quiet
   Revolution allowed the Québécois more narrative
   control over their sense of the past and their identity:
   "[the Revolution] allowed them to free themselves
   from this alienating [dispossessing] perspective and

to reinstall themselves as the true heroes of their own
liberation" (pp. 1052-53).

Jocélyn Létourneau, "The Current Great Narrative of
Québécois Identity" in *South Atlantic Quarterly* 94:4
(1995), pp. 1039-53.

5. In his article on "The Current Great Narrative of Québécois Identity," Létourneau also describes another
   shift in Québécois historiography: "Hence the persistent image of a homogeneous and static, egalitarian
   and immobile, enclosed and entrenched society has
   yielded to a new representation strongly anchored in
   the idea of movement, out of which general matrix
   such notions as dynamism, hierarchy, strategy, mobility, differentiation, and stratification may be derived"
   [Létourneau 1995, 1044]. Létourneau connects this
   shift with a new representation of the "New France
   subject," characterized as being linked to the Québécois contemporary subject ["being economics-minded,
   open to alien influences, in step with the times, and
   capable of engineering change" (p. 1045)].

6. "PM says Quebecers form nation within Canada,"
   CTV.ca http://www.ctv.ca/servlet/ArticleNews/
   story/CTVNews/20061122/harper_quebec_061122,
   [November 22, 2006], accessed December 14, 2006.

7. Page numbers for all citations from Lise Gauvin,
   Lettres d'une autre (Montréal: L'Hexagone, 1984)
   are placed parenthetically after the citation.

8. Jean-Pierre Lapointe, "L'Américanité du roman québécois contemporain: Altérité exotique ou endo-
   tique?" in *Etudes Canadiennes/Canadian Studies*
   33 (1992), 289-97, p. 291.

   In her analysis of Quebec as a postcolonial society,
   belonging to the phenomenon of *la Francophonie,*
   Katherine Roberts draws attention to critics and historians who replace the comparison of "Francophone" texts with other (North) American clusters.
   Gérard Bouchard's focus on the New World and on
   the similarities linking these New World societies
   connects his work with the ideology underpinning
   Poulin's novel.

9. Another cautionary example is the woman in the
   showcase window—a Québécoise who is reduced
   to making her living in San Francisco as a "live
   girl" [Poulin 1984, 302].

10. Another critic, Anne Marie Miraglia, has also focused
    attention on the distinction between *américanité* and
    américanisation. For Miraglia, *américanisation* "ex-
    prime ici un mode de vie—celui de la consommation
    à l'américaine (etats-unienne) ainsi que ses consé-
    quences sur la langue, la littérature et la culture qué-
    bécoise; le deuxième, par contre, signale un état
    d'esprit, c'est-à-dire la conscience d'appartenir au
    continent nord-américain, de jouer un rôle dans son

Histoire et de faire partie d'une nouvelle race humaine" ["Americanization describes here a way of life—that of consumerism in the American (U.S.) style as well as its influence on Québécois language, literature, and culture; the second [*américanité*] indicates, by contrast, a state of mind, that is to say, the consciousness of belonging to the North American continent, of playing a role in its History and belonging to a new human race"] (Miraglia, 34).

Anne Marie Miraglia, "L'Amérique et l'américanité chez Jacques Poulin" in *Urgences* 34 (1991), pp. 34-45.

In her article on Poulin's narratives, Miraglia investigates whether Poulin simply draws on U.S. cultural influences and allusions or whether he advocates a North American identity for his protagonists. On the one hand, she notes that Poulin excavates the *coureur de bois* figure, associated with *l'américanité,* in order to expand the sense of Québécois identity beyond the figure of the *habitant* or settler. On the other hand, she ends up concluding that the quest in *Volkswagen Blues* ultimately causes Jack Waterman to recognize the bankrupcty and illusion of the great American dream [Miraglia, 44].

11. Nora, Pierre, "Entre mémoire et histoire. La problématique des lieux," *Les Lieux de mémoire* (Paris: Gallimard, 1997), 40.

12. Ibid, 38.

13. It has become a commonplace that the explorer Jacques Cartier (1534) was preceded by Giovanni Caboto in 1492, not to mention Norse sailors around 1000 A.D.

14. One might expect that as the next stage of his quest, the protagonist might explore the topography of Quebec City. As, for instance, Aurélien Boivin has pointed out in his article on Quebec City and the contemporary novel, Québec's symbolic charge is multiple—as "*ville de contrastes*" (a space opposing the well-to-do and the poor), as "*ville du pouvoir*" (the location of Quebec's National Assembly, nationalist demonstrations, and acts of terrorism), and, most significantly, as "*ville du passé et de la mémoire.*" Boivin does end up noting, however, that contemporary representations of Quebec City tend to downplay the historical characteristics of the city and that it becomes simply the backdrop of narrative plot. In Poulin's *Volkswagen Blues,* moreover, the understated depiction of Québec seems to be part of his general demystification of origins already recognizable in the first chapter of the novel.

Aurélien Boivin, "La ville de Québec dans le roman contemporain" in *La Licorne* 27 (1993), pp. 119-34.

15. Joseph Brant (1743-1807) was a Mohawk who sympathized with the Loyalists during the American Revolution. According to the *Oxford Companion to Canadian History,* "Joseph was a military and diplomatic leader who fought the rebels in return for guarantees that London would protect Mohawk rights and lands at the return of peace" [83]. Brant attempted to create a pan-tribal confederacy across the lower Great Lakes while also promoting Anglicism and Euro-American farming techniques as a means to guarantee more independence among his people.

Gerald Hallowell (editor), *The Oxford Companion to Canadian History* (Don Mills: Oxford UP, 2004).

16. In a later chapter, Poulin has his protagonists meet briefly with Saul Bellow who remarks laconically: "When one is looking for one's brother, one is looking for everyone."

17. It is useful here to recall that Gauvin recently published two texts focusing on the interface of French/Francophone language and literature: an anthology of interviews with notable Francophone writers, *L'écrivain francophone à la croisée des langues* in 1997 and, in 2004, *La fabrique de la langue. De François Rabelais à Réjean Ducharme,* where she undertakes an analysis of French/Francophone writers' (self-reflexive) poetics of language.

18. In this context, it is interesting to consider Pierre Nepveu and Gilles Marcotte's anthology, *Montréal imaginaire. Ville et littérature,* where the Montreal cityscape is tracked over the 19th and 20th centuries. According to the two critics, a city may exist as a symbol of spirituality, materialism or decadence, but it only accesses the status of literariness when it triggers questions [*quand elle fait question*]. For Nepveu and Marcotte, Montreal takes on a literary quality in the 1960's: "Mais la voici, peu après la Deuxième Guerre mondiale, investie par les interrogations, toutes les interrogations de la vie collective. Les grands débats de la nation deviennent, sitôt que la ville s'en mêle, terriblement urgents, conflictuels, bruyants, confus. [...] le nouveau récit urbain, volubile, mobile, éclaté, ne peut se produire que dans une ville entrée dans l'ère de la mutation perpétuelle; [...] c'est dans un tissu serré (quoique souvent chaotique) de symboles, de métaphores, de noms et de références, creusant les profondeurs de la mémoire et de l'histoire, c'est dans cette textualité vivante (où les médias et les divers discours sociaux jouent forcément un rôle essentiel) que Montréal comme toute ville devient davantage qu'un simple lieu ou qu'un pur agglomérat d'objets et de réalités [...]" [Nepveu and Marcotte, 9-10]. [But here she is, shortly after the Second World War, charged with the questions, with all questions relating to collective life. The great

debates of the nation—once the city is involved—become terribly urgent, conflicted, noisy, confused [...] the new, voluble, mobile, shattered urban narrative can only take place in a city that has entered into the era of perpetual transformation; [...] it is a tightly woven (although often chaotic) network of symbols, metaphors, names and references, burrowing into the depths of memory and history; it is this living textuality (where the media and divers social discourses necessarily play an essential role) that Montreal—as any city—becomes more than simply a place or a pure cluster of objects and realities [...].]

Pierre Nepveu and Gilles Marcotte (editors), *Montréal imaginaire. Ville et littérature* (Montréal: Fides, 1992).

19. Karen Gould notes in her *Writing in the Feminine. Feminism and Experimental Writing in Quebec* that "writing in the feminine" within the Quebecois context connects the "political concerns of contemporary feminism" with "the experimental forms of literary modernity, and the question of the specificity of *difference* of women's writing" [xiv]. She continues: "Inspired by contemporary French, American, and Québécois feminisms, Brossard, Gagnon, Bersianik, and Théoret have used their experimental texts to theorize on the nature of women's oppression in patriarchal culture and to delegitimatize male authority by undermining the rigid, constricting forms of its discourse" [xv-xvi].

Karen Gould, *Writing in the Feminine. Feminism and Experimental Writing in Quebec* (Carbondale: Southern Illinois University Press, 1990).

20. Marine draws attention to the hardships associated with the emigration process, particularly as this affected the large emigrant population of the Irish in the mid-nineteeth century [Poulin 2006, 71]. By informing her readers that in 1847 there were 1,300 sick on the island where only 200 sickbeds were available and that fifty emigrés were dying per day after having successfully survived the harsh Atlantic crossing, Marine shifts the focus away from the Francophone agenda of Quebec and more on the diversity of the province's population.

21. Page numbers for all citations from Jacques Poulin, *La traduction est une histoire d'amour* (Montréal: Léméac, 2006) are placed parenthetically after the citation.

22. Certeau, Michel de, "Marches dans la ville," *L'invention du quotidien* (Paris: Folio, 1994), xlix.

23. Gauvin's narrative strategy calls to mind Monique Proulx's approach to representing the city in her *Les aurores montréales*. Anne de Vaucher describes how Proulx stages the gaze of the immigrant exile in Montreal: "[...] la représentation de Montréal va s'identifier à son regard, à sa mémoire, à sa double identité. Souvent il perçoit un profond décalage entre la ville nord-américaine dont il a rêvé [...] et la vie réelle [...] Rarement il voit Montréal dans sa globalité et dans son immensité—l'île, la montagne, le fleuve—comme les auteurs québécois. Ses coups d'oeil sont brefs, sa vue partielle et fragmentée: une rue, un carrefour, quelque maison basse et profonde, avec les escaliers tournants et "la galerie" (la terrasse), des magasins, une école grise, où l'impact est terrrible en raison des deux réalités linguistiques du Québec [...]" [[...] the representation of Montreal becomes identified with his gaze, his memory, his double identity. Often he perceives a profound gap between the North American city about which he has dreamed [...] and real life [...]. Rarely does he see Montreal in its global nature and immensity—the island, the mountain, the river—as do Québécois authors. His glances are brief; his vision partial and fragmented: a street, an intersection, some low and deep house with spiral staircases and "the gallery" (the terrace), stores, a grey school whose impact is terrible because of the two linguistic realities in Quebec [...].]

Anne de Vaucher, "Une ville, des mémoires. *Les aurores montréales* de Monique Proulx" in Anna de Luca and J-P Dufiet (editors), *Palinsesti culturali: Gli apporti delle immigrazioni alla letteratura del Canada* (Udine: Forum, 1999), pp. 113-23. Interestingly, Gauvin—writing as a Québécoise in Paris—makes use of similar strategies in that there is no attempt to reproduce a complete or totalizing image of the city being visited.

Susan L. Rosenstreich (essay date 2008)

SOURCE: Rosenstreich, Susan L. "God the Father or Mother Earth?: *Nouvelle France* in Two Quebec Novels of the 1980s." *esprit créateur* 48.1 (2008): 120-30. Print.

[*In the following essay, Rosenstreich explores the ways in which* Volkswagen Blues *and another Quebecois novel, Anne Hébert's* The First Garden, *address the matter of historical origins. Rosenstreich considers the two novels' treatment of origins in relation to the Quiet Revolution, Quebec's colonial past, and the development of Quebec's distinctive cultural identity, among other issues.*]

Studying his native Quebec along with other collectivities formed since the sixteenth century by Europeans who settled in territories they considered 'new,' historian Gérard Bouchard notes these New World societies' shared awareness of distance from a homeland, "separée géographiquement et socialement de la mère patrie."[1] What are we to understand by this "mother fatherland" supposedly imagined by Europeans settling in a category of territories that, for Boucher, includes the Americas, Australasia, and even Africa? What is the meaning of such an expression, embracing in its image of familial harmony competing conceptions of parental power and far-flung offspring? Two celebrated Québécois novelists ponder this same question in works published during the 1980s. By assimilating the representation of *Nouvelle France* and the processes of arrival and settlement in the New World of northeastern North America during the sixteenth and seventeenth centuries to the experience of family ties, Jacques Poulin's **Volkswagen Blues** and *Le Premier Jardin* by Anne Hébert focus our attention on the matter of origins.

This matter, Edward Saïd has maintained, is fraught with ambivalence toward what should be inarguable: origins are our past. But what is that past? Is the past a point of origin from which the future proceeds inevitably towards a predetermined present? Or has the present issued from a point of rupture with the past, a beginning chosen from many possibilities? Saïd puzzles over this distinction, struck by the difference between "an origin [that] centrally dominates what derives from it, [and] the beginning [. . . that] encourages nonlinear development."[2] In Saïd's formulation, we can discern the subtle gendering that differentiates an inexorable law of origins, embodied in paternal authority, and empowered by that law to name and place its subjects, from a provident maternity that observes its freely wandering progeny with benevolence. In her landmark work, *Écrire dans la maison du père: L'émergence du féminin dans la tradition littéraire du Québec*,[3] Patricia Smart demonstrated the power of the parent figure—in this case the father—to shape the way a literature represents the past. But is it possible to choose that figure? God the Father or Mother Earth: can we choose our past?

As part of the larger historical moment in which they appear, the novels **Volkswagen Blues** and *Le Premier Jardin* are hardly ambivalent in their response to the question. That moment, the 1980s in Quebec, can be considered from the perspective of the Quiet Revolution in the 1960s. A period that began with the installation of the Liberal Party's Jean Lesage as premier of Quebec in 1960, the Quiet Revolution, *la Révolution tranquille,* launched a modernization project to reform Quebec's institutions after decades of paternalist governance under Lesage's conservative predecessor, Maurice Duplessis. The Liberal Party's campaign slogan, "Maîtres chez nous!," expressed a rising nationalist sentiment in the province's francophone population, and the project reached deep into that population's notion of identity during the 1960s.

Yet the 1980s can also be read as a chapter in another project, this one shaped by artists and writers in Quebec. In 1948, Paul-Émile Borduas, an abstract artist on the faculty at the École du meuble, having grown impatient with a Quebec that held itself in thrall to tradition, repressing the cultural originality of its people, published *Le*

Refus global.[4] "Refus de toute INTENTION, arme néfaste de la RAISON" was Borduas's proclamation. By refusing its history as a "petit peuple," abandoned by the elite in 1760 when Quebec City fell to the British in the Seven Years' War, and orphaned when the Treaty of Paris of 1763 erased the official existence of Nouvelle France, Quebec would be able to "rompre définitivement avec toutes les habitudes de la société, se désolidariser de son esprit utilisateur" (Borduas). The fifteen signatories of the *Refus global,* which continues to be cited as a driving force in the modernization of Quebec, exhorted this "petit peuple" to shed its "morale simiesque, envoûtée par le prestige annihilant de souvenirs des chefs d'œuvres d'Europe, dédaigneuse des authentiques créations de ses classes opprimées" (Borduas).

In the populist language of such broadly appreciated authors in 1970s Quebec as Michel Tremblay and Gaston Miron, we hear the "authentic creations" Borduas hoped for in Quebec's arts and literature. At the same time, the echo of the *Révolution tranquille*'s new, robust *québécité* is audible in their work. Tremblay's *joual* performance of *Les Belles Sœurs* in 1968 in Montreal cast aside standard French for Quebec's version of the language. Miron's Quebec-specific vocabulary in *L'Homme rapaillé* of 1970 gives voice to a Quebec identity that had, in the words of the poet Michèle Lalonde in her linguistically nationalist *Défense et illustration de la langue québécoise,* broken free of the "cordon ombilical qui les relie à la Mère-patrie."[5] As Marc Plourde, a translator of Miron's poetry, observed, the poet is "not only specific in his terminology, but specifically Québécois,"[6] affirming the power of theatre and poetry to articulate a new, linguistically audible distinctiveness on behalf of Quebec's culture.

As the literary production of Quebec expanded in the 1970s, honoring the call to authenticity by the *Refus global,* growing recognition of this cultural distinctiveness posed another question. Must a distinctive culture own its destiny in order to maintain its specificity? By the 1980s, Quebec had developed another paradigm of identity by which the people "tried to make sense of their individual and collective existence in relation to a larger human endeavor, that of North America or of American civilization."[7] If Quebec was no longer the land of an orphaned "petit peuple," did the new paradigm of "*américanité*" mean it was just another sibling in the New World family? Politically viewed, Quebec's vote against the 1980 Referendum to negotiate "a new agreement with the rest of Canada, based on the equality of nations,"[8] signaled its hesitation to be identified in this way. The hesitation is understandable when taken as part of the process Saïd is describing, in which identity emerges from a vision of destiny, and destiny is linked to the past. At the beginning of the 1980s, the question of the decade seemed clear. Would the price of an enduring distinctive culture be the filial piety of Quebec to the past of *Nouvelle France,* or could that distinctive culture sound out the rhythm of a different drummer breaking step with

Quebec's sixteenth- and seventeenth-century sources? In the formula "mère-patrie," Boucher the historian and Lalonde the poet conceptualized two paths toward cultural specificity in the New World. God the Father or Mother Earth: by recirculating the memory of *Nouvelle France, **Volkswagen Blues*** and *Le Premier Jardin* struggle with the meaning of origins. The texts of Poulin and Hébert navigate tensely between past and future, providing an opportunity to witness a moment when a culture hesitates, and looks back. In its retrospective gaze, it reads once more the constraints of God the Father, and deliverance into Mother Earth's garden of beginnings. Will these figures compete once again in their claims to Quebec's destiny?

The writer Jack Waterman considers the question in ***Volkswagen Blues.*** Jack, one in a series of Jacks or near-Jacks in the text including Jacques Cartier, Jack Kerouac, and the author himself, decides, after a decade and a half of separation from his brother Théo, to seek him out. His travel companion is Pitsémine, a female motor mechanic who claims First Nation heritage through her *Montagnais* mother, and European descent through her father. Pitsémine's defiance of conventional stereotypes—neither European nor First Nation, both female and a car mechanic—is complemented by Jack's indecisive, often passive, but always tender nature, characteristics not associated with aggressive masculinity. The reversal of stereotypes is fundamental to the novel. Though the characters are together night and day for several months, sexual involvement is not the interest of their relationship. Instead their genuine concern for each other's destination increases as they travel. Undistracted by tensions inherent in sexually charged relationships, we concentrate on the characters' journey across the continent, overhearing their conversations as they consult place names on road maps, travel guides with chatty historical information, and history books that draw on oral tradition. Beneath this array of evidence of the past, we hear two motifs.

One of these is migration. Jack and Pitsémine have met by chance on the road from Montreal to Gaspé, and to explain the purpose of his trip Jack shows Pitsémine a post card he received from Théo, the last he has heard from him in about fifteen years. The two puzzle over the post card, its writing illegible, but recognize that its "texte ancien" is "une sorte de message"[9] from Théo. Pitsémine suggests that Jack seek additional information at the Museum of the Gaspé, which is her destination. As they enter the museum, Pitsémine approaches a cleaning woman, while Jack asks the clerk for information about the text on the post card. The clerk, occupied with an issue of a Superman comic, knows nothing about the text. On the other hand, the cleaning woman immediately recognizes the "message" as an excerpt from the report of Cartier's first expedition to North America in 1534, on prominent display in an enlarged facsimile version at the museum. Ironic as it may be that a cleaning woman in a museum knows more than a museum clerk about a document announcing the birth of

Nouvelle France, greater ironies overshadow this one. The cleaning woman at the museum, which in fact overlooks the site where Cartier erected the cross on July 24, 1534, that signified his claim to *Nouvelle France* in the name of the French king, is Pitsémine's mother, her *Montagnais* parent. As a *Montagnais,* this character brings into the novel the Algonquin-speaking peoples believed to have occupied the territory of present-day Quebec as early as 2000 B.C. Simply the presence of such an individual in the text exposes the unnatural claim of political dominion in Cartier's document.

Théo's post card contests in this way the monolithic history recorded in and by documents, at the same time as it provides a clue to his message. Pitsémine sets out with Jack in the Volkswagen bus to follow Théo's signs, guided across the continent by police records and news items of Théo's infractions, even by the memories of a park attendant who recalls seeing him years earlier. Such signs of Théo's journey run parallel to those of North American explorations and discoveries that set out in the name of the French throne following Cartier's declaration of *Nouvelle France* on the beach in present-day Gaspé. Samuel de Champlain, Étienne Brûlé, Jean Nicolet, Pierre Radisson, Louis Joliet, Père Marquette, Jean Baptiste de la Salle, Pierre LeMoyne d'Iberville are all mentioned, their names forming links in the lengthy chain of French interests in North America. Songs in both French and English, histories, legends from French, English, and First Nation traditions, place names sometimes given in alternative French or English or First Nation versions, even tracks laid down by the passage of wagon trains inform this second record of cross-continental movement. The third record, Poulin's novel, begins, as do the other two records, with the Gaspé peninsula, and, like them, leaves a trail as far as the westernmost edge of the continent.

While these collections of incidents document cross-continental journeys, the records of the journeys have no closure, the journeys seeming never to end. Each journey, like a wave, passes its migrant impetus along to the next. Cartier's explorations paved the way for later French explorers who penetrated further across the continent; Théo followed alongside them, then reached San Francisco. In the novel, Jack and Pitsémine drive alongside Théo's trail to San Francisco. Here, though the landmass ends, migration does not. Pitsémine plans to live in the Volkswagen bus in San Francisco for "un certain temps"; even Jack's return to Quebec City is an ongoing journey, his writing a "forme d'exploration." Embracing their migrant condition, they recognize it as the North American one: "[Daniel Boone] disait: 'Je me sens parfois comme une feuille sur un torrent. Elle peut tournoyer, tourbillonner et se retourner, mais elle va toujours vers l'avant,'" Pitsémine muses to Jack in the final pages of the novel (Poulin 319).

Yet Jack's search for his brother holds out the promise of an anchor in this migrant life. When the couple pauses in

Chicago, Jack sits transfixed for three hours at the Art Institute contemplating Renoir's 1881 painting, identified only as *On the Terrace,* though its full title in French is *Deux Sœurs sur la terrasse.* Though Jack may not know the full title of the painting, he suddenly recalls Théo's advice to Jack, that he see the painting if ever he were in Chicago. Siblings caring for siblings: the theme is underscored a few pages later when Saul Bellow appears in the novel. Jack explains to the author that he is looking for his brother. Bellow exclaims first in English, "When you're looking for your brother, you're looking for everybody!" and then utters the French version of the statement: "Quand vous cherchez votre frère, vous cherchez tout le monde!" (Poulin 119).

Phrasing the statement in both English and French, Bellow unifies the diversity of languages in one meaning. In this way, he has transformed the continent of many histories into a single dwelling, and its inhabitants into siblings. In the vast space of North America, Jack and Pitsémine form the anchors of this recomposed family and attend to each other as siblings ought to. Jack comforts the bereft Pitsémine, the self-described *métisse,* whose origin is neither *Montagnais* nor European but rather "quelque chose de neuf, quelque chose qui commence" (Poulin 247). Just as thoughtful, Pitsémine reminds Jack that his return to Quebec City is a continuation of a journey: "Vous avez dit que l'écriture est une forme d'exploration" (Poulin 319). The moment of their separation is the moment of their deepest intimacy, each bound for a different future, united as siblings would be in a shared past: "Alors ils se serrèrent l'un contre l'autre, assis au bord de leur siège, les genoux mêlés, et ils restèrent un long moment immobiles, étroitement enlacés comme s'ils n'étaient plus qu'une seule personne" (Poulin 320).

The migrant condition is complemented by a second motif, a sort of permanence, introduced at the outset of the novel, when Jack and Pitsémine, with the help of Pitsémine's mother, recognize the text of Théo's post card. The original cross Cartier claims to have planted has disappeared; the original manuscript reporting his act of possession has likewise vanished, known to us thanks to an Italian version published in 1556 in the third volume of Giovanni Battista Ramusio's *Delle Navigazioni et viaggi,* of which a French translation was published in 1598, and subsequently to the 1867 discovery of a manuscript copy of the original. But the events of July 24, 1534, have nonetheless come down to us, relayed, like a signal, from one set of records to another. Like the many signs inscribed along the cross-continental trajectories, including the novel itself, documents and artifacts pass along their records before they themselves disappear. In this way, they leave their trace and accomplish permanence.

There is, however, still another set of signs left by cross-continental journeys in the text. In addition to the trail left by Jack, by explorers, and by the novel, there is a set of signs decipherable only by Pitsémine. Raised in a trailer, she is denied identity as a *Montagnais* by her mother's society, and as a European by her father's. Yet through her First Nation identity, she is competent and authorized to read the record of the cross-continental journey of that heritage. At three sentinel moments, we are assured of the need for this authorized reader. In chapter seven, Pitsémine spends the night next to the tomb of Joseph Brant, whose stewardship as Chief Thayendanegea is associated in Mohawk tradition with deference to women. The following morning, Pitsémine explains why the experience has left her unchanged: "D'abord, il y a eu cette histoire de la femme de Thayendanegea qui … je veux dire, elle n'a pas de nom, et j'ai passé une partie de la soirée à me demander pourquoi et je me suis posé toutes sortes de questions sur le vieux chef" (Poulin 93). Questioning a traditional belief about Mohawk democracy, Pitsémine discards the abstraction of First American identity. That identity is further tested when Pitsémine tells Jack the story of *le Rocher de la famine* as the couple drives toward Starved Rock State Park. In her story, the members of the Illinois tribe were besieged and starved, not by Europeans, but by the Ottawa and their allies. On yet a third occasion, a traditional image of the impassive European slaughter of First Americans is corrected. Until the 1854 massacre of Indians at Fort Laramie, explains Pitsémine, the fort, established by trapper Jacques Laramée, was a peaceful trading post for First Nations and a large population of French Canadian descent. A missing cow is cited as the cause of the massacre, and when Pitsémine finds a Gatling machine gun on display in the fort she assumes it was the instrument of slaughter. To her relief, she learns from the fort commander's journal that this particular Gatling model malfunctioned chronically and was useless. How misconceived it is, then, to imagine that First Nations were passive targets for Europeans. Both sides must have struggled mightily on that day; both had a way of life to protect, both felt entitled to the land.

The abstraction of First Nations gradually dissipates as Pitsémine makes their experience concrete. But so, too, does the abstraction of Europeans as Jack and Pitsémine follow their many, often troubled passages across the North American landscape. At Fort Laramie, Pitsémine had resolved the uncomfortable disparity between her two heritages, and in San Francisco she has found "un bon endroit pour essayer de faire l'unité et de se réconcilier avec elle-même" (Poulin 318). Born a migrant, Pitsémine has become, by the novel's end, the permanent dwelling for the many histories of *Nouvelle France.* By imperceptible phases, Poulin's novel moves away from an original, prescriptive *Nouvelle France,* a patriotic reflection of its *"patrie."* The greater the distance of Jack and Pitsémine from this origin, the more histories of *Nouvelle France* emerge. In these histories, categories break down, names become ephemera, claims are discredited. In the process, Jack and Pitsémine rewrite *Nouvelle France,* and when they separate, each carries another history of it elsewhere.

Like **Volkswagen Blues,** *Le Premier Jardin* recomposes a broken family in the context of recovering Quebec's past. Flora Fontanges, a retired actress living in France, has returned to Quebec City after an absence of four decades to play the role of Winnie in Beckett's *Happy Days.* Also calling her back to Quebec is a cryptic message from her estranged daughter ("Envie de te voir. Viens. T'embrasse. Maud"[10]), a habitual runaway who has joined a commune in Quebec City. The commune of young Québécois invites Flora, four decades older than its members, into their circle. She enchants Raphaël, Maud's lover, with her voice of "un ventriloque" (Hébert 19), and soon they have joined talents, Flora's acting experience and Raphaël's scholarship in history, to "faire revivre les femmes de la ville" (Hébert 133). During recesses from Flora's rehearsals as Winnie, they present living tableaux of women in Quebec's past, drawing on museum displays, street names, and records of the *filles du Roy,* contingents of young women sent to seventeenth-century *Nouvelle France* as marriage partners for early *habitants.*

Flora and Raphaël are not alone in calling the city's past to life. Eric, the commune leader, is haunted "par les vivants et les morts. Toute la ville, à commencer par ses plus proches parents, semble l'avoir choisi comme porte-parole" (Hébert 71). Through Eric's ventriloquy, we hear the city's bourgeoisie bemoan the vanity of earthly wealth and yearn for eternal life. But eternal life, Eric claims, comes through the experience of the body at work in daily tasks. His followers in the commune, "lassés de l'intolérance dans laquelle leurs parents les avaient élevés" (Hébert 58), have renounced family ties and university studies to "respirer l'odeur de la ville, saisir le passage de la lumière sur le fleuve, communiquer directement avec la terre" (Hébert 73). Like Eric, they imagine that this renunciation will return them to life as a "nouveau-né dans le neuf absolu" (Hébert 57).

But for Flora and Raphaël, attempts to erase the city's past in order to regain the moment when Quebec was innocent are futile. Signs of that past are everywhere, even if, as Raphaël claims, the city was the casual result of mistaken explorers seeking the riches of the Orient. Those signs are not visible to everyone—tourists, businessmen, party-goers from elsewhere turn down a street or two, accomplish their tasks and leave. For Raphaël, "[i]l suffit d'être attentif," and one can see Quebec emerge as a "nouveau-né": "Est-ce donc si difficile de faire un jardin, en pleine forêt, et de l'entourer d'une palissade comme un trésor? Le premier homme s'appelait Louis Hébert et la première femme, Marie Rollet. Ils ont semé le premier jardin avec des graines qui venaient de France" (Hébert 77). *Nouvelle France,* the garden at first both French and without a country, blossoms at the hands of these initial *habitants,* a Parisian apothecary and his wife who, in 1617, settled in Quebec as its first acknowledged farmers. The Old World, old France, becomes an ambivalent place, "à cause de la distance qui est entre ce monde-ci et l'autre qui était le leur

et qui ne sera plus jamais le leur" (Hébert 77). As the generations succeed each other, they continue to plant gardens in the image of that first one, but little by little "l'image mère s'est effacée dans les mémoires," and it is only "l'Histoire," according to Raphaël, that can grasp that past life in all its freshness.

The problem is this "History." Where is it? Seeing a pair of scissors and a small hammer in a museum display of pious articles from the seventeenth century, Flora learns from the nun who is their guide that the metalsmith was also a nun. How might this be, Flora wonders. What might move a nun to forge these implements? Theatre furnishes the answer. Calling on her years of practice, Flora imagines the seventeenth-century nun as a young girl open to the world, anticipating her rightful title in the partnership of "Thibault et fille, forgerons" with her blacksmith father. But "il y a des ouvrages d'hommes et des ouvrages de femmes, et le monde est en ordre. Mariage ou couvent, pour une fille, il n'y a pas d'autre issue" (Hébert 87). Before renouncing the name of Guillemette Thibault, this long-silent figure forges exquisite instruments and, as Sister Agnès-de-la-Pitié, includes them in the dowry she brings to the convent. "On n'a plus jamais entendu parler de Guillemette Thibault" (Hébert 87), imagines Flora, never, that is, until Flora visits the museum.

Raphaël's "History" resides in the names and dates inscribed on the cityscape. Yet he and the commune are dissatisfied with that past. The history they yearn for must be heard, inhaled, seen. The past they seek is *Nouvelle France,* when arrival in the New World was fraught with excitement, fear, hope, and loss of the Old World. Flora the acclaimed actress is well-qualified to place this France before them, for she is more than an experienced actress. Taken from her unmarried mother at birth, she grew up as Pierrette Paul, nuns and orphans her only family until the convent they occupied burned to the ground. Monsieur and Madame Éventurel, her adoptive parents, named her Marie, hoping that, by having a daughter, they would confirm their middle-class status. But Marie, wounded by the family for whom she was nothing but the sign of a stultifying propriety, dreams of becoming someone else, of knowing what it is like elsewhere, "s'incarner à nouveau," no longer having to gnaw "sans cesse le même os de sa vie unique" (Hébert 63). At eighteen, she signs on as a maid aboard the *Empress of Britain* and sails for France. "[L]a rupture s'est faite" (Hébert 162). Flora, too, has known arrival in a new world.

She has also known loss and recovery. At the Éventurel home, speechless and nameless like the rural misses who, she imagines, came to the city as maids, fading anonymously into the bourgeois homes they so assiduously kept, Flora recovers her voice only to speak as the middle class aspirant she dreads to become. But the recovered voice strengthens as she matures, and in France she realizes her dream of becoming others by ventriloquizing the characters she portrays. The value of Flora for the Québécois members of Maud's commune is this voice, the instrument of ventriloquy for *Nouvelle France.*

Standing on the quay where the *filles du Roy* had arrived three centuries earlier, Flora and Raphaël read the names of those women, almost all young, without resources and unmarried, dowried by the king and sent to *Nouvelle France* to become wives and mothers. But these names are not all we hear. We hear the young men waiting on the quay, gazing at the first shipload of daughters: "Il a été entendu, entre M. le Gouverneur, M. l'Intendant et nous, garçons à marier, qu'on les prendrait comme elles sont, ces filles du Roi" (Hébert 97). The daughters open themselves to us, the readers, who then see them through the eyes of the waiting bachelors, "fraîches et jeunes, sans passé, purifiées par la mer, au cours d'une longue et rude traversée de voilier" (Hébert 97).

In the Flaubertian model of *style indirect libre,* readers hear a character's view of the world at the same time as the author ironically reveals his view of it. But in the version of the discourse we hear on the quay at Anse aux Foulons where the King's daughters had arrived centuries earlier, Hébert redirects the indirect trajectory of the discourse in the space of a single sentence to an immense choral vocalization in which separate voices are audible, yet simultaneously divulging their view of the world. Readers hear the views of successively imagined characters, but the characters, too, hear each other: "Un jour, notre mère Ève s'est embarquée sur un grand voilier, traversant l'océan, durant de longs mois, pour venir vers nous qui n'existions pas encore, pour nous sortir du néant et de l'odeur de la terre en friche" (Hébert 100).

Using the first person plural pronoun and steadily shifting the point of view during the course of the sentence, Hébert departs radically from conventional *style indirect libre.* She begins with Flora and Raphaël through whom we hear the first men awaiting the women on the quay three hundred years earlier, and soon the women, too. We hear next the members of Eric's commune, anxiously awaiting a past they can embrace, and finally the chorus swells to include the voice of the author herself.

In its choral dimension, the sentence gathers together the multiple experiences of arrival. Like the daughters of the King arriving in Quebec, Flora had arrived in France the servant of a commanding power. She arrives, as many of them did, an orphan. Even Flora's daughter Maud had arrived in Quebec bereft of support. And though the men on the quay are waiting for the daughters of the King, they, too, had once arrived there. Just as Flora, Maud, and the daughters arrive in new worlds as instruments of others, named by others, the men, too, were objects, in their case of the French colonial project. If Hébert exploits the irony in traditional *style indirect libre,* it is in moments like this one, when we hear the voices of the men of *Nouvelle*

France as they expose the shallow thought behind that project. For while the Intendant and the Governor of *Nouvelle France* are planning to deploy the new families of *habitants* in stable colonies, the men are busy planning otherwise. "L'état de coureur de bois nous conviendrait assez bien, quoique le bon vouloir du Roi soit de nous enchaîner sur une terre en bois debout avec une femme" (Hébert 97), they baldly state. As was true of these first *habitants,* Flora, Maud, and the *filles du Roy* escape, through a vitality unsuspected by those whose tools they are, the narrow confines to which others had assigned them. The moment of arrival is a liberation, a moment after which one will always be more than the name recorded on forms, more than the label allotted in documents, even more than another life lived within the walls of its "first garden." The *Nouvelle France* that emerges from Hébert's novel is no longer a geographical destination, but a world of possibilities.

Like Pitsémine and Jack, Hébert's characters, separated from the "mère-patrie," progressively lose awareness of *Nouvelle France* where the memory of that mother fatherland resides. They become conscious instead of a new order of history. In this new order, the geopolitical reality of Quebec is recast as Saïd's "beginning," a moment, not a place, when characters liberate themselves from the laws of their fathers and the gardens of their mothers to flourish in gardens of their own making. The process of recomposing families in the novels considered here keeps pace with the characters' recursion of *Nouvelle France,* from which both God the Father and Mother Earth slowly but surely disappear. Speaking into the interstices of an eroded classical family structure, the characters of Poulin and Hébert form new and more democratic networks through which the authority to rewrite *Nouvelle France* devolves equally to each participant. These novels extend an invitation to cultural production in which every destiny is possible.

Notes

1. Gérard Bouchard, *Génèse des nations et cultures du Nouveau Monde* (Montreal: Les Éditions du Boréal, 2001), 12.

2. Edward Saïd, *Beginnings: Intention and Method* (New York: Basic Books, 1975), 373.

3. Patricia Smart, *Écrire dans la maison du père: L'émergence du féminin dans la tradition littéraire du Québec* (Montreal: Québec-Amérique, 1988).

4. Paul-Émile Borduas, *Refus global,* http://www. dantaylor.com/pages/frenchrefusglobal.html (accessed December 23, 2007).

5. Michèle Lalonde, *Défense et illustration de la langue québécoise* (Paris: Seghers/Laffont, 1979), 12.

6. Marc Plourde, "On Translating Miron," in Gaston Miron, *Embers and Earth (Selected Poems), Bilingual*

Edition, D. G. Jones and Marc Plourde, trans. (Montreal: Guernica, 1984), 118.

7. Louis Dupont, "*L'Américanité* in Quebec in the 1980s: Political and Cultural Considerations of an Emerging Discourse," *American Review of Canadian Studies,* 25:1 (1995): 27.

8. Text of 1980 Referendum Province of Quebec, http://en.wikipedia.org/wiki/1980_Quebec_referendum (accessed December 23, 2007).

9. Jacques Poulin, *Volkswagen Blues* (1984) (Montreal: Leméac, 1998), 14.

10. Anne Hébert, *Le Premier Jardin* (Montreal: Les Éditions du Boréal, 2000) [Paris: Seuil, 1988], 12.

Robert Sapp (essay date 2008)

SOURCE: Sapp, Robert. "Linguistic Vagabondage: The Driving Force in Jacques Poulin's *Volkswagen Blues.*" *Romance Notes* 48.3 (2008): 345-53. Print.

[*In the following essay, Sapp considers Poulin's handling of the relationship between language and identity in* Volkswagen Blues, *arguing that the use of English by French-speaking characters represents a radical break from the notion that language is a link to a shared, coherent cultural past.*]

Moving across the world, the nomad carries his home in his native language. But, if he were to lose his language or if it were replaced, would he sever himself from his home? Drawing on this new language, could he create a new notion of self, and subsequently a new identity? For the exiled, language may bridge "the unhealable rift [...] between the self and its true home," described by Edward Saïd (49). While language can operate as a link to an idyllic personal past and a concrete notion of identity, it risks tying the speaker to a predetermined concept of self.

In fact, this view of language does not take into account the heterogeneous blending of language and culture that one encounters on the transcontinental journey depicted in Jacques Poulin's *Volkswagen Blues.* Here, Poulin explores the rapport between language and identity that emerges from the collusion of Anglophone and Francophone cultures in North America calling into question the notion of a homogeneous self derived from language. This study explores the ambiguous rapport between language and identity in *Volkswagen Blues* examining the use of English by otherwise Francophone characters within the context of Jacques Derrida's conception of the otherness of language developed in *Le Monolinguisme de l'autre.* Far from innocent, the choice of English is not merely a pragmatic recourse to the *langue vehiculaire* described by Deleuze and Guattari in *Kafka: Pour une littérature mineure*

(43), but a violent refusal of a past that has become unrecognizable.

Derrida explains that while the impossibility of possessing language permits the discourse between belonging and language, it becomes necessary to combat these ideologies in order for language to function properly (121). The transient nature of language described by Derrida reveals the plasticity of cultural identity derived from it. Since no person or collective culture can claim ownership of a language, it cannot be responsible for a single, unified notion of identity nor can it be appropriated as such. While language offers intimate access to previously foreign cultures, it is insufficient as a *carte d'identité.* That is, although a requirement for citizenship in many countries, knowledge of the native language, even the ability to speak it well,[1] is insufficient in terms of belonging to the culture in which it is spoken.

While Derrida maintains that language is insufficient as representative of a single unified sense of belonging, it has been suggested that some aspects of identity cannot be changed. As Tzvetan Todorov explains, we are far from the notion, alleged by some *Lumières* of the 18th century, of *perfectibilité* which maintains that the human spirit operated as a *tabula rasa,* capable of distancing itself from its native culture and consequently adopting whatever culture for which it was best suited (22). Certain indelible aspects of identity are linked to our own personal past. However, in a postcolonial context, one in which the gap between self and other has diminished if not disappeared, questions of language and identity inevitably arise.

The complex relation between language and identity drives Jacques Poulin's *Volkswagen Blues.* The Volkswagen itself is an ambulatory library that has travelled throughout Europe crossing geographic and linguistic borders. Traces of a previous life are found throughout the vehicle. For instance, a citation attributed to Heidegger inscribed in the driver's side sun visor, an indelible trace of past travels, expresses a particular sentiment with regard to language and identity: *Die Sprache ist das Haus des Seins.*[2] Interestingly this message etched in the Volkswagen, the means of propulsion for the transcultural journey the protagonists undertake, reaffirms the colonial imposition of language as source of identification that Derrida writes against. Indeed, while the transcontinental journey Poulin depicts exposes the instability of cultural identity by underscoring the disruptive nature of contact with a different language on a cohesive concept of self, the text, much like the Volkswagen, contains scars of a colonial past which views the other as threatening in that he challenges any notion of identity brokered by language.

In *Langagement,* Lise Gauvin explores the complex and polemical question of language in Quebec and its repercussions on the literature that it has produced. For Gauvin the québécois writer is not merely interested in language for language's sake, rather he is obligated each time he takes up his pen to reexamine and reconquer the language he is using. Language for the francophone writer is in no way a simple means of communication. On the contrary, it becomes a constant negotiation between not only the writer and the reader, but also the author and his text. Gauvin employs the term *surconscience linguistique* to explain the obsessive and inherent nature of the relationship between writer and language. For this reason a complete study of any québécois literature must take into account this *surconscience linguistique* and examine how the text makes use of language (Gauvin 13).

A source of inspiration for francophone writers, this inescapable *surconscience* acts also as a source of suffering. Indeed for postcolonial literature the language imposed by the colonizing country is naturally in opposition to the *langue natale* and, subsequently, a remnant of the colonizers oppressive patriarchal culture that the colonized people are forced to internalize. This forced internalization may be seen as a metaphorical rape in which the patriarchal culture's trace, in this case language, serves as an indelible reminder of the violence that was inflicted. Expounding on the colonizer's claim to ownership of his own language, Derrida sees the violent imposition of language as a tenet of the colonial practice: "il [the colonizer] peut historiquement, à travers le viol d'une usurpation culturelle, c'est à dire toujours d'essence coloniale, feindre de se l'approprier pour l'imposer comme 'la sienne'" (45). In *Volkswagen Blues* the threat of violence is personified in the character of Pitsémine, a young *métisse* who at once evokes the historical aggression inflicted on Native Americans by both French and English colonizers as well as the real threat of violence which obligates her to travel with a concealed knife. Violence begets violence.

Throughout *Volkswagen Blues* Jacques Poulin evokes a disdain for the encroachment of English into French speaking Canada while concurrently incorporating it into the vernacular of the text. The following proposes an exploration of this simultaneous refusal and appropriation of language by examining which characters make use of it, in which circumstances it is used and to what end it is effective.

For instance, Poulin draws attention to the aforementioned violence inherent to language in a postcolonial setting through his selective use of English throughout the novel. This violence is often contrasted by an appreciation for French. In fact, Poulin's protagonist Jack Waterman, who is coincidentally a québécois writer of francophone novels, thematizes the *surconscience linguistique* of the francophone writer. In this way Poulin amplifies the already important question of language by bringing the writer into the narration. As a result Jack Waterman's fascination (*surconscience*) with words and, specifically, the French language are played out within the novel.

Of equal importance is Jack's knowledge of language. Not merely his ability to speak or write correctly, but the fact

that, as Sherry Simon points out, his experience as a bilingual writer reflects a heightened awareness of the ambivalence of language (70). Jack's fondness for his native tongue as well as his heightened awareness of its polysemous nature are revealed in his exchange with a hitchhiking vagabond. Though a native speaker of English, the man communicates with Jack in French, pausing only occasionally to search for a word or to ask for a translation. For Jack Waterman the answer is rarely a simple, one-word transposition. For example when the old vagabond asks for a translation of the word steep, Jack initially offers *escarpé* then cannot stop himself from adding *à pic* and *en pente raide* (Poulin 252). Here, it is obvious that Jack, as a writer and a Québécois, wants to celebrate the polysemous potential of his language. However, the inherent ambivalence of language can also evoke tension.

In the following exchange, taken again from the scene with the Anglophone vagabond, the reader detects a palpable tension due to Jack's refusal of a simple translation that the vagabond seems to be imposing:

> Il y avait un mot en anglais pour dire ça et c'était le verbe *to ramble.*
>
> —On peut dire vagabonder, en français, dit Jack.
>
> —C'est vrai, dit le vieux sans grande conviction.
>
> —Ou encore se promener, errer à l'aventure, aller de-ci de-là …
>
> —Hum hum! fit le vieux et Jack n'insista pas.

> (251-252)

For the reader, this exchange takes on the form of a competition: the old vagabond proudly enunciates the English verb *to ramble,* which is promptly countered by Jack's suggestion *vagabonder* and immediately followed by other options alluding to the myriad possibilities that the French language offers. Furthermore, in this example, the vagabond does not even seem to be asking for a translation. In this case his vocalization of *to ramble* seems to be more pedantic in nature. Jack responds abruptly to this imposition of English. Subsequently, Jack's prompt suggestion comes across as an insistence on the use of French; a refusal of an English encroachment. The exchange between Jack and the vagabond highlights a disdain for the violent imposition of English, while celebrating the polysemous nature of the French language.

This love for the French language is evident not only in Jack's role as a writer, but also his role as an avid reader. In *Volkswagen Blues,* the narrator makes a distinction between the reading practices of Jack and his fellow traveler la Grande Sauterelle/Pitsémine noting that, "tandis que la Grande Sauterelle devorait tous les livres qui lui tombaient sous la main, Jack Waterman était un lecteur inquiet et parcimonieux" (42). Jack is evidently a discriminating reader; however, despite his selectivity, Jack's list of favorite authors also includes some Anglophone and French writers among his fellow Québécois: Hemingway, Ducharme, Roy, Vian, Salinger and others (42), which exhibits Jack's own, albeit slight, appropriation of English into his development.

Despite his disdain for English, Jack seems unable to avoid it. This is demonstrated elsewhere in the narration as the encounter with the vagabond is not his first English encounter. Early in their journey, Jack and Pitsémine stop at a museum in Gaspé hoping to find information about the indecipherable text that Jack's brother Théo had sent to him on the back of a postcard fifteen years ago. Yet, just as it seems to be gaining momentum, Jack's nascent quest is abruptly halted by an apathetic young man sitting behind the information desk reading a comic book. Initially, when questioned about the text, the youth responds in terse French. Finally unable, or unwilling, to offer any help, the exasperated young man, hoping to end the conversation and return to his comic book, answers Jack with a curt, "So what?" (16).

Poulin's first use of English in *Volkswagen Blues* is an expression of exasperation and apathy. Placed in the mouth of the youth, living in the city of Gaspé on the edge of francophone Canada, the young man's utterance signals to the reader an encroachment of English into Québec. Anglophone influence is further supported by the young man's choice of reading material: *Superman*. Here, Poulin introduces English as a violent means of dealing with an increasingly frustrating situation.

Interestingly, the unreadable text is revealed to be the copy of a 16th century document written in French, by Jacques Cartier as opposed to some obscure language. In this case, the young man's inability to recognize the ancient text on the postcard, presumably the language of his ancestors, evokes a recourse to English. Indeed, the use of English in this example is linked with an effacement of personal history. The young man's choice of English can be seen as a reference to violence, as a means of threatening Jack into silence, but also as a means of silencing filiation with his ancestral past. On the level of meaning, the young man's phrase indicates to Jack that he is not interested in helping Jack with his current search. His insistence on expressing himself in English represents a willful ignorance of the past.

Not long after the scene in the museum at Gaspé the text places the same expression in the mouth of Jack Waterman. It comes at a time when the character of Etienne Brûlé, Jack's childhood hero, is maligned. Making a stop in Toronto in the public library, Jack and Pitsémine encounter a history student who offers his own opinion of Etienne Brûlé: "Je pense qu'Etienne Brûlé était un *bum*" (76). For Jack, Brûlé represents the epitome of Québécois identity. He incarnated a spirit of adventure and familiarity with other cultures that made him an ideal guide through the "new" continent. The revelation of Etienne Brûlé as a "bum" contradicts the personal history Jack had created destroying the very foundation of his sense of self. Again English, in the form of the word *bum,* serves as the vehicle through which violence is carried out leaving Jack visibly shaken up: "Il avait l'air assommé, comme un home qui vient de recevoir un mauvaise nouvelle concernant un de ces proches" (82).

Interestingly, Jack, who defends the French language against the English imposed by the vagabond, now makes use of it. When Jack is presented with information justifying the student's claim, revealing the degree of his disillusionment, he instinctively responds in English. Like the young man at the museum when confronted with the illegible text, Jack vocalizes an exasperated "so what?" when forced to face the unexpected realities concerning his hero. Whereas the former was unable to recognize the ancient text, Jack's use of English stems from a refusal to recognize the implications of the sordid history of Etienne Brûlé narrated to him by Pitsémine. Jack momentarily draws upon the language of the other to ignore claims that threaten his personal history.

The revelation of Brûlé's betrayal uproots Jack from a filial connection as well. For Jack, Théo personifies Brûlé who, like the pioneers and *coureurs de bois* depicted in history, was "absolument convaincu qu'il était capable de faire tout ce qu'il voulait" (149). Memories of Théo blend with the history of Etienne Brûlé until the images fuse and are lost in each other. The frontier between truth and reality is unrecognizable. Later Jack admits that Théo is "à moitié vrai et à moitié inventé" (149).

Jack's recourse to English operates in reaction to this rupture with tradition. Derrida observes that in the absence of a stable model of identification a movement is provoked: a need for genealogy (116). While Derrida maintains that all language comes from the other, even the native language, Jack's use of English only highlights his need to reestablish a personal genealogy. Within the language of the other, Jack is able to negotiate the *illisibilité* of the facts that threaten his personal history. In this way the search for Théo, which started with the deciphering of the unreadable text on a postcard sent to Jack from his estranged brother, is a quest to reestablish genealogical ties which is facilitated and instigated by the otherness of language.

It is not until the confrontation with Théo, the very reason for his journey, that Jack's disillusionment is irrevocably confirmed. Even before the encounter with his brother, Jack's hope seems severely shaken as evident in the following statement: "Don't talk to me about heroes! [...] I've traveled a long way and all my heroes ..." (309). Again, Jack uses English at a point when the reality with which he is being presented does not correlate with his own concept of the past. At the moment when he is on the verge of vocalizing his own deception, he is interrupted by Pitsémine who has seen Théo.

Finally, in this long awaited encounter, Jack sees that his brother, who personified the indomitable spirit of adventure, has been reduced to a grey-haired man with a long beard confined to a wheel chair. However, it is not the sight of Théo that is the most troubling for Jack. When Jack addresses his brother in his "langue natale," Théo is unable to recognize him and recoils abruptly saying, "I don't know you" (314). Much like the young man in the museum when asked to identify an ancient text, and Jack when confronted with the treason of Etienne Brûlé, Théo responds in English. Whether, as in the case of the former, he truly did not recognize his brother or, as in the case of the latter, he refused to see the truth before his eyes, Théo's use of English is significant. It represents a complete cassation of filial ties: he recognizes neither the sound of his native tongue nor the image of his brother. In a reversal of the exchange with the vagabond, Théo rejects Jack's imposition of French.

Théo's refusal of the French language marks his own break with his personal history. In short, he renounces the image that Jack remembers while reinventing himself in the new language. For Théo the appropriation of English signifies a breaking of ties to the colonial identity. However, any notion of freedom gained from this break is illusory and comes at a cost. Reinventing himself in the language of the other, Théo must forgo any personal history tied to his native language, effectively swapping one colonial master for another. Théo adheres to an identity politics in which notions of self are thoroughly invested in the language.

Contrary to the nomadic thought that informs Jack and Pitsémine's use of language, frequently negotiating meaning between at least two different languages throughout their transcontinental journey, Théo represents a fixed notion of language and identity that maintains the dominant binary of self and other. His appropriation of English is absolute and cannot be reconciled with his francophone past. Reverting to the dominant culture's use of monolanguage, an important tenet of the colonial system (cf. Hedi, 1993) acts as a means of denying ambiguity. For Théo appropriation of language is possible because language exists as a unified whole. His use of English only reinforces the colonial discourse in which mastery, that is appropriation, of language demonstrates belonging to the hegemony which imposes it. Consequently Théo's multicultural past is replaced, erased and forgotten. Jack, however, displays a linguistic nomadism which upsets fixed notions of identity. His linguistic mobility, paralleled in the image of the rambling Volkswagen, is contrasted by Théo: an image of death and immobility.

Describing both Jack and Pitsémine's rupture with the oppressive memory of "mere-patrie," Susan Rosenstreich observes that, "they become conscious instead of a new order of history" (130). Indeed the encounter with Théo reaffirms this "new order of history" as well as a new order of language. Throughout the novel the characters must confront information that is often unrecognizable. That is, their concept of the past does not correspond to the history with which they are presented. It is at these moments, when recognition is not possible, that Poulin often chooses to place English in the mouths of otherwise francophone characters. Unable to reconcile the contradiction between a constructed past and suggested reality, the characters make use of the otherness of language in order to refute memories that have become unrecognizable or *illisible*.

The polyglot union of Jack and Pitsémine, and their journey across North America, represent a nomadic image of the francophone world that traverses linguistic borders opposing the monolinguistic practices of dominant hegemonies. While the otherness of language allows for a means to reestablish severed historical ties through anamnesis, the complete appropriation of language would only reinforce the dominant hegemony, nullifying the very process. To this end the monolingual, sedentary character of Théo serves as a warning against the limits of appropriation. While this study restricts itself to the analysis of the use of English by francophone characters within **Volkswagen Blues,** further examination of the character of Théo in relation to language and history would be beneficial to a clearer understanding of notions, language and identity represented in Québécois literature.

Notes

1. In Maryse Condé's *Le Coeur à Rire et à Pleurer,* the narrator witnesses firsthand the insufficiency of language as means of belonging when a Parisian waiter fails to recognize her family's presumed "Frenchness" despite their command of the French language: "Pourtant nous sommes aussi français qu'eux, soupirait mon père. Plus français, renchérissait ma mère avec violence. Elle ajoutait en guise d'explication: Nous sommes plus instruits" (13).

2. "Language is the home of being."

Works Cited

Condé, Maryse. *Le Coeur à rire et à pleurer.* Paris: R. Laffont, 1999.

Deleuze, Gilles and Felix Guattari. *Kafka: Pour une littérature mineure.* Paris: Editions de Minuit, 1975.

Derrida, Jacques. *Le Monolinguisme de l'autre.* Paris: Galilée, 1996.

Gauvin, Lise. *Langagement.* Montreal: Boréal, 2000.

Hedi, Abdel-Jaouad. "Isabelle Eberhardt: Portrait of the Artist as a Young Nomad." *Yale French Studies* 89.2 (1993): 93-117.

Poulin, Jacques. *Volkswagen Blues*. Montreal: Babel, 1999.

Rosenstreich, Susan L. "God the Father or Mother Earth?: *Nouvelle France* in Two Quebec Novels of the 1980's." *L'esprit créateur* 48.1 (2008): 120-30.

Saïd, Edward W. "The Mind of Winter: Reflections on Life in Exile." *Harper's* Sept. 1984: 49-55.

Simon, Sherry. "Translating and Interlingual Creation in the Contact Zone: Border Writing in Quebec." *Post-colonial Translation*. London: Routledge, 1999.

Todorov, Tzvetan. *Les Abus de la Mémoire*. Paris: Arléa, 2004.

Heather Macfarlane (essay date 2009)

SOURCE: Macfarlane, Heather. "*Volkswagen Blues* Twenty-Five Years Later: Revisiting Poulin's Pitsémine." *Studies in Canadian Literature/Études en littérature canadienne* 34.2 (2009): 5-21. Print.

[*In the following essay, Macfarlane contends that the novel* Volkswagen Blues *attempts to identify a way for a mixed culture to evolve in Canada that will allow for a more tolerant and diverse society. Macfarlane notes that Poulin settles on a hybrid of native and European origin because he sees native culture as dying or already dead.*]

The year 2009 marks the twenty-fifth anniversary of the publication of Governor General's Award-winner Jacques Poulin's popular novel *Volkswagen Blues*. The novel, dubbed "roman culte" by *Le Soleil* and "one of the best novels of the 1980s" by *Le Devoir*, was written in 1984 and translated into English by Sheila Fischman in 1988, after winning the Prix Québec-Belgique. Poulin later won the prestigious Prix Athanase-David for his contribution to Quebec literature, and *Volkswagen Blues*, further described by *Devoir* columnist François Hébert as "Un grand, un très beau livre," continues to hold a prominent position not only in Québécois but also in Canadian literary histories. The novel tells the story of a writer, Jack Waterman (a reference to Jack Kerouac and to Poulin himself), who takes to the road in an effort to find his wandering brother Théo and to overcome his writer's block. On the road, he picks up Pitsémine, nicknamed la Grande Sauterelle, who turns out to be half Québécois and half Innu and suffering from an identity crisis related to her mixed ancestry; she accompanies him on his odyssey from Gaspé to San Francisco via the Oregon Trail. Both the narrator and Pitsémine personify an uneasy and changing Quebec, and their search for Théo leads them to retrace historical migrations that parallel their quest for roots in the American landscape. Simon Harel's article "L'Amérique ossuaire" examines the pair's search for answers and for direction, revealing their disillusionment with an America that is empty and founded on violence. Their quest involves a nostalgic search for traces of the colonial French presence in North America, but it reveals nothing concrete. Harel sees this as an escapist search for the absolute that ultimately reconfirms the new reality of the hybrid nature of Quebec (165).

Profoundly influenced by the period in which it was written—four years after the 1980 referendum that determined Quebec's continued presence within Canada—the novel explores the possibility of a movement away from a "pure-laine," homogeneous, French-Canadian Quebec toward a nation characterized by hybridity in its attempts to deal with its ever-increasing immigrant population.[1] With postmodernism at its peak in Canada, the tools of the postmodern movement and its attempt to break down master narratives were the cornerstone of the political and artistic ideologies of the time, and it is, therefore, no surprise that Poulin chose to address Quebec's ambiguous position within the nation in the terms posited by the movement. Max Dorsinville, in his 1990 *ECW* review of the English translation, calls the book "an imaginative revisitation of the continent uniquely suited to postmodernism" (40). Brent Ledger also comments on the novel's postmodern elements in *Quill & Quire*, calling it "A nimble, witty performance, blending travelogue, conventional narrative, and odd bits of revisionist history to form a seamless, dazzling whole" (26). Hébert too comments on the intertexts that give the novel its depth: "Ce que vous lisez est la partie visible de l'iceberg, la façade de la maison; il y a toujours beaucoup plus, en dessous, derrière, dedans" (25). Largely characterized by its revisionist approach to North American history, *Volkswagen Blues* is an attempt to break down the master narrative of a superior pure laine culture via the character of Pitsémine, who is intent on reconciling the two halves of her mixed identity. In order to promote a move toward a more tolerant and diverse society, Poulin embraces the hybrid as an alternative for Quebec. Postmodernism, like postcolonialism, favours discussions of hybridity and ambiguity, and it is through the character of Pitsémine that Poulin promotes the hybrid as the only viable option for ensuring Quebec's future.

The promotion of tolerance through the breaking down of limiting master narratives is an important undertaking, and Poulin's use of revisionist history to question the so-called heroism of the colonizer no doubt explains why *Volkswagen Blues* continues to garner such significant support. The novel does, after all, acknowledge the violence and genocide that permitted the colonization and settlement of the Americas. It is important to acknowledge, however, that while this approach certainly has its value, it also has its limitations. Poulin's use of the mixed-blood or Metis identity as a vehicle to promote hybridity, while it appears to promote inclusion, arguably leads to erasure of Indigenous cultures and nations. By portraying Native culture as dying or dead and presenting hybrid culture as the only viable solution for Quebec, Poulin threatens to eliminate the Native, replacing it instead with a new, generic hybrid.

This, however, has obvious dangers; as Cherokee scholar Jace Weaver states, "To press everyone into a hybrid or mixed-blood mold is to consummate finally the as yet uncompleted enterprise of colonialism" (29).

Volkswagen Blues is valuable for its historical revisionism and its acknowledgement of a violent and genocidal past. Where it breaks down, however, is in its portrayal of Indigeneity. Poulin, like countless other writers in Canada and Quebec, and in spite of ostensibly good intentions, falls into the trap of using the figure of the Native to further his own ends—in this case, the promotion of a hybrid society. In doing so, he not only perpetuates stereotypes and the myth of the dead and dying Indian but also threatens to eliminate Native cultures altogether. Cherokee scholar and writer Daniel Heath Justice writes, "Indigenous peoples are read primarily as colourful contributors to the great Canadian socio-cultural mosaic. While this reading is generally intended by scholars and teachers to affirm the human dignity of Aboriginal peoples, it ironically erases one of the most fundamental aspects of Indigenous survival: the status of nationhood" (150). Continuing to celebrate the novel as *L'Actualité* did in December 2005, as "un des 20 livres pour comprendre le Québec d'aujourd'hui," consequently poses a risk to the survival of Indigenous cultures in Quebec. This essay seeks to re-examine Poulin's treatment of Indigeneity and its implications for Native populations rather than its function as a vehicle through which to promote the interests of the author. The value of both postmodern and postcolonial approaches to literature is undeniable, but, as with any movement, there are limits to what they can accomplish. Twenty-five years after its publication, it is important to look at *Volkswagen Blues* in a new light; the novel is a product of its time and should be examined as such.

Marie Vautier examines *Volkswagen Blues* in an essay on the figure of the "Amerindian" in the works of Francois Barcelo, George Bowering, and Jacques Poulin and makes the following statement: "Although the historical colonization of the Amerindian and Inuit peoples by the British and French is openly signalled in these contemporary texts, they sometimes use the figure of the Amerindian and/or the Metis to further the postcolonial arguments of the non-native cultural majorities of their traditions" (18). These books, she goes on to explain, "exploit stereotypes to subvert Eurocentric attitudes" (24). This is certainly the case in *Volkswagen Blues* since it is Pitsémine should this be "whom"? Poulin presents as a model of the new Quebecker. When Pitsémine states sadly that she is "ni une Indienne ni une Blanche," concluding that "finalement, elle n'était rien du tout," (224), Jack tells her she's "quelque chose de neuf, quelque chose qui commence. Vous êtes quelque chose qui ne s'est encore jamais vu" (224). Metis cultures are hardly new nor is Indigeneity, yet it seems that Pitsémine has no option but to become "something new"—the hybrid that will characterize the new Quebec. It is interesting to note that while the figure of

Pitsémine is reportedly suffering from an identity crisis and is something "entirely new," Poulin uses all the stereotypes of Native identity in order to describe her, giving her a distinctly Native character. At times these characteristics are so exaggerated that it seems his intent is humour; however, there is a contradiction here: Poulin gives her Native attributes but prevents her from living as a Native woman, thus engaging in what Vautier describes above as the "[exploitation of] stereotypes to subvert Eurocentric attitudes."

Poulin ensures, on the very first page of the novel, that we recognize Pitsémine's Indigeneity by describing the apparition that Jack sees from the window of his minivan: "il vit une grande fille maigre qui était vêtue d'une robe de nuit blanche et marchait pieds nus dans l'herbe en dépit du froid; un petit chat noir courait derrière elle. ... Les cheveux de la fille étaient noirs comme du charbon et nattés en une longue tresse qui lui descendait au milieu du dos" (9). One page later, when he picks her up on the side of the road, she is still barefoot and will not enter the van until the cat explores it and ensures that it is safe. There is nothing ambiguous about Pitsémine's identity.[2] She goes barefoot, even in the cold early spring; she has an Innu name and a nickname that plays on her Native identity; she wears her long black hair tied in a braid and carries a hunting knife. She also has a mysterious connection to nature and, as Jack points out, "un sens de l'orientation infaillible" (53). She is portrayed stereotypically as the perpetual nomad wandering freely and aimlessly; she explains to Jack, "'je ne sais jamais à l'avance ce que je vais faire'" (37). As in the parable of the grasshopper and the ant, Pitsémine, nicknamed "la Grande Sauterelle," plays the role of the carefree grasshopper while Jack is the industrious, domestic ant. In an apparent gender reversal[3] and a stereotyped image of the strong, stoic Indian at one with nature, Pitsémine stands by, barefoot, as Jack shivers under a blanket on the ferry to Quebec City: "Jack avait une couverture de laine autour des épaules. La fille, nu-pieds comme d'habitude, disait qu'elle n'avait pas froid" (31).

Pitsémine also disappears and reappears mysteriously and has a sort of sixth sense—it seems she can read Jack's mind. "Vous êtes capable de dire ce qui se passe dans ma tête," he tells her. She is always in some kind of reverie, and even her dreams are "Native"—she tells Jack, "Je rêvais aux grands canots d'écorce" (55). Pitsémine also conforms to the stereotype of a sexually free and open Native woman, answering, "Oui. Evidemment," to Jack's question, "Et les Indiens avaient des mœurs sexuelles plus libres que les Blancs, n'est-ce pas?" (76) It is also she who initiates a sexual encounter between the two characters on the continental divide, stripping by the road on the Oregon Trail. Terry Goldie, in his 1988 review of the novel's English translation in *Books in Canada*, writes, "La Grande Sauterelle is partly faithful Metis guide, partly the sexually attractive Indian maiden, temptress of the North American wilderness. She is also ... the spiritual teacher" (29). Significantly, like a guide, it is she who acts as a vehicle to help Jack awaken from stagnation; similarly, she acts as the tool with which Poulin constructs his proposal for a new Quebec. Ledger signals Pitsémine's broader function: "Her mini-lectures on the French voyageurs and extinct Indian tribes give the trip its larger social and historical dimension, turning Waterman's quest for Théo into French Canada's search for its place in North America" (26).

Poulin's use of the Native figure as a vehicle to promote change is not in itself damaging. What makes it destructive to Aboriginal culture is the misrepresentation of Native people through the reinforcement of stereotypes and myths concerning Indigenous populations. Poulin's use of Pitsémine is indicative of non-Native use of Native characters to further their own goals; in this case, the undermining of a pure, racist Quebec. Poulin describes a Quebec, in fact, that seems to identify with Native peoples, giving Quebec an air of authenticity and a sense of entitlement denied to Canada outside Quebec or the United States. It is interesting that *Volkswagen Blues,* celebrated for its questioning of history and undercutting of explorer Etienne Brulé, claims very little responsibility for colonization by the French, though they too are colonizers. The novel suggests that the French have a deep and respectful bond with Native peoples—arguably brought about by a shared sense of marginalization from the mainstream anglophone culture. There is no doubt that the Québécois have suffered from the dangers of assimilation and marginalization from the anglophone majority. However, the tendency to underline the working relationships between the coureurs de bois and Indigenous people as proof of shared solidarity denies the colonial role of the original French settlers and suggests that there was nothing exploitative about the voyageurs' relationship with their Native guides and lovers. Pitsémine highlights this exploitation, identifying herself as Native, and saying, "Moi, je n'ai rien en commun avec les gens qui sont venus chercher de l'or et des épices et un passage vers l'Orient. Je suis du côté de ceux qui se sont fait voler leur terres et leur façon de vivre" (28). Later, however, she contradicts herself, which demonstrates the extent to which she is a vehicle for the author. Reading a book, she explains an explorer's choice of a francophone guide and says to Jack, "On a choisi un francophone pour qu'il soit capable de s'entendre avec les Indiens" (177). Indigenous peoples who continue to suffer the effects of poverty and marginalization might say otherwise, but many Québécois claim to identify with Native peoples and often feature in their works Native characters that conform to their romantic ideals.[4] Such stereotypes, when employed in discussions of sovereignty, are highly problematic. Quebec is happy to promote Native peoples as a colourful part of its culture in order to further its own interests, providing those Native people co-operate and do not get in the way of the province's goals. (The same, of course, applies in Canada outside Quebec.) As Justice points out, this is highly hypocritical. "Although Quebec sovereigntists are quite articulate about their own desire for

sovereignty," he writes, "their dismissal of similar Indigenous assertions—which has a much longer genealogy that significantly predates that of Quebec—amounts to an ultimately indefensible hypocrisy" (157). This is not to say, however, that there are no examples of potential change. During the government's landmark 2008 apology for the residential schools that sought to destroy Native cultures, the leader of the Bloc Québécois, Gilles Duceppe, made a commitment to engage with Native peoples in Quebec on a "nation to nation" basis. To date, this has not been the case; it remains to be seen whether or not he will honour this commitment.

Poulin's use of the Indigenous female figure, well-meaning though it may be, is troubling since it perpetuates myths of the dead and dying Indian and ultimately reinforces misconceptions of Native peoples created by non-Natives. The reinforcement of stereotypes is a problem discussed during the appropriation-of-voice debates in the 1980s and early 1990s.[5] Even the best intentions, as we have seen, can reinforce stereotypes, since writers are basing their characters on attitudes informed by Western ideals and myths of Native people. These myths are often tied to nationhood since Indigeneity is frequently used by Canadian anglophones and francophones alike in order to create unique national identities that will distinguish them from Europeans, as well as Americans, and ultimately give them a greater sense of entitlement to the land. This results not only in misrepresentation but also in exploitation. Pitsémine, portrayed so consistently as Native, ultimately lacks agency, and it is this that is problematic. Without exception, the myth of the dead and dying Indian is alive and well in *Volkswagen Blues*; the novel ultimately relegates Indigeneity to the past and leaves Pitsémine no choice but to choose hybridity over her Innu identity. Throughout the novel, in fact, La Grand Sauterelle encounters numerous hybrid authors who serve as examples of what she can be. Pierre L'Hérault points out intertexts that highlight writers of mixed ancestry, including Kerouac (Québécois-American) and Saul Bellow (Jewish-Canadian-American-Québécois) (38). Significantly, neither of these examples has Aboriginal origins.

The myth of the vanishing Indian has long been used to marginalize Native peoples; it relegates them to museums and anthropological studies as artifacts. It is, of course, a very convenient conception since a dead or dying people does not need any consideration or rights. This perception also allows Euro-Canadians to feel a guilty nostalgia about the past and about the disappearance of Indigenous peoples rather than dealing with the effects of colonization in the present.[6] In *Volkswagen Blues,* though Pitsémine is travelling through Quebec and the United States ostensibly searching for her identity, she never encounters any living Native people. The only other Native person we see is her mother, who is herself portrayed as a kind of artifact since she works in a museum. In fact, the only Native figures that seem to offer any sense of community are themselves dead. Leaving Toronto, Pitsémine tells Jack that she wants to visit the Mohawk chief Joseph Brant's grave in order to give herself some kind of peace; presumably, she hopes to draw strength from a Native hero: "Se réconcilier avec elle-meme. Voilà ce que la Grande Sauterelle voulait faire et il fallait pour cela qu'elle dorme dans le cimetière à coté de la tombe du vieux chef Thayendanegea" (81). Though Brant is male, Mohawk, colonized by the British, and dead, Pitsémine—female, Innu, colonized by the French, and living—feels that she can "find herself" with his help: "d'une façon ou d'une autre, le vieux chef pouvait l'aider à se connaitre elle-meme" (82). It is hardly surprising when this plan fails—sleeping with dead Indians does not do much for her sense of self: "'Il ne s'est rien passé du tout,' dit-elle un peu tristement. 'Je veux dire; je me sens exactement comme je me sentais avant'" (86).

Similarly, on their travels along the Oregon Trail, the only stories we are told about Native peoples are those of their death and destruction. Pitsémine describes the disappearance of the Illinois and talks about the extermination of the bison population that led to the destruction of the Plains peoples. She describes the Sand Creek Massacre of 1864 and that at Wounded Knee in 1890. With no chance of building community in the present, la Grande Sauterelle suffers from a sort of nostalgic melancholia and spends a great deal of time looking off into the horizon: "Elle regardait dehors et son regard était perdu dans la nuit" (33), dreaming of "canots d'écorce" (55) and her mother's Native past (87). In spite of the existence of thriving Native populations in both Canada and the United States, Pitsémine encounters nothing but death on the trip; ultimately, she has no opportunity to live or identify herself as a Native woman. Bowing to the Indians who once occupied the island of Alcatraz, she resigns herself to the myth of the vanishing Indian: "Son geste semblait dire que les Indiens perdaient toujours, qu'ils avaient perdu cette fois encore et qu'il n'y avait rien à faire. C'était le destin ou quelque chose du genre" (257). This reaction is particularly significant since the occupation of Alcatraz is such a powerful symbol of resistance and so significant an event in Aboriginal claims for justice and sovereignty. Between November 1969 and June 1971, over 5,600 Native Americans from 20 different tribes occupied the island of Alcatraz, which had been left unused after its prison was closed in 1963. They were demanding rights for Native Americans and wanted the island to be returned to Indigenous peoples. The occupation was a turning point in Native claims for human rights; although the island was never returned, the occupation forced Americans to recognize and take the claims of Native peoples seriously. The fact that Pitsémine accepts defeat in bowing to the *memory* of Aboriginal peoples rather than celebrating Alcatraz as a symbol of resistance perpetuates the idea that there is no hope for Indigenous survival.

The myth of the vanishing Indian necessarily dictates nostalgia for things past. There is no room for thriving, evolving Native populations, and Pitsémine is therefore unable to find a place to exist. Indigeneity in *Volkswagen Blues* seems to exist only in pre-contact times, and it seems that it is impossible for Aboriginal peoples to embrace both a pre-contact and contemporary world. A pristine world untouched by Europeans is continually romanticized, and, seemingly unable to survive as a modern Indian, Pitsémine breaks down in tears. She is conflicted, once again, between the artificial binaries of the pre-modern Indian and the modern white man: "'Je trouve que la nature est plus belle quand il n'y a rien, je veux dire quand elle est restée comme elle était au début, mais j'aime aussi les lumières. Je suis partagée entre les deux et je sais que ca va durer toujours' ... sa voix se brisa" (57). Indigeneity is essentialized here to represent the opposite of the civilized and modern European; Native peoples seem incapable of adapting; they are portrayed as capable of thriving only in nature—without modern conveniences such as electricity. As Weaver points out, however, "Natives showed themselves adept at adopting and adapting anything that seemed to be useful or to have power ... each new item, tool, or technology was used to strengthen, not weaken, their people" (29).[7] This essentialism is also reflected in a 1999 essay on the novel by Roger Hyman, published in the *Journal of Canadian Studies*. Like *Volkswagen Blues,* Hyman seems to lament the disappearance of Native culture. In the novel, Poulin reveals La Grande Sauterelle's Innu name; he writes, "Pitsémine était le nom de la Grande Sauterelle en langue Innue" (42). Hyman states, however, that "though she is Metis, neither of her names, 'La Grande Sauterelle,' because of her long legs, or 'Pitsémine,' suggests her Innu background" (2). He seems reluctant to recognize adaptive and contemporary Indigenous societies, and further comments that "she has lost 2 of the key signs of her tribal inheritance, oral transmission of knowledge and her language" (3). In fact, Pitsémine does seem to have knowledge of native languages, and Jack comments on her capable pronunciation: "'Michillimakinac!' ... Elle le prononçait en faisant sonner toutes les voyelles et en faisant claquer la dernière syllabe comme un coup d'aviron à plat dans l'eau" (56). Hyman is quite right to signal the fact that the loss of Aboriginal languages has had a huge and negative impact on Native communities, but he does not acknowledge the fact that Indigenous cultures continue to survive and adapt in spite of this. Among many others, Cree scholar Emma LaRocque believes that English has become a Native language, since it has been used by Indigenous peoples for centuries and has been modified to suit their needs (xxvi). The same can be said of French for Native peoples in Quebec. I would also argue that Pitsémine's extensive knowledge of Indigenous culture, as well as her voracious appetite for literature and storytelling, demonstrate that, far from losing her oral culture, she is eager to keep it alive. The portrayal of print culture as foreign or not a part of Native cultures is an essentialization of Indigenous experience. Creek-Cherokee scholar Craig Womack writes, "One might even argue that some Native people versed in orality might be predisposed to novel writing or the reading of them rather than alienated by them. This seems to be the case, at the very least, for a number of American Indian authors" (119). It also seems to be the case for Pitsémine, who is constantly visiting libraries and bookstores, reading, and telling stories. A romanticized notion of what is authentic, Womack adds, "locks Native Studies [and Native people, too,] into a system that does not allow the discipline [or the people themselves] to evolve; it is the way in which we have inherited the vanishing mentality" (145).

With no access to living Native culture, Pitsémine, in spite of her desire to keep her culture alive, has no choice but to view herself as a hybrid. This is why she chooses to stay in the melting pot that is San Francisco instead of returning home: "Elle voulait rester un certain temps à San Francisco: elle pensait que cette ville, où les races semblaient vivre en harmonie, était un bon endroit pour essayer de faire l'unité et de se réconcilier avec elle-même" (287). In San Francisco, Pitsémine is no longer looked upon as Indigenous; she is ultimately identified as just another hybrid—a part of just another ethnic group. Immigrant and ethnic groups are certainly deserving of recognition, but their situation is altogether different from that of Aboriginal peoples. Pitsémine is likened, near the end of the novel, to a Chinese-Mexican-American clerk in a bookstore: "La bibliothécaire était une fille grande et maigre avec de longs cheveux noirs. Elle ressemblait curieusement à la Grande Sauterelle, sauf que ses traits étaient à demi chinois et à demi mexicains" (259). This woman is somehow moving for Jack and Pitsémine—presumably because she, like la Grande Sauterelle, represents the face of the future. There is one significant difference between the two that Poulin fails to signal, however. Pitsémine, far from being just another member of a hybrid, multicultural mosaic, undeniably identifies herself as Native; and Poulin, describing her black hair in braids, bare feet, and hunting knife, clearly presents her as such. In spite of ostensibly good intentions—and a discussion of the devastating effects of colonialism—the author's portrayal of Pitsémine as representative of a generic hybridity denies recognition of Aboriginal nationhood and promotes, instead, a model of assimilation. This move is demonstrated by the author's decision to leave Pitsémine in San Francisco. The author's portrayal of Pitsémine is, as we have seen, contradictory. He uses all the stereotypes of aboriginality to describe her; thus, he foregrounds her Native identity only to erase it later on; he removes her agency by leaving her in San Francisco with all the other hybrids. The categorization of Native people as one of the country's many "ethnic groups" is extremely damaging, since their situation and political status as first inhabitants of the land are altogether different from those of new immigrant groups. As Justice writes, "Indigenousness is *not* ethnic difference; it is both cultural and political distinctiveness, defined by land-based genealogical connections and obligations to human and nonhuman bonds of kinship"

(146). Denying Native communities First Peoples status suggests that they have no claim to their lands, history, memory, cultural continuity, or to their rights as original inhabitants of the land.

It is, therefore, essential to signal just to what extent *Volkswagen Blues* is a vehicle for the author rather than a representation of Native people. While it is true that this story is written from the perspective of a white Quebecker—and is therefore representative of a non-Native perspective—the representation of Aboriginal peoples by a non-Native author can, as we have seen, perpetuate damaging stereotypes. It is important to problematize the continuing domination of portrayals of Indigeneity by non-Aboriginals and to read such portrayals critically in order to deconstruct representations of Native experience that don't accurately reflect Indigenous world views. In *Volkswagen Blues,* contrary to many narratives authored by both full and mixed-blood Native peoples, Poulin's work takes Pitsémine *away* from home rather than toward it; there is, in fact, no other option for her since there is never any allusion made to a Native community she might return to. There is a long and very significant Aboriginal literary tradition of Indigenous peoples returning home with the goal of rebuilding community, however difficult this proves to be.[8] It is important that Poulin's work be read critically in this context since his description of Pitsémine's actions contradicts the portrayal of Indigenous experience by both Aboriginal and Metis authors. There is always the risk that books such as *Volkswagen Blues*—much more publicized and accessible than Native-authored works—might become the only portrayals of Aboriginal experience to which most non-Natives are exposed, leading to the perpetuation of the dangerous stereotypes and misconceptions we have seen. Speaking of her peoples' tendency to return to community, Abenaki scholar Lisa Brooks writes, "When calamity hits, families may disperse, but they never 'disappear.' Always, they end up gathering together when the storms clear" (229). This tendency in Native writing demonstrates an awareness on the part of the authors of the importance of community in the survival and continuing evolution of a people; it is a phenomenon recognized and referred to by both Native and non-Native critics of Aboriginal literature as a "homing narrative." William Bevis, in his essay, "Native American Novels: Homing In," uses the term "homing plot" to describe the traditional homeward movement of Native protagonists in narratives by Indigenous writers. Pitsémine's decision, in *Volkswagen Blues,* to remain in San Francisco rather than returning to her community can be misleading in this regard since it suggests that there is no community for her to return to and thus confirms the myth of the dead and dying Indian. There is also the implication, earlier in the book, that Pitsémine, because of her mixed blood, is rejected not only by the white community but also by her Native community. Poulin writes that "sa mere, en épousant un Blanc, avait perdu la maison qu'elle possédait sur la réserve de La Roumaine; elle avait été expulsée et elle avait perdu son statut d'Indienne. Mais les Blancs, de leur côté, la considéraient toujours comme une indienne et ils avaient refusé de louer ou de vendre une maison aux nouveaux mariés" (99). "De leur côté" here suggests that Native people were also hostile toward the couple when, in fact, it was the government's Indian Act that removed the status of any Native woman marrying a non-Native and was ultimately responsible for the mother's alienation. If anything, this government clause made Native women all the more determined to return to their communities, and many did return after it was reversed with Bill C-31. Aboriginal women themselves, along with the Native Women's Association of Canada, were instrumental in the creation of the bill.

As was the case with the Indian Act, the label "hybrid" threatens to erase Native identity altogether, completing the process of colonization. Interestingly, Pitsémine signals this erasure directly when she tells Jack that she is nothing: "Son sourire, toutefois, s'évanouit presque aussitôt et elle recommença à dire qu'elle n'était ni une Indienne ni une Blanche, qu'elle était quelque chose entre les deux et que, finalement, elle n'était rien du tout" (224). It is at this point, as we have seen, that Jack eliminates the Native completely by telling her that she is "something new" in an attempt to give her hope. Shortly after this, she gives in to the myth of the dead Indian, accepting elimination when she says, "C'était le destin ou quelque chose du genre" (257). Up to this point, it could be argued that these events are critical of hybridity—until La Grande Sauterelle announces how happy she is in San Francisco. "'Je me sens bien,'" she tells Jack. "'Ça fait longtemps que je ne me sens pas aussi bien'" (261). No longer an Aboriginal Metis but now a generic hybrid, Pitsémine is the archetype of the new Quebecker, signalling new hope for the province in a move away from a pure laine culture toward an open, progressive society where no one is marginalized and everyone is equal. As Pierre L'Hérault points out, division and conflict, represented at the beginning of the novel by two separate maps of Canada (one Native, the other non-Native), are in the past; the present unifies: "Du point de vue des rapports entre les personnages, on peut donc distinguer très clairement le passé qui les isole du présent qui les unit" (31). Where once Canada was divided into Native and non-Native maps of the country, now there is only one map in Jack and Pitsémine, the travelling pair. To say that this is unity, however, is false since, as we have seen, Indigeneity is ultimately removed. It would be a more accurate unity to promote a dialogue between two distinct individuals or nations, rather than combine them in one generic whole.

The discussion here is political for, as Justice argues, "to be a member of an Indigenous nation in a colonized country is a political act in itself, as the existence of such a collective is an embodied denial of the power of the State to claim either historical or moral inheritance of the land or its memories" (146). Replacing the Native with the hybrid amounts, therefore, to assimilation, and a failure to discuss these politics in *Volkswagen Blues* only perpetuates erasure. Saying we're all the same allows us to ignore imbalances of power—saying we're different allows us to address them. There is no doubt that cultures, particularly those that live side by side, influence each other profoundly, and this influence is even more pronounced in an age of globalization. The very persistence of Native cultures in such an era, however, is testament to their endurance. Hybridity, as Weaver explains, does not necessitate a loss of culture: "Native cultures have always been highly adaptive, and they continue to evolve constantly. To acknowledge the truth of hybridity, however, does not mean that we are globally merging into a single McCulture" (28). In *Volkswagen Blues,* however, the hybridity promoted for Pitsémine is a generic one since the Native side of her identity is ultimately lost in the melting pot of San Francisco; there she identifies more with a Chinese-Mexican-American bookstore clerk than with either the French-Canadian or Indigenous cultures she comes from. In order to survive, cultures must be able to adapt, and there is no reason not to acknowledge more than one cultural influence, or one influence in particular. This was arguably, after all, the goal of both the postmodern and postcolonial movements. Tired of being referred to as hybrids, many Native people have chosen to assert their Native status. Algonquin writer Bernard Assiniwi is just one example of this, and the force of his assertion of his Algonquin-Cree identity is evident from the title of his article, "Je suis ce que je dis que je suis."

Womack asks of the postmodern and postcolonial movements, "What happened to the promise, when we first started hearing all about hybridity, that this kind of theory was going to liberate us, free us from the dominance of master narratives? It seems like the freedom train pulled out of the station with no Indians on board" (168). Twenty-five years ago, Poulin undertook to demonstrate to what degree the continent was constructed on violence, and he produced a successful and popular work that continues to attract readers. A work so greatly admired clearly reaches many, and so to abandon its study is certainly not the answer—it is an artful assembly of postmodern intertexts and a telling portrait of the period it describes. What should be made clear, however, is the degree to which it is a product of its times and not a model for the future. Both the postmodern and postcolonial movements have served their purposes and have uncovered injustices and imbalances, but Indigenous cultures in Quebec and Canada are far from dying or dead, and concrete change is something that requires expression in culture and in literature. The best approach might be precisely the one Duceppe suggested in his apology to residential school survivors: nation to nation dialogue, characterized by respect.

Notes

1. For a discussion of the effects of changing demographics in Quebec, see Gérard Bouchard's "Pour une nation Québécoise."

2. See Robert Berkhofer, Thomas King, Daniel Francis and Philip Deloria for descriptions of stereotypes of Native peoples perpetuated by non-Natives.

3. See Janet Paterson's essay "Métissage et alterité" for an examination of gender in *Volkswagen Blues.*

4. For more information on Quebec-Native relations, see *Autochtones et Québécois: La rencontre des nationalismes,* ed. Pierre Trudel.

5. Appropriation of voice is a very complex and contentious issue in Canada and was the subject of considerable debate in the pages of Toronto's *Globe and Mail* newspaper in 1990. For an excellent examination of the issues involved, see Bruce Ziff and Pratima Rao's collection of essays, entitled *Borrowed Power.*

6. Artist Joane Cardinal-Schubert cites the example of nameless Native artists whose works are displayed under the banner "Native Art" rather than under the artist or collective's names. She writes, "As art that is viewed as primitive, we are dead makers of a dead art. As such, we are vulnerable to appropriation and vast pillaging by the dominant culture" (128). The myth of the dead and dying Indian is well established and has been examined by many writers. See Philip Deloria's *Indians in Unexpected Places* and *Playing Indian.* See also Daniel Francis's *The Imaginary Indian,* Pearce's *Savagism and Civilisation,* Robert Berkhofer's *The White Man's Indian,* Ward Churchill's controversial *Fantasies of the Master Race,* Thomas King's *The Native in Literature,* and Chrystos's poetry collection *Not Vanishing.*

7. Photographer Edward S. Curtis, famous for his portraits of Native peoples, actually removed all traces of modernity in his pictures. In his famous 1910 photogravure "Peigan Lodge," Curtis erased a clock from between the two men posing in order to portray them as "authentic."

8. This is the case in such works as Jeannette Armstrong's *Slash,* Laure Bouvier's *Une Histoire de Métisses,* Linda Hogan's *Solar Storms,* Lee Maracle's short story "Charlie," Armand Ruffo's "Homeward," N. Scott Momaday's *House Made of Dawn,* Sherman Alexie's *The Toughest Indian in the World,* Richard Van Camp's "Year of the Dog," Brian Maracle's *Back on the Rez: Finding the Way Home,* Tomson Highway's "The Rez Sisters," and Richard Wagamese's *Keeper 'n Me,* to name but a few.

Works Cited

Alexie, Sherman. "The Toughest Indian in the World." *The Toughest Indian in the World.* New York: Atlantic Monthly, 2000. 21-34.

Armstrong, Jeannette. *Slash.* Penticton: Theytus, 1988.

Assiniwi, Bernard. "Je suis ce que je dis que je suis." *Le Renouveau de la parole identitaire.* Ed. Mireille Calle-Gruber and Jeanne-Marie Clerc. Université Paul Valéry, Montpellier/Queen's University, Kingston: Centre d'Études littéraires françaises du XXe siècle, Groupe de recherche sur les expressions françaises, cahier 2 (1993): 101-06.

Berkhofer, Robert F. *The White Man's Indian.* New York: Knopf, 1978.

Bevis, William. "Native American Novels: Homing In." *Recovering the Word.* Ed. Brian Swann and Arnold Krupat. Berkeley: U of California P, 1987. 580-620.

Bouchard, Gérard. "Pour une nation Québécoise." *La Nation Québécoise au futur et au passé.* Montréal: VLB Editeur, 1999. 11-80.

Bouvier, Laure. *Une Histoire de Métisses.* Montréal: Leméac, 1995.

Brooks, Lisa. "At the Gathering Place." Weaver, Womack, and Warrior 225-52.

Cardinal-Schubert, Joanne. "In the Red." Ziff and Rao 122-33.

Cayouette, Pierre. "20 livres pour comprendre le Québec d'aujourd'hui." *L'Actualité* 15 décembre 2005: 174.

Chrystos. *Not Vanishing.* Vancouver: Press Gang, 1988.

Churchill, Ward. *Fantasies of the Master Race.* San Francisco: City Lights, 1998.

Deloria, Philip J. *Indians in Unexpected Places.* Kansas: UP of Kansas, 2004.

———. *Playing Indian.* New Haven: Yale UP, 1998.

Dorsinville, Max. "I Lost My Art in San Francisco." *Essays in Canadian Writing* 40 (1990): 40-4.

Francis, Daniel. *The Imaginary Indian.* Vancouver: Arsenal Pulp, 1992.

Goldie, Terry. "Transcontinental." *Books in Canada* 18.6 (1988): 29.

Harel, Simon. "L'Amérique ossuaire." *Le Voleur du parcours.* Montréal: Éditions du Préambule, 1989. 159-207.

Hébert, François. "Deux maîtres livres, issus de l'humour du cœur." *Le Devoir* 12 mai 1984: 25.

Highway, Tomson. *The Rez Sisters.* Saskatoon: Fifth House, 1988.

Hogan, Linda. *Solar Storms.* New York: Scribner, 1995.

Hyman, Roger. "Writing against Knowing, Writing against Certainty; or, What's Really under the Veranda in Jacques Poulin's *Volkswagen Blues." Journal of Canadian Studies* 34.3 (1999): 106-33.

Justice, Daniel. "The Necessity of Nationhood: Affirming the Sovereignty of Indigenous National Literatures." *Moveable Margins: The Shifting Spaces of Canadian Literature.* Ed. Chelva Kanaganayakam. Toronto: TSAR, 2005. 143-56.

King, Thomas, Cheryl Calver, and Helen Hoy, eds. *The Native in Literature: Canadian and Comparative Perspectives.* Toronto: ECW, 1987.

LaRocque, Emma. "Preface, or Here Are Our Voices—Who Will Hear?" *Writing the Circle: Native Women of Western Canada.* Ed. Jeanne Perreault and Sylvia Vance. Edmonton: NeWest, 1990. xv-xxx.

Ledger, Brent. "Poulin's Witty Trek: Quebec's Search for an American Home." *Quill & Quire.* 54.6: 26.

L'Hérault, Pierre. "*Volkswagen Blues*: Traverser les identités." *Voix & images* 43 (1989): 28-42.

Maracle, Brian. *Back on the Rez: Finding the Way Home.* Toronto: Penguin, 1997.

Maracle, Lee. "Charlie." *Sojourner's Truth.* Vancouver: Press Gang, 1990. 99-107.

Martel, Réginald. "Jacques Poulin et Marie-Claire Blais—L'Amérique entre rêve et violence." *La Presse* 12 mai 1984: D-3.

Momaday, N. Scott. *House Made of Dawn.* New York: Harper, 1977.

Paterson, Janet. "Metissage et altérité: *Volkswagen blues* et *La Petite fille qui aimait trop les allumettes.*" *Figures de l'autre dans le roman québécois.* Québec: Editions Nota bene, 2004. 105-36.

Pearce, Roy Harvey. *Savagism and Civilisation.* Baltimore: Johns Hopkins UP, 1967.

Poulin, Jacques. *Volkswagen Blues.* Montréal: Editions; Québec/Amérique, 1984.

Ruffo, Armand Garnet. "Homeward." *Outcrops.* Ed. Laurence Steven. Sudbury: Scrivener, 2005.

Trudel, Pierre, ed. *Autochtones et Québécois: La rencontre des nationalismes.* Montréal: Recherches amérindiennes au Québec, 1995.

Van Camp, Richard. "Year of the Dog." *Without Reservation: Indigenous Erotica.* Ed. Kateri Akiwenzie-Damm. Wiarton: Kegedonce, 2003. 170-99.

Vautier, Marie. "Postmodern Myth, Post-European History, and the Figure of the Amerindian: François Barcelo, George Bowering, and Jacques Poulin." *Canadian Literature* 141 (1994): 15-37.

Wagamese, Richard. *Keeper 'n Me.* Toronto: Doubleday, 1994.

Warrior, Robert. "Native Critics in the World." Weaver, Womack, and Warrior 179-224.

Weaver, Jace, Craig Womack, and Robert Warrior, eds. *American Indian Literary Nationalism.* Albuquerque: U of New Mexico P, 2006.

———. "Splitting the Earth." Weaver, Womack, and Warrior 1-90.

Womack, Craig. "The Integrity of American Indian Claims." Weaver, Womack, and Warrior 91-178.

Ziff, Bruce, and Pratima V. Rao, eds. *Borrowed Power.* New Brunswick: Rutgers UP, 1997.

Steven G. Kellman (review date 2009)

SOURCE: Kellman, Steven G. "Translation's Trail." Rev. of *Translation Is a Love Affair,* by Jacques Poulin. *American Book Review* 30.6 (2009): 17. Print.

[*In the following review, Kellman provides a generally negative assessment of Poulin's* Translation Is a Love Affair, *criticizing the author's "terse, limpid clauses" and finding the novel's romantic relationship "noticeably lacking in tension, anguish, and ecstasy."*]

If, as the Italian adage claims, *traduttore traditore,* translators might want to conceal their treachery. The owner's manual to a Toyota Prius or a Toshiba laptop does not identify the persons responsible for transposing turgid Japanese into turgid English. Even when title pages disclose the name of the translator, many translations aspire to invisibility, trying to lull readers into believing they are turning pages of the original text.

Not so *Translation Is a Love Affair,* whose very title puts the process of switching languages into question. Itself a translation of Jacques Poulin's 2006 novel *La traduction est une histoire d'amour,* it is a tender allegory about the relationship between a Quebecois author and the woman who translates him into English. Early in his career, Poulin, a leading French Canadian novelist, worked as a commercial translator, and he offers a translator, a free-spirited young woman named Marine as narrator of this, his eleventh novel. (His twelfth, not yet published in English, also sports a title that announces language as a theme; *L'Anglais n'est pas une langue magique* (2009) translates as *English Is Not a Magical Language.*) The ventriloquism of using a woman's voice to tell the story is yet another instance of Poulin in translation.

While studying translation at the University of Geneva, Marine acquired a copy of a novel written by a fellow Canadian publishing under the nom de plume Jack Waterman (who also happens to be a character in Poulin's best-known novel, *Volkswagen Blues* [1984]). Because it is about the Oregon Trail, which she had visited while hitchhiking alone across the US, Marine was especially drawn to the book and longed to translate it into English. When she returns to her native Quebec, Marine encounters Waterman in what Hollywood would call "meet cute." Standing before the graves of her mother, sister, and grandmother, she encounters an older man reading Ernest Hemingway on a cemetery bench. It is of course Waterman, and Marine, convinced that "If there was a way to get close to someone in this life—of which I was not certain—it might be through translation," elicits Waterman's permission to translate his Oregon Trail novel into English. He even sets her up to work in an idyllic chalet on Île d'Orléans, while he labors over *les mots justes* in the tower he inhabits in nearby Quebec City.

Lest readers get the wrong impression about the relationship between an elderly, ailing writer and the perky translator who imagines him as the father she never knew, Marine assures us: "The business of sex doesn't concern Monsieur Waterman and me." What do concern them are the delicacies of verbal expression and the construction of what Marine, a damaged, lonely soul, calls "the old house of language, midway between earth and heaven." Midway also between author and translator, it is "a place, a domain, a universe in which I was safe from the woes of this world, in which there was a possibility that Monsieur Waterman and I, in spite of our age difference, had the possibility of meeting."

As if translating, like acting, demanded surrender of personal identity and appropriation of another's, Marine wears the author's clothes while reworking his prose. Both agree that finding the precise words is not as crucial as getting the tone right. In translating, Marine insists, "We must *embrace* the author's style." She reinforces her view of translation as erotic exchange by recalling the title of a course she took at the University of Geneva, "Translation is a Love Affair," and quoting an apocryphal statement by Franz Kafka's translator, Milena Jesenská: "'Every day, to keep me faithful to your text, my words hug the curves of your writing, like a lover nestling in her sweetheart's arms.'" Yet the love affair that constitutes the substance of this novel is not only remarkably chaste; it occupies the borderland between the gentle and the bland.

We are told that a bad back, a heart condition, and literary perfectionism keep Waterman from writing more than a few sentences at a time. But in his dealings with Marine, he is invariably patient and compassionate. And, though she is haunted by her sister's suicide and the hardships of her Irish immigrant grandmother, Marine fits snugly into her new situation on the Île d'Orléans. If translation is a love affair, this one is noticeably lacking in tension, anguish, and ecstasy. Whatever drama the novel possesses is supplied by a shaggy cat story—how Marine and Waterman combine forces to solve the mystery of an abandoned feline named Famine. Attached to the cat, Marine discovers, is a plea for help from an adolescent damsel in distress. The plot devolves into a kind of Nancy Drew caper, and Poulin concludes his novel with a sentimental affirmation of the power of love.

If the Hemingway short stories, which Waterman is reading when Marine meets him in the cemetery, are the model for Poulin's terse, limpid clauses, John Irving, whom Marine invokes at one point, seems closer in spirit to this winsome but irksome work. Sheila Fischman is an accomplished translator of more than 125 French Canadian novels and is, like Poulin, a septuagenarian. Her seamless English version of his mellow fantasy creates the refuge that Marine calls the best definition of a novel: "'Small structure high in the mountains where climbers can spend the night.'" Yet how much larger would have been the structure, how many more nights it might have accommodated climbers, if only Jorge Luis Borges, Italo Calvino, or Vladimir Nabokov had taken on the premise of *Translation Is a Love Affair.*

Edith Biegler Vandervoort (essay date 2011)

SOURCE: Vandervoort, Edith Biegler. "Subverting the Masculine Image in Jacques Godbout's *Salut Galarneau!* and Jacques Poulin's *Volkswagen Blues.*" *Masculinities in Twentieth- and Twenty-First Century French and Francophone Literature.* Ed. Vandervoort. Newcastle upon Tyne: Cambridge Scholars, 2011. 305-24. Print.

[*In the following essay, Vandervoort discusses the portrayal of male characters in* Volkswagen Blues *and Godbout's novel* Hail Galarneau! *(1967). She suggests that both works subvert traditional conceptions of masculinity in ways that reflect the changes in social mores since the Quiet Revolution.*]

The way in which the male characters are depicted in novels written since the Quiet Revolution contrasts sharply with masculine depictions in earlier novels of the twentieth century. In early novels such as *Marie Chapdelaine* (published in 1916) or *Menaud, maître-draveur* (published in 1937), the male character plays an authoritative role in the family and he is the head of household. It is his responsibility to ensure that the family survives and he must work hard and make intelligent decisions so that he is respected by his family and the community. In novels of the 1950s and 1960s, this trend continues. Novels such as *Les temps des hommes* and *La bagarre* (both published in 1958) depict men who work hard and uphold patriarchal traditions as the dominant member of the family, in which it is the male member of the relationship who must support and protect the female member who is unable to earn enough money to support herself. As is often the case in the novels of this period, the women of the family have not had the educational and professional opportunities to earn a living. Thus, the wife and children look to the husband and father who proudly exhibit their skills to support the family.

There are several scenarios in this depiction of masculinity: Gabrielle Roy's *Bonheur d'occasion* (published in 1945) reveals men who are willing to work and support a family, but are unable to do so because of harsh economic conditions. The brave French-Canadian lumberjack or trapper represented in older novels is humiliated in Roch Carrier's novel, *La guerre, yes sir* (published in 1968). In this work, the author portrays Quebec's citizens forced to fight for the British army in World War II, but without the honor normally accorded to soldiers for their bravery and courage. These exceptions aside, however, the *roman de la terre* presents the father as the head of the household, who takes an authoritarian role in making decisions for the family. This genre provides the template for the Quebec man.

This trend begins to change around the late 1960s, or after the advent of the Quiet Revolution. Several novels describe men who no longer have the ambition to prepare themselves for the responsibilities they previously accepted and they readily relinquish them to women, who become increasingly better educated and competent. Such novels reveal men who are passive and uncertain of themselves and their roles in the family or society and their behavior even begins to blur the boundaries between genders. Two novels representing the changing role of men in French-Canadian society are Jacques Godbout's *Salut Galarneau!* and Jacques Poulin's **Volkswagen Blues**. In both of these novels, the male protagonists reflect the ways in which literary representations of men have changed since the early twentieth century, especially in the way in which they relate to other men and women.

Jacques Godbout's prize-winning novel, *Salut Galarneau!* is about François Galarneau and his reflections about his life, his occupation as the owner of a mobile hot dog stand and his desire to write. Published in 1967, the novel won the *prix du Gouverneur général.* Seen as a turning point in Godbout's style of writing, it is "une sculpture à laquelle on n'a plus le droit de toucher" and a work which Yvon Bellemare correctly evaluates as "une des belle réussites de la littérature québécoise des années soixante" (796). Indeed, François Galarneau's character, with all its weaknesses and shortcomings, is endearing and leaves the reader wanting to know what happens to him and the other characters long after the novel has ended. Fortunately, there is a sequence, *Le temps des Galarneau,* published by Seuil in 1993. *Salut Garlaneau!* is a humorous, but at times melancholy novel and is especially amusing to American readers because of the references to American culture, the many Anglicisms the author employs, as well as the French language one would only hear in Quebec. It is the first Godbout novel, in which the narrator has a real name, much less one which is typically *québécois,* an element which can particularly be interpreted as political (Bellemare 796). Another typically French-Canadian feature is that the city of Lowell in Massachusetts, where his mother lives, is in an area to which many of Quebec's citizens moved to work in the textile mills (Lemire xiv-xv).

In addition to language, the narrator evokes other elements typical of Quebec at the onset of his writing. For instance,

when he takes inventory of his soul, he mentions things which are characteristic of life in Canada and Quebec, such as "des décalques de Batman ... des saint-christophe aimantés à placer sur un dash ... des mouches artificielles pour la pêche, des rêves grands comme l'océan ..." (59). Although François discusses the failed war in Vietnam, the abusive regime in the Congo and the hostilities against those representing the Civil Rights movement in San Francisco, he does not speak about these political problems at length, nor does he have the mental awareness of a political activist. The only nationalist remark he makes is that he would like to improve Quebec's economy through commerce, as René Lévèsque, the Premier of Canada, has suggested in the media, by opening a chain of hot dog stands. The location of the novel does not serve to make a political statement, either (Smith 8). As André Smith argues, "le fait que *Salut Galarneau!* se déroule à île Perrot, à Montréal et à Lévis ne le transforme en hymne national" (8). In essence, this novel has little to do with political engagement and Quebec's movement towards sovereignty, as is the case in his novels *l'Aquarium* and *D'Amour P.Q.* (Smith 5). It is about François's desire to write and his failed relationships with women.

François's family plays an important role in his life, so much so that he often evokes the name of Galarneau, speaks at length about his ancestors and wants to become an ethnographer. His mother is present throughout his childhood, but she spends her days sleeping and her nights eating Black Magic chocolates and reading trashy Italian novels. Michael Klementowicz points out that he condemns his mother's lifestyle and that he feels abandoned and estranged from his mother throughout the novel (89). Indeed, she neglects her children and does not even remember to send them a Christmas card when she is away from them. It is the company of his brothers which provides François with his fondest memories. His childhood memories are falsely nostalgic, for his mother and father have no real relationship and it was François's grandfather Aldéric who financially supported the boys, because the father is irresponsible.

From the onset of the novel, François expresses interest in writing and is increasingly driven by the urge to write, but when he meets Marise, who wants him to be more ambitious, he is forced to think more seriously about completing a book. At the prospect of beginning this project, he shows signs of stress: he develops a fever and becomes mentally unstable, he becomes increasingly aggressive towards Marise, who is then tempted to accept advances from Jacques, for whom she eventually leaves François. Since childhood, François has admired Jacques, who is four years older and left Quebec to study in Paris. Often he wrote François about his life in Paris, his philosophical and educational development and his many girlfriends. Jacques has a domineering influence in François's life, offers to correct François's writing and both he and Marise give François advice. Marise, who, according to François, would like him to be "un écrivain avec une fossette en plein milieu du menton," believes he should write a detective novel "avec des hommes fatals, des femmes vénales, des chalets abondonnés piqués sur des rochers au bord de la mer, des histoires de collier" (57). Her idea of writing is to imitate and her literary ideas come from trivial novels and television magazines. Jacques, for his part, writes for Radio Canada and hides behind a pen name. Although he would like to write a serious novel some day, he cannot give up his materialistic lifestyle, which involves buying a new car every year. As a commercial writer, he gives his brother advice: "Tout ce que tu devrais écrire, c'est ce qui te tiens à cœur, pense pas à ceux qui vont te lire, il y a des gens qui comprendront" (58). This statement is ironic, for one cannot express what is in one's heart if one is thinking of the audience, but Jacques believes that he, who is experienced, is in a position to give such advice. Jacques also believes he must act as François's second father and treats him as one would treat a child, but the way in which he lures Marise from François indicates that he does not respect François. When the three of them go out together, Jacques tries to touch her breasts during their dinner. After dinner they all go to the cinema and in the dark, during the film, Marise, who has evidently anticipated Jacques's advances by wearing a sexy dress, tries to kiss him. François is aware of their flirtations, but decides to drown his disappointment in alcohol.

François has a weak and passive personality. He not only allows his male family members to dominate him, but also others. For instance, when he discovers his first wife Louise is pregnant, he accepts his responsibility, marries her and moves to Lévis. He does not realize, however, how much this entails also becoming a part of her family, the Gagnons, which involves buying a piece of land with a small fast-food restaurant. According to him, "[q]uand on épouse une Gagnon, c'est la tribu qui dirige!" (100). When François realizes that Louise is not pregnant, he must consult Aldéric for advice and he eventually leaves Louise. But on the trip back, he seems ambivalent about returning to Aldéric and his brothers again. He disembarks in Montreal and, in strolling through the city, buys a bus ticket to visit his mother, but he misses the bus. At this time, he fantasizes about meeting a captain of a ship to New Caledonia, who accepts him as "le marin qui manquait à notre équipage" or being hired as a trumpet player in a bar, because he tells the owner, "j'ai vécu déjà, et j'y mets toute cette souffrance, toute mon âme, when I blow, quand je joue ce n'est plus de la musique qui s'échappe du cuivre, c'est l'essence même du son ..." (105, 106). These excerpts reveal how much of a fantasy abandoning his family in Sainte-Anne is, for he depends on them too much to do so. François rarely has the courage to act alone and even his studies were forced on him. He attends the university while his father is alive, but abandons his studies on the day of his father's funeral to open the hot dog stand. For François, the day marks a change in his life, for

his mother leaves the family shortly thereafter to live with her sister in Lowell. He remarks: "Je suis entré à l'église derrière le cercueil avec un peu de pêche aux joues. Au sortir de la cérémonie, j'avais une moustache" (21). His immature attitude about his future contrasts with his brothers' ambitions: Arthur studies at the seminary in Sainte-Thérèse in France and Jacques in Paris.

François discovers that Marise has a car accident and, after making a great effort to find her in the hospital, he discovers that Jacques has already taken her home. Instead of confronting Jacques, François avoids his friends and family members and secretly commissions the building of a bunker, in which he secludes himself with limited food without notifying anyone. It is here that he commits himself to writing his book in isolation.

To be sure, François experiences an intimacy with his grandfather, his father and his brothers which is far stronger than what he feels for his former wife Louise, his girlfriend Marise and his mother. Toward these women he has thoughts which are misogynist and, because he often fantasizes about their demise, it appears that a positive relationship with women is impossible (Klementowicz 86). He wavers between the desire to love them and annihilate them and he is resentful toward the women he believes have caused him to suffer. Klementowicz writes that there are several passages in the novel, in which it is apparent that François does not view women as equals, for "he likes women for their company, their love, but regards them as inferior to men as people. He is looking for a woman who is pretty and liberated, but not too liberated. He sees women as possessions—they are a source of diversion" (Klementowicz 86). Indeed, François's opinions of women are influenced not only by his male family members, but also by society. François's father virtually ignores his wife and, instead of working, spends his time on his boat, drinks all day and pursues the affections of other women. The superficial Jacques uses his wealth to seduce women and, when he and François first meet Marise and her friend at a bar, it is clear that Jacques only wants a brief one-night stand. François's other brother, Arthur, is a priest and has nothing to do with women. The other men, with whom François comes into contact at the Canada Hotel, also speak of women as objects. On one occasion they joke about trading women in black jack games.

From François's narrative, it is apparent that he prefers the company of men and he often speaks about his childhood memories growing up with his brothers, Aldéric and his father. As a child, the brothers' sleeping arrangements reflect the close contact and shared experiences they had with each other:

> Nous couchions tous les trois dans la même chambre, les lits prenaient toute la place, il fallait se glisser entre eux comme dans un banc d'église. C'était plus un dortoir qu'une chambre, c'était un hôtel, une arène de boxe, un terrain d'aviation sur lequel on s'écrasait comme des

cf-104 en perdition. Le soir venu, maman au salon, la lumière fermée, nous lisions en cachette sous les draps avec des lampes de poche volées, piquées, raflées chez Handy Handy, à Cartierville, le samedi matin, quand Aldéric nous faisait faire un tour.

(89-90)

Despite the dysfunctional relationship of their parents, the three boys have a happy childhood and close relationship. François fondly remembers activities, such as boxing and aviation, which are typical interests of boys and men. Secretive reading in bed under the covers and trips to Cartierville with Aldéric and their illegal activities there increase their bonds as men and brothers. Indeed, these bonds between men are often created by activities used to define patriarchy, for they are formed by men, promote the interests of men and are "relations with men which have a material base, and which, though hierarchical, establish or create interdependence and solidarity among men that enable them to dominate women" (Hartman qtd. in Sedgewick 697). This display of affection between men should not be confused with homosexual love, for these bonds, which are instead homosocial, do not exclude hatred and fear of homosexuality (Sedgewick 696-98). As Eve Kosofsky Sedgwick argues, in homosocial relationships there is a continuum which exists between "men-loving-men and men-promoting-the-interests-of-men ..." which further strengthens the economic and social impact of patriarchy (698).

Examples of strong homosocial bonds between these men are seen in many instances in this novel. Despite his dependence on his brothers and Aldéric and their interference in his life, which he resents, he loves them. Furthermore, he has serious misgivings about trusting women. In an extensive essay about Jacques's relationship with his parents, Smith correctly argues that his erotic infatuation with his mother, who dresses only in translucent negligees, sleeps during the day and eats only chocolates leads to his inability to love another woman and transforms Louise and Marise into maternal figures (51). For this reason, he does not accord Louise an identity and mistrusts Marise, for he fears she will reject him when he does not show the ambition to become a writer. Marise's plans for him allow him to remember his parents' neglect and abandonment. Smith argues, "[e]nfant qu'on n'a pas voulu, puis adolescent incapable de surmonter le spectacle de l'irresponsabilité paternelle, François reste englué dans la conscience de son indignité" (61). The conflict he experiences between loving his mother and his resentment about her departure after his father's funeral results in descriptions of her, which alternate between adoration and hate. Nevertheless, it is clear that, in the same way that he is loyal to Aldéric, his brothers and his father, he is loyal to her; thus, he is confused by his love for her and he is distressed because of her departure after his father's funeral, when he still needed her. On the other hand, François does not recognize his resentment towards his father and romanticizes his memory. Indeed, his behavior leaves its mark, for he internalizes his father's promiscuity and disloyalty so much that he becomes interested in Marise only when she mentions that she has recently been abandoned by her former lover (Smith 59).

Not only is François prevented from loving other women by his mother, but Aldéric also encourages his mistrust of them. He strongly encourages him to divorce Louise, whom François finds extremely attractive before their marriage. Both Aldéric and Arthur are also suspicious about Louise's motives, but before the marriage, Arthur is especially opposed to their union and contends, "tu vas en province creuse; Lévis c'est au bout des glaces, méfie-toi des filles, ça sort du couvent, tu vas te retrouver un beau matin comme un cave avec un licou d'argent et un abonnement à *l'Anneau d'or,* dont tu ne voudras pas" (99).

Another instance which illustrates the strong bond between the male family members occurs while François is in the bunker. Here he fantasizes of an event with Aldéric, which is an unusual version of a rite of passage or initiation, and involves swimming in the nude through an ice cold lake with him. The imagined event takes place in the middle of the night, when Aldéric arrives to get François from the compound. They ride their bicycles to the lake, remove all their clothes and enter the water. At first, François is confused about their activity and believes it is a duck hunt. As François removes his clothes, he scrapes himself on his bicycle and the wound bleeds. They both swim out to the middle of the lake and back, François noting that Aldéric is extremely energetic and enthusiastic. François is relieved to finally return to the shore, but he is exhausted. Both men share a bottle of brandy and Aldéric tells François that he is now a man because he has survived the initiation. The rite of passage not only functions to mark the end of a boy's childhood and the beginning of his adulthood, it is to identify with other males and their activities, which are distinguishable from those of women, and to create a bond with other males.[1] Indeed, Aldéric, satisfied that François passed the test, states that he wishes his father could have been there to share in the noteworthy event. Aldéric is even pleased that François injured himself on the bicycle and began to bleed, for pain and an injury are parts of this ancient ceremony. The fact that the swim reminds François of a duck hunt is also important, because the passage to manhood involves hunting, an activity reserved for men in cultures where hunting provides the bulk of their food supply. This rite of passage is a very important stage in the initiation of a boy to manhood. Godbout describes this event with irony and humor because Aldéric has gotten the idea from a *Reader's Digest* article. Aldéric's pleasure at seeing François's injury adds to the irony, for it is a bicycle, not a wild beast, which injures him. Aldéric also feels justified in carrying through with this ritual, even though François is already sixteen and Aldéric is not his father. Drinking the large bottle of brandy completes the ceremony, further strengthens the bonds between them and assures that this event will be remembered for a long time. The entire ritual serves to illustrate the importance of the male characters in this novel and their importance in François's family. This rite of passage has another noteworthy aspect: the fact that it involves nudity adds a homoerotic element, which more significantly marks their intimacy in performing this ritual, thereby strengthening their homosocial bonds. In his noteworthy essay, the "Introduction to Guy Hocquengham's *Homosexual Desire*," Jeffrey Weeks states that homosexual desire is more than a sexual act. He writes, "[h]omosexuality expresses something—some aspect of desire—which appears nowhere else, and that something is not merely the accomplishment of the sexual act with a person of the same sex" (693).[2] Indeed, homosexuality, like homosocial desire, involves men loving men and men promoting each others' interests. Thus, nonsexual activities—participating in or watching sporting activities, fighting in battles, hunting and fishing, accomplishing productive or hard work, drinking alcohol—in which men often participate with other men, also lead to deep affection and love between men. The strong feelings resulting from these shared activities, which strengthen homosocial bonds between males, are a form of homosexual love which may or may not have an erotic element. In this novel, most demonstrations of homosocial love are nonsexual. However, because nudity and pain are part of the rite of passage, they not only create intimacy between the participants, but add an erotic element to the event.

After this fantasy with Aldéric, François accepts his break up with Marise, though instead of forgiving her, he wants to seek revenge by having his uncle stuff her with his poems. The male dominated society this novel depicts is not yet mature enough to have a vision that includes all of its members, argues Klementowicz: "The search for identity, whose voice is a supposedly collective *nous,* is in fact a male *nous* that excludes women from the dynamic historical process and which ignores the realities of women during one of the important decades in Quebec's recent history" (90). To be sure, François's attitude toward women is not unusual for the time in which this novel was written.[3] François displaces his anger toward Jacques onto Marise, an anger which is manifested in a violent way several times in this novel. François, to his detriment, is too submissive to confront Jacques about his comportment towards Marise, despite his macho attitude towards women. Nevertheless, even as he wastes away in his compound, he fondly thinks of his brothers. Near a state of delirium, he imagines Jacques and Arthur coming to the compound and coaxing him out of it; Arthur has the hot dog stand refurbished and brings it along to show it to him and they all go to visit their mother. Because his mother explains that his father will return later because he is fishing, this day dream is a nostalgic fantasy and reveals how much François

misses having a nuclear family. For François, the reunion with his family—Aldéric is missing, but is due to arrive on the next day—constructs his idea of happiness. Arthur even brags to their mother that François is writing his book and François tells her of his restaurant. This day dream has such an uplifting effect on him that, on the following day, his birthday, he decides to leave the compound. Thus, it is this fantasy which convinces him to forgive Jacques and indicates that he seeks reconciliation with his mother.

The break-up with Marise marks a turning point for François, but during this time alone in the compound—interrupted by fantasies and bouts of delirium—François finally begins to mature. It is Jacques's and Marise's disloyalty which cause François to isolate himself and finally remove himself from the influence of his brothers and Aldéric which leads to his desire to *vécrire,* a term he coins when he learns that writing and living form an inseparable combination. Thus, he begins to create an identity through writing. Indeed, as Bellamare states "[l]'activité littéraire engendre donc une valorisation qui rend François presque euphorique et le fait miser sur l'avenir, comme le suggèrent les dernières lignes du roman: 'À demain vieille boule, salut Galarneau! Stie'" (797). The end of the novel is optimistic, for he decides to abandon the memory of his past, represented by Louise, and his present, represented by Marise, and begins to move on with his life.

Volkswagen Blues was published fifteen years after Godbout's novel and one year after the first referendum of Quebec's separation from Canada in 1984. It is a complex, but simply written novel about the protagonist, Jack Waterman, and the search for his brother Théo, who has been missing for about twenty years and is thought to live in the United States. Jack travels the route of the explorers and pioneers in an old Volkswagen minibus in search of his brother, taking him and his companion from Gaspé through Quebec, Toronto, Chicago, Saint Louis and Kansas City before arriving in San Francisco. His companion is a young woman of mixed race, Pitsémine, whom he sees at a campground and picks up later on a nearby road. She is part French Canadian and part Montagnais Indian and hails from northern Quebec. The two of them set out not only to find Théo, but to discover America and eventually, their own identities.

Just like François in *Salut Galarneau!* who is limited by his provincial upbringing in a culture and economy which was not only dominated by the English Canadians, but overshadowed by Americans, Jack is restricted by his inability to speak English; therefore, he must piece together Théo's past through information he receives from French speakers he meets. The fact that he is often overheard speaking French to Pitsémine also causes him to meet French speakers haphazardly. Max Dorinville argues that "[s]tress is placed, undoubtedly, on language as the preeminent code girding the real nature of the search for Théo" and imperative is the "unveiling of masks and disguises" (42). These disguises contain within them the deeper meaning of the text. For instance, Pitsémine's and Jack's backgrounds say something about their identities: Pitsémine's as a reflection of Canada's past and Jack's background as a white man who is unaware of the suffering of Native Americans. Pitsémine's extensive reading uncovers the real truth of the historic sites they visit, both those who mark the tragedies of Native American people as well as landmarks indicating the accomplishments of French explorers like Etienne Brûlé, Laclède, Laramée, Louis Jolliet, Père Marquette and LaSalle.

In their travels, they uncover American myths with secretive histories. Among other facts, they learn the truth about Brulé and his shady relationship with Indians. The false myth of blues music as representative of America is also exposed, for the blues attack the linear authority of central musical and social interpretive tradition (Hyman 118). An anticapitalist work which subverts nationalism, a Diego Rivera mural they view in the Detroit Institute of Arts, suggests the danger to the critical awareness of goal-directed behavior (Hyman 118). Indeed, as Roger Hyman points out, Théo himself is Jack's construction and is one of the myths which are included among some of his other external validators, such as Sam Peckinpah, Gary Cooper and John Wayne (124). More importantly, Jack and Théo's childhood heroes—those they imitated in playing cowboys and Indians as children—are characters who have contributed to or have represented the downfall of Pitsémine's people, who not only lost their land and way of life, but whose legacy was erased (Hymen 115). Pitémine laments that these heroes and adventurers cost the indigenous people their blood. She remarks,

> [q]uand vous parlez des découvreurs et des explorateurs de l'Amérique ... Moi, je n'ai rien en commun avec les gens qui sont venus chercher de l'or et des épices et un passage vers L'Orient. Je suis du côté de ceux qui se sont fait voler leurs terres et leur façon de vivre.

(29)

Thus, the "uncovering masks and disguises" and the destruction of myths construct the recasting and subversion of patriarchal authority in this narrative (Dorinville 42).

Other elements, which represent the status quo of a society centering on the authority and importance of men, are also upset in this novel. One of these elements is apparent by Poulin's use of visual elements, or "a memory map" in the novel (Purdy). Anthony Purdy writes, "[a]t the heart of the series are three kinds of objects linked most immediately by a verbal echo: a postcard (or 'carte postale'), two text panels ('pancartes'), and two maps ('cartes geographiques')." Adam Paul Weisman points out that on one of the maps, the border between the United States and Canada are intact, as are the place names and geographic features, but the names of the provinces and states are delineated. This map is noteworthy because, in addition to these mark-

ings, the routes of the explorers are indicated in two languages, French and English: the place names in English, the mountain ranges and pioneering destinations in French. The map is nearly blank, which gives the impression that it was made before the two countries were completely explored. Some place names and geographic features are illogical; as Weisman states,

> it is as if English-speaking settlers left their mark upon the surface of the continent in the form of individual place names, but the continent itself, its mountain ranges (marked 'Rocheuses') for example, is French, as are its pioneering destinations, California and Oregon.

Noteworthy in Weisman's argument is the lack of state and provincial borders because it gives the reader an idea of how the continent looked before the United States and Canada were settled. Indeed, this map may resemble the way in which Native Americans viewed North America, as they would not have indicated borders between states and provinces or even between the United States and Canada. In fact, the omission of names on this map illustrates the lack of property and governmental jurisdiction of the states and provinces, for these regions are named depending on which of the European explorers happened upon them first and have nothing to do with the meaning, which was attributed to them by the indigenous populations. Jean-Pierre Lapointe notes that the myth of the lost paradise, prevalent in many nineteenth-century American novels, is also apparent in this narrative: "au fil du récit se succèdent et se superposent les 'paradis perdus' de l'Amérique autochtone, de l'Eldorado, de l'Amérique française, de la Prairie, de la Californie et autre plaies mal cicatrisées du *grand rêves de l'Amérique*" (17). Lapointe continues by remarking that the liberty and happiness, which should accompany this myth, is impossible to attain in Poulin's novels, for despite the suffering caused by the European explorers, conquerors and settlers, the result, according to Poulin, is a passive expectation of happiness (17).

The blurring of boundaries seen on the map is symbolic of other important delineations in this novel, such as those marked by Pitsémine's mixed race and Jack's background as a French Canadian; both characters represent the shared ancestry of Canadians and the indigenous populations. The author's choice of these characters is especially significant at this point in Quebec's history, when the idea of identity, nationality and origin are debated and at a time when the idea of separation is at the forefront. Poulin's characters not only retrace the path of the American settlers in the United States, but also the history of Quebec, its beginnings as a colony of France, then of England and finally as a province of an independent country. Théo's postcard, on which he rewrites an old text from Jacques Cartier, clearly illustrates this point.

Poulin's choice of characters is also significant because Jack and Pitsémine share a history, as well as an ancestry. It is a history which includes France's abandonment of

Quebec on the Plains of Abraham and French-Canadians' distinction from English-Canadians and Americans. As Weisman writes, "French Canadians … and Indians can both be seen as non-antagonistic residents of the New World, neither of whom is sustained by the colonial connection to Europe." He cites the historian Morisset, who does not argue that Canadians and Indians are the same, "merely that their role in North America after the conquest of 1759 is the same: groups indigenous to the continent who are under programmatic assault by British and American colonialism in North America." Because Jack and Pitsémine share the same heritage as members of a colonized territory and their lives are affected by this history, the fact that many Canadians are *métis* is as prevalent in this novel as the search of identity and origin.

The lack of distinct boundaries of gender roles is also obvious in this novel. Jack is portrayed in sharp contrast to the men who fought Indians and wild animals to protect their land on the prairies and high plains, who starved and froze to death on the Oregon Trail in conquest of a passage to the Pacific Ocean, or who fought in Custer's army at Wounded Knee. In reading this novel, one issue which comes to mind is Jack's masculinity. Jean-Pierre Lapointe writes that most male protagonists in Poulin's novels are not happy and, rather than seeking out their own happiness, await it passively. Like Jack, they are characterized by their dissatisfaction:

> C'est un inquiet, craintif par sentiment d'infériorité et méticuleux par insécurité. Mais il n'est pas malheureux non plus. Sa mélancolie est sereine, résignée, avec parfois plus qu'un soupçon d'ironie. Jamais il ne s'apitoie. Ses moments de tristesse, comme ses joies, sont éphémères.
>
> (17-18)

Indeed, it is clear why Pitsémine finds his company agreeable, for his gentleness, passivity, lack of aggression and his sense of inferiority and sadness are traits often found in women. In portraying a man who is uncertain, retrospective and mild-mannered, Poulin has created a character which subverts patriarchy.

Jack earns his living by writing and, perhaps because of his ambivalent feelings toward his writing, he embarks on the search for his brother, a symbol of his childhood and a dominant force in his past. It is as if he cannot continue to live as an adult and realize himself as a writer until he finds Théo, for he is too strongly linked with a time that was happy. Lapointe correctly argues that he speaks more of his childhood, or the past, than the present:

> dans l'intervalle, le personnage central est resté comme détaché du présent: son étrange passivité, sa douceur terne et mélancolique, son indifférence désabusée, masquent effectivement les souvenirs d'une enfance pourtant plus ardente, laquelle s'éveille à l'occasion en de belles images complexes de l'eau, du feu, de la maison.
>
> (19)

Moreover, he falls in a deep depression because he is having difficulty finding Théo and, because of this memory of Théo, he cannot continue with his own life. He cannot get out of bed and does not eat and it is only with Pitsémine's help that he recovers. It is clear that he believes he loves Théo and mourns because of the difficulty he has finding him. One manifestation of his grief is during a visit to the Art Institute of Chicago. In one of his letters, Théo mentions the museum and the Renoir paintings, because he knows that Jack likes Renoir. Jack goes to see the painting of the woman with the red hat, or the *On the Terrace,* painted in 1881. For three hours, Jack observes the picture, which he increasingly associates with Théo; as Nathalie Dolbec writes: "Théo lui-même est de plus en plus présent, de plus en plus *nommé* dans le tableau" (35). The passage describes the loss he feels for Théo and his disability to distance himself from an object, which represents Théo's presence. As the author describes, "Jack regardait la toile sans dire un mot. Il avait la bouche ouvert, le regard fixe et les yeux mouillés. Il était complètement immobile" (114). Pitsémine comes and goes, visiting other paintings in the museum. When she returns, he is still there: "Toujours immobile sur le banc en face de la femme au chapeau rouge, il grommela péniblement deux ou trois phrases indistinctes auxquelles la fille ne comprit rien à part les mots 'lumière' et 'harmonie' qu'elle parvint à saisir au passage" (114).

Jack has a number of favorite writers, such as Hemingway, Réjean Ducharme, Gabrielle Roy, Salinger, Boris Vian and Brautigan and he has read all of their works, but, in general, he has not read a great variety of literature. His romantic image of a model writer also comes from his youth and he involves his brother in his decision to write by asking him for a pen name. Because he does not keep to the standards of his model writer—whom he envisions as sitting in a bar in old Quebec and waiting for ideas to come to him, which he hastily writes on a paper napkin—he does not value himself very much as a writer. This is most apparent when he and Pitsémine visit the *Libraire Garlaneu* and he questions his ability to write. He tells Pitsémine that he does not believe that his writing is noteworthy. In another instance, when he is asked about what he writes, he is unable to answer the question directly, even though he has written several novels. With regret, Jack undermines his creative abilities in admitting how easy it is to shut oneself up in a room, away from people and events. In a passage describing how his wife left him, he complains, "[i]l y a des gens qui disent que l'écriture est une façon de vivre; moi, je pense que c'est aussi une façon de ne pas vivre" (148). He believes that he has failed as a writer because his books do not change the world, which he believes is requisite. In his lamentation, it is clear that he has used the search for Théo as an excuse to avoid living his life, but because he has not seen him for so long, Jack no longer has an accurate picture of who he really was.

Roger Hyman correctly argues that Jack lacks the authority of an author and "is unable to control or define his own work" (111-12). Indeed, Jack himself admits that he begins to write at a time when most people begin to live and he allows his characters to take over in his writing. He merely observes what his characters are doing and records their actions. In admitting his shortcomings as a writer, he is also relinquishing his hierarchy in a patriarchal world. He confesses his lack of control as a creator to Pitsémine, who listens to him, and tries to dissuade him from feeling uncertain. But patriarchy is defined as having a material base, which establishes or creates interdependence and solidarity among men that enable them to dominate women (Hartman 14). The latter element of this definition is important, for in confiding in Pitsémine, he is creating an interdependence and solidarity with a woman. In an ironic twist, it is Pitsémine who has a better idea of the role of an author and how books should be read. An avid reader, she often steals books from libraries and bookstores—with the intention of returning them—so that she can read them during their voyage and use them as guides. Pitsémine's past time adds to the intertextual quality of this novel, supplying excerpts from over forty other sources (Weisman). She wisely recognizes how books are written and tells Jack,

> [i]l ne faut pas juger les livres un par un. Je veux dire: il ne faut pas les voir comme des choses indépendantes. Un livre n'est jamais complet en lui-même; si on veut le comprendre, il faut le mettre en rapport avec d'autres livres, non seulement avec les livres du même auteur, mais aussi avec des livres écrits par d'autres personnes. Ce que l'on croit être un livre n'est la plupart du temps qu'une partie d'un autre livre plus vaste auquel plusieurs auteurs ont collaboré sans le savoir.

> (186)

Pitsémine has strong opinions about literature, but it is Jack who earns his living as a writer. It is he who records information, his novels are read and it is he who, in part, prevails over culture, even though he himself does not know the purpose his stories serve. Here, Poulin subverts traditional Eurocentric gender roles which hold that men are those who transmit culture and history—in the form of historians, journalists, authors and creators of literary canons—and avoid work which does not mark their achievements. Indeed, Hannah Arndt writes that, historically, "[c]ontempt for laboring originally [arose] out of a passionate striving for freedom from necessity and a no less passionate impatience with every effort that left no trace, no monument, no great work worthy of remembrance" (qtd. in Sedgwick 698). In another inversion of gender roles, therefore, Poulin allows Pitsémine to claim the role of literary critic normally left to men.

There are other instances in which Pitsémine takes the dominant role during their travels and Jack tends to the domestic details. An experienced mechanic, she knows how to maintain the Volkswagen when Jack demonstrates his helplessness in mechanical matters. She also takes care of him when he becomes too depressed to get out of the

van. Of the two travelers, Jack is stagnant and docile and does not attempt to court Pitsémine or lure her into his bed. It is clear that he is attracted to her, because he mentions her long black hair when he first sees the girl, but when Pitsémine allows him to observe her long legs he shows no reaction and behaves neutrally. On another occasion, she flirts with a parking attendant, which upsets Jack, but he does not try to stop her. They sleep together in the bus, but they do not have sex. Pitsémine would like to have a more intimate friendship, but when she follows him to his room in the YMCA, he does not invite her in it. Clearly, the gender roles are reversed. On several occasions, she dresses like a man, for instance when she spends the night in the cemetery on Joseph Bryant's grave and on another occasion, when she wears men's clothing so that she will go undetected on the men's floor of the YMCA. On a sexual level, the reversal of gender roles is significant. Dorsinville argues,

> [t]he juxtaposition of the two brothers' passivity (Jack's foreshadowing of Théo's paralysis conflating into a single image) and 'the girl's' vitality suggests that the upturning of sexual stereotyping stems from the undermining of a patriarchally defined and encoded heroic mythos reflected in the frail vestiges of the two brothers and their landscapes.

> (108 Dorinville)

To be sure, as Lapointe argues, women in Poulin's novels are often more fortunate than men. He writes,

> [c]haque roman toutefois est traversé par un personnage qui semble plus doué, instinctivement, pour le bonheur. Ce sont des êtres rares, des femmes exclusivement, qui réunissent confiance en soi, connaissance de soi, chaleur et généroisité, mais qui restent farouchement libres et indépendantes.

> (18)

Jack, like his brother Théo, is an emasculated figure, for he is unable to perform the most essential behavior of every animal: procreation. Later in the novel, Jack again has an opportunity to make love to Pitsémine and fails. Emboldened, Pitsémine suggests that they make love when they reach the Continental Divide, as a symbol of the divide itself and in honor of the explorers, guides and emigrants who passed this way. But Jack cannot manage the act, saying that he gets too excited when he makes love outdoors. The location is thus a symbol of the affinity Jack feels to the land itself, but it is yet another example of Jack's inability to fulfill his role as a man. The reason for his impotence may also be that the author would not like this act to occur for symbolic reasons, for the two of them share a similar ancestry. Jack and Pitsémine's Canadian history, which includes the close relationship between French Canadians and Native Americans—not only as fellow hunters and trappers, but also in the creation of familial ties through intermarriage—is symbolized at this moment at the Continental Divide. Not only do they have a similar history as colonized people, as mentioned above, they are descendants of the people who settled Quebec (Weisman). Taking these historical facts to an extreme, a sexual union between the two would be incestuous. Even on a behavioral level it would be incestuous, I believe, for based on the way in which they care for one another, they are more like siblings than lovers.

There may be another reason for Jack's impotence: Poulin is a product of North America and the white man's history and he does not want to include a love scene in his novel. Lapointe points out that American history is fraught with stories of unaccomplished love and, because of the strictly protestant religion, in which many North American writers are raised, a myth of chastity exists among men:

> Le climat moral d'une Amérique longtemps puritaine explique en partie la pudeur avec laquelle les écrivains traitent des passions. À cause de cela sans doute, il y a au fond de l'idéal américain un mythe de la chasteté mâle qui s'exprime dans des images insistantes de virilité. Les liens profonds du cœur se lient entre hommes, mais restent inavoués.
>
> (18)

The unrequited love, of which Lapointe writes, is the homosocial bond which exists between men and which is frequently depicted in American narratives. To be sure, writing of respect, admiration, shared adventures and heroic acts between men is much more acceptable to a strictly raised puritanical audience than narratives depicting passion and lovemaking. Furthermore, because these activities between men do not involve sexual intercourse and often are depicted in narratives of exploration and conquest, they are even more readily accepted by the public, for they augment the myth of the brave, righteous white male conquering savage Indians for the gain of territory and westward expansion. Central, however, to Jack's depression is his belief that he has never loved anyone, not even his brother, and this inability is always present. Thus, because he is preoccupied with his childhood memories, Jack cannot love Pitsémine, despite his sexual attraction to her.

Jack's childhood memories of Théo are tainted when he discovers that he has committed some violent crimes. Théo had been arrested for carrying a weapon without a permit and he was detained as a suspect in a burglary. Jack learns that he has become indigent and eventually finds Théo in San Francisco in the care of a nursing home. A broken man, he is mentally ill and cannot recognize Jack. Just as Théo's heroes, who were explorers, brave adventurers and heroes and who eventually became Jack's heroes, Théo's image is shattered. Poulin's portrayal of Jack and Théo has destroyed the myths surrounding masculine behavior and the heroes, who comprised the history of North America, and has subverted century-old patriarchal behavior. Having found Théo, Jack leaves San Franscisco, where Pitsé-

mine remains. The pair's parting is positive, for Pitsémine reminds Jack that no matter what happened in the past, the future awaits him. The realization that Jack's memories of Théo were myths and the optimism expressed as Jack and Pitsémine part serves as a defining moment for both of them: for Jack because he can now leave his memories behind, which hindered him as a writer and an individual, and for Pitsémine, because she is now able to discover her history and identity. Jack leaves her with the Volkswagen in San Francisco, where she will live, because it is a place where, she believes, many cultures live together harmoniously. She will continue to live in the minibus to try to "faire l'unité et de se réconcilier avec elle-même" (318).

Just like Jack, François also has difficulty loving women, is hindered from becoming an adult because of his childhood memories and is dependent on Aldéric and his older siblings. Indeed, Jack's passive and docile characteristics can be attributed to Théo's influence. Godbout's novel, like Poulin's, ends in self discovery after a long and painful process. The idea to leave the past behind and begin anew reflects the ideology of the Quiet Revolution, for the call to be "Masters in Our Own House" is a refusal to submit to an authoritarian government (Rocher 206). As in these novels, two father figures, the pope and Maurice Duplessis (former premier of Quebec) are the cause of poverty and backward thinking in Quebec before the Quiet Revolution. Quebec's newfound autonomy represents a desire to think about the future and is a call for the liberation of ideas. In subverting the ideas held by patriarchal leaders and rebelling against the symbols of patriarchy, these authors have paved the way for other means of self expression, which will ensure the distinct nature of this province.

Notes

1. The discussion of initiation rites is outlined by Victor-Laurent Tremblay, who applies René Girard's theories in his discussion of various aspects of the rite of passage in a group of hockey players. He argues, "l'initiation traditionnelle est de rigueur, comme elle l'est dans la plupart des autres sports, clubs, ou associations regroupant des hommes. Le rite de passage permet au jeune mâle de se départir de tout ce qui le rattache à l'enfance et au féminin pour accéder à la virilité, processus douloureux et souvent sanglant qui mime la quête du héros mythique devant tuer le dragon (le mal, le tabou, l'ennemi, le différent, le féminin ...) menaçant la communauté homosociale" (420-25).

2. Although homosexuality in the erotic sense may not be something which everyone has experienced, the thought of homosexual love evokes strong, familiar feelings. Weeks writes, "[i]f the homosexual image contains a complex knot of dread and desire, if the homosexual phantasy is more obscene than any other and at the same time more exciting, if it is impossible to appear anywhere as a self-confessed homosexual

without upsetting families, causing children to be dragged out of the way and arousing mixed feelings of horror and desire, then the reason must be that for us twentieth-century westerners there is a close connection between desire and homosexuality" (Weeks 693).

3. François's attitude towards women is similar to that of many male characters in the novels of the 1950s and 60s. For instance, Gérard Bessette's depiction of women in his novel *La bagarre* (published in 1958) is one of servitude and dependence; women did not work outside the home and, if they did, they had a job which did not pay much more than minimum wage. It was understood that, once they got married, that they would stop working all together. For the most part, they resembled the female figures in Michel Tremblays's play *Les belles sœurs,* who spent their time with other women during the day, while their husbands worked to support the family.

Works Cited

Bellamare, Yvon. "Salut Galarneau!" *Dictionnaire des Oeuvres Littéraires du Québec.* Vol. 4 1960-1969. Montréal: Fides, 1984. 796-97. Print.

Dolbec, Nathalie. "D'un tableau l'autre." *Canadian Literature.* 184 (2005): 27-43. Print.

Dorsinville, Max. "I Lost My Art in San Francisco." *Essays in Canadian Writing.* 40 (1990): 40-3. Print.

Godbout, Jacques. *Salut Garlaneau!* Paris: Seuil, 1967. Print.

Hartman, Heidi. "The Unhappy Marriage of Marxism and Feminism: Towards a More Progressive Union." *Women and Revolution. A Discussion of the Unhappy Marriage of Marxism and Feminism.* Ed. Lydia Sargent. Boston: South End, 1981. 1-41. Print.

Hyman, Roger. "Writing against Knowing, Writing against Certainty; or, What's Really under the Veranda in Jacques Poulin's *Volkswagen Blues.*" *Journal of Canadian Studies.* 34.3 (1999): 106-33. Print.

Klementowicz, Michael. Jacques Godbout's *Salut Galarneau!:* Identity and Violence towards Women. *Québec Studies.* 14 (1992): 83-91. Print.

Lapointe, Jean-Pierre. "Sur la piste américaine: Le statut des références littéraires dans l'oeuvre de Jacques Poulin." *Voix et Images.* 15.1 (1989): 15-27. Print.

Lemire, Maurice. "Introduction." *Dictionnaire des oeuvres littéraire quebecoise.* 2nd Ed. Vol 2. xi-lxix. Print.

Poulin, Jacques. *Volkswagen Blues.* Québec: Leméac Éditeur, 1988. Print.

Purdy, Anthony. "Memory Maps: Mnemotopic Motifs in Creates, Poulin, and Robin." *Essays on Canadian Writing.*

80 (2003): n. pag. *Academic One File.* Web. 10 March 2009.

Rocher, Guy. "Beyond the Quiet Revolution." *As I Recall.* Ed. The Institute for Research on Public Policy. Montreal: IRPP, 1999. 203-08. Print.

Sedgwick, Eve Kosofsky. "Introduction." *Between Men. English Literature and Male Homosocial Desire.* New York: UP Colombia, 1985. 1-20. Print.

Smith, André. *L'univers romanesque de Jacques Godbout.* Montreal: Aquila, 1976. Print.

Tremblay, Victor-Laurent. "Masculinité et hockey dans le roman québécois." *The French Review.* 78.6 (2005): 114-16. Print.

Weeks, Jeffrey. "Introduction to Guy Hocquengham's *Homosexual Desire.*" *Literary Theory: An Anthology.* Eds. Julie Rivkin and Michael Ryan. Malden, MA: Blackwell, 1998. 694-96. Print.

Weisman, Adam Paul. "Postcolonialism in North America: Imaginative Colonization in Henry David Thoreau's *A Yankee in Canada* and Jacques Poulin's *Volkswagen Blues.*" *The Massachusetts Review* 36 (1995): n.pag. *Humanities Full Text.* Web. 12 September 2008.

FURTHER READING

Biographies

Asselin, Viviane, and Camille Arpin. "Jacques Poulin." *Auteurs contemporains.* N.p., n.d. Web. 31 Aug. 2015.
> Offers an up-to-date biography of Poulin and a useful bibliography of criticism on his work. Not available in English.

Poulin, Jacques. "Un entretien avec l'écrivain Jacques Poulin." Interview by Jean-Denis Côté. *Études canadiennes/ Canadian Studies* 46 (1999): 77-92. Print.
> Investigates Poulin's life in Paris and his role in the literary scene in an interview with the author conducted in 1993. Not available in English.

Criticism

Bastien, Sophie. "*Les grandes marées,* dans le roman de Jacques Poulin: Phénomène naturel ou courant culturel?" *Canadian Literature* 198 (2008): 48-56. Print.
> Argues that wilderness in *Spring Tides* is reflective of a nature/culture dialectic. Not available in English.

Harel, Simon. "L'amérique ossuaire." *Le voleur de parcours: Identité et cosmopolitisme dans la littérature québécoise contemporaine.* Montreal: Préambule, 1989. 159-207. Print.
> Describes what Harel terms in French as "extraterritoriality" in *Volkswagen Blues* and how the Other has had a considerable influence on the French-language

population of Quebec. Harel argues that *Volkswagen Blues* demonstrates a broader acceptance of immigrant and indigenous populations in Quebec but that Poulin conflates the two. Not available in English.

Hébert, Pierre. *Jacques Poulin: La création d'un espace amoureux.* Ottawa: PU d'Ottawa, 1997. Print.
Examines the ethics and aesthetics of love in eight of Poulin's novels. Hébert demonstrates how Poulin deconstructs gender in order to create a dynamic space for love in each text. Not available in English.

Hyman, Roger. "Writing against Knowing, Writing against Certainty; or, What's Really under the Veranda in Jacques Poulin's *Volkswagen Blues.*" *Journal of Canadian Studies/ Revue d'études canadiennes* 34.3 (1999): 106-33. Print.
Examines the historical outlook expressed in *Volkswagen Blues,* noting the postcolonial ramifications of the novel's treatment of North America and its evocation of the tension between competing historical frameworks. Hyman argues that the novel warns against the destructive potential of totalizing, monolithic conceptions of history.

Lapointe, Jean-Pierre, ed. Spec. issue of *Voix et images* 15.1 (1989): 4-154. Print.
Features essays on *Volkswagen Blues, Spring Tides,* and intertextuality, as well as an interview with Poulin and a bibliography of critical essays on his works. Not available in English.

Lintvelt, Jaap. "Jacques Poulin's Novels: From Duality to Fusion of Identity." *Dynamics of Modernization: European-American Comparisons and Perceptions.* Ed. Tity de Vries. Amsterdam: VU UP, 1998. 135-45. Print.
Analyzes the gender duality and reversal of traditional gender roles in Poulin's works.

Miraglia, Anne Marie. *L'écriture de l'autre chez Jacques Poulin.* Montreal: Balzac, 1993. Print.
Explores what Miraglia calls in French Poulin's method of "literary communication" and the dialogic elements of his writing. Not available in English.

———. "Texts Engendering Texts: A Québecois Rewriting of American Novels." *Intertextuality in Literature and Film: Selected Papers from the Thirteenth Annual Florida State University Conference on Literature and Film.* Ed. Elaine D. Cancalon and Antoine Spacagna. Gainesville: UP of Florida, 1994. 49-60. Print.
Analyzes the role of intertextuality in *Volkswagen Blues.* Miraglia argues that the novel enacts a thematic

reading and rewriting of various American works in distinctively Quebecois terms.

Morency, Jean. "La thématique de la mer et la structuration de l'œuvre romanesque de Jacques Poulin." *Mer et littérature. Actes du colloque international sur "La mer dans les littératures d'expression française du XXe siècle": Moncton, les 22-23-24 août 1991.* Ed. Melvin Gallant. Moncton: Acadie, 1992. 327-36. Print.
Details the role of the sea in Poulin's work, describing how the author uses water and its double, the earth, to structure his novels. Not available in English.

Pedri, Nancy. "Cartographic Explorations of Self in Michael Ondaatje's *Running in the Family* and Jacques Poulin's *Volkswagen Blues.*" *International Journal of Canadian Studies* 38 (2008): 41-60. Print.
Compares the employment of maps and cartographic commentary in *Volkswagen Blues* and Ondaatje's *Running in the Family* (1982), observing that in both works, "readers of maps see in them—in the use of language, the selection of place names, and the map's changing topography—traces of their own selves." According to Pedri, the "cartographic representations of land" in these texts "prompt an autobiographical reading that ultimately informs configurations of self."

Purdy, Anthony. "Memory Maps: Mnemotopic Motifs in Creates, Poulin, and Robin." *Essays on Canadian Writing* 80 (2003): 261-81. Print.
Examines the many layers of cultural and individual memory present in the works of visual artist Marlene Creates and Quebec authors Régine Robin and Poulin. With particular reference to *Volkswagen Blues,* Purdy demonstrates the impact of the combined elements of history and geography on the experience of the protagonists.

Socken, Paul G. *The Myth of the Lost Paradise in the Novels of Jacques Poulin.* Rutherford: Fairleigh Dickinson UP, 1993. Print.
Investigates how seven of Poulin's novels reconfigure the long-established myth of paradise lost in order to define the quests of the various protagonists.

Vautier, Marie. "Canadian Fiction Meets History and Historiography: Jacques Poulin, Daphne Marlatt, and Wayson Choy." *Colby Quarterly* 35.1 (1999): 18-34. Print.
Discusses the dominant presence of historiography in several Canadian literary texts including Poulin's *Volkswagen Blues.* [Excerpted in the Marlatt entry in *CLC,* Vol. 168.]

Additional information on Poulin's life and works is contained in the following sources published by Gale: *Contemporary Authors,* **Vol. 165;** *Contemporary Authors New Revision Series,* **Vol. 216;** *Dictionary of Literary Biography,* **Vol. 60; and** *Literature Resource Center.*

Lygia Fagundes Telles

1923-

(Born Lygia de Azevedo Fagundes) Brazilian novelist and short-story and novella writer.

INTRODUCTION

Lygia Fagundes Telles is highly regarded in her native country for her novels and stories that intensely evoke the interior lives of female characters. Though often described as a member of the Generation of 1945, a loosely affiliated group of Brazilian writers who reacted against the modernist movement of the 1920s and 1930s by using more traditional literary forms, Telles does employ modernist techniques in her work. She has made extensive use of interior monolog and stream-of-consciousness narration, preferences she shares with the celebrated Brazilian author and journalist Clarice Lispector, to whom she is frequently compared.

Telles's work also bears the influence of non-realist literary movements, such as surrealism and Expressionism, and her narratives frequently blur the distinction between fantasy and reality, particularly in her short fiction. She has returned repeatedly to themes of solitude, alienation, and disillusionment. Her plots treat stifled women attempting to evade the expectations placed upon them by society and to establish free, comfortable identities for themselves, themes evident in Telles's best-known work, the novel *As meninas* (1973; published as *The Girl in the Photograph*). Critically acclaimed in Brazil and the winner of several prestigious literary prizes, Telles, though widely translated, remains relatively little-read outside the Portuguese-speaking world, but her centrality to contemporary Brazilian literature is widely acknowledged.

BIOGRAPHICAL INFORMATION

Telles was born Lygia de Azevedo Fagundes in São Paulo on 19 April 1923, the youngest of four children of Durval de Azevedo Fagundes, an attorney and police chief, and Maria do Rosário Azevedo Fagundes, a pianist. Largely as a result of her father's vocational restlessness, Fagundes's family moved frequently throughout her childhood, which she spent in several different towns within São Paulo state. As a child, Fagundes was fascinated by the ghost stories her nursemaid told her, and during her adolescence, she read primarily European and American authors, including Edgar Allan Poe, Virginia Woolf, and Franz Kafka, among others. At the age of fifteen, she self-published her first short-story collection, *Porão e sobrado* (1938; may be translated as

Basement and Two-Story House), with her father's help, though she later dismissed it as juvenilia. During this period, she studied at the Instituto de Educação Caetano de Campos, from which she graduated in 1939.

Thereafter, she studied at the Universidade de São Paulo, where she took a degree in physical education in 1941, followed by a law degree in 1946. During this time, she began to publish in various periodicals. Her first commercially published short-story collection, *Praia viva* (may be translated as *Living Beach*), appeared in 1943. A second collection, *O cacto vermelho* (1949; may be translated as *The Red Cactus*), received the Afonso Arinos Prize from the Brazilian Academy of Letters. In 1950, she married law professor Goffredo da Silva Telles, with whom she had one son. Four years later, she published her first novel, *Ciranda de pedra* (1954; published as *The Marble Dance*), regarded as her first mature work.

In 1961, Telles divorced her husband, and the following year, she married Paulo Emílio Salles Gomes, a film critic, professor, and founder of the Filmoteca do Museu de Arte de São Paulo (later the Cinemateca Brasileira). Around the time of her second marriage, Telles began working for the Social Security Institute of the State of São Paulo, where she remained for three decades. In the meantime, she maintained a steady output of stories and novels. Her third novel, *The Girl in the Photograph*, won the Coelho Neto Prize from the Brazilian Academy of Letters.

Critics admired *The Girl in the Photograph* for its engagement with the oppressive policies of Brazil's military dictatorship (1964-85). Sociopolitical critique of this type was risky at the time because of the cultural repression practiced by the dictatorship, which Telles continued to criticize in her subsequent works. She was elected to the Brazilian Academy of Letters in 1985, becoming only the third female member in the institution's history. In 2005, she received the Camões Prize, the most prestigious award for Portuguese-language literature.

MAJOR WORKS

The Marble Dance, Telles's first novel, exhibits many of the formal and thematic attributes of her subsequent work. Highly introspective and psychologically intense, the novel is a bildungsroman about an alienated, middle-class girl living in an emotionally difficult family situation. Unhappy in either of her divorced parents' households, the protagonist, Virgínia, tries with little success to establish a sense of her own identity while coping with patriarchal social expectations and sordid familial dramas. At the end of the novel, having fended off thoughts of suicide, Virgínia leaves for a period of travel. The nature of this conclusion, in which much of the protagonist's personal solace derives from physical escape in solitude, is typical of Telles's outlook on the realities of women's lives. The emphasis on solitude is also discernible in the lack of communication that characterizes Virgínia's relationship with her two sisters. Variations on this triad of unhappy female characters appear in each of Telles's subsequent novels.

Telles's second novel, *Verão no aquário* (1963; may be translated as *Summer in the Aquarium*), displays a similar focus on family matters, filtered this time through a psychoanalytic sensibility. Much of the narrative dwells on the narrator's troubled, obsessive relationship with her mother, whom she sees as a romantic rival. As in *The Marble Dance,* the protagonist has learned a great deal by the end of the narrative, but her personal relationships have not been happily resolved.

The Girl in the Photograph, Telles's third and most highly regarded novel, interweaves the stories of three discontented young women—a dreamer, a revolutionary activist, and a drug addict—living in a boardinghouse in the late 1960s. Hailed as Telles's most formally adventurous work, the novel extends beyond the thematic focus of her previous works on bourgeois family structures to address also the grim, occasionally brutal realities of life during the era of Brazil's military dictatorship. Telles's fourth novel, *As horas nuas* (1989; may be translated as *The Naked Hours*), revisits many of the themes and motifs of her earlier novels in its portrayal of the intense reflections of an aging actress on her career, her need for approval, and her relations with others. A testimony to Telles's interest in the fantastic and supernatural, the novel also features a wise cat, repeatedly reincarnated since its earlier life in ancient Egypt.

In addition to her novels, Telles has produced a vast body of short fiction. For the most part, these stories explore the same thematic territory as her novels, though they tend to make greater use of fantastic and supernatural narrative elements. Many of her short stories are straightforwardly mimetic, as is the title story of her collection *Antes do baile verde* (1970; may be translated as *Before the Green Dance*), which concerns the indecision of a young woman who wishes to join in a Carnival celebration but is obligated to stay at home to care for her dying father. Other tales introduce elements of fantasy into otherwise realistic settings, as in "Noturno amarelo" (published as "Yellow Nocturne"), a story collected in *Seminário dos ratos* (1977; published as *Tigrela and Other Stories*), whose protagonist is made to atone for her past sins in a sort of magical garden that appears to exist outside of ordinary time and space. The fabulist "Seminário dos ratos" (published as "Rat Seminar") uses a nationwide rat infestation as the narrative basis for a critique of Brazil's sociopolitical situation. The story begins with a bureaucratic seminar about how to deal with the rat problem; by the tale's end, the victorious rodents are overheard holding their own seminar.

CRITICAL RECEPTION

Despite the general acknowledgment of her literary stature, Telles remains a relatively obscure figure in the English-speaking world, and only three of her thirty books have been translated into English. Although her work has attracted scholarly attention, little criticism is available in English.

Scholarship on Telles's work situates her writing within the context of larger social, political, and ideological forces. Her treatment of gender issues is a particularly common topic, as in Cristina Ferreira-Pinto's 1993 analysis of the ways in which Telles's novels reflect the concerns of the Brazilian feminist movement. Ferreira-Pinto noted Telles's abiding interest in feminist issues and traced the evolution of her handling of these issues throughout her novels, calling attention to her increasingly pessimistic perspective and asserting that "the path the author traces in her novels goes from hope in the Brazilian woman to disbelief in her possibilities. It is thus that Telles fulfills her social role as a writer: by reflecting the present hopeless reality of her country and by inviting the reader to reflect on such a reality." Peggy Sharpe (1995) identified a recurring pattern of fragmented female identity across Telles's novels and analyzed the treatment of this motif in *The Naked Hours*. Richard L. Brown (1991) argued that Telles also depicts women who are able to prevail in a patriarchal society. He contended that she "diminishes the traditional concept of men as pillars of strength . . . to entities who are insecure, frequently demented, and otherwise morally and socially weak."

Other critics have focused on Telles's use of specific literary techniques and conventions. Ferreira-Pinto (1996) suggested that Telles uses the supernatural and the absurd to question the reality of her characters' situations. W. Martins (1978), reviewing *Tigrela and Other Stories,* regarded the volume as a turning point in her career, as it "expands her territory into the fantastic and into political satire." Renata R. Mautner Wasserman (2007), on the other hand, argued that Telles's work is usually characterized as psychologically intimate and unconcerned with larger political developments. Having pointed out the ways in which Telles's first two novels confirm this view, Wasserman contended that *The Girl in the Photograph* incorporates a greater degree of political engagement into its narrative framework and asserted that "the novel is almost forced to reveal the external pressure of politics upon a fictional form that had generally been seen as immune to politics so understood, or had been used to repel it." In a 2002 interview with Elzbieta Szoka (see Further Reading), Telles said that her hope is that her reader will "be my partner and accomplice in the act of creation which means anxiety and suffering. It's a search and a celebration."

James Overholtzer

PRINCIPAL WORKS

Porão e sobrado [may be translated as *Basement and Two-Story House*]. São Paulo: n.p., 1938. Print. (Short stories)

Praia viva [may be translated as *Living Beach*]. São Paulo: Martins, 1943. Print. (Short stories)

O cacto vermelho [may be translated as *The Red Cactus*]. Rio de Janeiro: Mérito, 1949. Print. (Short stories)

Ciranda de pedra [published as *The Marble Dance*]. Rio de Janeiro: O Cruzeiro, 1954. Print. (Novel)

Histórias do desencontro [may be translated as *Stories of a Missed Encounter*]. Rio de Janeiro: Olympio, 1958. Print. (Short stories)

As pérolas [may be translated as *Pearls*]. Sá da Bandeira: Imbondeiro, 1960. Print. (Novella)

Histórias escolhidas [may be translated as *Selected Stories*]. São Paulo: Boa Leitura, 1961. Print. (Short stories)

Os mortos [may be translated as *The Dead*]. Lisbon: Casa Portuguesa, 1963. Print. (Short story)

Verão no aquário [may be translated as *Summer in the Aquarium*]. São Paulo: Martins, 1963. Print. (Novel)

A confissão de Leontina [may be translated as *Leontina's Confession*]. Sá da Bandeira: Imbondeiro, 1964. Print. (Novella)

O jardim selvagem [may be translated as *The Wild Garden*]. São Paulo: Martins, 1965. Print. (Short stories)

*Antes do baile verde [may be translated as *Before the Green Dance*]. Rio de Janeiro: Bloch, 1970. Rev. and enl. ed. Rio de Janeiro: Olympio, 1971. Print. (Short stories)

Seleta [may be translated as *Selected Works*]. Ed. Nelly Novais Coelho. Rio de Janeiro: Olympio, 1971. Print. (Biography, interviews, and short stories)

As meninas [published as *The Girl in the Photograph*]. Rio de Janeiro: Olympio, 1973. Print. (Novel)

†Seminário dos ratos [published as *Tigrela and Other Stories*]. Rio de Janeiro: Olympio, 1977. Print. (Short stories)

Filhos pródigos [may be translated as *Prodigal Children*]. São Paulo: Cultura, 1978. Pub. as *A estrutura da bolha de sabão: Contos* [may be translated as *The Structure of the Soap Bubble: Short Stories*]. Rio de Janeiro: Nova Fronteira, 1991. Print. (Short stories)

A disciplina do amor: Fragmentos [may be translated as *The Discipline of Love: Fragments*]. Rio de Janeiro: Nova Fronteira, 1980. Print. (Sketches)

Lygia Fagundes Telles. Ed. Leonardo Monteiro. São Paulo: Abril, 1980. Print. (Criticism)

Mistérios: Ficções [may be translated as *Mysteries: Fictions*]. Rio de Janeiro: Nova Fronteira, 1981. Print. (Short stories)

10 contos escolhidos [may be translated as *10 Selected Short Stories*]. Brasília: Horizonte, 1984. Print. (Short stories)

Os melhores contos de Lygia Fagundes Telles [may be translated as *The Best Stories by Lygia Fagundes Telles*]. Ed. Eduardo Portella. São Paulo: Global, 1984. Print. (Short stories)

Venha ver o pôr-do-sol e outros contos [may be translated as *Come See the Sunset and Other Stories*]. São Paulo: Ática, 1988. Print. (Short stories)

As horas nuas [may be translated as *The Naked Hours*]. Rio de Janeiro: Nova Fronteira, 1989. Print. (Novel)

Capitu. With Paulo Emílio Salles Gomes. São Paulo: Siciliano, 1993. Print. (Screenplay)

A noite escura e mais eu: Contos [may be translated as *The Dark Night and More: Short Stories*]. Rio de Janeiro: Nova Fronteira, 1995. Print. (Short stories)

A confissão de Leontina e fragmentos [may be translated as *Leontina's Confession and Fragments*]. Ed. Maura Sardinha. Rio de Janeiro: Ediouro, 1996. Print. (Short stories and sketches)

Oito contos de amor [may be translated as *Eight Love Stories*]. São Paulo: Ática, 1996. Print. (Short stories)

Pomba enamorada, ou, Uma história de amor, e outros contos escolhidos [may be translated as *A Dove in Love; or, A Love Story, and Other Selected Short Stories*]. Ed. Léa Masina. Porto Alegre: L and PM, 1999. Print. (Short stories)

Invenção e memória [may be translated as *Invention and Memory*]. Rio de Janeiro: Rocco, 2000. Print. (Short stories)

Durante aquele estranho chá: Perdidos e achados [may be translated as *At That Strange Tea Party: Lost and Found*]. Ed. Suênio Campos de Lucena. Rio de Janeiro: Rocco, 2002. Print. (Biography)

Histórias de mistério [may be translated as *Mystery Tales*]. Rio de Janeiro: Rocco, 2004. Print. (Short stories)

Meus contos preferidos [may be translated as *My Favorite Short Stories*]. Rio de Janeiro: Rocco, 2004. Print. (Short stories)

Meus contos esquecidos [may be translated as *My Forgotten Short Stories*]. Rio de Janeiro: Rocco, 2005. Print. (Short stories)

Conspiração de nuvens [may be translated as *Cloud Conspiracy*]. Rio de Janeiro: Rocco, 2007. Print. (Reminiscences and short stories)

Principal English Translations

The Girl in the Photograph. Trans. Margaret A. Neves. New York: Avon, 1982. Print. Trans. of *As meninas*.

The Marble Dance. Trans. Neves. New York: Avon, 1986. Print. Trans. of *Ciranda de pedra*.

‡*Tigrela and Other Stories.* Trans. Neves. New York: Avon, 1986. Print. Trans. of *Seminário dos ratos*.

*Includes the short story "Antes do baile verde" [may be translated as "Before the Green Dance"].

†Includes the short stories "Noturno amarelo" [published as "Yellow Nocturne"] and "Seminário dos ratos" [published as "Rat Seminar"].

‡Includes the English translations "Yellow Nocturne" and "Rat Seminar."

CRITICISM

W. Martins (review date 1978)

SOURCE: Martins, W. Rev. of *Seminário dos ratos*, by Lygia Fagundes Telles. *World Literature Today* 52.2 (1978): 276. Print.

[*In the following review, Martins assesses Telles's* Tigrela and Other Stories, *contending that the contents of the collection "confirm her talent and distinguished place in the crowd of short story writers in contemporary Brazil." Martins considers the volume a turning point in her career, as it "expands her territory into the fantastic and into political satire."*]

Since the publication of her second volume of short stories, **O cacto vermelho,** in 1949 (the first one was **Praia viva** in 1944) Lygia Fagundes Telles has established herself as a master of modern Brazilian literature. Although tempted by the novel (**Ciranda de pedra,** 1954; **Verão no aquário,** 1963; and **As meninas,** 1973), she is fundamentally a short story writer; even her novels are in fact a succession of juxtaposed short stories sewn together by the unity of the characters.

Adding more than a title to her bibliography, **Seminário dos ratos** presents some novelty in themes, plots and style. Without really dropping her *intimiste* technique and her interest in slightly deranged feminine psychology, she expands her territory into the fantastic and into political satire, as represented by the piece that gives the volume its title. Of course any reader of Camus's *La peste* cannot avoid a feeling of déjà vu; but after all, *La peste* was published in 1947, and that kind of metaphor—be it rats, ants or a rhinoceros—is one of those immediately suggested by monstrous bureaucracies. So in a sense it is reusable, except that reusage is the capital sin in literature and art. Let us say in

all fairness that she has succeeded in making something new out of that well-worn material; the other short stories in the volume confirm her talent and distinguished place in the crowd of short story writers in contemporary Brazil.

Richard L. Brown (essay date 1991)

SOURCE: Brown, Richard L. "Lygia Fagundes Telles: Equalizer of the Sexes." *Romance Notes* 32.2 (1991): 157-61. Print.

[*In the following essay, Brown concentrates on Telles's depiction of women who are able to rise above their conventional role in a patriarchal society. In order to create her strong female characters, Brown observes, the author "diminishes the traditional concept of men as pillars of strength with unchallenged authority to entities who are insecure, frequently demented, and otherwise morally and socially weak." Through her attempts to equalize the sexes, Brown concludes that Telles has not only "captured the imagination of the Brazilian reading public" but also achieved "that nebulous, but coveted sense of universality."*]

Lygia Fagundes Telles exerts a notable equalizing force in her literary portrayal of the sexes. She elevates women from the traditional position of subservience and passivity to a position of stability, rationality, and, to a certain degree, social autonomy. She diminishes the traditional concept of men as pillars of strength with unchallenged authority to entities who are insecure, frequently demented, and otherwise morally and socially weak. Women, however, in the short stories of Fagundes Telles, are not anointed with sainthood, and men are neither ridiculed nor portrayed as imbeciles. The reading public can easily sympathize with most of her characters regardless of their sex or their dilemma. Over the years Fagundes Telles has consistently presented men and women as psychological and social equals in a maze of realistic and imaginary situations.

What Fagundes Telles has accomplished in literature has its greatest impact when viewed in the context of Brazilian norms. Brazil has a patriarchal society supported by a firm foundation of machismo, and the idea of personal and social equality of the sexes is still a nebulous concept. So to portray women as anything but dependent and men as anything but dominant is almost revolutionary. Fagundes Telles may be included among the few writers who have attempted to treat men and women as equals.

For the purpose of this study, machismo can be narrowly defined, but the implications can be far-reaching. Men are expected to be in control of their destinies, because they support their families financially and make all the major decisions concerning family security. This attitude places women and children in a position of obedience and acquiescence. To enhance his macho image, a man frequently smokes, drinks excessively, and curses. He feels compelled to brag about his sexual prowess and promiscuity.

The same attitudes are not tolerated in feminine counterparts. Men attempt to control women by limiting their social roles and responsibilities. Let us keep this in mind as we examine a few characters in *Antes do Baile Verde,* a volume of twenty selected short stories which were written by Lygia Fagundes Telles between 1943 and 1969.

In **"Os Objetos"** something is awry in Miguel's life. From the dialogue the reader can surmise that he is basically a good person, but he is now suffering from an emotional crisis which might lead to his commitment to an asylum. His mischievous nature becomes apparent when he taunts Lorena with his philosophical musings about the nature of objects, his visions in a crystal ball, his story of a dwarf strewn with roses, and his description of a picture depicting deceased love. He is childlike, and, because of his mental debilitation, he forces Lorena into the role of the protective mother figure.

Lorena accepts the maternal role and seems strong, but she is also cautious as she plays mental games with Miguel. More than once the reader is able to detect her carefully concealed fear, a fear contained by some remaining trust and loyalty. She wants him to recover from his malady. While Lorena is a stable and rational character, the emphasis in this episode is on the weakness and instability of Miguel. Miguel has lost the decision-making power in his life, and he has lost the control over his own destiny. The implication is that he will react by killing himself or someone else to atone for his failure as a macho. Lorena, on the other hand, is careful not to defy the macho honor code. She pretends that he is still psychologically coherent and trustworthy.

In **"Apenas um Saxofone"** Luisiana, a forty-four year old alcoholic, laments the passing of her youth. She addresses the reader in a prose narration that reveals her past and present. What makes Luisiana transcend the stereotypical woman is certainly not moral turpitude or stable rationality, but rather her fierce sense of feminine independence and her manipulative control over men. She insures her control by surrounding herself with weak (from a stereotypical point of view) men: a husband who does not seem to demand anything of her, a male homosexual who is non-threatening to her lifestyle, and a young derelict (who plays a saxophone) whose love she conquers and then rejects without consequence.

Luisiana blatantly violates almost every aspect of the macho honor code and survives it. She makes the decisions concerning her own destiny and is obedient to no one, not even the wealthy husband who supports her financially. She also violates the moral and sexual codes that govern most women in her society. In fact, her attitudes and actions represent an inversion of the values of the macho honor code. She does everything that a man is expected to do, but not a woman.

"A Janela" echoes the theme of male dementia found in **"Os Objetos."** **"A Janela"** is a story told through direct dialogue with infrequent, but effective, intrusions by the narrator, a writing technique also paralleled in **"Os Objetos."** The two main characters are simply referred to as "a mulher" and "o homem." The woman, a prostitute, finds a strange man in her room. Instead of screaming she reacts rationally by greeting him and offering him a seat. She is able to control her fears, because the man is docile, soft-spoken, and courteous. It is obvious, however, that something is wrong. The man glances around the room as if to inspect it, and then he tells the woman that this room is where his son died. Outside the window there used to be a rose bush which bestowed its fragrance upon the death bed of his child. The man stares at the window. A few minutes later the man is taken away to the insane asylum from which he has escaped. Then the woman sits and stares pensively at the open window.

The strength and independence of the woman is highlighted by the frivolous reactions of other women in the brothel. She is sympathetic to the debilitated intruder, an insane member of the opposite sex. She is a prostitute, but this does not preclude her from being a sympathetic, sensitive human being.

As we can see from these three stories, Fagundes Telles is primarily interested in the psychology of her characters and intentionally neglects their physical attributes, except to emphasize or contrast a psychological trait. All the stories in *Antes do Baile Verde* serve as a framework for psychological confrontations. These confrontations may be between men and women, women and women, men and men, or they may simply be self-confrontations. A confrontation, of course, implies some sort of conflict, and Fagundes Telles is a master at presenting conflicts, although she chooses not to resolve them.

In **"Os Objetos"** and **"A Janela"** we have examples of women confronting men. In **"Apenas um Saxofone"** Luisiana exemplifies self-confrontation in the form of a confession of her perversity toward men.

In **"Verde Lagarto Amarelo"** a psychological confrontation between men occurs: a case of adult sibling rivalry. Eduardo (his mother's favorite son) is tall, blonde, handsome, and highly competitive. Rodolfo is short, overweight, and has an inferiority complex. The latter has worked for years to improve his self-image by doing something that his brother cannot do. Rodolfo is writing a novel which he hopes to publish soon, and this will be his triumph, but his hopes are dashed when Eduardo appears one day with a completed manuscript of his own.

Eduardo is the embodiment of competitive machismo, which dictates that one man must destroy another man either physically or psychologically to ensure his own superiority. Rodolfo is, of course, psychologically devastated by the incident. He has been reduced from a macho to a weak, sensitive man who possesses numerous feminine characteristics. Eduardo is used only as a poignant contrast and a reminder of what machismo really is.

In **"Antes do Baile Verde"** (the story) a psychological confrontation occurs between women: responsibility versus irresponsibility. Lu, a responsible domestic servant, tries in vain to convince Tatisa to stay home to take care of her seriously ill father, but Tatisa is intent on going to a *carnaval* dance where everyone will be dressed in green. Besides, she is afraid of losing her macho boyfriend, who becomes angry when she disobeys him. She is excited as she rushes off to the dance unaware that her father has just died in the next room. Lu is left alone to deal with the situation. In this story Lu is emphasized as a strong, responsible woman, while Tatisa is the embodiment of a woman who is totally dependent on and obedient to the man who controls her.

In the twenty short stories of *Antes do Baile Verde,* women are more apt to be cast as principal characters than men. The most consistent characteristic of these female characters is their sense of psychological and social independence. While such women seem to control their own lives and destinies, they are not superwomen. Men, on the other hand, are frequently portrayed in some sort of personal crisis which causes them to lose control of their own lives and destinies. They seem to be searching for peace of mind, because of a lost sense of essence.

Whether by intent or coincidence, Fagundes Telles is a literary iconoclast. In the Brazilian context, she has to a great degree departed from the stereotyped portrayals of women and men. By doing so, she has contributed to the cultural liberation of her country and to the intellectual liberation of both sexes worldwide. The equalizing of the sexes in *Antes do Baile Verde* is subtle, so it is not clear that Fagundes Telles is an intentional iconoclast. It is very likely that her ability to destroy images is a by-product of her ability to invent extraordinary plots which tend to invert or modify the traditional roles of men and women.

Lygia Fagundes Telles has earned a well-deserved reputation as an innovator of contemporary Brazilian letters. She has won the hearts and captured the imagination of the Brazilian reading public. Now she is well along the way to international renown due to her keen sense of human nature and her polished manner of presenting it in literature. Lygia Fagundes Telles seems to have attained that nebulous, but coveted sense of universality.

Work Cited

Fagundes Telles, Lygia. *Antes do Baile Verde.* Rio de Janeiro: Livraria José Olympio Editõra, 1983 (8a edição).

Cristina Ferreira-Pinto (essay date 1993)

SOURCE: Ferreira-Pinto, Cristina. "Feminist Consciousness in the Novel of Lygia Fagundes Telles." *MLS: Modern Language Studies* 23.4 (1993): 4-17. Print.

[*In the following essay, Ferreira-Pinto discusses the interrelationship of Telles's novelistic output with the Brazilian feminist movement. Tracing the development of Telles's feminist consciousness throughout the course of her career, Ferreira-Pinto identifies in her work an increasingly pessimistic attitude toward the social plight of women.*]

In the 1940s, the social role of Brazilian women was still very much restricted to their family environment, where they were solely responsible for their family's wellbeing, seeing to their husband's and children's interests. Yet the Brazilian feminist movement had already accomplished some of its most important victories. Women had been given the right to higher education (1879) and the right to vote (1932); for the first time in Brazil a woman had been elected to the House of Representatives (Bertha Lutz in 1934) and a significant number of women had joined the labor force. The beginning of Getúlio Vargas's *Estado Novo* in 1937, however, along with a lack of unity within the feminist movement, brings to a halt women's social and political advancement in Brazil. Moreover, "a manutenção da discriminação de sexo" [the perpetuation of sexual discrimination] against women within society underlines the fact that the issue of "[a] emancipação da mulher não se limitava ao nível jurídico-institucional, atingindo raízes mais profundas, estabelecidas na própria cultura" [women's emancipation was not circumscribed to the sphere of legal-institutional decisions: it was deeply rooted in the culture itself (Fundação Carlos Chagas, 214)].[1] Nevertheless, one of the major accomplishments of the Brazilian feminist movement was to draw widespread attention to the social condition of women, especially after the last quarter of the nineteenth century. The ensuing debate about this issue brings to the fore many women who will emerge in the feminist cause, such as Maria Lacerda de Moura, or in politics, as is the case of Bertha Lutz. In the literary scene, many female voices will be heard, in the "crônica" genre (Eneida), in poetry (Gilka Machado) and in prose fiction (Júlia Lopes de Almeida, Lúcia Miguel Pereira, Raquel de Queiroz, etc.). This last kind of literary expression, particularly the novel, will become an important vehicle for discussing women's social situation in Brazil.

Lygia Fagundes Telles is among those female fiction writers whose first publications come to light in the 1940s (a few others are Clarice Lispector, Lúcia Benedetti and Ondina Ferreira). Her collection of short stories *Praia viva* [**Living Beach**] is published in 1944 and is usually considered her first book, even though another book of short stories, *Porões e sobrados* [**Cellars and Townhouses**], had been published in 1938, when Telles was only fifteen years old, paid for by the author herself with money she had been saving. Telles was brought up in the city of São Paulo, at a time when decisive events in the history of modern Brazil were taking place. The emergence of the *Estado Novo,* the dictatorship headed by Getúlio Vargas, is probably the most important of these events, one that "marcou uma geração" [left a mark on a generation], according to Brazilian writer Antônio Callado (personal interview), and will have a great impact on all sectors of Brazilian life up to the coup d'etat of 1964. During Vargas's tenure the country's process of industrialization accelerates, and a period of economic development starts for Brazil, bringing also a significant growth of the middle-class and the decline of the land-owning oligarchy. New means of production become important for the economy and Brazil becomes increasingly more urban in character. The arrival of European immigrants and the influence of American culture before the beginning of World War II create new habits and consumer needs among the population. The family structure is greatly affected by these changes, being exposed to customs that will lead to a clash between the traditional and the modern. A new family model emerges, one in which the old patriarch sees his heretofore absolute authority and social power erode little by little. Yet, despite some social gains, women are still discriminated against and have to fight deeply-rooted prejudices they themselves have incorporated.

It is in this context that Telles begins what we may call her social and political learning process. It is not a coincidence that during this same period she starts writing. It is as a law student at the Faculdade de Direito de São Paulo (São Paulo Law School) that she becomes increasingly aware of the social and political situation of Brazil and of her own situation as a woman in a patriarchal society. Attending Law School in the early 40s, Telles belongs to a tiny minority of female students: in the mid-1930s only six out of two hundred students at the Faculdade de Direito de São Paulo were women (Dulles, 80), and this situation had not improved significantly by the beginning of the next decade.

Telles did not conform to the traditional patterns of female behavior generally accepted by Brazilian society then, as her choices of law and literature—two traditionally "male" careers—make clear. In her book *A disciplina do amor* [**The Discipline of Love,** 1980] she records in many passages the discrimination that befalls a woman who chooses to write either as a profession or pastime. Her own encounter with discrimination early on in her career is a good example of how the issue "women and literature" was seen in Brazil. As she tells us in *A disciplina,* a certain critic had the following words to say about *Praia viva*: "Tem essa jovem páginas que apesar de escritas com pena adestrada, ficariam melhor se fossem de autoria de um barbado" [This young lady has produced some fine pages of literature which, although well written, would be better if authored by a man (73)]. Telles found herself then in a pioneering but rather marginalized position, having the beginning of her literary career inhibited by the patriarchal structure of Brazilian society. However, she feels that her own "timidez" [shyness (cf. *Review:* 31)] was also an obstacle that kept her from writing about

certain themes: "Naquela ocasião eu não sabia ou, pior ainda, não ousava escrever certas coisas, chegar a determinadas soluções" [At that time there were many things I did not know how to write about or, what is worse, I did not dare write about; I did not dare use certain [thematic and formal] strategies (*Seleta,* 146)]. Telles's development as a writer was a gradual process, simultaneous to her "liberation" as an individual. She believes that this liberation resulted from a series of changes within the Brazilian society that had been occurring since her adolescence (Bins, 4; "Truth," 269). Her works, particularly her novels, *reflect* this process of social transformation, since they are influenced by these changes, but they also try to make sense of this social process and thus are a *reflection* on these changes, a reflection the author encourages her readers to share.

* * *

Lygia Fagundes Telles believes in the author's role as a "testemunha do [seu] tempo" [a witness and recorder of her or his time (Bins, 4)]; she has discussed in several articles and interviews what she considers to be the writer's social function. For Telles, writers make use of words in order to depict their realities and to give voice to those who cannot—or are not allowed to—express themselves. The writer, she contends, "escreve por aqueles que não podem escrever. Fala por aqueles que esperam ouvir da nossa boca a palavra que não conseguem dizer" [writes for those who are prevented from writing, for those who expect to hear from our lips the words they cannot manage to utter (**"Depoimento,"** 7)]. Writing is thus the author's contribution to the transformation of his or her reality (Bins, 4). This does not mean, however, that Telles proposes a solution to all the social problems she raises in her novels. As Telles herself has stated, "a função do escritor não é corrigir, é denunciar" [it is not the writer's role to correct [the social reality] but rather to denounce [it] (personal interview)], and it would be unfair to expect writers to find an answer to social evils. They are, nevertheless, historical beings, and cannot possibly escape this fact, as the Brazilian novelist Érico Veríssimo already maintained in 1945 (140). In this sense, literature, and the arts in general, accomplishes an important function: to enlighten people as to what their historical past was, what their present represents and to make them aware of the perspectives and opportunities the future can hold for them. Literature, therefore, plays both a social and historical role, as states Nicolau Sevcenko in his book *Literatura como missão* [Literature as a Mission]:

> a criação literária revela todo o seu potencial como *documento,* . . . como uma instância complexa . . . que incorpora a história em todos os seus aspectos, . . . formais ou temáticos, reprodutivos ou criativos, de consumo ou produção. Nesse contexto globalizante, a literatura . . . implica uma comunidade envolvida por relações de produção e consumo, uma *espontaneidade de ação e transformacão* e um conjunto mais ou menos estável de códigos formais que orientam e definem o espaço da ação comum.

(246; my emphasis)

[literary creation reveals all its potential as a *document*, ... as a complex structure ... that incorporates history in different ways, ... [in its] form and content, creation and recreation, production and consumption. Seen within this all-encompassing context, literature ... entails the existence of a community based on relations of production and consumption, of a *spontaneous drive for action and transformation*, and of relatively stable formal codes that guide and circumscribe the field of common social practice.]

A literary work shares the social codes of the community it addresses, but it also suggests the adoption of new codes and thus points toward the transformation of that community. This is achieved by using the dominant discourse, that is, the "conjunto ... de códigos formais" [collection of formal codes] as an internal organizing principle of the text itself. At the same time, as John Brenkman has noted, the text advances a new discourse and proposes a new social order by pointing out novel codes of social behavior (Brenkman, 104). Literature then has a double character: a *critical* character, exactly because it criticizes the dominant social order from which it originates; and a *utopian* character, since it forecasts the coming of a new social order (Brenkman, 104). It is thus that we can read Telles's fictional work and understand her self-definition as a "testemunha" of her time and society. As a witness, her personal contribution to her society lies precisely in what she does through her literary work: to speak up, to express and discuss her reality, "refletir e levar o leitor à reflexão" [to think and make her readers think], as well as to suggest new modes of behavior which, despite their initial novel character, may eventually be assimilated by that society.

Lygia Fagundes Telles "escreve por aqueles que não podem escrever," for those who are not allowed to express themselves, those to whom the power of free expression is denied, whose voice, therefore, is not heard. It is hardly a coincidence, then, that most of her characters are women, including the protagonists of her four novels, for women have systematically had their attempts at self-expression either silenced or ignored. It is important to note, however, that most of her female characters are white middle-class women whose struggles revolve mostly around the issue of self-identity. There are a few important exceptions, though: Lião, from *As meninas* (1973; *The Girl in the Photograph*, 1982), whose father is German and whose mother is "baiana" (a native of the Northeastern state of Bahia) of African descent, and who is involved in the students' movement against the Brazilian military government in the late 60s; Ana Clara, also from *As meninas,* who comes from a lower class and whose mother was a prostitute, and who struggles to ascend socially on her good looks; and Dionísia, the black servant from *Verão no aquário* [**Summer in the Aquarium,** 1963] and *As horas nuas* [**The Naked Hours,** 1989] who appears briefly as Luciana in *Ciranda de pedra* (1954; *The Marble Dance,* 1986) and later as Lião's mother in *As meninas.* Telles acknowledges her "preferência por personagens femininas" [predilection for female characters] and finds

it a natural consequence "da [sua] condição de mulher" [of her female condition (**"Depoimento,"** 7)]. Focusing on the characters' situation within the social group and sharing their perspective of reality, Telles's reflections on Brazilian society are ultimately a mode of self-reflection, for the issues she raises are also her own. The writer sees herself in what she writes, places herself within her text, in a search for self-knowledge and an attempt to gain a better grasp of her reality.

Many of Telles's personal concerns find expression in her novelistic work, as the recurrence of certain themes in her novels, interviews, testimonies, and also in *A disciplina do amor* will show. Published in 1980, *A disciplina* is a collection of "fragmentos," short narrative pieces; it is a cross between a personal diary and fictional writing, or a collection of maxims and the recording of everyday life events. We can say that it is a direct descendant of her grandmothers' "cadernões de capa preta" [huge black-covered notebooks], the notebooks which Telles refers to in *A disciplina* as the "cadernos caseiros da mulher-goiabada" [the homey notebooks of the "goiabada" women] on which, says Telles, "de mistura com os gastos da casa cuidadosamente anotados e somados no fim do mês, elas ousavam escrever alguma lembrança ou uma confissão que se juntava na linha adiante com o preço do pó de café e da cebola" [they carefully entered and added the domestic expenses of each month, writing some poetic line or confession alongside the costs of onions or coffee (*A disciplina,* 16)].[2] In a manner akin to that of these old notebooks, then, *A disciplina* collects personal memories and confessions and, without concerning itself with the daily chores of domestic life, it does deal with other kinds of problems contemporary Brazilian women face. For example, Telles writes in a fragment of *A disciplina*:

[de] Simone de Beauvoir ... destaco esta frase ... : "Somente o trabalho fora do lar é capaz de ajudar a plena realização psíquica e social da mulher."

E a retaguarda dessa mulher que vai trabalhar fora?

... A professora Moema Toscano dá a resposta certa: "Enquanto não se superar a necessidade da empregada doméstica (como acontece nos países desenvolvidos) eu não acredito que possa haver um feminismo no Brasil."

(110)

[Let me quote Simone de Beauvoir: "Women can only achieve psychological and social fulfillment by engaging in some work outside the home."

But who will provide the support at home for this career woman?

... Professor Moema Toscano has the right answer: "As long as the need for the domestic servant is not abolished (as it has been in developed countries) the feminist movement will not go anywhere in Brazil."]

In this paragraph are raised several issues that personally concern the author and which she discusses in many of her works: the "psychological and social fulfillment" of Brazilian women, the feminist movement in Brazil, and the question of the domestic servant. This issue is present in all of Telles's novels with the exception of *As meninas,* although questions of race and class, which come up when the problem of the domestic servant is discussed, are also present.

The focus of Telles's novelistic work, however, is on the struggle of bourgeois women for psychological, emotional and social self-realization, and this is the main theme of her first novel, *Ciranda de pedra. Ciranda de pedra* is a "novel of apprenticeship," a "Bildungsroman," in which the reader follows the main character's development from childhood to early adulthood, witnessing the process of building a sense of identity and the obstacles she has to overcome during this process. In this novel Telles brings up, even if only in passing, a problem she herself faced at the beginning of her career: the discrimination against intelligent women who also had professional aspirations. The protagonist of *Ciranda de pedra,* Virgínia, who has a degree in languages, faces the mocking comments of both her sister and her brother-in-law when she tells them about her professional plans, "lecionar e trabalhar em traduções" [to teach and work on translations (114)]. Her brother-in-law tells her: ". . . [hão] de querer transformá-la numa Minerva, mas não invente de conhecer mais nada, você já é uma bela doutrina, deixe agora que a conheçam, a começar por este seu vizinho" [. . . people will certainly want to make a Minerva out of you, but do not think of learning any more, for you are quite a beautiful doctrine yourself. Let others learn (about) you now, and let me be the first one to do so (115)]. What becomes clear from this passage, besides the sexual innuendo, is the male vision of women not as active subjects who may search for and succeed in finding knowledge, but rather as passive objects, a field of knowledge in which he, the man, becomes an expert. The autobiographical nature of that passage becomes apparent when it is compared to the following fragment of *A disciplina do amor*:

> Me lembro do tio J. dizendo à minha mãe que rompera o noivado com M. I. porque ela era inteligente demais, culta demais, andava exausto com suas elocubrações intelectuais, queria uma gueixa e não uma Minerva: "Parece um homem falando! . . ." Minha mãe riu, eu fiquei rindo junto mas um tanto preocupada, era adolescente, com certos planos.

(89)

> [I remember Uncle J. telling my mother that he had broken up his engagement with M. I. because she was far too intelligent and learned, he had grown tired of her intellectual cogitations, he wanted a geisha girl, not a Minerva: "She sounded like a man whenever she spoke! . . ." My mother laughed, I laughed too but a bit worried, I was an adolescent and had some plans of my own.]

From this we may infer that that young woman writer who in 1954 published her first novel had certain concerns which could only be addressed fictionally, through her characters' voices, which allows some distance between the author and the issues raised. This situation is radically reversed by the time Telles publishes *A disciplina,* where we meet a mature writer who makes use of her own voice to express herself.

Lygia Fagundes Telles is also very concerned with feminism, not only as an organized movement, but also as an individual attitude, and as any social manifestation that somehow affects the self-realization of the female subject. Here it is possible to find a parallel between the evolution of the author's personal attitude concerning women's issues and that of the formal expression of these issues in her literary work. Thus one may find that in her first three novels—*Ciranda de pedra, Verão no aquário* and *As meninas*—there is no direct reference to feminism, although they focus on the emotional, psychological and social problems women have to face in a patriarchal society. In *A disciplina do amor* and in her last novel *As horas nuas,* however, feminism is dealt with in an explicit manner. In many fragments of *A disciplina* Telles discusses women's condition and in a number of them she comments on feminism, quoting feminists such as Simone de Beauvoir (110), pointing out the contradictions within the feminist movement in Brazil (91, 110), or reexamining her own position (73). The tone the author adopts here is generally positive, even when criticizing certain aspects of feminism, and at times it gets to be quite optimistic as, for example, when she mentions that the feminist movement in Brazil is a "revolução ainda no início . . . [em] tempo de espera" [revolution in its very beginnings . . . [in a] gestation period (91-92)]. This calm voice—critical and yet positive—who "speaks" in *A disciplina do amor* will be dichotomized in Telles's latest novel. One will be the subdued, quiet, almost silent voice—since she listens more than speaks—of Ananta, a feminist psychologist. Ananta is actively engaged in the feminist movement and defends it verbally, echoing the novelist's own words: "A revolução é recente" [The revolution is still recent (*As horas nuas,* 122)]. The other voice is quite bitter and belongs to the protagonist Rosa Ambrósio, who questions the achievements of the feminist movement and its validity in the context of Brazilian society. Rosa and Ananta will thus engage in a dialogue through which Telles raises once more the issue of feminism, in order to question, criticize and also defend it.

* * *

The importance of using a novel as the vehicle for discussing issues that had already been raised in a non-fictional work lies in the fact that the work of art may serve as a catalyst for social changes in a way that a book such as *A disciplina* will not. This catalysis coincides with the act of reading and interpretation of the text by the reader. "It is then that meanings and values are refashioned in the very process of being understood," says Brenkman (xi). The reader of a fictional work takes part in the critical process of questioning and analyzing the social group, and also participates in the utopian construction of a new social order, for there is a considerable degree of involvement between reader and text that does not take place when the reader is faced with the writer's own voice. Telles acknowledges that narrative fiction is more effective in enlisting the reader in a process of critical reading. Thus she states, in an interview with Paulo Rassolini in 1989:

> Quero mostrar a realidade deste País, mas *não diretamente,* como fiz antes. Assim eu acredito que funciona melhor.
>
> ... Acho que as metáforas exigem mais do leitor, mas ao mesmo tempo lhe dão mais prazer ao descobrir o que pode estar escrito por trás das palavras.
>
> (4; my emphasis)
>
> [I want to express my country's reality, but *not in an explicit manner,* as I have done before. I think that it works better this [indirect] way.
>
> ... I believe that metaphors demand more from the reader, but at the same time they provide more pleasure in the process of trying to decipher what is written behind the words.]

The work of fiction offers its readers a greater possibility of either identifying with or rejecting the protagonists. The reader would be inclined here to question, above all, not the author, but the fictional characters, their attitudes and the context in which they act. Upon reflecting on the characters and situations the fictional text presents, the reader will also reflect on her or his own situation and on the social group wherein she or he lives. The identification between reader and text is possible thanks to the usage of the dominant discourse as an organizing principle within the narrative (Brenkman, 120-121). This dominant discourse will be present not only as a linguistic code, but mainly as a socio-cultural one. It makes the literary work understandable for the reader, thus allowing an involvement between reader and text. In Telles's novels, one finds that the narrative's organizing principle is the bourgeois institution of the family in Brazil and its socio-political context.

* * *

Lygia Fagundes Telles's four novels are centered on the institution of the bourgeois family. This is apparent in *Ciranda de pedra* and *Verão no aquário*; in both novels the main theme is the protagonists' situation within the family and the relationship between the female subject, the mother and the father. *As horas nuas* is also centered on a nuclear family but it now constitutes a small community that is very different from the traditional family model. Here we find, not the oedipean triangle of Subject—Father—Mother, but the middle-aged protagonist Rosa Ambrósio, a nihilist cat and the faithful old maid; instead of a husband, a young lover. While in the first two novels the main characters play the daughter's role within the family structure, the protagonist of *As horas nuas* is a mother and the head of the household, although she is also in a daughter's position

when remembering her childhood, her youth and her parents. In *As meninas,* however, the family or, rather, the three protagonists' families, take on a background position in the narrative. The novel is nevertheless centered once again on a family structure—and a triangular one: the three girls, Lorena, Lião and Ana Clara. Having this female triangle as a basis, other relationships—often structured in a triangular manner—are built: Lião, her father and her mother; Ana Clara, her boyfriend and her older fiancé; and the larger triangle: the three girls—the outside world—the nuns' boardinghouse.

It is interesting to note that not until 35 years after the publication of her first novel does Telles allow the subject of the narrative discourse to "speak" from a mother's vantage point. It is true, though, that in *As horas nuas* the main narrative focus is not placed on the relationship between mother and daughter. This relationship represents only one aspect of Rosa Ambrósio's complex and problematic life. At any rate, *As horas nuas* represents a change that should not go unnoticed, for in Telles's previous novels the narrative perspective is always that of the daughter, despite the mother's importance in each work. This insight takes on more meaning when compared to what Marianne Hirsch says in her book *The Mother/Daughter Plot*: "Not surprisingly I find ... that mothers tend to be absent, silent, or devalued in novels by [late nineteenth-century women writers]" (14). During that period and even later, in the first five or six decades of our century, the maternal figure will frequently represent for her daughter a negative, "reverse model," to use the expression coined by Carolyn Heilbrun (123). Often the mother will also represent a role model that seems to be positive because it is idealized by the daughter. When this is the case, however, the mother is usually absent; she becomes then a role model that is out of reach, whose only value is that of being a disembodied ideal that does not exist in real life. Only in the post-modern novel of the 70s, according to Hirsch, do women as mothers occupy a more eminent position: "[These] fictional ... texts ... feature mothers prominently, and displace fathers, brothers, husbands, and male lovers. The text themselves, however, are still written from daughterly perspectives" (15). It will be in the following decade when the maternal voice finally "speaks" for herself, having been allowed to play the subject of the narrative discourse (Hirsch, 15-16). This seems also to be the case in Brazil, as novels such as *Mulher no espelho* (1983; *Woman between Mirrors,* 1989) by Helena Parente Cunha, *Jogo de fiar* [Spinning Game, 1983] by Patricia Bins, and *O quarto fechado* (1984; *The Island of the Dead,* 1986) by Lya Luft suggest.

The family structure as an organizing principle within the narrative—as well as the mother figure within that structure—is undeniably important in Telles's novelistic work. This is particularly true in *Ciranda de pedra* and *Verão no aquário,* where we find the traditional Oedipal family model. In these two novels a continuous affirmation of the "feminine" takes place, simultaneously with a decentering of the "masculine." This happens as women gradually step out of relationships with male characters—fathers, husbands, lovers. Virgínia, from *Ciranda de pedra,* and Raíza, from *Verão no aquário,* find themselves in a quest for self-knowledge as they try to build a sense of identity. Both the mother and the father play a determinant role in Virgínia's and Raíza's process of search and apprenticeship; but while the mother grows in importance in her daughter's development and in the narrative, the father becomes gradually less important and ends up being just a fading memory in *Verão no aquário.* At the beginning of the two novels, Virgínia and Raíza take their fathers' side in opposition to their mothers.' Eventually, however, the daughters will be able to reconsider their own and their mothers' situation and will learn to recognize positive role models in their mothers.

At the end of *Ciranda de pedra,* the protagonist breaks away from her social group's patriarchal values, and realizes that, before herself, her mother had already challenged the father's authority and for that reason had been punished. In *Verão no aquário,* however, the protagonist herself never acknowledges her mother as a woman who went against a patriarchal model of female behavior, but the text makes clear references to this. By the end of the narrative, however, Raíza begins to accept her mother in a positive way. Therefore, while the relationship between mother and daughter in *Verão no aquário* is at first highly problematic, as the narrative approaches its end there is a reconciliation between the two women, even though Raíza's mother does not comply with the traditional model of maternal behavior, which demands from the woman selflessness and self-sacrifice for the Other: husband, children and family. Thus in each of Telles's first two novels the reader witnesses the subject's building of an identity that will lead the daughter to acknowledge her mother as a positive role model. Simultaneously, the development of a feminist consciousness takes place in *Ciranda de pedra* and *Verão no aquário.* Beginning with these two texts, Telles's novelistic work will reflect an increasing awareness of her social environment and of women's situation in society, as the author starts to question more and more, both as an individual and a writer, the dominant social order. And it is precisely through her characters that the social awareness and feminist consciousness of Telles as an individual find expression.

Telles's protagonists will voice her personal and social concerns, and at the same time will act as precursors for the creation of new characters. For this reason, it is not incorrect to say that Telles's characters appear repeatedly in her subsequent works, something the author herself has acknowledged in an interview (*Review:* 32). Each new character incorporates others from previous narratives and may be regarded as representing an act of readdressing and rethinking issues the author raised before. Thus the recurrence of certain characters will mark the writer's intellectual evolution and the development of her social awareness. It will also point out those issues that concern Telles the most and

how she deals with certain themes and situations at different stages of her career. Considering the protagonists of Telles's novelistic works, it is apparent that they "voltam" [return] in subsequent novels. It is more important to note, however, that these characters do reappear but "speaking" in a very different key, if not in a different voice. If the reader is aware of this change, it becomes clear that Telles's characters go through an evolution, parallel to an evolution in the author's perception of women's situation and of Brazilian reality. Therefore, it is very revealing that *Ciranda de pedra* is the only novel in which Telles suggests a positive outcome, with the protagonist's self-realization. Many years after *Ciranda de pedra* is written and published, the protagonist of this text, Virgínia, will appear again in *As horas nuas.* However, the hopeful and even utopian denouement of the first novel will give way, in the 1989 work, to a pessimistic, negative tone. Here we find a limbo-like atmosphere reflecting the characters' inertia—their impossibility or incapacity for action.

* * *

In *The Mother/Daughter Plot,* Hirsch discusses the gradual construction of women as subjects of the narrative discourse, a process she calls "becoming-woman," and which "is intimately tied to the process of transmission and the relationship to previous and subsequent generations of women" (11).[3] This statement finds an echo in Telles's novels. On the one hand, each protagonist may be seen as representing a new generation of women. In this regard, it is interesting to note the chronological gap between the publication of each of the four novels: they were published in 1954, 1963, 1973 and 1989. A period of about ten years (or a little more) has elapsed between each work, marking the birth of another generation. On the other hand, however, we also find in these novels a force seeking connection with the past in hopes of finding positive role models there. In this respect, the maternal figure will often play a significant role, for the mother serves as a link between the protagonist and a previous generation of women, as we see, for example, in *Ciranda de pedra.* In this first novel the protagonist's mother is also a valuable model of female behavior, being the first one to go against the father's authority and eventually breaking away from the patriarchal values of her society. Laura leaves her repressive husband, refusing to restrict herself to the roles of wife and mother, and therefore becomes "guilty" of disobeying the patriarchal patterns of female behavior. She is not able, however, to free herself from her husband's threatening image and will eventually succumb to madness, which represents here the "quintessential female privacy" (Heilbrun, 183). In madness Laura seeks to create that which she is unable to find in reality: a space where she can express herself, where she can develop as an individual—in brief, the "room of one's own" recommended by Virginia Woolf. By way of setting an example that is eventually recognized and valued by her daughter, the mother will be of great importance in the main character's social and psychological development. By the end of the novel, Virgínia, the protagonist, is aware of her situation within her social group which, like her mother, she will choose to abandon in order to build her destiny with her own hands. At last she will be able to accept her past and her own contradictions, and will acknowledge her mother as a valuable role model through which she herself can grow as a new model of female behavior.

As an individual who eventually manages to step beyond all social limitations, the protagonist of *Ciranda de pedra* becomes a woman capable of designing her own future and of accomplishing self-realization. Thus Telles's first novel presents the double feature discussed here earlier: as critical of the dominant order (Brazilian patriarchal society) and as a utopian text that proposes a new social order in which women's self-realization would be possible. A positive, hopeful note marks the text's end. This however will not be repeated in the later novels. In *Verão no aquário* promising perspectives are still opening up for the female subject. Patrícia, the protagonist's mother, is shaped as an important model of female behavior. Through this character, Telles suggests that women can indeed refuse to restrict themselves to the roles society imposes on them and find instead self-realization in their own work, without being dependent on a man. It is not unimportant that Patrícia, like Telles, is a writer who has a number of novels published and owns her private room, a space that is only hers. Patrícia represents a major advance in relation to the maternal figure of the previous novel. Nevertheless, this does not mean that Patrícia is without problems. Quite the opposite, she pays a high price for her independence: loneliness, the criticism of her social group, and a very problematic relationship with her daughter, in part because Patrícia does not play the traditional role of the "good mother." While the mother is capable of realizing an authentic selfhood, fulfilling her literary and professional aspirations, the outcome of *Verão no aquário* is rather doubtful as to whether the protagonist will be able to follow her mother's example. Any doubts left from the reading of Telles's second novel, however, will dissipate in *As meninas* and *As horas nuas,* giving way to a more negative portrayal of the female subject. It is possible to regard these two works as offering the readers a warning: women—like Ana Clara from *As meninas* or Rosa from *As horas nuas*—are still seeking a relationship of dependence on men and on the patriarchal order as a way of self-definition. On the other hand, Virgínia from *Ciranda de pedra* lives again in Telles's last novel through the character Ananta. Like Virgínia, the psychoanalyst of *As horas nuas* will abandon everything—relationships, work, her participation in the feminist group of her community. However, what we see here is not the same hope for success and self-realization of the first novel but rather pessimism: women's self-realization within a slow-changing society is but a very remote possibility, barely discernible.

Upon examining Lygia Fagundes Telles's novelistic work, it becomes apparent that the author has developed a feminist consciousness and social awareness during her career. Throughout her work she has questioned the social condition of Brazilian bourgeois women; she has also made of her characters female role models that both criticize the dominant order and the behavior of women themselves, and at the same time point out new perspectives for the female subject. Nonetheless, the path the author traces in her novels goes from hope in the Brazilian woman to disbelief in her possibilities. It is thus that Telles fulfills her social role as a writer: by reflecting the present hopeless reality of her country and by inviting the reader to reflect on such a reality.

Notes

1. All translations following the Portuguese texts are mine.

2. "Mulher-goiabada" 'guava-paste woman' is an expression Telles uses in *A disciplina do amor* (16) and *As horas nuas* (17) referring to women of older generations who took care of the family and the household and did not work outside the home or had any non-domestic activity. The expression alludes to the process of making guava paste by way of slowly cooking the guava fruit in huge pots while constantly stirring it. It is an activity that demands much time and patience, and would keep the woman occupied for many hours. In a testimony published in *Jornal de Letras,* Telles says that the expression originated from her recollections of her own mother making "goiabada" when the author was a child.

3. Hirsch uses here an expression—"becoming-woman"—reminiscent of the expression used by Ellen Morgan in her ground-breaking essay "Humanbecoming: Form and Focus in the Neo-Feminist Novel" (1973). But while in her work Morgan examined the attempts by female protagonists to accomplish self-realization as individuals, i.e. outside traditional female social roles, Hirsch discusses a process of "en-genderment," through which women take on a sexual identity; as the author explains, this sexual identity may be based on a "desidentification from conventional constructions of femininity" (Hirsch, 11).

Works Cited

Bins, Patricia. *Jogo de fiar.* Rio: Nova Fronteira, 1983.

Brenkman, John. *Culture and Domination.* Ithaca: Cornell UP, 1987.

Callado, Antônio. Personal interview. July 15, 1991.

Cunha, Helena Parente. *Mulher no espelho.* 1983. *Woman between Mirrors.* Trans. Fred P. Ellison and Naomi Lindstrom. Austin: U of Texas P, 1989.

Dulles, John W. F. *A Faculdade de Direito de São Paulo e a resistência anti-Vargas: 1938-1945.* Rio: Nova Fronteira; São Paulo: Editora da Universidade de São Paulo, 1984.

Fundação, Carlos Chagas. *Mulher brasileira: Bibliografia anotada.* Vol. 1. São Paulo: Brasiliense, 1979. 2 vols.

Hahner, June E. *A mulher brasileira e suas lutas sociais e políticas: 1850-1937.* São Paulo: Brasiliense, 1981.

Heilbrun, Carolyn G. *Reinventing Womanhood.* New York, London: W. W. Norton, 1979.

Hirsch, Marianne. *The Mother/Daughter Plot: Narrative, Psychoanalysis, Feminism.* Bloomington: Indiana UP, 1989.

Luft, Lya. *O quarto fechado.* 1984. 3rd ed. Rio: Editora Guanabara, 1986. *The Island of the Dead.* Trans. Carmen Chaves McClendon and Betty Jean Craige. Athens, London: U of Georgia P, 1986.

Morgan, Ellen. "Humanbecoming: Form and Focus in the Neo-Feminist Novel." *Images of Women in Fiction: Feminist Perspectives.* Ed. Susan Koppelman Cornillon. Bowling Green: Bowling Green UP, 1973. 183-205.

Saffioti, Heleieth I. B. *A mulher na sociedade de classes: Mito e realidade.* São Paulo: Quatro Artes, 1969.

Sevcenko, Nicolau. *Literatura como missão: Tensões sociais e criação cultural na Primeira República.* 3rd ed. São Paulo: Brasiliense, 1989.

Telles, Lygia Fagundes. *Ciranda de pedra.* 4th ed. Rio: José Olympio, 1974.

———. "Depoimento." *Jornal de Letras* [Lisboa] April 13-26, 1982: 7.

———. *A disciplina do amor.* 6th ed. Rio: Nova Fronteira, 1980.

———. Interview. "Lygia Fagundes Telles. Ontem, hoje, sempre: A imortal." By Patricia Bins. *Suplemento Literário do Estado de São Paulo* Dec 14, 1985: 4.

———. Interview. "Política pelas linhas tortas." By Paulo Rassolini. *Correio Braziliense* May 28, 1989. "20. Caderno": 4.

———. Interview. By Edla Van Steen. *Review* 36 (1986): 30-3.

———. *As horas nuas.* Rio: Nova Fronteira, 1989.

———. *As meninas.* 4th ed. Rio: José Olympio, 1974.

———. Personal interview. July 1, 1991.

———. *Porões e sobrados.* São Paulo: n.e., 1938.

———. *Praia viva.* São Paulo: Livraria Martins Editora, 1944.

——— *Seleta.* Rio: José Olympio; Brasília: INL-MEC, 1971.

———. "Truth of Invention." *Lives on the Line: The Testimony of Contemporary Latin American Authors.* Ed. Doris Meyer. Los Angeles: U of California P, 1988. 265-71.

———. *Verão no aquário.* 8th ed. Rio: Nova Fronteira, 1984.

Veríssimo, Érico. *Brazilian Literature: An Outline.* New York: Macmillan, 1945.

Peggy Sharpe (essay date 1995)

SOURCE: Sharpe, Peggy. "Fragmented Identities and the Process of Metamorphosis in Works by Lygia Fagundes Telles." *International Women's Writing: New Landscapes of Identity.* Ed. Anne E. Brown and Marjanne E. Goozé. Westport: Greenwood, 1995. 78-85. Print.

[*In the following essay, Sharpe considers the fragmentation and metamorphosis of female identity in Telles's novels, noting that each depicts female characters who attempt to construct new, liberating identities for themselves before ultimately failing and reappearing, in a different form, in a later novel. Sharpe explicates this process as it plays out in the narrative of* The Naked Hours.]

> What is dark becomes clear only until the clarity returns to darken again; clarity is fleeting.
>
> [O que é escuro fica claro até que o claro volta a escurecer de novo, a claridade é provisória.]
>
> (Telles, *The Bare Hours* [*As Horas Nuas* (206)])[1]

In 1980, Lygia Fagundes Telles made the following observation concerning women's writing:

> It is natural for a woman author to lend a certain femininity to the work. But what ought to always prevail is the writer. That is, what she/he writes, independent of sex, social condition, etc. ... I do not accept prejudices of any kind. ... That is not to say that women should only speak about women, even though they might find it easier to describe women and feel their needs. I think that feminism is exactly the work that a woman must do. Her marked presence should be felt in all kinds of activities, hating each and every type of prejudice.
>
> (*O Globo,* July 4, 1974)

Although Telles admits that prejudice against women writers exists, she does not sanction the categorization of text or writer. As a result of her personal experience with marginalization in the fields of law and literature, she believes that each of us must undertake our own struggles with honesty and seriousness (*O Estado de São Paulo,* November 26, 1978).

Telles's struggle over the past forty-five years has produced a literary career of four novels and thirteen collections of short fiction. Although she was better known for her short stories during the beginning of her literary career, Telles's novelistic production has gained so much strength that she is now widely recognized as Clarice Lispector's successor. She was elected to the São Paulo Academy of Letters [Academia Paulista de Letras] in 1982 and to the Brazilian Academy of Letters [Academia Brasileira de Letras] in 1987. Her novelistic development began with the publication of **The Marble Dance** [*Ciranda de Pedra*] in 1954, followed by **Summer in the Fishbowl** [*Verão no*

Aquário] in 1963. *The Girl in the Photograph* [*As Meninas*] appeared in 1973, and in 1981 Telles began work on her most recent novel, *The Bare Hours* [*As Horas Nuas*], which was completed and published only in 1989.

With each successive novel, Telles hones her stylistic technique while creating and re-creating her cast of fragmented female characters that populate her fiction. Despite their strength and sheer courage, these characters are usually unable to complete the process of metamorphosis that would free them from their solitude, decadence, and lack of identity.[2] This discussion examines the interplay between the recurrent themes and characters of Telles's previous novels that constitute the narrative space of *The Bare Hours.*

Telles was born in the city of São Paulo but spent her childhood in the interior of the state. She returned to the capital to pursue her secondary education, remaining there for her university studies as well. In 1939, she received her first university degree in physical education, and during the same year she began her law degree. Against the backdrop of São Paulo's elitist social milieu, the author attests to her position as observer of a significant historical period characterized by the decline of the bourgeoisie and the rise of the values of capitalism. In the face of these complex sociohistorical realities, which Telles has often described as fitting subject matter to record the decadence of the bourgeoisie, she sets out to intermingle the real and the imaginative, stressing that she uses reality as a point of departure to speak for those who cannot express themselves (Pinto, 112). Telles views fiction as something real: "[T]he imaginary or what already happened, or is happening or will happen. You cannot set this apart from reality" (*Folha de São Paulo,* July 6, 1983).

When Telles writes about women, she does not attempt to define the concept of woman, to establish fixed definitions about what is or is not essentially feminine. Rather, she describes the ways in which women interact with what Alcoff calls the "network of elements involving others, the objective economic conditions, cultural and political institutions and ideologies" (323). Alcoff reminds us that the external context within which a person is situated determines her or his relative position, "just as the position of a pawn on a chessboard is considered safe or dangerous, powerful or weak, according to its relation to the other chess pieces" (323).

Individual identity, on the other hand, is constituted, as Teresa de Lauretis postulates, by a historical process of consciousness, a process in which one's history "is interpreted or reconstructed by each of us within the horizon of meanings and knowledge available in the culture at a given historical moment, a horizon that also includes modes of political commitment and struggle" (8). If we accept de Lauretis's definition, then we must accept her conclusion, that "consciousness is never fixed or attained once and for all because discursive boundaries change with historical conditions" (8).

Consciousness, if it is not something posited in an unchanging symbolic order, is a "fluid interaction in constant motion and open to alteration by self-analyzing practice" (Alcoff, 315). The explosion of the boundaries that enclose Telles's female characters in a world devoid of human feeling represents a dynamic attempt to break open the sociohistorical conditions that delimit their barren existence. Through their attempts at self-reflectiveness, they are involved at every moment in the futile project of reconstructing their own history. This process allows them agency as subjects at the same time that it places them within particular discursive configurations that are linked to their sociohistorical conditions (Alcoff, 315).

The concept of positionality reconfirms what Telles reveals about her own feminist intentions—that there are no universal maxims about the feminine. One's identity is a political point of departure, a motivation for action and a delineation of one's politics (Alcoff, 323). Alcoff's postulations show how women use their positional perspective as a place where values are interpreted and constructed as opposed to the concept of a place where meaning can be discovered. In other words, the positional perspective is not the locus of an already determined set of values. Thus, woman is involved in an active fashion in the construction of her identity because it is the product of her own interpretation and reconstruction of her history as mediated through the cultural discursive context to which she has access (de Lauretis, 8-9). She is the dynamic element in any attempt to alter the context that offers her limited power and mobility.

With the explosion of language and narrative style that Telles achieves in *The Bare Hours,* she continues and even surpasses the legacy of Clarice Lispector. Whereas Lispector avoids plot and incorporates unusual and lyrical language patterns, Telles breaks with convention at every aesthetic level. In retrospect, the following comment about *The Girl in the Photograph* is a better description of *The Bare Hours*: "I think rupture is important, to break the established, to break off with all that which is the easiest, the most predictable. It is difficult to explain. To forget what I already know, to invent a new adventure in language" (*O Estado de São Paulo,* May 9, 1987).

Analogous with the linguistic revolution undergone at the level of the word, signifying Telles's final break with aesthetic convention, is the complete fragmentation of the female characters that leaves them with only the core of a human identity. The novel is held together by the disparate fragments of language of what used to be considered Telles's "well-behaved prose" (Wasserman, 50) and fragments of characters who all share common experiences with separation, disappearance, solitude, loneliness, and death.

Like Telles's previous novels, *The Bare Hours* has three female protagonists, all of whom live on the periphery, outside the structure of the traditional family where the individuals' interests are mediated through the Law of the

Father. Telles's readers have already witnessed the destruction of the family as a social institution in her first novel, and the subsequent works have introduced us to a whole cast of female protagonists whose attempts at self-reflection are obstructed by the characters' incapacity to integrate the process of self-reflection with the external context of their lives. Since the protagonists are ultimately unable to fix anything more than their relative position in the process of identity making, they become like characters looking for an identity. Certain personalities are then reincarnated in subsequent novels, albeit with a different external context: "Until today, characters that I did not develop sufficiently, like Lorena from **'The Girl'** [*The Girl in the Photograph*], return to disturb me. They end up returning in another book, with another name. I am writing and I realize that I was already with that character in another book. It is her return, only that its camouflaged" (*O Globo,* August 7, 1984).

In **The Bare Hours,** the central female figure is Rosa Ambrósio, the author as Other, an actress who anesthetizes her solitude and fear of aging with alcohol.[3] Rosa's cat, Rahul, is an innovative narrator whose disclosures aid the reader in putting together the missing pieces of the puzzle of Rosa's life story that do not make up part of her interior monologues. Rosa's daughter, Cordélia, is the reincarnation of Ana Clara from **The Girl in the Photograph,** who continually attempts to escape from the solitude of her identity crisis by living out her attraction for older men. Ananta is the young feminist psychiatrist whose strange metamorphosis and subsequent physical disappearance, reminiscent of Virginia's voyage in **The Marble Dance,** bring the narrative to an end but leave the novel with no closure.

In contrast to the female characters' torment, over their lack of ability to establish an individual identity, Telles's male characters are mere puppets. Indeed, the masculine universe of Telles's entire novelistic production seems to exist solely as a point of reference for the female characters' discursive attempts to journey into the realm of self-knowledge: "In my condition as woman, I speak about woman because I don't know men as well as I know us, even though I try to penetrate the masculine universe. But it is as woman that I relate to myself and that I open myself up to all fears and the symptoms of the unknown" (*O Globo,* December 6, 1980).

In **The Bare Hours,** the male trinity consists of Renato, Gregório, and Diogo. Telles has remained loyal to her objective to interpret the world from the female point of view, and even the male characters are seen through feminine cycs:

> In my next book, the masculine characters are important because they are seen through the eyes of women. Of course, this does not take away their importance. We, women, cannot see ourselves. Somebody else is seeing us all the time: man, woman, elderly person, child. It doesn't matter. The whole time we are being analyzed by somebody, regardless of their condition. In this book, I consider the masculine characters as important as the feminine characters. Yes, there are masculine characters, but they do not act. It is the women who define these men. This is even a more truthful way of seeing. If the men were to define themselves, they would not be the same.

> (*O Estado de São Paulo,* May 9, 1987)

Renato is the stereotypical male aggressor who attempts to overpower everybody with his take-charge manner. However, his efficiency, organization, and self-confidence do not win him the affection of his cousin, Ananta. She is one female character who is an enigma to Renato. Alongside Renato Medrado are the three male figures of Rosa's past. Miguel was her first boyfriend, who died unexpectedly. Her husband, Gregório, was imprisoned and later also died. Diogo, the gigolo, is Rosa's third attempt at finding companionship. He was her lover even while Gregório was still alive, but Rosa dismisses him during one of his repeated instances of infidelity. His subsequent disappearance is a continual dilemma for Rosa, who uses the idea of his return as an escape to her encounter of self. In fact, beginning with Rosa's father, who disappeared mysteriously during her childhood, every intimate relationship Rosa has ever experienced with a man has ended in abandonment.

Rosa not only is abandoned by her father and her lovers but also experiences desertion by the women in her life. First, Cordélia announces that she is going to Australia with her elderly lover. With this, Rosa's imminent solitude is insufferable, and Telles focuses on her overpowering fear as Rosa seeks herself even more desperately in the Other. Finally, the asexual Ananta, Rosa's analyst, the ultimate knowing Other, also disappears in a strange metaphysical transformation with a third unknown Other who lives in the same apartment building as Rosa, Ananta, and Cordélia. In terms of companionship, only Rahul remains a constant, but he, just like everyone else in the novel, is unfaithful to Rosa. Rahul divulges Rosa's weaknesses and the inconsistencies of her character, stripping her of the rationalizations that prohibit her from discovering the hidden truths that would aid her in the process of self-acceptance. Instead, Rosa is left alone with her fear of the unknown.

Unable to withstand the loneliness, Rosa is incapable of anything productive, from the organization of events of her life to harnessing the creative and analytical powers of forging a true identity. This is reflected in the circular movement of her interior monologues, in the constant struggle to run from herself, in the fear of looking at herself in the mirror:

> I could use up all the saliva in the world explaining it and I would not have explained it; what is interesting is hidden. I Know Everything, my mother's magazine used to say. Now I answer, I know nothing. I know that the body belongs to the Devil because it was after I broke off with my body that I got close to God.

> [Eu poderia gastar todo o cuspe do mundo explicando e não explicava, o que interessa está escondido. Eu Sei

Tudo, dizia a revista da mamãe. Respondo agora, eu não sei nada. Sei que o corpo é do Diabo porque foi depois que rompi com meu corpo que me aproximei de Deus.]

(50)

There are both continuity and progression between the female characters of Telles's first two novels and Rosa and Ananta of *The Bare Hours.* However, unlike her spiritual sisters in *The Marble Dance* and *The Girl in the Photograph,* Rosa is older, more experienced, and aware that the enigma of life lies in the space beyond her body, beyond her lover, beyond her profession, even though she is unable to position herself effectually to reach and penetrate that space. Overwhelmed by fear, Rosa, as artist, would agree with Telles, as writer, that:

My only power is that of the word. I want to develop this up to the last drop that is not bitter. The truth is this: I am the fear, but I work with this fear. What's important is this, to work this fear with courage. I have moments of great courage; it is often necessary to treat the body like a horse that does not want to jump the fence, the whip. I whip myself, I beat myself, I try to overcome this fear and sometimes I win.

(*O Estado de São Paulo,* January 9, 1983)

Throughout the novel, Rosa's story is juxtaposed with a simultaneous discourse on the status of women in the 1980s. Although each character has a particular point of view to advance on this subject, the composite depiction for Brazilian women is far from encouraging. As a point of departure, Rosa comments on the bonding between mother and daughter, positing that although her mother is her best friend, she does not believe that women like other women: "I agree but women hate women, still that climate of competition like the king reigning amongst the odalisques. Only that story about mother and daughter works. Sometimes" [Concordo mas mulher detesta mulher, ainda aquele clima de competição com o rei reinando entre as odaliscas. Só essa história de mãe com filha é que funciona. Às vezes (17)].

Rosa also admits to having cried at childbirth when she gave birth to a daughter, instead of a son, supposedly because girls suffer more than boys. On the subject of abortion and modern technology's ability to discover the sex of unborn children, Rosa mimics the concerns of many feminists who are disturbed by the fact that, given a choice, many women still reflect their husbands' desires to have sons rather than daughters. Rosa observes that if this attitude were allowed to influence decisions on the desirability of unborn children, abortion could conceivably endanger the future of womankind.

Ananta responds to Rosa's concerns from a more rational stance: "The revolution is recent, Rosa. Think of a test tube that was shaken up, the water is murky but when the deposit settles, the water will clear up again. Even though the bottom is full of blood" [A revolução é recente, Rosa. Pense num tubo de ensaio que foi sacudido, a água fica turva mas quando o depósito se assentar essa água vai ficar límpida. Ainda que o fundo seja de sangue (122)].

Rosa counters Ananta's argument with a critique of the power structure that has corrupted woman's purity. Whereas women's choices are more open-ended today than they were in the past, self-knowledge is essential for resolving one's personal preferences. Rosa manifests the anguish of the process of self-acceptance when she admits that she was happier with herself back in the days when she was like:

those ancient women who used to embroider, [that] seemed so calm making pillows, rugs. Or was it all make-believe? Wouldn't the women be happier embroidering themselves? ... I used to like myself, Ananta. Now I hate myself ... to live with me, myself, horrible.

[aquelas antigas mulheres que bordavam [que] pareciam tão calmas fazendo almofadas, tapetes. Ou era tudo fingimento? As mulheres não seriam mais felizes se bordassem? ... Eu gostava de mim, Ananta. Agora me detesto ... conviver comigo mesma, horrível.]

(122)

Ananta responds calmly, as has Telles in numerous interviews, that those who like to embroider would certainly be happier doing so, but each woman must make her own choices.

In response to Rosa's and Ananta's views on the issues of selfhood, Renato offers the reader the masculine critique of the feminist movement. He views Ananta's nonthreatening behavior as an acceptable form of feminism, and he even falls in love with this nonaggressive feminist who is involved with organizations that give social and legal aid to the large numbers of needy women who are victims of the social transformations women have experienced over the past several decades. Renato's behavior suggests that the feminist movement is worthy of male support, as long as it stays within the limits of charitable acts and does not challenge the power structure.

Ananta's puzzling disappearance from her apartment one afternoon spurs Renato into beginning an extensive search for her. Always preoccupied with the traffic and her watch, Ananta is reminiscent of the city and its impact on our contemporary lifestyle. Renato imagines that Ananta's association with various feminist groups might even be responsible for her disappearance. The narration of Renato's interaction with the police department, his frustration at not being able to locate Ananta, and the declaration of his feelings of love for her conclude the novel in the fashion of a detective story that has no resolution.

Closure is unobtainable for Rosa, Cordélia, Ananta, and even Renato who is left with only the faintest hope of finding Ananta. In the last analysis, solitude, even among the many inhabitants of the colossal São Paulo, is inescapable, and sanctuary from solitude is only momentary, as we learn from Telles in the novel: "What is dark becomes clear until the clarity returns to darken again; clarity is fleeting" [O que é escuro fica claro até que o claro volta a escurecer de novo, a claridade é provisória (206)].

If the agony of the process of writing is a metaphor for darkness, as Telles has sometimes described it, then we can equate clarity with the interplay between the explosion of language and recurrent themes that constitute **The Bare Hours.** Caio Fernando Abreu has appraised Telles's contribution in a slightly different fashion: "The first lady went crazy. God bless her: this craziness is sacred" (88). Whether Telles's most recent novel is seen as another fleeting moment of clarity in her brilliant literary career or as the result of the craziness of creativity, the result is indeed sacred.

Notes

1. Except for quotes taken from *The Girl in the Photograph* [*As Meninas*], all translations are Susan Quinlan's and mine.

2. See Cristina Ferreira Pinto's discussion of the character Virginia in *The Marble Dance* [*Ciranda de Pedra*] in *O Bildungsroman feminino: Quatro exemplos brasileiros,* 109-50. Pinto establishes Virginia as an exception to this rule in Telles's fiction.

3. In a personal interview with Lygia Fagundes Telles in São Paulo in July 1988, she described the protagonist of her next novel as an aging woman, alone and uncomfortable with the process of growing old, and insinuated that some of the protagonist's concerns were autobiographical in nature.

References

PRIMARY

NOVELS BY TELLES

The Girl in the Photograph. Trans. Margaret A. Neves. New York: Avon Bard, 1973.

As Meninas. Rio de Janeiro: Nova Fronteira, 1985.

As Horas Nuas. Rio de Janeiro: Nova Fronteira, 1989.

The Marble Dance. Trans. Margaret A. Neves. New York: Avon Bard, 1986.

Ciranda de Pedra. Rio de Janeiro: José Olympio Editora, 1954.

Verão no Aquário. Rio de Janeiro: Editora Nova Fronteira, 1984.

INTERVIEWS

"Histórias do desencontro: Uma atmosfera de conflitos." Interview. *Última Hora,* July 17, 1958.

Medina, Cremilda. "Cinco escritoras questionam a literatura feminina." *O Estado de São Paulo,* November 26, 1978.

"Microentrevista com Lygia Fagundes Telles." Interview. *Folha de São Paulo,* July 6, 1983.

Paiva, Fernando, and Sílvio Cioffi. "Lygia: Meu único poder: A palavra." *O Estado de São Paulo,* January 9, 1983.

Priami, Elda. "Lygia Fagundes Telles." *O Globo,* December 6, 1980.

Ribeiro, Leo Gilson. "Lygia, imortal." *Jornal da Tarde,* May 9, 1987.

Schulke, Evelyn. "Lygia Fagundes Telles voltou a escrever um livro atual." *Jornal da Tarde,* December 7, 1973.

SECONDARY

Abreu, Caio Fernando. "As horas de Lygia." Review of *As horas nuas* by Lygia Fagundes Telles. *Isto É,* June 21, 1989.

Alcoff, Linda. "Cultural Feminism versus Post-Structuralism: The Identity Crisis in Feminist Theory." *Feminist Theory in Practice and Process.* Ed. Micheline Malson, Jean F. O'Barr, Sarah Westphal-Wihl, and Mary Wyer. Chicago: University of Chicago Press, 1989, 295-326.

de Lauretis, Teresa, ed. *Feminist Studies, Critical Studies.* Bloomington: Indiana University Press, 1986.

Pinto, Cristina Ferreira. *O Bildungsroman feminino: Quatro exemplos brasileiros.* São Paulo: Perspectiva, 1990.

Wasserman, Renata R. Mautner. "The Guerrilla in the Bathtub: Telles's *As Meninas* and the Eruption of Politics." *Modern Language Studies* 19.1 (1989): 50-65.

Cristina Ferreira-Pinto (essay date 1996)

SOURCE: Ferreira-Pinto, Cristina. "The Fantastic, the Gothic, and the Grotesque in Contemporary Brazilian Women's Novels." *Chasqui* 25.2 (1996): 71-80. Print.

[*In the following essay, Ferreira-Pinto includes Telles and her novel* The Naked Hours *in a discussion of fantastic, Gothic, and grotesque elements in the fictional works of contemporary Brazilian women writers, who are notable for their inventive and experimental narratives. According to Ferreira-Pinto, Telles employs aspects of the supernatural and the absurd to call into question the accuracy of her characters' reality.*]

Brazilian literature has long been characterized by linguistic and stylistic innovation and the construction of an ambiguous narrative viewpoint, characteristics derived from the authors' awareness of the fluid, shifting relationship between language and reality (cf. Payne and Fitz 5). Contemporary Brazilian women writers are part of this tradition, and have produced, in the last twenty or twenty-five years, a significant body of work, outstanding for its discourse experimentation and inventiveness in plot.[1] This includes the use of elements of the fantasy novel, a term that describes the novel of the fantastic, the gothic, the grotesque, the fairy tale, the utopian novel, etc. Sonia Coutinho (*O jogo de Ifá,*

1980, *O caso Alice,* 1991), Marilene Felinto (*As mulheres de Tijucopapo,* 1982), and Márcia Denser (*A ponte das estrelas,* 1990) are a few examples of this tendency. This study will focus on the use of the fantastic, the gothic and the grotesque in two novels by two of the most prominent Brazilian female writers today: Lya Luft's *O quarto fechado* (1984), and Lygia Fagundes Telles's *As horas nuas* (1989).

The gothic can be generally understood as a subgenre within the literature of the fantastic; however, Rosemary Jackson, in *Fantasy: The Literature of Subversion,* points out that the gothic in fact constitutes the more "immediate roots" of the fantastic, while its more remote origins could "be traced back to ancient myths, legends, folklore, carnival art" (95). Nevertheless, what will distinguish the gothic within the fantastic mode is its "preoccupation with the domestic realm" (Ellis ix), which is constructed as an oppressive environment, wherein a sense of terror or imminent danger looms over the protagonist. The gothic novel shows a "topography of enclosures, wastelands, vaults, dark spaces, to express psychic terrors and primal desires" (Jackson 108). Since its inception, it has been characterized by elements of horror and violence, and by supernatural effects. It emerges at the margins of the bourgeois culture, while at the same time representing a form of commentary and pressure against this culture. As the genre undergoes changes in the early nineteenth century, with the novels of Mary Shelley and others, the gothic becomes more concerned with psychological problems, often expressing the subject's conflicts within an inimical social situation. The modern gothic will then be an enactment of the split of the subject, and an expression of the subject's desire for unity (Jackson 97, 99-101). Thus the gothic is used by contemporary authors, particularly women, who have made effective use of the genre, developing and extending a tradition that has come to constitute "a literary form capable of more radical interrogation of social contradictions" (Jackson 97).[2]

In the modern and contemporary gothic, "the object of fear can have no adequate representation and is, therefore, all the more threatening" (Jackson 112). Fear emanates, not from physical characteristics, but rather from antagonistic social values thereby represented. Yet, the source of fear is barely perceived by the subject, never fully articulated through language. The object of fear, as Jackson says, is "unnameable" (112), it escapes language, and therefore appears frequently as a grotesque construct, for the grotesque is "beyond the reach of language," it defies "our conventional, language-based categories" (Harpham 3, 5).

The grotesque represents the physical and/or psychological distortion of human or animal forms, and can be seen also as a strategy of the literature of the fantastic, since exaggeration is one of the features constitutive of the fantastic figurative discourse (cf. Todorov 77). The grotesque appears often as metaphors that heighten the paltriness and absurdity of our lives, in a literary mode which is the genre

par excellence that allows for transgression, questioning—if not subverting—the value system supported by the dominant ideology (cf. Guerra-Cunningham 84). In addition, the fantastic mode "problematizes representation of the 'real,' . . . [by drawing] attention to difficulties of representation and to conventions of literary discourse" (Jackson 84). The fantastic, as Tzvetan Todorov explains, deals with the same subjects all literature deals with, but brings to this subject a *different intensity,* the superlative, the excessive; it represents "an experience of limits" (Todorov 93), and the transgression of these limits. The use of elements of the fantastic in women's literature, however, has another function as well: it serves to highlight the ambiguous position of women in a male-centered order, to underline their marginality. By the same token, contemporary female authors, from Brazil and elsewhere, have also favored the gothic novel as the vehicle for "an increasingly insistent critique of the ideology of separate spheres," male and female (Ellis xv). Gothic novels bring together "fantastic occurrences," cases of madness (either real or perceived as such), "ghostly images, eerie voices, . . . ethereal figures" (Quinlan 97), constructing thus a troubling portrayal of the inequalities and frustrations faced by contemporary women. The gothic novel, blurring the boundaries between the "natural" and the supernatural, serves the "purpose of journeying into the psyche" of the female subject, but is also "a way to dissect the silent, mad places of a collective consciousness" (Quinlan 83).

Lygia Fagundes Telles and Lya Luft, the two authors whose novels will be the object of my scrutiny, have shown common points in their fictional production. In both Telles's and Luft's fiction the reader often finds a gap between the expected, common logic and the characters' actual lives, and feels, along with the characters, the ambiguity caused by the merging of two worlds—"that of the real and that of the fantastic" (Todorov 26). Their novelistic works are characterized by a probing into the lives of middle-class women, constituting a study of the female subject in her relations with the Other within the context of Brazilian society—a society that continues to be inherently patriarchal, in spite of some relative freedoms that women from the upper classes have achieved.[3]

The focus on contemporary, middle-class, and most often urban, women leads to the questioning of the human condition within a world that is in transition, in a crisis "gerada pela desorientação de homens e mulheres diante de uma avalanche de interrogações impostas pelos novos tempos, pós-teológicos" (Coelho 13).[4] A recurrent theme in Telles's and in Luft's novels is precisely the decadence of the bourgeois order and, within it, the decadence of the family institution. It is the conflict between the characters' desires and aspirations, on one hand, and the demands and obstacles still imposed by the social order, on the other hand, that originates the ambiguity and absurdity highlighted by the use of the fantastic and the gothic, or metaphorized through the use of the grotesque. The fantastic, the gothic and the grotesque constitute thus strategies of estrangement which will lead to the revelation, in the lives of these otherwise ordinary women, the ruling of a different logic, or the lack of any logic altogether. In this respect, their novels can be seen as Kafkaesque narratives, in that the everyday, ordinary middle-class lives of the protagonists are revealed to obey an absurd order.

* * *

The intrusion of the supernatural in the daily life of the protagonist can be seen in Luft's *As parceiras* (1980), which has been studied as a contemporary example of the gothic novel in Susan Quinlan's *The Female Voice in Contemporary Brazilian Narrative. As parceiras* serves as a paradigm for the author's later novels, introducing many of the same thematic and formal elements found in *O quarto fechado*. Madness, death, the repression of desires, and aspirations, and the absurd logic of human life—all come to light as the middle-aged female protagonist delves into the absurdity of her own life, in a reassessment of her past, her frustrations and failures. Death is the starting point of the two novels, as the narrative compensates for the void left by the absence of the dead (in both novels, the protagonist's son). But while the narrative—in the form, mainly, of the characters' thoughts and memories—serves to fill in the space left by a loss, it will also reveal other losses and absences, the *death in life* experienced by each character in their daily existences.

In *O quarto fechado,* death is at the core of the text in several different ways. First, it is identified with one of the characters, Ella, whose strange name in Portuguese allows for this ambiguous identification, Ella—a woman's name—and "ela, a Morte," she—death (cf. McClendon and Craige xi). Death is a character in its own right, referred to as the "Lover" and the "Bride," whose presence in the house is first acknowledged by the external narrative voice. Death "holds the symbolic center for the narrative" (McClendon 24), and is also at the center of the text in a structural way, in the form of a casket holding the body of Camilo, in the center of a room, around which sit the various characters. Death is finally a central theme in the text, a leitmotif that appears intertwined with the life of each character as their existences are examined through the narrative.

In *O quarto fechado* Luft manipulates elements of the grotesque, the gothic, and of the fantastic in order to expose the conflicts of the characters and, by extension, the disintegration of the bourgeois family unit. According to Luft herself, the novel is about "the conflict of a woman who wants to have a career ... , and also wants to have the joys of a married life, of being a mother ... [and] how difficult it is to conciliate" (Payne 113). Giving up a satisfying but yet incomplete life as a famous pianist to become a wife and mother—roles which she does not find self-fulfilling—causes a split in the protagonist, Renata.[5] As a counterpoint

to her is Martim, her husband, whose attachment to the traditional male role of *material provider—emotional absentee* does not allow him true self-realization or a satisfying relationship with his wife and children. His clinging to a traditional, patriarchal order clashes with Renata's aspirations and her inability to submit to social expectations. Renata's conflicts, her sense of being incomplete, is thus similar to the split we see in Martim and also in the other characters, each one torn between roles they have to accept and desires that remain unfulfilled. In fact, very little distinguishes Renata as protagonist from the other characters; showing, one by one, the inner turmoils, frustrated expectations, and hidden selves of each family member, the novel plays and replays its main theme: the inner split experienced by every human being, and the desire for connection and unity each individual seeks to achieve in different— and most often failed—ways. Therefore, while we may accept Renata as the protagonist in a novel that presents multiple narrative viewpoints, it is Camilo, Renata's son, who in fact incarnates the novel's very theme.

Camilo's body in a casket opens the narrative. His presence/absence in the center of the room, and in the center of the text, creates the possibility for each family member to rethink his/her own process of destruction, their own paths towards death. Says Ruth Silviano Brandão: "É diante dele que todos revivem suas fantasias, fazem retornar seus fantasmas, penetrando mais na própria loucura, pois a loucura é a outra face da morte. Para todos ele começa a ser uma ausência que deve ser preenchida por palavras ..." (34).

Camilo's casket in the center of the room/text, his slow "death" within death, marked by subtle but regular changes in his face and appearance, the presence of death itself (herself?) as a character in the narrative—all this makes María Luisa Bombal's *La amortajada* (1938) an unavoidable reference for the reader of Spanish-American literature. As in many of Bombal's works, reality becomes an ambiguous concept, oscillating between what we usually call "real" and that which is undefinable, a dream-like, fantastic, or imaginary dimension. This ambiguity serves to highlight—in both Bombal's and Luft's works—the female problematic within a male-dominated order, as Lucía Guerra-Cunningham has asserted (82). In *O quarto fechado,* however, it is also used to underscore Camilo's quest for wholeness, his desperate search for unity, which becomes a troubling representation of every individual's search for him/herself. Camilo is the transgressive element, the one who dares search for the true meaning of existence beyond existence itself. He is aware of the emptiness in life and seeks to fulfill it, as he is attracted by the other, definitive, emptiness/absence—death. Death is the ultimate answer, the only possibility of achieving totality, the integration of the self with the self. It is by actively seeking death that Camilo becomes the transgressor. His death— actually his suicide—is the transgressive and epiphanic moment, the instant of knowledge:

Cavalgando o demônio do próprio sêmem misturado ao
de suor e imanações brutais, ele errara de prazer e medo,
ódio e vitória. Expelira fezes e urina, e despencara enfim
naquele abraço, onde seria unicamente Camilo: dissolvido
em beleza, liberado numa água sem margens ...

(11)

Camilo's suicide is described as an instant of liberation,
exuberance, excess—elements that also characterize eroti-
cism (Bataille 11). The description of Camilo's encounter
with death as sexual is not unintentional, precisely because
death is here the culmination of Camilo's search, a search
that before had taken him to other borders, to other possible transgressions as, for example, the possibility of incest
with his twin sister. Death is thus a dimension of the erotic
experience, both as transgression and as a moment of integration, when the subject feels complete, whole. Camilo is
also the transgressor in that he is an androgynous figure. In
fact, his characterization, particularly through his father's
eyes, implies the possibility that he is homosexual, or bi-
sexual, for that matter. But his sexual orientation is not
precisely the point; Camilo's importance here lies, rather,
in three aspects: first, as an androgynous figure, he represents the very totality he searches for; second, as a young
man who is "different," who may even be "effeminate"
(36), he is a challenge to the patriarchal order the father
stands for; and, third, in the characterization of Camilo we
find an example of the authorial manipulation which lends
to the narrative a tone of ambiguity and mystery.

This ambiguity is achieved through an abundance of certain
locutions, such as "maybe," "perhaps," "it seemed," "as if,"
and the recurrent use of the imperfect tense as well as of
questions that remain unanswered, as for example:

Clara saberia talvez das incursões ao quarto de Ella, mas
Renata não tinha coragem de indagar. A cunhada olharia,
sorrindo, que mal tinha isso? Um quarto de doente, apenas. Ella não era um bicho. *Ou era?* diria Clara, com seus
olhos bem abertos, de criança, de louca, de sábia?

(84-85)

The use of the imperfect tense and modalization are identified by Todorov as narrative strategies that contribute to the
construction of the fantastic. The imperfect tense, in particular, "introduces a further distance between the character
and the narrator, so that we are kept from knowing the
latter's position" (Todorov 38-39). The reader is kept "suspended" between everyday events and the supernatural,
and therefore in doubt as to what is actually taking place.
The intrusion of mystery in everyday life constitutes a
break in the common, acceptable order, and thus discloses
some hidden dimensions of "normal" life. As I noted before, the fantastic produces an effect of estrangement and
thereby serves to highlight and address the incongruities of
the established social order. Likewise, the grotesque (which
in Luft may reveal the influence of German writers such as
Thomas Mann and Günter Grass, whose works she has
translated into Portuguese) is also used as a social commen-

tary. In *O quarto fechado,* Ella's huge and lifeless body,
Mamãe's grotesquely made-up face, and Clara's daily routine of making up and dressing up in order to wait for a date
that never arrives, are all grotesque masks, caricatures that
hide a hollow body of unfulfilled desires, destitute of meaningful life. The three women are metaphors of everyone's
hopeless and absurd wait: they all wait or have once waited
for happiness, self-realization, wholeness, when the one
who *has* come indeed is death.

O quarto fechado offers an example of Luft's taste for the
fantastic and the supernatural as vehicles for denouncing
the failures and frustrations of the contemporary individual
within the chaos and uncertainties of a social order in crisis.
Although Luft's social commentary concerns everyone, regardless of sex, we cannot ignore the author's own remarks
about the novel's thematic (i.e. the conflicts of a female
protagonist), nor the fact that, of the only two male characters in the book, one, Martim, serves as a counterpoint to
Renata's conflicts, while at the same time representing the
very patriarchal order that engulfs her. The second male
character, Camilo, as an androgynous figure represents at
the same time the duality of human life, male and female,
and the desire for unity shared by all. The articulation of
elements of the fantastic and the grotesque, the themes of
death, suicide, madness, and transgression, along with an
imagery of spider-webs, closed spaces and the fog that
threatens to invade the house, creates a contemporary gothic novel "to demonstrate the author's contention that the
norms of ... [that society are] in and of themselves abnormal" (Quinlan 81). As in some of her other novels, Luft
illustrates here the difficulties faced by the female subject,
divided between her own aspirations and the demands of a
patriarchal social order within which self-realization and
integration are nearly impossible. Death, then, may seem
to be the only answer.

* * *

The obstacles faced by women in conflict with an inimical
society is also a recurrent theme in Lygia Fagundes Telles's
fiction. In *As horas nuas,* her latest novel, the author once
again places the female problematic as the center of the
narrative, from which point she raises pressing issues for
the contemporary subject, male and female. The use of the
fantastic and the supernatural in *As horas nuas* serves
similar purposes to those seen in Luft's *O quarto fechado,*
however with different results. This is in part due to the fact
that, while *O quarto fechado* leaves the reader with a deep
sense of the powerlessness experienced by the characters,
irony and a somewhat humorous sense of the absurd permeates Telles's novel.

Telles's use of the fantastic, the magic, and the supernatural has long been recognized and studied by the critics, but
mostly in reference to her short fiction, for it is in her stories
that these elements appear with more force and distinction.
Her novels, nevertheless, have also shown the author's skill

in creating an atmosphere wherein the boundaries between the real and the supernatural are broken. In her novelistic work, Telles often reveals her "strong inclination for exploring the manifestations of the unconscious" (Lucas 288), with dream fragments playing an important part in the narrative and character development. Telles utilizes dreams to create a sense of discontinuity in the characters' reality and thereby leads the reader to question the integrity of such reality. Likewise, the recurrence of omens, signs, visions, and memories, and the character's pursuit of their meaning and echoes in real life, produce an effect of ambiguity: did it happen or was it a subjective impression on the part of the character, an impression the reader is led to share? In fact, the reliance on memories in the construction of the narrative, as in *Verão no aquário* (1963), points to the very fragility of any categorization of what may be termed "real."

In the three novels written before *As horas nuas,* the most obvious sign of the fantastic is the ambiguity that results from the identification between reader and protagonist, as the reader follows the character in her hesitation before the probable occurrence of a dream or vision and its possible meanings. In this respect, *As horas nuas* represents a departure from the earlier novels, in that the fantastic is now fully developed, constituting a main element in the narrative structure. However, we may say that some of Telles's novels—most notably *Ciranda de pedra* (1954)—are set in a gothic-like oppressive environment, and thus *As horas nuas* does find a precedent within the novelist's work.

As horas nuas reworks the general conventions of the gothic novel, if we consider it, with Jameson, a genre "in which the dialectic of privilege and shelter is rehearsed: your privileges seal you off from other people, but by the same token constitute a protective wall through which you cannot see, and behind which, therefore, all kinds of envious forces may be imagined ... preparing to give assault" (528). In Telles's novel the protagonist hides in the confines of her upper-class apartment, protected and cared for by an old maid who also serves as a channel of communication with the outside world. Ironically, while the news brought in by the maid may be only reports about the weather or the day's patron saint read on the wall almanac, the "envious forces" threatening the protagonist are signs of the collapse, not only of her personal life—abandonment by her lover, aging, idleness—but also of the dominant social order—sexual liberation, feminist agendas—and of society in general—AIDS, urban chaos, violence. It is here that *As horas nuas* is able to give a "more substantive and formal leap" as a gothic novel, for, despite the protagonist's reactionary mentality, she nevertheless represents the crisis confronted by the individual within contemporary society; as the "victim," she is but a metonymy for the collectivity assaulted by similar problems (cf. Jameson 529).

As horas nuas has three main focuses, just as it has three narrative voices. The central focus is occupied by the protagonist-narrator, Rosa Ambrósio, an aging, alcoholic, and decadent actress who struggles with the spectrum of old age. The world she sees around her is equally decadent, a society in crisis. The two other focuses of the text are centered on two strange characters who function as Rosa's alter egos. Ananta, a psychoanalyst and feminist, is not a narrator, but the external, omniscient narrative voice lets the reader share her thoughts, uncovering desires and motives normally hidden behind her mask of cold and self-control, characteristics that contrast with Rosa's alcoholism and excess. As the protagonist's alter ego, Ananta serves as a voice to express opinions that are rebuffed by Rosa, thus establishing a dialogue that examines issues such as women's roles and feminism in Brazilian society. Rosa's second alterego, who is also a narrator in the text, is Rahul, a cat. Here comes into play the fantastic, no longer as "an uncanny event ... [that appears] following a series of indirect indications, as the climax of gradation" (Todorov 171), but as a reality the reader has to accept without further questioning: a cat who thinks and remembers, an ironic, cynical, "Machado-de-Assis-like" observer who critically watches Rosa, making her and the others characters of his own narrative.[6]

Rahul, a cat with a man's name, is a lucid but marginal voice, an outside observer in the line of Machado de Assis's Brás Cubas or Cyro dos Anjos's Belmiro. In fact, Rahul's detachment from his human "fellows" is very much the same one that comes to characterize Brás Cubas in his "life" after death. A comparison betweeen the last lines of *Memórias Póstumas de Brás Cubas* (1881) and the following excerpt from *As horas nuas* reveals an unexpected intertextuality:

> ... Não alcancei a celebridade do emplastro, não fui califa, não conheci o casamento. Verdade é que, ao lado dessas faltas, coube-me a boa fortuna de não comprar o pão como o suor do meu rosto ... ao chegar a este outro lado do mistério achei-me com um pequeno saldo, que é a derradeira negativa deste capítulo de negativas:—Não tive filhos, não transmiti a nenhuma criatura o legado da nossa miséria.

> (144)

> A única vantagem do bicho sobre o homem é a inconsciência da morte e da morte eu estou consciente. Resta-me o consolo da morte sem bagagem, deixo uma coleira antipulga. Duas vasilhas e uma almofada.

> (*As horas nuas* 114)

Rahul holds a privileged position as observer/narrator/comentator of the lives of those who inhabit Rosa Ambrósio's world, due to his double marginality, as a cat living among humans, and as a cat who does not participate in a feline mode of economic exchange: since he is declawed and castrated, Rahul neither hunts nor procreates. ...

As one of the narrative voices, Rahul allows the author a greater distance between herself and the events narrated and issues raised, making possible that otherwise too disturbing comments be made, while still keeping the reader's full attention. Rahul is also an obvious parallel to the protagonist, for as a cat he has nine lives to live, just as Rosa, an actress, has had several previous lives, having played different roles. The memories of their previous lives are a common point between the protagonist and her cat. In a world in decadence and, in Rosa's case, living an existence whose fragility is made obvious by the approach of old age and of death itself, memories are a recourse for postponing the inevitable. Memories serve to relieve the characters—as well as the reader—from a bleak reality, by bringing into it seemingly better and happier times. But the cat narrator will take away from the reader the possibility of relief when he begins to interpose within his own remembrances the painful doubt as to whether the memories he has been narrating are anything but fiction (53, 54-55, 59). According to Nancy A. Walker, it is not uncommon to find that, in writings by women, "the validity of the author's or the narrator's own perceptions is called into question and revised or reconstructed" (186). In a similar manner, Rahul questions the authenticity of his own discourse by shattering the "suspension of disbelief" that had been the contract established between the text and the reader.

This fantastic dimension of the novel, constructed around the figure of Rahul, is augmented by his narrating seeing visions, ghosts from recent times and from other lives (other incarnations) he had lived before. All this is narrated in a quite matter-of-fact tone, which demands that the reader accept the supernatural as normal. So we may say of *As horas nuas* what Todorov did of Kafka's *Metamorphosis* (1915): "the most surprising thing here is precisely the absence of surprise" regarding events that affect the character (Todorov 169).

The reference to Kafka here is not casual, for the Jewish writer was one of Telles's favorite readings at the beginning of her career, and has been an influence on her work (cf. Silva; Van Steen 30). Kafka's influence may be seen in the use of metamorphosis as a means to achieve a fantastic effect. The fantastic centers now on the character of Ananta and is used to shed a new light on such trivial things as somebody coming home after a workday to an empty room, or somebody disappearing in a big city without anyone ever knowing of his or her whereabouts. We come across facts like these, through the newspapers or in our own lives, with such frequency that we stop paying attention to them. Telles, however, makes clear that, while common, they are not "normal," but rather a reflection of the chaos of contemporary life. Likewise, Ananta's spartan and orderly lifestyle is revealed to be a mask hiding the fear of the outside reality (*As horas nuas* 78). It is in this light that we can read the metamorphosis of Ananta's neighbor in the upstairs apartment:

> [Ananta] ouviu os passos circulares na ronda da fatalidade, ainda o espanto. Ainda a contenção toda feita de cálculo,

ele se preparava. Quando a respiração se acelerou, vieram os espasmos, o corpo crescendo intenso com a música ... até estourar em focinho, cascos, crinas ... O úmido resfolegar soprando furioso por entre os dentes, as veias saltadas, os olhos. O latejamento crescendo na acomodação das carnes, peles ...

(70)

Undressing upon coming home, the man takes off clothes as well as skin, removing the human mask worn on the street in order to become a horse and thus liberate himself, within the confines of his lonely apartment, as energy, strength, fury. In her own home, Ananta, fascinated, listens to her neighbor's nightly routine, aware that he knows *she* knows (71). Later, when Ananta disappears at about the same time as the upstairs apartment is vacated, there is an implication that maybe she and the man-horse had in fact achieved some kind of true communication, breaking the isolation that is the norm in contemporary society. In this manner, here, as in Kafka, the fantastic object is the normal, everyday human being, and the supernatural becomes both a consequence of, or rather, a reaction to the dominant logic, and a way of highlighting the absurdity of our existence.

* * *

In Telles's *As horas nuas,* as in Luft's *O quarto fechado,* we have two examples of the use of elements of the fantasy novel by contemporary Brazilian women writers. While Luft's novel concludes on a much more pessimistic tone in regard to the perspectives (or lack thereof) that await the individual in contemporary society, both authors, nevertheless, find a common ground in their use of the fantastic, the gothic and the grotesque. As Anne Cranny-Francis points out, "fantastic elements or conventions ... disrupt the realist surface of narrative," and the lack of final resolution or explanation for events perceived as supernatural or "unnatural" maintains the disruption of the dominant discourse, which otherwise would have been reasserted, had a resolution been achieved (Cranny-Francis 100, 102). The fantastic and its allied genres, therefore, constitute effective vehicles to denounce the failure of traditional logic and the incongruities of the dominant value system. Focusing on problems affecting the female subject, Telles and Luft have been successful in exposing the many ways in which contemporary Brazilian society has failed to provide for the authentic self-realization of the individual.

Notes

1. Brazilian women's participation in this tradition is undeniable; it should not be ignored, however, that the relationship of the Brazilian female author to the literary canon has been very problematic, especially through the first five decades of this century. Up to then, women had been occasionally accepted in the canon on the basis of their "exceptionality" (e.g. Raquel de Queiroz, Clarice Lispector). More frequently,

however, "exceptional" women had been simply reduced to a name that would appear among a long ennumeration of male writers belonging to a particular literary period or movement (cf. Ferreira-Pinto 224-25). This situation begins to change in the 1970's, when the literary production by women starts to receive more recognition, a trend that is part of the larger recognition and acceptance of the Other, of those voices that had been systematically silenced or ignored by the dominant discourse (Coelho 11; see also Santiago 31-35).

2. On the use of the gothic by women writers, see, among others, Cranny-Francis, specially pages 99-103; Ellis; Fleenor.

3. See Gerda Lerner (215-17) on the issue of women's relative freedom and the distribution of power and responsibilities within the family and in society. Even though Lerner discusses women in modern industrial states such as the United States, her assertions are valid for Brazilian women of the middle and upper classes.

4. Whenever a text is available in English, I will quote from the English translation, unless an alternate version, which will appear in brackets, is deemed appropriate. Lacking an English translation, I will quote from the original in Portuguese.

5. The meaning of the name Renata is easily recognized: "re-nata," "born again," "reborn." McClendon found here a "first clue" for her reading of Luft's novel in "Theoretical dialogue in *O quarto fechado*" (25). I see the name's denotation as ironic, at the least, for what the reader witnesses here is not the character's rebirth to a new self, with the positive implications usually associated with "the beginning of a new life," but rather the slow death of the character, as her aspirations are, little by little, left unfulfilled.

6. The creation of a cat who thinks as a human being may be regarded as a grotesque construct, for it fuses in one character both animal and human traits. Nevertheless, Rahul evokes the fable, another subgenre within the fantastic mode, not only because he thinks and narrates, but also because his observations and remarks seem at times to convey a moral. A better example of the grotesque in this novel is Ananta's neighbor, whom nobody sees during the day, and whose movements at night are described as those of a horse.

Works Cited

Bataille, Georges. *Erotism: Death and Sensuality.* 1957. San Francisco: City Lights, 1986.

Bombal, María Luisa. *La amortajada.* 1938. Barcelona: Seix Barral, 1984.

Brandão, Ruth Silviano. "A fascinante (in)quietude do feminino." *A mulher escrita.* Lúcia Castello Branco and Ruth Silviano Brandão. Rio de Janeiro: Casa Maria Editorial/Livros Técnicos e Científicos, 1989. 25-35.

Coelho, Nelly Novaes. *A literatura feminina no Brasil contemporâneo.* São Paulo: Siciliano, 1993.

Coutinho, Sonia. *O caso Alice.* Rio de Janeiro: Rocco, 1991.

———. *O jogo de Ifá.* São Paulo: Atica, 1980.

Cranny-Francis, Anne. *Feminist Fiction. Feminist Uses of Generic Fiction.* New York: St. Martin's P, 1990.

Denser, Márcia. *A ponte das estrelas: Uma superprodução de aventuras.* São Paulo: Editora Best Seller, 1990.

Ellis, Kate Ferguson. *The Contested Castle: Gothic Novels and the Subversion of Domestic Ideology.* Urbana: U of Illinois P, 1989.

Fábio, Lucas. "Lygia Fagundes Telles." *Dictionary of Literary Biography. Modern Latin-American Fiction Writers.* Vol. 113. Detroit: Bruccoli Clark Layman Book, 1992. 287-92.

Felinto, Marilene. *As mulheres de Tijucopapo.* Rio de Janeiro: Paz e Terra, 1982.

Ferreira-Pinto, Cristina. "La mujer y el canon poético en Brasil a principios del siglo XX: Hacia una reevaluación de la poesía de Gilka Machado." *La torre* 34 (abril-junio 1995): 221-41.

Fleenor, Juliann E., ed. *The Female Gothic.* Montreal: Eden P, 1983.

Guerra-Cunningham, Lucía. "Estética fantástica y mensaje metafísico en 'Lo secreto' de María Luisa Bombal." *María Luisa Bombal: Apreciaciones críticas.* Eds. Marjorie Agosín, Elena Gascón and Joy Renjilian-Burgy. Tempe: Bilingual P/Editorial Bilingüe, 1987. 82-7.

Harpham, Geoffrey Galt. *On the Grotesque. Strategies of Contradiction in Art and Literature.* Princeton: Princeton UP, 1982.

Jackson, Rosemary. *Fantasy: The Literature of Subversion.* 1981. London: Routledge, 1988.

Jameson, Fredric. "Nostalgia for the Present." *South Atlantic Quaterly* 88.2 (1989): 517-37.

Lerner, Gerda. *The Creation of Patriarchy.* New York: Oxford UP, 1986a.

Luft, Lya. *As parceiras.* 5a ed. Rio de Janeiro: Guanabara, 1986. Orig. 1980.

————. *O quarto fechado.* 3a ed. Rio de Janeiro: Editora Guanabara, 1986. Orig. 1984.

Machado de Assis, Joaquim Maria. *Epitaph of a Small Winner.* Trans. William L. Grossman. 1952. New York: Avon, 1978.

————. *Memórias póstumas de Brás Cubas.* 6a ed. São Paulo: Atica, 1977.

McClendon, Carmen Chaves. "Theoretical Dialogue in *O quarto fechado.*" *Chasqui* 17.2 (1988): 23-6.

McClendon, Carmen Chaves, and Betty Jean Craige. "Translators' Preface." Lya Luft, *The Island of the Dead.* Trans. Carmen Chaves McClendon and Betty Jean Craige. Athens: U of Georgia P, 1986. ix-xii.

Payne, Judith A. "Lya Luft: Fiction and the Possible Selves." *Brasil/Brazil* 5 (1991): 104-14.

Payne, Judith A., and Earl E. Fitz. *Ambiguity and Gender in the New Novel of Brazil and Spanish America: A Comparative Assessment.* Iowa City: U of Iowa P, 1993.

Quinlan, Susan. *The Female Voice in Contemporary Brazilian Narrative.* New York: Peter Lang, 1990.

Santiago, Silviano. "Prosa literária atual no Brasil." *Nas malhas da letra.* São Paulo: Companhia das Letras, 1989. 24-37.

Silva, Vera Maria Tietzmann. *A metamorfose nos contos de Lygia Fagundes Telles.* Rio de Janeiro: Presença, 1985.

Telles, Lygia Fagundes. *Ciranda de pedra.* 20a ed. Rio de Janeiro: Nova Fronteira, 1984.

————. *As horas nuas.* Rio de Janeiro: Nova Fronteira, 1989.

————. *Verão no aquário.* 1963. 8a ed. Rio de Janeiro: Nova Fronteira, 1984.

Todorov, Tzvetan. *The Fantastic. A Structural Approach to a Literary Genre.* Trans. Richard Howard. Cleveland: Case Western Reserve UP, 1973.

Van Steen, Edla. "The Baroness of Tatuí [Interview with Lygia Fagundes Telles]." *Review: Latin American Literature and Arts* 36 (1986): 30-3.

Walker, Nancy A. *Feminist Alternatives: Irony and Fantasy in the Contemporary Novel by Women.* Jackson: U of Mississippi P, 1990.

Maria Manuel Lisboa (essay date 1999)

SOURCE: Lisboa, Maria Manuel. "Darkness Visible: Alternative Theologies in Lygia Fagundes Telles." *Brazilian Feminisms.* Ed. Solange Ribeiro de Oliveira and Judith Still. Nottingham: U of Nottingham, 1999. 133-54. Print.

[*In the following essay, Lisboa examines the portrayal of motherhood in Telles's short fiction, noting that the majority of her female protagonists exhibit "a reactive violence" in response to the societal pressure to bear and care for children. Commenting on Telles's depiction of society's "denial of a female role in reproduction," as promoted by Judeo-Christian theology, Lisboa argues that "through her onslaughts upon the male she at once aborts, castrates and kills, all actions which prematurely terminate life and pleasure."*]

The threatening power of a revisionist female womb capable of destabilizing the certainty of male input into personal and collective, or individual and national creation (or origin) will inform the consideration that follows of an important assumption at the heart of Brazilian cultural history from its early beginnings to contemporary writing. Specific attention will be focused here on this preoccupation as repeatedly observable in the narrative fiction of a contemporary Brazilian writer, Lygia Fagundes Telles.

The issue of motherhood, always problematic in Brazil whether in the light of imported psychoanalytic ideas or of national concerns with a European origin in conflict with the desire for American specificity, has always been at the heart of a complex phenomenon which, arising with the arrival of Romanticism in Brazil has, in the almost two centuries that have followed, characterized a variety of aspects of the Brazilian search for an emancipated cultural expression parallel to its political independence from Portugal in 1822. The mother or source of origin, whether understood as a national or an individual, an anthropomorphic or abstract concern, becomes central to an understanding of the Brazilian preoccupation with the metaphor of birth and the maternal body as the engendering origin of the individuality of the self and the collectivity of the nation. And whether all-powerful or disempowered within the nation or home, whether adored or vilified, the mother in the shape of either a person (woman) or continent (Europe) is always uncomfortably irreducible and perpetually dangerous.

The importation from Europe of thought paradigms across the spectrum of history, theology, literature and psychoanalysis in the last two centuries fed into a Brazilian cultural reality in the process of formation and caught up in the contradictory drives of a sought emancipation from European models in parallel with a clear dependence on these same models. It is the fields of psychoanalysis, theology, and certain other related disciplines whose effect has proved most enduring in the circumscription of a Brazilian cultural specificity which from Romanticism, through Naturalism and Modernism to contemporary writing has sustained a common thread or metaphor, that of a motherland to be invented anew by an exclusively national impetus acquitted of outside cultural influences. The process, however, does not appear devoid of ambivalence, since it implies on the part of that nation's cultural activists the necessity for the inversion of this national and aesthetic birthing process, whereby the nation's sons invent *her,* and thus usurp the originating power which they both fear in her and do not fully trust her to wield. In Brazil, therefore, a foreign—but as psychoanalytic theory would have it, universal—ambivalence towards the mother as source of life, but of a life which is *finite,* dovetails with a geographically specific preoccupation with the need for reinventing anew (and newly virginally) a maternal national body uncompromised by colonial influences, which together lend emphasis to the imperative of a denial of the originating (European) womb and a reversal of the mother-son order of creation. This denial, in turn, as I shall argue with specific reference to the writing of Lygia Fagundes Telles, leads, in the twentieth century, to a retaliatory response on the part of the mother figure, against the usurping sons who literarily and otherwise resorted, for the purposes of the shoring up of an individual and national cultural identity, to a variety of denials subsumed in the refusal of the inevitability of being of woman born, and through her endowed with the awareness of the finiteness of life and the certainty of death.

Julia Kristeva departs from Freudian Oedipal insights to develop a theory of the abject which she defines as 'the place where meaning collapses,'[1] 'the other side' (83) of orthodoxy, the site of disruption (psychic, social, communal), and locates it, more specifically, within psychosexual relations, as abiding 'within the mother woman' (83), a figure who thus emerges as a taboo object simultaneously of abhorrence and desire. An abhorrence and desire which relate to the way in which, through her mothering role, unorthodoxly performed, the woman is able to wreak widespread disruption upon a series of pre-existing status quos:

> The abject is perverse because it neither gives up nor assumes a prohibition, a rule, or a law; but turns them aside, misleads, corrupts; uses them, takes advantage of them, the better to deny them. It kills in the name of life— a progressive despot; it lives at the behest of death ... An unshakable adherence to Prohibition and Law is necessary if that perverse interspace of abjection is to be hemmed in and thrust aside. Religion, Morality, Law.

> (Kristeva, 15-16)

Kristeva underpins her development of the concept of abjectification in thought traditions ranging from Greek Antiquity, through Judaeo-Christian and Patristic writings to contemporary Western authorship. Some of these sources, I should wish to argue, are also the departure point for Lygia Fagundes Telles' fictional response to and reversal of a series of expectations which the former set up.

Throughout the two centuries since its independence, European inputs from a variety of sources have continued to feed into a Brazilian assimilation of the all-important metaphor of maternity as origin, and to contradict the Brazilian desire for cultural emancipation from these sources. Out-

side and prior to the impact of psychoanalysis upon the Western psyche, a suspicion regarding the originating power of the female womb has underpinned Judaeo-Christian thought from its earliest paradigmatic manifestations. The problems raised by Eve's theft of the apple in Genesis were only uneasily resolved by a reactive, antidotal Marian worship which promoted Mary's virginal womb as the empty vessel subject, from the moment of its inception to the occupancy of the Father and the tenancy of the Son as the sole active agents of gestation. Mary, therefore, theologically promoted as a female role model but contradictorily declared to be inimitable by other women ('mother and maiden, was never none but she'[2]), in fact reproblematizes the concept of origin as being one of gender separation and struggle for male monopoly over reproduction. The difficulties she gives rise to, as regards the remainder of her sex, are summed up by Marina Warner:

> Every facet of the Virgin had been systematically developed to diminish, not increase, her likeness to the female condition. Her freedom from sex, painful delivery, age, death, and all sin exalted her ipso facto above ordinary women and showed them up as inferior.[3]

Mary, the role model imposed upon women who are urged as a sex to emulate her while being told that they cannot do so, gives rise to an impasse which finds its counterpart in a male fear that rather than being like her, women as a whole are her antithesis.

Not surprisingly, then, in the Western imagination a long-traceable tradition emerges which, from the nightmare fantasies of the *vagina dentata* through medieval indictments of the female body as either the devil's gateway of Eve or the empty vessel of Mary and onto the comforting Freudian paradigm of early relegation of the mother to pre-Oedipal insignificance and her dismissal by father-oriented sons and daughters, articulates the need to contain and confine the dangers entailed in the figure of the mother.

Post-Freudian psychoanalytic theory, through the work of writers such as Melanie Klein, Karen Horney, Nancy Chodorow and Dorothy Dinnerstein,[4] has re-emphasized a consideration of the maternal figure as pivotal to an understanding of the psychosexual development of the sexes, a revival which by implication also resuscitates the older Greek and Judaeo-Christian nightmares of motherhood as an alternative dangerous creation, in opposition to divine Fatherly Creation, and the heresy of the slightly different, of which more later. The revisionist work of Chodorow and Dinnerstein argues that for the newly-born infant the mother, omnipotent mediator between the infant and all that is external to it, is the source of all that the latter experiences as good, but also all that is experienced as bad, her power gradually becoming comprehensible as the bounty of life but, additionally, as the terror of *finite* life, or death. The consciousness of this dual impact will persist in post-infancy stages and through into adult consciousness, as the divided desire for, but dread of, a return to the Nirvana-like womb which signals both binding pleasure and boundless dissolution. And the mother herself, as the possessor of that dangerous womb, triggers also the knowledge of the finiteness of life and the inevitability of death for all those for whom she signals the only available beginning: 'men have never tired of fashioning expressions for the violent force by which man feels himself drawn to the woman, and side by side with his longing, the dread that through her he might die and be undone' (Horney, 134).

The mother who reminds us of the pre-self state of utter disempowerment, the Lacanian Imaginary or the Kristevan Semiotic, all the more dangerous because bewitching as the last occasion of absolute psychic self-abandon, is, as post-Freudian theory clarifies, identified as that which needs to be jettisoned,[5] as the price of being granted access to the rational safety of the Symbolic Order. The mother signifies regression, lack of autonomy, the opposite of all that the Symbolic defines as the very essence of identity: 'absence, lack, inchoateness, insatiability, nothingness: it is a monstrous image of the feminine, yet it is also, astoundingly, the normative view presented in Freud (the castration complex), [and] Lacan [. . .]. Thus distance, separateness, objectivity, and rationality are the haven and 'escape' of masculinity,'[6] When, being all these things and nothing, the mother refuses to continue being the object, not subject, of a plethora of definitions of herself in which she bears no agency, she becomes synonymous with the threat of death for those upon whom, as the only available point of beginning, she bestowed both the gift of a life qualified by finiteness and therefore, cruelly, the inevitability of ultimate annihilation. And when those children so afflicted are the sons of the nation, the mother, rather than archetypal originator becomes instead possibly the purveyor of collective cultural, not merely personal, annihilation.

It is against this legacy of European intellectual (and anti-maternal) imports that one might seek to understand the Brazilian impetus towards self-creation as the desire for a cultural *tabula rasa* which would paradoxically deny the very legacy that drove that anti-maternal imperative and permit the nation's self-reinvention *ex nihilo*. A process which, moreover, would allow the murder of the post-lapsarian Eve-like or Freudian (European) mother, and her replacement by a Marian, empty vessel lookalike, such as for example, the eminently malleable, wholly re-imaginable because utterly lost and undocumented Indian motherland prior to European contact, beloved in Brazil by the Romantic *Indianista* tradition, as absolutely docile to imaginative remoulding by these loving and matricidal cultural sons.

Brazilian literature in all its important movements and schools has retained, across a rich and disparate spectrum, a shared impetus which runs from Romanticism through Naturalism, twentieth-century Regionalism, Modernism

and seamlessly into important strands of contemporary writing: namely the imperative to define, record, archive and articulate a specific *Brazilian* reality. And each movement, whether represented by the Romantic *Indianismo* of Gonçalves Dias and José de Alencar, or the minutely detailed Naturalism of Inglês de Sousa, or the Regionalism of Northeastern or Amazonian writers such as Graciliano Ramos and Ferreira de Castro, or the rural Modernism of Jorge Amado or the urban one of Manuel Bandeira, has grappled, sooner or later, with the complexity of feelings that accrue to a drive to national identification ultimately always contingent upon the metaphor of a *mother*land.

In the second half of the twentieth century, however, another variable has added complexity to this cultural reality, namely the increasingly important dimension of a wave of writing of female authorship for whom the clash between matrilinear and patrilinear interests presents a new set of problems and a new position from which to confront these problems. In a non-Portuguese-speaking international context the name that more immediately signals writing by Brazilian women is that of Clarice Lispector. Her grappling with notions of non-binary, fluctuating identity has made her an obvious focus for the deconstructive approval of a French feminist theory for which she represents the refusal to perpetuate binaries seen as subservient to a set of metaphysical assumptions impossible to sustain through deconstructive practice. I wish now, however, to illustrate a different response to the ambivalent tradition of individual or collective, national or geographical and spiritual or metaphysical identity, by reference to the work of Lispector's internationally less well-known contemporary, Lygia Fagundes Telles.

If motherhood, whether psychically or nationally understood, is the source of such ambivalence for the sons who are the recipients of its effects, the ambivalence, logically, must be understood as feeding back upon the deliverers of those self-same effects, producing in the women upon whom maternity is urged while being contradictorily feared, the discordant undertow of a path felt to be both a duty and an impertinence, and eliciting from these women (as is repeatedly the case in the writing of Fagundes Telles) a reactive violence.

The narrative fiction of this author demands an insight (and possibly invites reader collusion) into the potentially murderous nature of motherhood, since almost every one of Fagundes Telles' female protagonists in one way or another, through symbolic but more often real murder, commits a crime which has threefold implications: murder itself (whether fabricated or actually perpetrated, and of course in either case transgressive), is compounded by gender aggression, since the female in fact or fantasy invariably murders the male; and is further aggravated by its kin-slaying dimension, since the male victims are invariably infantilized by a variety of means, abducted from the Symbolic Order and snatched back into the non-speaking regressive, filial, or infantile status of these murderous women's sons. A reversal there and then revealed as lethal, and imperilling the status quo in its temporal, but sometimes also metaphysical and theological dimensions. The murderousness is, arguably, representative of a retaliatory growing tradition of female thinking and writing against the grain of centuries of male ambivalence concerning femaleness, and more specifically femaleness in its maternal and originating capacities.

I shall concentrate here on two short stories—**'Natal na Barca'** (**'Christmas on the Barge'**) and **'Missa do Galo'** (**'Midnight Mass'**)—which, in different ways, take the theme of the birth of Jesus and of Christianity as the departure point for the blocking of a variety of notions of origin as understood metaphysically and secularly through the agency of the concept of a divine and patriarchal Creation beginning with God-the-Father and transmitted to an inheriting Son. In the first story, **'Natal na Barca,'** a first-person narrator, only belatedly disclosed as female, travels on a mysterious barge on the night before Christmas, over a purgatorial stretch of water, with a demonic madonna figure who, holding her baby in her arms, spooks the mesmerized narrator with the tale of the death of her first child, here hijacked as the thematic propellant of her own murderous (yet creative) story-telling impetus.[7] As fear escalates, the narrator realizes that the child in the arms of the story-teller is also dead. The catastrophe of the second death, not birth, of this second Child on an improbably gory Christmas Eve, is not alleviated by the awareness on the part of the narrator, at the end, that she has been misled, and that the second child in this uncannily re-scripted Nativity is after all, and for the moment, alive.

'Natal na Barca,' within its own terms, 'replies to one question with another' ('respondi com uma outra pergunta' 136),[8] and the outcome, which is also the opening of the story, negates the barge as the site of any possibility other than silence: 'nem combinava mesmo com a barca tão despojada, tão sem artifícios, a ociosidade de um diálogo' ('in any case, the superfluousness of a dialogue was inappropriate to a barge such as this one, so spare, so devoid of artifice' 135). If the Judaeo-Christian imperative proclaims that in the beginning was the Word, here, already, we face an antithetical drive towards a silence which is not impotence on the part of the Madonna narrator-within-the-narrative, but rather the preliminary to a disruptive impetus that has at its heart the foundation moment of the sacred Western Nativity, namely the birth of Jesus. Thus, if the rudimentary barge is the re-rendering, and a deeply profane one at that, of the holy stable scenario, that stable is here translated into literally shifting terrain (the water upon which it floats), in effect destabilized and populated with protagonists no less disruptive of the original paradigm: a black-clad and as it will turn out unholy mother, a shrouded and near-invisible child, and a down-at-heel, drunken Joseph, all observed by the narrator (as it turns out female) of this scene, who will be press-ganged into the

role of reluctant (and terrified rather than triumphantly annunciatory) apostolic conveyor of the events to follow.

These events are declared, early on in the opening pages, to be unequivocally implicated in an anti-Nativity concern, a heretical Second Coming in the course of which divine birth is metamorphosed into death everlasting: 'ali estávamos os quatro, silenciosos como mortos num antigo barco de mortos deslizando na escuridão. Contudo, estávamos vivos. E era Natal' ('there we were, the four of us, silent as the dead in an old barge for the dead sliding through the darkness. Nonetheless, we were alive. And it was Christmas' 135-36). As the Virgin figure discloses her story to the first-person narrator, the heresy of a deserting God (husband to this ersatz Mary) and the ensuing Godless vacuum are established in a secular setting: 'meu marido me abandonou' ('my husband deserted me' 137). In a universe vacated of the absconding Father's presence, it soon becomes clear that female sorcery gains the day, or rather the night, and more to the point, the night before Christmas, holy of holies now desecrated. The victim of this new arrangement, not surprisingly, will turn out to be the divine Father's forgotten, or forsaken son.

The narrator remarks upon the calm, almost scandalous resignation with which the supposed *mater dolorosa*—already seen as that, in what again amounts to a heretical anticipation of the death of the Son of God at the moment of his birth—recounts her tragic story of desertion and bereft motherhood, faced with the death of her first son and the impending death of the second, and expresses 'uma obscura irritação' ('an obscure irritation,' 138) faced with what she knows is not explicable as maternal apathy, but might, instead, be understandable as 'a tal fé que removia montanhas . . .' ('that faith that moved mountains,' 139). The scenario that emerges from this narrative within a narrative, however, is, deceptively, that of an abolished male lineage. It outlines a female plot at war with the original patriarchal Judaeo-Christian faith, the spectacle of a vanished God, his dead first son, a perishing second, a negligible Joseph-substitute, and deaths accomplished or impending. And all this, furthermore, shrouded in suggestions of witchcraft whereby Jesus-like little boys who spent not forty days in the wilderness but four years in the world, unlike their precursor Gospel Christ fail to resist the Satanic temptation to throw themselves off high places in order to prove their divine (immortal) status, and in so failing, disprove it: 'o meu primeiro [filho] morreu o ano passado. Subiu no muro, estava brincando de mágico quando de repente avisou, vou voar! A queda não foi grande, o muro não era alto, mas caiu de tal jeito . . . Tinha pouco mais de quatro anos' ('my eldest [son] died last year. He climbed the garden wall, pretending to be a magician when suddenly he said, I am going to fly! The fall wasn't serious, the wall wasn't very high, but he fell in such a way . . . he was less than four years old,' 137).

In his trips down psychic and mythical memory lane Freud curiously omitted all mention of one destiny undoubtedly as striking, certainly more disturbing than that of Oedipus. I refer to Euripides' Medea, witch, sorceress, demon-woman and finally child-killer and kinslayer. Having destroyed her children in order to wreak revenge upon their father, and in particular upon his lineage, Medea exits with impunity to go and live in peace, of all places in Athens, the seat of masculinely conceived Justice.[9] At the hands of this Medea-like Virgin, typical of Lygia Fagundes Telles' gallery of malevolent motherhood, the sons of God, already heretical for being not *one* and unique but *two* and therefore replicable, or repeatable, incarnate the threat to the original creed by being also stripped of the gift of perpetuity, and proved to be mortal. The very declaration of faith on the part of this Virgin, once again 'that faith that moved mountains' (139), proves here to be earth-shattering in a different way, since the relocated mountains will literally rearrange the terrain upon which voice will be gendered anew, enabling a female version of the erstwhile male monopoly over speech to become possible. Thus, this deceptive Madonna recounts an apparently conventionally redeeming story of Christian resignation to her first child's death:

> Foi logo depois da morte do meu menino. Acordei uma noite tão desesperada que saí pela rua afora, enfiei um casaco e saí descalça e chorando feito louca, chamando por ele [...] Então sonhei e no sonho Deus me apareceu [...] senti que ele pegava na minha mão com sua mão de luz. E vi o meu menino brincando com o Menino Jesus no jardim do Paraíso. Assim que ele me viu, parou de brincar e veio rindo ao meu encontro e me beijou tanto, tanto ... Era tal sua alegria que acordei rindo também, com o sol batendo em mim.

> (139)

> (It was right after the death of my baby. I woke up one night, so desperate that I went out on the street, I pulled on a cardigan and walked out barefoot and crying my heart out, calling for him [...] Then I fell asleep and dreamed, and in the dream God came to me [...] I felt that he took my hand in his bright one. And I saw my boy playing with the baby Jesus in the garden of Eden. As soon as he saw me, he stopped playing and came to me laughing and kissed me so much, so much ... Such was his happiness that I too woke up laughing, with the sun shining on me.)

Any potential edification, however, is immediately threatened by the discovery, mistaken but nonetheless threatening while it lasts, on the part of her interlocutor, that while the story was being told by the mother, her second child had also died in her arms. At the moment when the kingdom of God appeared to have been reinstated on Earth through the agency of the female voice, therefore, that voice shows itself to herald instead the possibility of a second filial death. The Virgin's last words to the narrator, 'então bom Natal!' ('merry Christmas, then,' 140) before she disappears into the night are the final denial of a set of redemptory foundation premises of both religious and secular character and their replacement by an ironic, contrary vacuum; but a vacuum which is also, as I shall argue in

connection with the second story to be discussed here, the affirmation of an alternative heretical (because female) beginning.

If in the first-person narration of **'Natal na Barca'** the narrative's origins are thrown into question by the diegetic narrator herself ('não quero nem devo lembrar aqui porque me encontrava naquela barca. Só sei que em redor tudo era silêncio e treva' ['I neither want nor ought to recall here why I was on that barge. All I know is that around me all was silence and darkness'], 135), in **'Missa do Galo,'**[10] the second story to be considered, the process gains further complexity since the tale is the re-writing of an earlier narrative of the same title with an ostensibly similar plot and the same protagonists, by Machado de Assis,[11] Brazil's foremost man of letters in the nineteenth century, and himself responsible for the rooting in Brazilian literature of important intellectual imports from a variety of European sources. Whether homage, desecration, or mere sequel, however, the status and intent of Lygia Fagundes Telles' story must remain ambivalent, not least given her choice of an epigraph for her own narrative, drawn from the Machado original, but which circumscribes a space of absolute silence in/for her precursor's text: 'chegamos a ficar algum tempo—não posso dizer quanto—inteiramente calados' ('we even stayed absolutely silent for some time, I know not how long,' 121). The silencing of expectation and of the established word, in any case impels this narrative, also in the first-person, in the end establishing void, or silence, or nothingness, as central to a plot from which the possibility of a revelatory, Genesiacal Word is excluded. I will digress here briefly to consider a series of theoretical points which will become pertinent to the reading that follows of this second story.

The problem that the previously discussed dichotomy of Mary and Eve, good woman and loose woman, sets up, which is also the problem of obedience or disobedience to a series of Godly/Fatherly decrees including those governing the engendering of children, finds parallels in other preceding and subsequent traditions. In the contemplation of metaphors of creation, both cosmic and human, a helpful point of departure may be the consideration of the dilemma between the concepts of creation *ex nihilo* as opposed to creation from a preceding chaos, which is the dilemma between the Greek and Judaeo-Christian paradigms, and out of which implications arise regarding the conflict between human (female) versus divine (male) procreation, or between female (matrilinear) versus male (patrilinear) origin. Brian Rotman approaches the problem through a consideration of the significance of zero as a sign in Western mathematics, theology and aesthetics, and begins by raising the question of what it is precisely that can only find expression through the invention of such a sign, and is unsayable without it.[12] If, as he goes on to suggest, the sign zero is connected to the concept of nothing, the void, the place where no thing is, I shall attempt to connect it also to that preoccupation that has afflicted meditations concerning the question of the female role in reproduction from Plato to Freud and beyond, bearing in mind that the site before things become things or beings become beings, the point before origin, is also, biological-ly, the empty womb, the referent whose sign might be said to be that zero which mirrors the womb's ovoid shape. Rotman discusses the resistance encountered by the intro-duction of the sign zero within European Christian medie-val intellectual thought, a resistance based on the grounds that the assertion that the void can exist in God's world is blasphemous and heretical. This assertion itself, however, encountered difficulties faced with the Genesis affirmation of creation *ex-nihilo,* and required elaboration.

The tension between the two positions, indeed, com-pounded by the horror of the void inherited from the Greeks whose thought it permeates (Rotman, 60-61), leads, according to R. Colie,[13] to a dialectic between noth-ing and its opposite, which might be said to be All, the Cosmos or Infinity. These terms, as well as bearing upon scientific, philosophical and theological thought, 'impinge on questions of individual existence, survival, oblivion and annihilation' (Rotman, 59), from which, arguably, it is but a short step to the consideration of the connection between questions of birth and death through the originating body of the mother.

According to Colie (226) and Rotman (59-60), the sign zero can be linked to the ovoid shape of the egg, and to that egg's procreative function, through a principle of contra-diction. The egg's shape is the ovoid of zero, but is itself the symbol of generation and creation, and is further linked, in other theological traditions, to both *ex-nihilo* and female creation.

The links between *ex nihilo* creation—with all the contra-dictions associated to the uneasiness that attaches to it yet the inevitability of accepting it in Judaeo-Christian thought—and female creation, have, not surprisingly, re-sulted in a denial of the female procreative role which dates from antiquity and whose longevity equals, as well as being more than coincidentally analogous to, that *horror vacui* which Aristotle associated with a dangerous sick-ness or a God-denying madness (Rotman, 63). If the fe-male is associated with nothingness, her role, particularly in reproduction, must be itself denied, because being at once nothing and origin she threatens at once the Greeks' fear of the vacuum, which they transmitted to Christian mysticism in one of its strands, and the monopoly over procreation of God-the-Father which that mysticism inher-ited from its Jewish roots in Genesis.

The solution to the problem was traditionally undertaken in a variety of ways. At the level of human and female repro-duction, through the simple denial of the reality of it, from Aristotle through St. Thomas Aquinas to seventeenth-century biological empiricism (Warner, 40-42). This denial of a female role in reproduction is traced by Rosalind Miles

as the imperative whereby the various monotheisms, Juda-ism, Islam, Christianity and Buddhism usurped the prior understanding of a female-originated universe,[14] and be-comes translatable, in medieval Augustinian theology, into an association between female biology and nothing-ness, and between nothingness and the Devil, a syllogism which further links femaleness with the Devil as its third term. For St. Augustine Nothing is the Devil itself, 'the ultimate privation [...] that which was absent, lacking, lost, which had been subtracted and taken away from the original presence and fulness of God' (Rotman, 63). To be in a state of sin was to contain within oneself this absence of God which is Nothing, and which woman, both by being associated with emptiness or nothingness, and by being the gateway to evil (according to for example St. John Chry-sostom and Tertullian), by definition did contain.[15]

The danger, however, is rendered of further complexity by the fact that if the female body, as the antithesis of God, represents Nothing, which, according to the *ex nihilo* doc-trine comes before Being, the notion of a devilish female origin out of which Something—Being—by definition must be understood to arise, becomes always, by defini-tion the usurpation of a male/Godly origin. The connection between a dangerous female reproductive power and noth-ingness or zero, which is the proof of her wickedness, is thus somewhat circuitously established, while that repro-ductive role, contradictorily, is simultaneously denied (as being exclusively a paternal one).

In Fagundes Telles' **'Missa do Galo,'** the clash between metaphors of annihilatory voids and originating life under-pin the ambiguous encounter just before midnight on Christmas Eve, between a nameless young man who waits to be collected for midnight mass by a friend, and his landlady, Conceição. In the course of this encounter the possibility arises of the seduction of the young man by the older woman, habitually seen by him in daytime as a self-effacing, downtrodden, betrayed wife, but suddenly, in the course of this nocturnal meeting, unexpectedly and per-turbingly seductive. In both the Machado de Assis and the Fagundes Telles versions of the story the seduction re-mains unachieved, leaving open a space of unfulfilled ex-pectation. In Lygia Fagundes Telles, however, that space, which is also a vacuum, creates further and disturbing possibilities, announced already in the opening paragraphs which signal hidden implications in the 'superficies tão inocentes como essa noite diante do que vai acontecer. E do que não vai—precisamente o que não acontece é que me inquieta. E excita' ('surfaces as innocent as that night in the face of that which is about to happen. And that which will not happen—it is precisely what doesn't happen that worries me. And excites me,' 121-22). Echoing Machado who, in his best-known novel, *Dom Casmurro,* also a de-ceptive first-person narration by an unreliable narrator, famously extols the virtues of 'livros omissos'[16] ('books with omissions') which encourage between-the-lines read-er participation as the pre-requisite for any hope of textual signification, Lygia Fagundes Telles' text, too, stresses 'as omissões. Os silêncios tão mais importantes' ('ommisions. The oh-so-important silences,' 122). In this retelling of the Machado story, however, it is what is slightly altered, as well as what is not said or does not happen that pushes one step further the possibilities left open by the precursor tale.

Thus, while in the later version the physical environment is given early narrative attention, setting up a hierarchy of description in which the room's furniture and décor are given precedence over their youthful inhabitant ('por último há o jovem, há um jovem lendo dentro do círculo luminoso,' 'finally there is the young man, there is a young man reading within the circle of light,' 121), in the earlier Machado narrative this description is left till the end and prioritizes the young man until the last pages. Both stories pay attention to the detail of the paintings which decorate the walls, but the re-writing of their theme in the twentieth-century version introduces the typical Fagundes Telles theme of the fragilized, threatened child-man, which is not touched upon in the first. Thus in Machado we read that 'os quadros falavam do principal negócio [do marido]. Um representava "cleópatra"; não me recordo o assunto do outro, mas eram mulheres. Vulgares ambos' ('the paintings bespoke [the husband's] main business. One depicted "cleopatra"; I don't recall the theme of the other, but it was women. Both commonplace paintings,' 144). Machado here gestures towards female disempowerment as denoted by the lower-case 'c' of 'cleopatra,' and by implication to contrasting (Caesarean) male power. In contrast, in Lygia Fagundes Telles' version, men figure as well as women, but in a context which bespeaks male bondage (male slaves) both socially and within the picture plane, rather than signposting masculine power outside the universe of the painting, as did the first: 'Os quadros ingenuamente pretensiosos, não há afetação nos móveis mas os quadros têm aspirações de grandeza nas gravuras de mulheres imponentes (rainhas?) entre pavões e escravos transbordando até o ouro purpurino das molduras' ('The paintings naively pretentious, there is no affectation in the furniture but the paintings have grandiose aspirations in the prints of imposing women (queens?) amidst peacocks and slaves overflowing into the purple gold of the frames,' 121).

In the gap that separates Machado from Fagundes Telles, therefore, there develops a clear accentuation of the imagery of male confinement within the restrictions of a female optic which in that opening page allows the young man the status of 'um jovem nítido, próximo' ('a well-defined, young man in close proximity,' 121), only steadily to deprive him of definition or even, at the end, as we shall see, of visibility in a changed world in which masculine presence is subsumed by the female attributes of 'silêncio e treva' ('silence and darkness,' 135).

In Lygia Fagundes Telles the confusion of identity between the narrator as outside observer and Conceição as

protagonist is never fully resolved, both fusing into a co-participative process whereby the young man is ensnared by the words and gaze of one and the seduction of the other, as depicted by insistent images of ambush, spider webs and feral female sexuality:

> Ela adverte com um sorriso cálido que ele não retribui, nem pode, enredado como está naqueles cabelos, massa sombria tão mal arrepanhada como as saias, ameaçando desabar.
>
> (122-23)

> (She reassures him with a warm smile which he does not and cannot return, enmeshed as he is in her hair, a dark, disordered mass like her clothes, and threatening to break loose.)

> E do olhar que inesperadamente se concentrou inteiro nele, fechando-o: sentiu-se profundo através desse olhar. [...] Para encará-la de novo já sem resistência: pronto, aqui estou. Mas não disse nada nessa pausa que ela interrompeu, *a iniciativa nunca era dele.*
>
> (122, italics mine)

> (And the gaze which unexpectedly focused entirely on him, surrounding him: that gaze made him feel deep. [...] In order to be able to return her gaze, now without resisting it: right, here I am. But he said nothing in that pause which she interrupted, *the initiative never came from him.*)

His disempowerment is commensurate with Conceição's empowerment, the latter being compared to a caged beast ('com seu andar de jaula,' 'with her caged walk,' 122), but a beast possibly about to be released. And it evokes also, here, the theological and (within Christian monotheism) heretical possibility of a female deity ('como a deusa da gravura,' 'like the goddess in the print,' 122) whose hieratic power is underscored also by unmistakable sexual attraction ('magra, mas os seios altos como os da deusa da gravura, os cabelos quase num desalinho de travesseiro,' 'thin, but her breasts firm like those of the goddess in the print, her hair disordered as if from sleep,' 122). Breasts, of course, are the hallmark of lovers and here of goddesses, but also of older women who are nurturing and potentially lethal mothers, the act of mothering, or rather conception (origin) being in any case implied in the age difference between them, but more to the point in Conceição's very name: a name with associations of orthodox theology and engendering origin (Nossa Senhora da Conceição, Our Lady of the Conception) but here also of heterodoxy or heresy (female conception to the exclusion of any male/ divine input). The three female functions, mother, goddess and lover, therefore become inextricable in the figure of a woman who in the process of seduction of the younger man acquires, in the alternative realm of the night, an unearthly stature—'tão apaziguada (ou insignificante?) durante o dia, quase invisível no seu jeito de ir e vir pela casa. E agora ocupando todo o espaço, grande como um navio, a mulher era um navio' ('so serene (or insignificant?) during the day, almost invisible in her way of coming and going through the house. And now taking up all this space like a ship, the woman was a ship,' 125)—which also, through a process of infantilization which is disempowering, relegates the boy back to the helplessness of the pre-linguistic maternal, whose link to this worryingly libidinal moment, in attempting to deny it, he underlines:

> Nunca ele estivera com uma senhora assim na intimidade. Tinha a mãe. Mas mãe não tem esse olhar que se retrai e de repente avança, agrandado. Para diminuir até aquelas fendas que quase não alcança, o que o perturba ainda mais porque é à traição que se sente tomado. Inundado, oh Deus, o que é que ela está dizendo?
>
> (125-26)
>
> (He had never been like this in a lady's intimacy. There was his mother. But a mother never has that gaze which withdraws and then moves forward, grows deep. Probing even those orifices which it almost cannot reach, which disturbs him even more because he feels himself taken by treason. Flooded, oh Lord, what is it she is saying?)

Conceição, as mother, lover and goddess (or witch) seduces but simultaneously forbids access to her body of impenetrable orifices which he himself 'almost cannot reach' ('alcançar'), the verb 'alcançar' punning on the double meaning of the word, to reach but also to grasp or understand, that is, to dominate knowledge. Knowledge, purloined by Eve (first lover and first mother) in Genesis when she ate of the fruit of the tree, was at the root of Original Sin, and goes hand in hand with carnal knowledge, also acquired on the occasion of that trespass. Conceição, therefore, rather than signalling the contented oblivion and passivity of the Virgin Mother to whom her name deceptively alludes, joins instead the ranks of dangerously lapsing mothers who lure their progeny to perdition. Hers is a body which takes unilateral and treacherous possession of the boy, 'by treason,' leaving him linguistically at sea faced with this woman who resembles a ship or heretical 'barge.' The penetration, then, or violation, is in this case that of male by female, or of the son by a mother fearless of paternal or divine retaliation. The nameless boy concerning whom the narrative voice speculates 'será virgem?' ('might he be a virgin?' 127) becomes her target ('alvo,' 127), associated to the vulnerability of the Saint Sebastian penetrated by arrows of whom she speaks and to whom she claims to pray, while leaving her silent interlocutor speechless, reduced to head gestures of assent, and 'seteado de dúvidas como a imagem do santo, não é estranho?' ('punctured by arrow-sharp doubts like the image of the saint, isn't it strange?' 127).

Conceição's advantage over him, other than that of origin, is also the mesmeric power of the Word which in any case we know, in Judaeo-Christian understanding, to be that of origin, in the beginning. Here that power is hers ('a solução é falar, falar e ela estimula a prosa quando essa prosa vai desfalecendo,' 'the solution is to talk, talk and she stimulates chat when it threatens to slacken,' 125), a fact he

experiences equally as heresy and engulfing danger ('inundado, oh Deus, o que é que ela está dizendo?' 'flooded, oh Lord, what is it she is saying?' 125-26), and over which he attempts to gain control, only to be silenced again: 'ah, sempre gostei de ler, ele diz num tom alto e ela pede, mais baixo, por favor, mais baixo!' ('ah, I have always enjoyed reading, says he loudly and she begs, more softly, please, more softly,' 126). If 'the solution is to talk,' it is she who stimulates speech while he remains hypnotized by her mouth as yet another impenetrable orifice, 'branco, preto e vermelho, os lábios úmidos, de vez em quando ela os umedece com a ponta da língua' ('white, black and red, her lips moist, occasionally she moistens them with the tip of her tongue,' 125). It is Conceição who exercises control over both speech and silence in the narrative, a control which reaffirms her to him as, among other roles, occupying that of the psychoanalytic pre-Symbolic all-powerful mother, in equal proportions desirable and annihilatory, the representative of a world of suggestive 'porões indevassáveis, caves tão apertadas que nelas não caberia um camundongo' ('unfathomable shipholds, dungeons so narrow that you couldn't squeeze a mouse inside them,' 127).

Finally, however, in Lygia Fagundes Telles, it is the destructive role of Kristeva's mother-woman, both theologically, in antagonism to the paradigm of a male Creation, and secularly through the abolition of males and male lineages, which is reiterated in the story as one of this writer's habitual tropes. Whereas in Machado's story Conceição outlives her promiscuous husband and marries his clerk, here the possibility is vented only to be rejected in favour of the more satisfying activity of seducing, or stopping just short of the seduction of, vulnerable young boys whose potential destruction is always by association implied in the less equivocal one of the husband. The latter, Meneses, we are told, has a mistress 'teúda e manteúda' ('a kept woman,' 123), the very wording which the nineteeenth-century Brazilian penal code selected to describe the sole case of male adultery which justified a measure of wifely retaliation in the eyes of the law.[17] On this particular Christmas Eve, we are told, he left the conjugal home as was his habit, and is at the very moment of Conceição's encounter with the boy, 'montado na concubina' ('mounted on his concubine,' 123). At this point the narrative, while perpetuating the female monopoly over gaze, multiplies the optic position to include four women: Conceição herself, her mother who lies awake and listens in the dark, the mistress, and her *madrinha* or godmother, also listening in her room. Each of the two older women in what becomes tantamount to a female troika utters a death curse against Meneses: 'com o coração estropiado e ainda nessa vida, um dia ainda pode ter uma coisa quando estiver em cima da outra, credo' ('his heart worn-out and still leading that kind of life, one of these days something could happen to him when he is mounted on top of the woman, Heaven have mercy,' 123); 'bom para o fogo, esse Meneses' ('fit only for the fire, that Meneses,' 124). The latter, coming from the *madrinha*, leads her to a more general contemplation of the threat of death which, by a logical continuity from one sentence to another, links death itself (as ill-wished upon Meneses by the *madrinha*) to Conceição (in the following sentence) who, on this Christmas Eve is metamorphosed from downtrodden wife into avenging force in the lives, or deaths, of both man and boy, husband and son/lover: 'mas dormir se o sono é o irmão da morte? [...] um perigo dormir. A gente passa o ferrolho e [a morte] entra pelo vão das telhas feito um sopro, entra em tudo. Mas foi Conceição que entrou [...] num meneio de barco [...] eterna na essência como a noite' ('but sleep how, if sleep is the brother of death? [...] sleeping is dangerous. We bolt the door and [death] comes in through roof tiles like a breeze, it gets in everywhere. But it was Conceição who came in [...] swinging hips like a ship [...] eternal in essence like the night,' 124-25).

The daytime Conceição, like the Virgin Mary, queen of light in more orthodox moments, is here, like the counterfeit Virgin of **'Natal na Barca,'** transfigured into a nocturnal, vampiric operator of the dark, a disturbing *memento mori* whose coming into being as an alternative to the very concept of origin gestures to the end of masculine monotheistic monopoly over creation and presence. 'Eternal in essence like the night," that is, infinite and dark as the encapsulation of that shadow which the Oneness of God in Genesis separated from light, a fallen Daughter of Morning, Conceição is transformed, in her dealings with boyish innocence on the brink of the moment of Nativity, into non-perishable ('eternal') matter. A matter which is, by antithesis to the reality of human mortality, heretical anti-matter, the zero point of origin before finite life begins, but also infinity itself, or, in the story's terminology, 'the vacuum of dark emptiness between the stars' ('estrelas com os escuros pelos meios,' 126): a state which here, as in **'Natal na Barca,'** sees the lover and mother associated to unreadable darkness (absence of light), inexplicability (absence of meaning), and death (absence of life):

> Há um certo perfume (jasmim-do-imperador?) que vem de algum quintal. Está no ar como estão outras coisas—quais? Objetos Não Identificáveis. Matérias Perecíveis [...]. Agora tem o céu apertado de estrelas *com os escuros pelo meio—ocos que procuro preencher com minha verdade que já não sei se é verdadeira,* há mais pessoas na casa. E fora dela. Cada qual com sua explicação para a noite inexplicável, Matéria Imperecível no bojo do tempo.

> (126, italics mine)

> (There is a certain perfume (imperial jasmine?) which comes from a garden somewhere. It hovers in the air, like other things—which? Unidentifiable Objects. Perishable Matter [...]. Now there is the sky crammed with the vaccum of dark emptiness between the stars—*voids which I try to fill with my truth which I am no longer certain of being true,* there are more people inside the house. And outside it. Each with an explanation for the inexplicable night, non-perishable matter in the bosom of time.)

It is not a coincidence, therefore that her depiction as the female vacuum produces in the boy, the representative of

Greek and Judaeo-Christian *horror vacui,* a mesmerized disintegration of thought and reasoning powers, leaving him 'apalermado como esses voluntários de teatro, os ingênuos que se prontificam a ajudar o mágico: sobem no palco e ali ficam sujeitos ao magnetismo do olhar que manda e desmanda, um encantado que não pode mesmo raciocinar em pleno encantamento' ('foolish like those audience participants, the gullible ones who volunteer to help the magician: they climb on stage and there they remain subject to the magnetism of a gaze which commands and countermands, a creature under a spell who really cannot think for being caught up in that spell,' 126). Not surprisingly, therefore, the ostensible affirmation of her practicing Christianity is immediately followed by a doubt regarding her sincerity in general—'o conformismo, era cristã praticante. Seria real o seu interesse pelos objectos em redor?' ('her conformity, she was a practicing christian. Could her interest in the objects around her be real?' 125)—and by the apparently inapposite affirmation of a desire for change which approximates the language of revolution: 'numa das voltas, passou a mão pelo vidro do armário e queixouse do envelhecimento das coisas, chegou a ter um gesto de insatisfação, *tanta vontade de renovar!*' ('on one occasion she ran her hand over the glass of the cupboard and complained about the ageing of things, she even made a dissatisfied gesture, *such a longing to make things over!*' 125, italics mine).

Conceição, then, carrier of a perfume (or essence) which signals both transience (his) and nocturnal perpetuity (hers, 'eternal in essence like the night')—'pena que o perfume não dure. Falam sobre perfumes como se tivessem toda noite pela frente. E a eternidade' ('such a shame that the perfume does not last. They talk about perfumes as if they had the whole night ahead of them. And eternity,' 128)—becomes the point of conception of a new heretical and profane order, a demonic mother, clearly dangerous, like the Virgin in **'Natal na Barca,'** as regards both boys and the theological and social conventions whose certain durability those boys no longer represent.

In each of these stories the Nativity midnight is the cusp between the two orders, the old one which may or may not renovate itself through the yearly ritual of that Nativity, and the new one which ultimately declares that it cannot. As the clock strikes midnight in **'Missa do Galo,'** the sound of a desperate dog's barking and the woman's circling 'por detrás da cadeira onde está o jovem' ('behind the chair on which the young man sits,' 128) introduce a note of fear regarding the viability of little boys, divine and other: 'faça com que aconteça alguma coisa!—repito e meu coração está pesado diante desses dois indefesos no tempo, *expostos como o Menino Jesus*' ('make something happen!—I repeat and my heart is heavy faced with those two boys, helpless in time, *as vulnerable as the baby Jesus,*' 128, italics mine).

The hour of midnight, when the two hands of the clock are joined together, represents, paradoxically, the inauguration of fissure, the manichean duality of an alternative

Creation. It is the moment of heretical separation from the oneness of God and the uniqueness of his Genesiacal moment, towards the affirmation of a possible substitute origin, which, because it is essentially a female origin, leads, altogether properly, by a reverse route, from Male Being to the female Nothingness of Zero that fundamentally questions the possibility of that Being enduring:

> E o grande relógio empurrando seus ponteiros: quando ambos se juntarem, estarão se separando, ela no quarto, ele na igreja—tão rápido tudo, mais uns minutos e o vizinho virá bater na janela, hora da missa, vamos? Perdidos um para o outro, nunca mais aquela sala. Naquela noite. Vocês sabem que dentro de alguns minutos será o *nunca mais*?
>
> (128, original italics)
>
> (And the great clock pushing its hands onwards: when both come together, they will be parting, she to her room, he to church—everything so quick, a few more minutes and the neighbour will come knocking on the window, time for mass, shall we go? Lost to each other, never again in that room. In that night. Did you know that in a few minutes it will be the *never more*?)

The midnight mass (now black mass) that ushers in the two Christmases in these stories, therefore, becomes the ritual of a heterodoxy which disallows the cyclical rebirth of the Son of God and introduces instead, or in parallel, an upside down universe, the heresy of a difference which, it is declared, cannot be later unspoken: 'essa senhora é só bondade!—ele repetirá no dia seguinte, quando as coisas voltarem aos seus lugares, *tudo vai voltar aos lugares* quando todos estiverem acordados' ('that lady is all goodness!—he will repeat the following day, when everything has gone back to place, *everything is going to go back to its place* when everyone is awake,' 123, italics mine). The assurance that tomorrow everything will be back to normal becomes here a frantic and frightened case of protesting too much in the face of the accumulating evidence of irreversible change and profanity, such as the Advent calendar which now can only proclaim sacred texts clandestinely, under cover of little paper flaps ('cada dia arrancado trazia nas costas um trecho dos salmos' 'each day you pulled out had on its back a passage from the psalms,' 127), and the boy's own avowed inability, thenceforward, ever to contemplate the silk garments of an officiating priest without remembering the texture of Conceição's slippers, tempting him beneath the disarray of her revealing nightgown (128).

The story finaly concludes with a declaration of war on her part and against him. As the cockerel sings inappropriately to announce not dawn (light) but midnight (deepest darkness), the final statement of intent is made, with this sacrificial Saint Sebastian as the official target in her sights:

> Contradições, há momentos em que o sinto dissimulado, um jovem se fazendo tolo diante da mulher desafiante, provocativa. Com olhos que eram castanhos e agora ficaram pretos, mais uma singularidade dessa noite: não é que a simpática senhora ficou subitamente belíssima?

> Mas não, ele não dissimula, está em êxtase, atordoado com a descoberta, bruxa, bruxa! quer gritar. A hora é de calar. [...] Apago o lampião.
>
> (127, 129)
>
> (Contradictions, yes, moments in which I feel him to be dissimulated, a young man playing the fool for the challenging, provocative woman. With eyes that used to be brown and now have turned black, yet another peculiarity of that night: now would you believe that the homely lady suddenly has become beautiful? No, he is not pretending, he is in ecstasy, dizzy with the discovery, witch, witch! he wants to shout. The hour is for silence. [...] I turn off the lamp.)

Midnight, the most sacred moment of Christian ritual, is evoked and immediately denied in what now becomes the witching hour ('witch, witch!') and in **'Missa do Galo,'** as in **'Natal na Barca,'** what is left, after all, is the vacuum of disobedient, alternative anti-matter.

If the virginal Madonna in her various guises can become a killer of individuals and of theologies, and, in these two cases a speaking killer, an assassin mother/lover turned author and demiurge on the theme of her man-children's deaths, the fundamental question must remain that of who or what is erased, and what is substituted in its place. Lygia Fagundes Telles' writing utters all that is profane, transgressive and desecratory, and through her onslaughts upon the male she at once aborts, castrates and kills, all actions which prematurely terminate life and pleasure. Abortion is the wrecking of the possibility of new life. Castration is the wrecking of the possibility of pleasure. And murder is the wrecking of the possibility of ongoing life, or immortality. But all of them are merely *premature* wreckages, untimely anticipations of the death which in any case is inherent in the moment when the mother, in giving life, gives *finite* life, life without the promise of perpetuity or eternity or immortality, a life that is therefore poisoned, initiated by a birth quantitatively but not qualitatively different from its deformed avatars of abortion, castration and murder, to which it is linked by the common denominator of an inescapable end. Her writing, then, functions as 'indefinite catharsis' (Kristeva, 208), or, to put it differently, as an act of aesthetic *coitus interruptus,* which as everyone knows dislocates a number of orthodoxies, fertilizing, reproductive, proprietorial, pleasurable and other. And at the origin of this horrible truth, whether she be murderous or simply maternal, we find the mother.

In re-writing Machado de Assis' story, Lygia Fagundes Telles was also engaging, in the twentieth century, with the same doubts which, in a Brazil back then in the nineteenth century, in the grip of a conflict between two brands of certainty each admitting of no self-doubt (Romantic utopic nationalism informed by Western Judaeo-Christian religiosity on the one hand, and imported European optimism regarding the possibility of Positive scientific truth on the other), also preoccupied Machado. Preoccupied him in his capacity as a master of ambiguity and precursor author of a narrative itself ridden with equivocation, and which, rather than problematizing, Fagundes Telles here possibly contents herself with extending. Each, faced in a different century with the unresolved problem of desired intellectual Brazilian emancipation in the face of a sometimes only semi-consciously absorbed, often unacknowledged or denied panorama of European doctrines, raises questions which are inevitably left unanswered. The eventual answers, possibly, will need to include the contemplation of the non-enduring power, the feared mutability, of both theological and secular intellectual traditions which are also male lineages, and the interruption of rituals (for example, Nativity nights), formerly intended to usher in the light, (whether spiritual or scientific) of an original *fiat,* but which here are instead pushed aside, to vacate an alternative female space of questioning darkness:

I turn off the lamp.

Notes

1. Julia Kristeva, *Powers of Horror: An Essay on Abjection,* New York, Columbia University Press, 1982, 2.

2. 'I sing of a maiden' (Anon, music by Lennox Berkeley), *Chester Book of Carols,* London, Chester [n.d.].

3. Marina Warner, *Alone of All Her Sex: The Myth and Cult of the Virgin Mary,* London, Picador, 1985, 153.

4. Melanie Klein, *The Psychoanalysis of Children,* London, Virago Press Ltd, 1989. Karen Horney, 'The Dread of Woman' in *Feminine Psychology,* New York and London, W. W. Norton and Company, 1993. Nancy Chodorow, *The Reproduction of Mothering: Psychoanalysis and the Sociology of Gender,* Berkeley, Los Angeles and London, The University of California Press, 1979. Nancy Chodorow, *Feminism and Psychoanalytic Theory,* New Haven and London, Yale University Press, 1989. Dorothy Dinnerstein, *The Rocking of the Cradle and the Ruling of the World,* London, The Women's Press, 1987.

5. See, for example, Simone de Beauvoir, *The Second Sex,* London, Picador, 1988, 501-42.

6. Patricia Waugh, *Feminine Fictions: Revisiting the Postmodern,* London and New York, Routledge, 1989, 71.

7. Lygia Fagundes Telles, 'Natal na Barca' in *Antes do Baile Verde,* Rio de Janeiro, Nova Fronteira, 1986, first published in 1970, 135-41. All quotations in the text will refer to this edition.

8. In the absence of available published translations, all translations of quotations from 'Natal na Barca' and 'Missa do Galo' are my own.

9. Euripides, *Medea,* London, Penguin, 1963.

10. Lygia Fagundes Telles, 'Missa do Galo' in *Os Melhores Contos de Lygia Fagundes Telles,* São Paulo,

Global Editora, 1984 (first published in 1978), 121-129. All quotations in the text will refer to this edition.

11. Machado de Assis, 'Missa do Galo' in *Contos,* Porto, Lello & Irmão, 1985 (first published in 1899), 135-47.

12. Brian Rotman, *Signifying Nothing: The Semiotics of Zero,* Basingstoke, Macmillan, 1987, 2.

13. R. Colie, *Paradoxia Epidemica,* Princeton, Princeton University Press, 1966, 226.

14. Rosalind Miles, *The Women's History of the World,* London, Paladin, 1989, 19-145.

15. St. John Chrysostom, *On Virginity* and *To the Fallen Monk Theodore,* quoted in Warner, op.cit. 51-52, 58; Tertullian, *Disciplinary, Moral and Ascetic Works,* quoted in Warner, op.cit., 58.

16. Machado de Assis, *Dom Casmurro,* Rio de Janeiro, Editora José Aguilar, 1962, 868.

17. For a discussion of Brazilian legislation on crimes of passion see Ingrid Stein, *Figuras Femininas em Machado de Assis,* Rio de Janeiro, Editora Paz e Terra, Coleção Literatura e Teoria Literária, 1984, 29.

Renata R. Mautner Wasserman (essay date 2007)

SOURCE: Wasserman, Renata R. Mautner. "Lygia Fagundes Telles: Political and Intimate." *Central at the Margin: Five Brazilian Women Writers.* Lewisburg: Bucknell UP, 2007. 82-102. Print.

[*In the following essay, Wasserman discusses Telles's reputation as an author of psychological, inward-looking fiction that focuses on the exclusion of women's private lives to history and politics. Noting the ways in which Telles's first two novels abide by these conventions, Wasserman argues that* The Girl in the Photograph *represents a break from their limitations.*]

Lygia Fagundes Telles published her first book, a collection of short stories, in 1944, and has enjoyed constant public and critical respect and success ever since.[1] Her reputation is as solid as her writing is delicate. She is known for her nuanced, stylistically accomplished examination of the inner lives of mainly female protagonists. Her tone is restrained and cool and although she makes full use of the freedom of language and material secured by modernist rebels in the two decades before she began publishing, her own writing is well behaved. She moves among respected intellectuals and has collected honors and prizes with unhurried regularity. She was nominated for an opening in the Brazilian Academy of Letters, an official recognition pleasantly complementing the popular one of steady sales.

Telles's writing occupies a well-defined niche in Brazilian literature: with Clarice Lispector, and despite the differences between them, she is recognized as a leading practitioner of what Wilson Martins calls "intimist fictions."[2] Her work sounds the psychological depths of certain characters and, at its best, balances precariously between the dangers of solipsism and of collapse before the pressures of the outside world. In her fiction—as it conforms to the parameters of intimist writing, that world of historical events and economic forces, of mass media, scientific discovery and politics is admitted into the text's well-wrought language only as filtered through the narrowing and intensifying perception of individual characters interested in feelings, in personal and family history, and in relations with other characters. Concentration on these concerns can be judged negatively as a form of flight or defeat, but is generally seen as a positive sign of superior sensibility, and associated with the feminine. In different terminology from Martins's, but with reference to the same qualities, Adonias Filho remarked in 1958 that Telles was, among Brazilian writers, one of the creators of a "woman's novelistic tradition," at the center of which "the condition of women is the paramount problem," and "woman is the great, if not the only character."[3] He does not say women do, or must, confine themselves to writing about "the condition of women" and has high praise, in a previous chapter, for Dinah Silveira de Queiroz's historical novel, but he calls her a great "Brazilian" writer and does not correlate her work with her gender: a historical novel by a woman is not unnatural; it is, simply, unmarked as to the gender of its author. The label of woman writer—in this view—implicitly charges its carrier with a natural expertise in the private world of feelings, impressions, memory; it charges her with creating characters of whatever sex as nodes in complex systems of relationships, defined by the gossamer threads that link them to other characters, like super spiders quivering at the center of an intricate pattern of interwoven webs. This world of relations is not an exclusive domain of the woman writer since, at least according to Roberto DaMatta, it encompasses, in a form characteristic of Brazilian society, a domain in structural opposition to the world of the "street," where the garishness of history, the cruelty of the marketplace, the impersonality of the law negate personality and subsume personal relationships to the detriment of the individual, destroying rather than protecting him—or her.[4] In short, unlike that of Rachel de Queiroz, for whose characters the "relational" world crosses or disregards—often at great cost—any boundaries between the domestic and the public, Telles's work tends to be read as falling within a thus loosely defined category of "woman's" fiction that explores the "home" world of personal feelings and personal history, where systems of interpersonal relations seem to be rooted. Yet, while most of her fiction does center on the personal and on what can be called a culture-congruent "feminine" sensibility, the special character of the world she creates appears most clearly, by means of contrast, when her other novels are read with and against *As meninas* (*The Girls*; 1973), perhaps her most interesting and appreciated book, on which this chapter will

concentrate. It raises, for Telles, the following question: what happens when an "intimist" writer comes under an almost unbearable pressure from the politics of DaMatta's "street"?

The two novels Telles published before **As meninas, Ciranda de pedra** (**Stone Circle**, 1954) and **Verão no aquário** (**Summer in the Fishbowl,** 1963), fit easily under the rubric of "intimism." Their titles announce that they deal with limits and enclosures and will not stray from the thematic grounds of home and relation. They are examples of the fiction of personality for which Telles became known, and did not present her with more than the appropriate literary problems in periods of relative political normalcy; they established the expectations that would greet the third novel, and a brief examination will help trace the third novel's deviations from and continuities with them.

As meninas was published during the darkest times of a military dictatorship, when ordinary politics was forcefully suspended, making politics inescapable; when the law was refashioned into an instrument of subjection divested of the usual mitigation by social networks; when the person became unsafe and personal relations lost their customary power. Thus the novel is almost forced to reveal the external pressure of politics upon a fictional form that had generally been seen as immune to politics so understood, or had been used to repel it.[5]

The earlier **Ciranda de pedra** could spend its energy examining the inner life of its heroine, Virginia: sensitive and intelligent, like so many of Telles's heroines, she grows up painfully and rather neglected, shadowed by the unhappiness of adults whose history and relationships determine and explain her destiny. It is a melodramatic history, deftly filtered through the girl's imperfect perceptions so that its bluntest edges appear less crass. Virginia's mother is going mad. She has left her husband and her other two daughters and gone with Virginia to live with her doctor and lover, who cares for her, and is the girl's real father. As her mother's health deteriorates, Virginia is sent back to her first home, in whose garden stands the circle of stone dwarfs that provides the novel's title and represents, for the girl, all the systems of relationships from which she feels excluded: the man who is shy of showing his father's love for her so as not to jeopardize her legitimacy; the father who avoids her because of her illegitimacy; the siblings and their friends who refuse to admit her to their games or tell her their secrets. But it is also a circle that encloses and supports her. As her father's putative daughter she is admitted to a convent school, even though her mother's abandonment of the conjugal home prompts the nuns to make public the extent of their charity in discounting the scandal. In short, the stone circle marks the limits of the world of exclusion and protection in which her life seems mapped out. At the end of the novel, she has learned most of the secrets it keeps, has rejected suicide prompted by her earlier despair at breaking into it, and is ready to leave the house in whose garden it stands. But she has also learned that the stone of which the dwarfs were made is flawed and friable, and that she will carry with her the consequences of its defects: her mother's madness, her father's suicide, her legal father's coldness, the continuation of muted scandal in her own generation, her sister's adultery and promiscuity, her friend's homosexuality, and the impotence of the boy she had loved all her life. Her final decision to leave may be construed as a positive ending: she is shown capable of drawing strength from the negative conditions of powerlessness and exclusion, but neither she nor the reader are given an idea of how her exit can free her from the determination of the stone circle that has always enclosed her.[6]

Madness and death had followed upon, though not specifically from, her mother's escape from the circle, where she too had felt a stranger, but neither for her nor for Virginia does the question ever arise of the origin of their determination. If social or historical conditions ground their destinies, they are so completely embedded in their psychological makeup—their actions seem to flow so logically from personality—that no language can arise with which to view from the outside the stone circle that encloses the writing itself. "Intimist" fiction appears, in this example, as a discourse on inevitable, naturalized limits, a stoical overview of the individual's powerlessness before the vaguely adumbrated world, a courageous, clear-eyed look at defeat, whose clarity redeems it and disguises its incompleteness. But even that incompleteness only appears in the possibility of reading the plot also as a form of revenge: if it imprisons the women, checkmating their sensibility and intelligence, it also condemns the men to impotence and to various forms of self-destruction. The intimate attention to the home world reveals a refuge riddled with weakness, vice, and madness, where relations define the individual by fixing and isolating him or her, where fortresses turn into prisons and the threads that connect also throttle.

The heroine of the second novel (***Verão no aquário***—**Summer in the Fishbowl**), Raiza, spends a pivotal summer in her mother's home, haunted by imperfect memories of her father, who died an alcoholic, and locked in sexual rivalry with her mother for the attention of a lapsed seminarian who kills himself after the girl seduces him. Her mother suggests that she leave the "aquarium" of her childhood home and try swimming in the open ocean, but Raiza suspects this is a ruse to get her out of the young man's way, and the reader doubts whether she would be equipped to survive out there: the plausibility with which Telles presents Raiza's imprisonment in past and passion, through a sensibility that is one of her positive characteristics, makes it difficult to step back from, or out of, the metaphorical aquarium where she is shown.

These then are the girls of Telles's longer fiction before *As meninas*: children of old, generally dissipated wealth, with acute intelligence and feeling; existing amid decadence, madness, jealousy, sexual dissatisfaction; dependent on a past that cannot sustain them; prey to a world that does not accept them, their femininity making them exceptionally fit to understand their plight and exceptionally unfit to escape it. The respectful to enthusiastic acceptance of these novels indicates their congruence with a common notion of the proper forms and boundaries of fiction by and about women. It is not a sanitized territory: it encompasses vices and passions, but it excludes history, learning, money, and any kind of work. These girls don't even write poetry.

In *As meninas*, however, the characters seem different from those one had come to know in Telles's novels: the girls are students, away from home and family—though not too far away, since they are boarders in a convent.[7] And the story offers a number of topical details; most startlingly, it states very clearly at a dangerous time of intensifying censorship of news and opinions, that it is set in a contemporary world of political repression and that an authoritarian—as the nomenclature went then in the United States—regime rules the outside world. In this, it awakens hope by showing it is possible to write a character both sympathetic and politically subversive who does not land herself or her author in jail. One of the novel's early reviewers speaks repeatedly of its "courage," without daring to specify what such courage consisted of: whether of Telles's departure from customary situations and characterization, or of her taunting the authorities.[8] By leaving the question open, the critic shows herself constrained by the same conditions that call for courage in the text, and calls attention to an opening through which the political has invaded the literary undisguised, so that context threatens the text that would originate or shape it, and the text can be qualified by power relations in a world where it is likely to find itself irrelevant or compromised. The appearance of "courage" as a critical category marks the possibility of change in the relation between Telles's work and the extraliterary context in which it appears, and raises questions, such as whether author and character can be trusted even though they are in print, or whether publication is a sign that the subversion is innocuous and the text powerless. Reading under these circumstances becomes an act of both interpretation and collusion that of necessity goes beyond the purely "literary" to confirm the continued possibility of an unhampered discourse someplace where reader and text are unreachable by contingencies. It is also a reading-in-the-world, and the differences between *As meninas* and its predecessors seem to affirm that it would be so even if the text offered the same isolation from history that characterized the two former novels and their heroines. Once the conditions which called forth these two aspects of reading and writing under pressure have changed, another question arises—that of how great the intensity of reading that still attaches to the work twenty years after the end of the dictatorship and, linked to it, that of the resilience of the "intimist" mode under the pressure of politics.

In *As meninas* Telles compresses a picture of the contemporary situation into the lives of three girls from different backgrounds and social classes, who meet and befriend one another as pensioners in a student boarding house run in a convent. The main characters are "round" in that they have histories, contradictory traits, plausible indefinitions, but their traits are apportioned paradigmatically so that they also represent rural aristocracy, urban (sub-)proletariat, and middle class; North and South of the country; traditional Brazilian family and descendant of recent immigrants; various racial combinations, and different attitudes toward public and private morality. The story is filtered through the consciousness of the girls, complemented occasionally by an impersonal voice that blends into the interior monologue so seamlessly as to have the effect of widening the perceptions possible to individual characters while contributing to the paradigmatic tenor of their feelings and reasoning without exactly relying on the device of an omniscient narrator.[9] The world outside the girls' consciousness is introduced also through their encounters with a number of peripheral figures: nuns, drug dealers, urban guerrillas, bar flies, industrialists on the prowl for sex, which widen the experience of the usual Telles heroine. The girls themselves differ from that heroine too, at least in that they are not shown at home and in that two of them, Ana, the addict, and Lia, the revolutionary, seem to escape the usual model altogether in their makeup, background, actions, and convictions.

But not even the gallery of disreputable types, struggling youths, and wise and innocent nuns that fleshes out the novel quite answers the plausible question of whether the purely and topically political elements that provided the initial shock in the reading occupy the prominent position that seemed promised in the invention of Lia and her adventures. Political repression begins to look like just one item in a catalog of decay that embraces all aspects of urban life shown in the tale. The imprisonment of students, workers, and intellectuals, the official brutality to which the novel alludes, undergo something like normalization as expected forms of discomfort among the many difficult conditions of modern urban life. The generalized decay envelops the surprising topicality of the novel; it begins to sound like the familiar form of Telles's earlier fiction, extended outward from within the families in which it had formerly appeared, but not different in kind.

The sense of familiarity grows as one considers the main character, Lorena, whose monologue opens and closes the novel. She is the descendant of an old, rich family of landowners whose plantation was sold when no one was left to manage it. The family money has not yet been completely dissipated: part of it belongs to Lorena directly, who uses it to finance her studies and to help her friends; part belongs to her mother, who uses it to keep a charming younger lover (he likes to pinch Lorena's bottom when unobserved) and bankroll a succession of his glamorous and unprofitable business ventures. The mother has migraines, attentive servants and, more modern than Virginia's, a psychiatrist, but on the whole she lives in an old-fashioned kind of decadence, and establishes around her daughter some of the atmosphere of the earlier Telles novels. We also learn, in the course of Lorena's monologue, that her father has died in an insane asylum, his madness the probable effect of the tragedy in which one of her brothers killed his twin in a gunshot accident. In addition, we learn that she is in love with her gynecologist who is married and who avoids her after a couple of passionate embraces but sends her a drippingly romantic letter. We also learn that she is bothered by her virginity, so she courts and yet flees sex. She is intelligent and a law student; she loves cleanliness and order, regularly going into her friends' rooms to clean their combs and have their clothes laundered. She has gentrified the old porter's lodge at the convent, erasing in it the marks of coarser lives and loves, outfitting it with a luxurious bathroom. She spends the whole novel in her nest—though she is a student, the topically correct detail that her university is on strike allows Telles to keep her within the confines of her surrogate home and avoid showing her in action in the outside world.

At the center of Lorena's protective circle is her bathtub, refuge and antidote to the world. It is not unusual, especially in rural Brazil, to offer a travel-weary visitor a bath before any other type of refreshment, so that any metaphorical meaning of Lorena's tub is planted in solid cultural ground and carries connotations of traditional forms of hospitality in the precincts of a civilization that, for the wealthy, is peaceful and secure. This is the spirit Lorena evokes as she offers political baths to her friend Lia, to expose her to the delights of oils and perfumes, the comfort of clean feet and plush bourgeois towels, hoping to temper and supplement her absorption in finding solutions for the plights of the masses; or as she offers psychological baths to Ana, addicted to drugs and lies, hoping to convert her to the simpler pleasures of the affluent life. The tub is a refuge from the pressures and losses of Lorena's history, from her intelligence, sensitivity, inadequacy and self-awareness, from Ana's alienation and Lia's politics. It is also a sociable tub that washes away contingencies under which, it is implied, lies the essential person, defined by friendship, not by ideas or origins. Fairly explicitly, the tub is charged even further: the perfumed mists arising from it should be seen not only as defenses against the unpleasant realities of the street, but as carriers of civilization itself.

Lorena considers that she helps the other characters less by giving them money (which she does, often) than by offering them that which they lack and which makes up a civilized life, one equally free of drugs and politics. "The only way of helping them," she declares, "is to give them the things they do not have"—perfume, cleanliness, order, tea with biscuits, music by Brazilian composers and singers, poetry.[10] Annoyed when her efforts are greeted with an unopposed irony which also signals misgivings within the text about the appropriateness of the proposed solution to the problems it raises, Lorena promises (in italics) that some day she will put up a sign: "Please pardon the order, the cleanliness, the elegance and superfluity, but this is the residence of a civilized citizen of the most civilized city in Brazil."[11]

She does not mean it ironically. Yet that "civilization," as she sees and defends it, has lost both its material foundation and its appetite for the world it should transform. The aristocratic rural money and traditions are being overwhelmed in a city where industry and commerce amass new, still unrefined fortunes, and where the police are unleashed in defense of interests that may completely escape a discussion of the limits and future of a Brazilian civilization. But even Lorena's consumption is dispirited: she dreams of stepping into the streets, grabbing people and dancing with them, of "eating blood-red steaks, soups with octopuses in them, and fish swimming among braided onions at volcanic temperatures" (55), in what sounds almost like a wistful and unconscious echo of Jorge Amado's Gabriela. Instead, she squeezes a rubber duck until it squawks, thinks of how, despite affection and desire, she refused to sleep with the young man who gave her the squawker, and drinks a glass of milk. If she is emblematic of civilization, the image she proposes is marked by the conventionally female traits of passivity, restraint, and domesticity; she represents a place of retreat, not a force of transformation. She is a source of commodified generosity, transferred from person to thing. To friends involved in the various dangerous or unsavory aspects of life in that most civilized of cities, which the text itself shows to throb ceaselessly with public and private brutality, with poverty, beatings by spouses and by police, crime, drugs, and death, with perversion, prostitution, and political imprisonment, Lorena offers her tub and her books, her music and her poetry, Latin, English, and French quotations from law and literature, her oils and soap bubbles, perfumes and plush towels in colors matching the mood and character of the bather. It is an endeavor both heroic and ridiculous, necessary and misplaced. A reading of Lorena then begins to oscillate between the perception of a radically ironic view of a feminized and therefore weakened civilization engaged in avoidance, denial, and escape—a view that seems to go against the grain of the text—and a radically despairing vision of the possibility of civilization. With Lorena, Telles places the blocked female consciousness at the center of a tale ampler than her usual ones. But Lorena's verbal nimbleness, the clarity with which she sees and criticizes her position and limitations, and her humor, constitute only a pleasant and persuasive justification for the ease with which she glides through the unpleasant world of the street, avoiding or forgetting its threats.

One encouraging aspect of the character, however, is that she is open to attack from two flanks: Wilson Martins objects to Lorena's aiding those who, by vulgarity or subversion, are about to destroy Brazilian civilization[12] (a peculiar position in view of the events of the time), while from the other side Paulo Hecker Filho accuses her of

silliness, of throwing her money around like a crazy person, and of not having read all the Malraux, Barthes, and Mayakovsky (the reference is to *Meninas,* 215) from whom she quotes, in short, not as destructive of civilization, but as inadequate to represent it because not fully aware of what threatens it.[13] In fact, with Lorena, Telles raises the problem of the survival of a civilization that defines itself in terms of social relation when the inward world with which it is identified ceases to either complement or echo the world of the street, when the street invades and swallows the home and invalidates relation. The comforts Lorena provides are not so different from those available to her mother for giving or receiving. But while her mother's life was broken up by personal tragedy arising from disruptions in the relations between individuals (however conditioned by wider socioeconomic forces), or as the result of tragic configurations of individual traits, the troubles that stalk Lorena's friends arise from conditions that do not yield to individual efforts at correction and are largely independent of personality. One can ask then, how Telles's choice of setting and characters limits and determines the scope of their effectiveness in the world in which they are shown to move and, if they are taken as emblematic of personalities, classes, or configurations in the extraliterary world, how they determine the reading of that world. The insistence with which these questions pose themselves in the reading of *As meninas* is a measure of the strength with which extraliterary circumstances have pressed upon this novel and deflected it from the course of the preceding ones: the aquarium is cracked from the outside by politics suddenly made visible as it had not been in the previous works. But even so, if one looks at Lorena only, it is not clear that Telles has done much more than transfer her heroines to a larger tank. This conclusion is premature, however, if the two other characters with whom Lorena shares voice escape the constraints of the intimist novel and are capable of offering a coherent view of the world of the street and its relation with that of the home.

The portions of the novel spoken from Ana's point of view constitute a stylistic tour de force in which Telles grasps the skewed logic of a drugged consciousness and conveys in fragments of images and memories the brutality of the girl's earlier life, and the waste of her lover's. Ana's childhood was traumatic and poor; her mother had lived in insecure dependence on a series of working men who maltreated her and had escaped from their blows and from a late, unwanted pregnancy by drinking ant poison. Ana's lover, in an abridged variation on the fate of Telles's other dying families, had seen his sister carted away to an insane asylum and had himself drifted into drug taking and dealing after his home, the trees in his large garden, his entire former life, had been literally demolished and replaced by an apartment complex, swallowed up in the growth of São Paulo into a modern metropolis. The men who beat Ana's mother are the same ones who hammered down the house where her lover Max and his sister had lived and, by smashing the protective stones and trees on their land, exposed their frailty to an indifferent world, where personal tragedies have no repercussions.

The text dwells on the social and economic conditions at the root of the addict-lovers' situation to the point of privileging them as causes of their alienation over relations with parental figures that had played such a prominent role in the earlier novels. Yet, through this technique of psychological exploration, Telles calls up the readers' empathy for her characters by the skillful exploration of abysses of personal despair that fill the page until no other landscape seems possible. Plausibly lacking in will and insight, Max sinks without a struggle into deadly pleasure. Plausibly struggling for escape, Ana tears herself away from her lover's bed and apartment, dresses and paints herself to meet the man whom she hopes to persuade to marry her into respectability. Although their history is conditioned by social class and economic conditions, we see their destiny as psychologically determined; the social and economic determinants of their lives are thus consistently translated into emotions and placed beyond the reach of decision, will, or action. These determinants—the cancerous growth of the city, disruptive shifts in economic power, poverty and lower-class brutality—having absorbed the specifically political disruptions of the social fabric, are thus transformed and naturalized, and made fit for the form in which emotions, taken as natural and feminine, given and unchangeable, objects of passive contemplation, become the appropriate tools for the transposition of the man-made world of history and society into the home, the soul, and other categories of interiority.

Child of an unlikely marriage between Emile Zola and Virginia Woolf, Ana brings the life of the street and the category of the will into Telles's fiction of fenced-in sensibility. It is notable, however, that the instrument Ana is given for the exercise of her will is her beauty, which is more likely to make her the object of a gaze than the subject of action, and most likely to entangle her in contradictory cultural rules for the proper behavior of a woman. Hungry and beaten as a child, raped as a young girl, Ana slowly realizes that her beauty differentiates her from her mother and offers an escape from the poor woman's fate they would otherwise have shared. When she realizes the power of her beauty, Ana also gains a partial understanding of the place of the conventionally feminine in the world she wants to subdue; she decides to use it as an instrument for advancement and a weapon for revenge. She wants to be a model, to marry well, to dominate the men she grew up fearing, and to make them suffer in their desire for her. Convinced she can ride it, she becomes the strongest defender of the status quo, exclaiming indignantly to Lia: "Destroy the bourgeoisie! Not now, just as I. Wait a minute, I want some too, can't I?" (71). She is never allowed to realize, however—and this means the text does not confront the matter—that although the feminine can be objectified, it must not, according to the rules of the status quo,

be perceptibly instrumentalized; the "bourgeoisie" will reward beauty but forbids its obvious use as a tool.

Ana's miscalculation is fatal to her self, but her "I want" becomes the hard core against which the values of other characters break up. With it she disarms not only Lia's revolutionary theorizing, but also the religious charity and love with which the head nun at the convent hopes to lead her out of her alienation and to cure her of loathing self and others, that is, of her conviction that she must use self and others as instruments of pleasure or profit. At the same time, however, the plausibility of the shock she delivers illustrates the structure of the relational universe Telles creates. Martins complains about the absurdity of the nuns' harboring a penniless girl like Ana, but it is precisely the possibility of such vertical ties that defines the world the nuns defend; it is a world in which the classification of the self by attribute instead of relation is fatal, whether the attribute be beauty, class, or ideology. Ana's story illustrates serious malfunctions in this relational universe, while the failure of her attempt to fight dispossession in accordance with the expressed rules and values of those who have possession indicates its strength.

As a character, Ana illustrates the problems of enlarging the world of Telles's usual heroines. She differs from the girls we have met in other novels. Unlike Raiza, Virginia, or Lorena, she looks beyond the limits of her class, heredity, and economic situation, and does not take them as setting down the only terms in which her world can be defined. Also unlike them, she takes steps to move away from the circle into which she was born, to swim in the larger sea. However, like them, she cannot see further than the determination of sex. Her escape route, the weapons she uses, are those of conventional femininity: beauty and—stressing the point—artificial virginity (Lorena has paid for her abortions and is ready to pay for a virginity-restoration, spoken of as if it were an urban renewal project, "mending the South End" [58]). These are to help her attach herself to a powerful man whose power she can only envision as repellent. In that trap, however, she rejoins the other girls, and like them again, she "loves" a lost boy, whose weakness destroys her and in whose embrace her desire for control turns into a desire for death. In Max's apartment Ana is surrounded by the same atmosphere of despair that envelops the heroines of the other novels, and Telles's excursion into a different social class and a different personal history reveals itself as an illusory movement. Though free of family ties, Ana is as constrained by her sex and history as were Raiza and Virginia, and her freedom becomes a liability, depriving her of the protection an aquarium provides.

The presence of Ana also calls attention to the difficulty of speaking about power within the inner-directed text. The man Ana intends to marry may be entirely a figment of her imagination: we never see him. The lost boy, on the other hand, is fleshed out as clearly as the other ineffectual males of Telles's fiction, those pendants to her enclosed women who can never answer—or even ask—the question about the origin of the oppression that stifles them all and that becomes encoded as psychological barriers to action. Ana's "I want" addresses this unspoken source of power and in its directness confounds Lorena's politeness by short-circuiting her vocabulary of generosity in which demands appear as moves in a play of reciprocity between equals. It also confounds Lia's revolutionary rhetoric by individualizing Ana's desire, just as it confounds the rhetoric of individual relation in which the novel is embedded. The tip-off is Ana's voicing a racism that is taboo in polite society and that denies the existence of personal ties linking all the members of Brazilian society and making each individual into an exception to general rules governing the allotment of privilege in accordance with class or race.

Ana dies. After a night of dissipation from most of which we are kept discreetly away, she fetches up on the convent's doorstep, where Lorena collects her, washes her and leaves her to rest on a couch. There Ana overdoses, and the plot picks up her character's disruptiveness: if Ana is found dead of drugs in the convent, the scandal will jeopardize the nuns' private and religious lives as well as the public and secular good they are able to do. They will be hampered in their care for young girls, and they will lose the authority they derive from the Church—an authority the mother superior uses to intervene on behalf of those tortured and "disappeared" by the totalitarian regime. Ana's irregular death can thus introduce profound disturbances in the relational strategies the nuns employ to counteract a political process that aims to destroy the power of relation. Ana would like to exist for herself, but the plot emphasizes that her actions can have consequences derived from her position in the relational web, rather than from her personality or personal history. In this way any political implications of Ana's position and fate are translated into terms of relation and fail to introduce a significant change in the usual world of Telles's novels. Ana's death becomes topical in a very wide sense: her desires and transgressions are quite appropriately expressed in the Jimi Hendrix songs Lorena plays endlessly on her hi-fi; it is a cosmopolitan despair that haunts her and a transnational death that reaps her, in a play of causes and consequences that owes much to the psychologically and literarily documented course of twentieth-century lives turning against themselves in their alienation, but even more to nineteenth-century conventions for writing the trespassing heroine.

Enter Lia, the remaining girl. Her signature characteristic is her springy hair, a cross between mop and halo, indomitably escaping ribbons and headbands, leaping back into its full glory as soon as it is released from any attempted confinement that bows to Lorena's standards of order and elegance. Her hair links Lia with her mother, who is from the state of Bahia and "morena," a proper representative of the true, African-inflected Brazilianness from which the country is thought to draw its deepest strength and identity.[14] Her father, however, is German, a former Nazi, a curious touch which Telles hastens to neutralize with the information that he had joined the party in a fit of absentmindedness, fleeing immediately upon noticing what was up, and ending his escape in tolerant Bahia, where he attached himself to a family-surrounded woman on whom he could anchor his restless, rootless, conscience-stricken Europeanness, and with whom he could contribute to the ethnic brew Lia embodies, a strain of Teutonic toughness, energy and industriousness. Possibly, by marrying an ex-Nazi to a representative of Bilac's three sad races, named Dionisia, Telles means to indicate that even the most extreme European brutality can be humanized in Brazil (Brazilians like to stress the *relatively* lower incidence of violence in their history, often by de-emphasizing its bloodier episodes). It might also have amused her to give her Marxist heroine a Nazi father, in an ambiguous gesture implying either comparison or opposition. Or she might have wished to imply a kinship between the European forms of totalitarianism and its current Brazilian version, which had shocked the public by beating up and torturing students and intellectuals with foreign-seeming brutality.[15] Still, whatever its justification, it is a clumsy device. But it attaches itself to the most attractive of the novel's protagonists, one whose vitality, outer-directedness, and open political involvement do set her apart from other Telles heroines.

Lia is not imprisoned within the walls of family, tradition, or self. She is impatient with interiority, and has so much to do in the world that she cannot spare time for her studies, for her fears and suffering—her lover is a political prisoner and she herself may be in danger—or for the civilizing baths she should, after an initial pleasing trial, continue to enjoy by Lorena's courtesy and pedagogical generosity. Instead she has Lorena borrow her mother's car so she can transport her comrades to shadowy secret meetings, of which the reader learns very little. She has *Das Kapital* on her lips and a poster of Che Guevara on her wall. Her actions and pronouncements provide some of the funniest and most startling moments in the novel, delightful in their direct engagement with the world of actions and ideas, and in their disregard for convention. Telles seems not only to be getting away from the kind of protagonist she has used so far, but also to be getting away with her at a time when her creation constitutes both literary and political defiance.

However, a slightly different view of Lia as character and as statement begins to emerge if one pays attention to the situations in which she is shown rather than to the words she speaks. We see her as a revolutionary when she follows instructions to teach a new, young member of the group the theoretical underpinnings and the practical strategies of subversive action. Almost from the start, however, the conversation between them turns confessional, ending when Lia initiates the young man into sex, in a friendly manner, to prepare him for his next encounter with his girlfriend. Alone again, in her group's secret "cell," she reminisces about her own first romantic attachment, which was to another girl. On one hand, while both act and memory could be taken as negative indices of deviation, considering how Telles presents Lia as markedly nonneurotic (at the time of the novel the negative valuation would have been taken as a matter of course), they probably ought to be read as signs of liberation, of true freedom. On the other hand, it is significant that her politically subversive activity is translated into action and thought that hinges on, and questions, her gender and gender definition. The only other time we see her in her quality as a member of a "cell" is when she takes a ride with another comrade, who informs her that her lover has been released from prison and is being shipped to Algeria, in exchange for the American ambassador who had been kidnapped by guerrillas (a topical touch). Lia is to follow him, borrowing money from her family and from Lorena for the passage. All rejoice at the news of the trip, and Lorena's mother gives her, as a parting present, a luxurious coat, which she calls a *cache-misère,* and which is transformed, as it disguises the would-be harbinger of the new order into a representative of the exhausted old one, into a *cache-politique.*

One is happy that Lia's politics have not had the same end result as Ana's rebellion. But it also seems that Telles circumvents the implications of the choices she makes for her character. It is true that Lia is free from the weight of personal history that hobbles Lorena and from the sexual inhibitions that mark her friend's brand of civilized sensibility. She is also untouched by the pressures of the dark side of that civilization, in which Ana is abused. Lia's uninhibited, generous, "natural" sexuality appears in opposition both to Lorena's frightened virginity and to Ana's frigidity and promiscuity, just as her ability to turn energy and intelligence toward action in the world outside of self and family, the world said to be of men, appears in opposition to Lorena's passivity and to Ana's thwarted and wrong-headed attempts at manipulating that world by means of an imperfect understanding of its rules. But Lia's actions in the world consist, in the end, of one episode in which her sexuality is charged with bearing the entire weight of revolt, and of another in which her freedom consists of the possibility of following her man. The boundaries of her freedom are circumscribed by her femaleness, no less than those of other women in Telles's novels. The only way in which her active disposition affects the definition of her femininity is in tingeing it with ambiguity: the reported memory of her early infatuation, in which she appears to have taken the stronger role, and the misgivings Lorena's mother expresses about the true relations between her daughter and the energetic, outspoken girl from a different class, attach to Lia the signs of the masculine and cast doubt on the possibility of being out in

the world of men while not one of them, and on the possibility of redefining the feminine and redrawing the boundaries that enclose its representatives.

Undeniably, there is topical justification for the narrow scope and slight impact of Lia's revolutionary activity in the violent repression that reigned in the land when the novel was written and published. Within the novel itself, however, the presence of police violence is small and indirect, heard of as happening to others, who do not appear as characters or affect the plot. The result is that the realistic justification for Lia's ineffectiveness also serves to camouflage the fundamental distrust of direct forms of feminine power and action that underlies even the construction of a character like her, who seems at first an embodied challenge to the traditional gender definitions that inform other Telles works.

In the end, it is Lorena who has the last word and action of the story. She restores order in the convent and in her life by resolving to remove Ana's body from her room before anyone discovers it there, leaving it to be found in an anonymous little park. She dresses the body in some elegantly exotic clothes of her own, makes it up with great care and ability, and, by insisting she will complete her task alone, if need be, convinces Lia—whose physical strength and training in stealth become indispensable in the execution of the caper—to help her out. Lorena's decision to clothe the death of Ana in the trappings of her own station repeats the gesture with which her mother had clothed Lia's political exile, and arises out of the same system of values. Passive and introspective throughout the novel, Lorena becomes decisive and authoritative as soon as a dead body on her couch threatens to disturb the enclosures of family, religion, and class that protect her and allow her to extend protection to those of whatever station with whom she establishes personal relations.

Lorena's burst of activity and authority serves, in the end, as a necessary defense of the possibility of Lia's departure, and also of the nuns' continued ability to counteract some of the brutality of the police state. At an earlier point in the story, Lia had read to the mother superior a letter from the subject of one of the cases of torture on which her group was to work—a botanist found distributing pamphlets at the gates of a factory and subjected, in consequence, to electric shocks and other discomforts. She finds out that the mother superior not only knows the man but has sat up with his mother and gone with her to see the cardinal to exert pressure for his release. Lia, who had scoffed at the nun's earlier mention of a divine scheme of things and of spiritual reality, declares to Lorena, as she tells her the incident: "She plays innocent, but is as with it as we are. Or more, I don't know, the woman is something else" (244). The two conversations establish a series of mediations between the social and the ideological positions of the nuns, Lia, and Lorena, predicated on personal goodwill and the "dialogue" that Lia had proposed among different political factions as an alternative to both official repression and revolutionary resistance. The need for removing Ana, however, points up the impossibility of engaging in such a dialogue with those who hold political power, of extending the ties of relation into the realm of public action except under very special circumstances in which these are able to mobilize another established and empowered institution, like the Church. If the convent is linked with a criminal matter, the secular powers will be able to gain the upper hand; the nuns' authority in matters of conscience will be compromised; the webs of relation they are able to control will be weakened or torn; the conduits through which information about prisoners comes to them might be plugged. Neither Lorena nor even Lia have to think twice before going to work in defense of their domain, but it is significant that it is Lorena who asserts authority over her generally more determined and active friend. Telles's placement of the reins in Lorena's hands may also suggest something ritual about her heroines' banging against the walls of their aquaria: stone and glass are repaired and replaced when threatened from the outside—the unhappiness found in the ocean is for another kind of fish—and activity becomes simply a form of defending the possibility of continued passivity.

The pressure of extratextual politics made Telles, in this one novel, write characters as female hustlers and guerrillas. But in killing Ana, exiling Lia, and sending—as she does toward the end—Lorena back to her mother, Telles reaffirms the constraints that determined her earlier heroines and turned their energies back against themselves in their confinement. *As meninas* begins as if it would contradict Adonias Filho's statement that "women novelists prefer introspection."[16] Detached from their families and engaged in the affairs of the world, which exists beyond the front gates of family homes, Telles's three heroines start out claiming a stake in the "masculine" territories of learning, work, self-advancement, and political action, of those activities which lie outside the self and its relations with others. The three girls raise the possibility, for a while, that the self and its relations may also depend on the outside world, and that the separation between aquarium and open sea may be a permeable membrane, allowing for passage of more than just the longing glance of the enclosed.

As the novel develops, however, Telles rebuilds the barriers it had seemed to question. Of the three protagonists, Lia and Ana, who embody the strongest impulses toward bridging the separation between inner and outer, of passing back and forth through the membrane, lose themselves in distance and death. There remains the civilized and obedient virgin Lorena, pulsating in longing but imprisoned in a femininity affirmed once again as inward, and besieged in her retreat behind the gates of home. The interest of *As meninas* resides then not, as it seemed at first, in its breaking out of the mode assigned to the "woman's novel," but in how it defines its limits. It shows, on one hand, the susceptibility of these limits to the pressures of the generally excluded world of politics, when these pressures are sufficiently violent, and, on the other hand, their resistance even to such irruption. Under such pressure, Telles plants Lorena's bathtub in the world, and subjects Lia to its influence. But a tub is an intimate thing, and Lorena does not manage to make it function as a mediator between inner and outer; it reasserts its nature, Lia refuses it, and Lorena retreats. The experiment is interesting, amusing, and oddly inadequate.

In the years after the liberalization—and final democratization—of the government, a vast literature has appeared that tries to speak of the dark times: memoirs of imprisonment, accounts of exile, fictions of political violence, dystopias of totalitarianism, analyses of the causes and consequences of the events, witnesses of torture, and allegories of political and social upheaval, of powerlessness and exclusion.[17] Telles has the merit of having spoken up early and of not having made an alibi of the acceptable inwardness of the genre in which she usually works and excels.[18] Under the pressure of an untenable political situation (but using to advantage the protection she enjoyed by status), Telles wrote the least depressing of her novels, and the liveliest, most amusing of her heroines. She turned the situation into an opportunity to introduce variations in the guidelines defining "women's novels" in Brazilian literature, which her earlier works had helped codify, by inviting readers to look beyond the structures of the literary work and beyond the self, which in such works had come to occupy their entire scope. The differences between *As meninas* and her earlier novels became thus like the imprints of extraliterary conditions that, by subjecting literary creation to suddenly shifting forces, more or less make it acknowledge that it does not exist as an autonomous system of significations, responsive only to other systems of signification of the same kind.

Just as it is instructive to see *As meninas* in relation to the earlier novels, so it is to examine how Telles's work reacted once the pressure of politics lifted, and the nation returned to its more usual—and chaotic—form of democracy. To an extent, as one might have thought, Telles returned to the more accustomed preoccupations of her fiction. However, accustomed does not mean identical: the trauma of the '60s and '70s is still manifest, though no longer central to the plot. *As horas nuas* (**The Naked Hours**), published in 1989, once again centers on an enclosed woman. We are introduced to Rosa Ambrósio, famous actress, in a darkened room, drinking, and vaguely remembering headlines about how she was carried off a plane, completely soused. Her fame is fading; her lover has left her; she is terrified of old age. In her apartment, where she lives with a faithful maid and a cat, she drinks herself into frequent oblivion and dreams of making a comeback. Telles says that while *As meninas* and *Ciranda de Pedra* are "young," *As horas nuas* is a work of old age.[19] Whereas the problems are those of old age, we recognize the protagonist, suffering, paralyzed, holed up in her apartment, beating against the walls of her compulsions even though she is said to have been, at one point, out in the world and successful on the world's terms.[20]

And so the imprint of the recent past persists in the novel both at the level of fable and of discourse. In *As horas nuas,* as in *As meninas,* the narration is divided among the protagonists. From Rosa we get the kind of allusive, fragmented language that Telles had perfected for Ana. The omniscient narrator is there too, in free indirect discourse that tells us about some of the other people around Rosa, like her psychiatrist, Ananta.[21] We also hear the commentary of the castrated cat, Rahul, who has lived several lives—as a Roman youth with a homosexual lover and as a boy in an old house where his mother went mad and had to be put away—and who sees ghosts and sees through his mistress. Telles claims a certain freedom, of style, of detail (Rosa dyes her pubic hair; she is years past menopause; Ananta fantasizes ritually, perhaps masturbating before going to sleep, about a neighbor who turns into a horse), of plot (Ananta vanishes at one point, as does the neighbor, and though her disappearance is investigated, her fate is left suspended by the end of the novel), of characterization (the cat). And in Rosa's husband, Gregório, Telles keeps alive the force of the dictatorship: he was denounced—probably by Rosa's faithless lover—to the political police; he never recovered from being tortured, broken mentally and physically, and his death is a consequence of the beatings he suffered.

In short, the novel is as infused with death, abandonment, and decadence as its predecessors; the references to the recent historical past function then as markers of continuity with the times before the political break. Rosa's past is similar to the present of protagonists in Telles' "younger" novels: her father abandoned the family; the great love of her youth—and life—lived in a fog of drugs, left her for another girl, killed the girl in a car accident, and died young in his mother's arms. But while we left Virgínia and Raíza at the point where they were preparing—ready or not—to enter the wider world, we see in Rosa their avatar after she has not only lived in that world, but achieved what can be called success. One can say that Telles has abandoned the enclosures of her earlier fiction, and not only the reference to the continued pressure of politics, in the form of Gregório's fate, but also the striking stylistic freedom she achieved in *As meninas* signal a shift away from the forms with which she began her life as a writer. The aquarium is shattered; it turns out that the fragments are not just glass, but, as Peggy Sharpe sees it, "fragmented identities" through which Telles assesses the inescapable suffering of being-in-the-world, especially of a woman's being-in-the-world.[22] It is a radical and not simply physical fragmentation, which invades the animal and the inanimate world, creating observant, articulate cats, and, as Sandra Almeida observes, a garden full of triadic flowers that encapsulate both the tell-

ing and the tale.[23] Yet this vision of interpenetrations creates neither the sense of plenitude, nor the serenity that such a sense of the whole promises or, in some cases, seems to bring with it. For the landscape of Telles's fiction has not changed significantly, and though Rosa has been in the world, and suffered the losses it imposes, when we see her, she is as enclosed in her apartment, which she does not want to leave, as were earlier heroines in stone circles, aquaria, or bathtubs.

The continuities between Telles's novels signal the force of established conventions and of the limits imposed by social forms and literary models, normalized and naturalized as intrinsically appropriate to certain writers, certain subjects, and certain works. The strength of her novels lies in the insistence with which she marks these limits, so that one can not only see them but feel the shock of beating against them. It may well be in this awareness of limits and the suffering they impose that Telles rides "feminine" experience and sensibility into landscapes that are not inhabited by women only; it may be the resistance to such recognition that, in the views of so many critics, attempts to read her as confined, like her heroines in their enclosures, to the "feminine."

Notes

1. From 1958, when she received the prize of the Instituto Nacional do Livro, to 2005, when she was awarded the Camões Prize for the body of her work, Telles has garnered just about every literary award available in Brazil: she received the Jabuti prize for fiction three times. Her novels and short stories have been translated into at least eight languages and have been adapted for theater, film, and television.

2. Wilson Martins, "Ficção Intimista," in *O Estado de São Paulo, Suplemento Literário,* vol. 18, February 17, 1974.

3. Adonias Filho, "Um romance em crise," in *Modernos ficcionistas brasileiros* (Rio de Janeiro: O Cruzeiro, 1958), 162.

4. See Roberto DaMatta, *A casa e a rua* (São Paulo: Editora Brasiliense, 1985), for a discussion of the "relational" aspects of Brazilian culture and literature.

5. Lucia Helena Costigan refers to Emir Rodríguez Monegal, who argues that the dictatorship has a deep effect on works by the generation of Brazilian writers coming of age around that time, while the older writers tend to gloss it over; however, she thinks the statement, though generally accurate, is too sweeping: Telles, Nélida Piñon, and Rubem Fonseca certainly acknowledge the turbulence and oppression of the times in their fictions. Alhough Costigan argues

that *As meninas* is "a post-modern novel where the presence and elaboration of historical facts pertinent to the period are woven into the language" ("Literatura e ditadura," 143), that the pension where the girls live is a "metaphor for Brazil itself" (144), and quotes an extended passage in which torture is described (145), she still thinks that in Piñon's *Republica dos sonhos* the impact of the politics of the time is stronger and more direct, its expression more daring (146). When speaking of dictatorships, however, one should not forget that Brazil suffered under more than one of them: Telles began publishing in the late '40s—the dictatorship of Getúlio Vargas lasted until 1945; however, as a student in the prestigious and always democratically inclined law school of the University of São Paulo Telles was involved with anti-Vargas movements whose "silent march" in November of 1943 is remembered for the brutal reaction of the police, in which the cousin of her future husband was killed. The interest she shows in resistance to the later dictatorship in *As meninas* is not new to her. See Cristina Ferreira Pinto, *O Bildungsroman feminino*, 116-17.

6. For Ferreira Pinto, this is another example of the female *Bildungsroman* in Brazil; the lack of resolution at the end is one of the genre's characteristics. Its focus on the decadence of the coffee aristocracy, on the other hand, aligns it with the works of her contemporaries—the playwright Nelson Rodrigues and the novelist and short-story writer Dalton Trevisan—this is a useful reminder that the women writers of which she writes do not exist in a (female) social and historical vacuum.

7. This setting, of three girls as guests in a nunnery, is another "community of women," gathered together in a cohesive group which, from a culturally marginal position, is well placed both to reflect and to oppose a male-dominated world. However, what is characteristic of Telles is that, although she consistently constructs women-dominated communities, these are consistently presented—unlike those that appear in Lopes de Almeida, as accidental, almost unwilled: their constituents do not participate in them because they are women. They are pushed together by and for the culture around them, not against that culture, and do not necessarily derive strength from being in that community. And whereas these tend to be dominated by one stronger woman, like those of Rachel de Queiroz, they do not, except for the convent school in *As meninas,* open to the outside: the domination is directed entirely toward the participants in the community, some of whom are men.

8. Nelly Novaes Coelho, "*As meninas,* a crise das elites e da literatura," in *O Estado de São Paulo, Suplemento Literário,* vol. 17, December 23, 1973.

9. Telles is widely recognized as a master of form. See Martins, "Ficção Intimista"; Coelho; Vicente de Paula Ataíde's "A narrativa de Lygia Fagundes Telles," in *A narrativo de ficção* (Curitiba: Editora dos Professores, 1972); and Paulo Rónai, in "A arte de Lygia Fagundes Telles" in *Histórias escolhidas* (São Paulo: Martins, 1964); all have agreed, along the whole course of her career, that her writing is of highest formal quality, the result of specific attention to form. Mostly, however, questions of models have not arisen. It is interesting to note, in this respect, that the fourth voice in *As meninas* strongly resembles what Erich Auerbach has called the "multipersonal representation of consciousness" in his analysis of Virginia Woolf's *To the Lighthouse,* one of the benchmarks of the modern psychological realism that can also describe Telles's work (see ch. 20, "The Brown Stocking," trans. W. Trask [Princeton, NJ: Princeton University Press, 1953]). Erich Auerbach also observes, by the way, that Woolf's novel is "filled … in its feminine way, with irony, amorphous sadness and doubt of life" (487-88).

10. Lygia Fagundes Telles, *As meninas,* 3rd. ed. (Rio de Janeiro: José Olympio, 1974), 52. Further references will be cited parenthetically in the text.

11. Ibid.

12. See Martins, "Ficção Intimista," above. In his view, the political aspects of the novel are a clumsy addition to its basic intimist structure, which links it unambiguously to the two earlier works. Part of the difficulty, he says, in integrating the two themes, lies in Telles's lack of affinity with politics in general and revolution in particular; he expects that the true "novel of the Revolution" or of "youth" will someday be written, by someone other than Telles.

13. See Paulo Hecker Filho, "Atenção, saiu um romance," in *O Estado de São Paulo, Suplemento Literário,* vol. 18, June 16, 1974.

14. "Morena" refers to skin color—tan, as in suntanned, and can designate a person classified as racially white; it is also often used to indicate that some of the person's ancestors were of African origin.

15. See Roberto Schwarz, *O pai de família e outros estudos* (Rio de Janeiro: Paz e Terra, 1978), particularly the essay "Cultura e política" (Culture and Politics; 61-92), in which he discusses the phases of the dictatorship and its relation with cultural production and consumption (fiction, essays, films, cartoons), as well as its changeable position relative to different social classes.

16. See Adonias Filho, "Um romance de crise," 163. He gives as other examples Virginia Woolf and Françoise Sagan.

17. For an overview of literary production in the years of the dictatorship, see Flora Süssekind, *Literatura e vida literária: Polêmicas, diários e retratos* (Rio de Janeiro: Jorge Zahar, 1985). She discusses the relationship between censorship and literary production, arguing that the government censor was often replaced by internal controls. She also points out the various forms taken by literary responses to the dictatorship and their relation to a growing Brazilian publishing industry and reading public. She does not discuss *As meninas*.

18. In "Literatura e ditadura," Lúcia Helena Costigan makes a much stronger case than I do for the courageously political content of the novel, quoting several passages in which the omniscient narrator makes unambiguous—and in the context of the times, brave—statements about torture, repression, and the growing economic inequality that the dictatorship of '64 instituted in Brazil. A reading of *As meninas* as a text specifically about politics and its violence is, in the end, however, a question of emphasis; when emphasis matters, that is one indication of the richness of a text.

19. Interview with Patrícia Sobral, "Lygia Fagundes Telles," 85-95, 87.

20. Cristina Ferreira Pinto notes that the protagonist is hiding from personal decay brought with age as well as from a more general social decadence whose symptoms are urban violence, AIDS, and the rest of the catalog; more generally, however, she sees in the book a turn toward the Gothic mode by an author who had always shown an interest in inexplicable phenomena both physical (going all out in this novel with the cat Rahul) and psychological, the latter represented by the importance that dreams, premonitions, intuitions take on in all of Telles's fiction. Nevertheless, it seems to me that in whatever mode, Telles is consistent in her preoccupations with enclosure, isolation, and powerlessness, and it may well be that in her last book she does indeed what Fredric Jameson (quoted by Ferreira-Pinto, in "The Fantastic, the Gothic, and the Grotesque in Contemporary Brazilian Women's Novels," *Chasqui: Revista de Literatura Latinoamericana* 25, no. 2 [November 1996]: 71-80, 77) says the Gothic does: it rehearses the "'dialectic of privilege and shelter'" in which "'privileges seal you off from other people, but by the same token constitute a protective veil through which you cannot see, and behind which, therefore, all kinds of envious forces may be imagined … preparing to give assault'" (Fredric Jameson, "Nostalgia for the Present," *South Atlantic Quarterly* 82, no. 2 [1989]: 517-37, 529).

21. Sandra Regina Goulart Almeida examines *As horas nuas* in greater detail, and with resort to the ideas of Hélène Cixous, Julia Kristeva, and Claudine Herrmann on the constitution of a feminine consciousness. For her the novel's "treatment of women … reflects many ideas embodied by postmodern feminists on the plurality of women's nature and the impossibility of confining them to a fixed and absolute definition" ("Castration and Melancholia in Lygia Fagundes Telles," *Romance Languages Annual* 3 [1991]: 339-43, 43). Goulart is less interested in the continuity between this and Telles's other novels.

22. See "Fragmented Identities and the Progress of Metamorphosis in Works by Lygia Fagundes Telles," in Brown and Goozé, eds., *International Women's Writing: New Landscapes of Identity* (Westport, CT: Greenwood, 1995), 78-85.

23. Ibid., 343.

FURTHER READING

Biographies

Lucas, Fábio. "A ficção giratória de Lygia Fagundes Telles." *Travessia* 20 (1990): 60-77. Print.
> A short, literary biography of Telles. Lucas provides a thematic analysis of several of Telles's short stories and her most important novels and discusses her place in the Generation of 1945. Not available in English.

Telles, Lygia Fagundes. "The Baroness of Tatui." Interview by Edla Van Steen. Trans. Irene Matthews. *Review* 19.36 (1986): 30-3. Print.
> Relates Telles's experiences growing up as a girl in Brazil and discusses changes in the lives and opportunities for women during her lifetime. Van Steen also questions Telles on her writing process, how she thinks her writing has changed over the years, and how she feels about her characters, books, and work.

———. "Lygia Fagundes Telles: Esperança, pasárgada e vida literária no Brasil." Interview by Patrícia Sobral. *Brasil/Brazil* 16 (1996): 85-95. Print.
> An interview with Telles in which she discusses the difficulties of being a writer in Brazil. Sobral specifically addresses *A noite escura e mais eu* (1995; may be translated as *The Dark Night and More*), but the conversation also touches on social, political, and psychological matters. Not available in English.

Criticism

Bianchin, Neila Roso. "Espelho, espelho meu: Uma leitura de 'As horas nuas' de Lygia Fagundes Telles." *Travessia* 21 (1990): 133-42. Print.

Provides a discussion of *The Naked Hours* based heavily on Christopher Lasch's argument that narcissism is characteristic of our times. Bianchin analyzes the main character, Rosa, as representative of this concept in her obsession with youth and health and her need of affirmation from men, from her public, and from mirrors. Not available in English.

Bishop-Sanchez, Kathryn. "Entre a *décadence* e o imaginário: O caleidoscópio do envelhecimento em *As horas nuas* de Lygia Fagundes Telles." *Passo e compasso: Nos ritmos do envelhecer.* Ed. Maria José Somerlate Barbosa. Porto Alegre: EDIPUCRS, 2003. 175-89. Print.
Examines the various ways in which Rosa in *The Naked Hours* fails to reconcile herself to her increasing age. Not available in English.

Costigan, Lúcia Helena. "Literatura e ditadura: Aspectos da ficção Brasileira pós-64 em alguns dos escritos de Lygia Fagundes Telles e de Nelida Piñon." *Hispanic Journal* 13.1 (1992): 141-51. Print.
Discusses the political involvement of Brazilian authors through their literary works. Costigan starts in colonial times but focuses mainly on Telles and Piñon. Not available in English.

Gomes, Carlos Magno. "A culpa na ficção de Lygia Fagundes Telles." *Estudos de Literatura Brasileira Contemporânea* 30 (2007): 41-51. Print.
Asserts that an important and durable element in Telles's fiction is the guilt of its bourgeois protagonists in relation to the excluded. Gomes argues that this guilt infuses the narrative voice and characterizes the social dimension of Telles's art. Not available in English.

Hecker Filho, Paulo. "Atenção, saiu um romance." *Estado de São Paulo, Suplemento Literário* 16 June 1974: 6. Print.
Stresses that *The Girl in the Photograph* shows Telles's advance from competent literary dilettante to mature novelist worthy of attention and admiration. Hecker Filho is critical of the novel and its characters, but he also recognizes its value as an accurate rendering of a moment in Brazilian culture and society. Not available in English.

Jeftanovic, Andrea. "*As meninas* de Lygia Fagundes Telles: La infancia a tres voces." *Chasqui* 35.1 (2006): 22-34. Print.
Reads *The Girl in the Photograph* from the perspective of Sigmund Freud's idea of the family romance. Jeftanovic traces how the three girls in Telles's novel achieve maturity, outgrowing fantasies from their different culturally and historically determined childhoods into a present marked by the Brazilian dictatorship of the sixties. Not available in English.

Josef, Bella. "El arte de Lygia Fagundes Telles." *Nueva Narrativa Hispanoamericana* 5.1-2 (1975): 185-88. Print.

Places Telles in a wide movement of Brazilian authors who reject what Josef terms in Spanish "horizontal realism" and "discursive language." Josef notes that although Telles embeds the Brazilian dictatorship into the plot and setting of *The Girl in the Photograph,* she does not dwell on that historical background. Not available in English.

Quinlan, Susan Canty. "Revisando/revisualizando gêneros: *A noite escura e mais eu* e *Invenção e memória* de Lygia Fagundes Telles." *Revista Iberoamericana* 71.210 (2005): 275-87. Print.
Argues that while Telles's novels generally focus on the relation between fiction and reality and though her characters have trouble realizing themselves, her more recent works no longer fit that characterization. Quinlan discusses Telles's exploration of different ways of writing, specifically exploring transitional spaces. Not available in English.

Schwantes, Cíntia. "Preto no branco: As relações inter-raciais em *As horas nuas* e *O eco distante da tormenta.*" *Estudos de Literatura Brasileira Contemporânea* 28 (2006): 59-70. Print.
Compares Doris Lessing's *A Ripple from the Storm* (1958) and Telles's *The Naked Hours.* Schwantes notes that *The Naked Hours* examines domestic relations between blacks and whites in Brazil, where racism is more attenuated than in Lessing's South Africa. Not available in English.

Silva, Antonio Manoel dos Santos. "Existência e coisificação nos contos de Lygia Fagundes Telles." *Revista de Letras* 26-7 (1986-87): 1-16. Print.
Examines the relation between memories of the past and the everyday in *Before the Green Dance,* suggesting similarities between the narrations and the Brazilian historical and social processes between 1945 and 1969. Silva argues that Telles has been able to represent a complex universe without becoming a slave to ideological schemes. Not available in English.

Teixeira, Angela Enz. "Miscelânea discursiva em conto de Lygia Fagundes Telles." *Acta Scientiarum: Language and Culture* 31.1 (2009): 7-14. Print.
Discusses short stories by Telles with particular attention to discursive features and how these elements affect the understanding of their plots. Teixeira proposes to use stylistics as the theoretical ground on which to proceed with discussion. Not available in English.

Telles, Lygia Fagundes. "Lygia Fagundes Telles: Interview." Interview by Elzbieta Szoka. *Fourteen Female Voices from Brazil: Interviews and Works.* Ed. Szoka. Austin: Host, 2002. 19-30. Print.
Discusses how her childhood influenced her writing career, the impact of spirituality on her work, and the current challenges that Brazilian women authors face.

In response to a question about her intended audience and the concept of a "universal reader," Telles relates that she desires for her reader "to be my partner and accomplice in the act of creation which means anxiety and suffering. It's a search and a celebration."

Wasserman, Renata R. Mautner. "The Guerrilla in the Bathtub: Telles's *As meninas* and the Irruption of Politics." *MLS: Modern Language Studies* 19.1 (1989): 50-65. Print.

Examines the continuity between the central characters in Telles's early novels and *The Girl in the Photograph*, even as that work is affected by the political and moral pressures imposed by the Brazilian dictatorship.

Additional information on Telles's life and works is contained in the following sources published by Gale: *Contemporary Authors,* **Vol. 157;** *Contemporary World Writers,* **Ed. 2;** *Dictionary of Literary Biography,* **Vols. 113, 307;** *Encyclopedia of World Literature in the 20th Century,* **Ed. 3;** *Hispanic Writers,* **Ed. 2;** *Latin American Writers; Literature Resource Center;* **and** *Reference Guide to Short Fiction,* **Ed. 2.**

How to Use This Index

The main references

Calvino, Italo
1923-1985 .... CLC 5, 8, 11, 22, 33, 39,
73; SSC 3, 48

list all author entries in the following Gale Literary Criticism series:

AAL = *Asian American Literature*
BG = *The Beat Generation: A Gale Critical Companion*
BLC = *Black Literature Criticism*
BLCS = *Black Literature Criticism Supplement*
CLC = *Contemporary Literary Criticism*
CLR = *Children's Literature Review*
CMLC = *Classical and Medieval Literature Criticism*
DC = *Drama Criticism*
FL = *Feminism in Literature: A Gale Critical Companion*
GL = *Gothic Literature: A Gale Critical Companion*
HLC = *Hispanic Literature Criticism*
HLCS = *Hispanic Literature Criticism Supplement*
HR = *Harlem Renaissance: A Gale Critical Companion*
LC = *Literature Criticism from 1400 to 1800*
NCLC = *Nineteenth-Century Literature Criticism*
NNAL = *Native North American Literature*
PC = *Poetry Criticism*
SSC = *Short Story Criticism*
TCLC = *Twentieth-Century Literary Criticism*
WLC = *World Literature Criticism, 1500 to the Present*
WLCS = *World Literature Criticism Supplement*

The cross-references

See also CA 85-88, 116; CANR 23, 61;
DAM NOV; DLB 196; EW 13; MTCW 1, 2;
RGSF 2; RGWL 2; SFW 4; SSFS 12

list all author entries in the following Gale biographical and literary sources:

AAYA = *Authors & Artists for Young Adults*
AFAW = *African American Writers*
AFW = *African Writers*
AITN = *Authors in the News*
AMW = *American Writers*
AMWR = *American Writers Retrospective Supplement*
AMWS = *American Writers Supplement*
ANW = *American Nature Writers*
AW = *Ancient Writers*
BEST = *Bestsellers*
BPFB = *Beacham's Encyclopedia of Popular Fiction: Biography and Resources*
BRW = *British Writers*
BRWS = *British Writers Supplement*
BW = *Black Writers*
BYA = *Beacham's Guide to Literature for Young Adults*
CA = *Contemporary Authors*
CAAS = *Contemporary Authors Autobiography Series*
CABS = *Contemporary Authors Bibliographical Series*
CAD = *Contemporary American Dramatists*
CANR = *Contemporary Authors New Revision Series*
CAP = *Contemporary Authors Permanent Series*
CBD = *Contemporary British Dramatists*
CCA = *Contemporary Canadian Authors*

CD = *Contemporary Dramatists*
CDALB = *Concise Dictionary of American Literary Biography*
CDALBS = *Concise Dictionary of American Literary Biography Supplement*
CDBLB = *Concise Dictionary of British Literary Biography*
CMW = *St. James Guide to Crime & Mystery Writers*
CN = *Contemporary Novelists*
CP = *Contemporary Poets*
CPW = *Contemporary Popular Writers*
CSW = *Contemporary Southern Writers*
CWD = *Contemporary Women Dramatists*
CWP = *Contemporary Women Poets*
CWRI = *St. James Guide to Children's Writers*
CWW = *Contemporary World Writers*
DA = *DISCovering Authors*
DA3 = *DISCovering Authors 3.0*
DAB = *DISCovering Authors: British Edition*
DAC = *DISCovering Authors: Canadian Edition*
DAM = *DISCovering Authors: Modules*
    DRAM: *Dramatists Module;* ***MST:*** Most-studied Authors Module;
    MULT: *Multicultural Authors Module;* ***NOV:*** Novelists Module;
    POET: *Poets Module;* ***POP:*** Popular Fiction and Genre Authors Module
DFS = *Drama for Students*
DLB = *Dictionary of Literary Biography*
DLBD = *Dictionary of Literary Biography Documentary Series*
DLBY = *Dictionary of Literary Biography Yearbook*
DNFS = *Literature of Developing Nations for Students*
EFS = *Epics for Students*
EW = *European Writers*
EWL = *Encyclopedia of World Literature in the 20th Century*
EXPN = *Exploring Novels*
EXPP = *Exploring Poetry*
EXPS = *Exploring Short Stories*
FANT = *St. James Guide to Fantasy Writers*
FW = *Feminist Writers*
GFL = *Guide to French Literature, Beginnings to 1789; 1789 to the Present*
GLL = *Gay and Lesbian Literature*
HGG = *St. James Guide to Horror, Ghost & Gothic Writers*
HW = *Hispanic Writers*
IDFW = *International Dictionary of Films and Filmmakers: Writers and Production Artists*
IDTP = *International Dictionary of Theatre: Playwrights*
LAIT = *Literature and Its Times*
LAW = *Latin American Writers*
JRDA = *Junior DISCovering Authors*
MAICYA = *Major Authors and Illustrators for Children and Young Adults*
MAICYAS = *Major Authors and Illustrators for Children and Young Adults Supplement*
MAWW = *Modern American Women Writers*
MJW = *Modern Japanese Writers*
MTCW = *Major 20th-Century Writers*
NCFS = *Nonfiction Classics for Students*
NFS = *Novels for Students*
PAB = *Poets: American and British*
PFS = *Poetry for Students*
RGAL = *Reference Guide to American Literature*
RGEL = *Reference Guide to English Literature*
RGSF = *Reference Guide to Short Fiction*
RGWL = *Reference Guide to World Literature*
RHW = *Twentieth-Century Romance and Historical Writers*
SAAS = *Something about the Author Autobiography Series*
SATA = *Something about the Author*
SFW = *St. James Guide to Science Fiction Writers*
SSFS = *Short Stories for Students*
TCWW = *Twentieth-Century Western Writers*
WLIT = *World Literature and Its Times*
WP = *World Poets*
YABC = *Yesterday's Authors of Books for Children*
YAW = *St. James Guide to Young Adult Writers*

Literary Criticism Series
Cumulative Author Index

Aldanov, Mark (Alexandrovich)
1886-1957 .... **TCLC 23**
See also CA 118; 181; DLB 317

Alden, Jean François
See Twain, Mark

Aldhelm c. 639-709 .... **CMLC 90**

Aldington, Richard 1892-1962 .... **CLC 49;**
PC 134; TCLC 296
See also CA 85-88; CANR 45; DLB 20, 36,
100, 149; LMFS 2; RGEL 2

Aldiss, Brian W. 1925- .... **CLC 5, 14, 40,**
290; SSC 36
See also AAYA 42; BRWS 19; CA 5-8R; 190;
CAAE 190; CAAS 2; CANR 5, 28, 64, 121,
168; CLR 197; CN 1, 2, 3, 4, 5, 6, 7; DAM
NOV; DLB 14, 261, 271; MTCW 1, 2;
MTFW 2005; SATA 34; SCFW 1, 2; SFW 4

Aldiss, Brian Wilson
See Aldiss, Brian W.

Aldrich, Ann
See Meaker, Marijane

Aldrich, Bess Streeter
1881-1954 .... **TCLC 125**
See also CLR 70; TCWW 2

Alegria, Claribel 1924- .... **CLC 75;**
HLCS 1; PC 26, 150
See also CA 131; CAAS 15; CANR 66, 94,
134; CWW 2; DAM MULT; DLB 145,
283; EWL 3; HW 1; MTCW 2; MTFW
2005; PFS 21

Alegria, Claribel Joy
See Alegria, Claribel

Alegria, Fernando 1918-2005 .... **CLC 57**
See also CA 9-12R; CANR 5, 32, 72; EWL
3; HW 1, 2

Aleichem, Sholom 1859-1916 .. **SSC 33, 125;**
TCLC 1, 35
See also CA 104; DLB 333; TWA

Aleixandre, Vicente 1898-1984 ...... **HLCS 1;**
TCLC 113
See also CANR 81; DLB 108, 329; EWL 3;
HW 2; MTCW 1, 2; RGWL 2, 3

Alekseev, Konstantin Sergeivich
See Stanislavsky, Constantin

Alekseyev, Konstantin Sergeyevich
See Stanislavsky, Constantin

Alemán, Mateo 1547-1615(?) ..... **LC 81, 234**

Alencar, Jose de 1829-1877 .... **NCLC 157**
See also DLB 307; LAW; WLIT 1

Alencon, Marguerite d'
See de Navarre, Marguerite

Alepoudelis, Odysseus
See Elytis, Odysseus

Aleramo, Sibilla 1876-1960 .... **TCLC 312**
See also DLB 114, 264; WLIT 7

Aleshkovsky, Joseph
See Aleshkovsky, Yuz

Aleshkovsky, Yuz 1929- .... **CLC 44**
See also CA 121; 128; DLB 317

Alexander, Barbara
See Ehrenreich, Barbara

Alexander, Lloyd 1924-2007 .... **CLC 35**
See also AAYA 1, 27; BPFB 1; BYA 5, 6, 7, 9,
10, 11; CA 1-4R; 260; CANR 1, 24, 38, 55,
113; CLR 1, 5, 48; CWRI 5; DLB 52; FANT;
JRDA; MAICYA 1, 2; MAICYAS 1; MTCW
1; SAAS 19; SATA 3, 49, 81, 129, 135;
SATA-Obit 182; SUFW; TUS; WYA; YAW

Alexander, Lloyd Chudley
See Alexander, Lloyd

Alexander, Meena 1951- .... **CLC 121, 335**
See also CA 115; CANR 38, 70, 146; CP 5,
6, 7; CWP; DLB 323; FW

Alexander, Rae Pace
See Alexander, Raymond Pace

Alexander, Raymond Pace
1898-1974 .... **SSC 62**
See also CA 97-100; SATA 22; SSFS 4

Alexander, Samuel 1859-1938 .... **TCLC 77**

Alexander of Hales
c. 1185-1245 .... **CMLC 128**

Alexeiev, Konstantin
See Stanislavsky, Constantin

Alexeyev, Constantin Sergeivich
See Stanislavsky, Constantin

Alexeyev, Konstantin Sergeyevich
See Stanislavsky, Constantin

Alexie, Sherman 1966- ... **CLC 96, 154, 312;**
NNAL; PC 53; SSC 107, 189
See also AAYA 28, 85; BYA 15; CA 138;
CANR 65, 95, 133, 174; CLR 179; CN 7;
DA3; DAM MULT; DLB 175, 206, 278;
LATS 1:2; MTCW 2; MTFW 2005; NFS
17, 31, 38; PFS 39; SSFS 18, 36

Alexie, Sherman Joseph, Jr.
See Alexie, Sherman

al-Farabi 870(?)-950 .... **CMLC 58**
See also DLB 115

Alfau, Felipe 1902-1999 .... **CLC 66**
See also CA 137

Alfieri, Vittorio 1749-1803 .... **NCLC 101**
See also EW 4; RGWL 2, 3; WLIT 7

Alfonso X 1221-1284 .... **CMLC 78**

Alfred, Jean Gaston
See Ponge, Francis

Alger, Horatio, Jr.
1832-1899 .... **NCLC 8, 83, 260**
See also CLR 87, 170; DLB 42; LAIT 2;
RGAL 4; SATA 16; TUS

Al-Ghazali, Muhammad ibn Muhammad
1058-1111 .... **CMLC 50, 149**
See also DLB 115

Algren, Nelson 1909-1981 .... **CLC 4,**
10, 33; SSC 33
See also AMWS 9; BPFB 1; CA 13-16R;
103; CANR 20, 61; CDALB 1941-1968;
CN 1, 2; DLB 9; DLBY 1981, 1982, 2000;
EWL 3; MAL 5; MTCW 1, 2; MTFW
2005; RGAL 4; RGSF 2

al-Hamadhani 967-1007 .... **CMLC 93**
See also WLIT 6

al-Hariri, al-Qasim ibn 'Ali Abu Muhammad
al-Basri 1054-1122 .... **CMLC 63**
See also RGWL 3

Ali, Ahmed 1908-1998 .... **CLC 69**
See also CA 25-28R; CANR 15, 34; CN 1,
2, 3, 4, 5; DLB 323; EWL 3

Ali, Monica 1967- .... **CLC 304**
See also AAYA 67; BRWS 13; CA 219;
CANR 158, 205, 240; DLB 323

Ali, Tariq 1943- .... **CLC 173, 323**
See also CA 25-28R; CANR 10, 99, 161, 196

Alighieri, Dante
See Dante

Alkali, Zaynab 1950- .... **CLC 381**
See also CA 172; DLB 360

al-Kindi, Abu Yusuf Ya'qub ibn Ishaq
c. 801-c. 873 .... **CMLC 80**

Allan, John B.
See Westlake, Donald E.

Allan, Sidney
See Hartmann, Sadakichi

Allan, Sydney
See Hartmann, Sadakichi

Allard, Janet .... **CLC 59**

Allen, Betsy
See Harrison, Elizabeth (Allen) Cavanna

Allen, Edward 1948- .... **CLC 59**

Allen, Fred 1894-1956 .... **TCLC 87**

Allen, Paula Gunn 1939-2008 .... **CLC 84,**
202, 280; NNAL
See also AMWS 4; CA 112; 143; 272;
CANR 63, 130; CWP; DA3; DAM MULT;
DLB 175; FW; MTCW 2; MTFW 2005;
RGAL 4; TCWW 2

Allen, Roland
See Ayckbourn, Alan

Allen, Sarah A.
See Hopkins, Pauline Elizabeth

Allen, Sidney H.
See Hartmann, Sadakichi

Allen, Woody 1935- ... **CLC 16, 52, 195, 288**
See also AAYA 10, 51; AMWS 15; CA 33-
36R; CANR 27, 38, 63, 128, 172; DAM
POP; DLB 44; MTCW 1; SSFS 21

Allende, Isabel 1942- ... **CLC 39, 57, 97, 170,**
264, 350; HLC 1; SSC 65, 209; WLCS
See also AAYA 18, 70; CA 125; 130; CANR
51, 74, 129, 165, 208; CDWLB 3; CLR 99,
171; CWW 2; DA3; DAM MULT, NOV;
DLB 145; DNFS 1; EWL 3; FL 1:5; FW;
HW 1, 2; INT CA-130; LAIT 5; LAWS 1;
LMFS 2; MTCW 1, 2; MTFW 2005;
NCFS 1; NFS 6, 18, 29; RGSF 2; RGWL
3; SATA 163; SSFS 11, 16; WLIT 1

Alleyn, Ellen
See Rossetti, Christina

Alleyne, Carla D. .... **CLC 65**

Allingham, Margery (Louise)
1904-1966 .... **CLC 19**
See also CA 5-8R; 25-28R; CANR 4, 58;
CMW 4; DLB 77; MSW; MTCW 1, 2

Allingham, William 1824-1889 ..... **NCLC 25**
See also DLB 35; RGEL 2

Allison, Dorothy E. 1949- .... **CLC 78,**
153, 290
See also AAYA 53; CA 140; CANR 66, 107;
CN 7; CSW; DA3; DLB 350; FW; MTCW
2; MTFW 2005; NFS 11; RGAL 4

Alloula, Malek .... **CLC 65**

Allston, Washington 1779-1843 ...... **NCLC 2**
See also DLB 1, 235

Almedingen, E. M. 1898-1971 .... **CLC 12**
See also CA 1-4R; CANR 1; SATA 3

Almedingen, Martha Edith von
See Almedingen, E. M.

Almodovar, Pedro 1949(?)- ... **CLC 114, 229;**
HLCS 1
See also CA 133; CANR 72, 151; HW 2

Almqvist, Carl Jonas Love
1793-1866 .... **NCLC 42**

al-Mutanabbi, Ahmad ibn al-Husayn Abu al-
Tayyib al-Jufi al-Kindi
915-965 .... **CMLC 66**
See also RGWL 3; WLIT 6

Alonso, Dámaso 1898-1990 .... **CLC 14;**
PC 158; TCLC 245
See also CA 110; 131; 130; CANR 72; DLB
108; EWL 3; HW 1, 2

Alov
See Gogol, Nikolai

al'Sadaawi, Nawal
See El Saadawi, Nawal

al-Shaykh, Hanan
See Shaykh, Hanan al-

Al Siddik
See Rolfe, Frederick (William Serafino
Austin Lewis Mary)

Alta 1942- .... **CLC 19**
See also CA 57-60

Alter, Robert B. 1935- .... **CLC 34**
See also CA 49-52; CANR 1, 47, 100, 160, 201

Alter, Robert Bernard
See Alter, Robert B.

Alther, Lisa 1944- .... **CLC 7, 41**
See also BPFB 1; CA 65-68; CAAS 30;
CANR 12, 30, 51, 180; CN 4, 5, 6, 7;
CSW; GLL 2; MTCW 1

Althusser, L.
See Althusser, Louis

Althusser, Louis 1918-1990 .... **CLC 106**
See also CA 131; 132; CANR 102; DLB 242

Annunzio, Gabriele d'
See D'Annunzio, Gabriele
Anodos
See Coleridge, Mary E(lizabeth)
Anon, Charles Robert
See Pessoa, Fernando
Anouilh, Jean 1910-1987 .... **CLC 1, 3, 8, 13, 40, 50; DC 8, 21; TCLC 195**
See also AAYA 67; CA 17-20R; 123; CANR 32; DAM DRAM; DFS 9, 10, 19; DLB 321; EW 13; EWL 3; GFL 1789 to the Present; MTCW 1, 2; MTFW 2005; RGWL 2, 3; TWA
Anouilh, Jean Marie Lucien Pierre
See Anouilh, Jean
Ansa, Tina McElroy 1949- .... **BLC 2:1**
See also BW 2; CA 142; CANR 143; CSW
Anselm of Canterbury
1033(?)-1109 .... **CMLC 67**
See also DLB 115
Anthony, Florence
See Ai
Anthony, John
See Ciardi, John (Anthony)
Anthony, Peter
See Shaffer, Anthony; Shaffer, Peter
Anthony, Piers 1934- .... **CLC 35**
See also AAYA 11, 48; BYA 7; CA 200; CAAE 200; CANR 28, 56, 73, 102, 133, 202; CLR 118; CPW; DAM POP; DLB 8; FANT; MAICYA 2; MAICYAS 1; MTCW 1, 2; MTFW 2005; SAAS 22; SATA 84, 129; SATA-Essay 129; SFW 4; SUFW 1, 2; YAW
Anthony, Susan B(rownell)
1820-1906 .... **TCLC 84**
See also CA 211; FW
Antin, David 1932- .... **PC 124**
See also CA 73-76; CP 1, 3, 4, 5, 6, 7; DLB 169
Antin, Mary 1881-1949 .... **TCLC 247**
See also AMWS 20; CA 118; 181; DLB 221; DLBY 1984
Antiphon
c. 480B.C.-c. 411B.C. .... **CMLC 55**
Antoine, Marc
See Proust, Marcel
Antoninus, Brother
See Everson, William
Antonioni, Michelangelo
1912-2007 .... **CLC 20, 144, 259**
See also CA 73-76; 262; CANR 45, 77
Antschel, Paul
See Celan, Paul
Anwar, Chairil 1922-1949 .... **TCLC 22**
See also CA 121; 219; EWL 3; RGWL 3
Anyidoho, Kofi 1947- .... **BLC 2:1**
See also BW 3; CA 178; CP 5, 6, 7; DLB 157; EWL 3
Anzaldúa, Gloria (Evanjelina)
1942-2004 ...... **CLC 200, 350; HLCS 1**
See also CA 175; 227; CSW; CWP; DLB 122; FW; LLW; RGAL 4; SATA-Obit 154
Apess, William 1798-1839(?) .... **NCLC 73; NNAL**
See also DAM MULT; DLB 175, 243
Apollinaire, Guillaume 1880-1918 ...... **PC 7; TCLC 3, 8, 51**
See also CA 104; 152; DAM POET; DLB 258, 321; EW 9; EWL 3; GFL 1789 to the Present; MTCW 2; PFS 24; RGWL 2, 3; TWA; WP
Apollonius of Rhodes
See Apollonius Rhodius
Apollonius Rhodius
c. 300B.C.-c. 220B.C. .... **CMLC 28**
See also AW 1; DLB 176; RGWL 2, 3
Appelfeld, Aharon 1932- .... **CLC 23, 47, 317; SSC 42**

See also CA 112; 133; CANR 86, 160, 207; CWW 2; DLB 299; EWL 3; RGHL; RGSF 2; WLIT 6
Appelfeld, Aron
See Appelfeld, Aharon
Apple, Max 1941- .... **CLC 9, 33; SSC 50**
See also AMWS 17; CA 81-84; CANR 19, 54, 214; DLB 130
Apple, Max Isaac
See Apple, Max
Appleman, Philip (Dean) 1926- ...... **CLC 51**
See also CA 13-16R; CAAS 18; CANR 6, 29, 56
Appleton, Lawrence
See Lovecraft, H. P.
Apteryx
See Eliot, T. S.
Apuleius, (Lucius Madaurensis)
c. 125-c. 164 .... **CMLC 1, 84**
See also AW 2; CDWLB 1; DLB 211; RGWL 2, 3; SUFW 1; WLIT 8
Aquin, Hubert 1929-1977 .... **CLC 15**
See also CA 105; DLB 53; EWL 3
Aquinas, Thomas 1224(?)-1274 ... **CMLC 33, 137**
See also DLB 115; EW 1; TWA
Aragon, Louis 1897-1982 .... **CLC 3, 22; PC 155; TCLC 123**
See also CA 69-72; 108; CANR 28, 71; DAM NOV, POET; DLB 72, 258; EW 11; EWL 3; GFL 1789 to the Present; GLL 2; LMFS 2; MTCW 1, 2; RGWL 2, 3
Arany, Janos 1817-1882 .... **NCLC 34**
Aranyos, Kakay 1847-1910
See Mikszath, Kalman
Aratus of Soli
c. 315B.C.-c. 240B.C. .... **CMLC 64, 114**
See also DLB 176
Arbuthnot, John 1667-1735 .... **LC 1**
See also BRWS 16; DLB 101
Archer, Herbert Winslow
See Mencken, H. L.
Archer, Jeffrey 1940- .... **CLC 28**
See also AAYA 16; BEST 89:3; BPFB 1; CA 77-80; CANR 22, 52, 95, 136, 209; CPW; DA3; DAM POP; INT CANR-22; MTFW 2005
Archer, Jeffrey Howard
See Archer, Jeffrey
Archer, Jules 1915- .... **CLC 12**
See also CA 9-12R; CANR 6, 69; SAAS 5; SATA 4, 85
Archer, Lee
See Ellison, Harlan
Archilochus c. 7th cent. B.C. .... **CMLC 44**
See also DLB 176
Ard, William
See Jakes, John
Ardelia
See Finch, Anne
Arden, Constance
See Naden, Constance
Arden, John 1930-2012 .... **CLC 6, 13, 15**
See also BRWS 2; CA 13-16R; CAAS 4; CANR 31, 65, 67, 124; CBD; CD 5, 6; DAM DRAM; DFS 9; DLB 13, 245; EWL 3; MTCW 1
Arenas, Reinaldo 1943-1990 .... **CLC 41; HLC 1; TCLC 191**
See also CA 124; 128; 133; CANR 73, 106; DAM MULT; DLB 145; EWL 3; GLL 2; HW 1; LAW; LAWS 1; MTCW 2; MTFW 2005; RGSF 2; RGWL 3; WLIT 1
Arendt, Hannah 1906-1975 .... **CLC 66, 98; TCLC 193**
See also CA 17-20R; 61-64; CANR 26, 60, 172; DLB 242; MTCW 1, 2
Aretino, Pietro 1492-1556 .... **LC 12, 165**
See also RGWL 2, 3

Arghezi, Tudor 1880-1967 .... **CLC 80**
See also CA 167; 116; CDWLB 4; DLB 220; EWL 3
Arguedas, Jose Maria 1911-1969 ... **CLC 10, 18; HLCS 1; TCLC 147**
See also CA 89-92; CANR 73; DLB 113; EWL 3; HW 1; LAW; RGWL 2, 3; WLIT 1
Argueta, Manlio 1936- .... **CLC 31**
See also CA 131; CANR 73; CWW 2; DLB 145; EWL 3; HW 1; RGWL 3
Arias, Ron 1941- .... **HLC 1**
See also CA 131; CANR 81, 136; DAM MULT; DLB 82; HW 1, 2; MTCW 2; MTFW 2005
Ariosto, Lodovico
See Ariosto, Ludovico
Ariosto, Ludovico 1474-1533 .... **LC 6, 87, 206; PC 42**
See also EW 2; RGWL 2, 3; WLIT 7
Aristides
See Epstein, Joseph
Aristides Quintilianus
fl. c. 100-fl. c. 400 .... **CMLC 122**
Aristophanes 450B.C.-385B.C. ...... **CMLC 4, 51, 138, 164, 176; DC 2; WLCS**
See also AW 1; CDWLB 1; DA; DA3; DAB; DAC; DAM DRAM, MST; DFS 10; DLB 176; LMFS 1; RGWL 2, 3; TWA; WLIT 8
Aristotle 384B.C.-322B.C. .... **CMLC 31, 123; WLCS**
See also AW 1; CDWLB 1; DA; DA3; DAB; DAC; DAM MST; DLB 176; RGWL 2, 3; TWA; WLIT 8
Arlt, Roberto 1900-1942 .... **HLC 1; TCLC 29, 255**
See also CA 123; 131; CANR 67; DAM MULT; DLB 305; EWL 3; HW 1, 2; IDTP; LAW
Arlt, Roberto Godofredo Christophersen
See Arlt, Roberto
Armah, Ayi Kwei
1939- ... **BLC 1:1, 2:1; CLC 5, 33, 136**
See also AFW; BRWS 10; BW 1; CA 61-64; CANR 21, 64; CDWLB 3; CN 1, 2, 3, 4, 5, 6, 7; DAM MULT, POET; DLB 117; EWL 3; MTCW 1; WLIT 2
Armatrading, Joan 1950- .... **CLC 17**
See also CA 114; 186
Armin, Robert 1568(?)-1615(?) .... **LC 120**
Armitage, Frank
See Carpenter, John
Armstrong, Gillian 1950- .... **CLC 385**
See also AAYA 74; CA 173
Armstrong, Jeannette (C.) 1948- .... **NNAL**
See also CA 149; CCA 1; CN 6, 7; DAC; DLB 334; SATA 102
Armytage, R.
See Watson, Rosamund Marriott
Arnauld, Antoine 1612-1694 .... **LC 169**
See also DLB 268
Arnette, Robert
See Silverberg, Robert
Arnim, Achim von (Ludwig Joachim von Arnim) 1781-1831 .... **NCLC 5, 159; SSC 29**
See also DLB 90
Arnim, Bettina von
1785-1859 .... **NCLC 38, 123**
See also DLB 90; RGWL 2, 3
Arnold, Matthew 1822-1888 .... **NCLC 6, 29, 89, 126, 218; PC 5, 94; WLC 1**
See also BRW 5; CDBLB 1832-1890; DA; DAB; DAC; DAM MST, POET; DLB 32, 57; EXPP; PAB; PFS 2; TEA; WP
Arnold, Thomas 1795-1842 .... **NCLC 18**
See also DLB 55
Arnow, Harriette (Louisa) Simpson
1908-1986 .... **CLC 2, 7, 18; TCLC 196**

DA3; DLB 227; MAL 5; MTCW 2; MTFW 2005; SUFW 2; TCLE 1:1

Austin, Frank
See Faust, Frederick

Austin, Mary Hunter 1868-1934 ... **SSC 104; TCLC 25, 249**
See also ANW; CA 109; 178; DLB 9, 78, 206, 221, 275; FW; TCWW 1, 2

Avellaneda, Gertrudis Gomez de
See Gomez de Avellaneda, Gertrudis

Averroes 1126-1198 .... **CMLC 7, 104**
See also DLB 115

Avicenna 980-1037 .... **CMLC 16, 110**
See also DLB 115

Avison, Margaret 1918-2007 .... **CLC 2, 4, 97; PC 148**
See also CA 17-20R; CANR 134; CP 1, 2, 3, 4, 5, 6, 7; DAC; DAM POET; DLB 53; MTCW 1

Avison, Margaret Kirkland
See Avison, Margaret

Axton, David
See Koontz, Dean

Ayala, Francisco 1906-2009 .... **SSC 119**
See also CA 208; CWW 2; DLB 322; EWL 3; RGSF 2

Ayala, Francisco de Paula y Garcia Duarte
See Ayala, Francisco

Ayckbourn, Alan 1939- .... **CLC 5, 8, 18, 33, 74; DC 13**
See also BRWS 5; CA 21-24R; CANR 31, 59, 118; CBD; CD 5, 6; DAB; DAM DRAM; DFS 7; DLB 13, 245; EWL 3; MTCW 1, 2; MTFW 2005

Aydy, Catherine
See Tennant, Emma

Ayme, Marcel (Andre)
1902-1967 .... **CLC 11; SSC 41**
See also CA 89-92; CANR 67, 137; CLR 25; DLB 72; EW 12; EWL 3; GFL 1789 to the Present; RGSF 2; RGWL 2, 3; SATA 91

Ayrton, Michael 1921-1975 .... **CLC 7**
See also CA 5-8R; 61-64; CANR 9, 21

Aytmatov, Chingiz
See Aitmatov, Chingiz

Azorin
See Martinez Ruiz, Jose

Azuela, Mariano 1873-1952 .... **HLC 1; TCLC 3, 145, 217**
See also CA 104; 131; CANR 81; DAM MULT; EWL 3; HW 1, 2; LAW; MTCW 1, 2; MTFW 2005

Ba, Mariama 1929-1981 .... **BLC 2:1; BLCS**
See also AFW; BW 2; CA 141; CANR 87; DLB 360; DNFS 2; WLIT 2

Baastad, Babbis Friis
See Friis-Baastad, Babbis Ellinor

Bab
See Gilbert, W(illiam) S(chwenck)

Babbis, Eleanor
See Friis-Baastad, Babbis Ellinor

Babel, Isaac
See Babel, Isaak (Emmanuilovich)

Babel, Isaak (Emmanuilovich)
1894-1941(?) .... **SSC 16, 78, 161; TCLC 2, 13, 171**
See also CA 104; 155; CANR 113; DLB 272; EW 11; EWL 3; MTCW 2; MTFW 2005; RGSF 2; RGWL 2, 3; SSFS 10; TWA

Babits, Mihaly 1883-1941 .... **TCLC 14**
See also CA 114; CDWLB 4; DLB 215; EWL 3

Babur 1483-1530 .... **LC 18**

Babylas
See Ghelderode, Michel de

Baca, Jimmy Santiago
1952- .... **HLC 1; PC 41**

See also CA 131; CANR 81, 90, 146, 220; CP 6, 7; DAM MULT; DLB 122; HW 1, 2; LLW; MAL 5; PFS 40

Baca, Jose Santiago
See Baca, Jimmy Santiago

Bacchelli, Riccardo 1891-1985 .... **CLC 19**
See also CA 29-32R; 117; DLB 264; EWL 3

Bacchylides
c. 520B.C.-c. 452B.C. .... **CMLC 119**

Bach, Richard 1936- .... **CLC 14**
See also AITN 1; BEST 89:2; BPFB 1; BYA 5; CA 9-12R; CANR 18, 93, 151; CPW; DAM NOV, POP; FANT; MTCW 1; SATA 13

Bach, Richard David
See Bach, Richard

Bache, Benjamin Franklin
1769-1798 .... **LC 74**
See also DLB 43

Bachelard, Gaston 1884-1962 ..... **TCLC 128**
See also CA 97-100; 89-92; DLB 296; GFL 1789 to the Present

Bachman, Richard
See King, Stephen

Bachmann, Ingeborg 1926-1973 ... **CLC 69; PC 151; TCLC 192**
See also CA 93-96; 45-48; CANR 69; DLB 85; EWL 3; RGHL; RGWL 2, 3

Bacigalupi, Paolo 1973- .... **CLC 309**
See also AAYA 86; CA 317; SATA 230

Bacon, Delia 1811-1859 .... **NCLC 315**
See also DLB 1, 243

Bacon, Francis 1561-1626 .... **LC 18, 32, 131, 239**
See also BRW 1; CDBLB Before 1660; DLB 151, 236, 252; RGEL 2; TEA

Bacon, Roger
1214(?)-1294 .... **CMLC 14, 108, 155**
See also DLB 115

Bacovia, G.
See Bacovia, George

Bacovia, George 1881-1957 .... **TCLC 24**
See Bacovia, George
See also CA 123; 189; CDWLB 4; DLB 220; EWL 3

Badanes, Jerome 1937-1995 .... **CLC 59**
See also CA 234

Badiou, Alain 1937- .... **CLC 326**
See also CA 261

Baena, Juan Alfonso de
c. 1375-c. 1434 .... **LC 239**

Bage, Robert 1728-1801 .... **NCLC 182**
See also DLB 39; RGEL 2

Bagehot, Walter 1826-1877 .... **NCLC 10**
See also DLB 55

Bagnold, Enid 1889-1981 .... **CLC 25**
See also AAYA 75; BYA 2; CA 5-8R; 103; CANR 5, 40; CBD; CN 2; CWD; CWRI 5; DAM DRAM; DLB 13, 160, 191, 245; FW; MAICYA 1, 2; RGEL 2; SATA 1, 25

Bagritsky, Eduard
See Dzyubin, Eduard Georgievich

Bagritsky, Edvard
See Dzyubin, Eduard Georgievich

Bagrjana, Elisaveta
See Belcheva, Elisaveta Lyubomirova

Bagryana, Elisaveta
See Belcheva, Elisaveta Lyubomirova

Bail, Murray 1941- .... **CLC 353**
See also CA 127; CANR 62; CN 4, 5, 6, 7; DLB 325

Bailey, Paul 1937- .... **CLC 45**
See also CA 21-24R; CANR 16, 62, 124; CN 1, 2, 3, 4, 5, 6, 7; DLB 14, 271; GLL 2

Baillie, Joanna 1762-1851 .... **NCLC 71, 151; PC 151**
See also DLB 93, 344; GL 2; RGEL 2

Bainbridge, Beryl 1934-2010 .... **CLC 4, 5, 8, 10, 14, 18, 22, 62, 130, 292**

See also BRWS 6; CA 21-24R; CANR 24, 55, 75, 88, 128; CN 2, 3, 4, 5, 6, 7; DAM NOV; DLB 14, 231; EWL 3; MTCW 1, 2; MTFW 2005

Baker, Carlos (Heard) 1909-1987 ... **TCLC 119**
See also CA 5-8R; 122; CANR 3, 63; DLB 103

Baker, Elliott 1922-2007 .... **CLC 8**
See also CA 45-48; 257; CANR 2, 63; CN 1, 2, 3, 4, 5, 6, 7

Baker, Elliott Joseph
See Baker, Elliott

Baker, Nicholson 1957- .... **CLC 61, 165**
See also AMWS 13; CA 135; CANR 63, 120, 138, 190, 237; CN 6; CPW; DA3; DAM POP; DLB 227; MTFW 2005

Baker, Ray Stannard 1870-1946 ... **TCLC 47**
See also CA 118; DLB 345

Baker, Russell 1925- .... **CLC 31**
See also BEST 89:4; CA 57-60; CANR 11, 41, 59, 137; MTCW 1, 2; MTFW 2005

Baker, Russell Wayne
See Baker, Russell

Bakhtin, M.
See Bakhtin, Mikhail Mikhailovich

Bakhtin, M. M.
See Bakhtin, Mikhail Mikhailovich

Bakhtin, Mikhail
See Bakhtin, Mikhail Mikhailovich

Bakhtin, Mikhail Mikhailovich
1895-1975 .... **CLC 83; TCLC 160**
See Bakhtin, Mikhail Mikhailovich
See also CA 128; 113; DLB 242; EWL 3

Bakshi, Ralph 1938(?)- .... **CLC 26**
See also CA 112; 138; IDFW 3

Bakunin, Mikhail (Alexandrovich)
1814-1876 .... **NCLC 25, 58**
See also DLB 277

Bal, Mieke 1946- .... **CLC 252**
See also CA 156; CANR 99

Bal, Mieke Maria Gertrudis
See Bal, Mieke

Baldwin, James 1924-1987 .... **BLC 1:1, 2:1; CLC 1, 2, 3, 4, 5, 8, 13, 15, 17, 42, 50, 67, 90, 127; DC 1; SSC 10, 33, 98, 134, 199; TCLC 229; WLC 1**
See also AAYA 4, 34; AFAW 1, 2; AMWR 2; AMWS 1; BPFB 1; BW 1; CA 1-4R; 124; CABS 1; CAD; CANR 3, 24; CDALB 1941-1968; CLR 191; CN 1, 2, 3, 4; CPW; DA; DA3; DAB; DAC; DAM MST, MULT, NOV, POP; DFS 11, 15; DLB 2, 7, 33, 249, 278; DLBY 1987; EWL 3; EXPS; LAIT 5; MAL 5; MTCW 1, 2; MTFW 2005; NCFS 4; NFS 4; RGAL 4; RGSF 2; SATA 9; SATA-Obit 54; SSFS 2, 18; TUS

Baldwin, William c. 1515-1563 ... **LC 113, 209**
See also DLB 132

Bale, John 1495-1563 .... **LC 62, 228**
See also DLB 132; RGEL 2; TEA

Ball, Hugo 1886-1927 .... **TCLC 104**

Ballard, James G.
See Ballard, J.G.

Ballard, James Graham
See Ballard, J.G.

Ballard, J.G. 1930-2009 .... **CLC 3, 6, 14, 36, 137, 299; SSC 1, 53, 146**
See also AAYA 3, 52; BRWS 5; CA 5-8R; 285; CANR 15, 39, 65, 107, 133, 198; CN 1, 2, 3, 4, 5, 6, 7; DA3; DAM NOV, POP; DLB 14, 207, 261, 319; EWL 3; HGG; MTCW 1, 2; MTFW 2005; NFS 8; RGEL 2; RGSF 2; SATA 93; SATA-Obit 203; SCFW 1, 2; SFW 4

Ballard, Jim G.
See Ballard, J.G.

Balmont, Konstantin (Dmitriyevich)
1867-1943 .... **PC 149; TCLC 11**
See also CA 109; 155; DLB 295; EWL 3

Ballantyne, R. M. 1825-1894 ...... **NCLC 301**
  See also CLR 137; DLB 163; JRDA; RGEL
  2; SATA 24

Baltausis, Vincas 1847-1910
  See Mikszath, Kalman

Balwhidder, Rev. Micah
  See Galt, John

Balzac, Guez de (?)-
  See Balzac, Jean-Louis Guez de

Balzac, Honore de 1799-1850 .... **NCLC 5,**
  35, 53, 153, 273, 311; SSC 5, 59, 102, 153;
  WLC 1
  See also DA; DA3; DAB; DAC; DAM MST,
  NOV; DLB 119; EW 5; GFL 1789 to the
  Present; LMFS 1; NFS 33; RGSF 2;
  RGWL 2, 3; SSFS 10; SUFW; TWA

Balzac, Jean-Louis Guez de
  1597-1654 .... **LC 162**
  See also DLB 268; GFL Beginnings to 1789

Bambara, Toni Cade 1939-1995 .... **BLC 1:1,**
  2:1; CLC 19, 88; SSC 35, 107; TCLC
  116; WLCS
  See also AAYA 5, 49; AFAW 2; AMWS 11;
  BW 2, 3; BYA 12, 14; CA 29-32R; 150;
  CANR 24, 49, 81; CDALBS; DA; DA3;
  DAC; DAM MST, MULT; DLB 38, 218;
  EXPS; MAL 5; MTCW 1, 2; MTFW 2005;
  RGAL 4; RGSF 2; SATA 112; SSFS 4, 7,
  12, 21

Bamdad, A.
  See Shamlu, Ahmad

Bamdad, Alef
  See Shamlu, Ahmad

Banat, D. R.
  See Bradbury, Ray

Bancroft, Laura
  See Baum, L. Frank

Bandello, Matteo 1485-1562 .. **LC 212; SSC 143**

Banim, John 1798-1842 .... **NCLC 13**
  See also DLB 116, 158, 159; RGEL 2

Banim, Michael 1796-1874 .... **NCLC 13**
  See also DLB 158, 159

Banjo, The
  See Paterson, A(ndrew) B(arton)

Banks, Iain 1954-2013 .... **CLC 34, 356**
  See also BRWS 11; CA 123; 128; CANR 61,
  106, 180; DLB 194, 261; EWL 3; HGG;
  INT CA-128; MTFW 2005; SFW 4

Banks, Iain M.
  See Banks, Iain

Banks, Iain Menzies
  See Banks, Iain

Banks, Lynne Reid
  See Reid Banks, Lynne

Banks, Russell
  1940- .... **CLC 37, 72, 187; SSC 42**
  See also AAYA 45; AMWS 5; CA 65-68;
  CAAS 15; CANR 19, 52, 73, 118, 195,
  240; CN 4, 5, 6, 7; DLB 130, 278; EWL 3;
  MAL 5; MTCW 2; MTFW 2005; NFS 13

Banks, Russell Earl
  See Banks, Russell

Banti, Anna 1895-1985 .... **TCLC 303**
  See also CA 202; DLB 177; WLIT 7

Banville, John
  1945- .... **CLC 46, 118, 224, 315**
  See also CA 117; 128; CANR 104, 150, 176,
  225; CN 4, 5, 6, 7; DLB 14, 271, 326; INT
  CA-128

Banville, Theodore (Faullain) de
  1832-1891 .... **NCLC 9**
  See also DLB 217; GFL 1789 to the Present

Baraka, Amiri 1934-2014 ...... **BLC 1:1, 2:1;**
  CLC 1, 2, 3, 5, 10, 14, 33, 115, 213, 389;
  DC 6; PC 4, 113; WLCS
  See also AAYA 63; AFAW 1, 2; AMWS 2;
  BW 2, 3; CA 21-24R; CABS 3; CAD;
  CANR 27, 38, 61, 133, 172; CD 3, 5, 6;
  CDALB 1941-1968; CN 1, 2; CP 1, 2, 3, 4,

5, 6, 7; CPW; DA; DA3; DAC; DAM MST,
MULT, POET, POP; DFS 3, 11, 16; DLB
5, 7, 16, 38; DLBD 8; EWL 3; MAL 5;
MTCW 1, 2; MTFW 2005; PFS 9; RGAL
4; TCLE 1:1; TUS; WP

Baratynsky, Evgenii Abramovich
  1800-1844 .... **NCLC 103**
  See also DLB 205

Barbauld, Anna Laetitia
  1743-1825 .... **NCLC 50, 185; PC 149**
  See also CLR 160; DLB 107, 109, 142, 158,
  336; RGEL 2

Barbellion, W. N. P.
  See Cummings, Bruce F.

Barber, Benjamin R. 1939- .... **CLC 141**
  See also CA 29-32R; CANR 12, 32, 64, 119

Barbera, Jack 1945- .... **CLC 44**
  See also CA 110; CANR 45

Barbera, Jack Vincent
  See Barbera, Jack

Barbey d'Aurevilly, Jules-Amédée
  1808-1889 ... **NCLC 1, 213; SSC 17, 218**
  See also DLB 119; GFL 1789 to the Present

Barbour, John c. 1316-1395 .... **CMLC 33**
  See also DLB 146

Barbusse, Henri 1873-1935 .... **TCLC 5**
  See also CA 105; 154; DLB 65; EWL 3;
  RGWL 2, 3

Barclay, Alexander c. 1475-1552 ..... **LC 109**
  See also DLB 132

Barclay, Bill
  See Moorcock, Michael

Barclay, William Ewert
  See Moorcock, Michael

Barclay, William Ewert
  See Moorcock, Michael

Barea, Arturo 1897-1957 .... **TCLC 14**
  See also CA 111; 201

Barfoot, Joan 1946- .... **CLC 18**
  See also CA 105; CANR 141, 179

Barham, Richard Harris
  1788-1845 .... **NCLC 77**
  See also DLB 159

Baring, Maurice 1874-1945 .... **TCLC 8**
  See also CA 105; 168; DLB 34; HGG

Baring-Gould, Sabine 1834-1924 ... **TCLC 88**
  See also DLB 156, 190

Barker, Clive 1952- .... **CLC 52, 205;**
  SSC 53
  See also AAYA 10, 54; BEST 90:3; BPFB 1;
  CA 121; 129; CANR 71, 111, 133, 187;
  CPW; DA3; DAM POP; DLB 261; HGG;
  INT CA-129; MTCW 1, 2; MTFW 2005;
  SUFW 2

Barker, George Granville
  1913-1991 .... **CLC 8, 48; PC 77**
  See also CA 9-12R; 135; CANR 7, 38; CP 1,
  2, 3, 4, 5; DAM POET; DLB 20; EWL 3;
  MTCW 1

Barker, Harley Granville
  See Granville-Barker, Harley

Barker, Howard 1946- .... **CLC 37; DC 51**
  See also CA 102; CBD; CD 5, 6; DLB
  13, 233

Barker, Jane 1652-1732 ...... **LC 42, 82, 216;**
  PC 91
  See also DLB 39, 131

Barker, Pat 1943- .... **CLC 32, 94, 146**
  See also BRWS 4; CA 117; 122; CANR 50,
  101, 148, 195; CN 6, 7; DLB 271, 326;
  INT CA-122

Barker, Patricia
  See Barker, Pat

Barlach, Ernst (Heinrich)
  1870-1938 .... **TCLC 84**
  See also CA 178; DLB 56, 118; EWL 3

Barlow, Joel 1754-1812 .... **NCLC 23, 223**
  See also AMWS 2; DLB 37; RGAL 4

Barnard, Mary (Ethel) 1909- .... **CLC 48**
  See also CA 21-22; CAP 2; CP 1

Barnes, Djuna 1892-1982 .... **CLC 3, 4, 8,**
  11, 29, 127; SSC 3, 163; TCLC 212
  See also AMWS 3; CA 9-12R; 107; CAD;
  CANR 16, 55; CN 1, 2, 3; CWD; DLB 4,
  9, 45; EWL 3; GLL 1; MAL 5; MTCW 1,
  2; MTFW 2005; RGAL 4; TCLE 1:1; TUS

Barnes, Jim 1933- .... **NNAL**
  See also CA 108, 175, 272; CAAE 175, 272;
  CAAS 28; DLB 175

Barnes, Julian 1946- ...... **CLC 42, 141, 315**
  See also BRWS 4; CA 102; CANR 19, 54,
  115, 137, 195; CN 4, 5, 6, 7; DAB; DLB
  194; DLBY 1993; EWL 3; MTCW 2;
  MTFW 2005; SSFS 24

Barnes, Julian Patrick
  See Barnes, Julian

Barnes, Peter 1931-2004 .... **CLC 5, 56**
  See also CA 65-68; 230; CAAS 12; CANR
  33, 34, 64, 113; CBD; CD 5, 6; DFS 6;
  DLB 13, 233; MTCW 1

Barnes, William 1801-1886 ... **NCLC 75, 283**
  See also DLB 32

Barnfield, Richard 1574-1627 .... **LC 192;**
  PC 152
  See also DLB 172

Baroja, Pio 1872-1956 ..... **HLC 1; SSC 112;**
  TCLC 8, 240
  See also CA 104; 247; EW 9

Baroja y Nessi, Pio
  See Baroja, Pio

Baron, David
  See Pinter, Harold

Baron Corvo
  See Rolfe, Frederick (William Serafino
  Austin Lewis Mary)

Barondess, Sue K. 1926-1977 .... **CLC 3, 8**
  See also CA 1-4R; 69-72; CANR 1

Barondess, Sue Kaufman
  See Barondess, Sue K.

Baron de Teive
  See Pessoa, Fernando

Baroness Von S.
  See Zangwill, Israel

Barreto, Afonso Henrique de Lima
  See Lima Barreto, Afonso Henrique de

Barrett, Andrea 1954- .... **CLC 150**
  See also CA 156; CANR 92, 186; CN 7;
  DLB 335; SSFS 24

Barrett, Michele
  See Barrett, Michele

Barrett, Michele 1949- .... **CLC 65**
  See also CA 280

Barrett, Roger Syd
  See Barrett, Syd

Barrett, Syd 1946-2006 .... **CLC 35**

Barrett, William (Christopher)
  1913-1992 .... **CLC 27**
  See also CA 13-16R; 139; CANR 11, 67;
  INT CANR-11

Barrett Browning, Elizabeth
  1806-1861 .... **NCLC 1, 16, 61, 66,**
  170; PC 6, 62; WLC 1
  See also AAYA 63; BRW 4; CDBLB 1832-
  1890; DA; DA3; DAB; DAC; DAM MST,
  POET; DLB 32, 199; EXPP; FL 1:2; PAB;
  PFS 2, 16, 23; TEA; WLIT 4; WP

Barrie, Baronet
  See Barrie, J. M.

Barrie, J. M. 1860-1937 .... **TCLC 2, 164**
  See also BRWS 3; BYA 4, 5; CA 104; 136;
  CANR 77; CDBLB 1890-1914; CLR 16,
  124; CWRI 5; DA3; DAB; DAM DRAM;
  DFS 7; DLB 10, 141, 156, 352; EWL 3;
  FANT; MAICYA 1, 2; MTCW 2; MTFW
  2005; SATA 100; SUFW; WCH; WLIT 4;
  YABC 1

Barrie, James Matthew
  See Barrie, J. M.

See also CA 106; 153; DLB 56; EWL 3; RGWL 2, 3

Bennett, Alan 1934- .... **CLC 45, 77, 292**
See also BRWS 8; CA 103; CANR 35, 55, 106, 157, 197, 227; CBD; CD 5, 6; DAB; DAM MST; DLB 310; MTCW 1, 2; MTFW 2005

Bennett, (Enoch) Arnold
1867-1931 .... **TCLC 5, 20, 197**
See also BRW 6; CA 106; 155; CDBLB 1890-1914; DLB 10, 34, 98, 135; EWL 3; MTCW 2

Bennett, Elizabeth
See Mitchell, Margaret

Bennett, George Harold 1930- .... **CLC 5**
See also BW 1; CA 97-100; CAAS 13; CANR 87; DLB 33

Bennett, Gwendolyn B. 1902-1981 ... **HR 1:2**
See also BW 1; CA 125; DLB 51; WP

Bennett, Hal
See Bennett, George Harold

Bennett, Jay 1912- .... **CLC 35**
See also AAYA 10, 73; CA 69-72; CANR 11, 42, 79; JRDA; SAAS 4; SATA 41, 87; SATA-Brief 27; WYA; YAW

Bennett, Louise 1919-2006 .... **BLC 1:1; CLC 28**
See also BW 2, 3; CA 151; 252; CDWLB 3; CP 1, 2, 3, 4, 5, 6, 7; DAM MULT; DLB 117; EWL 3

Bennett, Louise Simone
See Bennett, Louise

Bennett-Coverley, Louise
See Bennett, Louise

Benoit de Sainte-Maure
fl. 12th cent. .... **CMLC 90**

Benson, A. C. 1862-1925 .... **TCLC 123**
See also DLB 98

Benson, E(dward) F(rederic)
1867-1940 .... **TCLC 27**
See also CA 114; 157; DLB 135, 153; HGG; SUFW 1

Benson, Jackson J. 1930- .... **CLC 34**
See also CA 25-28R; CANR 214; DLB 111

Benson, Sally 1900-1972 .... **CLC 17**
See also CA 19-20; 37-40R; CAP 1; SATA 1, 35; SATA-Obit 27

Benson, Stella 1892-1933 .... **TCLC 17**
See also CA 117; 154, 155; DLB 36, 162; FANT; TEA

Benet, Stephen Vincent 1898-1943 ... **PC 64; SSC 10, 86; TCLC 7**
See also AMWS 11; CA 104; 152; DA3; DAM POET; DLB 4, 48, 102, 249, 284; DLBY 1997; EWL 3; HGG; MAL 5; MTCW 1; MTFW 2005; RGAL 4; RGSF 2; SSFS 22, 31; SUFW; WP; YABC 1

Benet, William Rose 1886-1950 .... **TCLC 28**
See also CA 118; 152; DAM POET; DLB 45; RGAL 4

Bentham, Jeremy
1748-1832 .... **NCLC 38, 237**
See also DLB 107, 158, 252

Bentley, E(dmund) C(lerihew)
1875-1956 .... **TCLC 12**
See also CA 108; 232; DLB 70; MSW

Bentley, Eric 1916- .... **CLC 24**
See also CA 5-8R; CAD; CANR 6, 67; CBD; CD 5, 6; INT CANR 6

Bentley, Eric Russell
See Bentley, Eric

ben Uzair, Salem
See Horne, Richard Henry Hengist

Beolco, Angelo 1496-1542 .... **LC 139**

Beranger, Pierre Jean de
1780-1857 .... **NCLC 34; PC 112**

Berceo, Gonzalo de
c. 1190-c. 1260 .... **CMLC 151**

See also DLB 337

Berdyaev, Nicolas
See Berdyaev, Nikolai (Aleksandrovich)

Berdyaev, Nikolai (Aleksandrovich)
1874-1948 .... **TCLC 67**
See also CA 120; 157

Berdyayev, Nikolai (Aleksandrovich)
See Berdyaev, Nikolai (Aleksandrovich)

Berendt, John 1939- .... **CLC 86**
See also CA 146; CANR 75, 83, 151

Berendt, John Lawrence
See Berendt, John

Berengar of Tours
c. 1000-1088 .... **CMLC 124**

Beresford, J(ohn) D(avys)
1873-1947 .... **TCLC 81**
See also CA 112; 155; DLB 162, 178, 197; SFW 4; SUFW 1

Bergelson, David (Rafailovich)
1884-1952 .... **TCLC 81**
See also CA 220; DLB 333; EWL 3

Bergelson, Dovid
See Bergelson, David (Rafailovich)

Berger, Colonel
See Malraux, Andre

Berger, John 1926- .... **CLC 2, 19, 375**
See also BRWS 4; CA 81-84; CANR 51, 78, 117, 163, 200; CN 1, 2, 3, 4, 5, 6, 7; DLB 14, 207, 319, 326

Berger, John Peter
See Berger, John

Berger, Melvin H. 1927- .... **CLC 12**
See also CA 5-8R; CANR 4, 142; CLR 32; SAAS 2; SATA 5, 88, 158; SATA-Essay 124

Berger, Thomas 1924- .... **CLC 3, 5, 8, 11, 18, 38, 259**
See also BPFB 1; CA 1-4R; CANR 5, 28, 51, 128; CN 1, 2, 3, 4, 5, 6, 7; DAM NOV; DLB 2; DLBY 1980; EWL 3; FANT; INT CANR-28; MAL 5; MTCW 1, 2; MTFW 2005; RHW; TCLE 1:1; TCWW 1, 2

Bergman, Ernst Ingmar
See Bergman, Ingmar

Bergman, Ingmar
1918-2007 .... **CLC 16, 72, 210**
See also AAYA 61; CA 81-84; 262; CANR 33, 70; CWW 2; DLB 257; MTCW 2; MTFW 2005

Bergson, Henri(-Louis)
1859-1941 .... **TCLC 32**
See also CA 164; DLB 329; EW 8; EWL 3; GFL 1789 to the Present

Bergstein, Eleanor 1938- .... **CLC 4**
See also CA 53-56; CANR 5

Berkeley, George 1685-1753 .... **LC 65**
See also DLB 31, 101, 252

Berkoff, Steven 1937- .... **CLC 56**
See also CA 104; CANR 72; CBD; CD 5, 6

Berlin, Isaiah 1909-1997 .... **TCLC 105**
See also CA 85-88; 162

Bermant, Chaim (Icyk)
1929-1998 .... **CLC 40**
See also CA 57-60; CANR 6, 31, 57, 105; CN 2, 3, 4, 5, 6

Bern, Victoria
See Fisher, M. F. K.

Bernanos, (Paul Louis) Georges
1888-1948 .... **TCLC 3, 267**
See also CA 104; 130; CANR 94; DLB 72; EWL 3; GFL 1789 to the Present; RGWL 2, 3

Bernard, April 1956- .... **CLC 59**
See also CA 131; CANR 144, 230

Bernard, Mary Ann
See Soderbergh, Steven

Bernard of Clairvaux
1090-1153 .... **CMLC 71, 170**
See also DLB 208

Bernard Silvestris
fl. c. 1130-fl. c. 1160 .... **CMLC 87**
See also DLB 208

Bernardin de Saint-Pierre, Jacques-Henri
1737-1814 .... **NCLC 297**
See also DLB 313; GFL

Bernart de Ventadorn
c. 1130-c. 1190 .... **CMLC 98**

Berne, Victoria
See Fisher, M. F. K.

Bernhard, Thomas 1931-1989 .... **CLC 3, 32, 61; DC 14; TCLC 165**
See also CA 85-88; 127; CANR 32, 57; CDWLB 2; DLB 85, 124; EWL 3; MTCW 1; RGHL; RGWL 2, 3

Bernhardt, Sarah (Henriette Rosine)
1844-1923 .... **TCLC 75**
See also CA 157

Berni, Francesco c. 1497-1536 .... **LC 210**

Bernstein, Charles 1950- .. **CLC 142; PC 152**
See also CA 129; CAAS 24; CANR 90; CP 4, 5, 6, 7; DLB 169

Bernstein, Ingrid
See Kirsch, Sarah

Béroul fl. c. 12th cent. .... **CMLC 75, 148; PC 151**

Berriault, Gina 1926-1999 ...... **CLC 54, 109; SSC 30**
See also CA 116; 129; 185; CANR 66; DLB 130; SSFS 7, 11

Berrigan, Daniel 1921- .... **CLC 4**
See also CA 33-36R; 187; CAAE 187; CAAS 1; CANR 11, 43, 78, 219; CP 1, 2, 3, 4, 5, 6, 7; DLB 5

Berrigan, Edmund Joseph Michael, Jr.
1934-1983 .... **CLC 37; PC 103**
See also CA 61-64; 110; CANR 14, 102; CP 1, 2, 3; DLB 5, 169; WP

Berrigan, Ted
See Berrigan, Edmund Joseph Michael, Jr.

Berry, Charles Edward Anderson
See Berry, Chuck

Berry, Chuck 1931- .... **CLC 17**
See also CA 115

Berry, Jonas
See Ashbery, John

Berry, Wendell 1934- .... **CLC 4, 6, 8, 27, 46, 279; PC 28**
See also AITN 1; AMWS 10; ANW; CA 73-76; CANR 50, 73, 101, 132, 174, 228; CP 1, 2, 3, 4, 5, 6, 7; CSW; DAM POET; DLB 5, 6, 234, 275, 342; MTCW 2; MTFW 2005; PFS 30; TCLE 1:1

Berry, Wendell Erdman
See Berry, Wendell

Berry, William
See Harwood, Gwen

Berryman, John 1914-1972 ..... **CLC 1, 2, 3, 4, 6, 8, 10, 13, 25, 62; PC 64**
See also AMW; CA 13-16R; CABS 2; CANR 35; CAP 1; CDALB 1941-1968; CP 1; DAM POET; DLB 48; EWL 3; MAL 5; MTCW 1, 2; MTFW 2005; PAB; PFS 27; RGAL 4; WP

Berssenbrugge, Mei-mei 1947- .... **PC 115**
See also CA 104; DLB 312

Bertolucci, Bernardo 1940- ..... **CLC 16, 157**
See also CA 106; CANR 125

Berton, Pierre (Francis de Marigny)
1920-2004 .... **CLC 104**
See also CA 1-4R; 233; CANR 2, 56, 144; CPW; DLB 68; SATA 99; SATA-Obit 158

Bertrand, Aloysius 1807-1841 .... **NCLC 31**
See also DLB 217

Bertrand, Louis oAloysiusc
See Bertrand, Aloysius

Bertran de Born c. 1140-1215 .... **CMLC 5**

Berwick, Mary
See Adelaide Anne Procter

Bleeck, Oliver
  See Thomas, Ross (Elmore)
Bleecker, Ann Eliza 1752-1783 .... **LC 161**
  See also DLB 200
Blessing, Lee 1949- .... **CLC 54**
  See also CA 236; CAD; CD 5, 6; DFS 23, 26
Blessing, Lee Knowlton
  See Blessing, Lee
Blessington, Marguerite, Countess of
  1789-1849 .... **NCLC 297**
  See also DLB 166
Blight, Rose
  See Greer, Germaine
Blind, Mathilde 1841-1896 .... **NCLC 202**
  See also DLB 199
Blish, James 1921-1975 .... **CLC 14**
  See also BPFB 1; CA 1-4R; 57-60; CANR 3; CN 2; DLB 8; MTCW 1; SATA 66; SCFW 1, 2; SFW 4
Blish, James Benjamin
  See Blish, James
Bliss, Frederick
  See Card, Orson Scott
Bliss, Gillian
  See Paton Walsh, Jill
Bliss, Reginald
  See Wells, H. G.
Blixen, Karen 1885-1962 .... **CLC 10, 29, 95; SSC 7, 75, 191; TCLC 255**
  See also CA 25-28; CANR 22, 50; CAP 2; DA3; DLB 214; EW 10; EWL 3; EXPS; FW; GL 2; HGG; LAIT 3; MTCW 1; NCFS 2; NFS 9; RGSF 2; RGWL 2, 3; SATA 44; SSFS 3, 6, 13; WLIT 2
Blixen, Karen Christentze Dinesen
  See Blixen, Karen
Boll, Heinrich
  See Boell, Heinrich
Bloch, Robert (Albert) 1917-1994 ... **CLC 33**
  See also AAYA 29; CA 5-8R, 179; 146; CAAE 179; CAAS 20; CANR 5, 78; DA3; DLB 44; HGG; INT CANR-5; MTCW 2; SATA 12; SATA-Obit 82; SFW 4; SUFW 1, 2
Blok, Alexander (Alexandrovich)
  1880-1921 .... **PC 21; TCLC 5**
  See also CA 104; 183; DLB 295; EW 9; EWL 3; LMFS 2; RGWL 2, 3
Blom, Jan
  See Breytenbach, Breyten
Bloom, Harold 1930- .... **CLC 24, 103, 221**
  See also CA 13-16R; CANR 39, 75, 92, 133, 181, 238; DLB 67; EWL 3; MTCW 2; MTFW 2005; RGAL 4
Bloomfield, Aurelius
  See Bourne, Randolph S(illiman)
Bloomfield, Robert
  1766-1823 .... **NCLC 145; PC 160**
  See also DLB 93
Blount, Roy, Jr. 1941- .... **CLC 38**
  See also CA 53-56; CANR 10, 28, 61, 125, 176; CSW; INT CANR-28; MTCW 1, 2; MTFW 2005
Blount, Roy Alton
  See Blount, Roy, Jr.
Blowsnake, Sam 1875-(?) .... **NNAL**
Bloy, Leon 1846-1917 .... **TCLC 22**
  See also CA 121; 183; DLB 123; GFL 1789 to the Present
Blue Cloud, Peter (Aroniawenrate)
  1933- .... **NNAL**
  See also CA 117; CANR 40; DAM MULT; DLB 342
Bluggage, Oranthy
  See Alcott, Louisa May
Blume, Judy 1938- .... **CLC 12, 30, 325**
  See also AAYA 3, 26; BYA 1, 8, 12; CA 29-32R; CANR 13, 37, 66, 124, 186; CLR 2, 15, 69, 176; CPW; DA3; DAM NOV, POP;

DLB 52; JRDA; MAICYA 1, 2; MAI-CYAS 1; MTCW 1, 2; MTFW 2005; NFS 24; SATA 2, 31, 79, 142, 195; WYA; YAW
Blume, Judy Sussman
  See Blume, Judy
Blunden, Edmund (Charles)
  1896-1974 .... **CLC 2, 56; PC 66**
  See also BRW 6; BRWS 11; CA 17-18; 45-48; CANR 54; CAP 2; CP 1, 2; DLB 20, 100, 155; MTCW 1; PAB
Bly, Robert 1926- .... **CLC 1, 2, 5, 10, 15, 38, 128, 325; PC 39**
  See also AMWS 4; CA 5-8R; CANR 41, 73, 125, 235; CP 1, 2, 3, 4, 5, 6, 7; DA3; DAM POET; DLB 5, 342; EWL 3; MAL 5; MTCW 1, 2; MTFW 2005; PFS 6, 17; RGAL 4
Bly, Robert Elwood
  See Bly, Robert
Boas, Franz 1858-1942 .... **TCLC 56**
  See also CA 115; 181
Bobette
  See Simenon, Georges
Bobrowski, Johannes 1917-1965 ... **TCLC 319**
  See also CA 77-80; CANR 33; DLB 75; EWL 3; RGWL 2, 3
Boccaccio, Giovanni 1313-1375 ... **CMLC 13, 57, 140; PC 162; SSC 10, 87, 167**
  See also EW 2; RGSF 2; RGWL 2, 3; SSFS 28; TWA; WLIT 7
Bochco, Steven 1943- .... **CLC 35**
  See also AAYA 11, 71; CA 124; 138
Bock, Charles 1970- .... **CLC 299**
  See also CA 274
Bode, Sigmund
  See O'Doherty, Brian
Bodel, Jean 1167(?)-1210 ..... **CMLC 28, 162**
Bodenheim, Maxwell 1892-1954 ... **TCLC 44**
  See also CA 110; 187; DLB 9, 45; MAL 5; RGAL 4
Bodenheimer, Maxwell
  See Bodenheim, Maxwell
Bodin, Jean 1529/30?-1596 .... **LC 242**
  See also GFL
Bodker, Cecil
  See Bodker, Cecil
Boell, Heinrich 1917-1985 .... **CLC 2, 3, 6, 9, 11, 15, 27, 32, 72; SSC 23; TCLC 185; WLC 1**
  See also BPFB 1; CA 21-24R; 116; CANR 24; CDWLB 2; DA; DA3; DAB; DAC; DAM MST, NOV; DLB 69, 329; DLBY 1985; EW 13; EWL 3; MTCW 1, 2; MTFW 2005; RGHL; RGSF 2; RGWL 2, 3; SSFS 20; TWA
Boell, Heinrich Theodor
  See Boell, Heinrich
Boerne, Alfred
  See Doeblin, Alfred
Boethius c. 480-c. 524 .... **CMLC 15, 136**
  See also DLB 115; RGWL 2, 3; WLIT 8
Boff, Leonardo (Genezio Darci)
  1938- .... **CLC 70; HLC 1**
  See also CA 150; DAM MULT; HW 2
Bogan, Louise 1897-1970 .... **CLC 4, 39, 46, 93; PC 12**
  See also AMWS 3; CA 73-76; 25-28R; CANR 33, 82; CP 1; DAM POET; DLB 45, 169; EWL 3; MAL 5; MBL; MTCW 1, 2; PFS 21, 39; RGAL 4
Bogarde, Dirk 1921-1999 .... **CLC 14**
  See also CA 77-80; 179; DLB 14
Bogat, Shatan
  See Kacew, Romain
Bogomolny, Robert L. 1938- .... **SSC 41; TCLC 11**
  See also CA 121, 164; DLB 182; EWL 3; MJW; RGSF 2; RGWL 2, 3; TWA

Bogomolny, Robert Lee
  See Bogomolny, Robert L.
Bogosian, Eric 1953- .... **CLC 45, 141**
  See also CA 138; CAD; CANR 102, 148, 217; CD 5, 6; DLB 341
Bograd, Larry 1953- .... **CLC 35**
  See also CA 93-96; CANR 57; SAAS 21; SATA 33, 89; WYA
Boiardo, Matteo Maria 1441-1494 **LC 6, 168**
Boileau-Despreaux, Nicolas
  1636-1711 .... **LC 3, 164**
  See also DLB 268; EW 3; GFL Beginnings to 1789; RGWL 2, 3
Boissard, Maurice
  See Leautaud, Paul
Bojer, Johan 1872-1959 .... **TCLC 64**
  See also CA 189; EWL 3
Bok, Edward W(illiam)
  1863-1930 .... **TCLC 101**
  See also CA 217; DLB 91; DLBD 16
Boker, George Henry 1823-1890 ... **NCLC 125**
  See also RGAL 4
Boland, Eavan 1944- .... **CLC 40, 67, 113; PC 58**
  See also BRWS 5; CA 143, 207; CAAE 207; CANR 61, 180; CP 1, 6, 7; CWP; DAM POET; DLB 40; FW; MTCW 2; MTFW 2005; PFS 12, 22, 31, 39
Boland, Eavan Aisling
  See Boland, Eavan
Bolano, Roberto 1953-2003 .... **CLC 294**
  See also CA 229; CANR 175
Bolingbroke, Viscount
  See St. John, Henry
Bolt, Lee
  See Faust, Frederick
Bolt, Robert (Oxton) 1924-1995 .... **CLC 14; TCLC 175**
  See also CA 17-20R; 147; CANR 35, 67; CBD; DAM DRAM; DFS 2; DLB 13, 233; EWL 3; LAIT 1; MTCW 1
Bolivar, Simon 1783-1830 .... **NCLC 266**
Bombal, Maria Luisa 1910-1980 ... **HLCS 1; SSC 37; TCLC 296**
  See also CA 127; CANR 72; EWL 3; HW 1; LAW; RGSF 2; SSFS 36
Bombet, Louis-Alexandre-Cesar
  See Stendhal
Bomkauf
  See Kaufman, Bob (Garnell)
Bonaventura .... **NCLC 35, 252**
  See also DLB 90
Bonaventure 1217(?)-1274 .... **CMLC 79**
  See also DLB 115; LMFS 1
Bond, Edward 1934- ...... **CLC 4, 6, 13, 23; DC 45**
  See also AAYA 50; BRWS 1; CA 25-28R; CANR 38, 67, 106; CBD; CD 5, 6; DAM DRAM; DFS 3, 8; DLB 13, 310; EWL 3; MTCW 1
Bonham, Frank 1914-1989 .... **CLC 12**
  See also AAYA 1, 70; BYA 1, 3; CA 9-12R; CANR 4, 36; JRDA; MAICYA 1, 2; SAAS 3; SATA 1, 49; SATA-Obit 62; TCWW 1, 2; YAW
Bonnefoy, Yves 1923- .... **CLC 9, 15, 58; PC 58**
  See also CA 85-88; CANR 33, 75, 97, 136; CWW 2; DAM MST, POET; DLB 258; EWL 3; GFL 1789 to the Present; MTCW 1, 2; MTFW 2005
Bonner, Marita
  See Occomy, Marita (Odette) Bonner
Bonnin, Gertrude 1876-1938 .... **NNAL**
  See also CA 150; DAM MULT; DLB 175
Bontemps, Arna 1902-1973 .... **BLC 1:1; CLC 1, 18; HR 1:2; TCLC 292**
  See also BW 1; CA 1-4R; 41-44R; CANR 4, 35; CLR 6; CP 1; CWRI 5; DA3; DAM

Bradstreet, Anne 1612(?)-1672 .... **LC 4, 30, 130; PC 10, 139, 155**
See also AMWS 1; CDALB 1640-1865; DA; DA3; DAC; DAM MST, POET; DLB 24; EXPP; FW; PFS 6, 33, 42; RGAL 4; TUS; WP

Brady, Joan 1939- .... **CLC 86**
See also CA 141

Bragg, Melvyn 1939- .... **CLC 10**
See also BEST 89:3; CA 57-60; CANR 10, 48, 89, 158; CN 1, 2, 3, 4, 5, 6, 7; DLB 14, 271; RHW

Bragg, Rick 1959- .... **CLC 296**
See also CA 165; CANR 112, 137, 194; MTFW 2005

Bragg, Ricky Edward
See Bragg, Rick

Brahe, Tycho 1546-1601 .... **LC 45**
See also DLB 300

Braine, John (Gerard)
1922-1986 .... **CLC 1, 3, 41**
See also CA 1-4R; 120; CANR 1, 33; CDBLB 1945-1960; CN 1, 2, 3, 4; DLB 15; DLBY 1986; EWL 3; MTCW 1

Braithwaite, William Stanley (Beaumont)
1878-1962 .... **BLC 1:1; HR 1:2; PC 52**
See also BW 1; CA 125; DAM MULT; DLB 50, 54; MAL 5

Bramah, Ernest 1868-1942 .... **TCLC 72**
See also CA 156; CMW 4; DLB 70; FANT

Brammer, Billy Lee
See Brammer, William

Brammer, William 1929-1978 .... **CLC 31**
See also CA 235; 77-80

Brancati, Vitaliano 1907-1954 ...... **TCLC 12**
See also CA 109; DLB 264; EWL 3

Brancato, Robin F. 1936- .... **CLC 35**
See also AAYA 9, 68; BYA 6; CA 69-72; CANR 11, 45; CLR 32; JRDA; MAICYA 2; MAICYAS 1; SAAS 9; SATA 97; WYA; YAW

Brancato, Robin Fidler
See Brancato, Robin F.

Brand, Dionne 1953- .... **CLC 192**
See also BW 2; CA 143; CANR 143, 216; CWP; DLB 334

Brand, Max
See Faust, Frederick

Brand, Millen 1906-1980 .... **CLC 7**
See also CA 21-24R; 97-100; CANR 72

Branden, Barbara 1929- .... **CLC 44**
See also CA 148

Brandes, Georg (Morris Cohen)
1842-1927 .... **TCLC 10, 264**
See also CA 105; 189; DLB 300

Brandys, Kazimierz 1916-2000 .... **CLC 62**
See also CA 239; EWL 3

Branley, Franklyn M(ansfield)
1915-2002 .... **CLC 21**
See also CA 33-36R; 207; CANR 14, 39; CLR 13; MAICYA 1, 2; SAAS 16; SATA 4, 68, 136

Brant, Beth (E.) 1941- .... **NNAL**
See also CA 144; FW

Brant, Sebastian 1457-1521 ..... **LC 112, 206**
See also DLB 179; RGWL 2, 3

Brathwaite, Edward Kamau
1930- .... **BLC 2:1; BLCS; CLC 11, 305; PC 56**
See also BRWS 12; BW 2, 3; CA 25-28R; CANR 11, 26, 47, 107; CDWLB 3; CP 1, 2, 3, 4, 5, 6, 7; DAM POET; DLB 125; EWL 3

Brathwaite, Kamau
See Brathwaite, Edward Kamau

Braun, Volker 1939- .... **CLC 356**
See also CA 194; CWW 2; DLB 75, 124; EWL 3

Brautigan, Richard 1935-1984 .... **CLC 1, 3, 5, 9, 12, 34, 42; PC 94; TCLC 133**
See also BPFB 1; CA 53-56; 113; CANR 34; CN 1, 2, 3; CP 1, 2, 3, 4; DA3; DAM NOV; DLB 2, 5, 206; DLBY 1980, 1984; FANT; MAL 5; MTCW 1; RGAL 4; SATA 56

Brautigan, Richard Gary
See Brautigan, Richard

Brave Bird, Mary
See Crow Dog, Mary

Braverman, Kate 1950- .... **CLC 67**
See also CA 89-92; CANR 141; DLB 335

Brecht, Bertolt 1898-1956 ... **DC 3; TCLC 1, 6, 13, 35, 169; WLC 1**
See also CA 104; 133; CANR 62; CDWLB 2; DA; DA3; DAB; DAC; DAM DRAM, MST; DFS 4, 5, 9; DLB 56, 124; EW 11; EWL 3; IDTP; MTCW 1, 2; MTFW 2005; RGHL; RGWL 2, 3; TWA

Brecht, Eugen Berthold Friedrich
See Brecht, Bertolt

Brecht, Eugen Bertolt Friedrich
See Brecht, Bertolt

Bremer, Fredrika 1801-1865 .... **NCLC 11**
See also DLB 254

Brennan, Christopher John
1870-1932 .... **TCLC 17**
See also CA 117; 188; DLB 230; EWL 3

Brennan, Maeve 1917-1993 .... **CLC 5; TCLC 124**
See also CA 81-84; CANR 72, 100

Brenner, Jozef 1887-1919 .... **TCLC 13**
See also CA 111; 240

Brent, Linda
See Jacobs, Harriet A.

Brentano, Clemens (Maria)
1778-1842 .... **NCLC 1, 191; SSC 115**
See also DLB 90; RGWL 2, 3

Brent of Bin Bin
See Franklin, (Stella Maria Sarah) Miles (Lampe)

Brenton, Howard 1942- .... **CLC 31**
See also CA 69-72; CANR 33, 67; CBD; CD 5, 6; DLB 13; MTCW 1

Breslin, James
See Breslin, Jimmy

Breslin, Jimmy 1930- .... **CLC 4, 43**
See also CA 73-76; CANR 31, 75, 139, 187, 237; DAM NOV; DLB 185; MTCW 2; MTFW 2005

Bresson, Robert 1901(?)-1999 .... **CLC 16; TCLC 287**
See also CA 110; 187; CANR 49

Breton, Andre 1896-1966 ...... **CLC 2, 9, 15, 54; PC 15; TCLC 247**
See also CA 19-20; 25-28R; CANR 40, 60; CAP 2; DLB 65, 258; EW 11; EWL 3; GFL 1789 to the Present; LMFS 2; MTCW 1, 2; MTFW 2005; RGWL 2, 3; TWA; WP

Breton, Nicholas c. 1554-c. 1626 ..... **LC 133**
See also DLB 136

Breytenbach, Breyten
1939(?)- .... **CLC 23, 37, 126**
See also CA 113; 129; CANR 61, 122, 202; CWW 2; DAM POET; DLB 225; EWL 3

Bridgers, Sue Ellen 1942- .... **CLC 26**
See also AAYA 8, 49; BYA 7, 8; CA 65-68; CANR 11, 36; CLR 18, 199; DLB 52; JRDA; MAICYA 1, 2; SAAS 1; SATA 22, 90; SATA-Essay 109; WYA; YAW

Bridges, Robert (Seymour)
1844-1930 .... **PC 28; TCLC 1**
See also BRW 6; CA 104; 152; CDBLB 1890-1914; DAM POET; DLB 19, 98

Bridie, James
See Mavor, Osborne Henry

Brin, David 1950- .... **CLC 34**
See also AAYA 21; CA 102; CANR 24, 70, 125, 127; INT CANR-24; SATA 65; SCFW 2; SFW 4

Brink, Andre 1935- .... **CLC 18, 36, 106**
See also AFW; BRWS 6; CA 104; CANR 39, 62, 109, 133, 182; CN 4, 5, 6, 7; DLB 225; EWL 3; INT CA-103; LATS 1:2; MTCW 1, 2; MTFW 2005; WLIT 2

Brink, Andre Philippus
See Brink, Andre

Brinsmead, H. F(ay)
See Brinsmead, H(esba) F(ay)

Brinsmead, H. F.
See Brinsmead, H(esba) F(ay)

Brinsmead, H(esba) F(ay) 1922- .... **CLC 21**
See also CA 21-24R; CANR 10; CLR 47; CWRI 5; MAICYA 1, 2; SAAS 5; SATA 18, 78

Brittain, Vera (Mary)
1893(?)-1970 .... **CLC 23; TCLC 228**
See also BRWS 10; CA 13-16; 25-28R; CANR 58; CAP 1; DLB 191; FW; MTCW 1, 2

Broch, Hermann
1886-1951 ...... **TCLC 20, 204, 304, 307**
See also CA 117; 211; CDWLB 2; DLB 85, 124; EW 10; EWL 3; RGWL 2, 3

Brock, Rose
See Hansen, Joseph

Brod, Max 1884-1968 .... **TCLC 115, 305**
See also CA 5-8R; 25-28R; CANR 7; DLB 81; EWL 3

Brodber, Erna 1940- .... **CLC 379**
See also BW 2; CA 143; CN 6, 7; DLB 157

Brodkey, Harold (Roy)
1930-1996 .... **CLC 56; TCLC 123**
See also CA 111; 151; CANR 71; CN 4, 5, 6; DLB 130

Brodskii, Iosif
See Brodsky, Joseph

Brodskii, Iosif Alexandrovich
See Brodsky, Joseph

Brodsky, Iosif Alexandrovich
See Brodsky, Joseph

Brodsky, Joseph 1940-1996 .... **CLC 4, 6, 13, 36, 100; PC 9; TCLC 219**
See also AAYA 71; AITN 1; AMWS 8; CA 41-44R; 151; CANR 37, 106; CWW 2; DA3; DAM POET; DLB 285, 329; EWL 3; MTCW 1, 2; MTFW 2005; PFS 35; RGWL 2, 3

Brodsky, Michael 1948- .... **CLC 19**
See also CA 102; CANR 18, 41, 58, 147; DLB 244

Brodsky, Michael Mark
See Brodsky, Michael

Brodzki, Bella .... **CLC 65**

Brome, Richard 1590(?)-1652 ... **DC 50; LC 61**
See also BRWS 10; DLB 58

Bromell, Henry 1947- .... **CLC 5**
See also CA 53-56; CANR 9, 115, 116

Bromfield, Louis (Brucker)
1896-1956 .... **TCLC 11**
See also CA 107; 155; DLB 4, 9, 86; RGAL 4; RHW

Broner, E. M. 1930-2011 .... **CLC 19**
See also CA 17-20R; CANR 8, 25, 72, 216; CN 4, 5, 6; DLB 28

Broner, Esther Masserman
See Broner, E. M.

Bronk, William 1918-1999 .... **CLC 10**
See also AMWS 21; CA 89-92; 177; CANR 23; CP 3, 4, 5, 6, 7; DLB 165

Bronstein, Lev Davidovich
See Trotsky, Leon

Bronte, Anne 1820-1849 .... **NCLC 4, 71, 102, 235**
See also BRW 5; BRWR 1; DA3; DLB 21, 199, 340; NFS 26; TEA

Cavallo, Evelyn
  See Spark, Muriel
Cavanna, Betty
  See Harrison, Elizabeth (Allen) Cavanna
Cavanna, Elizabeth
  See Harrison, Elizabeth (Allen) Cavanna
Cavanna, Elizabeth Allen
  See Harrison, Elizabeth (Allen) Cavanna
Cave, Nick 1957- .... **CLC 379**
  See also CA 303
Cavendish, Margaret
  1623-1673 .... **LC 30, 132; PC 134**
  See also DLB 131, 252, 281; RGEL 2
Cavendish, Margaret Lucas
  See Cavendish, Margaret
Caxton, William 1421(?)-1491(?) ... **LC 17, 236**
  See also DLB 170
Cayer, D. M.
  See Duffy, Maureen
Cayrol, Jean 1911-2005 .... **CLC 11**
  See also CA 89-92; 236; DLB 83; EWL 3
Cela, Camilo Jose
  See Cela, Camilo Jose
Cela, Camilo Jose 1916-2002 ..... **CLC 4, 13,**
  59, 122; HLC 1; SSC 71
  See also BEST 90:2; CA 21-24R; 206;
  CAAS 10; CANR 21, 32, 76, 139; CWW
  2; DAM MULT; DLB 322; DLBY 1989;
  EW 13; EWL 3; HW 1; MTCW 1, 2;
  MTFW 2005; RGSF 2; RGWL 2, 3
Celan, Paul 1920-1970 .... **CLC 10, 19, 53,**
  82; PC 10
  See also CA 85-88; CANR 33, 61; CDWLB
  2; DLB 69; EWL 3; MTCW 1; PFS 21;
  RGHL; RGWL 2, 3
Cela y Trulock, Camilo Jose
  See Cela, Camilo Jose
Celati, Gianni 1937- .... **CLC 373**
  See also CA 251; CWW 2; DLB 196
Cellini, Benvenuto 1500-1571 .... **LC 7**
  See also WLIT 7
Cendrars, Blaise
  See Sauser-Hall, Frederic
Centlivre, Susanna 1669(?)-1723 ...... **DC 25;**
  LC 65, 221
  See also DLB 84; RGEL 2
Cernuda, Luis 1902-1963 .... **CLC 54; PC 62;**
  TCLC 286
  See also CA 131; 89-92; DAM POET; DLB
  134; EWL 3; GLL 1; HW 1; RGWL 2, 3
Cernuda y Bidon, Luis
  See Cernuda, Luis
Cervantes, Lorna Dee 1954- ... **HLCS 1; PC 35**
  See also CA 131; CANR 80; CP 7; CWP;
  DLB 82; EXPP; HW 1; LLW; PFS 30
Cervantes, Miguel de 1547-1616 ...... **HLCS;**
  LC 6, 23, 93; SSC 12, 108; WLC 1
  See also AAYA 56; BYA 1, 14; DA; DAB;
  DAC; DAM MST, NOV; EW 2; LAIT 1;
  LATS 1:1; LMFS 1; NFS 8; RGSF 2;
  RGWL 2, 3; TWA
Cervantes Saavedra, Miguel de
  See Cervantes, Miguel de
Cesaire, Aime 1913-2008 .... **BLC 1:1;**
  CLC 19, 32, 112, 280; DC 22; PC 25
  See also BW 2, 3; CA 65-68; 271; CANR
  24, 43, 81; CWW 2; DA3; DAM MULT,
  POET; DLB 321; EWL 3; GFL 1789 to the
  Present, MTCW 1, 2; MTFW 2005; WP
Cesaire, Aime Fernand
  See Cesaire, Aime
Cha, Louis
  See Jin Yong
Cha Leung-yung, Louis
  See Jin Yong
Cha, Theresa Hak Kyung
  1951-1982 .... **TCLC 307**
  See also CA 217; DLB 312

Chaadaev, Petr Iakovlevich
  1794-1856 .... **NCLC 197**
  See also DLB 198
Chabon, Michael 1963- .... **CLC 55, 149,**
  265; SSC 59
  See also AAYA 45; AMWS 11; CA 139;
  CANR 57, 96, 127, 138, 196; DLB 278;
  MAL 5; MTFW 2005; NFS 25; SATA 145;
  SSFS 36
Chabrol, Claude 1930-2010 .... **CLC 16**
  See also CA 110
Chacel, Rosa 1898-1994 .... **TCLC 298**
  See also CA 243; CANR 216; CWW 2; DLB
  134, 322; EWL 3
Chairil Anwar
  See Anwar, Chairil
Challans, Mary
  See Renault, Mary
Challis, George
  See Faust, Frederick
Chambers, Aidan 1934- .... **CLC 35**
  See also AAYA 27, 86; CA 25-28R; CANR 12,
  31, 58, 116; CLR 151; JRDA; MAICYA 1, 2;
  SAAS 12; SATA 1, 69, 108, 171; WYA; YAW
Chambers, James .... **CLC 21**
  See also CA 124; 199
Chambers, Jessie
  See Lawrence, D. H.
Chambers, Maria Cristina
  See Mena, Maria Cristina
Chambers, Robert W(illiam)
  1865-1933 .... **SSC 92; TCLC 41**
  See also CA 165; DLB 202; HGG; SATA
  107; SUFW 1
Chambers, (David) Whittaker
  1901-1961 .... **TCLC 129**
  See also CA 89-92; DLB 303
Chamisso, Adelbert von
  1781-1838 .... **NCLC 82; SSC 140**
  See also DLB 90; RGWL 2, 3; SUFW 1
Chamoiseau, Patrick 1953- ... **CLC 268, 276**
  See also CA 162; CANR 88; EWL 3; RGWL 3
Chance, James T.
  See Carpenter, John
Chance, John T.
  See Carpenter, John
Chand, Munshi Prem
  See Srivastava, Dhanpat Rai
Chand, Prem
  See Srivastava, Dhanpat Rai
Chandler, Raymond 1888-1959 ...... **SSC 23;**
  TCLC 1, 7, 179
  See also AAYA 25; AMWC 2; AMWS 4;
  BPFB 1; CA 104; 129; CANR 60, 107;
  CDALB 1929-1941; CMW 4; DA3; DLB
  226, 253; DLBD 6; EWL 3; MAL 5;
  MSW; MTCW 1, 2; MTFW 2005; NFS
  17; RGAL 4; TUS
Chandler, Raymond Thornton
  See Chandler, Raymond
Chandra, Vikram 1961- .... **CLC 302**
  See also CA 149; CANR 97, 214; SSFS 16
Chang, Diana 1934-2009 .... **AAL**
  See also CA 228; CWP; DLB 312; EXPP;
  PFS 37
Chang, Eileen 1920-1995 ...... **AAL; SSC 28,**
  169; TCLC 184
  See also CA 166; CANR 168; CWW 2; DLB
  328; EWL 3; RGSF 2
Chang, Jung 1952- .... **CLC 71**
  See also CA 142
Chang Ai-Ling
  See Chang, Eileen
Channing, William Ellery
  1780-1842 .... **NCLC 17**
  See also DLB 1, 59, 235; RGAL 4
Channing, William Ellery II
  1817-1901 .... **TCLC 306**

  See also CA 215; DLB 1, 223
Chao, Patricia 1955- .... **CLC 119**
  See also CA 163; CANR 155
Chaplin, Charles Spencer
  1889-1977 .... **CLC 16**
  See also AAYA 61; CA 81-84; 73-76; DLB 44
Chaplin, Charlie
  See Chaplin, Charles Spencer
Chapman, George 1559(?)-1634 .... **DC 19;**
  LC 22, 116; PC 96
  See also BRW 1; DAM DRAM; DLB 62,
  121; LMFS 1; RGEL 2
Chapman, Graham 1941-1989 .... **CLC 21**
  See also AAYA 7; CA 116; 129; CANR 35, 95
Chapman, John Jay 1862-1933 ...... **TCLC 7**
  See also AMWS 14; CA 104; 191
Chapman, Lee
  See Bradley, Marion Zimmer
Chapman, Maile .... **CLC 318**
Chapman, Walker
  See Silverberg, Robert
Chappell, Fred 1936- .... **CLC 40, 78, 162,**
  293; PC 105
  See also CA 5-8R, 198; CAAE 198; CAAS
  4; CANR 8, 33, 67, 110, 215; CN 6; CP 6,
  7; CSW; DLB 6, 105; HGG
Chappell, Fred Davis
  See Chappell, Fred
Char, Rene 1907-1988 ... **CLC 9, 11, 14, 55;**
  PC 56
  See also CA 13-16R; 124; CANR 32; DAM
  POET; DLB 258; EWL 3; GFL 1789 to the
  Present; MTCW 1, 2; RGWL 2, 3
Char, Rene-Emile
  See Char, Rene
Charby, Jay
  See Ellison, Harlan
Chardin, Pierre Teilhard de
  See Teilhard de Chardin, (Marie Joseph) Pierre
Chariton fl. 1st cent. (?) .... **CMLC 49**
Charke, Charlotte 1713-1760 .... **LC 236**
Charlemagne 742-814 .... **CMLC 37**
Charles I 1600-1649 .... **LC 13, 194, 237**
Charrière, Isabelle de
  1740-1805 .... **NCLC 66, 314**
  See also DLB 313
Charron, Pierre 1541-1603 .... **LC 174**
  See also GFL Beginnings to 1789
Chartier, Alain c. 1392-1430 .... **LC 94**
  See also DLB 208
Chartier, Emile-Auguste
  See Alain
Charyn, Jerome 1937- .... **CLC 5, 8, 18**
  See also CA 5-8R; CAAS 1; CANR 7, 61,
  101, 158, 199; CMW 4; CN 1, 2, 3, 4, 5, 6,
  7; DLBY 1983; MTCW 1
Chase, Adam
  See Marlowe, Stephen
Chase, Mary (Coyle) 1907-1981 .... **DC 1**
  See also CA 77-80; 105; CAD; CWD; DFS
  11; DLB 228; SATA 17; SATA-Obit 29
Chase, Mary Ellen 1887-1973 .... **CLC 2;**
  TCLC 124
  See also CA 13-16; 41-44R; CAP 1; SATA 10
Chase, Nicholas
  See Hyde, Anthony
Chase-Riboud, Barbara (Dewayne Tosi)
  1939- .... **BLC 2:1**
  See also BW 2; CA 113; CANR 76; DAM
  MULT; DLB 33; MTCW 2
Chateaubriand, Francois Rene de
  1768-1848 .... **NCLC 3, 134**
  See also DLB 119, 366; EW 5; GFL 1789 to
  the Present; RGWL 2, 3; TWA
Chatterje, Saratchandra -(?)
  See Chatterji, Sarat Chandra
Chatterji, Bankim Chandra
  1838-1894 .... **NCLC 19**

Churchill, Sir Winston
1874-1965 .... **TCLC 113**
See also BRW 6; CA 97-100; CDBLB 1890-1914; DA3; DLB 100, 329; DLBD 16; LAIT 4; MTCW 1, 2

Churchill, Sir Winston Leonard Spencer
See Churchill, Sir Winston

Churchyard, Thomas 1520(?)-1604 ... **LC 187**
See also DLB 132; RGEL 2

Chute, Carolyn 1947- .... **CLC 39, 322**
See also CA 123; CANR 135, 213; CN 7; DLB 350

Ciardi, John (Anthony) 1916-1986 .. **CLC 10, 40, 44, 129; PC 69**
See also CA 5-8R; 118; CAAS 2; CANR 5, 33; CLR 19; CP 1, 2, 3, 4; CWRI 5; DAM POET; DLB 5; DLBY 1986; INT CANR-5; MAICYA 1, 2; MAL 5; MTCW 1, 2; MTFW 2005; RGAL 4; SAAS 26; SATA 1, 65; SATA-Obit 46

Cibber, Colley 1671-1757 .... **LC 66, 211**
See also DLB 84; RGEL 2

Cicero, Marcus Tullius
106B.C.-43B.C. .... **CMLC 3, 81, 121, 175**
See also AW 1; CDWLB 1; DLB 211; RGWL 2, 3; WLIT 8

Cimino, Michael 1943- .... **CLC 16**
See also CA 105

Cioran, E(mil) M. 1911-1995 .... **CLC 64**
See also CA 25-28R; 149; CANR 91; DLB 220; EWL 3

Circus, Anthony
See Hoch, Edward D.

Cisneros, Sandra 1954- .... **CLC 69, 118, 193, 305, 352; HLC 1; PC 52; SSC 32, 72, 143, 187**
See also AAYA 9, 53; AMWS 7; CA 131; CANR 64, 118; CLR 123; CN 7; CWP; DA3; DAM MULT; DLB 122, 152; EWL 3; EXPN; FL 1:5; FW; HW 1, 2; LAIT 5; LATS 1:2; LLW; MAICYA 2; MAL 5; MTCW 2; MTFW 2005; NFS 2; PFS 19; RGAL 4; RGSF 2; SSFS 3, 13, 27, 32; WLIT 1; YAW

Cixous, Helene 1937- .... **CLC 92, 253**
See also CA 126; CANR 55, 123; CWW 2; DLB 83, 242; EWL 3; FL 1:5; FW; GLL 2; MTCW 1, 2; MTFW 2005; TWA

Clair, Rene
See Chomette, Rene Lucien

Clampitt, Amy 1920-1994 ... **CLC 32; PC 19**
See also AMWS 9; CA 110; 146; CANR 29, 79; CP 4, 5; DLB 105; MAL 5; PFS 27, 39

Clancy, Thomas L., Jr.
See Clancy, Tom

Clancy, Tom 1947-2013 .... **CLC 45, 112**
See also AAYA 9, 51; BEST 89:1, 90:1; BPFB 1; BYA 10, 11; CA 125; 131; CANR 62, 105, 132; CMW 4; CPW; DA3; DAM NOV, POP; DLB 227; INT CA-131; MTCW 1, 2; MTFW 2005

Clare, John 1793-1864 .... **NCLC 9, 86, 259; PC 23**
See also BRWS 11; DAB; DAM POET; DLB 55, 96; RGEL 2

Clare of Assisi 1194-1253 .... **CMLC 149**

Clarin
See Alas (y Urena), Leopoldo (Enrique Garcia)

Clark, Al C.
See Goines, Donald

Clark, Brian (Robert)
See Clark, (Robert) Brian

Clark, (Robert) Brian 1932- .... **CLC 29**
See also CA 41-44R; CANR 67; CBD; CD 5, 6

Clark, Curt
See Westlake, Donald E.

Clark, Eleanor 1913-1996 .... **CLC 5, 19**
See also CA 9-12R; 151; CANR 41; CN 1, 2, 3, 4, 5, 6; DLB 6

Clark, J. P.
See Clark-Bekederemo, J. P.

Clark, John Pepper
See Clark-Bekederemo, J. P.

Clark, Kenneth (Mackenzie)
1903-1983 .... **TCLC 147**
See also CA 93-96; 109; CANR 36; MTCW 1, 2; MTFW 2005

Clark, M. R.
See Clark, Mavis Thorpe

Clark, Mavis Thorpe 1909-1999 .... **CLC 12**
See also CA 57-60; CANR 8, 37, 107; CLR 30; CWRI 5; MAICYA 1, 2; SAAS 5; SATA 8, 74

Clark, Rev. T.
See Galt, John

Clark, Walter Van Tilburg
1909-1971 .... **CLC 28**
See also CA 9-12R; 33-36R; CANR 63, 113; CN 1; DLB 9, 206; LAIT 2; MAL 5; NFS 40; RGAL 4; SATA 8; TCWW 1, 2

Clark-Bekederemo, J. P. 1935- ..... **BLC 1:1; CLC 38; DC 5**
See also AAYA 79; AFW; BW 1; CA 65-68; CANR 16, 72; CD 5, 6; CDWLB 3; CP 1, 2, 3, 4, 5, 6, 7; DAM DRAM, MULT; DFS 13; DLB 117; EWL 3; MTCW 2; MTFW 2005; RGEL 2

Clark-Bekederemo, John Pepper
See Clark-Bekederemo, J. P.

Clark Bekederemo, Johnson Pepper
See Clark-Bekederemo, J. P.

Clarke, Arthur
See Clarke, Arthur C.

Clarke, Arthur C. 1917-2008 ...... **CLC 1, 4, 13, 18, 35, 136; SSC 3**
See also AAYA 4, 33; BPFB 1; BYA 13; CA 1-4R; 270; CANR 2, 28, 55, 74, 130, 196; CLR 119; CN 1, 2, 3, 4, 5, 6, 7; CPW; DA3; DAM POP; DLB 261; JRDA; LAIT 5; MAICYA 1, 2; MTCW 1, 2; MTFW 2005; SATA 13, 70, 115; SATA-Obit 191; SCFW 1, 2; SFW 4; SSFS 4, 18, 29, 36; TCLE 1:1; YAW

Clarke, Arthur Charles
See Clarke, Arthur C.

Clarke, Austin 1896-1974 .... **CLC 6, 9; PC 112**
See also BRWS 15; CA 29-32; 49-52; CAP 2; CP 1, 2; DAM POET; DLB 10, 20; EWL 3; RGEL 2

Clarke, Austin 1934- .... **BLC 1:1; CLC 8, 53; SSC 45, 116**
See also BW 1; CA 25-28R; CAAS 16; CANR 14, 32, 68, 140, 220; CN 1, 2, 3, 4, 5, 6, 7; DAC; DAM MULT; DLB 53, 125; DNFS 2; MTCW 2; MTFW 2005; RGSF 2

Clarke, Gillian 1937- .... **CLC 61**
See also CA 106; CP 3, 4, 5, 6, 7; CWP; DLB 40

Clarke, Marcus (Andrew Hislop)
1846-1881 .... **NCLC 19, 258; SSC 94**
See also DLB 230; RGEL 2; RGSF 2

Clarke, Shirley 1925-1997 .... **CLC 16**
See also CA 189

Clash, The
See Headon, (Nicky) Topper; Jones, Mick; Simonon, Paul; Strummer, Joe

Claudel, Paul (Louis Charles Marie)
1868-1955 .... **TCLC 2, 10, 268**
See also CA 104; 165; DLB 192, 258, 321; EW 8; EWL 3; GFL 1789 to the Present; RGWL 2, 3; TWA

Claudian 370(?)-404(?) .... **CMLC 46**
See also RGWL 2, 3

Claudius, Matthias 1740-1815 ...... **NCLC 75**
See also DLB 97

Clausewitz, Carl von 1780-1831 ... **NCLC 296**

Clavell, James 1925-1994 ..... **CLC 6, 25, 87**
See also BPFB 1; CA 25-28R; 146; CANR 26, 48; CN 5; CPW; DA3; DAM NOV, POP; MTCW 1, 2; MTFW 2005; NFS 10; RHW

Clayman, Gregory .... **CLC 65**

Cleage, Pearl 1948- .... **DC 32**
See also BW 2; CA 41-44R; CANR 27, 148, 177, 226; DFS 14, 16; DLB 228; NFS 17

Cleage, Pearl Michelle
See Cleage, Pearl

Cleaver, (Leroy) Eldridge 1935-1998 ... **BLC 1:1; CLC 30, 119**
See also BW 1, 3; CA 21-24R; 167; CANR 16, 75; DA3; DAM MULT; MTCW 2; YAW

Cleese, John (Marwood) 1939- .... **CLC 21**
See also CA 112; 116; CANR 35; MTCW 1

Cleishbotham, Jebediah
See Scott, Sir Walter

Cleland, John 1710-1789 .... **LC 2, 48, 235**
See also DLB 39; RGEL 2

Clemens, Samuel
See Twain, Mark

Clemens, Samuel Langhorne
See Twain, Mark

Clement of Alexandria
150(?)-215(?) .... **CMLC 41**

Cleophil
See Congreve, William

Clerihew, E.
See Bentley, E(dmund) C(lerihew)

Clerk, N. W.
See Lewis, C. S.

Cleveland, John 1613-1658 .... **LC 106**
See also DLB 126; RGEL 2

Cliff, Jimmy
See Chambers, James

Cliff, Michelle 1946- .... **BLCS; CLC 120**
See also BW 2; CA 116; CANR 39, 72; CDWLB 3; DLB 157; FW; GLL 2

Clifford, Lady Anne 1590-1676 .... **LC 76**
See also DLB 151

Clifton, Lucille 1936-2010 .... **BLC 1:1, 2:1; CLC 19, 66, 162, 283; PC 17, 148**
See also AFAW 2; BW 2, 3; CA 49-52; CANR 2, 24, 42, 76, 97, 138; CLR 5; CP 2, 3, 4, 5, 6, 7; CSW; CWP; CWRI 5; DA3; DAM MULT, POET; DLB 5, 41; EXPP; MAICYA 1, 2; MTCW 1, 2; MTFW 2005; PFS 1, 14, 29, 41; SATA 20, 69, 128; SSFS 34; WP

Clifton, Thelma Lucille
See Clifton, Lucille

Celine, Louis-Ferdinand
1894-1961 .... **CLC 1, 3, 4, 7, 47, 124**
See also CA 85-88; CANR 28; DLB 72; EW 11; EWL 3; GFL 1789 to the Present; MTCW 1; RGWL 2, 3

Clinton, Dirk
See Silverberg, Robert

Clough, Arthur Hugh
1819-1861 .... **NCLC 27, 163; PC 103**
See also BRW 5; DLB 32; RGEL 2

Clouts, Sydney 1926-1982 .... **TCLC 318**
See also CA 207; CP 1, 2, 3; DLB 225

Clutha, Janet
See Frame, Janet

Clutha, Janet Paterson Frame
See Frame, Janet

Clyne, Terence
See Blatty, William Peter

C. N.
See Naden, Constance

Cobalt, Martin
See Mayne, William

Cobb, Irvin S(hrewsbury)
1876-1944 .... **TCLC 77**
See also CA 175; DLB 11, 25, 86

Congreve, William 1670-1729 .... **DC 2;**
  LC 5, 21, 170; WLC 2
    See also BRW 2; CDBLB 1660-1789; DA;
    DAB; DAC; DAM DRAM, MST, POET;
    DFS 15; DLB 39, 84; RGEL 2; WLIT 3
Conley, Robert J. 1940- .... **NNAL**
    See also CA 41-44R, 295; CAAE 295; CANR
    15, 34, 45, 96, 186; DAM MULT; TCWW 2
Connell, Evan S. 1924-2013 ... **CLC 4, 6, 45**
    See also AAYA 7; AMWS 14; CA 1-4R;
    CAAS 2; CANR 2, 39, 76, 97, 140, 195;
    CN 1, 2, 3, 4, 5, 6; DAM NOV; DLB 2,
    335; DLBY 1981; MAL 5; MTCW 1, 2;
    MTFW 2005
Connell, Evan Shelby, Jr.
    See Connell, Evan S.
Connelly, Marc(us Cook) 1890-1980 ... **CLC 7**
    See also CA 85-88; 102; CAD; CANR 30;
    DFS 12; DLB 7; DLBY 1980; MAL 5;
    RGAL 4; SATA-Obit 25
Connelly, Michael 1956- .... **CLC 293**
    See also AMWS 21; CA 158; CANR 91,
    180, 234; CMW 4; LNFS 2
Connolly, Paul
    See Wicker, Tom
Connor, Ralph
    See Gordon, Charles William
Conrad, Joseph 1857-1924 ... **SSC 9, 67, 69,**
  71, 153, 169, 171, 174, 175, 177, 178, 185,
  188, 189, 193, 194, 197, 201, 203, 204, 206,
  219, 221; TCLC 1, 6, 13, 25, 43, 57, 291,
  293, 295, 297, 298, 301, 303; WLC 2, 193
    See also AAYA 26; BPFB 1; BRW 6; BRWC
    1; BRWR 2; BYA 2; CA 104; 131; CANR
    60; CDBLB 1890-1914; DA; DA3; DAB;
    DAC; DAM MST, NOV; DLB 10, 34, 98,
    156; EWL 3; EXPN; EXPS; LAIT 2;
    LATS 1:1; LMFS 1; MTCW 1, 2; MTFW
    2005; NFS 2, 16; RGEL 2; RGSF 2; SATA
    27; SSFS 1, 12, 31; TEA; WLIT 4
Conrad, Robert Arnold
    See Hart, Moss
Conroy, Donald Patrick
    See Conroy, Pat
Conroy, Pat 1945- .... **CLC 30, 74**
    See also AAYA 8, 52; AITN 1; BPFB 1;
    CA 85-88; CANR 24, 53, 129, 233; CN 7;
    CPW; CSW; DA3; DAM NOV, POP;
    DLB 6; LAIT 5; MAL 5; MTCW 1, 2;
    MTFW 2005
Consolo, Vincenzo 1933-2012 .... **CLC 371**
    See also CA 232; DLB 196
Constant (de Rebecque), (Henri) Benjamin
    1767-1830 .... **NCLC 6, 182**
    See also DLB 119; EW 4; GFL 1789 to the
    Present
Conway, Jill K. 1934- .... **CLC 152**
    See also CA 130; CANR 94
Conway, Jill Ker
    See Conway, Jill K.
Conybeare, Charles Augustus
    See Eliot, T. S.
Cook, Michael 1933-1994 .... **CLC 58**
    See also CA 93-96; CANR 68; DLB 53
Cook, Robin 1940- .... **CLC 14**
    See also AAYA 32; BEST 90:2; BPFB 1;
    CA 108; 111; CANR 41, 90, 109, 181, 219;
    CPW; DA3; DAM POP; HGG; INT CA-111
Cook, Roy
    See Silverberg, Robert
Cooke, Elizabeth 1948- .... **CLC 55**
    See also CA 129
Cooke, John Esten 1830-1886 .... **NCLC 5**
    See also DLB 3, 248; RGAL 4
Cooke, John Estes
    See Baum, L. Frank
Cooke, M. E.
    See Creasey, John
Cooke, Margaret
    See Creasey, John

Cooke, Rose Terry 1827-1892 ... **NCLC 110;**
  SSC 149
    See also DLB 12, 74
Cook-Lynn, Elizabeth 1930- **CLC 93; NNAL**
    See also CA 133; DAM MULT; DLB 175
Cooney, Ray .... **CLC 62**
    See also CBD
Cooper, Anthony Ashley 1671-1713 **LC 107**
    See also DLB 101, 336
Cooper, Dennis 1953- .... **CLC 203**
    See also CA 133; CANR 72, 86, 204; GLL 1;
    HGG
Cooper, Douglas 1960- .... **CLC 86**
Cooper, Henry St. John
    See Creasey, John
Cooper, J. California (?)- .... **CLC 56**
    See also AAYA 12; BW 1; CA 125; CANR
    55, 207; CLR 188; DAM MULT; DLB 212
Cooper, James Fenimore
    1789-1851 .... **NCLC 1, 27, 54, 203,**
  279, 312
    See also AAYA 22; AMW; BPFB 1; CDALB
    1640-1865; CLR 105, 188; DA3; DLB 3,
    183, 250, 254; LAIT 1; NFS 25; RGAL 4;
    SATA 19; TUS; WCH
Cooper, Joan California
    See Cooper, J. California
Cooper, Susan Fenimore
    1813-1894 .... **NCLC 129**
    See also ANW; DLB 239, 254
Coover, Robert 1932- ...... **CLC 3, 7, 15, 32,**
  46, 87, 161, 306; SSC 15, 101
    See also AMWS 5; BPFB 1; CA 45-48;
    CANR 3, 37, 58, 115, 228; CN 1, 2, 3,
    4, 5, 6, 7; DAM NOV; DLB 2, 227; DLBY
    1981; EWL 3; MAL 5; MTCW 1, 2;
    MTFW 2005; RGAL 4; RGSF 2
Copeland, Stewart 1952- .... **CLC 26**
    See also CA 305
Copeland, Stewart Armstrong
    See Copeland, Stewart
Copernicus, Nicolaus 1473-1543 .... **LC 45**
Coppard, A(lfred) E(dgar)
    1878-1957 .... **SSC 21; TCLC 5**
    See also BRWS 8; CA 114; 167; DLB 162;
    EWL 3; HGG; RGEL 2; RGSF 2; SUFW
    1; YABC 1
Coppee, Francois 1842-1908 .... **TCLC 25**
    See also CA 170; DLB 217
Coppola, Francis Ford 1939- ... **CLC 16, 126**
    See also AAYA 39; CA 77-80; CANR 40,
    78; DLB 44
Copway, George 1818-1869 .... **NNAL**
    See also DAM MULT; DLB 175, 183
Corbiere, Tristan 1845-1875 .... **NCLC 43**
    See also DLB 217; GFL 1789 to the Present
Corcoran, Barbara (Asenath)
    1911-2003 .... **CLC 17**
    See also AAYA 14; CA 21-24R, 191; CAAE
    191; CAAS 2; CANR 11, 28, 48; CLR 50;
    DLB 52; JRDA; MAICYA 2; MAICYAS
    1; RHW; SAAS 20; SATA 3, 77; SATA-
    Essay 125
Cordelier, Maurice
    See Giraudoux, Jean
Cordier, Gilbert
    See Rohmer, Eric
Corelli, Marie
    See Mackay, Mary
Corinna c. 225B.C.-c. 305B.C. ..... **CMLC 72**
Corman, Cid 1924-2004 .... **CLC 9**
    See also CA 85-88; 225; CAAS 2; CANR
    44; CP 1, 2, 3, 4, 5, 6, 7; DAM POET;
    DLB 5, 193
Corman, Sidney
    See Corman, Cid
Cormier, Robert 1925-2000 .... **CLC 12, 30**
    See also AAYA 3, 19; BYA 1, 2, 6, 8, 9; CA 1-
    4R; CANR 5, 23, 76, 93; CDALB 1968-

    1988; CLR 12, 55, 167; DA; DAB; DAC;
    DAM MST, NOV; DLB 52; EXPN; INT
    CANR-23; JRDA; LAIT 5; MAICYA 1, 2;
    MTCW 1, 2; MTFW 2005; NFS 2, 18; SATA
    10, 45, 83; SATA-Obit 122; WYA; YAW
Cormier, Robert Edmund
    See Cormier, Robert
Corn, Alfred (DeWitt III) 1943- .... **CLC 33**
    See also CA 179; CAAE 179; CAAS 25;
    CANR 44; CP 3, 4, 5, 6, 7; CSW; DLB
    120, 282; DLBY 1980
Corneille, Pierre 1606-1684 .... **DC 21;**
  LC 28, 135, 212, 217
    See also DAB; DAM MST; DFS 21; DLB
    268; EW 3; GFL Beginnings to 1789;
    RGWL 2, 3; TWA
Cornwell, David
    See le Carré, John
Cornwell, David John Moore
    See le Carré, John
Cornwell, Patricia 1956- .... **CLC 155**
    See also AAYA 16, 56; BPFB 1; CA 134;
    CANR 53, 131, 195; CMW 4; CPW; CSW;
    DAM POP; DLB 306; MSW; MTCW 2;
    MTFW 2005
Cornwell, Patricia Daniels
    See Cornwell, Patricia
Cornwell, Smith
    See Smith, David (Jeddie)
Corso, Gregory 1930-2001 .... **CLC 1, 11;**
  PC 33, 108
    See also AMWS 12; BG 1:2; CA 5-8R; 193;
    CANR 41, 76, 132; CP 1, 2, 3, 4, 5, 6, 7;
    DA3; DLB 5, 16, 237; LMFS 2; MAL 5;
    MTCW 1, 2; MTFW 2005; WP
Cortes, Hernan 1485-1547 .... **LC 31, 213**
Cortez, Jayne 1936- .... **BLC 2:1**
    See also BW 2, 3; CA 73-76; CANR 13, 31,
    68, 126; CWP; DLB 41; EWL 3
Cortázar, Julio 1914-1984 .... **CLC 2, 3, 5,**
  10, 13, 15, 33, 34, 92; HLC 1; SSC 7, 76,
  156, 210; TCLC 252
    See also AAYA 85; BPFB 1; CA 21-24R;
    CANR 12, 32, 81; CDWLB 3; DA3; DAM
    MULT, NOV; DLB 113; EWL 3; EXPS;
    HW 1, 2; LAW; MTCW 1, 2; MTFW
    2005; RGSF 2; RGWL 2, 3; SSFS 3,
    20, 28, 31, 34; TWA; WLIT 1
Corvinus, Jakob
    See Raabe, Wilhelm (Karl)
Corwin, Cecil
    See Kornbluth, C(yril) M.
Coryate, Thomas 1577(?)-1617 .... **LC 218**
    See also DLB 151, 172
Cosic, Dobrica 1921- .... **CLC 14**
    See also CA 122; 138; CDWLB 4; CWW 2;
    DLB 181; EWL 3
Costain, Thomas B(ertram)
    1885-1965 .... **CLC 30**
    See also BYA 3; CA 5-8R; 25-28R; DLB 9;
    RHW
Costantini, Humberto 1924(?)-1987 ... **CLC 49**
    See also CA 131; 122; EWL 3; HW 1
Costello, Elvis 1954(?)- .... **CLC 21**
    See also CA 204
Costenoble, Philostene
    See Ghelderode, Michel de
Cotes, Cecil V.
    See Duncan, Sara Jeannette
Cotter, Joseph Seamon Sr.
    1861-1949 .... **BLC 1:1; TCLC 28**
    See also BW 1; CA 124; DAM MULT;
    DLB 50
Cotton, John 1584-1652 .... **LC 176**
    See also DLB 24; TUS
Couch, Arthur Thomas Quiller
    See Quiller-Couch, Sir Arthur (Thomas)
Coulton, James
    See Hansen, Joseph

Crumb, Robert
  See Crumb, R.
Crumbum
  See Crumb, R.
Crumski
  See Crumb, R.
Crum the Bum
  See Crumb, R.
Crunk
  See Crumb, R.
Crustt
  See Crumb, R.
Crutchfield, Les
  See Trumbo, Dalton
Cruz, Victor Hernandez 1949- .... **HLC 1;
  PC 37**
    See also BW 2; CA 65-68, 271; CAAE 271;
    CAAS 17; CANR 14, 32, 74, 132; CP 1, 2,
    3, 4, 5, 6, 7; DAM MULT, POET; DLB 41;
    DNFS 1; EXPP; HW 1, 2; LLW; MTCW
    2; MTFW 2005; PFS 16; WP
Crevecoeur, J. Hector St. John de
  1735-1813 .... **NCLC 105**
    See also AMWS 1; ANW; DLB 37
Crevecoeur, Michel Guillaume Jean de
  See Crevecoeur, J. Hector St. John de
Cryer, Gretchen (Kiger) 1935- ...... **CLC 21**
    See also CA 114; 123
Csath, Geza
  See Brenner, Jozef
Cudlip, David R(ockwell) 1933- ..... **CLC 34**
    See also CA 177
Cuervo, Talia
  See Vega, Ana Lydia
Cullen, Countee 1903-1946 ... **BLC 1:1; HR
  1:2; PC 20; TCLC 4, 37, 220; WLCS**
    See also AAYA 78; AFAW 2; AMWS 4; BW
    1; CA 108; 124; CDALB 1917-1929; DA;
    DA3; DAC; DAM MST, MULT, POET;
    DLB 4, 48, 51; EWL 3; EXPP; LMFS 2;
    MAL 5; MTCW 1, 2; MTFW 2005; PFS 3,
    42; RGAL 4; SATA 18; WP
Culleton, Beatrice 1949- .... **NNAL**
    See also CA 120; CANR 83; DAC
Culver, Timothy J.
  See Westlake, Donald E.
Cum, R.
  See Crumb, R.
Cumberland, Richard 1732-1811 .... **NCLC 167**
    See also DLB 89; RGEL 2
Cummings, Bruce F. 1889-1919 ... **TCLC 24**
    See also CA 123
Cummings, Bruce Frederick
  See Cummings, Bruce F.
Cummings, E. E. 1894-1962 ... **CLC 1, 3, 8,
  12, 15, 68; PC 5; TCLC 137; WLC 2**
    See also AAYA 41; AMW; CA 73-76;
    CANR 31; CDALB 1929-1941; DA; DA3;
    DAB; DAC; DAM MST, POET; DLB 4,
    48; EWL 3; EXPP; MAL 5; MTCW 1, 2;
    MTFW 2005; PAB; PFS 1, 3, 12, 13, 19,
    30, 34, 40; RGAL 4; TUS; WP
Cummings, Edward Estlin
  See Cummings, E. E.
Cummins, Maria Susanna
  1827-1866 .... **NCLC 139**
    See also DLB 42; YABC 1
Cunha, Euclides (Rodrigues Pimenta) da
  1866-1909 .... **TCLC 24**
    See also CA 123; 219; DLB 307; LAW;
    WLIT 1
Cunningham, E. V.
  See Fast, Howard
Cunningham, J. Morgan
  See Westlake, Donald E.
Cunningham, J(ames) V(incent)
  1911-1985 .... **CLC 3, 31; PC 92**

See also CA 1-4R; 115; CANR 1, 72; CP 1,
2, 3, 4; DLB 5
Cunningham, Julia (Woolfolk) 1916- .. **CLC 12**
  See also CA 9-12R; CANR 4, 19, 36; CWRI
  5; JRDA; MAICYA 1, 2; SAAS 2; SATA
  1, 26, 132
Cunningham, Michael 1952- ... **CLC 34, 243**
  See also AMWS 15; CA 136; CANR 96,
  160, 227; CN 7; DLB 292; GLL 2; MTFW
  2005; NFS 23
Cunninghame Graham, R. B.
  See Cunninghame Graham, Robert Bontine
Cunninghame Graham, Robert Bontine
  1852-1936 .... **TCLC 19**
    See also CA 119; 184; DLB 98, 135, 174;
    RGEL 2; RGSF 2
**Cunninghame Graham, Robert Gallnigad
  Bontine**
  See Cunninghame Graham, Robert Bontine
Curnow, (Thomas) Allen (Monro)
  1911-2001 .... **PC 48**
    See also CA 69-72; 202; CANR 48, 99; CP
    1, 2, 3, 4, 5, 6, 7; EWL 3; RGEL 2
Currie, Ellen 19(?)- .... **CLC 44**
Curtin, Philip
  See Lowndes, Marie Adelaide (Belloc)
Curtin, Phillip
  See Lowndes, Marie Adelaide (Belloc)
Curtis, Price
  See Ellison, Harlan
Cusanus, Nicolaus 1401-1464
  See Nicholas of Cusa
Cutrate, Joe
  See Spiegelman, Art
Cynewulf fl. 9th cent. .... **CMLC 23, 117;
  PC 158**
    See also DLB 146; RGEL 2
Cyprian, St. c. 200-258 .... **CMLC 127**
Cyrano de Bergerac, Savinien de
  1619-1655 .... **LC 65**
    See also DLB 268; GFL Beginnings to 1789;
    RGWL 2, 3
Cyril of Alexandria c. 375-c. 430 ... **CMLC 59**
Czaczkes, Shmuel Yosef Halevi
  See Agnon, S. Y.
Dabrowska, Maria (Szumska)
  1889-1965 .... **CLC 15**
    See also CA 106; CDWLB 4; DLB 215;
    EWL 3
Dabydeen, David 1955- .... **CLC 34, 351**
    See also BW 1; CA 125; CANR 56, 92; CN
    6, 7; CP 5, 6, 7; DLB 347
Dacey, Philip 1939- .... **CLC 51**
    See also CA 37-40R; 231; CAAE 231;
    CAAS 17; CANR 14, 32, 64; CP 4, 5,
    6, 7; DLB 105
Dacre, Charlotte
  c. 1772-1825(?) .... **NCLC 151**
Dafydd ap Gwilym c. 1320-c. 1380 ... **PC 56**
Dagerman, Stig (Halvard)
  1923-1954 .... **TCLC 17**
    See also CA 117; 155; DLB 259; EWL 3
D'Aguiar, Fred 1960- ... **BLC 2:1; CLC 145**
    See also CA 148; CANR 83, 101; CN 7; CP
    5, 6, 7; DLB 157; EWL 3
Dahl, Roald 1916-1990 ... **CLC 1, 6, 18, 79;
  TCLC 173, 312**
    See also AAYA 15; BPFB 1; BRWS 4; BYA
    5; CA 1-4R; 133; CANR 6, 32, 37, 62;
    CLR 1, 7, 41, 111; CN 1, 2, 3, 4; CPW;
    DA3; DAB; DAC; DAM MST, NOV, POP;
    DLB 139, 255; HGG; JRDA; MAICYA 1,
    2; MTCW 1, 2; MTFW 2005; RGSF 2;
    SATA 1, 26, 73; SATA-Obit 65; SSFS 4,
    30; TEA; YAW
Dahlberg, Edward 1900-1977 ...... **CLC 1, 7,
  14; TCLC 208**

See also CA 9-12R; 69-72; CANR 31, 62;
CN 1, 2; DLB 48; MAL 5; MTCW 1;
RGAL 4
Dahlie, Michael 1970(?)- .... **CLC 299**
  See also CA 283
Daitch, Susan 1954- .... **CLC 103**
  See also CA 161
Dale, Colin
  See Lawrence, T. E.
Dale, George E.
  See Asimov, Isaac
d'Alembert, Jean Le Rond
  1717-1783 .... **LC 126**
Dalton, Roque 1935-1975(?) .... **HLCS 1;
  PC 36**
    See also CA 176; DLB 283; HW 2
Daly, Elizabeth 1878-1967 .... **CLC 52**
    See also CA 23-24; 25-28R; CANR 60; CAP
    2; CMW 4
Daly, Mary 1928-2010 .... **CLC 173**
    See also CA 25-28R; CANR 30, 62, 166;
    FW; GLL 1; MTCW 1
Daly, Maureen 1921-2006 .... **CLC 17**
    See also AAYA 5, 58; BYA 6; CA 253;
    CANR 37, 83, 108; CLR 96; JRDA; MAI-
    CYA 1, 2; SAAS 1; SATA 2, 129; SATA-
    Obit 176; WYA; YAW
Damas, Leon-Gontran
  1912-1978 .... **CLC 84; TCLC 204**
    See also BW 1; CA 125; 73-76; EWL 3
Damocles
  See Benedetti, Mario
Dana, Richard Henry Sr.
  1787-1879 .... **NCLC 53**
Dangarembga, Tsitsi 1959- .... **BLC 2:1**
    See also BW 3; CA 163; DLB 360; NFS 28;
    WLIT 2
Daniel, Laurent
  See Triolet, Elsa
Daniel, Samuel 1562(?)-1619 ...... **LC 24, 171**
    See also DLB 62; RGEL 2
Danielewski, Mark Z. 1966- .... **CLC 360**
    See also CA 194; CANR 170
Daniels, Brett
  See Adler, Renata
Dannay, Frederic 1905-1982 .... **CLC 3, 11**
    See also BPFB 3; CA 1-4R; 107; CANR 1,
    39; CMW 4; DAM POP; DLB 137; MSW;
    MTCW 1; RGAL 4
D'Annunzio, Gabriele
  1863-1938 .... **TCLC 6, 40, 215**
    See also CA 104; 155; EW 8; EWL 3;
    RGWL 2, 3; TWA; WLIT 7
Danois, N. le
  See Gourmont, Remy(-Marie-Charles) de
Dante 1265-1321 .... **CMLC 3, 18, 39, 70,
  142; PC 21, 108; WLCS**
    See also DA; DA3; DAB; DAC; DAM MST,
    POET; EFS 1:1, 2:1; EW 1; LAIT 1;
    RGWL 2, 3; TWA; WLIT 7; WP
d'Antibes, Germain
  See Simenon, Georges
Danticat, Edwidge 1969- .... **BLC 2:1;
  CLC 94, 139, 228; SSC 100**
    See also AAYA 29, 85; CA 152, 192; CAAE
    192; CANR 73, 129, 179; CN 7; DLB 350;
    DNFS 1; EXPS; LATS 1:2; LNFS 3;
    MTCW 2; MTFW 2005; NFS 28, 37;
    SSFS 1, 25, 37; YAW
Danvers, Dennis 1947- .... **CLC 70**
Danziger, Paula 1944-2004 .... **CLC 21**
    See also AAYA 4, 36; BYA 6, 7, 14; CA
    112; 115; 229; CANR 37, 132; CLR 20;
    JRDA; MAICYA 1, 2; MTFW 2005; SATA
    36, 63, 102, 149; SATA-Brief 30; SATA-
    Obit 155; WYA; YAW
Dao, Bei
  See Bei Dao

Da Ponte, Lorenzo 1749-1838 .... NCLC 50

d'Aragona, Tullia 1510(?)-1556 .... LC 121

Darko, Amma 1956- ...... BLC 2:1; CLC 341

Darley, George 1795-1846 .. NCLC 2; PC 125
See also DLB 96; RGEL 2

Dario, Ruben 1867-1916 ..... HLC 1; PC 15;
    TCLC 4, 265
See also CA 131; CANR 81; DAM MULT;
DLB 290; EWL 3; HW 1, 2; LAW;
MTCW 1, 2; MTFW 2005; RGWL 2, 3

Darrow, Clarence (Seward)
    1857-1938 .... TCLC 81
See also CA 164; DLB 303

Darwin, Charles 1809-1882 .... NCLC 57
See also BRWS 7; DLB 57, 166; LATS 1:1;
RGEL 2; TEA; WLIT 4

Darwin, Erasmus 1731-1802 .... NCLC 106
See also BRWS 16; DLB 93; RGEL 2

Darwish, Mahmoud 1941-2008 .... PC 86
See also CA 164; CANR 133; CWW 2;
EWL 3; MTCW 2; MTFW 2005

Darwish, Mahmud -2008
See Darwish, Mahmoud

Daryush, Elizabeth 1887-1977 .... CLC 6, 19
See also CA 49-52; CANR 3, 81; DLB 20

Das, Kamala 1934-2009 .... CLC 191; PC 43
See also CA 101; 287; CANR 27, 59; CP 1,
2, 3, 4, 5, 6, 7; CWP; DLB 323; FW

Dasgupta, Surendranath
    1887-1952 .... TCLC 81
See also CA 157

Dashwood, Edmee Elizabeth Monica de la
    Pasture 1890-1943 .... TCLC 61
See also CA 119; 154; DLB 34; RHW

d'Aubignac, François Hédelin, abbé
    1604-1676 .... LC 222

Daudet, (Louis Marie) Alphonse
    1840-1897 .... NCLC 1, 312
See also DLB 123; GFL 1789 to the Present;
RGSF 2

Daudet, Alphonse Marie Leon
    1867-1942 .... SSC 94
See also CA 217

d'Aulnoy, Marie-Catherine
    c. 1650-1705 .... LC 100, 216

Daumal, Rene 1908-1944 .... TCLC 14
See also CA 114; 247; EWL 3

Davenant, William 1606-1668 .... DC 48;
    LC 13, 166; PC 99
See also DLB 58, 126; RGEL 2

Davenport, Guy (Mattison, Jr.)
    1927-2005 .... CLC 6, 14, 38, 241;
    SSC 16
See also CA 33-36R; 235; CANR 23, 73;
CN 3, 4, 5, 6; CSW; DLB 130

David, Robert
See Nezval, Vitezslav

Davidson, Donald (Grady)
    1893-1968 .... CLC 2, 13, 19
See also CA 5-8R; 25-28R; CANR 4, 84;
DLB 45

Davidson, Hugh
See Hamilton, Edmond

Davidson, John 1857-1909 .... TCLC 24
See also CA 118; 217; DLB 19; RGEL 2

Davidson, Sara 1943- .... CLC 9
See also CA 81-84; CANR 44, 68; DLB 185

Davie, Donald (Alfred) 1922-1995 ... CLC 5,
    8, 10, 31; PC 29
See also BRWS 6; CA 1-4R; 149; CAAS 3;
CANR 1, 44; CP 1, 2, 3, 4, 5, 6; DLB 27;
MTCW 1; RGEL 2

Davie, Elspeth 1918-1995 .... SSC 52
See also CA 120; 126; 150; CANR 141;
DLB 139

Davies, Ray 1944- .... CLC 21
See also CA 116; 146; CANR 92

Davies, Raymond Douglas
See Davies, Ray

Davies, Rhys 1901-1978 .... CLC 23
See also CA 9-12R; 81-84; CANR 4; CN 1,
2; DLB 139, 191

Davies, Robertson 1913-1995 .... CLC 2, 7,
    13, 25, 42, 75, 91; WLC 2
See also BEST 89:2; BPFB 1; CA 1, 33-
36R; 150; CANR 17, 42, 103; CN 1, 2, 3,
4, 5, 6; CPW; DA; DA3; DAB; DAC;
DAM MST, NOV, POP; DLB 68; EWL
3; HGG; INT CANR-17; MTCW 1, 2;
MTFW 2005; RGEL 2; TWA

Davies, Sir John 1569-1626 .... LC 85
See also DLB 172

Davies, Walter C.
See Kornbluth, C(yril) M.

Davies, William Henry 1871-1940 ... TCLC 5
See also BRWS 11; CA 104; 179; DLB 19,
174; EWL 3; RGEL 2

Davies, William Robertson
See Davies, Robertson

Da Vinci, Leonardo 1452-1519 .... LC 12,
    57, 60
See also AAYA 40

Daviot, Gordon
See Mackintosh, Elizabeth

Davis, Angela Y. 1944- .... CLC 77
See also BW 2, 3; CA 57-60; CANR 10, 81;
CSW; DA3; DAM MULT; FW

Davis, Angela Yvonne
See Davis, Angela Y.

Davis, B. Lynch
See Bioy Casares, Adolfo; Borges,
Jorge Luis

Davis, Frank Marshall 1905-1987 .. BLC 1:1
See also BW 2, 3; CA 125; 123; CANR 42,
80; DAM MULT; DLB 51

Davis, Gordon
See Hunt, E. Howard

Davis, H(arold) L(enoir) 1896-1960 .... CLC 49
See also ANW; CA 178; 89-92; DLB 9, 206;
SATA 114; TCWW 1, 2

Davis, Hart
See Poniatowska, Elena

Davis, Lydia 1947- .... CLC 306, 370
See also CA 139; CANR 120, 171, 222;
DLB 130

Davis, Natalie Zemon 1928- .... CLC 204
See also CA 53-56; CANR 58, 100, 174

Davis, Rebecca Blaine Harding
See Davis, Rebecca Harding

Davis, Rebecca Harding 1831-1910 ... SSC 38,
    109, 192; TCLC 6, 267
See also AMWS 16; CA 104; 179; DLB 74,
239; FW; NFS 14; RGAL 4; SSFS 26; TUS

Davis, Richard Harding
    1864-1916 .... TCLC 24
See also CA 114; 179; DLB 12, 23, 78, 79,
189; DLBD 13; RGAL 4

Davison, Frank Dalby 1893-1970 ... CLC 15
See also CA 217; 116; DLB 260

Davison, Lawrence H.
See Lawrence, D. H.

Davison, Peter (Hubert)
    1928-2004 .... CLC 28
See also CA 9-12R; 234; CAAS 4; CANR 3,
43, 84; CP 1, 2, 3, 4, 5, 6, 7; DLB 5

Davys, Mary 1674-1732 .... LC 1, 46, 217
See also DLB 39

Dawe, Bruce 1930- .... PC 159
See also CA 69-72; CANR 11, 27, 52, 83;
CP 1, 2, 3, 4, 5, 6, 7; DLB 289; PFS 10

Dawson, (Guy) Fielding (Lewis)
    1930-2002 .... CLC 6
See also CA 85-88; 202; CANR 108; DLB
130; DLBY 2002

Day, Clarence (Shepard, Jr.)
    1874-1935 .... TCLC 25
See also CA 108; 199; DLB 11

Day, John 1574(?)-1640(?) .... LC 70
See also DLB 62, 170; RGEL 2

Day, Thomas 1748-1789 .... LC 1
See also DLB 39; YABC 1

Day Lewis, C. 1904-1972 ...... CLC 1, 6, 10;
    PC 11; TCLC 261
See also BRWS 3; CA 13-16; 33-36R;
CANR 34; CAP 1; CN 1; CP 1; CWRI
5; DAM POET; DLB 77; EWL 3; MSW;
MTCW 1, 2; RGEL 2

Day Lewis, Cecil
See Day Lewis, C.

Diaz, Junot 1968- .... CLC 258; SSC 144
See also AAYA 83; BYA 12; CA 161;
CANR 119, 183; LLW; NFS 36; SSFS 20

Diaz del Castillo, Bernal
    c. 1496-1584 .... HLCS 1; LC 31
See also DLB 318; LAW

Doblin, Alfred 1878-1957 .... TCLC 13, 269
See also CA 110; 141; CDWLB 2; DLB 66;
EWL 3; RGWL 2, 3

de Andrade, Carlos Drummond
See Drummond de Andrade, Carlos

de Andrade, Mario (?)-
See Andrade, Mario de

Deane, Norman
See Creasey, John

Deane, Seamus (Francis) 1940- .... CLC 122
See also CA 118; CANR 42

de Athayde, Alvaro Coelho
See Pessoa, Fernando

Deaver, Jeff
See Deaver, Jeffery

Deaver, Jeffery 1950- .... CLC 331
See also AAYA 41; CA 163; CANR 105,
151, 178, 236

Deaver, Jeffery Wilds
See Deaver, Jeffery

de Beauvoir, Simone
See Beauvoir, Simone de

de Beer, P.
See Bosman, Herman Charles

De Botton, Alain 1969- .... CLC 203
See also CA 159; CANR 96, 201

de Brissac, Malcolm
See Dickinson, Peter

de Campos, Álvaro
See Pessoa, Fernando

de Chardin, Pierre Teilhard
See Teilhard de Chardin, (Marie Joseph)
Pierre

de Conte, Sieur Louis
See Twain, Mark

de Crenne, Helisenne
    c. 1510-c. 1560 .... LC 113, 218

Dee, John 1527-1608 .... LC 20
See also DLB 136, 213

Deer, Sandra 1940- .... CLC 45
See also CA 186

De Ferrari, Gabriella 1941- .... CLC 65
See also CA 146

de Filippo, Eduardo 1900-1984 ... TCLC 127
See also CA 132; 114; EWL 3; MTCW 1;
RGWL 2, 3

Defoe, Daniel 1660(?)-1731 .... LC 1, 42,
    108, 180, 238; WLC 2
See also AAYA 27; BRW 3; BRWR 1; BYA
4; CDBLB 1660-1789; CLR 61, 164; DA;
DA3; DAB; DAC; DAM MST, NOV; DLB
39, 95, 101, 336; JRDA; LAIT 1; LMFS 1;
MAICYA 1, 2; NFS 9, 13, 30; RGEL 2;
SATA 22; TEA; WCH; WLIT 3

de Gouges, Olympe
See Gouges, Olympe de

de Gouges, Olympe 1748-1793 .. **LC 127, 214**
See also DLB 313
de Gourmont, Remy(-Marie-Charles)
See Gourmont, Remy(-Marie-Charles) de
de Gournay, Marie le Jars
1566-1645 .... **LC 98, 244**
See also DLB 327; FW
de Hartog, Jan 1914-2002 .... **CLC 19**
See also CA 1-4R; 210; CANR 1, 192; DFS 12
de Hostos, E. M.
See Hostos (y Bonilla), Eugenio Maria de
de Hostos, Eugenio M.
See Hostos (y Bonilla), Eugenio Maria de
Deighton, Len
See Deighton, Leonard Cyril
Deighton, Leonard Cyril 1929- ... **CLC 4, 7,**
22, 46
See also AAYA 57, 6; BEST 89:2; BPFB 1;
CA 9-12R; CANR 19, 33, 68; CDBLB
1960- Present; CMW 4; CN 1, 2, 3, 4,
5, 6, 7; CPW; DA3; DAM NOV, POP;
DLB 87; MTCW 1, 2; MTFW 2005
Dekker, Thomas 1572(?)-1632 .... **DC 12;**
LC 22, 159
See also CDBLB Before 1660; DAM
DRAM; DLB 62, 172; LMFS 1; RGEL 2
de Laclos, Pierre Ambroise Franois
See Laclos, Pierre-Ambroise Francois
Delacroix, (Ferdinand-Victor-)Eugene
1798-1863 .... **NCLC 133**
See also EW 5
Delafield, E. M.
See Dashwood, Edmee Elizabeth Monica de
la Pasture
de la Mare, Walter (John)
1873-1956 .... **PC 77; SSC 14;**
TCLC 4, 53; WLC 2
See also AAYA 81; CA 163; CDBLB 1914-
1945; CLR 23, 148; CWRI 5; DA3; DAB;
DAC; DAM MST, POET; DLB 19, 153,
162, 255, 284; EWL 3; EXPP; HGG;
MAICYA 1, 2; MTCW 2; MTFW 2005;
PFS 39; RGEL 2; RGSF 2; SATA 16;
SUFW 1; TEA; WCH
de Lamartine, Alphonse
See Lamartine, Alphonse de
Deland, Margaret(ta Wade Campbell)
1857-1945 .... **SSC 162**
See also CA 122; DLB 78; RGAL 4
Delaney, Franey
See O'Hara, John
Delaney, Shelagh 1939-2011 ... **CLC 29; DC 45**
See also CA 17-20R; CANR 30, 67; CBD;
CD 5, 6; CDBLB 1960 to Present; CWD;
DAM DRAM; DFS 7; DLB 13; MTCW 1
Delany, Martin Robison 1812-1885 .. **NCLC 93**
See also DLB 50; RGAL 4
Delany, Mary (Granville Pendarves)
1700-1788 .... **LC 12, 220**
Delany, Samuel R., Jr. 1942- .... **BLC 1:1;**
CLC 8, 14, 38, 141, 313
See also AAYA 24; AFAW 2; BPFB 1; BW
2, 3; CA 81-84; CANR 27, 43, 116, 172;
CN 2, 3, 4, 5, 6, 7; DAM MULT; DLB 8,
33; FANT; MAL 5; MTCW 1, 2; RGAL 4;
SATA 92; SCFW 1, 2; SFW 4; SUFW 2
Delany, Samuel Ray
See Delany, Samuel R., Jr.
de la Parra, Ana Teresa Sonojo
See de la Parra, Teresa
de la Parra, Teresa
1890(?)-1936 .... **HLCS 2; TCLC 185**
See also CA 178; HW 2; LAW
Delaporte, Theophile
See Green, Julien
De La Ramee, Marie Louise
1839-1908 .... **TCLC 43**
See also CA 204; DLB 18, 156; RGEL 2;
SATA 20

de la Roche, Mazo 1879-1961 .... **CLC 14**
See also CA 85-88; CANR 30; DLB 68;
RGEL 2; RHW; SATA 64
De La Salle, Innocent
See Hartmann, Sadakichi
de Laureamont, Comte
See Lautreamont
Delbanco, Nicholas 1942- ... **CLC 6, 13, 167**
See also CA 17-20R, 189; CAAE 189;
CAAS 2; CANR 29, 55, 116, 150, 204,
237; CN 7; DLB 6, 234
Delbanco, Nicholas Franklin
See Delbanco, Nicholas
del Castillo, Michel 1933- .... **CLC 38**
See also CA 109; CANR 77
Deledda, Grazia (Cosima) 1875
(?)-1936 .... **TCLC 23**
See also CA 123; 205; DLB 264, 329; EWL
3; RGWL 2, 3; WLIT 7
Deleuze, Gilles 1925-1995 .... **TCLC 116**
See also DLB 296
Delgado, Abelardo (Lalo) B(arrientos)
1930-2004 .... **HLC 1**
See also CA 131; 230; CAAS 15; CANR 90;
DAM MST, MULT; DLB 82; HW 1, 2
Delibes, Miguel
See Delibes Setien, Miguel
Delibes Setien, Miguel 1920-2010 ... **CLC 8, 18**
See also CA 45-48; CANR 1, 32; CWW 2;
DLB 322; EWL 3; HW 1; MTCW 1
DeLillo, Don 1936- .... **CLC 8, 10, 13, 27,**
39, 54, 76, 143, 210, 213, 336
See also AMWC 2; AMWS 6; BEST 89:1;
BPFB 1; CA 81-84; CANR 21, 76, 92,
133, 173, 240; CN 3, 4, 5, 6, 7; CPW;
DA3; DAM NOV, POP; DLB 6, 173; EWL
3; MAL 5; MTCW 1, 2; MTFW 2005;
NFS 28; RGAL 4; TUS
de Lisser, H. G.
See De Lisser, H(erbert) G(eorge)
De Lisser, H(erbert) G(eorge)
1878-1944 .... **TCLC 12**
See also BW 2; CA 109; 152; DLB 117
Della Casa, Giovanni 1503-1556 ..... **LC 220**
Deloire, Pierre
See Peguy, Charles (Pierre)
Deloney, Thomas 1543(?)-1600 .... **LC 41;**
PC 79
See also DLB 167; RGEL 2
Deloria, Ella (Cara) 1889-1971(?) ..... **NNAL**
See also CA 152; DAM MULT; DLB 175
Deloria, Vine, Jr. 1933-2005 ... **CLC 21, 122;**
NNAL
See also CA 53-56; 245; CANR 5, 20, 48,
98; DAM MULT; DLB 175; MTCW 1;
SATA 21; SATA-Obit 171
Deloria, Vine Victor, Jr.
See Deloria, Vine, Jr.
del Valle-Inclan, Ramon
See Valle-Inclan, Ramon del
Del Vecchio, John M(ichael) 1947- ... **CLC 29**
See also CA 110; DLBD 9
de Man, Paul (Adolph Michel)
1919-1983 .... **CLC 55**
See also CA 128; 111; CANR 61; DLB 67;
MTCW 1, 2
de Mandiargues, Andre Pieyre
See Pieyre de Mandiargues, Andre
DeMarinis, Rick 1934- .... **CLC 54**
See also CA 57-60, 184; CAAE 184; CAAS
24; CANR 9, 25, 50, 160; DLB 218;
TCWW 2
de Maupassant, Guy
See Maupassant, Guy de
Dembry, R. Emmet
See Murfree, Mary Noailles
Demby, William 1922- ...... **BLC 1:1; CLC 53**
See also BW 1, 3; CA 81-84; CANR 81;
DAM MULT; DLB 33

de Menton, Francisco
See Chin, Frank
Demetrius of Phalerum
c. 307B.C. .... **CMLC 34**
Demijohn, Thom
See Disch, Thomas M.
De Mille, James 1833-1880 .... **NCLC 123**
See also DLB 99, 251
Democritus
c. 460B.C.-c. 370B.C. .... **CMLC 47, 136**
de Montaigne, Michel
See Montaigne, Michel de
de Montherlant, Henry
See Montherlant, Henry de
Demosthenes 384B.C.-322B.C. ..... **CMLC 13**
See also AW 1; DLB 176; RGWL 2, 3;
WLIT 8
de Musset, (Louis Charles) Alfred
See Musset, Alfred de
de Natale, Francine
See Malzberg, Barry N(athaniel)
de Navarre, Marguerite
1492-1549 .... **LC 61, 167; SSC 85, 211**
See also DLB 327; GFL Beginnings to 1789;
RGWL 2, 3
Denby, Edwin (Orr) 1903-1983 ...... **CLC 48**
See also CA 138; 110; CP 1
de Nerval, Gerard
See Nerval, Gerard de
Denfeld, Rene 1967- .... **CLC 389**
See also CA 259
Denham, John 1615-1669 ... **LC 73; PC 166**
See also DLB 58, 126; RGEL 2
Denis, Claire 1948- .... **CLC 286**
See also CA 249
Denis, Julio
See Cortázar, Julio
Denmark, Harrison
See Zelazny, Roger
Dennie, Joseph 1768-1812 .... **NCLC 249**
See also DLB 37, 43, 59, 73
Dennis, John 1658-1734 ...... **LC 11, 154**
See also DLB 101; RGEL 2
Dennis, Nigel (Forbes)
1912-1989 .... **CLC 8**
See also CA 25-28R; 129; CN 1, 2, 3, 4;
DLB 13, 15, 233; EWL 3; MTCW 1
Dent, Lester 1904-1959 .... **TCLC 72**
See also CA 112; 161; CMW 4; DLB 306;
SFW 4
Dentinger, Stephen
See Hoch, Edward D.
De Palma, Brian 1940- .... **CLC 20, 247**
See also CA 109
De Palma, Brian Russell
See De Palma, Brian
de Pizan, Christine
See Christine de Pizan
De Quincey, Thomas
1785-1859 .... **NCLC 4, 87, 198**
See also BRW 4; CDBLB 1789-1832; DLB
110, 144; RGEL 2
De Ray, Jill
See Moore, Alan
Deren, Eleanora 1908(?)-1961 ... **CLC 16, 102**
See also CA 192; 111
Deren, Maya
See Deren, Eleanora
Derleth, August (William)
1909-1971 .... **CLC 31**
See also BPFB 1; BYA 9, 10; CA 1-4R; 29-
32R; CANR 4; CMW 4; CN 1; DLB 9;
DLBD 17; HGG; SATA 5; SUFW 1
Der Nister 1884-1950 .... **TCLC 56**
See also DLB 333; EWL 3
de Routisie, Albert
See Aragon, Louis

Dumas, Claudine
   See Malzberg, Barry N(athaniel)

Dumas, Henry L. 1934-1968 .... **BLC 2:1; CLC 6, 62; SSC 107**
   See also BW 1; CA 85-88; DLB 41; RGAL 4

du Maurier, Daphne 1907-1989 ...... **CLC 6, 11, 59; SSC 18, 129; TCLC 209**
   See also AAYA 37; BPFB 1; BRWS 3; CA 5-8R; 128; CANR 6, 55; CMW 4; CN 1, 2, 3, 4; CPW; DA3; DAB; DAC; DAM MST, POP; DLB 191; GL 2; HGG; LAIT 3; MSW; MTCW 1, 2; NFS 12; RGEL 2; RGSF 2; RHW; SATA 27; SATA-Obit 60; SSFS 14, 16; TEA

Du Maurier, George 1834-1896 .... **NCLC 86**
   See also DLB 153, 178; RGEL 2

Dummett, Michael 1925-2011 .... **CLC 384**
   See also CA 102; CANR 224; DLB 262

Dunbar, Alice
   See Nelson, Alice Ruth Moore Dunbar

Dunbar, Alice Moore
   See Nelson, Alice Ruth Moore Dunbar

Dunbar, Paul Laurence
   1872-1906 ...... **BLC 1:1; PC 5; SSC 8; TCLC 2, 12; WLC 2**
   See also AAYA 75; AFAW 1, 2; AMWS 2; BW 1, 3; CA 104; 124; CANR 79; CDALB 1865-1917; DA; DA3; DAC; DAM MST, MULT, POET; DLB 50, 54, 78; EXPP; MAL 5; PFS 33, 40; RGAL 4; SATA 34

Dunbar, William
   1460(?)-1520(?) .... **LC 20; PC 67**
   See also BRWS 8; DLB 132, 146; RGEL 2

Dunbar-Nelson, Alice
   See Nelson, Alice Ruth Moore Dunbar

Dunbar-Nelson, Alice Moore
   See Nelson, Alice Ruth Moore Dunbar

Duncan, Dora Angela
   See Duncan, Isadora

Duncan, Isadora 1877(?)-1927 ...... **TCLC 68**
   See also CA 118; 149

Duncan, Lois 1934- .... **CLC 26**
   See also AAYA 4, 34; BYA 6, 8; CA 1-4R; CANR 2, 23, 36, 111; CLR 29, 129; JRDA; MAICYA 1, 2; MAICYAS 1; MTFW 2005; SAAS 2; SATA 1, 36, 75, 133, 141, 219; SATA-Essay 141; WYA; YAW

Duncan, Robert 1919-1988 .... **CLC 1, 2, 4, 7, 15, 41, 55; PC 2, 75**
   See also BG 1:2; CA 9-12R; 124; CANR 28, 62; CP 1, 2, 3, 4; DAM POET; DLB 5, 16, 193; EWL 3; MAL 5; MTCW 1, 2; MTFW 2005; PFS 13; RGAL 4; WP

Duncan, Sara Jeannette 1861-1922 ... **TCLC 60**
   See also CA 157; DLB 92

Dunlap, William 1766-1839 .... **NCLC 2, 244**
   See also DLB 30, 37, 59; RGAL 4

Dunn, Douglas (Eaglesham) 1942- .. **CLC 6, 40**
   See also BRWS 10; CA 45-48; CANR 2, 33, 126; CP 1, 2, 3, 4, 5, 6, 7; DLB 40; MTCW 1

Dunn, Katherine 1945- .... **CLC 71**
   See also CA 33-36R; CANR 72; HGG; MTCW 2; MTFW 2005

Dunn, Stephen 1939- .... **CLC 36, 206**
   See also AMWS 11; CA 33-36R; CANR 12, 48, 53, 105; CP 3, 4, 5, 6, 7; DLB 105, 238; PFS 21

Dunn, Stephen Elliott
   See Dunn, Stephen

Dunne, Finley Peter 1867-1936 .... **TCLC 28**
   See also CA 108; 178; DLB 11, 23; RGAL 4

Dunne, John Gregory 1932-2003 ... **CLC 28**
   See also CA 25-28R; 222; CANR 14, 50; CN 5, 6, 7; DLBY 1980

Dunne, Mary Chavelita
   See Egerton, George

Duns Scotus, John
   See Scotus, John Duns

Dunton, John 1659-1733 .... **LC 219**
   See also DLB 170

Duong, Thu Huong 1947- .... **CLC 273**
   See also CA 152; CANR 106, 166; DLB 348; NFS 23

Duong Thu Huong
   See Duong, Thu Huong

du Perry, Jean
   See Simenon, Georges

Durang, Christopher 1949- .... **CLC 27, 38**
   See also CA 105; CAD; CANR 50, 76, 130; CD 5, 6; MTCW 2; MTFW 2005

Durang, Christopher Ferdinand
   See Durang, Christopher

Duras, Claire de 1777-1832 ... **NCLC 154, 304**

Duras, Marguerite 1914-1996 ...... **CLC 3, 6, 11, 20, 34, 40, 68, 100; DC 51; SSC 40, 206**
   See also BPFB 1; CA 25-28R; 151; CANR 50; CWW 2; DFS 21; DLB 83, 321; EWL 3; FL 1:5; GFL 1789 to the Present; IDFW 4; MTCW 1, 2; RGWL 2, 3; TWA

Durban, (Rosa) Pam 1947- .... **CLC 39**
   See also CA 123; CANR 98; CSW

Durcan, Paul 1944- .... **CLC 43, 70**
   See also CA 134; CANR 123; CP 1, 5, 6, 7; DAM POET; EWL 3

d'Urfe, Honore
   See Urfe, Honore d'

Durfey, Thomas 1653-1723 .... **LC 94**
   See also DLB 80; RGEL 2

Durkheim, Emile 1858-1917 .... **TCLC 55**
   See also CA 249

Durrell, Lawrence 1912-1990 .... **CLC 1, 4, 6, 8, 13, 27, 41; PC 142**
   See also BPFB 1; BRWR 3; BRWS 1; CA 9-12R; 132; CANR 40, 77; CDBLB 1945-1960; CN 1, 2, 3, 4; CP 1, 2, 3, 4, 5; DAM NOV; DLB 15, 27, 204; DLBY 1990; EWL 3; MTCW 1, 2; RGEL 2; SFW 4; TEA

Durrell, Lawrence George
   See Durrell, Lawrence

Dürrenmatt, Friedrich 1921-1990 ... **CLC 1, 4, 8, 11, 15, 43, 102**
   See also CA 17-20R; CANR 33; CDWLB 2; CMW 4; DAM DRAM; DLB 69, 124; EW 13; EWL 3; MTCW 1, 2; RGHL; RGWL 2, 3

Dutt, Michael Madhusudan
   1824-1873 .... **NCLC 118**

Dutt, Toru 1856-1877 .... **NCLC 29**
   See also DLB 240

Dwight, Timothy 1752-1817 ... **NCLC 13, 245**
   See also DLB 37; RGAL 4

Dworkin, Andrea 1946-2005 .... **CLC 43, 123**
   See also CA 77-80; 238; CAAS 21; CANR 16, 39, 76, 96; FL 1:5; FW; GLL 1; INT CANR-16; MTCW 1, 2; MTFW 2005

Dwyer, Deanna
   See Koontz, Dean

Dwyer, K.R.
   See Koontz, Dean

Dybek, Stuart 1942- .... **CLC 114; SSC 55**
   See also AMWS 23; CA 97-100; CANR 39; DLB 130; SSFS 23

Dye, Richard
   See De Voto, Bernard (Augustine)

Dyer, Geoff 1958- .... **CLC 149**
   See also CA 125; CANR 88, 209, 242

Dyer, George 1755-1841 .... **NCLC 129**
   See also DLB 93

Dylan, Bob 1941- .... **CLC 3, 4, 6, 12, 77, 308; PC 37**
   See also AMWS 18; CA 41-44R; CANR 108; CP 1, 2, 3, 4, 5, 6, 7; DLB 16

Dyson, John 1943- .... **CLC 70**
   See also CA 144

Dzyubin, Eduard Georgievich
   1895-1934 .... **TCLC 60**
   See also CA 170; DLB 359; EWL 3

E. V. L.
   See Lucas, E(dward) V(errall)

E. W.
   See Mangan, James Clarence

Eagleton, Terence
   See Eagleton, Terry

Eagleton, Terence Francis
   See Eagleton, Terry

Eagleton, Terry 1943- .... **CLC 63, 132**
   See also CA 57-60; CANR 7, 23, 68, 115, 198, 243; DLB 242; LMFS 2; MTCW 1, 2; MTFW 2005

Earl of Orrey
   See Boyle, Roger

Early, Jack
   See Scoppettone, Sandra

Early, Tom
   See Kelton, Elmer

East, Michael
   See West, Morris L(anglo)

Eastaway, Edward
   See Thomas, (Philip) Edward

Eastlake, William (Derry) 1917-1997 ... **CLC 8**
   See also CA 5-8R; 158; CAAS 1; CANR 5, 63; CN 1, 2, 3, 4, 5, 6; DLB 6, 206; INT CANR-5; MAL 5; TCWW 1, 2

Eastland, Sam
   See Watkins, Paul

Eastman, Charles A(lexander)
   1858-1939 .... **NNAL; TCLC 55**
   See also CA 179; CANR 91; DAM MULT; DLB 175; YABC 1

Eaton, Edith Maude
   1865-1914 ... **AAL; SSC 157; TCLC 232**
   See also CA 154; DLB 221, 312; FW

Eaton, (Lillie) Winnifred 1875-1954 .... **AAL**
   See also CA 217; DLB 221, 312; RGAL 4

Eberhart, Richard 1904-2005 .... **CLC 3, 11, 19, 56; PC 76**
   See also AMW; CA 1-4R; 240; CANR 2, 125; CDALB 1941-1968; CP 1, 2, 3, 4, 5, 6, 7; DAM POET; DLB 48; MAL 5; MTCW 1; RGAL 4

Eberhart, Richard Ghormley
   See Eberhart, Richard

Eberstadt, Fernanda 1960- .... **CLC 39**
   See also CA 136; CANR 69, 128

Ebner, Margaret
   c. 1291-1351 .... **CMLC 98**

Echegaray (y Eizaguirre), Jose (Maria Waldo)
   1832-1916 .... **HLCS 1; TCLC 4**
   See also CA 104; CANR 32; DLB 329; EWL 3; HW 1; MTCW 1

Echeverría, (Jose) Esteban (Antonino)
   1805-1851 .... **NCLC 18, 309**
   See also LAW

Echo
   See Proust, Marcel

Eckert, Allan W. 1931- .... **CLC 17**
   See also AAYA 18; BYA 2; CA 13-16R; CANR 14, 45; INT CANR-14; MAICYA 2; MAICYAS 1; SAAS 21; SATA 29, 91; SATA-Brief 27

Eckhart, Meister
   1260(?)-1327(?) .... **CMLC 9, 80, 131**
   See also DLB 115; LMFS 1

Eckmar, F. R.
   See de Hartog, Jan

Eco, Umberto 1932- .... **CLC 28, 60, 142, 248, 360**
   See also BEST 90:1; BPFB 1; CA 77-80; CANR 12, 33, 55, 110, 131, 195, 234; CPW; CWW 2; DA3; DAM NOV, POP; DLB 196, 242; EWL 3; MSW; MTCW 1, 2; MTFW 2005; NFS 22; RGWL 3; WLIT 7

Elliott, Sumner Locke
1917-1991 .... **CLC 38**
See also CA 5-8R; 134; CANR 2, 21; DLB 289
Elliott, William
See Bradbury, Ray
Ellis, A. E. .... **CLC 7**
Ellis, Alice Thomas
See Haycraft, Anna
Ellis, Bret Easton 1964- .... **CLC 39, 71,**
117, 229, 345
See also AAYA 2, 43; CA 118; 123; CANR
51, 74, 126, 226; CN 6, 7; CPW; DA3;
DAM POP; DLB 292; HGG; INT CA-123;
MTCW 2; MTFW 2005; NFS 11
Ellis, (Henry) Havelock
1859-1939 .... **TCLC 14**
See also CA 109; 169; DLB 190
Ellis, Landon
See Ellison, Harlan
Ellis, Trey 1962- .... **CLC 55**
See also CA 146; CANR 92; CN 7
Ellison, Harlan 1934- .... **CLC 1, 13, 42,**
139; SSC 14
See also AAYA 29; BPFB 1; BYA 14; CA 5-
8R; CANR 5, 46, 115; CPW; DAM POP;
DLB 8, 335; HGG; INT CANR-5; MTCW
1, 2; MTFW 2005; SCFW 4; SFW 4; SSFS
13, 14, 15, 21; SUFW 1, 2
Ellison, Ralph 1914-1994 .... **BLC 1:1, 2:2;**
CLC 1, 3, 11, 54, 86, 114; SSC 26, 79;
TCLC 308; WLC 2
See also AAYA 19; AFAW 1, 2; AMWC 2;
AMWR 2; AMWS 2; BPFB 1; BW 1, 3;
BYA 2; CA 9-12R; 145; CANR 24, 53;
CDALB 1941-1968; CLR 197; CN 1, 2, 3,
4, 5; CSW; DA; DA3; DAB; DAC; DAM
MST, MULT, NOV; DLB 2, 76, 227; DLBY
1994; EWL 3; EXPN; EXPS; LAIT 4; MAL
5; MTCW 1, 2; MTFW 2005; NCFS 3; NFS
2, 21; RGAL 4; RGSF 2; SSFS 1, 11; YAW
Ellison, Ralph Waldo
See Ellison, Ralph
Ellmann, Lucy 1956- .... **CLC 61**
See also CA 128; CANR 154
Ellmann, Lucy Elizabeth
See Ellmann, Lucy
Ellmann, Richard (David)
1918-1987 .... **CLC 50**
See also BEST 89:2; CA 1-4R; 122; CANR
2, 28, 61; DLB 103; DLBY 1987; MTCW
1, 2; MTFW 2005
Ellroy, James 1948- .... **CLC 215**
See also BEST 90:4; CA 138; CANR 74,
133, 219; CMW 4; CN 6, 7; DA3; DLB
226; MTCW 2; MTFW 2005
Ellroy, Lee Earle
See Ellroy, James
Elman, Richard (Martin)
1934-1997 .... **CLC 19**
See also CA 17-20R; 163; CAAS 3; CANR
47; TCLE 1:1
Elron
See Hubbard, L. Ron
El Saadawi, Nawal 1931- .... **BLC 2:2;**
CLC 196, 284
See also AFW; CA 118; CAAS 11; CANR
44, 92; CWW 2; DLB 360; EWL 3; FW;
WLIT 2
El-Shabazz, El-Hajj Malik
See Malcolm X
Elstob, Elizabeth 1683-1756 .... **LC 205**
Eltit, Diamela 1949- .... **CLC 294**
See also CA 253
Eluard, Paul
See Grindel, Eugene
Elyot, Thomas 1490(?)-1546 .... **LC 11, 139**
See also DLB 136; RGEL 2
Elytis, Odysseus 1911-1996 ...... **CLC 15, 49,**
100; PC 21

See also CA 102; 151; CANR 94; CWW 2;
DAM POET; DLB 329; EW 13; EWL 3;
MTCW 1, 2; RGWL 2, 3
Emecheta, Buchi 1944- .... **BLC 1:2;**
CLC 14, 48, 128, 214
See also AAYA 67; AFW; BW 2, 3; CA 81-
84; CANR 27, 81, 126; CDWLB 3; CLR
158; CN 4, 5, 6, 7; CWRI 5; DA3; DAM
MULT; DLB 117; EWL 3; FL 1:5; FW;
MTCW 1, 2; MTFW 2005; NFS 12, 14,
41; SATA 66; WLIT 2
Emecheta, Florence Onye Buchi
See Emecheta, Buchi
Emerson, Mary Moody 1774-1863 ... **NCLC 66**
Emerson, Ralph Waldo
1803-1882 **NCLC 1, 38, 98, 252; PC 18;**
WLC 2
See also AAYA 60; AMW; ANW; CDALB
1640-1865; DA; DA3; DAB; DAC; DAM
MST, POET; DLB 1, 59, 73, 183, 223, 270,
351, 366; EXPP; LAIT 2; LMFS 1; NCFS
3; PFS 4, 17, 34; RGAL 4; TUS; WP
Eminem 1972- .... **CLC 226**
See also CA 245
Eminescu, Mihail
1850-1889 .... **NCLC 33, 131**
Empedocles 5th cent. B.C. ... **CMLC 50, 171**
See also DLB 176
Empson, William 1906-1984 .... **CLC 3, 8,**
19, 33, 34; PC 104
See also BRWS 2; CA 17-20R; 112; CANR
31, 61; CP 1, 2, 3; DLB 20; EWL 3;
MTCW 1, 2; RGEL 2
Enchi, Fumiko 1905-1986 .... **CLC 31**
See also CA 129; 121; DLB 182; EWL 3;
FW; MJW
Enchi, Fumiko Ueda
See Enchi, Fumiko
Enchi Fumiko
See Enchi, Fumiko
Ende, Michael (Andreas Helmuth)
1929-1995 .... **CLC 31**
See also BYA 5; CA 118; 124; 149; CANR
36, 110; CLR 14, 138; DLB 75; MAICYA
1, 2; MAICYAS 1; SATA 61, 130; SATA-
Brief 42; SATA-Obit 86
Endo, Shusaku 1923-1996 ... **CLC 7, 14, 19,**
54, 99; SSC 48; TCLC 152
See also CA 29-32R; 153; CANR 21, 54,
131; CWW 2; DA3; DAM NOV; DLB 182;
EWL 3; MTCW 1, 2; MTFW 2005; RGSF
2; RGWL 2, 3
Endo Shusaku
See Endo, Shusaku
Engel, Marian 1933-1985 .... **CLC 36;**
TCLC 137
See also CA 25-28R; CANR 12; CN 2, 3;
DLB 53; FW; INT CANR-12
Engelhardt, Frederick
See Hubbard, L. Ron
Engels, Friedrich
1820-1895 .... **NCLC 85, 114**
See also DLB 129; LATS 1:1
Ennius, Quintus 239-169 BC .... **CMLC 169**
See also DLB 211; RGWL 1, 2
Enquist, Per Olov 1934- .... **CLC 257**
See also CA 109; 193; CANR 155; CWW 2;
DLB 257; EWL 3
Enright, D(ennis) J(oseph)
1920-2002 .... **CLC 4, 8, 31; PC 93**
See also CA 1-4R; 211; CANR 1, 42, 83;
CN 1, 2; CP 1, 2, 3, 4, 5, 6, 7; DLB 27;
EWL 3; SATA 25; SATA-Obit 140
Ensler, Eve 1953- .... **CLC 212; DC 47**
See also CA 172; CANR 126, 163; DFS 23
Enzensberger, Hans Magnus
1929- .... **CLC 43; PC 28**
See also CA 116; 119; CANR 103, 235;
CWW 2; EWL 3

Ephron, Nora 1941- .... **CLC 17, 31**
See also AAYA 35; AITN 2; CA 65-68;
CANR 12, 39, 83, 161, 236; DFS 22
Epictetus c. 55-c. 135 .... **CMLC 126**
See also AW 2; DLB 176
Epicurus 341B.C.-270B.C. ... **CMLC 21, 165**
See also DLB 176
Epinay, Louise d' 1726-1783 .... **LC 138**
See also DLB 313
Epsilon
See Betjeman, John
Epstein, Daniel Mark 1948- .... **CLC 7**
See also CA 49-52; CANR 2, 53, 90, 193, 236
Epstein, Jacob 1956- .... **CLC 19**
See also CA 114
Epstein, Jean 1897-1953 .... **TCLC 92**
Epstein, Joseph 1937- .... **CLC 39, 204**
See also AMWS 14; CA 112; 119; CANR
50, 65, 117, 164, 190, 225
Epstein, Leslie 1938- .... **CLC 27**
See also AMWS 12; CA 73-76, 215; CAAE
215; CAAS 12; CANR 23, 69, 162; DLB
299; RGHL
Equiano, Olaudah 1745(?)-1797 ... **BLC 1:2;**
LC 16, 143
See also AFAW 1, 2; AMWS 17; CDWLB 3;
DAM MULT; DLB 37, 50; WLIT 2
Erasmus, Desiderius
1469(?)-1536 .... **LC 16, 93, 228, 231**
See also DLB 136; EW 2; LMFS 1; RGWL
2, 3; TWA
Ercilla y Zuniga, Don Alonso de
1533-1594 .... **LC 190; PC 161**
See also LAW
Erdman, Paul E. 1932-2007 .... **CLC 25**
See also AITN 1; CA 61-64; 259; CANR 13,
43, 84
Erdman, Paul Emil
See Erdman, Paul E.
Erdrich, Karen Louise
See Erdrich, Louise
Erdrich, Louise 1954- ...... **CLC 39, 54, 120,**
176, 327, 354; NNAL; PC 52; SSC 121
See also AAYA 10, 47; AMWS 4; BEST
89:1; BPFB 1; CA 114; CANR 41, 62,
118, 138, 190; CDALBS; CN 5, 6, 7; CP 6,
7; CPW; CWP; DA3; DAM MULT, NOV,
POP; DLB 152, 175, 206; EWL 3; EXPP;
FL 1:5; LAIT 5; LATS 1:2; MAL 5;
MTCW 1, 2; MTFW 2005; NFS 5, 37,
40; PFS 14, 43; RGAL 4; SATA 94, 141;
SSFS 14, 22, 30, 37; TCWW 2
Erenburg, Ilya
See Ehrenburg, Ilya
Erenburg, Ilya Grigoryevich
See Ehrenburg, Ilya
Erickson, Stephen Michael
See Erickson, Steve
Erickson, Steve 1950- .... **CLC 64**
See also CA 129; CANR 60, 68, 136, 195;
MTFW 2005; SFW 4; SUFW 2
Erickson, Walter
See Fast, Howard
Ericson, Walter
See Fast, Howard
Eriksson, Buntel
See Bergman, Ingmar
Eriugena, John Scottus
c. 810-877 .... **CMLC 65**
See also DLB 115
Ernaux, Annie 1940- .... **CLC 88, 184, 330**
See also CA 147; CANR 93, 208; MTFW
2005; NCFS 3, 5
Erskine, John 1879-1951 .... **TCLC 84**
See also CA 112; 159; DLB 9, 102; FANT
Erwin, Will
See Eisner, Will

Eschenbach, Wolfram von
See von Eschenbach, Wolfram

Eseki, Bruno
See Mphahlele, Es'kia

Esekie, Bruno
See Mphahlele, Es'kia

Esenin, S.A.
See Esenin, Sergei

Esenin, Sergei 1895-1925 .... **TCLC 4**
See also CA 104; EWL 3; RGWL 2, 3

Esenin, Sergei Aleksandrovich
See Esenin, Sergei

Eshleman, Clayton 1935- .... **CLC 7**
See also CA 33-36R, 212; CAAE 212; CAAS
6; CANR 93; CP 1, 2, 3, 4, 5, 6, 7; DLB 5

Espada, Martin 1957- .... **PC 74**
See also CA 159; CANR 80, 241; CP 7;
EXPP; LLW; MAL 5; PFS 13, 16, 43

Espriella, Don Manuel Alvarez
See Southey, Robert

Espriu, Salvador 1913-1985 .... **CLC 9**
See also CA 154; 115; DLB 134; EWL 3

Espronceda, Jose de 1808-1842 ... **NCLC 39,
276**

Esquivel, Laura
1950- .... **CLC 141, 351; HLCS 1**
See also AAYA 29; CA 143; CANR 68, 113,
161; DA3; DNFS 2; LAIT 3; LMFS 2;
MTCW 2; MTFW 2005; NFS 5; WLIT 1

Esse, James
See Stephens, James

Esterbrook, Tom
See Hubbard, L. Ron

Esterhazy, Peter 1950- .... **CLC 251**
See also CA 140; CANR 137, 223; CDWLB
4; CWW 2; DLB 232; EWL 3; RGWL 3

Estleman, Loren D. 1952- .... **CLC 48**
See also AAYA 27; CA 85-88; CANR 27, 74,
139, 177, 240; CMW 4; CPW; DA3;
DAM NOV, POP; DLB 226; INT CANR-
27; MTCW 1, 2; MTFW 2005; TCWW 1, 2

Etherege, Sir George
1636-1692 .... **DC 23; LC 78**
See also BRW 2; DAM DRAM; DLB 80;
PAB; RGEL 2

Euclid 306B.C.-283B.C. .... **CMLC 25, 172**

Eugenides, Jeffrey 1960- ... **CLC 81, 212, 312**
See also AAYA 51; CA 144; CANR 120,
237; DLB 350; MTFW 2005; NFS 24

Euripides c. 484B.C.-406B.C. ...... **CMLC 23,
51, 169, 174, 176; DC 4; WLCS**
See also AW 1; CDWLB 1; DA; DA3; DAB;
DAC; DAM DRAM, MST; DFS 1, 4, 6,
25, 27; DLB 176; LAIT 1; LMFS 1;
RGWL 2, 3; WLIT 8

Eusebius c. 263-c. 339 .... **CMLC 103**

Evan, Evin
See Faust, Frederick

Evans, Caradoc
1878-1945 .... **SSC 43; TCLC 85**
See also DLB 162

Evans, Evan
See Faust, Frederick

Evans, Marian
See Eliot, George

Evans, Mary Ann
See Eliot, George

Evaristo, Bernardine 1959- .... **CLC 355**
See also CA 212, 275; CP 7; DLB 347

Evarts, Esther
See Benson, Sally

Evelyn, John 1620-1706 .... **LC 144**
See also BRW 2; RGEL 2

Everett, Percival 1956- .... **CLC 57, 304**
See also AMWS 18; BW 2; CA 129; CANR
94, 134, 179, 219; CN 7; CSW; DLB 350;
MTFW 2005

Everett, Percival L.
See Everett, Percival

Everson, R(onald) G(ilmour)
1903-1992 .... **CLC 27**
See also CA 17-20R; CP 1, 2, 3, 4; DLB 88

Everson, William 1912-1994 .... **CLC 1, 5,
14; PC 169**
See also BG 1:2; CA 9-12R; 145; CANR 20;
CP 1; DLB 5, 16, 212; MTCW 1

Everson, William Oliver
See Everson, William

Evtushenko, Evgenii Aleksandrovich
See Yevtushenko, Yevgenyn

Ewart, Gavin (Buchanan)
1916-1995 .... **CLC 13, 46**
See also BRWS 7; CA 89-92; 150; CANR 17,
46; CP 1, 2, 3, 4, 5, 6; DLB 40; MTCW 1

Ewers, Hanns Heinz 1871-1943 .... **TCLC 12**
See also CA 109; 149

Ewing, Frederick R.
See Sturgeon, Theodore (Hamilton)

Exley, Frederick 1929-1992 .... **CLC 6, 11**
See also AITN 2; AMWS 23; BPFB 1; CA
81-84; 138; CANR 117; DLB 143; DLBY
1981

Eynhardt, Guillermo
See Quiroga, Horacio (Sylvestre)

Ezekiel, Nissim (Moses) 1924-2004 ... **CLC 61**
See also CA 61-64; 223; CP 1, 2, 3, 4, 5, 6,
7; DLB 323; EWL 3

Ezekiel, Tish O'Dowd 1943- .... **CLC 34**
See also CA 129

Fadeev, Aleksandr Aleksandrovich
See Bulgya, Alexander Alexandrovich

Fadeev, Alexandr Alexandrovich
See Bulgya, Alexander Alexandrovich

Fadeyev, A.
See Bulgya, Alexander Alexandrovich

Fadeyev, Alexander
See Bulgya, Alexander Alexandrovich

Fagen, Donald 1948- .... **CLC 26**

Fagunwa, D. O. 1903-1963 .... **TCLC 295**
See also CA 116

Fainzil'berg, Il'ia Arnol'dovich
See Fainzilberg, Ilya Arnoldovich

Fainzilberg, Ilya Arnoldovich
1897-1937 .... **TCLC 21**
See also CA 120; 165; DLB 272; EWL 3

Fair, Ronald L. 1932- .... **CLC 18**
See also BW 1; CA 69-72; CANR 25;
DLB 33

Fairbairn, Roger
See Carr, John Dickson

Fairbairns, Zoe (Ann) 1948- .... **CLC 32**
See also CA 103; CANR 21, 85; CN 4, 5, 6, 7

Fairfield, Flora
See Alcott, Louisa May

Falco, Gian
See Papini, Giovanni

Falconer, James
See Kirkup, James

Falconer, Kenneth
See Kornbluth, C(yril) M.

Falkland, Samuel
See Heijermans, Herman

Fallaci, Oriana 1930-2006 .... **CLC 11, 110**
See also CA 77-80; 253; CANR 15, 58, 134;
FW; MTCW 1

Faludi, Susan 1959- .... **CLC 140**
See also CA 138; CANR 126, 194; FW;
MTCW 2; MTFW 2005; NCFS 3

Faludy, George
See Faludy, Gyorgy

Faludy, Gyorgy 1913-2006 .... **CLC 42**
See also CA 21-24R; CANR 243

Fanon, Frantz 1925-1961 .... **BLC 1:2;
CLC 74; TCLC 188**

See also BW 1; CA 116; 89-92; DAM
MULT; DLB 296; LMFS 2; WLIT 2

Fanshawe, Ann 1625-1680 .... **LC 11**

Fante, John (Thomas)
1911-1983 .... **CLC 60; SSC 65**
See also AMWS 11; CA 69-72; 109; CANR 23,
104; DLB 130; DLBY 1983

Farah, Nuruddin 1945- .... **BLC 1:2, 2:2;
CLC 53, 137, 344**
See also AFW; BW 2, 3; CA 106; CANR 81,
148, 243; CDWLB 3; CN 4, 5, 6, 7; DAM
MULT; DLB 125; EWL 3; WLIT 2

Fardusi
See Ferdowsi, Abu'l Qasem

Fargue, Leon-Paul 1876(?)-1947 ... **TCLC 11**
See also CA 109; CANR 107; DLB 258;
EWL 3

Farigoule, Louis
See Romains, Jules

Farina, Richard 1936(?)-1966 .... **CLC 9**
See also CA 81-84; 25-28R

Farley, Walter (Lorimer)
1915-1989 .... **CLC 17**
See also AAYA 58; BYA 14; CA 17-20R;
CANR 8, 29, 84; DLB 22; JRDA; MAI-
CYA 1, 2; SATA 2, 43, 132; YAW

Farmer, Philipe Jos
See Farmer, Philip Jose

Farmer, Philip Jose 1918-2009 .... **CLC 1,
19, 299**
See also AAYA 28; BPFB 1; CA 1-4R; 283;
CANR 4, 35, 111, 220; CLR 201; DLB 8;
MTCW 1; SATA 93; SATA-Obit 201;
SCFW 1, 2; SFW 4

Farmer, Philip Jose
See Farmer, Philip Jose

Farquhar, George 1677-1707 .... **DC 38;
LC 21**
See also BRW 2; DAM DRAM; DLB 84;
RGEL 2

Farrell, James Gordon
See Farrell, J.G.

Farrell, James T(homas)
1904-1979 .... **CLC 1, 4, 8, 11, 66;
SSC 28; TCLC 228**
See also AMW; BPFB 1; CA 5-8R; 89-92;
CANR 9, 61; CN 1, 2; DLB 4, 9, 86;
DLBD 2; EWL 3; MAL 5; MTCW 1, 2;
MTFW 2005; RGAL 4

Farrell, J.G. 1935-1979 .... **CLC 6**
See also CA 73-76; 89-92; CANR 36; CN 1,
2; DLB 14, 271, 326; MTCW 1; RGEL 2;
RHW; WLIT 4

Farrell, M. J.
See Keane, Mary Nesta

Farrell, Warren (Thomas) 1943- .... **CLC 70**
See also CA 146; CANR 120

Farren, Richard J.
See Betjeman, John

Farren, Richard M.
See Betjeman, John

Farrugia, Mario Benedetti
See Bentley, Eric

**Farrugia, Mario Orlando Hardy Hamlet
Brenno Benedetti**
See Benedetti, Mario

Fassbinder, Rainer Werner
1946-1982 .... **CLC 20**
See also CA 93-96; 106; CANR 31

Fast, Howard 1914-2003 .... **CLC 23, 131**
See also AAYA 16; BPFB 1; CA 1-4R, 181;
214; CAAE 181; CAAS 18; CANR 1, 33,
54, 75, 98, 140; CMW 4; CN 1, 2, 3, 4, 5,
6, 7; CPW; DAM NOV; DLB 9; INT
CANR-33; LATS 1:1; MAL 5; MTCW 2;
MTFW 2005; NFS 35; RHW; SATA 7;
SATA-Essay 107; TCWW 1, 2; YAW

Faulcon, Robert
See Holdstock, Robert

Ford, Ford Madox 1873-1939 .... **TCLC 1, 15, 39, 57, 172, 308, 309**
See also BRW 6; CA 104; 132; CANR 74; CDBLB 1914-1945; DA3; DAM NOV; DLB 34, 98, 162; EWL 3; MTCW 1, 2; NFS 28; RGEL 2; RHW; TEA

Ford, Helen
See Garner, Helen

Ford, Henry 1863-1947 .... **TCLC 73**
See also CA 115; 148

Ford, Jack
See Ford, John

Ford, John 1586-1639 .... **DC 8; LC 68, 153**
See also BRW 2; CDBLB Before 1660; DA3; DAM DRAM; DFS 7; DLB 58; IDTP; RGEL 2

Ford, John 1895-1973 .... **CLC 16**
See also AAYA 75; CA 187; 45-48

Ford, Richard 1944- .... **CLC 46, 99, 205, 277; SSC 143**
See also AMWS 5; CA 69-72; CANR 11, 47, 86, 128, 164; CN 5, 6, 7; CSW; DLB 227; EWL 3; MAL 5; MTCW 2; MTFW 2005; NFS 25; RGAL 4; RGSF 2

Ford, Webster
See Masters, Edgar Lee

Foreman, Richard 1937- .... **CLC 50**
See also CA 65-68; CAD; CANR 32, 63, 143; CD 5, 6

Forester, C. S. 1899-1966 .... **CLC 35; TCLC 152**
See also CA 73-76; 25-28R; CANR 83; DLB 191; RGEL 2; RHW; SATA 13

Forester, Cecil Scott
See Forester, C. S.

Forez
See Mauriac, Francois (Charles)

Forman, James
See Forman, James D.

Forman, James D. 1932-2009 .... **CLC 21**
See also AAYA 17; CA 9-12R; CANR 4, 19, 42; JRDA; MAICYA 1, 2; SATA 8, 70; YAW

Forman, James Douglas
See Forman, James D.

Forman, Milos 1932- .... **CLC 164**
See also AAYA 63; CA 109

Fornes, Maria Irene 1930- .... **CLC 39, 61, 187; DC 10; HLCS 1**
See also CA 25-28R; CAD; CANR 28, 81; CD 5, 6; CWD; DFS 25; DLB 7, 341; HW 1, 2; INT CANR-28; LLW; MAL 5; MTCW 1; RGAL 4

Forrest, Leon (Richard) 1937-1997 .... **BLCS; CLC 4**
See also AFAW 2; BW 2; CA 89-92; 162; CAAS 7; CANR 25, 52, 87; CN 4, 5, 6; DLB 33

Forster, E. M. 1879-1970 .... **CLC 1, 2, 3, 4, 9, 10, 13, 15, 22, 45, 77; SSC 27, 96, 201; TCLC 125, 264; WLC 2**
See also AAYA 2, 37; BRW 6; BRWR 2; BYA 12; CA 13-14; 25-28R; CANR 45; CAP 1; CDBLB 1914-1945; DA; DA3; DAB; DAC; DAM MST, NOV; DLB 34, 98, 162, 178, 195; DLBD 10; EWL 3; EXPN; LAIT 3; LMFS 1; MTCW 1, 2; MTFW 2005; NCFS 1; NFS 3, 10, 11; RGEL 2; RGSF 2; SATA 57; SUFW 1; TEA; WLIT 4

Forster, Edward Morgan
See Forster, E. M.

Forster, John 1812-1876 .... **NCLC 11**
See also DLB 144, 184

Forster, Margaret 1938- .... **CLC 149**
See also CA 133; CANR 62, 115, 175; CN 4, 5, 6, 7; DLB 155, 271

Forsyth, Frederick 1938- .... **CLC 2, 5, 36**
See also BEST 89:4; CA 85-88; CANR 38, 62, 115, 137, 183, 242; CMW 4; CN 3, 4,

5, 6, 7; CPW; DAM NOV, POP; DLB 87; MTCW 1, 2; MTFW 2005

Fort, Paul
See Stockton, Francis Richard

Forten, Charlotte
See Grimke, Charlotte L. Forten

Forten, Charlotte L. 1837-1914
See Grimke, Charlotte L. Forten

Fortinbras
See Grieg, (Johan) Nordahl (Brun)

Foscolo, Ugo 1778-1827 ... **NCLC 8, 97, 274**
See also EW 5; WLIT 7

Fosse, Bob 1927-1987 .... **CLC 20**
See also AAYA 82; CA 110; 123

Fosse, Robert L.
See Fosse, Bob

Foster, Hannah Webster 1758-1840 .... **NCLC 99, 252**
See also DLB 37, 200; RGAL 4

Foster, Stephen Collins 1826-1864 .. **NCLC 26**
See also RGAL 4

Foucault, Michel 1926-1984 .... **CLC 31, 34, 69**
See also CA 105; 113; CANR 34; DLB 242; EW 13; EWL 3; GFL 1789 to the Present; GLL 1; LMFS 2; MTCW 1, 2; TWA

Fountain, Ben 1958- .... **CLC 354**
See also CA 254; CANR 254

Fouqué, Caroline de la Motte 1774-1831 .... **NCLC 307**
See also DLB 90; RGWL 2, 3

Fouque, Friedrich (Heinrich Karl) de la Motte 1777-1843 .... **NCLC 2**
See also DLB 90; RGWL 2, 3; SUFW 1

Fourier, Charles 1772-1837 .... **NCLC 51**

Fournier, Henri-Alban
See Alain-Fournier

Fournier, Pierre 1916-1997 .... **CLC 11**
See also CA 89-92; CANR 16, 40; EWL 3; RGHL

Fowles, John 1926-2005 .... **CLC 1, 2, 3, 4, 6, 9, 10, 15, 33, 87, 287; SSC 33, 128**
See also BPFB 1; BRWS 1; CA 5-8R; 245; CANR 25, 71, 103; CDBLB 1960 to Present; CN 1, 2, 3, 4, 5, 6, 7; DA3; DAB; DAC; DAM MST; DLB 14, 139, 207; EWL 3; HGG; MTCW 1, 2; MTFW 2005; NFS 21; RGEL 2; RHW; SATA 22; SATA-Obit 171; TEA; WLIT 4

Fowles, John Robert
See Fowles, John

Fox, Norma Diane
See Mazer, Norma Fox

Fox, Paula 1923- .... **CLC 2, 8, 121**
See also AAYA 3, 37; BYA 3, 8; CA 73-76; CANR 20, 36, 62, 105, 200, 237; CLR 1, 44, 96; DLB 52; JRDA; MAICYA 1, 2; MTCW 1; NFS 12; SATA 17, 60, 120, 167; WYA; YAW

Fox, William Price, Jr.
See Fox, William Price

Fox, William Price 1926- .... **CLC 22**
See also CA 17-20R; CAAS 19; CANR 11, 142, 189; CSW; DLB 2; DLBY 1981

Foxe, John 1517(?)-1587 .... **LC 14, 166**
See also DLB 132

Frame, Janet 1924-2004 .... **CLC 2, 3, 6, 22, 66, 96, 237; SSC 29, 127**
See also CA 1-4R; 224; CANR 2, 36, 76, 135, 216; CN 1, 2, 3, 4, 5, 6, 7; CP 2, 3, 4; CWP; EWL 3; MTCW 1,2; RGEL 2; RGSF 2; SATA 119; TWA

Frame, Janet Paterson
See Frame, Janet

France, Anatole 1844-1924 .... **TCLC 9**
See also CA 106; 127; DA3; DAM NOV; DLB 123, 330; EWL 3; GFL 1789 to the

Present; MTCW 1, 2; RGWL 2, 3; SUFW 1; TWA

Francis, Claude .... **CLC 50**
See also CA 192

Francis, Dick 1920-2010 .... **CLC 2, 22, 42, 102**
See also AAYA 5, 21; BEST 89:3; BPFB 1; CA 5-8R; CANR 9, 42, 68, 100, 141, 179; CDBLB 1960 to Present; CMW 4; CN 2, 3, 4, 5, 6; DA3; DAM POP; DLB 87; INT CANR-9; MSW; MTCW 1, 2; MTFW 2005

Francis, Paula Marie
See Allen, Paula Gunn

Francis, Richard Stanley
See Francis, Dick

Francis, Robert (Churchill) 1901-1987 .... **CLC 15; PC 34**
See also AMWS 9; CA 1-4R; 123; CANR 1; CP 1, 2, 3, 4; EXPP; PFS 12; TCLE 1:1

Francis, Lord Jeffrey
See Jeffrey, Francis

Franco, Veronica 1546-1591 .... **LC 171**
See also WLIT 7

Frank, Anne 1929-1945 .... **TCLC 17; WLC 2**
See also AAYA 12; BYA 1; CA 113; 133; CANR 68; CLR 101, 189; DA; DA3; DAB; DAC; DAM MST; LAIT 4; MAICYA 2; MAICYAS 1; MTCW 1, 2; MTFW 2005; NCFS 2; RGHL; SATA 87; SATA-Brief 42; WYA; YAW

Frank, Annelies Marie
See Frank, Anne

Frank, Bruno 1887-1945 .... **TCLC 81**
See also CA 189; DLB 118; EWL 3

Frank, Elizabeth 1945- .... **CLC 39**
See also CA 121; 126; CANR 78, 150; INT CA-126

Frankl, Viktor E(mil) 1905-1997 .... **CLC 93**
See also CA 65-68; 161; RGHL

Franklin, Benjamin
See Hasek, Jaroslav

Franklin, Benjamin 1706-1790 .... **LC 25, 134; WLCS**
See also AMW; CDALB 1640-1865; DA; DA3; DAB; DAC; DAM MST; DLB 24, 43, 73, 183; LAIT 1; RGAL 4; TUS

Franklin, Madeleine
See L'Engle, Madeleine

Franklin, Madeleine L'Engle
See L'Engle, Madeleine

Franklin, Madeleine L'Engle Camp
See L'Engle, Madeleine

Franklin, (Stella Maria Sarah) Miles (Lampe) 1879-1954 .... **TCLC 7**
See also CA 104; 164; DLB 230; FW; MTCW 2; RGEL 2; TWA

Franzen, Jonathan 1959- .... **CLC 202, 309**
See also AAYA 65; AMWS 20; CA 129; CANR 105, 166, 219; NFS 40;

Fraser, Antonia 1932- .... **CLC 32, 107**
See also AAYA 57; CA 85-88; CANR 44, 65, 119, 164, 225; CMW; DLB 276; MTCW 1, 2; MTFW 2005; SATA-Brief 32

Fraser, George MacDonald 1925-2008 .... **CLC 7**
See also AAYA 48; CA 45-48; 180; 268; CAAE 180; CANR 2, 48, 74, 192; DLB 352; MTCW 2; RHW

Fraser, Sylvia 1935- .... **CLC 64**
See also CA 45-48; CANR 1, 16, 60; CCA 1

Frater Perdurabo
See Crowley, Edward Alexander

Frayn, Michael 1933- .... **CLC 3, 7, 31, 47, 176, 315; DC 27**
See also AAYA 69; BRWC 2; BRWS 7; CA 5-8R; CANR 30, 69, 114, 133, 166, 229; CBD; CD 5, 6; CN 1, 2, 3, 4, 5, 6, 7; DAM

DRAM, NOV; DFS 22, 28; DLB 13, 14, 194, 245; FANT; MTCW 1, 2; MTFW 2005; SFW 4

Fraze, Candida 1945- .... **CLC 50**
See also CA 126

Fraze, Candida Merrill
See Fraze, Candida

Frazer, Andrew
See Marlowe, Stephen

Frazer, J(ames) G(eorge)
1854-1941 .... **TCLC 32**
See also BRWS 3; CA 118; NCFS 5

Frazer, Robert Caine
See Creasey, John

Frazer, Sir James George
See Frazer, J(ames) G(eorge)

Frazier, Charles 1950- .... **CLC 109, 224**
See also AAYA 34; CA 161; CANR 126, 170, 235; CSW; DLB 292; MTFW 2005; NFS 25

Frazier, Charles R.
See Frazier, Charles

Frazier, Charles Robinson
See Frazier, Charles

Frazier, Ian 1951- .... **CLC 46**
See also CA 130; CANR 54, 93, 193, 227

Frederic, Harold
1856-1898 .... **NCLC 10, 175**
See also AMW; DLB 12, 23; DLBD 13; MAL 5; NFS 22; RGAL 4

Frederick, John
See Faust, Frederick

Frederick the Great 1712-1786 .... **LC 14**

Fredro, Aleksander 1793-1876 .... **NCLC 8**

Freeling, Nicolas 1927-2003 .... **CLC 38**
See also CA 49-52; 218; CAAS 12; CANR 1, 17, 50, 84; CMW 4; CN 1, 2, 3, 4, 5, 6; DLB 87

Freeman, Douglas Southall
1886-1953 .... **TCLC 11**
See also CA 109; 195; DLB 17; DLBD 17

Freeman, Judith 1946- .... **CLC 55**
See also CA 148; CANR 120, 179; DLB 256

Freeman, Mary E(leanor) Wilkins
1852-1930 ..... **SSC 1, 47, 113; TCLC 9**
See also CA 106; 177; DLB 12, 78, 221; EXPS; FW; HGG; MBL; RGAL 4; RGSF 2; SSFS 4, 8, 26; SUFW 1; TUS

Freeman, R(ichard) Austin
1862-1943 .... **TCLC 21**
See also CA 113; CANR 84; CMW 4; DLB 70

French, Albert 1943- .... **CLC 86**
See also BW 3; CA 167

French, Antonia
See Kureishi, Hanif

French, Marilyn 1929-2009 ...... **CLC 10, 18, 60, 177**
See also BPFB 1; CA 69-72; 286; CANR 3, 31, 134, 163, 220; CN 5, 6, 7; CPW; DAM DRAM, NOV, POP; FL 1:5; FW; INT CANR-31; MTCW 1, 2; MTFW 2005

French, Paul
See Asimov, Isaac

Freneau, Philip Morin
1752-1832 .... **NCLC 1, 111, 253**
See also AMWS 2; DLB 37, 43; RGAL 4

Freud, Sigmund 1856-1939 .... **TCLC 52**
See also CA 115; 133; CANR 69; DLB 296; EW 8; EWL 3; LATS 1:1; MTCW 1, 2; MTFW 2005; NCFS 3; TWA

Freytag, Gustav 1816-1895 .... **NCLC 109**
See also DLB 129

Friedan, Betty 1921-2006 .... **CLC 74**
See also CA 65-68; 248; CANR 18, 45, 74; DLB 246; FW; MTCW 1, 2; MTFW 2005; NCFS 5

Friedan, Betty Naomi
See Friedan, Betty

Friedlander, Saul
See Friedlander, Saul

Friedlander, Saul 1932- .... **CLC 90**
See also CA 117; 130; CANR 72, 214; RGHL

Friedman, Bernard Harper
See Friedman, B.H.

Friedman, B.H. 1926-2011 .... **CLC 7**
See also CA 1-4R; CANR 3, 48

Friedman, Bruce Jay 1930- ... **CLC 3, 5, 56**
See also CA 9-12R; CAD; CANR 25, 52, 101, 212; CD 5, 6; CN 1, 2, 3, 4, 5, 6, 7; DLB 2, 28, 244; INT CANR-25; MAL 5; SSFS 18

Friel, Brian 1929- .... **CLC 5, 42, 59, 115, 253; DC 8, 49; SSC 76**
See also BRWS 5; CA 21-24R; CANR 33, 69, 131; CBD; CD 5, 6; DFS 11; DLB 13, 319; EWL 3; MTCW 1; RGEL 2; TEA

Friis-Baastad, Babbis Ellinor
1921-1970 .... **CLC 12**
See also CA 17-20R; 134; SATA 7

Frisch, Max 1911-1991 .... **CLC 3, 9, 14, 18, 32, 44; TCLC 121**
See also CA 85-88; 134; CANR 32, 74; CDWLB 2; DAM DRAM, NOV; DFS 25; DLB 69, 124; EW 13; EWL 3; MTCW 1, 2; MTFW 2005; RGHL; RGWL 2, 3

Frischmuth, Barbara 1941- .... **CLC 372**
See also CA 178; DLB 85; SATA 114

Froehlich, Peter
See Gay, Peter

Fromentin, Eugene (Samuel Auguste)
1820-1876 .... **NCLC 10, 125**
See also DLB 123, 366; GFL 1789 to the Present

Frost, Frederick
See Faust, Frederick

Frost, Robert 1874-1963 ...... **CLC 1, 3, 4, 9, 10, 13, 15, 26, 34, 44; PC 1, 39, 71; TCLC 236; WLC 2**
See also AAYA 21; AMW; AMWR 1; CA 89-92; CANR 33; CDALB 1917-1929; CLR 67; DA; DA3; DAB; DAC; DAM MST, POET; DLB 54, 284, 342; DLBD 7; EWL 3; EXPP; MAL 5; MTCW 1, 2; MTFW 2005; PAB; PFS 1, 2, 3, 4, 5, 6, 7, 10, 13, 32, 35, 41; RGAL 4; SATA 14; TUS; WP; WYA

Frost, Robert Lee
See Frost, Robert

Froude, James Anthony
1818-1894 .... **NCLC 43, 311**
See also DLB 18, 57, 144

Froy, Herald
See Waterhouse, Keith

Fry, Christopher 1907-2005 .... **CLC 2, 10, 14; DC 36**
See also BRWS 3; CA 17-20R; 240; CAAS 23; CANR 9, 30, 74, 132; CBD; CD 5, 6; CP 1, 2, 3, 4, 5, 6, 7; DAM DRAM; DLB 13; EWL 3; MTCW 1, 2; MTFW 2005; RGEL 2; SATA 66; TEA

Frye, (Herman) Northrop
1912-1991 ...... **CLC 24, 70; TCLC 165**
See also CA 5-8R; 133; CANR 8, 37; DLB 67, 68, 246; EWL 3; MTCW 1, 2; MTFW 2005; RGAL 4; TWA

Fuchs, Daniel 1909-1993 .... **CLC 8, 22**
See also CA 81-84; 142; CAAS 5; CANR 40; CN 1, 2, 3, 4, 5; DLB 9, 26, 28; DLBY 1993; MAL 5

Fuchs, Daniel 1934-2012 .... **CLC 34**
See also CA 37-40R; CANR 14, 48

Fuentes, Carlos 1928- ...... **CLC 3, 8, 10, 13, 22, 41, 60, 113, 288, 354; HLC 1; SSC 24, 125; WLC 2**
See also AAYA 4, 45; AITN 2; BPFB 1; CA 69-72; CANR 10, 32, 68, 104, 138, 197; CDWLB 3; CWW 2; DA; DA3; DAB; DAC; DAM MST, MULT, NOV; DLB 113; DNFS 2; EWL 3; HW 1, 2; LAIT 3; LATS 1:2; LAW; LAWS 1; LMFS 2;

MTCW 1, 2; MTFW 2005; NFS 8; RGSF 2; RGWL 2, 3; TWA; WLIT 1

Fuentes, Gregorio Lopez y
See Lopez y Fuentes, Gregorio

Fuentes Macias, Carlos Manuel
See Fuentes, Carlos

Fuertes, Gloria
1918-1998 .... **PC 27; TCLC 271**
See also CA 178; 180; DLB 108; HW 2; SATA 115

Fugard, Athol 1932- .... **CLC 5, 9, 14, 25, 40, 80, 211; DC 3**
See also AAYA 17; AFW; BRWS 15; CA 85-88; CANR 32, 54, 118; CD 5, 6; DAM DRAM; DFS 3, 6, 10, 24; DLB 225; DNFS 1, 2; EWL 3; LATS 1:2; MTCW 1; MTFW 2005; RGEL 2; WLIT 2

Fugard, Harold Athol
See Fugard, Athol

Fugard, Sheila 1932- .... **CLC 48**
See also CA 125

Fuguet, Alberto 1964- .... **CLC 308**
See also CA 170; CANR 144

Fujiwara no Teika 1162-1241 ...... **CMLC 73**
See also DLB 203

Fukuyama, Francis 1952- ...... **CLC 131, 320**
See also CA 140; CANR 72, 125, 170, 233

Fuller, Charles (H.), (Jr.) 1939- .... **BLC 1:2; CLC 25; DC 1**
See also BW 2; CA 108; 112; CAD; CANR 87; CD 5, 6; DAM DRAM, MULT; DFS 8; DLB 38, 266; EWL 3; INT CA-112; MAL 5; MTCW 1

Fuller, Henry Blake 1857-1929 ... **TCLC 103**
See also CA 108; 177; DLB 12; RGAL 4

Fuller, John (Leopold) 1937- .... **CLC 62**
See also CA 21-24R; CANR 9, 44; CP 1, 2, 3, 4, 5, 6, 7; DLB 40

Fuller, Margaret
1810-1850 .... **NCLC 5, 50, 211**
See also AMWS 2; CDALB 1640-1865; DLB 1, 59, 73, 183, 223, 239; FW; LMFS 1; SATA 25

Fuller, Roy (Broadbent)
1912-1991 .... **CLC 4, 28**
See also BRWS 7; CA 5-8R; 135; CAAS 10; CANR 53, 83; CN 1, 2, 3, 4, 5; CP 1, 2, 3, 4, 5; CWRI 5; DLB 15, 20; EWL 3; RGEL 2; SATA 87

Fuller, Sarah Margaret
See Fuller, Margaret

Fuller, Thomas 1608-1661 .... **LC 111**
See also DLB 151

Fulton, Alice 1952- .... **CLC 52**
See also CA 116; CANR 57, 88, 200; CP 5, 6, 7; CWP; DLB 193; PFS 25

Fundi
See Baraka, Amiri

Furey, Michael
See Ward, Arthur Henry Sarsfield

Furphy, Joseph 1843-1912 .... **TCLC 25**
See also CA 163; DLB 230; EWL 3; RGEL 2

Furst, Alan 1941- .... **CLC 255**
See also CA 69-72; CANR 12, 34, 59, 102, 159, 193; DLB 350; DLBY 01

Fuson, Robert H(enderson) 1927- ... **CLC 70**
See also CA 89-92; CANR 103

Fussell, Paul 1924- .... **CLC 74**
See also BEST 90:1; CA 17-20R; CANR 8, 21, 35, 69, 135; INT CANR-21; MTCW 1, 2; MTFW 2005

Futabatei, Shimei 1864-1909 .... **TCLC 44**
See also CA 162; DLB 180; EWL 3; MJW

Futabatei Shimei
See Futabatei, Shimei

Futrelle, Jacques 1875-1912 .... **TCLC 19**
See also CA 113; 155; CMW 4

GAB
See Russell, George William

Gaberman, Judie Angell
See Angell, Judie

Gaboriau, Emile 1835-1873 .... **NCLC 14**
See also CMW 4; MSW

Gadamer, Hans-Georg
1900-2002 .... **CLC 376**
See also CA 85-88, 206; DLB 296

Gadda, Carlo Emilio 1893-1973 .... **CLC 11;**
TCLC 144
See also CA 89-92; DLB 177; EWL 3;
WLIT 7

Gaddis, William 1922-1998 ..... **CLC 1, 3, 6,**
8, 10, 19, 43, 86
See also AMWS 4; BPFB 1; CA 17-20R;
172; CANR 21, 48, 148; CN 1, 2, 3, 4, 5,
6; DLB 2, 278; EWL 3; MAL 5; MTCW 1,
2; MTFW 2005; RGAL 4

Gage, Walter
See Inge, William (Motter)

Gaiman, Neil 1960- .... **CLC 319**
See also AAYA 19, 42, 82; CA 133; CANR
81, 129, 188; CLR 109, 177; DLB 261;
HGG; MTFW 2005; SATA 85, 146, 197,
228; SFW 4; SUFW 2

Gaiman, Neil Richard
See Gaiman, Neil

Gaines, Ernest J. 1933- .... **BLC 1:2;**
CLC 3, 11, 18, 86, 181, 300; SSC 68, 137
See also AAYA 18; AFAW 1, 2; AITN 1;
BPFB 2; BW 2, 3; BYA 6; CA 9-12R;
CANR 6, 24, 42, 75, 126; CDALB 1968-
1988; CLR 62; CN 1, 2, 3, 4, 5, 6, 7; CSW;
DA3; DAM MULT; DLB 2, 33, 152;
DLBY 1980; EWL 3; EXPN; LAIT 5;
LATS 1:2; MAL 5; MTCW 1, 2; MTFW
2005; NFS 5, 7, 16; RGAL 4; RGSF 2;
RHW; SATA 86; SSFS 5; YAW

Gaines, Ernest James
See Gaines, Ernest J.

Gaitskill, Mary 1954- .... **CLC 69, 300;**
SSC 213
See also CA 128; CANR 61, 152, 208; DLB
244; TCLE 1:1

Gaitskill, Mary Lawrence
See Gaitskill, Mary

Gaius Suetonius Tranquillus
See Suetonius

Galdos, Benito Perez
See Perez Galdos, Benito

Gale, Zona 1874-1938 ...... **DC 30; SSC 159;**
TCLC 7
See also CA 105; 153; CANR 84; DAM
DRAM; DFS 17; DLB 9, 78, 228; RGAL 4

Galeano, Eduardo 1940- .... **CLC 72;**
HLCS 1
See also CA 29-32R; CANR 13, 32, 100,
163, 211; HW 1

Galeano, Eduardo Hughes
See Galeano, Eduardo

Galiano, Juan Valera y Alcala
See Valera y Alcala-Galiano, Juan

Galilei, Galileo 1564-1642 .... **LC 45, 188**

Gallagher, Tess 1943- ..... **CLC 18, 63; PC 9**
See also CA 106; CP 3, 4, 5, 6, 7; CWP;
DAM POET; DLB 120, 212, 244; PFS 16

Gallant, Mavis 1922- .... **CLC 7, 18, 38,**
172, 288; SSC 5, 78
See also CA 69-72; CANR 29, 69, 117;
CCA 1; CN 1, 2, 3, 4, 5, 6, 7; DAC; DAM
MST; DLB 53; EWL 3; MTCW 1, 2;
MTFW 2005; RGEL 2; RGSF 2

Gallant, Roy A(rthur) 1924- .... **CLC 17**
See also CA 5-8R; CANR 4, 29, 54, 117;
CLR 30; MAICYA 1, 2; SATA 4, 68, 110

Gallico, Paul 1897-1976 .... **CLC 2**
See also AITN 1; CA 5-8R; 69-72; CANR
23; CN 1, 2; DLB 9, 171; FANT; MAICYA
1, 2; SATA 13

Gallico, Paul William
See Gallico, Paul

Gallo, Max Louis 1932- .... **CLC 95**
See also CA 85-88

Gallois, Lucien
See Desnos, Robert

Gallup, Ralph
See Whitemore, Hugh (John)

Galsworthy, John 1867-1933 .... **SSC 22;**
TCLC 1, 45; WLC 2
See also BRW 6; CA 104; 141; CANR 75;
CDBLB 1890-1914; DA; DA3; DAB;
DAC; DAM DRAM, MST, NOV; DLB
10, 34, 98, 162, 330; DLBD 16; EWL
3; MTCW 2; RGEL 2; SSFS 3; TEA

Galt, John 1779-1839 ..... **NCLC 1, 110, 296**
See also DLB 99, 116, 159; RGEL 2; RGSF 2

Galvin, James 1951- .... **CLC 38**
See also CA 108; CANR 26

Gambaro, Griselda 1928- .... **CLC 380**
See also CA 131; CWW 2; DLB 305; EWL
3; HW 1; LAW

Gamboa, Federico 1864-1939 .... **TCLC 36**
See also CA 167; HW 2; LAW

Gandhi, M. K.
See Gandhi, Mohandas Karamchand

Gandhi, Mahatma
See Gandhi, Mohandas Karamchand

Gandhi, Mohandas Karamchand
1869-1948 .... **TCLC 59**
See also CA 121; 132; DA3; DAM MULT;
DLB 323; MTCW 1, 2

Gann, Ernest Kellogg 1910-1991 .... **CLC 23**
See also AITN 1; BPFB 2; CA 1-4R; 136;
CANR 1, 83; RHW

Gao Xingjian
See Xingjian, Gao

Garber, Eric
See Holleran, Andrew

Garber, Esther
See Lee, Tanith

Garcia Lorca, Federico 1898-1936 ..... **DC 2;**
HLC 2; PC 3, 130; TCLC 1, 7, 49, 181,
197; WLC 2
See also AAYA 46; CA 104; 131; CANR 81;
DA; DA3; DAB; DAC; DAM DRAM,
MST, MULT, POET; DFS 4; DLB 108;
EW 11; EWL 3; HW 1, 2; LATS 1:2;
MTCW 1, 2; MTFW 2005; PFS 20, 31,
38; RGWL 2, 3; TWA; WP

García Márquez, Gabriel
1927/28-2014 .... **CLC 2, 3, 8, 10,**
15, 27, 47, 55, 68, 170, 254, 389; HLC 1;
SSC 8, 83, 162, 217; WLC 3
See also AAYA 3, 33; BEST 89:1, 90:4;
BPFB 2; BYA 12, 16; CA 33-36R; CANR
10, 28, 50, 75, 82, 128, 204; CDWLB 3;
CPW; CWW 2; DA; DA3; DAB; DAC;
DAM MST, MULT, NOV, POP; DLB 113,
330; DNFS 1, 2; EWL 3; EXPN; EXPS;
HW 1, 2; LAIT 2; LATS 1:2; LAW; LAWS
1; LMFS 2; MTCW 1, 2; MTFW 2005;
NCFS 3; NFS 1, 5, 10; RGSF 2; RGWL 2,
3; SSFS 1, 6, 16, 21, 37; TWA; WLIT 1

García Márquez, Gabriel Jose
See Garcia Marquez, Gabriel

Garcia, Cristina 1958- .... **CLC 76**
See also AMWS 11; CA 141; CANR 73,
130, 172, 243; CN 7; DLB 292; DNFS 1;
EWL 3; HW 2; LLW; MTFW 2005; NFS
38; SATA 208

Garcilaso de la Vega, El Inca
1539-1616 .... **HLCS 1; LC 127**
See also DLB 318; LAW

Gard, Janice
See Latham, Jean Lee

Gard, Roger Martin du
See Martin du Gard, Roger

Gardam, Jane 1928- .... **CLC 43**
See also CA 49-52; CANR 2, 18, 33, 54,
106, 167, 206; CLR 12; DLB 14, 161, 231;
MAICYA 1, 2; MTCW 1; SAAS 9; SATA
39, 76, 130; SATA-Brief 28; YAW

Gardam, Jane Mary
See Gardam, Jane

Gardens, S. S.
See Snodgrass, W. D.

Gardner, Herb(ert George)
1934-2003 .... **CLC 44**
See also CA 149; 220; CAD; CANR 119;
CD 5, 6; DFS 18, 20

Gardner, John, Jr. 1933-1982 ...... **CLC 2, 3,**
5, 7, 8, 10, 18, 28, 34; SSC 7; TCLC 195
See also AAYA 45; AITN 1; AMWS 6;
BPFB 2; CA 65-68; 107; CANR 33, 73;
CDALBS; CN 2, 3; CPW; DA3; DAM
NOV, POP; DLB 2; DLBY 1982; EWL
3; FANT; LATS 1:2; MAL 5; MTCW 1, 2;
MTFW 2005; NFS 3; RGAL 4; RGSF 2;
SATA 40; SATA-Obit 31; SSFS 8

Gardner, John 1926-2007 .... **CLC 30**
See also CA 103; 263; CANR 15, 69, 127,
183; CMW 4; CPW; DAM POP; MTCW 1

Gardner, John Champlin, Jr.
See Gardner, John, Jr.

Gardner, John Edmund
See Gardner, John

Gardner, Miriam
See Bradley, Marion Zimmer

Gardner, Noel
See Kuttner, Henry

Gardons, S.S.
See Snodgrass, W. D.

Garfield, Leon 1921-1996 .... **CLC 12**
See also AAYA 8, 69; BYA 1, 3; CA 17-
20R; 152; CANR 38, 41, 78; CLR 21, 166;
DLB 161; JRDA; MAICYA 1, 2; MAI-
CYAS 1; SATA 1, 32, 76; SATA-Obit 90;
TEA; WYA; YAW

Garland, (Hannibal) Hamlin
1860-1940 ... **SSC 18, 117; TCLC 3, 256**
See also CA 104; DLB 12, 71, 78, 186;
MAL 5; RGAL 4; RGSF 2; TCWW 1, 2

Garneau, (Hector de) Saint-Denys
1912-1943 .... **TCLC 13**
See also CA 111; DLB 88

Garner, Alan 1934- .... **CLC 17**
See also AAYA 18; BYA 3, 5; CA 73-76,
178; CAAE 178; CANR 15, 64, 134; CLR
20, 130; CPW; DAB; DAM POP; DLB
161, 261; FANT; MAICYA 1, 2; MTCW 1,
2; MTFW 2005; SATA 18, 69; SATA-
Essay 108; SUFW 1, 2; YAW

Garner, Helen 1942- .... **SSC 135**
See also CA 124; 127; CANR 71, 206; CN
4, 5, 6, 7; DLB 325; GLL 2; RGSF 2

Garner, Hugh 1913-1979 .... **CLC 13**
See also CA 69-72; CANR 31; CCA 1; CN
1, 2; DLB 68

Garnett, David 1892-1981 .... **CLC 3**
See also CA 5-8R; 103; CANR 17, 79; CN
1, 2; DLB 34; FANT; MTCW 2; RGEL 2;
SFW 4; SUFW 1

Garnier, Robert c. 1545-1590 .... **LC 119**
See also DLB 327; GFL Beginnings to 1789

Garrett, Almeida 1799-1854 .... **NCLC 316**
See also DLB 287

Garrett, George 1929-2008 .... **CLC 3, 11,**
51; SSC 30
See also AMWS 7; BPFB 2; CA 1-4R; 202;
272; CAAE 202; CAAS 5; CANR 1, 42,
67, 109, 199; CN 1, 2, 3, 4, 5, 6, 7; CP 1,
2, 3, 4, 5, 6, 7; CSW; DLB 2, 5, 130, 152;
DLBY 1983

Garrett, George P.
See Garrett, George

See also AAYA 12, 59; AMWS 16; BPFB 2; CA 126; 133; CANR 52, 90, 106, 172, 229; CN 6, 7; CPW; DA3; DAM POP; DLB 251; MTCW 2; MTFW 2005; NFS 38; SCFW 2; SFW 4; SSFS 26

Gibson, William Ford
See Gibson, William

Gide, Andre 1869-1951 .... **SSC 13; TCLC 5, 12, 36, 177; WLC 3**
See also CA 104; 124; DA; DA3; DAB; DAC; DAM MST, NOV; DLB 65, 321, 330; EW 8; EWL 3; GFL 1789 to the Present; MTCW 1, 2; MTFW 2005; NFS 21; RGSF 2; RGWL 2, 3; TWA

Gide, Andre Paul Guillaume
See Gide, Andre

Gifford, Barry 1946- .... **CLC 34**
See also CA 65-68; CANR 9, 30, 40, 90, 180

Gifford, Barry Colby
See Gifford, Barry

Gilbert, Frank
See De Voto, Bernard (Augustine)

Gilbert, W(illiam) S(chwenck)
1836-1911 .... **TCLC 3**
See also CA 104; 173; DAM DRAM, POET; DLB 344; RGEL 2; SATA 36

Gilbert of Poitiers c. 1085-1154 ... **CMLC 85**

Gilbreth, Frank B., Jr. 1911-2001 ... **CLC 17**
See also CA 9-12R; SATA 2

Gilbreth, Frank Bunker
See Gilbreth, Frank B., Jr.

Gilchrist, Ellen 1935- .... **CLC 34, 48, 143, 264; SSC 14, 63**
See also BPFB 2; CA 113; 116; CANR 41, 61, 104, 191; CN 4, 5, 6, 7; CPW; CSW; DAM POP; DLB 130; EWL 3; EXPS; MTCW 1, 2; MTFW 2005; RGAL 4; RGSF 2; SSFS 9

Gilchrist, Ellen Louise
See Gilchrist, Ellen

Gildas fl. 6th cent. .... **CMLC 99**

Giles, Molly 1942- .... **CLC 39**
See also CA 126; CANR 98

Gill, Arthur Eric Rowton Peter Joseph
See Gill, Eric

Gill, Eric 1882-1940 .... **TCLC 85**
See Gill, Arthur Eric Rowton Peter Joseph
See also CA 120; DLB 98

Gill, Patrick
See Creasey, John

Gillette, Douglas .... **CLC 70**

Gilliam, Terry 1940- .... **CLC 21, 141**
See also AAYA 19, 59; CA 108; 113; CANR 35; INT CA-113

Gilliam, Terry Vance
See Gilliam, Terry

Gillian, Jerry
See Gilliam, Terry

Gilliatt, Penelope (Ann Douglass)
1932-1993 .... **CLC 2, 10, 13, 53**
See also AITN 2; CA 13-16R; 141; CANR 49; CN 1, 2, 3, 4, 5; DLB 14

Gilligan, Carol 1936- .... **CLC 208**
See also CA 142; CANR 121, 187; FW

Gilman, Caroline 1794-1888 .... **NCLC 302**
See also DLB 3, 73

Gilman, Charlotte Anna Perkins Stetson
See Gilman, Charlotte Perkins

Gilman, Charlotte Perkins
1860-1935 .. **SSC 13, 62, 182; TCLC 9, 37, 117, 201**
See also AAYA 75; AMWS 11; BYA 11; CA 106; 150; DLB 221; EXPS; FL 1:5; FW; HGG; LAIT 2; MBL; MTCW 2; MTFW 2005; NFS 36; RGAL 4; RGSF 2; SFW 4; SSFS 1, 18

Gilmore, Mary (Jean Cameron)
1865-1962 .... **PC 87**

See also CA 114; DLB 260; RGEL 2; SATA 49

Gilmour, David 1946- .... **CLC 35**

Gilpin, William 1724-1804 .... **NCLC 30**

Gilray, J. D.
See Mencken, H. L.

Gilroy, Frank D(aniel) 1925- .... **CLC 2**
See also CA 81-84; CAD; CANR 32, 64, 86; CD 5, 6; DFS 17; DLB 7

Gilstrap, John 1957(?)- .... **CLC 99**
See also AAYA 67; CA 160; CANR 101, 229

Ginsberg, Allen 1926-1997 ..... **CLC 1, 2, 3, 4, 6, 13, 36, 69, 109; PC 4, 47; TCLC 120; WLC 3**
See also AAYA 33; AITN 1; AMWC 1; AMWS 2; BG 1:2; CA 1-4R; 157; CANR 2, 41, 63, 95; CDALB 1941-1968; CP 1, 2, 3, 4, 5, 6; DA; DA3; DAB; DAC; DAM MST, POET; DLB 5, 16, 169, 237; EWL 3; GLL 1; LMFS 2; MAL 5; MTCW 1, 2; MTFW 2005; PAB; PFS 29; RGAL 4; TUS; WP

Ginzburg, Eugenia
See Ginzburg, Evgeniia

Ginzburg, Evgeniia 1904-1977 .... **CLC 59**
See also DLB 302

Ginzburg, Natalia 1916-1991 .... **CLC 5, 11, 54, 70; SSC 65; TCLC 156**
See also CA 85-88; 135; CANR 33; DFS 14; DLB 177; EW 13; EWL 3; MTCW 1, 2; MTFW 2005; RGHL; RGWL 2, 3

Gioia, (Michael) Dana
1950- .... **CLC 251**
See also AMWS 15; CA 130; CANR 70, 88; CP 6, 7; DLB 120, 282; PFS 24

Giono, Jean 1895-1970 .... **CLC 4, 11; TCLC 124**
See also CA 45-48; 29-32R; CANR 2, 35; DLB 72, 321; EWL 3; GFL 1789 to the Present; MTCW 1; RGWL 2, 3

Giovanni, Nikki 1943- ..... **BLC 1:2; CLC 2, 4, 19, 64, 117; PC 19; WLCS**
See also AAYA 22, 85; AITN 1; BW 2, 3; CA 29-32R; CAAS 6; CANR 18, 41, 60, 91, 130, 175; CDALBS; CLR 6, 73; CP 2, 3, 4, 5, 6, 7; CSW; CWP; CWRI 5; DA; DA3; DAB; DAC; DAM MST, MULT, POET; DLB 5, 41; EWL 3; EXPP; INT CANR-18; MAICYA 1, 2; MAL 5; MTCW 1, 2; MTFW 2005; PFS 17, 28, 35, 42; RGAL 4; SATA 24, 107, 208; TUS; YAW

Giovanni, Yolanda Cornelia
See Giovanni, Nikki

Giovanni, Yolande Cornelia
See Giovanni, Nikki

Giovanni, Yolande Cornelia, Jr.
See Giovanni, Nikki

Giovene, Andrea 1904-1998 .... **CLC 7**
See also CA 85-88

Gippius, Zinaida 1869-1945 ... **TCLC 9, 273**
See also CA 106; 212; DLB 295; EWL 3

Gippius, Zinaida Nikolaevna
See Gippius, Zinaida

Guiraldes, Ricardo (Guillermo)
1886-1927 .... **TCLC 39**
See also CA 131; EWL 3; HW 1; LAW; MTCW 1

Giraldi, Giovanni Battista
1504-1573 .... **LC 220**

Giraldi, William .... **CLC 334**
See also CA 329

Giraudoux, Jean 1882-1944 .... **DC 36; TCLC 2, 7**
See also CA 104; 196; DAM DRAM; DFS 28; DLB 65, 321; EW 9; EWL 3; GFL 1789 to the Present; RGWL 2, 3; TWA

Giraudoux, Jean-Hippolyte
See Giraudoux, Jean

Giraut de Bornelh
c. 1140-c. 1200 .... **CMLC 175**

Gironella, Jose Maria (Pous)
1917-2003 .... **CLC 11**
See also CA 101; 212; EWL 3; RGWL 2, 3

Gissing, George (Robert) 1857-1903 ..... **SSC 37, 113; TCLC 3, 24, 47; TCLC 310, 313**
See also BRW 5; CA 105; 167; DLB 18, 135, 184; RGEL 2; TEA

Gitlin, Todd 1943- .... **CLC 201**
See also CA 29-32R; CANR 25, 50, 88, 179, 227

Giurlani, Aldo
See Palazzeschi, Aldo

Gladkov, Fedor Vasil'evich
See Gladkov, Fyodor (Vasilyevich)

Gladkov, Fyodor (Vasilyevich)
1883-1958 .... **TCLC 27**
See also CA 170; DLB 272; EWL 3

Gladstone, William Ewart
1809-1898 .... **NCLC 213**
See also DLB 57, 184

Glancy, Diane 1941- .... **CLC 210; NNAL**
See also CA 136, 225; CAAE 225; CAAS 24; CANR 87, 162, 217; DLB 175

Glanville, Brian (Lester) 1931- .... **CLC 6**
See also CA 5-8R; CAAS 9; CANR 3, 70; CN 1, 2, 3, 4, 5, 6, 7; DLB 15, 139; SATA 42

Glasgow, Ellen 1873-1945 .... **SSC 34, 130; TCLC 2, 7, 239**
See also AMW; CA 104; 164; DLB 9, 12; MAL 5; MBL; MTCW 2; MTFW 2005; RGAL 4; RHW; SSFS 9; TUS

Glasgow, Ellen Anderson Gholson
See Glasgow, Ellen

Glaspell, Susan 1882(?)-1948 .... **DC 10; SSC 41, 132; TCLC 55, 175**
See also AMWS 3; CA 110; 154; DFS 8, 18, 24; DLB 7, 9, 78, 228; MBL; RGAL 4; SSFS 3; TCWW 2; TUS; YABC 2

Glassco, John 1909-1981 .... **CLC 9**
See also CA 13-16R; 102; CANR 15; CN 1, 2; CP 1, 2, 3; DLB 68

Glasscock, Amnesia
See Steinbeck, John

Glasser, Ronald J. 1940(?)- .... **CLC 37**
See also CA 209; CANR 240

Glassman, Joyce
See Johnson, Joyce

Gluck, Louise 1943- .... **CLC 7, 22, 44, 81, 160, 280; PC 16, 159**
See also AMWS 5; CA 33-36R; CANR 40, 69, 108, 133, 182; CP 1, 2, 3, .4, 5, 6, 7; CWP; DA3; DAM POET; DLB 5; MAL 5; MTCW 2; MTFW 2005; PFS 5, 15; RGAL 4; TCLE 1:1

Gluck, Louise Elisabeth
See Gluck, Louise

Gleick, James 1954- .... **CLC 147**
See also CA 131; 137; CANR 97, 236; INT CA-137

Gleick, James W.
See Gleick, James

Glendinning, Victoria 1937- .... **CLC 50**
See also CA 120; 127; CANR 59, 89, 166; DLB 155

Glissant, Edouard 1928-2011 ... **CLC 10, 68, 337**
See also CA 153; CANR 111; CWW 2; DAM MULT; EWL 3; RGWL 3

Glissant, Edouard Mathieu
See Glissant, Edouard

Gloag, Julian 1930- .... **CLC 40**
See also AITN 1; CA 65-68; CANR 10, 70; CN 1, 2, 3, 4, 5, 6

Glowacki, Aleksander
See Prus, Boleslaw

Glyn, Elinor 1864-1943 .... **TCLC 72**
See also DLB 153; RHW

Gosse, Edmund (William)
1849-1928 .... **TCLC 28**
See also CA 117; DLB 57, 144, 184; RGEL 2

Goto, Hiromi 1966- .... **CLC 338**
See also CA 165; CANR 142

Gotlieb, Phyllis 1926-2009 .... **CLC 18**
See also CA 13-16R; CANR 7, 135; CN 7; CP 1, 2, 3, 4; DLB 88, 251; SFW 4

Gotlieb, Phyllis Fay Bloom
See Gotlieb, Phyllis

Gottesman, S. D.
See Kornbluth, C(yril) M.; Pohl, Frederik

Gottfried von Strassburg
fl. c. 1170-1215 ...... **CMLC 10, 96, 132**
See also CDWLB 2; DLB 138; EW 1; RGWL 2, 3

Gotthelf, Jeremias 1797-1854 ...... **NCLC 117**
See also DLB 133; RGWL 2, 3

Gottschalk c. 804-c. 866 .... **CMLC 130**
See also DLB 148

Gottschalk, Laura Riding
See Jackson, Laura

Gottsched, Johann Christoph
1700-1766 .... **LC 207**
See also DLB 97

Gottsched, Luise Adelgunde Victoria
1713-1762 .... **LC 211**

Gouges, Olympe de
1748-1793 .... **LC 127, 214**
See also DLB 313

Gould, Lois 1932(?)-2002 .... **CLC 4, 10**
See also CA 77-80; 208; CANR 29; MTCW 1

Gould, Stephen Jay 1941-2002 ..... **CLC 163**
See also AAYA 26; BEST 90:2; CA 77-80; 205; CANR 10, 27, 56, 75, 125; CPW; INT CANR-27; MTCW 1, 2; MTFW 2005

Gourmont, Remy(-Marie-Charles) de
1858-1915 .... **TCLC 17**
See also CA 109; 150; GFL 1789 to the Present; MTCW 2

Gournay, Marie le Jars de
See de Gournay, Marie le Jars

Govier, Katherine 1948- .... **CLC 51**
See also CA 101; CANR 18, 40, 128; CCA 1

Gower, John c. 1330-1408 .... **LC 76; PC 59**
See also BRW 1; DLB 146; RGEL 2

Goyen, (Charles) William
1915-1983 .... **CLC 5, 8, 14, 40**
See also AITN 2; CA 5-8R; 110; CANR 6, 71; CN 1, 2, 3; DLB 2, 218; DLBY 1983; EWL 3; INT CANR-6; MAL 5

Goytisolo, Juan 1931- .... **CLC 5, 10, 23, 133; HLC 1**
See also CA 85-88; CANR 32, 61, 131, 182; CWW 2; DAM MULT; DLB 322; EWL 3; GLL 2; HW 1, 2; MTCW 1, 2; MTFW 2005

Gozzano, Guido 1883-1916 .... **PC 10**
See also CA 154; DLB 114; EWL 3

Gozzi, (Conte) Carlo 1720-1806 ... **NCLC 23**

Grabbe, Christian Dietrich
1801-1836 .... **NCLC 2**
See also DLB 133; RGWL 2, 3

Grace, Patricia 1937- .... **CLC 56, 337; SSC 199**
See also CA 176; CANR 118; CN 4, 5, 6, 7; EWL 3; RGSF 2; SSFS 33

Grace, Patricia Frances
See Grace, Patricia

Gracian, Baltasar 1601-1658 ..... **LC 15, 160**

Gracian y Morales, Baltasar
See Gracian, Baltasar

Gracq, Julien 1910-2007 ... **CLC 11, 48, 259**
See also CA 122; 126; 267; CANR 141; CWW 2; DLB 83; GFL 1789 to the present

Grade, Chaim 1910-1982 .... **CLC 10**
See also CA 93-96; 107; DLB 333; EWL 3; RGHL

Grade, Khayim
See Grade, Chaim

Graduate of Oxford, A
See Ruskin, John

Grafton, Garth
See Duncan, Sara Jeannette

Grafton, Sue 1940- .... **CLC 163, 299**
See also AAYA 11, 49; BEST 90:3; CA 108; CANR 31, 55, 111, 134, 195; CMW 4; CPW; CSW; DA3; DAM POP; DLB 226; FW; MSW; MTFW 2005

Graham, John
See Phillips, David Graham

Graham, Jorie 1950- **CLC 48, 118, 352; PC 59**
See also AAYA 67; CA 111; CANR 63, 118, 205; CP 4, 5, 6, 7; CWP; DLB 120; EWL 3; MTFW 2005; PFS 10, 17; TCLE 1:1

Graham, R. B. Cunninghame
See Cunninghame Graham, Robert Bontine

Graham, Robert
See Haldeman, Joe

Graham, Robert Bontine Cunninghame
See Cunninghame Graham, Robert Bontine

Graham, Tom
See Lewis, Sinclair

Graham, W(illiam) S(ydney)
1918-1986 .... **CLC 29; PC 127**
See also BRWS 7; CA 73-76; 118; CP 1, 2, 3, 4; DLB 20; RGEL 2

Graham, Winston (Mawdsley)
1910-2003 .... **CLC 23**
See also CA 49-52; 218; CANR 2, 22, 45, 66; CMW 4; CN 1, 2, 3, 4, 5, 6, 7; DLB 77; RHW

Grahame, Kenneth 1859-1932 ... **TCLC 64, 136**
See also BYA 5; CA 108; 136; CANR 80; CLR 5, 135; CWRI 5; DA3; DAB; DLB 34, 141, 178; FANT; MAICYA 1, 2; MTCW 2; NFS 20; RGEL 2; SATA 100; TEA; WCH; YABC 1

Granger, Darius John
See Marlowe, Stephen

Granin, Daniil 1918- .... **CLC 59**
See also DLB 302

Grannec, Yannick 1969- .... **CLC 389**

Granovsky, Timofei Nikolaevich
1813-1855 .... **NCLC 75**
See also DLB 198

Grant, Anne MacVicar
1755-1838 .... **NCLC 302**
See also DLB 200

Grant, Skeeter
See Spiegelman, Art

Granville-Barker, Harley 1877-1946 ... **TCLC 2**
See also CA 104; 204; DAM DRAM; DLB 10; RGEL 2

Granzotto, Gianni
See Granzotto, Giovanni Battista

Granzotto, Giovanni Battista
1914-1985 .... **CLC 70**
See also CA 166

Grasemann, Ruth Barbara
See Rendell, Ruth

Grass, Gunter 1927- ..... **CLC 1, 2, 4, 6, 11, 15, 22, 32, 49, 88, 207; WLC 3**
See also BPFB 2; CA 13-16R; CANR 20, 75, 93, 133, 174, 229; CDWLB 2; CWW 2; DA; DA3; DAB; DAC; DAM MST, NOV; DLB 330; EW 13; EWL 3; MTCW 1, 2; MTFW 2005; RGHL; RGWL 2, 3; TWA

Grass, Gunter Wilhelm
See Grass, Gunter

Grass, Guenter
See Grass, Gunter

Gratton, Thomas
See Hulme, T(homas) E(rnest)

Grau, Shirley Ann 1929- ..... **CLC 4, 9, 146; SSC 15**

See also CA 89-92; CANR 22, 69; CN 1, 2, 3, 4, 5, 6, 7; CSW; DLB 2, 218; INT CA-89-92; CANR-22; MTCW 1

Gravel, Fern
See Hall, James Norman

Graver, Elizabeth 1964- .... **CLC 70**
See also CA 135; CANR 71, 129

Graves, Richard Perceval
1895-1985 .... **CLC 44**
See also CA 65-68; CANR 9, 26, 51

Graves, Robert 1895-1985 .... **CLC 1, 2, 6, 11, 39, 44, 45; PC 6**
See also BPFB 2; BRW 7; BYA 4; CA 5-8R; 117; CANR 5, 36; CDBLB 1914-1945; CN 1, 2, 3; CP 1, 2, 3, 4; DA3; DAB; DAC; DAM MST, POET; DLB 20, 100, 191; DLBD 18; DLBY 1985; EWL 3; LATS 1:1; MTCW 1, 2; MTFW 2005; NCFS 2; NFS 21; RGEL 2; RHW; SATA 45; TEA

Graves, Robert von Ranke
See Graves, Robert

Graves, Valerie
See Bradley, Marion Zimmer

Gray, Alasdair 1934- .... **CLC 41, 275, 388**
See also BRWS 9; CA 126; CANR 47, 69, 106, 140; CN 4, 5, 6, 7; DLB 194, 261, 319; HGG; INT CA-126; MTCW 1, 2; MTFW 2005; RGSF 2; SUFW 2

Gray, Amlin 1946- .... **CLC 29**
See also CA 138

Gray, Francine du Plessix
1930- .... **CLC 22, 153**
See also BEST 90:3; CA 61-64; CAAS 2; CANR 11, 33, 75, 81, 197; DAM NOV; INT CANR-11; MTCW 1, 2; MTFW 2005

Gray, John (Henry) 1866-1934 ..... **TCLC 19**
See also CA 119; 162; RGEL 2

Gray, John Lee
See Jakes, John

Gray, Simon 1936-2008 .... **CLC 9, 14, 36**
See also AITN 1; CA 21-24R; 275; CAAS 3; CANR 32, 69, 208; CBD; CD 5, 6; CN 1, 2, 3; DLB 13; EWL 3; MTCW 1; RGEL 2

Gray, Simon James Holliday
See Gray, Simon

Gray, Spalding 1941-2004 ...... **CLC 49, 112; DC 7**
See also AAYA 62; CA 128; 225; CAD; CANR 74, 138; CD 5, 6; CPW; DAM POP; MTCW 2; MTFW 2005

Gray, Thomas 1716-1771 ..... **LC 4, 40, 178; PC 2, 80; WLC 3**
See also BRW 3; CDBLB 1660-1789; DA; DA3; DAB; DAC; DAM MST; DLB 109; EXPP; PAB; PFS 9; RGEL 2; TEA; WP

Grayson, David
See Baker, Ray Stannard

Grayson, Richard (A.) 1951- .... **CLC 38**
See also CA 85-88; 210; CAAE 210; CANR 14, 31, 57; DLB 234

Greeley, Andrew M. 1928-2013 ...... **CLC 28**
See also BPFB 2; CA 5-8R; CAAS 7; CANR 7, 43, 69, 104, 136, 184; CMW 4; CPW; DA3; DAM POP; MTCW 1, 2; MTFW 2005

Green, Anna Katharine
1846-1935 .... **TCLC 63**
See also CA 112; 159; CMW 4; DLB 202, 221; MSW

Green, Brian
See Card, Orson Scott

Green, Hannah
See Greenberg, Joanne (Goldenberg)

Green, Hannah 1927(?)-1996 .... **CLC 3**
See also CA 73-76; CANR 59, 93; NFS 10

Green, Henry
See Yorke, Henry Vincent

Gubar, Susan 1944- .... **CLC 145**
See also CA 108; CANR 45, 70, 139, 179;
FW; MTCW 1; RGAL 4

Gubar, Susan David
See Gubar, Susan

Gudjonsson, Halldor Kiljan
1902-1998 .... **CLC 25**
See also CA 103; 164; CWW 2; DLB 293,
331; EW 12; EWL 3; RGWL 2, 3

Guedes, Vincente
See Pessoa, Fernando

Guenter, Erich
See Eich, Gunter

Guest, Barbara 1920-2006 .... **CLC 34;**
PC 55
See also BG 1:2; CA 25-28R; 248; CANR
11, 44, 84; CP 1, 2, 3, 4, 5, 6, 7; CWP;
DLB 5, 193

Guest, Edgar A(lbert)
1881-1959 .... **TCLC 95**
See also CA 112; 168

Guest, Judith 1936- .... **CLC 8, 30**
See also AAYA 7, 66; CA 77-80; CANR 15,
75, 138; DA3; DAM NOV, POP; EXPN;
INT CANR-15; LAIT 5; MTCW 1, 2;
MTFW 2005; NFS 1, 33

Guest, Judith Ann
See Guest, Judith

Guevara, Che 1928-1967 .. **CLC 87; HLC 1**
See also CA 127; 111; CANR 56; DAM
MULT; HW 1

Guevara (Serna), Ernesto
See Guevara, Che

Guicciardini, Francesco 1483-1540 ... **LC 49**

Guido delle Colonne
c. 1215-c. 1290 .... **CMLC 90**

Guild, Nicholas M. 1944- .... **CLC 33**
See also CA 93-96

Guillemin, Jacques
See Sartre, Jean-Paul

Guillen y Alvarez, Jorge
See Guillen, Jorge

Guillevic, (Eugene) 1907-1997 .... **CLC 33**
See also CA 93-96; CWW 2

Guillen, Jorge 1893-1984 .... **CLC 11;**
HLCS 1; PC 35; TCLC 233
See also CA 89-92; 112; DAM MULT,
POET; DLB 108; EWL 3; HW 1; RGWL
2, 3

Guillen, Nicolas 1902-1989 .... **BLC 1:2;**
CLC 48, 79; HLC 1; PC 23
See also BW 2; CA 116; 125; 129; CANR
84; DAM MST, MULT, POET; DLB 283;
EWL 3; HW 1; LAW; RGWL 2, 3; WP

Guillen, Nicolas Cristobal
See Guillen, Nicolas

Guillois
See Desnos, Robert

Guillois, Valentin
See Desnos, Robert

Guimaraes Rosa, Joao
1908-1967 .... **CLC 23; HLCS 1**
See also CA 175; 89-92; DLB 113, 307;
EWL 3; LAW; RGSF 2; RGWL 2, 3;
WLIT 1

Guiney, Louise Imogen
1861-1920 .... **TCLC 41**
See also CA 160; DLB 54; RGAL 4

Guinizelli, Guido c. 1230-1276 .... **CMLC 49**
See also WLIT 7

Guinizzelli, Guido
See Guinizelli, Guido

Guma, Alex La
See La Guma, Alex

Gumilev, Nikolai (Stepanovich)
1886-1921 .... **TCLC 60**
See also CA 165; DLB 295; EWL 3

Gumilyov, Nikolay Stepanovich
See Gumilev, Nikolai (Stepanovich)

Gump, P.Q.
See Card, Orson Scott

Gunesekera, Romesh 1954- ..... **CLC 91, 336**
See also BRWS 10; CA 159; CANR 140,
172; CN 6, 7; DLB 267, 323

Gunn, Bill
See Gunn, William Harrison

Gunn, Thom 1929-2004 .... **CLC 3, 6, 18,**
32, 81; PC 26
See also BRWR 3; BRWS 4; CA 17-20R;
227; CANR 9, 33, 116; CDBLB 1960 to
Present; CP 1, 2, 3, 4, 5, 6, 7; DAM POET;
DLB 27; INT CANR-33; MTCW 1; PFS 9;
RGEL 2

Gunn, William Harrison
1934(?)-1989 .... **CLC 5**
See also AITN 1; BW 1, 3; CA 13-16R; 128;
CANR 12, 25, 76; DLB 38

Gunn Allen, Paula
See Allen, Paula Gunn

Gunnars, Kristjana 1948- .... **CLC 69**
See also CA 113; CCA 1; CP 6, 7; CWP;
DLB 60

Gurdjieff, G(eorgei) I(vanovich)
1877(?)-1949 .... **TCLC 71**
See also CA 157

Gurganus, Allan 1947- .... **CLC 70**
See also BEST 90:1; CA 135; CANR 114;
CN 6, 7; CPW; CSW; DAM POP; DLB
350; GLL 1

Gurnah, Abdulrazak 1948- .... **CLC 368**
See also CA 179; CANR 153; CN 7; EWL 3

Gurney, A. R.
See Gurney, A(lbert) R(amsdell), Jr.

Gurney, A(lbert) R(amsdell), Jr.
1930- .... **CLC 32, 50, 54**
See also AMWS 5; CA 77-80; CAD; CANR
32, 64, 121; CD 5, 6; DAM DRAM; DLB
266; EWL 3

Gurney, Ivor (Bertie) 1890-1937 ... **TCLC 33**
See also BRW 6; CA 167; DLBY 2002;
PAB; RGEL 2

Gurney, Peter
See Gurney, A(lbert) R(amsdell), Jr.

Guro, Elena (Genrikhovna)
1877-1913 .... **TCLC 56**
See also DLB 295

Gustafson, James M(oody) 1925- ... **CLC 100**
See also CA 25-28R; CANR 37

Gustafson, Ralph (Barker)
1909-1995 .... **CLC 36**
See also CA 21-24R; CANR 8, 45, 84; CP 1,
2, 3, 4, 5, 6; DLB 88; RGEL 2

Gut, Gom
See Simenon, Georges

Guterson, David 1956- .... **CLC 91**
See also CA 132; CANR 73, 126, 194; CN
7; DLB 292; MTCW 2; MTFW 2005;
NFS 13

Guthrie, A(lfred) B(ertram), Jr.
1901-1991 .... **CLC 23**
See also CA 57-60; 134; CANR 24; CN 1, 2,
3; DLB 6, 212; MAL 5; SATA 62; SATA-
Obit 67; TCWW 1, 2

Guthrie, Isobel
See Grieve, C. M.

Gutierrez Najera, Manuel
1859-1895 .... **HLCS 2; NCLC 133**
See also DLB 290; LAW

Guy, Rosa 1925- .... **CLC 26**
See also AAYA 4, 37; BW 2; CA 17-20R;
CANR 14, 34, 83; CLR 13, 137; DLB 33;
DNFS 1; JRDA; MAICYA 1, 2; SATA 14,
62, 122; YAW

Guy, Rosa Cuthbert
See Guy, Rosa

Gwendolyn
See Bennett, (Enoch) Arnold

H. D.
See Doolittle, Hilda

H. de V.
See Buchan, John

Haavikko, Paavo Juhani 1931- ... **CLC 18, 34**
See also CA 106; CWW 2; EWL 3

Habbema, Koos
See Heijermans, Herman

Habermas, Jurgen
See Habermas, Juergen

Habermas, Juergen 1929- ..... **CLC 104, 345**
See also CA 109; CANR 85, 162; DLB 242

Hacker, Marilyn 1942- .... **CLC 5, 9, 23,**
72, 91; PC 47
See also CA 77-80; CANR 68, 129; CP 3, 4,
5, 6, 7; CWP; DAM POET; DLB 120, 282;
FW; GLL 2; MAL 5; PFS 19

Hackleskinner, Fred
See Harwood, Gwen

Hadewijch of Antwerp
fl. 1250 .... **CMLC 61**
See also RGWL 3

Hadrian 76-138 .... **CMLC 52**

Haeckel, Ernst Heinrich (Philipp August)
1834-1919 .... **TCLC 83**
See also CA 157

Hafiz c. 1326-1389(?) .... **CMLC 34, 156;**
PC 116
See also RGWL 2, 3; WLIT 6

Hagedorn, Jessica 1949- .... **CLC 185**
See also CA 139; CANR 69, 231; CWP;
DLB 312; RGAL 4

Hagedorn, Jessica Tarahata
See Hagedorn, Jessica

Hagendoor, W. W.
See Harwood, Gwen

Haggard, H(enry) Rider
1856-1925 .... **TCLC 11**
See also AAYA 81; BRWS 3; BYA 4, 5; CA
108; 148; CANR 112; DLB 70, 156, 174,
178; FANT; LMFS 1; MTCW 2; NFS 40;
RGEL 2; RHW; SATA 16; SCFW 1, 2;
SFW 4; SUFW 1; WLIT 4

Hagiosy, L.
See Larbaud, Valery (Nicolas)

Hagiwara, Sakutaro 1886-1942 .... **PC 18;**
TCLC 60
See also CA 154; EWL 3; RGWL 3

Hagiwara Sakutaro
See Hagiwara, Sakutaro

Haig, Fenil
See Ford, Ford Madox

Haig-Brown, Roderick (Langmere)
1908-1976 .... **CLC 21**
See also CA 5-8R; 69-72; CANR 4, 38, 83;
CLR 31; CWRI 5; DLB 88; MAICYA 1, 2;
SATA 12; TCWW 2

Haight, Rip
See Carpenter, John

Haij, Vera
See Jansson, Tove (Marika)

Hailey, Arthur 1920-2004 .... **CLC 5**
See also AITN 2; BEST 90:3; BPFB 2; CA
1-4R; 233; CANR 2, 36, 75; CCA 1; CN 1,
2, 3, 4, 5, 6, 7; CPW; DAM NOV, POP;
DLB 88; DLBY 1982; MTCW 1, 2;
MTFW 2005

Hailey, Elizabeth Forsythe 1938- ... **CLC 40**
See also CA 93-96; 188; CAAE 188; CAAS
1; CANR 15, 48; INT CANR-15

Haines, John 1924-2011 .... **CLC 58**
See also AMWS 12; CA 17-20R; CANR 13,
34; CP 1, 2, 3, 4, 5; CSW; DLB 5, 212;
TCLE 1:1

Haines, John Meade
See Haines, John

Hocking, Mary 1921- .... **CLC 13**
See also CA 101; CANR 18, 40

Hocking, Mary Eunice
See Hocking, Mary

Hodge, Merle 1944- .... **BLC 2:2**
See also EWL 3

Hodgins, Jack 1938- .... **CLC 23; SSC 132**
See also CA 93-96; CN 4, 5, 6, 7; DLB 60

Hodgson, William Hope
1877(?)-1918 .... **TCLC 13**
See also CA 111; 164; CMW 4; DLB 70, 153, 156, 178; HGG; MTCW 2; SFW 4; SUFW 1

Hoeg, Peter
See Hoeg, Peter

Hoffman, Alice 1952- .... **CLC 51**
See also AAYA 37; AMWS 10; CA 77-80; CANR 34, 66, 100, 138, 170, 237; CN 4, 5, 6, 7; CPW; DAM NOV; DLB 292; MAL 5; MTCW 1, 2; MTFW 2005; TCLE 1:1

Hoffman, Daniel (Gerard)
1923- .... **CLC 6, 13, 23**
See also CA 1-4R; CANR 4, 142; CP 1, 2, 3, 4, 5, 6, 7; DLB 5; TCLE 1:1

Hoffman, Eva 1945- .... **CLC 182**
See also AMWS 16; CA 132; CANR 146, 209

Hoffman, Stanley 1944- .... **CLC 5**
See also CA 77-80

Hoffman, William 1925-2009 .... **CLC 141**
See also AMWS 18; CA 21-24R; CANR 9, 103; CSW; DLB 234; TCLE 1:1

Hoffman, William M.
See Hoffman, William M(oses)

Hoffman, William M(oses) 1939- ... **CLC 40**
See also CA 57-60; CAD; CANR 11, 71; CD 5, 6

Hoffmann, E(rnst) T(heodor) A(madeus)
1776-1822 ... **NCLC 2, 183; SSC 13, 92**
See also CDWLB 2; CLR 133; DLB 90; EW 5; GL 2; RGSF 2; RGWL 2, 3; SATA 27; SUFW 1; WCH

Hofmann, Gert 1931-1993 .... **CLC 54**
See also CA 128; CANR 145; EWL 3; RGHL

Hofmannsthal, Hugo von
1874-1929 .... **DC 4; TCLC 11**
See also CA 106; 153; CDWLB 2; DAM DRAM; DFS 17; DLB 81, 118; EW 9; EWL 3; RGWL 2, 3

Hoffmannswaldau, Christian Hoffmann von
1616-1679 .... **LC 237**
See also DLB 168

Hogan, Linda 1947- .... **CLC 73, 290; NNAL; PC 35**
See also AMWS 4; ANW; BYA 12; CA 120, 226; CAAE 226; CANR 45, 73, 129, 196; CWP; DAM MULT; DLB 175; SATA 132; TCWW 2

Hogarth, Charles
See Creasey, John

Hogarth, Emmett
See Polonsky, Abraham (Lincoln)

Hogarth, William 1697-1764 .... **LC 112**
See also AAYA 56

Hogg, James 1770-1835 .... **NCLC 4, 109, 260; SSC 130**
See also BRWS 10; DLB 93, 116, 159; GL 2; HGG; RGEL 2; SUFW 1

Holbach, Paul-Henri Thiry 1723-1789 .. **LC 14**
See also DLB 313

Holberg, Ludvig 1684-1754 .... **LC 6, 208**
See also DLB 300; RGWL 2, 3

Holbrook, John
See Vance, Jack

Holcroft, Thomas 1745-1809 .... **NCLC 85**
See also DLB 39, 89, 158; RGEL 2

Holden, Ursula 1921- .... **CLC 18**
See also CA 101; CAAS 8; CANR 22

Holdstock, Robert 1948-2009 .... **CLC 39**
See also CA 131; CANR 81, 207; DLB 261; FANT; HGG; SFW 4; SUFW 2

Holdstock, Robert P.
See Holdstock, Robert

Holinshed, Raphael fl. 1580 .... **LC 69, 217**
See also DLB 167; RGEL 2

Holland, Isabelle (Christian)
1920-2002 .... **CLC 21**
See also AAYA 11, 64; CA 21-24R; 205; CAAE 181; CANR 10, 25, 47; CLR 57; CWRI 5; JRDA; LAIT 4; MAICYA 1, 2; SATA 8, 70; SATA-Essay 103; SATA-Obit 132; WYA

Holland, Marcus
See Caldwell, (Janet Miriam) Taylor (Holland)

Hollander, John 1929-2013 ..... **CLC 2, 5, 8, 14; PC 117**
See also CA 1-4R; CANR 1, 52, 136; CP 1, 2, 3, 4, 5, 6, 7; DLB 5; MAL 5; SATA 13

Hollander, Paul
See Silverberg, Robert

Holleran, Andrew 1943(?)- .... **CLC 38**
See also CA 144; CANR 89, 162; GLL 1

Holley, Marietta 1836(?)-1926 .... **TCLC 99**
See also CA 118; DLB 11; FL 1:3

Hollinghurst, Alan 1954- ... **CLC 55, 91, 329**
See also BRWS 10; CA 114; CN 5, 6, 7; DLB 207, 326; GLL 1

Hollis, Jim
See Summers, Hollis (Spurgeon, Jr.)

Holly, Buddy 1936-1959 .... **TCLC 65**
See also CA 213

Holmes, Gordon
See Shiel, M. P.

Holmes, John
See Souster, (Holmes) Raymond

Holmes, John Clellon 1926-1988 .... **CLC 56**
See also BG 1:2; CA 9-12R; 125; CANR 4; CN 1, 2, 3, 4; DLB 16, 237

Holmes, Oliver Wendell, Jr.
1841-1935 .... **TCLC 77**
See also CA 114; 186

Holmes, Oliver Wendell
1809-1894 .... **NCLC 14, 81; PC 71**
See also AMWS 1; CDALB 1640-1865; DLB 1, 189, 235; EXPP; PFS 24; RGAL 4; SATA 34

Holmes, Raymond
See Souster, (Holmes) Raymond

Holt, Elliott 1974- .... **CLC 370**
See also CA 351

Holt, Samuel
See Westlake, Donald E.

Holt, Victoria
See Hibbert, Eleanor Alice Burford

Holub, Miroslav 1923-1998 .... **CLC 4**
See also CA 21-24R; 169; CANR 10; CDWLB 4; CWW 2; DLB 232; EWL 3; RGWL 3

Holz, Detlev
See Benjamin, Walter

Homer c. 8th cent. B.C. .... **CMLC 1, 16, 61, 121, 166; PC 23; WLC 3**
See also AW 1; CDWLB 1; DA; DA3; DAB; DAC; DAM MST, POET; DLB 176; EFS 1:1, 2:1,2; LAIT 1; LMFS 1; RGWL 2, 3; TWA; WLIT 8; WP

Hong, Maxine Ting Ting
See Kingston, Maxine Hong

Hongo, Garrett Kaoru 1951- .... **PC 23**
See also CA 133; CAAS 22; CP 5, 6, 7; DLB 120, 312; EWL 3; EXPP; PFS 25, 33, 43; RGAL 4

Honig, Edwin 1919-2011 .... **CLC 33**
See also CA 5-8R; CAAS 8; CANR 4, 45, 144; CP 1, 2, 3, 4, 5, 6, 7; DLB 5

Hood, Hugh (John Blagdon)
1928- .... **CLC 15, 28, 273; SSC 42**
See also CA 49-52; CAAS 17; CANR 1, 33, 87; CN 1, 2, 3, 4, 5, 6, 7; DLB 53; RGSF 2

Hood, Thomas 1799-1845 .... **NCLC 16, 242; PC 93**
See also BRW 4; DLB 96; RGEL 2

Hooft, Pieter Corneliszoon
1581-1647 .... **LC 214**
See also RGWL 2, 3

Hooker, (Peter) Jeremy 1941- .... **CLC 43**
See also CA 77-80; CANR 22; CP 2, 3, 4, 5, 6, 7; DLB 40

Hooker, Richard 1554-1600 .... **LC 95**
See also BRW 1; DLB 132; RGEL 2

Hooker, Thomas 1586-1647 .... **LC 137**
See also DLB 24

hooks, bell 1952(?)- .... **BLCS; CLC 94**
See also BW 2; CA 143; CANR 87, 126, 211; DLB 246; MTCW 2; MTFW 2005; SATA 115, 170

Hooper, Johnson Jones
1815-1862 .... **NCLC 177**
See also DLB 3, 11, 248; RGAL 4

Hope, A(lec) D(erwent)
1907-2000 .... **CLC 3, 51; PC 56**
See also BRWS 7; CA 21-24R; 188; CANR 33, 74; CP 1, 2, 3, 4, 5; DLB 289; EWL 3; MTCW 1, 2; MTFW 2005; PFS 8; RGEL 2

Hope, Anthony 1863-1933 .... **TCLC 83**
See also CA 157; DLB 153, 156; RGEL 2; RHW

Hope, Brian
See Creasey, John

Hope, Christopher 1944- .... **CLC 52**
See also AFW; CA 106; CANR 47, 101, 177; CN 4, 5, 6, 7; DLB 225; SATA 62

Hope, Christopher David Tully
See Hope, Christopher

Hopkins, Gerard Manley
1844-1889 .... **NCLC 17, 189; PC 15; WLC 3**
See also BRW 5; BRWR 2; CDBLB 1890-1914; DA; DA3; DAB; DAC; DAM MST, POET; DLB 35, 57; EXPP; PAB; PFS 26, 40; RGEL 2; TEA; WP

Hopkins, John (Richard) 1931-1998 ... **CLC 4**
See also CA 85-88; 169; CBD; CD 5, 6

Hopkins, Pauline Elizabeth
1859-1930 .... **BLC 1:2; TCLC 28, 251**
See also AFAW 2; BW 2, 3; CA 141; CANR 82; DAM MULT; DLB 50

Hopkinson, Francis 1737-1791 .... **LC 25**
See also DLB 31; RGAL 4

Hopkinson, Nalo 1960- .... **CLC 316**
See also AAYA 40; CA 196, 219; CAAE 219; CANR 173; DLB 251

Hopley, George
See Hopley-Woolrich, Cornell George

Hopley-Woolrich, Cornell George
1903-1968 .... **CLC 77**
See also CA 13-14; CANR 58, 156; CAP 1; CMW 4; DLB 226; MSW; MTCW 2

Horace 65B.C.-8B.C. .... **CMLC 39, 125; PC 46**
See also AW 2; CDWLB 1; DLB 211; RGWL 2, 3; WLIT 8

Horatio
See Proust, Marcel

Horgan, Paul (George Vincent O'Shaughnessy)
1903-1995 .... **CLC 9, 53**
See also BPFB 2; CA 13-16R; 147; CANR 9, 35; CN 1, 2, 3, 4, 5; DAM NOV; DLB 102, 212; DLBY 1985; INT CANR-9; MTCW 1, 2; MTFW 2005; SATA 13; SATA-Obit 84; TCWW 1, 2

Horkheimer, Max 1895-1973 ...... **TCLC 132**
See also CA 216; 41-44R; DLB 296

Horn, Peter
See Kuttner, Henry

Hugo, Victor Marie
    See Hugo, Victor
Huidobro, Vicente
    1893-1948 .... **PC 147; TCLC 31**
    See also DLB 283
    See also Huidobro Fernandez, Vicente Garcia
Huidobro Fernandez, Vicente Garcia
    1893-1948 .... **PC 147; TCLC 31**
    See also CA 131; DLB 283; EWL 3; HW 1; LAW
Hulme, Keri 1947- .... **CLC 39, 130, 339**
    See also CA 125; CANR 69; CN 4, 5, 6, 7; CP 6, 7; CWP; DLB 326; EWL 3; FW; INT CA-125; NFS 24
Hulme, T(homas) E(rnest)
    1883-1917 .... **TCLC 21**
    See also BRWS 6; CA 117; 203; DLB 19
Humboldt, Alexander von
    1769-1859 .... **NCLC 170**
    See also DLB 90, 366
Humboldt, Wilhelm von
    1767-1835 .... **NCLC 134, 256**
    See also DLB 90
Hume, David 1711-1776 .... **LC 7, 56, 156, 157, 197**
    See also BRWS 3; DLB 104, 252, 336; LMFS 1; TEA
Hum-ishu-ma
    See Mourning Dove
Humphrey, William 1924-1997 .... **CLC 45**
    See also AMWS 9; CA 77-80; 160; CANR 68; CN 1, 2, 3, 4, 5, 6; CSW; DLB 6, 212, 234, 278; TCWW 1, 2
Humphreys, Emyr Owen 1919- ..... **CLC 47**
    See also CA 5-8R; CANR 3, 24; CN 1, 2, 3, 4, 5, 6, 7; DLB 15
Humphreys, Josephine 1945- .... **CLC 34, 57, 335**
    See also CA 121; 127; CANR 97; CSW; DLB 292; INT CA-127
Huneker, James Gibbons
    1860-1921 .... **TCLC 65**
    See also CA 193; DLB 71; RGAL 4
Hungerford, Hesba Fay
    See Brinsmead, H(esba) F(ay)
Hungerford, Pixie
    See Brinsmead, H(esba) F(ay)
Hunt, E. Howard 1918-2007 .... **CLC 3**
    See also AITN 1; CA 45-48; 256; CANR 2, 47, 103, 160; CMW 4
Hunt, Everette Howard, Jr.
    See Hunt, E. Howard
Hunt, Francesca
    See Holland, Isabelle (Christian)
Hunt, Howard
    See Hunt, E. Howard
Hunt, Kyle
    See Creasey, John
Hunt, (James Henry) Leigh
    1784-1859 .... **NCLC 1, 70; PC 73**
    See also DAM POET; DLB 96, 110, 144; RGEL 2; TEA
Hunt, Marsha 1946- .... **CLC 70**
    See also BW 2, 3; CA 143; CANR 79
Hunt, Violet 1866(?)-1942 .... **TCLC 53**
    See also CA 184; DLB 162, 197
Hunter, E. Waldo
    See Sturgeon, Theodore (Hamilton)
Hunter, Evan 1926-2005 .... **CLC 11, 31**
    See also AAYA 39; BPFB 2; CA 5-8R; 241; CANR 5, 38, 62, 97, 149; CMW 4; CN 1, 2, 3, 4, 5, 6, 7; CPW; DAM POP; DLB 306; DLBY 1982; INT CANR-5; MSW; MTCW 1; SATA 25; SATA-Obit 167; SFW 4
Hunter, Kristin
    See Lattany, Kristin Hunter
Hunter, Mary
    See Austin, Mary Hunter

Hunter, Mollie 1922- .... **CLC 21**
    See also AAYA 13, 71; BYA 6; CANR 37, 78; CLR 25; DLB 161; JRDA; MAICYA 1, 2; SAAS 7; SATA 2, 54, 106, 139; SATA-Essay 139; WYA; YAW
Hunter, Robert (?)-1734 .... **LC 7**
Hurston, Zora Neale 1891-1960 ... **BLC 1:2; CLC 7, 30, 61; DC 12; HR 1:2; SSC 4, 80, 219; TCLC 121, 131, 285; WLCS**
    See also AAYA 15, 71; AFAW 1, 2; AMWS 6; BW 1, 3; BYA 12; CA 85-88; CANR 61; CDALBS; CLR 177; DA; DA3; DAC; DAM MST, MULT, NOV; DFS 6, 30; DLB 51, 86; EWL 3; EXPN; EXPS; FL 1:6; FW; LAIT 3; LATS 1:1; LMFS 2; MAL 5; MBL; MTCW 1, 2; MTFW 2005; NFS 3; RGAL 4; RGSF 2; SSFS 1, 6, 11, 19, 21; TUS; YAW
Husserl, E. G.
    See Husserl, Edmund (Gustav Albrecht)
Husserl, Edmund (Gustav Albrecht)
    1859-1938 .... **TCLC 100**
    See also CA 116; 133; DLB 296
Huston, John (Marcellus) 1906-1987 **CLC 20**
    See also CA 73-76; 123; CANR 34; DLB 26
Huston, Nancy 1953- .... **CLC 357**
    See also CA 145; CANR 102, 198
Hustvedt, Siri 1955- .... **CLC 76**
    See also CA 137; CANR 149, 191, 223
Hutcheson, Francis 1694-1746 .... **LC 157**
    See also DLB 252
Hutchinson, Lucy 1620-1675 .... **LC 149**
Hutten, Ulrich von 1488-1523 .... **LC 16**
    See also DLB 179
Huxley, Aldous 1894-1963 .... **CLC 1, 3, 4, 5, 8, 11, 18, 35, 79; SSC 39; WLC 3**
    See also AAYA 11; BPFB 2; BRW 7; CA 85-88; CANR 44, 99; CDBLB 1914-1945; CLR 151; DA; DA3; DAB; DAC; DAM MST, NOV; DLB 36, 100, 162, 195, 255; EWL 3; EXPN; LAIT 5; LMFS 2; MTCW 1, 2; MTFW 2005; NFS 6; RGEL 2; SATA 63; SCFW 1, 2; SFW 4; TEA; YAW
Huxley, Aldous Leonard
    See Huxley, Aldous
Huxley, T(homas) H(enry)
    1825-1895 .... **NCLC 67**
    See also DLB 57; TEA
Huygens, Constantijn 1596-1687 ..... **LC 114**
    See also RGWL 2, 3
Huysmans, Charles Marie Georges
    See Huysmans, Joris-Karl
Huysmans, Joris-Karl
    1848-1907 .... **TCLC 7, 69, 212**
    See also CA 104; 165; DLB 123; EW 7; GFL 1789 to the Present; LMFS 2; RGWL 2, 3
Hwang, David Henry 1957- .... **CLC 55, 196; DC 4, 23**
    See also AMWS 21; CA 127; 132; CAD; CANR 76, 124; CD 5, 6; DA3; DAM DRAM; DFS 11, 18, 29; DLB 212, 228, 312; INT CA-132; MAL 5; MTCW 2; MTFW 2005; RGAL 4
Hyatt, Daniel
    See James, Daniel (Lewis)
Hyde, Anthony 1946- .... **CLC 42**
    See also CA 136; CCA 1
Hyde, Margaret O. 1917- .... **CLC 21**
    See also CA 1-4R; CANR 1, 36, 137, 181; CLR 23; JRDA; MAICYA 1, 2; SAAS 8; SATA 1, 42, 76, 139
Hyde, Margaret Oldroyd
    See Hyde, Margaret O.
Hynes, James 1956(?)- .... **CLC 65**
    See also CA 164; CANR 105
Hypatia c. 370-415 .... **CMLC 35**
Ian, Janis 1951- .... **CLC 21**
    See also CA 105; 187; CANR 206

Ibanez, Vicente Blasco
    See Blasco Ibanez, Vicente
Ibarbourou, Juana de
    1895(?)-1979 .... **HLCS 2**
    See also DLB 290; HW 1; LAW
Ibarguengoitia, Jorge 1928-1983 ... **CLC 37; TCLC 148**
    See also CA 124; 113; EWL 3; HW 1
Ibn Arabi 1165-1240 .... **CMLC 105**
Ibn Battuta, Abu Abdalla
    1304-1368(?) .... **CMLC 57**
    See also WLIT 2
Ibn Hazm 994-1064 .... **CMLC 64**
Ibn Zaydun 1003-1070 .... **CMLC 89**
Ibsen, Henrik 1828-1906 .... **DC 2, 30; TCLC 2, 8, 16, 37, 52; WLC 3**
    See also AAYA 46; CA 104; 141; DA; DA3; DAB; DAC; DAM DRAM, MST; DFS 1, 6, 8, 10, 11, 15, 16, 25; DLB 354; EW 7; LAIT 2; LATS 1:1; MTFW 2005; RGWL 2, 3
Ibsen, Henrik Johan
    See Ibsen, Henrik
Ibuse, Masuji 1898-1993 .... **CLC 22**
    See also CA 127; 141; CWW 2; DLB 180; EWL 3; MJW; RGWL 3
Ibuse Masuji
    See Ibuse, Masuji
Ichikawa, Kon 1915-2008 .... **CLC 20**
    See also CA 121; 269
Ichiyo, Higuchi 1872-1896 .... **NCLC 49**
    See also MJW
Idle, Eric 1943- .... **CLC 21**
    See also CA 116; CANR 35, 91, 148; DLB 352
Idler, An
    See Mangan, James Clarence
Idris, Yusuf 1927-1991 .... **SSC 74; TCLC 232**
    See also AFW; DLB 346; EWL 3; RGSF 2, 3; RGWL 3; WLIT 2
Ignatieff, Michael 1947- .... **CLC 236**
    See also CA 144; CANR 88, 156; CN 6, 7; DLB 267
Ignatieff, Michael Grant
    See Ignatieff, Michael
Ignatow, David 1914-1997 ..... **CLC 4, 7, 14, 40; PC 34**
    See also CA 9-12R; 162; CAAS 3; CANR 31, 57, 96; CP 1, 2, 3, 4, 5, 6; DLB 5; EWL 3; MAL 5
Ignotus
    See Strachey, (Giles) Lytton
Ihimaera, Witi (Tame) 1944- .... **CLC 46, 329**
    See also CA 77-80; CANR 130; CN 2, 3, 4, 5, 6, 7; RGSF 2; SATA 148
Il'f, Il'ia
    See Fainzilberg, Ilya Arnoldovich
Ilf, Ilya
    See Fainzilberg, Ilya Arnoldovich
Illyes, Gyula 1902-1983 .... **PC 16**
    See also CA 114; 109; CDWLB 4; DLB 215; EWL 3; RGWL 2, 3
Imalayen, Fatima-Zohra
    See Djebar, Assia
Immermann, Karl (Lebrecht)
    1796-1840 .... **NCLC 4, 49**
    See also DLB 133
Ince, Thomas H. 1882-1924 .... **TCLC 89**
    See also IDFW 3, 4
Inchbald, Elizabeth 1753-1821 .... **NCLC 62, 276**
    See also BRWS 15; DLB 39, 89; RGEL 2
Inclan, Ramon del Valle
    See Valle-Inclan, Ramon del
Incogniteau, Jean-Louis
    See Kerouac, Jack
Infante, Guillermo Cabrera
    See Cabrera Infante, G.

James, M. R.
See James, Montague

James, Mary
See Meaker, Marijane

James, Montague 1862-1936 ..... **SSC 16, 93, 214; TCLC 6**
See also CA 104; 203; DLB 156, 201; HGG; RGEL 2; RGSF 2; SUFW 1

James, Montague Rhodes
See James, Montague

James, P. D. 1920- .... **CLC 18, 46, 122, 226, 345**
See also BEST 90:2; BPFB 2; BRWS 4; CA 21-24R; CANR 17, 43, 65, 112, 201, 231; CDBLB 1960 to Present; CMW 4; CN 4, 5, 6, 7; CPW; DA3; DAM POP; DLB 87, 276; DLBD 17; MSW; MTCW 1, 2; MTFW 2005; TEA

James, Philip
See Moorcock, Michael

James, Samuel
See Stephens, James

James, Seumas
See Stephens, James

James, Stephen
See Stephens, James

James, T. F.
See Fleming, Thomas

James, William 1842-1910 ...... **TCLC 15, 32**
See also AMW; CA 109; 193; DLB 270, 284; MAL 5; NCFS 5; RGAL 4

Jameson, Anna 1794-1860 .... **NCLC 43, 282**
See also DLB 99, 166

Jameson, Fredric 1934- .... **CLC 142**
See also CA 196; CANR 169; DLB 67; LMFS 2

Jameson, Fredric R.
See Jameson, Fredric

James VI of Scotland 1566-1625 .... **LC 109**
See also DLB 151, 172

Jami, Nur al-Din 'Abd al-Rahman 1414-1492 .... **LC 9**

Jammes, Francis 1868-1938 .... **TCLC 75**
See also CA 198; EWL 3; GFL 1789 to the Present

Jandl, Ernst 1925-2000 .... **CLC 34**
See also CA 200; EWL 3

Janowitz, Tama 1957- .... **CLC 43, 145**
See also CA 106; CANR 52, 89, 129; CN 5, 6, 7; CPW; DAM POP; DLB 292; MTFW 2005

Jansson, Tove (Marika) 1914-2001 ... **SSC 96**
See also CA 17-20R; 196; CANR 38, 118; CLR 2, 125; CWW 2; DLB 257; EWL 3; MAICYA 1, 2; RGSF 2; SATA 3, 41

Japrisot, Sebastien 1931-
See Rossi, Jean-Baptiste

Jarrell, Randall 1914-1965 ...... **CLC 1, 2, 6, 9, 13, 49; PC 41; TCLC 177**
See also AMW; BYA 5; CA 5-8R; 25-28R; CABS 2; CANR 6, 34; CDALB 1941-1968; CLR 6, 111; CWRI 5; DAM POET; DLB 48, 52; EWL 3; EXPP; MAICYA 1, 2; MAL 5; MTCW 1, 2; PAB; PFS 2, 31; RGAL 4; SATA 7

Jarry, Alfred 1873-1907 ...... **DC 49; SSC 20; TCLC 2, 14, 147**
See also CA 104; 153; DA3; DAM DRAM; DFS 8; DLB 192, 258; EW 9; EWL 3; GFL 1789 to the Present; RGWL 2, 3; TWA

Jarvis, E. K.
See Ellison, Harlan; Silverberg, Robert

Jawien, Andrzej
See John Paul II, Pope

Jaynes, Roderick
See Coen, Ethan

Jeake, Samuel, Jr.
See Aiken, Conrad

Jean-Louis
See Kerouac, Jack

Jean Paul 1763-1825 .... **NCLC 7, 268**

Jefferies, (John) Richard 1848-1887 .... **NCLC 47**
See also BRWS 15; DLB 98, 141; RGEL 2; SATA 16; SFW 4

Jefferies, William
See Deaver, Jeffery

Jeffers, John Robinson
See Jeffers, Robinson

Jeffers, Robinson 1887-1962 .... **CLC 2, 3, 11, 15, 54; PC 17; WLC 3**
See also AMWS 2; CA 85-88; CANR 35; CDALB 1917-1929; DA; DAC; DAM MST, POET; DLB 45, 212, 342; EWL 3; MAL 5; MTCW 1, 2; MTFW 2005; PAB; PFS 3, 4; RGAL 4

Jefferson, Janet
See Mencken, H. L.

Jefferson, Thomas 1743-1826 ... **NCLC 11, 103**
See also AAYA 54; ANW; CDALB 1640-1865; DA3; DLB 31, 183; LAIT 1; RGAL 4

Jeffrey, Francis 1773-1850 .... **NCLC 33**
See also DLB 107

Jelakowitch, Ivan
See Heijermans, Herman

Jelinek, Elfriede 1946- .... **CLC 169, 303; DC 53**
See also AAYA 68; CA 154; CANR 169; DLB 85, 330; FW

Jellicoe, (Patricia) Ann 1927- .... **CLC 27**
See also CA 85-88; CBD; CD 5, 6; CWD; CWRI 5; DLB 13, 233; FW

Jelloun, Tahar ben
See Ben Jelloun, Tahar

Jemyma
See Holley, Marietta

Jen, Gish 1955- ..... **AAL; CLC 70, 198, 260**
See also AAYA 85; AMWC 2; CA 135; CANR 89, 130, 231; CN 7; DLB 312; NFS 30; SSFS 34

Jen, Lillian
See Jen, Gish

Jenkins, (John) Robin 1912- .... **CLC 52**
See also CA 1-4R; CANR 1, 135; CN 1, 2, 3, 4, 5, 6, 7; DLB 14, 271

Jennings, Elizabeth (Joan) 1926-2001 .... **CLC 5, 14, 131**
See also BRWS 5; CA 61-64; 200; CAAS 5; CANR 8, 39, 66, 127; CP 1, 2, 3, 4, 5, 6, 7; CWP; DLB 27; EWL 3; MTCW 1; SATA 66

Jennings, Waylon 1937-2002 .... **CLC 21**

Jensen, Johannes V(ilhelm) 1873-1950 .... **TCLC 41**
See also CA 170; DLB 214, 330; EWL 3; RGWL 3

Jensen, Laura 1948- .... **CLC 37**
See also CA 103

Jensen, Laura Linnea
See Jensen, Laura

Jensen, Wilhelm 1837-1911 .... **SSC 140**

Jerome, Saint 345-420 .... **CMLC 30, 157**
See also RGWL 3

Jerome, Jerome K(lapka) 1859-1927 .... **TCLC 23**
See also CA 119; 177; DLB 10, 34, 135; RGEL 2

Jerrold, Douglas William 1803-1857 .... **NCLC 2**
See also DLB 158, 159, 344; RGEL 2

Jewett, Sarah Orne 1849-1909 ... **SSC 6, 44, 110, 138; TCLC 1, 22, 253**
See also AAYA 76; AMW; AMWC 2; AMWR 2; CA 108; 127; CANR 71; DLB 12, 74, 221; EXPS; FL 1:3; FW; MAL 5; MBL; NFS 15; RGAL 4; RGSF 2; SATA 15; SSFS 4

Jewett, Theodora Sarah Orne
See Jewett, Sarah Orne

Jewsbury, Geraldine (Endsor) 1812-1880 .... **NCLC 22**
See also DLB 21

Jhabvala, Ruth Prawer 1927-2013 ... **CLC 4, 8, 29, 94, 138, 284; SSC 91**
See also BRWS 5; CA 1-4R; CANR 2, 29, 51, 74, 91, 128; CN 1, 2, 3, 4, 5, 6, 7; DAB; DAM NOV; DLB 139, 194, 323, 326; EWL 3; IDFW 3, 4; INT CANR-29; MTCW 1, 2; MTFW 2005; RGSF 2; RGWL 2; RHW; TEA

Jibran, Kahlil
See Gibran, Kahlil

Jibran, Khalil
See Gibran, Kahlil

Jiles, Paulette 1943- .... **CLC 13, 58**
See also CA 101; CANR 70, 124, 170; CP 5; CWP

Jimenez, Juan Ramon 1881-1958 ... **HLC 1; PC 7; TCLC 4, 183**
See also CA 104; 131; CANR 74; DAM MULT, POET; DLB 134, 330; EW 9; EWL 3; HW 1; MTCW 1, 2; MTFW 2005; NFS 36; RGWL 2, 3

Jimenez, Ramon
See Jimenez, Juan Ramon

Jimenez Mantecon, Juan
See Jimenez, Juan Ramon

Jimenez Mantecon, Juan Ramon
See Jimenez, Juan Ramon

Jin, Ba 1904-2005 .... **CLC 18**
See Cantu, Robert Clark
See also CA 105; 244; CWW 2; DLB 328; EWL 3

Jin, Ha 1956- .... **CLC 109, 262**
See also AMWS 18; CA 152; CANR 91, 130, 184; DLB 244, 292; MTFW 2005; NFS 25; SSFS 17, 32

Jin, Xuefei
See Jin, Ha

Jin Ha
See Jin, Ha

Jin Yong 1924- .... **CLC 358**
See also DLB 370

Junger, Ernst
See Juenger, Ernst

Jobbry, Archibald
See Galt, John

Jodelle, Etienne 1532-1573 .... **LC 119**
See also DLB 327; GFL Beginnings to 1789

Joel, Billy 1949- .... **CLC 26**
See also CA 108

Joel, William Martin
See Joel, Billy

John, St.
See John of Damascus, St.

John of Damascus, St. c. 675-749 .... **CMLC 27, 95**

John of Salisbury c. 1120-1180 .... **CMLC 63, 128**

John of the Cross, St. 1542-1591 .... **LC 18, 146**
See also RGWL 2, 3

John Paul II, Pope 1920-2005 ...... **CLC 128**
See also CA 106; 133; 238

Johnson, B(ryan) S(tanley William) 1933-1973 .... **CLC 6, 9**
See also CA 9-12R; 53-56; CANR 9; CN 1; CP 1, 2; DLB 14, 40; EWL 3; RGEL 2

Johnson, Benjamin F., of Boone
See Riley, James Whitcomb

Johnson, Charles (Richard) 1948- .... **BLC 1:2, 2:2; CLC 7, 51, 65, 163; SSC 160**

See also AFAW 2; AMWS 6; BW 2, 3; CA 116; CAAS 18; CANR 42, 66, 82, 129; CN 5, 6, 7; DAM MULT; DLB 33, 278; MAL 5; MTCW 2; MTFW 2005; NFS 43; RGAL 4; SSFS 16

Johnson, Charles S(purgeon) 1893-1956 .... **HR 1:3**
See also BW 1, 3; CA 125; CANR 82; DLB 51, 91

Johnson, Denis 1949- .... **CLC 52, 160; SSC 56**
See also CA 117; 121; CANR 71, 99, 178; CN 4, 5, 6, 7; DLB 120

Johnson, Diane 1934- .... **CLC 5, 13, 48, 244**
See also BPFB 2; CA 41-44R; CANR 17, 40, 62, 95, 155, 198; CN 4, 5, 6, 7; DLB 350; DLBY 1980; INT CANR-17; MTCW 1

Johnson, E(mily) Pauline 1861-1913 ... **NNAL**
See also CA 150; CCA 1; DAC; DAM MULT; DLB 92, 175; TCWW 2

Johnson, Eyvind (Olof Verner) 1900-1976 .... **CLC 14**
See also CA 73-76; 69-72; CANR 34, 101; DLB 259, 330; EW 12; EWL 3

Johnson, Fenton 1888-1958 .... **BLC 1:2**
See also BW 1; CA 118; 124; DAM MULT; DLB 45, 50

Johnson, Georgia Douglas (Camp) 1880-1966 .... **HR 1:3**
See also BW 1; CA 125; DLB 51, 249; WP

Johnson, Helene 1907-1995 .... **HR 1:3**
See also CA 181; DLB 51; WP

Johnson, J. R.
See James, C.L.R.

Johnson, James Weldon 1871-1938 ...... **BLC 1:2; HR 1:3; PC 24; TCLC 3, 19, 175**
See also AAYA 73; AFAW 1, 2; BW 1, 3; CA 104; 125; CANR 82; CDALB 1917-1929; CLR 32; DA3; DAM MULT, POET; DLB 51; EWL 3; EXPP; LMFS 2; MAL 5; MTCW 1, 2; MTFW 2005; NFS 22; PFS 1; RGAL 4; SATA 31; TUS

Johnson, Joyce 1935- .... **CLC 58**
See also BG 1:3; CA 125; 129; CANR 102

Johnson, Judith 1936- .... **CLC 7, 15**
See also CA 25-28R, 153; CANR 34, 85; CP 2, 3, 4, 5, 6, 7; CWP

Johnson, Judith Emlyn
See Johnson, Judith

Johnson, Lionel (Pigot) 1867-1902 .... **TCLC 19**
See also CA 117; 209; DLB 19; RGEL 2

Johnson, Marguerite Annie
See Angelou, Maya

Johnson, Mel
See Malzberg, Barry N(athaniel)

Johnson, Pamela Hansford 1912-1981 .... **CLC 1, 7, 27**
See also CA 1-4R; 104; CANR 2, 28; CN 1, 2, 3; DLB 15; MTCW 1, 2; MTFW 2005; RGEL 2

Johnson, Paul 1928- .... **CLC 147**
See also BEST 89:4; CA 17-20R; CANR 34, 62, 100, 155, 197, 241

Johnson, Paul Bede
See Johnson, Paul

Johnson, Robert .... **CLC 70**

Johnson, Robert 1911(?)-1938 ...... **TCLC 69**
See also BW 3; CA 174

Johnson, Samuel 1709-1784 .... **LC 15, 52, 128, 249, 250; PC 81; WLC 3**
See also BRW 3; BRWR 1; CDBLB 1660-1789; DA; DAB; DAC; DAM MST; DLB 39, 95, 104, 142, 213; LMFS 1; RGEL 2; TEA

Johnson, Stacie
See Myers, Walter Dean

Johnson, Uwe 1934-1984 ..... **CLC 5, 10, 15, 40; TCLC 249**
See also CA 1-4R; 112; CANR 1, 39; CDWLB 2; DLB 75; EWL 3; MTCW 1; RGWL 2, 3

Johnston, Basil H. 1929- .... **NNAL**
See also CA 69-72; CANR 11, 28, 66; DAC; DAM MULT; DLB 60

Johnston, George (Benson) 1913- .... **CLC 51**
See also CA 1-4R; CANR 5, 20; CP 1, 2, 3, 4, 5, 6, 7; DLB 88

Johnston, Jennifer (Prudence) 1930- .... **CLC 7, 150, 228**
See also CA 85-88; CANR 92; CN 4, 5, 6, 7; DLB 14

Joinville, Jean de 1224(?)-1317 ... **CMLC 38, 152**

Jolley, Elizabeth 1923-2007 .... **CLC 46, 256, 260; SSC 19**
See also CA 127; 257; CAAS 13; CANR 59; CN 4, 5, 6, 7; DLB 325; EWL 3; RGSF 2

Jolley, Monica Elizabeth
See Jolley, Elizabeth

Jones, Arthur Llewellyn 1863-1947 .... **SSC 20, 206; TCLC 4**
See also CA 104; 179; DLB 36; HGG; RGEL 2; SUFW 1

Jones, D(ouglas) G(ordon) 1929- ... **CLC 10**
See also CA 29-32R; CANR 13, 90; CP 1, 2, 3, 4, 5, 6, 7; DLB 53

Jones, David (Michael) 1895-1974 ... **CLC 2, 4, 7, 13, 42; PC 116**
See also BRW 6; BRWS 7; CA 9-12R; 53-56; CANR 28; CDBLB 1945-1960; CP 1, 2; DLB 20, 100; EWL 3; MTCW 1; PAB; RGEL 2

Jones, David Robert
See Bowie, David

Jones, Diana Wynne 1934-2011 ..... **CLC 26**
See also AAYA 12; BYA 6, 7, 9, 11, 13, 16; CA 49-52; CANR 4, 26, 56, 120, 167; CLR 23, 120; DLB 161; FANT; JRDA; MAICYA 1, 2; MTFW 2005; SAAS 7; SATA 9, 70, 108, 160, 234; SFW 4; SUFW 2; YAW

Jones, Edward P. 1950- .... **BLC 2:2; CLC 76, 223**
See also AAYA 71; BW 2, 3; CA 142; CANR 79, 134, 190; CSW; LNFS 2; MTFW 2005; NFS 26

Jones, Edward Paul
See Jones, Edward P.

Jones, Ernest Charles 1819-1869 .... **NCLC 222**
See also DLB 32

Jones, Everett LeRoi
See Baraka, Amiri

Jones, Gail 1955- .... **CLC 386**
See also CA 188; CANR 193

Jones, Gayl 1949- .... **BLC 1:2; CLC 6, 9, 131, 270**
See also AFAW 1, 2; BW 2, 3; CA 77-80; CANR 27, 66, 122; CN 4, 5, 6, 7; CSW; DA3; DAM MULT; DLB 33, 278; MAL 5; MTCW 1, 2; MTFW 2005; RGAL 4

Jones, James 1921-1977 .... **CLC 1, 3, 10, 39**
See also AITN 1, 2; AMWS 11; BPFB 2; CA 1-4R; 69-72; CANR 6; CN 1, 2; DLB 2, 143; DLBD 17; DLBY 1998; EWL 3; MAL 5; MTCW 1; RGAL 4

Jones, John J.
See Lovecraft, H. P.

Jones, LeRoi
See Baraka, Amiri

Jones, Louis B. 1953- .... **CLC 65**
See also CA 141; CANR 73

Jones, Madison 1925- .... **CLC 4**
See also CA 13-16R; CAAS 11; CANR 7, 54, 83, 158; CN 1, 2, 3, 4, 5, 6, 7; CSW; DLB 152

Jones, Madison Percy, Jr.
See Jones, Madison

Jones, Mervyn 1922-2010 .... **CLC 10, 52**
See also CA 45-48; CAAS 5; CANR 1, 91; CN 1, 2, 3, 4, 5, 6, 7; MTCW 1

Jones, Mick 1956(?)- .... **CLC 30**

Jones, Nettie (Pearl) 1941- .... **CLC 34**
See also BW 2; CA 137; CAAS 20; CANR 88

Jones, Peter 1802-1856 .... **NNAL**

Jones, Preston 1936-1979 .... **CLC 10**
See also CA 73-76; 89-92; DLB 7

Jones, Robert F(rancis) 1934-2003 ... **CLC 7**
See also CA 49-52; CANR 2, 61, 118

Jones, Rod 1953- .... **CLC 50**
See also CA 128

Jones, Terence Graham Parry 1942- .... **CLC 21**
See also CA 112; 116; CANR 35, 93, 173; INT CA-116; SATA 67, 127; SATA-Brief 51

Jones, Terry
See Jones, Terence Graham Parry

Jones, Thom (Douglas) 1945(?)- .... **CLC 81; SSC 56**
See also CA 157; CANR 88; DLB 244; SSFS 23

Jones, Sir William 1746-1794 .... **LC 191**
See also DLB 109

Jong, Erica 1942- .... **CLC 4, 6, 8, 18, 83**
See also AITN 1; AMWS 5; BEST 90:2; BPFB 2; CA 73-76; CANR 26, 52, 75, 132, 166, 212; CN 3, 4, 5, 6, 7; CP 2, 3, 4, 5, 6, 7; CPW; DA3; DAM NOV, POP; DLB 2, 5, 28, 152; FW; INT CANR-26; MAL 5; MTCW 1, 2; MTFW 2005

Jonson, Ben 1572(?)-1637 .... **DC 4; LC 6, 33, 110, 158, 196, 227, 240, 248; PC 17, 146; WLC 3**
See also BRW 1; BRWC 1; BRWR 1; CDBLB Before 1660; DA; DAB; DAC; DAM DRAM, MST, POET; DFS 4, 10; DLB 62, 121; LMFS 1; PFS 23, 33; RGEL 2; TEA; WLIT 3

Jonson, Benjamin
See Jonson, Ben

Jordan, June 1936-2002 ...... **BLCS; CLC 5, 11, 23, 114, 230; PC 38**
See also AAYA 2, 66; AFAW 1, 2; BW 2, 3; CA 33-36R; 206; CANR 25, 70, 114, 154; CLR 10; CP 3, 4, 5, 6, 7; CWP; DAM MULT, POET; DLB 38; GLL 2; LAIT 5; MAICYA 1, 2; MTCW 1; SATA 4, 136; YAW

Jordan, June Meyer
See Jordan, June

Jordan, Neil 1950- .... **CLC 110; SSC 180**
See also CA 124; 130; CANR 54, 154; CN 4, 5, 6, 7; GLL 2; INT CA-130

Jordan, Neil Patrick
See Jordan, Neil

Jordan, Pat(rick M.) 1941- .... **CLC 37**
See also CA 33-36R; CANR 121

Jorgensen, Ivar
See Ellison, Harlan

Jorgenson, Ivar
See Silverberg, Robert

Joseph, George Ghevarughese ...... **CLC 70**

Josephson, Mary
See O'Doherty, Brian

Josephus, Flavius c. 37-100 ... **CMLC 13, 93**
See also AW 2; DLB 176; WLIT 8

Josh
See Twain, Mark

Josiah Allen's Wife
See Holley, Marietta

Josipovici, Gabriel 1940- .... **CLC 6, 43, 153**
See also CA 37-40R, 224; CAAE 224;
CAAS 8; CANR 47, 84; CN 3, 4, 5, 6,
7; DLB 14, 319

Josipovici, Gabriel David
See Josipovici, Gabriel

Joubert, Joseph 1754-1824 .... **NCLC 9**

Jouve, Pierre Jean 1887-1976 .... **CLC 47**
See also CA 252; 65-68; DLB 258; EWL 3

Jovine, Francesco 1902-1950 .... **TCLC 79**
See also DLB 264; EWL 3

Joyaux, Julia
See Kristeva, Julia

Joyce, James 1882-1941 .... **DC 16; PC 22;
SSC 3, 26, 44, 64, 118, 122, 172, 186, 188,
198, 222; TCLC 3, 8, 16, 35, 52, 159,
280; WLC 3**
See also AAYA 42; BRW 7; BRWC 1;
BRWR 3; BYA 11, 13; CA 104; 126;
CDBLB 1914-1945; DA; DA3; DAB;
DAC; DAM MST, NOV, POET; DLB
10, 19, 36, 162, 247; EWL 3; EXPN;
EXPS; LAIT 3; LMFS 1, 2; MTCW 1,
2; MTFW 2005; NFS 7, 26; RGSF 2; SSFS
1, 19, 32; TEA; WLIT 4

Joyce, James Augustine Aloysius
See Joyce, James

Joyce, Rachel 1962- .... **CLC 354**

Jozsef, Attila 1905-1937 .... **TCLC 22**
See also CA 116; 230; CDWLB 4; DLB 215;
EWL 3

Juana Inés de la Cruz, Sor
1651(?)-1695 .... **HLCS 1; LC 5, 136;
PC 24, 166**
See also DLB 305; FW; LAW; PFS 43;
RGWL 2, 3; WLIT 1

Juana Inez de La Cruz, Sor
See Juana Inés de la Cruz, Sor

Juan Manuel, Don 1282-1348 .... **CMLC 88**

Judd, Cyril
See Kornbluth, C(yril) M.; Pohl, Frederik

Juenger, Ernst 1895-1998 .... **CLC 125**
See also CA 101; 167; CANR 21, 47, 106;
CDWLB 2; DLB 56; EWL 3; RGWL 2, 3

Julian of Norwich
1342(?)-1416(?) .... **LC 6, 52**
See also BRWS 12; DLB 146; LMFS 1

Julius Caesar 100B.C.-44B.C. ..... **CMLC 47,
173**
See also AW 1; CDWLB 1; DLB 211;
RGWL 2, 3; WLIT 8

Jung, Patricia B.
See Hope, Christopher

Junger, Sebastian 1962- .... **CLC 109**
See also AAYA 28; CA 165; CANR 130,
171, 228; MTFW 2005

Juniper, Alex
See Hospital, Janette Turner

Junius
See Luxemburg, Rosa

Junzaburo, Nishiwaki
See Nishiwaki, Junzaburo

Just, Ward 1935- .... **CLC 4, 27**
See also CA 25-28R; CANR 32, 87, 219;
CN 6, 7; DLB 335; INT CANR-32

Just, Ward S.
See Just, Ward

Just, Ward Swift
See Just, Ward

Justice, Donald 1925-2004 .... **CLC 6, 19,
102; PC 64**
See also AMWS 7; CA 5-8R; 230; CANR
26, 54, 74, 121, 122, 169; CP 1, 2, 3, 4, 5,
6, 7; CSW; DAM POET; DLBY 1983;
EWL 3; INT CANR-26; MAL 5; MTCW
2; PFS 14; TCLE 1:1

Justice, Donald Rodney
See Justice, Donald

Juvenal c. 55-c. 127 .... **CMLC 8, 115**
See also AW 2; CDWLB 1; DLB 211;
RGWL 2, 3; WLIT 8

Juvenis
See Bourne, Randolph S(illiman)

K., Alice
See Knapp, Caroline

Kabakov, Sasha .... **CLC 59**

Kabir 1398(?)-1448(?) .... **LC 109; PC 56**
See also RGWL 2, 3

Kacew, Romain 1914-1980 .... **CLC 25**
See also CA 108; 102; DLB 83, 299; RGHL

Kacew, Roman
See Kacew, Romain

Kadare, Ismail 1936- ...... **CLC 52, 190, 331**
See also CA 161; CANR 165, 212; DLB
353; EWL 3; RGWL 3

Kadohata, Cynthia 1956(?)- .... **CLC 59, 122**
See also AAYA 71; CA 140; CANR 124, 205;
CLR 121; LNFS 1; SATA 155, 180, 228

Kadohata, Cynthia L.
See Kadohata, Cynthia

Kafu
See Nagai, Kafu

Kafka, Franz 1883-1924 .... **SSC 5, 29, 35,
60, 128, 184, 186; TCLC 2, 6, 13, 29, 47,
53, 112, 179, 288; WLC 3**
See also AAYA 31; BPFB 2; CA 105; 126;
CDWLB 2; CLR 193; DA; DA3; DAB;
DAC; DAM MST, NOV; DLB 81; EW 9;
EWL 3; EXPS; LATS 1:1; LMFS 2;
MTCW 1, 2; MTFW 2005; NFS 7, 34;
RGSF 2; RGWL 2, 3; SFW 4; SSFS 3, 7,
12, 33; TWA

Kahanovitch, Pinchas
See Der Nister

Kahanovitsch, Pinkhes
See Der Nister

Kahanovitsh, Pinkhes
See Der Nister

Kahn, Roger 1927- .... **CLC 30**
See also CA 25-28R; CANR 44, 69, 152;
DLB 171; SATA 37

Kain, Saul
See Sassoon, Siegfried

Kaiser, Georg 1878-1945 .... **TCLC 9, 220**
See also CA 106; 190; CDWLB 2; DLB 124;
EWL 3; LMFS 2; RGWL 2, 3

Kaledin, Sergei .... **CLC 59**

Kaletski, Alexander 1946- .... **CLC 39**
See also CA 118; 143

Kallman, Chester (Simon)
1921-1975 .... **CLC 2**
See also CA 45-48; 53-56; CANR 3; CP 1, 2

Kaminsky, Melvin
See Brooks, Mel

Kaminsky, Stuart
See Kaminsky, Stuart M.

Kaminsky, Stuart M. 1934-2009 .... **CLC 59**
See also CA 73-76; 292; CANR 29, 53, 89,
161, 190; CMW 4

Kaminsky, Stuart Melvin
See Kaminsky, Stuart M.

Kamo no Chomei 1153(?)-1216 ... **CMLC 66**
See also DLB 203

Kamo no Nagaakira
See Kamo no Chomei

Kandinsky, Wassily 1866-1944 ..... **TCLC 92**
See also AAYA 64; CA 118; 155

Kane, Francis
See Robbins, Harold

Kane, Paul
See Simon, Paul

Kane, Sarah 1971-1999 .... **DC 31**
See also BRWS 8; CA 190; CD 5, 6; DLB 310

Kanin, Garson 1912-1999 .... **CLC 22**
See also AITN 1; CA 5-8R; 177; CAD;
CANR 7, 78; DLB 7; IDFW 3, 4

Kaniuk, Yoram 1930- .... **CLC 19**
See also CA 134; DLB 299; RGHL

Kant, Immanuel 1724-1804 .... **NCLC 27,
67, 253**
See also DLB 94

Kant, Klerk
See Copeland, Stewart

Kantor, MacKinlay 1904-1977 .... **CLC 7**
See also CA 61-64; 73-76; CANR 60, 63;
CN 1, 2; DLB 9, 102; MAL 5; MTCW 2;
RHW; TCWW 1, 2

Kanze Motokiyo
See Zeami

Kaplan, David Michael 1946- .... **CLC 50**
See also CA 187

Kaplan, James 1951- .... **CLC 59**
See also CA 135; CANR 121, 228

Karadzic, Vuk Stefanovic
1787-1864 .... **NCLC 115**
See also CDWLB 4; DLB 147

Karageorge, Michael
See Anderson, Poul

Karamzin, Nikolai Mikhailovich
1766-1826 .... **NCLC 3, 173**
See also DLB 150; RGSF 2

Karapanou, Margarita 1946- .... **CLC 13**
See also CA 101

Karinthy, Frigyes 1887-1938 .... **TCLC 47**
See also CA 170; DLB 215; EWL 3

Karl, Frederick R(obert) 1927-2004 .. **CLC 34**
See also CA 5-8R; 226; CANR 3, 44, 143

Karnad, Girish 1938- .... **CLC 367**
See also CA 65-68; CD 5, 6; DLB 323

Karr, Mary 1955- .... **CLC 188**
See also AMWS 11; CA 151; CANR 100,
191, 241; MTFW 2005; NCFS 5

Kastel, Warren
See Silverberg, Robert

Kataev, Evgeny Petrovich
1903-1942 .... **TCLC 21**
See also CA 120; DLB 272

Kataphusin
See Ruskin, John

Katz, Steve 1935- .... **CLC 47**
See also CA 25-28R; CAAS 14, 64; CANR
12; CN 4, 5, 6, 7; DLBY 1983

Kauffman, Janet 1945- .... **CLC 42**
See also CA 117; CANR 43, 84; DLB 218;
DLBY 1986

Kaufman, Bob (Garnell)
1925-1986 .... **CLC 49; PC 74**
See also BG 1:3; BW 1; CA 41-44R; 118;
CANR 22; CP 1; DLB 16, 41

Kaufman, George S. 1889-1961 .... **CLC 38;
DC 17**
See also CA 108; 93-96; DAM DRAM; DFS
1, 10; DLB 7; INT CA-108; MTCW 2;
MTFW 2005; RGAL 4; TUS

Kaufman, Moises 1963- .... **DC 26**
See also AAYA 85; CA 211; DFS 22;
MTFW 2005

Kaufman, Sue
See Barondess, Sue K.

Kavafis, Konstantinos Petrov
See Cavafy, Constantine

Kavan, Anna 1901-1968 .... **CLC 5, 13, 82**
See also BRWS 7; CA 5-8R; CANR 6, 57;
DLB 255; MTCW 1; RGEL 2; SFW 4

Kavanagh, Dan
See Barnes, Julian

Kavanagh, Julie 1952- .... **CLC 119**
See also CA 163; CANR 186

Kavanagh, Patrick (Joseph)
1904-1967 .... **CLC 22; PC 33, 105**
See also BRWS 7; CA 123; 25-28R; DLB
15, 20; EWL 3; MTCW 1; RGEL 2

Kawabata, Yasunari 1899-1972 ... **CLC 2, 5,
9, 18, 107; SSC 17**

3; EXPN; LAIT 4; MAL 5; MTCW 1, 2; MTFW 2005; NFS 2; RGAL 4; SATA 66; SATA-Obit 131; TUS; YAW

Kesselring, Joseph (Otto)
1902-1967 .... **CLC 45**
See also CA 150; DAM DRAM, MST; DFS 20

Kessler, Jascha (Frederick) 1929- .... **CLC 4**
See also CA 17-20R; CANR 8, 48, 111; CP 1

Kettelkamp, Larry (Dale) 1933- ..... **CLC 12**
See also CA 29-32R; CANR 16; SAAS 3; SATA 2

Key, Ellen (Karolina Sofia)
1849-1926 .... **TCLC 65**
See also DLB 259

Keyber, Conny
See Fielding, Henry

Keyes, Daniel 1927- .... **CLC 80**
See also AAYA 23; BYA 11; CA 17-20R, 181; CAAE 181; CANR 10, 26, 54, 74; DA; DA3; DAC; DAM MST, NOV; EXPN; LAIT 4; MTCW 2; MTFW 2005; NFS 2; SATA 37; SFW 4

Keynes, John Maynard
1883-1946 .... **TCLC 64**
See also CA 114; 162, 163; DLBD 10; MTCW 2; MTFW 2005

Khanshendel, Chiron
See Rose, Wendy

Khatibi, Abdelkebir 1938- .... **CLC 327**
See also CA 250; EWL 3; RGWL 3

Khayyam, Omar
1048-1131 .... **CMLC 11, 137; PC 8**
See also DA3; DAM POET; RGWL 2, 3; WLIT 6

Kherdian, David 1931- .... **CLC 6, 9**
See also AAYA 42; CA 21-24R, 192; CAAE 192; CAAS 2; CANR 39, 78; CLR 24; JRDA; LAIT 3; MAICYA 1, 2; SATA 16, 74; SATA-Essay 125

Khlebnikov, Velimir
See Khlebnikov, Viktor Vladimirovich

Khlebnikov, Viktor Vladimirovich
1885-1922 .... **TCLC 20, 322**
See also CA 117; 217; DLB 295; EW 10; EWL 3; RGWL 2, 3

Khodasevich, V.F.
See Khodasevich, Vladislav

Khodasevich, Vladislav
1886-1939 .... **TCLC 15**
See also CA 115; DLB 317; EWL 3

Khodasevich, Vladislav Felitsianovich
See Khodasevich, Vladislav

Khoury, Elias 1948- .... **CLC 338**
See also CA 248; CANR 189

Kis, Danilo 1935-1989 .... **CLC 57**
See also CA 109; 118; 129; CANR 61; CDWLB 4; DLB 181; EWL 3; MTCW 1; RGSF 2; RGWL 2, 3

Kiarostami, Abbas 1940- .... **CLC 295**
See also CA 204

Kidd, Sue Monk 1948- .... **CLC 267**
See also AAYA 72; CA 202; LNFS 1; MTFW 2005; NFS 27

Kielland, Alexander Lange
1849-1906 .... **TCLC 5**
See also CA 104; DLB 354

Kiely, Benedict 1919-2007 .... **CLC 23, 43; SSC 58, 184**
See also CA 1-4R; 257; CANR 2, 84; CN 1, 2, 3, 4, 5, 6, 7; DLB 15, 319; TCLE 1:1

Kienzle, William X. 1928-2001 .... **CLC 25**
See also CA 93-96; 203; CAAS 1; CANR 9, 31, 59, 111; CMW 4; DA3; DAM POP; INT CANR-31; MSW; MTCW 1, 2; MTFW 2005

Kierkegaard, Soren 1813-1855 .... **NCLC 34, 78, 125, 265**

See also DLB 300; EW 6; LMFS 2; RGWL 3; TWA

Kieslowski, Krzysztof 1941-1996 ... **CLC 120**
See also CA 147; 151

Killens, John Oliver 1916-1987 .... **BLC 2:2; CLC 10**
See also BW 2; CA 77-80; 123; CAAS 2; CANR 26; CN 1, 2, 3, 4; DLB 33; EWL 3

Killigrew, Anne 1660-1685 .... **LC 4, 73, 221**
See also DLB 131

Killigrew, Thomas 1612-1683 .... **LC 57**
See also DLB 58; RGEL 2

Kim
See Simenon, Georges

Kincaid, Jamaica 1949- .... **BLC 1:2, 2:2; CLC 43, 68, 137, 234; SSC 72, 180**
See also AAYA 13, 56; AFAW 2; AMWS 7; BRWS 7; BW 2, 3; CA 125; CANR 47, 59, 95, 133; CDALBS; CDWLB 3; CLR 63; CN 4, 5, 6, 7; DA3; DAM MULT, NOV; DLB 157, 227; DNFS 1; EWL 3; EXPS; FW; LATS 1:2; LMFS 2; MAL 5; MTCW 2; MTFW 2005; NCFS 1; NFS 3; SSFS 5, 7; TUS; WWE 1; YAW

King, Francis 1923-2011 ..... **CLC 8, 53, 145**
See also CA 1-4R; CANR 1, 33, 86; CN 1, 2, 3, 4, 5, 6, 7; DAM NOV; DLB 15, 139; MTCW 1

King, Francis Henry
See King, Francis

King, Grace 1852-1932 .... **SSC 195**
See also CA 116; DLB 12, 78

King, Kennedy
See Brown, George Douglas

King, Martin Luther, Jr.
1929-1968 ... **BLC 1:2; CLC 83; WLCS**
See also BW 2, 3; CA 25-28; CANR 27, 44; CAP 2; DA; DA3; DAB; DAC; DAM MST, MULT; LAIT 5; LATS 1:2; MTCW 1, 2; MTFW 2005; SATA 14

King, Stephen 1947- ..... **CLC 12, 26, 37, 61, 113, 228, 244, 328, 378; SSC 17, 55**
See also AAYA 1, 17, 82; AMWS 5; BEST 90:1; BPFB 2; CA 61-64; CANR 1, 30, 52, 76, 119, 134, 168, 227; CLR 124, 194; CN 7; CPW; DA3; DAM NOV, POP; DLB 143, 350; DLBY 1980; HGG; JRDA; LAIT 5; LNFS 1; MTCW 1, 2; MTFW 2005; RGAL 4; SATA 9, 55, 161; SSFS 30; SUFW 1, 2; WYAS 1; YAW

King, Stephen Edwin
See King, Stephen

King, Steve
See King, Stephen

King, Thomas 1943- .... **CLC 89, 171, 276; NNAL**
See also CA 144; CANR 95, 175; CCA 1; CN 6, 7; DAC; DAM MULT; DLB 175, 334; SATA 96

King, Thomas Hunt
See King, Thomas

Kingman, Lee
See Natti, Lee

Kingsley, Charles 1819-1875 .... **NCLC 35**
See also BRWS 16; CLR 77, 167; DLB 21, 32, 163, 178, 190; FANT; MAICYA 2; MAICYAS 1; RGEL 2; WCH; YABC 2

Kingsley, Henry 1830-1876 .... **NCLC 107**
See also DLB 21, 230; RGEL 2

Kingsley, Sidney 1906-1995 .... **CLC 44**
See also CA 85-88; 147; CAD; DFS 14, 19; DLB 7; MAL 5; RGAL 4

Kingsolver, Barbara 1955- .... **CLC 55, 81, 130, 216, 269, 342**
See also AAYA 15; AMWS 7; CA 129; 134; CANR 60, 96, 133, 179; CDALBS; CN 7; CPW; CSW; DA3; DAM POP; DLB 206; INT CA-134; LAIT 5; MTCW 2; MTFW 2005; NFS 5, 10, 12, 24; RGAL 4; TCLE 1:1

Kingston, Maxine Hong 1940- ... **AAL; CLC 12, 19, 58, 121, 271; SSC 136; WLCS**
See also AAYA 8, 55; AMWS 5; BPFB 2; CA 69-72; CANR 13, 38, 74, 87, 128, 239; CDALBS; CN 6, 7; DA3; DAM MULT, NOV; DLB 173, 212, 312; DLBY 1980; EWL 3; FL 1:6; FW; INT CANR-13; LAIT 5; MAL 5; MBL; MTCW 1, 2; MTFW 2005; NFS 6; RGAL 4; SATA 53; SSFS 3; TCWW 2

Kingston, Maxine Ting Ting Hong
See Kingston, Maxine Hong

Kinnell, Galway 1927- ... **CLC 1, 2, 3, 5, 13, 29, 129; PC 26**
See also AMWS 3; CA 9-12R; CANR 10, 34, 66, 116, 138, 175; CP 1, 2, 3, 4, 5, 6, 7; DLB 5, 342; DLBY 1987; EWL 3; INT CANR-34; MAL 5; MTCW 1, 2; MTFW 2005; PAB; PFS 9, 26, 35; RGAL 4; TCLE 1:1; WP

Kinsella, John 1963- .... **CLC 384**
See also CA 189; CP 7; DLB 325; WWE 1

Kinsella, Thomas 1928- ..... **CLC 4, 19, 138, 274; PC 69**
See also BRWS 5; CA 17-20R; CANR 15, 122; CP 1, 2, 3, 4, 5, 6, 7; DLB 27; EWL 3; MTCW 1, 2; MTFW 2005; RGEL 2; TEA

Kinsella, William Patrick
See Kinsella, W.P.

Kinsella, W.P. 1935- .... **CLC 27, 43, 166**
See also AAYA 7, 60; BPFB 2; CA 97-100, 222; CAAE 222; CAAS 7; CANR 21, 35, 66, 75, 129; CN 4, 5, 6, 7; CPW; DAC; DAM NOV, POP; DLB 362; FANT; INT CANR-21; LAIT 5; MTCW 1, 2; MTFW 2005; NFS 15; RGSF 2; SSFS 30

Kinsey, Alfred C(harles)
1894-1956 .... **TCLC 91**
See also CA 115; 170; MTCW 2

Kipling, Joseph Rudyard
See Kipling, Rudyard

Kipling, Rudyard 1865-1936 .... **PC 3, 91; SSC 5, 54, 110, 207, 217, 222; TCLC 8, 17, 167; WLC 3**
See also AAYA 32; BRW 6; BRWC 1, 2; BRWR 3; BYA 4; CA 105; 120; CANR 33; CDBLB 1890-1914; CLR 39, 65, 199; CWRI 5; DA; DA3; DAB; DAC; DAM MST, POET; DLB 19, 34, 141, 156, 330; EWL 3; EXPS; FANT; LAIT 3; LMFS 1; MAICYA 1, 2; MTCW 1, 2; MTFW 2005; NFS 21; PFS 22; RGEL 2; RGSF 2; SATA 100; SFW 4; SSFS 8, 21, 22, 32, 42; SUFW 1; TEA; WCH; WLIT 4; YABC 2

Kircher, Athanasius 1602-1680 .... **LC 121**
See also DLB 164

Kirk, Richard
See Holdstock, Robert

Kirk, Russell (Amos) 1918-1994 ... **TCLC 119**
See also AITN 1; CA 1-4R; 145; CAAS 9; CANR 1, 20, 60; HGG; INT CANR-20; MTCW 1, 2

Kirkham, Dinah
See Card, Orson Scott

Kirkland, Caroline M.
1801-1864 .... **NCLC 85, 309**
See also DLB 3, 73, 74, 250, 254; DLBD 13

Kirkup, James 1918-2009 .... **CLC 1**
See also CA 1-4R; CAAS 4; CANR 2; CP 1, 2, 3, 4, 5, 6, 7; DLB 27; SATA 12

Kirkwood, James 1930(?)-1989 .... **CLC 9**
See also AITN 2; CA 1-4R; 128; CANR 6, 40; GLL 2

Kirsch, Sarah 1935- .... **CLC 176**
See also CA 178; CWW 2; DLB 75; EWL 3

Kirshner, Sidney
See Kingsley, Sidney

Kissinger, Henry A. 1923- .... **CLC 137**
See also CA 1-4R; CANR 2, 33, 66, 109; MTCW 1

See also AAYA 64; BRW 4; BRWC 2;
  CDBLB 1789-1832; DA; DA3; DAB;
  DAC; DAM MST, POET; DLB 96, 110;
  EXPP; LMFS 1; PAB; PFS 1, 14, 29, 35;
  RGEL 2; TEA; WLIT 3; WP
Lord Dunsany 1878-1957 .... **TCLC 2, 59**
  See also CA 104; 148; DLB 10, 77, 153,
  156, 255; FANT; MTCW 2; RGEL 2; SFW
  4; SUFW 1
Lorde, Audre 1934-1992 .... **BLC 1:2, 2:2;**
  CLC 18, 71; PC 12, 141; TCLC 173, 300
  See also AFAW 1, 2; BW 1, 3; CA 25-28R;
  142; CANR 16, 26, 46, 82; CP 2, 3, 4, 5;
  DA3; DAM MULT, POET; DLB 41; EWL
  3; FW; GLL 1; MAL 5; MTCW 1, 2;
  MTFW 2005; PFS 16, 32; RGAL 4
Lorde, Audre Geraldine
  See Lorde, Audre
Lord Houghton
  See Milnes, Richard Monckton
Lord Jeffrey
  See Jeffrey, Francis
Loreaux, Nichol .... **CLC 65**
Lorenzo, Heberto Padilla
  See Padilla (Lorenzo), Heberto
Loris
  See Hofmannsthal, Hugo von
Loti, Pierre
  See Viaud, Julien
Lottie
  See Grimke, Charlotte L. Forten
Lou, Henri
  See Andreas-Salome, Lou
Louie, David Wong 1954- .... **CLC 70**
  See also CA 139; CANR 120
Louis, Adrian C. .... **NNAL**
  See also CA 223
Louis, Father M.
  See Merton, Thomas
Louise, Heidi
  See Erdrich, Louise
Lounsbury, Ruth Ozeki
  See Ozeki, Ruth L.
Lovecraft, H. P. 1890-1937 .... **SSC 3, 52,**
  165, 200; TCLC 4, 22
  See also AAYA 14; BPFB 2; CA 104; 133;
  CANR 106; DA3; DAM POP; HGG;
  MTCW 1, 2; MTFW 2005; RGAL 4;
  SCFW 1, 2; SFW 4; SUFW
Lovecraft, Howard Phillips
  See Lovecraft, H. P.
Lovelace, Earl 1935- .... **CLC 51; SSC 141**
  See also BW 2; CA 77-80; CANR 41, 72,
  114; CD 5, 6; CDWLB 3; CN 1, 2, 3, 4, 5,
  6, 7; DLB 125; EWL 3; MTCW 1
Lovelace, Richard
  1618-1658 .... **LC 24, 158; PC 69**
  See also BRW 2; DLB 131; EXPP; PAB;
  PFS 32, 34; RGEL 2
Low, Penelope Margaret
  See Lively, Penelope
Lowe, Pardee 1904- .... **AAL**
Lowell, Amy 1874-1925 .... **PC 13, 168;**
  TCLC 1, 8, 259
  See also AAYA 57; AMW; CA 104; 151;
  DAM POET; DLB 54, 140; EWL 3; EXPP;
  LMFS 2; MAL 5; MBL; MTCW 2; MTFW
  2005; PFS 30, 42; RGAL 4; TUS
Lowell, James Russell
  1819-1891 .... **NCLC 2, 90**
  See also AMWS 1; CDALB 1640-1865;
  DLB 1, 11, 64, 79, 189, 235; RGAL 4
Lowell, Robert 1917-1977 ... **CLC 1, 2, 3, 4,**
  5, 8, 9, 11, 15, 37, 124; PC 3, 132; WLC 4
  See also AMW; AMWC 2; AMWR 2; CA 9-
  12R; 73-76; CABS 2; CAD; CANR 26, 60;
  CDALBS; CP 1, 2; DA; DA3; DAB; DAC;
  DAM MST, NOV; DLB 5, 169; EWL 3;

MAL 5; MTCW 1, 2; MTFW 2005; PAB;
  PFS 6, 7, 36; RGAL 4; WP
Lowell, Robert Trail Spence, Jr.
  See Lowell, Robert
Lowenthal, Michael 1969- .... **CLC 119**
  See also CA 150; CANR 115, 164
Lowenthal, Michael Francis
  See Lowenthal, Michael
Lowndes, Marie Adelaide (Belloc)
  1868-1947 .... **TCLC 12**
  See also CA 107; CMW 4; DLB 70; RHW
Lowry, (Clarence) Malcolm
  1909-1957 ... **SSC 31; TCLC 6, 40, 275**
  See also BPFB 2; BRWS 3; CA 105; 131;
  CANR 62, 105; CDBLB 1945-1960; DLB
  15; EWL 3; MTCW 1, 2; MTFW 2005;
  RGEL 2
Lowry, Mina Gertrude
  1882-1966 .... **CLC 28; PC 16**
  See also CA 113; DAM POET; DLB 4, 54;
  PFS 20
Lowry, Sam
  See Soderbergh, Steven
Loxsmith, John
  See Brunner, John (Kilian Houston)
Loy, Mina
  See Lowry, Mina Gertrude
Loyson-Bridet
  See Schwob, Marcel (Mayer Andre)
Lopez de Mendoza, Inigo
  See Santillana, Inigo Lopez de Mendoza,
  Marques de
Lopez Portillo (y Pacheco), Jose
  1920-2004 .... **CLC 46**
  See also CA 129; 224; HW 1
Eluard, Paul
  See Grindel, Eugene
Lucan 39-65 .... **CMLC 33, 112, 160**
  See also AW 2; DLB 211; EFS 1:2, 2:2;
  RGWL 2, 3
Lucas, Craig 1951- .... **CLC 64**
  See also CA 137; CAD; CANR 71, 109,
  142; CD 5, 6; GLL 2; MTFW 2005
Lucas, E(dward) V(errall)
  1868-1938 .... **TCLC 73**
  See also CA 176; DLB 98, 149, 153; SATA 20
Lucas, George 1944- .... **CLC 16, 252**
  See also AAYA 1, 23; CA 77-80; CANR 30;
  SATA 56
Lucas, Hans
  See Godard, Jean-Luc
Lucas, Victoria
  See Plath, Sylvia
Lucian c. 125-c. 180 .... **CMLC 32, 144**
  See also AW 2; DLB 176; RGWL 2, 3
Lucilius c. 180B.C.-102B.C. .... **CMLC 82**
  See also DLB 211
Lucretius c. 94B.C.-c. 49B.C. ...... **CMLC 48,**
  170; PC 143
  See also AW 2; CDWLB 1; DLB 211; EFS
  1:2, 2:2; RGWL 2, 3; WLIT 8
Ludlam, Charles 1943-1987 ...... **CLC 46, 50**
  See also CA 85-88; 122; CAD; CANR 72,
  86; DLB 266
Ludlum, Robert 1927-2001 .... **CLC 22, 43**
  See also AAYA 10, 59; BEST 89:1, 90:3;
  BPFB 2; CA 33-36R; 195; CANR 25, 41,
  68, 105, 131; CMW 4; CPW; DA3; DAM
  NOV, POP; DLBY 1982; MSW; MTCW 1,
  2; MTFW 2005
Ludwig, Ken 1950- .... **CLC 60**
  See also CA 195; CAD; CD 6
Ludwig, Otto 1813-1865 .... **NCLC 4**
  See also DLB 129
Lugones, Leopoldo 1874-1938 .... **HLCS 2;**
  TCLC 15
  See also CA 116; 131; CANR 104; DLB
  283; EWL 3; HW 1; LAW

Lu Hsun
  See Lu Xun
Lu Hsun
  See Shu-Jen, Chou
Lukacs, George
  See Lukacs, Gyorgy
Lukacs, Gyorgy 1885-1971 .... **CLC 24**
  See also CA 101; 29-32R; CANR 62;
  CDWLB 4; DLB 215, 242; EW 10; EWL
  3; MTCW 1, 2
Lukacs, Gyorgy Szegeny von
  See Lukacs, Gyorgy
Luke, Peter (Ambrose Cyprian)
  1919-1995 .... **CLC 38**
  See also CA 81-84; 147; CANR 72; CBD;
  CD 5, 6; DLB 13
Lumet, Sidney 1924-2011 .... **CLC 341**
Lunar, Dennis
  See Mungo, Raymond
Luo Guanzhong 1315(?)-1385(?) .... **LC 12, 209**
Lurie, Alison 1926- ... **CLC 4, 5, 18, 39, 175**
  See also BPFB 2; CA 1-4R; CANR 2, 17,
  50, 88; CN 1, 2, 3, 4, 5, 6, 7; DLB 2, 350;
  MAL 5; MTCW 1; NFS 24; SATA 46,
  112; TCLE 1:1
Lustig, Arnost 1926-2011 .... **CLC 56**
  See also AAYA 3; CA 69-72; CANR 47,
  102; CWW 2; DLB 232, 299; EWL 3;
  RGHL; SATA 56
Luther, Martin 1483-1546 ..... **LC 9, 37, 150**
  See also CDWLB 2; DLB 179; EW 2;
  RGWL 2, 3
Luxemburg, Rosa 1870(?)-1919 .... **TCLC 63**
  See also CA 118
Lu Xun 1881-1936 ... **SSC 158; TCLC 3, 289**
  See also CA 243; DLB 328; RGSF 2;
  RGWL 2, 3
Luzi, Mario (Egidio Vincenzo)
  1914-2005 .... **CLC 13**
  See also CA 61-64; 236; CANR 9, 70;
  CWW 2; DLB 128; EWL 3
Levi-Strauss, Claude
  1908-2008 .... **CLC 38, 302, 374**
  See also CA 1-4R; CANR 6, 32, 57; DLB
  242; EWL 3; GFL 1789 to the Present;
  MTCW 1, 2; TWA
L'vov, Arkady .... **CLC 59**
Lydgate, John c. 1370-1450(?) ... **LC 81, 175**
  See also BRW 1; DLB 146; RGEL 2
Lyly, John 1554(?)-1606 .... **DC 7; LC 41, 187**
  See also BRW 1; DAM DRAM; DLB 62,
  167; RGEL 2
L'Ymagier
  See Gourmont, Remy(-Marie-Charles) de
Lynch, B. Suarez
  See Borges, Jorge Luis
Lynch, David 1946- .... **CLC 66, 162**
  See also AAYA 55; CA 124; 129; CANR 111
Lynch, David Keith
  See Lynch, David
Lynch, James
  See Andreyev, Leonid
Lyndsay, Sir David 1485-1555 .... **LC 20**
  See also RGEL 2
Lynn, Kenneth S(chuyler) 1923-2001 .. **CLC 50**
  See also CA 1-4R; 196; CANR 3, 27, 65
Lynx
  See West, Rebecca
Lyons, Marcus
  See Blish, James
Lyotard, Jean-Francois 1924-1998 .. **TCLC 103**
  See also DLB 242; EWL 3
Lyre, Pinchbeck
  See Sassoon, Siegfried
Lytle, Andrew (Nelson) 1902-1995 .... **CLC 22**
  See also CA 9-12R; 150; CANR 70; CN 1,
  2, 3, 4, 5, 6; CSW; DLB 6; DLBY 1995;
  RGAL 4; RHW

Mahfouz, Najib
See Mahfouz, Naguib
Mahfuz, Najib
See Mahfouz, Naguib
Mahon, Derek 1941- .... **CLC 27; PC 60**
See also BRWS 6; CA 113; 128; CANR 88;
CP 1, 2, 3, 4, 5, 6, 7; DLB 40; EWL 3
Maiakovskii, Vladimir
See Mayakovski, Vladimir
Mailer, Norman 1923-2007 ..... **CLC 1, 2, 3,**
4, 5, 8, 11, 14, 28, 39, 74, 111, 234, 345
See also AAYA 31; AITN 2; AMW; AMWC 2;
AMWR 2; BPFB 2; CA 9-12R; 266; CABS
1; CANR 28, 74, 77, 130, 196; CDALB
1968-1988; CN 1, 2, 3, 4, 5, 6, 7; CPW; DA;
DA3; DAB; DAC; DAM MST, NOV, POP;
DLB 2, 16, 28, 185, 278; DLBD 3; DLBY
1980, 1983; EWL 3; MAL 5; MTCW 1, 2;
MTFW 2005; NFS 10; RGAL 4; TUS
Mailer, Norman Kingsley
See Mailer, Norman
Maillet, Antonine 1929- .... **CLC 54, 118**
See also CA 115; 120; CANR 46, 74, 77,
134; CCA 1; CWW 2; DAC; DLB 60; INT
CA-120; MTCW 2; MTFW 2005
Maimonides, Moses 1135-1204 .... **CMLC 76**
See also DLB 115
Mais, Roger 1905-1955 .... **TCLC 8**
See also BW 1, 3; CA 105; 124; CANR 82;
CDWLB 3; DLB 125; EWL 3; MTCW 1;
RGEL 2
Maistre, Joseph 1753-1821 .... **NCLC 37**
See also GFL 1789 to the Present
Maitland, Frederic William
1850-1906 .... **TCLC 65**
Maitland, Sara 1950- .... **CLC 49**
See also BRWS 11; CA 69-72; CANR 13,
59, 221; DLB 271; FW
Maitland, Sara Louise
See Maitland, Sara
Major, Clarence 1936- .... **BLC 1:2;**
CLC 3, 19, 48
See also AFAW 2; BW 2, 3; CA 21-24R;
CAAS 6; CANR 13, 25, 53, 82; CN 3, 4,
5, 6, 7; CP 2, 3, 4, 5, 6, 7; CSW; DAM
MULT; DLB 33; EWL 3; MAL 5; MSW
Major, Kevin (Gerald) 1949- .... **CLC 26**
See also AAYA 16; CA 97-100; CANR 21,
38, 112; CLR 11; DAC; DLB 60; INT
CANR-21; JRDA; MAICYA 1, 2; MAI-
CYAS 1; SATA 32, 82, 134; WYA; YAW
Makanin, Vladimir 1937- .... **CLC 380**
See also DLB 285
Maki, James
See Ozu, Yasujiro
Makin, Bathsua 1600-1675(?) .... **LC 137**
Makine, Andrei 1957- .... **CLC 198**
See also CA 176; CANR 103, 162; MTFW
2005
Makine, Andrei
See Makine, Andrei
Malabaila, Damiano
See Levi, Primo
Malamud, Bernard 1914-1986 ..... **CLC 1, 2,**
3, 5, 8, 9, 11, 18, 27, 44, 78, 85; SSC 15,
147; TCLC 129, 184; WLC 4
See also AAYA 16; AMWS 1; BPFB 2; BYA
15; CA 5-8R; 118; CABS 1; CANR 28, 62,
114; CDALB 1941-1968; CN 1, 2, 3, 4; CPW;
DA; DA3; DAB; DAC; DAM MST, NOV,
POP; DLB 2, 28, 152; DLBY 1980, 1986;
EWL 3; EXPS; LAIT 4; LATS 1:1; MAL 5;
MTCW 1, 2; MTFW 2005; NFS 27; RGAL
4; RGHL; RGSF 2; SSFS 8, 13, 16; TUS
Malan, Herman
See Bosman, Herman Charles; Bosman, Her-
man Charles
Malaparte, Curzio 1898-1957 .... **TCLC 52**
See also DLB 264

Malcolm, Dan
See Silverberg, Robert
Malcolm, Janet 1934- .... **CLC 201**
See also CA 123; CANR 89, 199; NCFS 1
Malcolm X 1925-1965 ... **BLC 1:2; CLC 82,**
117; WLCS
See also BW 1, 3; CA 125; 111; CANR 82;
DA; DA3; DAB; DAC; DAM MST, MULT;
LAIT 5; MTCW 1, 2; MTFW 2005; NCFS 3
Malebranche, Nicolas 1638-1715 ..... **LC 133**
See also GFL Beginnings to 1789
Malherbe, Francois de 1555-1628 .... **LC 5**
See also DLB 327; GFL Beginnings to 1789
Mallarme, Stephane 1842-1898 ..... **NCLC 4,**
41, 210; PC 4, 102
See also DAM POET; DLB 217; EW 7; GFL
1789 to the Present; LMFS 2; RGWL 2, 3;
TWA
Mallet-Joris, Francoise 1930- .... **CLC 11**
See also CA 65-68; CANR 17; CWW 2;
DLB 83; EWL 3; GFL 1789 to the Present
Malley, Ern
See McAuley, James Phillip
Mallon, Thomas 1951- .... **CLC 172**
See also CA 110; CANR 29, 57, 92, 196;
DLB 350
Mallowan, Agatha Christie
See Christie, Agatha
Maloff, Saul 1922- .... **CLC 5**
See also CA 33-36R
Malone, Louis
See MacNeice, (Frederick) Louis
Malone, Michael 1942- .... **CLC 43**
See also CA 77-80; CANR 14, 32, 57, 114, 214
Malone, Michael Christopher
See Malone, Michael
Malory, Sir Thomas
1410(?)-1471(?) .... **LC 11, 88, 229;**
WLCS
See also BRW 1; BRWR 2; CDBLB Before
1660; DA; DAB; DAC; DAM MST; DLB
146; EFS 1:2, 2:2; RGEL 2; SATA 59;
SATA-Brief 33; TEA; WLIT 3
Malouf, David 1934- .... **CLC 28, 86, 245**
See also BRWS 12; CA 124; CANR 50, 76,
180, 224; CN 3, 4, 5, 6, 7; CP 1, 3, 4, 5, 6,
7; DLB 289; EWL 3; MTCW 2; MTFW
2005; SSFS 24
Malouf, George Joseph David
See Malouf, David
Malraux, Andre 1901-1976 ..... **CLC 1, 4, 9,**
13, 15, 57; TCLC 209
See also BPFB 2; CA 21-22; 69-72; CANR
34, 58; CAP 2; DA3; DAM NOV; DLB 72;
EW 12; EWL 3; GFL 1789 to the Present;
MTCW 1, 2; MTFW 2005; RGWL 2, 3;
TWA
Malraux, Georges-Andre
See Malraux, Andre
Malthus, Thomas Robert
1766-1834 .... **NCLC 145**
See also DLB 107, 158; RGEL 2
Malzberg, Barry N(athaniel) 1939- ... **CLC 7**
See also CA 61-64; CAAS 4; CANR 16;
CMW 4; DLB 8; SFW 4
Mamet, David 1947- .... **CLC 9, 15, 34, 46,**
91, 166; DC 4, 24
See also AAYA 3, 60; AMWS 14; CA 81-84;
CABS 3; CAD; CANR 15, 41, 67, 72, 129,
172; CD 5, 6; DA3; DAM DRAM; DFS 2,
3, 6, 12, 15; DLB 7; EWL 3; IDFW 4; MAL
5; MTCW 1, 2; MTFW 2005; RGAL 4
Mamet, David Alan
See Mamet, David
Mamoulian, Rouben (Zachary)
1897-1987 .... **CLC 16**
See also CA 25-28R; 124; CANR 85
Man in the Cloak, The
See Mangan, James Clarence

Mandelshtam, Osip
See Mandelstam, Osip
Mandel'shtam, Osip Emil'evich
See Mandelstam, Osip
Mandelstam, Osip 1891(?)-1943(?) ... **PC 14;**
TCLC 2, 6, 225
See also CA 104; 150; DLB 295; EW 10;
EWL 3; MTCW 2; RGWL 2, 3; TWA
Mandelstam, Osip Emilievich
See Mandelstam, Osip
Mander, (Mary) Jane 1877-1949 ... **TCLC 31**
See also CA 162; RGEL 2
Mandeville, Bernard 1670-1733 .... **LC 82**
See also DLB 101
Mandeville, Sir John fl. 1350 ...... **CMLC 19**
See also DLB 146
Mandiargues, Andre Pieyre de
See Pieyre de Mandiargues, Andre
Mandrake, Ethel Belle
See Thurman, Wallace (Henry)
Mangan, James Clarence
1803-1849 .... **NCLC 27, 316**
See also BRWS 13; RGEL 2
Maniere, J. E.
See Giraudoux, Jean
Mankell, Henning 1948- .... **CLC 292**
See also CA 187; CANR 163, 200
Mankiewicz, Herman (Jacob)
1897-1953 .... **TCLC 85**
See also CA 120; 169; DLB 26; IDFW 3, 4
Manley, (Mary) Delariviere
1672(?)-1724 .... **LC 1, 42**
See also DLB 39, 80; RGEL 2
Mann, Abel
See Creasey, John
Mann, Emily 1952- .... **DC 7**
See also CA 130; CAD; CANR 55; CD 5, 6;
CWD; DFS 28; DLB 266
Mann, Erica
See Jong, Erica
Mann, (Luiz) Heinrich
1871-1950 .... **TCLC 9, 279**
See also CA 106; 164, 181; DLB 66, 118;
EW 8; EWL 3; RGWL 2, 3
Mann, Mary Tyler Peabody
1806-1887 .... **NCLC 317**
See also DLB 239
Mann, Paul Thomas
See Mann, Thomas
Mann, Thomas 1875-1955 .... **SSC 5, 80, 82,**
170, 172, 174; TCLC 2, 8, 14, 21, 35, 44,
60, 168, 236, 292, 293, 303, 312; WLC 4
See also BPFB 2; CA 104; 128; CANR 133;
CDWLB 2; DA; DA3; DAB; DAC; DAM
MST, NOV; DLB 66, 331; EW 9; EWL 3;
GLL 1; LATS 1:1; LMFS 1; MTCW 1, 2;
MTFW 2005; NFS 17; RGSF 2; RGWL 2,
3; SSFS 4, 9; TWA
Mannheim, Karl 1893-1947 .... **TCLC 65**
See also CA 204
Manning, David
See Faust, Frederick
Manning, Frederic 1882-1935 .... **TCLC 25**
See also CA 124; 216; DLB 260
Manning, Olivia 1915-1980 .... **CLC 5, 19**
See also CA 5-8R; 101; CANR 29; CN 1, 2;
EWL 3; FW; MTCW 1; RGEL 2
Mannyng, Robert c. 1264-c. 1340 **CMLC 83**
See also DLB 146
Mano, D. Keith 1942- .... **CLC 2, 10**
See also CA 25-28R; CAAS 6; CANR 26,
57; DLB 6
Mansfield, Katherine 1888-1923 .... **SSC 9,**
23, 38, 81; TCLC 2, 8, 39, 164; WLC 4
See also BPFB 2; BRW 7; CA 104; 134;
DA; DA3; DAB; DAC; DAM MST; DLB
162; EWL 3; EXPS; FW; GLL 1; MTCW
2; RGEL 2; RGSF 2; SSFS 2, 8, 10, 11,
29; TEA; WWE 1

Martines, Julia
See O'Faolain, Julia

Martinez, Enrique Gonzalez
See Gonzalez Martinez, Enrique

Martinez, Jacinto Benavente y
See Benavente, Jacinto

Martinez Ruiz, Jose 1873-1967 ...... **CLC 11**
See also CA 93-96; DLB 322; EW 3; EWL 3; HW 1

Martinez Sierra, Gregorio
1881-1947 .... **TCLC 6**
See also CA 115; EWL 3

Martinsen, Martin
See Follett, Ken

Martinson, Harry (Edmund)
1904-1978 .... **CLC 14**
See also CA 77-80; CANR 34, 130; DLB 259, 331; EWL 3

Martinez de la Rosa, Francisco de Paula
1787-1862 .... **NCLC 102**
See also TWA

Martinez Sierra, Gregorio
See Martinez Sierra, Maria

Martinez Sierra, Maria 1874-1974 ... **TCLC 6**
See also CA 250; 115; EWL 3

Martinez Sierra, Maria de la O'LeJarraga
See Martinez Sierra, Maria

Martyn, Edward 1859-1923 .... **TCLC 131**
See also CA 179; DLB 10; RGEL 2

Martyr, Peter 1457-1526 .... **LC 241**

Marut, Ret
See Traven, B.

Marut, Robert
See Traven, B.

Marvell, Andrew 1621-1678 .... **LC 4, 43, 179, 226; PC 10, 86, 144, 154; WLC 4**
See also BRW 2; BRWR 2; CDBLB 1660-1789; DA; DAB; DAC; DAM MST, POET; DLB 131; EXPP; PFS 5; RGEL 2; TEA; WP

Marx, Karl 1818-1883 .... **NCLC 17, 114**
See also DLB 129; LATS 1:1; TWA

Marx, Karl Heinrich
See Marx, Karl

Masaoka, Shiki -1902
See Masaoka, Tsunenori

Masaoka, Tsunenori 1867-1902 .... **TCLC 18**
See also CA 117; 191; EWL 3; RGWL 3; TWA

Masaoka Shiki
See Masaoka, Tsunenori

Masefield, John (Edward)
1878-1967 .... **CLC 11, 47; PC 78**
See also CA 19-20; 25-28R; CANR 33; CAP 2; CDBLB 1890-1914; CLR 164; DAM POET; DLB 10, 19, 153, 160; EWL 3; EXPP; FANT; MTCW 1, 2; PFS 5; RGEL 2; SATA 19

Maso, Carole 1955(?)- .... **CLC 44**
See also CA 170; CANR 148; CN 7; GLL 2; RGAL 4

Mason, Bobbie Ann 1940- .... **CLC 28, 43, 82, 154, 303; SSC 4, 101, 193**
See also AAYA 5, 42; AMWS 8; BPFB 2; CA 53-56; CANR 11, 31, 58, 83, 125, 169, 235; CDALBS; CN 5, 6, 7; CSW; DA3; DLB 173; DLBY 1987; EWL 3; EXPS; INT CANR-31; MAL 5; MTCW 1, 2; MTFW 2005; NFS 4; RGAL 4; RGSF 2; SSFS 3, 8, 20; TCLE 1:2; YAW

Mason, Ernst
See Pohl, Frederik

Mason, Hunni B.
See Sternheim, (William Adolf) Carl

Mason, Lee W.
See Malzberg, Barry N(athaniel)

Mason, Nick 1945- .... **CLC 35**

Mason, Tally
See Derleth, August (William)

Mass, Anna .... **CLC 59**

Mass, William
See Gibson, William

Massinger, Philip 1583-1640 .... **DC 39; LC 70**
See also BRWS 11; DLB 58; RGEL 2

Master Lao
See Lao Tzu

Masters, Edgar Lee 1868-1950 ..... **PC 1, 36; TCLC 2, 25; WLCS**
See also AMWS 1; CA 104; 133; CDALB 1865-1917; DA; DAC; DAM MST, POET; DLB 54; EWL 3; EXPP; MAL 5; MTCW 1, 2; MTFW 2005; PFS 37; RGAL 4; TUS; WP

Masters, Hilary 1928- .... **CLC 48**
See also CA 25-28R, 217; CAAE 217; CANR 13, 47, 97, 171, 221; CN 6, 7; DLB 244

Masters, Hilary Thomas
See Masters, Hilary

Mastrosimone, William 1947- .... **CLC 36**
See also CA 186; CAD; CD 5, 6

Mathe, Albert
See Camus, Albert

Mather, Cotton 1663-1728 .... **LC 38**
See also AMWS 2; CDALB 1640-1865; DLB 24, 30, 140; RGAL 4; TUS

Mather, Increase 1639-1723 .... **LC 38, 161**
See also DLB 24

Mathers, Marshall
See Eminem

Mathers, Marshall Bruce
See Eminem

Matheson, Richard 1926-2013 .. **CLC 37, 267**
See also AAYA 31; CA 97-100; CANR 88, 99, 236; DLB 8, 44; HGG; INT CA-97-100; SCFW 1, 2; SFW 4; SUFW 2

Matheson, Richard Burton
See Matheson, Richard

Mathews, Harry 1930- .... **CLC 6, 52**
See also CA 21-24R; CAAS 6; CANR 18, 40, 98, 160; CN 5, 6, 7

Mathews, John Joseph
1894-1979 .... **CLC 84; NNAL**
See also CA 19-20; 142; CANR 45; CAP 2; DAM MULT; DLB 175; TCWW 1, 2

Mathias, Roland 1915-2007 .... **CLC 45**
See also CA 97-100; 263; CANR 19, 41; CP 1, 2, 3, 4, 5, 6, 7; DLB 27

Mathias, Roland Glyn
See Mathias, Roland

Matshoba, Mtutuzeli 1950- .... **SSC 173**
See also CA 221

Matsuo Basho 1644(?)-1694 .... **LC 62; PC 3, 125**
See also DAM POET; PFS 2, 7, 18; RGWL 2, 3; WP

Mattheson, Rodney
See Creasey, John

Matthew, James
See Barrie, J. M.

Matthew of Vendome
c. 1130-c. 1200 .... **CMLC 99**
See also DLB 208

Matthew Paris
See Paris, Matthew

Matthews, (James) Brander
1852-1929 .... **TCLC 95**
See also CA 181; DLB 71, 78; DLBD 13

Matthews, Greg 1949- .... **CLC 45**
See also CA 135

Matthews, William (Procter III)
1942-1997 .... **CLC 40**
See also AMWS 9; CA 29-32R; 162; CAAS 18; CANR 12, 57; CP 2, 3, 4, 5, 6; DLB 5

Matthias, John (Edward) 1941- .... **CLC 9**
See also CA 33-36R; CANR 56; CP 4, 5, 6, 7

Matthiessen, F(rancis) O(tto)
1902-1950 .... **TCLC 100**
See also CA 185; DLB 63; MAL 5

Matthiessen, Francis Otto
See Matthiessen, F(rancis) O(tto)

Matthiessen, Peter 1927- .... **CLC 5, 7, 11, 32, 64, 245**
See also AAYA 6, 40; AMWS 5; ANW; BEST 90:4; BPFB 2; CA 9-12R; CANR 21, 50, 73, 100, 138; CN 1, 2, 3, 4, 5, 6, 7; DA3; DAM NOV; DLB 6, 173, 275; MAL 5; MTCW 1, 2; MTFW 2005; SATA 27

Maturin, Charles Robert
1780(?)-1824 .... **NCLC 6, 169**
See also BRWS 8; DLB 178; GL 3; HGG; LMFS 1; RGEL 2; SUFW

Matute (Ausejo), Ana Maria 1925- .. **CLC 11, 352**
See also CA 89-92; CANR 129; CWW 2; DLB 322; EWL 3; MTCW 1; RGSF 2

Maugham, W. S.
See Maugham, W. Somerset

Maugham, W. Somerset
1874-1965 .... **CLC 1, 11, 15, 67, 93; SSC 8, 94, 164; TCLC 208; WLC 4**
See also AAYA 55; BPFB 2; BRW 6; CA 5-8R; 25-28R; CANR 40, 127; CDBLB 1914-1945; CMW 4; DA; DA3; DAB; DAC; DAM DRAM, MST, NOV; DFS 22; DLB 10, 36, 77, 100, 162, 195; EWL 3; LAIT 3; MTCW 1, 2; MTFW 2005; NFS 23, 35; RGEL 2; RGSF 2; SATA 54; SSFS 17

Maugham, William S.
See Maugham, W. Somerset

Maugham, William Somerset
See Maugham, W. Somerset

Maupassant, Guy de 1850-1893 .... **NCLC 1, 42, 83, 234; SSC 1, 64, 132; WLC 4**
See also BYA 14; DA; DA3; DAB; DAC; DAM MST; DLB 123; EW 7; EXPS; GFL 1789 to the Present; LAIT 2; LMFS 1; RGSF 2; RGWL 2, 3; SSFS 4, 21, 28, 31; SUFW; TWA

Maupassant, Henri Rene Albert Guy de
See Maupassant, Guy de

Maupin, Armistead 1944- .... **CLC 95**
See also CA 125; 130; CANR 58, 101, 183; CPW; DA3; DAM POP; DLB 278; GLL 1; INT CA-130; MTCW 2; MTFW 2005

Maupin, Armistead Jones, Jr.
See Maupin, Armistead

Maurhut, Richard
See Traven, B.

Mauriac, Claude 1914-1996 .... **CLC 9**
See also CA 89-92; 152; CWW 2; DLB 83; EWL 3; GFL 1789 to the Present

Mauriac, Francois (Charles)
1885-1970 .... **CLC 4, 9, 56; SSC 24; TCLC 281**
See also CA 25-28; CAP 2; DLB 65, 331; EW 10; EWL 3; GFL 1789 to the Present; MTCW 1, 2; MTFW 2005; RGWL 2, 3; TWA

Mavor, Osborne Henry 1888-1951 ... **TCLC 3**
See also CA 104; DLB 10; EWL 3

Maxwell, Glyn 1962- .... **CLC 238**
See also CA 154; CANR 88, 183; CP 6, 7; PFS 23

Maxwell, William (Keepers, Jr.)
1908-2000 .... **CLC 19**
See also AMWS 8; CA 93-96; 189; CANR 54, 95; CN 1, 2, 3, 4, 5, 6, 7; DLB 218, 278; DLBY 1980; INT CA-93-96; MAL 5; SATA-Obit 128

May, Elaine 1932- .... **CLC 16**
See also CA 124; 142; CAD; CWD; DLB 44

Mayakovski, Vladimir
1893-1930 .... **TCLC 4, 18**

See also CA 104; 158; EW 11; EWL 3; IDTP; MTCW 2; MTFW 2005; RGWL 2, 3; SFW 4; TWA; WP

Mayakovski, Vladimir Vladimirovich
See Mayakovski, Vladimir

Mayakovsky, Vladimir
See Mayakovski, Vladimir

Mayhew, Henry 1812-1887 .... **NCLC 31**
See also BRWS 16; DLB 18, 55, 190

Mayle, Peter 1939(?)- .... **CLC 89**
See also CA 139; CANR 64, 109, 168, 218

Maynard, Joyce 1953- .... **CLC 23**
See also CA 111; 129; CANR 64, 169, 220

Mayne, William 1928-2010 .... **CLC 12**
See also AAYA 20; CA 9-12R; CANR 37, 80, 100; CLR 25, 123; FANT; JRDA; MAICYA 1, 2; MAICYAS 1; SAAS 11; SATA 6, 68, 122; SUFW 2; YAW

Mayne, William James Carter
See Mayne, William

Mayo, Jim
See L'Amour, Louis

Maysles, Albert 1926- .... **CLC 16**
See also CA 29-32R

Maysles, David 1932-1987 .... **CLC 16**
See also CA 191

Mazer, Norma Fox 1931-2009 .... **CLC 26**
See also AAYA 5, 36; BYA 1, 8; CA 69-72; 292; CANR 12, 32, 66, 129, 189; CLR 23; JRDA; MAICYA 1, 2; SAAS 1; SATA 24, 67, 105, 168, 198; WYA; YAW

Mažuranić, Ivan 1814-1890 .... **NCLC 259**
See also DLB 147

Mazzini, Guiseppe 1805-1872 .... **NCLC 34**

McAlmon, Robert (Menzies)
1895-1956 .... **TCLC 97**
See also CA 107; 168; DLB 4, 45; DLBD 15; GLL 1

McAuley, James Phillip 1917-1976 ... **CLC 45**
See also CA 97-100; CP 1, 2; DLB 260; RGEL 2

McBain, Ed
See Hunter, Evan

McBride, James 1957- .... **CLC 370**
See also BW 3; CA 153; CANR 113, 194, 266; CMTFW; MTFW

McBrien, William 1930- .... **CLC 44**
See also CA 107; CANR 90

McBrien, William Augustine
See McBrien, William

McCabe, Pat
See McCabe, Patrick

McCabe, Patrick 1955- .... **CLC 133**
See also BRWS 9; CA 130; CANR 50, 90, 168, 202; CN 6, 7; DLB 194

McCaffrey, Anne 1926-2011 .... **CLC 17**
See also AAYA 6, 34; AITN 2; BEST 89:2; BPFB 2; BYA 5; CA 25-28R, 227; CAAE 227; CANR 15, 35, 55, 96, 169, 234; CLR 49, 130; CPW; DA3; DAM NOV, POP; DLB 8; JRDA; MAICYA 1, 2; MTCW 1, 2; MTFW 2005; SAAS 11; SATA 8, 70, 116, 152; SATA-Essay 152; SFW 4; SUFW 2; WYA; YAW

McCaffrey, Anne Inez
See McCaffrey, Anne

McCall, Nathan 1955(?)- .... **CLC 86**
See also AAYA 59; BW 3; CA 146; CANR 88, 186

McCall Smith, Alexander
See Smith, Alexander McCall

McCann, Arthur
See Campbell, John W.

McCann, Colum 1965- ... **CLC 299; SSC 170**
See also CA 152; CANR 99, 149; DLB 267

McCann, Edson
See Pohl, Frederik

McCarthy, Charles
See McCarthy, Cormac

McCarthy, Charles, Jr.
See McCarthy, Cormac

McCarthy, Cormac 1933- .... **CLC 4, 57, 101, 204, 295, 310**
See also AAYA 41; AMWS 8; BPFB 2; CA 13-16R; CANR 10, 42, 69, 101, 161, 171; CN 6, 7; CPW; CSW; DA3; DAM POP; DLB 6, 143, 256; EWL 3; LATS 1:2; LNFS 3; MAL 5; MTCW 2; MTFW 2005; NFS 36, 40; TCLE 1:2; TCWW 2

McCarthy, Mary 1912-1989 .... **CLC 1, 3, 5, 14, 24, 39, 59; SSC 24**
See also AMW; BPFB 2; CA 5-8R; 129; CANR 16, 50, 64; CN 1, 2, 3, 4; DA3; DLB 2; DLBY 1981; EWL 3; FW; INT CANR-16; MAL 5; MBL; MTCW 1, 2; MTFW 2005; RGAL 4; TUS

McCarthy, Mary Therese
See McCarthy, Mary

McCartney, James Paul
See McCartney, Paul

McCartney, Paul 1942- .... **CLC 12, 35**
See also CA 146; CANR 111

McCauley, Stephen 1955- .... **CLC 50**
See also CA 141

McClaren, Peter .... **CLC 70**

McClure, Michael 1932- ... **CLC 6, 10; PC 136**
See also BG 1:3; CA 21-24R; CAD; CANR 17, 46, 77, 131, 231; CD 5, 6; CP 1, 2, 3, 4, 5, 6, 7; DLB 16; WP

McClure, Michael Thomas
See McClure, Michael

McCorkle, Jill 1958- .... **CLC 51**
See also CA 121; CANR 113, 218; CSW; DLB 234; DLBY 1987; SSFS 24

McCorkle, Jill Collins
See McCorkle, Jill

McCourt, Francis
See McCourt, Frank

McCourt, Frank 1930-2009 ... **CLC 109, 299**
See also AAYA 61; AMWS 12; CA 157; 288; CANR 97, 138; MTFW 2005; NCFS 1

McCourt, James 1941- .... **CLC 5**
See also CA 57-60; CANR 98, 152, 186

McCourt, Malachy 1931- .... **CLC 119**
See also SATA 126

McCoy, Edmund
See Gardner, John

McCoy, Horace (Stanley)
1897-1955 .... **TCLC 28**
See also AMWS 13; CA 108; 155; CMW 4; DLB 9

McCrae, John 1872-1918 .... **TCLC 12**
See also CA 109; DLB 92; PFS 5

McCreigh, James
See Pohl, Frederik

McCullers, Carson 1917-1967 ...... **CLC 1, 4, 10, 12, 48, 100; DC 35; SSC 9, 24, 99; TCLC 155; WLC 4**
See also AAYA 21; AMW; AMWC 2; BPFB 2; CA 5-8R; 25-28R; CABS 1, 3; CANR 18, 132; CDALB 1941-1968; DA; DA3; DAB; DAC; DAM MST, NOV; DFS 5, 18; DLB 2, 7, 173, 228; EWL 3; EXPS; FW; GLL 1; LAIT 3, 4; MAL 5; MBL; MTCW 1, 2; MTFW 2005; NFS 6, 13; RGAL 4; RGSF 2; SATA 27; SSFS 5, 32; TUS; YAW

McCullers, Lula Carson Smith
See McCullers, Carson

McCulloch, John Tyler
See Burroughs, Edgar Rice

McCullough, Colleen 1937- ..... **CLC 27, 107**
See also AAYA 36; BPFB 2; CA 81-84; CANR 17, 46, 67, 98, 139, 203; CPW; DA3; DAM NOV, POP; MTCW 1, 2; MTFW 2005; RHW

McCunn, Ruthanne Lum 1946- .... **AAL**
See also CA 119; CANR 43, 96; DLB 312; LAIT 2; SATA 63

McDermott, Alice 1953- .... **CLC 90**
See also AMWS 18; CA 109; CANR 40, 90, 126, 181; CN 7; DLB 292; MTFW 2005; NFS 23

McDonagh, Martin 1970(?)- .... **CLC 304**
See also AAYA 71; BRWS 12; CA 171; CANR 141; CD 6

McElroy, Joseph 1930- .... **CLC 5, 47**
See also CA 17-20R; CANR 149, 236; CN 3, 4, 5, 6, 7

McElroy, Joseph Prince
See McElroy, Joseph

McElroy, Lee
See Kelton, Elmer

McEwan, Ian 1948- .... **CLC 13, 66, 169, 269; SSC 106**
See also AAYA 84; BEST 90:4; BRWS 4; CA 61-64; CANR 14, 41, 69, 87, 132, 179, 232; CN 3, 4, 5, 6, 7; DAM NOV; DLB 14, 194, 319, 326; HGG; MTCW 1, 2; MTFW 2005; NFS 32; RGSF 2; SUFW 2; TEA

McEwan, Ian Russell
See McEwan, Ian

McFadden, David 1940- .... **CLC 48**
See also CA 104; CP 1, 2, 3, 4, 5, 6, 7; DLB 60; INT CA-104

McFarland, Dennis 1950- .... **CLC 65**
See also CA 165; CANR 110, 179

McGahern, John 1934-2006 .... **CLC 5, 9, 48, 156, 371; SSC 17, 181**
See also CA 17-20R; 249; CANR 29, 68, 113, 204; CN 1, 2, 3, 4, 5, 6, 7; DLB 14, 231, 319; MTCW 1

McGinley, Patrick (Anthony) 1937- ... **CLC 41**
See also CA 120; 127; CANR 56; INT CA-127

McGinley, Phyllis 1905-1978 .... **CLC 14**
See also CA 9-12R; 77-80; CANR 19; CP 1, 2; CWRI 5; DLB 11, 48; MAL 5; PFS 9, 13; SATA 2, 44; SATA-Obit 24

McGinniss, Joe 1942- .... **CLC 32**
See also AITN 2; BEST 89:2; CA 25-28R; CANR 26, 70, 152, 235; CPW; DLB 185; INT CANR-26

McGivern, Maureen Daly
See Daly, Maureen

McGivern, Maureen Patricia Daly
See Daly, Maureen

McGrath, Patrick 1950- .... **CLC 55**
See also CA 136; CANR 65, 148, 190; CN 5, 6, 7; DLB 231; HGG; SUFW 2

McGrath, Thomas (Matthew)
1916-1990 .... **CLC 28, 59**
See also AMWS 10; CA 9-12R; 132; CANR 6, 33, 95; CP 1, 2, 3, 4, 5; DAM POET; MAL 5; MTCW 1; SATA 41; SATA-Obit 66

McGuane, Thomas 1939- .... **CLC 3, 7, 18, 45, 127**
See also AITN 2; BPFB 2; CA 49-52; CANR 5, 24, 49, 94, 164, 229; CN 2, 3, 4, 5, 6, 7; DLB 2, 212; DLBY 1980; EWL 3; INT CANR-24; MAL 5; MTCW 1; MTFW 2005; TCWW 1, 2

McGuane, Thomas Francis III
See McGuane, Thomas

McGuckian, Medbh 1950- ...... **CLC 48, 174; PC 27**
See also BRWS 5; CA 143; CANR 206; CP 4, 5, 6, 7; CWP; DAM POET; DLB 40

McGuffin, P. V.
See Mangan, James Clarence

McHale, Tom 1942(?)-1982 .... **CLC 3, 5**
See also AITN 1; CA 77-80; 106; CN 1, 2, 3

McHugh, Heather 1948- .... **PC 61**
See also CA 69-72; CANR 11, 28, 55, 92; CP 4, 5, 6, 7; CWP; PFS 24

See also CA 9-12R; 260; CAAS 14; CANR
6, 40, 129; CP 1, 2, 3, 4, 5, 6, 7; DAM
POET; DLB 5; MAL 5

Meredith, William Morris
See Meredith, William

Merezhkovsky, Dmitrii Sergeevich
See Merezhkovsky, Dmitry Sergeyevich

Merezhkovsky, Dmitry Sergeevich
See Merezhkovsky, Dmitry Sergeyevich

Merezhkovsky, Dmitry Sergeyevich
1865-1941 .... **TCLC 29**
See also CA 169; DLB 295; EWL 3

Merezhkovsky, Zinaida
See Gippius, Zinaida

Merkin, Daphne 1954- .... **CLC 44**
See also CA 123

Merleau-Ponty, Maurice
1908-1961 .... **TCLC 156**
See also CA 114; 89-92; DLB 296; GFL
1789 to the Present

Merlin, Arthur
See Blish, James

Mernissi, Fatima 1940- .... **CLC 171**
See also CA 152; DLB 346; FW

Merrill, James 1926-1995 .... **CLC 2, 3,
6, 8, 13, 18, 34, 91; PC 28; TCLC 173**
See also AMWS 3; CA 13-16R; 147; CANR
10, 49, 63, 108; CP 1, 2, 3, 4; DA3; DAM
POET; DLB 5, 165; DLBY 1985; EWL 3;
INT CANR-10; MAL 5; MTCW 1, 2;
MTFW 2005; PAB; PFS 23; RGAL 4

Merrill, James Ingram
See Merrill, James

Merriman, Alex
See Silverberg, Robert

Merriman, Brian 1747-1805 .... **NCLC 70**

Merritt, E. B.
See Waddington, Miriam

Merton, Thomas 1915-1968 ... **CLC 1, 3, 11,
34, 83; PC 10**
See also AAYA 61; AMWS 8; CA 5-8R; 25-
28R; CANR 22, 53, 111, 131; DA3; DLB
48; DLBY 1981; MAL 5; MTCW 1, 2;
MTFW 2005

Merton, Thomas James
See Merton, Thomas

Merwin, W. S. 1927- .... **CLC 1, 2, 3, 5, 8,
13, 18, 45, 88; PC 45**
See also AMWS 3; CA 13-16R; CANR 15,
51, 112, 140, 209; CP 1, 2, 3, 4, 5, 6, 7;
DA3; DAM POET; DLB 5, 169, 342; EWL
3; INT CANR-15; MAL 5; MTCW 1, 2;
MTFW 2005; PAB; PFS 5, 15; RGAL 4

Merwin, William Stanley
See Merwin, W. S.

Metastasio, Pietro 1698-1782 .... **LC 115**
See also RGWL 2, 3

Metcalf, John 1938- .... **CLC 37; SSC 43**
See also CA 113; CN 4, 5, 6, 7; DLB 60;
RGSF 2; TWA

Metcalf, Suzanne
See Baum, L. Frank

Mew, Charlotte (Mary)
1870-1928 .... **PC 107; TCLC 8**
See also CA 105; 189; DLB 19, 135; RGEL 2

Mewshaw, Michael 1943- .... **CLC 9**
See also CA 53-56; CANR 7, 47, 147, 213;
DLBY 1980

Meyer, Conrad Ferdinand
1825-1898 .... **NCLC 81, 249; SSC 30**
See also DLB 129; EW; RGWL 2, 3

Meyer, Gustav 1868-1932 .... **TCLC 21**
See also CA 117; 190; DLB 81; EWL 3

Meyer, June
See Jordan, June

Meyer, Lynn
See Slavitt, David R.

Meyer, Stephenie 1973- .... **CLC 280**
See also AAYA 77; CA 253; CANR 192;
CLR 142, 180; SATA 193

Meyer-Meyrink, Gustav
See Meyer, Gustav

Meyers, Jeffrey 1939- .... **CLC 39**
See also CA 73-76, 186; CAAE 186; CANR
54, 102, 159; DLB 111

**Meynell, Alice (Christina Gertrude Thomp-
son)** 1847-1922 .... **PC 112; TCLC 6**
See also CA 104; 177; DLB 19, 98; RGEL 2

Meyrink, Gustav
See Meyer, Gustav

Mhlophe, Gcina 1960- .... **BLC 2:3**

Michaels, Leonard 1933-2003 .... **CLC 6, 25;
SSC 16**
See also AMWS 16; CA 61-64; 216; CANR
21, 62, 119, 179; CN 3, 45, 6, 7; DLB 130;
MTCW 1; TCLE 1:2

Michaux, Henri 1899-1984 .... **CLC 8, 19**
See also CA 85-88; 114; DLB 258; EWL 3;
GFL 1789 to the Present; RGWL 2, 3

Micheaux, Oscar (Devereaux)
1884-1951 .... **TCLC 76**
See also BW 3; CA 174; DLB 50; TCWW 2

Michelangelo 1475-1564 .... **LC 12**
See also AAYA 43

Michelet, Jules 1798-1874 .... **NCLC 31, 218**
See also EW 5; GFL 1789 to the Present

Michels, Robert 1876-1936 .... **TCLC 88**
See also CA 212

Michener, James A. 1907(?)-1997 ... **CLC 1,
5, 11, 29, 60, 109**
See also AAYA 27; AITN 1; BEST 90:1;
BPFB 2; CA 5-8R; 161; CANR 21, 45, 68;
CN 1, 2, 3, 4, 5, 6; CPW; DA3; DAM
NOV, POP; DLB 6; MAL 5; MTCW 1, 2;
MTFW 2005; RHW; TCWW 1, 2

Michener, James Albert
See Michener, James A.

Mickiewicz, Adam 1798-1855 .... **NCLC 3,
101, 265; PC 38**
See also EW 5; RGWL 2, 3

Middleton, (John) Christopher
1926- .... **CLC 13**
See also CA 13-16R; CANR 29, 54, 117; CP
1, 2, 3, 4, 5, 6, 7; DLB 40

Middleton, Richard (Barham) 1882-
1911 .... **TCLC 56**
See also CA 187; DLB 156; HGG

Middleton, Stanley 1919-2009 ..... **CLC 7, 38**
See also CA 25-28R; 288; CAAS 23; CANR
21, 46, 81, 157; CN 1, 2, 3, 4, 5, 6, 7; DLB
14, 326

Middleton, Thomas 1580-1627 .... **DC 5, 40;
LC 33, 123**
See also BRW 2; DAM DRAM, MST; DFS
18, 22; DLB 58; RGEL 2

Migueis, Jose Rodrigues
1901-1980 .... **CLC 10**
See also DLB 287

Mihura, Miguel 1905-1977 .... **DC 34**
See also CA 214

Mikszath, Kalman 1847-1910 .... **TCLC 31**
See also CA 170

Miles, Jack .... **CLC 100**
See also CA 200

Miles, John Russiano
See Miles, Jack

Miles, Josephine (Louise)
1911-1985 .... **CLC 1, 2, 14, 34, 39**
See also CA 1-4R; 116; CANR 2, 55; CP 1,
2, 3, 4; DAM POET; DLB 48; MAL 5;
TCLE 1:2

Militant
See Sandburg, Carl

Mill, Harriet (Hardy) Taylor
1807-1858 .... **NCLC 102**

See also FW

Mill, John Stuart 1806-1873 .... **NCLC 11,
58, 179, 223**
See also CDBLB 1832-1890; DLB 55, 190,
262, 366; FW 1; RGEL 2; TEA

Millar, Kenneth 1915-1983 ...... **CLC 1, 2, 3,
14, 34, 41**
See also AAYA 81; AMWS 4; BPFB 2; CA
9-12R; 110; CANR 16, 63, 107; CMW 4;
CN 1, 2, 3; CPW; DA3; DAM POP; DLB 2,
226; DLBD 6; DLBY 1983; MAL 5; MSW;
MTCW 1, 2; MTFW 2005; RGAL 4

Millás, Juan José 1946- .... **CLC 390**
See also DLB 322

Millay, E. Vincent
See Millay, Edna St. Vincent

Millay, Edna St. Vincent 1892-1950 ... **PC 6,
61; TCLC 4, 49, 169; WLCS**
See also AMW; CA 104; 130; CDALB
1917-1929; DA; DA3; DAB; DAC; DAM
MST, POET; DFS 27; DLB 45, 249; EWL
3; EXPP; FL 1:6; GLL 1; MAL 5; MBL;
MTCW 1, 2; MTFW 2005; PAB; PFS 3,
17, 31, 34, 41; RGAL 4; TUS; WP

Miller, Arthur 1915-2005 .... **CLC 1, 2, 6,
10, 15, 26, 47, 78, 179; DC 1, 31; WLC 4**
See also AAYA 15; AITN 1; AMW; AMWC
1; CA 1-4R; 236; CABS 3; CAD; CANR
2, 30, 54, 76, 132; CD 5, 6; CDALB 1941-
1968; CLR 195; DA; DA3; DAB; DAC;
DAM DRAM, MST; DFS 1, 3, 8, 27; DLB
7, 266; EWL 3; LAIT 1, 4; LATS 1:2;
MAL 5; MTCW 1, 2; MTFW 2005; RGAL
4; RGHL; TUS; WYAS 1

Miller, Frank 1957- .... **CLC 278**
See also AAYA 45; CA 224

Miller, Henry (Valentine)
1891-1980 .... **CLC 1, 2, 4, 9, 14, 43,
84; TCLC 213; WLC 4**
See also AMW; BPFB 2; CA 9-12R; 97-100;
CANR 33, 64; CDALB 1929-1941; CN 1,
2; DA; DA3; DAB; DAC; DAM MST,
NOV; DLB 4, 9; DLBY 1980; EWL 3;
MAL 5; MTCW 1, 2; MTFW 2005; RGAL
4; TUS

Miller, Hugh 1802-1856 .... **NCLC 143**
See also DLB 190

Miller, Jason 1939(?)-2001 .... **CLC 2**
See also AITN 1; CA 73-76; 197; CAD;
CANR 130; DFS 12; DLB 7

Miller, Sue 1943- .... **CLC 44**
See also AMWS 12; BEST 90:3; CA 139;
CANR 59, 91, 128, 194, 231; DA3; DAM
POP; DLB 143

Miller, Walter M(ichael, Jr.)
1923-1996 .... **CLC 4, 30**
See also BPFB 2; CA 85-88; CANR 108;
DLB 8; SCFW 1, 2; SFW 4

Millett, Kate 1934- .... **CLC 67**
See also AITN 1; CA 73-76; CANR 32, 53,
76, 110; DA3; DLB 246; FW; GLL 1;
MTCW 1, 2; MTFW 2005

Millhauser, Steven 1943- .... **CLC 21, 54,
109, 300; SSC 57**
See also AAYA 76; CA 110; 111; CANR 63,
114, 133, 189; CN 6, 7; DA3; DLB 2, 350;
FANT; INT CA-111; MAL 5; MTCW 2;
MTFW 2005

Millhauser, Steven Lewis
See Millhauser, Steven

Millin, Sarah Gertrude 1889-1968 ... **CLC 49**
See also CA 102; 93-96; DLB 225; EWL 3

Milne, A. A. 1882-1956 .... **TCLC 6, 88**
See also BRWS 5; CA 104; 133; CLR 1, 26,
108; CMW 4; CWRI 5; DA3; DAB; DAC;
DAM MST; DLB 10, 77, 100, 160, 352;
FANT; MAICYA 1, 2; MTCW 1, 2; MTFW
2005; RGEL 2; SATA 100; WCH; YABC 1

Naylor, Gloria 1950- ..... **BLC 1:3; CLC 28, 52, 156, 261, 375, 383; WLCS**
See also AAYA 6, 39; AFAW 1, 2; AMWS 8; BW 2, 3; CA 107; CANR 27, 51, 74, 130; CLR 202; CN 4, 5, 6, 7; CPW; DA; DA3; DAC; DAM MST, MULT, NOV, POP; DLB 173; EWL 3; FW; MAL 5; MTCW 1, 2; MTFW 2005; NFS 4, 7; RGAL 4; TCLE 1:2; TUS

Ni Chuilleanain, Eilean 1942- .... **PC 34**
See also CA 126; CANR 53, 83, 241; CP 5, 6, 7; CWP; DLB 40

Ndebele, Njabulo (Simakahle) 1948- .... **SSC 135**
See also CA 184; DLB 157, 225; EWL 3

Neal, John 1793-1876 .... **NCLC 161**
See also DLB 1, 59, 243; FW; RGAL 4

Neff, Debra .... **CLC 59**

Negri, Antonio 1933- .... **CLC 368**
See also CA 235

Neidhart von Reuental
c. 1185-c. 1240 .... **CMLC 145**
See also DLB 138

Neihardt, John Gneisenau
1881-1973 .... **CLC 32**
See also CA 13-14; CANR 65; CAP 1; DLB 9, 54, 256; LAIT 2; TCWW 1, 2

Nekrasov, Nikolai Alekseevich
1821-1878 .... **NCLC 11, 294**
See also DLB 277

Nelligan, Emile 1879-1941 .... **TCLC 14**
See also CA 114; 204; DLB 92; EWL 3

Nelson, Alice Ruth Moore Dunbar
1875-1935 .... **HR 1:2; SSC 132**
See also BW 1, 3; CA 122; 124; CANR 82; DLB 50; FW; MTCW 1

Nelson, Willie 1933- .... **CLC 17**
See also CA 107; CANR 114, 178

Nemerov, Howard 1920-1991 .... **CLC 2, 6, 9, 36; PC 24; TCLC 124**
See also AMW; CA 1-4R; 134; CABS 2; CANR 1, 27, 53; CN 1, 2, 3; CP 1, 2, 3, 4, 5; DAM POET; DLB 5, 6; DLBY 1983; EWL 3; INT CANR-27; MAL 5; MTCW 1, 2; MTFW 2005; PFS 10, 14; RGAL 4

Nemerov, Howard Stanley
See Nemerov, Howard

Nepos, Cornelius
c. 99B.C.-c. 24B.C. .... **CMLC 89**
See also DLB 211

Neruda, Pablo 1904-1973 .... **CLC 1, 2, 5, 7, 9, 28, 62; HLC 2; PC 4, 64; WLC 4**
See also CA 19-20; 45-48; CANR 131; CAP 2; DA; DA3; DAB; DAC; DAM MST, MULT, POET; DLB 283, 331; DNFS 2; EWL 3; HW 1; LAW; MTCW 1, 2; MTFW 2005; PFS 11, 28, 33, 35, 41; RGWL 2, 3; TWA; WLIT 1; WP

Nerval, Gerard de 1808-1855 .... **NCLC 1, 67, 250; PC 13; SSC 18**
See also DLB 217, 366; EW 6; GFL 1789 to the Present; RGSF 2; RGWL 2, 3

Nervo, (Jose) Amado (Ruiz de)
1870-1919 .... **HLCS 2; TCLC 11**
See also CA 109; 131; DLB 290; EWL 3; HW 1; LAW

Nesbit, Malcolm
See Chester, Alfred

Nessi, Pio Baroja y
See Baroja, Pio

Nestroy, Johann
1801-1862 .... **DC 46; NCLC 42**
See also DLB 133; RGWL 2, 3

Nethersole, Lady Olga
See Harwood, Gwen

Netterville, Luke
See O'Grady, Standish (James)

Neufeld, John (Arthur) 1938- .... **CLC 17**
See also AAYA 11; CA 25-28R; CANR 11, 37, 56; CLR 52; MAICYA 1, 2; SAAS 3; SATA 6, 81, 131; SATA-Essay 131; YAW

Neumann, Alfred 1895-1952 .... **TCLC 100**
See also CA 183; DLB 56

Neumann, Ferenc
See Molnar, Ferenc

Neville, Emily Cheney 1919- .... **CLC 12**
See also BYA 2; CA 5-8R; CANR 3, 37, 85; JRDA; MAICYA 1, 2; SAAS 2; SATA 1; YAW

Neville, Henry 1619-1694 .... **LC 244**

Newbound, Bernard Slade 1930- .. **CLC 11, 46**
See also CA 81-84; CAAS 9; CANR 49; CCA 1; CD 5, 6; DAM DRAM; DLB 53

Newby, P(ercy) H(oward)
1918-1997 .... **CLC 2, 13**
See also CA 5-8R; 161; CANR 32, 67; CN 1, 2, 3, 4, 5, 6; DAM NOV; DLB 15, 326; MTCW 1; RGEL 2

Newcastle
See Cavendish, Margaret

Newlove, Donald 1928- .... **CLC 6**
See also CA 29-32R; CANR 25

Newlove, John (Herbert) 1938- ...... **CLC 14**
See also CA 21-24R; CANR 9, 25; CP 1, 2, 3, 4, 5, 6, 7

Newman, Charles 1938-2006 .... **CLC 2, 8**
See also CA 21-24R; 249; CANR 84; CN 3, 4, 5, 6

Newman, Charles Hamilton
See Newman, Charles

Newman, Edwin 1919-2010 .... **CLC 14**
See also AITN 1; CA 69-72; CANR 5

Newman, Edwin Harold
See Newman, Edwin

Newman, John Henry
1801-1890 .... **NCLC 38, 99**
See also BRWS 7; DLB 18, 32, 55; RGEL 2

Newton, (Sir) Isaac 1642-1727 ..... **LC 35, 53**
See also DLB 252

Newton, Suzanne 1936- .... **CLC 35**
See also BYA 7; CA 41-44R; CANR 14; JRDA; SATA 5, 77

New York Dept. of Ed. .... **CLC 70**

Nexo, Martin Andersen
1869-1954 .... **TCLC 43**
See also CA 202; DLB 214; EWL 3; NFS 34

Nezval, Vitezslav 1900-1958 .... **TCLC 44**
See also CA 123; CDWLB 4; DLB 215; EWL 3

Ng, Fae Myenne 1956- .... **CLC 81, 379**
See also BYA 11; CA 146; CANR 191; NFS 37

Ngcobo, Lauretta 1931- .... **BLC 2:3**
See also CA 165

Ngema, Mbongeni 1955- .... **CLC 57**
See also BW 2; CA 143; CANR 84; CD 5, 6

Ngugi, James T.
See Ngugi wa Thiong'o

Ngugi, James Thiong'o
See Ngugi wa Thiong'o

Ngugi wa Thiong'o 1938- .... **BLC 1:3, 2:3; CLC 3, 7, 13, 36, 182, 275**
See also AFW; BRWS 8; BW 2; CA 81-84; CANR 27, 58, 164, 213; CD 3, 4, 5, 6, 7; CDWLB 3; CN 1, 2; DAM MULT, NOV; DLB 125; DNFS 2; EWL 3; MTCW 1, 2; MTFW 2005; RGEL 2; WWE 1

Niatum, Duane 1938- .... **NNAL**
See also CA 41-44R; CANR 21, 45, 83; DLB 175

Nichol, B(arrie) P(hillip)
1944-1988 .... **CLC 18; PC 165**
See also CA 53-56; CP 1, 2, 3, 4; DLB 53; SATA 66

Nicholas of Autrecourt
c. 1298-1369 .... **CMLC 108**

Nicholas of Cusa 1401-1464 .... **LC 80**
See also DLB 115

Nichols, John 1940- .... **CLC 38**
See also AMWS 13; CA 9-12R, 190; CAAE 190; CAAS 2; CANR 6, 70, 121, 185; DLBY 1982; LATS 1:2; MTFW 2005; TCWW 1, 2

Nichols, Leigh
See Koontz, Dean

Nichols, Peter (Richard) 1927- ... **CLC 5, 36, 65**
See also CA 104; CANR 33, 86; CBD; CD 5, 6; DLB 13, 245; MTCW 1

Nicholson, Linda .... **CLC 65**

Nicolas, F. R. E.
See Freeling, Nicolas

Ni Dhomhnaill, Nuala 1952- .... **PC 128**
See also CA 190; CWP

Niedecker, Lorine 1903-1970 .... **CLC 10, 42; PC 42, 163**
See also CA 25-28; CAP 2; DAM POET; DLB 48

Niekerk, Marlene van
See van Niekerk, Marlene

Nietzsche, Friedrich
1844-1900 ... **TCLC 10, 18, 55, 289, 290**
See also CA 107; 121; CDWLB 2; DLB 129; EW 7; RGWL 2, 3; TWA

Nietzsche, Friedrich Wilhelm
See Nietzsche, Friedrich

Nievo, Ippolito 1831-1861 .... **NCLC 22**

Nightingale, Anne Redmon 1943- .... **CLC 22**
See also CA 103; DLBY 1986

Nightingale, Florence 1820-1910 ... **TCLC 85**
See also CA 188; DLB 166

Nijo Yoshimoto 1320-1388 .... **CMLC 49**
See also DLB 203

Nik. T. O.
See Annensky, Innokenty (Fyodorovich)

Nin, Anais 1903-1977 .... **CLC 1, 4, 8, 11, 14, 60, 127; SSC 10; TCLC 224**
See also AITN 2; AMWS 10; BPFB 2; CA 13-16R; 69-72; CANR 22, 53; CN 1, 2; DAM NOV, POP; DLB 2, 4, 152; EWL 3; GLL 2; MAL 5; MBL; MTCW 1, 2; MTFW 2005; RGAL 4; RGSF 2

Nisbet, Robert A(lexander)
1913-1996 .... **TCLC 117**
See also CA 25-28R; 153; CANR 17; INT CANR-17

Nishida, Kitaro 1870-1945 .... **TCLC 83**

Nishiwaki, Junzaburo 1894-1982 .... **PC 15**
See also CA 194; 107; EWL 3; MJW; RGWL 3

Nissenson, Hugh 1933- .... **CLC 4, 9**
See also CA 17-20R; CANR 27, 108, 151; CN 5, 6; DLB 28, 335

Nister, Der
See Der Nister

Niven, Larry 1938- .... **CLC 8**
See also AAYA 27; BPFB 2; BYA 10; CA 21-24R, 207; CAAE 207; CAAS 12; CANR 14, 44, 66, 113, 155, 206; CPW; DAM POP; DLB 8; MTCW 1, 2; SATA 95, 171; SCFW 1, 2; SFW 4

Niven, Laurence Van Cott
See Niven, Larry

Niven, Laurence VanCott
See Niven, Larry

Nixon, Agnes Eckhardt 1927- ...... **CLC 21**
See also CA 110

Nizami Ganjavi c. 1141-c. 1209 .... **PC 165**

Nizan, Paul 1905-1940 .... **TCLC 40**
See also CA 161; DLB 72; EWL 3; GFL 1789 to the Present

Nkosi, Lewis 1936-2010 .... **BLC 1:3; CLC 45, 377**
See also BW 1, 3; CA 65-68; CANR 27, 81; CBD; CD 5, 6; DAM MULT; DLB 157, 225; WWE 1

Nodier, (Jean) Charles (Emmanuel)
1780-1844 .... **NCLC 19**
See also DLB 119; GFL 1789 to the Present
Noguchi, Yone 1875-1947 .... **TCLC 80**
Nolan, Brian
See O Nuallain, Brian
Nolan, Christopher 1965-2009 .... **CLC 58**
See also CA 111; 283; CANR 88
Nolan, Christopher John
See Nolan, Christopher
Noon, Jeff 1957- .... **CLC 91**
See also CA 148; CANR 83; DLB 267; SFW 4
Nooteboom, Cees 1933- .... **CLC 323**
See also CA 124; 130; CANR 120, 177;
EWL 3; RGWL 3
Nordan, Lewis 1939-2012 .... **CLC 304**
See also CA 117; CANR 40, 72, 121; CSW;
DLB 234, 350
Norden, Charles
See Durrell, Lawrence
Nordhoff, Charles Bernard
1887-1947 .... **TCLC 23**
See also CA 108; 211; DLB 9; LAIT 1;
RHW 1; SATA 23
Norfolk, Lawrence 1963- .... **CLC 76**
See also CA 144; CANR 85; CN 6, 7;
DLB 267
Norman, Marsha (Williams)
1947- .... **CLC 28, 186; DC 8**
See also CA 105; CABS 3; CAD; CANR 41,
131; CD 5, 6; CSW; CWD; DAM DRAM;
DFS 2; DLB 266; DLBY 1984; FW; MAL 5
Normyx
See Douglas, (George) Norman
Norris, Benjamin Franklin, Jr.
See Norris, Frank
Norris, Frank 1870-1902 .... **SSC 28;**
TCLC 24, 155, 211
See also AAYA 57; AMW; AMWC 2; BPFB
2; CA 110; 160; CDALB 1865-1917; DLB
12, 71, 186; LMFS 2; MAL 5; NFS 12;
RGAL 4; TCWW 1, 2; TUS
Norris, Kathleen 1947- .... **CLC 248**
See also CA 160; CANR 113, 199
Norris, Leslie 1921-2006 .... **CLC 14, 351**
See also CA 11-12; 251; CANR 14, 117;
CAP 1; CP 1, 2, 3, 4, 5, 6, 7; DLB 27, 256
North, Andrew
See Norton, Andre
North, Anthony
See Koontz, Dean
North, Captain George
See Stevenson, Robert Louis
North, Captain George
See Stevenson, Robert Louis
North, Milou
See Erdrich, Louise
Northrup, B. A.
See Hubbard, L. Ron
North Staffs
See Hulme, T(homas) E(rnest)
Northup, Solomon 1808-1863 ..... **NCLC 105**
Norton, Alice Mary
See Norton, Andre
Norton, Andre 1912-2005 .... **CLC 12**
See also AAYA 83; BPFB 2; BYA 4, 10, 12;
CA 1-4R; 237; CANR 2, 31, 68, 108, 149;
CLR 50; 184; DLB 8, 52; JRDA; MAI-
CYA 1, 2; MTCW 1; SATA 1, 43, 91;
SUFW 1, 2; YAW
Norton, Caroline 1808-1877 ... **NCLC 47, 205**
See also DLB 21, 159, 199
Norway, Nevil Shute
See Shute, Nevil
Norwid, Cyprian Kamil 1821-1883 .. **NCLC 17**
See also RGWL 3
Nosille, Nabrah
See Ellison, Harlan

Nossack, Hans Erich 1901-1977 .... **CLC 6**
See also CA 93-96; 85-88; CANR 156; DLB
69; EWL 3
Nostradamus 1503-1566 .... **LC 27**
Nosu, Chuji
See Ozu, Yasujiro
Notenburg, Eleanora (Genrikhovna) von
See Guro, Elena (Genrikhovna)
Nothomb, Amélie 1967- .... **CLC 344**
See also CA 205; CANR 154, 205
Nova, Craig 1945- .... **CLC 7, 31**
See also CA 45-48; CANR 2, 53, 127, 223
Novak, Joseph
See Kosinski, Jerzy
Novalis 1772-1801 .... **NCLC 13, 178; PC 120**
See also CDWLB 2; DLB 90; EW 5; RGWL
2, 3
Novick, Peter 1934-2012 .... **CLC 164**
See also CA 188
Novis, Emile
See Weil, Simone
Nowlan, Alden (Albert) 1933-1983 ... **CLC 15**
See also CA 9-12R; CANR 5; CP 1, 2, 3;
DAC; DAM MST; DLB 53; PFS 12
Nowra, Louis 1950- .... **CLC 372**
See also CA 195; CD 5, 6; DLB 325; IDTP
Noyes, Alfred 1880-1958 .... **PC 27; TCLC 7**
See also CA 104; 188; DLB 20; EXPP;
FANT; PFS 4; RGEL 2
Nugent, Richard Bruce 1906(?)-1987 ... **HR 1:3**
See also BW 1; CA 125; CANR 198; DLB
51; GLL 2
Nunez, Elizabeth 1944- .... **BLC 2:3**
See also CA 223; CANR 220
Nunn, Kem .... **CLC 34**
See also CA 159; CANR 204
Nussbaum, Martha 1947- .... **CLC 203**
See also CA 134; CANR 102, 176, 213, 241
Nussbaum, Martha Craven
See Nussbaum, Martha
Nwapa, Flora (Nwanzuruaha)
1931-1993 .... **BLCS; CLC 133**
See also BW 2; CA 143; CANR 83;
CDWLB 3; CLR 162; CWRI 5; DLB
125; EWL 3; WLIT 2
Nye, Robert 1939- .... **CLC 13, 42**
See also BRWS 10; CA 33-36R; CANR 29,
67, 107; CN 1, 2, 3, 4, 5, 6, 7; CP 1, 2, 3, 4,
5, 6, 7; CWRI 5; DAM NOV; DLB 14, 271;
FANT; HGG; MTCW 1; RHW; SATA 6
Nyro, Laura 1947-1997 .... **CLC 17**
See also CA 194
O. Henry
See Henry, O.
Oates, Joyce Carol 1938- .... **CLC 1, 2,**
3, 6, 9, 11, 15, 19, 33, 52, 108, 134, 228;
SSC 6, 70, 121; WLC 4
See also AAYA 15, 52; AITN 1; AMWS 2;
BEST 89:2; BPFB 2; BYA 11; CA 5-8R;
CANR 25, 45, 74, 113, 129, 165; CDALB
1968-1988; CN 1, 2, 3, 4, 5, 6, 7; CP 5, 6,
7; CPW; CWP; DA; DA3; DAB; DAC;
DAM MST, NOV, POP; DLB 2, 5, 130;
DLBY 1981; EWL 3; EXPS; FL 1:6; FW;
GL 3; HGG; INT CANR-25; LAIT 4;
MAL 5; MBL; MTCW 1, 2; MTFW
2005; NFS 8, 24; RGAL 4; RGSF 2; SATA
159; SSFS 1, 8, 17, 32; SUFW 2; TUS
Obradovic, Dositej 1740(?)-1811 .. **NCLC 254**
See also DLB 147
O'Brian, E.G.
See Clarke, Arthur C.
O'Brian, Patrick 1914-2000 .... **CLC 152**
See also AAYA 55; BRWS 12; CA 144; 187;
CANR 74, 201; CPW; MTCW 2; MTFW
2005; RHW
O'Brien, Darcy 1939-1998 .... **CLC 11**
See also CA 21-24R; 167; CANR 8, 59

O'Brien, Edna 1930- .... **CLC 3, 5, 8,**
13, 36, 65, 116, 237; SSC 10, 77, 192
See also BRWS 5; CA 1-4R; CANR 6, 41,
65, 102, 169, 213; CDBLB 1960 to Present;
CN 1, 2, 3, 4, 5, 6, 7; DA3; DAM NOV;
DLB 14, 231, 319; EWL 3; FW; MTCW 1,
2; MTFW 2005; RGSF 2; WLIT 4
O'Brien, E.G.
See Clarke, Arthur C.
O'Brien, Fitz-James 1828-1862 .... **NCLC 21**
See also DLB 74; RGAL 4; SUFW
O'Brien, Flann
See O Nuallain, Brian
Ono no Komachi fl. c. 850- .... **CMLC 134**
O'Brien, Richard 1942- .... **CLC 17**
See also CA 124
O'Brien, Tim 1946- ...... **CLC 7, 19, 40, 103,**
211, 305; SSC 74, 123
See also AAYA 16; AMWS 5; CA 85-88;
CANR 40, 58, 133; CDALBS; CN 5, 6, 7;
CPW; DA3; DAM POP; DLB 152; DLBD
9; DLBY 1980; LATS 1:2; MAL 5;
MTCW 2; MTFW 2005; NFS 37; RGAL
4; SSFS 5, 15, 29, 32; TCLE 1:2
O'Brien, William Timothy
See O'Brien, Tim
Obstfelder, Sigbjørn 1866-1900 .... **TCLC 23**
See also CA 123; DLB 354
Ocampo, Silvina 1906-1993 .... **SSC 175**
See also CA 131; CANR 87, CWW 2, HW
1, RGSF 2
O'Casey, Brenda
See Haycraft, Anna
O'Casey, Sean 1880-1964 .... **CLC 1, 5, 9,**
11, 15, 88; DC 12; WLCS
See also BRW 7; CA 89-92; CANR 62;
CBD; CDBLB 1914-1945; DA3; DAB;
DAC; DAM DRAM, MST; DFS 19; DLB
10; EWL 3; MTCW 1, 2; MTFW 2005;
RGEL 2; TEA; WLIT 4
O'Cathasaigh, Sean
See O'Casey, Sean
Occom, Samson 1723-1792 ... **LC 60; NNAL**
See also DLB 175
Occomy, Marita (Odette) Bonner
1899(?)-1971 .... **HR 1:2; PC 72;**
TCLC 179
See also BW 2; CA 142; DFS 13; DLB 51, 228
Ochs, Phil(ip David) 1940-1976 ...... **CLC 17**
See also CA 185; 65-68
O'Connor, Edwin (Greene)
1918-1968 .... **CLC 14**
See also CA 93-96; 25-28R; MAL 5
O'Connor, Flannery 1925-1964 .... **CLC 1,**
2, 3, 6, 10, 13, 15, 21, 66, 104; SSC 1, 23,
61, 82, 111, 168, 173, 190, 195, 196, 199;
TCLC 132, 305; WLC 4
See also AAYA 7; AMW; AMWR 2; BPFB
3; BYA 16; CA 1-4R; CANR 3, 41;
CDALB 1941-1968; DA; DA3; DAB;
DAC; DAM MST, NOV; DLB 2, 152;
DLBD 12; DLBY 1980; EWL 3; EXPS;
LAIT 5; MAL 5; MBL; MTCW 1, 2;
MTFW 2005; NFS 3, 21; RGAL 4; RGSF
2; SSFS 2, 7, 10, 19, 34; TUS
O'Connor, Frank 1903-1966 .... **CLC 14, 23;**
SSC 5, 109, 177
See also BRWS 14; CA 93-96; CANR 84;
DLB 162; EWL 3; RGSF 2; SSFS 5, 34
O'Connor, Mary Flannery
See O'Connor, Flannery
O'Dell, Scott 1898-1989 .... **CLC 30**
See also AAYA 3, 44; BPFB 3; BYA 1, 2, 3,
5; CA 61-64; 129; CANR 12, 30, 112;
CLR 1, 16, 126; DLB 52; JRDA; MAI-
CYA 1, 2; SATA 12, 60, 134; WYA; YAW
Odets, Clifford 1906-1963 .... **CLC 2,**
28, 98; DC 6; TCLC 244

See also AMWS 2; CA 85-88; CAD; CANR
62; DAM DRAM; DFS 3, 17, 20; DLB 7,
26, 341; EWL 3; MAL 5; MTCW 1, 2;
MTFW 2005; RGAL 4; TUS

O'Doherty, Brian 1928- .... **CLC 76**
See also CA 105; CANR 108

O'Donnell, K. M.
See Malzberg, Barry N(athaniel)

O'Donnell, Lawrence
See Kuttner, Henry

O'Donovan, Michael Francis
See O'Connor, Frank

Oe, Kenzaburo 1935- .... **CLC 10, 36, 86,**
187, 303; SSC 20, 176
See also CA 97-100; CANR 36, 50, 74, 126;
CWW 2; DA3; DAM NOV; DLB 182,
331; DLBY 1994; EWL 3; LATS 1:2;
MJW; MTCW 1, 2; MTFW 2005; RGSF
2; RGWL 2, 3

Oe Kenzaburo
See Oe, Kenzaburo

O'Faolain, Julia 1932- ... **CLC 6, 19, 47, 108**
See also CA 81-84; CAAS 2; CANR 12, 61;
CN 2, 3, 4, 5, 6, 7; DLB 14, 231, 319; FW;
MTCW 1; RHW

O'Faolain, Sean 1900-1991 ... **CLC 1, 7, 14,**
32, 70; SSC 13, 194; TCLC 143
See also CA 61-64; 134; CANR 12, 66; CN
1, 2, 3, 4; DLB 15, 162; MTCW 1, 2;
MTFW 2005; RGEL 2; RGSF 2

O'Flaherty, Liam 1896-1984 ...... **CLC 5, 34;**
SSC 6, 116
See also CA 101; 113; CANR 35; CN 1, 2, 3;
DLB 36, 162; DLBY 1984; MTCW 1, 2;
MTFW 2005; RGEL 2; RGSF 2; SSFS 5, 20

Ogai
See Mori Ogai

Ogilvy, Gavin
See Barrie, J. M.

O'Grady, Standish (James)
1846-1928 .... **TCLC 5**
See also CA 104; 157

O'Grady, Timothy 1951- .... **CLC 59**
See also CA 138

O'Hara, Frank 1926-1966 ..... **CLC 2, 5, 13,**
78; PC 45
See also AMWS 23; CA 9-12R; 25-28R;
CANR 33; DA3; DAM POET; DLB 5, 16,
193; EWL 3; MAL 5; MTCW 1, 2; MTFW
2005; PFS 8, 12, 34, 38; RGAL 4; WP

O'Hara, John 1905-1970 ..... **CLC 1, 2, 3, 6,**
11, 42; SSC 15
See also AMW; BPFB 3; CA 5-8R; 25-28R;
CANR 31, 60; CDALB 1929-1941; DAM
NOV; DLB 9, 86, 324; DLBD 2; EWL 3;
MAL 5; MTCW 1, 2; MTFW 2005; NFS
11; RGAL 4; RGSF 2

O'Hara, John Henry
See O'Hara, John

O'Hehir, Diana 1929- .... **CLC 41**
See also CA 245; CANR 177

O'Hehir, Diana F.
See O'Hehir, Diana

Ohiyesa
See Eastman, Charles A(lexander)

Okada, John 1923-1971 .... **AAL**
See also BYA 14; CA 212; DLB 312; NFS 25

O'Kelly, Seamus 1881(?)-1918 .... **SSC 136**

Okigbo, Christopher 1930-1967 ... **BLC 1:3;**
CLC 25, 84; PC 7, 128; TCLC 171
See also AFW; BW 1, 3; CA 77-80; CANR
74; CDWLB 3; DAM MULT, POET; DLB
125; EWL 3; MTCW 1, 2; MTFW 2005;
RGEL 2

Okigbo, Christopher Ifenayichukwu
See Okigbo, Christopher

Okri, Ben 1959- .... **BLC 2:3; CLC 87,**
223, 337; SSC 127

See also AFW; BRWS 5; BW 2, 3; CA 130;
138; CANR 65, 128; CN 5, 6, 7; DLB 157,
231, 319, 326; EWL 3; INT CA-138;
MTCW 2; MTFW 2005; RGSF 2; SSFS
20; WLIT 2; WWE 1

Old Boy
See Hughes, Thomas

Olds, Sharon 1942- .... **CLC 32, 39, 85, 361;**
PC 22
See also AMWS 10; CA 101; CANR 18, 41,
66, 98, 135, 211; CP 5, 6, 7; CPW; CWP;
DAM POET; DLB 120; MAL 5; MTCW 2;
MTFW 2005; PFS 17

Oldstyle, Jonathan
See Irving, Washington

Olesha, Iurii
See Olesha, Yuri (Karlovich)

Olesha, Iurii Karlovich
See Olesha, Yuri (Karlovich)

Olesha, Yuri (Karlovich) 1899-1960 ... **CLC 8;**
SSC 69; TCLC 136
See also CA 85-88; DLB 272; EW 11; EWL
3; RGWL 2, 3

Olesha, Yury Karlovich
See Olesha, Yuri (Karlovich)

Oliphant, Mrs.
See Oliphant, Margaret (Oliphant Wilson)

Oliphant, Laurence 1829(?)-1888 .. **NCLC 47**
See also DLB 18, 166

Oliphant, Margaret (Oliphant Wilson)
1828-1897 ... **NCLC 11, 61, 221; SSC 25**
See also BRWS 10; DLB 18, 159, 190;
HGG; RGEL 2; RGSF 2; SUFW

Oliver, Mary 1935- .... **CLC 19, 34, 98, 364;**
PC 75
See also AMWS 7; CA 21-24R; CANR 9,
43, 84, 92, 138, 217; CP 4, 5, 6, 7; CWP;
DLB 5, 193, 342; EWL 3; MTFW 2005;
PFS 15, 31, 40

Olivi, Peter 1248-1298 .... **CMLC 114**

Olivier, Laurence (Kerr) 1907-1989 ... **CLC 20**
See also CA 111; 150; 129

O.L.S.
See Russell, George William

Olsen, Tillie 1912-2007 ...... **CLC 4, 13, 114;**
SSC 11, 103
See also AAYA 51; AMWS 13; BYA 11; CA
1-4R; 256; CANR 1, 43, 74, 132; CDALBS;
CN 2, 3, 4, 5, 6, 7; DA; DA3; DAB; DAC;
DAM MST; DLB 28, 206; DLBY 1980;
EWL 3; EXPS; FW; MAL 5; MTCW 1, 2;
MTFW 2005; RGAL 4; RGSF 2; SSFS 1,
32; TCLE 1:2; TCWW 2; TUS

Olson, Charles 1910-1970 .... **CLC 1, 2, 5,**
6, 9, 11, 29; PC 19
See also AMWS 2; CA 13-16; 25-28R;
CABS 2; CANR 35, 61; CAP 1; CP 1;
DAM POET; DLB 5, 16, 193; EWL 3;
MAL 5; MTCW 1, 2; RGAL 4; WP

Olson, Charles John
See Olson, Charles

Olson, Merle Theodore
See Olson, Toby

Olson, Toby 1937- .... **CLC 28**
See also CA 65-68; CAAS 11; CANR 9, 31,
84, 175; CP 3, 4, 5, 6, 7

Olyesha, Yuri
See Olesha, Yuri (Karlovich)

Olympiodorus of Thebes
c. 375-c. 430 .... **CMLC 59**

Omar Khayyam
See Khayyam, Omar

Ondaatje, Michael 1943- .... **CLC 14,**
29, 51, 76, 180, 258, 322; PC 28
See also AAYA 66; CA 77-80; CANR 42,
74, 109, 133, 172; CN 5, 6, 7; CP 1, 2, 3,
4, 5, 6, 7; DA3; DAB; DAC; DAM MST;
DLB 60, 323, 326; EWL 3; LATS 1:2;

LMFS 2; MTCW 2; MTFW 2005; NFS 23;
PFS 8, 19; TCLE 1:2; TWA; WWE 1

Ondaatje, Philip Michael
See Ondaatje, Michael

Oneal, Elizabeth 1934- .... **CLC 30**
See also AAYA 5, 41; BYA 13; CA 106;
CANR 28, 84; CLR 13, 169; JRDA; MAI-
CYA 1, 2; SATA 30, 82; WYA; YAW

Oneal, Zibby
See Oneal, Elizabeth

O'Neill, Eugene 1888-1953 .... **DC 20;**
TCLC 1, 6, 27, 49, 225; WLC 4
See also AAYA 54; AITN 1; AMW; AMWC
1; CA 110; 132; CAD; CANR 131;
CDALB 1929-1941; DA; DA3; DAB;
DAC; DAM DRAM, MST; DFS 2, 4, 5,
6, 9, 11, 12, 16, 20, 26, 27; DLB 7, 331;
EWL 3; LAIT 3; LMFS 2; MAL 5;
MTCW 1, 2; MTFW 2005; RGAL 4; TUS

O'Neill, Eugene Gladstone
See O'Neill, Eugene

Onetti, Juan Carlos 1909-1994 ... **CLC 7, 10;**
HLCS 2; SSC 23; TCLC 131
See also CA 85-88; 145; CANR 32, 63;
CDWLB 3; CWW 2; DAM MULT, NOV;
DLB 113; EWL 3; HW 1, 2; LAW;
MTCW 1, 2; MTFW 2005; RGSF 2

Lonnrot, Elias 1802-1884 .... **NCLC 53**
See also EFS 1:1, 2:1

O'Nolan, Brian
See O Nuallain, Brian

O Nuallain, Brian 1911-1966 .... **CLC 1, 4,**
5, 7, 10, 47
See also BRWS 2; CA 21-22; 25-28R; CAP 2;
DLB 231; EWL 3; FANT; RGEL 2; TEA

Ophuls, Max 1902-1957 .... **TCLC 79**
See also CA 113

Opie, Amelia 1769-1853 .... **NCLC 65, 317**
See also DLB 116, 159; RGEL 2

Opitz, Martin 1597-1639 .... **LC 207**
See also DLB 164

Oppen, George 1908-1984 ... **CLC 7, 13, 34;**
PC 35; TCLC 107
See also CA 13-16R; 113; CANR 8, 82; CP
1, 2, 3; DLB 5, 165

Oppenheim, E(dward) Phillips
1866-1946 .... **TCLC 45**
See also CA 111; 202; CMW 4; DLB 70

Oppenheimer, Max
See Ophuls, Max

Opuls, Max
See Ophuls, Max

Ophuls, Max
See Ophuls, Max

Orage, A(lfred) R(ichard)
1873-1934 .... **TCLC 157**
See also CA 122

Oresme, Nicole 1320/1325?-1382 ..... **CMLC**
163

Origen c. 185-c. 254 .... **CMLC 19**

Orlovitz, Gil 1918-1973 .... **CLC 22**
See also CA 77-80; 45-48; CN 1; CP 1, 2;
DLB 2, 5

Orosius c. 385-c. 420 .... **CMLC 100**

O'Rourke, P. J. 1947- .... **CLC 209**
See also CA 77-80; CANR 13, 41, 67, 111,
155, 217; CPW; DAM POP; DLB 185

O'Rourke, Patrick Jake
See O'Rourke, P.J.

Orrery
See Boyle, Roger

Orris
See Ingelow, Jean

Ortega y Gasset, Jose 1883-1955 .... **HLC 2;**
TCLC 9
See also CA 106; 130; DAM MULT; EW 9;
EWL 3; HW 1, 2; MTCW 1, 2; MTFW 2005

See also AMWS 6; CA 25-28R; 263; CANR 13, 46, 74, 118; CN 2, 3, 4, 5, 6, 7; CPW; DA3; DAM POP; DLB 28, 218; EWL 3; EXPS; FW; INT CANR-13; MAL 5; MBL; MTCW 1, 2; MTFW 2005; RGAL 4; RGSF 2; SSFS 3, 20, 27

Paley, Grace Goodside
See Paley, Grace

Palin, Michael 1943- .... **CLC 21**
See also CA 107; CANR 35, 109, 179, 229; DLB 352; SATA 67

Palin, Michael Edward
See Palin, Michael

Palliser, Charles 1947- .... **CLC 65**
See also CA 136; CANR 76; CN 5, 6, 7

Palma, Ricardo 1833-1919 .... **SSC 175; TCLC 29**
See also CA 168; LAW

Palmer, Michael 1943- .... **PC 172**
See also CA 114; CANR 35, 150, 238; CP 3, 4, 5, 6, 7; CPW; DLB 169; DAM POET

Pamuk, Orhan 1952- .... **CLC 185, 288, 377**
See also AAYA 82; CA 142; CANR 75, 127, 172, 208; CWW 2; NFS 27; WLIT 6

Panbury, Theophilus
See Harwood, Gwen

Pancake, Breece Dexter
1952-1979 .... **CLC 29; SSC 61**
See also CA 123; 109; DLB 130

Pancake, Breece D'J
See Pancake, Breece Dexter

Panchenko, Nikolai .... **CLC 59**

Pankhurst, Emmeline (Goulden)
1858-1928 .... **TCLC 100**
See also CA 116; FW

Panko, Rudy
See Gogol, Nikolai

Papadiamantis, Alexandros
1851-1911 .... **TCLC 29**
See also CA 168; EWL 3

Papadiamantopoulos, Johannes
1856-1910 .... **TCLC 18**
See also CA 117; 242; GFL 1789 to the Present

Papadiamantopoulos, Yannis
See Papadiamantopoulos, Johannes

Papini, Giovanni 1881-1956 .... **TCLC 22**
See also CA 121; 180; DLB 264

Paracelsus 1493-1541 .... **LC 14, 228**
See also DLB 179

Parasol, Peter
See Stevens, Wallace

Pardo Bazan, Emilia 1851-1921 ...... **SSC 30, 158; TCLC 189**
See also EWL 3; FW; RGSF 2; RGWL 2, 3; SSFS 36

Paredes, Americo 1915-1999 .... **PC 83**
See also CA 37-40R; 179; DLB 209; EXPP; HW 1

Pareto, Vilfredo 1848-1923 .... **TCLC 69**
See also CA 175

Paretsky, Sara 1947- .... **CLC 135**
See also AAYA 30; BEST 90:3; CA 125; 129; CANR 59, 95, 184, 218; CMW 4; CPW; DA3; DAM POP; DLB 306; INT CA-129; MSW; RGAL 4

Paretsky, Sara N.
See Paretsky, Sara

Parfenie, Maria
See Codrescu, Andrei

Parini, Jay 1948- .... **CLC 54, 133**
See also CA 97-100, 229; CAAE 229; CAAS 16; CANR 32, 87, 198, 230

Parini, Jay Lee
See Parini, Jay

Paris, Matthew c. 1200-1259 ..... **CMLC 152**

Park, Jordan
See Kornbluth, C(yril) M.; Pohl, Frederik

Park, Robert E(zra) 1864-1944 .... **TCLC 73**
See also CA 122; 165

Parker, Bert
See Ellison, Harlan

Parker, Dorothy 1893-1967 ...... **CLC 15,68; DC 40; PC 28; SSC 2, 101; TCLC 143**
See also AMWS 9; CA 19-20; 25-28R; CAP 2; DA3; DAM POET; DLB 11, 45, 86; EXPP; FW; MAL 5; MBL; MTCW 1, 2; MTFW 2005; PFS 18, 43; RGAL 4; RGSF 2; TUS

Parker, Dorothy Rothschild
See Parker, Dorothy

Parker, Robert B. 1932-2010 ... **CLC 27, 283**
See also AAYA 28; BEST 89:4; BPFB 3; CA 49-52; CANR 1, 26, 52, 89, 128, 165, 200; CMW 4; CPW; DAM NOV, POP; DLB 306; INT CANR-26; MSW; MTCW 1; MTFW 2005

Parker, Robert Brown
See Parker, Robert B.

Parker, Theodore 1810-1860 .... **NCLC 186**
See also DLB 1, 235

Parkes, Lucas
See Harris, John (Wyndham Parkes Lucas) Beynon

Parkin, Frank 1940-2011 .... **CLC 43**
See also CA 147

Parkman, Francis, Jr. 1823-1893 ... **NCLC 12**
See also AMWS 2; DLB 1, 30, 183, 186, 235; RGAL 4

Parks, Gordon 1912-2006 .... **BLC 1:3; CLC 1, 16**
See also AAYA 36; AITN 2; BW 2, 3; CA 41-44R; 249; CANR 26, 66, 145; DA3; DAM MULT; DLB 33; MTCW 2; MTFW 2005; NFS 32; SATA 8, 108; SATA-Obit 175

Parks, Gordon Roger Alexander
See Parks, Gordon

Parks, Suzan-Lori 1964(?)- .... **BLC 2:3; CLC 309; DC 23**
See also AAYA 55; CA 201; CAD; CD 5, 6; CWD; DFS 22; DLB 341; RGAL 4

Parks, Tim 1954- .... **CLC 147**
See also CA 126; 131; CANR 77, 144, 202; CN 7; DLB 231; INT CA-131

Parks, Timothy Harold
See Parks, Tim

Parmenides c. 515B.C.-c. 450B.C. ... **CMLC 22**
See also DLB 176

Parnell, Thomas 1679-1718 .... **LC 3**
See also DLB 95; RGEL 2

Parr, Catherine c. 1513(?)-1548 .... **LC 86**
See also DLB 136

Parra, Nicanor 1914- .... **CLC 2, 102; HLC 2; PC 39**
See also CA 85-88; CANR 32; CWW 2; DAM MULT; DLB 283; EWL 3; HW 1; LAW; MTCW 1

Parra Sanojo, Ana Teresa de la 1890-1936
See de la Parra, Teresa

Parrish, Mary Frances
See Fisher, M. F. K.

Parshchikov, Aleksei 1954- .... **CLC 59**
See also DLB 285

Parshchikov, Aleksei Maksimovich
See Parshchikov, Aleksei

Parson, Professor
See Coleridge, Samuel Taylor

Parson Lot
See Kingsley, Charles

Parton, Sara Payson Willis
1811-1872 .... **NCLC 86, 257**
See also DLB 43, 74, 239

Partridge, Anthony
See Oppenheim, E(dward) Phillips

Pascal, Blaise 1623-1662 .... **LC 35**
See also DLB 268; EW 3; GFL Beginnings to 1789; RGWL 2, 3; TWA

Pascoli, Giovanni 1855-1912 .... **TCLC 45**
See also CA 170; EW 7; EWL 3

Pasolini, Pier Paolo 1922-1975 ...... **CLC 20, 37, 106; PC 17**
See also CA 93-96; 61-64; CANR 63; DLB 128, 177; EWL 3; MTCW 1; RGWL 2, 3

Pasquil
See Nashe, Thomas

Pasquini
See Silone, Ignazio

Pastan, Linda 1932- .... **CLC 27**
See also CA 61-64; CANR 18, 40, 61, 113, 233; CP 3, 4, 5, 6, 7; CSW; CWP; DAM POET; DLB 5; PFS 8, 25, 32, 40

Pastan, Linda Olenik
See Pastan, Linda

Pasternak, Boris 1890-1960 ... **CLC 7, 10, 18, 63; PC 6; SSC 31; TCLC 188; WLC 4**
See also BPFB 3; CA 127; 116; DA; DA3; DAB; DAC; DAM MST, NOV, POET; DLB 302, 331; EW 10; MTCW 1, 2; MTFW 2005; NFS 26; RGSF 2; RGWL 2, 3; TWA; WP

Pasternak, Boris Leonidovich
See Pasternak, Boris

Patchen, Kenneth 1911-1972 ... **CLC 1, 2, 18**
See also BG 1:3; CA 1-4R; 33-36R; CANR 3, 35; CN 1; CP 1; DAM POET; DLB 16, 48; EWL 3; MAL 5; MTCW 1; RGAL 4

Patchett, Ann 1963- .... **CLC 244**
See also AAYA 69; AMWS 12; CA 139; CANR 64, 110, 167, 200, 235; DLB 350; MTFW 2005; NFS 30

Pater, Walter (Horatio)
1839-1894 .... **NCLC 7, 90, 159**
See also BRW 5; CDBLB 1832-1890; DLB 57, 156; RGEL 2; TEA

Paterson, A(ndrew) B(arton)
1864-1941 .... **TCLC 32**
See also CA 155; DLB 230; RGEL 2; SATA 97

Paterson, Banjo
See Paterson, A(ndrew) B(arton)

Paterson, Katherine 1932- .... **CLC 12, 30**
See also AAYA 1, 31; BYA 1, 2, 7; CA 21-24R; CANR 28, 59, 111, 173, 196; CLR 7, 50, 127; CWRI 5; DLB 52; JRDA; LAIT 4; MAICYA 1; MAICYAS 1; MTCW 1; SATA 13, 53, 92, 133, 204; WYA; YAW

Paterson, Katherine Womeldorf
See Paterson, Katherine

Patmore, Coventry Kersey Dighton
1823-1896 .... **NCLC 9; PC 59**
See also DLB 35, 98; RGEL 2; TEA

Paton, Alan 1903-1988 .... **CLC 4, 10, 25, 55, 106; TCLC 165; WLC 4**
See also AAYA 26; AFW; BPFB 3; BRWS 2; BYA 1; CA 13-16; 125; CANR 22; CAP 1; CN 1, 2, 3, 4; DA; DA3; DAB; DAC; DAM MST, NOV; DLB 225; DLBD 17; EWL 3; EXPN; LAIT 4; MTCW 1, 2; MTFW 2005; NFS 3, 12; RGEL 2; SATA 11; SATA-Obit 56; SSFS 29; TWA; WLIT 2; WWE 1

Paton, Alan Stewart
See Paton, Alan

Paton Walsh, Gillian
See Paton Walsh, Jill

Paton Walsh, Jill 1937- .... **CLC 35**
See also AAYA 11, 47; BYA 1, 8; CA 262; CAAE 262; CANR 38, 83, 158, 229; CLR 2, 6, 128; DLB 161; JRDA; MAICYA 1, 2; SAAS 3; SATA 4, 72, 109, 190; SATA-Essay 190; WYA; YAW

Patsauq, Markoosie 1942- .... **NNAL**
See also CA 101; CLR 23; CWRI 5; DAM MULT

Patterson, (Horace) Orlando (Lloyd)
1940- .... **BLCS**
See also BW 1; CA 65-68; CANR 27, 84; CN 1, 2, 3, 4, 5, 6

Patton, George S(mith), Jr.
1885-1945 .... **TCLC 79**
See also CA 189

Paulding, James Kirke 1778-1860 ... **NCLC 2**
See also DLB 3, 59, 74, 250; RGAL 4

Paulhan, Jean 1884-1968 .... **TCLC 313**
See also CA 25-28R, 249; EWL 3

Paulin, Thomas Neilson
See Paulin, Tom

Paulin, Tom 1949- .... **CLC 37, 177**
See also CA 123; 128; CANR 98; CP 3, 4, 5,
6, 7; DLB 40

Paulinus of Nola 353?-431 .... **CMLC 156**

Pausanias c. 1st cent. .... **CMLC 36**

Paustovsky, Konstantin (Georgievich)
1892-1968 .... **CLC 40**
See also CA 93-96; 25-28R; DLB 272;
EWL 3

Pavese, Cesare 1908-1950 .... **PC 13;
SSC 19; TCLC 3, 240**
See also CA 104; 169; DLB 128, 177; EW
12; EWL 3; PFS 20; RGSF 2; RGWL 2, 3;
TWA; WLIT 7

Pavic, Milorad 1929-2009 .... **CLC 60**
See also CA 136; CDWLB 4; CWW 2; DLB
181; EWL 3; RGWL 3

Pavlov, Ivan Petrovich 1849-1936 ... **TCLC 91**
See also CA 118; 180

Pavlova, Karolina Karlovna
1807-1893 .... **NCLC 138**
See also DLB 205

Payne, Alan
See Jakes, John

Payne, John Howard 1791-1852 ... **NCLC 241**
See also DLB 37; RGAL 4

Payne, Rachel Ann
See Jakes, John

Paz, Gil
See Lugones, Leopoldo

Paz, Octavio 1914-1998 ..... **CLC 3, 4, 6, 10,
19, 51, 65, 119; HLC 2; PC 1, 48; TCLC
211; WLC 4**
See also AAYA 50; CA 73-76; 165; CANR
32, 65, 104; CWW 2; DA; DA3; DAB;
DAC; DAM MST, MULT, POET; DLB
290, 331; DLBY 1990, 1998; DNFS 1;
EWL 3; HW 1, 2; LAW; LAWS 1; MTCW
1, 2; MTFW 2005; PFS 18, 30, 38; RGWL
2, 3; SSFS 13; TWA; WLIT 1

p'Bitek, Okot 1931-1982 .... **BLC 1:3;
CLC 96; TCLC 149**
See also AFW; BW 2, 3; CA 124; 107;
CANR 82; CP 1, 2, 3; DAM MULT; DLB
125; EWL 3; MTCW 1, 2; MTFW 2005;
RGEL 2; WLIT 2

Peabody, Elizabeth Palmer
1804-1894 .... **NCLC 169**
See also DLB 1, 223

Peacham, Henry 1578-1644(?) .... **LC 119**
See also DLB 151

Peacock, Molly 1947- .... **CLC 60**
See also CA 103, 262; CAAE 262; CAAS
21; CANR 52, 84, 235; CP 5, 6, 7; CWP;
DLB 120, 282

Peacock, Thomas Love
1785-1866 .... **NCLC 22; PC 87**
See also BRW 4; DLB 96, 116; RGEL 2;
RGSF 2

Peake, Mervyn 1911-1968 .... **CLC 7, 54**
See also CA 5-8R; 25-28R; CANR 3; DLB
15, 160, 255; FANT; MTCW 1; RGEL 2;
SATA 23; SFW 4

Pearce, Ann Philippa
See Pearce, Philippa

Pearce, Philippa 1920-2006 .... **CLC 21**
See also BRWS 19; BYA 5; CA 5-8R; 255;
CANR 4, 109; CLR 9; CWRI 5; DLB 161;
FANT; MAICYA 1; SATA 1, 67, 129;
SATA-Obit 179

Pearl, Eric
See Elman, Richard (Martin)

Pearson, Jean Mary
See Gardam, Jane

Pearson, Thomas Reid
See Pearson, T.R.

Pearson, T.R. 1956- .... **CLC 39**
See also CA 120; 130; CANR 97, 147, 185;
CSW; INT CA-130

Peck, Dale 1967- .... **CLC 81**
See also CA 146; CANR 72, 127, 180; GLL 2

Peck, John (Frederick) 1941- .... **CLC 3**
See also CA 49-52; CANR 3, 100; CP 4, 5, 6, 7

Peck, Richard 1934- .... **CLC 21**
See also AAYA 1, 24; BYA 1, 6, 8, 11; CA
85-88; CANR 19, 38, 129, 178; CLR 15,
142; INT CANR-19; JRDA; MAICYA 1,
2; SAAS 2; SATA 18, 55, 97, 110, 158,
190, 228; SATA-Essay 110; WYA; YAW

Peck, Richard Wayne
See Peck, Richard

Peck, Robert Newton 1928- .... **CLC 17**
See also AAYA 3, 43; BYA 1, 6; CA 81-84,
182; CAAE 182; CANR 31, 63, 127; CLR
45, 163; DA; DAC; DAM MST; JRDA;
LAIT 3; MAICYA 1, 2; NFS 29; SAAS 1;
SATA 21, 62, 111, 156; SATA-Essay 108;
WYA; YAW

Peckinpah, David Samuel
See Peckinpah, Sam

Peckinpah, Sam 1925-1984 .... **CLC 20**
See also CA 109; 114; CANR 82

Pedersen, Knut 1859-1952 .... **TCLC 2, 14,
49, 151, 203**
See also AAYA 79; CA 104; 119; CANR 63;
DLB 297, 330; EW 8; EWL 8; MTCW 1,
2; RGWL 2, 3

Peele, George 1556-1596 ..... **DC 27; LC 115**
See also BRW 1; DLB 62, 167; RGEL 2

Peeslake, Gaffer
See Durrell, Lawrence

Peguy, Charles (Pierre) 1873-1914 .... **TCLC 10**
See also CA 107; 193; DLB 258; EWL 3;
GFL 1789 to the Present

Penninc fl. 13th cent. .... **CMLC 173**

Peirce, Charles Sanders
1839-1914 .... **TCLC 81**
See also CA 194; DLB 270

Pelagius c. 350-c. 418 .... **CMLC 118**

Pelecanos, George P. 1957- .... **CLC 236**
See also CA 138; CANR 122, 165, 194, 243;
DLB 306

Pelevin, Victor 1962- .... **CLC 238**
See also CA 154; CANR 88, 159, 197;
DLB 285

Pelevin, Viktor Olegovich
See Pelevin, Victor

Pellicer, Carlos 1897(?)-1977 .... **HLCS 2**
See also CA 153; 69-72; DLB 290; EWL 3;
HW 1

Pena, Ramon del Valle y
See Valle-Inclan, Ramon del

Pendennis, Arthur Esquir
See Thackeray, William Makepeace

Penn, Arthur
See Matthews, (James) Brander

Penn, William 1644-1718 .... **LC 25**
See also DLB 24

Penny, Carolyn
See Chute, Carolyn

PEPECE
See Prado (Calvo), Pedro

Pepys, Samuel 1633-1703 .... **LC 11, 58;
WLC 4**
See also BRW 2; CDBLB 1660-1789; DA;
DA3; DAB; DAC; DAM MST; DLB 101,
213; NCFS 4; RGEL 2; TEA; WLIT 3

Percy, Thomas 1729-1811 .... **NCLC 95**
See also DLB 104

Percy, Walker 1916-1990 ..... **CLC 2, 3, 6, 8,
14, 18, 47, 65**
See also AMWS 3; BPFB 3; CA 1-4R; 131;
CANR 1, 23, 64; CN 1, 2, 3, 4; CPW;
CSW; DA3; DAM NOV, POP; DLB 2;
DLBY 1980, 1990; EWL 3; MAL 5;
MTCW 1, 2; MTFW 2005; RGAL 4; TUS

Percy, William Alexander
1885-1942 .... **TCLC 84**
See also CA 163; MTCW 2

Perdurabo, Frater
See Crowley, Edward Alexander

Pereda (y Sanchez de Porrua), Jose Maria de
1833-1906 .... **TCLC 16**
See also CA 117

Pereda y Porrua, Jose Maria de
See Pereda (y Sanchez de Porrua), Jose
Maria de

Peregoy, George Weems
See Mencken, H. L.

Perelman, Bob 1947- .... **PC 132**
See also CA 154; CANR 85, 160; CP 5, 6, 7;
DLB 193; RGAL 4

Perelman, Robert
See Perelman, Bob

Perelman, S(idney) J(oseph)
1904-1979 ...... **CLC 3, 5, 9, 15, 23, 44,
49; SSC 32**
See also AAYA 79; AITN 1, 2; BPFB 3; CA
73-76; 89-92; CANR 18; DAM DRAM;
DLB 11, 44; MTCW 1, 2; MTFW 2005;
RGAL 4

Perets, Yitskhok Leybush
See Peretz, Isaac Loeb

Peretz, Isaac Leib (?)-
See Peretz, Isaac Loeb

Peretz, Isaac Loeb 1851-1915 .... **SSC 26;
TCLC 16**
See Peretz, Isaac Leib
See also CA 109; 201; DLB 333

Peretz, Yitzkhok Leibush
See Peretz, Isaac Loeb

Peri Rossi, Cristina 1941- .... **CLC 156;
HLCS 2**
See also CA 131; CANR 59, 81; CWW 2;
DLB 145, 290; EWL 3; HW 1, 2

Perkins, W. Epaminondas Adrastus
See Twain, Mark

Perlata
See Peret, Benjamin

Perloff, Marjorie G(abrielle)
1931- .... **CLC 137**
See also CA 57-60; CANR 7, 22, 49, 104

Perrault, Charles 1628-1703 .... **LC 2, 56;
SSC 144**
See also BYA 4; CLR 79, 134, 203; DLB
268; GFL Beginnings to 1789; MAICYA
1, 2; RGWL 2, 3; SATA 25; WCH

Perrotta, Tom 1961- .... **CLC 266**
See also CA 162; CANR 99, 155, 197

Perry, Anne 1938- .... **CLC 126**
See also CA 101; CANR 22, 50, 84, 150, 177,
238; CMW 4; CN 6, 7; CPW; DLB 276

Perry, Brighton
See Sherwood, Robert E(mmet)

Perse, St.-John
See Leger, Alexis Saint-Leger

Perse, Saint-John
See Leger, Alexis Saint-Leger

Persius 34-62 .... **CMLC 74**
See also AW 2; DLB 211; RGWL 2, 3

Perutz, Leo(pold) 1882-1957 .... **TCLC 60**
See also CA 147; DLB 81

Peseenz, Tulio F.
See Lopez y Fuentes, Gregorio

Pesetsky, Bette 1932- .... **CLC 28**
See also CA 133; DLB 130

Peshkov, Alexei Maximovich
See Gorky, Maxim

Pessoa, Fernando 1888-1935 .... **HLC 2;
PC 20, 165; TCLC 27, 257**
See also CA 125; 183; CANR 182; DAM
MULT; DLB 287; EW 10; EWL 3; RGWL
2, 3; WP

Pessoa, Fernando António Nogueira
See Pessoa, Fernando

Peterkin, Julia Mood 1880-1961 .... **CLC 31**
See also CA 102; DLB 9

Peter of Blois c. 1135-c. 1212 .... **CMLC 127**

Peters, Joan K(aren) 1945- .... **CLC 39**
See also CA 158; CANR 109

Peters, Robert L(ouis) 1924- .... **CLC 7**
See also CA 13-16R; CAAS 8; CP 1, 5, 6, 7;
DLB 105

Peters, S. H.
See Henry, O.

Petofi, Sandor 1823-1849 ...... **NCLC 21, 264**
See also RGWL 2, 3

Petrakis, Harry Mark 1923- .... **CLC 3**
See also CA 9-12R; CANR 4, 30, 85, 155;
CN 1, 2, 3, 4, 5, 6, 7

Petrarch 1304-1374 .... **CMLC 20; PC 8**
See also DA3; DAM POET; EW 2; LMFS 1;
PFS 42; RGWL 2, 3; WLIT 7

Petrarch, Francesco
See Petrarch

Petronius c. 20-66 .... **CMLC 34, 170**
See also AW 2; CDWLB 1; DLB 211;
RGWL 2, 3; WLIT 8

Petrov, Eugene
See Kataev, Evgeny Petrovich

Petrov, Evgenii
See Kataev, Evgeny Petrovich

Petrov, Evgeny
See Kataev, Evgeny Petrovich

Petrovsky, Boris
See Mansfield, Katherine

Petrushevskaia, Liudmila
1938- .... **CLC 387**
See also CWW 2; DLB 285; EWL 3

Petry, Ann 1908-1997 .... **CLC 1, 7, 18;
SSC 161; TCLC 112**
See also AFAW 1, 2; BPFB 3; BW 1, 3;
BYA 2; CA 5-8R; 157; CAAS 6; CANR 4,
46; CLR 12; CN 1, 2, 3, 4, 5, 6; DLB 76;
EWL 3; JRDA; LAIT 1; MAICYA 1, 2;
MAICYAS 1; MTCW 1; NFS 33; RGAL
4; SATA 5; SATA-Obit 94; TUS

Petry, Ann Lane
See Petry, Ann

Petursson, Halligrimur 1614-1674 .... **LC 8**

Peychinovich
See Vazov, Ivan (Minchov)

Phaedrus c. 15B.C.-c. 50 ..... **CMLC 25, 171**
See also DLB 211

Phelge, Nanker
See Richards, Keith

Phelps (Ward), Elizabeth Stuart
See Phelps, Elizabeth Stuart

Phelps, Elizabeth Stuart
1844-1911 .... **TCLC 113, 296**
See also CA 242; DLB 74; FW

Pheradausi
See Ferdowsi, Abu'l Qasem

Philip, M(arlene) Nourbese 1947 ... **CLC 307,
360**
See also BW 3; CA 163; CWP; DLB 157, 334

Philippe de Remi
c. 1247-1296 .... **CMLC 102**

Philips, Katherine
1632-1664 .... **LC 30, 145; PC 40**
See also DLB 131; RGEL 2

Philipson, Ilene J. 1950- .... **CLC 65**
See also CA 219

Philipson, Morris H. 1926-2011 ..... **CLC 53**
See also CA 1-4R; CANR 4

Phillips, Caryl 1958- ... **BLCS; CLC 96, 224**
See also BRWS 5; BW 2; CA 141; CANR
63, 104, 140, 195; CBD; CD 5, 6; CN 5, 6,
7; DA3; DAM MULT; DLB 157; EWL 3;
MTCW 2; MTFW 2005; WLIT 4; WWE 1

Phillips, David Graham 1867-1911 **TCLC 44**
See also CA 108; 176; DLB 9, 12, 303;
RGAL 4

Phillips, Jack
See Sandburg, Carl

Phillips, Jayne Anne 1952- ...... **CLC 15, 33,
139, 296; SSC 16**
See also AAYA 57; BPFB 3; CA 101;
CANR 24, 50, 96, 200; CN 4, 5, 6, 7;
CSW; DLBY 1980; INT CANR-24;
MTCW 1, 2; MTFW 2005; RGAL 4;
RGSF 2; SSFS 4

Phillips, Richard
See Dick, Philip K.

Phillips, Robert (Schaeffer) 1938- ... **CLC 28**
See also CA 17-20R; CAAS 13; CANR 8;
DLB 105

Phillips, Ward
See Lovecraft, H. P.

Philo c. 20B.C.-c. 50 .... **CMLC 100**
See also DLB 176

Philostratus, Flavius
c. 179-c. 244 .... **CMLC 62, 171**

Phiradausi
See Ferdowsi, Abu'l Qasem

Piccolo, Lucio 1901-1969 .... **CLC 13**
See also CA 97-100; DLB 114; EWL 3

Pickthall, Marjorie L(owry) C(hristie)
1883-1922 .... **TCLC 21**
See also CA 107; DLB 92

Pico della Mirandola, Giovanni
1463-1494 .... **LC 15**
See also LMFS 1

Piercy, Marge 1936- .... **CLC 3, 6, 14, 18,
27, 62, 128, 347; PC 29**
See also BPFB 3; CA 21-24R, 187; CAAE
187; CAAS 1; CANR 13, 43, 66, 111; CN 3,
4, 5, 6, 7; CP 1, 2, 3, 4, 5, 6, 7; CWP; DLB
120, 227; EXPP; FW; MAL 5; MTCW 1, 2;
MTFW 2005; PFS 9, 22, 32, 40; SFW 4

Pinero, Miguel (Antonio Gomez)
1946-1988 .... **CLC 4, 55**
See also CA 61-64; 125; CAD; CANR 29,
90; DLB 266; HW 1; LLW

Piers, Robert
See Anthony, Piers

Pieyre de Mandiargues, Andre
1909-1991 .... **CLC 41**
See also CA 103; 136; CANR 22, 82; DLB
83; EWL 3; GFL 1789 to the Present

Pilkington, Laetitia 1709?-1750 .... **LC 211**

Pil'niak, Boris
See Vogau, Boris Andreyevich

Pil'niak, Boris Andreevich
See Vogau, Boris Andreyevich

Pilnyak, Boris 1894-1938
See Vogau, Boris Andreyevich

Pinchback, Eugene
See Toomer, Jean

Pincherle, Alberto 1907-1990 .... **CLC 2, 7,
11, 27, 46; SSC 26**
See also CA 25-28R; 132; CANR 33, 63,
142; DAM NOV; DLB 127; EW 12; EWL
3; MTCW 2; MTFW 2005; RGSF 2;
RGWL 2, 3; WLIT 7

Pinckney, Darryl 1953- .... **CLC 76**
See also BW 2, 3; CA 143; CANR 79

Pindar 518(?)B.C.-438(?)B.C. ...... **CMLC 12,
130; PC 19**
See also AW 1; CDWLB 1; DLB 176;
RGWL 2

Pineda, Cecile 1942- .... **CLC 39**
See also CA 118; DLB 209

Pinero, Arthur Wing 1855-1934 ... **TCLC 32**
See also CA 110; 153; DAM DRAM; DLB
10, 344; RGEL 2

Pinget, Robert 1919-1997 ..... **CLC 7, 13, 37**
See also CA 85-88; 160; CWW 2; DLB 83;
EWL 3; GFL 1789 to the Present

Pink Floyd
See Barrett, Syd; Gilmour, David; Mason,
Nick; Waters, Roger; Wright, Rick

Pinkney, Edward 1802-1828 .... **NCLC 31**
See also DLB 248

Pinkwater, D. Manus
See Pinkwater, Daniel

Pinkwater, Daniel 1941- .... **CLC 35**
See also AAYA 1, 46; BYA 9; CA 29-32R;
CANR 12, 38, 89, 143; CLR 4, 175; CSW;
FANT; JRDA; MAICYA 1, 2; SAAS 3;
SATA 8, 46, 76, 114, 158, 210, 243; SFW
4; YAW

Pinkwater, Daniel M.
See Pinkwater, Daniel

Pinkwater, Daniel Manus
See Pinkwater, Daniel

Pinkwater, Manus
See Pinkwater, Daniel

Pinsky, Robert 1940- ...... **CLC 9, 19, 38, 94,
121, 216; PC 27**
See also AMWS 6; CA 29-32R; CAAS 4;
CANR 58, 97, 138, 177; CP 3, 4, 5, 6, 7;
DA3; DAM POET; DLBY 1982, 1998;
MAL 5; MTCW 2; MTFW 2005; PFS
18, 44; RGAL 4; TCLE 1:2

Pinta, Harold
See Pinter, Harold

Pinter, Harold 1930-2008 .... **CLC 1, 3, 6,
9, 11, 15, 27, 58, 73, 199; DC 15; WLC 4**
See also BRWR 1; BRWS 1; CA 5-8R; 280;
CANR 33, 65, 112, 145; CBD; CD 5, 6;
CDBLB 1960 to Present; CP 1; DA; DA3;
DAB; DAC; DAM DRAM, MST; DFS 3,
5, 7, 14, 25; DLB 13, 310, 331; EWL 3;
IDFW 3, 4; LMFS 2; MTCW 1, 2; MTFW
2005; RGEL 2; RGHL; TEA

Piozzi, Hester Lynch (Thrale)
1741-1821 .... **NCLC 57, 294**
See also DLB 104, 142

Pirandello, Luigi 1867-1936 .... **DC 5;
SSC 22, 148; TCLC 4, 29, 172; WLC 4**
See also CA 104; 153; CANR 103; DA;
DA3; DAB; DAC; DAM DRAM, MST;
DFS 4, 9; DLB 264, 331; EW 8; EWL 3;
MTCW 2; MTFW 2005; RGSF 2; RGWL
2, 3; SSFS 30, 33; WLIT 7

Pirdousi
See Ferdowsi, Abu'l Qasem

Pirdousi, Abu-l-Qasim
See Ferdowsi, Abu'l Qasem

Pirsig, Robert M(aynard)
1928- .... **CLC 4, 6, 73**
See also CA 53-56; CANR 42, 74; CPW 1;
DA3; DAM POP; MTCW 1, 2; MTFW
2005; NFS 31; SATA 39

Pisan, Christine de
See Christine de Pizan

Pisarev, Dmitrii Ivanovich
See Pisarev, Dmitry Ivanovich

Pisarev, Dmitry Ivanovich
1840-1868 .... **NCLC 25**
See also DLB 277

Pix, Mary (Griffith) 1666-1709 .... **LC 8,
149, 226**
See also DLB 80

Pixerecourt, (Rene Charles) Guilbert de
1773-1844 .... **NCLC 39**
See also DLB 192; GFL 1789 to the Present

Pizarnik, Alejandra
1936-1972 .... **TCLC 318**
See also DLB 283

2, 5, 33, 169, 227; DLBD 8; EWL 3;
LMFS 2; MAL 5; MSW; MTCW 1, 2;
MTFW 2005; PFS 6; RGAL 4; TCWW 2

Reed, Ishmael Scott
See Reed, Ishmael

Reed, John (Silas) 1887-1920 .... **TCLC 9**
See also CA 106; 195; MAL 5; TUS

Reed, Lou 1942- .... **CLC 21**
See also CA 117

Reese, Lizette Woodworth
1856-1935 .... **PC 29; TCLC 181**
See also CA 180; DLB 54

Reeve, Clara 1729-1807 .... **NCLC 19**
See also DLB 39; RGEL 2

Reich, Wilhelm 1897-1957 .... **TCLC 57**
See also CA 199

Reid, Christopher 1949- .... **CLC 33**
See also CA 140; CANR 89, 241; CP 4, 5, 6,
7; DLB 40; EWL 3

Reid, Christopher John
See Reid, Christopher

Reid, Desmond
See Moorcock, Michael

Reid, Thomas 1710-1796 .... **LC 201**
See also DLB 31, 252

Reid Banks, Lynne 1929- .... **CLC 23**
See also AAYA 6; BYA 7; CA 1-4R; CANR
6, 22, 38, 87; CLR 24, 86; CN 4, 5, 6;
JRDA; MAICYA 1, 2; SATA 22, 75, 111,
165; YAW

Reilly, William K.
See Creasey, John

Reiner, Max
See Caldwell, (Janet Miriam) Taylor (Holland)

Reis, Ricardo
See Pessoa, Fernando

Reizenstein, Elmer Leopold
See Rice, Elmer (Leopold)

Remark, Erich Paul
See Remarque, Erich Maria

Remarque, Erich Maria
1898-1970 .... **CLC 21**
See also AAYA 27; BPFB 3; CA 77-80; 29-
32R; CDWLB 2; CLR 159; DA; DA3; DAB;
DAC; DAM MST, NOV; DLB 56; EWL 3;
EXPN; LAIT 3; MTCW 1, 2; MTFW 2005;
NFS 4, 36; RGHL; RGWL 2, 3

Remington, Frederic S(ackrider)
1861-1909 .... **TCLC 89**
See also CA 108; 169; DLB 12, 186, 188;
SATA 41; TCWW 2

Remizov, A.
See Remizov, Aleksei (Mikhailovich)

Remizov, A. M.
See Remizov, Aleksei (Mikhailovich)

Remizov, Aleksei (Mikhailovich)
1877-1957 .... **TCLC 27**
See also CA 125; 133; DLB 295; EWL 3

Remizov, Alexey Mikhaylovich
See Remizov, Aleksei (Mikhailovich)

Renan, Joseph Ernest
1823-1892 .... **NCLC 26, 145**
See also GFL 1789 to the Present

Renard, Jules(-Pierre) 1864-1910 ... **TCLC 17**
See also CA 117; 202; GFL 1789 to the
Present

Renart, Jean fl. 13th cent. .... **CMLC 83**

Renault, Mary 1905-1983 ..... **CLC 3, 11, 17**
See also BPFB 3; BYA 2; CA 81-84; 111;
CANR 74; CN 1, 2, 3; DA3; DLBY 1983;
EWL 3; GLL 1; LAIT 1; MTCW 2;
MTFW 2005; RGEL 2; RHW; SATA 23;
SATA-Obit 36; TEA

Rendell, Ruth
See Rendell, Ruth

Rendell, Ruth
1930- .... **CLC 28, 48, 50, 295**

See also BEST 90:4; BPFB 3; BRWS 9; CA
109; CANR 32, 52, 74, 127, 162, 190, 227;
CN 5, 6, 7; CPW; DAM POP; DLB 87,
276; INT CANR-32; MSW; MTCW 1, 2;
MTFW 2005

Rendell, Ruth Barbara
See Rendell, Ruth

Renoir, Jean 1894-1979 .... **CLC 20**
See also CA 129; 85-88

Rensie, Willis
See Eisner, Will

Resnais, Alain 1922- .... **CLC 16**

Restif de la Bretonne, Nicolas-Anne-Edme
1734-1806 .... **NCLC 257**
See also DLB 314; GFL Beginnings to 1789

Reuental, Niedhart von
See Neidhart von Ruental

Rev. D Blair
See Fenwick, Eliza

Revard, Carter 1931- .... **NNAL**
See also CA 144; CANR 81, 153; PFS 5

Reverdy, Pierre 1889-1960 .... **CLC 53**
See also CA 97-100; 89-92; DLB 258; EWL
3; GFL 1789 to the Present

Reverend Mandju
See Su, Chien

Rexroth, Kenneth 1905-1982 .... **CLC 1,**
2, 6, 11, 22, 49, 112; PC 20, 95
See also BG 1:3; CA 5-8R; 107; CANR 14,
34, 63; CDALB 1941-1968; CP 1, 2, 3;
DAM POET; DLB 16, 48, 165, 212; DLBY
1982; EWL 3; INT CANR-14; MAL 5;
MTCW 1, 2; MTFW 2005; RGAL 4

Reyes, Alfonso 1889-1959 .... **HLCS 2;**
TCLC 33
See also CA 131; EWL 3; HW 1; LAW

Reyes y Basoalto, Ricardo Eliecer Neftali
See Neruda, Pablo

Reymont, Wladyslaw (Stanislaw)
1868(?)-1925 .... **TCLC 5**
See also CA 104; DLB 332; EWL 3

Reynolds, John Hamilton
1794-1852 .... **NCLC 146**
See also DLB 96

Reynolds, Jonathan 1942- .... **CLC 6, 38**
See also CA 65-68; CANR 28, 176

Reynolds, Joshua 1723-1792 .... **LC 15**
See also DLB 104

Reynolds, Michael S(hane)
1937-2000 .... **CLC 44**
See also CA 65-68; 189; CANR 9, 89, 97

Reza, Yasmina 1959- .... **CLC 299; DC 34**
See also AAYA 69; CA 171; CANR 145;
DFS 19; DLB 321

Reznikoff, Charles 1894-1976 .... **CLC 9;**
PC 124
See also AMWS 14; CA 33-36; 61-64; CAP
2; CP 1, 2; DLB 28, 45; RGHL; WP

Rezzori, Gregor von
See Rezzori d'Arezzo, Gregor von

Rezzori d'Arezzo, Gregor von
1914-1998 .... **CLC 25**
See also CA 122; 136; 167

Rhine, Richard
See Silverstein, Alvin; Silverstein, Virginia B.

Rhodes, Eugene Manlove
1869-1934 .... **TCLC 53**
See also CA 198; DLB 256; TCWW 1, 2

R'hoone, Lord
See Balzac, Honore de

Rhys, Jean 1890-1979 .... **CLC 2, 4, 6, 14,**
19, 51, 124; SSC 21, 76
See also BRWS 2; CA 25-28R; 85-88;
CANR 35, 62; CDBLB 1945-1960;
CDWLB 3; CN 1, 2; DA3; DAM NOV;
DLB 36, 117, 162; DNFS 2; EWL 3; LATS
1:1; MTCW 1, 2; MTFW 2005; NFS 19;
RGEL 2; RGSF 2; RHW; TEA; WWE 1

Ribeiro, Darcy 1922-1997 .... **CLC 34**
See also CA 33-36R; 156; EWL 3

Ribeiro, Joao Ubaldo (Osorio Pimentel)
1941- .... **CLC 10, 67**
See also CA 81-84; CWW 2; EWL 3

Ribeyro, Julio Ramón 1929-1994 ... **SSC 204**
See also CA 180, 181; DLB 145; EWL 3

Ribman, Ronald (Burt) 1932- .... **CLC 7**
See also CA 21-24R; CAD; CANR 46, 80;
CD 5, 6

Ricci, Nino 1959- .... **CLC 70**
See also CA 137; CANR 130; CCA 1

Ricci, Nino Pio
See Ricci, Nino

Rice, Anne 1941- .... **CLC 41, 128, 349**
See also AAYA 9, 53; AMWS 7; BEST 89:2;
BPFB 3; CA 65-68; CANR 12, 36, 53, 74,
100, 133, 190; CN 6, 7; CPW; CSW; DA3;
DAM POP; DLB 292; GL 3; GLL 2; HGG;
MTCW 2; MTFW 2005; SUFW 2; YAW

Rice, Elmer (Leopold) 1892-1967 .... **CLC 7,**
49; DC 44; TCLC 221
See also CA 21-22; 25-28R; CAP 2; DAM
DRAM; DFS 12; DLB 4, 7; EWL 3; IDTP;
MAL 5; MTCW 1, 2; RGAL 4

Rice, Tim 1944- .... **CLC 21**
See also CA 103; CANR 46; DFS 7

Rice, Timothy Miles Bindon
See Rice, Tim

Rich, Adrienne 1929-2012 .... **CLC 3, 6, 7,**
11, 18, 36, 73, 76, 125, 328, 354; PC 5, 129
See also AAYA 69; AMWR 2; AMWS 1;
CA 9-12R; CANR 20, 53, 74, 128, 199,
233; CDALBS; CP 1, 2, 3, 4, 5, 6, 7; CSW;
CWP; DA3; DAM POET; DLB 5, 67;
EWL 3; EXPP; FL 1:6; FW; MAL 5;
MBL; MTCW 1, 2; MTFW 2005; PAB;
PFS 15, 29, 39; RGAL 4; RGHL; WP

Rich, Adrienne Cecile
See Rich, Adrienne

Rich, Barbara
See Graves, Robert

Rich, Robert
See Trumbo, Dalton

Richard, Keith
See Richards, Keith

Richards, David Adams 1950- .... **CLC 59**
See also CA 93-96; CANR 60, 110, 156;
CN 7; DAC; DLB 53; TCLE 1:2

Richards, I(vor) A(rmstrong)
1893-1979 .... **CLC 14, 24**
See also BRWS 2; CA 41-44R; 89-92;
CANR 34, 74; CP 1, 2; DLB 27; EWL
3; MTCW 1; RGEL 2

Richards, Keith 1943- .... **CLC 17**
See also CA 107; CANR 77

Richards, Scott
See Card, Orson Scott

Richardson, Anne
See Roiphe, Anne

Richardson, Dorothy Miller
1873-1957 .... **TCLC 3, 203**
See also BRWS 13; CA 104; 192; DLB 36;
EWL 3; FW; RGEL 2

Richardson, Ethel Florence Lindesay
1870-1946 .... **TCLC 4**
See also CA 105; 190; DLB 197, 230; EWL
3; RGEL 2; RGSF 2; RHW

Richardson, Henrietta
See Richardson, Ethel Florence Lindesay

Richardson, Henry Handel
See Richardson, Ethel Florence Lindesay

Richardson, John 1796-1852 .... **NCLC 55**
See also CCA 1; DAC; DLB 99

Richardson, Samuel 1689-1761 ..... **LC 1, 44,**
138, 204; WLC 5
See also BRW 3; CDBLB 1660-1789; DA;
DAB; DAC; DAM MST, NOV; DLB 154;
RGEL 2; TEA; WLIT 3

Richardson, Willis 1889-1977 .... **HR 1:3**
　　See also BW 1; CA 124; DLB 51; SATA 60

**Richardson Robertson, Ethel Florence
　　Lindesay**
　　See Richardson, Ethel Florence Lindesay

Richler, Mordecai 1931-2001 .... **CLC 3, 5,
　　9, 13, 18, 46, 70, 185, 271**
　　See also AITN 1; CA 65-68; 201; CANR 31,
　　62, 111; CCA 1; CLR 17; CN 1, 2, 3, 4, 5,
　　7; CWRI 5; DAC; DAM MST, NOV; DLB
　　53; EWL 3; MAICYA 1, 2; MTCW 1, 2;
　　MTFW 2005; RGEL 2; RGHL; SATA 44,
　　98; SATA-Brief 27; TWA

Richter, Conrad (Michael)
　　1890-1968 .... **CLC 30**
　　See also AAYA 21; AMWS 18; BYA 2; CA
　　5-8R; 25-28R; CANR 23; DLB 9, 212;
　　LAIT 1; MAL 5; MTCW 1, 2; MTFW
　　2005; NFS 43; RGAL 4; SATA 3; TCWW
　　1, 2; TUS; YAW

Ricostranza, Tom
　　See Ellis, Trey

Riddell, Charlotte 1832-1906 .... **TCLC 40**
　　See also CA 165; DLB 156; HGG; SUFW

Riddell, Mrs. J. H.
　　See Riddell, Charlotte

Ridge, John Rollin 1827-1867 .... **NCLC 82;
　　NNAL**
　　See also CA 144; DAM MULT; DLB 175

Ridgeway, Jason
　　See Marlowe, Stephen

Ridgway, Keith 1965- .... **CLC 119**
　　See also CA 172; CANR 144

Riding, Laura
　　See Jackson, Laura

Riefenstahl, Berta Helene Amalia
　　See Riefenstahl, Leni

Riefenstahl, Leni
　　1902-2003 .... **CLC 16, 190**
　　See also CA 108; 220

Riefenstahl, Leni
　　See Riefenstahl, Berta Helene Amalia

Riera, Carme 1948- .... **CLC 368; SSC 177**
　　See also CA 254; DLB 322, EWL 3

Riffaterre, Michael 1924-2006
　　See also CA 183; 250; DLB 67

Riffe, Ernest
　　See Bergman, Ingmar

Riffe, Ernest Ingmar
　　See Bergman, Ingmar

Riggs, (Rolla) Lynn 1899-1954 .... **NNAL;
　　TCLC 56**
　　See also CA 144; DAM MULT; DLB 175

Riis, Jacob A(ugust) 1849-1914 .... **TCLC 80**
　　See also CA 113; 168; DLB 23

Rikki
　　See Ducornet, Erica

Riley, James Whitcomb 1849-1916 ... **PC 48;
　　TCLC 51**
　　See also CA 118; 137; DAM POET; MAI-
　　CYA 1, 2; RGAL 4; SATA 17

Riley, Tex
　　See Creasey, John

Rilke, Rainer Maria 1875-1926 .. **PC 2, 140;
　　TCLC 1, 6, 19, 195, 310**
　　See also CA 104; 132; CANR 62, 99;
　　CDWLB 2; DA3; DAM POET; DLB 81;
　　EW 9; EWL 3; MTCW 1, 2; MTFW 2005;
　　PFS 19, 27; RGWL 2, 3; TWA; WP

Rimbaud, Arthur 1854-1891 ... **NCLC 4, 35,
　　82, 227; PC 3, 57; WLC 5**
　　See also DA; DA3; DAB; DAC; DAM MST,
　　POET; DLB 217; EW 7; GFL 1789 to the
　　Present; LMFS 2; PFS 28; RGWL 2, 3;
　　TWA; WP

Rimbaud, Jean Nicholas Arthur
　　See Rimbaud, Arthur

Rinehart, Mary Roberts 1876-1958 .. **TCLC 52**
　　See also BPFB 3; CA 108; 166; RGAL 4;
　　RHW

Ringmaster, The
　　See Mencken, H. L.

Ringwood, Gwen(dolyn Margaret) Pharis
　　1910-1984 .... **CLC 48**
　　See also CA 148; 112; DLB 88

Rio, Michel 1945(?)- .... **CLC 43**
　　See also CA 201

Ritchie, Anne Thackeray
　　1837-1919 .... **TCLC 297**
　　See also CA 180; DLB 18

Ritsos, Giannes
　　See Ritsos, Yannis

Ritsos, Yannis 1909-1990 ...... **CLC 6, 13, 31**
　　See also CA 77-80; 133; CANR 39, 61; EW
　　12; EWL 3; MTCW 1; RGWL 2, 3

Ritter, Erika 1948- .... **CLC 52**
　　See also CA 318; CD 5, 6; CWD; DLB 362

Rivera, Jose Eustasio 1889-1928 ... **TCLC 35**
　　See also CA 162; EWL 3; HW 1, 2; LAW

Rivera, Tomas 1935-1984 .... **HLCS 2;
　　SSC 160**
　　See also CA 49-52; CANR 32; DLB 82; HW
　　1; LLW; RGAL 4; SSFS 15; TCWW 2;
　　WLIT 1

Rivers, Conrad Kent 1933-1968 .... **CLC 1**
　　See also BW 1; CA 85-88; DLB 41

Rivers, Elfrida
　　See Bradley, Marion Zimmer

Riverside, John
　　See Heinlein, Robert A.

Rizal, Jose 1861-1896 .... **NCLC 27**
　　See also DLB 348

Rolaag, Ole Edvart
　　See Rolvaag, O.E.

Rolvaag, O.E.
　　See Rolvaag, O.E.

Rolvaag, O.E. 1876-1931 ...... **TCLC 17, 207**
　　See also AAYA 75; CA 117; 171; DLB 9,
　　212; MAL 5; NFS 5; RGAL 4; TCWW 1, 2

Roa Bastos, Augusto 1917-2005 .... **CLC 45,
　　316, 355; HLC 2; SSC 174**
　　See also CA 131; 238; CWW 2; DAM
　　MULT; DLB 113; EWL 3; HW 1; LAW;
　　RGSF 2; WLIT 1

Roa Bastos, Augusto Jose Antonio
　　See Roa Bastos, Augusto

Robbe-Grillet, Alain 1922-2008 .... **CLC 1,
　　2, 4, 6, 8, 10, 14, 43, 128, 287**
　　See also BPFB 3; CA 9-12R; 269; CANR
　　33, 65, 115; CWW 2; DLB 83; EW 13;
　　EWL 3; GFL 1789 to the Present; IDFW 3,
　　4; MTCW 1, 2; MTFW 2005; RGWL 2, 3;
　　SSFS 15

Robbins, Harold 1916-1997 .... **CLC 5**
　　See also BPFB 3; CA 73-76; 162; CANR
　　26, 54, 112, 156; DA3; DAM NOV;
　　MTCW 1, 2

Robbins, Thomas Eugene
　　See Robbins, Tom

Robbins, Tom 1936- ...... **CLC 9, 32, 64, 362**
　　See also AAYA 32; AMWS 10; BEST 90:3;
　　BPFB 3; CA 81-84; CANR 29, 59, 95,
　　139; CN 3, 4, 5, 6, 7; CPW; CSW; DA3;
　　DAM NOV, POP; DLBY 1980; MTCW 1,
　　2; MTFW 2005

Robbins, Trina 1938- .... **CLC 21**
　　See also AAYA 61; CA 128; CANR 152

Robert de Boron fl. 12th cent. ..... **CMLC 94**

Roberts, Charles G(eorge) D(ouglas)
　　1860-1943 .... **SSC 91; TCLC 8**
　　See also CA 105; 188; CLR 33; CWRI 5;
　　DLB 92; RGEL 2; RGSF 2; SATA 88;
　　SATA-Brief 29

Roberts, Elizabeth Madox
　　1886-1941 .... **TCLC 68**

　　See also CA 111; 166; CLR 100; CWRI 5;
　　DLB 9, 54, 102; RGAL 4; RHW; SATA
　　33; SATA-Brief 27; TCWW 2; WCH

Roberts, Kate 1891-1985 .... **CLC 15**
　　See also CA 107; 116; DLB 319

Roberts, Keith (John Kingston)
　　1935-2000 .... **CLC 14**
　　See also BRWS 10; CA 25-28R; CANR 46;
　　DLB 261; SFW 4

Roberts, Kenneth (Lewis)
　　1885-1957 .... **TCLC 23**
　　See also CA 109; 199; DLB 9; MAL 5;
　　RGAL 4; RHW

Roberts, Michele 1949- .... **CLC 48, 178**
　　See also BRWS 15; CA 115; CANR 58, 120,
　　164, 200; CN 6, 7; DLB 231; FW

Roberts, Michele Brigitte
　　See Roberts, Michele

Robertson, Ellis
　　See Ellison, Harlan; Silverberg, Robert

Robertson, Thomas William
　　1829-1871 .... **NCLC 35**
　　See also DAM DRAM; DLB 344; RGEL 2

Robertson, Tom
　　See Robertson, Thomas William

Robeson, Kenneth
　　See Dent, Lester

Robinson, Eden 1968- .... **CLC 301**
　　See also CA 171

Robinson, Edwin Arlington
　　1869-1935 .... **PC 1, 35; TCLC 5, 101**
　　See also AAYA 72; AMW; CA 104; 133;
　　CDALB 1865-1917; DA; DAC; DAM
　　MST, POET; DLB 54; EWL 3; EXPP; PAB;
　　MAL 5; MTCW 1, 2; MTFW 2005; PAB;
　　PFS 4, 35; RGAL 4; WP

Robinson, Henry Crabb
　　1775-1867 .... **NCLC 15, 239**
　　See also DLB 107

Robinson, Jill 1936- .... **CLC 10**
　　See also CA 102; CANR 120; INT CA-102

Robinson, Kim Stanley 1952- .... **CLC 34, 248**
　　See also AAYA 26; CA 126; CANR 113,
　　139, 173; CN 6, 7; MTFW 2005; SATA
　　109; SCFW 2; SFW 4

Robinson, Lloyd
　　See Silverberg, Robert

Robinson, Marilynne
　　1943- .... **CLC 25, 180, 276**
　　See also AAYA 69; AMWS 21; CA 116;
　　CANR 80, 140, 192, 240; CN 4, 5, 6, 7;
　　DLB 206, 350; MTFW 2005; NFS 24, 39

Robinson, Mary 1758-1800 .... **NCLC 142**
　　See also BRWS 13; DLB 158; FW

Robinson, Smokey 1940- .... **CLC 21**
　　See also CA 116

Robinson, William, Jr.
　　See Robinson, Smokey

Robison, Christopher
　　See Burroughs, Augusten

Robison, Mary 1949- .... **CLC 42, 98**
　　See also CA 113; 116; CANR 87, 206; CN
　　4, 5, 6, 7; DLB 130; INT CA-116; RGSF
　　2; SSFS 33

Roche, Regina Maria 1764-1845 ... **NCLC 308**

Rochester
　　See Wilmot, John

Rod, Edouard 1857-1910 .... **TCLC 52**

Rodo, Jose Enrique 1871(?)-1917 ... **HLCS 2**
　　See also CA 178; EWL 3; HW 2; LAW

Roddenberry, Eugene Wesley
　　See Roddenberry, Gene

Roddenberry, Gene 1921-1991 .... **CLC 17**
　　See also AAYA 5; CA 110; 135; CANR 37;
　　SATA 45; SATA-Obit 69

Rodgers, Mary 1931- .... **CLC 12**
　　See also BYA 5; CA 49-52; CANR 8, 55, 90;
　　CLR 20; CWRI 5; DFS 28; INT CANR-8;
　　JRDA; MAICYA 1, 2; SATA 8, 130

Rodgers, W(illiam) R(obert)
1909-1969 .... **CLC 7**
See also CA 85-88; DLB 20; RGEL 2

Rodman, Eric
See Silverberg, Robert

Rodman, Howard 1920(?)-1985 ...... **CLC 65**
See also CA 118

Rodman, Maia
See Wojciechowska, Maia (Teresa)

Rodolph, Utto
See Ouologuem, Yambo

Rodoreda, Mercè 1908-1983 .... **SSC 221**
See also CA 243; DLB 322; EWL 3; RGSF 2

Rodriguez, Claudio 1934-1999 .... **CLC 10**
See also CA 188; DLB 134

Rodriguez, Richard 1944- .... **CLC 155, 321;**
HLC 2
See also AMWS 14; CA 110; CANR 66,
116; DAM MULT; DLB 82, 256; HW 1, 2;
LAIT 5; LLW; MTFW 2005; NCFS 3;
WLIT 1

Roethke, Theodore 1908-1963 ..... **CLC 1, 3,**
8, 11, 19, 46, 101; PC 15, 137
See also AMW; CA 81-84; CABS 2; CDALB
1941-1968; DA3; DAM POET; DLB 5,
206; EWL 3; EXPP; MAL 5; MTCW 1,
2; PAB; PFS 3, 34, 40; RGAL 4; WP

Roethke, Theodore Huebner
See Roethke, Theodore

Rogers, Carl R(ansom)
1902-1987 .... **TCLC 125**
See also CA 1-4R; 121; CANR 1, 18;
MTCW 1

Rogers, Samuel 1763-1855 .... **NCLC 69**
See also DLB 93; RGEL 2

Rogers, Thomas 1927-2007 .... **CLC 57**
See also CA 89-92; 259; CANR 163; INT
CA-89-92

Rogers, Thomas Hunton
See Rogers, Thomas

Rogers, Will(iam Penn Adair)
1879-1935 .... **NNAL; TCLC 8, 71**
See also CA 105; 144; DA3; DAM MULT;
DLB 11; MTCW 2

Rogin, Gilbert 1929- .... **CLC 18**
See also CA 65-68; CANR 15

Rohan, Koda
See Koda Shigeyuki

Rohlfs, Anna Katharine Green
See Green, Anna Katharine

Rohmer, Eric 1920-2010 .... **CLC 16**
See also CA 110

Rohmer, Sax
See Ward, Arthur Henry Sarsfield

Roiphe, Anne 1935- .... **CLC 3, 9**
See also CA 89-92; CANR 45, 73, 138, 170,
230; DLBY 1980; INT CA-89-92

Roiphe, Anne Richardson
See Roiphe, Anne

Rojas, Fernando de 1475-1541 ...... **HLCS 1,**
2; LC 23, 169
See also DLB 286; RGWL 2, 3

Rojas, Gonzalo 1917-2011 .... **HLCS 2**
See also CA 178; HW 2; LAWS 1

Rojas Zorrilla, Francisco de
1607-1648 .... **LC 204**

Roland (de la Platiere), Marie-Jeanne
1754-1793 .... **LC 98**
See also DLB 314

Rolfe, Frederick (William Serafino Austin
Lewis Mary) 1860-1913 .... **TCLC 12**
See also CA 107; 210; DLB 34, 156; GLL 1;
RGEL 2

Rolland, Romain 1866-1944 .... **TCLC 23**
See also CA 118; 197; DLB 65, 284,
332; EWL 3; GFL 1789 to the Present;
RGWL 2, 3

Rolle, Richard
c. 1300-c. 1349 .... **CMLC 21, 165**
See also DLB 146; LMFS 1; RGEL 2

Rolvaag, O.E.
See Rolvaag, O.E.

Romain Arnaud, Saint
See Aragon, Louis

Romains, Jules 1885-1972 .... **CLC 7**
See also CA 85-88; CANR 34; DLB 65, 321;
EWL 3; GFL 1789 to the Present; MTCW 1

Romero, Jose Ruben 1890-1952 ... **TCLC 14**
See also CA 114; 131; EWL 3; HW 1; LAW

Ronsard, Pierre de 1524-1585 ..... **LC 6, 54;**
PC 11, 105
See also DLB 327; EW 2; GFL Beginnings
to 1789; RGWL 2, 3; TWA

Rooke, Leon 1934- .... **CLC 25, 34**
See also CA 25-28R; CANR 23, 53; CCA 1;
CPW; DAM POP

Roosevelt, Franklin Delano
1882-1945 .... **TCLC 93**
See also CA 116; 173; LAIT 3

Roosevelt, Theodore 1858-1919 .... **TCLC 69**
See also CA 115; 170; DLB 47, 186, 275

Roper, Margaret c. 1505-1544 .... **LC 147**

Roper, William 1498-1578 .... **LC 10**

Roquelaure, A. N.
See Rice, Anne

Rios, Alberto 1952- .... **PC 57**
See also AAYA 66; AMWS 4; CA 113;
CANR 34, 79, 137; CP 6, 7; DLB 122;
HW 2; MTFW 2005; PFS 11

Rios, Alberto Alvaro
See Rios, Alberto

Rosa, Joao Guimaraes
See Guimaraes Rosa, Joao

Rose, Wendy 1948- .... **CLC 85; NNAL;**
PC 13
See also CA 53-56; CANR 5, 51; CWP;
DAM MULT; DLB 175; PFS 13; RGAL 4;
SATA 12

Rosen, R.D. 1949- .... **CLC 39**
See also CA 77-80; CANR 62, 120, 175;
CMW 4; INT CANR-30

Rosen, Richard
See Rosen, R.D.

Rosen, Richard Dean
See Rosen, R.D.

Rosenberg, Isaac 1890-1918 .... **PC 146;**
TCLC 12; 314
See also BRW 6; CA 107; 188; DLB 20,
216; EWL 3; PAB; RGEL 2

Rosenblatt, Joe
See Rosenblatt, Joseph

Rosenblatt, Joseph 1933- .... **CLC 15**
See also CA 89-92; CP 3, 4, 5, 6, 7; INT
CA-89-92

Rosenfeld, Samuel
See Tzara, Tristan

Rosenstock, Sami
See Tzara, Tristan

Rosenstock, Samuel
See Tzara, Tristan

Rosenthal, M(acha) L(ouis)
1917-1996 .... **CLC 28**
See also CA 1-4R; 152; CAAS 6; CANR 4,
51; CP 1, 2, 3, 4, 5, 6; DLB 5; SATA 59

Ross, Barnaby
See Dannay, Frederic; Lee, Manfred B.

Ross, Bernard L.
See Follett, Ken

Ross, J. H.
See Lawrence, T. E.

Ross, John Hume
See Lawrence, T. E.

Ross, Martin 1862-1915
See Martin, Violet Florence
See also DLB 135; GLL 2; RGEL 2; RGSF 2

Ross, (James) Sinclair 1908-1996 ... **CLC 13;**
SSC 24
See also CA 73-76; CANR 81; CN 1, 2, 3, 4,
5, 6; DAC; DAM MST; DLB 88; RGEL 2;
RGSF 2; TCWW 1, 2

Rossetti, Christina 1830-1894 .... **NCLC 2,**
50, 66, 186; PC 7, 119; WLC 5
See also AAYA 51; BRW 5; BRWR 3; BYA
4; CLR 115; DA; DA3; DAB; DAC; DAM
MST, POET; DLB 35, 163, 240; EXPP; FL
1:3; LATS 1:1; MAICYA 1, 2; PFS 10, 14,
27, 34; RGEL 2; SATA 20; TEA; WCH

Rossetti, Christina Georgina
See Rossetti, Christina

Rossetti, Dante Gabriel
1828-1882 .... **NCLC 4, 77; PC 44;**
WLC 5
See also AAYA 51; BRW 5; CDBLB 1832-
1890; DA; DAB; DAC; DAM MST, POET;
DLB 35; EXPP; RGEL 2; TEA

Rossi, Cristina Peri
See Peri Rossi, Cristina

Rossi, Jean-Baptiste 1931-2003 .... **CLC 90**
See also CA 201; 215; CMW 4; NFS 18

Rossner, Judith 1935-2005 .... **CLC 6, 9, 29**
See also AITN 2; BEST 90:3; BPFB 3; CA
17-20R; 242; CANR 18, 51, 73; CN 4, 5,
6, 7; DLB 6; INT CANR-18; MAL 5;
MTCW 1, 2; MTFW 2005

Rossner, Judith Perelman
See Rossner, Judith

Rostand, Edmond 1868-1918 .... **DC 10;**
TCLC 6, 37
See also CA 104; 126; DA; DA3; DAB;
DAC; DAM DRAM, MST; DFS 1; DLB
192; LAIT 1; MTCW 1; RGWL 2, 3; TWA

Rostand, Edmond Eugene Alexis
See Rostand, Edmond

Rostopchine, Sophie, Comtesse de Ségur
See Ségur, Sophie Rostopchine, Comtesse de

Roth, Henry 1906-1995 .... **CLC 2, 6, 11,**
104; SSC 134
See also AMWS 9; CA 11-12; 149; CANR
38, 63; CAP 1; CN 1, 2, 3, 4, 5, 6; DA3;
DLB 28; EWL 3; MAL 5; MTCW 1, 2;
MTFW 2005; RGAL 4

Roth, (Moses) Joseph
1894-1939 .... **TCLC 33, 277**
See also CA 160; DLB 85; EWL 3; RGWL 2, 3

Roth, Philip 1933- ...... **CLC 1, 2, 3, 4, 6, 9,**
15, 22, 31, 47, 66, 86, 119, 201, 336; SSC
26, 102, 176; WLC 5
See also AAYA 67; AMWR 2; AMWS 3;
BEST 90:3; BPFB 3; CA 1-4R; CANR 1,
22, 36, 55, 89, 132, 170, 241; CDALB 1968-
1988; CN 3, 4, 5, 6, 7; CPW 1; DA; DA3;
DAB; DAC; DAM MST, NOV, POP; DLB
2, 28, 173; DLBY 1982; EWL 3; MAL 5;
MTCW 1, 2; MTFW 2005; NFS 25; RGAL
4; RGHL; RGSF 2; SSFS 12, 18; TUS

Roth, Philip Milton
See Roth, Philip

Rothenberg, Jerome 1931- .... **CLC 6, 57;**
PC 129
See also CA 45-48; CANR 1, 106; CP 1, 2,
3, 4, 5, 6, 7; DLB 5, 193

Rotrou, Jean 1609-1650 .... **LC 241**
See also DLB 268; GFL

Rotter, Pat .... **CLC 65**

Roubaud, Jacques 1932- .... **CLC 358**
See also CA 249

Roumain, Jacques 1907-1944 .... **BLC 1:3;**
TCLC 19
See also BW 1; CA 117; 125; DAM MULT;
EWL 3

Roumain, Jacques Jean Baptiste
See Roumain, Jacques

Rourke, Constance Mayfield
1885-1941 .... **TCLC 12**
See also CA 107; 200; MAL 5; YABC 1

Rousseau, Jean-Baptiste 1671-1741 ..... **LC 9**

Rousseau, Jean-Jacques 1712-1778 ... **LC 14, 36, 122, 198; WLC 5**
See also DA; DA3; DAB; DAC; DAM MST; DLB 314; EW 4; GFL Beginnings to 1789; LMFS 1; RGWL 2, 3; TWA

Roussel, Raymond 1877-1933 .... **TCLC 20**
See also CA 117; 201; EWL 3; GFL 1789 to the Present

Rovit, Earl (Herbert) 1927- .... **CLC 7**
See also CA 5-8R; CANR 12

Rowe, Elizabeth Singer 1674-1737 ... **LC 44, 234**
See also DLB 39, 95

Rowe, Nicholas 1674-1718 .... **LC 8**
See also DLB 84; RGEL 2

Rowlandson, Mary 1637(?)-1678 .... **LC 66**
See also DLB 24, 200; RGAL 4

Rowley, Ames Dorrance
See Lovecraft, H. P.

Rowley, William
1585(?)-1626 .... **DC 43; LC 100, 123**
See also DFS 22; DLB 58; RGEL 2

Rowling, J.K. 1965- .... **CLC 137, 217**
See also AAYA 34, 82; BRWS 16; BYA 11, 13, 14; CA 173; CANR 128, 157; CLR 66, 80, 112, 183; LNFS 1, 2, 3; MAICYA 2; MTFW 2005; SATA 109, 174; SUFW 2

Rowling, Joanne Kathleen
See Rowling, J.K.

Rowson, Susanna Haswell
1762(?)-1824 .... **NCLC 5, 69, 182**
See also AMWS 15; DLB 37, 200; RGAL 4

Roy, Arundhati 1961- ... **CLC 109, 210, 364**
See also CA 163; CANR 90, 126, 217; CN 7; DLB 323, 326; DLBY 1997; EWL 3; LATS 1:2; MTFW 2005; NFS 22; WWE 1

Roy, Gabrielle 1909-1983 .... **CLC 10, 14; TCLC 256**
See also CA 53-56; 110; CANR 5, 61; CCA 1; DAB; DAC; DAM MST; DLB 68; EWL 3; MTCW 1; RGWL 2, 3; SATA 104; TCLE 1:2

Roy, Suzanna Arundhati
See Roy, Arundhati

Royko, Mike 1932-1997 .... **CLC 109**
See also CA 89-92; 157; CANR 26, 111; CPW

Rozanov, Vasilii Vasil'evich
See Rozanov, Vassili

Rozanov, Vasily Vasilyevich
See Rozanov, Vassili

Rozanov, Vassili 1856-1919 .... **TCLC 104**
See also DLB 295; EWL 3

Rozewicz, Tadeusz 1921- .... **CLC 9, 23, 139**
See also CA 108; CANR 36, 66; CWW 2; DA3; DAM POET; DLB 232; EWL 3; MTCW 1, 2; MTFW 2005; RGHL; RGWL 3

Ruark, Gibbons 1941- .... **CLC 3**
See also CA 33-36R; CAAS 23; CANR 14, 31, 57; DLB 120

Rubens, Bernice (Ruth)
1923-2004 .... **CLC 19, 31**
See also CA 25-28R; 232; CANR 33, 65, 128; CN 1, 2, 3, 4, 5, 6, 7; DLB 14, 207, 326; MTCW 1

Rubin, Harold
See Robbins, Harold

Rudkin, (James) David 1936- .... **CLC 14**
See also CA 89-92; CBD; CD 5, 6; DLB 13

Rudnik, Raphael 1933- .... **CLC 7**
See also CA 29-32R

Ruffian, M.
See Hasek, Jaroslav

Rufinus c. 345-410 .... **CMLC 111**

Ruiz, Jose Martinez
See Martinez Ruiz, Jose

Ruiz, Juan c. 1283-c. 1350 ... **CMLC 66, 143**

Rukeyser, Muriel 1913-1980 ...... **CLC 6, 10, 15, 27; PC 12, 137**
See also AMWS 6; CA 5-8R; 93-96; CANR 26, 60; CP 1, 2, 3; DA3; DAM POET; DLB 48; EWL 3; FW; GLL 2; MAL 5; MTCW 1, 2; PFS 10, 29; RGAL 4; SATA-Obit 22

Rule, Jane 1931-2007 .... **CLC 27, 265**
See also CA 25-28R; 266; CAAS 18; CANR 12, 87; CN 4, 5, 6, 7; DLB 60; FW

Rule, Jane Vance
See Rule, Jane

Rulfo, Juan 1918-1986 .... **CLC 8, 80; HLC 2; SSC 25**
See also CA 85-88; 118; CANR 26; CDWLB 3; DAM MULT; DLB 113; EWL 3; HW 1, 2; LAW; MTCW 1, 2; RGSF 2; RGWL 2, 3; WLIT 1

Rumi
See Rumi, Jalal al-Din

Rumi, Jalal al-Din 1207-1273 .... **CMLC 20; PC 45, 123**
See also AAYA 64; RGWL 2, 3; WLIT 6; WP

Runeberg, Johan 1804-1877 .... **NCLC 41**

Runyon, (Alfred) Damon 1884
(?)-1946 .... **TCLC 10**
See also CA 107; 165; DLB 11, 86, 171; MAL 5; MTCW 2; RGAL 4

Rush, Benjamin 1746-1813 .... **NCLC 251**
See also DLB 37

Rush, Norman 1933- .... **CLC 44, 306**
See also CA 121; 126; CANR 130; INT CA-126

Rushdie, Ahmed Salman
See Rushdie, Salman

Rushdie, Salman 1947- ...... **CLC 23, 31, 55, 100, 191, 272, 382; SSC 83, 183; WLCS**
See also AAYA 65; BEST 89:3; BPFB 3; BRWS 4; CA 108; 111; CANR 33, 56, 108, 133, 192; CLR 125; CN 4, 5, 6, 7; CPW 1; DA3; DAB; DAC; DAM MST, NOV, POP; DLB 194, 323, 326; EWL 3; FANT; INT CA-111; LATS 1:2; LMFS 2; MTCW 1, 2; MTFW 2005; NFS 22, 23, 41; RGEL 2; RGSF 2; TEA; WLIT 4

Rushforth, Peter 1945-2005 .... **CLC 19**
See also CA 101; 243

Rushforth, Peter Scott
See Rushforth, Peter

Ruskin, John 1819-1900 .... **TCLC 63**
See also BRW 5; BYA 5; CA 114; 129; CDBLB 1832-1890; DLB 55, 163, 190; RGEL 2; SATA 24; TEA; WCH

Russ, Joanna 1937-2011 .... **CLC 15**
See also BPFB 3; CA 25-28; CANR 11, 31, 65; CN 4, 5, 6, 7; DLB 8; FW; GLL 1; MTCW 1; SCFW 1, 2; SFW 4

Russ, Richard Patrick
See O'Brian, Patrick

Russell, Bertrand (Arthur William)
1872-1970 .... **TCLC 273**
See also CA 13-16; 25-28R; CANR 44; CAP 1; DLB 100, 262, 332; MTCW 1, 2; TEA

Russell, George William
1867-1935 .... **PC 133; TCLC 3, 10**
See also BRWS 8; CA 104; 153; CDBLB 1890-1914; DAM POET; DLB 19; EWL 3; RGEL 2

Russell, Henry Kenneth Alfred
See Russell, Ken

Russell, Jeffrey Burton 1934- .... **CLC 70**
See also CA 25-28R; CANR 11, 28, 52, 179

Russell, Karen 1981- .... **CLC 334**
See also CA 255

Russell, Ken 1927-2011 .... **CLC 16**
See also CA 105

Russell, William Martin 1947- .... **CLC 60**
See also CA 164; CANR 107; CBD; CD 5, 6; DLB 233

Russell, Willy
See Russell, William Martin

Russo, Richard 1949- .... **CLC 181**
See also AMWS 12; CA 127; 133; CANR 87, 114, 194; NFS 25

Rutebeuf fl. c. 1249-1277 .... **CMLC 104**
See also DLB 208

Rutherford, Mark
See White, William Hale

Ruysbroeck, Jan van 1293-1381 ... **CMLC 85**

Ruyslinck, Ward
See Belser, Reimond Karel Maria de

Ryan, Cornelius (John) 1920-1974 ... **CLC 7**
See also CA 69-72; 53-56; CANR 38

Ryan, Donal 1976- .... **CLC 370**

Ryan, Michael 1946- .... **CLC 65**
See also CA 49-52; CANR 109, 203; DLBY 1982

Ryan, Tim
See Dent, Lester

Rybakov, Anatoli (Naumovich)
1911-1998 .... **CLC 23, 53**
See also CA 126; 135; 172; DLB 302; RGHL; SATA 79; SATA-Obit 108

Rybakov, Anatolii (Naumovich)
See Rybakov, Anatoli (Naumovich)

Ryder, Jonathan
See Ludlum, Robert

Ryga, George 1932-1987 .... **CLC 14**
See also CA 101; 124; CANR 43, 90; CCA 1; DAC; DAM MST; DLB 60

Rymer, Thomas 1643(?)-1713 .... **LC 132**
See also DLB 101, 336

S. H.
See Hartmann, Sadakichi

S. L. C.
See Twain, Mark

S. S.
See Sassoon, Siegfried

Sa'adawi, al- Nawal
See El Saadawi, Nawal

Saadawi, Nawal El
See El Saadawi, Nawal

Saadiah Gaon 882-942 .... **CMLC 97**

Saavedra, Angel de 1791-1865 ... **NCLC 295**

Saba, Umberto 1883-1957 .... **TCLC 33**
See also CA 144; CANR 79; DLB 114; EWL 3; RGWL 2, 3

Sabatini, Rafael 1875-1950 .... **TCLC 47**
See also BPFB 3; CA 162; RHW

Sabato, Ernesto 1911-2011 **CLC 10, 23, 334; HLC 2**
See also CA 97-100; CANR 32, 65; CDWLB 3; CWW 2; DAM MULT; DLB 145; EWL 3; HW 1, 2; LAW; MTCW 1, 2; MTFW 2005

Sacastru, Martin
See Bioy Casares, Adolfo

Sacher-Masoch, Leopold von
1836(?)-1895 .... **NCLC 31**

Sachs, Hans 1494-1576 .... **LC 95**
See also CDWLB 2; DLB 179; RGWL 2, 3

Sachs, Marilyn 1927- .... **CLC 35**
See also AAYA 2; BYA 6; CA 17-20R; CANR 13, 47, 150; CLR 2; JRDA; MAICYA 1, 2; SAAS 2; SATA 3, 68, 164; SATA-Essay 110; WYA; YAW

Sachs, Marilyn Stickle
See Sachs, Marilyn

Sachs, Nelly 1891-1970 .... **CLC 14, 98; PC 78**
See also CA 17-18; 25-28R; CANR 87; CAP 2; DLB 332; EWL 3; MTCW 2; MTFW 2005; PFS 20; RGHL; RGWL 2, 3

Sackler, Howard (Oliver)
1929-1982 .... **CLC 14**
See also CA 61-64; 108; CAD; CANR 30; DFS 15; DLB 7

Schlesinger, Arthur M., Jr.
1917-2007 .... **CLC 84**
See Schlesinger, Arthur Meier
See also AITN 1; CA 1-4R; 257; CANR 1,
28, 58, 105, 187; DLB 17; INT CANR-28;
MTCW 1, 2; SATA 61; SATA-Obit 181

Schlink, Bernhard 1944- .... **CLC 174, 347**
See also CA 163; CANR 116, 175, 217;
RGHL

Schmidt, Arno (Otto) 1914-1979 .... **CLC 56**
See also CA 128; 109; DLB 69; EWL 3

Schmitz, Aron Hector 1861-1928 ... **SSC 25;
TCLC 2, 35, 244**
See also CA 104; 122; DLB 264; EW 8;
EWL 3; MTCW 1; RGWL 2, 3; WLIT 7

Schnackenberg, Gjertrud 1953- .... **CLC 40;
PC 45**
See also AMWS 15; CA 116; CANR 100; CP
5, 6, 7; CWP; DLB 120, 282; PFS 13, 25

Schnackenberg, Gjertrud Cecelia
See Schnackenberg, Gjertrud

Schneider, Leonard Alfred
See Bruce, Lenny

Schnitzler, Arthur 1862-1931 .... **DC 17;
SSC 15, 61; TCLC 4, 275**
See also CA 104; CDWLB 2; DLB 81, 118;
EW 8; EWL 3; RGSF 2; RGWL 2, 3

Schoenberg, Arnold Franz Walter
1874-1951 .... **TCLC 75**
See also CA 109; 188

Schonberg, Arnold
See Schoenberg, Arnold Franz Walter

Schopenhauer, Arthur
1788-1860 .... **NCLC 51, 157**
See also DLB 90; EW 5

Schor, Sandra (M.) 1932(?)-1990 ... **CLC 65**
See also CA 132

Schorer, Mark 1908-1977 .... **CLC 9**
See also CA 5-8R; 73-76; CANR 7; CN 1, 2;
DLB 103

Schrader, Paul (Joseph)
1946- .... **CLC 26, 212**
See also CA 37-40R; CANR 41; DLB 44

Schreber, Daniel 1842-1911 .... **TCLC 123**

Schreiner, Olive
1855-1920 .... **TCLC 9, 235, 309**
See also AFW; BRWS 2; CA 105; 154; DLB
18, 156, 190, 225; EWL 3; FW; RGEL 2;
TWA; WLIT 2; WWE 1

Schreiner, Olive Emilie Albertina
See Schreiner, Olive

Schulberg, Budd 1914-2009 .... **CLC 7, 48**
See also AMWS 18; BPFB 3; CA 25-28R; 289;
CANR 19, 87, 178; CN 1, 2, 3, 4, 5, 6, 7;
DLB 6, 26, 28; DLBY 1981, 2001; MAL 5

Schulberg, Budd Wilson
See Schulberg, Budd

Schulberg, Seymour Wilson
See Schulberg, Budd

Schulman, Arnold
See Trumbo, Dalton

Schulz, Bruno
1892-1942 ... **SSC 13; TCLC 5, 51, 273**
See also CA 115; 123; CDWLB 4; DLB 215; EWL 3; MTCW 2; MTFW
2005; RGSF 2; RGWL 2, 3

Schulz, Charles M. 1922-2000 .... **CLC 12**
See also AAYA 39; CA 9-12R; 187; CANR
6, 132; CLR 188; INT CANR-6; MTFW
2005; SATA 10; SATA-Obit 118

Schulz, Charles Monroe
See Schulz, Charles M.

Schumacher, E(rnst) F(riedrich)
1911-1977 .... **CLC 80**
See also CA 81-84; 73-76; CANR 34, 85

Schumann, Robert 1810-1856 ..... **NCLC 143**

Schuyler, George Samuel 1895-1977 **HR 1:3**
See also BW 2; CA 81-84; 73-76; CANR 42;
DLB 29, 51

Schuyler, James Marcus
1923-1991 .... **CLC 5, 23; PC 88**
See also CA 101; 134; CP 1, 2, 3, 4, 5; DAM
POET; DLB 5, 169; EWL 3; INT CA-101;
MAL 5; WP

Schwartz, Delmore (David)
1913-1966 .... **CLC 2, 4, 10, 45, 87;
PC 8; SSC 105**
See also AMWS 2; CA 17-18; 25-28R;
CANR 35; CAP 2; DLB 28, 48; EWL
3; MAL 5; MTCW 1, 2; MTFW 2005;
PAB; RGAL 4; TUS

Schwartz, Ernst
See Ozu, Yasujiro

Schwartz, John Burnham 1965- ..... **CLC 59**
See also CA 132; CANR 116, 188

Schwartz, Lynne Sharon 1939- ...... **CLC 31**
See also CA 103; CANR 44, 89, 160, 214;
DLB 218; MTCW 2; MTFW 2005

Schwartz, Muriel A.
See Eliot, T. S.

Schwartzman, Adam 1973- .... **CLC 318**
See also CA 307

Schwarz-Bart, Andre 1928-2006 ... **CLC 2, 4**
See also CA 89-92; 253; CANR 109; DLB
299; RGHL

Schwarz-Bart, Simone 1938- .... **BLCS;
CLC 7**
See also BW 2; CA 97-100; CANR 117;
EWL 3

Schwerner, Armand 1927-1999 .... **PC 42**
See also CA 9-12R; 179; CANR 50, 85; CP
2, 3, 4, 5, 6; DLB 165

**Schwitters, Kurt (Hermann Edward Karl
Julius)** 1887-1948 .... **TCLC 95**
See also CA 158

Schwob, Marcel (Mayer Andre)
1867-1905 .... **TCLC 20**
See also CA 117; 168; DLB 123; GFL 1789
to the Present

Sciascia, Leonardo
1921-1989 .... **CLC 8, 9, 41**
See also CA 85-88; 130; CANR 35; DLB
177; EWL 3; MTCW 1; RGWL 2, 3

Scoppettone, Sandra 1936- .... **CLC 26**
See also AAYA 11, 65; BYA 8; CA 5-8R;
CANR 41, 73, 157; GLL 1; MAICYA 2;
MAICYAS 1; SATA 9, 92; WYA; YAW

Scorsese, Martin 1942- ..... **CLC 20, 89, 207**
See also AAYA 38; CA 110; 114; CANR
46, 85

Scotland, Jay
See Jakes, John

Scott, Duncan Campbell
1862-1947 .... **TCLC 6**
See also CA 104; 153; DAC; DLB 92;
RGEL 2

Scott, Evelyn 1893-1963 .... **CLC 43**
See also CA 104; 112; CANR 64; DLB 9,
48; RHW

Scott, F(rancis) R(eginald)
1899-1985 .... **CLC 22**
See also CA 101; 114; CANR 87; CP 1, 2, 3,
4; DLB 88; INT CA-101; RGEL 2

Scott, Frank
See Scott, F(rancis) R(eginald)

Scott, Joan
See Scott, Joan Wallach

Scott, Joan W.
See Scott, Joan Wallach

Scott, Joan Wallach 1941- .... **CLC 65**
See also CA 293

Scott, Joanna 1960- .... **CLC 50**
See also AMWS 17; CA 126; CANR 53,
92, 168, 219

Scott, Joanna Jeanne
See Scott, Joanna

Scott, Paul (Mark) 1920-1978 ..... **CLC 9, 60**
See also BRWS 1; CA 81-84; 77-80; CANR
33; CN 1, 2; DLB 14, 207, 326; EWL 3;
MTCW 1; RGEL 2; RHW; WWE 1

Scott, Ridley 1937- .... **CLC 183**
See also AAYA 13, 43

Scott, Sarah 1723-1795 .... **LC 44, 233**
See also DLB 39

Scott, Sir Walter 1771-1832 .... **NCLC 15,
69, 110, 209, 241, 270; PC 13; SSC 32;
WLC 5**
See also AAYA 22; BRW 4; BYA 2; CDBLB
1789-1832; CLR 154; DA; DAB; DAC;
DAM MST, NOV, POET; DLB 93, 107,
116, 144, 159, 366; GL 3; HGG; LAIT 1;
NFS 31; RGEL 2; RGSF 2; SSFS 10;
SUFW 1; TEA; WLIT 3; YABC 2

Scotus, John Duns
1266(?)-1308 .... **CMLC 59, 138**
See also DLB 115

Scribe, Augustin Eugene
See Scribe, (Augustin) Eugene

Scribe, (Augustin) Eugene
1791-1861 .... **DC 5; NCLC 16**
See also DAM DRAM; DLB 192; GFL 1789
to the Present; RGWL 2, 3

Scrum, R.
See Crumb, R.

Scudery, Georges de 1601-1667 .... **LC 75**
See also GFL Beginnings to 1789

Scudery, Madeleine de 1607-1701 .. **LC 2, 58**
See also DLB 268; GFL Beginnings to 1789

Scum
See Crumb, R.

Scumbag, Little Bobby
See Crumb, R.

Sceve, Maurice c. 1500-c. 1564 ...... **LC 180;
PC 111**
See also DLB 327; GFL Beginnings to 1789

Schüler, Elisabeth
See Lasker-Schueler, Else

Seabrook, John
See Hubbard, L. Ron

Seacole, Mary Jane Grant
1805-1881 .... **NCLC 147, 305**
See also DLB 166

Sealsfield, Charles 1793-1864 ..... **NCLC 233**
See also DLB 133, 186

Sealy, I(rwin) Allan 1951- .... **CLC 55**
See also CA 136; CN 6, 7

Search, Alexander
See Pessoa, Fernando

Seare, Nicholas
See Whitaker, Rod

Sears, Djanet 1959- .... **DC 46**
See also CA 259

Sears, Janet
See Sears, Djanet

Sebald, W(infried) G(eorg)
1944-2001 .... **CLC 194, 296**
See also BRWS 8; CA 159; 202; CANR 98;
MTFW 2005; RGHL

Sebastian, Lee
See Silverberg, Robert

Sebastian Owl
See Thompson, Hunter S.

Sebbar, Leïla 1941- .... **CLC 365**
See also CA 199; CANR 177; EWL 3

Sebestyen, Igen
See Sebestyen, Ouida

Sebestyen, Ouida 1924- .... **CLC 30**
See also AAYA 8; BYA 7; CA 107; CANR
40, 114; CLR 17; JRDA; MAICYA 1, 2;
SAAS 10; SATA 39, 140; WYA; YAW

Author Index

Author Index

Smith, Woodrow Wilson
　　See Kuttner, Henry
Smith, Zadie 1975- .... **CLC 158, 306**
　　See also AAYA 50; CA 193; CANR 204;
　　DLB 347; MTFW 2005; NFS 40
Smolenskin, Peretz 1842-1885 .... **NCLC 30**
Smollett, Tobias (George)
　　1721-1771 ...... **LC 2, 46, 188, 247, 248**
　　See also BRW 3; CDBLB 1660-1789; DLB
　　39, 104; RGEL 2; TEA
Sanchez, Florencio 1875-1910 .... **TCLC 37**
　　See also CA 153; DLB 305; EWL 3; HW 1;
　　LAW
Sanchez, Luis Rafael 1936- .... **CLC 23**
　　See also CA 128; DLB 305; EWL 3; HW 1;
　　WLIT 1
Snodgrass, Quentin Curtius
　　See Twain, Mark
Snodgrass, Thomas Jefferson
　　See Twain, Mark
Snodgrass, W. D. 1926-2009 .... **CLC 2, 6,
　　10, 18, 68; PC 74**
　　See also AMWS 6; CA 1-4R; 282; CANR 6,
　　36, 65, 85, 185; CP 1, 2, 3, 4, 5, 6, 7; DAM
　　POET; DLB 5; MAL 5; MTCW 1, 2;
　　MTFW 2005; PFS 29; RGAL 4; TCLE 1:2
Snodgrass, W. de Witt
　　See Snodgrass, W. D.
Snodgrass, William de Witt
　　See Snodgrass, W. D.
Snodgrass, William De Witt
　　See Snodgrass, W. D.
Snorri Sturluson 1179-1241 **CMLC 56, 134**
　　See also RGWL 2, 3
Snow, C(harles) P(ercy)
　　1905-1980 .... **CLC 1, 4, 6, 9, 13, 19**
　　See also BRW 7; CA 5-8R; 101; CANR 28;
　　CDBLB 1945-1960; CN 1, 2; DAM NOV;
　　DLB 15, 77; DLBD 17; EWL 3; MTCW 1,
　　2; MTFW 2005; RGEL 2; TEA
Snow, Frances Compton
　　See Adams, Henry
Snyder, Gary 1930- .... **CLC 1, 2, 5, 9,
　　32, 120; PC 21**
　　See also AAYA 72; AMWS 8; ANW; BG
　　1:3; CA 17-20R; CANR 30, 60, 125; CP 1,
　　2, 3, 4, 5, 6, 7; DA3; DAM POET; DLB 5,
　　16, 165, 212, 237, 275, 342; EWL 3; MAL
　　5; MTCW 2; MTFW 2005; PFS 9, 19;
　　RGAL 4; WP
Snyder, Gary Sherman
　　See Snyder, Gary
Snyder, Zilpha Keatley 1927- .... **CLC 17**
　　See also AAYA 15; BYA 1; CA 9-12R, 252;
　　CAAE 252; CANR 38, 202; CLR 31, 121;
　　JRDA; MAICYA 1, 2; SAAS 2; SATA 1,
　　28, 75, 110, 163, 226; SATA-Essay 112,
　　163; YAW
Soares, Bernardo
　　See Pessoa, Fernando
Sobh, A.
　　See Shamlu, Ahmad
Sobh, Alef
　　See Shamlu, Ahmad
Sobol, Joshua 1939- .... **CLC 60**
　　See also CA 200; CWW 2; RGHL
Sobol, Yehoshua 1939-
　　See Sobol, Joshua
Socrates 470B.C.-399B.C. .... **CMLC 27**
Soderberg, Hjalmar 1869-1941 ..... **TCLC 39**
　　See also DLB 259; EWL 3; RGSF 2
Soderbergh, Steven 1963- .... **CLC 154**
　　See also AAYA 43; CA 243
Soderbergh, Steven Andrew
　　See Soderbergh, Steven
Sodergran, Edith 1892-1923 .... **TCLC 31**
　　See also CA 202; DLB 259; EW 11; EWL 3;
　　RGWL 2, 3

Soedergran, Edith Irene
　　See Sodergran, Edith
Softly, Edgar
　　See Lovecraft, H. P.
Softly, Edward
　　See Lovecraft, H. P.
Sokolov, Alexander V. 1943- .... **CLC 59**
　　See also CA 73-76; CWW 2; DLB 285;
　　EWL 3; RGWL 2, 3
Sokolov, Alexander Vsevolodovich
　　See Sokolov, Alexander V.
Sokolov, Raymond 1941- .... **CLC 7**
　　See also CA 85-88
Sokolov, Sasha
　　See Sokolov, Alexander V.
Soleather
　　See Twain, Mark
Soli, Tatjana .... **CLC 318**
　　See also CA 307
Solo, Jay
　　See Ellison, Harlan
Sologub, Fedor
　　See Teternikov, Fyodor Kuzmich
Sologub, Feodor
　　See Teternikov, Fyodor Kuzmich
Sologub, Fyodor
　　See Teternikov, Fyodor Kuzmich
Solomons, Ikey Esquir
　　See Thackeray, William Makepeace
Solomos, Dionysios 1798-1857 ...... **NCLC 15**
Solon c. 630-c. 560 BC .... **CMLC 175**
Solwoska, Mara
　　See French, Marilyn
Solzhenitsyn, Aleksandr 1918-2008 ... **CLC 1,
　　2, 4, 7, 9, 10, 18, 26, 34, 78, 134, 235; SSC
　　32, 105; WLC 5**
　　See also AAYA 49; AITN 1; BPFB 3; CA
　　69-72; CANR 40, 65, 116; CWW 2; DA;
　　DA3; DAB; DAC; DAM MST, NOV; DLB
　　302, 332; EW 13; EWL 3; EXPS; LAIT 4;
　　MTCW 1, 2; MTFW 2005; NFS 6; PFS
　　38; RGSF 2; RGWL 2, 3; SSFS 9; TWA
Solzhenitsyn, Aleksandr I.
　　See Solzhenitsyn, Aleksandr
Solzhenitsyn, Aleksandr Isayevich
　　See Solzhenitsyn, Aleksandr
Somers, Jane
　　See Lessing, Doris
Somerville, Edith Oenone
　　1858-1949 .... **SSC 56; TCLC 51**
　　See also CA 196; DLB 135; RGEL 2; RGSF 2
Somerville & Ross
　　See Martin, Violet Florence; Somerville,
　　Edith Oenone
Sommer, Scott 1951- .... **CLC 25**
　　See also CA 106
Sommers, Christina Hoff 1950- .... **CLC 197**
　　See also CA 153; CANR 95
Sondheim, Stephen 1930- .... **CLC 30, 39,
　　147; DC 22**
　　See also AAYA 11, 66; CA 103; CANR 47,
　　67, 125; DAM DRAM; DFS 25, 27, 28;
　　LAIT 4
Sondheim, Stephen Joshua
　　See Sondheim, Stephen
Sone, Monica 1919- .... **AAL**
　　See also DLB 312
Song, Cathy 1955- .... **AAL; PC 21**
　　See also CA 154; CANR 118; CWP; DLB
　　169, 312; EXPP; FW; PFS 5, 43
Sontag, Susan 1933-2004 .... **CLC 1, 2,
　　10, 13, 31, 105, 195, 277**
　　See also AMWS 3; CA 17-20R; 234; CANR
　　25, 51, 74, 97, 184; CN 1, 2, 3, 4, 5, 6, 7;
　　CPW; DA3; DAM POP; DLB 2, 67; EWL
　　3; MAL 5; MBL; MTCW 1, 2; MTFW
　　2005; RGAL 4; RHW; SSFS 10
Sophocles 496(?)B.C.-406(?)B.C. ... **CMLC 2,
　　47, 51, 86; DC 1; WLCS**

See also AW 1; CDWLB 1; DA; DA3; DAB;
DAC; DAM DRAM, MST; DFS 1, 4, 8,
24; DLB 176; LAIT 1; LATS 1:1; LMFS 1;
RGWL 2, 3; TWA; WLIT 8
Sor Juana
　　See Juana Inés de la Cruz, Sor
Sordello 1189-1269 .... **CMLC 15**
Sorel, Georges 1847-1922 .... **TCLC 91**
　　See also CA 118; 188
Sorel, Julia
　　See Drexler, Rosalyn
Sorokin, Vladimir 1955- .... **CLC 59, 374**
　　See also CA 258; CANR 233; DLB 285
Sorokin, Vladimir Georgievich
　　See Sorokin, Vladimir
Sorrentino, Gilbert 1929-2006 ..... **CLC 3, 7,
　　14, 22, 40, 247**
　　See also AMWS 21; CA 77-80; 250; CANR
　　14, 33, 115, 157; CN 3, 4, 5, 6, 7; CP 1, 2,
　　3, 4, 5, 6, 7; DLB 5, 173; DLBY 1980;
　　INT CANR-14
Soto, Gary 1952- .... **CLC 32, 80; HLC 2;
　　PC 28**
　　See also AAYA 10, 37; BYA 11; CA 119;
　　125; CANR 50, 74, 107, 157, 219; CLR
　　38; CP 4, 5, 6, 7; DAM MULT; DFS 26;
　　DLB 82; EWL 3; EXPP; HW 1, 2; INT
　　CA-125; JRDA; LLW; MAICYA 2; MAI-
　　CYAS 1; MAL 5; MTCW 2; MTFW 2005;
　　PFS 7, 30; RGAL 4; SATA 80, 120, 174;
　　SSFS 33; WYA; YAW
Soupault, Philippe 1897-1990 .... **CLC 68**
　　See also CA 116; 147; 131; EWL 3; GFL
　　1789 to the Present; LMFS 2
Souster, (Holmes) Raymond
　　1921- .... **CLC 5, 14**
　　See also CA 13-16R; CAAS 14; CANR 13,
　　29, 53; CP 1, 2, 3, 4, 5, 6, 7; DA3; DAC;
　　DAM POET; DLB 88; RGEL 2; SATA 63
Southern, Terry 1924(?)-1995 .... **CLC 7**
　　See also AMWS 11; BPFB 3; CA 1-4R; 150;
　　CANR 1, 55, 107; CN 1, 2, 3, 4, 5, 6; DLB
　　2; IDFW 3, 4
Southerne, Thomas 1660-1746 .... **LC 99**
　　See also DLB 80; RGEL 2
Southey, Robert 1774-1843 ..... **NCLC 8, 97;
　　PC 111**
　　See also BRW 4; DLB 93, 107, 142; RGEL
　　2; SATA 54
Southwell, Robert 1561(?)-1595 .... **LC 108**
　　See also DLB 167; RGEL 2; TEA
Southworth, Emma Dorothy Eliza Nevitte
　　1819-1899 .... **NCLC 26**
　　See also DLB 239
Souza, Ernest
　　See Scott, Evelyn
Soyinka, Wole 1934- .... **BLC 1:3, 2:3;
　　CLC 3, 5, 14, 36, 44, 179, 331; DC 2; PC
　　118; WLC 5**
　　See also AFW; BW 2, 3; CA 13-16R; CANR
　　27, 39, 82, 136; CD 5, 6; CDWLB 3; CN
　　6, 7; CP 1, 2, 3, 4, 5, 6 ,7; DA; DA3; DAB;
　　DAC; DAM DRAM, MST, MULT; DFS
　　10, 26; DLB 125, 332; EWL 3; MTCW 1,
　　2; MTFW 2005; PFS 27, 40; RGEL 2;
　　TWA; WLIT 2; WWE 1
Spackman, W(illiam) M(ode)
　　1905-1990 .... **CLC 46**
　　See also CA 81-84; 132
Spacks, Barry (Bernard) 1931- ...... **CLC 14**
　　See also CA 154; CANR 33, 109; CP 3, 4, 5,
　　6, 7; DLB 105
Spanidou, Irini 1946- .... **CLC 44**
　　See also CA 185; CANR 179
Spark, Muriel 1918-2006 .... **CLC 2, 3, 5,
　　8, 13, 18, 40, 94, 242; PC 72; SSC 10, 115**
　　See also BRWS 1; CA 5-8R; 251; CANR 12,
　　36, 76, 89, 131; CDBLB 1945-1960; CN 1,
　　2, 3, 4, 5, 6, 7; CP 1, 2, 3, 4, 5, 6, 7; DA3;

See also AAYA 64; AMW; AMWC 2; CA 104; 132; CANR 108; CDALB 1917-1929; DA; DA3; DAB; DAC; DAM MST, NOV, POET; DLB 4, 54, 86, 228; DLBD 15; EWL 3; EXPS; FL 1:6; GLL 1; MAL 5; MBL; MTCW 1, 2; MTFW 2005; NCFS 4; NFS 27; PFS 38; RGAL 4; RGSF 2; SSFS 5; TUS; WP

Steinbeck, John 1902-1968 ...... **CLC 1, 5, 9, 13, 21, 34, 45, 75, 124; DC 46; SSC 11, 37, 77, 135; TCLC 135; WLC 5**
See also AAYA 12; AMW; BPFB 3; BYA 2, 3, 13; CA 1-4R; 25-28R; CANR 1, 35; CDALB 1929-1941; CLR 172, 194, 195; DA; DA3; DAB; DAC; DAM DRAM, MST, NOV; DLB 7, 9, 212, 275, 309, 332, 364; DLBD 2; EWL 3; EXPS; LAIT 3; MAL 5; MTCW 1, 2; MTFW 2005; NFS 1, 5, 7, 17, 19, 28, 34, 37, 39; RGAL 4; RGSF 2; RHW; SATA 9; SSFS 3, 6, 22; TCWW 1, 2; TUS; WYA; YAW

Steinbeck, John Ernst
See Steinbeck, John

Steinem, Gloria 1934- .... **CLC 63**
See also CA 53-56; CANR 28, 51, 139; DLB 246; FL 1:1; FW; MTCW 1, 2; MTFW 2005

Steiner, George 1929- .... **CLC 24, 221**
See also CA 73-76; CANR 31, 67, 108, 212; DAM NOV; DLB 67, 299; EWL 3; MTCW 1, 2; MTFW 2005; RGHL; SATA 62

Steiner, K. Leslie
See Delany, Samuel R., Jr.

Steiner, Rudolf 1861-1925 .... **TCLC 13**
See also CA 107

Stendhal 1783-1842 .... **NCLC 23, 46, 178, 292; SSC 27; WLC 5**
See also DA; DA3; DAB; DAC; DAM MST, NOV; DLB 119; EW 5; GFL 1789 to the Present; RGWL 2, 3; TWA

Stephen, Adeline Virginia
See Woolf, Virginia

Stephen, Sir Leslie 1832-1904 .... **TCLC 23**
See also BRW 5; CA 123; DLB 57, 144, 190

Stephen, Sir Leslie
See Stephen, Sir Leslie

Stephen, Virginia
See Woolf, Virginia

Stephens, Ann Sophia 1810-1886 .. **NCLC 303**
See also DLB 3, 73, 250

Stephens, James 1882(?)-1950 .... **SSC 50; TCLC 4**
See also CA 104; 192; DLB 19, 153, 162; EWL 3; FANT; RGEL 2; SUFW

Stephens, Reed
See Donaldson, Stephen R.

Stephenson, Neal 1959- .... **CLC 220**
See also AAYA 38; CA 122; CANR 88, 138, 195; CN 7; MTFW 2005; SFW 4

Steptoe, Lydia
See Barnes, Djuna

Sterchi, Beat 1949- .... **CLC 65**
See also CA 203

Sterling, Brett
See Bradbury, Ray; Hamilton, Edmond

Sterling, Bruce 1954- .... **CLC 72**
See also AAYA 78; CA 119; CANR 44, 135, 184; CN 7; MTFW 2005; SCFW 2; SFW 4

Sterling, George 1869-1926 .... **TCLC 20**
See also CA 117; 165; DLB 54

Stern, Gerald 1925- ... **CLC 40, 100; PC 115**
See also AMWS 9; CA 81-84; CANR 28, 94, 206; CP 3, 4, 5, 6, 7; DLB 105; PFS 26; RGAL 4

Stern, Richard (Gustave) 1928- ... **CLC 4, 39**
See also CA 1-4R; CANR 1, 25, 52, 120; CN 1, 2, 3, 4, 5, 6, 7; DLB 218; DLBY 1987; INT CANR-25

Sternberg, Josef von 1894-1969 ..... **CLC 20**
See also CA 81-84

Sterne, Laurence 1713-1768 .... **LC 2, 48, 156; WLC 5**
See also BRW 3; BRWC 1; CDBLB 1660-1789; DA; DAB; DAC; DAM MST, NOV; DLB 39; RGEL 2; TEA

Sternheim, (William Adolf) Carl 1878-1942 .... **TCLC 8, 223**
See also CA 105; 193; DLB 56, 118; EWL 3; IDTP; RGWL 2, 3

Stesichorus 630?-555? BC .... **CMLC 167**

Stetson, Charlotte Perkins
See Gilman, Charlotte Perkins

Stevens, Margaret Dean
See Aldrich, Bess Streeter

Stevens, Mark 1951- .... **CLC 34**
See also CA 122

Stevens, R. L.
See Hoch, Edward D.

Stevens, Wallace 1879-1955 .... **PC 6, 110; TCLC 3, 12, 45; WLC 5**
See also AMW; AMWR 1; CA 104; 124; CANR 181; CDALB 1929-1941; DA; DA3; DAB; DAC; DAM MST, POET; DLB 54, 342; EWL 3; EXPP; MAL 5; MTCW 1, 2; PAB; PFS 13, 16, 35, 41; RGAL 4; TUS; WP

Stevenson, Anne (Katharine) 1933- .... **CLC 7, 33**
See also BRWS 6; CA 17-20R; CAAS 9; CANR 9, 33, 123; CP 3, 4, 5, 6, 7; CWP; DLB 40; MTCW 1; RHW

Stevenson, Robert Louis 1850-1894 ... **NCLC 5, 14, 63, 193, 274, 289, 292, 308; PC 84; SSC 11, 51, 126; WLC 5**
See also AAYA 24; BPFB 3; BRW 5; BRWC 1; BRWR 1; BYA 1, 2, 4, 13; CDBLB 1890-1914; CLR 10, 11, 107, 180, 204; DA; DA3; DAB; DAC; DAM MST, NOV; DLB 18, 57, 141, 156, 174; DLBD 13; GL 3; HGG; JRDA; LAIT 1, 3; MAICYA 1, 2; NFS 11, 20, 33; RGEL 2; RGSF 2; SATA 100; SUFW; TEA; WCH; WLIT 4; WYA; YABC 2; YAW

Stevenson, Robert Louis Balfour
See Stevenson, Robert Louis

Stewart, Douglas 1913-1985 .... **TCLC 317**
See also CA 81-84; CP 1, 2, 3, 4; DLB 260; RGEL 2

Stewart, J(ohn) I(nnes) M(ackintosh) 1906-1994 .... **CLC 7, 14, 32**
See also CA 85-88; 147; CAAS 3; CANR 47; CMW 4; CN 1, 2, 3, 4, 5; DLB 276; MSW; MTCW 1, 2

Stewart, Mary (Florence Elinor) 1916- .... **CLC 7, 35, 117**
See also AAYA 29, 73; BPFB 3; CA 1-4R; CANR 1, 59, 130; CMW 4; CPW; DAB; FANT; RHW; SATA 12; YAW

Stewart, Mary Rainbow
See Stewart, Mary (Florence Elinor)

Stewart, Will
See Williamson, John Stewart

Stifle, June
See Campbell, Maria

Stifter, Adalbert 1805-1868 .... **NCLC 41, 198; SSC 28**
See also CDWLB 2; DLB 133; RGSF 2; RGWL 2, 3

Still, James 1906-2001 .... **CLC 49**
See also CA 65-68; 195; CAAS 17; CANR 10, 26; CSW; DLB 9; DLBY 01; SATA 29; SATA-Obit 127

Sting 1951- .... **CLC 26**
See also CA 167

Stirling, Arthur
See Sinclair, Upton

Stitt, Milan 1941-2009 .... **CLC 29**
See also CA 69-72; 284

Stitt, Milan William
See Stitt, Milan

Stockton, Francis Richard 1834-1902 .... **TCLC 47**
See also AAYA 68; BYA 4, 13; CA 108; 137; DLB 42, 74; DLBD 13; EXPS; MAICYA 1, 2; SATA 44; SATA-Brief 32; SFW 4; SSFS 3; SUFW; WCH

Stockton, Frank R.
See Stockton, Francis Richard

Stoddard, Charles
See Kuttner, Henry

Stoker, Abraham
See Stoker, Bram

Stoker, Bram 1847-1912 .... **SSC 62; TCLC 8, 144; WLC 6**
See also AAYA 23; BPFB 3; BRWS 3; BYA 5; CA 105; 150; CDBLB 1890-1914; CLR 178; DA; DA3; DAB; DAC; DAM MST, NOV; DLB 304; GL 3; HGG; LATS 1:1; MTFW 2005; NFS 18; RGEL 2; SATA 29; SUFW; TEA; WLIT 4

Stolz, Mary 1920-2006 .... **CLC 12**
See also AAYA 8, 73; AITN 1; CA 5-8R; 255; CANR 13, 41, 112; JRDA; MAICYA 1, 2; SAAS 3; SATA 10, 71, 133; SATA-Obit 180; YAW

Stolz, Mary Slattery
See Stolz, Mary

Stone, Irving 1903-1989 .... **CLC 7**
See also AITN 1; BPFB 3; CA 1-4R; 129; CAAS 3; CANR 1, 23; CN 1, 2, 3, 4; CPW; DA3; DAM POP; INT CANR-23; MTCW 1, 2; MTFW 2005; RHW; SATA 3; SATA-Obit 64

Stone, Lucy 1818-1893 .... **NCLC 250**
See also DLB 79, 239

Stone, Miriam
See Harwood, Gwen

Stone, Oliver 1946- .... **CLC 73**
See also AAYA 15, 64; CA 110; CANR 55, 125

Stone, Oliver William
See Stone, Oliver

Stone, Robert 1937- .... **CLC 5, 23, 42, 175, 331**
See also AMWS 5; BPFB 3; CA 85-88; CANR 23, 66, 95, 173; CN 4, 5, 6, 7; DLB 152; EWL 3; INT CANR-23; MAL 5; MTCW 1; MTFW 2005

Stone, Robert Anthony
See Stone, Robert

Stone, Ruth 1915-2011 .... **PC 53**
See also CA 45-48; CANR 2, 91, 209; CP 5, 6, 7; CSW; DLB 105; PFS 19, 40

Stone, Zachary
See Follett, Ken

Stoppard, Tom 1937- .... **CLC 1, 3, 4, 5, 8, 15, 29, 34, 63, 91, 328; DC 6, 30; WLC 6**
See also AAYA 63; BRWC 1; BRWR 2; BRWS 1; CA 81-84; CANR 39, 67, 125; CBD; CD 5, 6; CDBLB 1960 to Present; DA; DA3; DAB; DAC; DAM DRAM, MST; DFS 2, 5, 8, 11, 13, 16; DLB 13, 233; DLBY 1985; EWL 3; LAIT 1:2; LNFS 3; MTCW 1, 2; MTFW 2005; RGEL 2; TEA; WLIT 4

Storey, David (Malcolm) 1933- .... **CLC 2, 4, 5, 8; DC 40**
See also BRWS 1; CA 81-84; CANR 36; CBD; CD 5, 6; CN 1, 2, 3, 4, 5, 6; DAM DRAM; DLB 13, 14, 207, 245, 326; EWL 3; MTCW 1; RGEL 2

Storm, Hyemeyohsts 1935- ... **CLC 3; NNAL**
See also CA 81-84; CANR 45; DAM MULT

Storm, (Hans) Theodor (Woldsen) 1817-1888 .... **NCLC 1, 195; SSC 27, 106**

Trout, Kilgore
See Farmer, Philip Jose
Trow, George William Swift
See Trow, George W.S.
Trow, George W.S. 1943-2006 .... **CLC 52**
See also CA 126; 255; CANR 91
Troyat, Henri
1911-2007 .... **CLC 23**
See also CA 45-48; 258; CANR 2, 33, 67,
117; GFL 1789 to the Present; MTCW 1
Trudeau, Garretson Beekman
See Trudeau, Garry
Trudeau, Garry 1948- .... **CLC 12**
See also AAYA 10, 60; AITN 2; CA 81-84;
CANR 31; SATA 35, 168
Trudeau, Garry B.
See Trudeau, Garry
Trudeau, G.B. 1948- .... **CLC 12**
See also AAYA 10, 60; AITN 2; CA 81-84;
CANR 31; SATA 35, 168
Truffaut, Francois
1932-1984 .... **CLC 20, 101**
See also AAYA 84; CA 81-84; 113; CANR 34
Trumbo, Dalton
1905-1976 .... **CLC 19**
See also CA 21-24R; 69-72; CANR 10; CN
1, 2; DLB 26; IDFW 3, 4; YAW
Trumbull, John
1750-1831 .... **NCLC 30**
See also DLB 31; RGAL 4
Trundlett, Helen B.
See Eliot, T. S.
Truth, Sojourner 1797(?)-1883 ..... **NCLC 94**
See also DLB 239; FW; LAIT 2
Tryon, Thomas
1926-1991 .... **CLC 3, 11**
See also AITN 1; BPFB 3; CA 29-32R; 135;
CANR 32, 77; CPW; DA3; DAM POP;
HGG; MTCW 1
Tryon, Tom
See Tryon, Thomas
Ts'ao Hsueh-ch'in 1715(?)-1763 .... **LC 1**
Toson
See Shimazaki, Haruki
Tsurayuki Ed. fl. 10th cent. .... **PC 73**
Tsvetaeva, Marina 1892-1941 .... **PC 14;**
TCLC 7, 35
See also CA 104; 128; CANR 73; DLB 295;
EW 11; MTCW 1, 2; PFS 29; RGWL 2, 3
Tsvetaeva Efron, Marina Ivanovna
See Tsvetaeva, Marina
Tuck, Lily 1938- .... **CLC 70**
See also AAYA 74; CA 139; CANR 90, 192
Tuckerman, Frederick Goddard
1821-1873 .... **PC 85**
See also DLB 243; RGAL 4
Tu Fu 712-770 .... **PC 9**
See also DAM MULT; PFS 32; RGWL 2, 3;
TWA; WP
Tulsidas, Gosvami 1532(?)-1623 ...... **LC 158**
See also RGWL 2, 3
Tunis, John R(oberts) 1889-1975 ... **CLC 12**
See also BYA 1; CA 61-64; CANR 62; DLB
22, 171; JRDA; MAICYA 1, 2; SATA 37;
SATA-Brief 30; YAW
Tuohy, Frank
See Tuohy, John Francis
Tuohy, John Francis 1925- .... **CLC 37**
See also CA 5-8R; 178; CANR 3, 47; CN 1,
2, 3, 4, 5, 6, 7; DLB 14, 139
Turco, Lewis 1934- .... **CLC 11, 63**
See also CA 13-16R; CAAS 22; CANR 24,
51, 185; CP 1, 2, 3, 4, 5, 6, 7; DLBY 1984;
TCLE 1:2
Turco, Lewis Putnam
See Turco, Lewis
Turgenev, Ivan 1818-1883 .... **DC 7;**
NCLC 21, 37, 122, 269; SSC 7, 57; WLC 6

See also AAYA 58; DA; DAB; DAC; DAM
MST, NOV; DFS 6; DLB 238, 284; EW 6;
LATS 1:1; NFS 16; RGSF 2; RGWL 2, 3;
TWA
Turgenev, Ivan Sergeevich
See Turgenev, Ivan
Turgot, Anne-Robert-Jacques
1727-1781 .... **LC 26**
See also DLB 314
Turlin, Heinrich von dem
See Heinrich von dem Tuerlin
Turner, Frederick 1943- .... **CLC 48**
See also CA 73-76, 227; CAAE 227; CAAS
10; CANR 12, 30, 56; DLB 40, 282
Turrini, Peter 1944- .... **DC 49**
See also CA 209; DLB 124
Turton, James
See Crace, Jim
Tutu, Desmond M. 1931- .... **BLC 1:3;**
CLC 80
See also BW 1, 3; CA 125; CANR 67, 81,
242; DAM MULT
Tutu, Desmond Mpilo
See Tutu, Desmond M.
Tutuola, Amos 1920-1997 ...... **BLC 1:3, 2:3;**
CLC 5, 14, 29; TCLC 188
See also AAYA 76; AFW; BW 2, 3; CA 9-
12R; 159; CANR 27, 66; CDWLB 3; CN
1, 2, 3, 4, 5, 6; DA3; DAM MULT; DLB
125; DNFS 2; EWL 3; MTCW 1, 2;
MTFW 2005; RGSF 2; RGWL 2; WLIT 2
Twain, Mark 1835-1910 ...... **SSC 6, 26, 34,**
87, 119, 210; TCLC 6, 12, 19, 36, 48, 59,
161, 185, 260; WLC 6
See also AAYA 20; AMW; AMWC 1; BPFB
3; BYA 2, 3, 11, 14; CA 104; 135; CDALB
1865-1917; CLR 58, 60, 66, 156, 187; DA;
DA3; DAB; DAC; DAM MST, NOV; DLB
11, 12, 23, 64, 74, 186, 189, 11, 343;
EXPN; EXPS; JRDA; LAIT 2; LMFS 1;
MAICYA 1, 2; MAL 5; NCFS 4; NFS 1, 6;
RGAL 4; RGSF 2; SATA 100; SFW 4;
SSFS 1, 7, 16, 21, 27, 33; SUFW; TUS;
WCH; WYA; YABC 2; YAW
Twohill, Maggie
See Angell, Judie
Tyard, Pontus de 1521?-1605 .... **LC 243**
See also DLB 327
Tyler, Anne 1941- .... **CLC 7, 11, 18, 28, 44,**
59, 103, 205, 265
See also AAYA 18, 60; AMWS 4; BEST
89:1; BPFB 3; BYA 12; CA 9-12R; CANR
11, 33, 53, 109, 132, 168; CDALBS; CN 1,
2, 3, 4, 5, 6, 7; CPW; CSW; DAM NOV,
POP; DLB 6, 143; DLBY 1982; EWL 3;
EXPN; LATS 1:2; MAL 5; MBL; MTCW
1, 2; MTFW 2005; NFS 2, 7, 10, 38;
RGAL 4; SATA 7, 90, 173; SSFS 1, 31;
TCLE 1:2; TUS; YAW
Tyler, Royall 1757-1826 .... **NCLC 3, 244**
See also DLB 37; RGAL 4
Tynan, Katharine
1861-1931 .... **PC 120; TCLC 3, 217**
See also CA 104; 167; DLB 153, 240; FW
Tyndale, William c. 1484-1536 .... **LC 103**
See also DLB 132
Tyutchev, Fyodor
1803-1873 .... **NCLC 34, 291**
Tzara, Tristan
1896-1963 .... **CLC 47;**
PC 27; TCLC 168
See also CA 153; 89-92; DAM POET; EWL
3; MTCW 2
Uc de Saint Circ
c. 1190B.C.-13th cent. B.C. .... **CMLC 102**
Uchida, Yoshiko
1921-1992 .... **AAL**
See also AAYA 16; BYA 2, 3; CA 13-16R;
139; CANR 6, 22, 47, 61; CDALBS; CLR

6, 56; CWRI 5; DLB 312; JRDA; MAI-
CYA 1, 2; MTCW 1, 2; MTFW 2005; NFS
26; SAAS 1; SATA 1, 53; SATA-Obit 72;
SSFS 31
Udall, Nicholas 1504-1556 .... **LC 84**
See also DLB 62; RGEL 2
Ueda Akinari
1734-1809 .... **NCLC 131**
Ugrešić, Dubravka 1949- .... **CLC 375**
See also CA 136, CANR 90, 159, 198;
CWW 2; DLC 181
Uhry, Alfred 1936- .... **CLC 55; DC 28**
See also CA 127; 133; CAD; CANR 112;
CD 5, 6; CSW; DA3; DAM DRAM, POP;
DFS 11, 15; INT CA-133; MTFW 2005
Ulf, Haerved
See Strindberg, August
Ulf, Harved
See Strindberg, August
Ulibarrí, Sabine R(eyes)
1919-2003 .... **CLC 83; HLCS 2**
See also CA 131; 214; CANR 81; DAM
MULT; DLB 82; HW 1, 2; RGSF 2
Ulyanov, V. I.
See Lenin, Vladimir
Ulyanov, Vladimir Ilyich
See Lenin, Vladimir
Ulyanov-Lenin
See Lenin, Vladimir
Unamuno, Miguel de
1864-1936 .... **DC 45;**
HLC 2; SSC 11, 69; TCLC 2, 9, 148, 237
See also CA 104; 131; CANR 81; DAM
MULT, NOV; DLB 108, 322; EW 8; EWL
3; HW 1, 2; MTCW 1, 2; MTFW 2005;
RGSF 2; RGWL 2, 3; SSFS 20; TWA
Unamuno y Jugo, Miguel de
See Unamuno, Miguel de
Uncle Shelby
See Silverstein, Shel
Undercliffe, Errol
See Campbell, Ramsey
Underwood, Miles
See Glassco, John
Undset, Sigrid 1882-1949 ...... **TCLC 3, 197;**
WLC 6
See also AAYA 77; CA 104; 129; DA; DA3;
DAB; DAC; DAM MST, NOV; DLB 293,
332; EW 9; EWL 3; FW; MTCW 1, 2;
MTFW 2005; RGWL 2, 3
Ungaretti, Giuseppe 1888-1970 .... **CLC 7,**
11, 15; PC 57; TCLC 200
See also CA 19-20; 25-28R; CAP 2; DLB
114; EW 10; EWL 3; PFS 20; RGWL 2, 3;
WLIT 7
Unger, Douglas 1952- .... **CLC 34**
See also CA 130; CANR 94, 155
Unsworth, Barry 1930-2012 .... **CLC 76, 127**
See also BRWS 7; CA 25-28R; CANR 30,
54, 125, 171, 202; CN 6, 7; DLB 194, 326
Unsworth, Barry Forster
See Unsworth, Barry
Updike, John 1932-2009 ..... **CLC 1, 2, 3, 5,**
7, 9, 13, 15, 23, 34, 43, 70, 139, 214,
278; PC 90; SSC 13, 27, 103; WLC 6
See also AAYA 36; AMW; AMWC 1;
AMWR 1; BPFB 3; BYA 12; CA 1-4R;
282; CABS 1; CANR 4, 33, 51, 94, 133,
197, 229; CDALB 1968-1988; CN 1, 2, 3,
4, 5, 6, 7; CP 1, 2, 3, 4, 5, 6, 7; CPW 1;
DA; DA3; DAB; DAC; DAM MST, NOV,
POET, POP; DLB 2, 5, 143, 218, 227;
DLBD 3; DLBY 1980, 1982, 1997; EWL
3; EXPP; HGG; MAL 5; MTCW 1, 2;
MTFW 2005; NFS 12, 24; RGAL 4; RGSF
2; SSFS 3, 19, 37; TUS
Updike, John Hoyer
See Updike, John

Upshaw, Margaret Mitchell
See Mitchell, Margaret
Upton, Mark
See Sanders, Lawrence
Upward, Allen
1863-1926 .... **TCLC 85**
See also CA 117; 187; DLB 36
Urdang, Constance (Henriette)
1922-1996 .... **CLC 47**
See also CA 21-24R; CANR 9, 24; CP 1, 2,
3, 4, 5, 6; CWP
Urfé, Honoré d'
1567(?)-1625 .... **LC 132, 232**
See also DLB 268; GFL Beginnings to 1789;
RGWL 2, 3
Uriel, Henry
See Faust, Frederick
Uris, Leon
1924-2003 .... **CLC 7, 32**
See also AITN 1, 2; AMWS 20; BEST 89:2;
BPFB 3; CA 1-4R; 217; CANR 1, 40, 65,
123; CN 1, 2, 3, 4, 5, 6; CPW 1; DA3;
DAM NOV, POP; MTCW 1, 2; MTFW
2005; RGHL; SATA 49; SATA-Obit 146
Urista, Alberto
See Alurista
Urmuz
See Codrescu, Andrei
Urquhart, Guy
See McAlmon, Robert (Menzies)
Urquhart, Jane 1949- .... **CLC 90, 242**
See also CA 113; CANR 32, 68, 116, 157;
CCA 1; DAC; DLB 334
Usigli, Rodolfo 1905-1979 .... **HLCS 1**
See also CA 131; DLB 305; EWL 3; HW 1;
LAW
Usk, Thomas
(?)-1388 .... **CMLC 76**
See also DLB 146
Ustinov, Peter (Alexander)
1921-2004 .... **CLC 1**
See also AITN 1; CA 13-16R; 225; CANR 25,
51; CBD; CD 5, 6; DLB 13; MTCW 2
U Tam'si, Gerald Felix Tchicaya
See Tchicaya, Gerald Felix
U Tam'si, Tchicaya
See Tchicaya, Gerald Felix
Vachss, Andrew 1942- .... **CLC 106**
See also CA 118, 214; CAAE 214; CANR
44, 95, 153, 197, 238; CMW 4
Vachss, Andrew H.
See Vachss, Andrew
Vachss, Andrew Henry
See Vachss, Andrew
Vaculik, Ludvik
1926- .... **CLC 7**
See also CA 53-56; CANR 72; CWW 2;
DLB 232; EWL 3
Vaihinger, Hans
1852-1933 .... **TCLC 71**
See also CA 116; 166
Valdez, Luis (Miguel) 1940- .... **CLC 84;
DC 10; HLC 2**
See also CA 101; CAD; CANR 32, 81; CD
5, 6; DAM MULT; DFS 5, 29; DLB 122;
EWL 3; HW 1; LAIT 4; LLW
Valenzuela, Luisa 1938- .... **CLC 31, 104;
HLCS 2; SSC 14, 82**
See also CA 101; CANR 32, 65, 123;
CDWLB 3; CWW 2; DAM MULT; DLB
113; EWL 3; FW; HW 1, 2; LAW; RGSF
2; RGWL 3; SSFS 29
Valera y Alcala-Galiano, Juan
1824-1905 .... **TCLC 10**
See also CA 106
Valerius Maximus .... **CMLC 64**
See also DLB 211
Valle-Inclan, Ramon del
1866-1936 .... **HLC 2; TCLC 5, 228**
See also CA 106; 153; CANR 80; DAM
MULT; DLB 134, 322; EW 8; EWL 3; HW
2; RGSF 2; RGWL 2, 3
Valle-Inclan, Ramon Maria del
See Valle-Inclan, Ramon del
Vallejo, Antonio Buero
See Buero Vallejo, Antonio
Vallejo, Cesar 1892-1938 .... **HLC 2;
TCLC 3, 56**
See also CA 105; 153; DAM MULT; DLB
290; EWL 3; HW 1; LAW; PFS 26;
RGWL 2, 3
Vallejo, Cesar Abraham
See Vallejo, Cesar
Vallette, Marguerite Eymery
1860-1953 .... **TCLC 67**
See also CA 182; DLB 123, 192; EWL 3
Valle Y Pena, Ramon del
See Valle-Inclan, Ramon del
Valles, Jules
1832-1885 .... **NCLC 71**
See also DLB 123; GFL 1789 to the Present
Valery, Ambroise Paul Toussaint Jules
See Valery, Paul
Valery, Paul 1871-1945 .... **PC 9; TCLC 4,
15, 231**
See also CA 104; 122; DA3; DAM POET;
DLB 258; EW 8; EWL 3; GFL 1789 to
the Present; MTCW 1, 2; MTFW 2005;
RGWL 2, 3; TWA
Van Ash, Cay 1918-1994 .... **CLC 34**
See also CA 220
Vanbrugh, Sir John 1664-1726 .... **DC 40;
LC 21**
See also BRW 2; DAM DRAM; DLB 80;
IDTP; RGEL 2
Van Campen, Karl
See Campbell, John W.
Vance, Gerald
See Silverberg, Robert
Vance, Jack 1916- .... **CLC 35**
See also CA 29-32R; CANR 17, 65, 154,
218; CMW 4; DLB 8; FANT; MTCW 1;
SCFW 1, 2; SFW 4; SUFW 1, 2
Vance, John Holbrook
See Vance, Jack
**Van Den Bogarde, Derek Jules Gaspard Ulric
Niven**
See Bogarde, Dirk
Vandenburgh, Jane .... **CLC 59**
See also CA 168; CANR 208
Vanderhaeghe, Guy 1951- .... **CLC 41**
See also BPFB 3; CA 113; CANR 72, 145;
CN 7; DLB 334
van der Post, Laurens (Jan)
1906-1996 .... **CLC 5**
See also AFW; CA 5-8R; 155; CANR 35;
CN 1, 2, 3, 4, 5, 6; DLB 204; RGEL 2
van de Wetering, Janwillem
1931-2008 .... **CLC 47**
See also CA 49-52; 274; CANR 4, 62, 90;
CMW 4
Van Dine, S. S.
See Wright, Willard Huntington
Van Doren, Carl (Clinton)
1885-1950 .... **TCLC 18**
See also CA 111; 168
Van Doren, Mark 1894-1972 ...... **CLC 6, 10**
See also CA 1-4R; 37-40R; CANR 3; CN 1;
CP 1; DLB 45, 284, 335; MAL 5; MTCW
1, 2; RGAL 4
Van Druten, John (William)
1901-1957 .... **TCLC 2**
See also CA 104; 161; DFS 30; DLB 10;
MAL 5; RGAL 4
Van Duyn, Mona 1921-2004 .... **CLC 3, 7,
63, 116**
See also CA 9-12R; 234; CANR 7, 38, 60,
116; CP 1, 2, 3, 4, 5, 6, 7; CWP; DAM
POET; DLB 5; MAL 5; MTFW 2005;
PFS 20
Van Dyne, Edith
See Baum, L. Frank
van Herk, Aritha
1954- .... **CLC 249**
See also CA 101; CANR 94; DLB 334
van Itallie, Jean-Claude
1936- .... **CLC 3**
See also CA 45-48; 311; CAAS 2, 311;
CAD; CANR 1, 48; CD 5, 6; DLB 7
Van Loot, Cornelius Obenchain
See Roberts, Kenneth (Lewis)
van Niekerk, Marlene
1954- .... **CLC 324**
See also CA 229
van Ostaijen, Paul
1896-1928 .... **TCLC 33**
See also CA 163
Van Peebles, Melvin 1932- .... **CLC 2, 20**
See also BW 2, 3; CA 85-88; CANR 27, 67,
82; DAM MULT
van Schendel, Arthur(-Francois-Emile)
1874-1946 .... **TCLC 56**
See also EWL 3
van Schurman, Anna Maria
1607-1678 .... **LC 199**
Van See, John
See Vance, Jack
Vansittart, Peter
1920-2008 .... **CLC 42**
See also CA 1-4R; 278; CANR 3, 49, 90;
CN 4, 5, 6, 7; RHW
Van Vechten, Carl
1880-1964 .... **CLC 33; HR 1:3**
See also AMWS 2; CA 183; 89-92; DLB 4,
9, 51; RGAL 4
van Vogt, A(lfred) E(lton)
1912-2000 .... **CLC 1**
See also BPFB 3; BYA 13, 14; CA 21-24R;
190; CANR 28; DLB 8, 251; SATA 14;
SATA-Obit 124; SCFW 1, 2; SFW 4
Vara, Madeleine
See Jackson, Laura
Varda, Agnes 1928- .... **CLC 16**
See also CA 116; 122
Vargas Llosa, Jorge Mario Pedro
See Vargas Llosa, Mario
Vargas Llosa, Mario 1936- ..... **CLC 3, 6, 9,
10, 15, 31, 42, 85, 181, 318; HLC 2**
See also BPFB 3; CA 73-76; CANR 18, 32,
42, 67, 116, 140, 173, 213; CDWLB 3;
CWW 2; DA; DA3; DAB; DAC; DAM
MST, MULT, NOV; DLB 145; DNFS 2;
EWL 3; HW 1, 2; LAIT 5; LATS 1:2; LAW;
LAWS 1; MTCW 1, 2; MTFW 2005;
RGWL 2, 3; SSFS 14; TWA; WLIT 1
Varnhagen von Ense, Rahel
1771-1833 .... **NCLC 130**
See also DLB 90
Vasari, Giorgio
1511-1574 .... **LC 114**
Vasilikos, Vasiles
See Vassilikos, Vassilis
Vasiliu, Gheorghe
See Bacovia, George
Vassa, Gustavus
See Equiano, Olaudah
Vassanji, M.G. 1950- .... **CLC 326**
See also CA 136; CANR 186; CN 6, 7; DLB
334; EWL 3
Vassanji, Moyez G.
See Vassanji, M.G.
Vassilikos, Vassilis 1933- .... **CLC 4, 8**
See also CA 81-84; CANR 75, 149; EWL 3
Vaughan, Henry
1621-1695 .... **LC 27; PC 81**
See also BRW 2; DLB 131; PAB; RGEL 2

Walser, Martin 1927- .... **CLC 27, 183**
See also CA 57-60; CANR 8, 46, 145;
CWW 2; DLB 75, 124; EWL 3

Walser, Robert 1878-1956 .... **SSC 20;**
TCLC 18, 267
See also CA 118; 165; CANR 100, 194;
DLB 66; EWL 3

Walsh, Gillian Paton
See Paton Walsh, Jill

Walsh, Jill Paton
See Paton Walsh, Jill

Walter, Villiam Christian
See Andersen, Hans Christian

Walter of Chatillon
c. 1135-c. 1202 .... **CMLC 111**

Walters, Anna L(ee) 1946- .... **NNAL**
See also CA 73-76

Walther von der Vogelweide
c. 1170-1228 .... **CMLC 56**

Walther von der Vogelweide c. 1170-c.
1230 .... **CMLC 147**
See also DLB 138; EW 1; RGWL 2, 3

Walton, Izaak 1593-1683 .... **LC 72**
See also BRW 2; CDBLB Before 1660; DLB
151, 213; RGEL 2

Walzer, Michael 1935- .... **CLC 238**
See also CA 37-40R; CANR 15, 48,
127, 190

Walzer, Michael Laban
See Walzer, Michael

Wambaugh, Joseph, Jr. 1937- .... **CLC 3, 18**
See also AITN 1; BEST 89:3; BPFB 3; CA
33-36R; CANR 42, 65, 115, 167, 217;
CMW 4; CPW 1; DA3; DAM NOV, POP;
DLB 6; DLBY 1983; MSW; MTCW 1, 2

Wambaugh, Joseph Aloysius
See Wambaugh, Joseph, Jr.

Wang Wei 699(?)-761(?) .... **CMLC 100;**
PC 18
See also TWA

Warburton, William 1698-1779 .... **LC 97**
See also DLB 104

Ward, Arthur Henry Sarsfield
1883-1959 .... **TCLC 28**
See also AAYA 80; CA 108; 173; CMW 4;
DLB 70; HGG; MSW; SUFW

Ward, Douglas Turner 1930- .... **CLC 19**
See also BW 1; CA 81-84; CAD; CANR 27;
CD 5, 6; DLB 7, 38

Ward, E. D.
See Lucas, E(dward) V(errall)

Ward, Mrs. Humphry 1851-1920
See Ward, Mary Augusta
See also RGEL 2

Ward, Mary Augusta
1851-1920 .... **TCLC 55**
See Ward, Mrs. Humphry
See also DLB 18

Ward, Nathaniel 1578(?)-1652 .... **LC 114**
See also DLB 24

Ward, Peter
See Faust, Frederick

Warhol, Andy 1928(?)-1987 .... **CLC 20**
See also AAYA 12; BEST 89:4; CA 89-92;
121; CANR 34

Warner, Francis (Robert Le Plastrier)
1937- .... **CLC 14**
See also CA 53-56; CANR 11; CP 1, 2, 3, 4

Warner, Marina 1946- .... **CLC 59, 231**
See also CA 65-68; CANR 21, 55, 118; CN
5, 6, 7; DLB 194; MTFW 2005

Warner, Rex (Ernest)
1905-1986 .... **CLC 45**
See also CA 89-92; 119; CN 1, 2, 3, 4; CP 1,
2, 3, 4; DLB 15; RGEL 2; RHW

Warner, Susan (Bogert)
1819-1885 .... **NCLC 31, 146**

See also AMWS 18; CLR 179; DLB 3, 42,
239, 250, 254

Warner, Sylvia (Constance) Ashton
See Ashton-Warner, Sylvia (Constance)

Warner, Sylvia Townsend
1893-1978 .... **CLC 7, 19; SSC 23;**
TCLC 131
See also BRWS 7; CA 61-64; 77-80; CANR
16, 60, 104; CN 1, 2; DLB 34, 139; EWL
3; FANT; FW; MTCW 1, 2; RGEL 2;
RGSF 2; RHW

Warren, Mercy Otis
1728-1814 .... **NCLC 13, 226**
See also DLB 31, 200; RGAL 4; TUS

Warren, Robert Penn 1905-1989 ..... **CLC 1,**
4, 6, 8, 10, 13, 18, 39, 53, 59; PC 37; SSC
4, 58, 126; WLC 6
See also AITN 1; AMW; AMWC 2; BPFB
3; BYA 1; CA 13-16R; 129; CANR 10, 47;
CDALB 1968-1988; CN 1, 2, 3, 4; CP 1, 2,
3, 4; DA; DA3; DAB; DAC; DAM MST,
NOV, POET; DLB 2, 48, 152, 320; DLBY
1980, 1989; EWL 3; INT CANR-10; MAL
5; MTCW 1, 2; MTFW 2005; NFS 13;
RGAL 4; RGSF 2; RHW; SATA 46;
SATA-Obit 63; SSFS 8; TUS

Warrigal, Jack
See Furphy, Joseph

Warshofsky, Isaac
See Singer, Isaac Bashevis

Warton, Joseph 1722-1800 .... **LC 128;**
NCLC 118
See also DLB 104, 109; RGEL 2

Warton, Thomas
1728-1790 .... **LC 15, 82**
See also DAM POET; DLB 104, 109, 336;
RGEL 2

Waruk, Kona
See Harris, (Theodore) Wilson

Warung, Price
See Astley, William

Warwick, Jarvis
See Garner, Hugh

Washington, Alex
See Harris, Mark

Washington, Booker T.
1856-1915 .... **BLC 1:3; TCLC 10**
See also BW 1; CA 114; 125; DA3; DAM
MULT; DLB 345; LAIT 2; RGAL 4;
SATA 28

Washington, Booker Taliaferro
See Washington, Booker T.

Washington, George 1732-1799 .... **LC 25**
See also DLB 31

Wassermann, (Karl) Jakob
1873-1934 .... **TCLC 6**
See also CA 104; 163; DLB 66; EWL 3

Wasserstein, Wendy 1950-2006 ...... **CLC 32,**
59, 90, 183; DC 4
See also AAYA 73; AMWS 15; CA 121;
129; 247; CABS 3; CAD; CANR 53, 75,
128; CD 5, 6; CWD; DA3; DAM DRAM;
DFS 5, 17, 29; DLB 228; EWL 3; FW;
INT CA-129; MAL 5; MTCW 2; MTFW
2005; SATA 94; SATA-Obit 174

Waterhouse, Keith 1929-2009 .... **CLC 47**
See also BRWS 13; CA 5-8R; 290; CANR
38, 67, 109; CBD; CD 6; CN 1, 2, 3, 4, 5,
6, 7; DLB 13, 15; MTCW 1, 2; MTFW
2005

Waterhouse, Keith Spencer
See Waterhouse, Keith

Waters, Frank (Joseph)
1902-1995 .... **CLC 88**
See also CA 5-8R; 149; CAAS 13; CANR 3,
18, 63, 121; DLB 212; DLBY 1986;
RGAL 4; TCWW 1, 2

Waters, Mary C. .... **CLC 70**

Waters, Roger 1944- .... **CLC 35**

Watkins, Frances Ellen
See Harper, Frances Ellen Watkins

Watkins, Gerrold
See Malzberg, Barry N(athaniel)

Watkins, Gloria Jean
See hooks, bell

Watkins, Paul 1964- .... **CLC 55**
See also CA 132; CANR 62, 98, 231

Watkins, Vernon Phillips
1906-1967 .... **CLC 43**
See also CA 9-10; 25-28R; CAP 1; DLB 20;
EWL 3; RGEL 2

Watson, Irving S.
See Mencken, H. L.

Watson, John H.
See Farmer, Philip Jose

Watson, Richard F.
See Silverberg, Robert

Watson, Rosamund Marriott
1860-1911 .... **PC 117**
See also CA 207; DLB 240

Watson, Sheila 1909-1998 .... **SSC 128**
See also AITN 2; CA 155; CCA 1; DAC;
DLB 60

Watts, Ephraim
See Horne, Richard Henry Hengist

Watts, Isaac 1674-1748 .... **LC 98**
See also DLB 95; RGEL 2; SATA 52

Waugh, Auberon (Alexander)
1939-2001 .... **CLC 7**
See also CA 45-48; 192; CANR 6, 22, 92;
CN 1, 2, 3; DLB 14, 194

Waugh, Evelyn 1903-1966 .... **CLC 1, 3, 8,**
13, 19, 27, 107; SSC 41; TCLC 229, 318;
WLC 6
See also AAYA 78; BPFB 3; BRW 7; CA
85-88; 25-28R; CANR 22; CDBLB 1914-
1945; DA; DA3; DAB; DAC; DAM MST,
NOV, POP; DLB 15, 162, 195, 352; EWL
3; MTCW 1, 2; MTFW 2005; NFS 13, 17,
34; RGEL 2; RGSF 2; TEA; WLIT 4

Waugh, Evelyn Arthur St. John
See Waugh, Evelyn

Waugh, Harriet 1944- .... **CLC 6**
See also CA 85-88; CANR 22

Ways, C.R.
See Blount, Roy, Jr.

Waystaff, Simon
See Swift, Jonathan

Webb, Beatrice 1858-1943 .... **TCLC 22**
See also CA 117; 162; DLB 190; FW

Webb, Beatrice Martha Potter
See Webb, Beatrice

Webb, Charles 1939- .... **CLC 7**
See also CA 25-28R; CANR 114, 188

Webb, Charles Richard
See Webb, Charles

Webb, Frank J. .... **NCLC 143**
See also DLB 50

Webb, James, Jr.
See Webb, James

Webb, James 1946- .... **CLC 22**
See also CA 81-84; CANR 156

Webb, James H.
See Webb, James

Webb, James Henry
See Webb, James

Webb, Mary Gladys (Meredith)
1881-1927 .... **TCLC 24**
See also CA 182; 123; DLB 34; FW; RGEL 2

Webb, Mrs. Sidney
See Webb, Beatrice

Webb, Phyllis 1927- .... **CLC 18; PC 124**
See also CA 104; CANR 23; CCA 1; CP 1,
2, 3, 4, 5, 6, 7; CWP; DLB 53

Yokomitsu, Riichi 1898-1947 .... **TCLC 47**
　See also CA 170; EWL 3
Yolen, Jane 1939- .... **CLC 256**
　See also AAYA 4, 22, 85; BPFB 3; BYA 9,
　10, 11, 14, 16; CA 13-16R; CANR 11, 29,
　56, 91, 126, 185; CLR 4, 44, 149; CWRI 5;
　DLB 52; FANT; INT CANR-29; JRDA;
　MAICYA 1, 2; MTFW 2005; NFS 30;
　SAAS 1; SATA 4, 40, 75, 112, 158,
　194, 230; SATA-Essay 111; SFW 4; SSFS
　29; SUFW 2; WYA; YAW
Yolen, Jane Hyatt
　See Yolen, Jane
Yonge, Charlotte 1823-1901 ... **TCLC 48, 245**
　See also BRWS 17; CA 109; 163; DLB 18,
　163; RGEL 2; SATA 17; WCH
Yonge, Charlotte Mary
　See Yonge, Charlotte
York, Jeremy
　See Creasey, John
York, Simon
　See Heinlein, Robert A.
Yorke, Henry Vincent
　1905-1974 .... **CLC 2, 13, 97**
　See also BRWS 2; CA 85-88, 175; 49-52;
　DLB 15; EWL 3; RGEL 2
Yosano, Akiko 1878-1942 .... **PC 11;**
　　TCLC 59
　See also CA 161; EWL 3; RGWL 3
Yoshimoto, Banana
　See Yoshimoto, Mahoko
Yoshimoto, Mahoko 1964- .... **CLC 84**
　See also AAYA 50; CA 144; CANR 98, 160,
　235; NFS 7; SSFS 16
Young, Al(bert James) 1939- .... **BLC 1:3;**
　　CLC 19
　See also BW 2, 3; CA 29-32R; CANR 26,
　65, 109; CN 2, 3, 4, 5, 6, 7; CP 1, 2, 3, 4,
　5, 6, 7; DAM MULT; DLB 33
Young, Andrew (John) 1885-1971 .... **CLC 5**
　See also CA 5-8R; CANR 7, 29; CP 1;
　RGEL 2
Young, Collier
　See Bloch, Robert (Albert)
Young, Edward 1683-1765 .... **LC 3, 40**
　See also DLB 95; RGEL 2
Young, Marguerite (Vivian)
　1909-1995 .... **CLC 82**
　See also CA 13-16; 150; CAP 1; CN 1, 2, 3,
　4, 5, 6
Young, Neil 1945- .... **CLC 17**
　See also CA 110; CCA 1
Young Bear, Ray A. 1950- .... **CLC 94;**
　　NNAL
　See also CA 146; DAM MULT; DLB 175;
　MAL 5
Yourcenar, Marguerite
　1903-1987 .... **CLC 19, 38, 50, 87;**
　　TCLC 193
　See also BPFB 3; CA 69-72; CANR 23, 60,
　93; DAM NOV; DLB 72; DLBY 1988; EW
　12; EWL 3; GFL 1789 to the Present; GLL
　1; MTCW 1, 2; MTFW 2005; RGWL 2, 3
Yuan, Chu
　340(?)B.C.-278(?)B.C. .... **CMLC 36**
Yu Dafu 1896-1945 .... **SSC 122**
　See also DLB 328; RGSF 2
Yurick, Sol 1925- .... **CLC 6**
　See also CA 13-16R; CANR 25; CN 1, 2, 3,
　4, 5, 6, 7; MAL 5
Zabolotsky, Nikolai
　See Zabolotsky, Nikolai Alekseevich
Zabolotsky, Nikolai Alekseevich
　1903-1958 .... **TCLC 52**
　See also CA 116; 164; DLB 359; EWL 3

Zabolotsky, Nikolay Alekseevich
　See Zabolotsky, Nikolai Alekseevich
Zagajewski, Adam 1945- .... **PC 27**
　See also CA 186; DLB 232; EWL 3; PFS 25,
　44
Zakaria, Fareed 1964- .... **CLC 269**
　See also CA 171; CANR 151, 189
Zalygin, Sergei -2000 .... **CLC 59**
Zalygin, Sergei (Pavlovich)
　1913-2000 .... **CLC 59**
　See also DLB 302
Zamiatin, Evgenii
　See Zamyatin, Evgeny Ivanovich
Zamiatin, Evgenii Ivanovich
　See Zamyatin, Evgeny Ivanovich
Zamiatin, Yevgenii
　See Zamyatin, Evgeny Ivanovich
Zamora, Bernice (B. Ortiz)
　1938- .... **CLC 89; HLC 2**
　See also CA 151; CANR 80; DAM MULT;
　DLB 82; HW 1, 2
Zamyatin, Evgeny Ivanovich
　1884-1937 ... **SSC 89; TCLC 8, 37, 302**
　See also CA 105; 166; DLB 272; EW 10;
　EWL 3; RGSF 2; RGWL 2, 3; SFW 4
Zamyatin, Yevgeny
　See Zamyatin, Evgeny Ivanovich
Zamyatin, Yevgeny Ivanovich
　See Zamyatin, Evgeny Ivanovich
Zangwill, Israel 1864-1926 .... **SSC 44;**
　　TCLC 16
　See also CA 109; 167; CMW 4; DLB 10,
　135, 197; RGEL 2
Zanzotto, Andrea 1921- .... **PC 65**
　See also CA 208; CWW 2; DLB 128; EWL 3
Zappa, Francis Vincent, Jr.
　See Zappa, Frank
Zappa, Frank 1940-1993 .... **CLC 17**
　See also CA 108; 143; CANR 57
Zaturenska, Marya 1902-1982 .... **CLC 6, 11**
　See also CA 13-16R; 105; CANR 22; CP 1,
　2, 3
Zayas y Sotomayor, Maria de
　1590-c. 1661 ...... **LC 102, 238; SSC 94**
　See also RGSF 2
Zeami 1363-1443 .... **DC 7; LC 86, 243**
　See also DLB 203; RGWL 2, 3
Zelazny, Roger 1937-1995 .... **CLC 21**
　See also AAYA 7, 68; BPFB 3; CA 21-24R;
　148; CANR 26, 60, 219; CN 6; DLB 8;
　FANT; MTCW 1, 2; MTFW 2005; SATA
　57; SATA-Brief 39; SCFW 1, 2; SFW 4;
　SUFW 1, 2
Zelazny, Roger Joseph
　See Zelazny, Roger
Zephaniah, Benjamin 1958- .... **BLC 2:3**
　See also CA 147; CANR 103, 156, 177; CP
　5, 6, 7; DLB 347; SATA 86, 140, 189
Azevedo, Angela de
　fl. 17th cent. - .... **LC 218**
Zhang Ailing
　See Chang, Eileen
Zhdanov, Andrei Alexandrovich
　1896-1948 .... **TCLC 18**
　See also CA 117; 167
Zhenkai, Zhao
　See Bei Dao
Zhou Shuren
　See Lu Xun
Zhukovsky, Vasilii Andreevich
　See Zhukovsky, Vasily (Andreevich)
Zhukovsky, Vasily (Andreevich)
　1783-1852 .... **NCLC 35, 292**
　See also DLB 205

Ziegenhagen, Eric .... **CLC 55**
Zimmer, Jill Schary
　See Robinson, Jill
Zimmerman, Robert
　See Dylan, Bob
Zindel, Paul 1936-2003 .... **CLC 6, 26; DC 5**
　See also AAYA 2, 37; BYA 2, 3, 8, 11, 14;
　CA 73-76; 213; CAD; CANR 31, 65, 108;
　CD 5, 6; CDALBS; CLR 3, 45, 85, 186;
　DA; DA3; DAB; DAC; DAM DRAM,
　MST, NOV; DFS 12; DLB 7, 52; JRDA;
　LAIT 5; MAICYA 1, 2; MTCW 1, 2;
　MTFW 2005; NFS 14; SATA 16, 58,
　102; SATA-Obit 142; WYA; YAW
Zinger, Yisroel-Yehoyshue
　See Singer, Israel Joshua
Zinger, Yitskhok
　See Singer, Isaac Bashevis
Zinn, Howard 1922-2010 .... **CLC 199**
　See also CA 1-4R; CANR 2, 33, 90, 159
Zinov'Ev, A.A.
　See Zinoviev, Alexander
Zinov'ev, Aleksandr
　See Zinoviev, Alexander
Zinoviev, Alexander 1922-2006 .... **CLC 19**
　See also CA 116; 133; 250; CAAS 10;
　DLB 302
Zinoviev, Alexander Aleksandrovich
　See Zinoviev, Alexander
Zizek, Slavoj 1949- .... **CLC 188**
　See also CA 201; CANR 171; MTFW 2005
Zobel, Joseph 1915-2006 .... **BLC 2:3;**
　　CLC 373
Zoilus
　See Lovecraft, H. P.
Zola, Émile Edouard Charles Antione
　See Zola, Émile
Zola, Émile 1840-1902 .... **SSC 109;**
　　TCLC 1, 6, 21, 41, 219; WLC 6
　See also CA 104; 138; DA; DA3; DAB;
　DAC; DAM MST, NOV; DLB 123; EW
　7; GFL 1789 to the Present; IDTP; LMFS
　1, 2; RGWL 2; TWA
Zoline, Pamela 1941- .... **CLC 62**
　See also CA 161; SFW 4
Zoroaster date unknown .... **CMLC 40, 154**
Zorrilla y Moral, Jose
　1817-1893 .... **NCLC 6, 298**
Zoshchenko, Mikhail
　1895-1958 .... **SSC 15; TCLC 15**
　See also CA 115; 160; EWL 3; RGSF 2;
　RGWL 3
Zoshchenko, Mikhail Mikhailovich
　See Zoshchenko, Mikhail
Zuckmayer, Carl 1896-1977 .... **CLC 18;**
　　TCLC 191
　See also CA 69-72; DLB 56, 124; EWL 3;
　RGWL 2, 3
Zuk, Georges
　See Skelton, Robin
Zukofsky, Louis 1904-1978 .... **CLC 1, 2,**
　　4, 7, 11, 18; PC 11, 121
　See also AMWS 3; CA 9-12R; 77-80;
　CANR 39; CP 1, 2; DAM POET; DLB 5,
　165; EWL 3; MAL 5; MTCW 1; RGAL 4
Zweig, Arnold 1887-1968 .... **TCLC 199**
　See also CA 189; 115; DLB 66; EWL 3
Zweig, Paul 1935-1984 .... **CLC 34, 42**
　See also CA 85-88; 113
Zweig, Stefan 1881-1942 .... **TCLC 17, 290**
　See also CA 112; 170; DLB 81, 118; EWL
　3; RGHL
Zwingli, Huldreich 1484-1531 .... **LC 37**
　See also DLB 179

Literary Criticism Series
Cumulative Topic Index

This index lists all topic entries in Gale's *Children's Literature Review* (CLR), *Classical and Medieval Literature Criticism* (CMLC), *Contemporary Literary Criticism* (CLC), *Drama Criticism* (DC), *Literature Criticism from 1400 to 1800* (LC), *Nineteenth-Century Literature Criticism* (NCLC), *Poetry Criticism* (PC), *Short Story Criticism* (SSC), and *Twentieth-Century Literary Criticism* (TCLC). The index also lists topic entries in the Gale Critical Companion Collection, which includes the following publications: *The Beat Generation* (BG), *Feminism in Literature* (FL), *Gothic Literature* (GL), and *Harlem Renaissance* (HR).

Topic Index

Topic Index

Topic Index

Topic Index

Topic Index

Topic Index

CLC Cumulative Nationality Index

Nationality Index

Nationality Index

Nationality Index

CLC-390 Title Index